The War of 1898 and U.S. Interventions 1898–1934

Military History of the United States
(Vol. 2)

Garland Reference Library of the Humanities
(Vol. 933)

The WAR of 1898 and U.S. INTERVENTIONS 1898–1934

An Encyclopedia

BENJAMIN R. BEEDE • *Editor*

GARLAND PUBLISHING, INC.
New York & London • 1994

Library of Congress Cataloging-in-Publication Data

The War of 1898, and U.S. interventions, 1898–1934 : an encyclopedia / Benjamin
R. Beede, editor.
    p.   cm. — (Military history of the United States ; v. 2)
(Garland reference library of the humanities ; vol. 933)
   Includes bibliographical references (p.   ) and index.
   ISBN 0-8240-5624-8
   1. United States—History, Military—20th century—Encyclopedias.
2. Spanish-American War, 1898—United States—Encyclopedias.
I. Beede, Benjamin R.   II. Series: Garland reference library of the humanities ;
vol. 933.   III. Series: Garland reference library of the humanities. Military
history of the United States ; v. 2.
E745.W37 1994
973.8'9'03—dc20   93-49579
                                                 CIP

Printed on acid-free, 250-year-life paper
Manufactured in the United States of America

Contents

Acknowledgments

My primary debt is, of course, to the many people who agreed to write entries for the encyclopedia. Some of the contributors also provided valuable comments on the project and suggested additional contributors. A number of specialists who could not write entries because of insufficient time, being located away from research facilities, or changing research interests gave me highly useful advice on the book and its organization or leads on recruiting other contributors.

Professor John Offner gave me much advice on entries to be included. Several noncontributors educated me through correspondence, especially about the more controversial topics covered. Professor James L. Abrahamson (Campbell University) offered significant comments on military and naval coverage of the Spanish-Cuban/American War. Professor Alice R. Wexler gave me important guidance on Cuba in the 1890s and discussed in considerable detail my plan for entries regarding Cuba between 1895 and 1898. Professor John A. Larkin (State University of New York at Buffalo) gave me a number of helpful criticisms on the work. He expressed considerable concern about more space being given to the Spanish-Cuban/American War than to the Philippine War, 1899–1902. As a result of his letters I made a greater effort to ensure that most topics relating to the Philippine War have been covered in one or more entries.

Numerous scholars suggested additional potential contributors. Those who provided such needed suggestions include Dr. Timothy K. Nenninger (National Archives) and Professors Glenn A. May (University of Oregon), Norman G. Owen (University of Hong Kong), Ben Kerkvliet (University of Hawaii at Manoa), Robert Van Niel (University of Hawaii at Manoa), Donald B. Dodd (Auburn University at Montgomery), Leslie E. Bauzon (Philippine National Historical Society), Bruce Cruikshank (Concordia College), Louis A. Pérez, Jr. (University of Florida), Willard B. Gatewood, Jr. (University of Arkansas), Rhett S. Jones (Brown University), Robert J. Alexander (Rutgers University), Bruce Calder (University of Illinois at Chicago), Michael P. Onorato (California State University, Fullerton), Vincent C. Peloso (Howard University), Douglas R. Reynolds (Georgia State University), Dean Rolando M. Gripaldo (Mindanao State University), and Joseph A. Caldon, S.J. (*Philippines Studies*).

I received helpful letters from various scholars at the historical centers maintained by the armed services, including Dr. Ronald H. Spector, Director of Naval History in the Department of the Navy.

Of special importance was the assistance generously provided by Brigadier General E.H. Simmons, Director of Marine Corps History and Museums at the Marine Corps Historical Center. General Simmons' staff reviewed a considerable number of the entries and gave me valuable comments on those that were examined. I took many of the suggestions offered, but for a variety of reasons could not follow all of them.

Acknowledgments

I wish to express my appreciation to Emma A. Warren, Director of the Kilmer Area Library at Rutgers—The State University of New Jersey, and to Dr. Joanne R. Euster, then University Librarian at Rutgers, for having approved my application for a research leave in 1989 to begin planning this encyclopedia and to carry out much of my recruiting for entry authors.

My wife, Anne Brugh, always works with me on my research and other publication projects, but her contribution to this volume has been outstanding in terms of both her personal efforts and her patience with me. She contributed to the editing of the volume and did much checking and rechecking of names and facts.

Dr. Richard L. Blanco, Professor Emeritus of History College at Brockport, the State University of New York, who is editing the series, Military History of the United States, of which this volume is a component, contributed importantly by working with me on the scope of the volume. At one time, I did not entirely agree with his views, but am now very much satisfied that changing the scope of the book was the right decision.

Garland Publishing has provided a considerable amount of editorial support for the book. Paula Grant worked extensively with me over a period of several months, and we exchanged numerous letters and telephone calls in the editing process. Her many questions and suggestions significantly improved this work. Phyllis Korper, Senior Editor at Garland, also provided me with much needed information and guidance on a regular basis while the volume was being compiled. Helga McCue, Managing Editor; Eunice Petrini, Production Manager; and Jennifer Brosious, Bruce Chambers, Patti Hefner, Dora Kubek, Sylvia Ploss, and Jennifer Sorenson of the Garland prepress staff worked steadily with me to improve and to expedite the book.

Finding a model for this volume was difficult because of the long period covered and the varied nature of the conflicts. Most military encyclopedias appear to cover either a long period of time, often several centuries, or deal with a particular war rather than a group of conflicts. David G. Chandler's *Dictionary of the Napoleonic Wars* (Macmillan, 1979) gave me some useful guidance on organizing the structure of this book.

Benjamin R. Beede

Introduction

Despite its brevity the Spanish-Cuban/American War of 1898 had a profound effect on the United States. Suddenly, the United States had worldwide responsibilities stretching from the Philippines and Guam to the Caribbean. It has become a cliché that the United States reached major power status in 1898. The political and diplomatic effects of the conflict were highly important, but it is the war's military influences that are briefly discussed in this introduction.

In terms of military resources, the Spanish-Cuban/American War, the Philippine War, and the new responsibilities in the Caribbean brought a significantly enlarged army, temporarily further swelled by thousands of federal volunteers for the Philippine War, and the building of a navy that eventually moved the United States into the ranks of the major naval powers. Organizational changes were probably more significant in the long run, however. The army was extensively reformed. The archaic structure of the War Department that institutionalized conflict between the secretary of war and the commanding general of the army was abolished. A General Staff and an Army War College were established for planning and other purposes. The National Guard was further coordinated with the army, with the federal government expanding its supervision of the guard.

The Spanish-Cuban/American War was a transitional conflict. In many respects the army resembled the army of the Civil War and represented a continuation of the frontier army of the years 1865 to 1898. As in the Civil War and earlier U.S. conflicts, most soldiers were combat troops. Table 1 shows how different the army in 1898 was in composition in terms of percentages of combat versus noncombat troops from the armies of the world wars and the Korean War era. After 1898 more and more soldiers became specialists, many of whose assignments were apparently far removed from the battlefield. In 1898, as in the Civil War, most soldiers who died were victims of disease, not enemy action. This pattern was consistent with U.S. wars through the end of the 19th century but was distinctly different from the world wars, the Korean War, and the Vietnam War. Table 2 shows in striking fashion the impact of disease on wartime soldiers before World War I.

The Spanish-Cuban/American War cannot be dismissed as a wholly traditional war, however. In some respects, it foreshadowed later and larger scale conflicts. As the encyclopedia entry on the Turpie-Foraker Amendment shows, there was a struggle in Congress and the executive branch at the very beginning of the war over presidential war powers that resulted in an early victory for President William McKinley and indirectly for his successors in the White House. In terms of raising troops, as the entry on United States Volunteers indicates, the army for the first time had the opportunity of recruiting, selecting, and training large numbers of men rather than simply accepting troops from the states. This was the pattern, of course, for the huge intakes of men and women from World War I on. As the entry on war finance in 1898 indicates, raising money for the Spanish-Cuban/American War broke new ground for the federal government. For the first time, small denomination bonds were offered to the public, thus involving many citizens in the war effort, thereby creating a precedent for World War I and later conflicts.

The Philippine War and the small wars between 1899 and the end of the occupation of Haiti in 1934 were also learning experiences for the U.S. armed forces. The entry on Small Wars, for example, describes the evolution of U.S. responses to guerrilla threats in the Far East and the Caribbean area, and other entries touch on this topic. The Philippine War and many of the smaller interventions remain highly controversial conflicts. Users of this volume should keep that in mind when reading entries. On the Philippine War, in particular, a variety of points of view are presented. The scholars who wrote the entries clearly do not agree wholly on interpretations and sometimes facts. Because of the controversial nature of the counterinsurgency campaigns, it is imperative that the entries reflect a diversity of opinion.

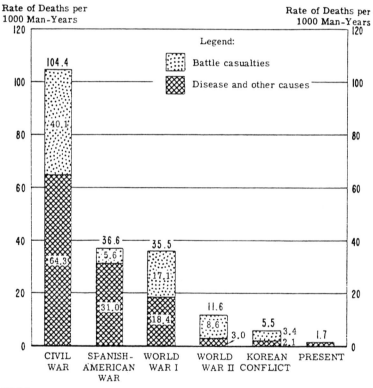

Table 1
Mortality Rates of Armed Services from the Civil War to 1956
Source: U.S. President's Commission on Veterans' Pensions, *Report: Findings and Recommendations* (1956), 82.

As the previous discussion suggests, the primary emphasis of the encyclopedia is on the Spanish-Cuban/American War of 1898. My decision to give the 1898 conflict such emphasis did not go unchallenged during my lengthy correspondence with specialists. One professor asserted that because of its importance and the loss of life the Philippine War should be stressed.

In the course of planning, collecting, and editing entries I was faced with several questions of terminology. It seemed unrealistic to perpetuate the use of the term "Spanish-American War." Such usage ignores the fact that the war in Cuba had been largely won by the Cuban revolutionaries before U.S. intervention. Therefore, using the term "Spanish-Cuban/American War" seemed appropriate, if a bit clumsy. Philip S. Foner uses "Spanish-Cuban-American War" in his important study, but the division of nationalities by dashes suggests to me a three-sided conflict. In a way events in Cuba during 1898 constituted such a three-way conflict, but nevertheless the Cuban revolutionaries and the United States were nominal allies against Spain.

Several scholars quickly called my attention to the unacceptability of the phrase "Philippine Insurrection." Use of this term connotes that the United States was the governing authority in the Philippines and that the Philippine nationalists rebelled against it. In reality, Philippine forces had taken most of the islands from Spain before U.S. ground forces arrived, and indeed, Philippine troops controlled much of the island group for a long time after the war began in February 1899. The term "Philippine-American War" is sometimes used instead of "Philippine Insurrection." It is quite appropriate, but I decided to employ the phrase "Philippine War." It seems sufficient and was much in vogue at the time of the conflict.

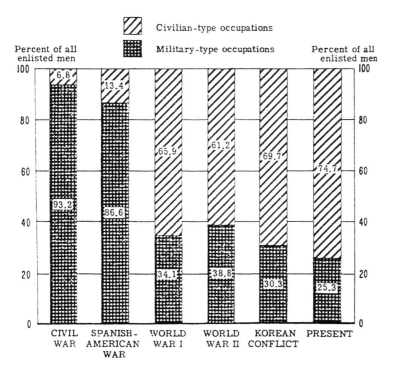

Table 2
Service Occupations of Enlisted Military Personnel from the Civil War to 1956
Source: U.S. President's Commission on Veterans' Pensions, *Report: Findings and Recommendations* (1956), 80.

I have generally tried to avoid the term "insurgents" to describe guerrilla forces opposing U.S. forces, although there is probably no serious problem with the word. Instead, the words "guerrillas" or "revolutionaries" are commonly employed. Such forces have often been dismissed as "bandits," but of course that has simply been to discredit them. The decision to use "blacks" to describe U.S. nationals of an African heritage was made by the publisher.

The decision to stress the Spanish-Cuban/American War shaped the configuration of entries significantly. Thus, there is an important entry on William McKinley, but none on the presidents between 1901 and 1934. A lengthy entry on McKinley was clearly essential. I strongly considered recruiting authors for entries on Theodore Roosevelt and Woodrow Wilson. However, if such entries were included, entries on Harding, Coolidge, Hoover, and Franklin D. Roosevelt might also be needed. These seemed inappropriate, however, for an encyclopedia on military history.

I planned most of the entries, but scholars suggested additional entries or modifications in projected entries. There would be little point in detailing here the negotiations involved with each entry author. I do very much appreciate the proposals I received. The book would be poorer without their inclusion.

Every effort has been made to verify the spelling and appropriate designation of personal names, geographical features, military organizations, and ships. Some variations occurred in the entries submitted, and, as editor, I had to assure that names and other designations were uniformly presented in this book. Sometimes, there were several ways to denote, in particular, geographical locations. Therefore, it is possible, for example, that some readers who are quite familiar with the Philippines may take issue with some spellings. As editor, I accept full responsibility for any nonstandard spellings that may have been used. It should also be noted that Professor Lewis Bernstein has used the Pinyin system for romanization of Chinese terms. In addition, some entries were edited extensively to make them fully comprehensible to nonspecialist readers. An effort was made to maintain the author's meaning, even though some wording had to be changed.

Indexing for this volume emphasizes names of persons and ships, geographical designations, and military organizations. An effort has been made to include the names of all individuals and ships mentioned in the text and most geographical designations are included. However, a few city names either have not been indexed or have been indexed sparingly. These are Havana, Cuba; Manila, The Philippines; New York City; and Washington, D.C. Military organizations from regiment to army are generally included, except that specific companies are not cited and battalions are generally, but not entirely, omitted. Large governmental agencies, such as the "United States Department of State," and branches of service, such as the "United States Navy," are generally omitted. Entries are included in the index with the page number(s) in bold.

Contributors

ABBOTT, RICHARD H., PROFESSOR OF HISTORY
Eastern Michigan University

ALVAREZ, DAVID, PROFESSOR OF GOVERNMENT
Saint Mary's College of California

ARNOLD, ALLAN A., HUMANITIES DEPARTMENT
United States Merchant Marine Academy, Kings Point, New York

BAILEY, JENNIFER, FOREIGN AFFAIRS SPECIALIST
National Marine Fisheries Service, National Oceanic and Atmospheric Administration

BEEDE, BENJAMIN R., COLLECTION DEVELOPMENT LIBRARIAN
Kilmer Area Library, Rutgers—The State University of New Jersey

BERNSTEIN, LEWIS, ASSISTANT PROFESSOR OF HISTORY
Boise State University

BIEDZYNSKI, JAMES C., PH.D.

BITTNER, DONALD F., PROFESSOR OF HISTORY
Marine Corps Command and Staff College

BRADFORD, RICHARD H., PROFESSOR OF HISTORY
West Virginia Institute of Technology

BUCKLEY, THOMAS H., PROFESSOR OF HISTORY
University of Tulsa

CARLSON, PAUL H., PROFESSOR OF HISTORY
Texas Tech University

CHAPUT, DONALD, CURATOR OF HISTORY
Los Angeles County Museum of Natural History

CHERNY, ROBERT W., PROFESSOR OF HISTORY
San Francisco State University

CHURCHILL, BERNARDITA REYES, PROFESSOR OF HISTORY
University of the Philippines

CLYMER, KENTON J., PROFESSOR OF HISTORY
University of Texas at El Paso

COERVER, DON M., PROFESSOR OF HISTORY
Texas Christian University

COLETTA, PAOLO E., PROFESSOR EMERITUS
United States Naval Academy, Annapolis

COOLING, B. FRANKLIN, CHIEF HISTORIAN
United States Department of Energy

CYR, ARTHUR, VICE PRESIDENT AND PROGRAM DIRECTOR
Chicago Council on Foreign Relations

DAWSON, JOSEPH G., III, ASSOCIATE PROFESSOR OF HISTORY
Texas A&M University

DEVINE, MICHAEL J., DIRECTOR
American Heritage Center, University of Wyoming

DOBSON, JOHN M., PROFESSOR OF HISTORY AND ASSOCIATE VICE PROVOST
Iowa State University of Science and Technology

DORWART, JEFFERY, PROFESSOR OF HISTORY
Rutgers—The State University of New Jersey, Camden

DOUGLAS, LAWRENCE H., PROFESSOR OF HISTORY
Plymouth State College

DRAKE, FREDERICK C., PROFESSOR OF HISTORY
Brock University

DRECHSLER, WOLFGANG, VISITING PROFESSOR OF POLITICAL SCIENCE
University of Tartu

Contributors

DUNAR, ANDREW J., ASSOCIATE PROFESSOR OF HISTORY
University of Alabama at Huntsville

EMCH, ERIC R., HISTORICAL RESOURCES INTERN
American Red Cross

FERENCE, GREGORY C., ASSISTANT PROFESSOR OF HISTORY
Salisbury State University

FLETCHER, MARVIN E., PROFESSOR OF HISTORY
Ohio University

GATES, JOHN MORGAN, PROFESSOR OF HISTORY
College of Wooster

GAY, THOMAS E., PROFESSOR OF HISTORY, EMERITUS
Edinboro University of Pennsylvania

GILBO, PATRICK F., MANAGER
Historical Resources, American Red Cross

GILMORE, GLENDA E., PH.D. CANDIDATE IN HISTORY
Princeton University

GRIEB, KENNETH J., PROFESSOR OF HISTORY AND COORDINATOR OF INTERNATIONAL STUDIES
University of Wisconsin—Oshkosh

HALL, LINDA B., PROFESSOR OF HISTORY
University of New Mexico

HAYNES, KEITH A., ASSOCIATE PROFESSOR OF HISTORY
College of St. Rose

HITCHMAN, JAMES H., PROFESSOR OF HISTORY
Western Washington University

HOFFMAN, JON T., MAJOR
United States Marine Corps Reserve

HOLBO, PAUL S., PROFESSOR OF HISTORY AND VICE PROVOST
University of Oregon

KAMMAN, WILLIAM, PROFESSOR OF HISTORY
University of North Texas

KEEFE, JOHN M., MAJOR
United States Army

KING, IRVING H., PROFESSOR OF HISTORY, DEPARTMENT OF HUMANITIES
United States Coast Guard Academy

KIRK, JOHN M., PROFESSOR OF LATIN AMERICAN STUDIES
Dalhousie University

KNOPP, ANTHONY K., PROFESSOR OF HISTORY
Texas Southmost College

KRAUS, THERESA L., HISTORIAN
Federal Aviation Administration

LAEL, RICHARD L., PROFESSOR OF HISTORY
Westminster College

LANGLEY, HAROLD D., CURATOR OF NAVAL HISTORY
Smithsonian Institution

LAURIE, CLAYTON D., HISTORIAN
United States Army Center of Military History

LIDE, JAMES H. L., DIRECTOR OF LITIGATION RESEARCH
History Associates Incorporated

LINN, BRIAN MCALLISTER, ASSISTANT PROFESSOR OF HISTORY
Texas A&M University

LIVINGSTON, JEFFERY C., ASSISTANT PROFESSOR OF HISTORY
California State University—Chico

LONG, JOHN W., PROFESSOR OF HISTORY
Rider College

LUX, WILLIAM, PROFESSOR OF HISTORY
New Mexico Highlands University

MACHADO, MANUEL A., JR., PROFESSOR OF HISTORY EMERITUS
University of Montana

McCARTHY, JOSEPH M., PROFESSOR OF HISTORY
Suffolk University

McFARLAND, GERALD W., PROFESSOR OF HISTORY
University of Massachusetts, Amherst

MADDOX, ROBERT JAMES, PROFESSOR OF HISTORY
The Pennsylvania State University

MAGDALENA, FEDERICO V., PROFESSOR OF SOCIOLOGY AND DIRECTOR OF RESEARCH
Mamitua Saber Research Center, Mindanao State University

MAHON, JOHN K., PROFESSOR OF HISTORY EMERITUS
University of Florida

MANDER, MARY S., ASSOCIATE PROFESSOR OF COMMUNICATION
The State University of Pennsylvania

MILLER, STUART CREIGHTON, PROFESSOR OF SOCIAL SCIENCE AND HISTORY EMERITUS
San Francisco State University

MUMME, STEPHEN P., PROFESSOR OF
POLITICAL SCIENCE
Colorado State University

MURRAY, DAVID R., PROFESSOR OF HISTORY
AND DEAN
University of Guelph

OFFNER, JOHN L., PROFESSOR OF HISTORY
Shippensburg University

PETERSON, DALE W., ASSOCIATE
PROFESSOR OF HISTORY
St. Cloud State University

PISANI, ANTHONY R., JR., A.B.

PITTMAN, WALTER E., JR., PROFESSOR OF
HISTORY
Livingston University

PLUMMER, BRENDA GAYLE, ASSOCIATE
PROFESSOR OF HISTORY
University of Wisconsin-Madison

RAUSCH, JANE M., PROFESSOR OF HISTORY
University of Massachusetts, Amherst

REED, JOHN SCOTT, PH.D. CANDIDATE IN
HISTORY
University of Southern California

RICE, C. DAVID, PROFESSOR OF HISTORY
Central Missouri State University

ROBERTSON, MICHAEL, ASSISTANT
PROFESSOR OF ENGLISH
Trenton State College

ROCA, SERGIO G., PROFESSOR OF
ECONOMICS
Adelphi University

ROSS, RODNEY J., PROFESSOR OF HISTORY/
GEOGRAPHY
Harrisburg Area Community College

RUSSELL, RICHARD A., HISTORIAN
*Contemporary History Branch, Naval Historical
Center*

SALISBURY, ROBERT S., VISITING ASSISTANT
PROFESSOR
University of the South

SARKESIAN, SAM C., PROFESSOR OF
POLITICAL SCIENCE
Loyola University Chicago

SCHIRMER, DANIEL B.
*Has taught at Boston University and in the
Goddard-Cambridge Graduate Program*

SIMS, HAROLD DANA, PROFESSOR OF
HISTORY
University of Pittsburgh

SMITH, JOSEPH, SENIOR LECTURER IN
HISTORY
University of Exeter

SMITH, ROBERT FREEMAN, DISTINGUISHED
UNIVERSITY PROFESSOR OF HISTORY
University of Toledo

STRAND, WILSON E.
National University, Osaka, Japan

STROBRIDGE, WILLIAM F., COLONEL
United States Army, Retired

STULTS, TAYLOR, PROFESSOR OF HISTORY
Muskingum College

TALBOTT, ROBERT D., PROFESSOR OF LATIN
AMERICAN HISTORY
University of Northern Iowa

TAN, SAMUEL K., PROFESSOR OF HISTORY
University of the Philippines

TATE, MICHAEL L., PROFESSOR OF HISTORY
University of Nebraska at Omaha

VENZON, ANNE CIPRIANO, PH.D.

WARNOCK, A. TIMOTHY, HISTORIAN AND
CHIEF
*Organizational History Branch, Air Force
Historical Research Agency*

WELLS, ALLEN, PROFESSOR OF HISTORY
Bowdoin College

WILLIAMS, VERNON L., ASSOCIATE
PROFESSOR OF HISTORY
Abilene Christian University

WOLFF, GERALD W., ASSOCIATE PROFESSOR
OF HISTORY
University of South Dakota

WOOSTER, ROBERT, ASSOCIATE PROFESSOR
OF HISTORY
Corpus Christi State University

YERXA, DONALD A., PROFESSOR OF HISTORY
Eastern Nazarene College

YOUNG, KENNETH RAY, PROFESSOR OF
HISTORY
Western Connecticut State University

ZABECKI, DAVID T., LIEUTENANT COLONEL
United States Army Reserve

List of Entries by Conflict or Occupation

General Topics

Bureau of Insular Affairs
Constabularies in the United States's Counterguerrilla Operations
The Monroe Doctrine and Its Corollaries
Moore, Dan Taylor
Pacification
Pensions and Other Benefits for Veterans of the Spanish-Cuban/American War and Other Conflicts
Small Wars
Small Wars Manual
Special Service Squadron, United States Navy
Utley, Harold Hickox

Spanish-Cuban/American War
General Topics

Spanish-Cuban/American War
American National Red Cross
Barton, Clara, in the Spanish-Cuban/American War
Bryan, William Jennings, and the Spanish-Cuban/American War
Chinese in the Spanish-Cuban/American War and the Phillippine War
Congress and the Spanish-Cuban/American War
The Cuban Bond "Conspiracy"
The Cuban Junta
Cuban Revolt (1895–1898)
Day, William Rufus
Dupuy de Lôme, Enrique, and the de Lôme Letter (1898)
France and the Spanish-Cuban/American War
Germany and the Spanish-Cuban/American War
Great Britain and the Spanish-Cuban/American War
Intelligence in the Spanish-Cuban/American War
McKinley, William, and the Spanish-Cuban/American War (1898)
Martí y Perez, José Julían
Motion Pictures in the Spanish-Cuban/American War
Nurses in the Spanish-Cuban/American War
Peace Commission (1898)
Press Censorship in the Spanish-Cuban/American War
Public Opinion and the Spanish-Cuban/American War
Railways in the Spanish-Cuban/American War
Sagasta, Práxedes Mateo
State of Texas
Teller Amendment (1898)
Treaty of Paris (1898)
Turpie-Foraker Amendment (1898)

Spanish-Cuban/American War
Land Operations

Spanish-Cuban/American War
Naval Operations

Cuba, Occupation (1898–1902)

Philippine War (1899–1902)

Samoa, Intervention (1899)

Boxer Uprising, China (1899–1901)

China, United States Military and Naval Presence (1901–1941)

Moro Campaigns (1902–1913)

Panama, Intervention (1903)

Cuba, Intervention (1906–1909)

Mexican Border Battles and Skirmishes (1911–1921)

Nicaragua, Intervention (1927–1933)

List of Maps

List of Maps

The Encyclopedia

A

Achuapa, Nicaragua, Battle (1930)

The engagement at Achuapa had the heaviest marine losses in Nicaragua in about two years and brought the U.S. intervention there back to the front pages of newspapers.

On 31 December 1930, 10 marines under the command of Sgt. Arthur Palrang were repairing a broken telephone line at Achuapa between Ocotal and San Fernando in the Department of Neuva Segovia, Nicaragua, when they were attacked by a band of Sandinistas commanded by Miguel Angel Ortez y Guillén, one of nationalist leader Augusto C. Sandino's chief aides. The attack lasted over two and a half hours; eight marines were killed and two who escaped were wounded. The marines killed an estimated 11 attackers and wounded four.

As a result, in the United States, there was a renewal of demands, supported by Senator William E. Borah, chairman of the Senate Foreign Relations Committee, for immediate withdrawal of marines from Nicaragua. President Herbert Hoover and his secretary of state, Henry L. Stimson, were responsive. By the end of January 1931, plans were laid to remove the last marines immediately after the supervised 1932 Nicaraguan elections; meanwhile, marine units were to be relieved of combat duties.

William Kamman

REFERENCES

William Kamman, *A Search for Stability: United States Diplomacy Toward Nicaragua, 1925–1933* (Univ. of Notre Dame Pr., 1968); Neill Macaulay, *The Sandino Affair* (Quadrangle, 1967); Vernon Edgar Megee, "United States Military Intervention in Nicaragua, 1909–1932," M.A. thesis, Univ. of Texas, 1963.

Aguinaldo y Famy, Emilio (1869–1964)

Emilio Aguinaldo y Famy, military leader and president of the short-lived Philippine Republic from 1898 to 1901, was a Chinese mestizo of relative wealth and provincial *gobernadorcillo* (justice of the peace) status. This young mayor of Kawit in Cavite Province was a latecomer to the revolutionary Katipunan, a working-class movement, which he joined after the execution of José Rizal y Mercado in 1896. Aguinaldo soon came into conflict with its founder, Andrés Bonifacio, over the pseudoreligious flavor of the organization. Aguinaldo favored the more secular *ilustrado* (intellectual) concept of nationalism. As the revolution unfolded, Bonifacio moved his headquarters to Cavite—Aguinaldo's bailiwick and the scene of Aguinaldo's impressive victory over the Spanish at the Imus River. In a power struggle, Aguinaldo outflanked Bonifacio by forming a revolutionary government to supersede the Katipunan and charged its leader with treason and sedition, for which Bonifacio was executed.

Greatly weakened by the desertion of Bonifacio's followers, and mauled by the Spanish, Aguinaldo was forced to retreat to a mountain redoubt at Biyak-na-bato, scarcely 30 miles from Manila. From there, he directed guerrilla operations until he was forced to negotiate with Spain. He and 40 followers were allowed to leave for Hong Kong in exile early in 1898 with $400,000 paid by Spain as a first installment of the negotiated settlement for their departure. Both sides flagrantly violated the truce, with Aguinaldo forming a junta to plan the next stage of the revolution, and Spain reneging on paying the second installment, along with other violations. When war between the United States and Spain seemed imminent, the revolutionary junta began to negotiate, first with Rounseville Wildman, the U.S. consul general in Hong Kong, and then with Adm. George Dewey and his staff when they arrived with an armada in anticipation of war. These U.S. officials encouraged the junta to return to the Philippines where the revolution had erupted again, if it had ever really ended. When one member of the junta sued to divide the $400,000 for personal use, Aguinaldo fled to Singapore, where he continued talks with E. Spencer Pratt, the U.S. consul general there. Unable to wait for Aguinaldo once war was declared, Dewey made his historic dash for Manila without him, but immediately after the battle he sent a ship back to pick up the exiled Filipino nationalists.

Once back in the Philippines, Aguinaldo took charge of the renewed rebellion, making his capital at Malolos, some 30 miles north of Manila. There, he drafted a declaration of independence; created a government; designed a flag; and called for a constitutional convention. His troops routed Spanish garrisons throughout the archipelago and bottled up the Spanish colonial leadership in Manila, all before U.S. troops landed in significant numbers. Like all revolutionary movements, his was sharply divided along class, regional, and ideological lines. In addition he had to deal with rival revolutionary movements,

mostly religious, as well as those military in nature, such as the Guardia de Honor in the Ilocos region, or the Pulahanes on Samar. *Ilustrados* dominated the constitutional convention to defeat more radical schemes of the Katipuneros and those of Aguinaldo's chief advisor, Apolinario Mabini.

Much was made of these divisions in Washington and in the nation's pro-imperialist press to create the impression that Aguinaldo was not in control and that his organization was little more than an opportunistic mob. To their credit, Dewey and Gen. Thomas M. Anderson, the first U.S. commander in the Philippines, attempted to counter this erroneous impression. Two naval officers traveled through Luzon in summer 1898 and reported very favorably on Aguinaldo's popular support. Dewey forwarded their report to the United States Navy Department with an enthusiastic endorsement, where it remained closeted until the authors published their account a year later. As the government moved closer to a decision to keep all of Luzon, and then the entire archipelago, it was less interested in changing its image and justification for annexing the Philippines. Both Wildman and Pratt were muzzled and also reprimanded for having encouraged Aguinaldo to think in terms of independence.

Once Gen. Wesley Merritt arrived to assume command on 25 July 1898, the United States had not only an imperious leader, but one who brought negative images of Aguinaldo as a "Chinese halfbreed adventurer" with no legitimate claim to govern the islands. One of Merritt's first orders was to forbid any communications with the Filipino nationalists. He then connived with the Spanish to arrange a sham battle for Manila on 13 August, allowing the U.S. troops, for whom Dewey had earlier persuaded Aguinaldo to make room on his line of siege, to take Manila, and excluded the Philippine army. Merritt left shortly after to misinform the U.S. peace commission in Paris about the nature of Aguinaldo's "pretentious government."

Merritt's successor, Gen. Elwell S. Otis, characterized Aguinaldo as little more than a "robber," whose armed mob was interested only in "looting" the islands. Otis managed a diplomatic offensive designed to humiliate Aguinaldo and his followers, and circumstantial evidence strongly suggests that he deliberately provoked warfare between the two armies. Otis launched his military offensive on 5 February 1899. Aguinaldo's army was no match for U.S. firepower. It fought largely delaying actions as Aguinaldo retreated to a mountain refuge by the end of 1899, this time at Palanan near the rugged mountainous coast of Isabela Province in northeastern Luzon.

Before that, Aguinaldo had been engaged in a power struggle with his very able general, António Narciso Luna de St. Pedro, who was critical of Aguinaldo's military leadership. Luna was an Ilocano, and Aguinaldo's army and government were both dominated by Tagalogs. Also, Luna was an *ilustrado*, and he may have looked down on Aguinaldo's lower social status. In June, as he was on his way to confer with Aguinaldo, Luna was assassinated by two soldiers from Cavite and loyal to Aguinaldo. Later, Mabini accused Aguinaldo of having ordered Luna's murder, attributing the defeat of the revolution to this despicable act.

Over the next 15 months, Aguinaldo seems to have been only a figurehead in his isolated headquarters. Actually, the guerrilla strength of the revolution was greatly enhanced by the decentralized leadership because local commanders could make immediate decisions based on local conditions without going through an elaborate chain of command that would have involved communicating with Aguinaldo in remote Palanan. On 24 March 1901 Aguinaldo was captured by Gen. Frederick Funston at Palanan, and transported to Manila the next day by the navy.

Almost immediately, Aguinaldo cooperated with his captors, signed an oath of allegiance to the United States, and urged his followers in the field to do the same. This did not help his historical image at the hands of more nationalistic Filipino historians, any more than did his execution of Bonifacio and his most probable murder of Luna. Ironically, his two victims rank much higher in the Philippines's pantheon of patriotic honor, just below that of the martyred José Rizal y Mercado. Aguinaldo was pretty much relegated to oblivion by the *ilustrado* leadership that dominated the postwar government, occasionally being called out to serve the oligarchy in a ceremonial capacity. His desperate attempt to persuade the Japanese to name him president of its puppet republic during the wartime occupation did not help him, even though the *ilustrado* leaders who had remained behind shamelessly collaborated with their new conquerors, leaving

resistance up to the lower classes. The Japanese wisely turned Aguinaldo down, sensing that he had no significant following. At best, Aguinaldo is, to this day, a tarnished Filipino hero. That might change with future historiographic revisionism.

Stuart Creighton Miller

REFERENCES

Teodoro Agoncillo, *Malolos: The Crisis of the Republic* (Univ. of the Philippines, 1960); Eufronio Melo Alip, *In the Days of General Emilio Aguinaldo: A Study of the Life and Times of a Great Military Leader, Statesman, and Patriot* (Alip, 1969); William B. Cochran, "The Wanderings of Emilio Aguinaldo," *Journal of the Military Service Institution of the United States*, 34 (1904), 454–466; S.V. Epistola, "The Hong Kong Junta," *Philippine Social Science and Humanities*, 26 (1961), 3–65; Peter Stanley, *A Nation in the Making: The Philippines and the United States, 1899–1921* (Harvard Univ. Pr., 1974).

See also Dewey, George; Funston, Frederick; Luna de St. Pedro, António Narciso; Manila, The Philippines, Battle (1899); Merritt, Wesley; Otis, Elwell Stephen; Philippine Revolution (1896–1899); Philippine Revolutionary Government; Philippine War (1899–1902).

Air Operations in China (1927–1928)

The operations by Marine Corps aviators in China were part of the activities of the 3rd Marine Brigade, West Coast Expeditionary Force—the first Marine Corps expeditionary force to be accompanied by aircraft squadrons—under the command of Brig. Gen. Smedley D. Butler. Butler had previously served in China, distinguishing himself in the Battle of Tianjin (Tientsin) and the Battle of Beijing (Peking) during the Boxer Uprising of 1900.

Most of the force was deployed after the 1927 Nanjing (Nanking) incident (an antiforeign episode in the Guomindang's [Kuomintang] Northern Expedition to unify China). To prevent a duplication of effort and unnecessary friction with other Treaty Powers, most of the U.S. expeditionary force was deployed around Beijing and Tianjin in North China. This was to enable the marines to reinforce the Beijing Legation Guard and the United States Army's 15th Infantry Regiment (stationed in Tianjin). The air units (three squadrons: one fighter, one scout, and one observer) arrived in late June and were flying by early July.

The marine squadrons served as airborne scouts and observers, providing advance warning of both Guomindang and northern warlord army advances and retreats. The primary function of both soldiers and marines in North China was defensive, the preservation of U.S. lives and property; they adroitly avoided offensive military actions.

That summer and the following winter, the marine squadrons operated a reconnaissance, mail, and passenger service for U.S. diplomats and military in the Beijing-Tianjin area. When the Guomindang offensive resumed in summer 1928, they kept track of the approximately 250,000 Chinese troops in the area.

By late July the goals of the Northern Expedition were accomplished: all of the major transportation and administrative nodes in North China were occupied by the Guomindang. No looting of foreign property or attacks on foreign nationals occurred. By September, the squadrons were being redeployed to Guam and the United States, the last aviators leaving China in late November.

In 17 months of air operations (July 1927–November 1928), the marines flew 3,100.7 hours during 4,565 flights. There were five crashes with no aircrew injuries. Despite being overshadowed by marine flyers in Nicaragua, the Marine Corps aviators in China were an integral part of a unified air-ground force very early in Marine Corps aviation history.

Lewis Bernstein

REFERENCES

Graham A. Cosmas, "The Formative Years of Marine Corps Aviation, 1912–1939," *Aerospace Historian*, 24 (June 1977), 82–93; Edward C. Johnson, *Marine Corps Aviation: The Early Years, 1912–1940* (History and Museums Division, Headquarters, U.S. Marine Corps, 1977); Gabrielle M. Neufeld and James S. Santelli, "Smedley Butler's Air Corps: The First Marine Aviators in China," *United States Naval Institute Proceedings*, 103 (1977), 48–59.

Air Operations in Nicaragua

Marine Corps aviation was used extensively in Nicaragua during the second intervention when it had its greatest test between the two world wars. The Nicaraguan experience served well many pilots who later were senior officers in World War II.

Marine Corps aviation performed many functions for the intervening troops and their Nicaraguan national guard allies, amply demonstrating its practicability in supporting ground operations. The first aviation unit (VO–1M) arrived in Nicaragua on 25 February 1927; a second squadron (VO–4M) arrived in May. Reportedly, VO–1M was the first fully manned, trained, and equipped U.S. air squadron to accompany an overseas expedition. Among the duties performed by the aviation units were transport service; observation, including contact, liaison, photographic, and reconnaissance missions; and attack aviation.

Conditions in Nicaragua were not conducive to flying aircraft. There were few landing fields. Trade winds frequently made air currents around the mountains rough for flying. The rainy season often had severe thunderstorms and a low ceiling. Low-flying airplanes had to contend with mountains, tall trees, and enemy fire. Tall grass and dense jungle often hindered reconnaissance.

Despite these obstacles, marine aviation played an important role during the intervention. Because the Nicaraguan terrain made supplying isolated units and small patrols by the usual pack train impractical, if not impossible in a reasonable time, air drops were used. The packers quickly learned the best way to wrap supplies to prevent loss or damage. Hauling cargo was a major contribution of marine aviation. Although the DeHavilands and the O2U Corsair biplanes could carry only a few hundred pounds of cargo each flight, they hauled many tons of supplies each week. Eventually, the marines acquired three tri-engine Fokker transports; the first arrived in December 1927. The second arrived in Managua in January 1928, making history in the first nonstop flight between the United States (Florida) and Nicaragua. The three transports enabled the military commander to place six tons of personnel and supplies in the northern insurgent areas every day. The top speed of 120 miles an hour and the 16-passenger capacity attracted the attention of commercial air transport. (The route from Florida across the Caribbean to Nicaragua was later followed by Pan American Airline flights.)

Another valuable function of aviation was communication. Although every plane had radio equipment and constant communication could be maintained when ground stations were properly equipped, the ground equipment was usually lacking. Therefore, planes had to drop messages. For ground-to-air communication, panel signals displayed in open areas on the ground conveyed short messages to planes overhead. For more detailed messages, planes trailing a long weighted line snagged a small leather bag fastened to string stretched between two tall poles and attached by headless nails.

Aviation support of ground fighting during the Nicaraguan air operations is illustrated by two often-cited encounters. The Battle of Ocotal saw the first important use of marine planes for tactical support in Nicaragua. Marines and national guardsmen in Ocotal, precariously defending themselves against a guerrilla assault by the followers of Augusto C. Sandino, were relieved when five DeHavilands, conducting the first organized dive-bombing attack, routed the Sandinistas. The relief of Quilali is another example of aviation's importance in the Nicaraguan campaign. Flying a modified Vought Corsair and using a short runway hastily constructed along the town's main street, 1st Lt. Christian F. Schilt flew 10 flights into Quilali to deliver hundreds of pounds of supplies and to evacuate the seriously wounded. Schilt received the Medal of Honor for these flights.

The marines would have been hard-pressed without air support. The airplanes and their crews provided many essential services to the ground operations, but there were limitations. A guerrilla war fought in mountainous, dense jungle terrain by insurgents living off the land and not needing extensive supply lines prevented the marines and the Nicaragua national guard from enjoying the full technological advantage of airpower.

William Kamman

REFERENCES

Charles R. Anderson, "The Supply Service in Western Nicaragua," *Marine Corps Gazette*, 17 (1932), 41–44; Edwin H. Brainard, "Marine Corps Aviation," *Marine Corps Gazette*, 13 (1928), 25–36; Frank G. Dailey, "Aircraft Squadrons, 2nd Marine Brigade, Managua, Nicaragua," *Leatherneck*, 15 (1932), 15–16, 61; Vernon E. Megee, "The Genesis of Air Support in Guerrilla Operations," *United States Naval Institute Proceedings*, 91 (1965), 48–59; Peter B. Mersky, *U.S. Marine Corps Aviation, 1912 to the Present* (Nautical & Aviation, 1983).

See also El Chipote, Nicaragua, Battle (1928); Ocotal, Nicaragua, Battle (1928); Quilalí, Nicaragua, Siege (1927).

Air Operations in the Dominican Republic

Air operations were not part of the initial U.S. landing in the capital, Santo Domingo, or involved in the deployment of troops around the Dominican Republic during 1916, but planes were used in the long campaign against the guerrillas in the eastern provinces.

In April 1919, the marine detachment in the East, having been frustrated in its efforts to find and to engage the guerrilla bands operating throughout that region, sought to break the deadlock by using airpower. This decision undoubtedly reflected the emergence and development of that relatively new weapon during World War I, as well as the postwar availability of air units. A marine air squadron of 130 men and six biplanes was deployed in Consuelo, and later moved to San Isidro.

Although the aircraft were used for both scouting and combat missions, their impact was decidedly limited. Despite the apparent need for more effective scouting, the guerrillas' greater familiarity with and ability to use the local terrain prevailed. Pierced only by small trails, the jungle effectively screened small ground units from aircraft, while the terrain made pursuit difficult even if the rebels were sighted. Consequently, the air effort did not result in a notable increase in engagements. Given the nature of small unit action, there were few suitable targets for bombing or strafing attacks. Infrequent air attacks were just as apt to threaten innocent civilians as combatants, particularly given the guerrillas' ability to blend in with the local populace. While the aircraft attracted much attention and the initial missions impressed the local populace, the guerrillas continued to operate effectively. They successfully countered the deployment of aircraft by spreading rumors that the occupation authorities planned to use the aircraft to attack civilians.

The air squadron was useful principally to improve communications among small garrisons scattered throughout the region. Although an important contribution given the absence of roads and the scarcity of radios, it did little in terms of combat effectiveness or the military balance.

The presence of the air squadron nonetheless left its mark on the Dominican Republic. Serving as couriers, the aircraft effectively established the first air mail service in the nation, connecting command posts in the eastern cities with the capital. The air squadron's relocation to San Isidro established a focus for military aviation, and San Isidro remained the location of the nation's principal air base long after the end of the occupation. Its role in subsequent coups was an unintentional legacy of the introduction of military airpower by the United States.

Kenneth J. Grieb

REFERENCES

Bruce J. Calder, *The Impact of Intervention: The Dominican Republic During the U.S. Occupation of 1916-1924* (Univ. of Texas Pr., 1984); Lester D. Langley, *The Banana Wars: An Inner History of the American Empire, 1900–1934* (Univ. of Kentucky Pr., 1983).

Air Operations in the Punitive Expedition

Irregular forces of Francisco "Pancho" Villa, Mexican revolutionary leader, raided the small town of Columbus, New Mexico, on 9 March 1916. The next day, the 1st Aero Squadron of the Aviation Section, Signal Corps, United States Army, was ordered to join the Punitive Expedition being formed by Brig. Gen. John J. Pershing.

The expedition's mission was to find and capture Villa in punishment for the raid on U.S. territory. It also was the first opportunity that the Aviation Section had since its establishment in 1907 to support combat operations.

The 1st Aero Squadron commander, Capt. Benjamin D. Foulois, took eight Curtiss JN–2 aircraft with the squadron from El Paso, Texas, to Columbus. Although the aircraft were underpowered, unreliable trainers, they were all the U.S. Army had available.

On 16 March, the day after its arrival, the squadron made its first flight into Mexico. Meanwhile, Pershing invaded Mexico and established his headquarters at Colonia Dublán, just outside of Casas Grandes, 125 miles south of Columbus.

Foulois received an order on 19 March 1916 from Pershing to go at once to Casas Grandes. Interpreting the order literally, Foulois ordered the pilots to fly at night, but the pilots became lost. Although one pilot crashed his airplane, eventually all the pilots and the remaining aircraft arrived at Casas Grandes.

The 1st Aero Squadron attempted to fly reconnaissance and liaison missions in support of the 7th, 10th, 11th, and 13th Cavalry Regiments but its underpowered airplanes could not fly over the rugged Sierra Madre Mountains to reach the cavalry columns moving rapidly southward. The squadron was reduced to carrying messages for Pershing. Foulois made two flights, on 7 April and 13 April, to Chihuahua City to deliver dispatches to the U.S. consul.

By 20 April 1916 the squadron had crashed all but two of the JN–2 airplanes; the pilots survived the crashes with only minor injuries. The squadron returned to Columbus to receive Curtiss N8 aircraft, which were no better than the JN–2. Foulois nevertheless sent a detachment to Pershing's headquarters at Colonia Dublán to continue flying messages and mail. In May, the Signal Corps replaced the N8 aircraft with Curtiss R2s, which were only slightly more powerful and reliable than the two previous types.

Foulois later reported that as of 15 August 1916, the pilots had made 540 flights covering 19,533 miles totaling 346 flying hours. The pilots had been injured in crashes, subjected to ground fire, kidnapped, and abused by the Mexicans. Foulois transferred in September; he was replaced as squadron commander by Maj. Ralph Royce.

The government of Mexico had from the beginning protested the U.S. incursion, and eventually the diplomatic protests and military confrontations convinced the United States to suspend operations even though Villa had not been found. In September 1916, Pershing concentrated his forces at Colonia Dublan. A 1st Aero Squadron detachment remained in Mexico through January 1917. At that time flying over Mexico apparently ended, although U.S. troops were not withdrawn until 5 February 1917.

During the Punitive Expedition, the 1st Aero Squadron carried out significant tasks. Even though it generally could not act as the "eyes" of the cavalry as intended, on several occasions the squadron's pilots located cavalry elements with which Pershing's headquarters had lost contact. It was also the first United States Army aviation unit to support combat operations. The squadron used photographic equipment for mosaic mapping, a first for U.S. aviation, and provided vital, albeit limited, messenger service for the expeditionary force.

The expedition found the army's aircraft far less capable and reliable than desired. The Signal Corps, concerned about the squadron's problems in Mexico, subsequently developed better equipment and more intensive training for aviators. As the historian Clarence C. Clendenen states, "The dozen pilots and less than a hundred soldiers of the 1st Aero Squadron were the seed from which the present United States Air Force has grown" (Clendenen, p. 322).

A. Timothy Warnock

REFERENCES

Clarence C. Clendenen, "Airplanes and Motors," chap. 17 in *Blood on the Border: The United States Army and the Mexican Irregulars* (Macmillan, 1969), 315–327; Juliette A. Hennessy, "The 1st Squadron With Pershing's Punitive Expedition, 1916," chap. 9 in *The United States Army Air Arm, April 1861 to April 1917* (U.S. Government Printing Office, 1985), 167–176; Herbert Molloy Mason, "No Eyes for the General," chap. 6 in *The Great Pursuit* (Random, 1970), 103–120; Frank Tompkins, "Report of the Operations of the 1st Aero Squadron, Signal Corps, With the Mexican Punitive Expedition," app. B in *Chasing Villa: Pershing's Expedition Into Mexico* (Military Service Pub. Co., 1935), 236–245.

See also Air Operations on the Mexican Border (1911–1921).

Air Operations on the Mexican Border (1911–1921)

Military aviation in the United States was in its infancy when revolution broke out in Mexico in 1910, ushering in a long military conflict on the U.S.-Mexican border. The total strength of the United States Army's "aeronautical division" in 1910 consisted of one pilot, one aircraft, and eight enlisted personnel. Much of the army's early aviation activity occurred in Texas, centering on Fort Sam Houston in San Antonio.

When the Maneuver Division was formed at San Antonio in 1911 in response to the worsening situation in Mexico, the increased military activity included a role for the limited aviation section. The one available aircraft was detailed for reconnaissance work along the border; because of its limited operational capabilities, the plane was shipped by rail to Laredo, Texas, where

it began its aerial scouting. During its second reconnaissance flight on 5 March 1911, the plane crashed into the Rio Grande after engine failure. Later, aerial operations continued in the San Antonio area in connection with Maneuver Division exercises, but there were no more flights along the border. When the division disbanded in August 1911, all aviation equipment and personnel were reassigned to College Park, Maryland.

New developments in Mexico in early 1913 led to renewed aerial operations in the border region. The overthrow and later assassination of Mexican President Francisco I. Madero in February 1913 led to another concentration of U.S. forces in Texas, this time in the Galveston-Texas City area. Included among the forces was a "provisional aero squadron" of nine officers, 21 enlisted men, and nine aircraft. Air activities, however, were limited to training exercises in ground-air operations. As the immediate crisis in Mexico passed, these troops were dispersed in summer 1913; by September, there were only two pilots and two aircraft at Texas City.

The U.S. occupation of the Mexican port of Veracruz in April 1914 led to a new phase of air operations along the border. Five pilots, 30 enlisted men, and three aircraft were transferred from California to Galveston, Texas, for service at Veracruz, Mexico. Because the personnel and equipment arrived in Galveston the day after the last transport ship had sailed for Veracruz, the aviation detachment never made it to Mexico, spending four months in Galveston without uncrating the planes.

By 1915 plans were well underway to make San Antonio, Texas, the Army's "main aeronautical center." New facilities were constructed, and the 1st Aero Squadron—15 officers, 19 enlisted personnel, and 6 operational aircraft—was established there in time to be drawn into extensive air operations along the border in conjunction with the Punitive Expedition into Mexico. The attack on Columbus, New Mexico, on 9 March 1916 by forces of the Mexican revolutionary Francisco "Pancho" Villa led to the incursion into northern Mexico of the Punitive Expedition under Brig. Gen. John J. Pershing. For the first time, the United States Army used its aviation branch in combat. On 12 March the squadron was directed to move by rail to Columbus, New Mexico, enroute to service with the expedition in Mexico.

On 19 March the eight aircraft of the squadron—Curtiss JN–2s, notoriously underpowered and particularly undependable in the high altitudes and turbulent winds of Chihuahua—attempted to fly from Columbus to Casas Grandes, Mexico, 125 miles away. None of the aircraft arrived at Casas Grandes on time, a portent of operational problems ahead; the squadron lost two aircraft to accidents in its first two days of operation. Not outfitted for attack, the squadron engaged in reconnaissance and communications, making 540 flights. Less than a month after arriving in Mexico, only two of the squadron's planes were operational. On 20 April 1916 what was left of the squadron returned to Columbus, where the remaining two planes were later burned by the pilots because they were deemed unfit for service.

While World War I brought a major expansion in military aviation in the border region, especially in Texas, it was not in connection with difficulties on the international boundary. The emphasis was on training fliers for a vastly expanded air service in Europe.

The postwar period saw a renewal of air operations along the border, with the formal establishment of an army border air patrol in June 1919. Eight squadrons patrolled the international boundary, operating out of bases stretching from Brownsville, Texas, to San Diego, California. Flights over Mexican territory were specifically prohibited, but by accident or by design this rule was often violated. Several aviators either crashed or made forced landings in Mexican territory. Two were killed by Mexican bandits after getting lost and landing in Baja California. Two others were held for ransom by bandits in Chihuahua, leading to a combination air and cavalry punitive expedition below the border in August 1919.

In 1920 a new administration in Mexico City led to improved relations between the United States and Mexico and a decline in border conflict. In 1920 and 1921, the border air patrol was even furnishing reconnaissance and courtesy flights for Mexican officers. In June 1921 the border air patrol was discontinued, ending a decade of air operations along the border.

Don M. Coerver

REFERENCES

Charles Deforest Chandler and Frank P. Lahm, *How Our Army Grew Wings: Airmen and Aircraft Before 1914* (Ronald Pr., 1943); Barney M. Giles, "Early Military Aviation Activities in Texas," *Southwestern Historical Quarterly*, 44 (1950), 143–158; Stacy C. Hinkle, *Wings Over the Border: The Army Air Service Armed Patrol of the United States-Mexico Border, 1919–1921* (Texas Western Pr., 1970); Stacy C. Hinkle, *Wings and Saddles: The Air and Cavalry Punitive Expedition of 1919* (Texas Western Pr., 1967); William C. Pool, "Military Aviation in Texas, 1913–1917," *Southwestern Historical Quarterly*, 49 (1956), 429–454.

See also Air Operations in the Punitive Expedition.

Alger, Russell Alexander (1836–1907)

Russell Alexander Alger was secretary of war during the Spanish-Cuban/American War of 1898. He became an increasingly controversial figure and finally was forced from office by President William McKinley.

Born in Medina County, the Western Reserve of Ohio, on 27 February 1836, Alger was orphaned at age 12. He supported himself, doing farm work and teaching school, among other jobs, while he read enough law to be admitted to the Ohio bar in 1857. Two years later, he moved to Grand Rapids, Michigan.

During the Civil War, Alger became a captain and recruited a company which became part of the 2nd Michigan Volunteer Cavalry Regiment. An able and brave field commander, by June 1863 he was colonel commanding the 5th Michigan Cavalry Regiment, in a brigade commanded by Brig. Gen. George A. Custer. Alger served with distinction in the major battles in the eastern theater, among them Gettysburg, the Wilderness, and the Shenandoah Valley. When he resigned from the army on 20 September 1864, debilitated by typhoid, he was a major general by brevet.

Alger's historical significance concerns his political activity. He founded the Michigan division of the Grand Army of the Republic, becoming national commander in 1889. He was governor of Michigan from 1885 to 1887, and Michigan's choice for president in 1888. When McKinley ran for president in 1896, Alger organized a group of Civil War veterans to campaign for him.

As president, McKinley appointed Alger to be secretary of war: that is, the civil head of the army advising the president. As U.S. involvement in the Cuban revolt against Spain and the consequent possibility of war between the United States and Spain increased, Alger's role as secretary of war became more difficult. It was apparent that the United States was ill-prepared for war. The department was organized to do no more than maintain a small army functioning as a domestic constabulary. Because Alger often turned for help to John D. Long, the secretary of the navy, Long concluded that Alger was not qualified for his position; in time the president reached the same conclusion.

The supply bureaus had three months' supply for the small army and no orders to increase it. Alger ordered in the early spring of 1898 accelerated output of weapons and accumulation of supplies; he also bargained with wagon makers and mule salesmen to replace the wagons the army had sold.

Congress on 9 March 1898 had made a special appropriation of $20 million for the army, which was restricted to strengthening defenses. No such restriction curbed the $30 million appropriated for the navy because, initially, the administration did not expect to have to raise a large army. It was obviously a naval war. But the National Guard had the political clout to push McKinley into calling for 200,000 volunteers instead of 60,000. Alger and Adj. Gen. Henry C. Corbin recommended the general officers whom the president appointed for the volunteers; McKinley appointed 26 major generals and 102 brigadier generals. Critics complained that Republicans were favored for the commands.

McKinley intended to avoid war, but Alger, the most anti-Spain member of the Cabinet, insisted that failure to liberate Cuba would wreck the Republican party. He said that Congress would declare war without the president if necessary. Consequently, McKinley recommended a declaration 11 April 1898, and Congress declared war retroactive to 21 April 1898.

Adm. George Dewey's destruction of the Spanish fleet at Manila on 1 May 1898 resulted in sending U.S. troops to the Philippines six weeks before any move was made against Spain in the Caribbean. In a conference on 2 May 1898, the president; Alger; Maj. Gen. Nelson A. Miles, the commanding general; Corbin; and other leaders decided to send a small army to land at Mariel, close to Havana, to penetrate inland far enough to establish contact with Cuban forces. Made up of regulars, it would succor the Cubans and withdraw. This strategy lasted only until

8 May, when Miles was ordered to take 70,000 troops and capture Havana. Because there were not 70,000 troops equipped at the time, that plan was abandoned. On 26 May a conference of the same planners decided to let Havana wait and attack Santiago de Cuba as well as Puerto Rico.

From the start of Alger's tenure as secretary of war, he clashed with Miles, the commanding general, who considered his authority equal to that of the secretary. Throughout the war they thwarted each other. Although Miles had to obey orders from the president through the secretary of war, he refused to carry out some orders originating with Alger, which he contended infringed his prerogatives.

Miles argued that Cuba should be left alone until the rainy, sickly season was over, but he was overruled by Alger and McKinley. When the attack at Santiago stalled, Miles wanted to leave it, attack Puerto Rico, and come back to Cuba. Alger overruled him on that, too. Miles proposed that a strike force of cavalry start from Santiago and go westward by land to attack Havana. This, too, was overruled. Alger claimed that Miles could have had the command in Cuba and had opted instead for Puerto Rico. Miles, for his part, believed that Alger conspired to frustrate him, whatever he proposed.

McKinley was the true director of the war effort. In the beginning he had Lt. Gen. John McC. Schofield as his military aide, but Miles resented his presence, and Alger snubbed him. In June McKinley let Schofield go. As friction between Alger and Miles rendered them less useful to him, McKinley increasingly relied on Corbin for the technical advice he needed to make military decisions. Nonetheless, McKinley retained Alger in the War Department long after he had become a liability to the administration, partly because Alger was a screen behind which he could direct the war effort while avoiding criticism for specific failures. Although Alger continued to convey orders through the chain of command, the major decisions were made by McKinley, often in consultation with Brig. Gen. Henry C. Corbin, adjutant general of the United States Army.

The expeditionary force to Cuba was commanded by Maj. Gen. William R. Shafter, commander of V Corps. Because Shafter came from Michigan, had a gallant Civil War record, and had performed outstandingly in actions against the Native Americans after the Civil War, Alger became a careful guardian of his interests. McKinley, Miles, and Corbin all concurred in the decision to select Shafter.

Alger favored Tampa, Florida, as the staging area for the departure to Cuba. He was pushed toward that decision by Henry B. Plant, whose railroad ran there. Despite Plant's assurances that the facilities at Tampa were more than adequate to move men and materiel, supplies remained unloaded in long trains of boxcars parked on the sidings because there was no place for the contents and because no one knew what was in the idle cars. Campgrounds were flooded by the heavy rains, and standing water provided a source of typhoid, the principal killer in the conflict. Alger did not fault Shafter for the tangle at the port.

On 31 May, Alger ordered Shafter to embark the troops at Tampa and steam toward Santiago. Once Shafter reached that area, Alger approved of his decision to make his landings at Daiquirí and Siboney. He curtly informed Long that the army could make the landings without naval aid, but he was obliged in the end to rely on the navy to bring in men and supplies.

When Maj. Gen. Joseph Wheeler, a former Confederate general, brought on a battle at Las Guásimas before Shafter was ready to take the offensive, Alger praised the action. When Shafter split his force to attack El Caney and San Juan Hill at the same time, Alger expressed approval. He sustained Shafter in his refusal to follow Sampson's request to storm the forts at the entrance to Santiago Bay. This task, Shafter said, belonged to the navy, and Alger agreed.

The heavy casualties at El Caney and San Juan Hill made Shafter cautious. The oppressive heat debilitated him. After reaching the rim of hills overlooking Santiago and looking down at the Spanish forces below entrenched and behind barbed wire entanglements, he wrote to Alger that he might have to draw back. This possibility stunned the administration. Alger ordered Miles on 8 July to take 3,500 men to Cuba, without making it clear what the relationship between Miles and Shafter was to be. Shafter, however, retained the command.

After the Spanish naval squadron left Santiago Bay and was annihilated, Alger allowed Shafter discretion on the way to capture Santiago. Public pressure to assault the place and be done with it was very heavy, but Shafter did not intend to make an assault. Instead, he began a series of negotiations with the Spanish commanders. From Alger came orders to accept only unconditional surrender. Shafter tightened his lines around the city until all access was cut off and threatened bombardment with naval guns if those terms were not accepted. Some bombardments occurred, the last on 11 July. Finally, with reluctant consent of the administration, Shafter received on 16 July the surrender of all the Spanish forces in the Santiago region. The condition was that the Spaniards could march out carrying arms, stack the weapons, and turn them over to the United States. The latter, in turn, would bear the cost of shipping all the soldiers from Spain back to Spain. Spain would help remove the mines in Santiago Bay.

Along with typhoid, malaria attacked U.S. forces, and yellow fever appeared. Alger believed that the troops were still needed on the island and that the fever would run its course, but most of the ranking officers in Cuba composed a letter (the "round robin"), pointing out that leaving U.S. soldiers there was to condemn them to die. The press printed this letter and castigated Alger for his policy. Recognizing that the troops had to come home, Alger selected Montauk Point, Long Island, to receive them. The Cuban expeditionary force staggered ashore at Montauk Point before the buildings, hospitals, and supplies needed for sick men were in place. This intensified the growing criticism of Alger. On 18 July the administration authorized Miles to open the Puerto Rico campaign. Shafter's men were too much spent; so Miles received other troops.

The critics coined the term "Algerism" to suggest corruption, although charges were never specific, and to indicate incompetence. They demanded that the president dismiss Alger to "remove the polluting influence of Michigan politics." Miles testified luridly before the War Department Investigating Commission (or "Dodge Commission"). The public focused on his accusation that the troops had been provided with inedible beef, which he called "embalmed," and with wormy bread. Crowds taunted Alger when he traveled with the president. By spring 1899 McKinley desperately needed a secretary of war better qualified than Alger to handle colonial problems. He subtly disassociated himself from Alger, leaving the latter bitter and confused. Knowing that the president wanted his resignation, Alger instead asked for a special commission to examine the conduct of the war. This resulted in the creation of the "Dodge Commission," which produced eight volumes of documents. Although the commission found Alger to be a conscientious official struggling to solve problems that he did not create, after an acrimonious interview with McKinley on 19 July 1899, Alger resigned.

Alger still retained political power in Michigan. When a U.S. senator died in 1902, Alger was appointed to succeed him. He was reelected at the end of the appointed term and continued as senator from Michigan until his death on 24 January 1907.

John K. Mahon

REFERENCES

Graham A. Cosmas, *An Army for Empire: The United States Army in the Spanish American War* (Univ. of Missouri Pr., 1971); *Dictionary of American Biography*, s.v. "Alger, Russell A."; *Dictionary of American Military Biography*, s.v. "Alger, Russell A."; Margaret Leech, *In the Days of McKinley* (Harper, 1959); David F. Trask, *The War with Spain in 1898* (Macmillan, 1981).

See also War Department in the Spanish-Cuban/American War (1898); War Department Investigating Commission.

Ali, Datu (? –1906)

The collapse of Datu Uttu's leadership in the Maguindanao anticolonial struggle in the Muslim area of the Philippines put the mantle of leadership on Datu Piang of Dulawan. A shrewd Chinese trader, Datu Piang had risen by the late 19th century from obscurity into prominence through political marriages and economic successes. When U.S. sovereignty was established in the islands in 1899, he was the logical choice of U.S. authorities to help integrate Maguindanao leadership into the new colonial government. The remaining obstacle in the Rio Grande was Datu Ali, son-in-law of Datu Piang, who had assumed the line of resistance Datu Uttu had begun against Spanish rule.

Datu Ali's movement became alarming to U.S. authorities when intelligence reports confirmed the active campaigns conducted by the *datu* (chief) to rally the Maranaos, a Muslim ethnic group politically and culturally related to the Maguindanaos and also known for its armed resistance to Spanish rule in the Lake Lanao region. Capt. Carl Reichmann, U.S. military governor of Cotabato, tried to prevent the Ali uprising from spreading to Lanao by sending troops to Kudarangan and Serenaya where Ali's forces were located. In an encounter on 3 March 1904 Datu Ali's fort, located between Kudarangan and Serenaya, was shelled, and several of the defenders were killed. This led to a radical change in Muslim strategy which called for a hit-and-run type of warfare.

The new tactics used by Datu Ali prolonged the conflict until 1906, by which time U.S. strategy had become more effective with the use of local allies, particularly Datu Piang, who provided accurate information and who were willing to suppress the uprising in exchange for lucrative political and economic advantages offered by the U.S. colonial government. In March 1906, a sizeable band of Datu Ali's men was at the Serenaya fort when U.S. troops attacked, killing many of the defenders and capturing Datu Djimbangan, leader and brother of Datu Ali. Djimbangan was used as a hostage in an attempt to force Datu Ali to surrender.

Ali refused to yield. He was encouraged to continue the resistance by *datus* of Upper Cotabato, including Datu Ampatuan of Maganoy, Datu Mopuk of Dapitan, Datu Tambilawan of Libungan, Datu Manalintao of Madridagao, Datu Argao of Silag, and Datu Sansaluna.

Despite the support from the inland *datus*, Ali's resistance was dwindling. Datu Piang's resources had already isolated him from the support of kinsmen and, on 22 October 1906, troops under Capt. Frank R. McCoy engaged Ali's band in Simpetan, killing the *datu* and several of his men. On 31 October, 13 of Ali's followers, including his three sons, were slain, thus ending one of the most famous uprisings in the first decade of U.S. rule in the Philippine Muslim South.

Samuel K. Tan

REFERENCES

Peter G. Gowing, *Mandate in Moroland: The American Government of Muslim Filipines, 1899–1920* (Univ. of the Philippines, 1977); Samuel K. Tan, *The Filipino Muslim Armed Struggle, 1900–1972* (Filipinas Foundation, 1977).

Allen, Henry Tureman
(1859–1930)

Henry Tureman Allen formed the Philippine Constabulary, a paramilitary police force under U.S. control that fought in the Philippine War and later against Moro troops in the southern Philippines. After graduating from the United States Military Academy at West Point in 1882 Allen spent 16 years as an explorer, a teacher, and an attaché at various U.S. legations in Europe. The outbreak of the Spanish-Cuban/ American War in April 1898 found him a first lieutenant on military assignment in Berlin. Leaving Germany to take part in the fighting, by June he was commander of Troop D of the 2nd Cavalry. Shortly after, as a major in the United States Volunteers, he sailed with his men for Cuba.

Initially, Allen's force performed escort and scouting duties in the Santiago campaign. In early July, it saw action in the Battle of El Caney on the outskirts of Santiago de Cuba. On 10 July Allen took command of the town of El Caney and its refugee camp with 20,000 people. With neither adequate food nor medicine, disaster was averted when Santiago surrendered six days later, thus enabling the refugees to return home. At this point, Allen caught malaria and convalesced in the United States.

In fall 1898, Allen was promoted to regular army captain and eventually returned to Berlin. The Philippine War, which had begun in 1899, allowed him to return to combat. That autumn he transferred to the 43rd Volunteer Regiment with the rank of major. Upon arriving in the Philippines on New Year's Eve, Allen took command of the 3rd Battalion. The 43rd Regiment moved to the islands of Leyte and Samar. After taking the chief town of Samar, Allen and his battalion remained there to set up a military government, with Allen as governor, and to track down guerrillas.

Perceiving the need for more troops in his operations to pacify Samar, Allen persuaded the government in Manila to allow him to establish a company of Filipino scouts. By July 1900, with Samar quiet, Allen and his men rejoined the other two battalions of the 43rd Regiment on Leyte, where Allen continued to recruit scouts.

While commanding one of the three sections of Leyte, Allen often personally commanded the patrol expeditions, which suffered only minor casualties while capturing many guerrillas and supplies. To create goodwill on the island, Allen decried the atrocities U.S. troops committed against the guerrillas. At the same time, he was one of the first U.S. commanders to adopt internationally recognized rules of warfare toward the guerrillas and the civilian population. To further his cause, he carried out numerous improvement projects, including repairing the roads for economic as well as strategic reasons. Due to his strict but humane policies on Leyte, the natives nicknamed him "Iron Commandante."

Believing that the war had ended in the district under his jurisdiction, Allen volunteered for the U.S. expedition going to China to quell the Boxer Uprising. His request was denied because his service in the Philippines was considered more valuable. In April, he became the military governor of Leyte. By the end of May 1901 the war on Leyte was largely over, and the 43rd Regiment returned to the United States, although Allen remained in the Philippines. In July, due to his successes on Leyte and Samar, his ability to speak Spanish, and his competency in recruiting and working with Filipino scouts, U.S. authorities selected Allen to establish and lead the Philippine Constabulary. This force was to fill the void between municipal police organizations and the U.S. military already in the archipelago. The functions of the constabulary included suppressing the last vestiges of the guerrilla movement, providing intelligence, guarding jails and escorting prisoners, protecting officials in unsafe areas, ending banditry, and restoring law and order.

Allen quickly began building a force. He recruited most of the officers of the constabulary from former commissioned officers and enlisted men of the U.S. military who had remained on the islands after their units had returned to the United States. Allen personally interviewed all applicants and rejected officers who viewed the Filipinos as racially inferior. Thus, in general, Allen selected excellent men.

Filipinos were also rigorously screened before being chosen as constables. Allen insisted that they learn infantry techniques to carry out their duties of keeping the peace on the islands. To further this goal, Allen usually stationed constables in their home provinces. By doing so, he hoped that these men, raised in the local customs and dialects, would develop goodwill between the regions and the Manila government.

As the chief of a paramilitary force, Allen often became the center of disputes between civilian and military authorities. He perceived that the army was trying to undermine his position by not adequately supplying his men and underplaying their role. Allen also annoyed many by advocating that the Filipinos could rule themselves on the local level. Unlike most U.S. soldiers, Allen not only socialized on an equal basis with the upper class but also attended festivals and other events that brought him into close contact with all classes.

In spring 1902, Allen further alienated himself from the military by proposing that he take control of the army's Filipino scouts. He argued that the scouts and constables, knowledgeable in the dialects, customs, and terrain of the islands, together could easily pursue bandits and guerrillas. Congress agreed and passed the "Scout Law" in January 1903, which gave temporary control of the scouts to the constabulary. As a result, Allen received the temporary rank of brigadier general and commanded a force of over 10,000 men. With increased manpower the constabulary began slowly to restore order in the archipelago, except in Moro Province, which remained under the control of the army.

Meanwhile, sensing a conflict was brewing in East Asia, Allen managed to be in Korea when the Russo-Japanese War broke out. He secured an appointment as military attaché at the U.S. mission in Seoul and became an official observer of the war. He saw little action, however, and returned to Manila on 1 April 1904.

While Allen was in Korea, one of his constabulary units in Northern Luzon mutinied. Although a minor incident and quickly suppressed, it gave his opponents and his force the means to charge the constabulary with disloyalty. Simultaneously, the war flared up again on Samar. By late fall it had become increasingly more violent, with the constabulary and scouts making little headway. By December, Allen took personal control of the operations.

On the advice of civilian authorities, Allen requested that the army garrison four towns to free more constables and scouts for action. In late spring 1905, Allen realized that his forces could not easily suppress the rebellion and asked that the army be responsible for the eastern half of the island. Despite Allen's predictions that the army would have difficulty pacifying its territory, the violence decreased. The constabulary did not resume control over the entire island until several months after Allen had been relieved of his command in 1907. The war, however, did not end until 1911.

The renewed violence on Samar and the army intervention allowed critics to charge again that incompetent personnel manned the constabulary, rendering it a useless force, and suggested that it be disbanded. Instead, the authorities reorganized it, decreasing its strength and returning all the scouts to the army. Allen oversaw the initial stages of these changes before departing for the United States on leave for the first time in five years. He remained there for nine months before coming back to Manila in June 1906. In the fall, he passed the promotion examination for army major. Shortly after he was notified that he would be replaced as the chief of the constabulary in spring 1907.

Allen left the Philippines on 15 April 1907 and returned to the United States with the rank of major. He was first assigned to Yellowstone Park, then to Fort Huachuca, Arizona, before accepting an appointment to the General Staff, where from 1910 to 1914 he specialized in cavalry matters. With the outbreak of war in 1914, Allen was sent to Europe to bring U.S. civilians safely back to the United States. In February 1915, the army transferred him to the 11th Cavalry at Fort Oglethorpe, Georgia. Thirteen months later Allen's unit moved to the Mexican border, joining the Punitive Expedition led by Brig. Gen. John J. Pershing against Francisco "Pancho" Villa, who had raided U.S. territory.

Allen's force entered Mexico on 17 March 1916. Pershing soon chose him as one of four commanders to lead small detachments of about 100 men to cut off Villa's expected escape from Chihuahua Province. While attempting, unsuccessfully, to capture the bandit leader, U.S. troops encountered minor fighting, snipers, and hostile civilians.

Following this futile foray, Pershing withdrew to the town of Colonia Dublán in northern Chihuahua. There, the general reorganized his force, appointing Allen the inspector general of the expedition. From 30 April to 21 June 1916, Allen carried out his tasks, and Pershing commended him highly for his work. On 21 June Pershing put Allen temporarily in charge of both the 11th Cavalry and the military camp at Colonia

Dublán. He was promoted to colonel on July 1. In mid-August Allen took command of the 13th Cavalry at Camp Stewart, Texas.

Among the many accomplishments of his long military career was Allen's role in establishing and directing the Philippine Constabulary during its crucial development stage. Despite criticism of the constabulary, he created a highly reliable force that became an instrument for creating stability on the islands.

Gregory C. Ference

REFERENCES

Robert Lee Bullard, *Fighting Generals: Illustrated Biographical Sketches of Seven Major Generals in World War I* (Edwards, 1944); Heath Twitchell, Jr., *Allen: The Biography of an Army Officer, 1859–1930* (Rutgers Univ. Pr., 1974).

See also Moro Campaigns (1902–1913); Philippine Constabulary; The Philippine Scouts.

American Expeditionary Force, North Russia (1918–1919)

The American Expeditionary Force, North Russia (AEFNR), was the final official designation for the land forces that participated in U.S. intervention in North Russia from 1918 to 1919. Organized in late summer 1918, the AEFNR served from September 1918 until July 1919. In direct violation of the express wishes of the U.S. government, the AEFNR engaged in sporadic clashes with units of the Soviet 6th Red Army and suffered casualties amounting to more than 500 men killed, wounded, or missing in action.

On 17 July 1918, in response to an urgent appeal from the Allied Supreme War Council, President Woodrow Wilson issued the famous aide-mémoire authorizing the dispatch to North Russia of three battalions of U.S. infantry together with appropriate ordnance and auxiliary forces. In taking this action, however, the president specifically stipulated that these troops were to be used only "to help the Czecho-Slovaks," an embattled pro-Allied force, part of which was then attempting to leave Russia via the North, and/or "to steady any efforts at self-government or self-defense in which the Russians themselves may be willing to accept assistance." Under no circumstances, insisted Wilson, were U.S. troops to be used for military intervention in Russia which, he emphasized, the United States rejected "in principle."

On 22 July, acting on the president's orders, the United States War Department directed Gen. John J. Pershing to detach from his command in France the necessary U.S. troops for service in North Russia. As selected by Pershing, these forces included the 339th Infantry Regiment (three battalions), the 1st Battalion 310th Engineers (two companies), the 337th Field Hospital, and the 337th Ambulance Company. Under the overall command of Col. George E. Stewart, these troops, totaling 4,487 officers and soldiers, were originally designated the "Murmansk Expedition." Hastily trained and equipped in Great Britain, these U.S. troops, more than half of whom were conscripts from Michigan and Wisconsin, set sail for North Russia on 27 August.

While the Murmansk Expedition was in course of preparation, developments in the North took a turn sharply at odds with U.S. intentions. This situation was largely the result of aggressive activities in the region controlled by Allied forces under the command of Maj. Gen. Frederick C. Poole, who had recently been appointed Allied commander in chief in the North. An ardent interventionist, Poole had at once begun to implement an extremely ambitious plan of operations in the region which called, in effect, for the virtual invasion of central Russia with a projected army of 5,000 Allied troops supplemented by an unexpected volunteer force of some 100,000 anti-Bolshevik Russians. On 2 August, as the first stage of this plan, Poole carried out the occupation of Archangel, employing for this purpose a polyglot force of just 1,500 Allied troops, including 54 sailors from the previously dispatched U.S. cruiser *Olympia*. Moving swiftly to the next stage of his plan, Poole began an energetic offensive to the south, with the cities of Kotlas and Vologda, deep in the interior, as his ultimate objectives.

In these circumstances, Poole greeted with great enthusiasm the arrival on 4 September of the 339th Infantry at Archangel. The next day he issued orders directing two of its three battalions to take up positions on the fighting fronts. These orders were in direct violation of Wilson's aide-mémoire and placed Stewart, whose command was redesignated the American North Russian Expeditionary Force, in a dilemma. Sensing that Poole's directives were not in accord with U.S. intentions but unable to obtain countervailing support from U.S. Ambassador

David R. Francis, his political counterpart in Archangel, Stewart withdrew to his headquarters and thereafter took little part in the strategic disposition of his troops. As a result, within days of their arrival in the North, U.S. soldiers, in direct contravention of their government's policies, were engaged in numerous small-scale combats with opposing units of the Bolshevik 6th Red Army.

Among the first U.S. soldiers to become involved in hostilities were the four companies of the 1st Battalion of the 339th, which had been transshipped directly from their transports in Archangel some 175 miles upstream to the so-called Northern Dvina River Front. There, after several sharp skirmishes, an Allied line was finally established at Tulgas, a little less than halfway down the river to Poole's ultimate objective at Kotlas. Then, beginning on 27 September, three of the four companies of the 1st Battalion were transferred westward to bolster the Allied position on the Vaga River Front, located on a swift-flowing tributary of the Northern Dvina. Headquartered at Shenkursk, the second largest city in the region, these U.S. troops alternated in outposting several villages some 20 miles below Shenkursk at the southernmost point ever occupied by Allied troops in the North.

Meanwhile, simultaneously with the 1st Battalion's dispatch down the Northern Dvina, the 3rd Battalion of the 339th (together with Company B of the 310th Engineers) was packed off to the Vologda Railroad Front, whose terminus, 400 miles to the south, was Poole's other chief objective in the North. Here again, after several sharp clashes, as well as the stabilization of a subsidiary so-called Seletskoe Column to the east, a front line was established just above Emtsa, not even one-quarter of the way to Poole's ultimate goal at Vologda. Finally, to protect the flanks of the invading forces, small contingents of U.S. troops were also detailed to create the Pinega and Onega river fronts, located, respectively, far east and west of the main lines of Allied advance.

The modest offensive that characterized Allied intervention in the North during its initial months soon ground to a halt. On 30 September, reinforcements arrived at Archangel in the form of an additional 503 U.S. soldiers and a sorely needed Canadian artillery brigade. More important, the new arrivals included British Maj. Gen. William Edmund Ironside, whose appearance was destined to alter completely Allied intervention in the North. On 26 October, Ironside replaced Poole as Allied commander in the region and at once abandoned his predecessor's offensive strategy in favor of a new scheme emphasizing the consolidation of a strong defensive position in the North. This approach, which prevailed throughout the long winter of 1918–1919, left U.S. troops, despite their orders to the contrary, as the majority of the fighting forces on virtually all of the region's far-flung fronts.

Coming in early November, the end of World War I did not resolve the U.S. military dilemma in North Russia. On the contrary, even as the unhappy Stewart sent a plaintive cable requesting the immediate withdrawal of his troops, U.S. soldiers on the Northern Dvina River were engaged in a savage, stand-off clash with the enemy at Tulgas, which its participants later ironically dubbed "the Battle of Armistice Day." At year's end, U.S. forces with the Seletskoe Column also fought gallantly at Kodysh in a failed attempt to capture Emtsa, which Ironside considered essential to the consolidation of a strong defensive position on the Vologda Railroad. Finally, in mid-January 1919 U.S. troops on the Vaga Front bore the brunt of the first significant Soviet counteroffensive in the North directed against the exposed Allied salient at Ust' Padenga, south of Shenkursk. This overwhelming assault, which entailed the most U.S. casualties of any single engagement in the entire North Russian campaign, resulted in an Allied retreat to Vystavka, some 50 miles to the north.

The Shenkursk debacle, which coincided with a rising tide of opposition in the United States to intervention as well as a general Allied failure to agree on any common Russian policy at the Paris Peace Conference, finally convinced Wilson to make a unilateral evacuation from North Russia. Thus, in mid-February, while acceding to a British request for the dispatch to the Murmansk Railroad Front of two companies of U.S. transportation troops, Wilson announced the withdrawal of all U.S. forces from the North "as soon as weather conditions will permit in the spring." Unfortunately, before this directive could be implemented, a wave of disaffection swept through U.S. ranks in the North, producing several incidents of antiwar protest and at least one brief episode of insubordination. In March and April 1919, the inability to effect an earlier departure from the region also drew U.S.

soldiers into the defense of Bol'shie Ozerki, west of the railroad, where, at some cost, they successfully contained the final phase of the Bolsheviks' midwinter counteroffensive.

The Battle of Bol'shie Ozerki was the last gasp of U.S. intervention in North Russia. In April 1919 Brig. Gen. Wilds P. Richardson, having been briefed personally by Wilson, arrived at Archangel to direct the final evacuation of the finally designated AEFNR. Beginning at once, the new commander presided over a phased withdrawal of U.S. forces from each of the various fighting fronts followed, in June and July, by their complete evacuation from the North. As a result, the unintentional U.S. war in North Russia officially ended.

John W. Long

REFERENCES

Daniel P. Bolger, "Cruel Russian Winter," *Military Review*, 67 (1987), 63–77; Dennis Gordon, *Quartered in Hell: The Story of the American North Russian Expeditionary Force, 1918–1919* (GOS, 1982); Joel Moore, Harry Mead, and Lewis Jahns, *The History of the American Expedition Fighting the Bolsheviki* (Polar Bear, 1920); Benjamin D. Rhodes, "The Anglo-American Intervention at Archangel, 1918–1919: The Role of the 339th Infantry," *International History Review*, 8 (1986), 367–388; U.S. War Department, *Order of Battle of the United States Land Forces in the World War; American Expeditionary Forces, General Headquarters, Armies, Army Corps, Services of Supply and Separate Forces* (U.S. Government Printing Office, 1937).

See also North Russia, Intervention (1918–1919); Richardson, Wilds Preston; Stewart, George Evans.

American Expeditionary Forces, Siberia (1918–1920)

The United States dispatched this force for several reasons. It did relatively little fighting, but its presence permitted the United States, for a time, to influence events in Siberia.

On 3 August 1918, the United States War Department ordered the 27th and 31st Infantry Regiments, United States Army, to proceed from their duty stations in the Philippines to the port city of Vladivostok on Russia's Pacific Coast. They arrived in mid-August. Because both regiments were understrength, they were reinforced a few weeks later with 5,000 men of the 8th Division from Camp Fremont, California. Together with a field hospital, an ambulance company, and a company from a telegraph battalion, these units composed the American Expeditionary Forces, Siberia. Many of these troops remained in Siberia for nearly two years.

When U.S. troops walked down the gangplanks at Vladivostok, they entered a world in which chaos reigned. Russia had been torn apart by civil war since the Bolshevik (Communist) revolution of November 1917. Although the Bolsheviks had seized power in most cities in European Russia, they were opposed in outlying areas by newly formed "governments" representing various ideological persuasions. These groups in turn had difficulty exercising authority in the regions they nominally controlled against rivals and bandit gangs. Civil authority, in short, was nonexistent.

U.S. troops were placed in an awkward position from the start. Their commander, Maj. Gen. William S. Graves, had been ordered to remain neutral with regard to the various Russian factions, but to defend Vladivostok and keep the Trans-Siberian Railway open to the interior against any challengers. The fact that the rail line became a pipeline to supply an anti-Bolshevik regime located at Omsk in western Siberia, however, meant that U.S. forces were taking sides regardless of their conduct. The situation was complicated further by the Japanese. They had sent a much larger military contingent to Siberia than had the other Allied powers, and frequently caused trouble to gain their own ends.

The Trans-Siberian Railway ran over 300 miles north to the city of Khabarovsk before turning west to the interior. U.S. troops were restricted to the Vladivostok-Khabarovsk sector during the first months and to guarding the Suchan coal mines (which provided fuel for the locomotives) east of Vladivostok. In March 1919, by agreement with the other intervening powers, U.S. forces also began occupying a section of the track just east of Lake Baikal, more than 1,000 miles from Khabarovsk. There they remained until spring 1920.

U.S. forces sent to the Baikal area quickly met resistance. A Cossack band headed by Gregori Semënov, abetted by the Japanese, had been marauding that section of the line, looting towns and hijacking trains. Semënov had been able to range freely because he had the largest fleet of armored trains in Siberia. Soon after two battalions of the 27th Infantry, commanded by Col. Charles H. Morrow, took up positions,

Semënov sent word that he would continue to do as he pleased. Morrow disagreed.

The situation reached a climax when Semënov tried to send his most powerful armored train, the Destroyer, through the U.S. sector. Morrow had a cannon set up along the track and informed Semënov that the Destroyer would be fired on if it moved beyond a certain point. The showdown grew more ominous when Japanese forces appeared in support of Semënov. Although his troops were outnumbered five to one, Morrow's obvious intention to carry out his threat impressed the Japanese and Semënov. The Destroyer puffed backward down the line. Fortunately, the consequences of a large-scale firefight between nominal allies can only be guessed.

Despite frequent clashes between Morrow—whom a fellow officer described as a bomb with a lighted fuse—and the Cossacks and Japanese, no large-scale fighting occurred in the Baikal region. There were incidents: a sentry killed, a patrol ambushed, shots fired at a passing train. The troops, many living in boxcars alongside the railway, had to endure searing heat in the summer and sub-zero temperatures in the winter. Everlasting boredom was their worst enemy.

The bloodiest engagement of the intervention occurred near the Suchan mines to the east. There, a large band of partisans mounted a surprise attack on an encampment of about 75 men. The unit would have been annihilated had it not been for the heroic action of a soldier who broke out of the trap, hailed an approaching train, and got reinforcements. Twenty-five men were killed, another 25 wounded in what became known as the "Romanovka massacre."

The political affiliation of the attackers at Romanovka was unknown, which was also true of other skirmishes. Among the men, however, it was assumed they were in Siberia to fight the Bolsheviks. As a popular refrain had it:

"Take me over the sea/ Where the Bolsheviks can't get at me/ Oh my, I don't want to die/ I want to go home."

The Siberian Expeditionary Force went home in spring 1920. Units were pulled back to Vladivostok to avoid being overrun by advancing Bolshevik armies. Evacuation was completed by April. Because some soldiers had established more than casual relationships with Russian women, a chaplain performed about 80 marriage ceremonies. There was little fanfare during the evacuation. Many of those who served in Siberia

regarded themselves as the forgotten men of World War I.

Robert James Maddox

REFERENCES

William S. Graves, *America's Siberian Adventure, 1918–1920* (Cape & Smith, 1931); Robert James Maddox, *The Unknown War with Russia: Wilson's Siberian Intervention* (Presidio Pr., 1977); Betty Miller Unterberger, *America's Siberian Expedition, 1918–1920: A Study of National Policy* (Duke Univ. Pr., 1956); John Albert White, *The Siberian Intervention* (Princeton Univ. Pr., 1950).

See also Emerson, George Henry; Graves, William Sidney; Interallied Relations in the Siberian Intervention; Naval Operations off Siberia (1918–1922); Public Opinion and the Siberian Intervention; Russian Railway Advisory Mission; Russian Railway Service Corps; Stevens, John Frank; Siberian Intervention (1918–1920).

American National Red Cross

An association founded in 1881 to aid the sick and wounded during wartime, the American Red Cross faced the first real test of its mission during the Spanish-Cuban/American War. Under the hands-on direction of its founder and president, Clara Barton, the American Red Cross became a vital national relief organization during the war, while at the same time it discovered some of the limits of, and problems in, coordinating a large-scale relief effort.

American Red Cross involvement in Cuba began shortly before the United States entered the war. On 24 December 1897 President William McKinley issued an appeal for civilian relief donations to aid those affected by the Cuban revolution; shortly after, the State Department asked Barton to set up a special committee to raise and accept contributions for Cuban relief. In early February 1898, Barton, and a staff of about 20 Red Cross workers, traveled to Havana where Barton supervised the distribution of food, clothing, and medicine.

The Red Cross mission withdrew in early April on the advice of the U.S. consul general when war between Spain and the United States seemed imminent. But the relief effort survived and actually expanded when the Red Cross chartered a ship, the *State of Texas*, to sail to Havana with 1,400 tons of food and additional staff. The United States Navy blockade of the coast of Cuba, which began three days before the U.S.

declaration of war against Spain, kept the ship at port in Key West and Tampa, Florida, for two months before it was allowed to sail to Guantánamo. In Cuba, Red Cross workers helped out in a hospital in the town of Siboney and furnished aid to the sick and wounded in the American Reserve Divisional Hospital. They eventually established a special Red Cross fever hospital while also providing supplementary aid to army medical facilities.

One grateful recipient of Red Cross aid was Col. Theodore Roosevelt, commander of the famed "Rough Riders." As the story goes, Roosevelt arrived at Red Cross Headquarters one day in search of supplies for his men. "Can I buy them from the Red Cross?" he asked.

"Not for a million dollars," Clara Barton replied.

"How can I get them?" Roosevelt insisted. "I must have proper food for my sick men."

"Just ask for them, colonel," she said.

The encounter closed with the future president of the United States trudging off into the jungle with a sack of supplies for his men slung over his shoulder.

The Red Cross had trouble coordinating with the Army Medical Corps throughout the war, but the cooperation of the War and Navy departments was secured early on. Shortly after the war broke out, the national society's offer to provide services to the government was accepted on 24 May 1898 when Secretary of State William R. Day announced that President McKinley had requested him to recognize the American Red Cross as "the proper and sole representative in the United States" of the International Red Cross Committee formed at the Geneva Conference in 1864. This long-awaited official recognition was a major step forward for the organization.

Red Cross stateside war relief began soon after the United States declared war on Spain and became one of the major components of its services during the war. The Red Cross national organization sent field agents to every military camp to find out what services were necessary and acceptable to those running the camp.

Materials provided by the American Red Cross included cots, clothes, canned goods, pajamas and night shirts, bed linen, groceries, hospital and camp equipment, and ice. The Red Cross formed rest and relaxation centers for soldiers, and its hospital visiting corps gave the sick and wounded in army camps milk and broth. The American Red Cross was also involved with relief of discharged and furloughed men and helped soldiers establish communication with their relatives.

One of the most significant services initiated by the Red Cross during the war was in providing trained nurses for base hospitals as well as the field hospitals. Some army commanders were initially skeptical of the value of female nurses, in general, and Red Cross nurses in particular. By the end of the war, however, the place of Red Cross nurses in assisting army medical staff was well established, and the stage was set for a future close relationship between the Red Cross and the military.

Congress officially thanked Barton for her work during the war (making her the first woman to receive that honor). McKinley commended the relief effort, and journalists waxed eloquent about the tireless Red Cross nurse—but the work of the Red Cross was not without its problems. Some of them stemmed from the personality of Barton, its leader, who insisted on being on the front lines of the relief effort and often left much of the management of the Red Cross to others during the war. Other problems resulted from the fact that the Red Cross was still defining its precise role in wartime relief and had to formulate through trial and error a division between its duties and those of the Army Medical Corps. Coordination among state and local societies, various relief committees, and the Red Cross national organization also proved difficult throughout the war. Divisions within the organization that had formed during the war increased in the years immediately following and ultimately led to a reorganization of the Red Cross in 1905 under new leadership.

Many of the services later provided by the Red Cross during wartime had their origins in the Spanish-Cuban/American War. Altogether, the group distributed supplies worth about half a million dollars, provided workers to help the soldiers at Army hospitals and camps, and recruited approximately 700 nurses for service in the war. These efforts were dwarfed by Red Cross activities during World Wars I and II, but were on a scale appropriate for a war that lasted only 10 weeks and had just 379 fatal battle casualties.

One other U.S. conflict attracted Red Cross relief before the association saw unprecedented growth during World War I. The Mexican Civil

War, which raged off and on from 1911 to 1920, attracted a mixed and sometimes confused Red Cross response. At issue were the responsibility of the American Red Cross to respond to a conflict carried out along the U.S. border but outside the country itself, and the safety of U.S. volunteers in war-torn Mexico, where both sides showed intermittent hostility toward the United States.

As a result, Red Cross operations in Mexico were neither sustained nor centrally organized. Throughout the conflict, Red Cross chapters along the border provided periodic relief for Mexican civilian refugees and wounded soldiers. The Red Cross also provided transportation money for U.S. citizens trying to leave Mexico and later chartered a steamer for that purpose. In later years, the Red Cross would periodically send food for famine relief, but Mexican leaders often opposed these efforts.

When the U.S. armed forces occupied Veracruz, the American Red Cross finally began a definite program of war relief, although the country was not formally at war with Mexico. For wounded soldiers, the Red Cross supplied nurses, as well as reading material, stationery, medicines and drugs, and ice cream. The organization also worked with military officials in preventing and combating various diseases in the area.

The American Red Cross program in Veracruz ended after four months, and events in Mexico began to be overshadowed by the war in Europe.

Eric R. Emch

REFERENCES

Lavinia Dock and others, *History of American Red Cross Nursing* (Macmillan, 1922); Foster Rhea Dulles, *The American Red Cross: A History* (Harper, 1950); Portia Kernodle, *The Red Cross Nurse in Action, 1882–1948* (Harper, 1949); U.S. Department of the Interior, *Clara Barton*, Handbook 110, National Park Handbook Series (U.S. Department of the Interior, 1981).

See also Barton, Clara, in the Spanish-Cuban/American War; Nurses in the Spanish-Cuban/American War; *State of Texas*.

American-Mexican Joint Commission (1916)

The American-Mexican Joint Commission, created in 1916, was the product of a deteriora- tion in relations between the United States and the Mexican government of Venustiano Carranza following the attack on Columbus, New Mexico, on 9 March 1916 by forces of Carranza's revolutionary rival, Francisco "Pancho" Villa. This attack led the United States to launch the Punitive Expedition into Mexico under the command of Gen. John J. Pershing with the aim of capturing Villa and dispersing his forces so that they would no longer be a threat to the U.S. border region.

With several thousand U.S. troops operating in northern Mexico, the possibility of a clash with forces loyal to Carranza was a major concern. Carranza's troops had originally not opposed the intrusion, but the growing size of the expedition and the expansion of the area of its operations led to formal protests from the Carranza administration and demands for the expedition's withdrawal. The first conflict between forces of the expedition and Carranza's troops occurred at Parral, Chihuahua, on 12 April; the encounter resulted in two U.S. dead and several wounded, with Mexican casualties estimated at 40. A more serious clash between Carranza's forces and Pershing's troops occurred at Carrizal, Chihuahua, on 21 June. Twelve U.S. soldiers were killed, 10 wounded, and 24 taken prisoner; Mexican casualties were at least 74. With war imminent, Carranza and President Woodrow Wilson made a last effort to resolve their differences peacefully by forming a joint commission.

In early July the United States had suggested establishing the commission as one of several approaches to a negotiated settlement. The Carranza administration responded on 12 July by formally recommending the creation of a joint commission, a proposal accepted by the United States on 28 July. Even before the commission convened, however, there was considerable wrangling over what issues would be discussed. Carranza wanted to restrict discussion to the status of the Punitive Expedition and border security; the United States wanted a broad agenda to include virtually any areas of disagreement between the two governments. Carranza forced the issue by announcing that he had already appointed his three commissioners to discuss the withdrawal of the Punitive Expedition and border security. The United States agreed to Carranza's agenda after informal promises that other matters would be discussed.

The joint commission was in trouble even

before its first meeting. The three Mexican commissioners—Luis Cabrera, Alberto J. Pani, and Ignacio Bonillas—all spoke English and were familiar with U.S. politics and customs. The three U.S. commissioners—Secretary of the Interior Franklin K. Lane, attorney George Gray, and prominent missionary John R. Mott—did not speak Spanish and had no special expertise in Mexican affairs. Wilson's choice of commissioners caused speculation that he was not interested in serious negotiation but was simply playing for time in the midst of a presidential campaign. Carranza's instructions to his delegation also limited the commission's hopes for success; he directed his representatives to place primary emphasis on the withdrawal of U.S. troops from Mexico and stressed that all tentative agreements be cleared with him in advance.

The joint commission met from September 1916 to January 1917 at three locations: New London, Connecticut; Atlantic City, New Jersey; and Philadelphia. The fundamental problem that would confront the commission was evident at the first session: the Mexican delegation insisted that an agreement be reached on the withdrawal of U.S. forces and border security before any other matters would be discussed. The U.S. delegation responded by trying to broaden the discussion to include topics ranging from financial claims against the revolutionary government to freedom of religion.

While the United States was willing to assign priority to Mexico's interest in troop withdrawal and border protection, the Wilson administration wanted to tie this to other matters relating to a broad range of topics that Carranza considered the "internal affairs" of Mexico. A series of proposals and counterproposals ensued, all of them undone by the inability of both parties to agree on the scope and priorities of the commission. The final session of the joint commission was held on 15 January 1917. The joint commission ended as it had begun, with the delegates unable to agree, this time on a closing statement; it simply adjourned indefinitely.

While the joint commission produced no agreements after months of negotiations, it had served a useful purpose. Its creation had helped to defuse a dangerous military confrontation that threatened to degenerate into a full-scale war. In June 1916 neither Carranza nor Wilson could afford a war. A war between the United States and Mexico might very well have led to the over-

throw of Carranza. Wilson was in the middle of a presidential campaign keyed to the issue that he had kept the United States out of the European conflict; it would have done him little political good to have avoided a European conflict while becoming embroiled in a Mexican war. Keeping the Punitive Expedition in Mexico while negotiating with Carranza undercut the criticism of Wilson's Mexican policy by Republicans who had chided him for inaction while drawing support from his fellow Democrats, many of whom were uneasy with the ongoing intervention in Mexico. The withdrawal of the Punitive Expedition came quickly even without an agreement by the joint commission. U.S. forces started moving out of Mexico in late January 1917 and completed their withdrawal by 5 February. The United States had unilaterally decided to remove the troops in the face of changing conditions in both Mexico and in Europe. The other issues that the joint commission had attempted to address would take years of negotiations before agreements would be reached.

Don M. Coerver

REFERENCES

Clarence C. Clendenen, *The United States and Pancho Villa* (Cornell Univ. Pr., 1961); Mark T. Gilderhus, *Diplomacy and Revolution: U.S.-Mexican Relations Under Wilson and Carranza* (Univ. of Arizona Pr., 1977); P. Edward Haley, *Revolution and Intervention: The Diplomacy of Taft and Wilson With Mexico, 1910–1917* (MIT Pr., 1970); Linda B. Hall and Don M. Coerver, *Revolution on the Border: The United States and Mexico, 1910–1920* (Univ. of New Mexico Pr., 1988); Arthur S. Link, *Wilson: Campaigns for Progressivism and Peace, 1916–1917* (Princeton Univ. Pr., 1965).

See also Mexican Border Battles and Skirmishes (1911–1921); Obregón, Álvaro; Punitive Expedition, Mexico (1916–1917); Scott, Hugh Lenox.

Antiguerrilla Operations in the Dominican Republic (1917–1922)

Almost from the inception of the occupation of the Dominican Republic in 1916, U.S. forces encountered resistance, ultimately leading to a protracted antiguerrilla campaign in the eastern part of the nation. A region of small towns and rugged terrain containing few roads, these provinces were remote from the rest of the country.

The area was populated mainly by small peasant subsistence farmers. The presence of recently established foreign-owned sugar plantations in this region led to some land concentration, with the displaced peasants becoming seasonal laborers on the sugar estates. This provided many grievances and made the region fertile ground for resistance to foreign presence, much less foreign occupation.

Traditionally in the Dominican Republic, the so-called national government controlled only the capital, with the interior regions divided into a series of fiefdoms each governed by a local *caudillo* (military dictator) who acted independently of the regime in the capital. This system was especially prevalent in the eastern provinces, where the absence of transportation facilities and the resulting isolation provided an ideal setting for the emergence of local loyalties and strongmen. The national government negotiated with the local potentates and was often dependent on their support, rather than exerting any control over them.

When U.S. forces launched the occupation of the Dominican Republic in May 1916, they initially took control only of the capital and the principal cities. The countryside remained beyond the reach of the limited forces involved in the first landings, just as it had traditionally remained autonomous from control by the central governments. Disregarding the complex system of balancing forces which prevailed in the Dominican Republic, U.S. officials immediately set out to establish the full authority of the central government throughout the nation. This involved changing the entire political structure of the country, a fact U.S. authorities failed to appreciate because they saw themselves as bringing order to chaos. Seeking to establish an effective and stable national government, they were not aware of the local traditions and unable to comprehend that all the local citizens might not perceive centralized control by a strong national government in the capital as a benefit. Instead, U.S. representatives installed their version of an efficient government, making no effort to understand the local situation or to consult the local citizens.

It was scarcely surprising that the combination of foreign conquest and the imposition of central control encountered resistance from the citizens and from the beneficiaries of the existing system. While the marines quickly established themselves in the city of San Pedro de Macorís, a "metropolis" of 12,000 which was the center of the sugar export industry, extending control to the numerous remote villages connected only by trails proved far more difficult.

After a brief period of conflict, the initial resistance was stamped out, and a period of calm caused the occupation authorities to conclude that they had successfully suppressed what they considered mere "banditry." New leaders and bands made their presence felt within six months, and the region was torn by almost constant conflict from 1918 to 1922.

The effort to control the region involved a series of campaigns against numerous small guerrilla units, led by up to a dozen distinct leaders, each commanding no more than 600 combatants. Among the principal leaders were Eustacio "Bullito" Reyes and Gen. Ramón Natera. Natera assembled the largest force and used the most sophisticated political tactics. While the combat was small scale, up to 2,500 marines were eventually assigned to the region. The Dominican struggle consequently ranked with the Nicaraguan campaign against Gen. Augusto C. Sandino as one of the largest U.S. military operations in Latin America.

Seeking to assert control, the occupation authorities increased the marine deployment in the eastern provinces from its initial 76 men in 1917, to 250 the same year, to over 1,000 by 1919, and reached 2,500 by 1920. The marines were supplemented by members of the newly formed Guardia Nacional Dominicana. These increases of manpower proved ineffective.

While the marines enjoyed an advantage in weaponry and organization, the guerrillas counted on the support of the local populace and a superior knowledge of the terrain to successfully control the countryside and conduct ambushes. The marines lacked training in tactics suitable for and experience in this type of small-unit combat. Their contempt for the local residents tinged with racist attitudes, their inability to speak the local language, and their lack of understanding of local customs and culture all contributed to alienating the local populace. The resulting sentiments strengthened support for the guerrilla bands. As is often the case in antiguerrilla campaigns, the marines had difficulty distinguishing active combatants from the local populace, frequently firing on all those who fled their approach and assuming that the entire populace in rural areas was part of the enemy. This resulted in the deaths of numerous innocent civilians, including women and children, becoming a self-fulfilling prophecy by enraging the local residents.

During the years of combat, the marines used diverse tactics under a succession of commanders, unsuccessfully seeking a method of dealing with the guerrillas. Initial occupation of the region's principal towns accomplished little. Seeking to emulate the Dominican tactics, the marines requested reinforcements to enable a switch to small patrols. Units of 20 to 30 men set out on daily patrol, in the difficult terrain where only narrow trails pierced the underbrush and at a time when the marines had very few radios and no means of rapid movement or communication. Patrols kept the marines occupied, but resulted in little contact with the guerrillas.

Adopting a new approach, the marines tried the reconcentration policy which had failed the Spanish in Cuba, seeking to separate the populace from the rebels. Campaign Order No. 1, issued in August 1918, ordered the temporary concentration of the populace in towns to enable sweeps in the rural areas. This short-lived effort had little effect on the guerrillas and served mainly to inconvenience and alienate the local citizens. The marines refocused by placing small garrisons in every village, seeking to identify the local populace to enable recognition of outsiders. This too proved ineffective. Even the introduction of a small air squadron failed to pinpoint the guerrilla camps, and its aerial bombardment of suspected guerrilla areas both intimidated and enraged the populace. Large-scale sweeps cordoning off extended sectors resulted in increased arrests of suspected guerrillas. Guerrilla raids continued at night, however, when the marines returned to their barracks. Counter ambush tactics which sought to hold key points where trails crossed proved only slightly more successful in limiting guerrilla movement.

The guerrillas clearly sought to minimize contact with the marines and remained able to hide, save for brief ambush fusillades, by simply fading into the brush. Indeed, the period 1917–1919 produced only 100 contacts with guerrillas, resulting in six marines being killed and 18 wounded. The guerrillas effectively controlled the interior and even many of the towns at night, conducting raids to secure supplies and to collect "contributions."

The various guerrilla leaders contended that they were revolutionaries fighting against foreign occupation of their nation, although they had no contact with the nationalist groups in the capital. In actuality, these chieftains were fighting as much to preserve their fiefdoms and their influence in the national political system as to resist a foreign occupation. The United States insisted that the disturbances were caused by lawless "bandits" and even alleged that the discontent was provoked by German propaganda seeking to distract the United States from World War I.

The situation changed only in September 1921, when guerrillas loyal to General Natera kidnapped Thomas J. Steele, a British sugar estate manager, producing a furor in the capital, the United States, and Great Britain. After holding Steele for a few days, the rebels released him on the condition that he and the other estate managers in the region communicate to the occupation authorities in the capital and to their home governments the guerrilla determination to continue fighting until the foreign invaders withdrew from their nation. This statement caused the U.S. occupation authorities to reassess their view of the guerrillas and contributed to the decision to seek a negotiated political solution rather than one imposed by military force.

During spring 1922, an amnesty program was announced, guaranteeing parole after trial to all rebels who surrendered, launching a new stage. At this same time the newly formed civil guards in the local towns enabled the marines to increase pressure on the rebels, while negotiations proceeded at the national level in the capital. Reflecting these developments, guerrilla groups surrendered throughout the spring, with military activity effectively ending by May 1922. By September 1922, the marines were concentrated in a few cities, as one of the preliminary steps under the newly announced withdrawal agreement. Control of the interior was turned over to the Guardia Nacional.

The U.S. military operations not only illustrated many of the problems of conducting an antiguerrilla campaign and of the attitudes of U.S. personnel, but also changed the Dominican Republic. After the withdrawal and the surrender of the rebel leaders, the eastern provinces came under effective control of the national government for the first time in Dominican history.

Kenneth J. Grieb

REFERENCES

Bruce J. Calder, *The Impact of Intervention: The Dominican Republic during the U.S. Occupation of 1916–1924* (Univ. of Texas Pr., 1984); Lester D. Langley, *The Banana Wars: An Inner History of the American Empire, 1900–1934* (Univ. of Kentucky Pr., 1983).

Anti-Imperialism

In the context of the late 19th-century history of the United States, anti-imperialism relates to the mass movement stimulated by the Anti-Imperialist League and to the political outlook that accompanied this movement, which developed primarily as a result of the U.S. acquisition of the Philippines.

The founders of the Anti-Imperialist League realized that to be effective they would have to enlist elements in the population beyond their urban middle-class base, and they sought to establish a broad, many-sided coalition. As a result, labor leader Samuel Gompers and the American Federation of Labor, farm editor Herbert Myrick, and the National Grange endorsed anti-imperialism in 1898. Many blacks expressed anti-imperialist views in their churches and newspapers, and in 1901 Reverend William H. Scott, a Boston black, became an anti-imperialist league vice president. German-Americans and Irish-Americans were strong supporters of the anti-imperialist movement and were represented in the league leadership by Carl Schurz of New York and Patrick A. Collins of Boston, both outstanding figures in their ethnic groups. Catholic, Protestant, and Jewish leaders lent their voices to the cause. Mark Twain, William Dean Howells, William James, and other literary and intellectual figures spoke out. Women participated (Jane Addams, a noted social worker, was active in Chicago, for instance), but were not brought into the organized leadership.

The political effect of this varied coalition was to be seen chiefly in its influence with Democratic members of Congress and with the Democratic presidential candidate of 1900, William Jennings Bryan, who championed anti-imperialism. While the Republican party as a whole identified with imperialism, a few Republican legislators, such as Senators George F. Hoar of Massachusetts and Richard F. Pettigrew of South Dakota, opposed imperialist policy. Conversely, several Democratic legislators supported imperialism.

The Anti-Imperialist League and the coalition it inspired engaged in four major campaigns from 1898 to 1902: (1) opposition to the treaty to annex the Philippines as well as (2) to the Philippine War, (3) the elections of 1900, and (4) protest against the conduct of the U.S. military in the Philippines.

In December 1898 the anti-imperialist movement engaged in a full-scale effort to prevent passage by the United States Senate of the treaty to annex the Philippines through petitions to the United States Senate and other forms of lobbying. The labor movement and farm organizations came out against the treaty, as did many prominent public figures.

There were heavy counterpressures by the administration of President William McKinley and the business and financial community, by Bryan's defection from antitreaty ranks, and by the start of the war with the Philippines. As a result, the Senate passed the treaty, but only by one vote, and a leading imperialist, Senator Henry Cabot Lodge of Massachusetts, complained that it was "the closest, hardest fight I have known" (Tompkins, p. 194).

Directly following treaty passage, the Anti-Imperialist League called for an end to the war on the basis of Philippine independence, and the movement propagated this demand nationwide.

Anti-imperialist agitation against the war influenced public opinion and so had some effect on government policy. Of the 30,000 U.S. troops first in the Philippines, 12,000 had volunteered to fight Spain, and Washington expected them to reenlist to fight the Filipinos. The families of these troops, however, particularly in the South and West, called for their return home, and volunteers, too, made this demand. Local newspapers took up the issue, as did the California Senate and the governors of Minnesota and South Dakota. As a result, in April 1899, the McKinley administration announced that the volunteers would be withdrawn and replaced by 14,000 other troops.

In 1900 the anti-imperialists' antiwar agitation merged with their participation in the presidential election of that year. On direct urging of anti-imperialist leaders and as the price for their support, Bryan, the Democratic presidential candidate, having recovered from his treaty deviation, declared imperialism the "paramount" issue of the campaign and spoke against the war (Foner and Winchester, Vol. 1, pp. 426, 439).

The election campaign of 1900 was the high point in the influence of the anti-imperialist movement, bringing its message to millions of voters. When the tally was made, however, McKinley had a popular vote of 7,263,543; Bryan had 6,360,796. Bryan thought that the main reason for his defeat was the country's return to prosperity after years of depression, not the imperialism issue.

After their defeats in the treaty fight and the elections of 1900, the anti-imperialist movement rallied for one more effort.

Following its election victory, the McKinley administration pressed the army in the field for what the general in charge, Arthur MacArthur, described as "very drastic" methods (Schirmer, p. 227). The U.S. press began to print reports of torture, "reconcentration" of rural population, scorched earth policy, and indiscriminate killing of civilians. Responding to all this, Boston leaders rallied those in New York and Chicago to demand a Senate investigation of the conduct of the United States Army in the Philippines.

The campaign the anti-imperialists engendered caused such public and congressional outcry that, in April 1902, the Republicans in the Senate agreed to an investigation, taking care to place it in charge of Senator Lodge. Lodge first presented the committee with witnesses to defend the army. Then, the anti-imperialists offered U.S. soldiers who testified to military atrocities they had seen in the Philippines.

President Theodore Roosevelt felt compelled to court-martial one of the worst military offenders, Gen. Jacob H. "Howling Jake" Smith. The general was given a light sentence, and Lodge closed the investigation in June.

What ideas motivated the anti-imperialist movement in all these campaigns? The movement generally supported the program of the Anti-Imperialist League. Bryan in 1900, for example, denounced colonial policy as the subversion of U.S. democratic ideals by commercial interests and opposed what he called the "war of conquest" (Foner and Winchester, vol. 1, pp. 438–439).

In addition, the varied elements in the coalition brought their own viewpoints to the movement. The German-Americans and the Irish-Americans identified U.S. imperialism with Prussian militarism and British rule in Ireland, respectively. Farmers feared the competition of colonial agricultural goods, and labor, the competition of cheap colonial labor. These views can be seen as complementary to those of the Boston anti-imperialists.

There were, however, other political tendencies in the anti-imperialist coalition that were contradictory to those of the Boston leaders. The Bostonians opposed indirect as well as direct, or colonial, forms of imperialism, while many others in the movement opposed the latter only. Thus, Washington's apparent rejection of formal empire in 1902 had a deleterious effect on the movement, splitting its heart and core, the Anti-Imperialist League itself.

Moreover, the Boston leadership, like the black anti-imperialists, condemned imperial policy as a racist policy. Other elements in the anti-imperialist coalition, especially among Southern Democrats, opposed U.S. colonial rule in the Philippines for racist reasons. They did not want the U.S. government to have anything to do with the Filipinos, whom they considered an inferior colored race.

Of all those in the anti-imperialist coalition, the Boston anti-imperialists stood out in their opposition to racism and diverse forms of imperialism. Perhaps it was these qualities that made them both the initiators and most persistent exponents of anti-imperialism at the time of the Philippine War.

Daniel B. Schirmer

REFERENCES

Robert L. Beisner, *Twelve Against Empire, The Anti-Imperialists, 1899–1900* (McGraw-Hill, 1968; rpt. Univ. of Chicago Pr., 1985); Philip S. Foner and Richard C. Winchester, eds., *The Anti-Imperialist Reader, A Documentary History of Anti-Imperialism in the United States* (Holmes & Meier, 1984), Vol. 1; Daniel B. Schirmer, *Republic or Empire, American Resistance to the Philippine War* (Schenkman Bks., 1972; rpt. 1990); E. Berkeley Tompkins, *Anti-Imperialism in the United States: The Great Debate, 1890–1920* (Univ. of Pennsylvania Pr., 1970); Richard E. Welch, *Response to Imperialism, The United States and the Philippine-American War* (Univ. of North Carolina Pr., 1979; rpt. 1987).

See also Anti-Imperialist League; Public Opinion and the Philippine War.

Anti-Imperialist League

In November 1898, three months after the U.S. victory over the Spanish land forces at Manila in the Philippines, some prominent Boston professional men and reformers met to oppose what they saw as preparations by the administration of President William McKinley to conquer and colonize the Philippines, Spain's former possession. To this end they formed a society called the Anti-Imperialist League.

Earlier in the 19th century Boston had been a center of the antislavery movement, in which many of the anti-imperialist organizers had been active. Boston anti-imperialists included men with pasts like Moorfield Storey, personal secretary to the abolitionist Senator Charles Sumner; Thomas Wentworth Higginson, a white officer in a black regiment, and Franklin B. Sanborn, an associate of John Brown. Men such as these saw Washington's attempt to colonize the Filipinos, a colored people of Asia, as a betrayal of principles they had worked to establish. All this may help explain the initial crystallization of U.S. anti-imperialist sentiment in Boston.

Its organizers announced the league's aims in "An Address to the People of the United States." This document took a stand against colonial policy, declaring that true republican principles rested on consent of the governed. It declared a "new imperialism" sought to set "the law of might and commercial gain" above the standards of the Republic and warned of foreign complications and ensuing neglect of pressing domestic social problems (Tompkins, p. 129).

Then, the Bostonians set about stimulating the growth of this organization nationwide: issuing voluminous printed matter, corresponding with and visiting residents of other cities, and appointing many prominent and like-minded men as vice presidents.

There was a rapid growth of the membership. In July 1899, the Boston office reported 40,000 members, and by November there were a hundred or more "active centers of anti-imperialist work," with the largest organizations in New York, Chicago, Philadelphia, Washington, D.C., Cincinnati, Portland (Oregon), Los Angeles, and Minneapolis (Schirmer, p. 175; Tompkins, p. 130).

In 1900 the Democratic presidential candidate, William Jennings Bryan, who espoused anti-imperialism, lost to the incumbent William McKinley. Shortly after, the U.S. military began finally to subdue nationalist resistance in the Philippines.

Moreover, closely following these events, the U.S. government showed signs of turning away from a policy of formal empire toward an empire of an informal sort (what is now often called neo-colonialism). Thus, in 1902 Washington granted independence to Cuba (another former Spanish colony), under the restrictions of the Platt Amendment.

The Boston chapter of the Anti-Imperialist League opposed this new policy as imperialism in another guise. Much of the membership, led by New York and Chicago, gave assent, however, and the national organization dissolved.

This left the Boston Anti-Imperialist League standing alone. It continued to speak for Philippine independence until its demise in 1920.

Daniel B. Schirmer

REFERENCES

E. Berkeley Tompkins, *Anti-Imperialism in the United States: The Great Debate, 1890–1920* (Univ. of Pennsylvania Pr., 1970); Daniel B. Schirmer, *Republic or Empire, American Resistance to the Philippine War* (Schenkman Publishing Co., 1972); Thompkins, *Anti-Imperialism in the United States*; Maria Carpio Lanzar, "The Anti-Imperialist League," *Philippine Social Science Review*, 3(1) (Aug. 1930), 7–41; 3(2) (Nov. 1930), 118–198; 4(3) (July 1932), 182–198; 4(4) (Oct. 1932), 239–254; 5(3) (July 1933), 222–230; 5(5) (Oct. 1933), 248–279.

See also Anti-Imperialism; Public Opinion and the Philippine War.

Apache Scouts in the Punitive Expedition

After forces of Francisco "Pancho" Villa attacked Columbus, New Mexico, on 9 March 1916, the United States sent a punitive expedition under the command of Gen. John J. Pershing into Mexico to capture the Mexican revolutionary. Because of the Punitive Expedition's inability to track Villista forces in the unmapped desert and mountain terrain of Chihuahua, Mexico, Gen. Frederick Funston, commander of the Southern Military Department, approved the enlistment of Company A Apache Scouts for border service. On 6 April 1916, the 20 Native Americans reached Columbus, New Mexico, by train and awaited the arrival of their horses and equipment from Fort Apache, Arizona. There, they also met the new commander, Lt. James A. Shannon of the 11th Cavalry, a respected veteran of Philippine service, but a man devoid of any knowledge of Native Americans. Shannon initially underestimated the reliability of his charges because of their aversion to rigid discipline. After assuming reconnaissance duties around the base camp at San Antonio de los Arenales, Chihuahua, however, the Apaches proved their courage, hardiness, and unmatched tracking abilities.

On 5 May 1916, the scouts joined six troops of the 11th Cavalry and a machine gun troop to attack Villista forces at Ojos Azules Ranch. Despite the rather chaotic execution of the attack, total victory was achieved within a half hour. The Apache scouts were praised for their significant role in the battle, which netted 61 Villistas killed and 70 captured, all accomplished without U.S. casualties. The scouts participated in one additional minor skirmish at Las Varas Pass on 1 June, and spent the rest of their service conducting routine reconnaissance missions, tracking down absent or deserting soldiers, and supplementing the soldiers' diet with wild game.

The Mexican government's allegations that these Indians had committed atrocities against civilians and captive soldiers were never proven, but strongly suspected by some of the U.S. officers. Company A was among the last units pulled out of Mexico during early February 1917, and General Pershing honored these men before returning the unit to Fort Apache, where it remained in service until 1947.

Michael L. Tate

REFERENCES

James A. Shannon, "With the Apache Scouts in Mexico," *Journal of the United States Cavalry Association*, 27 (1917), 539–557; Michael L. Tate, "'Pershing's Pets': Apache Scouts in the Mexican Punitive Expedition of 1916," *New Mexico Historical Review*, 66 (1991), 49–71; Harry Aubrey Toulmin, Jr., *With Pershing in Mexico* (Military Service Pub. Co., 1935); H. B. Wharfield, *With Scouts and Cavalry at Fort Apache* (Pioneers' Historical Society, 1965); S. M. Williams, "The Cavalry Fight at Ojos Azules," *Journal of the United States Cavalry Association*, 27 (1917), 405–408.

Army of Cuban Pacification

The United States Army General Staff received warning from the War Department on 25 September 1906 that an expeditionary force would soon be needed for a military action in Cuba. While the White House, the War Department, and the State Department labored fruitlessly to secure a negotiated settlement between the weakened government of Tomás Estrada Palma and the Liberal insurgents who opposed him, the United States Army began its preparations to transport thousands of soldiers to the island. When diplomatic efforts collapsed, the United States on 29 September 1906 officially intervened under the Platt Amendment to prevent anarchy from overtaking the island and to protect North American economic interests.

The Liberals' hostility toward the government began in September 1905 when Estrada Palma's Moderate party rigged the presidential and congressional elections to ensure victory over the opposition. Frustrated with the blatant political fraud committed by the president's administration, the Liberals fomented a revolt in August 1906 in hopes of provoking a U.S. intervention that would lead to a negotiated settlement favorable to the Liberals.

Ironically, Estrada Palma also wanted U.S. intervention. Unable to suppress the rebellion with his weak Guardia Rural (Rural Guard), Estrada Palma requested urgent military assistance from Washington. President Theodore Roosevelt, reluctant to respond militarily, sent a diplomatic mission led by Secretary of War William H. Taft and Assistant Secretary of State Robert Bacon. Ultimately, Estrada Palma, confident that the United States would intervene to uphold his corrupt government, refused to negotiate seriously with the Liberals. When the Cuban president finally realized that U.S. military support was not immediately forthcoming, he resigned from the presidency on 28 September 1906.

The next day, the United States seized political control of Cuba, naming Taft provisional governor. A provisional marine brigade, led by Col. Littleton W. T. Waller, was ordered ashore to patrol the island until the army arrived. At the first sight of U.S. soldiers, the Liberals, pleased with their success, laid down their weapons and cooperated with efforts to end hostilities. Under the supervision of Gen. Frederick

Funston, the rebels were quickly disarmed and dispersed.

The first U.S. troops arrived on 6 October 1906 on board the army transport *Sumner* to join the aptly named "Army of Cuban Intervention." On 15 October Provisional Governor Taft renamed the expedition the "Army of Cuban Pacification," opting for a more euphemistic title.

Deployment of U.S. troops was complete by late October 1906. Minor disruptions of the peace were handled by the Cuban Guardia Rural. Although original plans for the expedition called for a force of 18,000 men, troop strength in Cuba never exceeded 425 officers and 6,196 enlisted men. The Army of Cuban Pacification served as a strong "moral" presence on the island to encourage stability and obedience to the provisional government. The U.S. objectives were to keep the peace, hold free elections, and withdraw as soon as possible. The commanding officers, many of whom had previously served in the Philippines, emphasized the immense importance of exemplary behavior and strict discipline to their soldiers. With very few exceptions, the men of the Army of Cuban Pacification avoided serious misconduct. The army's most persistent enemy, in fact, seemed to be gonorrhea, which afflicted over 10 percent of the U.S. troops during the occupation.

The army spread across the island into 27 outposts, including the central headquarters at Camp Columbia, west of Havana. The Cuban treasury funded the construction and maintenance of the troops' quarters. The placement of the army garrisons left no doubt about U.S. priorities in Cuba. The highest concentration of outposts was in the sugar-rich province of Santa Clara. The troops were strategically located to protect North American-owned sugar *centrales* and to secure the railways, roads, and shipping lanes used to transport the valuable crop. Even in the large province of Camagüey, where only three U.S. garrisons were stationed, two were located at Ciego de Avila, where the North American-owned Stuart Sugar Company held properties.

Although most of the U.S. soldiers were stationed near population centers, the army occupied the rural areas of Cuba as well. Rural commanders used practice marches through the countryside to remind the Cubans of the powerful U.S. military presence. Soldiers also kept active by participating in the provisional

government's road-construction operations, building 92 kilometers of new roads in various locations throughout the island.

Very early in the occupation the Military Information Division was created to perform a wide variety of reconnaissance missions. The United States wanted to create a reliable intelligence network to prevent future uprisings. Comprehensive lists were amassed with the names of participants in the 1906 revolt. The army also gathered detailed photographic intelligence on every strategic railroad bridge and waterway in Cuba. Extraordinarily accurate maps and topographical surveys of Cuba were drafted by the army's Corp of Engineers to assure that the United States would be prepared if future military intervention became necessary. Since U.S. reconnaissance efforts were widely known throughout the island, the intelligence was also valuable as a deterrent to prospective insurgents who understood that the United States knew the Cuban terrain at least as well as they did.

Officers of the Army of Cuban Pacification were also extremely influential in the U.S. effort to strengthen and restructure the Cuban Guardia Rural. Acting as advisors, U.S. military experts recommended ways to enhance the effectiveness of the Guardia. Military training schools were set up in Havana and elsewhere to improve the skills, discipline, and morale of the soldiers. The advisors also sought to depoliticize the promotion and selection processes of the Guardia. By the end of the occupation, however, much of the army's effort to transform the Guardia Rural into a formidable military force had proved unsuccessful because of a political decision to create a stronger, permanent Cuban army. Members of the Moderate party and U.S. Army officers often warned that a permanent Cuban army would become a political instrument of the Liberals. Proponents of the new force argued that only a strong military presence would assure economic and financial stability in Cuba. Preferring to err on the side of law and order, U.S. politicians opted for a permanent Cuban army that would protect North American interests on the island.

By 1908, Provisional Governor Charles E. Magoon was confident that the country was stable enough for peaceful elections. He announced that regional and general elections would be held on 25 May 1908 and 14 November 1908. The elections, supervised by the Army of Cuban Pacification, proceeded without incident. Victorious Liberal presidential candidate José Miguel Goméz was inducted into office on 28 January 1909 as Magoon officially transferred power to the Cuban government. As if to reinforce U.S. faith in the Cubans' ability to rule themselves, Magoon set sail for the United States that afternoon aboard the new battleship *Maine*.

Some detachments of the Army of Cuban Pacification also left Cuba in January, but the bulk of the forces stayed behind to assure that nothing impeded the peaceful transition to Cuban rule. On 31 March 1909, amidst great ceremony, the U.S. flag was lowered from the flagstaff at Camp Columbia and replaced by the Cuban flag. The next day, the last of the U.S. troops evacuated the island, signaling the end of the military occupation.

The Army of Cuban Pacification received much praise from both the Cuban and North American press for its dedicated professional service because the military occupation was largely uneventful. No fighting occurred between U.S. and Cuban soldiers and no significant reforms were enacted by the United States Army. Unfortunately, no long-term policy objectives were met by the military presence. The only lasting change was the strengthening of the Cuban army, which foreshadowed the menacing growth of the military that culminated in the 1930s in the dictatorship of Fulgencio Batista y Zaldívar. The troops were sent to Cuba to protect U.S. economic investments and secure hegemony over an island whose political sovereignty had already been rendered meaningless by persistent U.S. involvement in Cuba's internal affairs. Once their limited objective had been met, the army withdrew from the island.

Anthony R. Pisani, Jr.
Allen Wells

REFERENCES

Allan R. Millett, *The Politics of Intervention: The Military Occupation of Cuba, 1906–1909* (Ohio State Univ. Pr., 1968); Louis A. Pérez, Jr., *Army Politics in Cuba, 1898–1958* (Univ. of Pittsburgh Pr., 1976); "Report of the Army of Cuban Pacification," in U.S. Department of War *Annual Reports, 1908–1909* (U.S. Government Printing Office, 1909), Vol. 3, pp. 229–270.

See also Bell, James Franklin; Cuba, Intervention (1906–1909).

Asiatic Squadron, United States Navy (1898)

The United States Navy's Asiatic Squadron emerged from the Spanish-Cuban/American War as the nucleus of naval power used in building a fleet to support the developing imperialistic designs of the United States. When Commodore George Dewey arrived in Japan early in January 1898, he assumed command of the remnants of a meager fleet used for years to show the flag in the Far East. On the day Dewey raised his flag aboard the *Olympia* (protected cruiser, 5,870 tons), the small fleet included only one other protected cruiser (*Boston*, 3,000 tons), one gunboat (*Petrel*, 892 tons) and an obsolete paddle-wheeler from the Civil War period (*Monocacy*, 1,370 tons). In February the *Raleigh* (protected cruiser, 3,213 tons) arrived from Europe, augmenting the fleet's cruiser strength significantly.

Dewey set to work at once to ready his fleet, believing that war was imminent. He moved his command to Hong Kong where the fleet could operate best against a Philippine target. Upon arrival in Hong Kong Dewey purchased two support vessels, the *Zafiro* (collier, 1,062 tons) and the *Nanshan* (steamer, 4,827 tons), to increase his logistical resources. By 23 April the *Baltimore* (protected cruiser, 4,413 tons), *Concord* (gunboat, 1,710 tons), and *McCulloch* (revenue cutter, 1,432 tons) arrived at Hong Kong, delivering desperately-needed ammunition and other supplies and bringing the flotilla to 10 ships. Leaving the aged *Monocacy* behind, the Asiatic Squadron steamed for the Philippines on 27 April. Approaching Manila Bay Dewey ordered the *Nanshan* and the *Zafiro* out of harm's way. In the ensuing battle near Cavite, the modest U.S. fleet destroyed the antiquated Spanish flotilla. The battle proved to be a turning point in the growth of the United States' world-power status.

In the years that followed the Spanish-Cuban/American War, the Asiatic Squadron grew rapidly as the demands of empire placed heavy burdens upon the fleet, first to secure the Philippines and later to protect the United States' position in Asia.

Vernon L. Williams

REFERENCES

Vernon L. Williams, "George Dewey: Admiral of the Navy," in James C. Bradford, ed., *Admirals of the*

New Steel Navy: Makers of the American Naval Traditions, 1880–1930 (U.S. Naval Institute Pr., 1990); Vernon L. Williams, "The U.S. Navy in the Philippine Insurrection and Subsequent Native Unrest 1898–1906," Ph.D. diss., Texas A&M Univ., 1985.

Atrocities in the Philippine War

Characteristic of guerrilla warfare, atrocities were committed by both sides in the Philippine War. A sense of innocence in the United States at this time made it extraordinarily difficult to come to grips with this reality. Indeed, a few U.S. historians even today attempt to deny that U.S. soldiers committed many atrocities against the Filipinos. Like them, pro-imperialist editors and spokesmen, who were mostly, but not all, Republicans at the turn of the century, initially denied this reality as anti-imperialist, largely Democratic, propaganda. By 1902, this tactic was virtually impossible in the face of overwhelming contradictory evidence from the testimony of veterans and from some painfully revealing court-martials of U.S. officers for such offenses, along with some damaging documents thought to be safely secured in the United States War Department that were leaked to the press. Imperialists then switched tactics, arguing that U.S. atrocities were rare compared with all those committed against Americans by the Filipinos. In declaring the war to be over on 4 July 1902, President Theodore Roosevelt expressed regret that "a few acts of cruelty" were carried out by U.S. troops to retaliate for "the hundreds committed by Filipinos against American soldiers" (Miller, p. 250). No doubt, Filipino atrocities were far more numerous, particularly if one adds those committed against their own people suspected of collaborating with U.S. forces. There were many more than just "a few" committed by U.S. soldiers, however, often against innocent civilians, certainly too many for a nation whose president claimed, as Roosevelt did, that it had fought the "most glorious war in American history for the triumph of civilization over the black chaos of savagery and barbarism" (Miller, p. 250).

U.S. atrocities were carried out even before the guerrilla phase of this war began at the end of 1899. The first news of these reached the United States in private letters sent home by soldiers because these letters were not rigidly censored as were the correspondents' stories transmitted via the cable terminal at Manila. As long as these private reports reached only small, localized audiences, the War Department was little concerned. Increasingly, however, such letters fell into the hands of anti-imperialist editors, who would publish them locally. They were then reprinted by other editors critical of the war, thereby reaching a national audience. Thus, citizens in one city or town after another read in the local newspaper horrifying testimonials from soldiers sometimes complaining about the conduct of their comrades, but more often bragging about their own lawless conduct, or that of others. One soldier called his letter "a report on the nigger fighting business" (Miller, p. 88):

> Last night one of our boys was found shot with his stomach cut open. Immediately orders were received from General [Loyd] Wheaton to burn the town and kill every native in sight; which was done to a finish. About 1,000 men, women and children were reported killed. I am probably growing hard-hearted, for I am in my glory when I can sight my gun on some dark skin and pull the trigger.

Executing prisoners and wounded was described in a number of such letters. Because "a Filipino is so treacherous 'even' when badly wounded, he has to be killed." Another soldier wrote (Miller p. 189):

> The old boys will say that no cruelty is too severe for these brainless monkeys, who can appreciate no sense of honor, kindness or justice . . . . With an enemy like this to fight, it is not surprising that the boys should adopt "No quarter" as a motto, and fill the blacks full of lead before finding out whether they are friends or enemies.

Other soldiers described widespread looting and the senseless destruction of property. Capt. Albert Otis boasted that he "had enough plunder for a family of six. The house I had at Santa Ana had five pianos. I couldn't take them, so I put a big grand piano out of a second story window. You can guess its finish" (Miller, p. 188). One Iowa volunteer expressed shock over such conduct: "You have no idea what a mania for destruction the average man has when the fear of the law is removed. I have seen them . . . knock chandeliers and plate glass mirrors to pieces just because they could not carry them. It is such a pity" (Miller, p. 187).

Once such letters were made public, the secretary of war had no choice but to order U.S. Commander Gen. Elwell S. Otis (no relation to

Captain Otis) to conduct an investigation. Otis's idea of an inquiry was to send a copy of the offending letter to the writer's commanding officer, who had little trouble wringing a retraction from him. It was just "a tall tale" written to thrill some "maiden aunt in Wichita," or some such excuse. This allowed imperialist editors to crow that "another atrocity fable failed the test of time." Their anti-imperialist counterparts rejected the coverup, insisting that "the real current history of the far war is being published all over Iowa, Kansas, Nebraska, and Minnesota" (Miller, p. 90).

One Kansas volunteer, Pvt. Charles N. Brenner, refused to play Otis's game, insisting that his regiment had been ordered to shoot prisoners, as he had reported to his parents. This forced Otis to order Gen. Arthur MacArthur to investigate. Brenner confronted that general's advocate general, Maj. John S. Mallory, with Pvt. William H. Putnam, who confessed to shooting two prisoners under orders. Mallory collected corroborative affidavits from several officers and enlisted men. Pvt. Harris O. Husky swore under oath that he witnessed Maj. Wilder S. Metcalf shoot a prisoner on his knees begging for mercy. MacArthur forwarded Mallory's report to Otis, who, amazingly, ordered Brenner court-martialed "for writing and conniving at the publication of an article which brought about this investigation" (Miller, p. 89). When his own judge advocate warned of the implications of following through with a trial, Otis let the matter drop, although it did not die. Once the regiment disbanded, veterans, including five officers, renewed the charges, and their commander, Col. Frederick Funston, later foolishly incriminated himself by bragging publicly about all the prisoners he had summarily executed.

Many letters of soldiers that were never publicized at the time survive in archives today, attesting to more atrocities. Perhaps one of the most valuable collections is a typescript copy of the many letters written by a regular officer, Capt. Matthew A. Batson, to his wife. He was initially rather sympathetic to the Filipinos and protested the widespread abuses and lawless conduct of U.S. troops. Much later, as commander of the Macabebe scouts, however, Major Batson did a complete reversal and bragged about ordering similar tactics for his native soldiers. Early in the war, he had protested privately to his wife about the army's senseless destruction of a beau-tiful and peaceful town in Pampanga Province; he expressed shock that soldiers looted extensively. "We come here as a Christian people to relieve them [the Filipinos] from the Spanish yoke and bear ourselves like barbarians" (Miller, p. 183). One reason these complaints did not reach the public eye at the time was that Batson warned his wife not to share them with anyone.

Random atrocities occur in every war, but they may have been more widespread in this conflict due to the army's extremely rapid expansion, which spread experienced junior and noncommissioned officers too thinly. Nevertheless, there is also evidence that senior officers ordered tactics inconsistent with most concepts of civilized warfare. Gen. Robert P. Hughes conceded as much before a Senate investigating committee, but argued that it could not have been otherwise because the Filipinos were not "civilized." Besides Generals Wheaton and Funston, already mentioned, along with Hughes, who literally left the island of Panay in flames, Gen. Jacob H. Smith was court-martialed for savage orders to pacify Samar. Smith ordered the marines serving with him "to kill and burn"; to "make Samar a howling wilderness"; to kill all males aged 10 and up found outside the coastal settlements, although the marine commander, Maj. Littleton W. T. Waller, refused to take such orders literally and told his officers that they were not to make war on women and children. Anti-imperialist propaganda made the Samar episode much more draconian than it actually was, choosing to confuse Smith's orders with what actually occurred on that island.

Gen. J. Franklin Bell should have been court-martialed for his brutal campaign in Batangas. Bell's orders for Batangas were not as bizarre as Smith's for Samar, but in some ways they were much more sinister and came closer to matching what actually occurred in the pacification of that province. He gave his officers "the right of retaliation," ordering whole towns to "be destroyed by fire as a measure of retaliation" for "treachery," singling out in particular the "wealthy and influential classes" as "a guilty class," directly "responsible" for the war. Punishing one man "of wealth and standing" is "of greater importance and will exercise greater influence than the punishment of a hundred ignorant hombres for whose suffering no principale cares a straw," he declared (Miller, p. 208). Even more shocking, Bell directed his station commanders "to execute a prisoner of war" for every assassination committed by guerrillas. "This prisoner of war will be selected by lot from among officers or prominent citizens held as prisoners of war, and will be chosen when practicable from those who belong to the town where the murder or assassination occurred," he stated (Miller, p. 207). Authorization for this extreme measure had to be made by "a superior officer," but because station commanders were often lieutenants, and sometimes sergeants, a junior officer could have provided such authorization. Indeed, in these same orders, Bell cautioned his senior commanders against restraining younger subordinate officers, who were much more likely to commit atrocities than they were.

No one knows whether this particularly draconian written order of Bell's to engage in retaliatory murder was ever carried out in Batangas: probably not, but nevertheless, it is a tactic associated only with the Nazi SS and terrorists in this century. Bell mentions no such retaliatory murder in his final report dated 1 July 1902, but then he does not mention any retaliatory burning either, which is well documented elsewhere. Maj. Cornelius Gardener, governor of neighboring Tayabas Province, publicized Bell's "extensive burning of barrios" in Batangas.

Bell's overall policy was to concentrate the population in designated centers outside of which a scorched earth would deny support to guerrillas. Bell also refused in his final report to discuss those concentration camps, in which more than 11,000 died, because they had become too controversial in the press, he declared. Given the climate of opinion in the United States at the time of his final report, Bell was not so foolish as to incriminate himself. Already headlines were comparing him to Lord Herbert H. Kitchener in South Africa and to the infamous "Butcher" Weyler (Valeriano Weyler y Nicolau) in Cuba, while editors were demanding that he and others follow General Smith to the dock, in a civilian court this time.

The year 1902 opened with an investigation of the conduct of the war by Senator Henry Cabot Lodge's Committee on the Philippines. For the first two months Lodge called only "safe" witnesses, such as Adm. George Dewey, Generals Otis, MacArthur, and Hughes, along with Governor William H. Taft. Sometimes even they made damaging concessions, such as when Taft conceded that the "water cure" was used to ex-

tract information from suspects. The victim was placed on his back and forced to drink huge amounts of water, sometimes salted, until he talked. In reality, it was a pretty mild form of torture picked up from the Spanish. None died from it or suffered any long-term consequences, but anti-imperialist propaganda made it infinitely worse in the public mind; so Taft was not wise in admitting this. The critics on Lodge's committee finally forced him to call lower ranking veterans of the war to the stand, many of them the letter writers who were once forced to recant their observations while on active duty.

Over the next weeks the public was treated to very painful daily litanies on U.S. atrocities. Former Corp. Richard T. O'Brien, for example, described the senseless destruction of a peaceful village ordered by former Capt. Fred McDonald, who spared no one save a beautiful mestizo mother whom he and his fellow officers repeatedly raped, before turning her over to the men for their pleasure. Lodge desperately summoned more friendly veterans, including McDonald, who denied O'Brien's charges, which Lodge could then immediately dismiss as "hearsay." Sometimes this, too, backfired, when a carefully selected veteran, like former Sgt. Mark H. Evans, testified that extermination of the natives was the only solution; he had to be hustled off the stand. To end on a better note for the administration, Lodge recalled Dewey, Otis, MacArthur, and Taft before abruptly ending the hearings in June over the protests of the anti-imperialists.

At one point, Secretary of War Elihu Root, in an attempt to mitigate the growing evidence of atrocities, rushed into print a document to demonstrate that in those allegedly "rare instances" when U.S. atrocities were committed the perpetrators were swiftly punished. He listed 44 specific crimes committed by U.S. soldiers, along with the punishments meted out. The latter were so ludicrously light that they soon evoked editorial chortles in the opposition press. Six officers received reprimands for such crimes as rape, torture, and the murder of prisoners. Lt. Bissell N. Thomas's own commanding officer recommended stiff punishment for him because of assaults on prisoners that were "so severe" that they "amounted to acute torture." Thomas was fined $300. The case of Lt. Preston T. Brown became the *cause célèbre* for anti-imperialists. He had been appropriately dismissed from the service and given five years at hard labor for murdering a prisoner, but President Roosevelt commuted it to the forfeiture of half his pay for nine months and a loss of 35 places on the promotion list.

On the heels of this disaster for the administration, a series of damaging documents thought to be safely closeted in Root's department were leaked to the press. These included the earlier investigations of Funston that had been so obviously covered up, Gardener's complaint against Bell, and an official report on hundreds of atrocities committed by the Macabebe scouts. The individual responsible for these leaks was unquestionably the army's top commander, Gen. Nelson A. Miles, to aid his own ambition to become president of the United States. To this end, he had unsuccessfully badgered Roosevelt to place him in command of the army in the Philippines. Finally, he went on his own "inspection tour," only to return agreeing with the anti-imperialists that his army had committed numerous atrocities in the Philippines. Roosevelt refused to make Miles a martyr for the anti-imperialists and permitted him to serve in his post until he reached retirement age in 1903.

The sensational trial of Waller and Smith followed, and Funston returned to the United States to brag continuously about and to escalate the number of prisoners he had summarily executed. He even suggested that some prominent war critics at home should meet the same fate, until Roosevelt muzzled him with an official reprimand. While anti-imperialist propaganda undoubtedly exaggerated the number of U.S. atrocities, the evidence strongly suggests that far too many were committed, many more than most U.S. officials cared to admit. Atrocities are endemic to guerrilla warfare; they were probably increased in the Philippines by a shortage of experienced junior officers. Moreover, most of the senior officers in this war had spent almost their entire careers fighting Native Americans in the West, which may have hardened them to a certain amount of cruelty. On top of this, a vicious racism permeated U.S. culture at the turn of the century; this zeitgeist permitted U.S. soldiers to view anyone with a darker skin as less than human, making it all the easier to carry out atrocities against Filipinos.

Stuart Creighton Miller

REFERENCES

Glenn Anthony May, "150,000 Missing Filipinos: A Demographic Crisis in Batangas, 1897–1903," in *Annales de Demographie Historique* (1985), 215–243; Glenn Anthony May, "Resistance and Collaboration in the Philippine-American War: The Case of Batangas," *Journal of Southeast Asian Studies*, 15 (1983), 69–90; Stuart Creighton Miller, *"Benevolent Assimilation": The American Conquest of the Philippines, 1899–1903* (Yale Univ. Pr., 1982); David R. Sturtevant, *Popular Uprisings in the Philippines, 1840–1940* (Cornell Univ. Pr., 1976); Richard E. Welch, "American Atrocities in the Philippines: The Indictment and the Response," *Pacific Historical Review*, 43 (1974), 233–255.

See also Public Opinion and the Philippine War; Samar Campaigns, Philippine War.

Auxiliary Naval Forces in the Spanish-Cuban/American War

The relatively small size of the United States Navy in 1898 necessitated its purchasing merchant ships for conversion to naval purposes; some of these vessels were organized into the United States Auxiliary Naval Forces.

Between 16 March and 12 August 1898 the United States Navy Department acquired 126 auxiliary vessels. It purchased 97 merchantmen as auxiliary cruisers, gunboats, and colliers; chartered 5 vessels as auxiliary cruisers, received on loan one iceboat and 2 yachts, and transferred from other government departments 15 revenue cutters, 4 lighthouse tenders, and 2 U.S. Fisheries Commission vessels. Together with 5 warship purchases, over 130 new vessels joined the fleet, which consisted of 73 fighting ships and 126 auxiliaries. The department spent in total $32,147,913 from funds made available to it under the $50 million bill, the $25 million emergency fund, and the $3 million auxiliary fund. To supplement the two major war squadrons (the North Atlantic Squadron and the Flying Squadron) a third, officially called the United States Auxiliary Naval forces but labeled "The Mosquito Squadron," was constituted mainly for coastal defense and mine protection, manned by naval militia.

Fast merchantmen supplemented the battle fleet. One vessel of the Pacific Mail Steamship Company, the *City of Pekin* (under Comdr. William C. Gibson) and four vessels of the International Navigation Company—*New York* (renamed *Harvard*) under Capt. Charles S. Cotton; *Paris* (renamed *Yale*) under Capt. William C. Wise; *St. Louis*, under Capt. Caspar F. Goodrich; and *St. Paul*, under Capt. Charles D. Sigsbee— were chartered. Between the end of April and 10 May they, and others, acted as scouts for Adm. William T. Sampson, searching for Adm. Pascual Cervera y Topete's squadron. These ships were assigned east of the Windward Islands as follows: passages between Jamaica, Cuba, and Haiti (*Yale* and *St. Paul*); the Mona passage between Santo Domingo and Puerto Rico (*Harvard*); and the Yucatan passage (*Cincinnati* and *Vesuvius*). Other duties included telegraphic services near Martinique and Guadaloupe, cruising off Puerto Rico and St. Thomas, and cutting cables.

By 19 May, when telegraphic news from Cuba established that Cervera was in Santiago harbor, the *St. Paul*, *Harvard*, *St. Louis*, *Minneapolis*, and *Yale* were ordered to maintain a close lookout in case Cervera's fleet came out. The *Yale* and *St. Paul* reconnoitered Santiago, Cuba, on 21 May, and the *Harvard* and *Minneapolis* were stationed off the port by 23 May. Three days later the *Yale*, *St. Paul*, and *Minneapolis* joined Adm. Winfield Scott Schley's Flying Squadron which left Santiago uncovered for a time. The auxiliary cruisers served as fast dispatch and communications boats for the squadrons, which were short of high-speed tonnage.

When Cervera's weak fleet was annihilated on 3 July 1898, the role of all auxiliaries changed to fleet support work, carrying rations from Tampa and Key West, Florida, blockading duties, and convoying troops (*Yale*, *Harvard*, and *Columbia*) for the land campaigns in Cuba and Puerto Rico. The *St. Louis* transported prisoners to Portsmouth and Long Island, and, later, with the *Yale*, brought reinforcements for marines and Cubans fighting at Guantánamo. The *Yale* later became the flagship of the Puerto Rican expedition when the battleship *Massachusetts* was no longer required. The *Harvard* was decommissioned 2 September 1898, and the remainder of the chartered merchantmen resumed their civilian Atlantic service in October and November 1898.

Frederick C. Drake

REFERENCES

French Ensor Chadwick, *The Relations of the United States and Spain: The Spanish-American War* (Scribner, 1911), vol. 1, 397–403; G. S. Clark, "Naval Aspects of the Spanish-American War," *Naval Annual, 1899* (J. Griffin, 1899); William H. Flayhart III, "Four Fighting Ladies," in *America Spreads Her Sails: U.S. Seapower in the 19th Century*, ed. by Clayton R. Barrow, Jr. (U.S. Naval Institute Pr., 1973), 195–214; John D. Long, *The New American Navy* (Outlook, 1903), 2 vols.; David F. Trask, *The War With Spain in 1898* (Macmillan, 1981).

B

Balangiga Massacre, The Philippines (1901)

On 28 September 1901, in the midst of the Philippine War, townspeople in Balangiga, on the Island of Samar, surprised members of Company C, 9th Infantry, United States Army, in a savage attack that left 48 dead and only 26 survivors. Over 28,000 rounds of ammunition fell into the hands of the Filipinos. The battle brought swift retaliation by U.S. authorities and hardened their policies on Samar.

Ironically, in August army intelligence had intercepted a letter addressed to Philippine independence leader Vicente Lukban that included clues about the attack planned by Balangiga's citizens. The letter informed Lukban that the Balangiga townspeople intended to feign loyalty and support of the U.S. occupation and lay in wait for the proper time to strike. Unfortunately for the men of Company C, the letter did not surface in time to alert them to the danger.

Under the command of Capt. Thomas W. Connell, Company C had recently arrived on Samar to assist in the suppression of Lukban's forces. Connell immediately set out to establish good relations with the townspeople, pushing for a works project to clean the town plaza and instill pride and civic responsibility among the Filipinos. Using Connell's project as an excuse to bring in support from the outside, Filipinos slipped into town posing as farmers working off delinquent tax bills.

On Saturday evening, 27 September 1901, U.S. guards noticed an unusual number of women carrying small coffins through the plaza. One woman explained that cholera had claimed the life of her child and many others in the village. While the soldiers stood watching the solemn procession, men dressed in women's clothing filed past, carrying coffins filled with bolo knives tucked under the bodies. The next morning the Filipinos struck without warning.

Most of the men of Company C rose early on Sunday morning, eager to read again mail from home they had received the previous afternoon. With the mail came news of President William McKinley's death, and Connell's men went to breakfast a subdued group, most reading letters and carelessly leaving their weapons behind. The Filipinos working nearby bided their time until most of the soldiers arrived in the mess areas. The attack caught the U.S. troops unaware and unarmed and the stunned soldiers were easy prey. The attacking Filipinos, lacking firearms, used axes, bolos, picks, and shovels to hack their quarry to pieces. A few of the soldiers rallied, grabbing crude weapons to defend themselves while others made their way to the rifle racks in the huts. They drove their attackers into the jungle with a withering fire. When it was apparent that the Filipinos were retreating, the surviving soldiers collected the wounded, tried unsuccessfully to destroy anything of military value, and loaded themselves into four Filipino boats near the town wharf, hoping to reach Basey 30 miles away. Using shell horns, Filipinos hiding in the surrounding jungle sounded the call for others to come to their assistance and continued to snipe at the soldiers from the undergrowth. All three officers had been killed early in the fight, and only a few noncommissioned officers were left to organize the withdrawal. Thirty-six U.S. soldiers escaped from Balangiga, but one boat drifted to the beach only 10 miles from camp, and pursuing Filipinos killed those too badly wounded to resist or flee. Others who reached safety later succumbed to their wounds, leaving only 26 survivors of the attack and desperate escape.

In the aftermath of the attack, army authorities embraced retaliatory policies against the inhabitants of Samar. Marines under the command of Maj. Littleton W.T. Waller arrived on Samar as U.S. forces moved swiftly to subdue the island. Army general Jacob H. Smith ordered Waller to "Kill and burn! Kill and burn! The more you kill and burn the better you will please me. I want no prisoners. Do you understand?" Waller eventually was tried for murder on Samar, although the military court acquitted him of all charges. Smith, too, faced a court-martial; he was convicted and retired from the service. Harsh treatment of Filipinos finally led to a Senate investigation over the U.S. presence in the Philippines.

Vernon L. Williams

REFERENCES

John M. Gates, *Schoolbooks and Krags: The United States in the Philippines, 1898–1902* (Greenwood Pr., 1973); Julius F. Hellweg, "Notes Made by Ensign Hellweg, Villalobos on Massacre at Balangiga," October 1901, Area 10 File, Record Group 45 National Archives, Washington, D.C.; Joseph L. Schott, *The Ordeal of Samar* (Bobbs-Merrill Co., 1964); James O. Taylor, *The Massacre of Balangiga, Being an Authentic Account By Several of the Few Survivors* (McCarn Printing Co., 1931).

Baldwin, Frank Dwight (1842–1923)

Frank Dwight Baldwin, a career United States Army officer, participated in the Philippine War and some campaigns against the Moros in addition to extensive service in the Civil War and in campaigns against Native Americans.

One of only two regular army officers to receive two Medals of Honor, Baldwin was born in 1842 in Manchester, Michigan. During the Civil War, he was twice captured by Confederate troops before proving himself during William T. Sherman's campaigns in Georgia. He received his regular army commission in February 1866, married Alice Blackwood, and was eventually posted to Kansas with the 5th Infantry Regiment.

During the Red River War of 1874–1875, his colonel, Nelson A. Miles, appointed Lieutenant Baldwin chief of scouts. Baldwin gained national acclaim by leading an audacious charge into Grey Beard's camp on McClellan Creek, Texas, and freeing two white children, Adelaide and Julia German. He also served with distinction during the Great Sioux War of 1876–1877 and in the capture of Chief Joseph in 1877. Promoted to captain, he was appointed by Miles to a board of inquiry into the Wounded Knee tragedy.

Baldwin enjoyed the patronage of Miles, who during the 1890s helped secure Medals of Honor for his actions at Peach Tree Creek (1864) and in rescuing the German girls (1874). Association with the controversial commander, however, risked the enmity of the general's many rivals. At the outset of the Spanish-Cuban/American War in 1898, Maj. Baldwin was detailed as inspector general. Upon promotion to lieutenant colonel of the 4th Infantry Regiment, he skillfully guided campaigns against Filipino revolutionaries in Cavite Province, forcing the surrender of Mariano Trías and Baldomero Aguinaldo in 1901. As colonel of the 27th Infantry Regiment, Baldwin forced several engagements with the Muslim *datus* (chiefs) of Mindanao. But his reluctance to implement the patient diplomacy advocated by Maj. Gen. Adna R. Chaffee put him in a tenuous position despite his having reduced the Moro stronghold at Binidayan. Appointed brigadier general in 1902, Baldwin was transferred to Iloilo and then commanded the Department of the Colorado until his retirement in 1906.

Baldwin later served as historical advisor to a western movie starring William F. ("Buffalo Bill") Cody and volunteered for active duty in World War I. Though his offer was denied, Baldwin was named Colorado state adjutant general, a position from which he retired in 1919 as major general. Baldwin died in 1923, leaving an unfinished autobiography.

Robert Wooster

REFERENCES

Robert C. Carriker, "Frank D. Baldwin," in *Soldiers West: Biographies from the Military Frontier*, ed. by Paul A. Hutton (Univ. of Nebraska Pr., 1987), 228–242; Nelson A. Miles, *Serving the Republic: Memoirs of the Civil and Military Life of Nelson A. Miles, Lieutenant-General, United States Army* (Harper, 1911); Robert H. Steinbach, *A Long March: The Lives of Frank and Alice Baldwin* (Univ. of Texas Pr., 1989).

Balloon Operations at Santiago, Cuba, During the Spanish-Cuban/American War

As the United States Army prepared for war with Spain in 1898, Lt. Col. Joseph E. Maxfield assumed command of an old and patched United States Army Signal Corps spherical silk balloon of 14,000 cubic feet capacity and its crew. Ordered to Cuba, Maxfield and his company, consisting of three officers and 24 enlisted men, loaded the balloon, renamed the *Santiago*, and all of the equipment on one of the transports carrying Maj. Gen. William R. Shafter's expeditionary force.

On 30 June 1898 Maxfield and his company, under the command of Shafter's chief engineer, Lt. Col. George M. Derby, made three ascents, reporting on the roads toward the front and confirming the presence of the fleet of Adm. Pascual Cervera y Topete in Santiago harbor. The following day, Maxfield and Derby made another flight nearer to El Pozo with Sgt. William Ivy observing the movement of troops at El Caney and on the road leading toward San Juan Hill.

Over Maxfield's objections, Derby ordered the balloon and its crew closer to the front line. When it reascended in a grove of trees, the tether and telephone lines became tangled, and the *Santiago* could rise no higher than 300 feet. While in flight, the aeronauts not only spotted a hidden road that would permit U.S. forces to ease

the congestion on the one road then in use, which was already under heavy fire, but also pinpointed strong Spanish entrenchments on the slopes of San Juan Hill.

As Maxfield feared, the balloon, only 650 yards from San Juan Hill, made an attractive target for enemy shooters, who damaged the craft. In addition, the craft had lost so much gas that it could not be properly reinflated without the use of the generator, which had been left on the transport. Without a way to repair the envelope in Cuba, the balloon was transported to Sibony, where it was left after the war. The United States Army did not use a balloon again in combat until World War I.

Theresa L. Kraus

REFERENCES

William E. Butterworth, *Flying Army: The Modern Air Arm of the U.S. Army* (Doubleday, 1971); Graham A. Cosmas, "San Juan Hill and El Caney, 1–2 July 1898," in *America's First Battles, 1776–1965*, ed. by Charles E. Heller and William A. Stoft (Univ. Pr. of Kansas, 1986); Tom D. Crouch, *The Eagle Aloft: Two Centuries of the Balloon in America* (Smithsonian, 1983); Russell J. Parkinson, "United States Signal Corps Balloons, 1871–1902," *Military Affairs*, 24 (Winter 1960–61), 189–202.

Bandholtz, Harry Hill (1864–1925)

Gen. Harry Hill Bandholtz was one of the leading officers of the Philippine Constabulary. Born in Michigan in 1864, Bandholtz attended the United States Military Academy at West Point, graduating in 1890. Between 1890 and 1898, he served on several army posts and taught at Michigan Agricultural College. During the Spanish-Cuban/American War, he saw service in Cuba. In early 1900, Bandholtz was transferred to the Philippines, serving first in Marinduque and later in Southern Luzon. In Tayabas Province, he was instrumental in suppressing resistance to U.S. rule and winning over Filipino leaders to U.S. sovereignty.

Bandholtz had keen political skills, which he used in the administration of Tayabas Province. Elected the province's governor in 1902, he resigned a year later to assume a post in the newly created Philippine Constabulary. Rising quickly through the ranks, he became chief of the constabulary in 1907.

Bandholtz played a role in Philippine politics until his departure from the Philippines in 1913. Most important, he advised Manuel L. Quezon, later president of the Commonwealth of the Philippines.

After attempting unsuccessfully to secure the post of chief of the Bureau of Insular Affairs in Washington in 1912, the following year Bandholtz began a four-year garrison duty in the United States. During World War I, he returned overseas, serving with the Allied and U.S. units in France. He also served briefly as the American Expeditionary Force's provost marshal. After the Armistice, Bandholtz was sent to Hungary as a member of an Inter-Allied Military Mission.

Bandholtz spent from 1920 until his retirement from the army in 1923 in the Washington area. He died in Michigan in 1925.

James C. Biedzynski

REFERENCES

Michael Cullinane, "Quezon and Harry Bandholtz," *Bulletin of the American Historical Collection*, 9 (1981), 79–90, 99–100; *Fifty-Ninth Annual Report of the Association of Graduates of the United States Military Academy At West Point, New York, June 8, 1928* (Seemann & Peters, 1929); Peter W. Stanley, ed., *Reappraising an Empire* (Harvard Univ. Pr., 1984).

See also Philippine Constabulary.

Barton, Clara, in the Spanish-Cuban/American War

Clara Barton, founder of the American Red Cross in 1881, put her fledgling organization to its first battlefield test during the Spanish-Cuban/American War. After convincing the surgeon general that women nurses could operate as well as men in combat situations, she recruited nurses from across the country and sent her first contingent to Cuba in 1898. Her mission was twofold: to succor the wounded and to boost the morale of U.S. soldiers by providing food and other supplies that were sorely lacking within the military expedition.

Barton, former schoolteacher and government clerk from Massachusetts, had gained her battlefield experience as a volunteer during the Civil War. Her pragmatic approach was to aid the troops at the front rather than waiting for them to return to the rear, as was the common practice among less adventuresome volunteers. She put this tactic to good use in Cuba.

Before the Spanish-Cuban/American War, Barton had been aiding *reconcentrados* (imprisoned Cuban insurrectionists), distributing food and medical supplies. Her volunteers had also set up hospitals and orphanages. After the battleship *Maine* sank in 1898, Barton and her volunteers turned their energies to the wounded. In her memoirs, she stated that after the explosion, "We proceeded to the Spanish hospital San Ambrosia, to find thirty to forty wounded—bruised, cut, burned . . . . Both men and officers are very reticent in regard to the cause, but all declare it could not have been the result of an internal explosion" (*Clara Barton, Handbook 110*, p. 55).

Army medical officers came to rely on the American Red Cross for help with victims of heat exhaustion, yellow fever, and typhoid fever. Recalling her Civil War voluntary work, Barton wrote of the scarcity of food and of the wounded who had not eaten for three or four days before going into battle. She wrote: "I had not thought to ever make gruel again over a camp-fire; I cannot say how far it carried me back in the lapse of time . . . . And when the nurses came back and told us of the surprise with which it was received and the tears that rolled down the sunburned, often bloody, face . . . I felt it was again the same old story, and wondered what gain there had been in the last thirty years" (Barton, p. 565).

Red Cross volunteers also served in the Philippines with the U.S. troops, using donated supplies collected and shipped by their colleagues in the United States. This operation was run independently of Barton, who busied herself at the Cuban front instead of remaining at the headquarters in Washington. Although President William McKinley expressed gratitude to Barton for the work of the American Red Cross, it became obvious that the organization could have accomplished much more in its service with the military had it been larger and better organized. This initial expedition laid the groundwork for vast changes in the organization's work in World War I.

Patrick F. Gilbo

REFERENCES

Clara H. Barton, *The Red Cross* (James B. Lyons, 1898); Patrick F. Gilbo, *The American Red Cross—The First Century* (Harper, 1981); U.S. Department of the Interior, *Clara Barton*, Handbook 110, National Park Handbook Series (U.S. Department of the Interior, 1981).

See also American National Red Cross.

Bates, John Coalter (1842–1919)

John Coalter Bates, United States Army officer, established U.S. authority in the Moro areas of the Philippines and negotiated the "Bates Treaty of 1899." He was born on 26 August 1842 in St. Charles County, Missouri, the son of Edward and Julia Davenport (Coalter) Bates. His father served as Abraham Lincoln's attorney general (1861–1864).

The young Bates was a student at Washington University, St. Louis, Missouri, when the Civil War broke out. In May 1861, at age 18, he volunteered for service in the Union Army and was commissioned a first lieutenant. During the war, he served in the Army of the Potomac and was present at most of its major engagements.

Remaining in the regular army after the Confederacy's defeat, Bates spent more than 30 years at various posts throughout the Southwest and Northwest. Initially, he held the rank of captain, but he was promoted to major in 1882, lieutenant colonel in 1886, and colonel in 1892. His length of service gave him considerable seniority, with the result that by 1898 only three colonels in the regular army ranked above him on the promotion list.

In May 1898, less than a month after the United States declared war on Spain, Bates was appointed a brigadier general of United States Volunteers in command of an independent brigade that was part of Gen. William R. Shafter's V Corps. During the subsequent invasion of Cuba, Bates served for a time as the commander of the army's base at Siboney. Then, on 1 July his independent brigade was present in support of Gen. Henry W. Lawton's 2nd Division during the attack on El Caney. Held in reserve through the morning hours, Bates's troops joined in the final assault that captured the Spanish stronghold in the afternoon. As participants in skirmishes that followed on 2 July Bates's men endured more than 24 hours of nearly continuous marching and fighting in hot, humid weather.

During the final weeks of the campaign against Santiago, Bates commanded the 3rd Division and was promoted to major general of volunteers. After the city's surrender on 17 July,

Bates's troops were put in charge of guarding thousands of captured Spanish soldiers. Intense heat and humidity took a severe toll on Bates's officers and men, and he was one of the U.S. commanders who signed the round robin of early August that described the deplorable health conditions found among U.S. occupying forces in Cuba. Bates's troops were among those ordered to transfer to Montauk Point, Long Island, New York, in mid-August 1898.

Bates returned to Cuba briefly in early 1899 as the commander of U.S. forces in the Santa Clara district. In April 1899 his commission as a major general expired, and he was reappointed brigadier general of volunteers. By midyear, however, he was on his way to the Philippines to assist in suppressing the Filipino nationalist movement led by Emilio Aguinaldo y Famy.

In July 1899 Gen. Elwell S. Otis, commander of U.S. forces in the Philippines, sent Bates to negotiate with the sultan of Sulu, the spiritual leader of the Moros (as Muslim residents of the southwestern part of the Philippines, including the Sulu archipelago and the island of Mindanao, were called). Bates artfully pressured the sultan and local *datus* (Moro chiefs) into signing a treaty (August 1899) that accepted U.S. sovereignty. In return, the Moros were allowed to retain most of their traditional customs, which included polygamy and slavery. Although the so-called Bates Treaty aided in the pacification of the southern islands, it received considerable criticism from church groups and humanitarians in the United States.

When General Lawton was killed in battle in late 1899, Bates was reassigned to a command responsible for the department of Southern Luzon, a huge area that included all of Luzon (the country's largest island) south of Manila. In early 1900 Bates, once again a major general of volunteers, launched an offensive against Filipino forces. His plan was basically one drawn up by Lawton in which the Filipinos would be encircled and suppressed. Although U.S. forces quickly won the conventional war, guerrilla resistance continued throughout the area that was under Bates's command.

Similar guerrilla activity on the island of Mindanao led to a hard-fought and often frustrating campaign by Bates's troops. Garrisons were established at key points along the island's coast, and military thrusts were made into the countryside from these strongpoints. The tenacity of Filipino resistance and the severity of U.S. casualties had a significant impact on Bates's thinking about how the war could be ended. In the debate among U.S. leaders regarding whether positive incentives—such as granting humanitarian aid and allowing Filipino participation in civil affairs—would be effective in weakening rebel support, Bates was one of the hard-liners who doubted the efficacy of benevolence and believed that only military force would accomplish the task of establishing U.S. control.

Bates's long and effective service won him promotion to regular brigadier general in 1901 and to major general in 1902. He became chief of staff of the army in January 1906 with the tank of lieutenant general, a post that only nine other officers had held. He retired in April 1906, having completed 45 years of military service.

Bates, who never married, died in San Diego, California, on 4 February 1919.

Gerald W. McFarland

REFERENCES

New York Tribune, 6 Feb. 1919; *New York Times*, 9 Feb. 1919; David F. Trask, *The War With Spain in 1898* (Macmillan, 1981); William T. Sexton, *Soldiers in the Sun: An Adventure in Imperialism* (Military Service Pub. Co., 1939).

See also Bates Treaty (1899).

Bates Treaty (1899)

After the withdrawal of Spanish sovereignty in 1898 from the Philippines, the enforcement of U.S. rule was interrupted by the Filipino resistance in the North. This led to the Philippine War in early 1899 and the chaotic withdrawal of Spanish troops in Mindanao and Sulu where a U.S. presence had to be established. Diplomacy to neutralize the Sulu Muslims was necessary, and the result was the conclusion of a treaty (the Bates Treaty) between Sulu and the United States on 20 August 1899. Brig. Gen. John C. Bates of the United States Volunteers represented the United States, and Sultan Jamalul Kiram II, Datu Rajah Muda, Datu Atik, Datu Kalbi, and Datu Julkanain signed for the Sulu Sultanate.

The provisions of the agreement were written in English and in Tausug, for which the old Malay script *jawi* was used. The English translation was provided by Dr. Najeeb M. Saleeby, a Syrian-American surgeon who had done scholarly studies on the history and culture

of the Moros. The treaty provided for:

- Recognition of U.S. sovereignty;
- Use of the "Stars and Stripes" in the Sulu archipelago;
- Recognition of certain rights and powers of the sultan, especially freedom of religion;
- Recognition of the U.S. occupation and control in Sulu;
- Regulation of commerce and trade;
- Right of the sultan to communicate with the governor general of the Philippines;
- A ban on the use of firearms;
- Joint cooperation against piracy;
- Trial of Muslims and foreigners;
- Rights of the slaves to freedom;
- Peaceful solution of disputes;
- Duty of the United States to protect Sulu from foreign dangers; and
- A prohibition against the disposition of any island without the consent of the Sultan.

It also provided for financial annuities as follows: the sultan (Mexican), $250; Datu Rajah Muda, $75; Datu Atik, $60; Datu Kalbi, $75; Datu Julkanain, $75; Datu Puyo, $60; Datu Amilhussin, $60; Hadji Butu, $50; Habib Mura, $40; and Sherif Saguin, $15.

The treaty lasted for slightly over five years. Political conditions in Sulu, particularly on Jolo Island, began to deteriorate, requiring more military attention from the government. Armed disturbances and revolts occurred in several areas, especially in strategic centers of population like Taglibi, Luuk, Lati, Parang, Indanan, and Patikul. These disturbances raised serious questions about the ability of the sultan and his *datus* (chiefs) to ensure peace or, alternatively, their possible connection with the uprisings and disturbances. One of the most serious was the Hassan uprising which threatened the security of Jolo City where the seat of U.S. authority had been established. Despite prodding from U.S. authorities, the sultan failed to bring in Panglima Hassan and suppress his revolt, prompting Moro Province Governor Leonard Wood to mount a major military operation against Hassan. Without any consultation or warning, the United States unilaterally abrogated the Bates Treaty on 2 March 1904 through Secretary of War

William H. Taft's instruction to Governor Luke W. Wright. On 21 March General Wood notified the sultan of the termination of the treaty.

Samuel K. Tan

References

Peter G. Gowing, *Mandate in Moroland: The American Government of Muslim Filipinos, 1899–1920* (Univ. of the Philippines, 1977), 31–37; Samuel K. Tan, *The Filipino Muslim Armed Struggle, 1900–1972* (Filipinas Foundation, 1977), chap. 3.

See also Bates, John Coalter; Moro Province, The Philippines (1903–1913).

Bayang, Moro Province, The Philippines, Battle (1902)

While the Philippine War raged between Philippine nationalists and U.S. forces in the northern islands, conditions in Mindanao and Sulu were deceptively quiet when U.S. troops set foot on these two islands in 1899. The first taste of war between the Moros (Philippine Muslims) and the United States came two years after the occupation in what is known as the Battle of Bayang in 1902. Thereafter, Moro resistance grew for the next 12 years until the end of the U.S. military regime in 1913. The Moros realized that they had driven away the Spanish only to find that the U.S. authorities had taken their place. The events that unfolded in Mindanao and Sulu were another version of the "Indian wars" in the eyes of U.S. personnel; to the Moro warriors, however, the fighting was a continuation of the holy war (*jihad*) which they had waged against foreigners.

As U.S. troops penetrated the interior, Gen. George W. Davis issued an order on 4 March 1902 enjoining them to use considerable care when entering areas inhabited by non-Christians ("General Davis' Order," *Washington Evening Star*, 22 April 1902). He also directed the officers who were brought into direct contact with the Moros to treat them kindly, not to molest peaceful inhabitants, and not to interfere with their religious practices or the observance of their tribal customs. Davis offered to buy their ponies and to employ such of the laborers as the army needed. Above all, he impressed on the Moros that the taking and selling of slaves were henceforth forbidden.

As if testing the limits of U.S. authority, Moros attacked a detachment of cavalry under Lt. William D. Forsyth in March 1902. It had been sent by General Davis to open a trail from Parang-Parang (Cotabato) to Lake Lanao, Mindanao. In that skirmish one cavalryman died in the first volley; the Moros lost five killed and three wounded; all of these Moros were identified as followers of the sultan of Bayang. While the U.S. detachment was retreating to Buldon, it lost 18 of its horses, which were presumably captured by the pursuing Moros. Previous acts of the Moros, such as the theft of U.S. government property, had already irked U.S. commanders; so this small fight led to a major battle. Earlier, Capt. Ernst Hagedorn had reported several cases of petty disturbances at Malabang and its vicinity: (1) a Marano woman was seized and sold by Jolo Moros, and similar incidents had occurred at remote points; (2) nine slaves escaped from their masters and had come to U.S. troops for assistance; (3) two rival Moro factions had a fight in the market; (4) a Moro thief was beheaded by his *datu* (chief); and (5) Bayang Moros stole four U.S. government-owned cows and "had a great feast eating them." The last item intensified the conflict.

Then, before March 1902 had ended, two U.S. soldiers were hacked to death. Earlier, Adjutant General Henry C. Corbin had sent a cable to Gen. Adna R. Chaffee, who commanded U.S. forces in the Philippines, stating "the President is anxious that no expedition be made against Moros until all efforts by negotiation have been exhausted" ("General Davis' Orders," *Washington Evening Star*, 23 April 1902). Chaffee responded to this with a long dispatch stating, among other things, that "to withdraw all our forces will ruin our prestige; to withdraw part of our forces will be dangerous."

Meanwhile, on 13 April 1902, Chaffee wrote the *datus* concerned (Sultan of Bayang, Datu Adta of Paigoay, and Amai Tampugao of Tubaran), asking them to deliver the "assassins" and "make restitution of the Government property which has been stolen by their followers" within two weeks. The message was carried by Sherif Mohammed Afdal, an Afghan high priest from Rio Grande, who persuaded the recalcitrant *datus* to yield to the demands of U.S. authorities (*Annual Reports of the War Department 1902*, vol. 9, p. 485). He was to explain to them how pleasantly the Maguindanao of the Pulangui Valley got along with the soldiers. The *datus*, however, were "insolent and stated that they would not give up their men and if we came there they would fight us." The sultan of Bayang wrote to Chaffee that he recognized nobody but the sultan of Turkey: "The word of the Colonel [Frank D. Baldwin] is not the law of the Sultan of Bayan [Bayang]; if the Colonel is a person under the Sultan of Stamboul, he will not change the laws or types [sic] of one another" (Chaffee to Corbin, 30 April 1902, Box 1, Corbin Papers).

Meanwhile, war preparations began. Col. Frank D. Baldwin (Pershing described him as a "fine soldier, with large experience in handling Indians, but was disposed to use force instead of diplomacy," Pershing, Unpublished Memoirs, Box 374, Pershing Papers) was authorized to mobilize 1,800 men in a punitive expedition. He moved his forces from Parang-Parang to Malabang camp. He then advanced from Malabang eight miles out to continue clearing the trail toward Lake Lanao. Part of the column was a battalion led by Maj. Hugh L. Scott of the 27th Infantry Regiment. It reached Lake Lanao without opposition, but found the trail badly obstructed by fallen timber. Another battalion with an accompanying artillery battery headed by Capt. George D. Moore was fired on from the hills. Baldwin arrived with three infantry battalions and the rest of the battery to reinforce the beleaguered troops. The U.S. mountain guns pounded away at close range and drove off the Moros, leaving seven Moro dead; there were no U.S. casualties ("General Chaffee's Orders," *Washington Evening Star*, 23 April 1902). Baldwin easily destroyed the smaller *cottas* (forts) of Pualas and Ganassi as soon as his troops moved out from Malabang. During this fighting the sultan of Pualas was killed.

Two weeks elapsed. On 1 May 1902 an ultimatum was sent to the Baynag *datus* to give up the murderers within 24 hours, or else "the consequences would be bad for the Moros" (*Annual Reports of the War Department 1902*, vol. 9, p. 488). Baldwin positioned his forces around the *cotta* (fort) of Pandapatan, where the Bayang warriors and their allies from nearby Binidayan, 975 yards away, had grouped for defense. On their way, the U.S. troops had shelled and destroyed the Binidayan *cotta*. Fort Pandapatan, or Padang Karbala to the Maranao Moros, was reputed to be one of the strongest *cottas* in the area. This fort was estimated to be over 100 years old (Chaffee to Corbin, 27 May 1902, Box 1, Corbin papers). It was constructed mainly of sod, faced

with rock on the outside on 2 sides. The interior was about 80 feet square with various holes around the walls for serving the *lantacas* (brass cannon) which were laid on the ground. The exterior side of the fort was completely hidden by live bamboo so thick that a field mouse could hardly get through it. Outside the walls about 12 feet from them was a large ditch probably 10 feet deep and 12 feet wide at the top, then a space of undisturbed ground about 10 feet wide. On this ground was driven split bamboo slanting outward very close together, perhaps 6 or 8 inches apart and about 3 feet high. With red flags flying in defiance, the fort was defended by a combined force of some 600 Moro warriors, mostly from Bayang, with some fighters from Bacolod, Butig, Paigoay, Maciu, and Dirimuyud.

On 2 May 1902, between 1:30 and 2:00 p.m., U.S. troops began shelling Pandapatan with their mountain guns. They then surrounded the fort and showered it with rapid fire which kept the Moros from firing much. Night, and heavy rain, fell; the U.S. troops prepared to scale the high walls of the fort in a final assault the following day. Before daybreak, however, white flags were hoisted by the Moros. For U.S. forces, one officer and nine enlisted men were killed, and three officers and 37 enlisted men were wounded. Three of the wounded died within a few days. On the Moro side, casualties were severe, with as many as 300 to 400 dead according to surviving Moros. Among the slain was the sultan of Bayan. Eighty-three of the Moro warriors surrendered, but shortly after made a dash for freedom that brought death to many of them.

In General Chaffee's view the battle had favorable results because it asserted U.S. authority in the Moro area. Jacob G. Schurman, president of Cornell University and first head of the Philippine Commission, which prepared the way for civil government in the Philippines, criticized the actions of the military, however, believing that it "might be guilty of the original provocation which ended in murderous retaliation" (Schurman, p. 1105).

The Battle of Bayang meant the opening of the Lake Lanao area of Mindanao to trade and its absorption into a Western political and economic system. The centuries of insularity for the Maranaos (as the Moros near the lake were sometimes called) was broken for good. For U.S. authorities, who had gained ground in Mindanao, there was no other way but to go deeper into the heart of this frontier. "It would make an awful mistake to withdraw therefrom" (Chaffee to Corbin, 27 May 1902, Box 1, Corbin Papers). The deadly encounters between the *kris* (the sword used by the Moros) and the Krag rifle had just begun. Then, in early 1903, Capt. John J. Pershing moved from Lake Lanao to Iligan to relieve Baldwin who had been promoted to brigadier general and was assigned elsewhere. Pershing took command of the newly built Camp Vicars (named for Lt. Thomas A. Vicars, who had been killed in the Bayang affair), half a mile south of Bayang. During the next 12 months several campaigns were launched from this military post.

Federico V. Magdalena

REFERENCES

Annual Reports of the War Department for the Fiscal Year Ending June 30, 1902 (U.S. Government Printing Office, 1902), vol. 9, App. G [reports of Gen. George W. Davis], App. 10 [reports of Col. Frank D. Baldwin]; Henry Clark Corbin papers, Manuscript Division, Library of Congress; John J. Pershing papers, Manuscript Division, Library of Congress; Jacob G. Schurman, "The Philippines Again," *Independent*, 54 (May 8, 1902), 1104–1107.

Beadle, Elias Root (1878–1946)

Brig. Gen. Elias Root Beadle (lieutenant colonel, United States Marine Corps) served as chief of the Guardia Nacional de Nicaragua from 11 July 1927 until 10 March 1929. Before his duty in Nicaragua, Beadle served in the Philippines and Haiti, and during World War I was chief of staff of the marine corps base at Parris Island, South Carolina. He directed the early development of the Guardia, during which it grew to a force of about 2,000 men. During Beadle's tenure, nationalist leader Augusto C. Sandino launched his guerrilla war against the Nicaraguan government and the intervening U.S. Marines.

Beadle's relationship with Nicaraguan President Adolfo Díaz was amicable and cooperative; Díaz later commended him for splendid service. The friendly relationship between the Guardia and the government changed after José María Moncada won the presidency in the election of 1928. Moncada proposed creation of a force separate from the national guard to help in the fight against Sandino; such a force would favor Moncada and would undermine the U.S.

government's intention to create a nonpartisan national constabulary as the sole military and police force in Nicaragua. General Beadle and the U.S. minister in Nicaragua, Charles C. Eberhardt, opposed the president's plan while Gen. Logan Feland, commander of the 2nd Marine Brigade in Nicaragua, supported it. At the same time, Feland was using his influence with Moncada to have the national guard placed under his command, a change opposed by Beadle, Eberhardt, and the Department of State. There was also disagreement on proposed changes to legislation authorizing the national guard, which until then was based on presidential decree. Beadle and Eberhardt thought the changes backed by Moncada would allow greater political interference in administering the Guardia. The friction caused by these differences was probably sharpened by Feland virtually acting, according to Eberhardt, as Moncada's minister of war and by the president's view that Beadle had been too close to his predecessor, Adolfo Díaz, a member of the opposition Conservative party.

After charges of lavish spending on social functions by the Guardia and demands for an audit of its accounts, which indicated no wrongdoing, Beadle wanted to be relieved of duty because he believed these were efforts to lessen esteem of the national guard and indicative of personal grievances against him. Although believing that Beadle had done an excellent job under very difficult circumstances, Eberhardt recommended that both Beadle and Feland be replaced. Both officers left Nicaragua in March 1929. Beadle returned to Washington, D.C., where he served in Marine Corps headquarters.

Adm. David Foote Sellers, Feland's immediate superior, believed that the Guardia chief had shown a considerable lack of discretion in dealing with Moncada and Feland.

William Kamman

REFERENCES

Robert Debs Heinl, Jr., *Soldiers of the Sea: The United States Marine Corps, 1775–1962* (U.S. Naval Institute Pr., 1962); William Kamman, *A Search for Stability: United States Diplomacy Toward Nicaragua, 1925–1933* (Notre Dame Univ. Pr., 1968); Neill Macaulay, *The Sandino Affair* (Quadrangle, 1967); Richard Millett, *Guardians of the Dynasty: A History of the U.S. Created Guardia Nacional de Nicaragua and the Somoza Family* (Orbis, 1977).

See also Feland, Logan; Guardia Nacional de Nicaragua.

Beijing (Peking), China, Battle (1900)

The battle for Beijing, China, and the relief of the Beijing legations occurred on 14–16 August, 1900. It was the culmination of a march from Tianjin (Tientsin) to Beijing that began on 4 August during the Boxer Uprising.

Allied troops rested at Tianjin for three weeks after its seizure, receiving reinforcements and more supplies. Their commanders debated whether they should wait for more troops and supplies and the onset of the autumn rains (which would raise the level of the river and make the march to the capital more difficult) or leave immediately for Beijing. Initially, there was no sense of urgency because it was assumed all the foreigners in the capital were dead. When news was received that the foreigners in the Legation Quarter were still alive and their situation was critical, the Allied expedition hastened to start.

The Allied strategy for the approach march to Beijing was simple. The international relief force was divided into two mutually supporting columns advancing on both banks of the Beiho (Pei Ho). The river was used to ferry supplies and replacements to the relief force. The Allied commander, British Gen. Alfred Gaselee, proposed to strike directly for the capital, stopping only to fight the main body of the Chinese army and bypassing fortified strong points, leaving them for the rear echelon to subdue.

On 5 August and 6 August, the Allied forces defeated the Chinese army in two battles, at Beicang (Pei Tsang) and at Yangcun (Yang Tsun). On 12 August, the Allies occupied Tongzhou (T'ungchow), completing the rape and despoliation of the city begun by the Boxers after the retreat of the Imperial army. Filled with impatience, they prepared for the assault on the capital.

The plan was direct. To damp down some of the national rivalries, the relieving force was divided into four columns which were to attack simultaneously the four gates in Beijing's eastern wall: the Dongzhi (Tung Chih), Qihua (Ch'i Hua), Dongbian (Tung Pien), and Shahuo (Sha Huo) gates. (Beijing was divided into three cities: the Chinese City, the Tartar City, and the Imperial, or Forbidden, City. The Legation Quarter was located in the southeastern corner of the Tartar City; its southern boundary was the Tartar City's south wall.)

The Russians were to advance along the road and north of the Tongzhou-Beijing extension of the Grand Canal while the Japanese were to advance to the Russians' left, but still north of the canal. At the same time, British and U.S. forces were to attack on the south side of the canal in two columns a mile and a half apart. The other nationalities were to follow in their wake. The attack was supposed to begin at dawn on 14 August.

At the appointed time it was discovered that the Russians had started early. In their zeal to be the first to relieve the legations, they began their advance before midnight. The rest of the Allied force learned of the Russian advance only when they heard their preliminary artillery bombardment of the city gate.

However, in the dark, the Russians got lost and strayed from their original objective. Instead of attacking the Dongzhi Gate, the northernmost gate, they wandered diagonally across the front to the left and attacked the Dongbian Gate, the original objective of the U.S. forces. When the other detachments realized the Russians had stolen a march on them, they, too, abandoned the plan for a coordinated assault on the city gates and rushed to rescue the besieged foreigners. The coordinated attack of the international relief force turned into a road race as each detachment tried to beat the others into the capital.

The Russian assault on the Dongbian Gate began about dawn. At first it appeared the Russians would be the first foreigners into the city. The assault force succeeded in forcing the outer gates, but were caught between the two walls in what Chinese troops were able to turn into a killing ground.

The Japanese also met heavy resistance at their objective, the Qihua Gate. Stalled in front of it most of the day, their combat engineers eventually blew the gate open at 5:00 p.m. but only after the Japanese had brought up their artillery (five batteries of 54 guns) and had fired approximately 1,000 shells into the Chinese defenses. They were not able to enter Beijing until 15 August.

U.S. troops were also moving forward. Instead of their original objective, the Dongbian Gate, which was occupying the Russians, they attacked the wall itself between it and the original British objective, the Shahuo Gate. They ran into a problem: how to assault a 30-foot-high wall without ladders or grappling hooks. A volunteer, a bugler in the 14th Infantry Regiment, climbed the wall, using as handholds and footholds the spaces where mortar had eroded from between the bricks. When he reached the top, he found that particular section of the wall to be undefended. The Chinese defense was as disorganized as the Allied assault.

By noon, enough men had succeeded in climbing the wall to assist the Russians at the Dongbian Gate. As U.S. reinforcements arrived, they surged through the disorganized debris of the Russian attack and began fighting in the southeastern part of the city, advancing toward the Legation Quarter. At about 4:00 p.m., they reached the southern wall of the Tartar City and the U.S. Legation. They were inside the wall within half an hour and discovered the legations had already been relieved by the British.

While the Russians, Japanese, and the U.S. forces were occupied by the Chinese, a British artillery battery blew a hole in the Shahuo Gate. At the same time, a sepoy from the 24th Rajputs scaled the wall and opened the gate from the inside. British and Indian troops then entered the city. (The British had not yet arrived when U.S. troops began their assault on the wall.)

Once inside the city, they advanced to the Hata (Ha Ta) Gate. A British sentry on the south wall gestured for them to enter the Legation Quarter through the Imperial Canal water gate, which ran through the center of the Legation Quarter. They met a party of U.S. marines who were sawing through the bars of the sluice gate and squeezed into the Legation Quarter. They succeeded in relieving the legations at about 2:00 p.m. The main body of U.S. forces followed them about two hours later while the Russians and Japanese arrived later that evening and the next morning, respectively. The British, Russians, and the U.S. troops then proceeded to clear the area around the Legation Quarter of Chinese troops. After relieving the legations, the looting of Beijing began.

The next day, 15 August, U.S. troops, acting on orders from the U.S. Minister Edwin H. Conger, began an assault on the Forbidden City. U.S. infantry, supported by U.S. artillery firing from the top of the Chien (Ch'ien) Gate, began their attack shortly after dawn. U.S. artillery blew open one of the gates to the Forbidden City and the infantry surged in, only to be trapped in a courtyard. U.S. troops slowly fought their way through a series of courtyards toward the Imperial palace. As they neared their objective, they were recalled and returned to the Legation Quarter.

In retrospect, this last operation was militarily pointless because the Chinese were abandoning their positions. It also contravened Russian and French policy, which called for conciliation toward the court. It would have also failed to capture the dowager empress and the emperor because they had fled the city earlier that morning.

It was not until late in the afternoon of 15 August, 24 hours after the relief of the Legation Quarter, that the Allied commanders and the foreign diplomats remembered the siege of the Beidang (Pei Tang) Cathedral, two miles from the legations. Close to 4,000 people—Chinese Christian refugees and Catholic clergy, under the leadership of Monsignor Alphonse-Pierre Favier, vicar apostolic of Beijing and North Zhili (Chihli)—sought refuge in and fortified the cathedral on 16 June. They were defended by only 46 French and Italian sailors. They had little food, but plenty of water from the wells on the cathedral's grounds. At times more than 2,000 Boxers and Imperial troops, assisted by artillery fire, attacked the cathedral.

On 16 August, a combined force of French, British, and Russian troops left the legations to clear the area around the cathedral. When they arrived, they found the Japanese had already liberated the area. The 57-day siege of the cathedral was lifted.

With the relief of the legations and the cathedral the battle for Beijing was over. On 16 August 1900 in the immediate aftermath of the fighting, while looting and fires were still raging out of control, the Allies established a provisional occupation government for the city and set about restoring order.

Lewis Bernstein

REFERENCES

James A. Bevan, "With the Marines on the March to Peking, China—1900," *Leatherneck*, 18 (1935), 5–7, 55–56; Aaron S. Daggett, *America in the China Relief Expedition: An Account of the Brilliant Part Taken by United States Troops in the Memorable Campaign in the Summer of 1900 for the Relief of the Besieged Legations in Peking, China* (Hudson-

Kimberley, 1903); William J. Duiker, *Cultures in Collision: The Boxer Rebellion* (Presidio Pr., 1978); Peter Fleming, *The Siege at Peking* (Harper, 1959); Richard O'Connor, *The Spirit Soldiers: A Historical Narrative of the Boxer Rebellion* (Putnam, 1973).

See also Beijing (Peking) Legations, China, Siege (1900).

Beijing (Peking) Legations, China, Siege (1900)

The siege of the foreign legations in Beijing (Peking), China, began 20 June 1900 and lasted until the Allied relief force reached the legations on 14 August 1900, 55 days later. It may be divided into two parts: (1) 20 June to 14 July, when the Legation Quarter was attacked by artillery and infantry; and (2) 14 July to 14 August, when the legations were attacked only by infantry.

Although the siege began on 20 June 1900, tension had been increasing between foreign diplomats and missionaries and the Qing (Ch'ing) Court since 1898. The failure of the reform movement, the German seizure of Qingdao (Tsingtao) in retaliation for the murder of two missionaries, and the foreign Scramble for Concessions (Slicing the Chinese Melon) exacerbated Sino-foreign relations. The spread of the Boxer movement to Zhili (Chihli) from Shandong (Shantung) and the court's inability to control the Boxers' antiforeign activities heightened tensions in spring 1900.

The murder by Chinese soldiers of the Japanese legation's chancellor, Sugiyama Akira, on 11 June spread fear among Beijing's foreign residents. On 9 June, the British minister, Sir Claude M. Macdonald, requested reinforcements for the legation guards from the British naval squadron at Dagu (Taku). The following day, a relief column commanded by Adm. Edward H. Seymour set off for Beijing. It never arrived owing to heavy Chinese resistance. By 13 June, the legations were guarded by small troop contingents sent at the end of May. Armed guards were also sent to the Beidang (Pei T'ang) Catholic cathedral.

There were two groups of foreigners in Beijing: those in the legations and those at the cathedral. The latter group, under the leadership of Monsignor Alphonse-Pierre Favier, vicar apostolic of Beijing and North Zhili, fortified the church and held out until rescued by the relief force. The only armed defenders were two officers and 44 French and Italian sailors. There were approximately 3,900 people in the cathedral, mostly Chinese Christian refugees.

Between 14 June and 16 June, foreigners living in Beijing were brought into the Legation Quarter. In 1900, it measured about 2,000 feet square. It was bounded on the south by a city wall (50 feet high and approximately 40 feet thick). The other three sides were open to the city streets, although there were buildings strong enough to serve as fortified defensive anchors on two sides. On the east, such anchors included the Imperial Maritime Customs building and the French and German legations. On the west, the British and Russian legations and the Russo-Chinese Bank served the same purpose. On the north the Legation Quarter faced a major Beijing avenue, Changan Street, which passed in front of it and could be used as an attack route. If Chinese troops used this street to advance along the Imperial Canal, the Legation Quarter would be cut in two, and no effective defense could be maintained.

The legations were not fortified, nor had stocks of food, ammunition, and water been accumulated. On 16 June, tensions escalated as antiforeign rioters burned the Chien Men market; approximately 4,000 shops were set on fire.

The Allied attack on the Dagu Forts (17 June) precipitated an ultimatum which was presented to the foreign ministers on 19 June (when the Seymour Column was attempting to return to Tianjin [Tientsin]) demanding foreigners leave Beijing within 24 hours. The diplomats decided to delay by asking for an interview with the Zongli Yamen (Tsungli Yamen, the Chinese Foreign Office) the next day. They also stated that given the unsettled condition of the countryside and the unreliability of the Chinese army, they would not move until foreign guards arrived to escort them to Tianjin.

The next day, 20 June, the German minister, Baron Klemens von Ketteler, went to the Zongli Yamen to inquire about a reply to their message. Chinese soldiers murdered him on his way from the Legation Quarter. The Chinese reply, received that afternoon, did not mention the murder, but asked the ministers to reconsider their refusal to evacuate Beijing. The note was ignored, and at 4:00 p.m. Chinese artillery opened fire on the legations.

The total armed strength of the Legation Guards was 409 officers and soldiers. Contingents from eight nations were represented: Austria-Hungary, France, Germany, Great Britain, Italy, Japan, Russia, and the United States. There were also two categories of foreign volunteers: one consisted of about 75 men with previous military training or experience, the other, of about 50 civilians who had no military training.

Because of national rivalries, there was no centralized command and control structure. Responsibility for defending the Legation Quarter was divided among the different contingents. Each nationality guarded the area around its own legation wherever possible. The Russians and U.S. elements guarded the south; the French, Germans, and Austrians protected the east; the British, the northwest; while the Japanese stood watch in the northeast.

There were also 473 foreign civilians (men, women, and children) within the perimeter, as well as approximately 3,000 Christian Chinese refugees (Giles, p. 131). Most of them were sheltered in the Su Wang Fu (Prince Su's Palace).

Foreign noncombatant men organized committees to supervise Chinese labor, fortifications, and food rationing as well as fire fighting. The foreign women also organized committees, including a nursing committee and a sewing committee. Many women worked in the hospital as volunteer nurses, and others sewed sandbags for the barricades. All types of materials were used: bed linen, jute sacking, and blankets as well as fine silks.

A rationing system was organized, but food and water for the foreigners was not an immediate problem. There were several wells in the British Legation compound and several hundred tons of grain. In addition, large stocks of canned goods were found in the abandoned shops surrounding the Legation Quarter. A large number of ponies and mules were available to supply fresh meat.

No rations were allocated to the Chinese refugees, who survived by eating whatever they could find. In addition, every able-bodied Chinese was required to work two hours daily for the general good; that is, grave digging, building barricades, and clearing rubble. No such service was required of the foreigners; customary class distinctions would not permit it. Most survivors stated that most of the organizational work and physical labor was done by the missionaries, the least by the diplomats.

Ammunition supplies were low, and because each nationality used a different type of rifle,

there was no common ammunition reserve. There were two machine guns and two pieces of light artillery. There were originally supposed to be three, but the Russians left their field piece at Tianjin and brought only the ammunition. All the contingents were short of ammunition. Hand tools, fire fighting equipment, and medical supplies were also in short supply.

The military detachments were originally commanded by Capt. Eduard von Thomann, of the Austrian cruiser *Zenta*, sightseeing in Beijing when the siege began. As the senior officer present, he assumed command of the Legation Guards. On the first day of the siege (21 June), he ordered the troops back to their final defensive positions after the Chinese began firing, and there were unfounded rumors of a Russian and U.S. withdrawal from the city wall.

An immediate meeting was called by the ministers, and von Thomann was relieved of command. Sir Claude M. Macdonald was then given general command responsibility. Everyone was ordered back to his original position. Macdonald was titular commander in chief because he was the senior minister of all countries having troops in Beijing. However, he could neither command nor control the national contingents, only make requests for assistance. The Chinese were not able to take advantage of the premature withdrawal of the contingents and succeeded in burning only the Italian Legation, which had been abandoned.

On 23 June the Chinese set fire to the Mongol Market and the Hanlin Academy, which bordered the legations. This was the first of a series of fires set by the Chinese in an attempt to destroy the foreigners. The fires were all contained and served only to clear fields of fire for the defenders as well as provide positions of concealment for Chinese snipers. The fires burned out of control but did not spread.

Over the next two days the Allies counterattacked. The Japanese, Germans, and U.S. troops made separate attacks on the Chinese and killed large numbers of them. Large portions of the city wall were cleared of Chinese, and temporary barricades were erected by Chinese laborers.

More serious than the fires and the mass infantry attacks was the Chinese artillery bombardment. The Chinese artillery fire was accurate, and the besieged foreigners had no artillery with which to reply. Their only remedy was to use

Chinese labor to build bomb shelters covered with sandbags. Bags were made by the women on the sewing committee; the rate of production of the best workers was one every four minutes.

The pattern of the siege emerged in the first few days: constant sniping and intermittent artillery fire punctuated by violent assaults by both Boxers and Imperial Chinese troops.

The foreign defenders were forced to abandon the Austrian and Italian legations as well as the Imperial Maritime Customs building. This left the Chinese free to concentrate their energies on seizing the French Legation and the Su Wang Fu. The Chinese also attacked along the city wall and almost succeeded in dislodging U.S. and Russian forces from it.

The Chinese announced a truce in the late afternoon of 25 June; it lasted until the following morning. Before that, fighting had been heavy along the Legation Quarter's perimeter. The foreigners assumed the truce presaged the arrival of a relief force. At this time, however, the Seymour Column was struggling to fortify an arsenal between Beijing and Tianjin and waited for relief itself. In fact, it appears the dowager empress ordered the truce in a fit of pique against Prince Duan (Tuan). After hearing of the Chinese success against the Seymour Column, the truce was canceled.

The siege was rapidly becoming less of a lark to the inmates of the Legation Quarter. It was extremely hot, and the smell of gunpowder as well as of the fetid stench of unburied, decaying human and animal corpses added to the normally ripe smell of a North China city in the summer. After the first week, it was realized relief was not to be immediately forthcoming.

Desultory fighting continued through the first week of July. By this time the foreign contingents suffered casualties of 40 dead and 72 wounded (Giles, p. 2). In addition, squabbles were breaking out among the nationalities in the Legation Quarter. Charges and countercharges concerning various nationalities' bravery, cowardice, discipline, and indiscipline were bandied about. Smallpox and scarlet fever were rampant among the Chinese refugees and this added to the other continuing problems of inadequate food, potable water, and the growing incidence of dysentery.

On 7 July, a party of Chinese refugees digging a shelter uncovered a cannon barrel buried since the Anglo-French occupation of Beijing in 1860. It was removed and cleaned by two U.S. Marines and mounted on a gun carriage donated by the Italians. The ammunition for the Russian cannon left at Tianjin fitted it, more or less. It was christened the International Gun: an Anglo-French barrel, mounted on an Italian carriage, shooting Russian ammunition, served by two U.S. citizens. It was used by the foreigners for the rest of the siege.

On 13 July, there was a bitter battle for the French Legation. The Chinese succeeded in blowing up part of it by planting explosives under it. This was followed by a second attempt to negotiate a cease-fire. On 14 July, after the fall of Tianjin, the Qing Court sent a message offering the foreigners refuge in the Zongli Yamen, several blocks away, under the protection of the Chinese army. The diplomats were wary and replied they preferred to remain in their present positions.

The Yamen replied by suspending hostilities. During the cease-fire, which lasted from 14 July until 4 August, soldiers on both sides laid down their arms and traded food and souvenirs. On 18 July, the Japanese minister received a message stating Tianjin had fallen to the Allies and a relief force was on its way to Beijing. On 27 July, the dowager empress sent gifts of fruit, rice, melons, and ice to the besieged foreigners.

This truce reflected the ambivalence of the Qing Court toward the foreigners. While it wished to punish them for their real and imagined crimes, it also seemed to be sincerely concerned for their welfare. Both moderates and antiforeign radicals vied for the ear of the dowager empress. Even at this late date she had not committed herself to either side.

Her indecision was based on hatred and fear of the foreigners, as well as on her practicality and ability to dissemble. She hated the incursions of foreign missionaries. The government was powerless to prevent the Chinese Christians and foreign missionaries from becoming local rivals to the Confucian elite (Esherick, pp. 68–95, 167–205; Tan, pp. 97–104). It was impossible to completely suppress the Boxers without arousing the Shandong peasants against the dynasty. She also believed the Allied powers wished to replace her with her nephew, the Guangxu (Kuang-hsu) emperor, whom she had overthrown in 1898.

Peace feelers, made by Chinese officials in the South through the United States, were not deemed sincere because the southern officials could not guarantee the safety of the foreigners in Beijing. In fact, the war party was still in control of the capital.

The Chinese attacks continued after the truce. Between 10 August and 14 August, fighting slackened as Chinese troops withdrew from the area around the Legation Quarter in order to stop the Allied advance from Tianjin. They were unsuccessful, and the siege of the legations was raised on 14 August. Two days later, almost as an afterthought, Allied troops cleared the area around the Beidang Cathedral and raised the siege. It had lasted 57 days.

During the siege, 76 foreigners were killed and 169 were wounded. More than half of the military men were casualties. No records of the casualties among the Chinese Christians were kept; estimates ranged from several hundred to about one thousand dead and wounded.

Lewis Bernstein

REFERENCES

Aaron S. Daggett, *America in the China Relief Expedition: An Account of the Brilliant Part Taken by United States Troops in the Memorable Campaign in the Summer of 1900 for the Relief of the Besieged Legations in Peking, China* (Hudson-Kimberley, 1903); William J. Duiker, *Cultures in Collision: The Boxer Rebellion* (Presidio Pr., 1978); Joseph Esherick, *The Origins of the Boxer Uprising* (Univ. of California Pr., 1987); Peter Fleming, *The Siege at Peking* (Harper, 1959); Lancelot Giles, *The Siege of the Peking Legations: A Diary*, edited by L.R. Marchant (Univ. of Western Australia Pr., 1970); A. Henry Savage Landor, *China and the Allies* (Scribner, 1901), 2 vols.; Chester C. Tan, *The Boxer Catastrophe* (Octagon Books, 1967).

See also Beijing (Peking), China, Battle (1900).

Bell, James Franklin (1856–1919)

Gen. James Franklin Bell actively participated in military expeditions to suppress anti-imperialist movements among Native Americans, Filipinos, and Cubans. Perhaps more important were his substantial contributions to the turn-of-the-century effort to reorganize the U.S. military and improve its capacity for counterinsurgency, a tactic civilian government leaders increasingly relied on to secure the property, markets, and labor resources of U.S. corporations as they expanded abroad after 1898.

Born 9 January 1856 to a Kentucky farm family, Bell graduated from the United States Military Academy at West Point in 1878, whereupon he was assigned to Gen. George Armstrong Custer's famous (or infamous) 7th Calvary at Fort Abraham Lincoln in the Dakota Territory. For the next 12 years, Bell served with distinction in a series of counterinsurgency wars against Native Americans, learning the importance of military intelligence in defeating an enemy that used the "hit and run" tactics commonly associated today with Third World guerrilla movements. In 1882, his troops were assigned to protect the private property of the Northern Pacific Railway. These invaluable experiences later served him well in military interventions to safeguard foreign investments against Cuban and Filipino popular guerrilla campaigns.

After a brief leave of absence to pursue business opportunities in Mexico, Bell returned to garrison duty at Fort Apache, Arizona. In April 1898, the United States declared war on Spain, and Bell immediately requested assignment to Cuba, but was ordered to the Philippines. There, he deepened his experience in the tactics of counterinsurgency, which came to include public diplomacy, economic reconstruction projects, and public health campaigns to win the hearts and minds of the local population. He organized the "fighting 36th" regiment, better known in military circles as the "suicide club," and engaged in counterinsurgency campaigns against the peoples of Vigan, Luzon, Batangas, Laguna, and Tayabas—exploits that won him a Medal of Honor and promotion to brigadier general in the regular army.

On 14 April 1906, President Theodore Roosevelt, perhaps sensing the new counterinsurgency mission of the United States's military forces and recognizing Bell's extraordinary record of achievements in that area, appointed him army chief of staff. Scarcely six months later, Secretary of War William H. Taft directed the general to command the First Expeditionary Brigade, subsequently rechristened the "Army of Cuban Pacification" after the secretary rejected as politically dangerous a far more honest and revealing name, the "Army of Cuban Intervention."

Although Roosevelt and Taft were committed to a policy of military intervention "to preserve life, liberty, and property" in Cuba, both men feared that this would quickly become politically unpopular in the United States and throughout Latin America. Given the political parameters of Roosevelt's mission, Bell was sanguine about the military prospects for success. Ordinarily, the deployment of 15,000 troops in three coordinated expeditions would be more than sufficient to overwhelm and destroy a conventional force structure with the size and equipment of Cuba's insurrectionary movement.

But Bell, like his counterparts during the war against Vietnam, worried that U.S. troops would quickly become frustrated and demoralized as they sought to engage an enemy that refused to fight a conventional war. He feared a long-term military occupation in a forbidding climate, facing unfamiliar terrain and a hostile civilian population that would likely provide military intelligence, logistical support, and even soldiers to the rebel forces. Thus, Bell recommended that U.S. war plans include a deployment of 18,000 highly mobile troops with complete freedom of action to suppress the rebellion. Specifically, he warned that this would include unpopular "reconcentration" policies reminiscent of the notorious Spanish General Valeriano Weyler y Nicolau who, in his effort to smash the Cuban independence movement in 1896, aroused considerable public outrage in Cuba and the United States. Interestingly, Bell neglected to mention that the United States Army had used similar policies to crush Native American and Filipino resistance to the United States's expanding empire.

Drawing on his personal experience in the U.S. war against the Filipinos, Bell further recommended preparations for a counterinsurgency campaign that relied heavily on sophisticated, thorough military intelligence and an extensive network of spies so that the U.S. military command could target individual subversives, their families, their clandestine political organizations, and their services for supply, information, and communication (Millett, *Politics of Intervention*, p. 66).

To this end, Bell appointed Maj. Eugene F. Ladd and Capt. Dwight E. Aultman to survey the politico-military landscape and to establish a reliable source of military intelligence. Both had substantial in-country contacts, the result of long experience accumulated during service in Gen. Leonard Wood's military government after the defeat of Spanish forces in 1898. In the ensuing months, the Army of Cuban Pacification's Military Information Division divided Cuba into 26 intelligence districts, each of which was staffed by an intelligence officer who "supervised mapping, compiled an extensive file of photos and personality sketches, and wrote extensive descriptions of the terrain, towns, and communications system" (Millett, *Politics of Intervention*, p. 130).

Finally, Bell advised the president and secretary of war to approve a tactical war plan that would provide a relatively low profile for U.S. combat units which would serve primarily as a moral force to secure political and economic order. Roosevelt and Taft, who both sought to avoid the expense and potentially negative political fallout of a long-term military conflict, agreed. Contrary to long-standing interpretations of the Platt Amendment, which had placed primary responsibility on U.S. forces for the guarantee of Cuba's internal political and social order, Roosevelt expected that burden to fall on the Guardia Rural (Rural Guard), but this would require substantial reorganization of Cuba's constabulary force. This was the last task to which Bell committed himself before his promotion to major general and his resumption of duties as chief of staff in Washington in 1907.

Four years later, Bell returned to the Asian theater of U.S. military operations where he took command of the Philippine Department until 1914. After ill health cut short his service in World War I, Bell died of angina pectoris on 8 January 1919.

Keith A. Haynes

REFERENCES

Jules Robert Benjamin, *The United States and Cuba: Hegemony and Dependent Development, 1880–1934* (Univ. of Pittsburgh Pr., 1977); David A. Lockmiller, *Magoon in Cuba: A History of the Second Intervention, 1906–1909* (Univ. of North Carolina Pr., 1938); Allan R. Millett, "The General Staff and the Cuban Intervention of 1906," *Military Affairs*, 31 (1967), 113–119; Allan R. Millett, *The Politics of Intervention: The Military Occupation of Cuba, 1906–1909* (Ohio State Univ. Pr., 1968); Louis A. Pérez, Jr., *Army Politics in Cuba, 1898–1958* (Univ. of Pittsburgh Pr., 1976).

See also Cuba, Intervention (1906–1909).

Black Militia in the Spanish-Cuban/American War

The experience of blacks in state militias in the Spanish-Cuban/American War shaped blacks' political attitudes both during and after the war. Initially, blacks deplored Spain's subjugation of Cuba, promoted its liberation, and advocated the creation of what they believed would be a "Negro Republic." By the end of the war, most blacks saw the U.S. occupation of the Philippines as domination over darker peoples and derided the "White Man's Burden." The ideological change owed a great deal to the wartime experience of black volunteers.

Black participation in the state militias mustered into federal service was a political issue from the outset. President William McKinley understood the political capital that he would gain by calling up the state militias. By involving the civilian populace in the war, he could minimize fears of the regular army's power and raise support on the home front for the conflict. Service would offer upward mobility and possible federal benefits to state political figures. Thus, McKinley called for large numbers of troops from each governor, more troops than necessary to fight the war.

Because McKinley, a Republican, owed a political debt to blacks, and blacks saw service as a way to prove their capability for combat in a cause in which they believed, the issue of using black volunteers came up immediately. In some states, black volunteers had already participated in segregated companies in the state militia; in other cases, entirely new volunteer companies formed.

McKinley's first call for volunteers from state militias brought forth two preexisting black units in the North: Company L of the 6th Massachusetts Regiment and the 9th Ohio Battalion. Company L had black captains, and 1st Lt. Charles Young, a graduate of the United States Military Academy at West Point, commanded the 9th Ohio. At the same time, the Alabama governor, in an effort to meet his volunteer quota, expanded an existing black battalion into a regiment and replaced its black officers with whites. In North Carolina, Governor Daniel Russell responded by using the one black company in the state militia, the Charlotte Light Infantry, as the nucleus of a black battalion. A Republican, Russell owed a political debt to the state's blacks. Like the 9th

Ohio, all of the battalion officers were blacks, a pathbreaking departure for a southern governor.

McKinley's second appeal for volunteers pressured governors to contribute more men. Governor Russell expanded the black battalion into a regiment under the command of black officers, the 3rd North Carolina. Kansas created the 23rd Kansas Regiment, and Illinois the 8th. As in North Carolina's regiment, black officers led those of Kansas and Illinois. Virginia formed the 6th Regiment, made up of state militia members, with black officers, except for the white commanding colonel. Indiana added two black companies under black captains.

The total fighting strength of blacks in state militias called into federal service numbered 6,000. Three states had inducted blacks into companies or battalions. Five states had formed regiments, with only one led by white officers exclusively. Thus, most blacks mustered into federal service from the state militias served under 300 black officers, at a time when there was only one black officer in the regular army.

The 23rd Kansas and the 8th Illinois deployed to San Luis, Cuba, on garrison duty from August 1898 until mustered out in March 1899. Company L of the 6th Massachusetts was the only former black militia unit that saw action in Cuba.

The other troops never left the southern United States and suffered much abuse at the hands of white southerners and fellow white soldiers. The 3rd Alabama never left its home state. The North Carolina and Virginia forces were stationed at Fort Poland in Knoxville, Tennessee, where they expected to be mobilized for service in the Philippines. The 6th was drawn from large groups of men who had served together in companies in the state militia under black officers. They had volunteered with the understanding that black officers would directly command them, under the leadership of a white colonel. However, as the white colonel increased pressure on the black officers of his staff, nine of them resigned. Through the governor of Virginia, he replaced them with white officers, whom the soldiers refused to obey, and contemporary white observers termed the regiment the "Mutinous Sixth."

Both the 3rd North Carolina and the 6th Virginia experienced harassment and physical abuse from white soldiers and local whites who deplored the idea of black officers and armed blacks.

When the 3rd North Carolina and the 6th Virginia deployed to Camp Haskill, near Macon, Georgia, late in 1898, four members of the 3rd North Carolina died in a fight with whites. White troops kept Gatling guns fixed on the 6th Virginia. Finally, in early 1899, the 3rd North Carolina was mustered out of service, and the soldiers returned home on trains. At every station, rowdy whites boarded the trains and fought with the black soldiers.

The tilt in political thinking occasioned by the acquisition of territory with people of color and the occupation of the Philippines resulted in tacit federal approval of disfranchisement and racial violence in the South. When members of the 3rd North Carolina returned to their home state, they lost the right to vote in a matter of months. Across the South, governors abolished black companies of the state militia, even in Georgia, where they had not been permitted to enter federal service. White supremacists capitalized on whites' fear of armed blacks serving under black leadership, and they quickly made state militias lily-white by act and statute.

Whites' violent treatment of blacks in the state militias during the Spanish-Cuban/American War caused many blacks to question minority participation in the armed forces. Their patriotism and volunteerism resulted in more, not less, discrimination in the South upon their return to civilian life.

Glenda E. Gilmore

REFERENCES

Willard B. Gatewood, Jr., "Alabama's Negro Soldier Experiment, 1898–1899," *Journal of Negro History,* 57 (1972), 333–351; Willard B. Gatewood, Jr., "Black Americans and the Quest for Empire, 1898–1903," *Journal of Southern History,* 37 (1972), 545–566; Willard B. Gatewood, Jr., "Kansas Negroes and the Spanish-American War," *Kansas Historical Quarterly,* 37 (1971), 300–313; Willard B. Gatewood, Jr., *"Smoked Yankees" and the Struggle for Empire: Letters from Negro Soldiers, 1898–1902* (Univ. of Illinois Pr., 1971); Edward A. Johnson, *History of the Negro Soldiers in the Spanish-American War* (Capitol Printing Co., 1899); Bernard C. Nalty, *Strength for the Fight: A History of Black Americans in the Military* (Free Pr., 1986); T.S. Steward, *The Colored Regulars in the United States Army* (A.M.E. Book Concern, 1904; rpt. Arno Pr., 1969).

See also Militia in the Spanish-Cuban/American War.

Black Regular Troops in the Philippine War

In 1899 the United States annexed the Philippines, and U.S. troops, both black and white, took to the field to defeat Philippine troops who were determined to fight for their country's independence. In July 1899, the first black troops arrived in Manila, veterans of the regular army's 24th and 25th Infantry Regiment, that had fought in the Spanish-Cuban/American War in Cuba. In mid-September 1900, eight troops of the 9th Cavalry disembarked, and nine months later units of the 10th Cavalry arrived. The War Department also recruited two regiments of black volunteers, the 48th and 49th Infantry Regiments, which arrived in the Philippines early in 1900 and remained until their periods of service expired 18 months later. By December 1900, when U.S. total troop strength in the islands was at its peak of 70,000 men, their numbers included over 6,000 black regulars and volunteers.

In fall 1899 the men of the 24th and 25th Infantry Regiments were assigned to the perimeter of Manila; they also helped to protect a strategic railroad line heading north. The black soldiers engaged in some small skirmishes around Manila before joining in a major offensive into the interior of Northern Luzon, where United States Army commanders hoped to trap the bulk of the Philippine forces and capture their leader, Emilio Aguinaldo y Famy. In mid-November men of the 25th conducted a long march to the town of O'Donnell, where they captured over 100 Filipino troops and a large amount of supplies. At the same time, a battalion of the 24th undertook an extraordinary march of 300 miles through difficult terrain, penetrating areas not previously reached by U.S. troops. Although they failed in their effort to cut off Aguinaldo, they captured some Filipino installations and freed Spanish prisoners.

Early in 1900 the Filipinos abandoned conventional tactics in favor of guerrilla warfare, and black and white troops alike suffered from the frustrations of attempting to locate and defeat scattered bands of Filipino guerrillas. Throughout the year black units ranged widely across Luzon and fought dozens of skirmishes. They also garrisoned towns, built and maintained telegraph lines, scouted for the enemy, provided protection for work crews building roads, and escorted supply trains. By the end of the year

Philippine resistance was fading, but throughout 1901 black troops, as well as their white counterparts, continued to conduct endless marches through rice paddies, mountains, and forests, fighting few pitched battles. Diseases and the climate posed more severe problems than Filipino bullets.

By mid-1901 fighting shifted southward to Batangas and the island of Samar. By this time the two black volunteer regiments had returned to the United States, and the 24th and 25th Infantry Regiments and most of the 9th Cavalry remained in Luzon on garrison duty. When the second squadron of the 10th Cavalry arrived in the Philippines, it was sent to Samar, along with some units of the 9th Cavalry; these men served there from May through August. By mid-autumn 1902, all of the black troops in the Philippines had been sent home.

Most observers, whether military or civilian, black or white, praised the combat effectiveness of the black troops. Officers of the black units recommended several of their men for Medals of Honor. Although stories abounded in the Philippines concerning atrocities committed by U.S. troops against the Philippine population, no black unit was ever charged with such activity. Generally, black troops treated the Filipinos with more consideration than their white comrades, and the towns they garrisoned rarely had problems.

In addition to occupying villages and mounting marches into the interior in search of guerrillas, black troops shared in other duties assigned to their white counterparts, including supervising elections, establishing schools and courts, and combating public health problems. Black troops were especially proud of these nonmilitary activities. Filipinos came to respect the black soldiers, and in their turn, many of the soldiers came to identify with another nonwhite race. The men of the black regiments faced prejudice and discriminatory treatment from the whites they soldiered with, and facilities in Manila were often closed to them. Turnover among the white officers of the black regiments was high, and the black soldiers especially resented the insults and mistreatment they received from some of their commanders. Since whites often referred to Filipinos as "niggers," many black soldiers felt a bond with the Filipino population, which helps to account for the mutual respect and goodwill that prevailed between the two groups.

Blacks at home were divided over the advisability of having black troops assist in crushing the Filipinos' bid for independence. As the war in the islands continued, more and more black spokespersons condemned it. Black troops in the Philippines were aware of these questions being raised at home. Some fully endorsed the U.S. mission in the Philippines, but many felt ambivalent about their role. Filipino guerrillas sought to appeal to race issues in an attempt to encourage black troops to desert; they told the blacks that they were fighting a white man's war to subdue a nonwhite population, at a time when at home they were denied any semblance of equality. Although black troops were sensitive to this argument, only about a dozen deserted. Instead, the vast majority ignored the appeals and regarded their assignment as a duty they were expected to fulfill as U.S. citizens. They hoped that by serving with honor and valor in the Philippines, as they had done previously in Cuba, they would win recognition and equal rights at home. In particular, they hoped that the regular army would agree to organize more black regiments and would commission black officers.

None of these hopes were to be realized, although the army did agree to expand the four existing black regiments in order to incorporate veterans of the two volunteer regiments who had served in the Philippines and who wished to remain in uniform. On their return to the United States, the black veterans received none of the publicity and attention that they had found upon their return from Cuba a few years before. They came back to a nation where racism and injustice were still pervasive; as a vivid reminder of this, in fall 1902 the white leaders of the Spanish-American War Veterans Association sought to deny membership to black veterans.

A few black soldiers decided to remain in the Philippines and were mustered out there; they took jobs in hotels and restaurants, and a few worked for the civil government. Many of the veterans who went home carried with them some positive memories of the islands and contended that enterprising black Americans could find abundant economic opportunities there. Their stories encouraged a short-lived movement in the United States to send black colonists to the islands, but this came to naught. In 1906, some U.S. blacks did embark for the Philippines as part of the 24th and 25th Infantry Regiments which were sent there to help quash a rebellion of Moros on the island of Mindanao.

Richard H. Abbott

REFERENCES

Willard B. Gatewood, Jr., *Black Americans and the White Man's Burden, 1898–1903* (Univ. of Illinois Pr., 1975); Willard B. Gatewood, Jr., *"Smoked Yankees" and the Struggle for Empire: Letters From Negro Soldiers, 1898–1902* (Univ. of Illinois Pr., 1971).

See also Black Volunteer Troops in the Spanish-Cuban/American War and Philippine War (1898–1901).

Black Regular Troops in the Spanish-Cuban/American War

The first black soldiers mobilized for service in Cuba during the Spanish-Cuban/American War of 1898 were the four black regiments of the regular army: the 24th and 25th Infantries and the 9th and 10th Cavalries. The War Department's decision to commit all the black regiments to the Cuban campaign rested on a belief that blacks could withstand the Cuban climate better than whites and were less likely to succumb to tropical disease. Accordingly, the 25th Infantry was the first regiment assembled at Chickamauga Park, Georgia, to prepare for the Cuban campaign. The black regiments were commanded by white officers because the army did not have black commissioned officers, even for black regiments. Very few black officers served in the army. Moreover, there were no black artillery units.

Along with the other troops assigned to Cuba, the black regiments gathered in Tampa, Florida, where the black soldiers discovered that even their uniforms were no protection against discrimination and overt racism. The prejudice they experienced in Florida made them determined to gain the respect of their country on the battlefield in order to return home and carry on the continuing struggle for equality. The chaplain of the 9th Cavalry described their mission as "going to help free Cuba, and they will return to their homes, some then mustered out and begin again to fight the battle of American prejudice" (Gatewood, *"Smoked Yankees,"* p. 29).

The racial tension in Florida escalated when black soldiers refused to submit meekly to racism and challenged discriminatory practices. The most serious incident before embarkation occurred during a night of rioting in Tampa on 6 June 1898; at least 27 black soldiers and three white volunteers were seriously injured.

The black regiments saw most of their action in the Santiago campaign, beginning at the battle of Las Guásimas where the troopers of the 10th Cavalry distinguished themselves, and then at the major Battles of El Caney and San Juan Hill which led to the fall of Santiago.

George Kennan, another U.S. war correspondent, was impressed by the fighting ability of "Uncle Sam's black boys in blue," as one of the black volunteers labeled them. After the Battle of San Juan Hill, Kennan wrote:

> It is the testimony of all who saw them under fire that they fought with the utmost courage, coolness and determination, and Colonel Roosevelt said to a squad of them in the trenches, in my presence, that he never expected to have, and could not ask to have, better men beside him in a hard fight (Kennan, p. 144).

Black soldiers received 26 Certificates of Merit for heroism in the Santiago campaign. Troop M of the 10th Cavalry fought for three months with the Cuban army commanded by Gen. Máximo Gómez y Baez. The troopers participated in several military engagements, including the capture of El Hebro and a rescue at Tayabocoa. Four soldiers of the troop received Medals of Honor for bravery in this operation. Members of the 24th Infantry also volunteered to serve in the yellow fever hospital at Siboney, adding a reputation for selfless humanitarianism to their military service.

The performance of the black regulars in the Santiago campaign made them heroes in the eyes of the public during summer 1898, but especially so to the readers of the black newspapers. This no doubt was a powerful reason for the large number of blacks who volunteered for service. President William McKinley's first call for volunteers saw black units mustered in only three states: Alabama, Ohio, and Massachusetts. Some states, notably Georgia and Mississippi, refused to mobilize black militia units; other states refused to accept black volunteers. Most of the black volunteers served for a year, after which they were mustered out. Company L of the 6th Massachusetts Regiment took part in the invasion of Puerto Rico, the only black volunteer unit to see any action.

Later in the summer the president's second call for volunteers expanded the list of states where black units were created to include Illinois, Kansas, Virginia, Indiana, and North Carolina. Three regiments were brought in as federal units, and each had black officers. The colonel of the 8th Illinois, conscious of their pioneering role, rallied his men.

In summer 1898 Congress authorized the War Department to add 10 additional volunteer regiments. Four of these so-called immune regiments—because they were to recruit men who were ostensibly immune to yellow fever—were black. The army, responding to an active campaign by black soldiers and the black civilian community, commissioned black lieutenants for these regiments, including some 30 regular army enlisted soldiers who received commissions as a reward for their Cuban service. Officers above the rank of lieutenant in these regiments were white. One of the "immune" regiments, the 9th Volunteer Infantry, and two state units, the 8th Illinois and 23rd Kansas, performed garrison duty in Cuba during 1898–1899. By 1898 the volunteer army included over 6,000 blacks and another 4,000 who had enlisted in the four "immune" regiments.

When the black regiments returned to the United States following the war, the soldiers campaigned with even greater determination for their right to hold commissions in the army. Their hope that their contribution to victory would erase or reduce discrimination at home turned out to be misplaced. Pride in what they had accomplished was tested following the war when an article by Theodore Roosevelt in *Scribner's* magazine in 1899 implied cowardice among the black soldiers, a charge completely refuted by both the soldiers themselves and the correspondents who described the action. The article contradicted Roosevelt's earlier statements in 1898. He later modified his charges, again praising black troops, during the 1900 national election. The volunteers left their units when their terms of service expired, many disillusioned about their earlier belief that military service would improve their situation.

David R. Murray

REFERENCES

George Kennan, *Campaigning in Cuba* (Charles Scribner's Sons, 1898); Willard B. Gatewood, Jr., *Black Americans and the White Man's Burden, 1898–1903* (Univ. of Illinois Pr., 1975); Willard B. Gatewood, Jr., *"Smoked Yankees" and the Struggle for Empire: Letters from Negro Soldiers, 1898–1902* (Univ. of Illinois Pr., 1971).

Black Volunteer Troops in the Spanish-Cuban/American War and the Philippine War (1898–1901)

Although black soldiers have fought in all of the wars of the United States since the Revolution, their separate service in segregated "colored" regiments dates from the Civil War. In 1862, on a local basis, Gen. Benjamin F. Butler in Louisiana and David Hunter in the Carolinas had enlisted free blacks and ex-slaves into provisional units without approval from the United States War Department. That approval was granted in 1863, after President Abraham Lincoln expanded on these efforts and enlisted large numbers of black soldiers into the Union Army.

By April 1865, over 186,000 blacks were serving in 166 regiments: 145 infantry, 7 cavalry, 13 artillery, and one engineer. Earlier in the war black troops had been used as laborers or garrison troops along the Union's long lines of communication. Eventually, however, 60 black regiments went into the line of battle, most notably in the trenches around Petersburg, Virginia, and in the earlier assaults on Charleston's Battery Wagner and Port Hudson, Louisiana. Three regiments—the 8th and 79th United States Colored Infantry Regiments and 54th Massachusetts—earned inclusion in William F. Fox's 1888 list of "Three Hundred Fighting Regiments," all of which suffered over 100 combat deaths. In all, 33,380 black troops died during the war: 3,274 in battle and 30,106 from disease and other causes.

In 1869, after the army's massive postwar reduction, four black regiments, the 24th and 25th Infantries and the 9th and 10th Cavalries, remained in the regular establishment. These regiments served throughout the Indian wars, being particularly active against the nontreaty southwestern tribes. Soldiers of the 10th Cavalry, popularly known as the "Buffalo Soldiers," earned several Medals of Honor during this period. Blacks proved to be very cost-effective soldiers: they deserted less often and reenlisted more often than white troops and were court-martialed less frequently. In May 1898 after the outbreak of the Spanish-Cuban/American War, all four black regiments were concentrated in Gulf Coast ports for the invasion of Cuba.

These regiments fought with great efficiency and distinction during the Santiago campaign: the 9th, 10th, and 24th at Kettle Hill and San Juan Hill, and the 25th at El Caney. Less well known, however, are the contributions of the black volunteer soldiers of the Spanish-Cuban/American War and the Philippine War.

During the decade of the 1890s mob violence against blacks rose in many southern states, along with a movement to deprive blacks of the voting rights they had gained during Reconstruction. These were the years of "Jim Crow." Nevertheless, in the patriotic enthusiasm of 1898 at least nine state governors enrolled black as well as white volunteer soldiers.

While it is difficult to arrive at a total percentage of the 216,000 state volunteers who were blacks, it is known that blacks served in at least nine regiments: the 3rd Alabama, 8th Illinois, 1st Indiana, 23rd Kansas, 6th Massachusetts, 3rd North Carolina, 9th Ohio, 2nd Tennessee, and 6th Virginia. The army also organized a separate force of 10,000 volunteers in 10 infantry regiments, men who were thought to be biologically resistant to tropical diseases. At least four of these "immune regiments," the 7th through 10th, were composed of black soldiers and company officers (captains and lieutenants). This alone was a significant departure from previous regular army practice: before 1898 blacks had not served as company-grade officers except in very small numbers.

None of the state volunteer regiments that enrolled black soldiers are known to have fought in the Philippines or in the Caribbean, except for several of the immune regiments that saw garrison and antibandit duty in Cuba. However, this was not their only chance for active service during this period. In March 1899, shortly after the outbreak of the Philippine War, Congress authorized the enlistment of 35,000 two-year federal volunteers to replace the 11,000 state troops sent to the islands the previous summer. These men were formed into one cavalry and 24 infantry regiments that began to arrive in the Philippines in October 1899.

Two of these United States Volunteer (USV) regiments, the 48th and 49th, were composed of black soldiers and company-grade officers drawn from the immunes and state volunteers of 1898. A number of commissions were also awarded to noncommissioned officers (sergeants) from regular army black regiments who had distinguished themselves in Cuba.

One example of an officer in the volunteers of 1898–1901 is Stephen Galveston Starr of the 9th immunes and 48th USVs. At age 16 a cowboy on the Mexican border, Starr enlisted in the 65th United States Colored Infantry in December 1864 and was wounded in action. After the Civil War he served five separate enlistments in the 24th Infantry and 10th Cavalry, as a private, corporal, musician, messenger, and sergeant. During his final enlistment he saw action at San Juan Hill. In December 1898 he became a second lieutenant in the 9th immunes and returned with them to Cuba. After the 9th was mustered out in May 1899 he was awarded a captain's commission in the 48th, formed that September. In a thumbnail sketch that appeared in a history of the 9th immunes he took equal pride in his service during "all the Indian Wars of the United States from 1868 to 1885" and having had "but one court-martial recorded against him in all his service," presumably as a younger enlisted man (Coston, p. 112).

The 48th and 49th USVs arrived in the Philippines in January 1900 and were stationed in the Department of Northern Luzon. They served there throughout the early stages of the army's two-year pacification of the island, not returning to the United States until June 1901. They were among the four best USV regiments with respect to desertions, at four and 10 men respectively. In contrast, one white regiment had 110 desertions and another 104, of an authorized strength of 1,200. Several contemporary observers recorded that the USVs were better behaved toward the Filipinos than the regulars who replaced them, with the black volunteers thought to be the least abusive of all.

The black regulars of the 24th and 25th Infantries also served in the Philippines after August 1899. Throughout the counterguerrilla campaign they and their USV comrades were rarely mentioned in allegations of torture leveled at U.S. troops, especially numerous during the final pacification campaigns of 1901 and 1902.

The United States was soon to cease making efforts to integrate significant numbers of blacks into combat roles in its armed forces. Neither during World War I or World War II were blacks routinely given combat missions, except in a small number of specialist formations: armored battalions, field artillery regiments, and air force fighter-bomber squadrons. It was not until the Korean and Vietnam wars that they achieved what some might consider a hard form of equality: the opportunity to die interchangeably with white soldiers in the same battalions, companies, platoons, and squads.

John Scott Reed

REFERENCES

William Hilary Coston, *The Spanish-American War Volunteer* (Published by the author at Camp Meade, Maryland, 1899; 2nd ed. rpt. by Books for Libraries Pr., 1971); Marvin E. Fletcher, *The Black Soldier and Officer in the United States Army, 1891–1917* (Univ. of Missouri Pr., 1974); Jack D. Foner, *Blacks and the Military in U.S. History: A New Perspective* (Praeger, 1974); Willard B. Gatewood, Jr., *Black Americans and the White Man's Burden, 1898–1903* (Univ. of Illinois Pr., 1975); Willard B. Gatewood, Jr., *"Smoked Yankees" and the Struggle for Empire: Letters from Negro Soldiers, 1898–1902* (Univ. of Illinois Pr., 1971).

See also United States Volunteers in the Spanish-Cuban/American War and Philippine War (1898–1902).

Bliss, Tasker Howard (1853–1930)

Tasker Howard Bliss, United States Army officer, was an effective governor of Moro Province in the Philippines. Bliss, a highly sophisticated and scholarly man, graduated from the United States Military Academy at West Point in 1875. By 1897, he held the rank of commissary captain and went to Spain as the U.S. military attaché. His reports to Washington concerned all aspects of the Spanish army and were of major importance during the Spanish-Cuban/American War. While in Madrid, Bliss quickly became the chief diplomatic advisor to the U.S. minister, Gen. Stewart L. Woodford. Bliss counseled caution in dealing with the Spanish government, attempting to prevent a conflict in the tense months before the outbreak of war. In this manner he received his first training as a diplomat, which helped him throughout his career.

With the U.S. declaration of war against Spain in April 1898, Bliss returned to the United States. He became the chief of commissary and chief of staff of Maj. Gen. James H. Wilson's 1st Division stationed at Chickamauga, Georgia. In midsummer the division left for Puerto Rico to engage the Spanish. The troops disembarked at Ponce on 28 July 1898. From there the 1st Division followed the military road to San Juan through Aibonito, linking up with another force at Cayey.

The troops met very little resistance until Aibonito. There, on 11 August 1898 under a flag of truce made from a bedsheet, Bliss tried to persuade the Spanish to surrender, explaining that peace negotiations were underway. The Spanish had to relay his request to their superiors in San Juan, and, while the U.S. force awaited an answer, the war ended the next day.

In fall 1898 Bliss went to Cuba. As a member of a board to select campsites for the U.S. occupation forces he insisted that the healthiest locations be chosen and that every precaution be taken to prevent an outbreak of yellow fever. Following this, due to his experience in Cuba and his fluency in Spanish, the military selected him to become the collector of customs and the chief of customs services of Cuba, a position he assumed on 1 January 1899.

Bliss intently studied customs duties and went personally to the Cuban docks to learn about trade and the notorious corruption of the service. He was also allocated $65,000 to clean up and renovate the Havana customs house. Under his watchful eye the work was completed, and the laws were carried out to their fullest extent, with unscrupulous officials either dismissed or jailed. He thereby created a customs service that for decades prided itself on its honesty.

At the same time Bliss was asked to help reform the Cuban treasury. By the end of his second year in Cuba he had become a member of Governor General Leonard Wood's staff that was preparing the island for civilian government. Meanwhile, when the Philippine War, and later the Boxer Uprising, broke out Bliss requested active duty, only to be turned down because his work in Cuba was deemed more important.

On 26 April 1901, Bliss was promoted to brigadier general of the volunteers for his excellent work in Cuba; the single star became permanent in 1902. In that year Bliss returned to the United States when he accepted an appointment to the Army War College Board. Shortly after, he went back to Havana as a special envoy and negotiated a treaty of reciprocity between the United States and Cuba, which remained unchanged for years.

After serving as the Army War College's first president, Bliss went to the Philippines as the commander of the Department of Luzon in late 1905. Before arriving he traveled to Japan as part of a diplomatic team headed by Secretary of War William H. Taft. During his eight months as commander on the main island of the Philippines no major confrontations between U.S. forces and the Filipinos occurred. Again, his knowledge of Spanish assisted him in understanding the territory and the people of the Philippines.

In 1906, Bliss replaced Wood as the military commander, civilian governor, and chief of the Legislative Council of Moro Province, a volatile region with its headquarters at Zamboanga. Bliss's mission was to develop and to extend further the civil administration set up by Wood, while simultaneously acting as the peacekeeper in the province. To aid him in governing and comprehending the Moros as a people, Bliss studied their folklore and language. He also respected their religion and culture and tried to treat them justly. Bliss sent agents to investigate the treatment of plantation workers and urged better care and working conditions. He cooperated with the *datus* (Moro chieftains) wherever possible and simultaneously tried to keep the balance of power between the various Moro tribes.

While in the Philippines Bliss was one of a handful of people who viewed the fledgling Philippine Assembly optimistically. He thought it capable of achieving independence for the northern islands. For the southern Philippines and Moro Province in particular, Bliss regarded a continued U.S. presence as necessary to "civilize" the people. He saw his role as the difficult task of "Americanizing" the populace.

Bliss decided that for his plans to be effective the region required extensive economic progress. He advocated the construction of railways, roads, and schools; better sanitary conditions; improved agricultural techniques; and vocational training. Lack of funds hindered his attempts to achieve these goals.

At the same time, in order not to provoke the Moros, Bliss relied on the Philippine Constabulary and Philippine Scouts to extend U.S. control to the restless areas. Bliss realized that the local men in these organizations had the necessary language and cultural skills to bring order

to the turbulent regions of the province. U.S. troops, he concluded, were not trained in these tasks and could incite hostilities. Bliss believed that the best course of action in Moro Province was for the military to do little. He thereby discounted rumors and calls for action whenever he saw no reason for operations, sending troops only when the situation warranted it.

For its endeavors Bliss praised the constabulary as an auxiliary of his forces. In 1908, he recommended an increase in its numbers and posts to "insure maximum effectiveness to their facilities" (Forbes, vol. 1, p. 215), while opposing attempts to reduce U.S. forces due to the quiet conditions. Although he did not believe in using U.S. soldiers on every occasion, he feared that a reduction in the number of troops might tempt the Moros back into a fight. Still, Bliss thought the Moros to be generally peaceful.

Some U.S. civilian and military authorities in the Philippines criticized Bliss for his lack of action in Moro Province. They felt that he did too little by keeping his forces at their bases. Thus, Brig. Gen. John J. Pershing succeeded Bliss on 28 November 1908. Bliss went to Manila, where he became the commanding general of the U.S. forces in the Philippines from 14 December 1908 to 5 April 1909.

Nonetheless, for his actions in the Philippines, Bliss was lauded by his superiors, especially for the relative peacefulness of the Moros. When he left the Philippines much goodwill remained, especially in Moro Province. Due to his emphasis on commerce, industry, and agriculture, the province slowly began to develop. The Moros called his years the "peace era" because no major confrontations occurred.

Bliss returned to the United States to resume his post as president of the Army War College, while also becoming a member of the general staff. In August 1910, at his request he was relieved of this position, taking command of the Department of California with orders to improve military preparedness because of the Mexican Revolution. Bliss formed a provisional brigade and took command when it moved to Southern California in order to protect the border. He was cautious not to raise the suspicions of or to enrage the Mexicans by the presence of this force. He also toured the border area to assess the situation and found that most U.S. citizens were sympathetic to the revolution.

From summer 1911 until February 1913, Bliss commanded the Department of the East. As the Mexican Revolution grew more violent, the authorities felt that he had the skills necessary to keep the matter under control at the border. Commanding the Southern Department, with its headquarters at San Antonio, Texas, Bliss suggested establishing a buffer zone by occupying Mexican territory south of the Rio Grande. He concluded that even if it meant war U.S. interests and communities along the border would be safeguarded from the turmoil. However, no action was taken on his proposal. Instead, he was ordered to patrol the border, which his troops were forbidden to cross or to fire over unless provoked. In February 1915, Bliss was recalled to the nation's capital, becoming assistant chief of staff and the chief of the Mobile Army Division.

From 1897 to 1915 Bliss participated in almost every major military action of the United States. Yet, his successes did not stem from the battlefield, but rather from his skills as a diplomat, scholar, and organizer.

Gregory C. Ference

REFERENCES

W. Cameron Forbes, *The Philippine Islands* (Houghton Mifflin, 1928), 2 vols.; Frederick Palmer, *Bliss, Peacemaker: The Life and Letters of General Tasker Howard Bliss* (Dodd, Mead, 1934); Wayne Wray Thompson, "Governors of the Moro Province: Wood, Bliss, and Pershing in the Southern Philippines, 1903–1913," Ph.D. diss., Univ. of California, San Diego, 1975.

See also Moro Campaigns (1902–1913); Moro Province, The Philippines (1903–1913); Puerto Rico Campaign (1898).

Blockades in the West Indies During the Spanish-Cuban/American War

Under international law, a blockade is an act of war. To have legal force, a blockade must be declared (a "formal" blockade) and must be effective in keeping most ships from entering or leaving port. On the evening of 21 April 1898 Acting Adm. William T. Sampson received orders from the United States Navy Department to move his squadron from Key West, Florida, to the northern coast of Cuba and to begin the blockade of that island from Cárdenas on the East to Bahía Honda on the West. It was left to Sampson's discretion and the availability of a sufficient force whether he would also blockade the port of Cienfuegos on the southern coast of Cuba. The next morning Sampson's force headed for Havana. Enroute it captured two Spanish merchant ships, the *Buenaventura* and the *Pedro*. Arriving off Havana on the evening of 22 April, the squadron was dispersed to its various blockade assignments. The *Iowa*, *Indiana*, and *New York* remained off Havana along with the gunboat *Wilmington* and the torpedo boats *Porter* and *Cushing*. Cruising close to the harbor entrance on 23 April, the *Porter* captured a schooner and, in cooperation with the *Wilmington*, two small fishing smacks. The next day the blockading force captured three merchant steamers.

Congress declared war on Spain on 25 April, but because ships had already been captured, the declaration was made retroactive to 21 April. The cruisers *New York* and *Cincinnati* and the monitor *Puritan* bombarded the shore batteries at the port of Matanzas, east of Havana, on 27 April, but made no serious effort to reduce the earthworks. The United States Navy briefly considered seizing Matanzas, establishing a base for the blockading force, and opening up communications with the Cuban revolutionaries, but decided against it. On the same day that Matanzas was bombarded, the blockading force off Havana captured a merchant steamer.

Beyond Matanzas the torpedo boat *Winslow* streamed into Cárdenas Bay on 8 May and fired 60 rounds at the Spanish gunboats there in an effort to draw them out of the bay and into a battle. The gunboats did not take up the challenge. Therefore, on 11 May the gunboat *Wilmington*, the revenue cutter *Hudson*, and the gunboat *Machias*, along with the *Winslow*, entered the bay. The *Winslow* was the only ship with a draft shallow enough to approach a Spanish gunboat lying at a wharf. As the *Winslow* drew near, the gunboat fired. Shots struck the steam pipe connection with the engine, knocked out the wheel, wounded the lieutenant in command, and started a fire. Another hit disabled the engine. The *Hudson* then approached, fastened a line to the *Winslow* and towed it out of danger. The effort resulted in the deaths of five men and the wounding of five others in the *Hudson*. The *Machias* shelled a Spanish signal station at Diana Cay, landed men to destroy it, and disabled an old armed tug. U.S. ships also shelled Cárdenas and started fires.

Meanwhile, on the southern coast of Cuba, a blockade of the port of Cienfuegos had been imposed on 21 April. Nevertheless, the Spanish liner *Monsterrat* ran the blockade and delivered soldiers, provisions, and gold to that port. By 27 April, when it was clear to Sampson that there were a great many difficulties associated with a blockade of this port, he telegraphed the Navy Department that he could not maintain the blockade of Cienfuegos without colliers. When these were sent Sampson found that the high seas made it difficult to use them effectively. U.S. naval forces then turned their attention to an effort to cut the five submarine cables linking Cienfuegos with other parts of Cuba. Launches filled with men from the *Nashville* and *Marblehead* moved out in a heavy swell on 11 May and sought to retrieve the cables. They came under heavy fire, and four men were killed or died of wounds; five others were seriously wounded. Only two of the five cables were cut. Later, the revenue cutter *Windom* destroyed a lighthouse that sheltered a Spanish machine gun. Before the blockade could be improved, more pressing matters demanded the attention of the Navy Department.

Capt. Charles S. Cotton of the auxiliary cruiser *Harvard* telegraphed the Navy Department on 11 May that the Spanish squadron under the command of Adm. Pascual Cervera y Topete had reached the island of Martinique. This news prompted the Navy Department to order the Flying Squadron under Commodore Winfield Scott Schley from Norfolk, Virginia, to Key West to await further orders. While he was enroute to Florida, the U.S. consul at Curaçao in the Dutch West Indies telegraphed on 14 May that Cervera's squadron was there. The Navy Department believed that once Cervera had coaled his ships, he would head for Santiago or Cienfuegos. This information was sent to Admiral Sampson in a letter on 16 May. Schley reached Key West about midnight on 17 May, and the next day he received orders from the Navy Department to take his force to Havana and blockade that port. Before this order could be carried out, Sampson's squadron returned from Puerto Rico. He countermanded the orders of the Navy Department and sent Schley to Cienfuegos to establish a close blockade. While Schley was watching Cienfuegos, Sampson would take his squadron to Havana and watch for any attempt by Cervera to enter that port.

Schley's squadron arrived off Cienfuegos about midnight on 21 May. That afternoon Schley heard gunfire, which he interpreted as a salute to Cervera's squadron. From the information he received he believed the Spanish squadron was in the port and did not learn otherwise until the afternoon of 23 May. Sampson's order of 21 May ran that when Schley was satisfied that the Spaniards were not in port, he was to "proceed with all dispatch, but cautiously, to Santiago de Cuba, and if the enemy is there blockade him in port" (Chadwick, vol. 1, p. 272). Accompanying this order was a memorandum from Sampson stating that it was assumed that the foregoing orders would be received by 23 May so that he could reach Santiago by the morning of 24 May: "It is thought that the Spanish squadron would probably be still at Santiago, as they must have some repairs to make and coal to take" (Chadwick, vol. 2, p. 274). Schley was also informed that the auxiliary cruiser *St. Paul* and the protected cruiser *Minneapolis* had been ordered to scout off Santiago, and if the Spanish squadron left, one of these ships would attempt to reach him. It was possible that when the Spanish learned of Schley's departure from Cienfuegos they would attempt to go there. Therefore, if Schley received this message after daylight, he was to mask his real direction as much as possible and follow the Spanish squadron wherever it went. So, at 7:00 p.m. on 24 May the Flying Squadron moved toward Santiago at a pace geared to the speed of its slowest collier. The cruiser *Castine* was left to watch Cienfuegos. Breakdowns in the collier delayed Schley's arrival off Santiago until 26 May.

Meanwhile, Cervera's squadron reached Santiago de Cuba on the morning of 19 May. A Cuban agent at Havana sent a message to the Navy Department that same day reporting this development. The auxiliary cruiser *St. Louis*, which had been ordered to watch the port, had been off cable-cutting on 18–19 May and missed the arrival of the Spaniards. Two days later the auxiliary cruisers *St. Paul* and *Yale* arrived and took stations off the port. The *Harvard* and the *Minneapolis* arrived on 23 May. All were unaware of Cervera's presence in Santiago. Therefore, when Schley reached Santiago and conferred with Capt. Charles D. Sigsbee of the *St. Paul*, he was informed that Cervera's squadron was not in that port. Furthermore, Schley interviewed a man who had served as a pilot at Santiago for many years. The pilot said that the Spanish squadron could not enter the harbor except on smooth water days and then only with the assistance of tugs. In light of the information he had received from both Sigsbee and the pilot, Schley began to wonder if the reports of Cervera's presence at Santiago were not ruses intended to draw off the Flying Squadron and to deceive Sampson so that Cervera could steam around the rear of the admiral's force and reach Havana. On the other hand, if the Spaniards had not yet arrived, there was time for Schley to attend to the coal supply of his squadron so it would be ready to pursue or blockade the enemy force. The sea and the projecting sponsons of some of the big ships made it difficult to coal off Santiago. Therefore, Schley decided on the evening of 26 May to take his squadron to Key West to recoal in that protected environment.

Before knowing of the arrival of the Flying Squadron off Santiago, the secretary of the navy sent a message on 25 May to the *Harvard* at Haiti that it was to proceed at once to inform Schley and the senior officer off Santiago that the Navy Department's information was that Cervera's squadron was in that port. This was to be investigated, and if true, the enemy was not to leave without a battle. Schley replied on 27 May that he was forced to proceed to Key West for coal and that he regretted that he could not obey the department's orders. He had not been able to learn anything positive about the enemy's presence in Santiago. As it turned out, the ocean calmed, coaling was carried out by a collier, and Schley's force was back in position before Santiago on the evening of 28 May.

The secretary of the navy and President William McKinley were shocked by Schley's message of 27 May. They were more certain of Cervera's presence in Santiago than the secretary's earlier messages had conveyed. It seemed as though Schley was leaving his post of duty at a crucial time. Schley was ordered back to Santiago to ascertain if the Spanish squadron was there. By the time these urgent messages had reached Schley he was already where they wanted him to be. On 24 May Schley reported to the Navy Department on the definite presence of two cruisers and two destroyers of Cervera's squadron and his belief that the rest of the force was also in the harbor.

Schley brought the commanding officers of his squadron together in a meeting on the flag-ship *Brooklyn*, where he explained his blockade arrangements and the method of attack if the Spanish ships emerged. The squadron, formed in a line of battle, was to cruise slowly before the harbor entrance. If the Spanish ships emerged, most of the guns were to concentrate on the leading ships, other fire was to be directed at the vessels that followed. If any Spanish ships escaped from this concentration of fire, they were to be pursued as far as coal supplies would permit.

Meanwhile, the Navy Department, unaware that Schley was back before Santiago, had ordered Sampson to Key West where he was able to answer many of the secretary's questions. Before Sampson departed for Santiago it was learned that Schley had established a blockade, and Sampson ordered him to maintain a close watch, especially at night. Sampson arrived off Santiago on the evening of 1 June and took charge of U.S. forces, although for some reason a blockade was never formally declared.

Sampson divided his force into two groups. One, under Schley's command, consisted of the battleships *Massachusetts* and *Texas*, the cruiser *Brooklyn*, and the unprotected cruiser *Marblehead*. The second group, under Sampson, consisted of the *New York*, *Iowa*, *Oregon*, the auxiliary cruiser *Mayflower*, and the torpedo boat *Porter*. Both groups were placed in an arc around the harbor entrance, with Schley on the east and Sampson on the west. The blockading ships were to remain six miles from the shore during the day and move closer during the night. An attempt to block the harbor entrance by sinking the collier *Merrimac* on 3 June was unsuccessful. On 7 June Sampson tightened the nighttime disposition by ordering three picket launches to a position within a mile of the fortifications at Morro Castle at the entrance to the harbor. Two miles beyond them was a line of three small vessels, and the rest of the ships were in an arc four miles out.

The next day, 8 June, Sampson ordered the *Iowa*, *Oregon*, and *Massachusetts* to move within two miles of the channel opening and to take turns every two hours in focusing their powerful searchlights on the entrance. Similar two-hour sweeps of the coastline on both sides of the harbor entrance were to be made by the *Brooklyn* and *Texas* on the west and the *New York* and the *New Orleans* on the east. These activities had an important effect in deterring any attempt by the Spaniards to escape at night.

When the blockade of Santiago was imposed there was a demand for more ships than were available. Plans had to be made for ships to depart from the blockade for coaling, water, or other duties without greatly diminishing its effectiveness. For example, navy ships supported the landing of U.S. troops at Daiquirí and at Siboney on 22–23 June. The army then began its advance on Santiago. One result of the shortage of ships was that it was sometimes necessary to leave Cienfuegos unguarded for several days at a time. Technically, such departures ended the blockade, and a new proclamation was needed to notify neutrals and others that restricted access to the port had been reimposed, but this was not done. It was not until after the Battle of Santiago on 3 July that the situation improved. By the middle and end of July the concentration of many ships led to a strict blockade.

From the beginning Havana also posed special problems. To keep up the blockade and to supply reliefs when vessels had to depart for water or coal would have required 40 ships, but Commodore John A. Howell had only 26. As a result, the nearby smaller ports of Santa Clara Bay, Sagua la Grande, and Caibarien all remained open and all had railroad connections with Havana over which supplies were shipped to that city. Howell recognized the problem, but it was not until July that he was able to blockade these ports. He does not seem to have issued a proclamation announcing the blockade before actually imposing it. On 10 July Sampson ordered Howell to watch the ports of Nipe and Nuevitas and to blockade the north coast of Cuba as far as possible. Again, these ports were not included in the formal proclamations of blockades, nor were the various foreign powers notified. On 8 August the Navy Department notified Howell that he could not capture vessels going to Sagua la Grande and asked him by what authority he was blockading that port. Howell replied that there was little practical use in blockading Havana if other ports were kept open. Actually, Spain made little use of Sagua. In the last analysis, Howell had too few ships for the job he was asked to do. Most of the ships in his force were slow, lightly armed, and subject to machinery and maintenance problems. His total effective force was only about 14 ships with which he was to watch 400 miles of coastline.

Despite its flaws, the blockade did have an effect on Havana. By the end of June it was necessary to open free food kitchens for the poor, and large quantities of fruit and vegetables were grown under government auspices. In July, however, the food kitchens were not able to supply all the food that they needed, and there was a threat of famine. At the end of the war a newspaper correspondent estimated that 45 percent of the deaths among the poor white population were the result of inadequate food.

The problem of too few ships for the blockading duties increased in late June as the result of a naval reorganization and new demands. On 21 June the Navy Department made changes in the command structure of its forces in the West Indies. The North Atlantic Squadron under Sampson became the North Atlantic Fleet. Howell was named as Sampson's deputy, and on 7 July relieved Commodore John C. Watson, then in charge of the Caribbean blockade, and assumed command of the newly designated First North Atlantic Squadron. Watson became commander of the navy's Eastern Squadron with a mission of threatening the Spanish coast. Schley was given the command of the Second North Atlantic Squadron. The Navy Department wanted to send Watson's squadron to Europe to harass Spain. In preparation for this, it increased the strength of his force over Sampson's objections. The admiral argued that the battleships *Iowa*, *Indiana*, and cruiser *New York* had been at sea for six months and needed extensive overhauling before undertaking a long sea voyage. There was also the matter of the pending invasion of Puerto Rico which required naval support. To give Howell what was proposed would mean that a large part of the blockade would have to be abandoned. Sampson succeeded in delaying the departure of the squadron until the end of the war.

Another demand on Sampson's force was the State Department's announcement on 28 June of a new restriction on commerce. This declared that the southern coast of Cuba from Cape Francés to Cape Cruz was under blockade, as well as the port of San Juan, Puerto Rico. During May and June, San Juan was blockaded by a single U.S. warship. Rough seas made it difficult to board incoming merchant ships, and the blockader was always exposed to hostile fire from the shore. Sigsbee had reported to the Navy Department that a considerable force of ships would be needed to maintain an effective blockade, and such a force was not forthcoming. Under the 28 June blockade proclamation, neutral ships were given 30 days to clear the areas involved; so the blockade was never completely effective. In addition, Sampson did not have enough ships to enforce an effective blockade.

All these matters soon became academic. On 26 July a letter of the queen regent of Spain to President McKinley asking for peace terms was decoded. Negotiations began in earnest. By 12 August Spain had accepted all the U.S. demands except the one concerning the cession of the Philippines. On that basis, all military and naval operations were suspended. The blockade of the northern coast of Cuba did not end until 14 August. The peace treaty was not signed until 10 December.

Harold D. Langley

REFERENCES

French Ensor Chadwick, *The Relations of the United States and Spain: The Spanish-American War* (Scribner, 1911), 2 vols.; David F. Trask, *The War With Spain in 1898* (Macmillan, 1981), 108–144; Henry Watterson, *History of the Spanish-American War Embracing a Complete Review of Our Relations with Spain* (Werner, 1898), 124–151.

See also Cienfuegos, Cuba, Naval Battle (1898).

Borno, (Joseph) Louis (1865–1942)

Joseph Louis Borno was president of Haiti for much of the period of the U.S. occupation, 1915–1934. Borno was born in 1865 into the mulatto elite in Port-au-Prince, Haiti. He studied law in Paris and became fluent in English and Spanish. He was a keen botanist, distinguished poet, lawyer, and legal scholar. As a diplomat, he represented Haiti in the Dominican Republic and at the Permanent Court of International Justice. He held almost every position in President Philippe Sudre Dartiguenave's cabinet and was minister of foreign affairs on three occasions. In this capacity he signed the Treaty of 16 September 1915 that reduced Haiti to a protectorate. Although at first Borno so opposed the U.S. intervention that his obstructive attitude led to U.S. demands in 1918 for his removal as minister of finance, he came to believe that more could be gained for his country through conciliation than by resistance. He was

elected president by the Council of State on 10 April 1922 and assumed office a month later.

President Borno cooperated closely with the U.S. high commissioner, Gen. John H. Russell, forming what critics called a "joint dictatorship." While some historians dismiss him as a "puppet ruler," others point out that his attitude was by no means servile. He expressed his own ideas forcefully and in some cases insisted on their adoption. He refused to call the Assembly and ruled instead through the Council of State whose members, removed and appointed at his pleasure, reelected him to a second four-year term in 1926. Borno was in a position to compel the enactment of the essential features of any project of law. Sensitive to criticism, he promulgated a new press law in December 1922 setting heavy penalties for insults made by the media against government officials or foreign diplomats and forbidding the courts to grant bail to persons accused of such offenses. These provisions enabled his government to regulate the publication of opposition newspapers and to deal harshly with unfriendly critics.

During the tranquil, comparatively prosperous era of Borno's presidency, much of the material progress experienced as the result of the U.S. occupation occurred, financed entirely from efficiently managed Haitian revenues. With Borno's cooperation replacing Dartiguenave's intransigence, $16 million in Haitian bonds were floated in 1922 by the National City Bank. The Gendarmerie d'Haiti, renamed Garde d'Haiti in 1928, took over the functions of urban and rural police, prison administration, fire protection, and the coast guard, and its officers were financial supervisors to communal governments.

The public works administration constructed thousands of miles of highway, 210 bridges, and nine air fields. It erected public buildings, renovated municipal water works, and repaired ancient irrigation systems. Telephone subscribers in Port-au-Prince grew from 450 in 1924 to 1,200 in 1929, while the number of automobiles increased from virtually none in 1915 to 3,000 in 1929. The public health service with the cooperation of the Rockefeller Foundation established 12 modern hospitals and 147 rural clinics. It examined and vaccinated schoolchildren, distributed quinine, drained swamps, attended to street cleaning and garbage disposal, constructed latrines, and carried on a general campaign of sanitation.

In April 1923 Borno approved the formation of the Service Technique, which was to begin programs of agricultural and vocational education. A central school of agriculture opened in Damien in June 1924. By 1930 there were 65 rural farm schools with 7,493 pupils, and the Service had carried out nationwide soil surveys, reintroduced tobacco as a money crop, and created a successful sisal plantation. Despite these gains, the Service Technique proved the most controversial of the occupation programs, drawing bitter criticism from elites who opposed any tampering with the traditional educational system and who specifically objected to the U.S. teachers and the vocational slant of the instruction.

Borno's autocratic rule and willing collaboration with the United States were offensive to Haitian nationalists. His manipulated reelection in 1925 drew protests from people of all classes, and when he left Port-au-Prince to visit New York, he was publicly booed. His decision in November 1929 to postpone national elections until 1932 sparked riots in the capital at Cayes, where a marine patrol fired on an advancing mob and killed 21 people. These events led to President Herbert Hoover's appointment in 1930 of an investigating commission headed by W. Cameron Forbes. After holding public hearings in Port-au-Prince, the commission recommended that a neutral candidate be selected temporary president until the Assembly could be elected to choose a permanent president. Reluctantly, Borno accepted Eugéne Roy, who succeeded him on 15 May 1930. Among the few men who left the presidency alive and constitutionally, Borno was the only incumbent who neither sought nor was granted a pension. He lived peacefully in Pétionville until his death in 1942.

Jane M. Rausch

REFERENCES

Emily Green Balch, *Occupied Haiti* (Writers Pub. Co., 1927); Robert Debs Heinl, Jr., and Nancy Gordon Heinl, *Written in Blood: The Story of the Haitian People, 1492–1971* (Houghton Mifflin, 1978); Arthur C. Millspaugh, *Haiti Under American Control, 1915–1930* (World Peace Foundation, 1921); Dana G. Munro, *The United States and the Caribbean Republic, 1921–1933* (Princeton Univ. Pr., 1974); Robert I. Rotberg, *Haiti: The Politics of Squalor* (Houghton Mifflin, 1971).

See also Haiti, Occupation (1915–1934).

Boxer Uprising, China (1899–1901)

The Boxer Uprising against foreign imperialism is one of the best known events in modern Chinese history. Thanks to the efforts of novelists, popularizing historians, and motion pictures, it is possibly the most publicized episode in the history of foreign imperialism in China. However, it is still misunderstood. The majority of non-Chinese accounts concentrate on the ways in which foreign powers reacted to it. The Chinese side is treated as a whole, not as a part of a complex process.

Many, but not all, foreign contemporaries viewed it as a psychotic episode; part of the "Oriental mentality." Today, after experiences with national liberation movements and religious fundamentalism, it should be viewed beyond the notion of Chinese antiforeign feelings and actions as a form of psychosis. When reading about it, one should try to imagine what it was like to be a Chinese set upon by powerful foreigners in one's own country.

Boxer studies around the world usually focus on one of five areas. Scholars (as well as some contemporary observers) consider it one of the first examples of a popular Chinese nationalist movement. This is the favored interpretation in the People's Republic of China in both the scholarly and popular literature. Another line of study deals with the origins of the Boxers. This has always fascinated Chinese and foreign scholars and has been written about since the Boxers first appeared.

A third investigative area is the relationship between the Boxers and various members of the Qing (Ch'ing) court. No one has yet presented a satisfactory explanation of the linkages, though there is much speculation. Another facet of study is the connection between the Boxers and heterodox folk religious sects. This subject has intrigued Chinese and Japanese scholars of late, but has been of little interest to Western scholars.

Finally, there is the history of the activities of Christian missionaries and their converts in North China. This topic is attracting more interest in the West as Chinese archivists release more records of missionary cases. Western scholars are also excited about material on the relationships between missionaries, converts, and local societies available in the relatively unexplored missionary archives in the United States and Western Europe.

The foreign military and diplomatic reactions to the Boxers are not on this list of areas of study. These subjects have been neglected of late due to lack of interest, partly because it is thought that they have already been analyzed, and partly because of the existence of an enormous amount of primary and secondary material in seven languages. Coming to grips with these various languages daunts even the most valiant researcher. However, neither the official records of the foreign expeditionary forces nor the oral history collections nor the foreign ministry archives have been fully exploited by investigators.

Although sometimes referred to as the Boxer Rebellion, the uprising was not directed against the Qing Dynasty. Rather, it was an outbreak of populism and xenophobia, rooted in religious traditionalism and peasant unrest in reaction to foreign and Christian influence. The dynasty supported the movement as a way to secure its own popular support.

This antiforeign, anti-Christian movement began to assume an organized form in North China in 1899 after floods, famine, aggressive Christian proseletyzation, and foreign intervention on behalf of missionaries and converts. The Boxers appear to have been rooted in secret societies and in the activities of itinerant entertainers who performed at local market fairs. They were proficient in the traditional martial arts and conducted secret rituals that guaranteed the believer immunity from death in battle against foreigners (see Esherick for a definitive discussion of the movement's origins).

However, popular religion and antiforeign agitation are not the only contexts in which the Boxers must be viewed. The years 1895–1900 are fraught with significance. China was defeated in the Sino-Japanese War (1894–1895), losing territory to Japan. This marked the end of the Self-Strengthening Movement (a conservative attempt designed to import foreign technology into China). Military failure signaled the start of a foreign Scramble for Concessions (Slicing the Chinese Melon) to secure economic and political spheres of influence if China was to be split up.

These events also helped create a social reform movement that captured the attention of the emperor in the "One Hundred Days Reform" in summer 1898. The movement failed when reactionary elements at court rallied behind the dowager empress and mounted a *coup d'état* to eliminate the emperor's power.

In 1897, the German seizure of Qingdao (Tsingtao) and Jiaozhou (Kiaochow) Bay in Shandong (Shantung), and aggressive German backing of missionaries in Shandong Province brought matters to a boil. When foreign intrusions combined with elite and popular resentment against Chinese Christians and a spate of natural disasters, the Shandong peasantry was brought to a state of near panic.

Part of the court was predisposed to believe in and support the Boxers for its own reasons. Giving the Boxers, or any private group, official permission to organize in self-defense was an extraordinary departure from imperial policy. Chinese law prohibited this type of organization because it was seen as a potential center of subversion and armed rebellion. However, foreign pressure on the dynasty, not only in Shandong but also in Hubei (Hupei) and Sichuan (Szechuan), in central and western China, where other groups were organizing similar organizations, seemed to justify this unprecedented, extraordinary measure by the court (*see* Li Chiennung).

There were also signs of anti-imperial sentiment among the elite. The dynasty felt particularly vulnerable to charges that it wished to stay in power regardless of the cost to the Chinese sovereignty.

There was a split at court, which divided those who supported the dowager empress in her coup against the emperor and the reform party. The former had the upper hand after summer 1898. Its leadership consisted of antiforeign Manchu princes and their Chinese supporters. Their opponents, although not as powerful, were men who owed allegiance to the more progressive Guangxu (Kuang-hsu) emperor. By late 1899 they had been dispersed; many were given official posts outside North China.

By the beginning of 1900 the Boxers were spreading from northern Shandong into southern Zhili (Chihli) Province. By April and May, Boxer bands were active in the areas around Beijing (Peking) and Tianjin (Tientsin). The spread of the Boxers in Zhili was aided by the divisions within the provincial bureaucracy on the question of suppression, the mediocre governor general of the province, and the shortage of troops available for Boxer suppression duties.

This was compounded by Treaty Power displeasure with the measures taken by the court to eliminate the Boxer threat. Predictably, foreign hectoring strengthened the antiforeign, pro-Boxer faction at court. Divisions among the dowager empress's advisors meant that policy oscillated from one extreme to another.

In late May 1900, given the destruction of foreign property, especially the Beijing-Tianjin railway, and the danger to foreign lives, the diplomats at Beijing informed the Zongli Yamen (Tsungli Yamen, the Chinese Foreign Office) that additional legation guards were being summoned from the coast. The Chinese agreed to this extra-treaty reinforcement as long as the reinforcements were limited to 30 men per legation. More than these were sent and by the beginning of June two dozen warships were gathered in the Dagu (Taku) Roads. This was viewed as a provocation by the antiforeign faction at court.

On June 10, further reinforcements were sent to the legations from Tianjin under the command of Adm. Edward H. Seymour. Heavy Chinese resistance blocked the passage of the column to Beijing. That same day, Boxers burned the British Summer Legation in the West Hills outside the capital. The next day, the Japanese Legation's chancellor was murdered by Imperial troops. On 20 June 1900, the German minister was murdered by Chinese troops as he went to the Zongli Yamen. It appeared to both the court and the foreign ministers that a state of war existed.

Both the pro-emperor and pro-Boxer court factions saw that the dynasty's military suppression of the Boxers would leave the Qing facing a popular rebellion with strong grass roots support in North China. The only difference between the two court factions was that the conservatives believed suppression would make the boxers rebellious while the reformers thought they always were a subversive organization.

But with foreign warships massing off the coast and foreign troops advancing toward the capital, neither faction wished to add to China's problems by starting an internal rebellion. However, the actions of the Treaty Powers and the growth of the Boxer strength had foreclosed other options. If the dynasty was to survive, suppression and pacification were the only paths left to take.

The bombardment and seizure of the Dagu Forts (17 June) as well as the beginnings of the sieges of the foreign legations at Beijing (20 June) and the Tianjin concessions (17 June) made war

a foregone conclusion. The court declared war on the Treaty Powers on 21 June 1900 (Yishan, pp. 196–198).

This declaration of war is an interesting document. It was one of a number of edicts issued that day and was not sent directly to the foreign ministers. Foreigners were blamed for initiating hostilities; resisting troops were praised and were urged to stop the foreigners. Officials and the people were warned against retreating or becoming traitors; there was no clear statement of a formal declaration of war, however.

The vagueness of the terms used in this document permitted the viceroys outside the capital to interpret the edict in any way they wished. Many were opposed to the Boxers and had been sent away from the capital because of their views. Zhang Zhidong (Chang Chih-tung) at Wuhan, Yuan Shikai (Yuan Shih-k'ai) in Shandong, Li Hongzhang (Li Hung-chang) in Canton, and Liu Kunyi (Liu K'un-i) in Nanjing (Nanking) chose to disregard and suppress the edict. They claimed it was an improperly issued, illegitimate order. They used it as a pretext to suppress antiforeign organizations in the Yangzi (Yangtze) Valley and southeast China.

In concert with Sheng Xuanhuai (Sheng Hsuan-huai), director of Imperial Railways and Telegraphs, Zhang and Lin (governors general in the Yangtze Valley) entered into an agreement with the Treaty Powers at Shanghai. In return for a pledge of nonintervention they promised to suppress Boxers and other antiforeign organizations and to protect foreigners living in areas under their jurisdiction. Li and Yuan also abided by this agreement. Southeastern China was saved from antiforeign disturbance and foreign invasion.

After the seizure of Dagu and Tianjin in June and July 1900, the Treaty Powers gathered reinforcements for their drive to Beijing. Their lightning campaign lifted the siege of the foreign legation quarter in the middle of August. Shortly before the Allied expeditionary forces reached Beijing, the dowager empress and the court fled westward and reestablished the court in Xian (Sian) near the end of October.

The Russians used the confusion and chaos engendered by the uprising to seize Manchuria. Hoping to make the area a part of the Russian Empire, they attempted to wrest it from Chinese jurisdiction using methods similar to those used to seize the Maritime Province (1860) and to crush the independent khanate of Bukhara (1850). However, Russian occupation of Manchuria aroused the ire and suspicions of the other Treaty Powers, especially the United States and Japan, for varying reasons (*see* Hunt).

In the aftermath of the uprising, the court appointed Li Hongzhang chief negotiator with the Allies. Negotiations began that fall.

The Allied coalition, with the immediate antiforeign threat gone, splintered, with each power following its own perceived interests. The Germans favored harsh punishment. The British supported the Germans in an attempt to check the Russian occupation of Manchuria. The Japanese, angry and wary of Russian expansion, were conciliatory to the Chinese. The French announced they had no territorial designs on China, while the United States announced a second Open Door policy, supporting Chinese administrative and territorial integrity and advocating peace and safety for all in China.

The Allies were eventually able to agree on terms, and the Boxer Protocols were signed in September 1901. They consisted of 12 articles and 19 annexes and represented a high point of foreign imperialism in China (*see* Kelly). The main features were as follows:

1. Culpable officials were to be punished by the court under the direction of the Treaty Powers. More than 100 provincial and central government officials were punished. Penalties ranged from official reprimands to internal exile to posthumous degradation to death.

2. Huge indemnities were established. The final figure decided on by the Treaty Powers was 450 million taels (U.S. $70.905 billion) payable over 39 years (to 1940) at 4 percent annual interest. Security for payment was the revenue generated by the maritime customs, the transit taxes, the native customs, and the salt gabelle. In addition, the existing tariff was raised to 5 percent and extended to what had been duty-free merchandise.

3. Apology missions were to be sent to Japan and Germany to atone for the deaths of the Japanese legation's chancellor and the German minister.

4. A permanent foreign military presence, the legation guards, was to be permitted in Beijing.

5. All fortifications and arsenals between Beijing and the sea were to be destroyed, including the Dagu Forts, the Tanggu (Tang-ku) shipyard, the arsenals near Tianjin, and the walls of Tianjin.

6. Foreign troops could be stationed at all strategic points between Beijing and the sea.

7. China was forbidden to import arms for two years.

8. The Legation Quarter was to be turned into a fortified foreign enclave.

9. Official examinations were suspended for five years in cities where the Boxers were active.

10. An Allied occupation of Beijing and Tianjin was established.

11. The river between Tianjin and the sea was to be dredged and straightened, ensuring easy access for foreign ships.

The Boxer Uprising had domestic and international ramifications. The majority of foreign observers saw it as the blind, bigoted, uncivilized reaction of the Chinese against Western civilization. Even though the superiority of Western arts, sciences, and technology was reestablished, foreigners felt they could never feel as at home in their concessions as they had before.

Foreigners were also faced with the uncomfortable realization that Chinese adoption of Western technology did not mean they would adopt Western mores. It also showed just how much the foreign presence was resented and disliked.

At the same time, foreign dreams about the impending dissolution of the Chinese Empire were also shown to be fantasies. Emergent Chinese nationalism made a territorial division of China among the Treaty Powers impossible.

A new imperialist consensus of opinion was reached that coincided with the U.S. propositions in the Open Door notes (which enunciated the Open Policy): China should be open to all powers, in thrall to none, with its territorial integrity preserved. The Open Door notes had been sent to other major powers by Secretary of State John Hay in 1899–1900. This point of view was dominant until the collapse of the imperialist system and the emergence of radical Chinese nationalism in the 1920s.

The uprising also had an enormous domestic impact. The immediate effect left no Chinese with any doubts as to the efficacy of Western science and technology. Blatant foreign interference in China's domestic affairs compromised its sovereignty in many ways. The most obvious included the prohibition against importing foreign armaments, the imposition of heavy indemnities, the permanent stationing of foreign troops in North China, and the destruction of fortifications and arsenals between Beijing and the sea.

The uprising helped discredit the dynasty among the elite. Two villains emerged: reactionary Manchus and ignorant and credulous peasants. Those who had opposed the 1898 reforms were totally discredited. Although the dynasty undertook many reforms in its last decade of existence, it had lost its hold on the elite because of its backing of the uprising. Westernization and revolution began to appear as credible alternatives to conservative reform.

The Boxer Uprising also made the elite very wary of any popular participation in government. Early republican theorists called for political revolution among the elite, but assiduously avoided encouraging popular participation in politics. Both revolutionaries and reformers feared the participation of the peasant majority in politics because of the events of summer 1900. Not even the most radical were willing to harness popular discontent against social institutions in an attempt to change them. Not until Mao Tse-Tung's vision of communism took hold in parts of rural China in the 1930s did anyone try to harness the populist resentment of China's peasantry to force political change.

Lewis Bernstein

REFERENCES

David D. Buck, ed., *Recent Chinese Studies of the Boxer Movement* (M.E. Sharpe, 1987); Li Chien-nung, *The Political History of China, 1840–1928* (Princeton Univ. Pr., 1956); William J. Duiker, *Cultures in Collision: The Boxer Rebellion* (Presidio Pr., 1978); Joseph W. Esherick, *The Origins of the Boxer Uprising* (Univ. of California Pr., 1987); Michael H. Hunt, *Frontier Defense and the Open Door: Manchuria in Chinese-American Relations, 1895–1911* (Yale Univ. Pr., 1973); John S. Kelly, *A Forgotten Conference: The Negotiations at Peking, 1900–1901* (Librairie E. Droz, 1963); A. Henry Savage Landon, *China and the Allies* (Scribner, 1901), 2 vols.; Chester C. Tan, *The Boxer Catastrophe* (Octagon, 1967); Xiao Yishan, *Qingdai tongshi* (General History of the Qing), rev. ed. (Taibei, 1962), 4:2.

See list of entries at front of book for Boxer Uprising.

Brooke, John Rutter (1838–1926)

Maj. Gen. John Rutter Brooke served as military governor of Cuba in 1899, a critical period in the transition from Spanish rule to temporary U.S. rule of the island in the wake of a hard-fought war of independence between 1895 and 1898.

Brooke was a career army officer who had served with distinction in the Civil War, rising from captain to brigadier general of volunteers by its end. He resigned from the army in 1866 but soon returned to service with an appointment as lieutenant colonel. In 1898, at the outset of the war with Spain, Brooke assumed command of I Corps and the army training camp at Chickamauga, Georgia. In July, he was reassigned to Puerto Rico, where he took part in the fighting before the armistice with Spain was declared in August. He served as military governor of Puerto Rico for a few months before assuming his duties as governor general of Cuba.

The Spanish forces in Cuba formally surrendered to Brooke on 1 January 1899, and he subsequently became the head of the U.S. military government of Cuba: the first U.S. governor general of Cuba. The last Spanish troops left Cuba on 6 February 1899. Under U.S. military rule, Cuba was divided into four civil departments based on geography. The military governors of these departments reported to Brooke, whose headquarters was located in the city of Havana. Brooke served as the commanding general of the U.S. troops stationed on the island as well as governor general. Among Brooke's more notable appointments was that of Lt. Col. Tasker H. Bliss to be chief of the customs service. Maj. Gen. Leonard Wood was appointed commander of the Department of Santiago, later combined with the province of Puerto Príncipe.

Brooke's first tasks were to care for refugees and the destitute and to restore order and public services to an island devastated by nearly four years of vicious warfare. In his annual report of 30 June 1899, he wrote of a Cuba in which "a state of desolation, starvation, and anarchy prevailed almost everywhere" (Brooke, *Civil Report*,

p. 9). Brooke had to move quickly to distribute food throughout the island to alleviate acute hunger. The war had devastated Cuban commerce, agriculture, and dwellings. Fevers and other diseases were a major problem made worse by the breakdown in public services and the poor health of the population. Local and provincial governments were bankrupt or in total disarray.

Brooke turned over nearly 5 million complete rations to department commanders for distribution in the first half of 1899 and recorded that by June, the situation had improved such that regular food distribution to the population at large was no longer necessary. After meeting the most immediate needs of the population, Brooke then moved to more complex and long-range projects. His military government conducted an islandwide census; reestablished local and municipal governments; revived and revised the tax and customs systems; improved roads and bridges; began improvements to harbors, sanitation systems, and public buildings; and effectively separated church from state. Brooke saw a critical need for the creation of a public school system, the codification and revision of the laws, and the reorganization of the court systems, but had only begun such projects before his administration ended. Brooke's efforts laid the foundation for the later, more famous accomplishments of his successor, Leonard Wood.

The Cuban Liberation Army presented a difficult problem for the United States in general and for Brooke in particular. The war that broke out in Cuba in 1895 was only the latest in a series of Cuban independence struggles which had begun in 1868. When the United States entered the war in Cuba in April 1898 as part of a larger war against Spain, it found an extant although faltering indigenous Cuban army that had already been fighting Spain for three years. Despite the notorious inefficiencies of the U.S. war effort in the Spanish-Cuban/American War, the United States quickly defeated the Spanish in Cuba and elsewhere.

While many Cubans, notably the revolutionary exile committee that had carried on the war effort from New York, had lobbied for and welcomed U.S. involvement in the Cuban fight for independence, others had adamantly opposed it, fearing it to be the first step toward U.S. annexation. The army, in particular, resented U.S. intervention in the struggle for national independence, feared annexation, and saw the dissolution of its forces as the loss of nascent Cuban independence to the United States. Many independence-minded Cubans were insulted, angered, and worried by the exclusion of the Cuban army from the ceremony which marked the formal surrender of the Spanish forces to U.S. forces.

The continued presence of armed Cuban troops posed a problem for the imposition of order under the U.S. military government. The problem was particularly acute because the discipline of the troops was uncertain, the material conditions of the island were desperate, and elements of the Cuban army had taken over local administration and police duties in many rural areas as the Spanish army withdrew.

It fell to Brooke to oversee the dismantling of the Cuban army. Gen. Máximo Gómez y Baez agreed to disband the army in exchange for the distribution of $3 million among its soldiers. The opposition of the Cuban Assembly, a fledgling would-be Cuban government that controlled the necessary rolls, delayed the payment. Further delays came from the difficulty of compiling a list of recipients acceptable to the United States. In May 1898, 33,930 men received $75 each, with the remaining balance reverting to the U.S. treasury. The Assembly's conflict with the very popular General Gómez led to the dissolution of this center of independence sentiment as well.

Brooke's administration tended to be bureaucratic and stodgy. However, he relied much on Cubans to govern the island, thereby co-opting many whose opposition could have thwarted his efforts to govern. Brooke clashed with the younger, energetic, and annexationist-minded Leonard Wood, then one of the four military governors. At the end of December 1899, Wood replaced him as military governor, and Brooke returned to the United States to assume command of the Department of the East.

In his final report as governor general, Brooke wrote with pride of the achievements of the U.S. occupation under his administration, contrasting the very serious economic and health problems existing when Brooke became military governor with the prosperous appearance of Cuba after U.S. military rule and the provision by the U.S. of food and employment for the Cubans.

Jennifer Bailey

REFERENCES

Dictionary of American Biography, s.v. "Brooke, John Rutter"; Russell H. Fitzgibbon, *Cuba and the United States, 1900–1935* (Russell & Russell, 1964 [1935]); Louis A. Pérez, Jr., *Cuba Between Empires* (Univ. of Pittsburgh Pr., 1983); U.S. War Department, *Annual Report of the War Department for the Fiscal Year Ended June 30, 1898* (U.S. Government Printing Office, 1899), part I; U.S. War Department, *Civil Report of Major-General John R. Brooke, U.S. Army, Military Governor, Island of Cuba, 1900* (U.S. Government Printing Office, 1900).

See also Cuba, Military Government (1898–1902); Cuba, Occupation (1898–1902).

Bryan, William Jennings, and the Spanish-Cuban/American War

William Jennings Bryan, Democratic party leader, sympathized with the Cuban revolutionaries in their uprising against Spanish colonial rule, and their aspiration for Cuban independence, as did most of his supporters. Bryan held back from jingoism, however, and supported President William McKinley's cautious approach. After war was declared in 1898, Bryan entered the army over the objections of political advisors; the Populist governor of Nebraska named him colonel of the 3rd Nebraska Volunteer Regiment. Before going on duty, Bryan expressed the fear that the war, undertaken for humanity, might become "a war of conquest" aimed at acquisition of territory, but he made no more political speeches until he left the service.

With no military experience, Bryan conducted his colonelcy with a minimum of military protocol and drew few distinctions between officers and enlisted men, preferring to entrust some decisions to a vote of his unit. He left most military matters to Victor Vifquain, his lieutenant colonel, a long-time Nebraska Democrat who had been a brevet brigadier general during the Civil War.

Bryan's regiment arrived in Florida in mid-July 1898 and was still there two months later, devastated by typhoid and other sicknesses; Bryan, too, came down with typhoid before leaving uniform. Rumors flourished that the administration intended to keep Bryan's regiment in service but out of action in order simultaneously to deny Bryan military laurels and to keep him off the fall campaign hustings. In late September, a month after the armistice and two months after the end of the fighting, Bryan appealed directly to McKinley to muster out his unit, arguing that his men had not enlisted to support imperialistic aims. McKinley refused, specifying that the request go through proper channels. Bryan resigned his commission as soon as the peace treaty with Spain was signed and hastened to Washington to lobby the Senate during its consideration of the treaty ending the Spanish-Cuban/American War in favor of passage.

Robert W. Cherny

REFERENCES

Robert W. Cherny, *A Righteous Cause: The Life of William Jennings Bryan* (Little, Brown, 1986); Paolo E. Coletta, *William Jennings Bryan* (Univ. of Nebraska Pr., 1964–1969), 3 vols.; J.C. Coovert, comp., *Historical Sketch and Scenes of Camp Life of the 3d Regiment Nebraska Volunteer Infantry Commanded by Colonel William Jennings Bryan* (J.C. Coovert, 1898); J.R. Johnson, "William Jennings Bryan: The Soldier," *Nebraska History*, 31 (1950), 95–106; Louis W. Koenig, *Bryan: A Political Biography of William Jennings Bryan* (Putnam, 1971).

Bud Bagsak, Moro Province, The Philippines, Battle (1913)

By 1912, U.S. disarmament efforts in Sulu had neutralized the opposition in Jolo Island, the Philippines, especially in the eastern part where resistance was very strong. The peace was short-lived because Moros (Philippine Muslims) of Lati and Luuk started to defy openly the disarmament policy. They harassed villages that had earlier been pacified and disarmed. U.S. troops were attacked by Moros whenever opportunities occurred. This renewed violence against U.S. authority prompted a military operation in January 1913 by a combined force of Philippine Constabulary and Philippine Scouts on orders of Governor John J. Pershing. The Lati Moros were led by Naquib Amil, Datu Jami, and Datu Sahipa. Two fierce engagements occurred in Lati, but U.S. troops, assisted by scouts, destroyed two Moro *cottas* (forts), resulting in several casualties on both sides. Reinforcements were sent to augment the troops. This induced the Lati Moros to take practically all the population of the place, between 6,000 to 10,000, to Bud Bagsak, a strategic peak a few kilometers from the historic Bud Daju, site of a bloody massacre in 1906. The presence of about nine-tenths noncombatants on the mount posed a serious problem to Governor Pershing and Sulu district governor Lt. William W. Gordon. Pershing, in a letter to the governor general of the Philippines, W. Cameron Forbes, revealed that the armed Moros were estimated to be only 300 and that any military operation to crush the resistance would surely result in the killing of many women and children. Pershing knew this because he was personally leading the troops in the campaign.

With the assistance of local leaders like Charles Schück, a prominent Joloano of German extraction, the Moros agreed to return to their homes provided the troops were withdrawn. The agreement was reached, and the noncombatants, especially women and children, returned to their farms. The leaders and their armed followers, however, refused to surrender and remained ready to return to Bud Bagsak. In fact, they sent word to Pershing that they would never lay down their arms. It was this final word of defiance that gave Pershing the basis for ordering the scouts and constabulary troops to move against 300 to 400 Moros on 11 June 1913.

The troops swiftly cut off the noncombatants on the slope of the mount, thus isolating the combatants for easy and convenient assault. Fighting immediately erupted, and hand-to-hand combat marked the five days of fierce fighting. On 15 June the Moro forts were bombarded, rendering Moro defense futile. As expected and true to the Moro character, *kris*-swinging Moros tried to attack the troops but were repelled. In the evening of the same day, a final assault was made on the mount, killing the remaining rebels. On the government side, 14 were killed, and 13 were wounded. Later reports revealed that some Moros escaped through underground passageways, but others were killed, including Naquib Amil and Datu Jami. Among those who escaped were Datu Sahipa, Datu Tahil, Datu Tambuyong, and Datu Japal.

As expected, the reaction to the bloodbath at Bud Bagsak from both the colony and the United States was both positive and negative. Critical comments in the Philippines came from the nationalist sector, which tended to view disturbances throughout the archipelago as basically anticolonial, that is, against U.S. domination. The *politicos*, as some of the nationalists were popularly called because of their keen political interest, were quick to regard the U.S. campaigns in Moroland as part of the "imperialist" approach

to colonial rule. U.S. authorities, especially Pershing, were also as quick to point out that the Moro *datus* (chiefs), and even the sultan of Sulu himself, supported U.S. military operations in the district.

Although not as adverse as the reaction to Gen. Leonard Wood's handling of the Bud Daju battle in 1906, U.S. newspapers, particularly in California, gave space to those who tried to dramatize the atrocities in Moroland. For instance, John McLean, who had served in the army in the Philippines, told a San Francisco reporter that 2,000 Moros, including 196 women and 340 children, were killed in Bud Bagsak. Pershing became the object of severe criticisms for the Bagsak massacre. For some time, the prospect of a congressional inquiry into the Moro affair loomed. But the investigation did not materialize because no less than the secretary of war and colonial authorities in the Philippines provided accurate accounts of what had happened in Bud Bagsak. However, according to Richard O'Connor's biographical sketch of Pershing, three correspondents who witnessed the Bagsak battle were ordered arrested by Pershing, thus reinforcing the picture of what Governor General of the Philippines Francis B. Harrison referred to five months later as "thousands of fighting Mohammedans, men, and women (who) were killed" in Bud Bagsak.

The adverse reactions in the United States against Pershing were similar to those raised against Wood after Bud Daju, but the Bud Bagsak massacre was successfully justified by no less than Governor General Forbes. Forbes affirmed that Pershing exhausted all the "virtues of patience" before taking the drastic action. He considered the action "necessary in the interests of good government." Pershing reported that the "entire population of the Sulu Archipelago" approved of the action taken.

The U.S. military success in Bud Bagsak sent clear warnings to other rebellious elements in the Sulu archipelago, including several small bands that continued to resist U.S. authority. By 15 June the bands had been dispersed, and 500 more guns were added to the disarmament campaign. From then on, relative peace settled on the troubled island of Jolo. Although the unsubdued elements continued to foment trouble, they were no longer capable of posing serious threats to U.S. rule as in the previous period. One unmistakable indication of this trend toward an enduring peace was the subsequent abolition of the Moro Province on 20 December 1913 by Philippine Commission Act No. 2309, changing the name of the province to the Department of Mindanao and Sulu. This marked the formal beginning of civil government in Mindanao and Sulu under Frank W. Carpenter as the first civil governor.

Samuel K. Tan

REFERENCES

Peter G. Gowing, *Mandate in Moroland: The American Government of Muslim Filipinos, 1899–1920* (Univ. of the Philippines, 1977); Richard O'Connor, *Black Jack Pershing* (Doubleday, 1961); Donald Smythe, "Pershing and the Mount Bagsak Campaign of 1913," *Philippine Studies*, 12 (1964), 3–31; Samuel K. Tan, *Sulu Under American Military Rule, 1899–1913* (Univ. of the Philippines, 1967).

Bud Daju, Moro Province, The Philippines, Battle (1906)

After the abrogation of the Bates Treaty, which had governed relations between the United States and the Sulu Moros, disturbances and incidents occurred in Jolo that necessitated the use of U.S. troops. As early as January 1905, Datu Usap of Luuk challenged U.S. troops that were sent to destroy his *cotta* (fort) on 9 January. In summer a more serious movement was led by Datu Pala, who had returned from Pulu Sekar, Borneo, in December 1904 after a series of killing incidents made him a fugitive from British law. In November 1905, he was killed near Maimbung, as were several of his men in the U.S. attacks on his stronghold. By 1906, the mainland of Jolo had literally become a trouble spot with the northern areas preparing for attacks on U.S. troops, including those in Jolo City. Muslims trekked to historic Bud Daju, an extinct volcano that had been regarded in local traditions as an abode of ancestral spirits which could provide warriors with mystical help in times of battle. The trek was caused by rumors that U.S. forces were planning to annihilate the Muslims in the outlying towns of Jolo. Although denied by U.S. authorities, the rumors became truth.

Bud Daju could be reached only by three small trails about two feet wide leading to the crater which occupied about 15 acres. The crater was well provisioned with fresh water and food. As described by Gen. Leonard Wood, Bud Daju

was "an ugly and difficult place to take" because the "lava ridges were probably, on the average, not more than eight feet wide, and in many places the fall off would land on the tops of tall trees" (Hagedorn, vol. II, p. 65). Before military assaults were ordered, attempts were made to convince the rebels to surrender. Col. Hugh L. Scott, military governor of Sulu, sent Datu Kalbi, Datu Julkanain, and Panglima Bandahala to Bud Daju to persuade the Muslims to abandon their resistance. After two days of talks, the *datus* (Moro chiefs) returned to Jolo to inform Governor Scott of the failure of the negotiations. The sultan of Sulu did not help in bringing the rebels to yield.

On 5 March, military operations began with about 800 officers and soldiers involved. The overall command was given to Col. Joseph W. Duncan. The *cotta* was bombarded from the southeast where Colonel Duncan took his position. Muslim casualties were heavy in an almost hopeless situation which forced the defenders to change strategy. Feigning corpses wrapped in white, as was the Muslim custom, when they were within striking distance, they jumped at their intended victims and slashed them. Several on the U.S. side were either killed or wounded. By the end of the operations the estimated 600 Muslims in Bud Daju were wiped out. There were no prisoners or wounded. On the U.S. side, 18 were killed, and 52 were wounded. The governor of Moro Province, Leonard Wood, believed the massacre could have been avoided had there been cooperation and assistance from the sultan and the local *datus*. The reactions from both the colony and the United States were both encouraging and damaging to Wood's military and political image.

In the Philippines, the Bud Daju affair evoked a mixture of opinions. The governor general commended Wood for his success in the Jolo campaigns. Scott looked at the bloody incident as resulting in an apparent climate of peace in Jolo, "the best in the Philippines." Victor Hurley, the author of several popular books on the Moros, did not share the same sentiment. While admitting that the Moros had broken the law and some form of punishment was necessary "if America was to maintain her prestige in the East," he believed that there was "unnecessary bloodshed at Bud Daju" (Hurley, *Swish of the Kris*, p. 374).

In the United States, the reactions were more critical of the army in dealing with the Moros as seen from a cross section of U.S. private and public opinion, official and unofficial. The *Washington Post* referred to Wood as the "blood-thirsty monster." A New York *World* cartoon showed Wood standing beside his victims with blood-dripping sword. *Pro Bono Publico* considered the Bud Daju slaughter a "disgrace to the country" and an indication of the lack of wisdom in holding the Philippines as a colony. Erving Winslow of the Anti-Imperialist League regarded the affair as a case of U.S. soldiers shooting "a lot of human game." A veteran of the Bud Daju massacre, Rowland Thomas, in an article for the *Boston Transcript*, stated that the killing of 600 Moros had no great significance; it was merely a "piece of public work" that the army had to do. Senator John S. Williams of Mississippi compared the 600 dead Moros to the charge of the Light Brigade.

More important for long-range U.S. colonial policies were reactions from the academic and intellectual sector, especially those who were intimately involved in the internal and general affairs of the Philippine colony. David P. Barrows, an educator and scholar, viewed the policy inaugurated by General Wood in Moroland as conflicting with the traditional authority of the sultans and *datus*. The local leaders found for the first time that their internal affairs and government were seriously threatened by the new colonial system. Barrows also related the Moro resistance to the "problem of the non-Christian peoples" posing obstacles to the Filipinos advocating the early independence of the Philippines. James H. Blount, who served as judge in the colonial judiciary and was well-known for his straightforward views, commented that the situation of the non-Christian tribes had negatively affected the U.S. view of Filipino capacity for self-government and independence.

To General Wood and decisionmakers, the reaction of the sultan of Sulu and his local *datus* was quite significant. On 16 April 1906, during the turnover of the Moro Province to the new governor, Gen. Tasker H. Bliss, Wood received encouraging and conciliatory remarks from the sultan and local leaders who were invited to Wood's last conference as outgoing governor. Prominent leaders like the sultan, Datu Kalbi, Datu Julkanain, Datu Indanan, Hadji Butu, and Datu Japal expressed the view that Wood had done what was best in the Bud Daju incident and, in fact, had eliminated the bad elements from the island, thus ensuring the peace and order for the inhabitants.

Samuel K. Tan

REFERENCES

"A Battle in Jolo," *Outlook*, 82 (1906), 582–583; Peter G. Gowing, *Mandate in Moroland: The American Government of Muslim Filipinos, 1899–1920* (Univ. of the Philippines, 1977); Hermann Hagedorn, *Leonard Wood: A Biography* (Harper & Brothers, 1931); Victor Hurley, *Swish of the Kris* (Dutton, 1936); "Mt. Dajo a Lesson," *Manila Times*, 20 July 1906; Samuel K. Tan, *Sulu Under American Military Rule, 1899–1913* (Univ. of the Philippines, 1967); "Why Moros Run Amuck," *Manila Times*, 3 Jan. 1907.

Bullard, Robert E. Lee (1861–1947)

General Robert E. Lee Bullard was the first governor of Lanao District, Mindanao, home of the Maranao Moros (Muslims) who defiantly stood in the way of the new U.S. rulers of the Philippines following the Spanish-Cuban/American War. Previously, in 1902–1904 Bullard had accomplished an important service in directing construction of a road from Iligan to the heart of the Lake Lanao region in Mindanao.

Bullard was born in Alabama in 1861. He was a teacher before he chose a military career. After he graduated from the United States Military Academy at West Point, he served in various capacities, including service in the campaign against Apache chief Geronimo. Later, he organized the 39th United States Volunteer Infantry for Philippine service. The regiment fought in the Philippines and earned the name "Bullard's Indians."

Under orders from Gen. George W. Davis, Bullard went into Moro country on a delicate peace-making mission with the "fiercest, fightingest savages" known in the history of the Philippines to enlist them for building a civilized life (unpublished book, Box 9, Bullard papers). The Lanao Moros numbered some 80,000 and were one of the three large Moro groups the United States Army had yet to pacify. William H. Taft's Philippine Commission realized that constructing a road from Iligan to Marahui, Mindanao, was a key to the military pacification and successful governance of the Moro region.

Bullard sailed into Iligan port at the northern end of Mindanao on 8 October 1902 (Diary,

Box 1, Bullard papers). Upon landing, he immediately sensed hostility, not from the Moros, but rather "envy and obstruction" from Col. Charles H. Noble, commander of the U.S. garrison in Iligan. Perhaps fearing competition from Bullard, Noble either delayed or did not deliver supplies intended for Bullard's battalion which was building a road to Marahui. At times he even withheld mail for Bullard.

The road work proceeded nonetheless. Bullard successfully avoided open warfare with the hostile Moros, many of whom he recruited as hired laborers for his construction project. The road cut across the mountain vastness and virgin rain forest of the Maranao country some 25 miles deep into the interior of central Mandanao. Despite the noncooperation of U.S. forces in Iligan, Bullard completed the road in only 10 months. It was a feat even the Spanish had not accomplished during their previous 300 years of attempts to subjugate the Moros. The Spanish soldiers were only able to begin a trail, which had become impassable, leading to Momungan, less than half the distance between Iligan and Marahui. To Bullard the road was the "gateway to modern government and civilization." He believed that savagery and civilization could not co-exist ("Road Building Among the Moros," Box 6, Bullard papers):

> Because they [the Moros] are part of us, we must fetch them forward with us; we cannot leave them behind. Because savagery and civilization cannot exist side by side; either all Mindanao must be turned over to the aggressive Moros, or all be taken over to civilization.

The odds were against Bullard in this project. Fighting was occurring in Mindanao. Capt. John J. Pershing, although also trying to win Moro friendship, marched around the Lake Lanao region in 1902–1903 with his cavalry to bring the racalcitrant Moros into submission. The Battle of Bayang in May 1902 was still fresh in the minds of many Moros, as were the campaigns in Butig, Maciu, Bacolod, and Calahui during the same period. Finally, when the Iligan-Marahui road was finished, it broke the shell of centuries of isolation in the Lake Lanao country. It allowed direct access for communication and trade from Manila. The long detour to Zamboanga in western Mindanao and then to Malabang to enter the Lanao area became a relic of the past.

While the road was being constructed, Bullard also studied the Maranao language. He found it to be similar in "roots and genus" to the Tagalog language, which he had learned in Luzon. He read about the Moros and tried to acquaint himself with their unique Oriental customs and traditions. Aware that the failure of the Spanish government to pacify Mindanao ultimately resulted from the effort to convert the Moros to Christianity, Bullard eschewed the idea of religious conversion of the Moros. When he discussed religion with the Moros he talked with authority and wisdom. For this he earned their respect and awe.

As he was gaining the confidence of the Moros at the close of 1902, cholera struck the Lake Lanao area. The Moros blamed the white men for bringing the dreaded disease; others even suspected that the whites were in league with the disease because U.S. troops, officials, and citizens lived while the Moros died by the hundreds ("Road Building Among the Moros," Box 6, Bullard papers). It took an unnamed Moro chief to realize that this was not the case. He observed that Bullard and his men boiled their water before drinking it. Asked why they did so, Bullard replied: "to drive away the *nonoks* (bad spirits)." That reassured the Moros, validating their beliefs about evil spirits causing sickness, and won a measure of admiration for U.S. forces. What made Bullard even more admirable in the eyes of the Moros was his dedication to learning from the Koran, the Moro's holy book, and his keen interest in knowing the customs and traditions of the Maranao Moros. His ability, although limited, to speak to them in Maranao eliminated the need for an interpreter. The Moros' respect for him was such that a Moro high priest, Nuska Alim, conferred the title of *imam* (Muslim pious man) on him ("How I Became a Mohammedan Priest," Box 9, Bullard papers).

Recognizing Bullard's work and his knowledge of Moro society, Gen. Leonard Wood, then governor of Moro Province, appointed Bullard head of Lanao District in November 1903, a post he held for less than a year because of his "broken health" (Diary, Box 1, Bullard papers). Bullard believed that the Moros could be won over by tact and diplomacy rather than by brute force, the usual military approach to pacifying the Moros. During the brief period he was governor, Bullard conducted some punitive expeditions when necessary. Shortly before his appointment as governor of Lanao, Bullard even joined, although reluctantly, General Wood in some of the expeditions around the lake area, such as the Taraca campaign of November 1903 and the expedition against Panglima Hassan of Sulu that same year. Among the actions he engaged in later were the campaigns in Lati, Toros, Birimbingan, and Maranatao, where he marched his troops at night to eliminate the chiefs of those *rancherias* (settlements) for repeatedly causing trouble for the U.S. authorities (Diary, Box 6, Bullard papers). These chiefs did not merely fail to express friendship for the United States, they also attacked small parties of soldiers, shot into U.S. military camps at night, and stole property available for the taking, usually firearms or horses that wandered close to their territory. Moreover, friendly *datus* (Moro chiefs) told Bullard that continued U.S. inaction threatened the U.S. mission in Mindanao and threatened the peaceful *datus*'s survival.

The last expedition Bullard carried out on General Wood's orders was a fruitless hunt for another hostile *datu*. Bullard returned to the barracks at Camp Vicars near Malabang tired, sick, and frustrated. Not long after, he resigned as district governor. He left Manila in July 1904 for San Francisco.

To Moros who knew Bullard well, he was "Bullug." He had tried to understand the Moros. He had studied their language and customs so well that he was canonized as a venerable priest like their own *imams* whose profound knowledge of Islam was held sacred. While he launched numerous military expeditions against hostile Moros, he was generally recognized by the Moros as a gallant soldier and officer.

When the United States entered World War I Bullard joined the American Expeditionary Force in France. He earned the Distinguished Service Medal and other decorations. Promoted to brigadier general in command of the 2nd Brigade, 1st Division, in 1917, rapid subsequent promotions brought him to the rank of lieutenant general. He briefly commanded the IX Army Corps. Bullard retired from the army in 1925 and died in 1947.

Federico V. Magdalena

REFERENCES

Robert L. Bullard, "Military Pacification," *Journal of the Military Service Institution of the United States*, 46 (1910), 1–24; unpublished book, chap. 9, Box 9, Robert L. Bullard papers, Manuscript Division, Library of Congress; Diary, Box 1, Robert L. Bullard papers, Manuscript Division, Library of Congress; "Road Building Among the Moros," Box 6, Robert L. Bullard papers, Manuscript Division, Library of Congress; Lester D. Langley, *The Banana Wars: An Inner History of American Empire, 1900–1914* (Univ. Pr. of Kentucky, 1983); Allan R. Millett, *The General: Robert L. Bullard and Officership in the United States Army, 1881–1925* (Greenwood Pr., 1975).

Bundy, Omar (1861–1940)

Omar Bundy, United States Army officer, distinguished himself at the Battle of Bud Daju one of the most notable engagements of the Moro campaigns. Bundy was born on 17 June 1861 in New Castle, Indiana. After attending Asbury College (now DePauw University) for one year, he entered the United States Military Academy at West Point, graduating in 1883 with a commission in the 2nd Infantry. His first active service was against the Crow Indians in the 1887 Montana campaign. He was promoted to first lieutenant in May 1890 and saw service against the Sioux in South Dakota in 1890–1891. In April 1898, he advanced to captain in the 6th Infantry. He participated in the Battle of El Caney (for which he was later awarded the Silver Star and cited for gallantry) and the siege of Santiago (where he was brevetted major) during the Spanish-Cuban/American War. He served in the Philippines from 1899 to 1902, first in the field against the revolutionaries and later on staff duty. After three years (1902–1905) of duty at Fort Leavenworth, Kansas, he returned to the Philippines.

While operating against the Moro rebels in March 1906, Bundy won high commendation and special distinction from his superior officers for his conduct in the battle of Bud Daju on Jolo Island. An extinct volcano some 2,100 feet high, Bud Daju was fortified by Moros who had entrenched themselves in its crater, after erecting barricades along the mountainside. The terrain did not favor an attacker since the ascent averaged some 45 degrees. Major Bundy commanded one of six attacking columns in the assault, which began on the afternoon of 6 March and ended on the morning of 8 March. Under Bundy's command were 2 companies of the 6th Infantry Regiment, 2 troops of the 4th Cavalry Regiment, and 50 Moro scouts. After a bitter round of mainly hand-to-hand combat amid the mountainside tangle of brush and bamboo, the Moro rebels were defeated. U.S. losses amounted to 18 killed and 52 wounded, while the Moros lost some 600 killed. This battle engendered a fierce controversy because Moro women and children died in the assault. Gen. Leonard Wood, the U.S. commander in the Philippines, was accused by some of ordering an unnecessary attack that resulted in the wanton butchery of innocent civilians. Both Secretary of War William H. Taft and President Theodore Roosevelt strongly defended Wood against these charges. Defenders of the Bud Daju assault asserted that the women were dressed like men and fought with them, while the children were frequently used as shields by the Moros. It was also alleged that the Moro women as well as the men had been whipped into a fighting frenzy by their priests.

After returning to the United States in 1907, Bundy served at various posts. Promoted to brigadier general in May 1917 after the United States entered World War I, he was ordered to France as commander of the 1st Brigade, 1st Division. In August 1917, he was placed in charge of preparing the training areas in France for the incoming American Expeditionary Force troops. He was given command of the 2nd Division in November 1917. In August 1918, he was promoted to command of the 6th Army Corps, and in September, he was transferred to command of the 7th Army Corps. In November 1918, he took command of Camp Lee, Virginia. Advanced to major general in 1921, he was commander of the Philippine Division from 1922 to 1924. He was then transferred to command the V Corps area at Columbus, Ohio, until his retirement in June 1925. Bundy died in Washington, D.C. on 21 January 1940.

Robert S. Salisbury

REFERENCES

National Cyclopaedia of American Biography, s.v. "Bundy, Omar"; "Our Generals in the Big Battle," *New York Times Magazine*, July 21, 1918, pp. 1, 8–9; Russell Roth, *Muddy Glory: America's "Indian Wars" in the Philippines, 1899–1935* (Christopher, 1981), 30–31; *Webster's American Military Biographies*, s.v. "Bundy, Omar"; John R. White, *Bullets and Bolos: Fifteen Years in the Philippine Islands* (Century, 1928), 299–313.

Bureau of Insular Affairs

The Bureau of Insular Affairs was the *de facto* colonial ministry of the United States. Its status as such resulted from the United States acquisition of the Philippines, Puerto Rico, and Guam after the Spanish-Cuban/American War. The War Department was assigned to administer the Philippines and Puerto Rico because the government had no agency to supervise colonies. In December 1898, the Division of Customs and Insular Affairs was established in the War Department to handle colonial matters. In 1900, it was renamed the Division of Insular Affairs. Two years later, Congress created the Bureau of Insular Affairs (BIA).

From the beginning, much was expected of the bureau. It was in charge of colonial policy for the Philippines and Puerto Rico (except from 1905 until 1909) and was required to supervise the customs receivership in the Dominican Republic. On occasion the BIA was called on for assignments with Cuba, Haiti, and Panama. Thus, the bureau functioned much as a European colonial ministry did, but without the formal trappings that signified ownership of an overseas empire. Indeed, most people in the United States of the time were generally unaware that their nation possessed an island empire halfway around the world.

The BIA was constantly hampered by various problems: a small staff, inadequate office space, and vaguely defined powers. Because Congress never precisely defined its functions, it could either obey its superiors or ignore them. The secretary of war, in addition to supervising the army, was responsible for federal works projects and colonies under the War Department. As it happened, most of the secretaries of war knew little about colonial matters and relied on the BIA for advice to formulate policy. With the White House and Congress ignorant and apathetic concerning the Philippines and Puerto Rico, presidents and congressmen often solicited the BIA's help. Indeed, the BIA was the silent partner in making U.S. colonial policy, working decisively behind the scenes.

The bureau performed a wide variety of functions. It was the link between Washington, Manila, and San Juan. Philippine and Puerto Rican governmental funds in the United States were placed in its care. It supervised Filipino students studying in the United States. It also kept records of most of the important documents pertaining to the Philippines and Puerto Rico and prepared legislation for congressmen and successive presidential administrations concerning them. Most legislation pertinent to the Philippines between 1902 and 1939 was either written by or partially drafted by BIA officials.

The BIA's chiefs were its driving force. They were expected to provide expert advice on colonial subjects, to deal with influential people, and to create policy when their superiors were unable to do so. Because the bureau was part of the War Department, every BIA chief was an army officer. The two most prominent chiefs were Gens. Clarence R. Edwards and Frank McIntyre. Edwards, chief from 1902 to 1912, was political and highly abrasive. McIntyre, who was his assistant chief after 1905, succeeded him. Except for service in World War I, McIntyre ran the BIA until 1929. He was genial, low-keyed, and somewhat secretive. He had more factual data about the Philippines than any other U.S. figure before World War II, and he shaped colonial policy. After he retired in 1929, the Philippine government hired him as its lobbyist in Washington.

Beginning in 1920, attempts to create a civilian agency to supervise all U.S. possessions meant that the War Department and the Navy Department, which governed Samoa, Guam, and the Virgin Islands, would have to yield their imperial jurisdictions. Congressional action gradually accomplished this. The BIA lost control over Puerto Rico in 1934 and was abolished five years later. To date, historians have not adequately investigated the United States's colonial experiment in the Pacific and the Caribbean.

James C. Biedzynski

REFERENCES

Any study on the Bureau of Insular Affairs must rely heavily on *The Records of the Bureau of Insular Affairs* (RG-350), at the United States National Archives in Washington, D.C. These records contain considerable material on American colonial rule in the Philippines and Puerto Rico, as well as some documents on American interaction with the Dominican Republic; Romeo V. Cruz, *America's Colonial Desk and the Philippines, 1898–1934,* Quezon City: Univ. of the Philippines Pr., 1974; James Christopher Biedzynski, *Frank McIntyre and the Philippines,* Ph.D. diss., Ohio Univ., 1990; Truman R. Clark, *Puerto Rico and the United States, 1917–1933,* Pittsburgh: Univ. of Pittsburgh Pr., 1975.

Butler, Smedley Darlington (1881–1940)

Smedley Darlington Butler was a controversial, colorful, and paradoxical general. A great Marine Corps combat hero and one of the United States's most highly decorated fighting men, he spent the last nine years of his life criticizing war and the United States's use of military power for imperialistic purposes after he retired from the military. Born a Quaker, Butler came from an upper-class Republican family; nonetheless he embraced a wide range of populist causes and constantly spoke out against both big business and big labor. He obtained his commission in the Marine Corps through the political influence of his congressman father, Thomas Butler, yet he spent most of his career fighting political insiders in the Navy Department, whom he called "swivel-chair admirals."

Butler was born in West Chester, Pennsylvania, on 30 July 1881. When the Spanish-Cuban/American War erupted in 1898, he tried to join both the army and the navy, but he was rejected because he was only 16 years old. Through his father's influence, however, he secured a temporary war-time commission as a second lieutenant on 20 May 1898. After a few weeks of training at the marine barracks in Washington, Butler went to Cuba, but he arrived too late to take part in the hostilities; he was discharged in February 1899.

When the regular Marine Corps, which then numbered only about 2,000 men, was authorized to expand threefold, Butler was reappointed first lieutenant in April 1899. In May he shipped out for the Philippines, where he had his first combat experience during the capture of Noveleta. He celebrated his initiation by having a huge Marine Corps emblem tattooed across his chest.

In summer 1900, Butler volunteered to join the force sent to China to rescue Westerners trapped by the Boxer Uprising. His company was first sent to relieve Tientsin. On 21 June, Butler, another lieutenant, and four enlisted men rescued a wounded marine private. While doing so, they held off several thousand Boxers for four hours. Butler and the other lieutenant were nominated for brevet promotions. (Marine and naval officers did not become eligible for the Medal of Honor until 1914.) In 1921, the Marine Corps created its short-lived Brevet Medal to recognize marine officers who had won brevet promotions for combat heroism. The medal, which ranked above the Navy Cross and below the Medal of Honor, was awarded to only 23 officers; Butler was one of them.

On 13 July, Butler led his company in the attack at Tientsin, during which he was wounded while rescuing one of his men. Ten days later, while convalescing in the hospital, he was promoted to captain—one week before his 19th birthday. In early August he joined the relief column marching on Peking. During the attack he was again wounded, this time by a bullet that drove his uniform button into his chest, thereby obliterating South America from his tattoo.

Butler spent 18 of the next 30 years in foreign service. In 1903 he participated in the expedition to Honduras. From 1905 to 1907 he was back in the Philippines. In 1909 he was promoted to major and took a battalion to Panama. He next participated in two expeditions to Nicaragua in 1910 and a third in 1912. It was during this period that Butler started his long-running feud with the admirals and others in the Navy Department. Whenever he felt his marines were being misused or abused by the navy, he immediately complained to his father, then chairman of the House Naval Affairs Committee.

In January 1914 Butler took his battalion to Veracruz, Mexico, aboard the USS *Minnesota*. While the U.S. force, under Adm. Frank Friday Fletcher, sat anchored in the bay, Butler, wearing civilian clothes, went deep into the Mexican interior on an intelligence-gathering mission. Posing as a U.S. railroad official, Butler spent three days in Mexico City mapping important military sites before the local police got suspicious. He arrived back in Veracruz one step ahead of the Mexican secret service, and he had to fight his way through a local mob before he reached the U.S. launch at the docks.

U.S. forces landed at Veracruz in April 1914, and Butler went ashore with a company of sailors and a company of marines not from his own battalion. With his troops pinned down by snipers in the town, Butler took his famous walk down the main street. Armed with only a swagger stick, he drew fire and pointed out the snipers' positions to his men. Awarded his first Medal of Honor for his actions in Veracruz, he refused to accept it. The Navy Department returned it to him with orders to wear it.

During the Haiti campaign in 1915, Butler led a 27-man reconnaissance force deep into the interior to locate the bases of the *Caco* bandits. Butler's top sergeant on the patrol was Medal of Honor recipient Daniel J. Daly. Butler's men located their objectives, but the *Caco* ambushed them. After fighting their way out without losing a man, Butler recommended Daly for a second Medal of Honor. The following month Butler led a 100-man force against the *Caco* strongholds, Fort Capois and Fort Rivière. During the 17 November attack on Fort Rivière, Butler and two of his men got inside the supposedly impregnable position by crawling through a drainage culvert. Once inside they caused so much confusion that the *Cacos* guarding the outer walls were drawn off and the fort was easily breached by the attacking marines. Butler received his second Medal of Honor for his actions at Fort Rivière.

In December 1915 Butler was ordered to go to Port-au-Prince to organize and command the Gendarmerie d'Haiti. He was by then a lieutenant colonel in the marines, but he was given the constabulary rank of major general. The marines supplied all 120 officers for the 2,600-man force. Most were sergeants who had officer privileges under their dual status. Butler's responsibilities went far beyond running the police force to include maintaining many key elements of the island's infrastructure. One of his major accomplishments was the construction of a 170-mile road from Port-au-Prince to Cap Haïtien. Butler got his labor force by envoking Haiti's 1864 *corvée* law, which required peasants to work on local roads in lieu of paying taxes. At any given time Butler had up to 6,000 men working on the roads. During this two-year tenure the *corvée* system was well administered, and the peasants were treated fairly. Under Butler's successors, however, the *corvée* system was corrupt and abused.

After the United States entered World War I, Butler flooded the Navy Department with requests for a combat assignment. He was finally assigned in France as the head of the 13th Marines. Much to Butler's disgust, Gen. John J. Pershing appointed him commander of Camp Pontanezen in Brest, the major U.S. replacement center in France. The job carried the rank of brigadier general, and at 38, Butler became the youngest general officer in Marine Corps history.

Camp Pontanezen was a disease-infested mud hole with no sanitation facilities. The camp held close to 100,000 U.S. troops, and an average of 25 were dying each day from the flu when Butler took over. Butler turned Pontanezen into a model camp. After the Armistice, Pontanezen became the major debarkation station for homeward-bound U.S. troops. Butler's actions undoubtedly saved thousands of U.S. lives. Both the army and the navy awarded him their Distinguished Service Medals, and France gave him the Order of the Black Star.

In 1924 Butler was granted a two-year leave of absence from the marines to serve as director of public safety in the reform administration of Philadelphia Mayor W. Freeland Kendrick. Butler shook up the administration of the police department, sacked corrupt and incompetent captains and lieutenants, and increased liquor arrests sixfold. The number of convictions, however, actually went down because Butler alienated the judges and political bosses. Butler lost Kendrick's support when the police started hitting the big hotels as hard as the corner speakeasies. The mayor fired him at the end of 1925, but the experience made Butler a life-long prohibitionist.

In 1926 Butler took command of the marine base at San Diego, California. From 1927 to 1929 Butler commanded the marine expeditionary force sent to Shanghai to protect U.S. interests during the period of the Chinese nationalist revolution. Rather than a military expedition in the sense of the Boxer Uprising or the "banana wars," the China mission turned into one of the first U.S. experiences in what was later called "peacekeeping." Uncharacteristically, Butler showed much restraint and diplomatic skill in that assignment. The Chinese twice presented him with their "Umbrella of Ten Thousand Blessings," and Butler is thought to be the first foreigner to receive such an honor.

The China expedition was Butler's last overseas assignment, and the experience altered his view of U.S. military interventions. In 1929 he was promoted to major general and reassigned as commander of Quantico, Virginia. When he started openly criticizing U.S. military policy, he incurred the wrath of the administration of President Herbert Hoover. Butler's father, who had died in 1928, could no longer run interference in Congress. In 1929 Butler infuriated Secretary of State Henry L. Stimson by publicly stating that the marines, under State Department orders, had used strong-arm methods to rig the 1912 elections in Nicaragua. In reaction, the administration passed Butler over for the post of commandant, even though he was the senior major general in the corps.

Butler decided to retire, but before the paperwork went through he was in trouble again. In a 1931 speech he accused Italian Prime Minister Benito Mussolini of killing a child in a hit-and-run accident. When stories about Butler's speech appeared in U.S. newspapers, the Italian government protested, and Stimson issued a formal apology from the U.S. government. Butler was arrested and confined to his quarters pending court-martial. The court-martial never happened because popular support of Butler was swift and overwhelming. Butler was allowed to retire as a major general on 1 October 1931.

Once he was no longer an active duty officer, Butler turned into a vigorous and outspoken critic of U.S. military policy and advocated a wide number of populist causes. Often associated briefly with various organizations, he never committed to any. He essentially remained a loner.

Butler advocated neutrality and isolationism. He eventually came to regard his military career as an effort to make the world safe for U.S. business. Butler turned antiwar, but he did not turn antimilitary. He was not a pacifist, and he opposed disarmament. He supported an armed-neutrality with the United States having an "iron-clad defense a rat couldn't crawl through."

After almost nine years on the lecture circuit, Butler entered the Philadelphia Naval Hospital in May 1940 for a medical examination and a rest. Four weeks later he died of an intestinal ailment, probably cancer. He was 58 years old. Two years later the United States Navy named a destroyer after one of its most outspoken critics.

David T. Zabecki

REFERENCES

Smedley D. Butler, *Old Gimlet Eye: The Adventures of Smedley D. Butler as Told to Lowell Thomas* (Farrar & Rinehart, 1933); rpt., Marine Corps Assoc., 1981); Smedley D. Butler, *War is a Racket* (Round Table Pr., 1935); Hans Schmidt, *Maverick Marine* (Univ. Pr. of Kentucky, 1987).

See also Fort Rivière, Haiti, Battle (1915).

Caco Campaigns, Haiti (1918–1920)

The 1918–1920 Second *Caco* War was initially instigated by Charlemagne Masséna Péralte. A former general in the Haitian army, Péralte was a supporter of Dr. Rosalvo Bobo, the exiled leader of the mulattoes in the north, and an enemy of President Philippe Sudre Dartiguenave, a southern Haitian black. Sentenced to five years' hard labor on the *corvée* for revolutionary activity, Péralte escaped on 3 September 1918 and issued a call to rebellion, styling himself general-in-chief of the revolution. The *corvée*, a system of forced labor for road building and repair, was widely resented among the Haitian population, and Péralte used it to ignite rebellion. In reality, however, the outbreak was another episode in the long struggle of the mulattoes against black rule; its true aim was to topple Dartiguenave and bring Bobo to power.

On 17 October a force of 100 *Cacos* attacked the barracks of the Gendarmerie d'Haiti in Hinche and was beaten off with a loss of 35 lives. The officer in charge, gendarmerie Lt. Patrick F. Kelly (a U.S. Marine sergeant) earned the Haitian *Medaille Militaire* and a captaincy for his role in the skirmish. On 10 November a *Caco* force drove the Gendarmerie garrison away from Maissade and burned the barracks. Numerous attacks ensued, and by March 1919 Péralte had about 5,000 men in arms. He commanded in the northern part of the island, while Benoît Batraville, former police chief of Mirebalais, now chief minister of the revolution, operated in central Haiti. The *chef de gendarmerie*, Col. Alexander S. Williams (a U.S. Marine major) was forced to request the assistance of the marine brigade commanded by Brig. Gen. Albertus W. Catlin. Five companies, half the brigade, were sent to occupy towns near Hinche and the Dominican border to free the Gendarmerie for field operations, in addition to which one-fourth of the brigade was ordered on patrol at all times. Four more companies came to Haiti from Guantánamo, Cuba, as well as 13 aircraft.

In May the new *chef de gendarmerie*, Lt. Col. Frederic M. Wise, inaugurated a training program to improve the Gendarmerie's morale and combat readiness. He also replaced the short-service marines in the Gendarmerie with long-service regulars. An increasingly aggressive Gendarmerie clashed frequently with the increasingly active *Cacos* throughout the summer, a total of 131 actions from April through September. Despite all measures the rebellion flourished, although it never moved out of its central and northern enclaves and never mobilized the allegiance of more than a fraction of the populace.

Early in the morning of 6 October 1919 the *Cacos* risked an assault on Port-au-Prince. Though it was a military failure, the attack on the capital bolstered the reputation of the revolutionaries. U.S. authorities decided to decapitate the movement by killing or capturing Péralte. A former *Caco* general, Jean-Baptiste Conzé, was lured by the promise of a reward to raise his own guerrilla band and establish contact with Péralte. This ruse was to culminate in a joint attack by Conzé and Péralte on Grande-Rivière-du-Nord during which Péralte could be taken. When Péralte did not arrive for the attack, two marines and 16 gendarmes disguised as *Cacos* went to his camp, ostensibly to provide an honor guard for his triumphal entry into Grande-Rivière-du-Nord. On the night of 30–31 October their leader, Gendarmerie Capt. Herman H. Hanneken (a U.S. Marine sergeant), who knew Péralte because he had succeeded him in command of Port-de-Paix at the beginning of the occupation, shot the *Caco* leader and brought his body back, an action for which he and his second-in-command, Gendarmerie Lt. William R. Button (a U.S. Marine corporal), received the Medal of Honor. A cordon was established to prevent the leaderless troops in the North from joining Batraville.

The struggle against Batraville in central Haiti had already produced the first coordinated air-ground combat operation in Marine Corps history, which had a relatively limited impact on Marine Corps doctrine as compared to similar operations against guerrillas in Nicaragua during the late 1920s and early 1930s. Capt. Edward A. Ostermann, commandant at Mirebalais, had been sending air patrols to track *Caco* movements. Late in the summer, learning that Batraville was hosting a night-long drinking party on a mountain, Ostermann covered the trails leading from the place and sent planes to strafe the gathering at first light. More than 200 *Cacos* were killed or wounded on the mountaintop or fleeing down the trails.

Early in October 1919, Col. John H. Russell became the new brigade commander and began reorganizing operations and improving intelligence. In December, the 8th Regiment was reconstituted and sent to Haiti, bringing brigade strength to 83 officers and 1,263 men under the operational command of Col. Louis McC. Little,

an aggressive officer fluent in French. Gendarmerie strength was at 2,700. On New Year's Day 1920, operations began south of Hinche against Batraville's 2,500 *Cacos*. The marines were successful in using small patrols to provoke attacks which they could suppress with superior firepower and marksmanship. In retaliation, Batraville, with a force of 300, raided Port-au-Prince before dawn on 15 January 1920. The marines and gendarmes had been warned and repulsed the attackers, killing 66 and wounding or capturing many more. The *Cacos* afterward referred to this defeat by a term evoking the Franco-Prussian War: *la débacle*. Batraville's support began to dwindle and many chiefs surrendered, among them Péralte's brother. In a last-ditch effort to retrieve momentum, Batraville consulted a sorcerer and, following a skirmish on 4 April, killed a prisoner, Gendarmerie 2nd Lt. Lawrence Muth (a U.S. Marine sergeant), ate his heart and liver, and smeared Muth's brains on a rifle to ensure accuracy. Only 45 days later, his camp was overrun and he was killed by Sgts. William F. Passmore and Albert A. Taubert. With his death the rebellion ended. It had cost the lives of 23 marines, 75 gendarmes, and an unknown number of *Cacos*. Estimates of 2,250 *Cacos* killed between 1915 and 1920 have been suggested. Although these are doubtless exaggerated, the disproportion in discipline, firepower, and marksmanship between the *Cacos* and the U.S. Marine/Gendarmerie force suggests high losses among the *Cacos*. The *corvée* had been officially abolished on 1 October 1918, less than a month after the start of the rebellion.

Joseph M. McCarthy

REFERENCES

Edgard Gausse, *Non a une intervention americaine en Haiti* (Éditions du Progrès, 1988); Robert Debs Heinl, *Soldiers of the Sea: The United States Marine Corps, 1775–1962* (U.S. Naval Institute Pr., 1962; rpt. ed. Nautical & Aviation, 1991); Robert Debs Heinl and Mary Gordon Heinl, *Written in Blood: The Story of the Haitian People, 1492–1971* (Houghton Mifflin, 1978); Allan R. Millett, *Semper Fidelis: The History of the United States Marine Corps* (rev. and enl. ed.; Free Pr., 1991); Ivan Musicant, *The Banana Wars: A History of United States Military Intervention in Latin America From the Spanish-American War to the Invasion of Panama* (Macmillan, 1990).

See also Hanneken, Herman Henry; Péralte, Charlemagne Masséna; Port-au-Prince, Haiti, Battles (1919, 1920); Wise, Frederick May.

Caco War, Haiti (1915–1916)

Cacos was the name given to Haitian peasants who historically had provided the irregular forces used by Haiti's political elite to topple regimes in Port-au-Prince. Between 1908 and 1915 they were the force behind seven *coups-d'état*, and, as the country degenerated into anarchy, their number and importance grew.

When the U.S. marines landed in Port-au-Prince on 4 August 1915, their initial goal was to keep the peace and to protect foreign interests after a particularly bloody coup toppled President Vilbrun Guillaume Sam. After considerable palaver with various Haitian interests, U.S. authorities installed a client chief executive, Philippe Sudre Dartiguenave, expecting the *Cacos* to abandon their candidate, Dr. Rosalvo Bobo, and fade back into the hills. Had this been a "normal" coup that probably would have happened. But the occupation had added the issue of nationalism to the traditional mercenary/bandit interests. *Cacos* lashed out at U.S. citizens, particularly in northern Haiti. The conflict between Haitian irregulars and U.S. Marines, sometimes called the First *Caco* War, lasted until September 1916.

From the first, Adm. William B. Caperton, commander of the Atlantic Fleet's Cruiser Squadron, and as such, commander of all U.S. forces in Haiti, wanted to disarm the *Cacos* peacefully, to implement a cease-fire, and to reconcile the many disaffected elements in Port-au-Prince. Some progress was made in accomplishing these objectives in and around the capital, but northern Haiti, particularly the Cap Haïtien district and the area between Grande-Rivière-du-Nord, Fort Liberté, and Ouanaminthe, was in turmoil.

On 20 September 1915 a marine unit was ambushed while on patrol south of Cap Haïtien. When Col. Eli K. Cole, commander of the 1st Regiment, then stationed at Cap Haïtien, ordered two additional patrols to their aid, *Cacos* attacked them as well. Cole finally called in the USS *Connecticut*'s landing party to maintain order in the town. He then led the rest of his regiment in pursuit of the *Cacos*, who seemed to vanish in the face of a large U.S. force.

The following week the marines drove a number of small *Caco* bands away from Quartier Morin. Cole secured the town and continued to send patrols farther into the countryside.

Gonaïves also suffered from *Caco* attention; so Cole sent Maj. Smedley D. Butler after Pierre Benoît Rameau, a *Caco* leader responsible for cutting the water supply to Gonaïves and harassing the local population. The bantam Butler caught up with Rameau at Poteau. Butler yanked the Haitian from his horse, forced him and his men to surrender, and sent him under guard to Port-au-Prince.

Disturbances were also reported from the interior around Petite Rivière. Cole responded by ordering detachments of marines to occupy the town. The marines also drove *Cacos* from Haut-du-Cap and pursued them along the rail line from Grande Rivière to Bahon. The remaining guerrillas fled into the northeastern mountains.

Col. Littleton W.T. Waller, commander of the 1st Provisional Brigade of marines in Haiti, came north to survey the situation. Unlike the courtly Caperton, Waller was known for his tenacious, sometimes brutal, methods of suppressing rebellious peoples. Nonetheless, Waller bowed to his chief's wishes and concluded an agreement with *Caco* Gen. Jean-Baptiste Pétion and Antoine Morency on 29 September 1915. The guerrillas promised to disband and relinquish their arms and ammunition to the marines who would pay 50 gourdes (about U.S. $10) for each rifle. *Cacos* who complied would be granted amnesty. Those who did not would be treated as criminals. The cease-fire lasted only a few weeks. With its lapse, Waller felt justified in implementing what Butler called the "roughneck" approach to pacification of the countryside.

Waller's first move was to order increased patrols and reconnaissance activity throughout northern Haiti to locate and neutralize the remaining *Cacos*. On 22 October Butler and a detachment of over 40 men began a six-day reconnaissance to locate the *Caco* stronghold. The marines marched from Fort Liberté to Le Trou, and from there to Grande Rivière and La Vallière via Bahon and Grosse Roche.

While fording the Grande Rivière on the evening of 24 October, about 400 *Cacos* ambushed the patrol. The marines fought their way to a secure position, which they held that night despite continued, but erratic sniping. At daybreak, three squads under Capt. William P. Upshur, 1st Lt. Edward A. Ostermann, and Sgt. Daniel J. Daly advanced against the *Cacos* from different directions, forcing them to retreat to their base at Fort Dipitié. The marines pursued the *Cacos*, drove them from the wooden stockade, and burned it to the ground. Upshur, Ostermann, and Daly received the Medal of Honor for their roles in the action.

Another patrol stumbled across old Fort Rivière, perched atop Montagne Noire, where a large band of *Cacos* had taken refuge. On 17 November, Butler took three companies of marines and the landing party from the USS *Connecticut* to seize the fort. They drove out or killed the *Caco* defenders and razed the dilapidated citadel, bringing a temporary halt to *Caco* activities. Butler, Sgt. Ross L. Iams, and Cpl. Samuel Gross received the Medal of Honor for their participation in the raid.

Violence erupted again in early January 1916, when François Antoine Simon, one-time president of Haiti, financed a coup attempt masterminded by Antoine Pierre-Paul, a long-time political associate of Simon's. The plot called for the assassination of Dartiguenave and the installation of the anti-United States Pauléus Sannon as president. At 2:30 a.m. on 5 January, about 80 *Cacos* led by Mizaël Codio, Annabel V. Hilaire, Seymour Pradel, and Generals Metallus and Philogne attacked the provost marshal's office and the marine corral. A handful of marines and Haitian gendarmes drove them off within an hour, and by 16 January all the leaders except Pierre-Paul (to whom Waller granted amnesty) were in custody.

At this time, the marines began turning over the job of keeping the peace to the Gendarmerie d'Haiti, trained and officered by U.S. Marines. The gendarmes assumed their new duties on 1 February 1916 and faced their first challenges in early March. *Cacos* attacked gendarme stations at Cerca-la-Source, and Lamielle on 3 March, at Castelleur on 4 March, and at Acul-Samedi on 6 March. The guerrillas' only success came at Cerca-la-Source, where they temporarily routed the six-man detachment from its barracks.

Codio, Rameau, and a group of *Cacos* continued to scheme even while in the national penitentiary. They took advantage of a Decoration Day ceremony held by the marine garrison in Port-au-Prince on 30 May 1916 to escape. Between 7:00 p.m. and 2:00 a.m. they swept through the capital, using the arms and ammunition they had taken from the prison detachment to fire indiscriminately at shops and buildings in the business district near the U.S. Legation. They then seemed to evaporate into the countryside.

Betrayed by Haitian peasants who were generally sick of the constant violence and turmoil, the fugitives were captured near Fond des Verrettes on 4 June. When they attempted to escape, the marines opened fire and shot them.

The denouement of the First *Caco* War began on 1 September 1916 when Butler led over 100 gendarmes and marines, the Provisional Mounted Company, on a three-week trek through northern Haiti to the Dominican border. They were searching for a few die-hard *Cacos* and Pierre-Paul, who had fled Port-au-Prince, as well as for arms and ammunition supposedly belonging to the Dominican bandit Celidiano Pantilion.

In an astounding exhibition of endurance they covered 406 tortuous miles through jungles and over mountains without losing a man or an animal—although they never caught up with their quarries. That march, in effect, marked the end of the First *Caco* War, for although there were occasional acts of violence directed against the marines, there was no further organized resistance until 1918.

Anne Cipriano Venzon

REFERENCES

David Healy, *Gunboat Diplomacy in the Wilson Era: The U.S. Navy in Haiti, 1915–1916* (Univ. of Wisconsin Pr., 1976); Robert D. Heinl, Jr., *Soldiers of the Sea: The United States Marine Corps, 1775–1962* (U.S. Naval Institute Pr., 1962); J. Robert Moskin, *The Story of the U.S. Marine Corps* (Paddington Pr., 1979); Anne Cipriano Venzon, "The Papers of Maj. Gen. Smedley D. Butler, 1915–1918," Ph.D. diss., Princeton Univ., 1982.

See also Cole, Eli Kelley; Fort Rivière, Haiti, Battle (1915).

Cailles, Juan (1871–1951)

Juan Cailles of Laguna Province, the Philippines, stands out as one of the most skillful and merciless guerrilla leaders of the Philippine War. Slender and mustachioed, the erstwhile Cavite educator, a descendant of maternal British-Indian and paternal French parents, possessed a disposition both impulsive and hot-tempered.

An early supporter of the Katipunan, a secret Philippine political society, Cailles warred against

Spanish forces in neighboring Cavite Province. In 1896 his inability to protect the back road into Lian brought about the defeat of revolutionaries commanded by Santiago Alvarez. Two years later, he mustered to Emilio Aguinaldo y Famy's summons for war against Spain and led liberation forces south of Manila.

When the Spanish-Cuban/American War started, Lieutenant Colonel Cailles served under Gen. Mariano Noriel at the siege of Manila. Assigned to the *primera zona* (a position closest to the Spanish stronghold), Cailles warned of a U.S. troop buildup and defied U.S. forces' attempt to persuade him to retreat. His daring won the praise of Aguinaldo.

In 1899, the 33-year-old Cailles became a brigadier general and governor of Laguna Province. He exerted rigorous rule over underlings and affairs, not hesitating to use coercion as well as appeals. Indeed, he exercised the power of supreme military leader, but his authority rarely stretched beyond his province.

When U.S. troops invaded the Second District, Department of Southern Luzon, which included Laguna, in 1900, Cailles turned to guerrilla strategy. Reflecting a knowledge of irregular warfare, he avoided large-scale engagements and subverted U.S. occupation authorities. He maintained popular support with the help of able subordinates and, when necessary, the use of ruthless measures. His reversion to conventional battlefield tactics came only for reasons of political expediency or military opportunity.

Unable to match the United States Army's resources as well as firepower, Cailles's guerrillas husbanded their weaponry, even producing crude munitions much as the National Liberation Front did later during the Vietnam War. Again like the Vietnamese, Filipino revolutionaries sought an extended conflict by surviving as a force in being. Avoiding regular warfare and fighting a *guerra de emboscadas* (war of ambushes) came to fatigue U.S. troops both physically and politically.

Cailles showed no reluctance to use terrorism ruthlessly. The property and persons of suspected collaborators were targeted, both to eliminate hostile Filipinos and to discourage waverers. Although the revolutionaries victimized mostly Filipinos, occasionally U.S. soldiers became prey in efforts to undermine their morale. In spite of a Tayabas Province commander's distaste for political assassination, Cailles commanded death

sentences for 29 persons in a nine-month period.

As the guerrillas stepped up their harassment tactics, Cailles's base became subject to U.S. raids. Sharp clashes ensued, and the guerrilla leader defeated the invaders at Mabitac in Laguna. Despite sweeps by the United States Army, he remained active and retained the province's loyalty.

Factionalism, weariness, and a loss of will weakened the revolutionaries by mid-1901. With a compromised guerrilla infrastructure and many defections, Cailles's failure to revive the resistance in neighboring Tayabas Province resulted in his surprising surrender on 24 June 1901, ending the career of one of the major leaders of Filipino guerrillas during the Philippine War.

Rodney J. Ross

REFERENCES

Teodoro A. Agoncillo, *Malolos: The Crisis of the Republic* (Univ. of the Philippines, 1960); Brian McAllister Linn, *The U.S. Army and Counterinsurgency in the Philippine War, 1899–1902* (Univ. of North Carolina Pr., 1989); William T. Sexton, *Soldiers in the Sun: An Adventure in Imperialism* (Military Service Pub. Co., 1939); John R.M. Taylor, *History of the Philippine Insurrection Against the United States* (Eugenio Lopez Foundation, 1971); U.S. War Department, *Annual Report of the War Department for the Fiscal Year Ending June 30, 1902* (U.S. Government Printing Office, 1902).

Cámara y Libermoore, Manuel de la (1836–1920)

Adm. Manuel de la Cámara y Libermoore commanded a Spanish fleet which was sent to the Philippines during the Spanish-Cuban/American War, but which had to be recalled far short of its destination because of Spanish fears that U.S. naval forces were going to attack in Spanish waters. He was commander of the Cádiz-based Spanish fleet in 1898. Cámara's earlier career included commands of the corvette *Vencedora* in the Mexican expedition of 1861–1862 which bombarded Callao, and later of the corvette *Africa* and the steamer *Tornado*. In the 1890s, he took out the *Castilla*, *Don Antonio de Ulloa*, and *Don Juan de Austria* to the Philippines and following that headed naval commissions to Washington and London, and as a rear admiral headed the general staff at Havana.

During the Spanish-Cuban/American War, on 6 June 1898, the minister of the marine in Madrid, Ramón Auñón y Villalón, directed Cámara, then commanding at Cádiz, to proceed through the Suez Canal and the Indian Ocean. In June 1898, the fleet consisted of two armored cruisers, six converted cruisers, and four destroyers. Under his command were the battleship *Pelayo*; the armored cruiser *Carlos V*; the auxiliary cruisers *Patriota* and *Rápido* purchased from Germany; three torpedo boats, *Audaz*, *Proserpina*, and *Osado*; and the former liner transport the *Buenos Aires* with 4,000 troops. The fleet was to be accompanied by the destroyer escorts *Isla de Panay*, *San Francisco*, *Covadonga*, and *Colón* to Suez, but the destroyers were then to return. Four colliers carrying 20,000 tons of coal accompanied the small fleet. Cámara was directed to exercise due caution not to sacrifice the fleet "and always to leave the honor of the troops without injury." But he was also ordered to ensure the security of Spanish sovereignty in the archipelago, which would have brought him into conflict with Adm. George Dewey's squadron.

Cámara's voyage began 16 June. U.S. navy Ens. William H. Buck tracked the fleet off Ceuta, Spain, and followed Cámara's fleet to Port Said, Egypt, telegraphing details of its movements. The United States Navy Department passed on the warning to Dewey at Manila Bay. After the naval victory at Santiago de Cuba on 3 July 1898 the United States Navy Department began to mature plans to assemble a powerful squadron, the "Eastern Squadron," under Commodore John C. Watson, to harass the coast of Spain and counter Cámara's movement. Two slow but powerful monitors, *Monterey* and *Monadnock*, were sent as reinforcements to Dewey at Manila.

When Cámara arrived at Port Said, he had difficulty getting through the Suez Canal. The British delayed his coaling operations in Egypt, and Cámara was not allowed to refuel from Egyptian lighters. On 29 June he was asked to depart within 24 hours of arrival. As a result Cámara was prepared to tow the disabled *Pelayo* through the Suez Canal. On 3 July he received orders to proceed through the canal to the Red Sea. He completed the journey by 5–6 July. On the 6th he was ordered to keep up steam ready to proceed, but on the 7th orders came for him to return immediately to Spain. Although Cámara's fleet was theoretically stronger than Dewey's Asiatic Squadron, the United States Navy Department's Eastern Squadron's anticipated movement across the Atlantic led the Spanish government to recall Cámara's fleet from the Red Sea through the Suez Canal into the Mediterranean Sea.

Cámara's original orders specified he was to rendezvous at Mindanao, the Philippines. The voyage from Suez to Mindanao for his fleet, cruising at 10 knots, would have taken about 30 days, and longer if repairs and coaling had caused delays. Had he left Suez on 8 July Cámara would have arrived about mid-August. Sooner or later he would have had to engage the U.S. squadron, but Mindanao was 700 miles from Manila. Historian David Trask has argued that "[w]hatever other motives there might have been for his return to Spain, the American victory at Santiago de Cuba rendered his further movement eastward a strategic and political absurdity" (Trask, p. 277).

Frederick C. Drake

REFERENCES

French Ensor Chadwick, *The Relations of the United States and Spain: The Spanish American War* (Scribner, 1911), vol. 2, 388–390; Spain, Ministry of Marine, *Correspondencia oficial referente a las operaciones navales durante la guerre con los Estados Unidos en 1898* (1899), 287–296; David F. Trask, *The War With Spain in 1898* (Macmillan, 1981), chap. 12; U.S. Navy Department, *Annual Report of the Navy Department for the Year 1898* (U.S. Government Printing Office, 1898), 2 vols.

See also Eastern Squadron, Spanish Navy (1898).

Camino Real, Nicaragua, Battle (1927)

In December 1927, the U.S. Marines began an offensive to drive Augusto C. Sandino from his elusive mountain fortress, El Chipote, which had just been located by U.S. aircraft, in northern Nicaragua. Two strong marine and *guardia* columns left Jinotega and Telpaneca to rendezvous at Quilalí for an assault on Sandino. Capt. Richard Livingston commanded the Jinotega column of 115 men and over 200 pack mules. As the column approached Quilalí from the south on 30 December along a narrow trail, the Camino Real, bordered by the Jícaro River to the left and a steep slope to the right, a Sandinista force estimated at 200–400 men struck suddenly with machine gun and rifle fire and dynamite bombs from both sides and the front. Captain Livingston was hit with the first volley and relinquished command to lst Lt. Moses J. Gould, who was slightly wounded. The frightened pack animals scattered, taking supplies with them. The Sandinistas did not rush the column, and the marines were able to counter with their own machine gun fire and to launch a flanking movement to the right, forcing evacuation of enemy foxholes on that side. After 80 minutes of heavy firing, the attackers retired. Two marine planes appeared to strafe enemy positions and withdrawal routes. Five marines and two national guardsmen were killed, and 23 marines and two members of the *guardia* were wounded.

The column limped into Quilalí as did the one from Telpaneca, which had also been hit by guerrillas. These encounters near the end of 1927 surprised Washington and helped correct some of the underestimates of Sandino's potential. The marines in Nicaragua were reinforced to subdue Sandino.

William Kamman

REFERENCES

Harold Norman Denny, *Dollars for Bullets: The Story of American Rule in Nicaragua* (Dial Pr., 1929); Robert Debs Heinl, Jr., *Soldiers of the Sea: The United States Marine Corps, 1775–1962* (U.S. Naval Institute Pr., 1962); Neill Macaulay, *The Sandino Affair* (Quadrangle, 1967); Vernon Edgar Megee, "United States Military Intervention in Nicaragua," M.A. thesis, University of Texas, 1963; Clyde H. Metcalf, *A History of the United States Marine Corps* (Putnam, 1939); Bernard C. Nalty, *The United States Marines in Nicaragua*, rev. ed., Marine Corps Historical Reference Series, No. 21 (Historical Branch, G-3 Division Headquarters, U.S. Marine Corps, 1962).

Caperton, William Banks (1855–1941)

The naval officer who commanded the occupations of Haiti (1915) and the Dominican Republic (1916), was William Banks Caperton, a native Tennessean who was born in 1855. Caperton served on vessels in the North Atlantic and Far East after graduating from the United States Naval Academy at Annapolis, Maryland, in 1875. Following brief assignments with the Office of Naval Operations and the Naval War College, in the mid–1890s, he served in the commissioning crews of the armored cruiser *Brooklyn* and the gunboat *Marietta*. He was on board the *Marietta* when the gunboat accompanied the battleship *Oregon* on its historic run around South America during the Spanish-Cuban/American War.

Caperton's career advanced rapidly during the naval expansion that followed the war with Spain. He was promoted to lieutenant commander in 1899, commander in 1904, and captain in 1908. Caperton, who became a rear admiral in March 1913, spent four years (1909–1913) ashore in a variety of administrative assignments before assuming command of the Atlantic Reserve Fleet in November 1913. One year later, he took over the Atlantic Fleet's Cruiser Squadron (later Force) and raised his flag on the armored cruiser *Washington*, then stationed off Veracruz, Mexico.

Soon after Caperton assumed his new command, he had to deal with a crisis in Haiti, where political chaos had reigned since 1911. By mid-summer 1915, particularly gruesome political violence prompted a full-fledged U.S. intervention. Initially, the U.S. forces occupied only Port-au-Prince and Cap Haïtien and oversaw the installation of the State Department's candidate for the Haitian presidency. But in mid-August 1915, the admiral used the five warships then stationed in Haitian waters for transporting marines to occupy most of the principal ports. These operations were generally uneventful, but Haitian guerrillas resisted the occupation in the northern interior provinces. As pacification operations continued on land, Caperton's vessels conducted antismuggling patrols, transported marines, and mounted occasional riverine expeditions.

By spring 1916, Caperton was able to withdraw all but three ships of marginal fighting value. But by then, political turmoil in the neighboring Dominican Republic led to another U.S. intervention in the Caribbean. In May, the navy dispatched Caperton and a variety of vessels (numbering 14 at one point) to the Dominican coast. There, Caperton followed essentially the same pattern of occupation as in Haiti the previous year. Covered by warships, marines occupied the capital city and then the main seaports, which became staging areas for pacification operations in the interior. The landings were unopposed except at Puerto Plata, where Haitian forces inflicted several casualties on the marines.

By midsummer 1916, most resistance had been stilled, although an August squall off Santo Domingo drove the cruiser *Memphis* onto the rocks, and 40 sailors died.

Shortly after the occupation of the Dominican Republic's ports, Caperton became commander in chief of the Pacific Fleet, with the rank of admiral. In May 1919, on the eve of his retirement, Caperton submitted a lengthy report that stressed the importance of the navy's diplomatic mission, particularly in Latin American waters, where a permanent squadron would be helpful in cultivating friendly relations. This proved to be a seminal document instrumental in the formation of the Special Service Squadron in 1920.

Caperton retired in June 1919 with the rank of rear admiral. In 1930, the navy advanced him on the retired list to the rank of admiral. Caperton died in 1941.

Donald A. Yerxa

REFERENCES

David Healy, *Gunboat Diplomacy in the Wilson Era: The U.S. Navy in Haiti, 1915–1916* (Univ. of Wisconsin Pr., 1976); Robert Debs Heinl, Jr., and Nancy Gordon Heinl, "The American Occupation of Haiti: Pacification, 1915–1921," *Marine Corps Gazette*, 62 (1978), 28–41; Clark G. Reynolds, *Famous American Admirals* (Van Nostrand, 1978); Hans Schmidt, *The United States Occupation of Haiti, 1915–1934* (Rutgers Univ. Pr., 1971); Donald A. Yerxa, *The United States Navy and the American Empire in the Caribbean, 1898–1945* (Univ. of South Carolina Pr., 1991).

See also Caco War, Haiti (1915–1916); Haiti, Occupation (1915–1934).

Carlson, Evans Fordyce
(1896–1947)

Although Evans Fordyce Carlson is best remembered for his service in China and for organizing and leading the 2nd Marine Raider Battalion in World War II, it was in Nicaragua that after 18 years of being in and out of military service he experienced his first taste of battle and his introduction to guerrilla warfare.

Carlson, by lying about his age, joined the army in 1912. Eventually he rose to the rank of captain; arrived in France just as World War I ended; and resigned from the army in 1919 to take a sales position. In 1922 he enlisted in the marines, attended officers' school, and was commissioned a second lieutenant. He was in China from 1927 to 1929 and arrived in Nicaragua in May 1930. There, he was commissioned a captain in the U.S.-trained *guardia nacional*. Carlson was initially assigned to head a guard post at Jicaro and then at Jalapa, where his duties included settling disputes among the citizenry. In July he led a small patrol to Portillo to fight off a guerrilla band of about a hundred men headed by Simon González. Although the guerrillas had left Portillo when Carlson's patrol arrived, he pursued and surprised them in their retreat. After his early success in the engagement, the jungle seemed to absorb the guerrillas, and the patrol lost contact, much to Carlson's disgust. The experience spurred him to learn more about guerrilla warfare.

In December 1930, Carlson was transferred to Managua, where he became the department commander for Managua-Carazo, a post he held when a strong earthquake destroyed the capital in March. He and his comrades worked feverishly for several days to bring relief and order to the stricken city. He was hospitalized from the strain and malaria after which he returned as Managua's chief of police, a position he held until the marine intervention ended in January 1933. For service in Nicaragua, Carlson received the Navy Cross and the Nicaraguan Medal of Merit and the Medal of Distinction.

William Kamman

REFERENCES

Michael Blankfurt, *The Big Yankee: The Life of Carlson of the Raiders* (Little, Brown, 1947); Karl Schuon, *U.S. Marine Corps Biographical Dictionary* (Franklin Watts, 1963).

Carranza, Venustiano
(1859–1920)

Although not always known for taking decisive action, Governor Venustiano Carranza of Coahuila, Mexico, refused to recognize the usurpation of the Mexican presidency by the dictator Victoriano Huerta in 1913. By continuing to support the democratic cause of the deposed President Francisco I. Madero and urging other governors to do the same, Carranza began his claim to leadership of the Constitutionalist revolution, which eventually succeeded in ousting Huerta in 1914. As "first chief" of the Constitutionalists, Carranza was the political leader, but not a military commander.

Autocratic and aloof, Carranza often clashed with his field commanders, especially Francisco "Pancho" Villa, who had his own base of support in Chihuahua. Huerta's departure led to an open rupture between Carranza and Villa. Thanks largely to the military tactics of his field commander, Álvaro Obregón, Carranza ultimately gained control of most of Mexico and was granted *de facto* recognition by the United States.

Then came Villa's raid on Columbus, New Mexico, in 1916, and the U.S. response in the form of Gen. John J. Pershing's Punitive Expedition. Carranza's dilemma: how to maintain the territorial integrity of Mexico while avoiding a war with the powerful United States. Adding to this dilemma was the strong nationalistic sentiment in Mexico against U.S. intervention. Carranza could not afford to do nothing.

The Mexican president would have been pleased to see the end of his rival, Villa, and he responded to news of the Columbus raid by ordering his military to intercept Villa's forces during their retreat and to free U.S. hostages. But Carranza prepared for the worst by apprising his military commanders of the possibility of a U.S. invasion. Despite receiving recognition from President Woodrow Wilson's administration Carranza distrusted the U.S. government, and especially the Wilson administration, which had previously encouraged the Villista faction.

Carranza warned the United States that pursuit of the "bandits" would not be tolerated unless mutual permission for forces to cross borders was agreed to. U.S. Secretary of State Robert Lansing accepted this condition and chose to misconstrue the Mexican proposals as approving the Punitive Expedition. Carranza, however, did not consider this proposal retroactive.

Indeed, President Carranza never authorized Pershing's expeditions, but neither did he take a firm stance against them during the first month. He even grudgingly allowed the expedition to be resupplied by rail. For their part, U.S. officials sought to avoid any appearance of hostility toward Carranza or his government. The U.S. War Department, having sent Pershing to attack the Villista bands, instructed him to cooperate with Mexican government forces.

Both sides were constrained by political considerations. In an election year U.S. public opin-

ion demanded action against Villa; the shaky Carranza regime faced adamant opposition to any U.S. intervention. The atmosphere of mutual distrust and suspicion intensified with the initial clash of U.S. and Mexican forces at Parral on 12 April 1916. While General Pershing suspected Mexican authorities were planning to create an incident, Carranza blamed the trouble on the U.S. detachment for entering the town without permission. A personal message from Carranza himself demanded immediate removal of Pershing's forces before more serious incidents could occur.

The Parral episode shattered the lingering notion that the Carrancistas could be persuaded to cooperate with Pershing. A cordial reception accorded Special Representative James L. Rodgers by President Carranza, however, seemed to offer hope for negotiation. When Secretary of State Lansing in April 1916 proposed a meeting between army Chief of Staff Hugh L. Scott and Obregón, the new Mexican Secretary of War, Carranza eagerly accepted.

The agreement reached by the military negotiators failed to specify a date for U.S. withdrawal from Mexico. This, together with a new U.S. incursion in the Big Bend country, caused Carranza to reject the proposed protocol. Diplomatic hostility increased when an unfriendly note from Carranza on 22 May demanded immediate withdrawal and implied a threat of war. A month later the U.S. government responded in kind. The U.S. note directly blamed Carranza for the failure to reach an agreement and rejected the demand for withdrawal.

The fuse to set off a powderkeg of war was ignited by the most serious military engagement of the expedition at Carrizal the day after the delivery of the U.S. note. Conflicting reports and interpretations of the events at Carrizal resulted in considerable bluster from both sides, but the lack of action demonstrated that neither Wilson nor Carranza wanted war. Carranza defused the crisis by ordering the release of U.S. soldiers captured at Carrizal and suggesting mediation.

On 3 July 1916 Secretary of State Lansing responded by proposing the establishment of a joint commission to deal with the conflict. Carranza accepted and appointed three civilians with close political ties to himself. When the American-Mexican Joint Commission presented a draft protocol to Carranza, it was rejected; but the commission served to preserve the peace until Wilson elected to remove the Punitive Expedition unilaterally.

While Carranza had been unable to force the withdrawal of the Punitive Expedition, neither did he acquiesce in its presence, thus maintaining his good standing as an ardent nationalist. Relations between the United States and Carranza's government continued to be abrasive.

Anthony K. Knopp

REFERENCES

Clarence C. Clendenen, *The United States and Pancho Villa: A Study in Unconventional Diplomacy* (Cornell Univ. Pr., 1961); Mark T. Gilderhus, *Diplomacy and Revolution: U.S.-Mexican Relations Under Wilson and Carranza* (Univ. of Arizona Pr., 1977); Linda B. Hall and Don M. Coerver, *Revolution on the Border: The United States and Mexico, 1910–1920* (Univ. of New Mexico Pr., 1988); Arthur S. Link, *Wilson: Confusions and Crises, 1915–1916* (Princeton Univ. Pr., 1964); Frank E. Vandiver, *Black Jack: The Life and Times of John J. Pershing* (Texas A&M Univ. Pr., 1977), vol. 20.

See also Punitive Expedition, Mexico (1916–1917); Veracruz, Mexico, Occupation (1914).

Carrizal, Mexico, Battle (1916)

Ever since March 1916, when President Woodrow Wilson had ordered Gen. John J. Pershing's Punitive Expedition into Mexico, hostility between the United States and Mexican governments had increased. Wilson, intent on driving Francisco "Pancho" Villa's troops away from the international boundary and restoring order to the border region, worked to establish a reciprocal crossings agreement with his southern neighbor. But Mexican President Venustiano Carranza felt that he would lose domestic support for his shaky government if he caved in to U.S. demands. Furthermore, he feared that the Punitive Expedition would become an army of extended occupation and intimidation if he allowed its continued presence.

Although Mexico's official displeasure with the expedition had been stated previously through Ambassador Eliseo Arredondo, it was the blunt declaration of Gen. Jacinto B. Treviño to General Pershing on 16 June 1916 that signaled an end to Mexican patience. Treviño warned that if U.S. troops moved in any direction other than northward toward the border, their conduct would be construed as an act of war, and the federal army would resist them with their full might. On the same day a second Carrancista courier delivered the same emphatic message. Pershing responded with an equally curt reply that he took orders only from Washington, and that he would continue operations until instructed differently by his superiors. He repeated orders to all patrols that they avoid direct contact with Carrancista soldiers where possible, but if fired on they were to protect themselves with all means at their disposal. Pershing also informed Gen. Frederick Funston, commander of the Southern Military Department, of the deteriorating situation, adding that he was prepared for offensive operations if war erupted between the two nations.

The series of events that almost triggered that full-scale confrontation began on 17 June when Capt. Charles T. Boyd received orders directly from Pershing to reconnoiter the area around Villa Ahumada, on the Mexican Central Railroad. Intelligence indicated a large Carrancista troop concentration there, and Pershing needed more information on their deployment, strength, and intentions. Pershing's orders allowed the captain a great deal of latitude: ". . . I want you to avoid a fight if possible. Do not allow yourself to be surprised by superior numbers. But if wantonly attacked, use your own judgment as to what you shall do, having due regard for the safety of your command" (Clendenen, p. 279).

Under command of Captain Boyd and Capt. Lewis S. Morey, 84 officers and men of the 10th Cavalry and two civilian guides set out from Casas Grandes the following day. The route of march toward Ahumada skirted the smaller town of Carrizal, which was occupied by a Carrancista garrison under Gen. Felix U. Gómez. Unknown to U.S. forces, Gómez had received telegraphed instructions from his superiors in Ciudad Juárez to hold the position and resist any U.S. effort to enter the town. Upon reaching a point just southwest of Carrizal, Boyd sent forward a brief message stating that he was on a peaceful reconnaissance mission and merely wished to pass through the village on his way to Ahumada. On the previous day, civilian scouts W.P. McCabe and Lemuel Spillsbury had advised Boyd to bypass Carrizal because of the 400-man garrison there, and Morey agreed with that assessment, but Boyd insisted that his orders necessitated that the troops ride through the center of town.

Just at sunrise on 21 June the U.S. cavalrymen reached the irrigation ditches one mile south of town, watered their horses, and surveyed the scene through binoculars. Boyd rode forward to confer with a dozen Mexican officers who had ridden out under a flag of truce. They indicated that the U.S. commander could proceed to the municipal square to discuss arrangements with Gómez. Fearing a possible ambush, Boyd elected to parley in a more open area. During the hour-long meeting Gómez remained adamantly opposed to the 10th Cavalry passing through the town, and, amid the tense negotiations, some of his troops began to take up flanking positions among the trees bordering the irrigation ditches. Boyd, aware of his untenable position in the open field, broke off negotiations and ordered a dismounted advance across 300 yards of unprotected plain. Shots rang out from the Mexican positions, soon joined by the deadly fire of machine guns that raked the field. Nearly all members of C troop were wounded, including Boyd who was hit in the shoulder, but most made it back to a hastily improvised defensive position along the irrigation ditches. Upon reaching that point, Boyd took two more wounds and fell dead across the dirt emplacement, as did Lt. Henry R. Adair. On the other side of the ill-defined battle line, Gómez also died within the first minutes of combat.

Morey, who also had been wounded, ordered the only three unwounded soldiers of his command to escape as best they could and deliver his distress message to the first U.S. troops they encountered. Ironically, their mission was unnecessary because earlier some soldiers had panicked and had fled eastward beyond the Santo Domingo Ranch where they contacted a U.S. patrol which subsequently rescued Morey and four of his men who were wandering in the desert.

Mexican authorities later admitted the loss of 30 killed and 40 wounded in the fierce combat, while the United States Army officially had 12 soldiers killed and 10 wounded. The larger tragedy seemed to be played out in the respective newspapers of the two nations and the martial bombast from some government leaders in both capitals. Minister of War Álvaro Obregón bragged that the Carrizal affair would give him the authority to drive the invaders out of Chihuahua, and he would march through Texas to seize San Antonio. Pershing initially contended that the Carrancistas had deliberately plotted this cowardly act to precipitate war, and he prepared for full-scale military operations.

Luckily, cooler heads prevailed in both capitals. Carranza ordered Treviño to release the 23 black soldiers of the 10th Cavalry and their Mormon guide Lemuel Spillsbury who had been captured at Carrizal. Although these men had been treated badly by their captors, U.S. authorities chose not to make this a major issue even after the soldiers were safely delivered to El Paso, Texas, on June 29. U.S. judgments had been tempered by further news about the provocative nature of Boyd's original demands, and Pershing's condemnation of the officer's impetuous behavior.

In a final bit of irony, the Carrizal tragedy helped create a more positive environment for international diplomacy. President Wilson and Secretary of State Robert Lansing accepted the Mexican proposal for a joint U.S.-Mexican Commission of four to six members to solve the problems between the two countries. Secretary of War Newton D. Baker expressed similar sentiments in an article for *Outlook* magazine by declaring that his government had unfairly expected the impossible from Carranza's government ever since it granted *de facto* recognition. At this point, Carranza responded favorably to U.S. specifications for a joint commission, which resulted in the formation of the American-Mexican Joint Commission, and he ended his demands for immediate removal of Pershing's Punitive Expedition. He further offered to accept either direct negotiations or mediation by other Latin American governments on the future date of withdrawal, whichever method the United States favored. Certainly, the two nations did not solve all of their problems or lay aside all of their old animosities in the coming months, but never again did they come so close to full-scale war as in the dark days immediately after the Carrizal tragedy.

Michael L. Tate

REFERENCES

Haldeen Braddy, *Pershing's Mission in Mexico* (Texas Western Pr., 1966); Clarence C. Clendenen, *The United States and Pancho Villa: A Study in Unconventional Diplomacy* (Cornell Univ. Pr., 1961); Lewis S. Morey, "The Cavalry Fight at Carrizal," *Journal of the United States Cavalry Association*, 27 (Jan. 1917), 426–433; Frank Tompkins, *Chasing*

Villa (Military Service Pub. Co., 1934); H.B. Wharfield, "The Affair at Carrizal," *Montana*, 8 (Oct. 1968), 24–39; Karl Young, "A Fight That Could Have Meant War," *American West*, 3 (Spring 1966), 17–23, 90.

See also American-Mexican Joint Commission (1916).

Carter, Calvin Brooks (1887?–)

On 10 June 1925 the Nicaraguan chargé d'affaires in Washington, José Antonio Tijerino, signed a contract with Calvin Brooks Carter appointing him chief of the Nicaraguan constabulary and of the school of instruction. Carter arrived in Managua on 16 July to assume his duties, and he remained in that position until February 1927.

Carter, a Texan and graduate of Southwestern University in Georgetown, Texas, served in the Philippine Constabulary for several years before his appointment as provincial governor of the province of Cotabato, the Philippines. His placement in Nicaragua came after the Managua government requested a recommendation from the State Department, which in turn approached Maj. Gen. Frank McIntyre, chief of the Bureau of Insular Affairs. Carter was recommended because he was available, having recently returned from the Philippines, had many years of constabulary training, and spoke Spanish.

The national guard Carter was to head was legislated by the Nicaraguan Congress in May 1925 at the urging of the State Department. Although the law differed from Washington's proposal, it was hoped that the new constabulary would preserve Nicaragua's political stability as the marine legation guard departed the country in August, ending the first intervention.

Upon arrival in Managua, Carter and two other U.S. citizens, David Rodriquez and Louis F. Shroeder, hired as instructors, found some 200 men enlisted in the new organization. Of these, about 80 were soon rejected as unfit for service. Carter praised the men but bemoaned the lack of officers and noncommissioned officers and the lack of clothing and equipment. Carter planned a two-year training program before his men would begin to replace the Nicaraguan police, but calls to provide a guard for the president's house, patrol the capital and its outskirts, and lend assistance, if needed, to protect Managua's fortress, La Loma, interfered with his plans. Nonetheless, there was soon progress

in enlisting additional men and preserving the guard's nonpartisan makeup. By the end of August, however, Carter witnessed rising political instability in which Conservative party members pressured President Carlos Solórzano to rid his coalition government of Liberal influence. In one incident involving the president's brother-in-law, Carter urged Solórzano to have a showdown, and he offered to accompany the president and shoot the brother-in-law if he misbehaved. The president declined. Later, Gen. Emiliano Chamorro Vargas, former Conservative president and perennial revolutionary, appeared in Managua and seized La Loma. Lacking machine guns and having only 30 rounds of ammunition per man, Carter asked for additional arms and offered to defend the president, but again Solórzano declined.

After Chamorro's successful *coup d'état* in which some guard members were wounded, Chamorro became a supporter of the national guard, wanting to use it against a Liberal counterrevolution. When many Liberal members of the constabulary refused to go along and resigned, it became clearly a partisan Conservative force battling Chamorro's Liberal opponents. Carter loyally served the Chamorro government, as he had Solórzano's, despite Washington's refusal to recognize Chamorro. When Charles C. Eberhardt, the U.S. minister, with whom Carter had good relations, took leave and a young legation secretary, Lawrence Dennis, became chargé d'affaires, there was criticism from the legation of Carter's actions. Dennis used extraordinary diplomatic pressure to remove Chamorro, and he disliked Carter's support of the unrecognized president. As a result, the chargé wrote a scathing report of Carter's actions to the State Department.

When Chamorro was forced out by diplomatic pressure and growing Liberal opposition, his successor Adolfo Díaz wanted Carter replaced. He resigned in early February 1927, and other U.S. citizens serving with the national guard departed by June.

William Kamman

REFERENCES

Calvin B. Carter, "The Kentucky Feud in Nicaragua," *World's Work*, 54 (1927), 312–321; Harold Norman Denny, *Dollars for Bullets: The Story of American Rule in Nicaragua* (Dial Pr., 1929); Richard Millett, *Guardians of the Dynasty: A History of the U.S.*

Created Guardia Nacional de Nicaragua and the Somoza Family (Orbis, 1977).

See also Guardia Nacional de Nicaragua.

Cavite, The Philippines, U.S. Seizure (1898)

On 1 May 1898, the Battle of Manila Bay, the Philippines, was fought off Cavite, a peninsula that juts into the bay from the southwestern end. The town housed a Spanish naval base, battery, and arsenal. During the battle, Commodore George Dewey sent the *Petrel* into Cavite harbor, where it fired a few shots from its six-inch guns at the government buildings. Soon the Spanish flag was hauled down and the white flag of surrender raised. At 12:30 p.m. the *Petrel* ceased firing and sent a small group of sailors to set fire to a number of Spanish boats which, though badly damaged and abandoned in shallow water, had not been completely destroyed.

The following day, much to the surprise of the U.S. forces, the Spanish flag was again hoisted over the Cavite arsenal. Capt. Benjamin P. Lamberton of the *Petrel* went back to Cavite to make inquiries and to demand a formal surrender. The Spanish commander, Capt. Enrique Sostoa y Ordõnez, told the U.S. officer that raising the white flag the previous day had signaled only a temporary truce, not a surrender. Lamberton then demanded that Sostoa surrender and denied his requests to consult with Spanish authorities in Madrid or in Mania, or with Adm. Patricio Montojo y Pasarón, his immediate superior. He did give Sostoa two hours to consult with his officers and insisted that he would open fire if the white flag was not raised by 12:00 noon.

Lamberton then returned to the *Petrel* and reported to Dewey, who approved his actions. Well before noon the white flag was again raised, and Lamberton returned to Cavite, only to find that the entire Spanish naval contingent had left. He locked the arsenal, and soon encountered Col. Pazos, who was in charge of two regiments of Spanish troops in Cavite town. Pazos asked for permission to remove his troops, and Lamberton advised him to go immediately to Manila. Filipino troops captured Pazos on his retreat but reportedly did him no harm. U.S. forces subsequently occupied Cavite.

Because he allowed the Spanish to withdraw, Lamberton was criticized, but in doing so he had saved Dewey the problems of caring for prisoners and also took into account Spain's practice of punishing severely officers who had surrendered.

Kenton J. Clymer

REFERENCES

French Ensor Chadwick, *The Relations of the United States and Spain: The Spanish-American War* (Scribner, 1911), 2 vols.; George Dewey, *Autobiography of George Dewey* (Scribner, 1913); Henry B. Russell, *An Illustrated History of Our War With Spain* (Worthington, 1898); Joseph L. Stickney, *War in the Philippines and the Life and Glorious Deeds of Admiral Dewey* (Bell, 1899); Richard H. Titherington, *A History of the Spanish-American War of 1898* (Books for Libraries, 1971).

See also Manila Bay, The Philippines, Naval Battle (1898).

Cayes, Haiti, Riot (1929)

The 1929 Cayes riot, also known as the "Cayes massacre," was one of several public disturbances that set off a chain of events leading to the withdrawal of U.S. occupation forces from Haiti.

The crisis began when President (Joseph) Louis Borno affronted Haitian nationalists by announcing on 5 October 1929 that he was cancelling popular elections scheduled for the following year, leaving the selection of his successor to his hand-picked Council of State. Reaction was swift. On 31 October 200 students from the Service Technique agricultural college at Damien went on strike, ostensibly because the bonus paid them for attending school had been reduced. Borno's opponents embraced their cause, as did students from the law school. By the end of November 20,000 people were holding peaceful demonstrations in the streets of Port-au-Prince. At first the authorities did not interfere, but as unrest continued and rumors spread of plans for a general strike of government employees, Gen. John H. Russell, who was U.S. high commissioner in Haiti, requested Washington to send 500 marines. On 4 December customs workers in the capital walked off their jobs, and by afternoon the city's streets were thronged with Haitians hurling rocks at marines. Russell declared martial law and placed the Garde d'Haiti under the marine brigade commander.

Meanwhile, anti-Borno agitators had extended their activities to the country districts which were less effectively policed. In the region surrounding Cayes, conditions were particularly conducive to discontent because peasant cane growers, who were hard-pressed by a poor harvest, resented the high taxes placed on alcohol and the competition from a U.S. distillery that had opened in Port-au-Prince. The peasants blamed a newly imposed standardization law for falling coffee prices and objected to the government's attempt to prevent seasonal emigration. Thus, when longshoremen and customs workers in Cayes halted the unloading of two ships on 4 December, they were ready to push their own demands. The next day Garde commander Lt. Fitzgerald Brown reported that the situation was getting out of hand and ordered U.S. women and children to assemble in the casern. Marine reinforcements were sent from Port-au-Prince, while three naval airplanes made dummy passes over Cayes discharging machine guns and dropping shell cases before flying out over the bay to unload live 25-pound bombs. This inane display of force lasted an hour, terrifying the inhabitants who ran out into the streets where the strikers were shouting, "Down with the Occupation! Down with Borno!" The marines remained in their barracks, allowing the people to rage through the town until they calmed down from sheer exhaustion.

On 6 December Cayes was peaceful until late afternoon when a crowd of 1,500 peasants from the plain of Torbeck approached carrying machetes, clubs, and stones. Believing that the dock strikers had obtained satisfaction, they had decided to press for abolition of the alcohol tax and removal of seals placed by the tax office on local distilleries. Twenty marines armed with machine guns and rifles confronted the peasants at a bridge outside the town. The peasants agreed to return home if the strike was over, and the marines permitted some of their leaders to enter Cayes to assure themselves on this point. When the leaders returned, they conceded that the strike had ended but demanded the release of three companions who had been detained as well as the removal of the seals on the distilleries. Leading citizens of the district came out to the bridge to persuade the mob to go home, but without success. Instead, the peasants milled about, hurling stones at the patrol and trying to creep past the blockade until the marines forced them back by firing over their heads. Finally, one man, stepping forward across the narrow interval to talk, grappled suddenly with a marine and bit him. As another marine prodded him off with a bayonet, the mob charged. This time the marines fired 600 rounds into the crowd, aiming low in an attempt to check the assault with as few fatalities as possible. In the midst of horrible screams, the peasants dispersed, leaving 21 dead and 51 wounded, and the riot was over.

The loss of life at Cayes tragically revealed the weakness of the occupation and its widespread unpopularity. By 1929 the U.S. populace had come to regard the killing of Haitians by marines unconscionable even in self-defense. President Herbert Hoover on 7 December asked Congress for authority to send a commission to Port-au-Prince to investigate the recent events and to ascertain when and how the United States might withdraw from the island. The commission headed by W. Cameron Forbes conducted hearings and defused a potentially explosive situation by convincing Borno to hand over the presidency to businessman Eugène Roy until the legislature could elect a successor in accordance with the constitution. Its report, submitted to Hoover on 26 March 1930, laid the groundwork for dismantling the U.S. protectorate.

Jane M. Rausch

REFERENCES

L.J. Bekker, "The Massacre at Aux Cayes," *Nation* 130 (1930), 308–310; Robert Debs Heinl, Jr., and Nancy Gordon Heinl, *Written in Blood: The Story of the Haitian People, 1492–1971* (Houghton Mifflin, 1978); James H. McCrocklin, *Garde d'Haiti, 1915–1934* (U.S. Naval Institute Pr., 1956); Arthur C. Millspaugh, *Haiti Under American Control, 1915–1930* (World Peace Foundation, 1931); Dana G. Munro, *The United States and the Caribbean Republics, 1921–1933* (Princeton Univ. Pr., 1974).

See also President's Commission on Conditions in Haiti (1930); Forbes Commission.

Cervera y Topete, Pascual (1833–1909)

Pascual Cervera y Topete, Spanish naval officer, commanded the Spanish fleet that was decisively defeated by the United States Navy during the Spanish-Cuban/American War.

Born in Medina-Sidonia, Spain, on 18 February 1833, into a noble family, Cervera y Topete began his education as an officer at age 12 when he entered a naval cadet school. Rising gradually through the officer ranks, he became highly regarded in the navy and was trusted by his subordinates. He took command of the Spanish squadron based at Cadiz on 30 October 1897. That same year he became the minister of marine, the Spanish equivalent of the U.S. secretary of the navy, in the government of Prime Minister Praxedas Mateo Sagasta, but resigned when he did not get support for his efforts to reform the navy.

Spain's efforts to end a civil war on the island of Cuba led to policies that increased tensions. As the crisis in Spanish-U.S. relations deepened, Cervera expressed concern to the minister of marine about how unprepared the Spanish navy was for war. He said that even if the Spanish navy won a battle, it would only postpone an inevitable defeat because Spain had no facilities in the Caribbean where it could repair damaged ships whereas the United States had efficient shipyards and plenty of money. These facts were not faced by his superior. After the destruction of the *Maine* in Havana harbor in February 1898, Cervera pointed out the disparity in strength between the Spanish and U.S. navies and urged that this information be forwarded to the queen regent and the cabinet. This suggestion was rejected by the new minister of marine, who replied that Cervera overestimated the strength of the United States. As the two nations drifted toward war, Cervera did his best to prepare for it while at the same time hoping that a peaceful resolution could be found. Finding that there were no war plans, he urged that such be prepared. He was concerned that the United States might seize the Canary Islands and use them as a base for operations against the Spanish mainland. He wanted to place his ships there to defend the islands.

Instead, Cervera was ordered to take the armored cruisers *Infanta María Teresa* and *Cristóbal Colón* to the Cape Verde Islands, where he was to meet a torpedo boat flotilla and await further instructions. Enroute Cervera found that the engines of the two ships were not functioning properly and that 700 tons of coal were consumed before the ships reached the port of St. Vincent in the Cape Verde Islands. At St. Vincent he discovered that the U.S. consul there had bought up most of the available coal; Cervera needed 1,000 tons for his ships but could only buy 700 tons at an inflated price. He still hoped

his force would be sent to the Canary Islands, but after the United States declared war on Spain he was ordered to Puerto Rico. Cervera complied but disclaimed responsibility for the consequences. He touched at Martinique on 13 May and then headed for Curaçao in the Dutch West Indies where he hoped to find a collier waiting for him. No collier was there, and neutrality regulations permitted only two ships to enter the harbor and to remain there for 48 hours. As a result, Cervera could do only limited coaling.

Meanwhile, the governor general of Cuba had urged the minister of marine to send Cervera's squadron there. With limited coal, Cervera had few options, and his six-ship force reached Santiago de Cuba on 19 May. Cervera had finally decided on Santiago because his fleet would be less vulnerable than in other Cuban or Puerto Rican ports. Subsequently, Cervera informed the minister of marine that he intended to recoal and to leave Santiago as quickly as he could before the port was blockaded. The coal intended for Cervera was lost when the collier carrying it was captured off Santiago on 25 May. On the evening of 27 May, the Flying Squadron under Commodore Winfield Scott Schley arrived off Santiago and began the blockade of that port.

When U.S. troops landed in Cuba on 22–23 June and advanced on Santiago, Cervera was ordered to escape at the first opportunity. He called a meeting of his captains and read to them the order. They all agreed that an escape was impossible and that they should resist as long as possible at Santiago. These sentiments were sent to the minister of marine. He informed Cervera that he had been placed under the orders of the captain general of Cuba. That official ordered Cervera to try to escape because he believed it better for national honor that the squadron be lost in battle than scuttled or surrendered. Accordingly, Cervera tried to run the blockade on 3 July. The result was the Battle of Santiago and the loss of all the ships under Cervera's command.

After the battle Cervera and his surviving crew were picked up on the beach by the yacht *Gloucester* and later transferred to the battleship *Iowa*. When he came on board the battleship Cervera was received with full military honors and greeted by Capt. Robley D. Evans. Later, Schley called on him and offered his personal funds for anything Cervera might need. The admiral politely declined the offer. Cervera was held at the United States Naval Academy, Annapolis, Maryland, until the war ended. While he was there he became aware that his bravery was much admired and that he was a popular hero. When he returned to Spain, Cervera was subjected to court-martial proceedings on the loss of his squadron but was honorably acquitted. Promoted to vice admiral in 1901, he became the chief of staff of the Spanish navy a year later. In 1903 he was made a senator for life. This honor lasted until 3 April 1909, when he died in Puerto Real, Spain.

Harold D. Langley

REFERENCES

Pascual Cervera y Topete, *The Spanish-American War: A Collection of Documents Relative to the Squadron Operations in the West Indies*, in U.S. Office of Naval Intelligence, *Information from Abroad, War Notes, No.* 7 (U.S. Government Printing Office, 1899); French Ensor Chadwick, *The Relations of the United States and Spain: The Spanish-American War* (Scribner, 1911), 2 vols.; Jose Cervera Pery, *El Admirante Cervera; Vida y Aventura de un Marino Español* (Editorial "Prensa Española," 1972); Victor María Concas y Palau, *La Escuadra del Almirante Cervera*, 2d ed., corr. and enl. (San Martin, 1899).

See also Santiago, Cuba, Naval Battle (1898).

Chaffee, Adna Romanza (1842–1914)

Gen. Adna Romanza Chaffee commanded U.S. forces in China during the Boxer Uprising and participated in many other wars and campaigns.

Brought up on his father's farm in Ohio, Chaffee was on his way to join an Ohio volunteer regiment in July 1861 to fight in the Civil War when he met a recruiting party from the newly formed 6th Cavalry Regiment. He joined that regiment as a private and served in it continuously for the next 26 years.

During the Civil War, Chaffee served with the Army of the Potomac, eventually becoming a first lieutenant in the regular cavalry. He participated, altogether, in 54 battles and engagements and was wounded three times.

In 1867, Chaffee resigned his commission to enter private business, but persuaded to reconsider, he was reinstated on the urging of his commanding officer. For the next 25 years, he served in the 6th and the 9th Cavalry Regiments in the Southwest. Except for the brief periods spent serving as a recruiting officer and temporary Indian agent, he fought in summer and winter campaigns against the Comanche, Cheyenne, Kiowa, and Apache.

In 1890, Chaffee became the inspector general of the Department of Arizona. Four years later he rejoined the 6th Cavalry at Fort Robinson, Nebraska. In 1896, he was an instructor at the Infantry and Cavalry School for Officers at Fort Leavenworth (Kansas). The following year, he commanded the 3rd Cavalry and was commandant of the Cavalry School at Fort Riley, Kansas.

In 1898, at the outbreak of the Spanish-Cuban/American War, Chaffee was commissioned a brigadier general of volunteers. He was assigned to command a brigade in Gen. William R. Shafter's V Corps in the invasion of Cuba. He commanded his brigade with distinction in the Battle of El Caney (1 July 1898) after making the only map and survey of the Spanish position. Following a brief period in the United States, he returned to Cuba after the end of hostilities as the military governor's chief of staff.

After the outbreak of the Boxer Uprising, Chaffee was assigned to command the U.S. China Relief Expedition by Secretary of War Elihi Root. He was the first U.S. general to participate in coalition warfare since George Washington.

In his official instructions from the secretary of war, Chaffee was encouraged to confer with his foreign counterparts and collaborate with them if doing so was consistent with U.S. interests. He was also instructed to preserve the government's freedom of action and was therefore forbidden to engage in activities that would limit the political or military flexibility of the United States (U.S., *Military Operations in South Africa and China*, p. 8).

Chaffee arrived in Tianjin (Tientsin) on 1 August 1900 after the fall of the city and took command of the U.S. contingent for the rest of the campaign. He was one of the proponents of a rapid advance to the capital. Collaborating with the rest of the Allied force, troops under his command took part in the advance to Beijing (Peking) and the Battles of Beicang (Pei-ts'ang), Yangcun (Yang-ts'un), and Tungzhou (T'ungchow).

U.S. troops played a key role in the seizure of Beijing: both the rescue of the legations and the capture of the Forbidden City. The original plan for a coordinated assault was abandoned because each contingent strove to be the first to enter the city and rescue its own nationals. U.S. troops entered Beijing shortly after the British on 14 August.

After the foreigners were rescued, the rest of the city had to be cleared of Chinese forces. The U.S. contingent under Chaffee was given the task of seizing the Forbidden City, the seat of dynastic power. The assault began on 15 August, but was stopped shortly after it began.

Historians have advanced several reasons for the halting of the U.S. advance. These include a Franco-Russian desire not to humiliate and alienate the dynasty completely, French anger at Chaffee's refusal to allow them to participate in the assault, and the fear of the other powers that the U.S. troops would get all the loot. A combination of all three was probably at work.

After the fall of Beijing, Chaffee telegraphed, "Purpose of expedition being accomplished, what is the further wish of Government as regards the use of troops? No more will be required as a relief force . . . . Suggest withdrawal . . . as soon as practicable" (U.S., *Military Operations in South Africa and China*, p. 180). He remained in Beijing commanding the U.S. occupation forces until May 1901. He and the troops under his command won praise for the relative restraint with which they conducted themselves during the campaign and the occupation. Chaffee performed well despite the lack of communication with and guidance from the president, Congress, and the War Department.

Promoted to lieutenant general in February 1901, Chaffee's next post was military governor of the Philippines, where he served until October 1902. He was then made commander of the Department of the East and finally, chief of staff, in January 1904. He served in that capacity until his retirement in January 1906.

Chaffee was part of the transitional generation of the United States Army. He was known to his contemporaries as a hard-bitten, Indian-fighting cavalryman and a strict disciplinarian. He was not overly enthusiastic about coalition warfare nor did he care much for interservice cooperation; he feuded with the marines in China and carried this dislike to the Philippines. Nev-

ertheless, he served well as the commander of a U.S. contingent of an Allied force.

Although an instructor in one and a commandant of another army school, he was not a graduate of the United States Military Academy, nor did he receive any formal education beyond elementary school. He has been the only chief of staff to enlist in the army as a private and hold every rank from private to lieutenant general. Despite his long and significant service, he remains a relatively unknown figure in U.S. military history.

Lewis Bernstein

REFERENCES

James B. Agnew, "Coalition Warfare—Relieving the Peking Legations, 1900," *Military Review*, 56 (1976), 58–70; William H. Carter, *The Life of Lieutenant General Chaffee* (Univ. of Chicago Pr., 1917); U.S., Department of War, Adjutant General's Office, *Reports on Military Operations in South Africa and China* (U.S. Government Printing Office, 1901).

See also Boxer Uprising, China (1899–1901).

Chichester, Edward (1849–1906)

Edward Chichester, a Royal naval captain, stepped into legend as part of the myth that Germany had designs on the Philippines during the period marked by the Spanish-Cuban/American War.

Chichester commanded the British squadron of three ships, including the heavy cruiser *Immortalité* and the gunboat *Linnet* in Manila Bay, the Philippines, during summer 1898. He was punctilious in observing the U.S. blockade established by Adm. George Dewey and the rules of war in a war zone, more so than the German Adm. Otto von Diederichs, who also commanded a squadron (five ships, including two battleships) in Manila Bay.

Chichester achieved misplaced fame after Henry Cabot Lodge claimed Chichester had deliberately intervened between von Diederichs's and Dewey's squadrons as Dewey's squadrons moved toward the bombardment of Manila in August. That legend, magnified into an act of Anglo-American friendship, found its way into many historical texts. It was long ago proved incorrect, however, by Thomas A. Bailey's researches into German and English archives.

Chichester was friendly with Dewey in China, paid courtesy visits in Manila Bay, and did move two of his vessels before the bombardment of Manila, but most likely to escape any field of fire and to improve his view. The myth is embroidered in Laura Hall Healy and Luis Kutner's account of an alleged partial understanding between Chichester and Dewey and is dealt with adequately in Ronald Spector's study of Dewey, and David Trask's study of the war.

Frederick C. Drake

REFERENCES

Thomas A. Bailey, "Dewey and the Germans at Manila Bay," *American Historical Review*, 45 (Oct. 1939), 58–81; William R. Braisted, *The United States Navy in the Pacific, 1897–1909* (Univ. of Texas Pr., 1958), 48–50; Laura Hall Healy and Luis Kutner, *The Admiral* (Ziff-Davis, 1944), 203–211; Ronald Spector, *Admiral of the New Empire: The Life and Career of George Dewey* (Louisiana State Univ. Pr., 1974), 72–79; David F. Trask, *The War With Spain in 1898* (Macmillan, 1981), 377–381.

See also German Naval Operations in the Philippines (1898–1899); Germany and the Spanish-Cuban/American War.

China, United States Military and Naval Presence (1901–1941)

The permanent U.S. military and naval presence in China between 1901 and 1941 was small and exposed; a military liability. It was a visible symbol of U.S. interest in and commitment to the *status quo* in East Asia. Its purpose was always political, never military.

Forces were concentrated at Beijing (Peking), Tianjin (Tientsin), Shanghai, and on the Yangzi (Yangtze) River. They consisted of the Beijing Legation Guard (soldiers, 1901–1905; marines, 1905–1941), the 15th Infantry (Tianjin, 1912–1938), the 4th Marines (Shanghai, 1927–1941) (*see* Condit), and the Yangzi Patrol (in one form or another, 1853–1941).

In times of crisis, these contingents were reinforced. In 1927–1929, during the Guomindang (Kuomintang) Northern Expedition, when Chinese nationalist forces sought the unity of China and an end to foreign imperialism, the 3rd Marine Expeditionary Brigade was sent to North China; its strength was concentrated around Tianjin. In 1932, the 31st Infantry and, in 1937–1938, the 2nd Marine Brigade were sent to Shanghai to reinforce the 4th Marines at the outbreak of different phases of the undeclared Sino-Japanese War.

The contingents' stated purpose changed over time, but the underlying reason for their existence remained constant. Through the 1920s their presence was a sign of the government's commitment to protect U.S. lives and property in the face of militant Chinese antiforeignism (thus to guard against a repetition of the Boxer Uprising), as well as a symbol of U.S. commitment to the Open Door policy. The Open Door policy had been proposed by the United States in 1899–1900 and sought to encourage keeping foreign spheres of influence in China open to trade and to discourage the seizure of any more Chinese territory by Japan or European powers. After 1931 the latter point was emphasized; the troops were supposed to aid in stopping Japanese expansionist aggression.

Withdrawing the force was debated in Washington throughout the 1920s as it became obvious the troops in North China would be inadequate to assert foreign rights under the Boxer Protocols. After the beginning of Japanese Army insubordination (the Jinan [Tsinan] incident, 1928), the debate continued, and it was decided withdrawal would have unfortunate political implications. The Department of State, acting in concert with the War and Navy departments, could not decide between withdrawal and reinforcement—withdrawal would be seen as weakness while reinforcement would be seen as provocative. This whole question was intimately tied to the ambiguous nature of U.S. economic and national security interests in East Asia; the mutual popular images held by the Japanese, the Chinese, and the United States of themselves and each other; and U.S., Japanese, and Chinese ambiguity about their relationships with each other, the rest of Asia in general, and other imperial powers.

Decisions were finally made after the expansion of the undeclared Sino-Japanese War in 1937 and the *Panay* incident. The 15th Infantry was redeployed to Fort Lewis, Washington, in 1938; it was replaced by a contingent from the marine legation guard. The 4th Marines were evacuated to the Philippines in November 1941 at about the same time the remaining Yangzi gunboats were withdrawn. The legation guard was taken prisoner by the Japanese following the Pearl Harbor attack in World War II.

Lewis Bernstein

REFERENCES

Howard F.K. Cahill, "The Thirty-First Infantry in Shanghai," *Infantry Journal*, 39 (May–June 1932), 165–175; Bernard D. Cole, *Gunboats and Marines: The United States Navy in China, 1925–1928* (Univ. of Delaware Pr., 1983); Kenneth W. Condit and Edwin T. Turnbladh, *Hold High the Torch: A History of the 4th Marines* (Historical Branch, G–3 Division, Headquarters, Marine Corps, 1960); Joe C. Dixon, ed., *The American Military and the Far East: Proceedings of the Ninth Military History Symposium, United States Air Force Academy, 1–3 October 1980* (U.S. Air Force Academy and Office of Air Force History, Headquarters, U.S. Air Force, 1981); Louis Morton, "Army and Marines on the China Station: A Study in Political and Military Rivalry," *Pacific Historical Review*, 29 (1960), 51–73; William L. Neumann, "Ambiguity and Ambivalence in Ideas of National Interest in Asia," in Alexander De Conde, ed., *Isolation and Security: Ideas and Interests in Twentieth Century American Foreign Policy* (Duke Univ. Pr., 1957).

See also list of entries at front of book for China, United States Military and Naval Presence.

China Relief Expedition

In the midst of U.S. diplomatic maneuvers regarding China, a nationalist Chinese movement threatened to overturn the efforts of President William McKinley's administration to create an "Open Door" policy for China. Long interested in forcing open trade for the Chinese market, Secretary of State John Hay had convinced the world that the major powers had agreed to a new era of cooperation with China. In early 1900, the Boxers, a group of aggressive young nationalist Chinese, launched a campaign to end foreign occupation in their country, initially targeting foreign missionaries and their Chinese converts. In the beginning, Chinese imperial military forces attempted to stop the Boxer rampage to maintain order, but the Boxers increased in strength during the spring and gained public support for their anti-foreign crusade. The Chinese government then began to support the Boxers by openly escalating the violence and creating a crisis for all foreigners living in China. Faced with increasing violence in the countryside, the murder of the German minister to China on 20 June 1900, and determined attacks in a number of Chinese cities, many foreign legations in Beijing (Peking) sent urgent petitions for increased military and naval support. By the end of June, Beijing was in a state of siege, and those foreigners fortunate enough to find themselves inside the legation quarter mounted a desperate defense against increasing attacks.

In response to this situation, foreign warships attacked the Dagu (Taku) forts on the outskirts of Tianjin (Tientsin). Subsequently, a small landing party from the U.S. squadron and other naval assets became part of an international rescue force (the Seymour Column) that sought to reach the legations in Beijing. Fighting against overwhelming numbers, the Seymour Column failed to break through and retreated to Tianjin, where plans were made to assemble a more formidable international army.

Drawing from its large complement of soldiers and marines in the Philippines, the United States contributed a significant portion of the Allied force. Maj. Gen. Adna R. Chaffee commanded the U.S. contingent, designated the China Relief Expedition, which eventually included the 9th and 14th Infantry Regiments, the 1st Marines, army artillery units, all from the Philippines and the 6th Cavalry Regiment from the United States. U.S. marines under Maj. Littleton W.T. Waller left the Philippines while the army's 9th Infantry Regiment prepared for departure. By 1 July the 9th Infantry was still not ready, so additional marines were sent from the Philippines to augment Waller's force.

On 13 July U.S. forces participated in the attack on Tianjin. The senior Allied officer, British Brig. Gen. A.R.F. Dorward, held a meeting in which he pointed in the direction of the Chinese section of Tianjin (also referred to as the Walled City) and told the Russians that they would form the right flank, while the French, Germans, Japanese, English, and Americans would take the left in the order named. The Walled City fell after a night of heavy fighting. One marine officer, upon reaching the inner city, observed that the Chinese civilian population suffered terribly with whole families executed and laid dead side by side. Although Boxers continued sniping at the Allied forces, the battle was won. Many Allied soldiers looted, often explaining their activities as "saving valuables" from the fires. Col. Robert L. Meade, commander of the marines, found two officers "saving valuables" and informed them that he, too, wanted to save "a few things from the flames" and suggested that they use the same trunk for safekeeping. One of the officers complained afterward that he never saw the trunk again. Later in Beijing, looting became so widespread that General Chaffee appointed marine Major Waller as provost of the city and ordered him to stop the looting.

By August 1900 the international relief expedition of almost 20,000 men had assembled at Tianjin and prepared to begin the 70-mile march on Beijing. It included forces from the United States, Japan, Great Britain, Germany, Austria-Hungary, Italy, and France. The march began on the morning of 4 August with the Boxers contesting the progress of the Allied army through pitched battles along the way. The expedition, under the command of Brig. Gen. Sir Alfred Gaselee, reached Beijing on 12 August and prepared to storm the city. By 14 August the relief of Beijing was ensured with the U.S. 14th Infantry Regiment providing covering fire from atop the city walls while the British fought their way through the gates. This action marked the end of the most significant U.S. participation in the suppression of the Boxer Uprising. U.S. forces returned to the Philippines to continue the campaign against the Filipino nationalists while other foreign troops remained in China to mop up scattered Boxer resistance and to restore order in China. U.S. casualties in the China campaign numbered less than 200 killed or wounded. At a comparatively small cost, U.S. operations in China effectively guaranteed the United States a voice in Chinese affairs. With the acquisition of the Philippines and a significant contribution to the rescue of foreign nationals in China and the suppression of the Boxers, the United States emerged as a player in politics in Asia.

Vernon L. Williams

REFERENCES

William R. Braisted, *The United States Navy in the Pacific, 1897–1909* (Univ. of Texas Pr., 1958); Robert D. Heinl, "Hell in China," *Marine Corps Gazette*, 39 (Nov. 1959), 55–68; Michael H. Hunt, "The Forgotten Occupation: Peking, 1900–1901," *Pacific Historical Review*, 48 (Nov. 1979), 501–529; John T. Myers, "Military Operations and Defenses of the Siege of Peking," *United States Naval Institute Proceedings*, 28 (Sept. 1902), 541–551; Boxer Rebellion File, U.S. Marine Corps Historical Center, personal papers, Washington, D.C.

Chinese in the Spanish–Cuban/ American War and the Philippine War

Commodore George Dewey told Hearst news correspondent John Barrett that the Battle of Manila Bay in May 1898 had been won in Hong Kong harbor. Acquiring quick fame from this Philippine naval engagement, Dewey attributed success to fleet rehearsals held before he upped anchor for Manila. With no reinforcements expected after he sailed, Dewey needed full crews of trained, "high grade" sailors to man every battle position (Barrett, pp. 59, 66, 80, 83).

What is startling about the capable navy crews who served under Dewey in 1898 is the number of Chinese-born. At a time when Chinese were generally barred from U.S. citizenship and military enlistments were normally denied to non-whites, Dewey skirted policy to raise his crews to authorized strength. Lacking sufficient white volunteers, the navy's Asiatic Squadron had enlisted aliens at least several years before the Manila Bay battle to overcome manpower shortages. The need for all hands to operate powerful new steel warships quashed objections to any good sailor's racial background. At the Battle of Manila Bay, 5 percent of Dewey's sailors were of Chinese heritage.

When the smoke of battle cleared, 29 Chinese sailors stood muster in uniform on Dewey's flagship, the *Olympia*. Likewise, roll calls on the other warships at Manila—the *Boston*, *Baltimore*, *Concord*, *Petrel*, and *Raleigh*—revealed names such as Foy, Gee, Li, Sou, Woo, Wing, and Young. Of the 88 Chinese aboard Dewey's fighting ships, one was a naturalized U.S. citizen, two were legal alien residents, and the rest classified simply as aliens. They had joined the navy at San Francisco, Mare Island, Bremerton, Norfolk, Honolulu, Shanghai, Hong Kong, Yokohama, and Nagasaki. Twenty-two signed up for the U.S. colors in March and April 1898, when war seemed imminent. A navy lieutenant observed that the Chinese sailors at Manila—Chinese-American was not a term then—"showed no fear in action and could bear comparison with any other race for cool industry" (Freidel, p. 24).

Chinese seamen proved important in settling Dewey's logistics situation, too. Dewey purchased two British-owned steamers, the *Nanshan* and *Zafiro*, before leaving Hong Kong. He registered the two steamers as U.S. merchant ships, converted them to supply vessels, and assigned two officers and four sailors to the pair. No other U.S. naval personnel were needed. The British captains and Chinese crews agreed to sail with the United States Navy for the duration of the combat operation. Carrying coal and ammunition, the *Nanshan* and *Zafiro* headed for Manila, adding another 100 Chinese to Dewey's squadron.

A grateful United States rewarded Dewey for his decisive Manila victory, promoted him to rear admiral, and voted him a gold sword. Furthermore, every sailor in Dewey's small fleet received a special medal for his part in the stunning action. Cognizant of the United States's racist Chinese exclusion laws, the admiral requested that the Chinese who had fought under his command at Manila be given the right to enter the United States. He pointed out that Chinese sailors had taken a "prominent and creditable" part in the fighting, yet they asked no special favor for their service to the country. Despite public support from the *New York Times*, Dewey's goal for his Chinese sailors remained unattainable.

In contrast with the navy, the army made no attempt to enlist Chinese-Americans for the Spanish-Cuban/American War. New Yorker Charlie Gong tried to join the Volunteer Reserve. Denied entry, Gong wondered aloud why he could not fight for his country the same as immigrants from France, Italy, and Ireland. In Portland, Oregon, local Chinese organized a semi-official fighting unit under a white officer. Described as the "American-born Chinese brigade," trained in military marching, the group drilled one evening a week. The 43-man unit paraded in National Guard uniforms, but saw no active service.

The army's racial attitude gradually changed when the Philippine War placed new demands on manpower. Mistrust between U.S. forces and their Filipino allies turned to open warfare in 1899. Both sides suffered casualties. Short of enlisted medical service personnel, the United States Army in the Philippines turned to local, apolitical Chinese for help.

On Luzon, officers of Maj. Gen. Arthur MacArthur's division recommended that the army hire "Chinese litter bearers" to meet the need for medical corpsmen. Beginning in March 1899, over two hundred Chinese residents of the Philippines went into the field as medical assistants. They administered first aid to U.S. troops and carried the wounded from the firing line to medical facilities in the rear. Army Surgeon General Brig. Gen. George M. Sternberg and Medal of Honor winner Brig. Gen. Frederick Funston both praised the Chinese litter bearers for their bravery (Funston, pp. 246, 301).

Successful in field service, men of Chinese parentage substituted for army medical personnel in the kitchens of military hospitals around Manila. Skilled Chinese cooks conserved army manpower and whetted hospital patients' appetites. At the army's 920-bed Santa Mesa hospital, for instance, 34 Chinese served as cooks and dining room attendants.

Other combat support services decided to seek Chinese help. Seventy-two Chinese were added to United States Signal Corps companies. In concert with regular army soldiers, the Chinese strung telegraph wire and built additional communications lines on Luzon. Twice they came under Filipino rifle fire. At Manila logistics stations, Chinese loaded supplies, ammunition, and coal, important tasks for which no soldiers had been allocated in departmental organization. By the end of 1899 quartermaster officers had organized carrying parties of the better acclimated Chinese to support each regiment of infantry. Charged with keeping troop formations supplied, the Chinese were extremely helpful during field operations.

For two years Chinese auxiliaries supported the United States Army in the Philippines. More troops arrived. The manpower situation improved. Some officers questioned the wisdom of employing Chinese auxiliaries. The military governor ordered U.S. exclusion laws placed in effect throughout the islands. Peace and Chinese bias returned under the U.S. flag. All Chinese auxiliaries of the medical and quartermaster departments were ordered discharged in February 1900.

By serving in the United States Navy and augmenting the United States Army, Chinese-American residents won the confidence and respect of their military comrades. Twenty years after the Spanish-Cuban/American War another generation of Chinese-Americans served their country in World War I, winning decorations ranging from the Distinguished Service Cross to the Purple Heart.

William F. Strobridge

REFERENCES

Annual Reports of the War Department, 1899, 1900, 1901 (U.S. Government Printing Office, 1899, 1900, 1901); *Annual Reports of the Navy Department*, 1898 (U.S. Government Printing Office, 1898); John Barrett, *Admiral George Dewey* (Harper, 1899), pp. 59, 66, 80, 83; Frank Freidel, *The Splendid Little War* (Little, Brown, 1958); Frederick Funston, *Memories of Two Wars: Cuban and Philippine Experiences* (Scribner, 1911); *New York World*, 25 April 1898; information on Portland Chinese furnished by Dr. Judy Yung; Ronald Spector, *Admiral of the New Empire: The Life and Career of George Dewey* (Louisiana State Univ. Pr., 1974).

Cienfuegos, Cuba, Naval Battle (1898)

On 11 May 1898 elements of the United States Navy's North Atlantic Squadron under the immediate command of Comdr. Bowman H. McCalla engaged Spanish land forces in a battle at Cienfuegos, a sugar port on the southern shore of Cuba. The three-hour battle resulted in the awarding of 54 Medals of Honor—the second largest number ever earned in a single engagement in U.S. military history.

In an attempt to disrupt the communications between Havana and Madrid and the Spanish fleet, Adm. William T. Sampson ordered the fourth division of his fleet under McCalla to cut the undersea cables at Cienfuegos. The division—comprising the light cruiser *Marblehead*, the gunboat *Nashville*, and the converted yacht *Eagle*, accompanied by the revenue cutter *Windom* and the collier *Saturn*—blockaded Cienfuegos on 7 May. In the early morning of 11 May two steam cutters and four sailing launches carrying 56 sailors and marines under the command of Lt. Cameron McRae Winslow left the protection of the warships and headed for shore. This small force came under intense fire from an estimated 1,500 enemy troops as they closed to within 50 feet of the shore line while they used grapnels to snag the cables, hoisted them aboard the small boats, and cut sections out of the cables so they could not easily be repaired. Supported by the main and secondary batteries of the *Marblehead* and the *Nashville* and firing at the enemy with pistols, rifles, and machine guns when necessary, Lt. Winslow and his men destroyed two of the three cables before withdrawing to the safety of the ships. U.S. casualties were two killed and 10 wounded

while the Spanish lost almost 300 men in the engagement. Although the mission was not a complete success—the remaining cable provided a line of communication from Cuba to Spain through Jamaica for the rest of the war—the Battle of Cienfuegos stands as an amazing example of the bravery of men under fire.

Lawrence H. Douglas

REFERENCES

Evelyn M. Cherpak, "Cable Cutting at Cienfuegos," *United States Naval Institute Proceedings*, 113 (1987), 119-122; Paolo E. Coletta, *Bowman Henry McCalla: A Fighting Sailor* (Univ. Pr. of America, 1979); David Trask, *The War With Spain in 1898* (Macmillan, 1981); Cameron McRae Winslow, "Cable-Cutting at Cienfuegos," *Century Magazine*, 57 (1899), 708–717.

Ciudad Juárez, Mexico, Battle (1919)

Mexico lay bleeding, bereft of almost two million people; its economy and society in shambles; its body politic still showing the signs of corruption in spite of the revolutionary rhetoric that had pushed the nation toward the overthrow of an old regime in 1910 and the latter's replacement by a regime that claimed to represent and benefit the Mexican people. Conflict with its neighbors and the massive global imbroglio in Europe also cast Mexico in the dubious role of neutral. The triumphant Venustiano Carranza, first chief of the Constitutionalist Army, had ascended to the presidential throne at Chapultepec Castle over the opposition of revolutionary stalwarts Francisco "Pancho" Villa and the "Attila of the South," Emiliano Zapata.

In reaching his lofty position, Carranza had reached an impasse in relations with the United States and took steps which were to prove at least an irritant to the professorial President Woodrow Wilson. Carranza showed definite pro-German tendencies throughout World War I, and the arrival in Mexico of the notorious Zimmerman telegram offering a German military alliance to Mexico led the United States to believe that Mexico planned to give aid and comfort to the Central Powers.

The conclusion of World War I and Wilson's campaign for the Treaty of Versailles left Mexican policy generally in the hands of the Department of State under the strong leadership of

Robert Lansing. Troops continued to dot the border between Mexico and the United States, for although Carranza was president of Mexico, he did not control the country. In early 1919, Zapata and Villa continued to bedevil Carranza.

The Zapata problem was quickly handled. By mid-April 1919, Zapata lay dead at the *hacienda* in Chinameca, Morelos. Villa, however, remained free with his diminished band of *guerrilleros* in the hills and plains of Chihuahua.

Villa, who had been the revolutionary *wunderkind* in the early years of the revolution, was, at this point, an outsider. Carranza had assumed national power; the United States treated Villa as an outlaw; and Villa, the former head of the División del Norte, wanted to prove that he was still a viable force in Mexico.

Much bandit activity continued along the U.S.-Mexico border, and the possibility of war with Mexico seemed strong by mid–1919. U.S. troops returning from World War I as well as those already stationed along the border seemed primed for a fight with Mexico. Contingency plans in the United States War Department indicated that a strong possibility for a fight remained. One member of the general staff suggested that points of supply be maintained at San Antonio, Galveston, and El Paso, Texas. Each of these should be ready to supply one division each, including a cavalry division. Texas Governor William P. Hobby, reflecting the views of his constituency, asked that the War Department incorporate the Texas National Guard into the regular army as a part of the concerted pressure to maintain a tranquil border zone. Secretary of War Newton D. Baker refused Hobby's request and noted pointedly that the regular army could handle any contingency.

News leaks from the War Department indicated that its views were not unanimous and did not share Baker's confidence. Press reports hinted bluntly that there did exist a distinct possibility that Villista forces could strike at Ciudad Juárez, right across the border from El Paso, Texas. Gen. DeRosey C. Cabell, commander of the Southern Department, received orders that if rebel shots penetrated into El Paso, he should move across the border with his forces to scatter Villa's troops but without mounting a major incursion into Mexico.

Press reports soon proved correct. By 14 June a substantial band—supposedly Villista—moved aggressively toward Juárez. Villistas soon took positions around Juárez, seizing the U.S.-owned race track and surrounding buildings. They began an artillery battering of Carrancista troops forming the garrison at Ciudad Juárez. Unfortunately, some shots crossed the border and killed U.S. citizens.

U.S. response was swift. In accordance with his orders, Gen. James B. Erwin, commander of the El Paso district, ordered an attack after informing Carrancista commander Gen. Francisco González that such action did not imply U.S. intervention in Mexican affairs.

On the night of 15 June 3,600 U.S. troops, including infantry, cavalry, and artillery, crossed the border. Within 11 hours, Erwin and his troops had the Villistas in full retreat. U.S. forces returned to El Paso with nine prisoners. Ciudad Juárez, moreover, seemed to bear no ill-will toward Erwin and the United States. General González moved his troops to nearby Fort Hidalgo, and according to one newspaper, had become a real friend of the United States to the point of "preaching American propaganda."

The lightning strike on Juárez in mid-June touched off an intervention fever in the United States. Carranza initially argued that such action constituted a prelude to full intervention, but within three days of the withdrawal of U.S. forces from Juárez (16 June), Carranza informed his son-in-law and special ambassador Cándido Aguilar that the incident was closed. The U.S. reaction, however, was not quite as forgiving.

Members of Congress, most of them Republicans opposed to Wilson's foreign policy in general, were jubilant over the attack on Juárez. Senator Albert B. Fall of New Mexico, who chaired the Senate Foreign Relations Committee's Subcommittee on Mexican Affairs later in the summer, claimed that the invasion aimed to save U.S. lives in Mexico and was, therefore, justified. Fall pointed out that Carranza "did not control Mexico and could not offer protection to U.S. citizens." Fall welcomed the expedition, especially if it preceded a full-scale invasion of Mexico. Congressman Norman J. Gould of New York denigrated the Carranza regime as just another element in unsettled Mexico even though his government had been recognized by the United States. Congressman Claude B. Hudspeth of Texas claimed that Carranza had no intention of protecting U.S. lives. Carranza's initial demand for an apology called forth more of Hudspeth's vitriol.

Carranza's inability to keep Villa from raiding Juárez and the concomitant intervention gave impetus to a conservative junta in exile in the United States which demanded a return to the Constitution of 1857. Moreover, alleged the junta, Carranza had failed to live up to his campaign promises. Further, it alleged that the Mexican people desired to see him overthrown and replaced by a more effective leader.

At the same time, the State Department insisted that threats to U.S. citizens on their own soil should cease. Yet, no large military movements into Mexico were anticipated, and any further forays would hinge on future events.

Wilson, in spite of preoccupation with the Versailles Treaty, reassumed a firm position on Mexico. Motivated in part by his antagonism toward Carranza, he reinstituted the arms embargos that had been applied earlier in the decade. He also informed all diplomatic officers of the United States:

> You will further state that should the lives of American citizens continue to remain unsafe, and these murders continue by reason of the unwillingness or the inability of the Mexican Government to afford adequate protection, this Government [the United States] may be forced to adopt a radical change in its policy with regard to Mexico.

The final major U.S. foray into Mexico was fraught with implications for future U.S.-Mexican relations and reflected many of the antagonisms of the past. Carranza had proved incapable of controlling the Villista threat in the North. More than once, Villa had tweaked Carranza's beard by showing he still remained a commanding guerrilla figure. Carranza never controlled Villa. It would take more skillful and crafty politicians like Álvaro Obregón and P. Elías Calles to arrange Villa's permanent exit from the Mexican stage in July 1923. The United States, once the friend of Villa, would welcome the news that the "Centaur of the North" was gone.

Manuel A. Machado, Jr.

REFERENCES

Linda B. Hall and Donald Coerver, *Texas and the Mexican Revolution: A Study in State and National Border Policy, 1910–1920* (Trinity Univ. Pr., 1984); Friedrich Katz, *The Secret War in Mexico: Europe, the United States, and the Mexican Revolution* (Univ. of Chicago Pr., 1981); Manuel A. Machado, Jr., *Centaur of the North: Francisco Villa, the Mexican Revolution, and Northern Mexico* (Eakin, 1988); Manuel A. Machado, Jr., and James T. Judge, "Tempest in a Teapot? The Mexican-United States Intervention Crisis of 1919," *Southwestern Historical Quarterly*, 74 (1970), 1–23; Roberto Blanco Moheno, *Pancho Villa, Que es su padre* (Editorial Diana, 1969).

See also Villa, Francisco "Pancho."

Civic Action at Veracruz, Mexico (1914)

When U.S. troops occupied Veracruz, Mexico, from 21 April to 23 November 1914, military officers found it necessary to assume complete control and to reestablish virtually all public services from scratch. The 7,150 troops were under the command of Gen. Frederick Funston, of the United States Army's 5th Brigade.

Military officers assumed control of virtually all departments and used uniformed personnel to carry out their functions. This was necessary because Mexicans refused to work for or be associated with the occupation authorities because, reflecting previous military interventions in that country, Mexican law provided severe penalties for any citizens associated with or facilitating a foreign occupation. As a result, local officials and civil servants abandoned their posts when the troops landed, refusing all efforts to persuade them to return to their duties. In this situation it was impossible to establish a civilian administration or enable input by the local citizens. A complete military regime, operating under martial law, was the only alternative.

It was necessary to reestablish all services under the command of U.S. military officers. The range included postal services, the customs house, water, electricity, schools, courts, and police, as well as tax collection. A new police force was recruited, with a Cuban as head; and a postal official was brought in from Texas. These constituted the only civilian presence. Justice was provided by provost courts, often operating informally and seeking to stay within the tradition of local law. Local court officials refused to work with the invaders. Drastic measures, such as water rationing, became necessary. Efforts also included the refurbishing of many public buildings and an extensive road construction program. In their only triumph over the refusal of the local citizens to cooperate, U.S. authorities were successful in reopening the school system.

Health and sanitation received high priority. Many of the initial steps involved massive cleanup operations to remove debris and refuse accumulated over years of neglect. Particularly notable in the initial stages were the efforts to enclose, clean up, and improve sanitation at the central market, and a massive project to remove centuries of grime and filth from the fortress of San Juan de Ulloa, which had been used as a prison for decades. These involved thousands of troops and as time went on also employed many local day laborers, particularly in collecting and hauling refuse. Virtually every street and open space was swept and flushed, and tons of refuse were hauled out of the city to dumps and burned, along with accumulated refuse. Screens were installed in many public buildings, in particular the city's central market. Sanitary laws were strictly enforced.

Particularly notable was the campaign by the Department of Public Works to eradicate malaria by eliminating the many stagnant pools of water that served as breeding grounds for mosquitos. This effort involved digging 61 miles of drainage ditches and consumed 69,000 gallons of crude oil poured in stagnant ponds. Other health measures included the enforced vaccination of 46,000 people, virtually the entire population. The scope of the effort was immense and drastically reduced the normal death rates in the city. Indeed, it was so successful that the vultures, which normally were present in large numbers, abandoned the port to search elsewhere for food.

Reestablishing the local tax collection system, relying on the efficient collection of traditional taxes, was successful. This rendered the occupation largely self-financing in terms of local public services, although the cost of maintaining the troops that comprised the occupation force was met by the U.S. government.

The emphasis on health, sanitation, public services, and roads paralleled the actions of U.S. officials in other interventions throughout the Caribbean and Central America, even though the decisions were made locally without any central plan or instructions, and the occupation was regarded as temporary. The accomplishments were considerable, given the short duration of the occupation.

Kenneth J. Grieb

REFERENCES

Kenneth J. Grieb, *The United States and Huerta* (Univ. of Nebraska Pr., 1969); Robert E. Quirk, *An Affair of Honor: Woodrow Wilson and the Occupation of Veracruz* (Univ. of Kentucky Pr., 1962).

Civic Action in Cuba (1898–1902)

See Cuba, Military Government (1898–1902).

Civic Action in Cuba (1906–1909)

See Public Works in Cuba (1906–1909).

Civic Action in Haiti

The United States occupied Haiti in 1915 in response to a local crisis and the collapse of the government, and hence began the occupation with few specific objectives. The initial focus of the occupation regime was the reorganization of the government and the establishment of order. The restructuring of the foreign debt and stabilization of the governmental finances became the next priorities.

It is instructive that even at the conclusion of the occupation, the U.S. authorities considered their major contributions to Haiti to be the establishment of law and order, the introduction of civil service reform, the elimination of graft, and the regularization of the government finances and foreign debt. The attraction of additional loan funds into the island nation was considered part of the above priorities. The dismal state of the Haitian economy was indicated by the necessity of arranging new foreign loans during the occupation.

As the occupation dragged on, gradually attention to so-called civic action efforts increased as the initial crises were surmounted and as the U.S. authorities realized that they were likely to remain in Haiti for a long time. Public works received major attention only after the 1922 elections in Haiti and the installation of a new and more pliant Haitian regime willing to formalize the protectorate arrangement with the United States. Despite an increased priority for public works after 1922, the program hardly constituted the major focus of either the Haitian regime or of the occupation authorities.

Even when transforming the nation by introducing modern techniques became a larger concern, this was often pursued in a manner that smacked of the prevailing "white man's burden" outlook. All too many of the occupation authorities, appalled by the backwardness and conditions they found in Haiti, viewed themselves as assuming a "civilizing" function.

The initial action, taken at the start of the occupation, was the formal establishment of a Department of Public Works, an action that occupation authorities found necessary because Haiti had previously had no such department. The creation of the Service Technique to promote rural vocational and agricultural education also dates to the initial days of the occupation.

All efforts to improve the economy and services suffered because of limited funding and the virtually total absence of facilities. The government and the Gendarmerie d'Haiti (later Garde d'Haiti) (constabulary) absorbed most of the available funds, and what remained could barely begin to meet the immense needs. Of the $16 million raised through the major foreign loan in 1922, only $2.4 million was assigned to public works and construction. One-quarter of this amount was directed toward irrigation projects. While the resulting 100 miles of completed irrigation ditches constitute a major contribution to the nation, they can scarcely be called a large-scale project. Hence, even when civic action became a higher priority, funding was very limited, and this was reflected in the accomplishments.

Throughout the occupation the Service Technique remained a priority, receiving more funding than the regular school system. Its programs were directed toward basic vocational education, principally on agriculture. This program reflected the U.S. conviction that the regular Haitian educational system was too focused on France and impractical educational subjects, such as literature and culture.

The Service Technique constituted a major portion of the U.S. effort to establish the basis for economic growth. The focus was on improving agriculture, the mainstay of the economy and the main activity of the overwhelming majority of the populace. Despite the budgetary favoritism, even its activities were limited by a shortage of available funding. By the end of the intervention, the Service Technique operated five experimental farms seeking to promote new crops to wean the nation from its dependence on coffee and placed agricultural agents and veterinary

clinics in many portions of the interior not previously reached by governmental services. The impact was limited, but still constituted a dramatic change in the availability of government services to the rural populace.

Between 1922 and the U.S. withdrawal from Haiti in 1934, additional efforts were devoted to the development of infrastructure. As was often the case in developing nations at this time, Haiti suffered from an almost total absence of transportation and communications facilities. Not surprisingly, this also became a focus of the occupation authorities. The United States constructed the nation's first comprehensive road system. During the occupation, 1,075 miles of roads were built, though only five of these miles were paved. Construction included 210 bridges. However limited, this road system constituted the first comprehensive national transportation in Haiti and continued to serve as the backbone of the national transportation system long after the U.S. withdrawal. The resulting increase in the number of automobiles in the nation was cited as evidence of the success of this campaign. Nine rudimentary airfields were also built.

Efforts were also made to rehabilitate public buildings and to establish parks in the capital and villages throughout the nation. Unfortunately, such efforts often focused on refurbishing. New construction included barracks for the Garde, a limited number of schools, and lighthouses to aid navigation, reflecting the focus on order and transportation. The occupation authorities built 12 of the nation's 16 lighthouses. Occupation authorities also cited a substantial expansion of the telephone system as one of their major accomplishments. By the end of the occupation, it included over 1,000 miles of lines reaching about 1,200 subscribers.

Health service was a considerable success, with the establishment of 12 hospitals, a training school to provide personnel for them, and many rural clinics. An extensive vaccination program and a swamp drainage effort, both assisted by the Rockefeller Foundation, improved health conditions in the island nation.

In the field of education, 65 rural schools were established, most of them under the Service Technique. Another 4,000 students were enrolled in a series of industrial or manual arts schools set up in the capital and major cities. These efforts increased the number of Haitian students enrolled in schools by about 50 percent. While this was a dramatic increase in available education, especially in rural areas, the educational system still reached only about 10 percent of the nation's school-age children.

Civic action in Haiti received attention only after the stabilization of the regime, and that attention consisted of a limited vision and scant funding in the face of overwhelming needs. Its impact was considerable yet limited, providing the initial such services in the nation and establishing the basis of the national transportation system, while meeting only a small portion of the existing needs. The fact that subsequent regimes failed to maintain even these rudimentary services indicated the scope of the accomplishment, in spite of the limited impact.

Kenneth J. Grieb

REFERENCES

Arthur C. Millspaugh, *Haiti Under American Control, 1915–1930* (World Peace Foundation, 1931); Dana G. Munroe, *The United States and the Caribbean Republics, 1921–1933* (Princeton Univ. Pr., 1974); Hans Schmidt, *The United States Occupation of Haiti, 1915–1934* (Rutgers Univ. Pr., 1971).

Civic Action in the Dominican Republic

Shortly after they landed in 1916, U.S. military officers assumed complete control of all governmental functions in the Dominican Republic, ultimately launching a major governmental reorganization and financial reform program. The decision to take full control of the government was compelled by the refusal of the Dominican president, cabinet, and all officials to associate with the occupation regime. Cabinet posts were filled by U.S. Marine officers, reporting to the military governor, a post occupied by the U.S. naval commander in the region.

The disputes that led to the occupation focused strongly on chronic government deficits and the resulting need for external borrowing, resulting in the United States taking charge of the customs receipts, the nation's principal source of revenue, through a customs receivership in 1905. By 1916, the United States extended its control to all internal revenues even before the troops landed. U.S. authorities were convinced that governmental inefficiency and corruption constituted the nation's principal problems.

The occupation regime launched a broad program to improve health service, education, and transport facilities, and a more limited effort to stimulate agriculture. Yet paradoxically, the efforts of the military government were limited by financial difficulties, which ultimately determined the pace of the civic action programs.

Indicating the high priority placed on health and sanitation, and given the virtual absence of sanitation facilities, a United States Navy surgeon, Dr. Philip E. Garrison, was appointed chief of sanitation within a month of the establishment of the military government. He faced a grim task in a nation with a ratio of trained medical personnel (including both physicians and licentistes in medicine) to populace of one to 8,500. The military regime devoted considerable efforts to projects to clean up the cities and streets, directing all local governmental units to allocate a fixed percentage of their annual budgets to such endeavors as establishing regular garbage disposal systems. A national sanitary code was promulgated in 1919, establishing a regulatory system covering everything from hospitals, medical institutions, and pharmacies to plumbing and sewerage. A smallpox vaccination program was launched, quarantines introduced, and prostitution banned.

The effort focused mainly on establishing regulations and gathering statistics, however, with only a few new institutions being formed. During the entire occupation, only two new hospitals were added to the five already existing; a national laboratory was also established. No efforts were made to train additional physicians; thus, the nation remained dependent on foreign medical personnel. The military government did establish the nation's first training program for nurses, although its initial graduating class of only four nurses did not complete their studies until after the marines withdrew. Hence, the impact of the health effort was quite limited, although the sanitation and cleanup program did have some rudimentary success.

Education became the focus of a massive effort; the Dominican Republic had a literacy rate of 10 percent. The program was devoted almost entirely to establishing primary education and to spreading educational opportunities into the rural areas. Secondary education and university education were neglected because all available resources were focused on basic literacy. There was considerable success, with school enrollments rising from 14,000 in 1916 to 100,000 in 1920, and the school system reaching 647 rural schools and 164 urban schools by 1920; unfortunately, numbers declined after 1920. Despite considerable accomplishment, there was little construction of school buildings and little provision of supplies or texts. Establishing such a system rapidly meant relying on inadequately trained teachers, who supplemented their background through summer teacher training. In spite of the limited results, the establishment of a national primary education system with regulations and a standard curriculum constituted one of the principal and most visible accomplishments of the occupation regime.

A public works program begun in 1918 focused on the construction of major and secondary roads and port improvements. The north-south highway was virtually completed by the end of the occupation, connecting Santo Domingo to Santiago and Monte Cristi. The East-West highway was less successful, reaching only Azua in the West and El Seibo in the East. These two roads became the backbone of the nation's transportation system, providing the first effective linkages between key parts of the island state. By enabling access to previously remote regions, they contributed to the nationalization of power by facilitating greater control from the capital. Port facilities at several locations were also improved, most notably at San Pedo de Macorís in the East.

An agricultural extension program was also established, including experimental demonstration farms and agricultural agents. It sought to promote the cultivation of cotton and wheat and to improve the methods of peasant farmers. The peasants proved resistant to change, however, and the program's impact was limited.

Unfortunately, the financial problems that were the source of the initial U.S. involvement also reduced the effectiveness of the intervention regime's civic action programs because uncertain financing frequently delayed projects. The wartime global economic disruption affected the Dominican Republic initially through shortages of shipping and materials and inflation; later through a postwar depression which occurred when commodity prices returned to prewar levels. As a result, the military government found itself preoccupied with financial shortages, just as had been the case with earlier Dominican governments before the intervention. Repeat-

edly, plans were delayed while permission was obtained from Washington for new bond issues for external loans; these loans were also major points of contention in negotiations with the local elite for eventual withdrawal.

Several new external loans proved necessary, particularly after a financial crisis compelled a 50 percent cut in the national budget in 1921, which virtually halted the road construction and drastically reduced the educational budget and teachers' salaries. Bond issues were necessary in 1921, 1922, and 1924, but most of these funds were absorbed in maintaining normal governmental functions, leaving little for civic action. Only the north-south road received significant funding from the loan proceeds.

The civic action program's principal benefit to the Dominican Republic was the road system, which enabled more efficient and rapid transportation through the heart of the republic. The educational program was a major success, but involved only primary education and even then suffered cuts after 1920. The remaining programs had less impact, save for the systematic establishment of codes, regulations, and systems. Some of these efforts were continued under later regimes, while others were regarded as a legacy of foreign intervention with little relation to local needs and methods. Hence, the overall civic action program in the Dominican Republic had only limited success.

Kenneth J. Grieb

REFERENCES

Bruce J. Calder, *The Impact of Intervention: The Dominican Republic During the U.S. Occupation of 1916–1924* (Univ. of Texas Pr., 1984); Dana G. Munro, *Intervention and Dollar Diplomacy in the Caribbean, 1900–1921* (Princeton Univ. Pr., 1964).

Civic Action in the Philippines

See Military Government and Civic Action in the Philippines.

Coast Guard Operations in the Philippine War

On 5 May 1898, following Commodore George Dewey's victory over Rear Adm. Patricio Montojo y Pasarón's Spanish squadron at Manila Bay, the U.S. revenue cutter *McCulloch* was dispatched to Hong Kong. It arrived on 7 May and wired news of Dewey's victory to Washington. On its return trip to Manila the next day, *McCulloch* carried supplies, mail, and word of Dewey's promotion to rear admiral.

Emilio Aquinaldo y Famy, leader of the Philippine independence movement, petitioned for a ride on the *McCulloch* when it was in Hong Kong, but Dewey's aide, Lt. Thomas M. Brumby, refused him. He did, however, carry Aquinaldo's message to Dewey, who authorized passage on the *McCulloch*'s second trip to Hong Kong. The *McCulloch* sailed with Aquinaldo and 13 of his followers on 16 May 1898 and arrived at Cavite three days later. Dewey hoped that Aquinaldo would help the U.S. cause by leading a revolt against Spain. He gave little thought to the long-range consequences of encouraging Aquinaldo to attack the Spanish. But when the United States established sovereignty over the Philippines, Aquinaldo decided to resist U.S. control.

After Dewey's victory over Montojo's fleet, the *McCulloch* cruised on blockade duty and served as the boarding vessel for the Asiatic Squadron. On 25 May it moved to an anchorage berth next to the *Olympia*. Thereafter, it kept up steam and was prepared to get underway at short notice, especially in response to orders from the flagship. The *McCulloch* intercepted all vessels sailing into Manila Bay to enforce the blockade.

All neutral nations but Germany respected the U.S. blockade of the Philippines. The German fleet anchored where it chose to, ships sailed into the blockading squadron at night, and its commander, Vice Adm. Otto von Diederichs, did as he pleased. Since his fleet was larger than the U.S. squadron, his assertiveness was most objectionable. Finally, antagonized by von Diederichs's behavior, Dewey made a personal reconnaissance of the German position. According to Nathan Sargent, he hoisted "his flag on *McCulloch*, he steamed down to Marweles Bay, passed around the German ships anchored there, and left again without communicating with them, allowing them to draw their own conclusions from his visit" (Sargent, pp. 69-70). It is significant that Dewey chose to make this reconnaissance run in the *McCulloch*. The Revenue Cutter Service had a long history of combining naval power with peaceful humanitarian service, and the government has often chosen to use cutters to make a diplomatic point where use of a naval vessel might convey too much hostility.

During the prelude to the Philippine War, Dewey planned to use the *McCulloch* to attack the new enemy's towns, vessels, and strongholds if such attacks were necessary. The only significant operation occurred late in September. The *McCulloch* was ordered to capture the Filipino's gunrunning steamer *Pasig*, which it accomplished without a fight, despite Dewey's apprehension that a sharp battle was inevitable.

An executive order dated 29 October returned the *McCulloch* to the Treasury Department. It sailed from Manila on 6 November and continued its trip to San Francisco, arriving on 4 January 1899, just 8 days short of a year after leaving Hampton Roads, Virginia.

Irving H. King

REFERENCES

Randolph Ridgely, "The Coast Guard Cutter *McCulloch* at Manila," *United States Naval Institute Proceedings*, 55 (1929), 417–426; Nathan Sargent, *Admiral Dewey and the Manila Campaign* (Naval Historical Foundation, 1947); *The United States Revenue Cutter Service in the War With Spain, 1898* (U.S. Government Printing Office, 1899).

See also Coast Guard Operations in the Spanish-Cuban/American War.

Coast Guard Operations in the Spanish-Cuban/American War

When Cuba revolted against Spanish rule in 1895, a Cuban underground in the United States prepared to smuggle arms and to organize filibustering expeditions to the island. In response, President Grover Cleveland ordered the United States Revenue Cutter Service to establish a neutrality patrol. Between 1895 and 1898 eight cutters cruised in the Florida straits and adjacent waters, seized 29 ships for violating U.S. neutrality, detained in port another dozen smugglers, and broke up two filibustering expeditions.

When Congress declared war on Spain in April 1898, the Revenue Cutter Service was transferred to the navy. Cutters served in all theaters of combat. Eight served with Rear Adm. William T. Sampson's North Atlantic Squadron on blockade duty in Cuban waters. One was with Commodore George Dewey's Asiatic Squadron at Manila Bay. Seven served with the United States Army, guarding principal U.S. harbors and ports from Boston to the Mississippi Passes, and four patrolled against Spanish raiders on the Pacific Coast.

While Dewey was at Hong Kong preparing his attack on the Spanish Pacific Fleet, the Department of the Navy sent him the revenue cutter *McCulloch*. It arrived at Hong Kong on 17 April.

Six days later Great Britain ordered Dewey to leave Hong Kong within 48 hours. On the following two days his fleet sailed to Mirs Bay, 30 miles north of Hong Kong. The *McCulloch*, acting as the squadron's dispatch boat, carried word of hostilities from Hong Kong to Mirs Bay and orders for Dewey to proceed to the Philippines to destroy the Spanish Pacific Fleet.

The Asiatic Squadron steamed toward the Philippines at eight knots, arriving off the entrance to Manila Bay just before midnight, 30 April 1898. The cruiser *Olympia* led the squadron into the bay in single file with *McCulloch* taking its position third from the end. As the cutter passed El Fraile its stack caught fire. From nearby Corregidor a rocket went up. Shortly after, guns of the El Fraile battery opened fire on the squadron, and were silenced by the guns of *Concord*, *McCulloch*, *Boston*, and *Raleigh*. The next day Dewey totally destroyed the Spanish squadron without losing a man to battle. The only serviceman to lose his life in the Manila campaign was Frank B. Randall, chief engineer on board the *McCulloch*. Minutes after the cutter's smokestack caught fire on entering the bay, Randall collapsed and died of heat prostration in his 170-degree engine room.

Following Dewey's victory *McCulloch* was sent to Hong Kong to wire the news to Washington. On the return trip, it carried word of Dewey's promotion to rear admiral. The *McCulloch* stayed in the Philippines and served on blockade duty and as boarding vessel for the squadron. It participated in amphibious operations when the army took the city of Manila, and after the victory, its crew restored the lighthouse on Corregidor.

Meanwhile, halfway round the world the revenue cutter *Hudson* was winning great acclaim.

On 22 April 1898 President William McKinley ordered a blockade of the ports between Cárdenas and Bahía Honda on Cuba's northern coast. That same day, Sampson led the North Atlantic Squadron to Cuba, where he employed revenue cutters on the blockade. While using the mouth of Cárdenas Bay, a shoal water lagoon with islands obstructing the entrance, as a rendezvous, vessels on blockade duty were harassed by three Spanish gunboats in Cárdenas. In addition, the ship channel was mined.

Just before noon on 11 May, Comdr. John F. Merry sent three of his vessels into the bay. The *Winslow* and the *Hudson*, drawing the least water, led the way, followed by the *Wilmington*.

Comdr. Chapman C. Todd of the *Wilmington* ordered the torpedo boat *Winslow* to capture one of the gunboats. After it had gone one-half mile, a battery east of the city opened fire with deadly accuracy. The first shell just missed *Winslow*; the second crashed through its bow, destroying the steering gear. A round crashed into the deck, wounding the *Winslow*'s captain. Another wrecked the hand steering-gear, leaving the *Winslow* helpless. The *Winslow* was totally disabled and drifting toward shore in shallow water. Lt. Frank H. Newcomb maneuvered the revenue cutter *Hudson* close enough to throw a line to the crippled vessel, and as the cutter approached Lt. Worth Bagley and four men gathered along the *Winslow*'s rail. The next instant they were gone. With rounds falling all around, the *Hudson* towed the *Winslow* out of harm's way. Five men were killed, and another five were wounded aboard the *Winslow*. That was nearly one-third of the U.S. personnel killed afloat in the Spanish-Cuban/American War.

Not all revenue cutter assignments were as glamorous as those of the *McCulloch* and the *Hudson*. The 40-year-old paddle-wheeler *McLane* guarded the telegraph cable linking Key West and Sanibel Island. Seven cutters patrolled mine fields in U.S. harbors. Eight cutters spent months on blockade duty in Cuban waters, escorted troop transports, performed scouting missions, carried army dispatches, guarded army supplies, provided gunfire support for landing operations, and rescued U.S. soldiers from enemy gunfire on Cuban beaches.

Participation in the war led to greater recognition of the Revenue Cutter Service and to acceptance of its value to the nation in wartime.

Irving H. King

REFERENCES

Ernest E. Mead, "The Rescue of the Winslow," *Harper's Monthly* 98 (1898), 123–129; Randolph Ridgely, "The Coast Guard Cutter *McCulloch* at Manila," *United States Naval Institute Proceedings*, 55 (1929), 417–426; Nathan Sargent, *Admiral Dewey and the Manila Campaign* (Naval Historical Foundation,

1947); John Spears, *Our Navy in the War With Spain* (Scribner, 1898); *The United States Revenue Cutter Service in the War With Spain, 1898* (U.S. Government Printing Office, 1899).

Coastal Defense in the Spanish-Cuban/American War

The Spanish-Cuban/American War came at a time when army and navy planners in the United States were redefining their services' roles in defending the country. Traditionally, the navy had provided the first line of defense, supplemented by the army, which manned forts protecting major ports and coastal cities from attack. By the 1880s, however, naval theorists wanted the navy to concentrate on engaging enemy battle fleets in order to gain control of the seas, giving the army major responsibility for coastal defense. Unfortunately, in the years following the U.S. Civil War, rapidly changing military technology, both in fort construction and especially in the design of heavy ordnance, had rendered most of the nation's coastal fortifications obsolete. In 1886, a board chaired by Secretary of War William C. Endicott produced a comprehensive report recommending the expenditure of $125 million over the next 15 years to replace old masonry forts with modern concrete and earthen structures containing heavy-caliber breechloading steel rifles and mortars capable of driving away enemy battleships.

In response to this report, the army was authorized to establish a foundry that could produce the necessary mortars and cannon. Meanwhile, engineers solved the technical problems associated with redesigning the fortifications and emplacing the new weapons. Given the lack of a significant threat from abroad, however, and facing public pressure to reduce spending, Congress appropriated only about 10 percent of the requested funds and construction lagged. By 1898, the War Department had emplaced only 151 of the 2,000 heavy guns and mortars called for and could supply them with only 20 rounds of ammunition each. Congress also failed to provide the army with sufficient troops to man the new batteries.

The approach of war with Spain changed congressional attitudes. On 9 March 1898, the legislature appropriated $50 million to improve the nation's military readiness; $15 million was allotted to improving coastal fortifications. Congress also agreed to add two regiments of artillery to the regular army, which provided a sufficient cadre to operate the defenses completed by 1898. In January 1898, the War Department had ordered the emplacement of all available coastal guns as soon as possible; with the new funds, engineers hired more workers and defied winter conditions to push construction of 90 new emplacements. The War Department began extra shifts at federal ordnance factories and arsenals, ordered light rapid-fire cannons from U.S. and foreign suppliers, and pressed munitions makers to increase production. The United States Signal Corps began installing the electrical communications systems the new weapons required, and engineers began to lay mine fields in the principal harbors, which were then patrolled by naval militia, dubbed the "Mosquito Squadron." When representatives from coastal communities not included in the Endicott plan pressed for protection, the administration improvised with temporary batteries and obsolete guns and mortars. Secretary of War Russell A. Alger also sent army siege guns to coastal forts, removing them after any threats had passed.

The work of reinforcing coastal defenses continued throughout the war. By midsummer, the War Department had installed 185 cannon and mortars, completed emplacements for 550 more, tripled ammunition reserves, and blocked every major port with mines. Still, defenses were incomplete, and in April, when fears swept East Coast cities regarding the intentions of a Spanish fleet then crossing the Atlantic, U.S. naval commanders had to send a strong squadron to Hampton Roads, Virginia, to protect the Atlantic seaboard. Fortunately for the United States, the Spanish fleet was too weak to take advantage of this diversion of U.S. sea power from waters around Cuba. Had the United States faced a stronger naval power, it might well have had cause to regret its previous neglect of coastal fortifications. By the war's end, however, the nation was well on the way to establishing a modern system of seacoast defenses.

Richard H. Abbott

REFERENCES

Graham A. Cosmas, *An Army for Empire: The United States Army in the Spanish-American War* (Univ. of Missouri Pr., 1971); Emanuel Raymond Lewis, *Seacoast Fortifications of the United States: An Introductory History* (Smithsonian, 1970); Edward Ranson, "The Endicott Board of 1885–1886 and the Coast Defenses," *Military Affairs*, 31 (1967), 74–84.

Coco River Patrols, Nicaragua (1928–1929)

As U.S. Marine reinforcements arrived in early 1928 to combat Augusto C. Sandino's operations in northern Nicaragua, many of the Sandinistas moved eastward. The area of the country between the eastern littoral and the western third was sparsely settled—a few Indians—and practically unmapped. It included the Pis Pis mining district which, along with Caribbean coastal towns, offered the attractions of money and supplies for raiders. Protecting the region from such depredations posed large problems for the marine commander of the eastern area, Maj. Harold H. Utley. 1st Lt. Merritt A. Edson proposed a plan that concentrated on the Coco River, which originated in southwestern Honduras and flowed to the Caribbean in large part along the Nicaraguan-Honduran border. When the plan proposing the garrisoning of the lower river valley and sending combat patrols from the east to operate in conjunction with marines from the west was accepted, Edson, who later won the Medal of Honor for his actions on Guadalcanal in World War II, became a major player in the 1928–1929 marine operations along the Coco River basin.

To gain more knowledge about the river valley, Edson led a small reconnaissance patrol in March 1928 up the Coco from the mouth at Cabo Gracias a Dios in extreme northeast Nicaragua to the Karasus Rapids about 260 miles from the coast. In April Edson was again on patrol to block the reported advance of Marcos Aguerro, a Nicaraguan guerrilla leader, down the Coco at the conjuncture of the Huaspuc and Coco rivers. While at Huaspuc, Edson learned of Sandinista raids on the Neptune Mine and moved to Kuabul to intercept any raiders moving northward. Finding none, Edson's patrol went to Musahuas, an Indian village to the northwest. There, he exchanged his flotilla of boats for a pack train of 36 mules belonging to Capt. Wesley W. Walker's patrol and set out with a patrol under Capt. Henry D. Linscott for Bocay in the direction the Sandinistas had gone. They arrived at Bocay on the banks of the Bocay and Coco rivers on 2 June 1928, one day after the Sandinistas had passed through. Edson at this point planned to take his patrol southward to pick up the Sandinista trail and move toward Poteca, but he and his patrol were ordered back to Puerto Cabezas, ending the first Coco patrol. He had had little success in engaging the enemy but had helped to prevent a Sandinista move on the East Coast and had helped to push garrisoned outposts of the eastern area farther to the west.

On 28 June 1928, Gen. Logan Feland, commander of the 2nd Marine Brigade in Nicaragua, consulted Utley about airplane reconnaissance reports of Sandinista concentrations at Poteca and decided to send a combat patrol to disperse the enemy forces. Because northern area marines reported that there were no trails from the west leading into Poteca and because he had earlier requested the opportunity to occupy the settlement, Edson was selected to lead a patrol into the territory more than 400 miles up the Coco River at its junction with the Poteca River and to continue southward beyond that point to join with patrols from the west. Along the way he was to destroy or drive out any enemy forces encountered in the river valley.

The patrol assembled at Bocay for departure on 26 July in the midst of the rainy season. The river was at a 30-year high level, swift and full of debris; rapids had to be portaged; the almost constant rain kept everybody wet; insects and poisonous snakes were common companions; overturned boats and lost supplies were almost everyday occurrences. By 2 August the patrol had reached Callejon Canyon, where the Indian boatmen expected an ambush which did not occur. Nonetheless, from this point on small shore patrols were kept on each bank of the river to precede the boats by 50 to 100 yards. At Mustahuas on 4 August the patrol surprised two Sandinistas who escaped into the bush. Beyond Mustahuas there was increasing evidence of recent Sandinista presence. At one point a small patrol of Sandinistas was sighted coming down the river and shots were fired, but the patrol escaped. On 7 August planes dropping mail and rations for Edson's patrol spotted suspicious activity along the river above the village of Ililiquas and dropped two bombs. There followed an engagement between the patrol and Sandinistas led by Gen. Manuel M. Girón Ruano, south of the village. After the bombing Sandino had, unbeknown to Girón, withdrawn his men. Yet the fight lasted three hours before Girón withdrew to the west. The marines had one dead and three wounded; the Sandinista casualties were 10 dead and three wounded.

The advance up the river was resumed on 10 August. Two more enemy contacts were made four days later, allowing capture of much needed clothing and shoes for the marines. The patrol reached Poteca on 17 August. Evidence indicated that the Sandinistas had been scattered in small groups and driven from the valley. A report to the major general commandant called attention to the difficulty, danger, isolation, and accomplishments of the patrol's work and said it was without parallel in the brigade. The marines remained in the area until April 1929, when orders were issued for discontinuance of all marine posts on the Coco River from the Poteca River eastward as part of a reduction of marine forces in Nicaragua.

William Kamman

REFERENCES

Lejeune Cummins, *Quijote on a Burro: Sandino and the Marines, A Study in the Formulation of Foreign Policy* (La Impresora Azteca, 1958); Merritt A. Edson, "The Coco Patrol: Operations of the Marine Patrol Along the Coco River in Nicaragua," *Marine Corps Gazette*, 20 (Aug. 1936), 18–23, 38–48; (Nov. 1936), 40–41, 60–72; 21 (Feb. 1937), 35–43, 57–63; Robert Debs Heinl, Jr., *Soldiers of the Sea: The United States Marine Corps, 1775–1962* (U.S. Naval Institute Pr., 1962); J. Robert Moskin, *The U.S. Marine Corps Story* (McGraw-Hill, 1977); Bernard C. Nalty, *The United States in Nicaragua*, rev. ed. Marine Corps Historical Reference Series, No. 21 (Historical Branch, G-3 Division, Headquarters, U.S. Marine Corps, 1962).

See also Edson, Merritt Austin.

Cole, Eli Kelley (1867–1929)

Eli Kelley Cole, a marine officer, participated in the Caco War in Haiti, 1915–1916. Cole, son of Oncken W. and Cornelia Walker Cole, was born on 1 September 1867 in Carmel, New York, and was graduated from the United States Naval Academy at Annapolis, Maryland, in 1888. After serving for two years he accepted a commission as a second lieutenant in the U.S. Marine Corps. He served in various posts, including those at the Philippines and Panama. He also served as the first assistant to the commandant from April 1911 to January 1915.

On 4 August 1915, Cole led five companies of the 2nd Regiment to Haiti, where he assumed command ashore until Col. Littleton W.T.

Waller arrived on 15 August. Faced with active *Caco* resistance in northern Haiti, Waller sent Cole to Cap Haïtien to pacify the area. Cole ordered a series of patrols crisscrossing the Plaine du Nord while, with Waller, he negotiated a tenuous cease-fire with the *Cacos*.

Cole commanded the 1st Regiment of the 1st Provisional Brigade of Marines in Haiti until 22 November 1916, when he assumed command of the 1st Provisional Brigade. He remained at that post until his reassignment to the marine barracks at Parris Island, South Carolina, on 11 January 1918.

Cole served in France during World War I and held numerous posts in the United States after the war. He died in San Francisco, California, on 4 July 1927.

Anne Cipriano Venzon

Columbus, New Mexico, Battle (1916)

When Mexican dictator Gen. Victoriano Huerta fled Mexico in the face of growing successes of the Constitutionalist rebels in 1914, the internal dissension among rebel commanders quickly became apparent. Gens. Francisco "Pancho" Villa and Emiliano Zapata gained the upper hand militarily and seized control of Mexico City. Ill-suited for governance and administration, the two generals soon abandoned the capital to the forces of Constitutionalist leaders Venustiano Carranza and Gen. Álvaro Obregón. In a crucial battle at Celaya in April 1915, Obregón badly defeated Villa, who was forced to retreat northward to his home state of Chihuahua.

In October 1915, President Woodrow Wilson decided to extend diplomatic recognition to the Carranza regime. Villa, who had previously received encouragement and some support from the U.S. government, was enraged. Seeking vengeance against U.S. citizens, a Villista band stopped a train at Santa Ysabel, Chihuahua, and murdered 15 U.S. engineers. Soon rumors spread along the Chihuahua-U.S. border that Villa was en route to the United States to defend himself against charges that he had instigated the Santa Ysabel killings. U.S. officials, however, were not alarmed at reports that Villa and his band were moving toward the border because lacking any secret intelligence service, they were unable to determine Villa's objective.

In 1916, Columbus, New Mexico, located just north of the international boundary, had 700 inhabitants plus over 400 troopers of the 13th Cavalry, under the command of Col. Herbert J. Slocum, who were stationed there. Slocum found it extremely difficult to ascertain the true situation concerning Villa's movements and intentions. Although Slocum received some accurate eyewitness reports of Villa's approach toward Columbus, he also received contradictory reports from others, including Mexican military officers. On 6 March Slocum received a telegram from his superior, Maj. Gen. Frederick Funston, reporting supposedly reliable information that Villa intended to surrender to U.S. authorities, as well as a rumor that Villa was planning a raid. Uncertain as to what, if anything, might transpire, Slocum increased the guard and sent out additional patrols.

In the darkness of the early morning of 9 March 1916, Villa, with approximately 450 men, invaded the United States at Columbus. Whether Villa entered the town with his men or remained outside has never been determined. The attack was well planned, and the attackers were clearly knowledgeable about the layout of the town and surroundings. U.S. authorities later concluded that Villista spies had infiltrated Columbus in the days before the assault. Utilizing the cover of a deep ditch, the Mexicans were able to attack the town and the army camp, known as Fort Furlong, simultaneously.

The Mexican attack was a complete surprise. At 4:00 a.m. the officer of the day, Lt. James P. Castleman, heard a cry and a shot as a bullet shattered the glass of a window near his head. Opening the door, Castleman confronted an armed Mexican; Castleman fired first, killing the raider. Under heavy fire Castleman crossed the parade ground to organize a response from the guard and then moved on to deploy his own unit, Troop F.

The attack on the town itself consisted of looting, burning, and killing. Shouts of "Viva Villa" resounded through the streets. Some of the Villistas seized kerosene from a hardware store and used it to set fire to the central part of town. Five of the nine guests at the Commercial Hotel were murdered. Confusion reigned as the only purpose of the raiders seemed to be acts of violence and mayhem, perhaps as intended.

Most of the cavalry officers resided with their families in the town proper. Consequently, these officers were in no position to organize a counterattack and could not even find their own units in the confusion. In addition, the cavalry's arms and ammunition, including machine guns, were locked in the guard tent. When the second column of raiders galloped into Fort Furlong, only the cooks preparing breakfast and the stableboys were awake. The cooks fought back with kettles of scalding water, potato mashers, knives, cleavers, and bare fists, disrupting the initial assault.

In a surprisingly brief time U.S. forces recovered from the initial confusion, began to return fire, and organized sufficiently to repulse a Villista attempt to stampede the cavalry's horses. This last failure on the part of the raiders was particularly costly later. At daybreak Mexican bugles called the raiders to retreat to Mexico, leaving 67 of their number fallen in Columbus besides the 17 U.S. dead.

As the Villistas evacuated Columbus, U.S. forces began to assume the offensive. In only 20 minutes Maj. Frank Tompkins led 32 mounted troopers against Villa's rear guard, which was holding a hill some 300 yards south of the border. Tompkins's attack caused the Mexicans to flee, but the pursuers killed 30 raiders before the rest escaped. Tompkins had no authority to proceed into Mexico, but Slocum quickly approved continued pursuit. Meanwhile, Tompkins's small force was augmented by the arrival of an additional 28 officers and men. Tompkins led his men some 15 miles into Mexico, engaging the rear guard of the enemy three more times. The cavalry inflicted sufficient casualties to bring the total Villista dead from the raid to perhaps as many as 170.

The immediate result of the Columbus raid was the Punitive Expedition into Mexico under the command of Gen. John J. Pershing. This U.S. intervention led to speculation and investigation concerning the motives of the instigator, Villa. The generally accepted explanations attribute Villa's actions to a desire for revenge for the U.S. recognition of Carranza's government or a hope of provoking U.S. action which might enable Villa to seize power. Other possibilities suggested by professional and popular historians, as well as by journalists and others, include plots by Germans, U.S. capitalists, and Mexican counterrevolutionaries to use Villa as a tool for their own special interests. Still others have claimed that Villa was motivated by a desire to restore morale for his men, a need for supplies, or an attempt to exact retribution from particular citizens of Columbus. In all likelihood Villa was inspired by the mixed and even contradictory motivations that seemed to underlie all of his revolutionary actions.

Anthony K. Knopp

REFERENCES

Clarence C. Clendenen, *The United States and Pancho Villa: A Study in Unconventional Diplomacy* (Cornell Univ. Pr., 1961); Linda B. Hall and Don M. Coerver, *Revolution on the Border: The United States and Mexico, 1910–1920* (Univ. of New Mexico Pr., 1988); Frank Tompkins, *Chasing Villa: The Story Behind the Story of Pershing's Expedition Into Mexico* (Military Service Pub. Co., 1934); Paul J. Vanderwood and Frank Samponaro, *Border Fury: A Picture Postcard Record of Mexico's Revolution and U.S. War Preparedness, 1910–1917* (Univ. of New Mexico Pr., 1988); E. Bruce White, "The Muddied Waters of Columbus, New Mexico," *The Americas*, 32 (1975), 72–98.

See also German Involvement With Francisco "Pancho" Villa; Villa, Francisco "Pancho."

Committee on the Philippines

The United States Senate Committee on the Philippines came into existence on 15 December 1899 as a standing committee (similar to one established on the Pacific Islands and Puerto Rico and another on Cuban Relations) to handle the problems of territories acquired during the Spanish-Cuban/American War. Unrest in the Philippines added to the debate between senators, largely Republican, who wanted to bring the Philippines under U.S. sovereignty and senators, largely Democratic, who opposed imperial responsibilities and wanted an investigation of both the acquisition of the Philippines and the Philippine War. While some matters on the Philippine conflict were sent to the Senate Committee on Foreign Relations, the Senate Committee on the Philippines conducted extensive hearings in 1902 on affairs in the Philippine Islands, attracting national attention and reflecting the bitter split in the Senate. The committee also dealt with questions of Philippine independence, administration by the Philippine Commission, and tariff and trade issues. It survived as a committee until 1921, when its jurisdiction over legislative matters concerning the Philippines was transferred to the newly created Committee on Territories and Insular Possessions.

The committee in 1902 was headed by Henry Cabot Lodge, Republican senator from Massachusetts, and was composed of eight Republicans, one Silver Republican, and four Democrats. The Republicans were Lodge, William B. Allison (Iowa), Eugene Hale (Maine), Redfield Proctor (Vermont), Albert J. Beveridge (Indiana), Julius C. Burrows (Michigan), Louis E. McComas (Maryland), and Charles H. Dietrich (Nebraska); Fred T. Dubois (Idaho) was the Silver Republican. Democrats were Joseph L. Rawlins (Utah), Charles A. Culberson (Texas), Edward W. Carmack (Tennessee), and Thomas M. Patterson (Colorado). The committee membership reflected general party positions. With the exception of Hale, who was a Republican anti-imperialist, the most bitter partisanship was indulged in by Patterson and Carmack on the Democratic side and Beveridge of the Republicans; Patterson and Carmack constantly attacked the U.S. position in the Philippines, especially the conduct of the army, and Beveridge defended the administration of Theodore Roosevelt. Lodge, as chairman, kept a tight grip on the committee and ruled far more often against Democratic initiatives than Republican ones.

Among the important witnesses who appeared before the committee were the civil governor of the Philippines, William H. Taft; Maj. Gen. Elwell S. Otis; Maj. Gen. Arthur MacArthur; and Adm. George Dewey. Most of the testimony supported the major Republican positions.

Major debates occurred over whether U.S. authorities had misled Philippine leaders about independence and whether U.S. or Filipino forces had taken the first steps that caused the war. Also debated were whether U.S. troops had practiced deliberate cruelty against the Filipinos by burning villages, reconcentrating segments of the population, and using the water-cure torture; and whether Filipinos were capable of self-government. Also of concern were U.S. goals in the Philippines.

The administration led off with Taft, who noted that while he had originally opposed the acquisition of the Philippines, preferring first to solve domestic problems of the United States, "chance" had thrown the United States there; the United States should remain "for the good of the Filipino people" (U.S., *Affairs in the Philippine Islands*, pt. 1, p. 406) because no "safe and honorable" (*Affairs in the Philippine Islands*, pt. 1, p. 411) way to withdraw immediately could be devised. No matter how long it would take, Taft stated it was "the duty of the United States to continue a government there which shall teach those people individual liberty, which shall lift them up to a point of civilization of which . . . they are capable, and which shall make them rise to call the name of the United States blessed" (*Affairs in the Philippine Islands*, pt. 1, p. 322). Filipinos, he suggested, would find the association with the United States so valuable "both in a business and a political way" (*Affairs in the Philippine Islands*, pt. 1, p. 349), that they would not want to see the United States leave. Immediate independence would "consign the 90 percent of uneducated people" (*Affairs in the Philippine Islands*, pt. 1, p. 333) to the same position they had held under the Spanish. The greatest difficulty he found was "the ease with which an educated Filipino who has any wealth can control and oppress his own people" (*Affairs in the Philippine Islands*, pt. 1, p. 51).

Taft's views on the war were similar. He noted that he had heard stories of both mutilations by Filipino guerrilla fighters of U.S. soldiers and the use by U.S. troops of the water-cure torture on Filipinos. "The guerrilla campaign (*Affairs in the Philippine Islands*, pt. 1, p. 69) rested necessarily on a system of terrorism" (*Affairs in the Philippine Islands*, pt. 1, p. 69) and "war . . . provokes some cruelty in everyone." (*Affairs in the Philippine Islands*, pt. 1, p. 77). Nevertheless, he argued there "never was a war conducted, whether against inferior races or not, in which there were more compassion and more restraint and more generosity . . . than there have been in the Philippine islands" (*Affairs in the Philippine Islands*, pt. 1, p. 77–78). U.S. soldiers who strayed would be properly tried and punished.

Brig. Gen. Robert P. Hughes argued the virtue of burning homes in villages supporting the nationalists as punishment. He agreed that it was not civilized warfare but that "In order to carry on civilized warfare both sides have to engage in such warfare" (*Affairs in the Philippine Islands*, pt. 1, p. 559). He became convinced that the Filipinos "would not follow the rules of war." Nor did they have any more "idea what it [independence] means than a shepherd dog" (*Affairs in the Philippine Islands*, pt. 1, p. 581). He said that U.S. soldiers felt that they were "simply fighting children. There is neither honor nor glory in it, and I never have had to make an attack I did not regret" (*Affairs in the Philippine Islands*, pt. 1, p. 659). His colleague, Maj. Gen. Elwell S. Otis, believed that Emilio Aguinaldo y Famy "never wanted self-government without outside protection . . . they [the Filipinos] know very well that other nations would divide up those islands" if the United States let them go (*Affairs in the Philippine Islands*, pt. 1, p. 739).

The articulate Maj. Gen. Arthur MacArthur stated that he was far more interested in the spread of "republicanism in the East" (*Affairs in the Philippine Islands*, pt. 2, p. 1921) than he was in either the commercial or strategic importance of the Philippines. Nor did MacArthur find that there had been "any unusual destruction of life in the Philippine islands" (*Affairs in the Philippine Islands*, pt. 2, p. 1922). Adm. George Dewey, easily the most outspoken military officer, said he had promised Aguinaldo nothing about independence. He concluded that the Filipino leader was there "for loot and money" (*Affairs in the Philippine Islands*, pt. 3, p. 2155) and stated that he thought neither the Cubans nor the Filipinos were capable of self-government. The military, in general, strongly defended its actions in the face of persistent questioning.

Soldiers of all ranks testified on the water-cure torture, which involved the forced funneling of water into the mouths of Filipinos and often hitting their distended stomachs until they gagged. There was no doubt that it occurred; too many cases appeared. By the time of the hearings in 1902, over 350 U.S. soldiers had been tried at court-martials for offenses committed against natives. Even Senator Beveridge, a staunch defender of the army, was reduced to arguing that the water-cure neither killed nor did more than temporary damage. No Filipinos were interviewed.

The Senate Committee on the Philippines conducted its hearings in a highly charged, partisan atmosphere which did not lend itself to finding ultimate truth. Despite that failing, the hearings provide the student of the Philippine War with valuable reports, documents, and, most important, attitudes of the participants in the war and its aftermath.

Thomas H. Buckley

REFERENCES

U.S. Congress, Senate, *Affairs in the Philippine Islands: Hearings Before the Committee on the Philippines of the United States Senate*, Senate Document No. 331, 57th Congress, 1st Session (1902); U.S. Congress, Senate, *Correspondence Relating to the Philippines Customs Tariff*, 57th Congress, 1st Session (1902), Senate Document No. 205 [papers of the committee are in Record Group 46 of the National Archives, Washington, D.C.]; Brian McAllister Linn, *The U.S. Army and Counterinsurgency in the Philippine War, 1899–1902* (Univ. of North Carolina Pr., 1989).

See also Public Opinion and the Philippine War.

Congress and the Spanish-Cuban/American War

When the 55th Congress of the United States convened on 4 March 1897, the Republican party had retained its majority in both chambers. This majority was solid in the House but tenuous on currency issues in the Senate. It was also the party of the new president, William McKinley, which meant that Congress could usually endorse rather than fight, White House policy.

The Republican leaders in the Senate were known as the "Big Four": William B. Allison of Iowa, Orville H. Platt of Connecticut, John C. Spooner of Wisconsin, and Nelson W. Aldrich of Rhode Island (who was considered the leader of the group). The Big Four seems to have exerted considerable influence over House members as well because they were key party figures with command of campaign resources. The Speaker of the House, "Czar" Thomas B. Reed of Maine, detested the Senate and accordingly tried to curtail the Big Four's power in the House of Representatives. Reed's importance in national and party politics has been debated in the very sparse scholarship there is about Congress at the turn of the century; it appears, however, that his control of the House, up to this point, was as considerable as his nickname suggests.

The possibility of U.S. intervention in Cuba, where a group of revolutionaries fought for independence from Spain, had long been the subject of animated discussion in the United States. Following the explosion of the USS *Maine* in Havana harbor on 15 February 1898, many in the United States cried out for war. It is a matter of much controversy where this sentiment originated, but it is probably safe to say that neither Congress, nor the president, nor business inter-

ests were to blame. All of them viewed such a war as foolish and unnecessary. It is certain, on the other hand, that long before the *Maine* incident, there had been a vicious campaign against Spain in the newspapers which at this point culminated in a frenzy of pro-war propaganda.

Public opinion rapidly turned against those who wanted to exercise caution, particularly against McKinley, who still refused to approve a war. Like his predecessor, Grover Cleveland, McKinley had continually opposed intervention in Cuba. Cleveland, a Democrat, had often clashed with Congress, especially when the Republicans gained a majority in both chambers during the latter part of his second term in 1895. McKinley was a 14-year veteran of the House and a president of the majority party. He always took into account the presidency's importance for congressional elections and the problems a Democratic majority would cause him.

The Republican leadership in Congress did not want a war with Spain any more than the president did, even after the *Maine* incident. Initially, in the Senate, only a few Republican jingoes—such as Henry Cabot Lodge of Massachusetts, William E. Chandler of New Hampshire, William P. Frye of Maine, and Cushman K. Davis of Minnesota—were in favor of war. But as the sentiment of the public changed, so did that of the Senate.

On 1 March 1898, Redfield Proctor of Vermont, a highly respected senator without jingoistic affiliations, reported on his recent trip to Cuba. He depicted the Spanish regime as insufferably atrocious. During the following days, it became probable that the "hawks" would have a majority. This new attitude clearly reflected the mood of the country, and many senators considered aiding the Cuban revolutionaries a humanitarian obligation as well. The Big Four, while typically uninterested in public opinion, realized how important it was this time. Speaker Reed and the Big Four presumably felt the same ideological and moral doubts about a war with Spain; they believed it to be wrong and the gradual Republican espousal of it not much better. But Aldrich in particular realized that war would happen in any case, and he always accepted a political *fait accompli*. So the Senate leadership slowly but skillfully gave in. Reed refused; he fought against the coming of the war as much as he could, but his options were limited and by no means sufficient.

After careful consideration, McKinley joined the Big Four in opting for war. His reasons have been likened to President James Madison's for entering the War of 1812, namely that the president had to heed public opinion in such a situation if he and his party wanted to maintain control. Thus, on 23 March 1898, McKinley expanded previous demands from Cuban autonomy to Cuban independence in a message to Madrid that constituted an ultimatum.

It appears that the president, who had planned to send a war message to Congress on 4 April, learned that Spain would meet his demands, but that he was persuaded by Senators Aldrich and Lodge to call for war regardless because it would be political suicide not to. The president's message of 11 April 1898 did acknowledge recent information of Spanish concessions, but nevertheless asked Congress to permit him "to use the military and naval forces of the United States" to pacify the island and "to secure in the island the establishment of a stable government" (*Congressional Record*, pp. 3699–3702, 3704–3707).

Congress debated a joint resolution on Cuba for a week. Its original three parts constituted

> [a] joint resolution for the recognition of the independence of the people of Cuba, demanding that the Government of Spain relinquish its authority and government in the Island of Cuba and to withdraw its land and naval forces from Cuba and Cuban waters, and directing the President of the United States to use the land and naval forces of the United States to carry these resolutions into effect (*Congressional Record*, p. 4062).

Many amendments were proposed to this resolution, but the only one that carried was offered by Senator Henry M. Teller of Colorado. The Teller Amendment added

> [t]hat the United States hereby disclaims any disposition or intention to exercise sovereignty, jurisdiction, or control over said island except for the pacification thereof, and asserts its determination when that is accomplished to leave the government and control of the island to its people (*Congressional Record*, p. 4062).

On 18 April 1898, the Senate passed the final resolution 42 to 35, 12 not voting. Less than a third of the Republicans voted for it, but with solid Democratic support, the resolution passed anyway.

The House took its final vote around 2:00 a.m. on 19 April, technically still the legislative day of 18 April. It supported war 311 to 6, one present, 38 not voting. Speaker Reed reportedly told a friend that he would have voted with the six opponents.

McKinley signed the resolution on 20 April, and one day later, diplomatic relations between Spain and the United States were severed. Upon a presidential request of 25 April 1898, Congress officially and unanimously recognized the state of war, retroactive to 21 April.

After the United States won the war, it faced the problem of annexation. Adm. George Dewey's victory in Manila had unleashed a strong expansionist movement. McKinley realized the great popular support for annexation of the Philippines, and, accordingly, resolved to take them. The U.S. victory had, indeed, caused a vacuum of power in the Philippines, and to McKinley, as to many others, annexation seemed the cheapest and most humanitarian solution to the problem at hand.

As a result of this decision, an expansionist peace treaty with Spain was signed in Paris on 10 December 1898. It included a provision that the United States would acquire the Philippines for $20 million.

The 55th Congress reconvened for the lame-duck session, its third and last, on 5 December 1898. The Big Four, especially Aldrich and Platt, was at this time of the annexationist persuasion, apparently again for the same pragmatic reasons as the president. But ratification of the treaty in the Senate required a two-thirds majority, and Senator Lodge, who served as whip for this endeavor, had good reason to worry about mustering enough votes. The treaty was opposed by several anti-expansionist Republican senators, mainly from New England. They were led by George F. Hoar of Massachusetts, who thereby disregarded the wishes of his constituents.

Most Democrats were opposed as well. Among the Democrats voting for the treaty, many were following the advice of William Jennings Bryan. Bryan wanted to use expansion as an issue in his second campaign against McKinley, in the 1900 elections. Bryan was not even a member of Congress at that time, but nonetheless wielded substantial influence with many Senate Democrats. His strategy failed; McKinley won in 1900 with a greater margin than in 1896, mainly, it seems, because of the success of the Spanish-Cuban/American War and the economic prosperity of the era.

The Paris Peace Treaty was ratified by the Senate in Executive Session on 6 February 1899. The anti-expansionists were only 2 votes short, since the treaty passed 57 to 27. The deciding factor, it is often claimed, was Bryan's influence.

After the long 1899 summer recess, the 56th Congress opened its first session on 4 December with gains for the Republicans in the Senate rendering solid their majority. In the House, Speaker Reed had voluntarily retired on 4 September, perhaps not wishing to preside over a House he could not control.

Toward the end of the 56th Congress, in early 1901, Sen. Orville H. Platt introduced an amendment to the army appropriation bill which tacitly reversed the Teller Amendment. It turned Cuba into what has been called anything from a quasi-protectorate to a colony of the United States, stating, *inter alia*, "[t]hat the government of Cuba consents that the United States may exercise the right to intervene for the preservation of Cuban independence" (*Congressional Record*, p. 3145). The Platt Amendment passed the Senate 43 to 20, 25 not voting, on 27 February. In the House of Representatives, it passed 161 to 137, 4 present, 51 not voting, on 1 March 1901.

Politically skilled, the Republican leaders in the Senate did not allow the effects of public opinion to dilute their power. It is generally agreed that, by joining the flow, the Big Four actually emerged strengthened from what its critics called a capitulation to public demand.

The Spanish-Cuban/American War is often cited as an example of undesirable jingoism and of a system that is too democratic: a system in which the leaders' good reason is swept aside by an unscrupulous yellow press and an ill-advised, fanatical public. However, it is not obvious that the Spanish-Cuban/American War, from a purely national point of view, was an unprofitable enterprise for the United States, even in the long run.

It could also be argued that both the president and Congress should be delegates, rather than trustees, of those they represent. Accordingly, their job would be to exercise the will of the people of the United States. In this case, presidential as well as congressional action in the Spanish-Cuban/American War would actu-ally exemplify a well-functioning representative government.

Wolfgang Drechsler

REFERENCES

Robert C. Byrd, "Currency, Foreign Affairs, and Party Organization, 1893–1900" (11 Nov. 1983), in *The Senate, 1789–1989* (U.S. Government Printing Office, 1988), vol. 1, 351–368; *Congressional Record*, Fifty-Fifth Congress, Second Session, vol. 31, pt. 4, pp. 3699–3702, 3704–3707; *ibid.* pt. 5, p. 4062; *ibid.* Fifty-Sixth Congress, Second Session, vol. 34, pt. 4, p. 3145; Brian P. Damiani, *Advocates of Empire: William McKinley, the Senate and American Expansion, 1898–1899* (Garland, 1987); Horace S. and Marion G. Merrill, *The Republican Command, 1897–1913* (Univ. Pr. of Kentucky, 1971); Barbara W. Tuchman, "End of a Dream—The United States, 1890–1902," in *The Proud Tower: A Portrait of the World Before the War, 1890–1914* (Macmillan, 1966), 117–167.

See also McKinley, William, and the Spanish-Cuban/American War (1898); Public Opinion and the Spanish-Cuban/American War; Teller Amendment (1898); Turpie-Foraker Amendment (1898).

Constabularies in the United States's Counterguerrilla Operations

Political and military planners in the United States have long recognized the importance of police forces in combating insurgency in friendly nations. While it would be a very serious error to regard insurgencies as banditry (as has often been done in particular historical situations), there are similarities and overlaps between banditry and guerrilla strategies and tactics. Consequently, between 1898 and the mid–1920s the United States established paramilitary police forces in Puerto Rico, the Philippines, Cuba, Haiti, the Dominican Republic, and Nicaragua.

The Philippine Constabulary helped suppress small units still fighting after the formal end of the Philippine War in 1902; control restive groups, such as the Muslims of the southern Philippines; and combat banditry. The function of the constabularies established in the Caribbean countries was to provide nonpolitical, relatively economical, internal security forces to replace expensive armies that had been prone to making coups.

Inspiration for the U.S.-sponsored constabularies seems to have come primarily from the Mexican *rurales* of the late 19th century, but knowledge of other foreign paramilitary police forces may also have helped encourage U.S. political and military leaders to rely on such units to bring stability to certain countries of strategic importance to the United States. Militarized police forces were widely used in the British Empire, for example. In the United States, Native American reservation police functioned very much like the overseas constabularies, supplementing the army by controlling hostile elements and performing law enforcement and civic action duties.

Another possible precedent for the constabularies was the evolution of the state police concept in the United States during the late 19th and early 20th centuries. There certainly seems to have been a parallel between the call in the United States for nonpolitical, paramilitary police to deal with labor unrest in place of the army and national guard and the U.S. insistence on the establishment of constabularies in the Philippines and some Caribbean nations.

In the Caribbean, recruiting for the constabularies proceeded slowly because these forces were closely associated with the U.S. occupation regimes or local governments that were under considerable U.S. influence. The more nationalistic an individual, apparently the less likely the person was to join the constabulary. Officer procurement was a serious problem, especially because of the general U.S. desire to avoid employing officers from the defunct, discredited local armies. Training and equipping the constabularies were retarded by limited funds and by language and cultural differences between U.S. military advisors and their Latin American or Haitian students.

Despite the obstacles referred to, U.S. advisors seem generally to have been enthusiastic about their assignments and to have worked hard to train the personnel needed to handle internal security and law enforcement. In terms of enlisted training, they seem to have been relatively successful. These advisors may have tried too hard to make the constabularies copies of the United States Army or the United States Marine Corps, however. Some problems occurred because training became more hurried as the time for a U.S. withdrawal from a particular country drew close. More serious was the rapid formation of officer corps that helped politically ambitious leaders to establish power bases in the constabularies and to use the forces to topple civilian governments after the U.S. withdrawals.

Despite the difficulties in training and equipping the constabularies, the lessons about the usefulness of paramilitary police forces in counterinsurgency do not seem to have been totally forgotten. As the United States began to assist friendly governments to combat insurgencies in the 1950s, it devoted some of its attention and funding to the strengthening of police forces in Third World nations. Much of this assistance went through the Agency for International Development and its predecessor organizations. The International Police Academy was established, and many police officials were trained in the United States and overseas. After much controversy developed about the kinds of training given to police, Congress in 1975 prohibited further funding of foreign police forces.

Benjamin R. Beede

REFERENCES

Marvin Goldwert, *The Constabulary in the Dominican Republic and Nicaragua: Progeny and Legacy of United States Intervention* (Univ. of Florida Pr., 1962); Ralph Stover Keyser, "Constabularies for Latin America," *Marine Corps Gazette*, 11 (1926), 89–97; Harold L. Oppenheimer, "Command of Native Troops," *Marine Corps Gazette*, 10 (1951), 50–59; U.S. Marine Corps, *Small Wars Manual, 1940* (U.S. Government Printing Office, 1940), chap. 12, section 2, "Organization of a Constabulary."

See also Garde d'Haiti/Gendarmerie d'Haiti; Guardia Nacional de Nicaragua; Guardia Nacional Dominicana; Guardia Rural, Cuba; Philippine Constabulary.

Corbin, Henry Clark (1842–1909)

Gen. Henry Clark Corbin contributed significantly to the U.S. military effort in the Spanish-Cuban/American War by coordinating the mobilization of U.S. forces and by counseling President William McKinley on military matters.

Corbin was born on 18 September 1842 on a farm near Cincinnati, Ohio. He attended local schools from December through March when the schools closed to free the pupils for farm work. Briefly, he enrolled in Parker's Academy, a bastion of abolitionism and a station on the underground railroad.

At age 16, Corbin taught school for three months a year. At the same time he read law with a local practitioner, spending Saturdays and Sundays in the office. The Civil War shifted him away from the law and from civil life. A committee in his district offered him a commission as second lieutenant if he recruited 30 men who could be accepted into military service. He raised the 30 at his own expense, and at age 19 became an officer in the 83rd Ohio Volunteer Infantry Regiment.

Corbin soon transferred to the 79th Ohio, commanded by Rutherford B. Hayes, who would loom large in his life later on. He described Hayes as absolutely fearless in all ways. The army placed him in contact, too, with another president-to-be Benjamin Harrison, whom he sometimes served as aide.

Corbin skipped the rank of captain by passing an examination that qualified him to become a major in the 14th U.S. Colored Infantry Regiment. He became lieutenant colonel on 4 March 1864, subordinate in the 14th to Col. Thomas Jefferson Morgan. Late in 1864 Morgan stated in an official report that Corbin was not fit to command brave men. Morgan and Corbin had been at odds over Morgan's fierce piety. He had objected when the colonel held prayer service while the men were in line under fire, some being hit. Such a report could have ruined Corbin's career, but he secured permission to appear in person before Gen. George H. Thomas, commander of the Army of the Cumberland. Thomas authorized a court of inquiry which fully exonerated Corbin.

The 14th engaged in its hardest fighting at the battle of Nashville, 15 and 16 December 1864. As part of two black brigades commanded by Ohio Maj. Gen. James B. Steedman, they held an entire Confederate corps on the right, while Thomas threw an overpowering attack at the left flank of John B. Hood's army. Corbin said that his men had marched and fought every day for five months. In March 1865 he became colonel and brigadier general of volunteers for meritorious service.

On 6 September 1865, Corbin married Frances Strickle. This new responsibility drew him again toward the study of law, but a chance encounter with Gen. Ulysses S. Grant changed that. Grant urged him to stay in the army. Be-

cause he considered Grant the greatest general ever to have lived, he accepted that advice, and received a commission as second lieutenant in the 17th U.S. Infantry on 11 May 1866. He had been a civilian only 45 days but wavered once more in that direction. Promotion to captain in the 38th Infantry kept him in. He spent the next 14 years of his life as an infantry officer, 10 of them in the Southwest.

The 38th was a black regiment, commanded by white officers. In the reduction of the army in 1869 it combined with the 41st Regiment, also black, to become the 24th Infantry. The colonel commanding the consolidated regiment was William R. Shafter, who reentered Corbin's life during the Spanish-Cuban/American War 29 years later. In the immediate postwar years, Corbin and his regiment moved often and over vast distances. Ordered to Fort Hays, Kansas, they traveled by rail to Fort Riley, the end of the line, then marched 210 miles through dry, harsh land. From the age of 23 to 34, Corbin wrote later, he had been separated from all the conveniences of civilization.

In 1876 Captain Corbin was sent to Columbia, South Carolina, to keep order during the tense presidential election between Republican Rutherford B. Hayes and Democrat Samuel J. Tilden. While on recruiting duty at some past time, he had met and impressed Hayes, who attached him to the party traveling with him by rail. Corbin was present when word was delivered to the train that Hayes had won the election. He journeyed to New York with Hayes, James A. Garfield, William McKinley, and Gen. George Crook. For a time he was assigned to the White House, but was transferred because it seemed inappropriate for the president to have a military officer close to him at the time when troops were being withdrawn from the former Confederate States.

For sometime, therefore, Corbin returned to field service, in this case to aid Gen. Alfred H. Terry to subdue the Nez Percé Indians in Idaho and Montana. In the fall of 1877 he served on the Sitting Bull Commission to determine what should be done about the Sioux who crossed back and forth over the U.S.-Canadian border.

President Hayes interested himself in Corbin's career. In 1880 he removed Gen. Edward D. Townsend as adjutant general, and had Corbin transferred into the adjutant general's department, as the lowest ranking major. Thus ended 14 years during which Corbin had been a captain. Regardless of rank he had become one of the inner circle of Ohioans who controlled the Republican party. When Garfield was nominated for president, Corbin was his roommate at the convention. Corbin was referred to as part of Garfield's kitchen cabinet. Often he played cards and pool with the president. He was present at Garfield's death. Although not close to Chester A. Arthur, he was useful to Arthur, who relied on Corbin in military matters.

Corbin's professional service continued to alternate between tours as an adjutant general and periods as a field officer against Native Americans. He became assistant adjutant general of the Department of the South in September 1882, but in 1885 he was campaigning in the West with Gens. Winfield S. Hancock, John M. Schofield, and Crook. He received a commission as lieutenant colonel in 1889. As adjutant general for the Department of the Missouri, he was present during the ghost dance troubles in 1890. He was associated with Gen. Nelson A. Miles here, and although he stated that there was never conflict between them, neither was there any friendliness. He and Miles would be thrown soon into close contact. In 1891 he was transferred to the Department of Arizona where the Native Americans were refusing to send their children to U.S. schools. Corbin arrested the leaders and resolved the issue without any fighting.

In Washington Republican presidents continued to use Corbin for consultation and for meticulous detail work. Corbin's life was permanently altered by the death of his wife of 28 years in 1893. Because one daughter was in Ohio, the other in school, and his son at Princeton, he lived alone in Washington, dedicated to his military duties as assistant adjutant general since 1882. Finally, in 1896 he attained once more the rank of colonel in the regular army, a grade which he had briefly held at the end of the Civil War, 31 years earlier.

On 25 February 1898 Corbin became adjutant general of the army with the rank of brigadier general. The officers of the line approved of him because he had spent more time with troops in the field than other adjutants before him. His civilian superiors appreciated his ability to make military arrangements clear to them. The United States was within two months of being at war with Spain. Corbin believed that

the United States Army was little more than a frontier constabulary that was quite unready for major military operations. It was up to him as much as to any individual to try to make what he referred to as a constabulary into an army. But everything had to be created. He did not expect very much help either from Brig. Gen. Charles P. Eagan, the commissary general, whom he regarded as irascible and erratic, or from the inspector general, Joseph C. Breckinridge, who seemed to him egotistical and overly ambitious. On the other hand he had a longstanding working relationship with President McKinley and quickly established one with Secretary of War Russell A. Alger. Relations with the commanding general, Nelson A. Miles, were less smooth.

Representative John A.T. Hull introduced a bill in March 1898 which received the support of the president, the secretary of war and the commanding general. The bill was based on John C. Calhoun's concept of an expansible regular army. Hull's version would bring the army to 104,000 men, considered enough for the impending war with Spain, without calling up hordes of volunteers. Corbin, too, liked the bill and became its legislative manager. It never became law, however.

McKinley wanted a short war, terminated, of course, with a quick victory. With the advice of a war council, he settled on a strategy to attack Cuba via Santiago. General Miles could not reconcile himself to this strategy, offering instead plans that focused on Puerto Rico. His persistence annoyed McKinley, and coupled with other incidents, caused McKinley to lose confidence in Miles's judgment. He turned more and more to Corbin, who became in all but name chief of staff. Corbin wrote later that he attempted to soften the president's attitude toward Miles, without effect, but Miles believed that the adjutant general intrigued against him.

Corbin tried to block concentration of the invasion force at Tampa, Florida. He knew that the last 10 miles of railroad to the wharf was only a single track and that the terrain was subject to flooding. He believed that the expedition should have sailed from New York or New Jersey, where it could have been properly supplied. Henry B. Plant, whose railroad ran to Tampa, convinced Alger that Tampa was the right place. Accepting the Tampa decision and others made by his superiors, Corbin was proud that by 25 May the first shiploads were able to sail for the

Philippines and that, by 1 August, 275,000 men were ready. Although the focus of U.S. military operations was the Caribbean area, troops had to be sent to the Philippines to hold the islands after the U.S. Navy destroyed the Spanish fleet at Manila Bay. Corbin concurred with the president, the secretary of war, and the commanding general that Shafter, major general of volunteers, should command the expedition to Cuba. Corbin and Shafter had had a long association in the field; Shafter had been lieutenant colonel of the 24th Infantry Regiment when Corbin was a captain in it.

All orders to the army, whether in the Caribbean or the Far East, had to pass through the adjutant general's office. Corbin kept the office open around the clock, often spending the night there, and he and the staff worked on Sundays and holidays.

The ultimate decisions were not his to make, but he was a member of the conferences during which they were made. He never forgot the military served civilian superiors and never intrigued against them. Often McKinley directed persons seeking decisions or benefits to see what Corbin thought of their requests. Graham A. Cosmas, the definitive historian of the United States Army in the Spanish-Cuban/American War, wrote of Corbin's contribution to the war effort: "Amid changing plans, conflicting orders, and clashing personalities, Corbin's calm, tact, physical endurance, and administrative efficiency held the creaking military machine on course" (Cosmas, p. 145).

Criticism of the conduct of the war was loud, praise nearly mute. Congress held interminable hearings trying to place the blame for the congestion that had delayed the departure of the expeditionary force for Cuba; for having to leave essential supplies, needed in Cuba, in the United States; for the shortage of food at the front and the almost inedible quality of what got there; and finally for the lack of judgment that had permitted sickness almost to destroy the army in Cuba. Even though the criticism was nearly all-embracing, Corbin stayed free of it.

Peace with Spain was signed on 10 December 1898 after which the United States faced the problems of organizing governments for its new empire. Corbin thought the man to take on that responsibility was a prominent lawyer, Elihu Root. McKinley persuaded Root to become secretary of war. Root knew little about the army,

but he tackled the reorganization of it along with the creation of new governments for the possessions acquired by conquest. Although Corbin had had little previous personal contact with Root, the two at once established an efficient working relationship. Root relied on Corbin to supply the military knowledge he lacked. Corbin, therefore, had much to do with the shape of the new army that emerged after the reorganization of 1903.

For his contributions to the service, Corbin received a commission as major general on 6 June 1900. His work on reorganization finished, the War Department sent Corbin on an extended mission to China, Japan, and the Philippines in 1901. On 6 September 1901 McKinley was assassinated; thus when Corbin returned to the United States he was serving under Theodore Roosevelt, who was little more than an acquaintance. In 1902, along with Gens. Leonard Wood and Samuel B.M. Young, he was the personal guest of Kaiser Wilhelm II to observe the maneuvers of the German army.

As a consequence of the reorganization of the army, Corbin left the adjutant general's department to serve as commanding general first of the Department of the East and then in 1904 as commanding general of the Department of the Atlantic. In the latter department, he supervised the first large-scale maneuvers involving both regulars and National Guard. Twenty-six thousand men assembled at Manassas, Virginia, four-fifths of them by law guardsmen. Later, in 1904, he assumed command of the Department of the Philippines. Wood, expecting to receive the post, resented its going to Corbin, although Wood did receive the assignment in 1906. Corbin retired on 15 September 1906 with the grade of lieutenant general. He died in New York on 8 September 1909. Few high ranking officers have exerted as much influence on national affairs as Corbin did and received so little notice in history. He was close and useful to three presidents, all of whom felt most comfortable when he was close by to give advice. He had a similar relationship with Elihu Root. Corbin had recommended William H. Taft to head the commission to establish civil government in the Philippines and had recommended Adna R. Chaffee to command the U.S. contingent sent to China in 1900 because of the Boxer Uprising.

Tall, erect, heavily built, Corbin was a splendid military figure. His bearing reflected an unusually strong constitution which had been tested both in the field and in the office. He had been oriented to work as a child, remaining tireless throughout his active life. Contemporaries described him as direct in speech, but also as having charm, tact, and forcefulness. Elihu Root's principal biographer called him blunt, rugged, fierce, and vigorous. Those historians that have noticed him considered him brilliantly able.

John K. Mahon

REFERENCES

Graham A. Cosmas, *An Army for Empire: The United States Army in the Spanish American War* (Univ. of Missouri Pr., 1971); Philip C. Jessup, *Elihu Root* (Dodd-Mead, 1938), 2 vols.; Jack C. Lane, *Armed Progressive: General Leonard Wood* (Presidio Pr., 1978); Margaret Leech, *In the Days of McKinley* (Harper, 1959); David F. Trask, *The War With Spain in 1898* (Macmillan, 1981).

See also Alger, Russell Alexander; Miles, Nelson Appleton; War Department in the Spanish-Cuban/American War (1898); War Department Investigating Commission.

Crane, Stephen (1871–1900)

Internationally famous as the author of the Civil War novel *The Red Badge of Courage* (1895), Stephen Crane served as a celebrity correspondent for both Joseph Pulitzer's New York *World* and William Randolph Hearst's *New York Journal* during the Spanish-Cuban/American War. Energetically throwing himself into the assignment, the 26-year-old writer witnessed every significant engagement of the Cuban and Puerto Rican campaigns, wrote almost 50 dispatches, and gained praise as the author of the best accounts of the fighting.

Crane signed on with the *World* before the official declaration of war and spent four weeks aboard the newspaper's tugboat covering the preliminary naval campaign. He was with the marines at Guantánamo, Cuba, during the war's first land battle, accompanied the Rough Riders during their first skirmish at Las Guásimas, and witnessed the fighting at San Juan Hill. Critically ill with fever, he was sent back to the United States in July 1898, but returned to the Caribbean in time to cover the Puerto Rican campaign for the *Journal*, then slipped illegally into Havana and stayed there for four months during the peace negotiations.

Hired as a "special correspondent," Crane sent a few brief cabled reports of spot news, but most of his dispatches were long, descriptive articles. In many of his dispatches, Crane served as self-appointed champion of the regular army soldier. Disgusted with the lavish attention given to the Rough Riders and other volunteer regiments, Crane charged in one article that the U.S. public wanted to hear only about "the gallantry of Reginald Marmaduke Maurice Montmorenci Sturtevant, and for goodness sake how the poor old chappy endures that dreadful hard-tack and bacon." In contrast, he wrote, "the name of the regular soldier is probably Michael Nolan and his life-sized portrait was not in the papers in celebration of his enlistment" (Stallman and Hagemann, p. 188).

After the war's conclusion, "Michael Nolan" became the hero of one of Crane's short stories about the Spanish-Cuban/American War, "The Price of the Harness." That story, along with other fiction and nonfiction about the war, was collected in *Wounds in the Rain* (1900). The longest and most distinguished of the pieces, "War Memories," is a memoir of Crane's experiences in Cuba. While "War Memories" emphasizes the primary theme of Crane's war dispatches, the stoic nobility of the regular army soldier, it also attacks the jingoism that marked virtually all of the U.S. reporting of the war—including Crane's own dispatches—and grapples with the inability of language to convey the reality of war, a theme that reappeared later in Vietnam War literature, such as Michael Herr's *Dispatches* (1977) and Tim O'Brien's *The Things They Carried* (1990).

Michael Robertson

REFERENCES

Fredson Bowers, ed., *Reports of War*, vol. 9 of *The University of Virginia Edition of the Works of Stephen Crane* (Univ. Pr. of Virginia, 1971); Stephen Crane, *Wounds in the Rain* (Frederick A. Stokes Co., 1900); R.W. Stallman and E.R. Hagemann, eds., *The War Dispatches of Stephen Crane* (New York Univ. Pr., 1964).

Creelman, James (1859–1915)

James Creelman was one of the best-known U.S. war correspondents during the Spanish-Cuban/American War.

A Canadian by birth, Creelman (born on 12 November 1859) journeyed to New York City, mostly on foot, at age 12, to live with his mother after his parents' divorce. He refused to go to school, taking odd jobs instead, until he was hired at age 18 by one of the most respected newspapers of its day, the *New York Herald*. By the onset of the Spanish-Cuban/American War he had worked for both Joseph Pulitzer's New York *World* and William Randolph Hearst's *New York Journal*, as well as several magazines. He had covered the Hatfield-McCoy feud, and had conducted interviews with such divergent notables as Sitting Bull, Pope Leo XIII, and the novelist Tolstoy.

Creelman came of age as a newspaper reporter at a time in journalism history when the reporter was getting his own byline and replacing the editor in public consciousness. He was sent by Pulitzer to report on the Cuban uprising against Spanish rule in 1895. His first dispatches from Havana described in detail the execution of war prisoners by the Spanish. His account set the pattern for all subsequent reporters in Cuba, who routinely witnessed executions.

The leader of the Spanish forces, Gen. Valeriano Weyler y Nicolau, threatened to deport Creelman because he reported the massacre of Cuban civilians, who were executed without trial. The reporter's attention to fact, and his penchant for thorough recitation of the details, including names, occupations, and ages of those who were murdered, all contributed to the believability of the story. It is a credit to his professional standing that Weyler, in summarizing his feelings about Creelman in particular and journalists in general, called reporters meddlesome scribblers.

When Weyler followed through on this threat, Hearst hired him away from the *World* to be his correspondent in Madrid. It was Creelman who recorded Hearst's most famous statement, one made in reply to the artist Frederic Remington, who had written from Cuba that there was no war. According to Creelman, Hearst cabled back: "You furnish the pictures and I'll furnish the war" (Brown, p. 78). No other evidence of the telegram has ever surfaced.

After the United States entered the war in 1898, Creelman returned to Cuba as one of Hearst's men. In the Spanish-Cuban/American War it was not unusual for reporters to participate in the fighting as well as to report it. Creelman led troops up the hill at El Caney. Finding Spaniards waiting in trenches, he or-

dered them to surrender. They did, but not before Creelman was wounded in the shoulder. He was evacuated to the rear to the cheers of U.S. soldiers.

His work in reporting the war was praised by many contemporaries, including one writer who described him as the most notable correspondent covering the conflict. By his own account, he wanted only to write something interesting, something reflecting the finest elements of human experience.

After 1898 Creelman had a varied career, working for the *World* again and later for *Pearson's Magazine*. He was active in the presidential campaign of Williams Jennings Bryan in 1900 and in education. He died suddenly on 12 February 1915 in Berlin, where he had been sent to report on World War I for the *New York American*.

Mary S. Mander

REFERENCES

Charles Brown, *The Correspondent's War: Journalists in the Spanish American War* (Scribner, 1967); James Creelman, *On the Great Highway: The Wanderings and Adventures of a Special Correspondent* (Lothrop Pub., 1901); Mary S. Mander, "Pen and Sword: Problems in Reporting the Spanish American War," *Journalism History*, 9 (1982), 2–9, 28; Joyce Milton, *The Yellow Kids: Foreign Correspondence in the Heyday of Yellow Journalism* (Harper, 1989); "Newspaper Correspondents in War," *Review of Reviews*, 9 (1898), 538–541.

Crowder, Enoch Herbert (1859–1932)

Enoch Herbert Crowder, an army legal specialist, had a long history of important assignments in Cuba.

Born a Missourian in 1859, Crowder was fortunate to have been reared in a social and economic environment that provided him with the personal qualities that resulted in his graduation from the United States Military Academy at West Point in 1881 as a second lieutenant. His first military assignment was in Texas, where he began to follow his avid interest in legal studies by reading military and civil law while carrying out his duties. In 1884 he was licensed to practice law in Texas and was soon given the same privilege in Missouri. This led to a new military assignment at the University of Missouri which provided him with the opportunity to enroll as a full-time law student. In 1886 Crowder received a law degree.

Crowder's army career took many twists and turns before a Cuban assignment in 1906–1909. He remained at the University of Missouri where he taught law until 1889. Meanwhile, he joined his regiment in the Apache campaign and for that he received a promotion. In 1889 he was reassigned to Fort Yates in Dakota Territory which led to a legal career in the army. Two years later he was appointed captain and acting judge advocate. After a two-year apprenticeship, Crowder, at age 36, was given the rank of major and made judge advocate.

Between 1893 and 1898, Crowder worked hard and cultivated friendships with the "right" people. The Spanish-Cuban/American War provided him with the opportunity for which he was looking. As judge advocate, he was sent to Manila which offered a fine chance for service and advancement. He served in various capacities, including legal advisor to the military governor of the Philippines and associate justice of the civil division of the Philippine Supreme Court. In this latter position, Crowder established himself as a jurist-legislator by writing a new code of criminal procedure. Upon completion of the code, he was relieved of court duties and became civil administrator of the Philippines and second-in-command to the military governor before returning to the United States in 1901.

Crowder's rank at this point was lieutenant colonel judge advocate, and he was given a permanent detail as deputy judge advocate general and chief of the first division of the General Staff. This detail gave him the responsibilities of tracking military legislation, reorganization plans, and general administrative matters affecting the army. In 1904, Crowder was on special assignment in the Far East as senior U.S. observer with the Japanese army during the Russo-Japanese War of 1904–1905.

Shortly after Crowder's return from his Japanese assignment, Secretary of War William H. Taft sent him to Cuba to serve as a personal advisor to Provisional Governor Charles E. Magoon, who was legal advisor to the provisional government and supervisor of the Departments of State and Justice of Cuba. In 1906, the United States, under the terms of the Platt Amendment, had been forced to intervene in Cuba with the collapse of the government of President Tomás Estrada Palma to protect U.S.

lives, property, and business interests. Magoon, who had served as U.S. minister to the Republic of Panama, was sent to administer a civilian government under the Cuban flag with the ultimate objective of restoring the Cuban government. Crowder and Magoon had earlier served together on the General Staff and in the Philippines.

Under the provisional government Crowder's duties ran far and wide. As supervisor of the State Department he was involved with nine divisions and bureaus concerned with such matters as overseeing political affairs, claims against the government, foreign commerce, department appointments, the translation of documents, the foreign press, the collection of general information, and the maintenance and updating of the departmental library. However, Crowder made his greatest contribution as chairman of the Advisory Law Commission and head of the Justice Department established under the provisional government to reform the legal system. Because the Palma administration had failed to enact new codes and to modernize the judicial system to support the Constitution of 1901, the Cuban government was still trying to function under Spanish law. It was the lack of a workable electoral law that had been largely responsible for the revolution of 1906.

Before legal reform could begin, emergency decrees had to be prepared, claims against the Cuban government had to be settled, and the Cuban Congress had to be reorganized following an election. Crowder divided the Department of Justice into two sections: one dealing with judicial and legislative matters and the other dealing with the registries of property. He wanted to reform the judicial system by drafting a law that would make the courts independent of all government departments and the congress. In addition, pardons, reprieves, and commutations were made on his recommendations. Decrees were issued in support of public works, and Crowder advised the Departments of Agriculture, Education, and Health and Sanitation on how these agencies could be more effective. In addition, he resolved the property issues between the Catholic Church and the Cuban government.

As chair of the Advisory Law Commission, Crowder charged the members to draft several laws that would not only prevent future political revolutions but would also regulate other segments of society and accord with the Cuban Constitution of 1901. These included an electoral law, municipal and provincial laws, a law providing for the reorganization and independence of the judiciary, a civil service law, and tax and accounting laws. In addition, the Advisory Law Commission prepared laws relating to executive power, the armed forces, telephones, juvenile courts, notaries, drainage and irrigation, and property registration.

Drafting the laws was time-consuming and complicated, especially the one pertaining to election reform which was the most important if progress was to be made to ensure political stability. Consequently, Crowder assumed responsibility for constructing the first draft of the election code. His objective was to eliminate the possibility of fraud and electoral abuses. He hoped to accomplish this feat with several provisions:

- By creating permanent electoral boards in the municipalities controlled by a central board in Havana;
- By providing equal representation of the principal political parties on all boards;
- By providing that the boards would keep an up-to-date registration list of eligible voters;
- By providing that nomination procedures would be established;
- By setting requirements pertaining to literacy, age, and place of birth as conditions for public office; and
- By establishing a proportional representation formula to decide the number of votes needed for elections.

The electoral code was finally promulgated on 1 April 1908. Local elections were held in August 1908, and the national election followed in November. The elections were closely supervised by Crowder. He considered them fair and orderly, and the reins of government were turned over to the Liberal president-elect, José Miguel Gómez, on 28 January 1909.

Between Crowder's first assignment in Cuba (1906–1909), his second (1919), and his third (1921–1927), his public service involved a variety of duties. Upon his return from Cuba in 1909 he was made temporary judge advocate of the Department of California. This led to his appointment as first assistant to the judge advocate general in Washington. As a result of his knowledge of Latin America, Crowder was delegated

by the Taft administration to attend the Fourth Conference of American States and inspect the Panama Canal. In fall 1910, he was sent on a special mission to Great Britain and France to study their systems of military justice. In 1911, he was appointed judge advocate general of the United States Army. In this position he proceeded to promote the reform of the system of military justice. A new general code became law in 1916. Crowder had planned to codify the military law of the United States, but these plans had to be delayed because of the United States's entry into World War I. However, under his direction a digest of the important opinions of the judge advocate general dating back to the Civil War was prepared. It contained several volumes and was still in use as of 1993.

In 1915, Crowder, on the basis of his legal reputation, was reappointed judge advocate general by President Woodrow Wilson. Crowder's membership on the International Preparatory Committee was continued. He played a part in drafting the National Defense Act of 1916 which helped to establish a legal foundation for a truly national army. He was also called on to prepare a plan that would mobilize the nation's manpower in the event of war. After war was declared in 1917, Crowder authored and administered the Selective Service Act, and in 1919 he was reappointed judge advocate general.

Meanwhile, the deteriorating condition of politics and elections in Cuba was about to take Crowder back to Cuba. Since the second intervention (1906–1909), the United States had followed a "preventive policy" toward Cuba. The U.S. government encouraged its citizens to invest in Cuba and tried to keep intermeddling to a minimum to avoid another formal intervention. However, the results of the hotly contested elections of 1916 led to another political crisis. The Liberals, headed by Dr. Alfredo Zayas y Alfonso, accused President Mario García Menocal and the Conservatives of depriving them of victory and raised the banner of revolt which Menocal, with the aid of U.S. Marines, quickly suppressed. At the time, the Department of State offered to send Crowder to help with the dispute, but the Menocal government refused the offer. During World War I marines remained in Cuba for "training purposes," and an uneasy truce prevailed between the two political factions. Meanwhile, the Liberal leadership began to demand that the United States guarantee an honest presidential election in 1920. The gravity of the political situation and pressure from Washington finally led the Cuban government to grant an invitation in spring 1919 for Crowder to come to Cuba to assist in preparing an electoral code which would take care of all exigencies.

With the approval of President Wilson and the Departments of State and War, Crowder accepted. His task of framing a code that would assure honest elections was not an easy one, especially in such a short time. However, within several weeks he presented several electoral reform bills to President Menocal for congressional approval. After some delay and much lobbying by Crowder, the Cuban Congress in August 1919 adopted a revised electoral code. The need for this new code was an indictment of Cuba and its political parties, and the question remained whether it would cure the deep-rooted political evils.

Crowder then returned to Washington to resume his duties as judge advocate general only to find himself caught up in a congressional debate, along with the secretary of war, over army recommendations for reforming the U.S. system of military justice and revision of the Articles of War. The issues were finally resolved in June 1920 when Congress enacted the National Defense Act and related measures sustaining Crowder's position. This kind of political turmoil and the deteriorating health of his mother probably would have resulted in Crowder's resignation from the army had it not been for his concern that he would be needed in Cuba again if his revised Electoral Code of 1919 was not enforced during the upcoming presidential election.

As events unfolded in Cuba, his concerns proved legitimate. The election of November 1920 was held against a background of unprecedented prosperity, the so-called dance of the millions, which suddenly turned into an economic disaster leaving many individuals, corporations, and the government of Cuba bankrupt. During the elections, President Menocal and the Conservatives paid little attention to the provisions of Crowder's revised code. In many cases, the code was either ignored or flagrantly violated. As a result, the Liberals, who were supporting former President Gómez, threatened to withdraw from the campaign and again sought

U.S. intervention unless an honest election could be assured. Zayas, a former Liberal, was the nominee of the Conservatives and supported by the Menocal government. The United States took an impartial position and sent observers. What they found was a stolen election. The Cuban military controlled the votes in the rural areas, some polls were not allowed to open, and voters were intimidated by violence. Even though Zayas had a small lead in a vast majority of the provinces, he needed a settlement of the contested elections in his favor to win. Wilson, fearing that Menocal's term would expire before elections could be decided, sent Crowder to Cuba as his personal representative in an attempt to solve the election dispute and to prevent further violence which could lead to civil war and a third U.S. intervention.

Crowder arrived for the third time in Cuba on 6 January 1921. He was acclaimed by the Liberals and denounced by the Conservatives. His first orders to the Menocal government were to continue the moratorium on financial obligations, to appoint a bank liquidation commission to administer payment of the debt, and to clear the docket of the Supreme Court so that final decisions could be rendered. To resolve the disputed election, Crowder ordered new elections in the contested districts and extracted a promise from Menocal, Gómez, and Zayas that they would honor the results. The Liberals refused to vote, and their actions resulted in the election of Zayas. Recognition of Zayas as the president-elect by the United States concluded the first phase of Crowder's mission.

Meanwhile, President Warren G. Harding had succeeded Wilson, and because Crowder had solved neither the constitutional question nor the financial one, Harding was determined to keep Crowder in Cuba. It was agreed that if Crowder would remain he would be appointed ambassador at the end of his third term as judge advocate general. After careful consideration, Crowder decided to stay on to work with President Zayas even though he found Zayas to be unethical, egotistical, power-hungry, and resentful of his subordinate position to Crowder. However, the fact that reforms were a prerequisite for a badly needed loan from the United States forced Zayas to cooperate.

After a thorough study of the political and economic ills and support from the State Department, Crowder made recommendations for reform in nearly every aspect of Cuban life, including electoral reform, grafts, auditing, lottery, and commercial and financial reform. Crowder insisted that the reforms be carried out before the badly needed loan could be negotiated. Zayas was more than willing to cooperate in order to receive the loan, but his ministers proved recalcitrant. Consequently, Crowder insisted that they be replaced from his list of "honest men." As a result, some progress was made toward reform: Cuba's credit was saved; the budget was reduced; illegal contracts were canceled; criminals were prosecuted; and other essential reforms were enacted and decreed. As a result, the moral tone of government was improved, civil war and military intervention were avoided, and the loan was approved.

As promised, Crowder, following completion of his term as judge advocate general, was appointed the first U.S. ambassador to Cuba effective 14 February 1923. In his new position he was governed by a new set of regulations and instructions which lessened his control over the Zayas administration. The new rules reflected a new attitude in Washington toward involvement in Cuban politics. The Cubans would henceforth be allowed to work out their own political problems in their own way as long as the lives and property of U.S. citizens were not endangered. This relaxation of control meant that Crowder's program of reform was lost, allowing Zayas to revert to his corrupt ways. Crowder warned his superiors of the consequences if his reforms were not continued. However, largely to Crowder's credit, the elections of 1924 resulted in a peaceful transfer of power to Gen. Gerado Machado y Marales, the Liberal candidate, and revolution by force of arms was delayed until 1933.

Crowder decided to resign his ambassadorship in 1927. Although his relationship with the Machado regime was basically routine, he saw political difficulties developing that he could not prevent or control. Provisions of his electoral code were being repealed, and the constitution was amended to extend Machado's term two years while providing for a six-year presidential term. He wanted to leave Cuba under peaceful and prosperous conditions. In addition, he was approaching age 70, in poor health, and wanted to practice law and to improve his financial condition. He accomplished this by representing selected U.S. and Cuban clients. Crowder's work as attorney and lobbyist was successful until the stock market crash in 1929. The crash, and old age, forced his retirement. Crowder died in 1932 at age 73 and was buried in Arlington National Cemetery.

Thomas E. Gay, Jr.

REFERENCES

Charles E. Chapman, *A History of the Cuban Republic* (Macmillan, 1927); Leland Hamilton Jenks, *Our Cuban Colony* (Vanguard Pr., 1928); David A. Lockmiller, *Enoch H. Crowder* (Univ. of Missouri Pr., 1955); Hugh Thomas, *Cuba: The Pursuit of Freedom* (Harper, 1971); Bryce Wood, *The Making of the Good Neighbor Policy* (Columbia Univ. Pr., 1961).

Cuba, Intervention (1906–1909)

On 29 September 1906 the United States seized political control of Cuba under Article III of the Platt Amendment. The military intervention, which lasted until early 1909, came only four years after the end of the first U.S. occupation of 1899–1902. Although the intervention lasted only three years, the United States remained entangled in Cuban politics for several decades in an unsuccessful effort to forge a formal democracy.

When the United States invaded and occupied Cuba in 1898 ostensibly to rescue its inhabitants from the tyranny of Spanish colonial rule, no one in the United States War Department or in the White House anticipated the consequences the occupation would have. Before the U.S. government relinquished control of the island to the Cubans, it demanded assurance that U.S. economic and political interests in Cuba be secured. In 1901 the Cuban Constitutional Convention appended the Platt Amendment to the new constitution, empowering the United States to "exercise the right to intervene for the maintenance of a government adequate for the protection of life, property, and individual liberty."

When the U.S. occupation ended in May 1902 Tomás Estrada Palma became president of the republic. During the first three years under Estrada Palma, Cubans enjoyed relative tranquility. Pervasive political corruption, however, debilitated Estrada Palma's administration. Many politicians saw public office as a way to amass private fortunes. Government fraud reached its peak during the 1905 reelection campaign of Estrada Palma. Through political violence and a comprehensive purge of opposition Liberal party members from the government, the president's Moderate party denied the Liberals any legitimate means of gaining office. Not surprisingly, Moderate candidates swept to victory in the rigged September elections, and Estrada Palma was reelected president.

Frustrated, the Liberals took up arms against the government in mid-August 1906. The revolt, which began in western Pinar del Río Province, quickly spread to Havana and Las Villas. Led by Gen. Faustino "Pino" Guerra, the insurgents deliberately threatened to destroy U.S. property in order to provoke a U.S. intervention. Once the United States intervened on the grounds that the Estrada Palma government was incapable of protecting U.S. property, the Liberals reasoned, the two sides would negotiate a settlement favorable to the Liberals. Ironically, the Platt Amendment served as an incentive to attack U.S. property in Cuba.

Moreover, the prospect of imminent U.S. intervention under the Platt Amendment also discouraged Estrada Palma from making concessions to the Liberals. Confident of U.S. support for his government, he believed that intervention would be beneficial to his party's interests. The president responded to the Liberal revolt by suspending civil liberties in three provinces and recruiting additional soldiers to his Guardia Rural (Rural Guard). Estrada Palma then sent his first request for military intervention to U.S. President Theodore Roosevelt on 8 September 1906. Estrada Palma and the Moderates hoped that U.S. military support would strengthen their tenuous position and quell the growing Liberal insurrection.

Faced with imminent chaos in Cuba, Roosevelt had to act decisively. Sixty percent of rural holdings on the island were in the hands of North American business interests which sought protection from the U.S. government in the face of Cuban unrest. Estrada Palma's unpopular government represented the only semblance of order in the country. Still, Roosevelt was extremely reluctant to commit U.S. troops to a potentially bloody guerrilla war with the Liberal insurgents.

Roosevelt responded to Moderate requests militarily and diplomatically. After insisting that full U.S. intervention was "out of the question," he curiously ordered two navy vessels, the *Denver* and the *Marietta*, to sail for Cuba. The ships arrived in Havana on 12 September to the cheers of grateful North American planters. The president also appointed Secretary of War William H. Taft and Assistant Secretary of State Robert Bacon to investigate the tense situation. The Taft-Bacon Peace Mission arrived in Cuba on 19 September on board the cruiser *Des Moines*, which joined the growing naval fleet stationed in Cuban waters.

The failure of the Taft-Bacon Peace Mission was a foregone conclusion because Roosevelt's military response precluded the success of his diplomatic efforts. Taft and Bacon found a stubborn Estrada Palma unwilling to concede any power to the Liberal rebels. The Cuban president interpreted the growing naval presence around the island as a signal that U.S. intervention was forthcoming. U.S. military analysts, however, had determined that Estrada Palma's government enjoyed very little popular support and that a large-scale military effort to uphold it would be far too costly. Nevertheless, Estrada Palma reiterated his demands for armed intervention and threatened to resign if the United States did not fulfill its obligations under the Platt Amendment.

The U.S. diplomats suggested a compromise to end the revolt, which would keep Estrada Palma in office, while satisfying many of the Liberals' demands, including the nullification of the recent elections. For the United States, the compromise seemed ideal: it assured political continuity while defusing a volatile situation without bloodshed or long-term military involvement. For Estrada Palma, however, the compromise represented not only a political defeat, but also betrayal by the United States. He defiantly rejected the initiative and notified Taft and the Cuban Congress of his resignation on 28 September 1906.

With the Cuban government momentarily decapitated and anarchy imminent, Secretary Taft issued a proclamation on behalf of President Roosevelt informing the Cuban people of the U.S. intervention "to restore order, protect life and property in the island of Cuba." Roosevelt appointed Taft as provisional governor of Cuba and ordered the Provisional Marine Brigade to protect North American property and the Cuban treasury until the first of the 6,000 troops of the Army of Cuban Pacification arrived on 6 October.

Rebel leaders cooperated with U.S. officials to facilitate a peaceful end to the insurrection. The U.S. Marines engaged in very little fighting. Disarmament and dispersal of the rebels, supervised by Gen. Frederick Funston, was complete by mid-October, just in time for the sugar harvest. A few U.S. and Cuban officials worried that the rebels had retained many of their arms and horses, but most were pleased with the ease of the pacification.

On 13 October 1906 civilian Charles E. Magoon replaced Taft as provisional governor. Magoon, an unenlightened bureaucrat who had previously served as governor of the Panama Canal Zone, was committed to continuing the plan devised by Taft to revise Cuba's political and economic system. New laws were required for the municipal, civil service, electoral, judicial, and provincial systems in order to guarantee future stability in Cuba. Magoon chose not to convene the Cuban Congress to enact the new laws. Instead, he retained greater control over the legislation by appointing the Advisory Law Commission, which drafted the new laws and submitted them for the governor's approval.

Rebuilding the Cuban economy was an equally complex task. Vast amounts of money were required to pay for reconstruction of the island. Previously accumulated debt had to be liquidated, damage inflicted during the revolt had to be paid for, and a multiplicity of public works programs had to be funded. The suppression of the yellow fever epidemic, which hit the island in fall 1905, unexpectedly depleted the treasury of over U.S. $4 million. Due to the seasonal nature of the sugar crop, unemployment remained a chronic problem in Cuba before, during, and after the occupation.

The provisional government also invested money in the reorganization of the military. President Roosevelt and Governor Magoon agreed that the Cuban military needed to be bolstered. If Estrada Palma had been equipped with a powerful army in 1906, they reasoned, he might have suppressed the Liberal revolt himself and freed the United States from any involvement whatsoever. The 5,000 member Guardia Rural was reorganized into 320 detachments and, more significantly, a new permanent army was created with plans to expand it in the future. Some United States Army personnel and Cuban Moderates warned that the new army, composed largely of Liberal commanders, would become a powerful tool for the Liberal party to secure power unlawfully, but U.S. politicians determined that economic and political stability in Cuba could best be assured by a government with military muscle behind his decrees.

With these modest reforms in place, Magoon set the date for regional and general elections to be held on 25 May 1908 and 14 November 1908. After Estrada Palma's resignation in 1906, the Moderate party had dissolved and re-formed as the Conservative party. The conservatives nominated Gen. Mario García Menocal for the presidency. The Liberals, who suffered from a debilitating schism during the regional elections, united to support José Miguel Gómez and Alfredo Zayas y Alfonso for the top executive offices.

The general elections yielded a decisive victory for the Liberal candidates, who then controlled both houses of Congress and received over 60 percent of the 331,455 votes cast for the presidency. On 28 January 1909, Governor Magoon officially transferred power to the newly chosen government amidst great fanfare and left Cuba that afternoon aboard the battleship *Maine*. The Army of Cuban Pacification remained on the island until April to make certain that the transfer progressed smoothly.

Although the U.S. officials departed in 1909, Cuba was still no closer to achieving sovereignty than it had been 11 years earlier when the United States intervened in its war with Spain. Under the Platt Amendment, Cuba had become a protectorate of the United States. Reluctant U.S. officials had become prisoners of their own short-sighted policy which sought to protect U.S. interests, but instead encouraged political instability in Cuba. In a country where public office served as an *entrée* to private enterprise, local politicians used the Platt Amendment to fulfill their own aspirations. During the 1906–1909 occupation, the modest reforms enacted by the United States did little to reverse this trend. Instead, U.S. policy makers perpetuated political strife by creating a strengthened permanent army, which repeatedly meddled in Cuban politics and ultimately served as an instrument of repression during the dictatorships of Gerardo Machado y Marales and Fulgencio Batista y Zaldívar.

Anthony R. Pisani, Jr.
Allen Wells

REFERENCES

Russell H. Fitzgibbon, *Cuba and the United States, 1900–1935* (Russell & Russell, 1964); David A. Lockmiller, *Magoon in Cuba: A History of the Second Intervention, 1906–1909* (Univ. of North Carolina Pr., 1938); Allan R. Millett, *The Politics of Intervention: The Military Occupation of Cuba, 1906–1909* (Ohio State Univ. Pr., 1968); Louis A. Pérez, Jr., "Indisposition to Intervention: The United States and the Cuban Revolution of 1906," *South Eastern Latin Americanist*, 28 (1984), 1–19; "Annual Report of Charles E. Magoon, Provisional Governor of Cuba, to the Secretary of War 1908," in U.S. Congress, House of Representatives, *House Document 145*, 60th Congress, 2d Session (U.S. Government Printing Office, 1909).

See also list of entries at front of book for Cuba, Intervention (1906–1909).

Cuba, Intervention (1912)

The administration of President William H. Taft ordered "preventive" intervention in Cuba in May 1912 because of concern that the government of Cuban President José Miguel Gómez could not protect U.S. property from a threat posed by a rebellion of Cuban blacks.

Blacks complained of social injustice, racism, and exclusion from politics in spite of their contributions in the battle for Cuban independence. Insurgent leader Evaristo Estenoz organized Partido Independiente de Color (Independent Party of Color) in 1907, but the party had only modest support from blacks. The 1910 Morúa law, introduced by a black senator, forbade parties organized on the basis of race. In 1912, when Gómez refused to support repeal of the Morúa law unless the party dropped the word "color" from its name, Estenoz organized a rebellion, perhaps hoping to provoke U.S. intervention and thereby hasten the fall of the government. By 21 May the government's rural guards clashed with armed blacks near the Guantánamo naval base in Oriente and Santa Clara provinces, where several U.S. companies operated.

U.S. minister Arthur M. Beaupré had a low regard for both the leaders of the revolt and the Cuban government. He considered Estenoz a "troublesome negro agitator" leading "irresponsible negroes . . . of a very ignorant class," and doubted that the leaders of the party were "capable of engineering a movement on this scale" (*Foreign Relations 1912*, pp. 243, 247). Nonetheless, in spite of repeated assurances from Gómez, Beaupré had little confidence that the Cuban government could control the rebels. His alarmist dispatches heightened concern in Washington throughout the crisis.

Secretary of State Philander C. Knox implemented a preventive policy to protect U.S. interests. On 23 May, the navy sent the *Prairie*, with 500 marines, to join two U.S. warships at Guantánamo. Two days later, the navy sent the *Nebraska* to Havana, and a gunboat to Nipe Bay. Knox claimed the vessels were to provide support in case the government was unable to protect U.S. lives or property, but insisted, "This is not intervention" (*Foreign Relations 1912*, p. 248). Gómez replied that it did not seem to be "anything else," and suggested that if troops landed it would accentuate the character of intervention (*Foreign Relations 1912*, p. 248). He claimed to have called 3,000 troops into action against the rebels and to have the situation under control. President Taft reiterated that naval vessels were meant to protect U.S. life and property, echoing Knox by insisting the precautions were "entirely disassociated from any question of intervention" (*Foreign Relations 1912*, p. 249).

Beaupré alerted Washington that destruction of foreign property began on 31 May, and the commandant of Guantánamo naval station landed four companies of marines. Knox sent four more warships from Key West. Beaupré called the situation in Oriente "extremely serious" and claimed Gómez understated the problem (*Foreign Relations 1912*, p. 255). At this point, the U.S. government accepted the presence of U.S. troops as providing an opportunity to withdraw forces that had been guarding foreign property and to employ them against the rebels. When Beaupré warned of a "race war" in Havana on 9 June Knox sent two more vessels, but insisted the action "indicates no change in this Government's policy of nonintervention" (*Foreign Relations 1912*, pp. 260–261). The British chargé d'affaires requested U.S. protection for British property in Cuba, and Knox assented.

As many as 3,000 Cubans may have died in the fighting between the government and the insurgents, but few foreigners suffered injury. The rebellion wilted quickly after Estenoz died in battle on 27 June, and the United States began withdrawing its larger warships two days later. Even Beaupré acknowledged that the Cuban government had "the upper hand" (*Foreign Relations 1912*, p. 267). The marines received orders on 25 July to leave Guantánamo, ending this "preventive" intervention. Historian Hugh Thomas has suggested that a consequence of the revolt was the reluctance of Cuban blacks to challenge the established political order until 1959 (Thomas, pp. 523–524).

Andrew J. Dunar

REFERENCES

Russell H. Fitzgibbon, *Cuba and the United States, 1900–1935* (Russell & Russell, 1964), 148–150; *Foreign Relations of the United States, 1912* (U.S. Government Printing Office, 1919), 242–268; Dana G. Munro, *Intervention and Dollar Diplomacy in the Caribbean, 1900–1921* (Princeton Univ. Pr., 1964), 477–480; Louis A. Pérez, Jr., *Cuba Under the Platt Amendment, 1902–1934* (Univ. of Pittsburgh Pr., 1986), 146–152; Hugh Thomas, *Cuba: The Pursuit of Freedom* (Harper, 1971), 419, 512–524.

See also Marine Operations in Cuba (1912); Naval Operations off Cuba (1912).

Cuba, Intervention (1917–1922)

The 1916 elections in Cuba involving President Mario García Menocal and the Liberal party led by José Miguel Gómez were marked by violence and fraud. The losing Liberal party began to plot a revolution complete with army defections and burning sugar cane fields. Some of the Liberal leaders hoped that President Woodrow Wilson would see the justice of their cause, intervene, and give them power in Cuba. Early in February 1917, Gómez raised the flag of insurrection and was joined by several other Liberal party leaders. Two army commanders joined the revolt, and several party officials sent a letter to Wilson requesting U.S. intervention.

Meanwhile, President García Menocal ordered the destruction of a key railroad bridge to hinder Gómez's advance and called for volunteers. The U.S. government announced its support for Menocal and denounced the Liberal revolution. In addition, the U.S. sold 10,000 rifles and two million cartridges to the Cuban government.

Beginning in early February small detachments of U.S. Marines and sailors were landed at various sites in response to requests from U.S. property owners for protection. On 4 March a six-company battalion was formed out of the force in Haiti and dispatched to Cuba. To protect the water supply of the U.S. naval base, 220 marines went to Guantánamo City, and compa-

nies were sent to protect the iron mines and ore docks at Daiquirí and facilities at Nipe Bay.

On 8 March the governor of Oriente Province requested Commodore Reginald R. Belknap to send a force of 500 men to protect the city of Santiago. The naval officer sent a force from his ships, and they were joined by the 43rd and 51st companies of marines from Haiti. Most were quickly withdrawn, but their presence allowed government troops to enter the city unopposed.

The United States had entered World War I in April 1917, and due to mobilization pressure, the marines were withdrawn on 23 May. Destruction of property in Cuba increased during April, however, and by May there was talk of sending a large body of U.S. soldiers. By the latter part of May the State Department had definitely decided to proceed with this plan and requested the War Department to begin preparations. Although most of the rebel leaders had given up by early May because the revolt was failing and because of peace-making efforts by U.S. naval commanders, sporadic violence continued in the eastern parts of the island. The potential of continued violence was enough to cause the United States to intervene in Cuba once again, especially in view of Washington's fear of German involvement. To salve Cuban feelings, and possibly the feelings of U.S. citizens who might disagree with a policy of occupying a friendly country, an artful plan was worked out. It was arranged for President Menocal to "offer" to the United States "sites for training camps . . . if it should be considered desirable to send troops to train in mild winter climate." This would make it possible to "impress eastern Cuba with [the] fact of [the] presence of United States troops" through the guise of "extensive practice marches" (Smith, p. 18). The people of the United States were informed that the "friendly offer" had been accepted and that it was proof of Cuba's desire to assist in the war with Germany.

Camp sites were rented in Oriente and Camagüey provinces, and on 16 August 1917 it was decided to send a regiment of marines rather than a cavalry regiment. The 7th Marine Regiment arrived later that month, and the 9th Regiment joined it in December. Together, they formed a brigade commanded by Col. James E. Mahoney. The commander regularly reported about the areas covered by marine patrols and the activities of the force. These reports were sent to the State Department.

Some historians contend that this intervention was due to fear of German attempts to create trouble. There was one report of possible German activity, but it was received almost two months after the decision to send troops had been made. Frank L. Polk, the acting secretary of state in July 1917, stated that troops were being sent "to aid in the protection of sugar properties and mining properties and in restoring complete order in the Oriente Province" (Smith, p. 19). In addition, the marines acted as strikebreakers and strike preventers for the Cuba railroad.

By April 1921 the marine force had been reduced to 350 men, but the presence of U.S. troops on Cuban soil was a constant source of irritation to the Cubans. The 1917 pretense that the marines were "training" on the island as part of the "war effort" had worn rather thin by 1921. The marines remained, however, and continued to fulfill the mission for which they had been sent. Herbert C. Lakin, president of the Cuba railroad, make a special trip to Washington to counteract Cuban requests for the removal of the marines. Secretary of State Charles E. Hughes later informed the secretary of the navy that he wanted the marine force retained at Camagüey.

The marines, however, wanted to withdraw the force to Guantánamo Bay for reasons of economy. Hughes was informed of this recommendation and referred the request to Gen. Enoch H. Crowder, special representative of the president of the United States. The general had been provost marshall of the United States Army and had served as the U.S. advisor to the Cuban government since 1919. The general reported that the marine force was needed to protect U.S. property, and Hughes informed the Navy Department that "General Crowder states that at the present time railroad labor troubles are again threatening, particularly on the Cuban-American Railroad [the Cuba railroad]" (Smith, p. 105). Thus, Secretary Hughes again asked the Navy Department to continue the maintenance of the Camagüey garrison.

On 5 December 1921 the Cuban House of Representatives passed a resolution calling on the United States to withdraw the marines. Crowder also reported that several newspapers had attacked the marine "intervention" as well

as his mission and that these attacks could not be "entirely disregarded." In a memorandum concerning the issue, General Crowder stated that he had advised against removal in June 1921 because he believed that the "dead season" between cane harvests would be a period of strikes and disorders. The season had passed, however, with no disturbances so Crowder wrote that it was no longer necessary to keep the marines at Camagüey. He did advise the department not to relieve the garrison immediately because this might be interpreted as a victory for anti-U.S. propaganda. Crowder concluded that the department should wait until a "more opportune moment" and that it should advise the Cuban government that public agitation concerning the question would only delay such action.

General Crowder returned to the United States in January 1922 to prepare for the forthcoming campaign to try to force various political reforms on the Cuban government (a "moralization" program as it was called). On 23 January, Crowder informed Sumner Welles, chief of the Latin American Division of the State Department, that he was anxious for the withdrawal instructions to go into effect before he returned to Cuba. The obvious implication of Crowder's recommendation was that the marine withdrawal would make the "moralization" program more palatable to the Cuban government. The general stated that there were no disturbances in Camagüey, and that if any developed, the marines could be rushed back from Guantánamo within 48 hours. Thus, the Cuba railroad would still have recourse to marine protection, if needed.

The State Department requested the withdrawal of the marine garrison on 24 January, and on 26 January 1922 the Navy Department replied that such orders would be issued immediately. On 6 February 1922 the last marine detachment sailed for Guantánamo Bay, and the intervention came to an end.

Robert Freeman Smith

REFERENCES

J. Robert Moskin, *The United States Marine Corps Story* (McGraw Hill, 1982); Ivan Musicant, *The Banana Wars: A History of United States Military Intervention in Latin America From the Spanish-American War to the Invasion of Panama* (Macmillan, 1990); Louis A. Pérez, Jr., *Intervention, Revolution, and Politics in Cuba, 1913–1921* (Univ. of Pittsburgh Pr., 1978); Robert F. Smith, *The United States and Cuba:*

Business and Diplomacy, 1917–1960 (Bookman Assocs., 1960); Hugh Thomas, *Cuba: The Pursuit of Freedom* (Harper, 1971).

See also Cuban Revolt (1916).

Cuba, Military Government (1898–1902)

At the end of the Spanish-Cuban/American War in 1898, the United States occupied Cuba with a temporary military government. Authority to pacify Cuba was given to President William McKinley by the congressional joint resolution of 20 April 1898 and the Treaty of Paris of 10 December 1898. These instruments indicated the intention of the United States not to annex Cuba but rather to administer the island's government until the Cuban people could govern themselves. The prerequisite for withdrawal was the establishment of an independent republic whose stability would satisfy the requirements of the United States. The Teller Amendment to the joint resolution bound the United States to depart Cuba.

The military government of Cuba undertook the reform of various institutions. As administered by Gen. Leonard Wood, it attempted to build a stable, independent republic by renovating the educational and legal systems, improving the public works infrastructure, and training the Cubans in self-government. In pursuing this course, the administrations of McKinley and Theodore Roosevelt steered between evacuation and annexation. Small groups in both the United States and Cuba demanded immediate evacuation; others desired ultimate annexation. The majority in both countries, however, supported the U.S. policy of remaining in Cuba for a few years to establish a durable government that would render future intervention unnecessary.

In addition to the educational, legal, economic, and governmental foundations, the United States desired a security safeguard from the Cubans. This instrument came to be known as the Platt Amendment of 1901, which was passed by the United States Congress, accepted by the Cuban constitutional convention and made into a treaty between the two nations until abrogated in 1934. The Platt Amendment, written mainly by Secretary of War Elihu Root and steered through Congress by Senator Orville H. Platt as a rider to the annual army appropriation bill of 1901, contained eight clauses. Among

these clauses were provisions for naval bases in Cuba (the origin of the present Guantánamo Bay naval base), sanitation, avoidance of debts or other agreements that might impair Cuban sovereignty, and, most important, the right for the United States to intervene to protect Cuban independence. The Cuban constitutional delegates did not like the Platt Amendment and tried to negotiate a different treaty, but were forced to accept it in order to establish their republic and to get U.S. authorities off of the island.

Thus, while the U.S. authorities and Cubans worked on internal reforms for a republic, Cuba started nationhood with a protectorate status that foreshadowed trouble. The Platt Amendment never worked as intended. Cuban political irresponsibility and U.S. meddling made for a dreary succession of official plunderers and commercial exploiters until the alienation of Cuba under the communist caudillo, Fidel Castro.

In 1898, however, few persons could peer that far into the future. The immediate situation demanded attention because Cuba was exhausted. A decade of depression and revolution had reduced the island's population by 12 percent and destroyed two-thirds of its wealth. While the countryside lay ravaged, towns and cities suffered from famine and pestilence. Water systems and sewers were destroyed, while malaria, dysentery, typhoid, smallpox, and yellow fever stalked the population. Deaths in Santiago alone exceeded 200 a day out of a population of less than 50,000. Enmity continued due to a basic divisiveness where black and white Cuban insurgents opposed Spaniards, neutralists, and autonomists, distinctions dating from the era of the Cuban War of Independence (1895–1898). Of the island's 1.5 million people, two-thirds were illiterate and unemployed. The courts had ceased to function, and public funds vanished with the departing Spaniards.

Maj. Gen. John R. Brooke, the first U.S. governor general of the island, made a needed start with measures to feed and clothe destitute victims of the war. He also opened schools, collected customs revenues, and appointed a cabinet of Cubans to begin the functions of civil government. The time seemed propitious for moving toward a contented Cuba. But nothing happened. In a few months, Brooke came under criticism from Cubans and U.S. authorities alike. His Cuban cabinet failed to cope with the problems of constructing a new society. Business stagnated; officials took bribes; prisons, hospitals, and asylums were neglected; and schools failed to operate. In late 1899, to avoid a major scandal in Cuba and further incompetence in the United States War Department, McKinley forced his secretary of war, Russell A. Alger, from office, and his general in Cuba, Brooke, replacing them with, respectively, Elihu Root, a corporation lawyer, and Leonard Wood, a general of army volunteers.

Root became the architect of United States's colonial policy, and Wood became Root's administrator in Cuba. Root appointed Wood military governor of Cuba because he believed Wood had the patience and imperturbability to carry out policy and get along with the Cubans. McKinley simply told Wood to prepare Cuba for a republican form of government, provide good schools and courts, put them on their feet, and leave the island as soon as possible. Root's program, carried out by Wood, envisioned supervising the Cubans as they governed the island. The steps were to include a census, municipal elections, insular administration, a convention to frame a new constitution and determine future Cuban-U.S. relations, and tariff reduction to give Cuba a market for sugar.

Wood, who could read, write, and speak Spanish, changed the pace and focus of government activity in Cuba. He reduced the size of the United States Army in Cuba to about 3,000 officers and men, gathered a capable staff of young officers, and appointed Cubans of high ability to civil offices. Most of his appointees were former rebels or autonomists; Wood did not appoint many conservatives or radicals to office. He formed the Guardia Rural (rural guard) of 1,300 Cubans to supervise law and order. Up at 5:30 a.m. and never in bed before midnight, Wood visited prisons, inspected hospitals, investigated courts, stopped by schools, and viewed public works projects. He worked his staff in shifts around the clock and expected an arduous eight-hour day from Cuban civil officials, different from the previous, leisurely, four-hour days. He talked with everyone he could from merchants and mayors to farmers and priests, showing them he cared and persuading them to join in the task of building Cuba.

Wood's actions were promulgated in a series of executive orders sent to his military and civil staffs. Col. Hugh L. Scott served as his second-in-command; Frank Steinhart ramrodded the busy clerks; and aides such as Lt. Frank R. McCoy coped with a wide array of problems. Wood appointed José Ramón Villalón, secretary of public works; Diego Tamayo y Tejera, secretary of state and government; Enriqué José Varona, secretary of finance, then public instruction, replaced by Leopoldo Cancio in the former office; Luis Estevez y Romero became secretary of justice, followed by Miguel Gener and José Varela y Jado. Juan Ruíz Rivera, the first secretary of agriculture, was replaced by Perfecto Lacosta. These appointments met with approval from most Cubans.

The military government took charge of a devastated island and left it in less than four years with freely elected officials, $1.7 million in the treasury, 82 self-supporting municipalities, 300 post offices, a telegraph system, sewers, roads, bridges, railroads, and ports. Higher courts in 21 judicial districts disposed of cases quickly and fairly, and the number of prisoners was reduced by two-thirds. Three thousand schools were built and remodeled for 256,000 pupils, and 3,600 teachers were employed at high wages by 121 local boards. Curricula and facilities of the University of Havana and the six provincial high schools were modernized. Thirty-nine hospitals, twelve orphan training schools, four vocational trade schools, six nursing schools, six homes for the aged, and one insane asylum operated where virtually none had existed before. Of 207 sugar plantations, 194 resumed production, and 38 new mines were located. The church property question was settled with a compromise, and a survey of land titles started. Yellow fever was eradicated and other diseases attacked as public health improved. The Cubans achieved these results themselves, with U.S. supervision.

In regard to the courts, the United States deemed the Spanish law excellent and its enforcement deplorable. So Wood made administrative changes. He simply released prisoners whose sentences had expired or had no charges against them. He took judges and clerks off the notorious fee system and paid them salaries. A civil marriage law appeared with much approval from Cubans who objected to Catholic Church control. To expedite cases, the military government established courts for minor infractions decided by a maximum penalty of 30 days or $30. It proved impossible, however, to institute *habeas corpus* and the jury system as other disturbing signs appeared. Many cases were dismissed by these lower courts without decisions, and judges suffered threats of intimidation by some Cubans as the military government prepared to lift its protective umbrella and depart. Nevertheless, two striking cases set a necessary, if temporary, example. Cubans were amazed to find that a coterie of prominent merchants was tried and convicted for defrauding the customs house of proper revenues. The postal frauds case involved extradition of three U.S. citizens to Cuba for trial in a Cuban court. The men, Estes G. Rathbone, Charles F. Neely, and W.H. Reeves, were convicted, fined, and imprisoned. Thus, the Cubans could see that the law pertained to all persons regardless of status.

Lts. Matthew E. Hanna, Enriqué José Varona, Alexis E. Frye led the reform of Cuban education. In addition to improving basic studies and providing adequate facilities, they stressed a curriculum to prepare Cubans in the technical skills and literate awareness needed to build a nation. No attempt was made to indoctrinate Cuba's youth in the English language or U.S. history. Such classes were elective, not required. The teachers were Cuban. The University of Havana was modernized as well: professors who sojourned in Spain or who had fewer than five students enrolled were fired; the curriculum was changed to coincide with the changes in universities elsewhere; laboratories and archives were established. Still, worrisome characteristics remained: low attendance, absence of teachers, corruption on local boards.

Cuba was an agricultural country with only 3 percent of its 28 million acres under production. Wood relied on Cuban initiative to begin raising crops and assisted the process by reducing taxes and building a transportation system and communications network to link farmers with markets. In all this, the possibility loomed that the attempt to rebuild Cuba's economy might degenerate into exploiting the island's resources for the benefit of U.S. entrepreneurs. However, the Foraker Amendment of March 1899 prevented the military government from granting any franchises in Cuba and Wood stopped carpetbaggers from plundering the island. For example, he refused to allow the firm of Michael Dady to cheat the city of Havana in a sewering and paving contract. The case dragged on so long in the courts that Havana did not receive a sewer system during the military occupation. Sir William C. Van Horne, of Canadian Pacific

Railway fame, built the Cuban national railway connecting the eastern end of the island to the center and west, without bribery and with excellent materials. He financed the project with New York investors and purchased property in Cuba. However, the only way he could cross public property was with a device of Root's, a revocable permit, which meant the Cuban government could revoke the right of passage at any time.

The military government lowered the tariff, which still provided most of the income, and genuinely collected the revenues which were spent in Cuba for Cubans, about $17 million a year. The military government received $57 million in its tenure and spent most of it on schools, courts, charities, and public works, leaving nearly $1.8 million for the new Cuban government in 1902.

Cuba depended on sugar exports to survive, with tobacco a second source of income and other products of negligible importance. Land ownership resided in the hands of a few men, Cubans, Spaniards, British, and U.S. citizens. Wood did not try to diversify the economy or redistribute the land. His Cuban advisors deterred him from taxing unused land, but he did work out a compromise between creditors and debtors regarding mortgages.

In the matter of U.S. economic control of Cuba, it may be asserted that while Cuba moved into the U.S. economic sphere and left Spain's, the United States invested less in Cuba during the military government than either before or after. By 1898, U.S. citizens had invested some $50 million in Cuba; by 1902 another $30 million, by 1906, another $80 million. This was less than one-half the foreign investment in Cuba and less than 2 percent of U.S. foreign trade. In 1902, U.S. interests produced about 13 percent of the Cuban sugar crop, owning all or part of some 12 out of 184 sugar *centrales*. However, the United States controlled nearly half of Cuba's imports and exports. The dominant U.S. investment in Cuba came after World War I, when the United States became a creditor nation and the world's banker.

The military government concentrated on public works in order to provide employment, improve public health, and create a transportation network linking producers and markets. Of the roughly $55 million spent by the military government, over $22 million was expended on varied public works. Cuba needed a public works program because there were no paved roads or railroads outside of the main cities and plantations, shallow ports discouraged shipping, and broken sanitation systems afflicted many Cubans.

The organization of public works was divided between the United States Army Engineers and the civilian department of public works. The army engineers, under Maj. William M. Black and Lt. William J. Barden, supervised public works and sanitation in Havana and larger towns. Secretary of Public Works José R. Villalón presided over works in the provinces. Care was exercised in awarding contracts, controlling profit, accounting for funds, and using materials. In general, the military government insisted on durable, efficient, prompt work at the lowest possible cost. All contracts were let for bid and awarded to the lowest competent bidder, allowing cost plus 10 to 25 percent profit. Wherever possible, they went to Cuban contractors. Administrative overhead was low, from 5 to 6 percent. Some U.S. contractors went into Cuba to provide expertise Cubans lacked, but they found only hard work under difficult conditions and insistence on a job well done. Villalón and Black employed Cuban labor wherever possible at $1 a day for unskilled and $4 for foremen and skilled workers. The military government was the largest steady employer on the island.

The necessary projects were severely limited by lack of funding, yet the accomplishments were impressive. Wood and Villalón believed that Cuba needed 2,200 kilometers of new roads at a cost of $15 million. From 1899 to 1902, the Department of Public Works erected 52 new bridges and repaired 40 others, built 99 kilometers of new roads, and repaired and maintained 350 kilometers of existing roads. There were some large projects as well, such as deepening Cárdenas harbor, to avoid costly lighterage fees.

The work in Havana received about as much funding as all the provinces together and consisted of road repair; sanitation; trolley lines; park and waterfront beautification; water supply; and surveys of service connections, fire hydrants, and existing lines. There were 99 projects for renovating buildings, such as the Pirotecnica Militar for the University of Havana and the National Archives at La Fuerza. The port went through a cleaning operation as well. Refuse was either dumped at sea or burned outside of town. Work in other cities consisted of street repair, sanita-

tion, and water supply. The usual ingredients for disinfecting edifices were electrozone, chloride of lime, sulphur, and bichloride of mercury.

Medical officers changed Cuba from one of the unhealthiest places in the world to one of the healthiest, reducing the death rate in Havana from 91.3 per 1,000 to 20 per 1,000. General Wood, a medical doctor, provided the funds for doctors Walter Reed, James Carroll, and Jesse W. Lazear to combat the dreaded yellow fever. Their experiments with the theory of Dr. Carlos J. Finlay that the *Stegomiya* mosquito carried the disease proved so successful that Dr. William C. Gorgas and the Sanitary Department eradicated yellow fever in Cuba. Next, a vaccination program stopped smallpox, but a sanitary and educational effort failed to reduce tuberculosis, also a lethal killer at the time.

Maj. Edwin St. John Greble carried out supervision of charitable work. After four years, with hospitals, training schools, leper asylums, and orphanages staffed by trained personnel with modern equipment, Cubans could consider hospitals and asylums as havens for help instead of dens of death. As with educational facilities, the state also paid for medical and welfare operations.

With public works and health organized, the economy revived, the courts reformed, and schools opened, the military government also began to prepare Cubans for self-government. Elections were held in June 1900 for municipal officials, based on a restricted suffrage: only Cubans born on the island, 21 years old, literate or owner of real or personal property valued at $250, or holder of honorable discharge from the Cuban army prior to 18 July 1898, could vote. Root wanted a capable electorate, not a mass, uninformed vote; nevertheless, the suffrage restriction still left native Cuban revolutionaries in control of politics. About one-third of adult Cuban males was eligible to vote, and about 68 percent of those registered did so in Cuba's first free election.

As mayors and city councils took hold in the towns, Wood called for a convention that would frame a constitution and establish the pattern of future Cuban-U.S. relations. In fall 1901, 31 delegates were elected by restricted manhood suffrage to meet in Havana. Most were former revolutionaries, with a sprinkling of conservatives present. Wood left them alone as they prepared a constitution, based on the principles of checks and balances, separation of powers, and recognition of the right of private property.

The *convencionales* delayed the dreaded question of future relations with the United States, hoping to avoid it until after U.S. troops departed. Root and Wood realized this when they met in Cuba in fall 1900; so Root penned the Platt Amendment upon his return to Washington, and Congress accepted it in March. The Cuban convention passed its own resolutions and tried to negotiate them with Root through the means of sending a special delegation to Washington. Finally, in June 1901, at Wood's suggestion, an ultimatum was delivered to the convention: either accept the Platt Amendment verbatim or the occupation would continue. Reluctantly, the Cuban delegates voted to accept it, 15–11, in order to end the intervention. Demonstrations and petitions indicated sizeable, but peaceful, public opposition to the law. If left to their own devices, the delegates would have preferred U.S. departure and an eventual treaty that embodied reciprocal trade relations and mutual defense.

For the next year, Wood prepared to transfer control to the Cubans. Elections were held in December, and Tomás Estrada Palma, a Cuban patriot sympathetic to friendly relations with the United States, defeated Bartolomé Masó, who was backed by opponents of the United States. Men such as Máximo Gómez y Baez, general in chief of the Cuban army during the war; Domingo Méndez Capote, chairman of the constitutional convention; and José Miguel Gómez, governor of Santa Clara Province and later president of the republic, supported Estrada Palma. Opponents included Juan Gualberto Gómez, the leading black politician; Salvador Cisneros Betancourt, large landholder and former president of the revolutionary republic; and José Lacret Morlet, general in the rebel army and later senator. Senators and representatives were also elected to form the new government, with the majority of members from various regional political factions supporting Estrada Palma. On 20 May 1902, after impressive ceremonies, the military government departed and the Cuban republic commenced.

In 1903, after a year of campaigning for a sugar treaty against U.S. beet sugar interests, the Roosevelt administration concluded a reciprocity agreement with Cuba to provide a market for Cuban sugar, not to control indirectly but to help ensure political stability in the island. Thus, the initial U.S. program for Cuba was completed, but events of the years that followed belied initial hopes for success.

Scholarship on the question of U.S. intervention in Cuba and the Philippines generally dwells on the motives of strategic security, self-determination, native adaptation, and economic exploitation. Few scholars would agree that either occupation proved to be a success in the long run. The most disputatious argument revolves around whether the interventionist governments promoted Cuban and Filipino independence or U.S. control.

Historical writing depends in part on the personality of the author, previous literature of the subject, and the times in which a person writes. After world wars, a depression, a cold war, thermonuclear stalemate, and the Vietnam War, it is still evident that some writers support and others oppose U.S. intervention overseas. Looking back at the Cuban and Filipino occupations, it is clear U.S. authorities did not believe either the Cubans or Filipinos were cohesive or experienced enough to manage republics at that time. The weight of evidence regarding cultural divisions and political favoritism in those islands indicates that U.S. officials were correct. Certainly most Cubans and Filipinos supported the initial U.S. programs because they were reformist in nature and resistance was hopeless. However, U.S. officials failed to consider three serious questions: the tendency toward politicking and corruption in later U.S. colonial administrations, the baleful effect of denying pure sovereignty to those who wanted it, and U.S. beliefs that made permanent political colonies impossible. During the ensuing clash of cultures, the United States acceded to independence demands, dropped economic ties with Cuba and maintained them with the Philippines, and exhibited strategic concerns for both nations, an uneasy practice which continued for the remainder of the 20th century.

James H. Hitchman

REFERENCES

Jules R. Benjamin, *The United States and Cuba: Hegemony and Dependent Development, 1880–1934* (Univ. of Pittsburgh Pr., 1974); Philip S. Foner, *The Spanish-Cuban-American War and the Birth of American Imperialism, 1885–1902* (Monthly Review Pr., 1972); David F. Healy, *The United States in Cuba, 1898–1902* (Univ. of Wisconsin Pr., 1963); James H. Hitchman, *Leonard Wood and Cuban Independence*,

1898–1902 (Nijhoff, 1971); Louis A. Pérez, Jr., *Cuba Between Empires, 1878–1902* (Univ. of Pittsburgh Pr., 1983).

See also Cuba, Occupation (1898–1902).

Cuba, Occupation (1898–1902)

On 10 December 1898 the United States and Spain signed a peace treaty ending the Spanish-Cuban/American War. In Cuba, only one theater of U.S. activities against the Spanish, Spanish forces surrendered to the U.S. commander, Maj. Gen. John R. Brooke, who then became the first U.S. governor general of the island. U.S. occupation of the island continued, under the auspices of the United States Army and the War Department, until the inauguration of the Cuban Republic on 20 May 1902. The Cuban Liberation Army as an organization was excluded from the military government just as it had been excluded from the ceremony marking the end of Spanish rule of the island.

Brooke was confronted with immediate, pressing tasks. Three years of vicious warfare had left the island devastated. Hunger, disease, and the collapse of basic services and order threatened the lives of those who had survived the war. Brooke immediately set to work to remedy the crisis and reported that by midyear, the worst had passed. The easing of the immediate crisis raised the question of the long-term objective of the occupation. Brooke acknowledged the general need for reform in Cuba, but he lacked guidance from Washington for such work. He operated under general orders to run a just and stable government, to maintain order, and to protect the liberties and property of the islands' residents.

The lack of instructions for Brooke reflected indecision in Washington. A long-standing expansionist impulse in the United States, made stronger over time as U.S. wealth and industrial power increased and impelled by the sinking of the battleship *Maine* in Havana harbor in February 1898, had pushed the administration of President William McKinley to intervene in Cuba, inaugurating the Spanish-Cuban/American War. Cuba, already the object of significant U.S. foreign investment, had long been coveted by U.S. annexationists. In opposition to annexation, however, stood a remarkably strong and very diverse anti-imperialist sentiment. The Teller Amendment to the joint resolution of

Congress authorizing the president to use military force against Spain was the price the McKinley administration had to pay to intervene in Cuba. The amendment proclaimed that the "people of Cuba are and of right ought to be free and independent" and that the United States "disclaims any disposition or intention to exercise sovereignty, jurisdiction, or control over said island except for the pacification thereof, and asserts its determination when that is accomplished to leave the government and control of the island to its people." The subsequent U.S. occupation of the island, however, strengthened the hand of those who favored annexation, leaving the fate of the island initially in doubt.

Opinion was also divided in Cuba. The Spanish-Cuban/American War was from the Cuban perspective only the latest outbreak of a war of independence that first began in 1868. Veterans of the Cuban Liberation Army, who had carried on the struggle for independence since 1895, resented the intervention of U.S. troops in April 1898 even as their own military effort faltered. Many affluent Cubans, resident Spaniards, and Cuban exiles, however, had advocated U.S. intervention or saw the U.S. occupation as protection from the more radical elements of the Cuban army that had agendas for social reform.

As the fate of the island was being decided elsewhere, Brooke took measures compatible with his vague general orders. His military government ran the island with the help of prominent Cubans, and, although he introduced some reforms (such as the creation of a system of public education), did not seek to transform the habits or customs of the Cuban people. A notable accomplishment of Brooke's administration was the carrying out of a thorough census of the island.

Most important for the political future of the island, Brooke oversaw the dissolution of the Cuban army. In 1899, U.S. emissary Robert P. Porter negotiated an agreement with the commander of the Cuban army, Gen. Máximo Gómez, to pay $75 to each veteran of the war up to the sum of $3 million. The Santa Cruz Assembly, the political arm of the indigenous revolutionary effort, strongly opposed this arrangement and attempted to dismiss Gómez. The enormously popular Gómez, who felt that the agreement ultimately represented the best strategy of preserving a chance for Cuban independence, prevailed over the Assembly and the army disbanded. The controversy fragmented the Assembly, and it too dissolved, leaving no organized force to press for Cuban independence. From the veteran officers and men of the Cuban army, Brooke and his lieutenants fashioned rural guards that saved the United States Army from having to perform police duties in a culture where laws and norms of behavior differed from those of the United States. The outbreak of war in the Philippines in February 1899 made the United States Army particularly determined to rely on indigenous forces to keep the peace.

Brooke found himself increasingly at odds with the four generals who served as his civil departmental commanders: Fitzhugh Lee (Pinar del Río and rural Havana departments), William Ludlow (city of Havana), James H. Wilson (Matanzas and Santa Clara departments), and Leonard Wood (Santiago and Puerto Principe departments). Brooke particularly clashed with Wood, many years his junior and representative of the new reforming spirit within the United States Army. Wood favored the annexation of Cuba and began his own program of improvements and reforms in Santiago and Puerto Príncipe. Well-connected in Washington, Wood developed a habit of appealing directly to the secretary of war to counter the orders of his commanding officer. Among Wood's criticisms of Brooke was that the governor general's policies were destructive of the annexation goal by allowing the island to slip back into the degenerate politics and practices that had prevailed under the Spanish. Wood replaced Brooke as governor general of the island on 20 December 1899.

Wood's strategy was to achieve Cuban annexation by creating the irresistible desire for it among the Cubans themselves. From his perspective, honest and efficient government combined with extensive social reforms would reinvigorate a decadent population and convincingly illustrate the benefits of association with the United States to Cuban citizens of substance.

There were few aspects of Cuban life that Wood's reforms did not touch. Building on the educational reforms begun by Brooke, Wood's administration opened many new public schools, enacted an education law modeled on that of the state of Ohio, introduced textbooks that were direct translations of texts used in the United States, and instructed Cuban teachers in the U.S. teaching techniques. Wood oversaw extensive public works projects, particularly relating to the improvement of harbors and roads, sanitation, public health, and the repair of public buildings. The military government also attempted extensive reforms of the Cuban judicial system, although the difficulties of conforming Spanish laws based on Roman law to U.S. laws based on Anglo-Saxon common law defeated many of the attempted reforms. The military government did succeed in reforming prisons. Wood furthered the separation of church from state by introducing civil marriage and divorce. Wood's new electoral law defined the eligible electorate as adult, Cuban males possessing either the ability to read and write, or real or personal property worth $250, or an honorable service record with the Cuban army. Wood also reorganized the rural guards established by Brooke, making them into the Guardia Rural of the Island of Cuba, a national police force under uniform regulation. Despite the Foraker Amendment, which prohibited the military government from granting economic concessions, Wood facilitated the construction of a trans-Cuba railway line by U.S. interests and other U.S. investments on the island.

The success of the military government in combating yellow fever stands out as a particularly impressive achievement. In 1901, a medical team under the command of Maj. Walter Reed confirmed Cuban physician Carlos J. Finlay's theory that mosquitos transmit yellow fever. After the military government took vigorous steps to eradicate the carrier mosquito, yellow fever, endemic to the island, virtually disappeared from Havana.

Wood simultaneously served as the commander of the Department of Cuba, a geographic division of the active United States Army. By June 1901, Wood's force had declined in number from approximately 11,000 U.S. officers and enlisted men in January 1900 to 4,914 officers and enlisted men, including two cavalry regiments and eight companies of coastal artillery. These were professional soldiers. The volunteers who had fought in the Spanish-Cuban/American War had been mustered out of the army by mid-1901, while the size of the regular army was increased in February 1901 to meet the needs of the Philippine War and the defense of the newly acquired U.S. territories.

The announcement in July 1900 that Cuba was to be given independence left Wood with the task of overseeing the transition, including the drafting of a Cuban constitution. Wood conducted elections for Cuban representatives to a constituent assembly in September 1900, and it convened 5 November. Wood, as instructed by the United States War Department, charged its delegates with the task of drafting a constitution that would not only establish the political system of the island but would also establish the future relationship between the United States and the Republic of Cuba. The result was the inclusion in the Cuban Constitution of the U.S.-drafted Platt Amendment which limited the authority of the Cuban government in the conduct of foreign affairs and gave the United States the duty and the right to intervene in the island in the event that the Cuban government failed to maintain order.

The military government held elections for the first president of the Cuban Republic on 31 December 1901, and Tomás Estrada Palma took office on 20 May 1902. The formal end of the U.S. occupation left behind a Cuba much improved in material conditions and infused with substantial U.S. investment. One legacy of the occupation and the Platt Amendment, however, was a political system that had to take root in the shadow of a United States still very actively interested in the affairs of the island and prone to involvement in them.

Jennifer Bailey

REFERENCES

Russell H. Fitzgibbon, *Cuba and the United States, 1900–1935* (Russell & Russell, 1964); Military Governor of Cuba, 1899–1902 [Leonard Wood], *Report of the Military Governor of Cuba on Civil Affairs, January 1, 1902–May 20, 1902* (U.S. Government Printing Office, 1902); Louis A. Pérez, Jr., *Cuba Between Empires, 1878–1902* (Univ. of Pittsburgh Pr., 1983); Hugh Thomas, *Cuba: The Pursuit of Freedom* (Harper, 1971); U.S., War Department, *Civil Report of Major General Leonard Wood, Military Governor of Cuba, for the Period from December 20, 1899, to December 31, 1900* (U.S. Government Printing Office, 1901); U.S. War Department, *Civil Report of Brigadier General Leonard Wood, Military Governor of Cuba for the Period from January 1 to May 20, 1902* (U.S. Government Printing Office, 1902).

See also list of entries at the front of book for Cuba, Occupation (1898–1902).

Cuban Army, Establishment

The surrender of Spanish forces in Cuba to the United States Army on 1 January 1899 left well over 40,000 Cuban soldiers under arms in the Cuban Liberation Army (*Ejercito Libertador*). What was for the United States the Spanish-Cuban/American War was for Cubans the third installment of a war for independence that had first broken out in 1868. The Cuban Liberation Army carried on the fight for three years before U.S. intervention.

The end of hostilities against Spain and the inauguration of a U.S. military government in Cuba raised the question of the fate of the Cuban Liberation Army. Many Cuban army leaders strongly favored independence and resented the U.S. intervention, the subordination of the Cuban army to U.S. forces during the war, the exclusion of the Cuban Liberation Army from the surrender ceremony, and the subsequent U.S. military government. In October 1898, Cubans favoring independence, including many army leaders, formed a fledgling government, the Santa Cruz Assembly. Units of the Cuban army took over many municipalities after the Spanish withdrew. In addition, the collapse of civilian order and the withdrawal of Spanish forces left substantial unrest in the countryside. In this situation, the Cuban army was an obvious potential threat to the U.S. military government, a situation well appreciated within the United States Army after the outbreak of war in the Philippines in February 1899.

The United States moved quickly to demobilize the Cuban army. In early 1899, U.S. emissary Robert P. Porter secured Gen. Máximo Gómez y Baez's agreement to a plan for demobilization. The United States would pay $75 to each Cuban veteran, up to $3 million, in exchange for demobilization. The Santa Cruz Assembly strongly opposed this plan and fired Gómez. The enormously popular Gómez prevailed over the Assembly, however, and the plan was carried out.

The money was to be paid according to rolls put together by the Assembly, and the military government could not act until the Assembly released them. Once the Assembly released the records, they indicated that 45,000 men were to be paid. The U.S. military government, convinced that the number was greatly inflated, reduced the number to under 40,000, in part by excluding soldiers by then employed by the military government from the payment. The first military governor of the island, Gen. John R. Brooke, reported that the first installment of $2,544,750 was paid out to 33,930 soldiers on 27 May 1899. The records were generally inadequate, including men who were not veterans of the war and excluding others who were. In his 1902 final report, the second governor general of Cuba, Leonard Wood, noted that Cuban officers had completed their work toward producing a more reliable roll of deserving veterans and recommended a final payment be made after careful U.S. review.

Some Cuban army veterans were absorbed into civilian occupations under the U.S. military government. The military government organized municipal police forces to fill the vacuum created by the withdrawal of the Spanish and recruited Cuban veterans to fill the ranks and officer the forces. Gen. Mario García Menocal, for example, took the position of chief of police in Havana in 1899. The military governor of Havana, Brig. Gen. William Ludlow, organized a rural guard to keep the peace outside the city limits, recruiting the force of approximately 350 officers and men from Cuban veterans. As military governor of Santiago and Puerto Príncipe provinces in 1899, Wood also formed municipal police forces and a rural guard. He found the mountainous district of Santiago to be particularly plagued by organized bands of bandits, an endemic problem in the area made worse by the existence of idle armed men. The U.S. military governors of the departments of Santa Clara and Pinar del Río created similar forces. Each provincial rural guard force was separate, had distinct uniforms, and operated according to similar, but not the same, regulations.

When Wood took Brooke's place as governor general of Cuba at the end of 1899, he quickly established the single, island-wide Guardia Rural (Rural Guard) under a unified command. On 26 February 1900, Wood issued Order No. 90 which established the Guardia Rural of the Island of Cuba, a uniform mounted force modeled on the U.S. cavalry. It was divided into companies consisting of one captain, one first lieutenant, one second lieutenant, one first sergeant, seven sergeants, eight corporals, and a minimum of 59 privates. Wood initially assigned 500 of-

ficers and men to the province of Santa Clara, 360 to Santiago Province, 250 to Puerto Principe Province, and Pinar del Río and Havana shared a force of 200. By the end of the year, Wood had shifted the number and posting of the force somewhat, and it numbered about 1,200. The Guardia Rural was designed to be and was shifted about the island as circumstances required.

Wood recruited members for the Guardia Rural from Cuban veterans who could produce two letters of recommendation from men of substance, that is, people with a local reputation and usually possessing some property. The men were clothed in cotton khaki uniforms with hats similar to the United States Army's campaign hat and armed with 7.7-mm Remington carbines. The men owned their own horses but found their salary substantially reduced if the animal became unfit through neglect or preventable injury. The requirements set by the United States produced a predominantly white Guardia Rural, particularly with respect to its officer corps.

Wood wrote in glowing terms about the excellent discipline and appearance of the Guardia Rural in his 1902 Civil Report of the Military Governor. The Guardia kept public order so well that Wood noted in his final report as governor general that U.S. troops never had to be deployed against Cuban civilians during the U.S. occupation of Cuba. Wood publicly judged this force to be capable of preserving order even when U.S. forces withdrew, although he privately but unsuccessfully recommended leaving behind a small detachment of U.S. troops to support the Guardia Rural after the formal U.S. withdrawal.

The Guardia Rural was formally a police force rather than an army. It was fashioned to keep internal order while U.S. troops were on hand during the occupation to meet any external threat to the island. However, while its size and armament were suited to this domestic role, the members of Guardia Rural were recruited from Cuban army veterans, organized along the lines of the U.S. cavalry, and its regulations and discipline were more military than civilian in nature. As the United States prepared to leave the island, Wood described the men of the Guardia Rural as "soldiers" and emphasized the military characteristics of the force.

On 20 May 1902, Wood turned over to the new Cuban Republic a Guardia Rural of 15 companies consisting of 1,604 officers and men stationed at 247 posts around the island. Cuban Brig. Gen. Alejandro Rodríguez commanded the Guardia Rural, with a lieutenant colonel responsible for the troops within each province. The Guardia had maintained its rural character, and its troops were stationed in small posts that were often built on private land and supported by local landowners to ensure order in their area.

The United States also turned over three companies of newly formed Cuban coast artillery companies to the new republic. A fourth company was planned, and U.S. coast artillery companies were left behind in Cuba to supplement the Cuban force until it was complete. Wood modeled the Cuban artillery on U.S. artillery forces, including U.S. racial segregation: two of the three organized companies were composed of white soldiers, the third was composed of Afro-Cubans. All officers were white.

The Cuban artillery was more directly intended for defense of the republic but it remained a small force. Under the Platt Amendment, forcibly appended to the Cuban Constitution, the United States continued to assume the task of defending the island from external aggression after the formal occupation of the island ended. The United States retained a military base at Guantánamo, a symbol to third powers and to the Cubans of the special relationship between the United States and the Republic of Cuba.

Jennifer Bailey

REFERENCES

Allan R. Millett, *The Politics of Intervention: The Military Occupation of Cuba, 1906–1909* (Ohio State Univ. Pr., 1968); Louis A. Pérez, Jr., *Army Politics in Cuba, 1898–1958* (Univ. of Pittsburgh Pr., 1976); Hugh Thomas, *Cuba: The Pursuit of Freedom* (Harper, 1971); U.S. War Department, *Annual Report of the War Department for the Fiscal Year ended June 30, 1899, Report of the Major General Commanding the Army*, part 1 (U.S. Government Printing Office, 1899); U.S. War Department, *Civil Report of Major General Leonard Wood, Military Governor of Cuba, for the Period from December 20, 1899, to December 31, 1900* (U.S. Government Printing Office, 1901); U.S. War Department, *Civil Report of Brigadier General Leonard Wood, Military Governor of Cuba, for the Period from January 1 to May 20, 1902* (U.S. Government Printing Office, 1902).

See also Cuban Army, Reconstitution; Guardia Rural, Cuba.

Cuban Army, Reconstitution

As the United States expanded its empire of trade and investment after 1898, it identified new political economic imperatives and developed corresponding institutions designed to secure them. Among these new needs was the capacity to govern efficiently the colonial lands and peoples seized in the aftermath of the Spanish-Cuban/American War. Because U.S. strategic and economic interests were not always popular among these conquered peoples, this required the creation of an effective local military capability.

Under the terms of the Platt Amendment, U.S. policy makers originally assumed that the U.S. military establishment would be sufficient to provide strategic defense of the island and protect against "domestic disorder." Hence, for U.S. officials, the Cuban independence movement's nationalistic *Ejército Libertador* (Cuban Liberation Army) only threatened U.S. hegemony. They therefore sought to demobilize the Cuban army. But the Philippine War of 1899–1902 undermined this theory and demonstrated to the United States the wisdom of reconstituting a Cuban army, albeit one in the service of U.S. strategic and economic interests.

Initially, these discussions focused on the creation of a colonial army, modeled on the experience of the British in Egypt. It would be composed of Cuban soldiers, with U.S. sergeants, and Cuban captains and lieutenants, all commanded by U.S. field-grade officers. Such a force would use Cuban resources, effectively reduce U.S. costs, permit greater tactical flexibility in the dispatch of U.S. troops, develop "native regiments" responsive to U.S. interests, and facilitate the demobilization of the *Ejército Libertador* by incorporating selected officers and enlisted men into the U.S. command structure.

Ultimately, however, this proposal was rejected in favor of a more limited project—the establishment of the Guardia Rural (Rural Guard), a domestic police force whose first responsibility was the protection of large corporations like those of the Chaparra Sugar Company, the Juragua Iron Company, and the United Fruit Company. The Guardia also promoted the political agenda of Tomás Estrada Palma, the Cuban president installed by the U.S. intervention.

But, as the Liberal revolt of 1906 quickly showed, the Guardia was utterly incapable of suppressing an organized insurrection. Its 1,500 officers and men, later expanded to 3,000, were still numerically insufficient to this task and far too spread out in relatively isolated rural areas to be militarily effective. Its political partisanship and lack of centralized coordination or uniform military discipline also undermined popular respect for its authority. Because Cuban revolutionaries did not seem to be sufficiently intimidated by the threat of U.S. armed intervention under the terms of the Platt Amendment, Governor Charles E. Magoon's provisional government searched for a more efficient means to stabilize the Cuban social order.

Given the deplorable state of the Guardia Rural in 1906, U.S. efforts naturally focused on rehabilitating it as the best way to secure a social stability that would preserve U.S. economic and strategic interests. Magoon ordered officers of the U.S. Army of Cuban Pacification to serve the Guardia Rural in various advisory capacities while Gen. J. Franklin Bell and a board of General Staff Corps officers carried out a review of the Guardia Rural's strengths and weaknesses.

These advisors—Maj. Herbert J. Slocum and Capts. Powell Clayton, Jr., James A. Ryan, George C. Barnhardt, Andrew J. Dougherty, Charles F. Crain, Cary I. Crockett, and Edmund Wittenmyer—attempted to transform the Guardia Rural from a police force hired to secure the political and economic interests of particular individuals into a professional organization capable of broadly defending "life, property, and individual liberty," the basic requirements of a stable capitalist social order. They recommended a substantial increase in the size of the force to 10,000 officers and men. They redistributed weapons and upgraded communications. They concentrated troops in fewer garrison outposts, increased supervision, and improved discipline, training, and morale. They initiated a program of regular patrols designed to establish an armed presence throughout the nation and to familiarize the Guardia with the surrounding countryside, its logistical possibilities, and political complexions. In effect, the force was being prepared to assume essential counterinsurgency responsibilities.

But leaders of the Liberal revolt against Estrada Palma—including Faustino Guerra, José de Jesus Monteagudo, Carlos García Velez, and Juan Gualberto Gómez—opposed the U.S. plan for reorganizing the Guardia. They doubted the force's capacity to extricate itself from political partisanship and distrusted its officer corps whom the provisional government reinstated despite its allegiance to the discredited Estrada Palma regime. Moreover, the Liberals sought to reward their political supporters and attract new recruits. Thus, they proposed the creation of a permanent army which would be responsible for national defense and the maintenance of public order.

Magoon's provisional government faced a dilemma. To approve the Liberal plan would empower a political constituency whose interests and objectives were not necessarily consistent with U.S. hegemony. To implement the U.S. plan would arouse widespread Cuban opposition and require a very expensive—both fiscally and politically—long-term U.S. military occupation of the island.

So the War Department set to work on a compromise plan approved by General Bell and authored by Maj. Frank McIntyre of the Bureau of Insular Affairs. After some discussion within the Advisory Law Commission, this proposal emerged on 4 April 1908 as a decree establishing the Armed Forces of Cuba.

It divided the Cuban military forces into two separate institutions: a rural guard and a permanent army, both of which were to adopt organizational structures recommended by the United States Army General Staff. The Guardia Rural would continue to implement earlier reforms, and the permanent army would receive extensive U.S. training. The Guardia Rural's authorized force levels would be increased by 700, but the combined force would not exceed 10,000 officers and men. Gen. Alejandro Rodríguez would continue to command the Guardia Rural, and General Guerra would assume command of the permanent army. Each would serve as a political check on the other. But both organizations were to pursue policies that served U.S. strategic objectives and protected the long-term class interests of private property, investment, and production in Cuba.

Keith A. Haynes

REFERENCES

Jules R. Benjamin, *The United States and Cuba: Hegemony and Dependent Development, 1880–1934* (Univ. of Pittsburgh Pr., 1977); David A. Lockmiller, *Magoon in Cuba: A History of the Second Intervention, 1906–1909* (Univ. of North Carolina Pr., 1938); Allan R. Millett, *The Politics of Intervention: The Military*

Occupation of Cuba, 1906–1909 (Ohio State Univ. Pr., 1968); Louis A. Pérez, Jr., *Army Politics in Cuba, 1898–1958* (Univ. of Pittsburgh Pr., 1976); Teresita Yglesia Martinez, *Cuba: primera republica, segunda intervencion* (Editorial de Ciencias Sociales, 1976).

See also Cuban Army, Establishment; Guardia Rural, Cuba.

The Cuban Bond "Conspiracy"

A mood of protest reform in the United States represented by the Populist and Bryanite revolts of the 1890s and a mood of assertive nationalism converged in 1898 into widespread suspicions of financial conspiracy. An elaborate theory developed among Silver Republicans, Bryanite Democrats, and Populists that Cuban bondholders, international bankers, and the William McKinley administration were conspiring to deprive the Cuban people of their freedom and to burden the United States with a substantial debt. The myths that developed inspired anti-imperialistic proclivities in Congress toward Cuba and expansionist aims toward the Philippines.

In spring 1898 a private poll of 4,000 editors told McKinley that his administration was seen very favorably. The only cloud on the Republican political horizon was the issue of the Cuban revolution against Spain that was taking so many lives on the island. Until the end of March 1898 McKinley hoped to reach a diplomatic resolution with Spain. Prominent Republicans in the House and the Senate supported the president's cautious policy.

Many Democrats by contrast were jingoistic. This was a substantial change from the party's views in 1896 and revealed the influence of Populists, such as Senator William V. Allen of Nebraska, the original congressional champion of Cuban independence. In 1896 the Populist convention had favored "free Cuba." After 1896, other Populist congressmen spoke on the subject, as did the six Silver Republican senators: Henry M. Teller of Colorado, Richard F. Pettigrew of South Dakota, Lee Mantle of Montana, Frank J. Cannon of Utah, and William M. Stewart and John P. Jones of Nevada. They were frustrated over the defeat in 1896 of William Jennings Bryan, and they looked to "free Cuba" as a new issue against the administration. They also became fearful that a financial conspiracy would attempt to forestall Cuban freedom and shackle U.S. citizens with a heavy debt transferred from the holders of Cuban bonds. These were bonds issued by Spain over the centuries to meet various colonial obligations and in the 19th century for costs of suppressing repeated insurrections.

Senator Stewart, who also published a prominent Washington bimetallic newspaper, charged that President McKinley and Speaker of the House Thomas B. Reed were blocking efforts at intervention because of the influence of "the money power." By March, Stewart came to fear that the "Wall Street assignees of the Republican party" might try to buy Cuba through a gigantic "bond deal," or, in case of war, to issue gold bonds instead of the bonds payable in silver that he and Senator Teller advocated. By late March, Democratic congressmen were making similar charges.

At this time Washington newspapers, such as the *Evening Times* and the *Post* conjured up a tale of conspiracy. Their raw material consisted of reports of congressmen, cabinet members, and other prominent visitors to the White House over the weekend of 26–27 March and of a dramatic rise in the value of the stock of the American Sugar Refining Company on 29 March. It is known today that McKinley consulted with the White House visitors over a Cuban relief bill and routine administrative matters and that some of them urged him to continue diplomatic negotiations with Spain. The increase in the price of sugar stock was probably due to market forces, a report the president intended to pursue peace, and an encouraging report on the money supply. But, at the time, pro-war editors and Bryanite congressmen charged that a clique of cabinet members was staging a bull raid.

A third story, in the Washington *Evening Times*, reported that an international syndicate had purchased $200 million of the Cuban bonds and that it would also buy Cuba for $200 million. The United States would presumably supervise the collection of funds to liquidate the debt. This paper and the *Washington Post* identified Col. John J. McCook as the central figure in the deal and as an opponent of Cuban independence. McCook was a prominent New York lawyer, a director of banks, insurance companies, and railroads, and had family connections to J.P. Morgan. A former Ohioan, he was close to the president, Senator Marcus A. (Mark) Hanna, and various members of the cabinet.

McCook had talked of a financial deal but did so with approval of the Cuban revolutionary junta, which he served as a legal advisor. He also helped the Cubans raise money, urged U.S. intervention in Cuba, argued that the Cuban bonds could not be charged against Cuba, and advocated immediate recognition of an independent republic of Cuba.

McKinley strongly disagreed with this last point. Moreover, although the president had several times explored the possibility of a financial deal, he had given up on the idea by 25 March 1898 because he had heard that Spain would not agree.

The Populists and Silver Republicans in Congress, however, introduced a resolution demanding the recognition of the "Republic of Cuba" in order to invalidate the Cuban bonds. Bryanite Democratic members followed suit, among them J. Hamilton Lewis of Washington who charged that the financiers had threatened McKinley that they would bring down the government if he did not follow their lead. Others argued that McKinley was part of the conspiracy. The Bryanite Omaha *World-Herald* fixed the chief blame on an insurance conglomerate and on Speaker Reed.

On 11 April the president asked Congress for authority, including the power to use military force, to halt the fighting in Cuba. He also argued vigorously against recognizing Cuban independence. Democratic, Populist, Silver Republican, and some other Republicans misunderstood his purpose. They argued that the "bond sharks" were at work, that Hanna was manipulating McKinley, and even that Catholic Archbishop John Ireland was the mastermind for the "Spanish bond conspirators."

McKinley and his supporters in Congress immediately turned back the effort to recognize Cuban independence (the Turpie-Foraker Amendment). But they gave way on a portion of an amendment introduced by Silver Republican Senator Teller—a qualifying clause that became known as the Teller Amendment.

Teller, an avowed expansionist who had long advocated annexing Cuba and Hawaii and later favored acquiring the Philippines, wanted to recognize Cuban independence because he believed this would invalidate the Cuban bonds. Congress accepted only his language disclaiming United States intent "to exercise sovereignty, jurisdiction or control" over Cuba. Teller's purpose was to prevent the United States from exercising legal authority over Cuba and from becoming a guarantor of the Cuban bonds or originator of new bonds. The Teller Amendment, which has gone into the history books as an idealistic statement, was actually the product of an expansionist senator and various other silverite members fearful of an imaginary bond conspiracy.

Later in 1898, the silverites feared a similar conspiracy involving the Philippines. Stewart then argued that there was no danger because Adm. George Dewey had conquered the islands and extinguished Spain's title.

Meanwhile, Spain had not given up its hopes of recovering some of its financial investments in Cuba and the Philippines. Spanish diplomats worked hard at the Paris Peace Conference to have the United States assume some responsibility for the debt or at least for certain legitimate obligations assumed with a transfer of sovereignty. They also proposed placing the subject of the entire debt before an arbitration tribunal. McKinley directed the U.S. commissioners that "under no circumstances will the Government of the United States assume any part of what is known as the Cuban debt."

Spanish Ambassador Fernando León y Castillo then gave up on the debt issue, but sought to have the United States pay something for the Philippines. The U.S. commissioners offered $20 million, a proposal Spain considered a "miserable sum" that covered only half of its obligations for the Philippines and would leave nothing for the Cuban debt. After intense internal debate and under U.S. pressure, Spain accepted the offer. The Treaty of Paris, moreover, explicitly limited the financial obligations of the United States with regard to Cuba "to the time of its occupancy thereof."

The Cuban bonds were a key practical issue for the United States and Spain. The bonds and the conspiracy theories about these obligations were also an important determinant of psychological attitudes, political alignments, and foreign policy statements in both countries before, during, and after the Spanish-Cuban/American War.

Paul S. Holbo

REFERENCES
Paul S. Holbo, "The Convergence of Moods and the Cuban-Bond 'Conspiracy' of 1898," *Journal of*

American History, 55 (1968), 54–72; John Stover, "Negotiating the 1898 Treaty of Paris: The British Connection," paper presented at Society for Historians of American Foreign Relations Conference, Washington, D.C., June 20, 1991.

See also Congress and the Spanish-Cuban/American War; Treaty of Paris (1898).

The Cuban Junta

The Cuban Junta was the active, notably visible fund-raising arm of the Cuban revolution in the United States. Like the revolution itself, the group proved to be remarkably durable. The revolt which began in October 1868 in the mountains of Oriente Province generated sympathy in the United States. The administration of Ulysses S. Grant in Washington remained formally committed to diplomatic ties with Spain, but nonetheless the Cuban Junta, an insurgent legation based in New York, had some success in raising funds. This in turn underwrote shipments of men and weapons to support the rebellion.

Predictably, the existence of the Junta led to various problems between the United States and Spain. An 1873 incident involved the boarding in international waters of the U.S. ship *Virginius*, originally a Civil War blockade runner, by the Spanish ship, the *Tornado*, and the capture and subsequent execution of members of the crew.

The Junta remained an influential, long-term lobby on behalf of the cause of Cuban independence through 1898, aided no doubt by congruence between this goal and the interests and opinions of a range of U.S. citizens.

Arthur Cyr

Cuban Revolt (1895–1898)

The Cuban revolt, beginning in 1895, may have been the first social revolution in modern Latin American history. Following several failed uprisings earlier in the century, Cuban creole planters had opted for autonomy within the Spanish empire. When Spain reneged on autonomy and on promised reforms, the autonomist cause was seriously weakened. Planters were questioning allegiance to Spain by 1895, and by February the war had begun anew for *Cuba Libré* (free Cuba). The struggle faltered in several provinces but held firm in Oriente Province, with its preponderantly black population. Planters wavered, many professing loyalty to Spain once

again. Autonomists denounced the rebellion as "criminal" and pleaded, fruitlessly, for reforms. Spain, as always, did not comply.

In April 1895, the Spanish government named Arsenio Martínez de Campos governor general of Cuba. He sought reconciliation through reform, which seemed possible at this juncture. Autonomist hopes were bolstered. But the Spanish cortes would not legislate reforms as long as Cuba was in rebellion. In Autumn 1895, the rebels marched west, disrupting harvest preparations. By early 1896, rebels were present in every province. The sugar harvest fell to less than a quarter of its 1894 level. As a result, economic collapse neared, with the prospect of unemployment. On one hand, autonomist hopes were dashed once again. On the other hand, conservatives blamed Martínez Campos, excoriating him for his search for a political solution and neglecting a military response.

The rebellion of 1895 differed substantially from all previous efforts. It benefited from careful planning and a high degree of unity among participating groups, stimulated by José Martí Julian y Perez's Partido Revolucionario Cubano (PRC) (Cuban Revolutionary Party), and it had a coherent ideology. As historian Louis A. Pérez has noted, a social imperative with much mass appeal was a part of that nationalist ideology. Revolutionary populism had taken shape, and the rebels spoke of a social transformation that would follow victory. The revolutionary program was left intentionally vague to avoid division. The result was a radical political movement of considerable force. Not only independence but a social revolution became the goal. New sectors were attracted, including displaced planters, professionals, farmers, ex-slaves, exiled workers, and the poor in general. As Máximo Gómez y Baez, one of the major leaders of the Cuban revolutionary movement, noted, it had become a "bottom up" revolt. About 40 percent of commissioned officers were men of color, and the PRC and the provisional government established by the revolutionaries had men of color in their leaderships.

Antonio Maceo, a black general, and second in command, estimated that by entering the West, the rebels added 10,000 men to their ranks. The number of regiments rose from 30 to 86, and the *pacíficos*, who supported the rebels, multiplied accordingly. Unfortunately for the rebels, the two heroic figures of the cause, Martí and

Maceo, were killed in 1895 and 1896, respectively. As Pérez has argued, until 1896 the conflict focused on sovereignty; after 1896, the struggle was for hegemony between the island's creole elite and the rebels' populist coalition. The defeat of the creole elite had become a necessity if Cuba was to attain independence. The geographical center of conflict moved to the central-west where the large sugar plantations were located. In the rebel view, it was no longer to be a war against the Spanish army. Instead, just as in modern guerrilla warfare, property and production were to be sabotaged. The colonial system would be ended by attacks on the sugar fields and the planters. In October 1895 the rebel general Máximo Gómez "outlawed" production, which was henceforth defined as treason. The new weapon of the social revolt became *la tea* (the torch). By April 1896, the rebel general Maceo had ordered all sugar estates destroyed. The planters faced calamity and, at first, hired armies of guards to defend their properties. But their ruin was inevitable. The result was economic hardship, even disaster, for all, not just the landlords. Planter debts mounted and led to the abandonment of estates. The rebels did not look on this as an unmitigated disaster; they contemplated the future division of the estates. A rebel decree of July 1896 promised land reform at the expense of loyalists and traitors, based on services rendered to the revolution.

Rebel successes produced a shock reaction in Spain. It was incumbent on the Spaniards to demonstrate that they could protect landowners from rebel depredations. The financial solvency of the colonial government was also at stake. The rebel strategy did not require victory, noted Pérez, but only to avoid losing. Spain responded with three important measures: it reorganized the army command, enlarged its forces to 200,000 men, and appointed Valeriano Weyler y Nicolau governor general. Weyler implemented a new and drastic strategy in late 1896; he responded to rebel destruction with a war on the peasantry, a "total war." The countryside would be forcibly evacuated; all *campesinos* (peasants) would become *reconcentrados*, residing henceforth in fortified towns under army control. The Spanish army occupied the countryside, destroying and plundering all small holdings. The rural population became refugees in their own country. The policy was ill-conceived and badly implemented. Town dwellers did not welcome these *campesinos* with

open arms. Tens of thousands died of epidemics and hunger. Weyler's policy was aimed at undermining rebel morale by dooming their families and relatives. The initial rebel response was to view Weyler as their best ally. By the end of 1896, there were some 50,000 rebels confronting roughly 200,000 Spanish troops. The latter were now lodged in cities or in fortified areas. The rebels controlled the depopulated countryside. The war had become a stalemate with both sides concentrating on destruction.

The political thrust of the Weyler regime was to restore unfettered Spanish rule. Large numbers of Cubans chose emigration. Autonomists were banished from government posts. Reaction was the official doctrine. All criticism was barred, and the government employed calculated terror. All activity by political parties was banned. Political prisoners were either jailed in Cuba or sent by the hundreds to the African colonies or to Cádiz, Spain. Creoles—planters and nonplanters alike—were caught in the middle. Moderates lost all faith in Spain as the repression of autonomists shocked creoles. By late 1897, even conservatives began to despair. Weyler, in desperation, ordered all cattle to the cities, in order to deny them to the rebels. He also prohibited the shipment of all tobacco leaf to Florida, where exiles made cigars and supported the rebellion. All rural-urban trade ceased, and labor for the sugar harvest vanished. As inflation mounted rapidly throughout 1897, it became apparent that Weyler had also failed. When Weyler printed paper currency, merchants rejected it and came under his persecution as well. There seemed no end to the protracted war, and autonomist exiles began joining separatist organizations abroad.

The Spanish government had itself become a threat to stability. The conservative consensus was collapsing in 1897. Spain had failed. The United States was seen by creole elites as the only viable alternative power that might offer its protection. President Grover Cleveland was petitioned by over 100 prominent creoles to intervene, and petitions became common as the war dragged on. The first petition for a "protectorate" was sent in December 1897. Even the Conservative party abandoned Spain and opted for U.S. assistance.

A Cuban victory seemed at hand in late 1897 and early 1898, as the rebel army prepared for an assault on the cities of the center and west.

Several cities in the East were already in rebel hands. By April 1898, Calixto García was ready to attack Santiago, and Spanish troops were abandoning smaller cities for the safety of provincial capitals. Máximo Gómez was confident that the end was at hand.

The U.S. administration was challenged by rebel gains and convinced that an independent Cuba in the hands of rebel leaders was inimical to U.S. interests. It recognized by early 1898 that Spain's cause was hopeless. U.S. planters in Cuba and U.S. sugar interests were chagrined at the thought of another ruined harvest. In April 1898, President William McKinley requested Congress to give him authority to intervene militarily. His message contained no mention of Cuban independence. The stated goal was to stop the war. He was proposing, in effect, a neutral intervention aimed at acquiring *de facto* sovereignty over Cuba. The United States would enter as a third force, as it were, hostile to both parties. Congressional supporters of *Cuba Libré* won a compromise: the Teller Amendment to the appropriation bill allowed McKinley to forgo a declaration of independence in exchange for a disclaimer of U.S. sovereignty over Cuba.

U.S. intervention altered everything, which was precisely its purpose. The U.S. figures disparaged Cuban rebel achievements and removed the Cuban Liberation Army from the front line. U.S. commanders showed ill-disguised disdain for the Cuban revolutionary leadership, especially its men of color, and denied the rebel army access to the cities, to positions of authority, and even to the Paris Peace Conference. The U.S. purpose was clear: to dictate unilateral peace terms with Spain, to determine who gained authority at the outset in the new Cuba, and to establish a claim on the supervision of future Cuban governments. The United States declared that the rebellion had "stalled" and that this had been not a Cuban revolution but a "Spanish-American War." As a result, the rebels lost their historic claim to sovereignty.

Harold Dana Sims

REFERENCES

Ramon de Armas, *La Revolucion Pospuesta* (Editorial de Ciencias Sociales, 1975); Philip S. Foner, *The Spanish-Cuban-American War and the Birth of American Imperialism* (Monthly Review Pr., 1972), 2 vols.; Araceli Garcia Carranza, ed., *Bibliografia de la Guerra de Independencia* (Editorial Orbe, Instituto Cubano del Libro, 1976); Louis A. Pérez, Jr., *Cuba Between Empires, 1878–1902* (Univ. of Pittsburgh Pr., 1983); Louis A. Pérez, Jr., *Cuba Between Reform and Revolution* (Oxford Univ. Pr., 1988), chap. 7.

See also Gómez y Báez, Máximo; Martí y Perez, José Julián; Weyler y Nicolau, Valeriano, Marques de Tenerife.

Cuban Revolt (1916)

The Cuban revolt of 1916 was in effect one violent incident in an ongoing series which defined, disrupted, and drove Cuban-U.S. relations during the last part of the 19th century and a good part of the early 20th century. Understanding this event is, therefore, directly useful to understanding broader relations between Cuba and the United States over time.

The summer of 1916 was highly turbulent, reflecting political instability and considerable alienation on the part of Cuban voters and political activists. The campaign for the reelection of the president, Gen. Mario García Menocal, was launched in January. The established Conservative party remained in office partly through active corruption; while the Liberal party was also guilty of widespread corruption, discontent among those out of power was reaching a peak.

Relative economic prosperity seemed only to fuel this discontent, providing confidence and resources to underwrite protest, as well as a reminder that major gaps remained between rich and poor.

The November 1916 elections brought victory for the ruling Conservatives, but only with considerable effort. García Menocal ensured that "military supervisors" would handle election rigging in various parts of the country. The voting process was accompanied by considerable violence. Three Conservative heads of election boards were shot. Gunfire at times seemed to be everywhere. Although there were only 500,000 eligible voters, a total of 800,000 ballots were cast. Only in December were the election results announced, affirming García Menocal in office.

The Liberals immediately protested and began planning another revolution. Information was gathered on Liberal supporters in the military. Violent actions, including burning sugar cane fields, were planned. José Miguel Gómez, a major opposition figure, and others worked to encourage Washington to intervene on the Liberals' behalf and also to stir revolt in the countryside. Two army commanders, in Camagüey and Santiago, opposed García Menocal.

The new administration of President Woodrow Wilson in Washington was ambivalent, and hence ambiguous in its communications. In mid-February 1917, the U.S. government declared foursquare in favor of constitutional governments and added that unconstitutional regimes should be opposed.

García Menocal had reacted to the Liberal revolt by moving to strengthen both his military and his political positions, solidifying his hold in Havana in particular. Liberals refused to participate in supplementary elections held in Santa Clara, opening the door to a smashing Conservative victory at the polls.

On 19 February another U.S. government communication condemned the Liberal revolt and stressed support for García Menocal's regime. The note stated that leaders of the attempted revolution would be held responsible for any property damage. Washington also sold the regime 10,000 rifles and a vast supply of ammunition. U.S. forces landed in Santiago on 8 March 1917. They were primarily valuable as a U.S. show of force.

Formal U.S. government support turned the tide in favor of García Menocal. Cuban government troops crushed the rebellion and leaders were jailed.

To some extent, U.S. actions and attitudes reflected preoccupation with events elsewhere. President Wilson and his government were pressured by a range of different developments connected with U.S. entry into World War I, which culminated in the U.S. declaration of war against Germany on 6 April 1917. To these policy makers in Washington, the actions of Liberals in Cuba seemed only to be helping the German cause. The result was that long-term U.S.-Cuban understanding was hurt, not helped.

Arthur Cyr

REFERENCES

Victor Hugo Gibean, Jr., "Relations of Cuba with the United States, 1916–1921," Ph.D. diss., Univ. of North Carolina, 1953; Leo J. Meyer, "United States and the Cuban Revolution of 1917," *Hispanic-American Historical Review*, 10 (1930), 138–166; Louis A. Pérez, Jr., *Intervention, Revolution, and Politics in Cuba, 1913–1921* (Univ. of Pittsburgh Pr., 1978); Robert Freeman Smith, *The United States and Cuba: Business and Diplomacy, 1917–1960* (Bookman Assoc., 1960).

See also Cuba, Intervention (1917–1922).

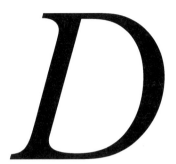

Dagu (Taku) Forts, China, Battle (1900)

The battle and capture of the Dagu (Taku) Forts in North China during the Boxer Uprising was of great importance in the campaign to liberate the besieged foreigners in the Beijing (Peking), China, legations because it was the starting line and the supply depot for the North China campaign that led to the capture of Tianjin (Tientsin) and later Beijing. It was also the first example of Treaty Power cooperation to maintain foreign privileges in China since 1860.

The problem confronting the Allied admirals at Dagu was how to maintain communications with and to protect their nationals in North China, especially in Beijing. Ultimately, if communications with their superiors in the capital were cut off they were supposed to restore them "and to resort to any and all means to accomplish this objective. If the Taku Forts were in the way, they must be taken out of the way" (Daggett, p. 15).

On 15 June 1900, after communications with the capital were cut off, the Allied admirals sent an ultimatum to the Chinese general commanding the forts stating that "if they were not evacu-

ated by midnight 16th June, the allied forces would bombard and storm them" (Dix, p. 25).

The forts at Dagu guarded the approaches to the city of Tianjin, one of the capital's ports of entry. There were four forts: two on the north side of the Bei (Pei) River and two on the south side. They were ideally sited for defense: the landward approaches were a flat plain intersected by numerous drainage canals and the seaward approach was dominated by a sandbar and mudflats stretching 11.5 miles out to sea. The Chinese were also aided by the narrowness and shallowness of the channel making escape virtually impossible if the attack failed. This meant the forts could be approached only by shallow-draft ships.

The assault in 1900 was the third time foreign powers made a landing under fire at Dagu. The first was in 1859. The Anglo-French expeditionary force was driven off in ignominious retreat, defeated by Chinese firepower and natural conditions. The British and the French returned the following year, captured the forts and the city of Tianjin, and proceeded to Beijing. Between 1860 and 1900 the forts were rebuilt and were well supplied with ordnance, ammunition, and supporting infantry.

The Allied admirals did not have to fight a naval battle to land troops. Before the expiration of the ultimatum, they moved their ships, torpedo boat destroyers, and gunboats into the river and occupied positions between the village of Dagu and the river's mouth. Their ships were deployed in a line-ahead column and were to provide gunfire support to the landing force that was to seize the forts. At the same time, to forestall the danger of a torpedo attack, two British and two Russian ships approached the Dagu Navy Yard to seize four Chinese torpedo boats there.

The assault started shortly before 1:00 a.m. Shell fire was quite intense because both the gunners in the forts and on the ships were firing at each other at point-blank range. When the firing started, the four Allied ships detailed to seize the torpedo boats at the Dagu Navy Yard secured them "after a trifling resistance and the exchange of a few shots" (Dix, pp. 36–37).

Simultaneously, the landing force was embarked and landed at about 2:30 a.m. The gunboats then bombarded the northwestern and the southern forts and blew up the latter's powder magazine about dawn. The ground assault on the northwestern fort then proceeded according to plan. After the seizure of the northern and the new forts, the Chinese evacuated the southern fort. By 7:00 a.m., the action was over.

This area provided the Allies with a secure, easily reinforceable bridgehead in North China. However, the ferocity of the Chinese resistance and the casualties inflicted on the gunboat crews gave the Allies pause. It was evident that the relief of the Beijing legations would be difficult. In fact, it was not known whether the foreigners in Tianjin and Beijing were still alive. Regardless of their status, it would be impossible to reach Tianjin, and then Beijing, without more men and supplies. All the seizure of the Dagu forts did or could do was to provide a starting place and a supply depot for the march to Tianjin and Beijing.

Lewis Bernstein

REFERENCES

"Capture of the Taku Forts by the Allied Forces, 17th June 1900," *United Service Magazine*, 28 (1903), 11–17; Aaron S. Daggett, *America in the China Relief Expedition: An Account of the Brilliant Part Taken by United States Troops in the Memorable Campaign in the Summer of 1900 for the Relief of the Besieged Legations in Peking, China* (Hudson-Kimberley, 1903); W. C. Davidson, "Operations in North China," *United States Naval Institute Proceedings*, 26 (1900), 637–646; C. C. Dix, *The World's Navies in the Boxer Rebellion (China 1900)* (Digby, Long, 1905); Myakishev, "The Capture of the Taku Forts," *Journal of the Royal United Service Institute*, 45 (1901), 730-744.

Daly, Daniel Joseph (1873–1937)

Daniel Joseph Daly was a career marine enlisted man who won the Medal of Honor during U.S. interventions.

Daly was born in Glen Cove, New York, on 11 November 1873. Although he stood only five feet, six inches and weighed 130 pounds, he won the Medal of Honor twice. Daly shunned publicity his entire life, and he rarely talked about his actions. As a result, many of the facts of his remarkable career are mixed with legend, and it is sometimes difficult to distinguish the difference.

Daly enlisted in the United States Marine Corps in January 1899 at age 26. In the spring of the following year he was assigned to the U.S. Legation Guard at Beijing, China. He won his first Medal of Honor during the 56-day siege by the Boxers. In the late afternoon of 13 July 1900 one flank of the U.S. defensive position became dangerously exposed when the Boxers drove a German unit from its position. To secure the flank until protective barricades could be erected, Private Daly volunteered to take a lone post on the Tartar Wall, about 100 yards in front of the marine's line. He spent the night in that exposed position and repelled numerous Boxer attacks. In the morning Daly was still there, and his position was surrounded with dead Boxers. Legend puts the number at 200—an exaggeration, but probably not by much.

After China, Daly served on a number of ships in the Pacific and Caribbean. One night in early 1911 he spotted a gasoline fire near the powder magazine on the USS *Springfield*. Daly put the fire out and saved the ship, but he was severely burned in doing so. That act of heroism brought him commendations from the secretary of the navy and the commandant of the Marine Corps. In 1914 Daly led a platoon of marines ashore at Veracruz, Mexico.

In 1915 the 42-year-old gunnery sergeant was sent to Haiti. On 22 October Daly accompanied a reconnaissance force of 27 marines sent into the interior of the island to locate Forts Dipitié and Capois, strongholds of the *Cacos*. The tiny force, commanded by Maj. Smedley D. Butler, was ambushed during a river crossing on the third day out. The marines got ashore without losing a man, but they lost 12 horses and the mule carrying their only machine gun. Butler formed his troops in a defensive perimeter on the far side of the river and dug in to repel attack from the 400 *Cacos*.

After darkness fell Daly slipped away from the position and returned to the river. The *Cacos* tried to ambush him along the way, but he killed several of them with his knife. When Daly reached the water he made repeated dives in the darkness to find the dead mule. Under fire from the *Cacos*, he cut away the machine gun and most of the ammunition. Once he got the 200-pound load on shore, he staggered with it a mile back through the jungle to the marine position, where he set up the machine gun in the dark. The following morning the marines attacked Fort Dipitié, using the machine gun for a base of fire. They killed 75 *Cacos* and scattered the rest without losing a man. Butler later recommended Daly for his second Medal of Honor.

Daly also fought in France in World War I as a first sergeant in charge of the 73rd Machine Gun Company of the 6th Marines.

On 10 June a German machine gun crew sneaked close to Daly's company and pinned it down. Characteristically, the 45-year-old Daly charged the Germans with hand grenades and a .45-caliber pistol. Daly was recommended for his third Medal of Honor—but higher authorities did not think it was right for any man to have three. Instead, Daly was awarded the Distinguished Service Cross, the Navy Cross, and the French *Medaille Militaire*.

Near the end of World War I Daly led one more attack during the Meuse-Argonne offensive. He was wounded in the shoulder and the leg, which ended his fighting career. He retired from active duty in 1919 and spent the rest of his life shunning publicity. He lived with his sister in New York City, where he worked as a bank guard. Daly died of a heart attack on 27 April 1937. During World War II, the navy named a destroyer after him.

David T. Zabecki

REFERENCES

Smedley D. Butler, "The 'Fightingest' Man I Know," *American Magazine*, 112 (Sept. 1931), 34–35, 82, 84; U.S. Congress, *Medal of Honor Recipients, 1863–1978* (U.S. Government Printing Office, 1979).

Dartiguenave, Philippe Sudre (1863–1926)

Born in 1863 in Anse-à-Veau in Sud Department, Haiti, Philippe Sudre Dartiguenave distinguished himself as a lawyer before entering the Haitian Senate in 1910. He was president of that body when the U.S. intervention occurred on 28 July 1915. Once it became clear that the U.S. government would not accept Dr. Rosalvo Bobo as Haiti's next president, Dartiguenave emerged as the candidate favored by the Haitian Senate and was duly elected on 10 August. A devout Catholic, dignified, cultured, and urbane, he was the first president since 1879 to come from Haiti's light-skinned southern elite.

The United States expected Dartiguenave to give it servile cooperation, but he resisted being a "puppet" president while strengthening control over what remained of the independent Haitian government. Forced to accept the Treaty of 1915, he protested vigorously when he realized that the officials appointed under it expected to dictate policy and to control all appointments. In April 1916 he dissolved the Senate and called on the deputies to serve as a constituent assembly to draw up a new constitution. Meeting the following year, the Assembly demonstrated its hostility toward the occupation by endorsing a charter directly counter to the known desires of the United States. Dartiguenave played a double game, subtly inciting the legislature to resist, while suggesting to U.S. authorities the desirability of suppressing that body and ruling with an appointed Council of State. The Haiti Constitution of 1918 that was eventually adopted by a rigged plebiscite contained such a provision and granted the president power to decide when legislative elections should take place. Subsequently, Dartiguenave postponed elections, ruling without a congress until his term expired in May 1922.

Ceaseless friction rather than constructive achievement marked Dartiguenave's seven-year administration. Criticism from the elites stymied judicial and educational reforms. The construction of highways provoked the peasants who, angered by widespread abuses of the *corvée* (a compulsory system for labor service), joined in the Caco rebellion of 1918–1920. Contributing to the lack of progress was the chaotic condition of Haiti's finances. Under U.S. control the nation defaulted on interest as well as on amortization payments on its foreign debt, and lower coffee imports by France during World War I aggravated the situation. No loan could be had until a settlement was reached with the national bank, and even when a claims protocol and loan agreement were finally negotiated in 1919, Dartiguenave delayed their execution. In 1920 he clashed with the U.S. legation and with financial advisor John A. McIlhenny by promulgating several laws against their wishes and by refusing to approve a new charter for the national bank recently acquired by the National City Bank of New York. To force compliance, McIlhenny stopped payment of the salaries of the president, his cabinet, and Council of State. Grudgingly, Dartiguenave rescinded the objectionable laws, but he was adamant about the bank charter and refused to authorize any loan contract signed by McIlhenny.

Dartiguenave protested frequently to Washington about the intransigence of U.S. officials, but President Woodrow Wilson paid little heed to his appeals. The Haitian leader sent a letter to Warren G. Harding on the day of his inauguration, urging that the Treaty of 1915 be given "a thorough and loyal execution," that the military occupation be withdrawn as soon as possible, and that U.S. officials be prevented from interfering in the administration of judicial matters. Harding was impressed with the letter but sent a noncommittal reply on 12 April. Later that year after holding exhaustive hearings on U.S. activities in Haiti, a U.S. Senate committee recommended the naming of a U.S. high commissioner with plenipotentiary powers to supervise all treaty officials. Harding accepted this recommendation, and in January 1922 he appointed Gen. John H. Russell to the new post.

Dartiguenave was eager for reelection, but he lacked Haitian support and was on bad terms with U.S. authorities as well. When he announced his candidacy, Russell refused to endorse him, and the Port-au-Prince press was fervent in stating its objections. A vote by the Council of State on 10 April 1922 produced only four ballots out of 21 for the president even though he had packed that body with his own sympathizers. Bowing to the inevitable, he withdrew

from the contest, allowing the election of his rival, Joseph Louis Borno. He retired to his native town of Anse-à-Veau, where he died in 1926.

Jane M. Rausch

REFERENCES

Dantes Bellegard, *Histoire du peuple haitien, 1492–1952* (Port-au-Prince, 1953); David Healy, *Gunboat Diplomacy in the Wilson Era: The U.S. Navy in Haiti, 1915–1916* (Univ. of Wisconsin Pr., 1976); Ludwell Lee Montague, *Haiti and the United States, 1714–1938* (Duke Univ. Pr., 1940); Dana G. Munro, *The United States and the Caribbean Republics, 1921–1933* (Princeton Univ. Pr., 1971).

See also Treaty of 1915: United States-Haiti.

Davis, Richard Harding (1864–1916)

For a quarter century, a generation in the United States viewed reporter and novelist Richard Harding Davis as the *beau ideal* of war correspondents.

In 1896 Davis covered the Cuban revolution against Spain and was converted to the cause of U.S. intervention. In "The Death of Rodriquez," he reported a young rebel's execution, an eloquent tribute that swayed readers in favor of *Cuba Libré*.

Following the U.S. declaration of war on Spain in April 1898, the government offered Davis a captaincy in the army. He declined in favor of going to the front as representative of the *New York Herald* and *Scribner's Magazine*.

Davis attached himself to Theodore Roosevelt's Rough Riders. During the regiment's first fight at Las Guásimas, Cuba, on 24 June, in defiance of his correspondent's status, he became so caught up in the fighting that he fired on the enemy, in addition to acting as a corpsman and scout. In the attack on San Juan Hill and Kettle Hill, Davis again charged the Spaniards. In the aftermath, Roosevelt made him an honorary member of the Rough Riders, as much for his glowing dispatches as for his help in combat. Following the surrender of Santiago, Davis transferred to Puerto Rico where he witnessed Gen. Nelson A. Miles's rapid conquest of the island.

Davis later covered the Boer and Russo-Japanese wars, as well as the early fighting in World War I.

Richard H. Bradford

REFERENCES

Richard Harding Davis, *The Cuban and Puerto Rican Campaigns* (Scribner, 1898); Charles Belmont Davis, ed., *Adventures and Letters of Richard Harding Davis* (Scribner, 1917); Fairfax Downey, *Richard Harding Davis, His Day* (Scribner, 1933), 144–163; Arthur Lubow, *The Reporter Who Would be King: A Biography of Richard Harding Davis* (Scribner, 1992); Scott Osborn and Robert L. Phillips, Jr., *Richard Harding Davis* (Twayne, 1978), 73–77.

Day, William Rufus (1849–1923)

William Rufus Day, a lawyer and close personal friend of President William McKinley, served as secretary of state from 28 April 1898 to 16 September 1898. He was born in Ravenna, Ohio, where his father, Luther Day, was a prominent jurist who served as chief justice of the Ohio Supreme Court. Educated at the University of Michigan, where he graduated in 1870, Day spent a year studying law before his admission to the Ohio bar in 1872. He began practice in Canton, Ohio, and there he became acquainted with McKinley, then the county prosecutor, and established a lasting friendship with him.

Successful in his profession, in which he was known for his reasoned oratory and extensive knowledge of law, Day was elected judge of the Court of Common Pleas in 1886. In 1889 he was appointed U.S. district judge for northern Ohio by President Benjamin Harrison, but because of frail health, a problem throughout his long life, he resigned before taking office. Day maintained a successful private practice and was a confidential legal, financial, and political advisor to McKinley while McKinley served in Congress and as governor of Ohio.

Day refused McKinley's offer of an appointment as U.S. attorney general following McKinley's election to the presidency in 1896. In April 1897, he agreed to serve as assistant secretary of state to John Sherman of Ohio, a former senator, whose failing mental and physical condition caused the president considerable distress. Although he had no formal training in diplomacy, Day was familiar with international law and knew national politics. He held the complete trust and confidence of the president. Furthermore, he quickly demonstrated discretion, tact, and organizational skills that enabled him to serve effectively during a time of crisis.

In his seventies, Sherman was appointed to the cabinet to allow McKinley's political bene-factor, Marcus A. (Mark) Hanna, to be appointed to the vacant seat in the United States Senate. It soon became apparent that Sherman was failing physically and mentally. Fortunately, the senior staff in the Department of State, in particular the meticulous but nearly deaf Alvey A. Adee, covered up for the frequently forgetful secretary. Still, foreign policy was on occasion handled unprofessionally, leading one critic to observe that "The head of the department knows nothing; the first assistant says nothing, the second assistant hears nothing" (McLean, p. 33). Even Day became frustrated with the situation, remarking to a friend, "I see that the newspapers talk about the diplomacy of this administration as 'amateurish,' and I must confess that it is" (Shippe and Way, p. 29).

Day soon began attending cabinet meetings with the secretary and was in direct communication with the president on all important issues related to the Department of State. Among Day's duties as assistant secretary was the drafting of a treaty to annex the Hawaiian Islands. This task Day assigned to former Secretary of State John W. Foster, who had been involved in the annexation effort in 1893. Sherman was either uninformed or simply forgot about Foster's role and his behind-the-scenes work with Hawaiian treaty commissioners in Washington. When Sherman assured the Japanese minister that there was nothing to the rumor of a new effort to annex Hawaii just as the treaty was being presented to the Senate, the Japanese, already concerned about the treatment of immigrants from their country in Hawaii, lodged a protest, which was later withdrawn. Day was also deeply involved in all matters related to the deteriorating relationship with Spain over the situation in Cuba, and he frequently received correspondence directly from Minister Stewart L. Woodford in Madrid and Consul General Fitzhugh Lee in Havana. Day also met directly with the Spanish minister to the United States, Enrique Dupuy de Lôme, during the crucial months of January and February 1898, when Lee was reporting that efforts to provide Cuba with autonomy were doomed and that rioting in Havana seemed to indicate that Spain could not control the situation. The assistant secretary also met directly with Dupuy de Lôme to arrange for the battleship *Maine* to visit Havana on a goodwill visit. Day likewise handled the recall of Minister Dupuy de Lôme following the public exposition of a personal letter Dupuy de Lôme had written the previous December in which he criticized McKinley as "weak and a popularity hunter."

Following the explosion of the *Maine* on 15 February, Day worked closely with leaders in congress and reported directly to the president on efforts to find a solution, short of war, to the crisis with Spain. However, both he and the president became increasingly suspicious of Spanish intentions and distrustful of proposals for mediation by the European powers and the pope. Meanwhile, pressure for the administration to take action against Spain mounted in Congress and in the press. In late March, Day informed Minister Woodford that the United States would not consider purchasing the island from Spain, an idea the minister had put forth, and stated emphatically, "We do not want Cuba." Day also made it clear to Woodford that the administration rejected any Spanish authority over Cuba and considered "full self-government with indemnity would mean Cuban independence."

Four days after the outbreak of the war, and following an embarrassing loss of memory in conversation with the Austrian minister, Secretary Sherman, who opposed any acquisition of foreign territory and was distressed at the prospect of war, resigned his office on 25 April. Day took the office three days later, Adee serving as acting secretary in the interim. Although he had been performing many of the duties of secretary of state for nearly a year, Day seemed to have no ambition to hold cabinet rank. It appears that he accepted the secretaryship only with the understanding that he would depart once the crisis of war had ended.

During his brief tenure, Day skillfully managed to maintain the neutrality of the European powers. He also directed the successful efforts to secure the annexation of Hawaii through a joint resolution in Congress, while keeping Japanese and European protests against this action at a minimum. When in summer 1898 the French ambassador in Washington, Jules M. Cambon, served as intermediary and proposed a cessation of hostilities between Spain and the United States, Day made U.S. terms known to Spain on 30 July and directed the drafting of the protocol, which was signed on 12 August.

On 1 September 1898 Day announced his resignation from the cabinet to serve as head of the U.S. commission appointed to make peace with Spain. He was succeeded by John Hay, then the ambassador to Great Britain. As a member of the commission, Day tended to mediate between those who desired the complete cession of the Philippines (Whitelaw Reid, publisher of the *New York Tribune* and former ambassador to France; and Republican Senators Cushman K. Davis of Minnesota and William P. Frye of Maine) and Democratic Senator George Gray of Delaware, who opposed acquisition of any part of the islands. Day, by holding that the United States had made no conquest that justified a demand for cession from Spain and, as an ethical nation, would not seek territory through conquest, opened the way for a provision in the treaty under which the United States would purchase the islands from Spain for $20 million.

Day won praise for his service as secretary of state because of his diligence and skill. Day, said McKinley, "Never made a single mistake." Members of the peace commission commended him for his negotiating skills. Reid noted that "Judge Day, in particular, has shown great clearness, precision of view, and well-balanced judgment." Gray was also generous in his praise, declaring "No State in this Union could have contributed . . . a mind and a character more equipoised, settled, clear and strong than was contributed by Ohio when she sent that quiet, sensible, strong statesman William R. Day to Paris to conclude the treaty of peace."

Upon his return from the work of the peace commission, Day was appointed to the United States Court of Appeals for the Sixth Circuit, succeeding William H. Taft. In 1903 President Theodore Roosevelt appointed Day to the United States Supreme Court, where he served until 1922 when he resigned to become umpire in the Mixed Claims Commission selected to judge claims of U.S. citizens against Germany. He resigned because of poor health in 1923 and died at his summer home in Mackinac Island, Michigan, the same year.

Always a frail man, Day was quiet, courteous, and scholarly. Reserved and dignified, but not without a keen sense of humor, he avoided participation in strenuous activity and all sports. However, he was an avid baseball fan and was known to have staff assistants report up-to-the-minute World Series scores to him even while sitting in session on the nation's highest court.

Michael J. Devine

REFERENCES

Dictionary of American Biography, s.v. "Day, William R."; Joseph E. McLean, *William R. Day: Supreme Court Justice from Ohio* (Johns Hopkins Univ. Pr., 1946); Louis Martin Sears, "John Sherman," *American Secretaries of State and Their Diplomacy*, ed. by Samuel Flagg Bemis (Cooper Square, 1963), vol. 9, 1–23; Lester B. Shippee and Royal B. Way, "William R. Day," *American Secretaries of State and Their Diplomacy*, vol. 9, 25–112.

See also Peace Commission (1898); Treaty of Paris (1898).

Dewey, George (1837–1917)

On 1 May 1898, as dawn was breaking across the gleaming waters of Manila Bay in the Philippines, Commodore George Dewey began military operations in the Spanish-Cuban/American War by turning to Capt. Charles V. Gridley and saying, "You may fire when you are ready, Gridley" (Dewey, p. 214). That moment put the United States on a course which would take it to the pinnacle of empire and world power. For Dewey it was a turning point in a career that began in the years preceding the Civil War.

Born on 26 December 1837 in Montpelier, Vermont, Dewey was the son of a prosperous physician and businessman, who made a profound impression on him. Determined to have a military education, Dewey was disappointed to learn that appointments to both service academies were filled. His father, Julius Dewey, appealed to political friends for consideration as a substitute, and when an appointee backed out, Dewey was named the substitute by Senator Solomon Foote.

Entering the United States Naval Academy in 1854, Dewey spent four years at Annapolis amassing a record of adequate scholarship tempered with disciplinary infractions. Nothing in his academy record indicated any extraordinary expectation for the young officer. Graduating in 1858, Dewey later spoke of his time at Annapolis as pure "hell" and was not unhappy to leave it.

Dewey filled a billet aboard the *Wabash* bound for Europe as flagship of the Mediterranean Squadron. During the next three years, he served on the *Wabash*, the *Powhatan*, and the *Pawnee*, learning the craft of seamanship and becoming acquainted with the diplomatic responsibilities of officers in naval service. These years served

Dewey well, giving him experience in the world of diplomacy and taking him to ports of call throughout Europe. In 1861 he returned to Annapolis to take the examination for lieutenant and receive his first leave.

While in Montpelier, word reached Dewey that Fort Sumter had been attacked and that war had begun with the South. He left immediately for his new assignment, the *Mississippi*, a veteran of the Mexican War and Matthew Perry's voyage to Japan eight years earlier. The *Mississippi* left Boston in May 1861 heading for the Florida Keys, where it took up blockading duties. During the rest of the year Dewey and his ship conducted operations against Confederate forces along the Gulf coastal area.

On the morning of 24 April 1862 the *Mississippi* received orders to follow the *Cayuga* and the *Pensacola* in the first division in an early morning strike up the Mississippi river as part of the attack on New Orleans. Adm. David G. Farragut's strategy was to bypass the rebel gun positions and to attack New Orleans. He hoped to get his fleet past the forts without having to take the two positions, which would require too much ammunition and take valuable time.

The *Mississippi* captain, Melancthon Smith, ordered Dewey to take the conn, explaining that his night vision was not good.

During the ensuing action, Dewey saw the Confederate ram *Manassas* appear nearby and ordered his ship to change course to intercept and ram the rebel vessel. The Confederate captain, seeing that the collision would be fatal for his ship, quickly ordered a change of course.

As morning broke the *Manassas* was again sighted astern of the fleet moving determinedly to stop the Union attack. Smith was back on the bridge when the flagship *Hartford* appeared with Farragut hanging out of the rigging screaming to Smith to attack the ram. Smith turned to Dewey and asked him if he thought he could turn the ship around so Smith could get an angle on the ram. Dewey replied in the affirmative, later confessing that he did not have the slightest idea whether or not he could.

Dewey maneuvered the *Mississippi* around, forcing the Confederate captain to avoid the fatal collision by running the ram on the river bank.

Dewey received valuable commendations from Smith in reports to Farragut and the Navy Department. Perhaps more importantly, the experience made a permanent impression on Dewey. He confessed that in the early morning hours of his approach to Manila Bay, he was thinking of Farragut and those tension-filled hours below New Orleans three decades earlier, wondering what Farragut would do in his place. During the rest of the Civil War, Dewey continued his service on the Mississippi River and along the Gulf coast, bringing him new combat opportunities, commendations, and promotion. He ended the war in blockade duty on the North Carolina coast at the rank of a lieutenant commander.

In the first 10 years of postwar service, Dewey served as flag lieutenant to Adm. Louis M. Goldsborough in the European Squadron and taught at Annapolis. He enjoyed an advantage over many of his classmates after the war: his promotion in 1865 to lieutenant commander gave him a head start on many of them who were still lieutenants and lieutenant commanders in the 1890s. In addition, his father's financial position enabled him to endure long years of slow promotion and small naval budgets in relative comfort.

In 1875 Dewey was ordered to Washington, D.C., to serve as a member of the Lighthouse Board. This began a long tenure of service in Washington where Dewey made the most of social and political opportunities. After seven years on the Lighthouse Board, Dewey commanded the sloop *Juniata* bound for assignment to the Asiatic Station. During the voyage, Dewey became ill and was hospitalized at Malta for what at first appeared to be a fatal disorder. After a two-year recovery he returned to take command of the *Dolphin* in 1884 which was still under construction. Delays in commissioning the ship led Dewey to request another command.

Dewey commanded the *Pensacola*, flagship on the European Station, for the next four years before returning to Washington as chief of the Bureau of Equipment. His leadership in the bureau came at a time when the navy was undergoing a dramatic change. New technology was applied to the construction of a fleet based on steel-hulled, steam-powered ships. Dewey oversaw the incorporation of innovative applications into the new emerging fleet. His administrative expertise brought together radical, impulsive, impatient technocrats and the intransigent, traditional, conservative leadership in the navy. Under Dewey's leadership, the bureau was successful

in assimilating many of the new inventions, while cushioning much of the opposition of the more orthodox officers.

In 1895 Dewey became president of the Board of Inspection and Survey. Continuing his service in Washington, Dewey won promotion to commodore soon after his appointment and became eligible for command of a squadron at the first vacancy. By fall 1897 Dewey was aware that the first vacancy would occur in the Asiatic Squadron and realized the importance of such a command if relations with Spain continued to deteriorate. President William McKinley and Secretary of the Navy John D. Long were concerned that if war with Spain occurred, Spanish naval forces in the Philippines would endanger U.S. operations against the Spanish in Cuban waters. Both McKinley and Long wanted a commander of the Asiatic Squadron who would be aggressive and would prevent the Spanish fleet in the Philippines from reinforcing the Spanish fleet in the Caribbean.

Dewey turned to Assistant Secretary of the Navy Theodore Roosevelt. Roosevelt liked and championed Dewey for the assignment. Commodore John A. Howell also wanted the post and enjoyed support within the political arena. Roosevelt warned Dewey that Howell had the inside track and suggested that Dewey use every political contact he could marshal. With the help of Vermont Senator Redfield Proctor, Dewey won the assignment, arriving in Japan in early January 1898 to command the small fleet.

Dewey moved the fleet to Hong Kong and began making preparations for war. He received an ominous telegram from Roosevelt, acting secretary of the navy for one day, warning Dewey that hostilities were imminent. Dewey acquired two small vessels to serve as supply ships, instituted a training program for crews, and purchased provisions adequate for operations against the Philippines.

On 23 April British authorities in Hong Kong ordered the U.S. fleet out of British waters in compliance with neutrality statutes. It was Dewey's first notice that the nation was at war. Moving to Mirs Bay, China, he received official word from Long on 25 April that the United States was at war with Spain. Long ordered Dewey to sail against the fleet in the Philippines and "capture vessels or destroy." After receiving intelligence on the Spanish fleet from the U.S. consul at Manila, Dewey sailed for the Philippines on 27 April, arriving off Bataan three days later. His fleet included four protected cruisers, two gunboats, one collier, one transport steamer, and one revenue cutter.

After making sure the Spanish fleet was not at Subig Bay, Dewey ordered the transoceanic cable cut and moved his fleet into the Boca Grande Passage near Corregidor. Confident that the Spanish waited for him in Manila Bay, Dewey ordered his ships to slow down so they would arrive off the city of Manila during the hours of darkness. After making a sweep of the city's wharf, Dewey altered course to starboard finding the Spanish fleet off Cavite. The Spanish admiral, Patricio Montojo y Pasarón, placed his ships so that he could take advantage of gun support from batteries at Cavite and carefully kept the city of Manila out of the line of fire.

At 5:40 a.m. Dewey opened fire with the U.S. fleet making five passes across the front of the Spanish ships. At 7:30 a.m. Dewey ordered a cease-fire and a temporary withdrawal from the range of Spanish guns. His captains had sent an erroneous report that their ships were low on ammunition. While Dewey met with his captains, the U.S. crews ate breakfast and rested from the morning's arduous activities. At 11:16 a.m. Dewey attacked again, pouring an unrelenting fire against the Spanish ships. By 12:30 p.m. the battle was over, and the Spanish ships lay sunk or burning, the surviving Spaniards scrambling to reach shore. Dewey's victory signaled the end of the Spanish fleet in the islands, which had losses of seven ships and 370 men killed. Dewey lost no ships and no men to enemy action, although one man died from heat exhaustion.

Dewey had completed his mission to eliminate the threat from the Spanish fleet, but he could not take the Philippines or even begin offensive operations ashore. His small force had to wait for army reinforcements to arrive later in the summer before the islands could begin to be secured. In August Manila surrendered, and an uneasy peace fell over the archipelago until the Treaty of Paris ended the war in December. Dewey remained in the islands only months longer, leaving for a hero's welcome in May 1899 as the nation's only admiral of the navy. Congress created the new rank for Dewey one week after the Battle of Manila Bay.

Dewey's arrival in the United States triggered an almost universal expression of support for the admiral. "Deweymania" brought offers of speeches, gifts, and even a proposed presidential nomination. Dewey was mystified by the attention, and eventually the public grew impatient with his ineffective responses and apparent indifference, leaving Dewey to ponder over a public angry at an ungrateful hero. While Dewey's public image grew tarnished, perhaps his most important contribution to the navy began in 1900 when he assumed the post of president of the newly formed General Board of the Navy.

Under President Theodore Roosevelt, the board initiated studies and made recommendations on questions relating to naval construction, personnel expansion, naval bases, strategy and war plans, and the role the navy would play in the emerging empire. In the years before World War I Dewey dominated naval planning as the United States became more concerned with growing tension in the world and anxious to take its place as a major world power.

In 1902 Dewey faced his first important crisis when Britain, Italy, and Germany blockaded Venezuela over a debt default. Roosevelt ordered Dewey to take personal command of U.S. training exercises then underway in the area, hoping the veiled threat would have effect. Over the years Dewey had gained the reputation for hating the Germans, and Roosevelt hoped that Dewey's presence with the fleet would force the Germans to back down. Tension eventually dissipated, although it is difficult to assess the role Dewey's presence played in ending the crisis. At least three important consequences resulted from the crisis. First, the navy emerged from the incident appearing able to enforce U.S. policy at will, gaining for itself essential goodwill and popular support in future budget battles in Congress. Second, Roosevelt demonstrated an aggressive foreign policy in Latin America and confirmed that the Monroe Doctrine was to be enforced through U.S. military and political power. Third, Dewey found his public reputation renewed.

During the next few years, the General Board under Dewey's leadership debated questions of fleet preparedness, deployment strategy, the creation of a battleship fleet and other ambitious building programs, reorganization of the Navy Department, naval bases in the Pacific, and war plans.

In 1916 reporter George Creel interviewed Dewey for the New York *World*. In the published interview, Dewey rebutted critics who charged that the navy was inefficient, demoralized, lacked a focused leadership, and was insufficient to meet the demands placed on it by the nation. In his statement, Dewey argued that the navy in 1916 was as efficient as it had been in any other era. Equipment and new technology made the navy and its ships more efficient and capable of completing its mission than at any other time in history. He contended that "our officers are as good as any, and our enlisted men are the finest in the world." The interview was Dewey's last public pronouncement and his last attack on what he saw as his greatest opponents: critics of the navy. On 11 January 1917 Dewey became bedridden, complaining of chest and back pains. Over the next several days, Dewey's condition worsened, and on 16 January 1917 he died.

Dewey's death concluded six decades of service to the navy from the Civil War to World War I. During his tenure as a flag officer, the United States had acquired an empire, and the navy had assumed a larger mission in protecting U.S. interests abroad. Dewey's aggressive leadership and commitment to change and modernization ensured that the navy completed the transition from 19th-century navy to a modern 20th-century naval force capable of enforcing U.S. policy anywhere in the world.

Vernon L. Williams

REFERENCES

George Dewey, *Autobiography of George Dewey: Admiral of the Navy* (Scribner, 1913); Laurin Hall Healy and Luis Kutner, *The Admiral* (Ziff-Davis, 1944); Ronald Spector, *Admiral of the New Empire: The Life and Career of George Dewey* (Louisiana State Univ. Pr., 1974); Vernon L. Williams, "George Dewey: Admiral of the Navy," in James C. Bradford, ed., *Admirals of the New Steel Navy: Makers of the American Naval Tradition, 1880–1930* (U.S. Naval Institute Pr., 1990); Vernon L. Williams, "The U.S. Navy in the Philippine Insurrection and Subsequent Native Unrest, 1898–1906," Ph.D. diss., Texas A&M Univ., 1985.

See also Manila Bay, The Philippines, Naval Battle (1898).

Disarmament of the Moros

Disarmament was one of the policies colonial powers tried to realize in the non-Christian areas of the Philippine archipelago. Only U.S. rule succeeded in achieving a measure of disarmament during the turbulent first decade of the 20th century. Several factors were responsible for effective U.S. enforcement of disarmament, especially in Moroland where it was a serious, persistent problem. First, U.S. diplomacy separated a number of influential *datus* (chiefs) and sultans with their followers or subjects from the recalcitrants, thus limiting the disarmament campaigns to the latter group. In fact, in Sulu, Cotabato, and Lanao the sultanates were supportive or, at least, neutral toward U.S. efforts to subdue the defiant *datus* and their men. The three governors of the Moro Province, Leonard Wood, Tasker H. Bliss, and John J. Pershing, pursued disarmament against the Moros, but the increasing seriousness of the disturbances, uprisings, and individual attacks on persons and properties, especially U.S. citizens and their property, necessitated the strongest possible enforcement of disarmament policies. Particularly noteworthy were the Hassan uprising (1903–1905), the Bud Daju battle (1906), the Jikiri depredations (1907–1909), the Subanun Buburan incident (1909), and the numerous challenges to peace and order in Jolo (1911). The same situation was also found in Cotabato where Datu Ali (1903) and Datu Alamada (1911–1912) were leading opponents of the colonial authorities, as well as in the Lanao lake region where several *datus* and sultans, such as Sajiduciman, Ganduli, Tanagan, and Ampuanagus were leading several pocket uprisings.

Consequently, on 8 September 1911 Pershing issued Executive Order No. 24 of the Moro Province which gave more teeth to the earlier 1908 Act No. 221 of the Legislative Council. The executive order was more comprehensive and punitive. It banned the possession, acquisition, and carrying of firearms of whatever kind and bladed weapons of whatever type without the permission and/or authorization of the governor. This order gave Pershing such vast powers of government in Moroland that he could apprehend any Moro with arms or weapons. He could also induce the *datus* to apply to U.S. authorities, especially the governor, for the privilege of keeping their arms upon proper registration. However, the order, as a new basis of disarmament, also pushed the recalcitrants to the other extreme— open and violent challenge to colonial rule. This was what occurred in the eastern part of the Jolo Island, specifically in the communities of Lati and Luuk. The series of outbreaks, which inflicted more casualties on U.S. troops than elsewhere in Moroland, but which also resulted in thousands of Tausugs killed, culminated in the decisive battle of Bud Bagsak in 1913.

Although criticism in the United States was severe because of the cost in lives of Moro disarmament, the campaigns resulted in the capture and surrender of 5,861 firearms in Sulu by 14 October 1913. Undoubtedly, this was a significant cache of arms in the history of the Moro campaigns and a serious blow to the Sulu Moros' capacity to resist after 1913. The relative peace in the following period proved that disarmament was the best policy for Moroland.

Samuel K. Tan

REFERENCES

Peter G. Gowing, *Mandate in Moroland: The American Government of Muslim Filipinos, 1899–1920* (Univ. of the Philippines, 1977); Donald Smythe, "Pershing and the Disarmament of the Moros," *Pacific Historical Review*, 31 (1962), 241–256.

Dodge Commission

See War Department Investigating Commission.

Dominican Republic, Occupation (1916–1924)

The United States was gradually drawn into the affairs of the Dominican Republic, through financial supervision and customs receiverships, until U.S. troops landed on 15 May 1916. Under the administration of President Woodrow Wilson, the United States assumed full control of the nation, seeking to end political turmoil and impose financial and political stability. U.S. authorities encountered a complex situation and considerable resistance to the occupation regime. Washington decision makers had little understanding of Dominican politics, and eventually the occupation became a controversial political issue in the United States during the election of 1920.

Initially, U.S. involvement resulted more from concerns about protecting the Caribbean from potential European bases than from interest in the Dominican Republic itself. The United States had long perceived the potential of Samaná Bay as a naval base, seeking to gain control of the bay as early as 1869. Although efforts to arrange a lease failed, the United States remained firmly committed to eventual use of the bay and in particular to preventing its use by any European power, citing the Monroe Doctrine as justification. This attitude led to the establishment of a series of financial protectorates throughout the Central American and Caribbean region, and in several cases to armed intervention, extending throughout the administrations of Theodore Roosevelt, William H. Taft, and Wilson.

A financial protectorate in 1905 and a treaty in 1907, established as part of the United States's extension of U.S. power into the Caribbean under the Roosevelt Corollary to the Monroe Doctrine, constituted the initial steps for direct U.S. involvement in Dominican government operations. Under these arrangements, the United States assumed control of the collection and disbursement of customs revenue, the nation's principal source of funds, in order to guarantee the payment of foreign loans and to prevent European intervention. A U.S.-appointed customs administrator collected and disbursed the funds, stemming losses from corruption and assuring payments to foreign lenders. This procedure provided the Dominican government with more revenue than it had previously received. The United States viewed this as a mutually beneficial arrangement, although the Dominicans felt that foreign control of their government's principal source of income restricted their government's ability to make decisions. Dominicans considered the resulting U.S. right of approval over the nation's major expenses an infringement on their sovereignty.

U.S. involvement increased due to a political deadlock in the Dominican Republic which resulted in governmental instability. The United States firmly believed that elections would solve all problems in all nations and was convinced that providing fair elections and maintaining respect for their outcome were essential for all governmental functioning. U.S. authorities were unable to understand the system of personalistic leadership through a *caudillo* (strongman) system, which prevailed in the Dominican Republic.

During the early 20th century two strong parties, each following its own strongman, dominated the Dominican Republic. The two factions were the Jimenistas, followers of Juan Isidro Jiménez, and the Horacistas, followers of Horacio Vásquez. At the national level the two groups split every vote, assuring that elections did not yield clear results. Fraud was always suspected, and each party rejected the results of any election won by the other. To the United States, this amounted to anarchy. Beyond the Dominican capital, the situation was even more complex. The entire nation was controlled by a series of local strongmen who ran the interior regions as fiefdoms. These factions were too powerful to be challenged by any regime; thus, the so-called national government controlled only the capital.

Consequently, politics in the Dominican Republic consisted of a constantly shifting set of alliances among regional *caudillos* and the leaders of the parties in the capital city of Santo Domingo. Governmental changes in the capital reflected revolutions and shifting political alliances, which seldom affected the situation in the countryside, but resulted in frequent turnovers in the national government.

A renewed outburst of revolts after the Wilson administration conducted a supervised election provided the immediate stimulus for the initial landing of troops. Exasperated with continuing turmoil and constant changes of government, U.S. forces took control of the capital during May 1916, only shortly after occupying the neighboring republic of Haiti. The United States cited its "rights and obligations" under the 1907 accord to justify this decision to impose "stability."

U.S. authorities apparently envisioned a limited intervention in which they would govern through a puppet regime, as in Haiti. This view was reckoned without the Dominicans, who were fiercely nationalistic. Attempts to manipulate the Dominican Congress, even to the extent of marines arresting senators to prevent a quorum, proved futile. Provisional President Francisco Henríquez y Carvajal and his entire cabinet refused to serve the invaders, with the president going into exile to launch a propaganda and political campaign seeking to regain his nation's independence.

In this situation, the United States was compelled to assume complete control of the nation, with marine officers holding all cabinet posts, and a naval officer serving as military governor. Decisions were issued by the military governor as executive orders. Throughout the occupation the refusal of Dominicans to cooperate forced the United States to bring in foreign personnel, often those with previous experience in the Philippines and Puerto Rico, to staff the government. These individuals were sometimes regarded as "colonial officials," though they were employed principally because of their experience abroad and knowledge of Spanish. A constant shortage of qualified personnel impeded the programs of the occupation regime.

The United States encountered resistance from guerrilla forces controlled by regional chieftains and a considerable international campaign by the former president and the elite. The marines occupied all the nation's cities, but failed to control the countryside, where they faced a prolonged guerrilla conflict for which they were not prepared or trained.

It quickly became apparent that governing the Dominican Republic was not as easy as the U.S. authorities had supposed; they faced the same problems that had plagued Dominican leaders and were unprepared to deal with them. Limited finances continued to render it impossible to carry out many of the plans prepared by the military government.

Because the military officers sent to the Dominican Republic came predominantly from the southern United States and prevailing attitudes of the day in the United States were ethnocentric, there was considerable friction between the occupiers and the local citizens. Imbued with attitudes of Anglo-Saxon superiority, U.S. leaders believed that they were carrying out a "civilizing mission" and disdained the locals, considering them lazy and lacking skills. Racial stereotypes played a role. These attitudes, when added to the marines' lack of training for guerrilla warfare and the general lack of understanding of the political situation of the Dominican Republic by U.S. figures, produced numerous disputes and several ugly incidents between the military authorities and the local residents.

Given the origins of the intervention, it is scarcely surprising that the United States sought to establish the primacy of the national government in the Dominican Republic. From the U.S. perspective the inability of the central government to implement its policies constituted the main problem. The occupation authorities sought to stamp out local *caudillos* and centralize power. Unlike Dominican regimes, the occupation government was not beholden to local power brokers and could summon sufficient military power to overcome local resistance in the nation's principal cities. Although the marines never fully controlled the countryside and the effort required far more troops than originally planned, they were able to establish control over most of the population. National finances were reorganized, and the tax system was reformed to provide new revenue sources from personal property and land taxes to reduce the importance of indirect taxation and, in particular, customs revenue. A road-building program, while achieving only limited success, provided the nation with the means of reaching into most of the hinterland from the capital, changing both the lines of authority and internal trade patterns. Major attention was devoted to drafting and enacting national law codes covering a variety of fields, including health and sanitation. In the process, the occupation regime established the basis for national government operations, while the marines imposed the most thorough and effective dictatorship the island nation had yet experienced. This effort refocused all political and economic activity on the capital.

Among the occupation regime's most controversial actions were placing civilians under the jurisdiction of military provost courts and establishing press censorship. The military government regarded the use of provost courts as essential in reforming a corrupt system of justice in the island nation and was convinced that only U.S. military courts offered a means of maintaining order until the reconstitution of the local judiciary. Dominicans saw this as an illegal extension of military jurisdiction over civilians and perceived no distinction between the U.S. courts and the actions of domestic revolutionaries because in both cases military victors imposed their own system of control. Press censorship by the military authorities constituted another source of constant friction. At its height, military authorities required prior clearance before publication of any statements about the occupation regime, banning the publication of "violent" or "inflammatory" articles and even any comments "unfavorable to the government of the United States of America or to the military government." Several Dominican editors were arrested and convicted under the censorship regime. The restrictions prevented the local press from reprinting items that routinely appeared in the domestic press in the United States and in several instances even compelled the occupation authorities to seize publications from the United States to prevent their circulation in the occupied nation. This situation became a major focus of Dominican propaganda abroad, causing the United States considerable embarrassment.

The U.S. military regime sought to improve the conditions of life in the Dominican Republic through extensive educational and health programs and a national road construction campaign. It modernized the financial system and standardized legislation, although providing only limited training to Dominicans.

To stabilize domestic politics, U.S. forces disarmed the nation and created a new constabulary, named the Guardia Nacional Dominicana, to serve as a police force that also replaced the army. They sought to form an apolitical police force that would be truly responsive to the national government by establishing law and order while separating law enforcement from politics.

World War I distracted Washington officials during the initial years of the occupation and disrupted the island republic's trade by causing shortages of materials and commodity price fluctuations which buffeted the nation. A postwar depression left occupation officials with a cash-flow shortage that required canceling planned projects and drastically reducing all government expenses, thus causing the collapse of some of the institutions already established. To their chagrin, U.S. authorities found it necessary to negotiate additional foreign loans on behalf of the island nation, in spite of vigorous objections by the local politicians.

Opposition to the occupation continued in the Dominican Republic, and the republic's plight became an important issue in U.S. politics. Dominican leaders launched highly successful propaganda, lobbying, and diplomatic efforts throughout the world which embarrassed the United States, while serving to keep the issue under consideration in Washington. Warren G. Harding made the Wilsonian intervention in the Caribbean an issue during the 1920 election campaign, criticizing the occupations as unnecessary. This stand reflected prevailing postwar isolationist attitudes and the economic crisis which caused the United States to seek to reduce its commitments abroad. A congressional investigation followed, concluding that while prolonged occupation was necessary in Haiti, withdrawal from the Dominican Republic was practical under certain conditions.

In the postwar atmosphere, Harding rectified the Wilsonian policy by reasserting State

Department control over the various Caribbean occupations, thereby establishing that foreign policy considerations would prevail. Under Harding, the Navy Department, which had been allowed to run these regimes during World War I, no longer controlled the occupation authorities. The military governors were detailed to the State Department and instructed to take their orders from it rather than from the Navy Department.

Withdrawal proved to be a protracted process, achieved only after extended negotiations with Dominican representatives. The Dominicans resisted U.S.-imposed conditions, disdaining several initial plans and forcing the occupation authorities to contract new loans before the occupation was concluded. The process begun by Harding eventually led to a withdrawal agreement and the installation of a provisional government in October 1922, culminating in elections during March 1924. U.S. forces left the island nation by September 1924, returning control to the local elite.

The results of the occupation changed Dominican politics drastically in ways which U.S. officials had not foreseen. The establishment of a single military/police force and the disarming of the nation ended the power of local factions and regional strongmen. The U.S. reforms refocused national politics on the capital, enabling tight centralized control, which strengthened the position of the capital's elite. While this did reduce revolts in the interior, it did not alter the power of the two principal parties or end the uprisings of the past. The political struggles continued, centering on domination of the capital, the only important location in the nation. The supposedly apolitical police force eventually moved into the power vacuum and became the instrument that enabled its commander, Gen. Rafael Leonidas Trujillo Molina, to seize control of the nation in May 1930 and impose a centralized dictatorship.

Kenneth J. Grieb

REFERENCES

Bruce J. Calder, *The Impact of Intervention: The Dominican Republic During the U.S. Occupation of 1916–1924* (Univ. of Texas Pr., 1984); Kenneth J. Grieb, *The Latin American Policy of Warren G. Harding* (Texas Christian Univ. Pr., 1976); Melvin M. Knight, *The Americans in Santo Domingo* (Vanguard Press, 1928); Dana G. Munro, *Intervention and Dollar Diplomacy in the Caribbean, 1900–1921* (Princeton Univ. Pr., 1964); Dana G. Munro, *The United States and the Caribbean Republics, 1921–1933* (Princeton Univ. Pr., 1974).

See also list of entries at front of book for Dominican Republic, Occupation (1916–1924).

Dunlap, Robert Henry (1879–1931)

Col. Robert Henry Dunlap arrived in Nicaragua early in 1928 as commander of the 11th Regiment, a U.S. Marine unit returning to counter the increasing hostile activity of nationalist leader Augusto C. Sandino and his followers.

Dunlap had entered the marines in 1898 for the Spanish-Cuban/American War. Before going to Nicaragua he served in the Philippines; in China during the Boxer Uprising; in Panama, Haiti, and the Dominican Republic. During World War I, he had participated in the Meuse-Argonne offensive.

Dunlap's arrival in Nicaragua coincided with the arrival of marine commandant, Maj. Gen. John A. Lejeune, and the return of Brig. Gen. Logan Feland to assume command of the marine 2nd Brigade. The reduction of marine forces in late summer 1927 because of mistaken optimism about handling Sandino had been reversed. Dunlap's command was first stationed along Nicaragua's Pacific Railway, but, after Feland divided the guerrilla-occupied parts of the nation into three areas, the 11th Regiment went to the northern area where Sandinistas seemed most active at the time. Dunlap believed that he and his officers should be in close contact and thoroughly familiar with operations against the rebels.

Headquarters for the 11th Regiment was established at Ocotal. Marines garrisoned many of the towns of the area, prepared landing fields to improve communication, and instituted extensive patrolling through the countryside. Dunlap believed that such aggressive actions would prevent further large-scale operations by Sandino. He and his staff officers accompanied patrols. On one occasion Dunlap led a patrol on an 11-day trip covering 250 miles of rugged terrain. Dunlap's tactics seemed to have, at least for the time, some success in quieting the northern area but not because Sandino was destroyed; he moved further east.

The Nicaraguan war, isolated and irregular, brought allegations of mistreatment of civilians and their property. In the northern area, opportunities for such violations seemed particularly rife. To curb such possibilities, Dunlap issued specific orders for protecting property of innocent people. The effect of such orders is difficult to assess, but Harold N. Denny, *New York Times* reporter in Nicaragua, believed that despite mistakes there was general compliance. On one occasion, however, a Nicaraguan volunteer force, operating in the northern area and accompanied by marines, executed a Sandinista chief taken prisoner by marines and turned over to the volunteers. The execution occurred after a questionable court-martial and allegedly with the approval of Dunlap.

By 1929, when the insurgency seemed greatly reduced and Sandino went to Mexico for about a year, much of the marine force returned to the United States. Colonel Dunlap and the 11th Regiment left Nicaragua in August. Dunlap at this point minimized the guerrilla threat and believed it did not require a large number of marines in that Central American nation. Interestingly, he suggested that golf and baseball may have awakened in the Nicaraguan people an appreciation of sportsmanship which might eventually be reflected in their political controversies.

After commanding the Marine Corps base at San Diego, California, in 1930, Dunlap took a course at French École de Guerre. While in France he tried to rescue a woman caught in a landslide and was killed. He died on 19 May 1931.

William Kamman

REFERENCES

Robert Debs Heinl, Jr., *Soldiers of the Sea: The United States Marine Corps, 1775–1962* (U.S. Naval Institute Pr., 1962); "In Memoriam, Brigadier General Robert Henry Dunlap, U.S.M.C.," *Marine Corps Gazette*, 26 (1931), 5–7; Neill Macaulay, *The Sandino Affair* (Quadrangle, 1967); Vernon Edgar Megee, "United States Military Intervention in Nicaragua, 1909–1932," M.A. thesis, Univ. of Texas, 1963; Clyde H. Metcalf, *A History of the United States Marine Corps* (Putnam, 1939).

Dupuy de Lôme, Enrique, and the de Lôme Letter (1898)

Enrique Dupuy de Lôme was the Spanish minister to the United States before the Spanish-Cuban/American War. He created a major diplomatic incident in 1898 by criticizing President William McKinley and belittling Spanish governmental reforms.

When the Cuban revolution began in 1895, Madrid assigned Dupuy de Lôme, a distinguished Spanish diplomat, to Washington to prevent U.S. intervention. Dupuy de Lôme worked closely with the administration of Grover Cleveland to stop the Cuban Junta from sending men and arms to Cuba and to preclude Washington's recognition of Cuban belligerency.

When the McKinley administration began in March 1897, it was more favorable to the Cuban revolution than the Spanish position. In July President McKinley criticized Spanish policies, particularly inhumane military actions. When a new Spanish government decreased its military campaign in Cuba and attempted political reforms, Dupuy de Lôme expected them to fail.

In November 1897 José Canalejas, a prominent Spanish politician, visited the United States and Cuba to assess the situation. Dupuy de Lôme introduced him to McKinley and other U.S. leaders. A few weeks later McKinley delivered his annual message, which examined Cuban developments, to Congress.

Displeased by McKinley's message, Dupuy de Lôme criticized it in a private letter to Canalejas. He accused McKinley of politically motivated attacks on Spanish policies, ascribing them to a weak president who was attempting to win popular and congressional approval. The Spanish minister also belabored Spanish policies. He characterized upcoming tariff negotiations with the United States as propaganda designed to win Republican support. He described Spain's offer of autonomy to Cuba as a means of diverting U.S. attention from the military campaign.

The Cuban Junta stole the letter and on 9 February 1898 released it through the *New York Journal*. The letter caused enormous public outrage in the United States. Its unflattering description of McKinley and cynical treatment of Madrid's reforms ended Dupuy de Lôme's diplomatic usefulness. Most newspaper editors demanded his immediate dismissal. The McKinley administration asked Madrid to recall Dupuy de

Lôme and to disavow his words. Before Washington's protest reached Madrid, the Spanish government removed him from office.

The de Lôme letter had two important results. McKinley and Congress concluded that Spanish political reforms were failing to end the fighting in Cuba, and therefore, Washington moved closer to direct intervention to end Spanish rule. The letter also tended to confirm U.S. suspicions that the Spanish were hypocritical and devious. As a result, when the *Maine* exploded on 15 February, many believed that Spaniards sank the ship.

John L. Offner

REFERENCES

Jerónimo Bécker, *Historia de la relaciones exteriores de España* (Editorial Voluntad, 1926), vol. 3; Gerald D. Eggert, *Richard Olney: Evolution of a Statesman* (Pennsylvania State Univ. Pr., 1974); Carlos García Barrón, "Enrique Dupuy de Lôme and the Spanish American War," *The Americas*, 36 (1979), 39–58; Ernest R. May, *Imperial Democracy: The Emergence of America as a Great Power* (Harcourt, 1961); H. Wayne Morgan, "The DeLôme Letter: A New Appraisal," *The Historian*, 26 (Nov. 1963), 36–49.

E

Eastern Squadron, Spanish Navy (1898)

At the beginning of 1898 Spain had three naval squadrons. The two commanded by Adm. Pascual Cervera y Topete and Adm. Manuel de la Cámara y Libermoore were in the port of Cádiz, Spain. The third was in Manila Bay, Philippine Islands. How these squadrons should be used if war with the United States erupted because of a U.S. demand that Spain free Cuba was debated among leading Spanish naval and diplomatic leaders. On 13 March it was decided that Cervera would prepare a squadron to defend Spain and another to strengthen Spanish forces in Cuba. Options available for Cámara were to defend the homeland, raid the East Coast of the United States or in the West Indies, or augment Spanish power in the Philippines. The Spanish government chose the last option. As Capt. French Ensor Chadwick, United States Navy, and historian of the war, put it, Cámara's was a "useless promenade" (Chadwick, vol. 2, p. 389).

Cámara's fleet consisted of the battleship *Pelayo*, the armored cruiser *Carlos V*, and auxiliary (unprotected) cruisers *Patriota* and *Rápido* of no fighting value. There were also destroyers *Audaz*, *Proserpina*, and *Osado*, which were towed

with great difficulty; two transports carrying 4,000 troops; and four colliers with 20,000 tons of coal. The colliers were to return home when empty; the destroyers, after reaching Suez. Only the four main ships were to follow the Mediterranean-Suez-Red Sea route to Socotra and the Laccadive Islands, the Dutch East Indies, and on to Mindanao, Philippines. From Mindanao, Cámara was to either support Spanish troops in the Visayan Islands or go some 700 miles farther on to Subig Bay or Manila Bay. However, he was to exercise caution with regard to Adm. George Dewey's ships in the latter, where U.S. expeditionary forces were landing and two 15-inch gun monitors, the *Monterey* and the *Monadnock*, were expected.

Cámara left Gibraltar Strait on 17 June and headed at about 10 knots for the Suez Canal. Upon reaching that point, his escorting destroyers returned home. Meanwhile, U.S. Secretary of the Navy John D. Long leaked information about the Eastern Squadron he was forming from the North Atlantic Fleet. Its purpose was to bombard Spain's coast if Cámara passed Suez, the objective being to frighten Spain into recalling him. Long also directed U.S. consular officers to try to impede Cámara from coaling or obtaining supplies from neutral nations. In this they were aided by British officials. When told by Egypt on 29 June that he could not coal in its territorial waters and must, according to international law, leave Port Said within 24 hours, Cámara passed through the canal to coal in the Red Sea.

Cámara's venture was thwarted after Rear Adm. William T. Sampson's forces destroyed Cervera's in the Battle of Santiago, Cuba, on 3 July. Upon reaching the Red Sea on 5 July, Cámara had been directed to keep steam up so that if necessary he could quickly return to defend Spain against a threatened attack by the newly formed U.S. Eastern Squadron. He had proceeded but seven miles into the Red Sea on 7 July when he attempted to coal. The same day he was recalled home while still 6,300 miles from the Philippines.

Cámara's brief voyage caused considerable discomfiture to U.S. leaders because the United States would have had to weaken its forces in the Caribbean if it wished to augment those in the Philippines. It would have also had to send the as-yet paper organization, the Eastern Squadron, to bombard Spanish coastal cities and then make passage to the Philippines. Given the option of strengthening the Philippines or defending the homeland, Spain chose the latter. Cámara's recall relieved Dewey from having to confront a superior Spanish force. On the other hand, after Cervera's defeat, the United States had ample naval strength to defeat the remnants of Spain's fleet in its home waters and, with the U.S. Eastern squadron forces joined to Dewey's, to defeat Cámara if he intruded into Manila Bay. These factors were among those that caused Spain to send a peace feeler to the United States through France on 22 July.

Paolo E. Coletta

REFERENCES

French Ensor Chadwick, *The Relations of the United States and Spain: The Spanish-American War* (Scribner, 1911), 2 vols.; Margaret Leech, *In the Days of McKinley* (Harper, 1959); John D. Long, *The New American Navy* (Outlook, 1903), 2 vols.; David F. Trask, *The War With Spain in 1898* (Macmillan, 1981).

See also Cámara y Libermoore, Manuel de la; Eastern Squadron, United States Navy (1898).

Eastern Squadron, United States Navy (1898)

For war with the United States in 1898 Spain had three naval squadrons: two at home and one in the Philippines. On 1 May 1898, Commodore (later Admiral) George Dewey destroyed the marine antiquities Adm. Patricio Montojo y Pasarón commanded in Manila Bay, the Philippines. This left Adm. Pascual Cervera y Topete with four armored cruisers and three torpedo boat destroyers, and Adm. Manuel de la Cámara y Libermoore's fleet. The latter, at Cádiz, Spain, consisted of the battleship *Pelayo*, the armored cruiser *Carlos V*, and the auxiliary (unprotected) cruiser *Alfonso XII*.

On 13 March 1898 the Spanish minister of marine, Adm. Segismundo Bermejo y Merelo, directed Cervera to prepare a squadron to defend the homeland and another for a voyage to the Caribbean. Though it was to be joined at the Cape Verde Islands by the armored cruisers *Vizcaya* and *Almirante Oquendo*, the fleet would still be much weaker than Rear Adm. William T. Sampson's North Atlantic Squadron, then exercising in Florida Bay and soon to be joined by the battleship *Oregon*.

On 23 April 1898, when Spain declared war on the United States, Cervera was granted discretion on how to reach Puerto Rico and, evading Sampson's blockade of that island, to seek to succor Cuba. On 29 April he left the Cape Verde Islands and by an evasive movement put in at Santiago de Cuba on 19 May. Sampson thus concentrated his forces there. This gave Cámara the options of remaining on the defensive at home, raiding the East Coast of the United States or the West Indies, or strengthening Spanish forces in the Philippines. His original orders, issued on 27 May, to raid the East Coast of the United States, were changed to support the Spanish garrison in the Philippines.

To Capt. Alfred Thayer Mahan, the leading member of the Naval War Board that advised Secretary of the Navy John D. Long, "The general military situation, constituted by Cámara's movement eastward, is to my apprehension the most important and instructive of the whole war" (Trask, p. 277). As Mahan reasoned, Dewey had no major armed vessel except monitors to counter Cámara's large ship, and Sampson lacked a sufficient number of ships to perform his multifarious tasks. Weakening Sampson might allow Cervera to escape while leaving Dewey to face a superior force. Cámara's eastern voyage left Spain open to attack, however. Therefore, the Naval War Board recommended the formation of an Eastern Squadron. If the squadron merely threatened to bombard Spanish cities, Spain would have to recall Cámara.

Cámara's voyage was short-lived. Spain had not given serious thought to the coal Cámara's ships would need for their extended journey. Upon learning that these ships had passed through the Strait of Gibraltar and sailed eastward into the Mediterranean, Secretary Long directed Sampson to detail seven ships—the United States Navy's Eastern Squadron—to descend on the Spanish coast if Cámara proceeded farther than Suez and then make for the Philippines to reinforce Dewey. When it was reported that Cámara had passed Pantelleria Island, Long ordered early movement by the Eastern Squadron. He leaked this order, which gave Spain the alternative of recalling its admiral or suffering attacks on its homeland.

Long's order would have seriously weakened Sampson's squadron (fleet after 21 June). Sampson's report that his destruction of Cervera's squadron might end the war caused Long to take no action for the moment. When the fleet was reorganized, Commodore John A. Howell commanded the First North Atlantic Squadron and took charge of the Cuban blockade. The man he relieved, Commodore John C. Watson, commanded the Eastern Squadron. Commodore Winfield Scott Schley commanded the Second North Atlantic Squadron.

Although Sampson's forces were strained to extend the blockade along Cuba's coast and around Puerto Rico, on 8 July Secretary Long urged haste in forming the Eastern Squadron and directed that the battleships *Iowa* and *Oregon*; the heavy cruiser *Brooklyn*; and three auxiliary cruisers be transferred to Watson's command. On the next day Watson hoisted his broad pennant on the *Oregon* and planned to sortie two days later. When Sampson objected to his being left with only four armored ships, Long relented and allowed him to retain the *Iowa* and *Oregon*—but only until Watson's ships were coaled and ready to depart. Colliers would deliver 40,000 tons of coal to him in the Azores. Although some of Sampson's ships would be detached to undertake the conquest of Puerto Rico, on 12 July

Long directed Sampson to prepare all his armored ships and use them as a covering force for Watson's squadron as far as Port Said. From there, he was to return to the United States. Sampson replied that ships that had served at sea for six months badly needed overhauling, but that Watson's *Oregon, Massachusetts, Newark*, and *Dixie* would be ready to sail on 19 July. To these were added the *Yosemite* and food ships. Sampson's covering squadron was to consist of two battleships (*Indiana* and *Iowa*), two heavy cruisers (*Brooklyn* and *New York*), and five cruisers (*Newark, New Orleans, Badger, Yankee*, and *Mayflower*).

Encountering great interference from U.S. and British consular officials and from the Egyptian government in obtaining coal and arranging passage through the Suez Canal, Cámara planned to coal from lighters after passing through the Canal and reaching the Red Sea. Upon learning of Sampson's defeat of Cervera on 3 July in the Battle of Santiago, Spain ordered Cámara to return home.

Although it continued to prepare for distant service and was strengthened so that it could sail via the Mediterranean to reinforce Dewey, the U.S. Eastern Squadron remained with Sampson, who was similarly prepared to sail with it as a covering force. In any event, Spain made peace overtures to the United States through France on 22 July. Knowledge that the U.S. Eastern Squadron was preparing to sail further stimulated Spanish peace efforts. Orders of 2 August to Sampson to sail with both the Eastern Squadron and his covering force were canceled on the 4th. With the peace protocol signed on 12 August, the Eastern Squadron was no longer needed, and it was disbanded.

Paolo E. Coletta

REFERENCES

French Ensor Chadwick, *The Relations of the United States and Spain: The Spanish-American War* (Scribner, 1911), 2 vols.; Margaret Leech, *In the Days of McKinley* (Harper, 1959); John D. Long, *The New American Navy* (Outlook, 1903), 2 vols.; Alfred Thayer Mahan, "Narrative Account of the Work of the Naval War Board of 1898," 29 Oct. 1906, NARG 7: Intelligence and Technological Archives, 1894–1945, Archives of the Naval War College; David F. Trask, *The War With Spain in 1898* (Macmillan, 1981).

See also Eastern Squadron, Spanish Navy (1898); Watson, John Crittenden.

Edson, Merritt Austin (1897–1955)

As a junior captain, Merritt Austin Edson led marine detachments from the USS *Denver* and USS *Galveston* in attacks against followers of Augusto C. Sandino in Nicaragua in 1928–1929. His three lengthy forays into the interior became known as the Coco River patrols. The initial effort was a daring reconnaissance by Edson and five men that penetrated 260 miles along the major water route between the coast and the rebel-dominated central highlands. In the second operation, a combat patrol covered about one thousand miles by boat and on foot over an eight-week period, but failed to catch its quarry.

Soon after its return, brigade headquarters launched the small detachment yet again in an effort to finally destroy Sandino and his band. Edson was chosen for the mission because of his demonstrated aggressiveness and his eagerness to penetrate the most difficult terrain. This third patrol lasted from July 1928 to March 1929. For much of this period, the unit operated from a primitive patrol base deep in the wilderness at the junction of the Coco and Poteca rivers.

During these difficult operations, Edson maintained close communications with his commander, Maj. Harold H. Utley. Both men supplemented the normal channels of radio and written message traffic with frequent personal notes. In this private correspondence and in the official after-action reports, the young captain developed strong views about methods for waging a counterinsurgency campaign.

Edson consistently pushed for a more offensive approach based on the concept of a roving patrol that would operate like a guerrilla unit. He opposed many of the methods used elsewhere in Nicaragua: the arming of point men with automatic weapons; the use of reconnaissance by fire; the reliance on volume, rather than accuracy of fire; and the tendency to make short patrols bound by geographic objectives. In some cases he was able to implement his views, but often his efforts were handicapped by the operational directives of brigade headquarters.

When the Coco patrols ended, Edson returned to the United States and assumed duties as a tactics instructor in the basic school for new lieutenants. There, he tried to reform the curriculum to increase the emphasis on bush warfare, even making it the core of the program. He continued his private correspondence with Ma-jor Utley and aided him in developing his manuscript on small wars.

In 1939 Major Edson was appointed to a board to revise the Corps' *Small Wars Operations*. Of the four officers involved in the project, Edson was the only one with infantry tactical experience against guerrillas; the others had seen service as an aviator, intelligence specialist, and a gendarmerie police chief. As a consequence, the 1940 version of the *Small Wars Manual* incorporated Edson's ideas about counterguerrilla operations, including verbatim selections from his earlier writings on the subject. In February 1942 the Corps acknowledged his leadership in this specialty and charged him with forming the 1st Marine Raider Battalion.

Jon T. Hoffman

REFERENCES

David C. Brooks, "U.S. Marines, Miskitos, and the Hunt for Sandino: The Rio Coco Patrol in 1928," *Journal of Latin American Studies*, 21 (1989), 311–342; Merritt A. Edson, "The Coco Patrol," *Marine Corps Gazette*, 20 (Aug. 1936), 18–23, 38–48, 20 (Nov. 1936), 40–41, 60–72, 21 (Feb. 1937), 35–43, 57–63; Jon T. Hoffman, "The Coco River Patrol and the *Small Wars Manual*," M.A. Thesis, Ohio State University, 1989; Jon T. Hoffman, "Edson's First Raiders," *Naval History*, 5 (1991), 20–25.

See also Coco River Patrols, Nicaragua (1928–1929)

El Caney, Cuba, Battle (1898)

This hard-fought battle between U.S. and Spanish forces during the Spanish-Cuban/American War, along with the Battle of San Juan Hill, threatened Santiago, Cuba, and helped prompt the Spanish fleet at Santiago to depart and be decisively defeated by the United States Navy.

Gen. Arsenio Linares Pomba disposed 4,760 of his 10,429 men in an arc around Santiago de Cuba, but he placed 520 soldiers under Gen. Joaquín Vara del Rey in the hamlet of El Caney, outside the arc, six miles northeast of the city. He did so because El Caney straddled the important road from Santiago to Guantánamo and because it was close to the reservoir which supplied water to the city and had to be protected.

Maj. Gen. William R. Shafter had landed most of his troops by 26 June 1898, but supplies came ashore erratically and not in the order they were needed. The general intended to gather his army at Siboney and hold it there until it was well supplied and well organized. This would take time because transport from ship to shore was not efficient and because the roads were unfit to handle any transport but pack mule trains.

Maj. Gen. Joseph Wheeler upset Shafter's timing by involving his division of dismounted cavalry in an unauthorized fight on 24 June. But what pushed Shafter into attacking before he was ready was word that 8,000 men were on their way to reinforce Santiago; he did not know that the number was actually only 3,700. Therefore, he ordered a two-pronged attack for the morning of 1 July. The left prong was aimed at San Juan Hill and Kettle Hill; the right at El Caney. Brig. Gen. Henry W. Lawton commanded the latter operation with a force of one division of two brigades plus two separate brigades, totaling 6,653 men.

Lawton's men marched all night to reach the vicinity and then had to scramble, sometimes crawling, their way up a slope thick with brush. Because of the difficulties of transportation, the troops had inadequate food.

There were six wooden blockhouses at El Caney but the strong point was El Viso, a stone fort. Brig. Gen. Adna R. Chaffee had the 7th, 12th, and 17th Regiments of regulars in his brigade, and he placed them northeast of El Caney, close to El Viso. Brig. Gen. William Ludlow put his three regiments southwest of the hamlet, beside the main road. He had the 8th and 22nd Regiments of regulars and the 2nd Regiment of Massachusetts volunteers. Capt. Allyn K. Capron put his battery of four 3.2-inch guns a mile and one half south of El Caney.

The U.S. timetable allotted two hours to overrun El Caney, after which Lawton was to move his troops the six miles southwestward to join in the attack on San Juan/Kettle Hill. However, it required two hours just to overcome the wooden blockhouses. Firing began at 6:30 a.m. and continued until late afternoon. The defenders had no artillery, but they had deadly Mauser rifles and the will to fight. Although Shafter's corps had a few heavy field pieces, they could not be brought into the action because the paths and roads would not support them. Capron's battery was out of range until 2:00 p.m. when it moved within 1,000 yards and began to breach the stone fort.

Shafter, suffering from the gout and from the heat (he weighed 300 pounds) attempted to direct the battle from a hill three miles south of El Caney and five miles east of San Juan/Kettle Hill. Shortly after noon he sent Lawton an order to halt the El Caney attack and move at once to join the other battle. Lawton protested this so vigorously that Shafter permitted him to stay until he had subdued El Caney.

Around 1:00 p.m. Lawton ordered his reserve (Col. Evan Miles's separate brigade, the 1st, 4th, and 24th infantry regiments; and Brig. Gen. John C. Bates's 3rd and 20th regular infantry regiments) to advance and take position between Chaffee's and Ludlow's brigades. Close to 3:00 p.m. Lawton ordered the 12th Regiment to charge El Viso, which was breached by artillery, and Miles sent in the 24th Regiment to support the 12th. Men of the 2nd Massachusetts, at this point out of the line, were impressed by the courage and discipline of the black soldiers of the 24th.

This battle, including San Juan/Kettle Hill, was the first in which both sides fired small-bore-magazine rifles using jacketed bullets (a coating of hard metal surrounded the lead core) propelled by smokeless powder. The 27.6-caliber Spanish Mauser was a better weapon than the 30-caliber Krag-Jorgensen of the U.S. regulars. One-seventh of all men hit were killed, but the wounded recovered more fully from small-bore wounds than from heavier caliber hits.

Col. Embury P. Clark of the 2nd Massachusetts stated that no unit had ever gone into combat under worse conditions. Fifty-five percent of his men were untrained, and all of them were armed with the single-shot, .45-caliber Springfield rifle which the inspector general called a "suicidal blunderbuss." It burned black powder, and the smoke from it made the riflemen easy targets. General Ludlow pulled the regiment out of the line.

Around noon Vara del Rey was killed and by midafternoon the Spanish soldiers were running out of ammunition. Finally, when only 80 soldiers were left, they retreated. Near 5:00 p.m. U.S. forces occupied El Caney. They took 125 prisoners during the day and killed or wounded 235 Spaniards. The Spanish casualties were 49 percent; U.S. forces lost 4 officers and 77 men killed, 25 officers and 335 men wounded, 11 percent of Lawton's command. The 520 defenders had made a gallant stand, but in the end the victors cut off the water supply into Santiago and closed the roads on which food reached the city.

Latter-day critics have blamed Shafter for devoting too many soldiers to El Caney. He could have used them better at San Juan/Kettle Hill. The artillery support was ineffective during most of the day. El Caney was in the range of the ship's guns, but Shafter turned down the offer to use them. The general's battle station was too far away, obliging unit commanders to make decisions without direct orders. Thus, V Corps fought as it had been trained, not as a cohesive force, but as an aggregation of individual units.

There have been critics of General Linares, too. He concentrated only 13 percent of his troops, holding 3,400 of them, nearly one-third, west of the city where there was no action at all. Some of these could have been more effective at El Caney.

John K. Mahon

REFERENCES

French Ensor Chadwick, *The Relations of the United States with Spain: The Spanish-American War* (Scribner, 1911), 2 vols.; Graham A. Cosmas, *An Army for Empire: The United States Army in the Spanish American War* (Univ. of Missouri Pr., 1971); David F. Trask, *The War With Spain in 1898* (Macmillan, 1981); *West Point Atlas of American Wars*, Vincent J. Esposito, chief ed. (Praeger, 1959), 2 vols.

See also San Juan Hill, Cuba, Battle (1898).

El Chipote, Nicaragua, Battle (1928)

After Henry L. Stimson's mission in 1927 to end the Liberal revolution against Nicaraguan President Adolfo Díaz and the arrangement for both sides to surrender arms to U.S. Marines, one Liberal general, Augusto C. Sandino, refused to comply and retreated into the jungle and mountain vastness of the Department of Nuevo Segovia. Following a period of uncertainty about Sandino's intentions, marines and Nicaraguan national guardsmen moved into Nueva Segovia to restore the government's control. There were hit-and-run encounters between Sandinista followers and the marines and their *guardia* allies. The marines hoped to find Sandino's base of operations to end the deadly, annoying, and embarrassing forays. Rumor told of a fortress at El Chipote but its location was a mystery. Some people said El Chipote was a myth

or only a symbol for the strength of Sandino's movement, but continued Sandinista attacks indicated that a place of concentration for the rebel leader and his men did exist. By late November 1927, marine planes had located El Chipote, an isolated mile-high mountain surrounded by jungle, not far from the Honduran border; the approaches were dense forests and the peak was often cloud-covered. The Sandinistas had constructed quarters and storehouses and had extensive trenches and machine gun nests for protection. Earlier in September it had been the site at which Sandino and his followers had signed the "Guidelines for the Organization of the Army in Defense of the National Sovereignty of Nicaragua" with Sandino as supreme commander.

Marine aviation began almost daily bombing and strafing raids on El Chipote, but Sandino had learned the essentials of air defense from his encounter with aircraft at Ocotal. The defenders were too well dug in to be easily driven out. Meanwhile, Sandinistas ambushed and badly mauled two strong patrols near Quilalí as they moved on El Chipote.

Following this unsuccessful beginning, a new air-ground operation against El Chipote began in the middle of January 1928. Maj. Archibald Young commanded the ground patrol while Maj. Ross E. Rowell led the air attack. The bombings took a heavy toll on El Chipote. In reports of the siege, Sandino denied the loss of many followers but did complain of dead animals whose decomposition and stench, he said, finally forced the evacuation of the mountain fortress. Although air observers reported the deserted appearance of the fortress, when Major Young's patrol began a cautious advance on 20 January it met some opposition. The patrol reached the crest on 26 January, but the main guerrilla force had escaped. In an interview years later, Sandino referred to the siege of El Chipote as the Sandinistas' real "Nicaraguan guerrilla academy" where his followers honed their skills of ambush, retreat, dispersion, and other important guerrilla tactics.

William Kamman

REFERENCES

Robert Edgar Conrad, ed. and trans., *Sandino: The Testimony of a Nicaraguan Patriot, 1921–1934* (Princeton Univ. Pr., 1990); Neill Macaulay, *The Sandino Affair* (Quadrangle, 1967); Bernard C. Nalty, *The United States Marines in Nicaragua*, rev.

ed., Marine Corps Historical Reference Series, No. 21 (Historical Branch, G-3 Division Headquarters, U.S. Marine Corps, 1962).

El Saraguazca, Nicaragua, Battle (1930)

Augusto C. Sandino's return to Nicaragua in May 1930, after an almost year-long absence, brought renewed fighting between his followers and the U.S. marines and their Nicaraguan national guard allies. He met with Pedro (Pedrón) Altamirano, a guerrilla colleague, at El Chipote and discussed a plan to attack Jinotega in the central area of operations. On 18 June 1930 Sandino and 400 men armed with 10 machine guns as well as rifles occupied the mountain, El Saraguazca, north of Jinotega, in preparation for the attack. Sandino's plans were upset the following day when two marine aircraft discovered the large concentration of Sandinistas on the mountain and attacked. After expending all of their ammunition, the pilots returned to Managua, dropping a warning message to the marines at Jinotega on the way. Marine planes in Managua were readied for a mission against El Saraguazca that afternoon, while a national guard force at Jinotega prepared for a ground assault. A national guard patrol already in the area had made contact when the planes arrived. The Sandinistas, well concealed and protected by trees and rocks, withstood the heavy bombing and strafing. The *guardia* unit out of Jinotega arrived as the planes had depleted their ammunition and bombs were on their way back to Managua. Darkness came before the national guard was able to encircle Sandino and his men, and they slipped away during the night. Sandino claimed to have inflicted heavy casualties on the *guardia* forces, but casualties were in fact light on both sides. Sandino was wounded by bomb shrapnel in the left leg during the engagement. He did not personally lead his troops into battle from this time until the end of the guerrilla war more than two and a half years later.

Examination by the air crews after the battle of El Saraguazca found evidence that the Sandinistas were using U.S.-manufactured ammunition not yet available to the marines in Nicaragua. It was apparently being provided by Sandino's network of suppliers, probably in Mexico.

William Kamman

REFERENCES

Robert Edgar Conrad, ed. and trans., *Sandino: The Testimony of a Nicaraguan Patriot, 1921–1934* (Princeton Univ. Pr., 1990); Neill Macaulay, *The Sandino Affair* (Quadrangle, 1967); Vernon Edgar Megee, "United States Military Intervention in Nicaragua, 1909–1932," M.A. thesis, Univ. of Texas, 1963); Bernard C. Nalty, *The United States in Nicaragua*, rev. ed., Marine Corps Historical Reference Series, No. 21 (Historical Branch, G-3 Division Headquarters, U.S. Marine Corps, 1962).

Emerson, George Henry (1869–1950)

George Henry Emerson, a U.S. railroad expert, supervised the effort to improve transportation systems during the Russian Civil War (1918–1920).

Born in St. Paul, Minnesota, in 1869, Emerson spent 60 years in a railroad career rising from menial jobs in the early 1880s through technical and administrative positions to the post of general manager (1912) of the Great Northern Railway. His expertise led to his appointment in fall 1917 by the U.S. government to go to Russia with a group of trained U.S. railroad personnel to undertake the task of restoring and improving railway systems, especially in Siberia and northern Manchuria. Under his direction, the Russian Railway Service Corps was created in September, and the first contingent left San Francisco in November 1917 with 350 men. Upon arrival in Vladivostok in late December, unsettled political conditions prevented landing, and the group sailed on to Japan. The group remained in Japan until March 1918, when Emerson reached Harbin, Manchuria, with the immediate assignment of improving the Chinese Eastern Railway, a vital line linking Vladivostok with western Siberia and European Russia.

Emerson's work was soon diverted, upon the request of U.S. Ambassador David R. Francis, by being ordered in April 1918 to go to Vologda (northeast of Moscow) to consult with Francis and Soviet authorities about railroad needs and supervisory control in European Russia.

Emerson left Harbin in early May and traveled West via Vladivostok. He and his party became involved on this trip in the dangerous confrontation between Bolshevik authorities and the Czech military forces in central Siberia along the Trans-Siberian line, and Emerson suddenly and unexpectedly emerged as a mediator between the two groups. He arrived in Omsk toward the end of June but was unable to reach Vologda as ordered because of the unfavorable military situation; so he returned to his earlier post to continue supervising the repair of rolling stock and the railroad lines themselves.

Emerson and the Russian Railway Service Corps valiantly attempted to increase the carrying capacity of the Chinese Eastern Railway and the Trans-Siberian Railway. Repair shops added to the limited and worn rolling stock, coordination of the railway system led to greater volume, and training of Russian personnel also resulted in the increase in the flow of goods.

Col. Benjamin O. Johnson was designated in December 1919 to replace Emerson, and the Russian Railway Service Corps was ordered to return to the United States in June 1920. Upon his return, Emerson joined the Baltimore and Ohio Railroad, working there from 1920 until his retirement in 1941. He died in 1950.

Taylor Stults

REFERENCES

Foreign Relations of the United States, 1918, 1920 (U.S. Government Printing Office, 1931, 1932, 1936); David R. Francis, *Russia From the American Embassy, April 1916–November 1918* (Scribner, 1921); Frederic C. Giffin, "Russian Railway Service Corps," *Modern Encyclopedia of Russian and Soviet History* (Academic International Pr., 1983), vol. 32, 149–153; William S. Graves, *America's Siberian Adventure, 1918–1920* (Cape & Smith, 1931); George F. Kennan, *Soviet-American Relations, 1917–1920: Russia Leaves the War* (Princeton Univ. Pr., 1956); George F. Kennan, *Soviet-American Relations, 1917–1920: The Decision to Intervene* (Princeton Univ. Pr., 1958); *New York Times*, 14 Jan. 1950, p. 15; Betty M. Unterberger, *America's Siberian Expedition, 1918–1920: A Study of National Policy* (Duke Univ. Pr., 1956).

See also Russian Railway Service Corps; Stevens, John Frank.

Estrada Palma, Tomás (1835–1908)

Tomás Estrada Palma struggled for over 30 years, along with José Martí Julian y Perez and other Cubans, to gain independence from Spain. After the Spanish-Cuban/American War in 1898 and the subsequent U.S. military occupation of Cuba that lasted until 1902, he served as president of the first Cuban Republic. In 1905 his bid for reelection incited political unrest, which led to a U.S. military intervention under the provisions of the Platt Amendment.

Born on 9 July 1835, Estrada Palma lived with his parents in Bayamo, Oriente Province, until he was old enough to travel to Havana to complete his secondary schooling. He then began studying law in Seville, but was forced to withdraw from the university and to return home to Cuba when his father suddenly died.

After the Ten Years War against Spain began in 1868, Estrada Palma joined the rebels and quickly became an integral part of the leadership. Dedicated to freeing Cuba from colonial rule, he became president of the provisional government in March 1876. He was captured by Spanish forces in October 1877 and was exiled to Spain, where he spent several months in prison until he was released at the conclusion of hostilities in 1878.

Estrada Palma then traveled to France, the United States, and Honduras before residing in Central Valley, New York. During his several years in Honduras, he served as postmaster general and married the daughter of the ex-president of Honduras. In New York he founded a high school for Latin American students named the Tomás Estrada Palma Institute.

During the 1880s political activity in the Cuban exile community in New York flourished. Political activists, led by José Martí and Estrada Palma, created the Partido Revolucionario Cubano (PRC) (the Cuban Revolutionary Party) in 1892. When Martí left the United States in 1895 to lead the rebellion in Cuba, Estrada Palma stayed behind and became chief of the PRC, with responsibilities ranging from fund-raising to propaganda.

Estrada Palma felt very comfortable in the United States, where he had become a naturalized citizen. Unlike his compatriot Martí, Estrada had long considered annexation by the United States a viable option for Cuba. He supported the U.S. intervention in 1898 and the inclusion of the Platt Amendment in the Cuban Constitution in 1901.

The first presidential election in the Republic of Cuba was held in 1901. When war hero Gen. Máximo Gómez y Báez rejected the Nationalist party nomination, the party turned to Estrada Palma, who accepted the nomination and ran a campaign that promised economic prosperity, close ties with the United States, and national unity.

Estrada Palma was not the obvious choice for the nomination. Due to his 25-year absence from Cuba, he was a relatively obscure figure. But thanks to strong endorsements of his candidacy by influential delegates to the Constitutional Convention and by U.S. President William McKinley, and the weak opposition offered from other parties in Cuba, Estrada Palma was elected president on 31 December 1901 (while still living in the United States). When the U.S. military occupation ended in May 1902, Estrada Palma, almost 67 years old, returned to Cuba to assume the presidency.

During his first term, Estrada Palma's administration was remarkably nonpartisan. Politically and economically conservative, Estrada Palma had been freed by his years in exile from the factionalism that plagued the revolutionary leadership in Cuba. He met with modest success during his first years. By 1906 he had reduced the public debt; created a $25 million budget surplus; and expanded upon the achievements of the U.S. military government in education, public works, and sanitation. Estrada Palma also signed a reciprocity treaty with the United States that enlarged Cuba's share of the U.S. sugar market, diminished duties on U.S. imports, reduced the number of naval bases the United States demanded to two, and gave Cubans sovereignty over the Isle of Pines.

The president also had political setbacks. The Estrada Palma government set a dangerous precedent for political corruption in the first republic. In the struggling economy, public office became a sure path to personal enrichment. The Cuban Congress, deeply involved in the growing political scandal, passed six amnesty bills for corrupt officeholders during Estrada Palma's presidency.

Sentiment for annexation was still very high among elites, suggesting that Estrada Palma's government failed to inspire confidence in the Cuban capacity to govern effectively. The reciprocity treaty also met with opposition from critics who considered the agreement harmful because it discouraged economic diversification.

At the end of his first term, Estrada Palma decided to seek reelection. Many of the delegates at the Constitutional Convention in 1901 had profound concerns that presidential reelection would lead to electoral abuse. The 1905–1906

Estrada Palma reelection campaign proved that their fears were well-founded. Once Estrada Palma decided to seek a second term with his newly named Moderate party, all members of the opposition Liberal party were purged from the government. At every level of the national, provincial, and municipal governments, Liberals were replaced by Moderates. When elections were held in September 1905 the polls were rife with fraud and political violence. As a result, a decisive Moderate victory was a foregone conclusion.

This blatant fraud represented a perplexing change from Estrada Palma's previous nonpartisanship. There is some historical debate about Estrada Palma's participation in the Liberal purge and the ensuing electoral impropriety. Many scholars contend that Estrada Palma participated in the Moderate plan because he believed that he was the best president for Cuba at that juncture.

The Liberals' reaction was understandable. Prohibited from gaining power through legitimate means, they organized a revolt in August 1906 designed to provoke U.S. intervention on the grounds that Estrada Palma's fraudulently elected government was too weak to protect U.S. "life, property, and individual liberty" as Article III of the Platt Amendment stipulated.

Estrada Palma's first reaction to the Liberal violence was to respond in kind. The government suspended civil liberties in cities where the revolt had become uncontrollable, and Liberals were indiscriminately arrested. Unable to quell the resistance on his own, Estrada Palma felt confident that U.S. military intervention would not be long in coming. This misplaced confidence proved to be one of the great mistakes of his presidency.

The U.S. government was reluctant to become mired in Cuban internal political squabbling. Estrada Palma's first requests for military assistance in early September 1906 were spurned by President Theodore Roosevelt. Estrada Palma then repeated his call for U.S. intervention and threatened to resign if no support came.

Roosevelt responded by sending Secretary of War William H. Taft and Assistant Secretary of State Robert Bacon to Cuba to investigate the nature and cause of the uprising. Taft and Bacon were disappointed to find that the source of the problem had been Moderate electoral corruption. Interestingly, they judged that Estrada

Palma was not directly responsible for the Moderate excesses and that he would have been legitimately reelected even if the elections had not been rigged.

The U.S. diplomats proposed a compromise which would keep Estrada Palma in office while satisfying many of the Liberals' demands. Estrada Palma stubbornly rejected the compromise, demanding that the United States intervene militarily to uphold his government. In desperation, Secretary Taft beseeched Estrada Palma, "Mr. President, there comes a time when patriotism demands a sacrifice." "Mr. Secretary," interrupted the bitter Cuban nationalist, "I do not intend to take any lesson in patriotism from you" (Pérez, *Cuba*, pp. 101–102).

True to his earlier threat, Estrada Palma angrily resigned from his presidency on 28 September 1906, leaving Cuba with no successor. To prevent anarchy, Roosevelt announced that the United States would intervene in Cuba under the provisions of the Platt Amendment. Roosevelt appointed Taft provisional governor of Cuba.

Estrada Palma's recalcitrance in the face of U.S. pressure gained him praise from many nationalistic Cuban historians. Few have claimed that he acted as a puppet of the United States, despite his consistent support for U.S. involvement in Cuba and for the Platt Amendment. Historians have generally painted Estrada Palma as a victim of a U.S. policy which promised him assistance, but never delivered it. Curiously, Estrada Palma has emerged from history as a genuine patriot.

After delivering his resignation to Congress, Estrada Palma retired to his Oriente birthplace where he lived until his death on 4 November 1908. He died in Santiago de Cuba, where he was buried next to the tomb of José Martí.

Anthony R. Pisani, Jr.
Allen Wells

REFERENCES

Pánfilo D. Camacho, *Estrada Palma: el gobernante honrado* (Editorial Trópico, 1938); Russell H. Fitzgibbon, *Cuba and the United States, 1900–1935* (Russell & Russell, 1964); Allan R. Millett, *The Politics of Intervention: The Military Occupation of Cuba, 1906–1909* (Ohio State Univ. Pr., 1968);

Louis A. Pérez, Jr., *Cuba Under the Platt Amendment, 1902–1934* (Univ. of Pittsburgh Pr., 1986); Louis A. Pérez, Jr., "Indisposition to Intervention: The United States and the Cuban Revolution of 1906," *South Eastern Latin Americanist*, 28 (1984), 1–19.

See also Cuba, Intervention (1906–1909).

Evans, Robley Dunglison (1846–1912)

In the Spanish-Cuban/American War, Robley Dunglison Evans commanded the battleship *Iowa*, leading the attack on the Spanish fleet at Santiago de Cuba.

Evans entered the United States Naval Academy in 1859 at age 13 by falsifying documents, thus beginning a career that spanned over half a century. Graduating in 1863, Evans entered active service in time to compile a remarkable record of bravery and leadership in the Civil War. Wounded four times at the battle for Fort Fisher, North Carolina, Evans led a party of marines ashore where he refused medical assistance and fought until relieved.

After a brief stint out of the navy, Evans spent the next several decades advocating the transition to a steel navy and producing technological improvements for the operation of ships at sea.

In 1891 he earned his nickname "Fighting Bob" when he used forceful measures to deal with mob violence in Chile where U.S. sailors had been killed. The next year, he added to his reputation by dealing effectively with a dispute over seal hunting in the Bering Sea.

Appointed rear admiral in 1901, Evans held station commands in the Far East and in the Atlantic, ending his career in command of the Great White Fleet in 1907. Evans fell ill on the Pacific Coast below California and was forced to relinquish his command when the fleet arrived in San Francisco on 8 May 1908. He died four years later in Washington, D.C.

Vernon L. Williams

REFERENCES

Robley D. Evans, *An Admiral's Log* (Appleton-Century, 1901); Robley D. Evans, *A Sailor's Log* (Appleton-Century, 1901); Clark G. Reynolds, *Famous American Admirals* (Van Nostrand, 1978).

Fall, Albert Bacon (1861–1944)

Albert Bacon Fall is best known for his bribery conviction in the Teapot Dome scandal in the 1920s. After seven years of court battles, he paid a $100,000 fine and served a year and a day in the Santa Fe State Penitentiary. For the purposes of this book, his importance is as an advocate of intervention in Mexico.

Fall was born in 1861 in Kentucky, where he read some law. He moved to New Mexico in 1883 and worked in the mines. Soon after, he opened a law practice in Dona Ana County and quickly became active in Democrat party politics. With a reputation as more of a frontier fighter than a legal scholar, Fall became a prominent figure in both political parties. He was elected twice to the Territorial Legislature, first as a Democrat and then as a Republican. He was appointed a New Mexico associate supreme court justice by President Grover Cleveland, earning for the rest of life the title "judge." The remainder of his political career was as a Republican. He was appointed attorney general of New Mexico in 1897 and in 1907.

When President William McKinley called for troops from the Territory of New Mexico to fight the Spanish-Cuban/American War, Fall, like many other New Mexicans, quickly volunteered. At the request of southern New Mexico Republicans, Governor Miguel Otero appointed Fall, still a Democrat, captain in the 1st Territorial Regiment. A proviso the Republicans included in their endorsement, which Governor Otero refused to accept, was that Fall, the effective politico, not return to New Mexico after the war. His personal and political enemies were glad to see him go. Fall, commission in hand, did not see action in Cuba, however, but was held in reserve in Georgia.

When President William H. Taft passed through New Mexico in 1909, the local politicos lobbied for his support for New Mexico statehood. To the chagrin of most at a banquet (and very characteristic of Judge Fall), Fall gave a fiery speech accusing the president of making hollow promises on the statehood cause.

Fall served in the 1910 constitutional convention (again creating controversy) and was chosen in 1912 by the first state legislature to be a U.S. senator. In the Senate, Fall constantly criticized President Woodrow Wilson's Mexican policy. Familiar with border politics and having allied himself with the exiled Felix Díaz faction, Fall faulted all Mexican presidential leaders as being too radical: specifically Francisco I. Madero, Venustiano Carranza, Álvaro Obregón, and social reformer Ricardo Flores-Magón. He urged Wilson to withdraw recognition of the Carranza administration. Between August 1919 and May 1920, Fall headed a Senate subcommittee which held hearings in border cities and took testimony from more than 250 witnesses. Finally, in December 1919 Wilson publicly reprimanded Fall, bringing to an end Fall's would-be interventionist activity while Wilson was in office. During the administration of William G. Harding, Fall continued his role as self-appointed expert on Mexican affairs.

In 1921, Fall was appointed secretary of the interior in the Harding administration, the first New Mexican to be so honored. From 1932 to 1944, when he died in El Paso, he worked to clear his name from the stigma of the Teapot Dome scandal.

It is important that Fall be placed within the historical context of his era: this prominent New Mexican, who made history on the border, was much like dozens of other rugged individualists who developed southern New Mexico. Fall was a rancher (he said he borrowed the $100,000 from Edward L. Doheny for his Three Rivers ranch) as well as lawyer-politician.

William Lux

REFERENCES

William A. Keleher, *The Fabulous Frontier* (Univ. of New Mexico Pr., 1962); Burl Noggle, *Teapot Dome: Oil and Politics in the 1920's* (Louisiana State Univ. Pr., 1962); C.L. Sonnichsen, *Tularosa: Last of the Frontier West* (Univ. of New Mexico Pr., 1980); David H. Stratton, ed., *The Memoirs of Albert B. Fall* (Univ. of Texas Pr., 1966); Ralph Emerson Twitchell, *Leading Facts of New Mexico History* (Horn & Wallace, 1963), vol. 2.

Feland, Logan (1869–1936)

Brig. Gen. Logan Feland arrived in Nicaragua on 7 March 1927 to take command of about 2,000 U.S. Marines composing the 2nd Brigade. The marines were creating neutral zones and protecting foreign lives and property in the midst of the Liberal revolution led by Juan B. Sacasa against Nicaraguan President Adolfo Díaz. Born in Hopkinsville, Kentucky, on 18 August 1869, Feland graduated from Massachusetts Institute of Technology and had been in the marines since

his appointment as a first lieutenant in 1899, following a year in the army during the Spanish-Cuban/American War. He served in Cuba, the Philippines, the Dominican Republic, and France during World War I before going to Nicaragua.

Feland arrived in Nicaragua about a month before Henry L. Stimson's mission ended the fighting by promising U.S.-supervised elections in 1928 and creation of a nonpartisan national constabulary trained by U.S. forces. Following Stimson's negotiations, Feland's men had the task of collecting arms from the disbanding Liberal and Conservative armies. One Liberal general, Augusto C. Sandino, refused to disarm, but the marine command in Nicaragua did not consider him a serious threat to Washington's peace arrangements. Sandino's withdrawal into northern Nicaragua did not trigger an immediate marine offensive, but by June Feland had decided to occupy major towns of Nueva Segovia, the northern province where Sandino seemed most entrenched. There followed Sandino defeats at Ocotal, San Fernando, and Santa Clara; by August 1927, the area was quiet and seemingly under control. The marine brigade was reduced, and Feland returned to the United States.

Sandino was not finished, however, and the increased marine activity against him brought General Feland and marine reinforcements back to Nicaragua in early 1928. Under Feland's command, the marines controlled most of the settled areas of Nicaragua and were able to move about the country without great opposition, but they never eliminated the Sandinistas and were never able to provide the desired security in northern and eastern Nicaragua.

After José María Moncada's presidential election victory in 1928, Feland used personal influence to encourage the new president to place the Nicaraguan national guard under his direction as commander of the 2nd Brigade. He also supported Moncada's plans for creating an armed force other than the *guardia* to fight the Sandinistas and for amending the *guardia* legislation to allow greater political influence in its operation. The State Department, the U.S. minister in Nicaragua, and marine Col. Elias R. Beadle, who headed the Guardia Nacional de Nicaragua, opposed these proposals. There evolved a personal animosity between Feland and Beadle which led to their reassignments in March 1929.

Feland irritated the U.S. legation and the State Department further by his sensitivity to seating arrangements when he attended Nicaraguan social and governmental functions. He seemed to encourage Nicaraguan legislation to grant him ministerial rank for ceremonial purposes. The State Department also indicated concern when Feland's former *aide de camp* and later aide to President Moncada recommended the aide's father-in-law for a position with the Nicaraguan Pacific Railroad. In addition Feland reportedly voiced open disapproval of a contract that Pan American Airways was negotiating with Nicaragua.

General Feland left Nicaragua on 27 March 1929. He retired as a major general in 1933 and died in Columbus, Ohio, on 18 July 1936.

William Kamman

REFERENCES

Harold Norman Denny, *Dollars for Bullets: The Story of American Rule in Nicaragua* (Dial Pr., 1929); Robert Debs Heinl, Jr., *Soldiers of the Sea: The United States Marine Corps, 1775–1962* (U.S. Naval Institute Pr., 1962); William Kamman, *A Search for Stability: United States Diplomacy Toward Nicaragua, 1925–1933* (Univ. of Notre Dame Pr., 1968); Richard Millett, *Guardians of the Dynasty: A History of the U.S. Created Guardia Nacional de Nicaragua and the Somoza Family* (Orbis, 1977).

See also Beadle, Elias Root; Guardia Nacional de Nicaragua; *Voluntario* Force, Nicaragua (1929).

15th Infantry Regiment, United States Army, Tianjin (Tientsin), China (1912–1938)

The 15th Infantry Regiment, United States Army, first came to China in 1900 to help suppress the Boxer Uprising as part of the American China Relief Expedition. It was withdrawn from North China with the rest of the U.S. contingent in 1901 after the conclusion of fighting in the Boxer Uprising.

The regiment returned to Tianjin (Tientsin) in 1912. It was sent in the aftermath of the 1911 revolution in China and the staged military riots of 29 February near the Beijing (Peking) Legation Quarter that prevented the transfer of the capital to Nanjing (Nanking). Two battalions of the regiment were stationed in Tianjin until 1938.

The United States and other Treaty Powers were given the right under Articles 7 and 9 of the Boxer Protocols (1901) to station troops in Beijing to guard their legations as well as along the Beijing-Tianjin railroad line between Beijing and the coast. The 15th Infantry, along with the marine legation guard, was supposed to defend U.S. lives and property in the event of another antiforeign uprising until reinforcements arrived.

Tianjin, the regimental headquarters, had long been a focal point of economic and political power in North China. It was North China's industrial center, the northern coasting trade terminus, and the major treaty port in North China.

It was China's second largest treaty port, with the largest foreign enclave outside Shanghai, including six major territorial concession areas (three after 1919) and 22 foreign consuls. In terms of economic and intellectual power it was China's second city, exceeded only by Shanghai and Beijing, respectively.

For the most part, duty in Tianjin was mornings spent drilling and afternoons spent off duty. Part of this time was devoted to language study. The regiment maintained a program in spoken Chinese. Officers were required, and noncommissioned officers encouraged, to attain proficiency in the language. Those who passed a special examination wore a sleeve patch designating them as interpreters. However, the social aspects of life predominated over the military. This was true for most of the regiment's tenure. The only serious sustained military exertions occurred in 1924–1928, the era of the Nationalist Revolution and the Northern Expedition.

The recurring civil wars in China between 1917 and 1928 were a source of Chinese humiliation and foreign trepidation. The regiment's primary duty was to protect Tianjin and its immediate hinterland from despoliation by marauding bands of warlord troops by disarming them before they entered the city or, if they could not be disarmed, diverting them from the city. Accomplishing this mission called for a mixture of diplomacy and military display.

The first incident occurred during the Second Fengtian-Zhili (Fengtien-Chihli) War (1923–1924). The situation worsened during the Northern Expedition, the Guomindang's (Kuomintang) attempt to unify and to oppose foreign imperialism in China. Because of the fear of Bolshevik influence over the Guomindang and because of a series of antiforeign attacks culminating in the Nanjing incident, U.S. and other foreign reinforcements were sent to China. The U.S. contingent included a reinforced legation guard and the West Coast Expeditionary Force (3rd Marine Brigade). After leaving a regiment at Shanghai, the bulk of the brigade was deployed in and around Tianjin. Unlike the marine brigade, the 15th and the legation guard were committed to cooperation with the other Treaty Powers and could not act unilaterally.

Military duty in China was relatively easy, if not especially prized by officers because it was perceived as a slow track for promotion. Nonetheless, many officer veterans of the regiment achieved high rank, including George C. Marshall, Joseph W. Stilwell, and Matthew B. Ridgway. The social whirl could be hectic; officers and enlisted men were rich by Chinese standards. In the 1920s, the favorable exchange rates magnified their salaries by 350 percent. Officers and their wives could maintain substantial households while enlisted men had barracks servants who cleaned equipment and uniforms (Noble, pp. 109–142).

The regiment's job in China changed between 1912 and 1937. When first deployed it was supposed to cooperate with other foreign units to protect and defend foreign lives and property in the face of possible resurgent Chinese xenophobia. By the late 1920s, the functions of maintaining U.S. prestige and preventing Japanese expansion were added to its mission. The regiment was finally withdrawn in 1938, after the *Panay* incident, when it became obvious it could no longer satisfy its political purpose in the face of overall U.S. military weakness, U.S. isolationism, and Japanese expansionism.

Lewis Bernstein

REFERENCES

Louis Morton, "Army and Marines on the China Station: A Study in Military and Political Rivalry," *Pacific Historical Review*, 29 (1960), 51–73; Louis Morton, "Interservice Cooperation and Political-Military Collaboration, 1900–1938," in Harry L. Coles, ed., *Total War and Cold War: Problems in Civilian Control of the Military* (Ohio State Univ. Pr., 1962); Dennis L. Noble, *The Eagle and the Dragon: The United States Military in China, 1901–1937* (Greenwood Pr., 1990).

1st United States Volunteer Cavalry (The Rough Riders)

The 1st United States Volunteer Cavalry, popularly known as the Rough Riders, is forever identified with Theodore Roosevelt. Following the declaration of war on Spain in 1898, Congress passed a volunteer army bill calling for three regiments composed of frontiersmen from the West. Offered command of one regiment, Roosevelt declined in favor of Leonard Wood, a regular army officer. Wood became colonel and Roosevelt lieutenant colonel of the 1st Volunteer Cavalry.

The majority of men were from the western territories, but the regiment also included Easterners who were athletes and aristocrats. They, paired with western miners and cowboys, captured the public's imagination. The Rough Riders trained for two weeks at San Antonio, Texas. Favorites of journalists, the regiment acquired several alliterative nicknames before the press settled on the "Rough Riders." The unit went to war like a college football team complete with its own cheer: "Rough, tough, we're the stuff. We want to fight, and we can't get enough. Woopee." "There'll Be A Hot Time in the Old Town Tonight" became the regiment's unofficial theme song.

Arriving in Tampa, Florida, for embarkation, the troops found themselves given low priority for transportation to Cuba. Finally assigned to the transport *Yucatan*, the regiment had to leave its horses and many men behind. The United States Army landed at Daiquirí, Cuba, on 22 June. In its first skirmish at Las Guásimas on 24 June the Rough Riders suffered eight men killed and 34 wounded.

On 30 June upon Wood's promotion to brigadier general, Roosevelt assumed command of the regiment. The next day the Rough Riders assaulted Spanish positions on Kettle Hill in the San Juan range. With little artillery support, they moved ahead on foot. Roosevelt was mounted until he encountered barbed wire half way up the hill; then he, too, advanced on foot. Arriving at the summit, Roosevelt killed a Spaniard with a pistol recovered from the *Maine*. U.S. troops chased the fleeing Spaniards nearly to the walls of Santiago. This action cost the regiment 15 men killed and 76 wounded.

Afterward, the army settled down in trenches where fever hit it harder than Spanish bullets.

Fortunately the war ended on 12 August. The Rough Riders went to Montauk Point, Long Island, for demobilization. The men mustered out, and on 15 September 1898 their colors were taken down for the last time.

Richard H. Bradford

REFERENCES

Richard Harding Davis, *The Cuban and Porto Rican Campaigns* (Scribner, 1898), 120–123; Virgil Carrington Jones, *Roosevelt's Rough Riders* (Doubleday, 1971); Edward Marshall, *The Story of the Rough Riders* (G. W. Dillingham Co., 1899); Edmund Morris, *The Rise of Theodore Roosevelt* (Coward, McCann & Geoghegan, 1979), 593–661; Theodore Roosevelt, *The Rough Riders* (Corner House, 1971, rpt. of 1899 ed.).

Fletcher, Frank Friday (1855–1928)

Rear Adm. Frank Friday Fletcher was completing a long distinguished naval career when he commanded the Fifth Division of the United States Atlantic Fleet, stationed at Veracruz, Mexico, during 1914, and in this capacity commanded the landing of U.S. forces to seize that port. Fletcher was considered an expert in naval ordnance and had been responsible for several developments and techniques which improved the accuracy of naval gunnery. He had commanded each of the divisions of the Atlantic Fleet during his career. The presence of the squadron in Mexican waters reflected the tensions between the United States and Mexico and the turmoil within Mexico resulting from the civil war in progress. President Woodrow Wilson, who strongly opposed the government of Gen. Victoriano Huerta and was actively campaigning diplomatically for Huerta's removal from the Mexican presidency, stationed U.S. warships in Mexican waters in large numbers to exert pressure on the Huerta regime. Naturally, the units were stationed principally at the two major ports, Veracruz and Tampico.

Ships were shuttled back and forth between Fletcher's squadron and the Fourth Division, stationed at Tampico, as needed. While Fletcher and Rear Adm. Henry T. Mayo at Tampico were equals, the uncertain state and limited range of radio communication in those years required that communications be passed through Veracruz. Only newer battleships were equipped with an tennae of sufficient height to give a range long enough to reach the naval station at Key West, Florida, the only means of reaching Washington for instructions. The battleship *Florida*, stationed at Veracruz, constituted the communications link between the ships off the coast of Mexico and their superiors.

The Fourth Division at Veracruz consisted of two battleships, the *Florida* and the *Utah*, both with a draft too deep to enter the inner harbor within the breakwaters, and the gunboat *Prairie*. While a small squadron to be stationed at Mexico's principal port, its firepower was sufficient to provide a formidable presence because the Mexican Navy consisted entirely of gunboats. The battleships, moreover, provided superiority over any other ships in the area because European squadrons stationed in Mexican waters usually consisted only of cruisers.

The Tampico incident of 9 April 1914 increased tensions between the United States and Mexico, and although the crisis initially occurred in Tampico, the focus of attention abruptly shifted to Veracruz when Wilson decided to use the incident as a pretext to intercept an arms shipment en route to the Huerta government from Europe. On 21 April Fletcher was suddenly directed to land troops in Veracruz and seize the customs house and dock area to prevent the German vessel *Ypiranga*, which was due to arrive within a few hours, from landing the arms. Thus, Fletcher had only three hours to plan and launch the landing at Veracruz. That he was able to act on such short notice and carry out his orders successfully demonstrated his considerable ability.

Fletcher conducted the planning and retained overall command throughout the battle to secure control of Veracruz. In accordance with his plan, the initial landing party, consisting only of 787 men, including 502 marines stationed on the warships and a company of bluejackets, came ashore at 11:20 a.m. on 21 April 1914. While reinforcements were en route, Fletcher was compelled to act with the forces at hand because the help would arrive too late to prevent delivery of the arms shipment. Landing by small boat, the troops initially seized the docks and the adjoining railroad terminal, without incident, although they failed to capture the trains awaiting the arms shipment, which departed as the landing began. As the troops advanced toward the customs house they were fired on at 11:57 a.m. by a small unit of about 100 Mexican troops and civilians who had rushed to the harbor to resist the landing. Mexican resistance was limited because the commander of the Veracruz Garrison, Gen. Gustavo Maass, was ordered to withdraw his troops a few miles inland. He never fully committed the main body of his troops, although Fletcher was not aware of this at the time.

The resistance made the seizure of the entire city necessary, in spite of the original intention to seize only the port area. Only the initial objective was secured the first day. Reinforcements appeared during the evening, when the *San Francisco* and *Chester* arrived from Tampico. Throughout the night the ships of the Atlantic Fleet, which President Wilson had earlier sent to Mexican waters, entered the harbor. Arriving singly as they rushed to reach the port at top speed, each landed the ship's company of marines and hastily formed detachments of bluejackets from the ships' crews. By the early morning the transport *Hancock* arrived with a detachment of 1,000 marines.

The U.S. force ashore reached 3,000 men by the time the battle resumed the next morning. Using house-to-house tactics, it overcame sporadic resistance and sniper fire to take control of the entire city. By 11:00 a.m. on 22 April 1914 Veracruz was completely in U.S. hands. U.S. forces had suffered 19 dead and 47 wounded. While Mexican casualties could not be accurately determined due to the burning of bodies, at least two hundred died defending the city; the casualties were overwhelmingly civilian.

Having commanded the invasion, Admiral Fletcher turned control of the city over to Gen. Frederick Funston, who arrived with an army infantry brigade on 27 April to conduct the longer term occupation and who was soon named as military governor.

Kenneth J. Grieb

REFERENCES

Kenneth J. Grieb, *The United States and Huerta* (Univ. of Nebraska Pr., 1969); Robert E. Quirk, *An Affair of Honor: Woodrow Wilson and the Occupation of Veracruz* (Univ. of Kentucky Pr., 1962).

See also Veracruz, Mexico, Battle (1914).

Flying Squadron, United States Navy (1898)

When a Cuban revolt against Spain began in 1895, the United States urged Spain to provide relief for suffering Cubans, if not grant them autonomy. While the threat of war increased, especially after the destruction of the *Maine* in Havana harbor on 15 February 1898, Secretary of the Navy John D. Long worried about the health of the commander of the North American Squadron, Rear Adm. Montgomery Sicard, who suffered from chronic malaria. Long ordered a medical examination of the admiral that resulted in his detachment on 26 March. Sicard's successor was Capt. William Thomas T. Sampson, who was due for promotion to commodore. Sampson was frail of health but austerely dedicated to duty. He doubled as commander of the heavy cruiser *New York*. His chief of staff was Capt. French E. Chadwick.

On 18 April Congress authorized President William McKinley to use his naval and military forces to force Spain to free Cuba. While waiting to hear from Spain, on 21 April McKinley sent Sampson to establish a blockade about Cuba. On the 25th, having heard nothing from Spain, Congress declared war and made it retroactive to 21 April, when the blockade order had been issued.

In violation of the Mahanian dictum that the fleet remain concentrated, the Navy Department answered demands from panic-stricken inhabitants along the East Coast for protection against Spanish warships by dividing the North Atlantic Squadron into thirds. Commodore John A. Howell was to defend north of the Delaware; Commodore Winfield Scott Schley was to have a Flying Squadron at Norfolk, Virginia; and Sampson, with the bulk of the ships, was to patrol the coast to the south and also cover Cuba from Key West.

On the evening of 21 April, Chadwick and Sampson reviewed the situation. Spanish Adm. Pascual Cervera y Topete was forming a squadron in the Cape Verde Islands; Adm. Manuel de la Cámara y Libermoore had a squadron in Cádiz, Spain; and Adm. Patricio Montojo y Pasarón was in Manila Bay, the Philippines. The major danger came from Cervera's four cruisers, armed with 11-inch rifles and capable of a speed of 20 knots. The most likely Caribbean sites from which they could operate were San Juan, Puerto Rico, and Havana, Cuba.

Spreading his ships about Havana and the Cuban coast to the northeast, Sampson after nine days returned to Key West. There, he learned that Cervera had left the Cape Verde Islands on 29 April and that on 1 May Commodore (soon Admiral) George Dewey had destroyed Montojo's ships in Manila Bay. Where could Cervera be headed? He had the options of trying to destroy the battleship *Oregon*, making passage from Bremerton, Washington, to the Caribbean; striking U.S. coastal cities; or heading for the most likely coal ports in the Caribbean— Havana, Cienfuegos, and Santiago, Cuba or San Juan, Puerto Rico. Desiring to at least damage San Juan before Cervera's arrival in the Caribbean, Sampson obtained permission to bombard it and to use Schley's Flying Squadron if he wished. On 12 May, with Cervera nowhere to be seen, Sampson bombarded San Juan with little effect and returned to blockade Havana.

During his retreat to Havana, Sampson was informed by Secretary Long that Cervera had reached Curaçao, West Indies, on 14 May, "destination unknown." Sampson was to go to Key West, where Schley would join him with his Flying Squadron. Sampson's intuition was that Cervera would deliver arms and obtain coal along Cuba's southern coast, most likely at Havana or Cienfuegos, the latter connected by rail with Havana. Choosing Cienfuegos, Sampson sent Schley to engage Cervera or blockade him there. Schley, in the heavy cruiser *Brooklyn*, also had the battleship *Massachusetts*, second-class battleship *Texas*, two cruisers, and two torpedo boats.

The choice of Schley to command the Flying Squadron, most likely on the advice of Assistant Secretary of the Navy Theodore Roosevelt, jumped him over at least a dozen admirals and senior commodores. Moreover, even if Secretary Long did not believe him to be as professionally qualified as Sampson and certain other officers, he authorized him to act independently until he joined Sampson and served as his subordinate. Another problem was that Sampson, who also had been jumped over a number of others, including Schley, was junior to Schley in rank but superior to him in command. These arrangements very much violated naval precepts, but as Chadwick said, "It is a business matter only." He believed Schley when the latter told Sampson that he would be "loyal, absolutely and unreservedly, to the cause that we are both representing" (Coletta, p. 77).

If Schley left Key West in the morning of 19 May, Sampson believed Schley could blockade Cienfuegos on the morning of the 20th. On that morning, intelligence reached Long that Cervera

had put into Santiago the day before. Long therefore directed Schley to leave a small ship off Cienfuegos and "proceed off Santiago," a day's sail at 15 knots. Sampson added that if Cervera really was in Santiago, he would join Schley there on the 24th. On the 23rd, Schley told Sampson that he was unsure that Cervera was at Cienfuegos and that he would have trouble coaling in heavy swells. Although he believed that Cervera would make for either Cienfuegos or Havana, he nevertheless would proceed to blockade Santiago on the 25th unless prevented from coaling.

Schley's conviction that Cervera was in Cienfuegos, his hesitancy to move toward Santiago, and his preoccupation with coaling distressed Sampson and Chadwick. Where was the aggressiveness and good judgment that had thus far marked his career? Sampson therefore repeated his orders: Schley was to hasten at full speed to Santiago, blockade Cervera if he were there, and pursue him if he had left. A message dated the 24th from Schley then shook Sampson's confidence: Schley would start for Santiago on the 25th, but "on account of short coal supply on ships, cannot blockade them if in Santiago" (Chadwick, vol. 1, p. 293).

Schley moved eastward on the morning of the 25th, but because two small ships that were with him could not make much headway in heavy weather he slowed from 18 to 12 knots. Meanwhile, Sampson decided to return to Key West and obtain Long's permission to blockade Santiago himself. He sent Schley a collier and directed him to blockade Santiago regardless of all hazards and also block the Santiago channel by sinking a collier in it. Long sent a similar message: one demanding prompt action.

After coming within 20 miles of Santiago on the 26th, Schley terribly shocked Sampson by telling him that he must return to Key West. Rather than "flying" after Cervera he was flying home—a move soon characterized as "retrograde" and "renegade" (Coletta, p. 77). His captains responded to his asking if they had enough coal by saying they did. However, Schley told Long that he was forced to return to Key West for coal and "can not ascertain anything myself enemy positive." Long showed the message to President McKinley, whose face fell. Long later said, "It was the darkest day of the war," adding that he should have relieved Schley at once and ordered an investigation into his actions (Coletta, p. 81).

Upon his return to Key West on the 28th, Sampson again directed Schley to take all measures needed to learn if Cervera were in Santiago and to pursue him if he had left. When Long asked him how long it would take Sampson to coal, to wait for Schley, and to reach Santiago, Sampson replied that he would not wait for Schley. He would coal, meet Schley, turn him around, and reach Santiago in two days. On 29 May Sampson told Schley to coal when conditions permitted and keep Santiago blockaded. He should also send a ship to Guantánamo Bay "with a view to occupying it as a base" (Coletta, p. 82). On the same day Long granted Sampson permission to proceed to Santiago. Would Cervera be there when he arrived? And where was Schley? After having delayed reaching Santiago for four days, Schley finally reported that he had seen Spanish ships in the Santiago Channel. Because of difficulties in coaling, he recommended that Sampson's squadron relieve his. Meanwhile, instead of a close blockade he was standing from 11 to 40 miles off the entrance to the channel, leaving Cervera ample room to escape. Moreover, during the two days that his ships fired at the *Cristóbal Colón*, his speed of 10 knots and distance of 9,000 yards permitted him to get off very few shells. He thus laid the basis for the charge that he had not done his utmost to destroy enemy ships.

On 31 May Sampson joined Schley's flying squadron to his own forces, thus ending its separate existence. However, to understand the subsequent Sampson-Schley controversy, the story must continue to the end of the war and beyond.

Sampson clamped a tight semicircular blockade about the mouth of the Santiago Channel. He kept command of the first squadron but gave Schley command of the second, with the flagship of each positioned so that it would be the first to intercept any Spanish ship that sortied. Sampson then ordered Lt. Richmond P. Hobson, Construction Corps, to sink the collier *Merrimac* in the channel. Hobson tried to do so on 3 June, but failed; it sank parallel to rather than across the channel. A happier note was that Guantánamo Bay, useful as a logistic support base, was taken by forces commanded by Comdr. Bowman H. McCalla of the cruiser *Newark*. From there Sampson scouted for beaches suit-

able for landing expeditionary forces and chose the beach at Daiquirí.

Meanwhile, on 2 July, the captain general of Cuba ordered Cervera to "go out immediately." Not expecting a Spanish sortie by day, some of Sampson's ships kept up only enough steam to enable them to maintain station. They could at best make 10 knots, and it would take 10 minutes to "get way on." Early in the morning of 3 July Sampson sailed eastward to confer with Brig. Gen. William R. Shafter. The signal he flew, "Disregard the movements of the commander in chief," meant that he had not relinquished or transferred command but merely left his blockade station. When the *New York* was about seven miles east of the Santiago Channel entrance at 9:30 a.m., a signalman shouted "Smoke in the harbor," then "The fleet's coming out." Sampson had signal 250 hoisted: "Close toward harbor entrance and attack vessels" (Coletta, p. 89). If the first Spanish ships turned eastward, the *New York* would soon engage. If they turned westward, it would miss the fight and Schley's *Brooklyn* would be the first to engage.

The first Spanish ship to clear the channel, Cervera's *Infanta Maria Teresa*, steered so as to ram the *Brooklyn*. Fire from four U.S. battleships and an armored cruiser dissuaded it from so doing. To the astonishment of all witnesses, Schley turned the *Brooklyn* away to starboard and across the bow of the *Texas*, which to avoid collision backed down full. He then made a great loop to southward and westward, joined other U.S. ships, and was most efficient in helping to destroy all the Spanish ships in a four-hour battle. Schley then sent Sampson two victory messages. When he boarded the *New York* he commiserated about Sampson's failure to have engaged "in the glories of that day's work" (Coletta, p. 91). Sampson prepared a message to Long reading, "The fleet under my command offers the nation as a 4th of July present the whole of Cervera's fleet" (Coletta, p. 92). When Sampson's flag lieutenant went to Siboney to send the message, he met Schley's flag lieutenant, there for the same purpose. The latter was forbidden to send it until approved by Sampson.

Had Sampson left Schley in command? Was not the victory Schley's? After Sampson spoke with him, Schley withdrew the pretentious report he had written. Further, when most of the U.S. press credited him with the victory, he personally denied that fact to Sampson.

Two controversies mushroomed from the Battle of Santiago, one between Sampson and Shafter, which is not important here, the other between Sampson and Schley. Part of the latter stemmed from differences in personalities. Sampson was older, sober, modest, restrained; Schley was younger, flamboyant, vain, and a talented publicist. The main reason for the controversy, however, was the seeking by the press and personal friends to name their man as the hero. Another was the unhappiness of Schley's supporters for Sampson's having been given higher rank and command.

Among the many counts against Schley were his great vacillation in seeking Cervera in Cienfuegos and Santiago and his disputing Sampson's claim that his ships could not enter the mined channel at Santiago. A third was his turning the *Brooklyn* away from Cervera's ship in violation of Sampson's directive that it was the "duty of every United States vessel to close in, immediately engage, and pursue" (Coletta, p. 100). So raucous did the battle between "Sampsonites" and "Schleyites" become that Congress refused to promote anyone who had participated in the Santiago campaign. Long's recommending the advancement of Sampson by eight numbers and Schley by six heightened the controversy. The board of officers Long asked to investigate and report on the conduct of the two principals upheld Sampson. More faggots were thrown on the fire when Schleyites claimed that Schley had been "banished" and "persecuted" when given command of the South Atlantic Squadron late in 1899. When Chadwick publicly criticized Schley, Long severely reprimanded him. Chadwick rebutted that Schley should ask for a court of inquiry and so clear his name and the honor of the service.

Not Chadwick but Edgar Stanton Maclay caused Schley to request a court of inquiry. In bringing his naval history text up to date, Maclay wrote that Schley was timid if not cowardly, a perverter of facts if not a liar, and a "caitiff" who turned away from danger. In 1901 Long appointed a court headed by Adm. George Dewey that heard testimony for 40 days. Schley said that he had done everything possible to coal and that his "loop" had been correct because the first and second Spanish ships that sortied intended to ram. On 11 November the court delivered its opinion that Schley had been dilatory while off Cienfuegos, slow in reaching Santiago, and

wrong in making his retrograde movement. He had turned his *Brooklyn* away to the eastward and caused the *Texas* to back down to avoid collision. The only member of the court to uphold Schley was Dewey. When Schley offered exceptions to the court's findings, Long sent them to President Theodore Roosevelt. On 18 February 1902, saying that with both Sampson and Schley retired and the court having recommended that no further action be taken, Roosevelt decided that the matter should be put to rest. In his autobiography, published in 1904, Schley stood his ground—but he has remained discredited.

Paolo E. Coletta

REFERENCES

French Ensor Chadwick, *The Relations of the United States and Spain: The Spanish-American War* (Scribner, 1911), 2 vols.; Paolo E. Coletta, *French Ensor Chadwick: Scholarly Warrior* (Univ. Pr. of America, 1980); Margaret Leech, *In the Days of McKinley* (Harper, 1959); John D. Long, *The New American Navy* (Outlook, 1903), 2 vols.; David F. Trask, *The War With Spain in 1898* (Macmillan, 1981).

See also Schley, Winfield Scott.

Forbes Commission

See President's Commission on Conditions in Haiti (1930); Forbes Commission.

Fort Rivière, Haiti, Battle (1915)

After a brief cease-fire in early October 1915, *Caco* forces (Haitian peasant guerrillas) in northern Haiti renewed their assaults against government-held towns and the occupying U.S. forces. Col. Littleton W.T. Waller, commander of the 1st Provisional Brigade of U.S. Marines in Haiti, ordered increased patrols and reconnaissance activity to locate and neutralize those forces. On 28 October, one of these marine patrols, following a tip from a guerrilla-turned-guide, stumbled across Fort Rivière while pursuing a small force of *Cacos* near Montagne Noire.

Fort Rivière was an old French bastion fort about 200 feet square with 25-foot-high walls built at the summit of Montagne Noire. Decrepit and overgrown with trees and brush, the original entrance in the northern wall had been blocked with rubble. To gain access to the fort the *Cacos* had slashed a narrow, jagged 15-foot-long passage in the western wall. "General" Josephette, a former cabinet minister leading a party of *Cacos*, used the fort as his headquarters. To Maj. Smedley D. Butler went the task of driving the guerrillas out of the fort and eliminating it as a possible *Caco* haven.

To accomplish his objectives Butler planned an early morning assault on the fort, using units from the 5th, 13th, and 23rd Companies, the marine detachment from USS *Connecticut*, and the ship's landing party. At 4:00 a.m. on 17 November this force, armed with Springfield '03 rifles and Benet-Mercié automatic guns, split into three parties and began their ascent of the mountain. By 7:40 a.m. Butler, with four squads of the 5th Company, was in position 800 yards southwest of the fort. Elements of the 13th Company under Capt. Chandler Campbell, and the marine detachment from *Connecticut* under Capt. Frederick A. Barker, were about 800 yards southeast of the fort. The sailors from the *Connecticut*, led by Lt. (j.g.) Scott D. McCaughey, covered the northern face of Fort Rivière.

Shortly after 7:45 a.m. the wiry major gave three blasts on his whistle, signaling the marines and sailors to begin the attack. Campbell's and Barker's men leveled a steady fire at the *Caco* stronghold. Meanwhile, under heavy but inaccurate fire from the guerrillas, Butler led his men across the open field which rose slightly toward the ramshackle fort and took shelter in the dead space at the base of the wall beside the sally port.

Despite heavy fire through the entrance by a *Caco* defender, Sgt. Ross L. Iams, of the 5th Company, bolted through the narrow tunnel with Cpl. Samuel Gross of the 23rd Company on his heels, closely followed by Butler. A wild hand-to-hand struggle ensued between the guerrilla defenders and the marines, with the Haitians resorting to clubs and machetes after emptying their rifles at their attackers. Desperate *Cacos* tried to escape from the fort by jumping from the walls, but most were cut down by Campbell's and McCaughey's men as they advanced on the fort. A few of the guerrillas escaped by climbing down trees which overhung the crumbling parapets. About 50 *Cacos* were killed. There were no marine casualties.

Immediately after its capture, Butler and navy Lt. Homer C. Wick, with the blasting squad of the 5th Company, rushed back to Cap Haïtien for a ton of dynamite. They returned to the fort before first light and on the morning of 18 November the marines finally demolished Fort Rivière.

Gross, Iams, and Butler each received the Medal of Honor for their actions in this engagement.

Anne Cipriano Venzon

REFERENCES

Smedley D. Butler, *Old Gimlet Eye: The Adventures of Smedley D. Butler as Told to Lowell Thomas* (Farrar & Rinehart, 1933); Robert D. Heinl, Jr., *Soldiers of the Sea: The United States Marine Corps, 1775–1962* (U.S. Naval Institute Pr., 1962); Anne Cipriano Venzon, "The Papers of Maj. Gen. Smedley D. Butler, 1915–1918," Ph.D. diss., Princeton Univ., 1982.

France and the Spanish–Cuban/American War

France played an important role in assisting Spain and the United States to end the Spanish-Cuban/American War. Although the French were pro-Spanish and held large amounts of Spanish government bonds, the French government pressured Spain to end the war on U.S. terms.

French involvement in Spanish-U.S. diplomatic relations fell into two phases because of a change in government. Gabriel Hanotaux was foreign minister until 28 June 1898 when Théophile Delcassé replaced him. Hanotaux's role in the diplomatic negotiations was not as large as that of Delcassé.

As the war crisis developed between the United States and Spain, the Spanish government attempted to obtain diplomatic support from Europe's Great Powers. Hanotaux resisted Madrid's attempts to persuade France to abandon neutrality in favor of Spain's position in Cuba. He refused because Russia, France's ally, wanted to avoid involvement, because he worried that Great Britain would obtain an advantage with the United States, and because he did not believe that France had any means of influencing Washington's attitude toward Cuba.

After the war started, Hanotaux cooperated with Spain in attempts to start peace talks. He met separately several times with U.S. and Spanish diplomats, but his efforts failed.

When Delcassé became foreign minister, he took an important part in ending the Spanish-Cuban/American War. He was ably assisted by French Ambassador Jules M. Cambon in Washington. Delcassé and Cambon worried about the military growth of the United States and the possibility that the U.S. government might annex Spanish colonies near Europe, such as the Canary Islands, Ceuta, and the Balearic Islands. They were also troubled by the growing friendship between Great Britain and the United States. By pressuring Spain to end the war quickly, they hoped to limit U.S. military growth, its territorial expansion, and the growing Anglo-Saxon rapprochement.

When Spain was ready to end the war, it asked Delcassé to use Cambon as the Spanish negotiator in Washington. The French represented Spanish interests in the United States during the war, and Spain considered France more friendly than Great Britain.

Although Cambon was supposed to be only a messenger for Madrid, he played a larger role. He defined the French position during the negotiations, and he influenced Spanish policy. On Spain's behalf, Cambon attempted to soften U.S. President William McKinley's demands for ending the war, but he was unsuccessful. At the same time he regularly applied pressure either directly or through Paris on the Spanish government to accept U.S. terms. Cambon also helped to draw up the protocol which ended the Spanish-Cuban/American War, and on 12 August he signed it at the White House on behalf of Spain.

As a result of French assistance in ending the war, President McKinley agreed to have the peace conference meet in Paris. Delcassé hosted the conference, which held its formal sessions at the French foreign ministry. Although France was outwardly neutral on the key issue of the Philippines, Delcassé strongly urged the Spanish government to cede the islands to the United States and sign the treaty which formally ended the war.

John L. Offner

REFERENCES

Christopher Andrew, *Théophile Delcassé and the Making of the Entente Cordiale: A Reappraisal of French Foreign Policy, 1898–1905* (Macmillan, 1968); Ernest R. May, *Imperial Democracy: The Emergence of America as a Great Power* (Harcourt, 1961); John Offner, "The United States and France: Ending the Spanish-American War," *Diplomatic History*, 7 (1983), 1–22; Louis M. Sears, "French Opinion of the Spanish-American War," *The Hispanic American Historical Review*, 7 (1927), 25–44; Geneviève Tabouis, *The Life of Jules Cambon*, translated by C.F. Atkinson (Jonathan Cape, 1938).

Funston, Frederick (1865–1917)

Frederick Funston was the most touted hero of the Philippine War, virtually a national idol, who seemed highly likely to occupy the White House at some point. He was born in 1865 in Kansas, the son of a Civil War hero who was later a congressman representing that state. Because of his five-foot, four-inch height and lackluster academic record, he was turned down by the United States Military Academy at West Point. He attended the University of Kansas without earning a degree. After a succession of jobs, he joined the revolutionary army in Cuba with the rank of captain, returning to Kansas 18 months later, in 1898, to recover from wounds and malaria. With the declaration of war against Spain, he was offered the command of the 20th Kansas Volunteer Regiment with the rank of colonel. His regiment was ordered to the Philippines after a training stint in San Francisco. It anchored in a semicircular line around Manila facing the Filipino nationalists, erstwhile *de facto* allies of the United States in the war with Spain. When war broke out between these two armies on 4 February 1899, Funston's regiment was part of Gen. Arthur MacArthur's division that pursued the nationalist leader, Gen. Emilio Aguinaldo y Famy, who fought delaying actions as he retreated to a mountain refuge in northeastern Luzon.

Funston was highly skilled at advertising himself as a hero in the national press, firing off almost as many press releases as he did bullets. Often this process involved personal histrionics to impress correspondents on hand, but which had little military value. Almost always, his actions violated army regulations that required he remain with the bulk of his command at all times. Instead, he led a charge with 13 men into an already abandoned and burning Malolos, Aguinaldo's capital. At Calacoon, he was in the vanguard of three companies in a bayonet charge. He swam across the Bagbag River with three of his men to take a deserted redoubt on the opposite bank, although MacArthur had already forded that river elsewhere and much closer to the retreating enemy. He was the first to cross a bridge spanning the Guiguintó River and was on the first raft with 21 men to cross the Tulliajan River. Again, he swam across the Rio Chico with four men, leaving his entire regiment on the other side. As a brigadier general commanding an entire brigade during his second tour, Funston led a company of cavalry on an all-night ride to surprise a small guerrilla encampment. Such maneuvers should have been, at best, led by a captain, more often by a sergeant, or even by a corporal, not by a "bird colonel," or a one-star general. At Calumpit on the Rio Grande de Pampanga, however, Funston's heroism was quite significant for the military operation. Two Kansans swam a line across and secured it to the opposite bank. Funston and eight others were on the first raft propelled across by means of that line. More trips augmented his force to 41, with which he surprised Gen. António Narciso Luna de St. Pedro, who quickly retreated before discovering just how small was the colonel's contingent and before completing the destruction of a railroad bridge much coveted by MacArthur to haul artillery and supplies across. Funston and the two swimmers were awarded Medals of Honor, and Funston was also promoted to brigadier general of volunteers for this impressive feat.

The state volunteer regiments returned to the United States in summer 1899 and disbanded. In Kansas, a number of former officers and soldiers in the regiment made serious charges against Funston: that he had "commanded, condoned, and rewarded rapine and murder." Even before he left the Philippines, a soldier's letter reporting that Funston had ordered prisoners to be shot fell into the hands of an anti-imperialist editor who published it, forcing an investigation. MacArthur's advocate general collected a number of damaging affidavits from officers and men corroborating the initial complaint, but Gen. Elwell S. Otis let the matter drop. A former civilian teamster had a letter published describing Funston leading a mock mass in stolen ecclesiastical garb to amuse his soldiers from the "Bible belt," while a former nurse accused Funston of looting two silver chalices from a church and removing a lavishly embroidered robe from a statue of the Madonna to give to his wife. All this quickly followed a Funston speech at Stanford University in which he had blamed the friars for the war, calling for their expulsion from the islands and the confiscation of their property. He launched a suit against the Catholic *Monitor* in San Francisco for charging him with religious bigotry and threatened one against Archbishop John Ireland merely for demanding an investigation into these charges.

Under such clouds of suspicion, Funston returned to Luzon at the end of 1899 to command a brigade of three national volunteer regiments. By then, the Filipino nationalists were resorting exclusively to guerrilla tactics, a mode of warfare not entirely suited to Funston's impetuous personality. He soon announced at a press conference that he had summarily executed some prisoners in retaliation for a successful ambush of some of his Macabebe Scouts. Such self-incrimination confirmed the worst rumors he had left behind, but when anti-imperialists demanded that he be indicted, and *The Call* in San Francisco ran a large headline that "Funston May Be Court-Martialed," he beat a quick retreat, claiming that he had been misquoted: the prisoners were killed "while attempting to escape."

A year later, having survived yet another army inquiry that was more of a cover-up than an investigation, Funston again became the hero of the hour in spring 1901 when he masterminded a brilliant and daring maneuver to capture Aguinaldo at his remote, carefully guarded headquarters in Palanan, just off the rugged northeastern coast of Luzon. Soldiers in his command had captured a courier bearing a coded message from Aguinaldo to his cousin requesting reinforcements. Once deciphered and once the courier had been persuaded to reveal his commander's location, Funston recruited 80 Tagalog-speaking Macabebe volunteers serving in the Philippine Scouts to pose as the requested troops. Four renegade "insurgent" officers plus a former Spanish secret agent in Funston's employ agreed to play their officers, while the general and four other officers, dressed as enlisted men, went along as "prisoners," captured en route to Palanan. The navy landed them far enough away to avoid detection, and Funston's group trekked over 100 miles to grab the astonished Aguinaldo and take him back to the coast for a prearranged rendezvous with the USS *Vicksburg* on 25 March 1901.

Funston dominated the national headlines for weeks as editors compared his coup to Adm. George Dewey's victory at Manila Bay and to Theodore Roosevelt's charge up San Juan Hill. Roosevelt was one of Funston's more partisan fans and persuaded President William McKinley to reward him with a regular commission at his present rank despite opposition from within the army. Funston was too much of a national idol to be denied, however. The nation, moreover, wished to believe that he had single-handedly ended a vexatious war with his brilliant stroke, a view he encouraged by entitling a rendition of his feat for a popular magazine: "The Exploit Which Ended the War in the Philippines."

Nine months later, Funston came home to recover from a botched appendectomy and was given a hero's welcome. He soon embarked on a cross-country speaking marathon at banquets held in his honor. Adoring crowds blocked his train at whistle stops until he emerged to say a few words. Essentially, his standard speech included mocking Governor William H. Taft's "misguided" attempts to install democracy in pacified areas, veterans who testified before the committee chaired by Henry Cabot Lodge concerning U.S. atrocities in the Philippine War, and anti-imperialists to whom he attributed the war and its continuation by giving the Filipinos false hopes. "We believe everything and everybody should have a vote, down to cattle and horses," he scoffed (Miller, p. 233). Instead, Filipinos respect only force and need more "bayonet rule," he asserted. He also began to brag about the number of prisoners he had summarily executed to deter guerrilla activity in his sector, escalating the number of his victims up to 200 before President Roosevelt muzzled him with an official reprimand. He would also interrupt his speeches to shout, "Bully for Waller!" the marine major facing a court-martial, and then "Hooray for Smith!" the general commanding Waller who followed Waller to the dock (Miller, p. 234). More ominously, Funston suggested hanging some U.S. critics of the war and finally decided that the prominent U.S. citizens who recently signed a peace petition to Congress would be ideal candidates for this noose. Demands for his court-martial emanated not only from the press, but also from the halls of Congress.

Funston lived a charmed life, however, and he escaped into the shadows for the next four years with no further damage beyond Roosevelt's reprimand. In 1906, he was suddenly thrust back into the limelight as the hero of the great earthquake in San Francisco, where he was temporarily in command of the Department of the Pacific while his commander was en route to Washington. In effect, Funston immediately established martial law without consulting any higher authority, civilian or military. Armed patrols were ordered to "shoot immediately any person caught looting, or committing any serious misdemeanor" (Miller, p. 266). All vehicles were subject to army control, and his engineers were instructed to dynamite buildings to create fire lanes. He was severely criticized for this, but much of this criticism seems unfair; most of it emanated from Irish labor leaders in response to the general's well-known antilabor and anti-Catholic biases.

Funston justified labor and Catholic fears a year later when he was given command of the Department of the Pacific, just as a streetcar strike in San Francisco turned violent. He lectured a group of prominent citizens on the dangers afflicting the city. He assured astonished reporters on hand that he could take action against the strikers on his own authority. While his partisans cheered this lawless assertion, his old *bête noire* in the Philippines, Governor William Howard Taft, then the secretary of war, quickly intervened, issuing an order that he could not use troops in the manner described without the express approval of the president.

Months later, Roosevelt did order Funston to send troops to Goldfield, Nevada, at the request of Governor John Sparks, who was concerned about the role of the Industrial Workers of the World in a strike at the mines. Funston followed three companies of the 22nd Infantry Regiment to Goldfield on a personal fact-finding mission. Naturally, he agreed with the mine owners that violent anarchy was threatening the area and so advised Roosevelt. The president's own investigative team reached the opposite conclusion, so Funston was ordered to withdraw the troops before he could put into effect his proposed military solution to such strikes and the impending anarchy he perceived to have been "engulfing the nation."

Over the next eight years, Funston and his ardent champions labored to win a promotion for him. Roosevelt and then Taft would not dream of it, but Woodrow Wilson finally rewarded him with a second star in 1915, after Funston had done a creditable job commanding the U.S. forces of occupation at Veracruz, Mexico, in 1914. He was given command on the Mexican border, where he supervised the Punitive Expedition after Francisco "Pancho" Villa, led by Brig. Gen. John J. Pershing. Funston dropped dead in San Antonio on 19 February 1917. The watch officer on duty at the War Department that evening, Maj. Douglas

MacArthur, brought the news to President Wilson, who was dining with Secretary of War Newton D. Baker, and it was made clear to young MacArthur, or so he later claimed, that Funston had already been selected to lead an American Expeditionary Force to France if the nation entered the Great War. Only months later, Funston's newly promoted subordinate, John J. Pershing, commanded that army in France.

Stuart Creighton Miller

REFERENCES

Thomas W. Crouch, *A Yankee Guerrillero: Frederick Funston and the Cuban Insurrection, 1896–1897* (Memphis State Univ. Pr., 1975); Frederick Funston, *Memories of Two Wars: Cuban and Philippine Experiences* (Scribner, 1911); Brian M. Linn, "Guerrilla Fighter: Frederick Funston in the Philippines, 1900–1901," *Kansas History*, 10 (1987), 2–16; Stuart Creighton Miller, *"Benevolent Assimilation": The American Conquest of the Philippines* (Yale Univ. Pr., 1982).

See also Public Opinion and the Philippine War.

García, Calixto (c. 1839–1898)

Probably best known in the United States from Elbert H. Hubbard's essay, "A Message to Garcia," Calixto García rose to prominence during the Cuban struggle for independence. He was one of the most important military leaders in the Cuban revolutionary armies and also played an important role as an intermediary between the United States government and the anti-Spanish Cuban revolutionaries during the Spanish-Cuban/American War.

Born in Holguín, Santiago Province, García served as an apprentice in his uncle's Havana law office, but returned to his native eastern Cuba to manage the family land and business before he completed his studies. In 1868 he joined the anti-Spanish movement organized by Carlos Manuel de Céspedes. That movement had the support of wealthy landowners in the eastern provinces who wanted political and economic independence from Spain. On 10 October 1868, in the town of Yara in Oriente Province, Céspedes and his followers proclaimed Cuban independence and began an unsuccessful 10-year struggle against the Spanish forces in Cuba.

During the Ten Years War (1868–1878) the Cuban leadership quickly recognized Calixto García as an excellent soldier and a keen strategist. He initially served as second-in-command to Gen. Máximo Gómez y Báez, the commander in chief of the rebel army. In mid-1872 García took command of the forces in Oriente Province. In late 1874 Spanish forces captured and sent García to Spain, where he remained imprisoned until hostilities ended in February 1878.

Upon his release from prison, García settled in New York, where he organized the Comite Revolucionario Cubana to continue the struggle for independence. With the support of Antonio Maceo, García planned another insurrection. In August 1878 the two men released their "Kingston Proclamation" claiming that Spain had not fulfilled its obligations under the 1878 Pact of Zanjon.

In May 1880 García and his followers made an ill-prepared invasion of Cuba. Three months later, García surrendered to the Spanish and was again imprisoned in Spain. This brief episode became known as *La Guerra Chiquita* (the Little War). Eventually freed from prison, he returned to the United States to continue his revolutionary agitation.

In 1895 García returned to Cuba to join Máximo Gómez and Antonio Maceo in a renewed struggle for independence. General García assumed his former role as second-in-command to Gómez. Relying on guerrilla tactics, the rebels quickly seized control of the eastern provinces. With José J. Martí as their spiritual leader, the revolutionaries declared the Republic of Cuba in September. By mid-January 1896 the dissidents controlled most of the island.

In early 1896 a new Spanish commander, Gen. Valeriano Weyler y Nicolau, instituted a new counterinsurgency strategy against Cuban forces. When the new Spanish offensive began to falter, García, the new military chief of Oriente Province, regained the initiative. García attacked and quickly captured the important towns of Jiguaní and Victoria de las Tunas. García's army, by now the largest and best trained of the rebel forces, soon had firm control of eastern Cuba.

Throughout 1897 and 1898, García and the other rebel leaders carried out continued guerrilla warfare against the entrenched Spanish forces. Years of warfare began to take its toll on the poorly equipped and under-supplied revolutionaries whose initiative began to languish. Despite such problems, García's army, receiving occasional support from the United States, remained the only rebel force capable of more than small-unit action. Because of that fact, military planners in the United States bypassed the Cuban commander-in-chief, Máximo Gómez, and opened direct negotiations with García to obtain his help in preparing for a U.S. invasion of Cuba.

On 9 April 1898, two weeks before the U.S. declaration of war on Spain, Secretary of War Russell A. Alger and Maj. Gen. Nelson A. Miles, commanding general of the United States Army, sent army Lt. Andrew S. Rowan to Cuba to establish contact with García. Rowan finally made his way to García's mountain camp, and on 1 May, after the U.S. declaration of war, the rebel leader promised cooperation with the United States and sent three of his officers to Washington to discuss the situation in Cuba with the War Department. In doing so, García committed himself independently of the other Cuban rebel leaders.

On 2 June General Miles requested García's help in facilitating the arrival of Maj. Gen. William R. Shafter and his U.S. expeditionary force. In preparation for the U.S. landing, García's troops besieged major Spanish posts in eastern Cuba, making it impossible for the Spanish to reinforce Santiago. The Cuban general also deployed troops to the coast to protect Shafter's troops as they arrived.

Shafter met with García and Rear Adm. William T. Sampson, commander of the U.S. naval squadron stationed off the coast of Cuba, to discuss operational plans. During the 20–21 June meeting, Shafter adopted García's suggestion that he land his force at Daiquirí, east of Santiago Bay, and then to move on Santiago. On 22 June Shafter's V Corps, supported by naval gunfire and by a simultaneous land attack by García's force, went ashore.

Before he ordered the frontal attack on San Juan Heights, Shafter ordered Brig. Gen. Henry W. Lawton to seize quickly the fortified village of El Caney, cutting off Santiago's water supply and, if necessary, intercepting rumored Spanish reinforcements. García's troops supported Lawton's drive, which began on 1 July. The Cuban troops followed Lawton to seal off the northwest side of Santiago.

Despite Lawton's inability to take El Caney rapidly, García's force performed admirably. Though of little value in frontal attacks throughout the rest of the campaign, García and his force harassed Spanish garrisons and furnished invaluable aid in scouting enemy positions for the expeditionary force and screening its front and flanks. When Santiago fell, despite García's aid in winning the battle, Shafter kept the Cuban revolutionaries out of Santiago and prohibited them from participating in its occupation. Relations between Shafter and García worsened when the U.S. commander did not invite the Cuban general to take part in the negotiations that ended the campaign, or to attend the formal capitulation ceremonies on 17 July.

On the day of the capitulation García sent a long letter to Shafter outlining his grievances. Later, after Shafter left Cuba, Gen. Leonard Wood tried to placate García with an invitation to visit the United States. García accepted Wood's offer and was subsequently honored with a public ceremony in New York City and a meeting with President William McKinley. While in Washington, García suddenly died on 11 December 1898, the day after the Spanish and U.S. governments signed the Treaty of Paris officially terminating the Spanish-Cuban/American War.

Theresa L. Kraus

REFERENCES

Leslie Bethell, ed., *The Cambridge History of Latin America* (Cambridge Univ. Pr., 1986), vol. 5; French Ensor Chadwick, *The Relations of the United States and Spain: The Spanish-American War* (Scribner, 1911), 2 vols.; Graham A. Cosmas, *An Army for Empire: The United States Army in the Spanish-American War* (Univ. of Missouri Pr., 1977); Jose M. Hernandez, "The Role of the Military in the Making of the Cuban Republic," Ph.D. diss., Georgetown Univ., 1970; Jaime Suchlicki, *Historical Dictionary of Cuba* (Scarecrow Pr., 1988); David F. Trask, *The War With Spain in 1898* (Macmillan, 1981).

See also Military Cooperation of the United States With the Cuban Revolutionaries (1898).

Garcia, Pantaleon T. (1856–1936)

Pantaleon T. Garcia was a prominent military and political leader in the Philippine nationalist movement that battled first Spain and later the United States.

Garcia was born in Imus, Cavite, the Philippines, on 17 July 1856. After finishing the teacher's course at age 19, he taught at Silang, Cavite. In 1896 he joined the secret revolutionary society, the Katipunan, which aimed at separating the Philippines from Spain. When the revolution against Spain broke out in August 1896, Garcia immediately joined the armed resistance with his fellow Caviteno, Emilio Aguinaldo y Famy, in the Battles of Binakayan in Kawit, Pasong Santol in Imus, and Naic, where he received a slight head wound during the first phase of the revolution between August 1896 and December 1897. Garcia was later promoted to brigadier general, and he was entrusted with the defense of Imus by Aguinaldo. General Garcia's wife, Valeriana Elises, also took part in the many military operations he led.

One of the most controversial and tragic events of the revolution was the execution of Andrés Bonifacio, founder of the Katipunan in 1892, and his brother, Procopio, by the Aguinaldo revolutionary government established in March 1897. The board that conducted the pretrial hearing on the Bonifacio brothers, who were charged with sedition and treason, was presided over by General Garcia. It heard testimony from witnesses between April and May 1897. General Garcia recommended a court-martial, which sentenced the Bonifacio brothers to death. They were executed in May 1897.

Shortly after this, the battle began to turn against the Filipino revolutionaries, and Aguinaldo retreated to Biak-na-bato in Bulacan, north of Manila. He took with him, among others, General Garcia, who figured in the victorious Battle of Puray in June 1897. At Biak-na-bato, a truce was concluded between the Spanish forces and the Filipino revolutionaries in December 1897, temporarily ending the revolution.

With the outbreak of the Spanish-Cuban/American War and the likely involvement of the Philippines, the Spanish governor general, Basilio Augustin, organized a consultative assembly of Filipinos in April 1898 in a desperate attempt to win the Philippine people's support in the fight against the United States. Pantaleon Garcia was one of two high-ranking Katipunan generals appointed to this assembly in May 1898.

The revolution against Spain resumed on the return of Aguinaldo in 1898 from exile in Hong Kong, where he stayed under the terms of the 1897 truce. Aguinaldo immediately organized military areas in each province under rebel control. General Garcia was appointed one of the zone commanders in Morong, the politico-military district adjacent to the province of Manila. In July 1898 Generals Garcia and Artemio Ricarte were issued credentials by Aguinaldo to negotiate the capitulation of the Spanish in Manila, already surrounded by Filipino rebels. Nothing came of these negotiations, and the Spanish eventually surrendered to U.S. forces in August 1898. In September 1898 General Garcia was appointed a delegate to the Malolos Congress, a constitutional assembly established to draft a constitution for a Philippine republic.

After the outbreak of the Philippine War in February 1899, General Garcia was made general of division in March 1899, and in July he was made army chief of staff. In November 1899, Aguinaldo, fleeing from U.S. pursuit, created the politico-military government of Central Luzon and ordered his troops to fight as roving guerrillas. Garcia was appointed supreme politico-military commander of the Central Luzon government.

In a battle fought in February 1900, the revolutionaries defended the important maintenance plant of the Manila-Dagupan railroad line in

Caloocan against a U.S. assault by land and sea. General Garcia was wounded in this battle and became seriously ill. He was taken to Jaen, Nueva Ecija, for treatment, and while still confined in bed, he was captured by Capt. Erneste Virgil Smith in May 1900. In June 1900 he took advantage of an amnesty issued by Military Governor General Arthur MacArthur and took the oath of allegiance to the United States.

After the Philippine War, General Garcia occupied several positions in the government as first municipal president of Imus (1903–1905), justice of the peace (1906–1907), and superintendent of the Colonia Agricola in Cavite. He died on 16 August 1936.

Bernardita Reyes Churchill

Garde d'Haiti/Gendarmerie d'Haiti

The Gendarmerie d'Haiti, later renamed Garde d'Haiti, was a constabulary organized and trained by U.S. Marines to keep order and to perform other public services during and after the occupation of Haiti from 1915 to 1934.

Restoration of public order in Haiti was a primary objective of the U.S. intervention on 28 July 1915. The marines disbanded the old army of 9,000 men which included 208 generals and 50 colonels, and under Article X of the Treaty of 1915 the Haitian government agreed to replace it with a constabulary of native Haitians organized and officered by U.S. personnel. Immediately, a marine, Maj. Smedley D. Butler, began recruiting for the new force that was originally limited to 336 men but later expanded to 2,500. On 1 February 1916 Adm. William B. Caperton announced that thereafter all military and police duties would be performed by the Gendarmerie d'Haiti supported by the expeditionary force. Six months later, on 24 August, the United States and Haiti signed the Gendarmerie Agreement which set forth in detail the organization and duties of the constabulary and placed it directly under the president of Haiti, although in practice the marine officer in command continued to exercise exclusive authority.

The development of the Gendarmerie falls into three periods corresponding to the presidencies of Philippe Sudre Dartiguenave (1915–1922), Louis Borno (1922–1930), and Sténio Joseph Vincent (1930–1941). During the Dartiguenave years, emphasis was placed on recruiting, maintaining public order, and suppressing the Caco War of 1918–1920. From the first, peasants proved eager to join the new constabulary, attracted by prompt payment of salaries and decent rations. Their officers were U.S. marines on temporary duty in the service of Haiti who were awarded Haitian rank and modest stipends from the Haitian government in addition to their regular pay. Since few of the marines spoke French, and even those who did could not easily communicate with the creole-speaking troops, they drilled their men in English by rote out of U.S. drill regulations and equipped them with surplus marine gear and old-model Krag rifles. It was hoped that the language problem would ease when Haitian aristocrats became officers, but the French-speaking elite knew as little creole patois as the U.S. personnel, and their overall performance in the first years was disappointing. Therefore, when the European war drained the contingent of U.S. officers, noncommissioned marines were upgraded and assigned to Gendarmerie units as officers.

For military purposes Haiti was divided into three departments—Port-au-Prince, Cap Haïtien, and Cayes—with general headquarters in Port-au-Prince. Each department was divided into districts commanded by captains. The districts were further broken down into subdistricts commanded by lieutenants. The U.S. officers were veritable potentates within their districts. They exercised normal police functions, supervised travel and traffic, regulated weights and measures, prevented smuggling, collected vital statistics, enforced the sanitation code, and administered prisons. They served as judges of all civil and criminal cases. As "communal advisors," they collected taxes and controlled the financial activities of mayors and town councils. The Haitians soon discovered that these white commandants could be just as arbitrary in their actions as their black predecessors, but in many communities the marines did bring about positive changes. They cleaned up the prisons, taught useful trades, rationalized tax assessments, and made a stab at improving sanitation.

Pending the organization of a department of public works, the government placed the Gendarmerie in charge of road construction and repair. Since funds were not available to pay for this work, the marines resorted to the *corvée*—a provision of the Haitian Code Rural that required the men of each district to work for free for a certain number of days each year on local roads. The peasants accepted the *corvée* as a legitimate obligation when it was fairly administered, and by the end of 1917 they had completed the highway between Port-au-Prince and Cap Haïtien as well as 100 miles of other roads. By mid–1918 however, there was mounting evidence that the gendarmes were routinely abusing the *corvée* by forcing men to work outside their own district and conscripting them for more than the legal number of days.

Outrage at these excesses induced many peasants to join the *Caco* revolt against Dartiguenave's government and his U.S. supporters that broke out in September 1918. The violence overwhelmed the resources of the gendarmes. Therefore, the marines, formerly restricted to reinforcing units in the coastal towns, took charge of restoring peace. The revolt at its height involved 15,000 rebels and one-quarter of the national territory, but after the death of *Caco* leader Charlemagne Masséna Péralt in October 1919, its fury abated. By mid–1920 when the last *Caco* surrendered, rebel casualties stood at 2,250 dead against 98 dead or wounded marines and gendarmes.

Rumors of widespread atrocities committed by government forces against the *Cacos* prompted the United States to hold two inquiries into the conduct of the war. The first undertaken by a Naval Court of Inquiry in October 1920 exonerated the marines. The second, conducted by the United States Senate between August and December 1921, concluded that the use of the *corvée* had been a "blunder" on the part of the marines and that especially in the first six months of the revolt, atrocities had occurred when the gendarmes lost control of the situation. The senators went on to point out other weaknesses in the occupation rule, such as the rapid turnover of U.S. officials. They recommended the creation of the office of high commissioner to coordinate all treaty services and enable the United States to exercise control more effectively.

The restoration of peace in Haiti began the second period in the development of the Gendarmerie—a decade of unbroken tranquility undergirded by close collaboration between Gen. John H. Russell, the high commissioner appointed by President Warren G. Harding in January 1922, and Louis Borno, elected presi

dent of Haiti by the Council of State in April of the same year. Martial law remained in force, but was applied only on rare occasions. Public works and road-building projects flourished while the gendarmes pursued their tasks as police, fire fighters, communal advisors, and coast guards, as well as in the administration of prisons, customs and immigration, emergency communications, light houses, and rural medicine. In recognition that these duties were much broader than the name "gendarmerie" or "police" implied, the force was renamed Garde d'Haiti on 1 November 1928.

Organization and discipline improved. Schools for enlisted men stressed marksmanship, and in 1924 a Haitian rifle team composed of gendarmes tied with France for second place in the Olympic games. In 1922 General Russell inaugurated the École Militaire to train Haitian officers in a course of study modeled on the United States Naval Academy. Some of the cadets found the military discipline, the hard work required of junior officers, and service outside Port-au-Prince too demanding, but most stuck it out. By 1929 Haitians made up just under 40 percent of the 197 Garde officers.

Borno's announcement on 5 October 1929 that he was canceling popular elections for the next president touched off a series of strikes and demonstrations. In Cayes on 7 December, a marine patrol attempting to control a mob of angry peasants, fired into the crowd, leaving 25 dead and many wounded. This tragedy convinced President Herbert Hoover that it was time to get out of Haiti. He appointed a commission headed by W. Cameron Forbes to investigate when and how the United States might withdraw from the island. After holding hearings in Port-au-Prince, the commission called for the resignation of President Borno, rapid Haitianization of the Garde, and the evacuation of marines as soon as possible.

Under intense U.S. pressure, Borno stepped down, permitting an interim president, Eugéne Roy, to oversee the election in May 1930 of a new chief-of-state, Sténio Joseph Vincent. Vincent's 11-year administration marked the final stage in the evolution of the Garde. On 1 December 1930 the government relieved the constabulary of the obligation of serving as communal advisor to the towns, but it continued to perform its other multifarious functions. Vincent spared no pains in enhancing the scope and efficiency of the École Militaire, as each year its graduates replaced U.S. marines whose tours of duty had expired as officers of the Garde. On 1 August 1934, when the marines withdrew, all 199 officers were Haitians. Col. Démosthènes P. Calixte assumed the duties of commandant over the most formidable force postrevolutionary Haiti had ever seen. The Garde had modern weapons, a serviceable communications systems, and its officers, who exhibited a degree of discipline rare in civil services, ranked among the best-educated and most able Haitians of their generation.

In evaluating the role played by the Gendarmerie/Garde during the occupation, most scholars agree that the marines did an excellent job. They replaced the old, corrupt army with a trained constabulary that kept the peace for most of the period of U.S. rule and made possible progress in other areas such as highway construction and improved sanitation. Yet, like the Dominican Republic and Nicaragua, where similar forces were created, once the U.S. presence ended, it was only a matter of time before the officers began to meddle in the political processes. As long as Colonel Calixte remained its commander, the Garde held fast to its professional ideals and its prestige survived even after its failure to retaliate when Leonidas Rafael Trujillo Molina massacred 20,000 Haitian cane cutters in the western provinces of the Dominican Republic in 1937. The dismissal of Calixte the following year, however, and a purge of the better-trained officers led to their replacement by younger, less experienced men who were loyal to Vincent rather than to the republic. By 1939 the Garde was thoroughly politicized. "Thereafter it played a role analogous to the military machines in the neighboring Caribbean republics" (Rotberg, p. 158).

Jane M. Rausch

REFERENCES

Robert Debs Heinl, Jr., and Nancy Gordon Heinl, *Written in Blood: The Story of the Haitian People, 1492–1971* (Houghton Mifflin, 1978); Lester D. Langley, *The United States and the Caribbean in the Twentieth Century*, rev. ed. (Univ. of Georgia Pr., 1985); James H. McCrocklin, *Garde d'Haiti, 1915–1934* (U.S. Naval Institute Pr., 1956); Dana G. Munro, *The United States and the Caribbean Republics, 1921–1933* (Princeton Univ. Pr., 1974); Robert I. Rotberg, *Haiti: The Politics of Squalor* (Houghton Mifflin, 1971).

See also Caco Campaigns, Haiti (1918–1920).

German Involvement With Francisco "Pancho" Villa

One intriguing aspect of Francisco "Pancho" Villa's raid on Columbus, New Mexico, in March 1916, is his motivation. Among the theories suggested is that the raid was instigated by a German agent, Felix Sommerfeld, as part of a master plan to provoke a war between Mexico and the United States.

When World War I began, Germany decided to divert U.S. attention from itself by creating a situation in which the United States was involved with Mexican problems. Germany promised money and weapons to the exiled Victoriano Huerta, but this effort was foiled when U.S. authorities arrested him before he could return to Mexico. Germany also planned to support Pancho Villa through Sommerfeld.

Felix Sommerfeld had been born in Germany but had immigrated to the United States in 1896. After extensive travels, he turned up in Mexico and became a confidant of a number of revolutionary leaders, including Francisco I. Madero and Villa. In 1914 and 1915 Sommerfeld was able to purchase arms for the Villa forces with funds partially provided by the German government and apparently laundered through a bank in St. Louis, Missouri. In addition, he was in a position to have collaborated with Lyman B. Rauschbaum, another German who was an aide to Villa.

In 1915 Bernhard Dernburg, German propaganda chief in the United States, received a proposal from Sommerfeld that he, Sommerfeld, could use his influence with Villa to instigate a border raid. After discussions with officials in Germany, Sommerfeld's plan was approved. However, he ran into problems with U.S. authorities at this time, and the German government disassociated itself from him.

It is possible that German assistance or suggestions helped Villa decide to raid Columbus, but there is no direct evidence to make such a link.

Marvin E. Fletcher

REFERENCES

Friedrich Katz, *The Secret War in Mexico: Europe, the United States, and the Mexican Revolution* (Univ. of Chicago Pr., 1981); Michael C. Meyer, "Felix Sommerfeld and the Columbus Raid of 1916," *Arizona and the West*, 25 (1983), 213–228; Francis J. Munch, "Villa's Columbus Raid: Practical Politics or German Design?" *New Mexico Historical Review*, 44 (1969), 189–214; James A. Sandos, "German Involvement in Northern Mexico, 1915–1916: A New Look at the Columbus Raid," *Hispanic American Historical Review*, 50 (1970), 60–88.

See also Columbus, New Mexico, Battle (1916); Villa, Francisco "Pancho."

German Naval Operations in the Philippines (1898–1899)

Shortly after Commodore George Dewey's victory at the Battle of Manila Bay in the Philippine Islands, Prince Heinrich of Prussia sent a report to Berlin indicating that the end of Spanish rule in the archipelago opened certain opportunities for Germany. Prince Heinrich, who was commander of the German Asiatic fleet, reported that the Filipino people wished to have the islands become a protectorate of one of the European powers, particularly Germany.

German Foreign Secretary Prince Bernhard von Bülow ordered Adm. Otto von Diederichs to relieve Heinrich and directed him to proceed to the Philippines, where he interfered with Dewey's operations, violated the U.S. blockade, and frustrated Dewey, who relied on naval customs and etiquette to obtain respect for the U.S. position.

Von Diederichs was unaware of Foreign Ministry plans to take the Philippines as a protectorate or alternatively if Germany was unable to stop the U.S. acquisition of the islands, it would insist on some compensation for its loss of the islands.

The first German ship to arrive in the Philippines, the cruiser *Irene*, sailed into Manila harbor on 6 May without stopping to receive observer instructions from the blockade commander. Dewey dismissed the incident as an omission, suggesting that the *Irene*'s captain had little experience with blockades and that the episode should not be taken too seriously. Dewey's sense of fairness quickly evaporated as the Germans became more aggressive.

During the next three months, von Diederichs moved ships during night hours, interfered with Filipino operations against the Spanish, refused to cooperate with U.S. efforts to identify German movements, and landed men at former Spanish positions and engaged in maneuvers and training—all without Dewey's permission. By the end of June, the Germans outnumbered Dewey in men and ships, causing Dewey increased concern over Germany's objectives.

In July the situation came to a crisis when the Germans landed and evacuated Spanish women and children from Grande Island, clearly in violation of U.S. blockade regulations. Dewey was outraged and in an altercation with von Diederichs's representative, he threatened war with Germany if the German admiral did not comply with Dewey's directives. At this point the Germans backed away, gradually decreasing naval forces in the area, partly in response to Dewey's intemperate remarks and partly in the realization that earlier expectations of pro-German sentiment among the Filipinos were unfounded. After the fall of Manila to the United States in August, Germany played no role in the islands.

In secret negotiations with Spain after the United States signed the Treaty of Paris with the Spanish, Germany acquired the Caroline Islands, the Palau Islands, and the Mariana Islands for approximately five million United States dollars.

Vernon L. Williams

REFERENCES

Vernon L. Williams, "The U.S. Navy in the Philippine Insurrection and Subsequent Native Unrest, 1898–1906," Ph.D. diss., Texas A&M Univ., 1985.

See also Chichester, Edward; Germany and the Spanish-Cuban/American War.

Germany and the Spanish-Cuban/American War

Confronted with the outbreak of the Spanish-Cuban/American War and the U.S. invasion of Cuba, the German emperor, Wilhelm II, and his government faced a dilemma. They were unwilling to take the first steps to support Spain and antagonize the United States, yet neither were they interested in the weakening of the monarchic principle nor in a shift of spheres of economic influence, which a U.S. victory would produce.

The German government consequently adhered to a policy of nonintervention throughout the war. Nevertheless, due to the influence of the U.S. ambassador to Berlin, Andrew D. White, German authorities detained and searched a Spanish ship in Hamburg harbor which had been suspected of transporting weapons (the suspicion proved unfounded). The German press and public opinion, however, sided emphatically with Spain, a fact well known and strongly resented in the United States.

Germany and the United States were the last Western nations to enter the race for overseas colonies. In 1897, Adm. Alfred von Tirpitz had launched a great new German naval program, but the German navy posed no threat to the United States. The imperial government lacked even a theoretical concept for war with the United States. However, this was not known on the other side of the Atlantic, and the German naval buildup was viewed with unease in the United States.

While Germany never had any interest in Cuba, the Philippines was a different matter. Germany refused Filipino applications for help against Spain and even for a German regent in 1896, 1897, and 1898; finally, the emperor prohibited the reception of Filipino envoys. Yet, Foreign Minister Bernhard von Bülow took some of these requests fairly seriously but, with the emperor's consent, sent Adm. Otto von Diederichs to Manila with instructions to observe the situation.

Diederichs's deployment unnerved the commander of the U.S. fleet, Commodore George Dewey, and led to the so-called Manila incident. Diederichs's questioning of Dewey's blockade of Manila, as well as rumors of additional approaching German ships and German hostile intentions, finally caused some clashes between the two admirals and allegedly even some minor military episodes.

Although these occurrences were not taken very seriously by anyone involved, the U.S. public reacted with great excitement. Between the two governments, there was no serious conflict, but on the level of public opinion, the Manila incident sparked a decisive and harmful change in German-U.S. relations.

In several conferences with the German deputy foreign minister, Oswald von Richthofen,

Ambassador White tried to balance the German interest in "gratis" colonies with the U.S. fear of German intervention. Richthofen assured White that Germany did not wish to interfere with U.S. operations in the Philippines, but at that point it still looked as if the United States would not annex the Philippines. Only if there was no annexation would Germany step in and acquire the islands.

U.S. Secretary of State, William R. Day, did not understand White's position and criticized his careful diplomacy, but White pointed out that he had successfully attempted to "minimize any temptation to interfere" without even considering German intervention as an option. White had tried to gain the Germans' confidence and to remove any bitterness until the military success of the United States was assured, thus carrying the situation "fully past the danger point."

It may be assumed that a military conflict between Germany and the United States caused by the Spanish-Cuban/American War or by the Manila incident was never imminent, but impulsive actions on either side could have caused such a collision. That peace prevailed might be ascribed to careful bilateral diplomacy.

Wolfgang Drechsler

REFERENCES

Wolfgang J.M. Drechsler, *Andrew D. White in Deutschland: Der Vertreter der USA in Berlin, 1879–1881 und 1897–1902* (Hans-Dieter Heinz, 1989); Reiner Pommerin, *Der Kaiser und Amerika: Die USA in der Politik der Reichsleitung, 1890–1917* (Boehlau, 1986); Lester Burrell Shippee, "Germany and the Spanish-American War," *American Historical Review*, 30 (1925), 754–777; David F. Trask, *The War With Spain in 1898* (Macmillan, 1981); Alfred Vagts, *Deutschland und die Vereinigten Staaten in der Weltpolitik* (Macmillan, 1935), 2 vols.

See also German Naval Operations in the Philippines (1898–1899).

Girón Ruano, Manuel María (? –1929)

Manuel María Girón Ruano, one of Nicaraguan nationalist leader Augusto C. Sandino's most able officers, was finally captured by a U.S. marine patrol in 1929 and was subsequently killed by Nicaraguan forces that were independent of the marines. A Guatemalan, he had received military training in Europe and at one time had been commandant of Petén, Guatemala. About age 50 at the time of his service to Sandino, Girón was among the Sandinistas who moved into eastern Nicaragua around the Pis Pis mining region in March and April 1928. General Girón commanded a group that occupied and looted La Luz and Los Angeles gold mines, both owned by U.S. citizens. One citizen, George B. Marshall, who was assistant superintendent of La Luz Mine and taken prisoner at the time, remained in Girón's custody and died of malaria. Girón's dependability was demonstrated in May 1928, when he successfully defended a Sandinista rest area by persistently attacking a marine patrol at La Flor and again in August when he ambushed a force of marines along the Coco River. The latter operation was bungled when Sandino, unknown to Girón, withdrew his supporting troops and another Sandinista chief failed to protect Girón's left flank. To assuage Girón's anger over these mistakes, Sandino made him chief of staff.

On 3 February 1929 near San Albino, a marine patrol headed by 1st Lt. Herman H. Hanneken spotted a lone rider, Girón, who was headed out of the country for a period of rest. He was captured and taken to marine headquarters at Ocotal where Girón refused Col. Robert H. Dunlap's offer of freedom for leading a Nicaraguan volunteer force, commanded by Gen. Juan Escamilla, to Sandino's camp. He was released into Escamilla's custody on 2 March and was tried by court-martial. Despite Girón's challenge to the proceedings, he was found guilty and executed by a Nicaraguan firing squad.

William Kamman

REFERENCES

Carleton Beals, *Banana Gold* (Lippincott, 1932); Lejeune Cummins, *Quijote on a Burro: Sandino and the Marines, A Study in the Formulation of Foreign Policy* (La Impresora Azteca, 1958); Herman H. Hanneken, "A Discussion of the Voluntario Troops in Nicaragua," *Marine Corps Gazette*, 26 (1942), 120, 247–248, 250–254, 256, 258, 260, 262, 264, 266; Neill Macaulay, *The Sandino Affair* (Quadrangle, 1967); Vernon Edgar Megee, "United States Military Intervention in Nicaragua, 1909–1932," M.A. thesis, Univ. of Texas, 1963.

Glenn Springs, Texas, Skirmish (1916)

On 5 May 1916, approximately 80 Mexican raiders under the command of Natividad Álvarez crossed the Rio Grande into the Big Bend district of Texas and set off a chain of events that led to a brief U.S. military intervention into Coahuila, Mexico, and a crisis between the U.S. and Mexican governments. Although Álvarez held the rank of lieutenant colonel in the Villista army, his motivations for assaulting the isolated settlements appeared to have no political context, but simply rested on his need for supplies.

The bandits separated into two parties as they crossed the river under the cover of darkness to attack the villages at Glenn Springs and Boquillas, Texas. The former, consisting of a wax factory and a general store to supply the workers, was the initial target. Arriving at Glenn Springs a few minutes before midnight, the attackers achieved total surprise, killing a young boy and three of the nine soldiers stationed there. After looting the store, they returned to the rendezvous point on the river to await the second group, which had attacked the Deemer store at Boquillas, 10 miles to the east. The second band encountered no resistance because troops were not stationed there, and it withdrew from the settlement with supplies, money, and two captives, Jesse Deemer and Monroe Payne. During their retreat southward, the bandits seized additional hostages at a U.S.-managed silver mine south of the Rio Grande.

Three days later Maj. George T. Langhorne arrived from El Paso with two troops of 8th Cavalry and, with approval from the secretary of war, crossed into Mexico on 11 May. Following a 22-hour grueling march, the troops reached El Piño, where they liberated Deemer and Payne but were unable to catch the bandits. On 15 May Lt. Stuart W. Cramer, Jr. surprised the raiders at Castillon, killing and wounding several in a brief firefight. The Langhorne expedition had achieved all of its stated goals within two weeks by driving the attackers from the border, rescuing all prisoners, and restoring order to the Big Bend. A larger issue, however, compelled a quick end to this operation. Mexico's President Venustiano Carranza, already threatening military action against the much longer expedition of Gen. John J. Pershing that had been in neighboring Chihuahua since March, complained that this "little punitive expedition" from the Big Bend was pushing the two nations toward war. Hopeful of restoring diplomatic negotiations through the El Paso conference between Gen. Hugh L. Scott and Gen. Álvaro Obregón, the United States ordered the immediate withdrawal of Langhorne's force. They had been in Mexico for 16 days, had traveled more than 550 miles, and had performed their difficult task honorably.

Michael L. Tate

REFERENCES

Stuart N. Cramer, Jr., "The Punitive Expedition from Boquillas," *Journal of the United States Cavalry Association*, 27 (1916), 200–227; Carlysle Graham Raht, *The Romance of the Davis Mountains and Big Bend Country* (Rahtbooks Co., 1919); W.D. Smithers, "Bandit Raids in the Big Bend Country," *Publications of the West Texas Historical and Scientific Society* (1963), 74–105; Ronnie C. Tyler, *The Big Bend: A History of the Last Texas Frontier* (National Park Service, 1975); Ronnie C. Tyler, "The Little Punitive Expedition in the Big Bend," *Southwestern Historical Quarterly*, 78 (1975), 271–291.

Gómez y Báez, Máximo (1836–1905)

Máximo Gómez y Báez, together with Antonio Maceo and José Martí Julian y Perez, was one of the most important leaders in the struggle for the independence of Cuba. Indisputably the greatest military strategist among the revolutionaries, Gómez's astuteness and tactics—and unsurpassed knowledge of guerrilla tactics—brought many crucial military victories for the Cubans. A participant in both the Ten Years War (1868–1878) and the Cuban War of Independence (1895–1898), this professional soldier dedicated three decades of his life to the Cuban cause.

The story of Gómez is extraordinary. Born in 1836 in Baní, the Dominican Republic, he pursued a military career there, reaching the rank of captain. In 1865 he moved to Cuba, where he worked as a small businessman in the lumber industry. The outbreak of war in 1868 and his belief in the cause led him to devote his talents to the war against Spain. He was subsequently appointed general and for a decade was active in the struggle against Spain.

A common characteristic of Gómez's participation in both the 1868–1878 and 1895–1898 wars was his conviction that the way to defeat the Spanish control over Cuba was through a policy of economic sabotage. Sugar, he later said, was "the principal enemy of independence" because it provided funds for the metropolis (and hence paid the expenses of the occupying army), while making the retention of the Cuban colony an attractive policy for Spain. Common to his participation in both epic struggles was his determination to force all sugar estates and mills to cease production. Any landowners who rejected orders from the revolutionaries to do so automatically saw their properties put to the torch. In one successful campaign in 1875 Gómez was reputed to have destroyed in this fashion some 83 plantations in just six weeks.

Following the truce arranged in 1878, Gómez withdrew from military life and lived in Jamaica and later Honduras; yet he remained interested in an honorable Cuban victory over the Spanish forces. In 1879 he criticized new plans for armed opposition to Spain, the ill-fated *Guerra Chiquita* (Small War), claiming that the time for renewing the struggle had not arrived. Approached by the new generation of revolutionary leaders, he subsequently met José Martí in New York in 1884. The meeting was not successful; Martí publicly excoriated Gómez for both his authoritarian and overly military approach to the liberation struggle and his unrestrained scorn for civilian politicians.

Both men shortly overcame their differences, seeing the necessity of the other's cooperation. There followed a decade of planning, conspiring, and fund-raising during which time Gómez traveled tirelessly throughout the United States, the Dominican Republic, Jamaica, Panama, and Peru. This stage of laying a solid base for the revolution was crucial, yet, it was not the Dominican's strong suit. Gómez was widely recognized as being intolerant and irascible, autocratic in his military manners, and frequently contemptuous of his civilian colleagues, who were often wealthy settlers.

In 1893 the Partido Revolucionario Cubano (Cuban Revolutionary Party) named him general-in-chief of the rebel army, and once again his military prowess was called on. A brilliant strategist, he successfully used the same strategy as before in burning down dozens of plantations which had continued to operate. This time, however, he also took the war successfully to the west of Cuba—and wore out the Spanish forces by obliging them to chase him (under the blistering sun) following innumerable guerrilla attacks. By 1895 he headed an army of some 50,000 people, and Spanish morale—in the wake of this extremely successful campaign—was disastrously low.

The U.S. military intervention, following the mysterious destruction in Havana harbor of the *Maine*, ended the rebels' war. Gómez seemed unsure how to react to U.S. forces in Cuba. On one hand, he feared that resistance to the occupying forces might jeopardize the standing agreement and cause Washington to abrogate the pact; on the other hand, he could clearly see the dangers of exchanging one political master for another. The racism of the occupying troops, combined with the arrogance and scorn of U.S. leaders toward Cuban forces, was also deeply troubling to Gómez because it was the Cubans who had virtually defeated the Spanish forces before Washington decided to enter the fray.

Eventually, in the wake of further difficulties with Cuban civilian politicians, Gómez retired from the political scene. Occasionally writing stirring articles on the danger of U.S. designs on Cuba, the 70-year-old former general-in-chief decided that it was up to the new generation to wrestle with such concerns. He rejected an invitation in 1900 to run for the Cuban presidency, claiming that he had fulfilled his obligations. For 30 years he, a foreigner, had devoted his life to the revolutionary cause; since the successful military campaign had defeated the Spanish forces, it was time for the Cubans to wrestle with the political problem inherent in the growing U.S. control of the island. He died in Havana in 1905.

John M. Kirk

REFERENCES

Charles E. Chapman, *A History of the Cuban Republic: A Study in Hispanic American Politics* (Macmillan, 1927); Philip S. Foner, *Antonio Maceo: The "Bronze Titan" of Cuba's Struggle for Independence* (Monthly Review Pr., 1977); Philip S. Foner, *The Spanish-Cuban-American War and the Birth of American Imperialism, 1895–1902* (Monthly Review Pr., 1972); *Maximo Gomez Aproximacion a su Cronlogia, 1836–1905* (Editorial Academia, 1986); *Maximo Gomez y Baez Sus Campanas Militares* (Editora Politica, 1986).

Gorgas, William Crawford (1854–1920)

William Crawford Gorgas, a career officer in the United States Army Medical Corps, was one of the leaders in the fight against yellow fever in U.S.-occupied Cuba and led medical and sanitation programs in Panama and other tropical countries.

Gorgas was born on 3 October 1854, in Mobile, Alabama. He was the son of Lt. Josiah and Amelia Gayle Gorgas, the daughter of a former governor of Alabama. His early life was spent at various army posts in Maine, South Carolina, and Kentucky. In 1861 when war between the North and South seemed imminent, William's father resigned his army commission and offered his services to the Confederacy. Jefferson Davis appointed him chief of ordnance with the rank of brigadier general.

After the war the Gorgas family moved from Virginia to Brierfield, Alabama, where Gorgas attended the local school. In 1868, Josiah Gorgas was appointed headmaster of the junior department of the newly opened Episcopal University of the South in Swanee, Tennessee. William transferred to Swanee and graduated with a B.A. in 1875.

Gorgas had been thinking of an army career for many years, and after an unsuccessful attempt to gain an appointment to the United States Military Academy at West Point, he decided to become an army doctor. He entered Bellevue Medical College in New York City in 1876 and graduated in 1879. After an internship of one year at Bellevue Hospital, he entered the United States Army Medical Department.

While stationed at Fort Brown, Texas, in 1882, he treated Marie Doughty, the sister-in-law of the post commander, for yellow fever and developed the disease himself. The two were convalescent at the same time, and in 1884, they were married.

Those experiences with yellow fever spurred Gorgas to study the disease, and he became recognized as a yellow fever expert. He was placed in charge of the yellow fever camp at Siboney near Havana during the Spanish-Cuban/American War. Refusing to accept the mosquito theory of transmission, he fought the disease by burning all materials that were suspected of being contaminated.

In 1898 Major Gorgas was named sanitary officer of the city of Havana. Under his orders, the streets and parks were cleaned up, as well as private residences and businesses. The general health of the city residents improved measurably. Small pox disappeared, and typhoid and dysentery showed marked declines. Yellow fever, however, increased.

When the Reed Commission conclusively proved the mosquito theory of transmission of yellow fever, Gorgas changed his methods and began a new clean-up campaign. He experimented unsuccessfully with vaccination and also unsuccessfully attempted a reporting system. Then, he eliminated the breeding places for mosquitoes. By 1901 yellow fever no longer existed in Havana. Gorgas and Maj. Walter Reed received worldwide recognition for their work in discovering the transmission and control of yellow fever.

Gorgas became the choice of several factions in the United States to assume charge of the sanitation for the construction of the Panama Canal, and although he was not appointed to the Canal Commission, he was placed in charge of sanitation in 1904. In spite of obstacles in his path, such as the canal authorities's unwillingness to face the seriousness of the health problem in Panama and their unwillingness to spend adequate amounts of money on sanitation, Gorgas was able to clean up the Canal Zone and to establish disease control measures and a hospital system. As in Havana, there was a remarkable decline in all tropical diseases, including yellow fever. In 1907 Gorgas was appointed to the Canal Commission. The American Medical Association recognized Gorgas in 1908 by electing him its president, and several universities awarded him honorary degrees.

In 1913 Gorgas was invited by the South African Chamber of Mines to investigate the health conditions in South Africa. While Gorgas was in South Africa President Woodrow Wilson appointed him Surgeon General with the rank of brigadier general. After writing his report on health conditions in South African mines, Gorgas returned to the United States to assume his new duties. By special act of Congress, he was promoted to major general in 1915. He supervised the medical mobilization of the army before and during World War I. As a result of his work, the death rate from disease in the army camps was drastically reduced.

Gorgas retired in 1918 and became director of the yellow fever work of the Rockefeller Foundation. The cleanup of Guayaquil, Ecuador, and Guatemala were two projects he directed. In 1920 he left for Belgium and England to receive medals. While in London, Gorgas became ill and died on 3 July. After a funeral held in St. Paul's Cathedral, Gorgas was buried in Arlington National Cemetery. A hospital in the Canal Zone, a medical library in Panama, and the medical library at the University of the South have been named in his honor.

Robert D. Talbott

REFERENCES

John M. Gibson, *Physician to the World: The Life of General William C. Gorgas* (Duke Univ. Pr., 1950); Marie D. Gorgas and Burton J. Hendrick, *William Crawford Gorgas: His Life and Work* (Doubleday, 1924); William Crawford Gorgas, *Sanitation in Panama* (Appleton, 1915).

See also Cuba, Military Government (1898–1902); Reed, Walter; Reed Commission.

Graves, William Sidney (1865–1940)

Maj. Gen. William Sidney Graves commanded U.S. troops in Siberia from 1918 to 1920. His father and grandfather had both served in the army, and as a young man Graves sought and received an appointment to the United States Military Academy at West Point, from which he graduated in 1889. He performed in various capacities as he made his way up the ranks and was cited for bravery during the Philippine War. Except for a few short tours elsewhere, he was assigned to the army General Staff from 1909 until 1918. When the United States entered World War I, Graves requested a command assignment but was unable to secure one until June 1918. At that time he was promoted to major general and given command of the 8th Division at Camp Fremont, California. The division was scheduled to leave for France in October.

On 2 August Graves received a coded message from Washington, which began "you will not tell any member of your staff or anybody else of the contents of this message." He was ordered to take the first available train to Kansas City where he was to meet Secretary of War Newton D. Baker at the Baltimore Hotel. On arrival, Graves was notified that Baker, who had his own train to catch, was waiting for him in a room at the station. During a brief conversation, Baker told Graves he was to command the U.S. expedition to Siberia. The secretary then handed him a sealed envelope, saying: "This contains the policy of the United States in Russia which you are to follow. Watch your step; you will be walking on eggs loaded with dynamite. God bless you and good-bye" (Graves, p. 4).

The envelope contained an *aide-mémoire* written by President Woodrow Wilson explaining his purpose in sending troops to Russia. The gist of it was that the United States was acting solely to help the Russian people defend themselves against the Germans. The message called on those who participated to refrain from "any interference of any kind with the political sovereignty of Russia," or from "any intervention in her internal affairs." Receiving no further instructions from the president during the entire affair, Graves hewed to his instructions (as he interpreted them) to the letter. In so doing, he was bitterly denounced by representatives of other nations and by numerous officials in the Wilson administration. Only strong support by Secretary Baker, by Army Chief of Staff Peyton C. March and, in the end, by the president himself, kept Graves from losing his command.

The situation Graves found in eastern Siberia was chaotic. Civil war raged between Bolshevik forces loyal to Moscow and various "White" regimes in the area. Several Cossack bands roamed almost at will, often raiding trains and supply depots the expeditionary forces were assigned to protect. Finally, other participating nations—France, Great Britain, and especially Japan—jockeyed endlessly for influence.

President Wilson's statement against meddling in Russia's internal affairs was compromised by the fact that U.S. troops were assigned to protect rail lines over which passed supplies and equipment from the port city of Vladivostok to the anti-Bolshevik government of Adm. Aleksandr V. Kolchak in Omsk. Within this framework, however, Graves maintained strict neutrality toward the competing factions. He refused to lend himself to British and French designs and brooked no interference from the Cossacks or the Japanese. Friction with the latter two groups on several occasions almost led to armed clashes. Above all, he refused to cooperate militarily with the Kolchak regime, which

he regularly reported to Washington was brutal, corrupt, and inefficient.

Several militantly anti-Bolshevik members of the State Department, who believed that Graves interpreted his orders too literally, worked to have him relieved. Acting Secretary of State Frank L. Polk referred to him as a "useless old woman." On one occasion, when Kolchak's government refused to intervene on behalf of two U.S. soldiers kidnapped by a Cossack group, Graves on his own initiative held up arms shipments as a means of applying pressure. "It ought to cost the General his head" (Maddox, p. 98) one official wrote to Polk, and another noted in his diary "We have recommended Graves' recall" (Maddox, p. 108). Although Graves's order to hold up the arms delivery was overridden, he continued to act with strict impartiality.

There is abundant evidence that President Wilson did hope that the intervention would unseat the Bolsheviks by bolstering the "White" governments. Graves's conduct, however, at least maintained the facade of neutrality the president had called for in his *aide-mémoire*. For this reason Wilson steadfastly refused to recall the general. Graves kept his command until U.S. troops were withdrawn from Siberia in April 1920.

Graves retired from the army in 1928 to write his own account of the Siberian intervention. It is a blunt, unsparing criticism of the entire operation and shows that he was well aware of the machinations of the State Department to have him relieved. He remained proud of his conduct, yet professed bewilderment over President Wilson's intentions. "I was in command of the United States troops sent to Siberia," he wrote, "and, I must admit, I do not know what the United States was trying to accomplish by military intervention."

Robert James Maddox

REFERENCES

William S. Graves, *America's Siberian Adventure* (Cape & Smith, 1931); Robert James Maddox, *The Unknown War with Russia: Wilson's Siberian Intervention* (Presidio Pr., 1977); Betty Miller Unterberger, *America's Siberian Expedition, 1918–1920: A Study of National Policy* (Duke Univ. Pr., 1956); John Albert White, *The Siberian Intervention* (Princeton Univ. Pr., 1950).

See also American Expeditionary Forces, Siberia (1918–1920); Interallied Relations in the Siberian Intervention; Siberian Intervention (1918–1920).

Great Britain and the Spanish-Cuban/American War

Great Britain played a significant role in European diplomacy during the Spanish-Cuban/American War crisis and the Paris peace negotiations. The British government sympathized with U.S. efforts to end the Cuban revolution, and it countered Spanish requests to rally the European powers to its side. Once the war began, it encouraged U.S. expansion.

Although Prime Minister Lord Salisbury was foreign secretary, Arthur James Balfour, his nephew and head of the treasury department, often directed British foreign relations. Joseph Chamberlain, colonial secretary, also took part. Both Balfour and Chamberlain were pro-United States.

During the three-year Spanish-Cuban conflict (1895–1898), the Spanish government repeatedly asked the European powers for support against U.S. intervention. Spain wanted the powers to argue its case in Washington and to urge the government to suppress the Cuban Junta.

Britain and the other European powers fended off Spain's requests for help. Most believed that Europe's efforts would be fruitless. Also, the continental powers would not act except in concert with Britain, and the British government refused to do anything unless the United States approved in advance.

During early April 1898, the administration of President William McKinley requested the British ambassador, Julian Pauncefote, to assist in preparing a joint six-power note to present to McKinley. The president hoped that a European appeal for a peaceful resolution of the crisis would slow the congressional rush toward war. Assistant Secretary of State William R. Day worked with Pauncefote to write the note, and the latter, doyen of the diplomatic corps, convened the other diplomats to arrange the presentation. On 7 April the six diplomats, led by Pauncefote, delivered the note to McKinley. It had little effect on congress.

When it appeared that the McKinley administration was preparing to go to war, Pauncefote became angry with the president and congress for dismissing Europe's appeal and Spanish efforts to avoid war. Pauncefote was upset by McKinley's statement that the civilized world supported the U.S. cause. The British ambassador attempted to organize a European demarche to criticize the U.S. government for aggression. Surprised by the request, Balfour refused to authorize this step, and the German, French, and Russian governments also demurred.

During the war British diplomacy also favored the United States. In a speech Chamberlain proposed an Anglo-Saxon alliance against Spain which shocked the Spanish government. Spain feared that Great Britain wanted some of the spoils of war, perhaps the Canary Islands or the Philippines.

When the British government offered to assist in negotiating a settlement of the war, the Spanish government, distrusting London, turned to Paris instead. At the close of the war London encouraged Washington to annex the Philippines.

When the Spanish-Cuban/American War ended in August, diplomatic relations between Britain and Spain had deteriorated to the point of a minor war scare over Gibraltar. By December British hostility and fear of British intentions pressured Madrid to sign the Treaty of Paris with the United States.

John L. Offner

REFERENCES

Lewis Einstein, "British Diplomacy in the Spanish-American War," *Proceedings of the Massachusetts Historical Society*, 76 (1964), 30–54; Ernest R. May, *Imperial Democracy: The Emergence of America as a Great Power* (Harcourt, 1961); Robert G. Neale, "British-American Relations During the Spanish-American War: Some Problems," *Historical Studies: Australia and New Zealand*, 6 (1953), 72–89; Robert G. Neale, *Great Britain and United States Expansion, 1898–1900* (Michigan State Univ. Pr., 1966); Rosario de la Torre del Río, *Inglaterra y España en 1898* (Peñalara, 1988).

Guam, Seizure (1898)

As the Spanish-Cuban/American War began in 1898, a U.S. fleet under the command of Capt. Henry Glass, bearing troops headed for the fighting in the Philippines, gathered in Honolulu. It consisted of the flagship *Charleston* and three transports.

Instructed to open his sealed orders only after leaving port, Captain Glass dramatically assembled his men, broke the seal, and informed them that they were to capture Guam, capturing all Spanish military stationed there and taking them to the Philippines.

Few on board knew anything of Guam, but an encyclopedia informed them that there were three Spanish forts on the island. Expecting fierce resistance, Glass drilled his men in preparation for battle.

On 20 June 1898 the fleet entered Apia Harbor, passing under Fort Santiago without being fired on. It then approached Fort Santa Cruz, situated on a small island at the entrance to the inner harbor, immediately firing on it. There was no return fire.

From the shore a small boat bearing three men hurried to greet the new arrivals. They were astonished to learn that Spain and the United States were at war. The last ship had arrived 11 days before war had been declared.

The U.S. naval officers asked about the island fortifications. Without hesitation, the islanders replied that none of the forts had been manned for years. Their cannons were all considered unsafe. As for the size of the army: there were only 54 Spanish soldiers, the naval officers were told, and a similar number of Chomorro militiamen.

Despite doubts, Captain Glass released his first prisoners, so that they could carry ashore his demand that the governor surrender the island. On shore Juan Marina, the newly arrived governor, consulting his manual, learned that as governor he was not permitted to step foot on a foreign ship. Captain Glass would have to come ashore.

Suspecting a trap, Captain Glass informed the governor that he would meet with him only the next morning. That night he prepared a landing party to take the coast by assault, instructing it to capture everyone Spanish and to destroy all military supplies.

The next morning Lt. William Braunersreuther, with an armed escort, met the Spanish governor and a small group of officials, all unarmed, on the shore. The governor wrote the formal surrender document on the spot and sent orders for all military personnel to report. On the way back to the *Charleston* the lieutenant met the landing party and instructed it to return to the ships.

That afternoon, the Spanish and Chomorro soldiers were found waiting on shore. The Spanish, complaining about being separated from their families, were taken on board as prisoners; the Chomorros were dismissed.

The U.S. fleet, with its Spanish captives, continued on as ordered to the Philippines only two days after arriving at Guam. The only shots fired during the "invasion of Guam" were at an abandoned fort. There was no fighting. No U.S. sailor or marine was left behind. Frank Portusach, the only U.S. citizen on the island, casually told Captain Glass not to worry; he would look after things until U.S. forces returned.

Wilson E. Strand

REFERENCES

Charles Beardsley, *Guam: Past and Present* (Charles E. Tuttle Co., 1964); Paul Carano and Pedro Sanchez, *Complete History of Guam* (Charles E. Tuttle Co., 1964); Robert E. Coontz, *From the Mississippi to the Sea* (Dorrance & Co., 1930); Earl S. Pomeroy, *Pacific Outpost: American Strategy in Guam and Micronesia* (Russell & Russell, 1951).

Guantánamo Bay, Cuba, Battle (1898)

The first two months of the war with Spain in Cuba were strictly a naval conflict. This was primarily due to the lack of readiness of the United States Army and to the fact that a Spanish fleet was operating in the Caribbean. The first act of war in the Cuban theater was a naval blockade of the island in April 1898. By June 1898 Rear Adm. William T. Sampson quickly realized he must look for a safe harbor in order to continue the blockade, since the hurricane season was about to begin. Moreover, Sampson needed a suitable area for coaling operations. Sampson's requirement for a safe harbor precipitated the first land action in Cuba, which was carried out by the marines.

The use of Guantánamo Bay for U.S. naval operations had already been discussed by U.S. naval leaders during May 1898. On 7 June the *Marblehead* and the *Yankee* under the command of Comdr. Bowman H. McCalla left the blockading squadron and headed for Guantánamo Bay. One small Spanish gunboat, the *Sandoval*, was in the bay when the two U.S. ships entered; it soon left the area without firing a shot. Guantánamo Bay was also protected by a few old smoothbore artillery pieces on Cayo Toto, a small island that separated the inner bay from the outer bay. These guns presented no threat, and no shots were fired.

The first land action occurred when a small detachment of sailors and marines landed at Playa del Este and destroyed a small cabling station. The detachment soon returned to the *Marblehead* and awaited the arrival of the marine battalion. On 10 June the 1st Marine Battalion was landed with no resistance. The battalion, commanded by Lt. Col. Robert W. Huntington, consisted of 647 men, organized into five rifle companies and an artillery battery. Landing on the east side of the outer harbor, they established Camp McCalla, the first base on Cuban soil, on a hill about 150 feet high (Trask, p. 140). Camp McCalla was defensible with the aid of naval gunfire. The marines' mission was to protect U.S. ships from Spanish artillery or rifle fire during coaling operations. Huntington intended to accomplish this by occupying the high ground and sending patrols into the surrounding area as required.

On the night of 11 June the camp was attacked; the fighting lasted three days and nights. During the attack the navy protected the marines with naval gunfire. Although there were few casualties, the continuous firing was wearing on the marines. The problem of sustaining and protecting the camp was solved when Huntington moved it to the beach after the attack. Later, the marines were reinforced by about 60 Cuban revolutionaries. One Cuban guerrilla recommended eliminating the Spanish threat by attacking the Cuzco Well, the only well in the area, which was being used by the Spanish.

On 14 June, Capt. George F. Elliott was given command of two rifle companies and a detachment of Cubans with the mission to attack and destroy the well, located about two miles from their present position. Moving in a circuitous route, Elliott and his men reached the vicinity of the well undetected by the Spanish battalion guarding it. Meanwhile, the U.S.-Cuban force gained a foothold on a hill dominating the Spanish camp in the valley below. Another marine platoon moved to the sound of the gunfire and closed off the exit to the valley. The Spanish were then caught in a cross fire aided by shells from the *Dolphin* (Millett, pp. 133–134). This fight lasted four hours on a very hot afternoon. The Spanish suffered over 160 casualties. The marines and Cubans prevailed, destroying the camp and the well, suffering only a few casualties.

By 15 June the eastern shore of Guantánamo Bay had been cleared of the Spanish. Although about 6,000 Spanish troops remained in the vicinity, they made no attempt to attack. Guantánamo Bay proved to be a very good coaling station, and the marines remained at Camp McCalla until 5 August, protecting the blockading squadron as the ships shuttled in from their positions outside of Santiago. During that time only two percent of the marines contracted any disease, and there were no deaths at the camp. These are astonishing figures when compared with the overall statistics for the war.

The fight at Guantánamo Bay was important because it allowed the blockade of Cuba to continue uninterrupted. It also belied earlier U.S. opinion that the Spanish were bad marksmen and fighters. Although the fight was only a small skirmish, it was the first on Cuban soil and generated a great deal of publicity for the marines.

John M. Keefe

References

Donald Barr Chidsey, *The Spanish American War* (Crown, 1971); Frank Freidel, *The Splendid Little War* (Little, Brown, 1958); Maurice Matloff, *American Military History* (U.S. Army Center for Military History, 1985); Allan R. Millett, *Semper Fidelis: The History of the United States Marine Corps* (Macmillan, 1980); David F. Trask, *The War With Spain in 1898* (Macmillan, 1981).

Guardas Campestres

Guardas Campestres was the term for the private security forces employed by the sugar haciendas of the eastern provinces of the Dominican Republic. While considered special police forces under the 1907 Dominican law that sanctioned their creation, the members of these forces were employees of the owners of the sugar estates, and their jurisdiction was limited to those estates.

These forces were expanded in 1920 during the U.S. Marine campaign against the eastern guerrillas. Forces of the Guardas Campestres were often used along with the police and the Guardia Nacional Dominicana to supplement the marines, reflecting the limited number of marines available and the effort to use local citizens more extensively. They were later replaced by civil guard units composed of residents in each village, which proved far more effective.

Kenneth J. Grieb

REFERENCES

Bruce J. Calder, *The Impact of Intervention: The Dominican Republic During the U.S. Occupation of 1916–1924* (Univ. of Texas Pr., 1984).

Guardia Nacional de Nicaragua

As the United States's first Nicaraguan intervention neared its end, Washington hoped to maintain political stability in that country by the creation of an efficient constabulary to replace the old partisan army. In the 1923 Central American treaty on the limitation of armaments, signed in Washington, D.C., there was reference to such organizations for the preservation of order, and in November of that year the United States offered its assistance to Nicaragua in organizing and training a constabulary. The offer included the possibility of members of the Marine Corps entering Nicaraguan service. Pending congressional action on this matter, the State Department indicated that marine officers of the legation guard already in Managua could volunteer their services. For a variety of reasons—Nicaraguan nationalism, a shortage of funds, and the Nicaraguan government's fear that a constabulary might be used to supervise the upcoming elections in 1924—nothing was done.

After the elections, President-elect Carlos Solórzano agreed to the formation of a constabulary with U.S. assistance, and he became alarmed after his inauguration when it appeared that the legation guard would withdraw before the new force was formed. Piqued by the new president's alarm after more than a year's delay by the Nicaraguan government, the State Department found itself in the awkward position of withdrawing the marines and perhaps appearing responsible for the instability in the republic for reluctantly delaying departure of the legation guard. Acceding to Solórzano's request, the State Department agreed to delay the departure for three to six months on condition that the Nicaraguan government move energetically in creating the national guard.

The State Department proposed a force designed to replace Nicaragua's national police, army, and navy, to be trained initially by U.S. officers and enlisted men of the legation guard, to place the training branch of the proposed constabulary directly under the Nicaraguan president, and to empower the training branch commander to recall individuals and units of the constabulary for further instruction and training. The Nicaraguan Congress countered with proposals which further delayed implementation. It said nothing about abolition of the army, it curtailed the power of the training branch, increased political meddling in its affairs, and seemed to indicate that the services of the legation guard were unwelcome. By that time (July, 1925) the United States citizen, hired directly by the Nicaraguan Government as chief of the constabulary and of the school of instruction, Maj. Calvin B. Carter, was in Nicaragua with one of his assistants. Carter's presence and the State Department's unhappiness with the Nicaraguan proposals moved the United States to have the marines in the legation guard depart in early August.

Carter soon learned the political intricacies and problems of his job. Despite political interference and shortages of money and equipment, he developed a force of around 200 men, eventually 400. Political developments in Nicaragua, however, provided the major hindrance to Carter's work. President Solórzano proved to be a weak executive in the face of armed Conservatives demanding changes in his coalition government. Solórzano feared bloodshed and refused to give adequate arms and ammunition to the national guard to oppose General Emiliano Chamorro Vargas's coup d'etat of 25 October 1925. As Chamorro's revolution developed, the Liberal Vice President, Juan B. Sacasa, fled; President Solórzano eventually resigned; and the national guard lost its nonpartisan character. Although he originally opposed the guard's formation, Chamorro now found it a useful weapon to fight the Liberal opposition. Carter and other U.S. instructors of the guard remained on, but the refusal of the United States to recognize Chamorro and the growing political complications forced them to terminate their relations with the Nicaraguan Government by the early months of 1927.

When Henry L. Stimson arranged an end to the Liberal counterrevolution against Chamorro and his successor Adolfo Díaz, he promised U.S. assistance in recreating a nonpartisan Nicaraguan national guard. United States Marines would command and instruct the new force. The remnant of the old guard was discharged, but some of them reenlisted when recruitment of the new guard began. Within four and a half months the new force had over 480 officers and men. Over the years of the second U.S. intervention, the size of the national guard changed because of increased duties and the threat of Augusto C. Sandino. At the end of 1932, on the eve of marine departure, there were approximately 2,500 officers and men in the Nicaraguan Guardia Nacional.

The early organization, administration, and duties of the guard were defined by executive orders and decrees of President Adolfo Díaz. In the summer, 1927, the United States offered a draft proposal for the formal basis of the national guard. The United States wanted the proposed 1,229-man body to be the sole military and police force of the republic, subject only to the direction of the Nicaraguan president. The chief of the guard (a marine officer) would have jurisdiction over recruiting, appointment, instruction, promotion, discipline, and operation. The agreement was designed to minimize political interference. After weeks of discussion, the United States *charge d'affaires*, Dana G. Munro, and the Nicaraguan foreign minister, Carlos Cuadra Pasos, signed the agreement on 22 December 1927. The Nicaraguan senate quickly passed the proposal, but the chamber of deputies, under influence of Emiliano Chamorro Conservatives, raised objections similar to those in 1925. After José María Moncada assumed the presidency, a revised national guard agreement passed on 19 February 1929, but the changes which opened the way for greater political interference were unacceptable to the United States. Despite failure of formal ratification of the agreement, the Nicaraguan Guardia Nacional continued its development under President Díaz's decree of 30 July 1927.

From the beginning, the guard's commissioned officers were primarily United States Marines. The commanding officers (*Jefe Directors*) were Lt. Colonel Robert Y. Rhea (May–June, 1927); Major Harold C. Pierce, acting (June–July, 1927); Lt. Colonel Elias R. Beadle (July, 1927–March, 1929); Colonel Douglas C. McDougal (March, 1929–February, 1931); Lt. Colonel Calvin B. Matthews (February, 1931–January, 1933); Major Julian C. Smith, acting (August–October, 1931). The officers had the task of developing and training a force to protect the government against revolution and to assume police duties of the nation as well as devising numerous administrative details. In the beginning there was an attempt to have a cen-

tralized recruiting and training center in Managua, but these functions were soon decentralized to meet the needs of isolated parts of the nation. Training included instruction by marine officers and attachment of *guardia* units to marine contingents for learning through emulation. Patrols through the countryside and town garrisons usually included a mix of marines and *guardia* units. The objective was for the Nicaraguan national guard to gradually replace the marine units in combating the guerrilla activities of Augusto C. Sandino and his followers, particularly after the 1928 Nicaraguan elections. By early 1930 the transfer was essentially accomplished with marines pulled back to the larger towns while the *guardia* conducted patrols and offensive operations. The United States marines and the Nicaraguan Guardia Nacional were unable to quash Sandino's insurgency which began with his attack on the town of Ocotal and continued until a negotiated settlement was arranged shortly after the marine departure in early 1933.

Besides problems caused by Sandino, there were also the financial woes of the government and attempts of President José María Moncada (1929–1933) to politicize the national guard. The Great Depression made funding for the *guardia* campaign against Sandino increasingly difficult. Hoping to find a cheaper way to fight the guerrilla war and at the same time to have an armed force personally loyal to him, President Moncada organized the *voluntarios* over which the *guardia* would have some control in financing and training but which would operate independently in the field and would not have the restrictions on nonpartisanship. Because the *voluntarios* caused numerous problems and were more expensive than anticipated, they were disbanded in a few months. Later Moncada proposed another force, *auxiliares*, that the United States also opposed but came to accept after some success.

As the United States planned marine withdrawal to come shortly after the U.S.-supervised 1932 elections, replacement of U.S. officers in the *guardia* with Nicaraguans became a major consideration. On 1 April 1930, a Nicaraguan military academy was formally inaugurated to train Nicaraguan officers. Applicants had to pass physical and mental examinations and finally pass presidential approval which allowed some political favoritism. Before the marines left, there were four graduating classes totaling 169 officers. Because these young graduates lacked experience, special arrangements were made to fill the *guardia*'s higher ranks. The presidential nominees of the Liberal and Conservative parties each prepared a list of persons for appointment to the national guard's higher ranks. Other than the *Jefe Director* the lists were to be equally Liberal Party and Conservative Party members. After the Liberal victory, President Juan B. Sacasa's list was appointed with Anastasio Somoza García selected as *Jefe Director*. There is some question whether Somoza was Sacasa's first choice, but he was favored by the out-going President Moncada and the United States minister in Managua, Matthew E. Hanna.

About a month after the last marines left Nicaragua in January 1933, Sandino and Sacasa negotiated an end to the guerrilla war. There followed a year of distrust and recrimination between the Somoza-led *guardia* and the Sandinistas who kept their arms and settled on uncultivated territory in northern Nicaragua. Sandino charged that the national guard was unconstitutional because it had never been approved by the Nicaraguan Congress, and Somoza viewed the Sandinista enclave as a state within a state and perhaps a barrier to his own political ambitions. In February 1934, Somoza ordered the abduction and execution of Sandino who was visiting in Managua. The national guard then killed or scattered the remaining Sandino followers. With Sandino out of the way, Somoza used his *guardia* base to maneuver his rise to presidency. Fearing that Nicaraguan political leaders would deny him the presidency in the 1936 election, he used the national guard to oust Sacasa and to rule through a provisional government until a controlled-election voted him for the high office beginning in 1937.

Many commentators have noted Washington's role in creating the Nicaraguan national guard and its use as a vehicle for Somoza's rise to power. It was not the intended result, but it is probably, as one U.S. diplomat in Managua said, a sorry example "of our inability to understand that we should not meddle in other people's affairs." The national guard remained the backbone of the Somoza dynasty until it was overthrown in 1979 by the Sandinista Front for National Liberation.

William Kamman

REFERENCES

Marvin Goldwert, *The Constabulary in the Dominican Republic and Nicaragua: Progeny and Legacy of United States Intervention* (Univ. of Florida Pr., 1962); William Kamman, *A Search for Stability: United States Diplomacy Toward Nicaragua* (Notre Dame Univ. Pr., 1968); Richard Millett, *Guardians of the Dynasty: A History of the U.S. Created Guardia Nacional de Nicaragua and the Somoza Family* (Orbis, 1977); Julian C. Smith and others, *A Review of the Organization and Operations of the Guardia Nacional de Nicaragua* (n.p., n.d.).

Guardia Nacional Dominicana

During the U.S. occupation of the Dominican Republic from 1916–1924, stabilizing the nation was a primary U.S. aim. Applying a formula reflecting U.S. attitudes toward Latin America, U.S. occupation authorities in several nations sought to depoliticize the armed forces as a means of providing political stability.

Applying U.S. values to Latin cultures which they scarcely understood, the U.S. authorities concluded that what they regarded as political anarchy reflecting the use of armed confrontation as the means of governmental change stemmed from the fact that the military was not under the control of the civilian government. The authorities concluded that the political system could be stabilized if a nonpolitical police force replaced the local military. This, it was assumed, would provide a force that would follow the instructions of the government, confine itself to preserving law and order, and remain totally outside politics. These policies were enforced during the administration of President Woodrow Wilson, which sought to spread democracy in the region by acting for the good of the locals, who were perceived as incapable of reforming themselves and receptive to a U.S.-style system.

To carry out this objective, the United States applied a standard formula to all the Caribbean nations it occupied militarily. Whenever U.S. authorities assumed complete control of the government, as in Nicaragua, Haiti, and the Dominican Republic, they disbanded the local military, disarmed the local citizenry, and established an entirely new force, usually called a national guard or constabulary. This force consisted entirely of newly recruited personnel, trained and initially commanded by marines. It was naively assumed that marine training would produce a force that thought like U.S. troops and acted on U.S. values rather than those of their native culture. This attitude ignored Latin attitudes and traditions and the strength of the local culture. The imposition of this "cure all" formula in several different nations was based on the assumption of Anglo-Saxon superiority and a disdain for other peoples. It reflected a total lack of appreciation of local cultures that the United States considered inferior and entailed ignoring what the U.S. authorities regarded as unstable political systems which rendered countries ungovernable. This U.S. solution created new problems.

The occupation of the Dominican Republic and the complete U.S. assumption of control in 1916 provided an opportunity to establish such a constabulary, and its creation became the centerpiece of U.S. policy in the island nation. The United States had called for the formation of a new military force in the island nation for several years and at this point had the power to carry out such a reform. Executive Order No. 47, dated 7 April 1917, established the Guardia Nacional Dominicana, and appropriated funds for its training and equipping.

The Guardia was conceived primarily as an internal police force, designed to bring chronic rebellions under control and to maintain law and order. It was initially authorized for a strength of 1,200 men, although its organization and recruiting proceeded slowly. The United States had sufficient control to assure the disbanding of the previously ill-trained military and police forces and to enforce the disarming of the local populace. These measures alone reduced the incidence of violence in the nation.

Establishing the Guardia proved complex. The Dominican elite had rejected the military government and refused to cooperate with the conquerors in any way, refusing to serve in the new police force. This deprived the Guardia of leadership by the most educated members of the society. Recruiting problems compelled U.S. leaders to induct individuals with questionable backgrounds and to enlist individuals who had previously been members of the local Republic guard to bring the Guardia to its targeted strength. This reduced the distinction between the new Guardia and earlier forces, thereby diminishing the effectiveness of the plan. With the elite that normally provided leadership in the society refusing to serve, officers were drawn

from the middle class, who often viewed the military as a means to achieve power and status. Even securing sufficient numbers of enlisted men proved problematical, despite the attractions of a regularly paid position in the face of widespread unemployment. Unfortunately, the individuals who agreed to serve were often illiterate and ill-prepared.

Although the force was initially commanded by marine officers, World War I caused a shortage, requiring that noncommissioned officers be put on temporary duty with the Guardia as officers. Hence, a newly commissioned Dominican was limited to the rank of second lieutenant and often found himself reporting to a marine sergeant or corporal, temporarily commissioned as a captain or major in the Dominican Guardia. This was an unattractive position and resulted in poor training for the Dominicans. The marine officers and enlisted men assigned to this duty were ill-prepared for their tasks and responsibilities, lacking a knowledge of the local culture, training in combating guerrillas, and in many cases even a knowledge of the Spanish language.

The situation was further complicated when the revolt in the East compelled the occupation authorities to rush newly recruited Guardia units into the field after only brief training. The result was an unruly force leading to charges of abuses and a high number of court-martials.

Recognizing the problems resulting from poor training and reflecting political negotiations that resulted in orders to "Dominicanize" the Guardia, the force was reorganized in 1921, under the auspices of Brig. Gen. Harry Lee, who commanded the marine brigade in the Dominican Republic. The changes included the establishment of a military school in Haina for training officers and renewed recruiting efforts, along with an authorization to expand the force, renamed the Policia Nacional Dominicana, to 3,000 men. A second training center was established in Santiago.

The reorganization and training were shortened because of the negotiations to arrange the end of the occupation. The withdrawal agreements established deadlines for control of the force by the government and the Dominicanization of the officer corps that were more rapid than marine officers desired. Control of the force was turned over to the Dominican government at the time of the U.S. withdrawal in 1924, at which time the force numbered 1,300 men.

After the U.S. withdrawal, the new regime of Horacio Vásquez lost little time changing the command of the force, installing officers associated with its political party. One of the officers involved was Rafael Leonidas Trujillo Molina, whose rise in the Guardia was meteoric. Originally commissioned as a second lieutenant in January 1919, he rose within five years to the rank of major and commander of the North. By 1928 Vásquez named Trujillo chief of staff of the force, renamed the national army. Trujillo used the power of command to thoroughly personalize the force, gaining full control of the nation's only armed force. His efforts were facilitated by earlier U.S. decisions which, in seeking to screen the force from local politics, invested the commander with full control of promotions.

In 1930, Trujillo used the army to seize control of the nation, thus employing the U.S.-designed "depoliticized" force to establish the tightest military dictatorship in the nation's history. His control of the army and its monopoly of power enabled him to perpetuate himself in power and to hold the nation in an iron grip from 1930 until 1961. This effort also benefited from the U.S. centralization of authority and control in the national government and the U.S. disarming of the rest of the population.

Hence, their efforts did provide peace and stability, but in a very different fashion from that envisioned by the U.S. authorities. These efforts certainly did not depoliticize the military in the Dominican Republic, although they did centralize political control, cement the power of the national government, and produce a new military force that changed the nature of Dominican politics. The result was not democracy, but a new dictatorship.

Kenneth J. Grieb

REFERENCES

Bruce J. Calder, *The Impact of Intervention: The Dominican Republic During the U.S. Occupation of 1916–1924* (Univ. of Texas Pr., 1984); Marvin Goldwert, *The Constabulary in the Dominican Republic and Nicaragua: Progeny and Legacy of United States Intervention* (Univ. of Florida Pr., 1962).

See also Dominican Republic, Occupation (1916–1924); Lee, Harry.

Guardia Rural, Cuba

Cuba's Guardia Rural resulted from the U.S. occupation of 1898–1902. It survived until 1909, when it was replaced by the Permanent Army, also at the instigation of the United States. The task assigned to the Guardia Rural by occupation authorities was to protect rural properties. In 1899 U.S. policy planners sought to disband the Cuban Liberation Army, which had fought the Spanish, replacing it with a new body that would provide employment for veterans and prevent banditry in rural areas. The Guardia fulfilled these needs. It served to maintain order in the interior, exercising the police power denied to U.S. forces. Also, it bridged the cultural gap between the occupiers and the local citizenry. This opening in the colonial system was made in reaction to the Philippine War (1899–1902), which caused the U.S. government to hesitate to confront local peoples directly.

In constructing the Guardia, U.S. officials chose officers and men from the Cuban Liberation Army, with an eye to their sympathy for the occupation. U.S. commanders retained overall responsibility and stressed loyalty to the provisional government. Capt. Herbert J. Slocum was named advisor to the force. The Guardia's authority depended on U.S. backing, and U.S. authorities feared that a pullout of troops might find the Guardia's authority lacking in credibility. As the end of occupation neared, the United States acted to make its commitment to support the force more evident.

Arrangements for U.S. withdrawal included reorganizing the Guardia Rural in preparation for its role after Cuban independence. In February 1900 the Guardia was declared to be a national organization with a unified command. In April 1901 the Organic Law of the Rural Guard was issued. Four chiefs were placed in charge of the six provinces, and an artillery corps was created to serve in coastal fortifications. Gen. Alejandro Rodríguez assumed command of the Guardia in April 1902.

The Guardia Rural, for the most part, was dispersed throughout the countryside at the insistence of local landowners, who often provided land, supplies, telephone services, and whatever else was needed to maintain outposts. By 1905, just 28 of the 288 such posts were state-owned. The Guardia was clearly linked to prominent rural sectors, and its recruitment system reflected that fact. Nonwhites were excluded from the officer corps; members had to pay for their own uniforms, and letters of recommendation from landowners were required for entry. In contrast to the Cuban Liberation Army, the Guardia became an elite organization. In the artillery corps, U.S. authorities prescribed that "all officers will be white." As historian Louis A. Pérez has noted, the Guardia was not an "institutional expression of Cuban nationalism."

The Guardia had just 1,250 men in its ranks. In August 1902, the Cuban Congress authorized the formation of four artillery companies to replace departing U.S. forces. The Guardia was too small to secure the entire island, especially during the period following harvests when the numbers of unemployed mounted. Expansion of the Guardia was demanded by property owners, and their cause was taken up by Herbert G. Squiers, the U.S. minister in Havana. Squiers favored abolishing the artillery units, devoting the funds they required to expanding rural components. The United States came to view the Guardia as an integral part of a U.S. defense strategy, and Cuba as its "Southern frontier." By the end of Tomás Estrada Palma's administration in 1906, the Guardia had doubled in size, with over 3,000 personnel and an artillery corps of 700 men. Plans were afoot to add 1,000 more men.

The Guardia proved inadequate to the task of confronting a serious rebellion against the conservative political order. On 16 August 1906, an armed protest was launched in Pinar del Río Province, led by Congressman Faustino Guerra. Liberal party leaders from several other provinces quickly joined. Their purpose was to denounce fraud in the recent reelection of Estrada Palma. Liberal presidential candidate José Miguel Gómez was the beneficiary. The Guardia's inability to withstand the Liberal "Constitutionalist Army" that resulted showed the flaws in the Guardia Rural concept. Rebel ranks grew rapidly and, by late August, 15,000 armed supporters were in the field. Guardia outposts were isolated by the destruction of transport and communication. On 20 August Estrada Palma sanctioned a 2,000-man increase in the Guardia. Then, on 25 August, he created a national militia, under General Rodríguez, and an artillery unit commanded by foreigners.

On 8 September Estrada Palma, unable to sustain his government, called for U.S. military assistance. President Theodore Roosevelt sent William H. Taft and Robert Bacon to find a peaceful solution. When that effort failed, Taft headed a provisional administration. As Pérez has pointed out, the failure of the Guardia stemmed from its mission: the maintenance of rural law and order. As Provisional Governor Charles E. Magoon soon learned, the dispersal of the 5,300-man Guardia among 250 rural posts precluded its functioning as a military organization. The political nature of the Guardia under the Estrada Palma administration had also deprived it of credibility, especially among Liberals.

Washington decided the time had come to create a national army in Cuba. The first step contemplated was doubling the size of the guard, authorized in January 1907. Next, Cuban troops were to be concentrated, not dispersed on rural estates. Soon, army schools were opened in four provinces. Care in recruitment was stressed, and the Guardia was purged of "undesirable" members. Magoon attempted to remove "politics" from the military and assure that merit was the sole criterion for promotion.

The Liberals never accepted the Guardia, however, and it was doomed due to its support for Estrada Palma in 1905–1906. Liberals petitioned Magoon to create a regular army while retaining the Guardia in a police capacity. A regular army would be cheaper than a guard equipped as a cavalry, they argued. U.S. advisors suspected the Liberals of wanting an army for their own uses. U.S. authorities were finally persuaded by the argument that only an army could make it difficult to launch another revolution, Magoon's paramount concern. Magoon decided against an expansion and reorientation of the Guardia Rural. The provisional government created a dual military force that could protect both government and property. Statutes organizing a permanent army were approved by the provisional government in April 1908. The Guardia Rural was salvaged as a police force, and its original mission was maintained. It consisted of 5,180 personnel distributed among 380 detachments, and its command was separate from that of the new army.

Harold Dana Sims

REFERENCES

David A. Lockmiller, *Magoon in Cuba: A History of the Second Intervention, 1906–1909* (Univ. of North

Carolina Pr., 1938); Allan R. Millett, *The Politics of Intervention: The Military Occupation of Cuba, 1906–1909* (Ohio Univ. Pr., 1968); Louis A. Pérez, Jr., *Army Politics in Cuba, 1898–1958* (Univ. of Pittsburgh Pr., 1976), chaps. 1, 2; Elihu Root, *The Military and Colonial Policy of the United States*, ed. by Robert Bacon and James Brown Scott (Harvard Univ. Pr., 1916).

See also Cuban Army, Establishment

Guerra, Faustino "Pino"

Faustino "Pino" Guerra, one of the "Heroes of 1906," was a prominent political and military leader in Cuba. In the aftermath of the Spanish-Cuban/American War, Cuba's overwhelming economic, political, and military dependence on the United States encouraged leaders, such as Guerra, to rely on U.S. intervention to secure their own personal and political objectives.

A former guerrilla colonel, Guerra had served with Antonio Maceo in the Ejército Libertador (Cuban Liberation Army). After the first U.S. military occupation of Cuba between 1898 and 1902, he became a Liberal congressman from his home province of Pinar del Río. On 16 August 1906, he led a Liberal revolt against Tomás Estrada Palma, the U.S.-installed president. In the wake of a series of spectacular military victories over a disorganized and politically corrupt Guardia Rural (Rural Guard), Guerra's movement quickly blossomed into a national insurrection. He assumed command of the Liberal "Constitutionalist Army," which soon numbered 15,000 troops, and devised a successful guerrilla strategy that targeted transportation and communication facilities. Although he promised to protect the great sugar estates, Guerra nonetheless threatened to destroy foreign-owned properties in order to induce U.S. intervention against Estrada Palma.

After the United States intervened to establish a provisional government, Guerra played a prominent role in the institutionalization of Cuba's counterinsurgency capability. In November 1906, he, along with Liberal leaders Carlos García Velez and José de Jesus Monteagudo, met with the provisional governor, Charles E. Magoon, to oppose U.S. plans to increase the size of the Guardia Rural and to vest it with a monopoly of military authority in Cuba. Guerra proposed the creation of a military force structure which included both a permanent army and a Guardia Rural. Based on his own experience in

the 1906 revolt, he defended the Liberal proposal as the most efficient means of suppressing armed insurrections before they developed into national revolutions.

During the second intervention (1906–1909), Guerra helped to strengthen the Liberal party and facilitated its growing collaboration with the U.S. occupation. He served as president of the Committee for Appointments which worked with Magoon's provisional government to control patronage for the Liberals. Later, as a party leader committed to protecting private property and securing a stable social order, Guerra led Liberal opposition to the revolutionary Afro-Cuban movement championed by Evaristo Estenoz and Luis Pena. The Military Information Division, the counterinsurgency intelligence agency of the U.S. Army of Cuban Pacification, commended Guerra for his "excellent work" in suppressing an Afro-Cuban revolt in Pinar del Río (Millett, pp. 177–183).

As the 1908 elections approached, longstanding divisions between followers of Alfredo Zayas y Alfonso (Zayistas) and José Miguel Gómez (Miguelistas) reappeared and threatened to weaken the Liberals. Under Guerra's leadership, however, Zayistas and Miguelistas united to sweep to victory. President Gómez, in recognition of his political and military talents, immediately appointed Guerra to command the newly created Permanent Army. Shortly after, as political factionalism among the Liberals reemerged, Gómez increasingly pressured Guerra, a loyal Zayista, to resign. Guerra was stripped of most of his authority, surrounded with Miguelista officers, and offered an overseas post, which he declined.

Finally, in 1910 after a failed assassination attempt, Guerra resigned, opening the way for Gómez to merge the Guardia Rural and Permanent Army under the command of a Miguelista general, José de Jesus Monteagudo. This partisan politicization of the armed forces set the stage for continuing instability as political rivals recurrently appealed alternatively to the Cuban army and to the United States to protect their interests. As president of the Liberal party in 1920, Guerra led the effort to secure U.S. supervision for presidential elections pitting Zayas, the candidate of the incumbent Conservative, Mario García Menocal, against José Miguel Gómez. Guerra thus continued the "turncoat" tradition denounced in 1897 by the great Cuban independence fighter General Máximo Gómez y Báez, for whom advocacy of U.S. intervention was tantamount to treason (Pérez, p. 113).

Keith A. Haynes

REFERENCES

Jules Robert Benjamin, *The United States and Cuba: Hegemony and Dependent Development, 1880–1934* (Univ. of Pittsburgh Pr., 1977); David A. Lockmiller, *Magoon in Cuba: A History of the Second Intervention, 1906–1909* (Univ. of North Carolina Pr., 1938); Allan R. Millett, *The Politics of Intervention: The Military Occupation of Cuba, 1906–1909* (Ohio State Univ. Pr., 1968); Louis A. Pérez, Jr., *Army Politics in Cuba, 1898–1958* (Univ. of Pittsburgh Pr., 1976); Teresita Yglesia Martinez, *Cuba: primera republica, segunda intervencion* (Editorial de Ciencias Sociales, 1976).

Guerrero, Mexico, Battle (1916)

In the days immediately following the 9 March 1916 attack on Columbus, New Mexico, Francisco "Pancho" Villa's whereabouts remained a mystery, not only to Gen. John J. Pershing who led the Punitive Expedition sent to capture Villa, but also to the officers of President Venustiano Carranza's army stationed in Chihuahua. On 27 March Villa suddenly made his presence known with a three-pronged attack on the towns of Miñaca, Guerrero, and San Ysidro. Using the cover of darkness, Gen. Francisco Beltrán completely surprised the sleeping Carrancista garrison at Miñaca and captured it without a shot. The same fate befell the federal garrison at Guerrero, where Col. Candelario Cervantes captured all the soldiers, three machine guns, and a supply of ammunition. The attack on San Ysidro by Col. Jesús María Ríos, however, failed to overwhelm the reinforced federal garrison, and instead turned into a rout. Carrancista cavalrymen pursued the raiders all the way back to the original rendezvous point, where they, in turn, were repulsed by the reformed Villista squadrons. During the melee, Villa was shot in the right leg by a stray bullet, possibly from the gun of one of his recently conscripted soldiers. The painful injury limited Villa's activities during the following three weeks and almost resulted in his capture by U.S. forces. After Villa had again been located, Pershing gave specific orders to Col. George A. Dodd to move elements of the 7th Cavalry into the area and meticulously seek out their wounded prey.

Unfortunately, Dodd had to operate across the rocky slopes of the Sierra Madre and through endless gullies that seemed to lead nowhere. Without adequate maps of the region, he had to depend totally on a civilian guide, J.B. Barker, who led U.S. troops on a circular march that doubled the actual 55–mile route. Valuable time was lost in this fruitless endeavor, and the men suffered from the icy wind blasts that froze their facial hair and the contents of their canteens.

On 29 March 1916, the 370-man column reached a point three miles south of Guerrero. Facing a broad plain which made a direct advance impossible, Dodd divided his squadrons for a coordinated attack. Efforts to gain information on Villista troop strength in the town further delayed the battle order, so not until 8:00 a.m. was the command finally given. The element of surprise had been lost because the town was alive with awakened soldiers, many of whom already had their horses saddled. Hostilities erupted simultaneously at three separate points as U.S. troops tried to corral the Villistas and cut off their lines of retreat. Despite their valiant efforts and willingness to engage in close combat, Dodd's soldiers were too few to cut off the numerous avenues of escape, especially because mountains ran along both sides of the town and they provided a means of instant concealment for many Villistas. Part of the operation, however, resulted in a 10–mile running fight through a valley east of town, an avenue by which most of the Villistas made their escape by outdistancing their pursuers. Another group escaped to the north by calmly riding under the protection of a Mexican national flag and convincing the U.S. force that they were Carrancistas.

Even though the 7th Cavalry failed to capture Villa or the majority of his Guerrero-based army, Colonel Dodd could take justifiable pride in his accomplishment. He had killed at least 30 Villistas and wounded as many more, in addition to capturing 36 horses and mules, assorted supplies, small arms, and two machine guns. One of those casualties was Villa's trusted aide Gen. Elicio Hernandez who died in the early moments of the fighting. Although five U.S. soldiers were wounded, none were killed in the one-sided battle. More importantly, the Villistas were compelled to disperse, and during the following three months they virtually disappeared from the scene as significant players in international events. Although limited in numbers and scope, the battle for Guerrero proved to be the most successful single engagement of Pershing's Punitive Expedition. Congressmen cheered news of the victory, newspapers applauded the colonel's bravery, and the Senate authorized Dodd's promotion to brigadier general. Henceforth, the Punitive Expedition was more concerned with evacuation ultimatums from President Carranza than with the toothless military threats of General Villa.

Michael L. Tate

REFERENCES

Ronald Atkin, *Revolution! Mexico, 1910–1920* (John Day Co., 1969); Jerome W. Howe, "Campaigning in Mexico, 1916," *Journal of Arizona History,* 7 (1966), 123–137, 168–181; Herbert Molloy Mason, Jr., *The Great Pursuit* (Random, 1970); Donald Smythe, *Guerrilla Warrior: The Early Life of John J. Pershing* (Scribner, 1973); Robert S. Thomas and Inez V. Allen, *The Mexican Punitive Expedition Under Brigadier General John J. Pershing United States Army, 1916–1917* (War Histories Division, Office of the Chief of Military History, Department of the Army, 1954).

H

Haiti, Occupation (1915–1934)

In July 1915 rebels overthrew the government of Haitian President Vilbrun Guillaume Sam. They planned to liberate hostages that Sam had detained as a guarantee of his political survival. Sam, driven from office, ordered jailers to slaughter the detainees, who included prominent citizens. Vengeful partisans routed Sam from his refuge in the French legation and murdered him on the street outside. The violence left Haiti without a government. On 28 July 1915 the United States Navy landed 330 marines at Port-au-Prince.

The disorder following Sam's assassination was not the only factor in the U.S. decision to intervene. President Woodrow Wilson's administration had long regarded Haiti's political instability as a source of regional insecurity. The debts to European creditors that short-lived Haitian governments incurred, sporadic lawlessness, and a tradition of foreign merchant-bankers financing insurgencies could lead to European domination. Preservation of the Monroe Doctrine, concern for the newly completed Panama Canal, and the prevention of encroachment by great powers, then at war, all played a role.

After the initial pacification, the State Department and U.S. field representative Adm. William B. Caperton conferred with top Haitian leaders to identify a presidential successor that Washington deemed acceptable. In the armed presence of the U.S. Marines, the national legislature voted Philippe Sudre Dartiguenave, president of the Haitian senate, into office. U.S. and Haitian officials then drafted a Haitian-U.S. treaty, ratified by the United States Senate in February 1916. The treaty provided for U.S. fiscal management, settlement of foreign claims, U.S. oversight of public works, and establishment of a U.S.-officered Haitian police force. Washington believed that control of customs receipts, the largest single source of state revenue, and the restriction of European credit operations would end Haitian turmoil. It accordingly held the country to a program of strict financial austerity, where debt servicing took priority over economic development needs.

U.S. reformers then rewrote the Haitian Constitution. They specifically abolished a law that prohibited foreign land ownership, hoping thereby to attract capital investment. The Haitian legislature in 1917 refused to approve a draft constitution written within the U.S. State Department. A marine officer, acting under Dartiguenave's orders, subsequently dispersed the legislature, which remained suspended for 12 years. The Dartiguenave government meanwhile authorized a referendum in which only 5 percent of the electorate approved the new constitution.

From the Haitian viewpoint, other inequities accompanied the "protectorate." Expatriate functionaries received generous salaries, while local personnel made little money for doing comparable work. U.S. authorities also insisted on drawing the color line in a country where racial segregation had not existed. A police state apparatus emerged with the establishment of censorship and surveillance systems directed particularly at Haitian dissidents and European residents. As the United States prepared for World War I, attention turned toward German nationals, perceived as a subversive influence.

In August 1915 peasant insurgents attempted to effect the withdrawal of U.S. troops. Unable to dislodge the better-armed invaders, they signed an armistice in September. Grievances against U.S. control nevertheless continued. Peasants especially resented forced labor on road gangs (the *corvée*) and rural authorities' abuses of power. Continued mistreatment led to further armed resistance in 1918. The guerrillas, called *Cacos*, received clandestine support from urban elements.

The native police force that occupation authorities had organized proved unequal to meet this challenge. The ensuing counterinsurgency campaign of 1918–1920 pitted U.S. forces, often unable to distinguish guerrillas from civilians, against rural Haitians. Haitian deaths are conservatively estimated at 3,000 out of a population of 1.5 million. A notable Haitian figure of the campaign, Charlemagne Masséna Péralte, became legendary for his military exploits and a bold escape to the mountains from where he rallied the resistance.

Marines ultimately tracked down Péralte and killed him in October 1919, thus striking a major blow against Haitian morale. U.S. forces had ended all significant opposition by mid-June 1920, but the ruthless character of the campaign had incurred criticism in the United States. Detractors included Republicans, hoping to profit during an election year; those uncomfortable with a U.S. colonialist posture; and civil rights activists. The United States Senate nevertheless waited until after the 1920 presidential election to begin investigating Haitian conditions. Senator Joseph Medill McCormick (Republican from Illinois) chaired subcommittee hearings which resulted in mild reforms. The occupation would continue under a so-called high commission. The high commissioner, responsible to the State Department, had diplomatic powers. The first commissioner, John H. Russell, was a marine officer with a juridical background. Formerly brigade commander in 1918–1922, Russell, a southern white man, held racial attitudes that reflected his times and circumstances. The high commission directed several technical bureaucracies, including a respected public health service. Most of these aimed to complement political reform with improved infrastructure. Industry would supposedly flock to Haiti once sound government, decent port facilities, and good roads were a reality. This capital influx did not, however, occur. Washington, sensitive to criticism, would not extend guarantees to prospective investors, who also encountered local resistance. Occupation officials retarded economic change through the alternate favoritism and hostility they showed to stateside firms. In general, plans to develop Haiti remained hostage to rigid financial policies.

U.S. agricultural experts advised both the Haitian government and the largely rural population. Most expatriate agronomists understood little, however, about local farming and peasant life. Their techniques and counsel were often inappropriate. Traditional land tenure patterns disfavored large plantations and even removing the ban on foreign proprietorship did not solve the problem of fragmented holdings.

Several events in 1929 precipitated an essential change in the direction and operation of the protectorate. The first, a student strike in 1929 at the Damien agricultural training college, quickly spread to law and medical students nationwide. On 4 December customs employees, protesting a dismissal, walked off the job in Port-au-Prince, instigating an impromptu general strike. While authorities declared martial law and temporarily restored order, Aux Cayes peasants marched on 6 December to express their grievances over poor prices for sugar cane products. Some 25 persons died when marines fired on the demonstrators.

Following extensive publicity, the administration of Herbert Hoover appointed a commission headed by former governor-general of the Philippines W. Cameron Forbes to investigate the causes of unrest. To placate blacks in the United States, he named a second commission to study Haitian education, in the vain hope that the conservative black educators named would reach conclusions favorable to continued U.S. domination. The Forbes Commission criticized the undemocratic character of the regime but had little confidence that Haiti could sustain itself without U.S. soldiers. Washington officials should refrain from undermining the efforts of Haitian authorities, the commissioners felt, and the military should lower its profile in Haiti. They believed the time had come to restore parliamentarism and normal diplomatic relations.

The commissioners' views reflected depression era realities. Policy makers realized that no quick remedy existed for Haiti's economic problems, difficulties that other Latin American republics shared to varying degrees. Haitian policy thus changed in tandem with a general Latin American policy review. The new policy substituted local constabularies for U.S. troops, limiting U.S. military personnel to training and advising. Hoover in 1930 appointed an ambassador to Haiti. Before the occupation, the ranking U.S. official had been a minister. The new ambassador did not have a high commissioner's unquestioned authority, but nevertheless exercised extraordinary powers, including selecting Haitian functionaries. Washington and Port-au-Prince concluded a new treaty that preserved the U.S. right to intervene in Haitian financial affairs. It forbade Haitian treaty making with European powers and the denial of land ownership to foreigners.

During the last four years of the occupation, attention turned to effecting a transition between foreign and indigenous control. Transition involved replacing top U.S. functionaries with Haitians, including military officers, and the evacuation of foreign troops. The Haitian and U.S. governments reached a mutually satisfactory agreement in the Executive Accord of 7 August 1933, and on 15 August 1934, the last marines departed.

Ultimately, the occupation proved of little value to Haiti. U.S. policies had emphasized order and control at the expense of development. Racism and ethnocentrism often blinded officials to opportunities to make a cultural impact. U.S. refusal to support Haitian bids for needed

credits after the occupation belied the decades of probity and financial sacrifice. Washington lacked the capacity to transform the country, a task that Haitians in the future would have to perform themselves.

Brenda Gayle Plummer

REFERENCES

Kethly Millet, *Les Paysans Haitiens et l'Occupation Américaine, 1915–1930* (collectif paroles, 1978); Arthur C. Millspaugh, *Haiti Under American Control* (World Peace Foundation, 1931); Hans Schmidt, *The United States Occupation of Haiti, 1915–1934* (Rutgers Univ. Pr., 1971).

See also list of entries at front of book for Haiti, Occupation (1915–1934).

Hanneken, Herman Henry (1893–1986)

Herman Henry Hanneken, a career marine, won fame by killing Charlemagne Masséna Péralte, a major Haitian guerrilla leader, in 1919.

Hanneken was born on 23 June 1893, in St. Louis, Missouri. He served 34 years in the United States Marine Corps, of which five were in the ranks. Enlisting on 14 July 1914, he reached the rank of sergeant before being commissioned on 29 January 1920, accepting the appointment on 10 February 1920 with a date of rank of 23 December 1919. Retiring in the grade of colonel on 26 July 1948, Hanneken was advanced to the rank of brigadier general because of commendation for actions in combat. He died on 23 August 1986.

Hanneken represents an officer whose career started in the "small wars" but culminated in World War II, a conflict requiring skill and expertise in amphibious operations and major ground operations ashore against a highly professional foe in the Pacific. He also epitomizes a shift in modern officer recruitment: a former noncommissioned officer who succeeded as an officer in a military service undergoing major changes in its organization and mission.

Before enlisting, Hanneken had studied for the priesthood. Later, he traveled west, working as a cowboy. Both experiences served him well after he enlisted in the marines and became involved in military operations in Haiti and Nicaragua. While in Haiti, Hanneken earned his reputation as a leader against "bandits." His most notable achievement occurred on the evening of

30 October 1919. That night he and another marine, disguised as Haitian guerrillas, plus 20 Haitian gendarmes, penetrated the camp of the *Caco* leader, Charlemagne Masséna Péralte, killed him, dispersed his followers, and held the camp against counterattack. For this action, he received the Medal of Honor and the Haitian *Médaille Militaire*, plus a commission in the United States Marine Corps. Five months later, Hanneken, again disguised as a Haitian, entered the camp of another *Caco* leader, Osiris Joseph, approached within 15 feet of him and killed the rebel leader. For this exploit, Hanneken received the Navy Cross.

In the 1920s and 1930s, Hanneken's career was normal for a marine officer: professional military schools, sea duty, and service at naval bases and marine barracks. He was also one of the marine representatives at Brazil's Centennial Exposition in 1922. Hanneken returned to the "small wars" in 1928, serving in Nicaragua. He repeated his Haitian successes, capturing Gen. Manuel María Girón Ruano, chief of staff to Augusto C. Sandino in February 1929. Later that spring he effectively operated in isolated areas, foiling enemy attempts to defeat his small force of marines and Nicaraguan volunteers. On 27 April 1929, his unit defeated a larger enemy force which had planned to ambush his. Summarizing these operations, his brigade commander stressed Hanneken's "intelligence, initiative, excellent judgment, powers of leadership, and fortitude."

During World War II, General Hanneken exhibited success in another type of conflict. Having passed through the three-tiered professional military education system of the Marine Corps, he joined the 1st Marine Division in June 1941. While commanding the 2nd Battalion, 7th Marines, he was awarded the Silver Star for action on Guadalcanal; he later received the Bronze Star on Cape Gloucester, and, while commanding the 7th Marines on Peleliu, he earned the Legion of Merit.

General Hanneken was one of the United States Marine Corps' most highly decorated officers. He received the Medal of Honor (Haiti), two Navy Crosses (Haiti and Nicaragua), the Silver Star (Guadalcanal), the Bronze Star (Cape Gloucester), and the Legion of Merit (Peleliu), plus the Good Conduct Medal (for enlisted service), in addition to appropriate campaign medals. He was also awarded the Haitian *Médaille Militaire* with two gold stars and the Nicaraguan Medal of Merit.

Donald F. Bittner

REFERENCES

Robert Debs Heinl, Jr., *Soldiers of the Sea: The United States Marine Corps, 1775–1962* (U.S. Naval Institute Pr., 1962); Robert Debs Heinl, Jr., and Nancy Gordon Heinl, *Written in Blood: The Story of the Haitian People, 1492–1971* (Houghton Mifflin, 1978); Lester D. Langley, *The Banana Wars: An Inner History of American Empire, 1900–1934* (Univ. Pr. of Kentucky, 1983); Allan R. Millett, *Semper Fidelis: A History of the United States Marine Corps* (Macmillan, 1980).

See also Péralte, Charlemagne Masséna.

Harding Plan for U.S. Withdrawal From the Dominican Republic

The so-called Harding plan constituted the initial effort of newly inaugurated President Warren G. Harding to establish a basis for withdrawal of U.S. forces from the Dominican Republic. The plan was announced by the newly dispatched military governor, Rear Adm. Samuel S. Robison, in a proclamation issued on 14 June 1921, shortly after his arrival in Santo Domingo, in accordance with the instructions he brought from Washington.

Harding entered the White House committed to reexamining the U.S. occupations in the Caribbean, having strongly criticized the Wilsonian interventions during the campaign of 1920. His inauguration was consequently welcomed by Dominicans. The new military governor was carefully selected for the task of improving contacts with the Dominicans. The specifics of the plan reflected a reassessment by the new administration.

The Harding plan was designed to establish the basis for negotiations with Dominicans to arrange for a withdrawal and publicly committed the United States "to inaugurate the simple process of its rapid withdrawal from the responsibilities assumed in connection with Dominican Affairs." Unfortunately, the terms it proposed were unacceptable to Dominicans, and hence the announcement demonstrated the need for further study and negotiation.

Admiral Robison's proclamation announcing the plan called for Dominican elections under

U.S. supervision via an indirect electoral college procedure to establish a government to which the United States could turn over authority. The proclamation announced the U.S. intent to withdraw U.S. forces eight months after the formation of such a government. The plan required prior Dominican agreement to several conditions to which the local nationalists objected, however. Specifically, it called for prior endorsement and acceptance by the Dominicans of the loan negotiated by the occupation regime, ratification by the provisional congress of all acts of the occupation regime, and the negotiation and ratification of a convention extending the powers of the customs receiver and the length of the receivership, all as preconditions for a withdrawal.

The Dominicans rejected these terms, which they found offensive. Party leaders informed Admiral Robison that they preferred continued occupation to terms they regarded as an infringement on their sovereignty. The admiral was outraged and became less willing to negotiate arrangements for withdrawal.

The Harding administration attempted to mollify the Dominicans by issuing "clarifications" to the plan, which failed to break the deadlock. This ultimately forced withdrawal of the plan. Robison was directed to inform the Dominicans that if they rejected the terms, the occupation regime would proceed with the negotiation of a badly needed foreign loan to keep the government afloat financially. Despite their objection to the loan, the Dominicans still considered the plan unacceptable. On 23 February 1922 Robison announced the extension of the military occupation until 1924, clearing the way for the loan negotiations.

Despite the lack of results, this constituted a preliminary step that led to future negotiations in which both the Dominicans and the U.S. representatives came to better understand each other's viewpoints. The Harding administration remained committed to arranging a withdrawal, and the proclamation of the plan had publicly committed it to this goal. The continued talks were protracted, but eventually did lead to withdrawal.

Kenneth J. Grieb

REFERENCES

Bruce J. Calder, *The Impact of Intervention: The Dominican Republic During the U.S. Occupation of 1916–1924* (Univ. of Texas Pr., 1984); Kenneth J. Grieb, *The Latin American Policy of Warren G. Harding* (Texas Christian Univ. Pr., 1976); Kenneth J. Grieb, "Warren G. Harding and the Dominican Republic U.S. Withdrawal, 1921–1923," *Journal of Inter-American Studies*, 11 (1969), 425–440; Dana G. Munro, *The United States and the Caribbean Republics, 1921–1933* (Princeton Univ. Pr., 1974).

See also Hughes-Peynado Plan for U.S. Withdrawal from the Dominican Republic.

The Hawaiian Islands and the Spanish-Cuban/American War

The Spanish-Cuban/American War served as a catalyst to bring about the annexation by the United States of the Hawaiian Islands in 1898. Previous attempts to annex the Pacific archipelago had failed because of strong public and political opposition to the acquisition of territory so distant from the North American continent and because of the efforts of the powerful U.S. sugar producers. Throughout the second half of the 19th century, U.S. influence and interests in Hawaii had steadily increased. In the early months of 1893, following a successful revolution led by white planters and business leaders in the islands to overthrow the regime of Queen Liliuokalani, John W. Foster, secretary of state in the final months of President Benjamin Harrison's administration, made a determined effort to push a treaty of annexation through the Senate. Time ran out for the administration, and President Grover Cleveland withdrew the treaty, criticized his predecessor for the involvement of U.S. naval forces in the Hawaii revolt, and, amid considerable confusion and indecisiveness within his administration, even considered restoring the queen to her throne.

The years that followed were a time of intrigue and uncertainty in the islands. The revolutionists established a republic in Hawaii under the presidency of Sanford B. Dole, successfully put down an abortive counterrevolution in January 1895, and awaited the election of an administration in the United States favorable to annexation. Meanwhile, leaders of the Hawaiian government became increasingly alarmed by the steady rise in the Japanese population, which amounted to 24,000, or a quarter of the population in 1896, and by the tiny island's vulnerability to attack by the Japanese or European naval powers. In January 1897 the *Hawaii Star* editorialized, "It's either annexation or a feeble state that's anybody's meat."

In 1896 the Republican National Committee had endorsed the annexation of Hawaii. Following the inauguration of President William McKinley, former secretary of state Foster and delegates from the Hawaiian government approached the president and his secretary of state, John Sherman, about annexation and received a favorable response. Indeed, at the request of Assistant Secretary of State William R. Day, Foster immediately set about drafting a treaty of annexation, soon producing a document with virtually the same language as the 1893 treaty, except that sections concerning compensation to the queen were deleted. Upon receiving Foster's draft document rolled up in a rubber band, Day stated, "that little roll can change the destiny of a nation" (Shippee, p. 33).

The treaty of annexation was introduced in the Senate on 16 June 1897, but it languished there for months. As reported in the 11 January 1898 issue of the *Washington Evening Star*, McKinley reiterated his support for annexation, stating, "We need Hawaii just as much and a good deal more than we did California. It is manifest destiny." Nevertheless, it appeared that those who opposed annexation for economic, moral, or political reasons would easily prevent the treaty from securing the two-thirds vote needed for passage. Influential Republican Carl Schurz, the editor of *Harper's Weekly*, believed McKinley had sent the treaty to the Senate merely as a test of public opinion.

Following the explosion of the battleship *Maine* in Havana harbor and the approach of war, annexationist strategy abruptly shifted. While the treaty was still being considered in the Senate, a joint resolution for annexation offered by Senator John T. Morgan was reported by the Senate Committee on Foreign Relations on 16 March. This tactic would overcome opponents because only a simple majority in each house would be required for passage. The resolution pointed to the danger of Japanese influence and the necessity of acquiring the "Key to the Pacific" in terms of naval importance and the "Crossroads of the Pacific" as far as commercial matters. This resolution failed to stir any action until Adm. George Dewey's victory at Manila focused new attention on the Pacific. On 4 May Representative Francis Newlands introduced a resolution for annexation in the House which was reported favorably out of the Committee on Foreign Affairs on 17 May. House

speaker Thomas B. Reed, an opponent of annexation, kept the issue from the floor until 10 June. Then, following heated debate, the resolution passed the House on 15 July in a vote of 201–91. Newlands's resolution then moved to the Senate where an intense final stand by anti-annexationists failed to prevent passage by a vote of 42–21 with 26 abstentions. Clearly, even with the pressures and anxieties created by war with Spain, the forces opposed to annexation remained strong enough to have prevented annexation by treaty.

The opponents of annexation argued that such an acquisition was a departure from U.S. tradition because the islands were distant from the mainland and populated in large measure by non-Caucasians. They also questioned the constitutionality of annexation by joint resolution. Schurz advised against annexation because he felt it would only confirm European suspicions that a war with Spain was being fought for territory rather than for humanitarian concerns. Proponents maintained that the islands had significant strategic importance and should be annexed lest Japan, recently emboldened following its victory in the Sino-Japanese War, or some European power, seize the islands. Some, like Senator Henry Cabot Lodge, saw Hawaii as an important station for supplying Admiral Dewey's fleet in the Philippines, and Lodge raised this issue in secret Senate debates on the annexation resolution. Meanwhile, as the debate proceeded, McKinley considered using executive action, if necessary, to bring about annexation. Lodge wrote to his close friend Theodore Roosevelt on 13 June that "the President has been very firm about it and means to annex the Islands any way. I consider the Hawaiian business as practically settled" (Pratt, p. 322).

In Hawaii the government at no time considered neutrality as an option and decided to do all it could to actively support the United States once war with Spain was declared. A bill authorizing the United States to use Hawaii for military purposes was drafted by Hawaiian officials in Washington and sent to Honolulu for consideration, but the administration in Hawaii never presented it to the island's legislature. A treaty of alliance was considered even before Dewey's victory at Manila; and, before the actual outbreak of hostilities, Lorin A. Thurston, Hawaiian treaty commissioner in Washington, suggested to the United States Navy Department that all available coal in Honolulu be bought for war needs. Roosevelt, then assistant secretary of the navy, followed up on Thurston's recommendation and consummated the purchases on 12 April. The Hawaiian executive council quickly voted to allow four additional lots for storage of the coal, an action not unnoticed by the Spanish vice consul in Honolulu.

Annexation ended uncertainty about Hawaii's future and conferred territorial status upon what in actuality was already a U.S. outpost in the Pacific. The annexation also opened the way for expansion-minded political leaders to urge the acquisition of additional overseas possessions at the end of the war with Spain.

The argument arising after the victory in Manila that Hawaii was necessary for the war effort carried much weight in Congress, but the islands were of far less importance strategically in the war with Spain than they were in future conflicts. However, had the war not arisen when it did, Hawaii would probably not have been annexed for many years, and its precarious status and the United States's unofficial protectorate over the islands might have continued until another international crisis brought the issue to a head.

Michael J. Devine

REFERENCES

Thomas A. Bailey, "The United States and Hawaii During the Spanish-American War," *American Historical Review*, 36 (1931), 552–560; Michael J. Devine, "John W. Foster and Struggle for the Annexation of Hawaii," *Pacific Historical Review*, 46 (1977), 29–50; Julius W. Pratt, *Expansionists of 1898: The Acquisition of Hawaii and the Spanish Islands* (Johns Hopkins Univ. Pr., 1936); William A. Russ, *The Hawaiian Republic, 1893–1898* (Susquehanna Univ. Pr., 1961); Lester B. Shippee and Royal B. Way, "William Rufus Day," in *American Secretaries of State and Their Diplomacy* (Knopf, 1929), vol. 9, p. 33; Merze Tate, *The United States and the Hawaiian Kingdom: A Political History* (Yale Univ. Pr., 1965).

Henríquez y Carvajal, Francisco (1859–1933)

Dr. Francisco Henríquez y Carvajal was elected provisional president of the Dominican Republic by the Dominican Congress in July 1916 shortly after U.S. Marines landed in the capital city of Santo Domingo. He took the oath of office on 31 July 1916. His election in the face of opposition by the United States and the occupation of his nation rendered his tenure in office short-lived, although he served his nation well from exile.

The United States occupied Santo Domingo amid political turmoil which had created a crisis in the Dominican Republic due to the stalemate between several political factions. When U.S. forces landed, President Juan Isidro Jiménez resigned in protest. The Dominican Congress met as U.S. warships took up positions at each of the nation's principal ports, and after extensive maneuvering among the various power brokers, decided to elect Federico Henríquez y Carvajal, the chief justice of the Dominican Supreme Court, as provisional president. U.S. occupation officials objected and sought to block the election by arresting seven senators to prevent a quorum. After a public outcry in Santo Domingo resulted in release of the detained lawmakers, the Dominican Congress reconvened. Just as its term was about to expire, the Congress unexpectedly elected Federico's brother, Dr. Francisco Henríquez y Carvajal, provisional president in spite of the objections of the United States.

A member of the Dominican educated elite with an international reputation, Henríquez y Carvajal held a doctorate in medicine from the University of Paris and a law degree from the University of Havana. His career included service as a physician, university professor, and diplomat. A strong nationalist, he firmly defended his nation's independence, and while negotiating with the U.S. occupation authorities he refused to surrender ultimate control of his nation, rejecting any continued U.S. oversight.

When it proclaimed a full military government on 29 November 1916, the United States apparently assumed that it could follow the model employed in Haiti and rule through the provisional government. The occupation authorities reckoned without the provisional president, however. Henríquez y Carvajal refused to serve as the puppet of the invaders and went into exile on 8 December 1916. His action deprived the military government of legitimacy and seriously weakened its position. Because all members of his cabinet followed his example, the conquerors could find no one to serve as a figurehead for their regime. This compelled the United States to assume complete control of all governmental offices and functions, with U.S. Marine officers holding all cabinet portfolios and the naval commander serving as military governor.

After leaving his country, Henríquez y Carvajal launched a tireless propaganda campaign to end the occupation, traveling to the United States and other nations speaking and focusing attention on the plight of his nation, styling himself as the head of the "deposed Constitutional Government." Discovering that U.S. officials refused to meet with him due to their preoccupation with the European conflict when he visited New York and Washington, he traveled to Havana and later to South America, seeking support against the occupation. He established his headquarters in Cuba, where he was well known and had practiced medicine, resuming his practice while continuing his political efforts. He succeeded in focusing considerable attention on the plight of his nation during the 1917 meeting of the American Institute of International Law held in Havana, causing the United States considerable embarrassment.

Together with his brother, sons, and several other nationalists, Henríquez y Carvajal was instrumental in forming a series of *juntas nacionalistas* in his home nation to raise funds for the propaganda effort and a network of committees in various cities throughout the world linking Dominican exiles. The group operated under the umbrella name of the Comisión Nacionalista Dominicana. It later combined with other nationalists to form the Unión Nacional Dominicana.

In 1919, Henríquez y Carvajal attended the Versailles Peace Conference, seeking to have his nation's plight considered at the peace conference by requesting classification of the Dominican Republic as one of the "oppressed nationalities." Though failing to gain admission to the formal conclave due to the efforts of President Woodrow Wilson, his lobbying efforts further embarrassed the United States and secured pledges of support from several Latin American nations.

A pragmatist, Henríquez y Carvajal avoided a full confrontation with the United States, focusing instead on keeping the issue before the public. At times he was distracted by personal problems, and ultimately his influence waned due to splits among the Dominican factions as prospects for an end to the occupation improved. One of his associates, Francisco J. Peynado, played a key role in later negotiations with U.S.

authorities that arranged the terms of the eventual U.S. withdrawal. Ironically, Henríquez y Carvajal opposed the Hughes-Peynado Plan of compromise with the United States that resulted from the talks.

Kenneth J. Grieb

REFERENCES

Bruce J. Calder, *The Impact of Intervention: The Dominican Republic During the U.S. Occupation of 1916–1924* (Univ. of Texas Pr., 1984); Kenneth J. Grieb, *The Latin American Policy of Warren G. Harding* (Texas Christian Univ. Pr., 1976); Dana G. Munro, *Intervention and Dollar Diplomacy in the Caribbean, 1900–1921* (Princeton Univ. Pr., 1964).

See also Dominican Republic, Occupation (1916–1924); Public Opinion and the Intervention in the Dominican Republic.

Hobson, Richmond Pearson (1870–1937)

In the early morning of 3 June 1898, a national hero was created in the narrow, twisting entrance to the harbor at Santiago de Cuba during the Spanish-Cuban/American War. The attempt to scuttle the obsolete collier *Merrimac* across the harbor entrance to bottle up Spanish naval forces failed when the intense cross fire of Spanish batteries severed several electrical detonating cords and the channel current proved stronger than expected. The ship came to rest, half afloat, well inside the harbor. Adm. Pascual Cervera y Topete's Spanish fleet remained free to sortie, which it did to its inevitable destruction under U.S. naval guns on 3 July. The abortive effort to trap Cervera catapulted navy Lt. Richmond P. Hobson, the leader of the volunteer crew of the *Merrimac*, from the obscurity of the regular navy to international fame. A sensation-hungry world press turned the 28-year-old, intelligent, and articulate Hobson into an overnight celebrity. The navy capitalized on the publicity and assigned him to make a series of public appearances which further enhanced his public image.

Command of the *Merrimac* had been no accident but was the result of persistent efforts by Hobson to put himself at the center of action. Born in 1870 and heir of an aristocratic Greensboro, Alabama, family, Hobson graduated first in his class at the U.S. Naval Academy in 1889. His academy career was marked by a strange interlude; the entire student body refused to speak to him for two years because of his overly zealous adherence to the honor code. Selected by the navy for postgraduate schooling, Hobson was trained as a naval architect in France. When the Spanish-Cuban/American War broke out, he hurriedly volunteered to accompany the fleet into combat. Then, he succeeded in convincing Adm. William T. Sampson that he was the best qualified officer to command the *Merrimac* on its suicide cruise.

Hobson retired from the navy at the height of his fame in 1902 to become a lecturer on the booming Chautauqua circuit. A brilliant speaker, he became one of the most popular Chautauqua attractions and was probably the highest paid of all.

He also turned to politics. In 1906, Hobson was elected from his home district in Alabama and began a decade long career in the House of Representatives. Almost immediately he emerged as the nation's leading navalist and spokesman for the navy. Furthermore, he came to serve as President Theodore Roosevelt's congressional leader on naval questions, a unique position for a freshman Southern Democrat. A special relationship existed between Hobson and the navy. His relationship with the navy's ranking officers was intimate, but usually secret. It was often the source of suspicion, jealousy, and antagonism between Hobson and the civilian leadership of the executive branch. Hobson covertly worked with the professional naval leaders to circumvent the small navy policies of the civilian leaders. Because of Hobson, the navy was able to take its arguments directly into the political forum bypassing the efforts of the administrations of Presidents William H. Taft and Woodrow Wilson to muzzle them.

Hobson also emerged as the congressional leader of the Prohibition movement and became one of its most important national spokesmen. After retiring from politics he created and led several international organizations which spearheaded the League of Nations' efforts to control the world narcotics trade.

Shortly before his death in 1937, Hobson was belatedly awarded the Medal of Honor for his exploits in Cuba.

Walter E. Pittman, Jr.

REFERENCES

Richmond Pearson Hobson, *The Sinking of the "Merrimac": A Personal Narrative of the Adventure in the Harbor of Santiago de Cuba and of the Subsequent Imprisonment of the Survivors* (Century, 1899); Walter E. Pittman, Jr., "Echoes of the Future," *United States Naval Institute Proceedings*, 111 (1985, Supplement), 32–37; Walter E. Pittman, Jr., "Richard P. Hobson and the Sinking of the *Merrimac*," *Alabama Historical Quarterly*, 38 (1976), 101–111; Barton C. Shaw, "The Hobson Craze," *United States Naval Institute Proceedings*, 102 (1976), 54–60.

See also *Merrimac*, Scuttling of (1898).

Hospital Ships in the Spanish-Cuban/American War

In the United States the use of vessels assigned to hospital duty occurred infrequently before the Spanish-Cuban/American War. One of the first, a captured Confederate sidewheeler, *Red Rover*, served the Union army from late 1862 as a "floating hospital." Nevertheless, the concept of a modern ocean-going hospital ship was not adopted until Congress, contemplating a war fought at great distances from U.S. shore-based medical facilities, voted on the eve of war with Spain funds for both the army and navy to furnish ships for hospital duty. During the war the navy operated one hospital ship and the army perhaps as many as five—the record is unclear—with a few transports doubling in hospital duty.

Navy officials required just 16 days to purchase and prepare the steamer *Creole* for hospital duty. The ship could accommodate 200 patients and offered the latest appliances for modern antiseptic surgery, including steam disinfecting apparatus, steam laundry plant, an ice machine, and cold-storage rooms. This feat of bureaucratic dexterity required the conspicuous aid of the Red Cross which donated the majority of the specialized equipment. On 14 April 1898, the navy commissioned the *Solace*, the first vessel in the United States Navy to fly the Geneva Red Cross flag. This "ambulance ship," reported the navy surgeon general, marked "a new departure in the care of the sick and wounded in naval warfare." Its modern facilities compared favorably to Japan's *Kobe Maru*, which employed modern methods to treat its wounded from the Sino-Japanese War in 1894–1895.

The *Solace* transported sick and wounded sailors to naval hospitals at Norfolk, Virginia; New

York, and Boston in continuous duty between Cuba and the East Coast. The ship also cared for army casualties "whenever practicable." Following the Battle of Santiago on 3 July, the *Solace* and several other U.S. ships carried some of the wounded from the Spanish fleet to the hospital at Norfolk.

The activities of army hospital ships are not as well-documented. The steamer *Olivette* supported the early landings of U.S. forces in Cuba and cared for Adm. Pascual Cervera y Topete and other Spanish survivors of the Battle of Santiago. In the Pacific, a former passenger liner, renamed *Relief*, carried soldiers to the West Coast. Other vessels identified with hospital duty for the army included the *Missouri*, *Bay State*, and *Vigilancia*. Another ship, the *Terry*, appeared on a list of hospital ships operated by the quartermaster corps of the army in the 1898–1899 fiscal year, although the wartime disposition of this ship is not clear.

After the war the services adopted the British practice, in which the fleet would always deploy hospital ships while the army would place them in service only when needed.

Richard A. Russell

REFERENCES

W.L. Mann, "The Origin and Early Development of Naval Medicine," *United States Naval Institute Proceedings*, 55 (1929), 772–782; John H. Plumridge, *Hospital Ships and Ambulance Trains* (Seeley, Service & Co., 1975); Milt Riske, "A History of Hospital Ships," *Sea Classics* (1973), 16–24; U.S. Navy Department, *Annual Reports of the Surgeon-General, USN, 1866–1929*; U.S. Navy Department, *Dictionary of American Naval Fighting Ships* (U.S. Government Printing Office, 1976), vol. 6.

Huerta, Victoriano (1854–1916)

Gen. Victoriano Huerta was president of Mexico from 19 February 1913 to 15 July 1914, a period of turmoil during the era of the Mexican Revolution. Because he opposed the eventually victorious revolutionaries, Huerta is often vilified in Mexican literature.

A career army man, Huerta entered the Mexican Military Academy as a youth and rose to the highest rank in the Mexican army, general of division. As a military engineer, he played a key role in preparing the official military map of Mexico and was one of the organizers of the general staff. Short and stocky and of Indian descent, this native of Colotan, Jalisco, was well known for his bravery, stoicism, fatalism, and capacity for alcohol. His early combat experience came from service in military campaigns which suppressed several rebellions.

In 1912 President Francisco I. Madero called on Huerta to assume command of the government forces when faced with the greatest threat to his regime, a revolt by Gen. Pascual Orozco, Jr. A former supporter of Madero, Orozco had defeated a government army commanded by the minister of war. Carefully building up his forces and using his superiority in artillery effectively, Huerta routed the rebels at the second battle at Rellano and the battle at Bachimba Pass, thereby suppressing the revolt.

A rebellion in Mexico City during February 1913, led by Gen. Felix Díaz, caused Madero again to call on Huerta to save the government. The rebels seized the government arsenal, securing a tactical advantage. The result was 10 days of combat, called the *La Decena Trágica*, during which artillery fire raked the heart of the capital, leading to a stalemate. Huerta and Díaz conducted secret negotiations, culminating in the Pact of the Embassy under the mediation of U.S. Ambassador Henry Lane Wilson, who sought to end the destructive combat. Through this agreement Díaz recognized Huerta as interim president in return for the right to select the cabinet and for Huerta's pledge to support Díaz in the election which the Constitution required within a year. Troops loyal to Huerta then seized the president and vice president, and Huerta proclaimed himself president with the approval of the Mexican Congress. The subsequent assassination of President Madero and his vice president, who had submitted their resignations, caused the supporters of Madero to condemn Huerta and rise in revolt, plunging the nation into civil war.

U.S. President Woodrow Wilson, who took office a few days after Huerta seized power, opposed the Mexican general, denied diplomatic recognition to his regime, and opened the border to shipments of arms to the northern revolutionaries.

While relying on the federal army to impose stability and adopting the methods of a traditional dictatorship, Huerta proved an adept politician. He showed skill in outmaneuvering his opponents and in arranging his own reelection despite the Constitution. To be sure, power was concentrated in the chief executive. Huerta used troops to close Congress when it opposed his efforts to perpetuate himself in power. Initially securing British support, he effectively resisted the efforts and political manipulations of the Wilson administration, which sent a long string of envoys to seek his ouster. Huerta's ability to continue in office in spite of the opposition of the United States demonstrated considerable skill.

Often characterized by his opponents as a counterrevolutionary who wished to reinstate the practices of Porfirio Díaz favoring the wealthy landowners, Huerta in fact promoted considerable reform. Although Huerta sought to restore the stability of the old regime and attract foreign investment, he rejected many of its policies. He was the first president in Mexican history to establish a ministry of agriculture and a ministry of labor. These acts constituted a sharp break with previous Mexican governments, including those of Díaz and revolutionary leader Madero. Huerta launched a program of rural school construction to provide the Indians with education and purged Positivist philosophy from the secondary school curriculum. The impact of these programs was restricted by the necessity to divert efforts and resources to combating the revolutionaries. Rejecting the corruption of the Porfirio Díaz years, Huerta continued to live simply in his own house throughout his tenure as president.

As Huerta proved adept at clinging to power, the United States became more supportive of the revolutionaries and eventually landed troops at Veracruz to prevent the delivery of a shipment of European arms. The occupation of Veracruz in April 1914 weakened the Huerta regime, but the general continued to hold the capital until July 1914 when he fled into exile.

Huerta later entered the United States, seeking to launch a new rebellion from the northern border. U.S. authorities arrested him, and he died in custody at Fort Bliss, Texas.

Kenneth J. Grieb

REFERENCES

Kenneth J. Grieb, *The United States and Huerta* (Univ. of Nebraska Pr., 1969); Michael C. Meyer, *Huerta: A Political Portrait* (Univ. of Nebraska Pr., 1972).

See also Niagara Falls Conference (1914); Veracruz, Mexico, Occupation (1914).

Hughes-Peynado Plan for U.S. Withdrawal From the Dominican Republic

Following the breakdown of initial efforts of President Warren G. Harding's administration to end the U.S. occupation of the Dominican Republic, sometimes called the "Harding plan," further talks ensued to find a more acceptable approach. The initial discussions took place in Washington when Francisco J. Peynado traveled to that city during March 1922. Peynado met with officials who included members of the Senate Foreign Relations Subcommittee investigating the U.S. occupation of Haiti and the Dominican Republic, Secretary of State Charles Evans Hughes, and the chief of the Latin American Division of the State Department, Sumner Welles.

A prominent Dominican political figure, Peynado had previously served as finance minister in the cabinet of Dr. Francisco Henríquez y Carvajal and represented his nation in Washington. He represented the pragmatic nationalists, who saw the need to compromise rather than to remain intransigent, a view shared by President Harding. Peynado was willing to accept a foreign loan as something that the Dominicans could not change and for which the United States was responsible, recognizing the advantages of letting the United States take the initiative in and bear the responsibility for new foreign borrowing. In his discussions with Hughes and other State Department officials he stressed the need to modify the customs receivership in the Dominican Republic, while showing a willingness to ratify certain actions by the occupation regime.

The Hughes-Peynado talks identified the basis for further negotiations and began contacts which brought the moderate nationalists to the fore, resulting in a new negotiation effort. Peynado was joined by Horacio Vásquez, Federico Velásquez, and Elías Brache, all major political party leaders in the Dominican Republic, and they signed a memorandum with Hughes on 30 June 1922 establishing the basis for withdrawal. Further negotiations were needed to complete the details. To conduct the talks, President Harding wisely selected Sumner Welles, the chief of the State Department's Latin American Division, who had been a participant in the Washington meetings. A diplomat with wide experience in Latin America, Welles was sent to the Dominican Republic as President Harding's "personal representative," thus effectively bypassing local occupation officials with an individual able to negotiate effectively with the Dominicans.

Welles and the four Dominican leaders worked diligently and patiently to undermine the local nationalists, while Welles also countered the recalcitrance of U.S. military governor Rear Adm. Samuel S. Robison and Minister William W. Russell. Harding and Hughes supported Welles in all disputes with the military governor, while a series of understandings and compromises were negotiated modifying and clarifying the initial accord. Among the agreements was the provision that the Dominican constabulary, renamed the Policia Nacional, would be under the full control of the provisional government once the latter was installed, without the presence of U.S. officers. While Admiral Robison objected, he was overruled by Harding. In return, the Dominicans recognized the loan and a specific list of occupation laws.

This agreement led to the eventual U.S. withdrawal. The Dominicans selected Juan Bautista Vicini Burgos as provisional president, and he assumed office 21 October 1922 to begin the transition process. Under the accord, the marines were concentrated in the principal cities during September 1922 while the electoral process moved forward, with security in the interior turned over to the Policia Nacional. The election of 15 March 1924 resulted in the selection of Horacio Vásquez as president. Vásquez was inaugurated 12 July 1924 as the marines left, thus completing the long process of withdrawal.

Kenneth J. Grieb

REFERENCES

Bruce J. Calder, *The Impact of Intervention: The Dominican Republic During the U.S. Occupation of 1916–1924* (Univ. of Texas Pr., 1984); Kenneth J. Grieb, *The Latin American Policy of Warren G. Harding* (Texas Christian Univ. Pr., 1976); Kenneth J. Grieb, "Warren G. Harding and the Dominican Republic U.S. Withdrawal, 1921–1923," *Journal of Inter-American Studies*, 11 (1969), 425–440; Dana G. Munro, *The United States and the Caribbean Republics, 1921–1933* (Princeton Univ. Pr., 1974).

See also Harding Plan for U.S. Withdrawal From the Dominican Republic.

I

Intelligence in the Philippine War

The history of military intelligence in the Philippines can be divided into three phases: from mid–1898 to early in 1900, when intelligence activities were sporadic and uncoordinated; from 1900 to 1901, when individual officers developed their own networks; and from mid–1901 to July 1902, when a reciprocal system of data collection and distribution between headquarters and the field emerged.

The first U.S. intelligence reports on the Philippines were the reports of naval and consular officers in May 1898, who gave a fragmented and confused version of events in the archipelago. Using these poor sources, President William McKinley ordered the United States Army to send an expedition to Manila, an order which revealed that the Military Information Division (MID), the army's general intelligence organization, had virtually no information on the islands in its files. Early arrivals among the army officers began sending back information, but because most of it consisted of field reports and summaries of conferences with a few Filipino and Spanish collaborators, they did little to clarify the confusing situation in the Philippines. Dur-

ing the critical months after the Spanish surrendered Manila in August 1898, neither President McKinley nor the War Department received accurate or adequate details from military or diplomatic sources. Partially as a result of this poor information, McKinley was convinced that the Filipinos would welcome U.S. sovereignty and discounted Philippine President Emilio Aguinaldo y Famy's demand for immediate independence for the Philippines.

After the outbreak of fighting between Filipino and U.S. forces on 4 February 1899, U.S. intelligence developed along two lines: the centralized, Manila-based official military organizations and the local networks established by garrison officers and tactical commands. The United States commander in the Philippines, Maj. Gen. Elwell S. Otis, ordered the creation of the Bureau of Insurgent Records (BIR), both to provide intelligence on enemy activities and to justify army policies in the islands. The BIR also became the eventual repository of thousands of captured documents seized from the Filipino revolutionaries; documents which often provided meticulous records of military forces, plans, finances, and so forth. This plethora of information swamped the understaffed BIR, and as a result it was unable to do more than sort and translate a small percentage of the material. Because Otis was convinced that the war was over by February 1900, he made little effort to increase either the size of the BIR or to expand its duties to include the collection and dissemination of tactical intelligence. Consequently, throughout its tenure, the BIR had virtually no contact with the majority of U.S. field officers stationed in the archipelago.

The failure of the army high command to establish a centralized intelligence apparatus threw the burden of gathering information on officers in the countryside. They resorted to a variety of means to develop intelligence networks and often secured significant successes. The most important source of information was Filipino collaborators, who, because of local feuds, of mistrust toward Aguinaldo or his lieutenants, or in reaction to guerrilla terrorism, preferred U.S. rule to that of the revolutionaries. An excellent source of intelligence resulted from the creation of paramilitary forces among ethnic groups hostile to the predominantly Tagalog leadership of the revolutionary movement. Where information was not freely tendered, officers hired spies and guides by use of "secret service" funds distributed by army quartermasters, or they used their own local powers to allocate political offices and military contracts to the loyal and compliant. Increasingly, information was obtained through field operations—from the interrogation of prisoners, from captured documents, and through the dispatch of special raiding forces. Unfortunately, information was also secured through other, illegal means. Ignoring frequent warnings against physical abuse, some soldiers mistreated captives or burned houses and fields in their efforts to extract information about the guerrillas. But despite their ingenuity and occasional successes in obtaining information, throughout 1900 the intelligence-gathering process remained local and sporadic.

Maj. Gen. Arthur MacArthur, who replaced Otis in mid–1900, recognized the importance of improving army intelligence organizations. Believing that the guerrillas' strength lay in their ability to secure information and supplies from clandestine networks located in U.S.-occupied towns, he directed officers to devote their full attention to rooting out the guerrilla infrastructure. On 13 December 1900, he reorganized the BIR into the Division of Military Information (DMI) of the army in the Philippines, and shifted its emphasis from translating documents into the dissemination of information to field commands. To take advantage of the existing local intelligence networks, he supported the DMI's orders that garrison commanders fill out identity cards not only on guerrilla officers, but also on priests, civic officials, and all other important people in their communities. These identity cards, first issued on 11 March 1901, gave the army material for a central file on guerrilla organizations as well as invaluable details on local conditions. The collapse of most Filipino resistance and the withdrawal of many military garrisons left the project incomplete, but it marked an important step toward creating a central military intelligence agency.

MacArthur's successor, Maj. Gen. Adna R. Chaffee, further extended the DMI's authority on 28 September 1901, when he ordered each garrison and field command to appoint a special intelligence officer charged with the collection and direct transmission of all military information to the DMI. This officer's first task was to make a detailed report on conditions in the area, paying special attention to topography, communications, the local economy, and transportation facilities. In addition, he was to report on the native officials and their political sympathies and give the names and addresses of guides. These reports provided the DMI with an overview of conditions in the archipelago and could be used later to track down the bandits and rebels who remained in officially pacified areas.

Chaffee's reforms mark the final phase of army intelligence activities in the Philippine War. With the official end of hostilities on 4 July 1902, the DMI was placed under the Army War College and soon became a major center for intelligence outside the continental United States. As a listening post for U.S. interests in the Far East, it sponsored numerous mapping trips and reconnaissance missions into Asia. Much of its attention after 1902 was directed at counterespionage, and the DMI's pursuit of ephemeral conspiracies involving expatriate revolutionaries and Japanese spies lined the pockets of a host of imaginative Filipino agents. The attempts by one BIR veteran, John R.M. Taylor, to write a history of the Philippine War based on material he had obtained as an intelligence officer were frustrated by Secretary of War William H. Taft's opposition and a lack of support from his military superiors. With the suppression of

Taylor's work, there appears to be no further effort to draw lessons from either the guerrilla war or the U.S. military intelligence effort.

Brian McAllister Linn

REFERENCES

Brian McAllister Linn, "Intelligence and Low-Intensity Conflict in the Philippine War, 1899–1902," *Intelligence and National Security*, 6 (1991), 90–114; John R.M. Taylor, *The Philippine Insurrection Against the United States* (Eugenio Lopez Foundation, 1971), 5 vols.

Intelligence in the Spanish-Cuban/American War

The U.S. government temporarily expanded its intelligence organization during the Spanish-Cuban/American War. The Treasury, War, and Navy departments developed spy networks, counterespionage, and communications intelligence, and collated information for war planners and field officers. Three tiny agencies provided intelligence for the U.S. war effort: the Secret Service (established in 1865) supervised by the Treasury Department; the Office of Naval Intelligence (formed in 1882) under the bureau of Navigation in the Navy Department; and the Military Information (Intelligence) Division (organized in 1885) of the War Department in the adjutant general's Office.

The Office of Naval Intelligence (ONI) had collected information about Spain and the Spanish colonies since the early 1880s. U.S. naval attachés in the major European capitals provided data about Spanish war ships, resources, and politics. In 1896–1897, chief intelligence officer Lt. Comdr. Richard Wainwright, and his staff officer Lt. William W. Kimball, expanded a war plan begun at the Naval War College, Newport, Rhode Island, for a two-front war against Spain that included operations in the Caribbean and the Philippines. Wainwright also sent Lt. Comdr. George L. Dyer in 1897 as the first full-time U.S. naval attaché to Madrid. Wainwright collaborated closely with Assistant Secretary of the Navy Theodore Roosevelt in developing clandestine U.S. war preparations, the secret purchase of armaments and warships overseas, and development of a spy network in Europe. Roosevelt corresponded with naval attachés Lt. Comdr. John C. Colwell in London and Lt. William S. Sims in Paris. Colwell and Sims operated a string of civilian spies with a "Secret Service Emergency Fund" sent directly by Assistant Secretary of the Navy Roosevelt, probably without the knowledge of either the secretary of the navy or the president.

During the war, ONI director Comdr. Richardson Clover joined Roosevelt, Capt. Alfred Thayer Mahan, and other top naval planners on a Naval War Board, providing information for war plans. The Naval War Board sent several naval secret agents disguised as civilian vacationers to Spain, the Mediterranean, and the Spanish colonies. Naval War Board and ONI informants, spies, and naval attachés collected little useful information, however. Colwell and Sims feuded continually over the operation of their makeshift intelligence operation. More successfully, ONI operated a ciphering and decoding room during the war, intercepting and reading Spanish cable and telegraphic communications and releasing false cables of its own to confuse Spain about U.S. ship movements and intentions to invade Cuba.

The Military Information (Intelligence) Division (MID) also operated an attaché and civilian informant network during the war. Capt. Tasker H. Bliss, the military attaché in Madrid, supplied information about Spanish war plans and troop deployments. Maj. Arthur L. Wagner, MID head and author of a text on tactical intelligence, prepared maps and information about Spanish fortifications and troop strength. Wagner also sent Lt. Andrew S. Rowan to Cuba for a secret rendezvous with Cuban revolutionary leader Gen. Calixto García (of the "Message to Garcia" fame), and sent Lt. Harry H. Whitney, disguised as a British seaman, on a covert operation to Puerto Rico. Most army commanders failed to consult MID. In the Philippines, the Bureau of Insurgent Records had to be established because of dissatisfaction with MID. This bureau's information became the basis for MID's Philippine Division and provided data for Lt. Col. Joseph T. Dickman and Capt. Ralph H. Van Deman to prepare "Notes on Philippines" as a supplement to MID's intelligence studies on Cuba and Puerto Rico. The United States Army Signal Corps assisted MID. Like the Navy, the Army Signal Corps carried out communications intelligence with its key operative a telegraph agent in Havana, who supplied critical cables about Spanish fleet movements in Cuban waters.

The United States Secret Service, founded at the end of the Civil War primarily to investigate counterfeiting and other Treasury crimes, became the government's counterespionage agency during the Spanish-Cuban/American War. Secret Service operatives launched several hundred investigations against suspected foreign agents in the United States and in Canada. In Canada a spy ring was headed by a former Spanish naval attaché to Washington, Ramón Carranza. Apparently, Secret Service detectives captured few actual enemy spies, but gained experience in domestic surveillance, which was greatly expanded during World War I.

There was no centralized coordination of intelligence and only minimal cooperation among the various intelligence organizations during the war. The intelligence agencies made some contributions to war planning, purchase of weapons overseas, collection of information, and military operations. ONI and MID provided information to planners and commanders about enemy terrain, fortifications, troop deployment, and fleet strength and movement. The importance of communications intercepts was clearly demonstrated by the Signal Corps. Intelligence expert Brig. Gen. Frederick Funston led the force that captured Emilio Aguinaldo y Famy, the major Filipino nationalist leader. U.S. commanders may have used ONI and MID notes, studies, and information in preparing operations. Certainly, Maj. Gen. Wesley Merritt recognized the importance of intelligence, organizing his own agency and seeking information from the State Department and other agencies.

The Spanish-Cuban/American War provided an intelligence legacy. The war stimulated ONI and MID reorganizations after its close and more closely tied intelligence to the development of a general staff and war planning mechanism. The Secret Service experience during the war demonstrated the federal government's willingness to expand domestic surveillance and to develop counterespionage methods against internal enemies.

Jeffery M. Dorwart

REFERENCES

William R. Corson, *The Armies of Ignorance: The Rise of the American Intelligence Empire* (Dial Pr., 1977); Graham A. Cosmas, *An Army for Empire: The United States Army in the Spanish-American War* (Univ. of Missouri Pr., 1971); Jeffrey M. Dorwart, *The Office of Naval Intelligence: The Birth of America's First Intelligence Agency, 1881–1918* (U.S. Naval Institute Pr., 1979); Rhodri Jeffreys-Jones, *American Espionage From Secret Service to CIA* (Free Pr., 1977); Marc B. Powe, *The Emergence of the War Department Intelligence Agency, 1885–1918* (Military Affairs for the American Military Institute, 1975).

Interallied Relations in the Siberian Intervention

The seizure of power in Petrograd in November 1917 by V.I. Lenin and the efforts to extend Bolshevik power throughout Russia quickly involved Russia's wartime partners. By early 1918 the Supreme War Council discussed sending Allied contingents to Siberia, especially to protect Allied supplies at Vladivostok and other storage depots. The Treaty of Brest-Litovsk (March 1918) took Russia out of World War I and raised fears that the Bolsheviks might aid the Germans materially in their campaigns on the Western Front. Deteriorating conditions in Russia and the outbreak of the civil war between Whites and Reds convinced the Allied powers to take steps to implement an intervention policy.

Differences among the Allies soon appeared, after the Supreme War Council on 15 March 1918 authorized Japanese intervention in Siberia. The United States was reluctant to support unilateral action by one nation. As a result, British forces landed at Vladivostok in April 1918 along with Japanese troops. President Woodrow Wilson finally agreed in mid-July that U.S. forces would be sent to eastern Siberia as well. A few U.S. troops landed at Vladivostok in mid-August, but the first major contingent did not arrive there until early September under the command of Gen. William S. Graves. By late September Wilson decided not to increase the size of U.S. forces in Siberia (scheduled to be approximately 7,000). The British and French had somewhat fewer, but the Japanese sent more than 70,000 soldiers to the region.

Allied intervention soon revealed differences, and occasionally serious disputes reduced Allied effectiveness. The size of the Japanese forces greatly concerned the United States, which feared the creation of a Japanese sphere of influence in eastern Siberia. The French and British were usually more tolerant of the Japanese presence, wanting to make sure the Bolsheviks did not gain control of the region.

Misunderstanding and competition developed over Japanese and U.S. interests in the two major railroad systems in the area: the Trans-Siberian Railway, linking Vladivostok to the West, and the Chinese Eastern Railway in northern Manchuria, which also served Vladivostok and other vital points. The Japanese believed that the United States intended to take over all the railroads and were unhappy that the United States signed agreements with Chinese and Russian officials giving U.S. technical personnel extensive administrative and operational control of the system. U.S. assurances to the contrary did not assuage the Japanese concerns.

The purposes of the intervention shifted after the end of the war in late 1918. Germany's defeat removed the threat of Allied supplies in Vladivostok falling into German hands. The new objective was to keep them out of the hands of the Bolsheviks as the civil war continued. Different priorities quickly emerged among the Allied governments. British and French policy strongly supported the White military effort against the Reds, and they were committed to military victory. Japan hoped to solidify its hold on the Siberian area. United States's policy was to maintain strict neutrality in the civil war, neither helping nor opposing the several factions fighting in Siberia. The U.S. commander, General Graves, faced an impossible task of doing nothing to help one side or the other. He was forced to exist in the middle of a very unstable situation, but prohibited from doing more than guarding railroad lines and supply depots. In fact, Washington's policy was fundamentally anti-Bolshevik, but Wilson did not want to take an active part in the civil war. U.S. partners criticized the United States for inaction and even hypocrisy.

The continuation of the civil war and the increase of military operations in Siberia eventually led the Allied governments to take a more active role in supporting one side. Adm. Aleksandr V. Kolchak became the dominant leader of White forces in Siberia after his rise to power with the overthrow of the Omsk Directory, consisting of moderate elements, in November 1918. His military successes, nearly reaching the Volga River in April 1919, led the Allied governments in late May to offer conditions for recognition of his regime and a com-

mitment to supply his forces. Kolchak accepted the conditions in early June, but by the fall of the year his system was in retreat and disintegration. Military and diplomatic support for Kolchak was very uneven, and the major powers could not reach a consistent and solid agreement on civil war issues. The collapse of Kolchak's movement ended the major White operation in Siberia.

Smaller, independent "war lord" Russian armies complicated Allied consensus and unity, the notable case being Grigori Semënov in northern Manchuria and the vicinity of Chita. Japanese support for Semënov, both with military supplies and advisers, created ill-will with U.S. authorities who correctly interpreted Semënov as undercutting their efforts to keep railroad lines open and traffic moving.

Another divisive and complicating problem was the presence of the Czech Legion in Siberia, which periodically opposed all other elements in the area: Reds, Whites, and the Allies. The major powers wished to help the Czechs leave Siberia in 1918, but could not agree on a common policy when the Czechs became an active military player in the Siberian conflict.

A final issue complicating Allied relations was that the major diplomatic personnel were in European Russia (first at Petrograd, then Moscow, then Vologda, and even Archangel). This forced political negotiations and decisions to be made by lesser officials in Siberia, or after delayed messages from their home governments. Military leaders of the Allied powers possessed extensive authority to make policy in Siberia. This often resulted in unevenness of high-level coordination and cooperation.

Public opinion and parliamentary debate within the western democracies pressured governments to remove the national contingents from the Russian morass, and gradually the forces withdrew from Siberia. The last British troops left Vladivostok in November 1919, and the last U.S. forces departed from Vladivostok in April 1920. Japanese forces remained in Siberia until October 1922.

Observers at the time and scholars of the topic generally agree that the intervention might have succeeded if full Allied support had been given to the White movement. This required better coordination and unity of purpose to achieve Allied objectives. Lacking these, the partial and competing efforts created a muddled situation which prolonged the civil war and had little chance for success.

Taylor Stults

REFERENCES

Peter Fleming, *The Fate of Admiral Kolchak* (Harcourt, 1963); William S. Graves, *America's Siberian Adventure, 1918–1920* (Cape & Smith, 1931); James W. Morley, *The Japanese Thrust into Siberia, 1918* (Columbia Univ. Pr., 1957); George Stewart, *The White Armies of Russia: A Chronicle of Counter-Revolution and Allied Intervention* (Macmillan, 1933); Betty M. Unterberger, *America's Siberian Expedition, 1918–1920: A Study of National Policy* (Duke Univ. Pr., 1956).

See also Graves, William Sidney; Siberia, Intervention (1918–1920).

Ironside, William Edmund, 1st Baron of Archangel and Ironside (1880–1959)

Maj. Gen. William Edmund Ironside was the British commander in chief of the Allied forces in North Russia, including the American Expeditionary Force, North Russia, from 14 October 1918 to 11 August 1919. Judged a success under trying circumstances, Ironside's service in the North was an early episode in one of the most brilliant military careers in modern British history.

Born in Scotland in 1880, "Tiny" Ironside, who was six feet, four inches tall and weighed some 250 pounds, joined the Royal Artillery in 1899 and served with distinction in the South African War of 1899–1902. In 1914, having achieved the rank of major, Ironside entered World War I as a general staff officer and, by mid-September 1918, was brigadier general commanding the British 99th Infantry Brigade on the Western Front. At that point, owing perhaps to his proficiency in foreign languages (he knew at least six), the 38-year-old commander was abruptly sent to North Russia to become chief of staff to the multinational force of Allied Commander in Chief Maj. Gen. Frederick C. Poole.

On 14 October, just two weeks after his arrival at Archangel, Ironside suddenly found himself thrust into the position of acting commander in chief in the region when General Poole unexpectedly left the North ostensibly on leave but, in fact, never to return. Shocked by what he perceived as the prevailing conditions of military and administrative disarray in the North, the new commander at once embarked on a dual campaign to consolidate Allied defenses in the region and hasten the recruitment of a local North Russian Army. Almost immediately, however, both of these efforts suffered setbacks in the form of a local Russian mutiny and a failed Allied offensive on the Vologda Railroad Front.

In mid-January 1919, in addition to his internal problems, Ironside was also confronted by a completely unexpected series of Bolshevik counteroffensives all across the Archangel front. In these circumstances, by employing a combination of strategic withdrawals and the skillful shifting of his limited reserves, Ironside succeeded, during the late winter and early spring of 1919, in holding his ground in the North. At the same time, thanks especially to the efforts of newly arrived Russian Gen. Eugene K. Miller, some success was achieved in the formation of a small but apparently reliable North Russian Army.

In late May, coincident with the final evacuation of his U.S. forces, Ironside was reinforced by the arrival at Archangel of an 8,000-man British relief force. Originally intended as part of a renewed Allied offensive in the North, these troops were at once faced with a crippling series of local Russian mutinies as a result of which, rather than an offensive, they were used to implement a spectacularly successful disengagement operation on the Northern Dvina River Front. Carried out in early August, this operation was promptly followed by Ironside's replacement as commander in chief by Gen. Henry C. Rawlinson, who then directed the final Allied evacuation of the North in September and October 1919.

After the North Russian episode, General Ironside held a succession of significant posts both at home and abroad, including, among others, Lieutenant of the Tower of London, aide to King George VI, quartermaster general of India, and governor general of Gibraltar. In 1939 he became chief of the Imperial General Staff, the highest position in the British armed forces. Stepping down from this position just after the evacuation from Dunkirk, Ironside was promoted field marshal and retired as commander in chief of the Home Forces in July 1940. Created a peer in 1941, he chose the title Baron Ironside of Archangel. He died in 1959.

John W. Long

REFERENCES

Lord Ironside of Archangel, *Archangel, 1918–1919* (Constable, 1953); Sir Edmund Ironside, "The North Russian Campaign," *Journal of the Royal Artillery*, 53 (1926), 307–319; Andrew Soutar, *With Ironside in North Russia* (Hutchinson, 1940).

Jikiri (? –1909)

By the middle of 1907, the armed and violent activities of Jikiri, a Sama pirate and rebel, had become a serious concern for both U.S. colonial authorities and the local leaders on Jolo Island in the Philippines. There is no clear record of Jikiri's birthplace, but he spent much time in Parang, Maimbung, and islands south of Jolo. He and his ragtag band of rebels, bandits, brigands, and pirates became notorious for attacks on villages on Jolo Island, ranging from as far as Zamboanga to the Bornean coast.

On 22 March 1908 Jikiri and his band attacked a Chinese store in Maimbung, seat of the sultanate, and killed several people. This incident prompted the authorities to raise the reward money on Jikiri's head to P4,000 (about two thousand United States dollars). On 9 November Jikiri and four of his men were thought to have passed the night in a hut in Parang. Informed of Jikiri's presence, the following morning Capt. Frank DeWitt and five Tausug constables surrounded the hut. When the outlaws refused to surrender, a firefight lasting five minutes ensued. All of Jikiri's men were killed, but Jikiri was not among the dead. The authorities learned later that he had gone to Borneo on 2 November and had been reported to the British government for many piratical attacks and killings in several villages on the Bornean coast.

Because of pressures from the British lawmen, Jikiri sneaked back into Sulu. On the way, he raided the island of South Ubián. His target was the store of Kong Bu Wa, a Chinese trader. Kong Bu Wa engaged Jikiri in hand-to-hand combat forcing him to abandon his intention. In Jolo, he spent some time on Cabingaan Island, where he had kept some of his booty and the women he had taken for wives or concubines.

In response to both British requests and local security, a search for Jikiri and his band was ordered by Brig. Gen. Tasker H. Bliss, governor of the Moro Province. Col. Jacob A. Augur and Lt. Arthur Poillon conducted on-the-spot investigations of the islands south of Jolo. The pirates were located on 2 July 1909 at Patián Island, south of Jolo. U.S. troops from cavalry, infantry, and artillery units were sent to the island where they cornered Jikiri and his eight men. After two days of fighting, the whole band was killed in the hand-to-hand fray on 4 July 1909, thus ending the exploits of one of the most notorious Sama in Western Mindanao.

Samuel K. Tan

REFERENCES

W. H. Davison, "Jikiri's Last Stand: Moro Uprising in the Philippines, 1907," *Quartermaster Review* (July-Aug. 1935); Peter G. Gowing, *Mandate in Moroland: The American Government of Muslim Filipinos, 1899–1920* (Univ. of the Philippines, 1977); Samuel K. Tan, *Sulu Under American Military Rule, 1899–1913* (Univ. of the Philippines, 1967).

Jolo, Moro Province, The Philippines, Battles (1905)

After the 1898 encounter between Spanish troops and the Moros in Busbus, a district in the town of Jolo, the Philippines, there were no serious engagements in the capital of Moro Province during the period of U.S. rule until early 1903. In that year the town of Jolo became somewhat disturbed by rumors of Moro leader Panglima Hassan's impending attack. The Hassan uprising, which started in Luuk in the east and spread to about two-thirds of the island, did not end with the death of Hassan in March 1904. Another revolt in Luuk started on 9 January 1905 when Datu Usap and his followers ignored U.S. peace overtures and refused to surrender. Maj. Hugh L. Scott ordered an assault on Usap's fort and ended the revolt.

Toward the summer of 1905, Datu Pala, an old slave trader and a strong supporter of Panglima Hassan, returned from Borneo and started to stir up people for a *jihad* (holy war) against U.S. rule. He attacked U.S. authorities as *kapil* (an infidel; one who has no God), an appeal to Koranic injunction to get into "Muslim psychology." The authorities did not move against him until British diplomatic pressures were exerted on the Jolo authorities to apprehend Pala for several murderous episodes in Borneo. This was stressed by Sandakan chief of police, A. T. Wardrop, who had arrived in Jolo. The U.S. response to British overtures was cautious because the collection of cedula tax (head tax) on the island, in recognition of U.S. sovereignty, might be jeopardized. The foot-dragging in Pala's capture was criticized in the *Singapore Free Press*.

The decisive U.S. move came after a series of killings by Pala's men, including Major Scott's stenographer, Ferdinand T. Vering, on 10 April and in response to the impending threats against the security and peace of Jolo itself, the seat of U.S. authority. In fact, within three miles of the town, Pala's men attacked Edward Schück's plantation, burning houses and killing a Muslim girl. On 6 April, the walled district of the town was attacked by Pala's men shouting defiance and invectives. On 13 April, two of Pala's men disguised as Christians eluded sentries and were about to murder Major Scott when they were caught. On 19 April a Chinese storekeeper was slashed to death, and a band of 40 men killed an entire pro-U.S. Muslim family in their home. Outside of Jolo town, Pala's men were attacking those who supported the cedula tax. The situation prompted the detail of 700 U.S. troops in Jolo. The number gradually increased to about 1,100 plus 160 local scouts and militiamen. To enable the authorities to conduct the operation, the campaign in Cotabato against Datu Ali had to be postponed.

On 1 May U.S. troops engaged the Pala rebels. The battle started with the attack on Paruka Utik's fort by two squadrons of the 14th Cavalry Regiment and two crack companies of the 22nd Infantry Regiment. Although hampered by trenches and pits, artillery bombardment wiped out the 100 Muslim defenders, including Utik who refused to surrender. On the U.S. side three were killed and 17 were wounded, the most severe loss since the battle at Bayan in Lanao. On 4 May U.S. troops overran and destroyed another interior fort of Pala. The following day, Pala and his 20 men were cornered in their coastal fort by Gen. Leonard Wood's pursuing columns. The rebels were all killed; U.S. troops sustained 28 casualties: 8 killed and 20 wounded.

The liquidation of Pala and his band did not end trouble for colonial rule. Subsequent disturbances continued to plague Jolo Island, culminating in one of the best remembered battles in local tradition and one of the most controversial in U.S. colonial history—the Battle of Bud Daju in 1906.

Samuel K. Tan

REFERENCES

Peter G. Gowing, *Mandate in Moroland: The American Government of Muslim Filipinos, 1899–1920* (Univ. of the Philippines, 1977); Victor Hurley, *Swish of the Kris* (Dutton, 1936); Samuel K. Tan, *Sulu Under American Military Rule, 1899–1913* (Univ. of the Philippines, 1967).

Junta Consultiva, Dominican Republic

In November 1919, after injudicious remarks by Rear Adm. Thomas Snowden about the duration of the U.S. occupation of the Dominican Republic produced a rash of protests, Snowden, the military governor, was directed to form a Junta Consultiva of prominent Dominican politicians by the State Department. The Junta was to propose reforms to be carried out by the U.S. occupation authorities that would show the United States intended to occupy the island nation only long enough for changes in the Dominican governmental structure to be implemented. The commission consisted of Archbishop Adolfo A. Nouel, and three prominent political figures: Francisco J. Peynado, Federico Velásquez, and Jacinto R. de Castro.

The commission prepared three memoranda during November and December 1919, proposing (1) the codification of electoral laws, (2) the reorganization of the treasury and of the various local communal and provincial governments, and (3) the abolition of the two most controversial policies of the occupation regime (i.e., press censorship and the jurisdiction of provost courts over civilians).

Admiral Snowden rejected these proposals, and the Junta members resigned in protest on 7 January 1920, ending the initial attempt to initiate negotiations to establish a basis for withdrawal. Attacks on the Junta Consultiva by Dominican political leaders and the Dominican press made it clear that the local citizens were not yet prepared to accept cooperation or negotiation with the invaders.

Kenneth J. Grieb

REFERENCES

Bruce J. Calder, *The Impact of Intervention: The Dominican Republic During the U.S. Occupation of 1916–1924* (Univ. of Texas Pr., 1984).

See also Snowden, Thomas.

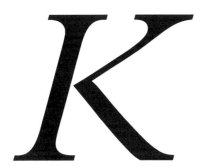

Kennan, George (1845–1924)

In 1898, George Kennan had a reputation as a Russian expert, based on travel and two books recording his experiences. One, a two-volume study entitled *Siberia and the Exile System* published in 1891, revealed the horrors of the tsarist prison system in Siberia.

A week after the outbreak of war between the United States and Spain, Kennan accepted an invitation to go to Cuba as a war correspondent for *The Outlook* of New York to report on the work of the American National Red Cross in Cuba. Kennan's dispatches covering the Santiago campaign during the summer of 1898 highlighted the inadequacy of military preparations to feed and care for the wounded. He strongly criticized the commissary and medical departments of the United States Army for bad management and poor planning. Within a month of the beginning of the campaign, half the V Army Corps was out of action with yellow fever, which Kennan attributed to neglect by senior officers. After Kennan caught malaria, he left Cuba in August 1898. He returned in December 1898 and reported on the U.S. military occupation until his departure in February 1899. He wrote a book about his experiences, *Campaigning in Cuba*.

David R. Murray

REFERENCES

George Kennan, *Campaigning in Cuba* (Century, 1899).

Knapp, Harry Shepard (1856–1923)

Rear Adm. Harry Shepard Knapp, commander of the United States Navy's Atlantic Cruiser Squadron from November 1916 to February 1919, established a U.S. military government in the Dominican Republic on 29 November 1916, and became its first military governor. Knapp had previously served as chief of staff of the Pacific Fleet and as a member of the General Board of the Navy. Later, he was detailed to the U.S. delegation at the Versailles Peace Conference.

The initial U.S. landing in the Dominican Republic occurred a few months before Knapp's arrival in 1916 when the Atlantic Cruiser Squadron was technically under the command of Rear Adm. William B. Caperton. By the time Knapp arrived, the situation had reached a critical point, and Knapp established the military government. Even though both Haiti and the Dominican Republic were nominally under the same command, in practice the principal naval officer in the region governed the Dominican Republic while the marines administered neighboring Haiti. Because the Dominicans refused to serve in the cabinet of the military government, the vacant posts were filled by marine officers, thus establishing a full military government.

With officials in Washington distracted by World War I, Knapp and U.S. Minister William W. Russell were left with considerable discretion and responsibility in the Dominican Republic. Knapp's executive orders determined the scope and organization of the military regime governing the Dominican Republic. But in establishing a full government, Knapp had to deal with establishing, maintaining, and staffing the entire range of governmental and civil services on a daily basis. This was a task of considerable detail for which he was not prepared. Despite his extensive naval experience, Knapp had no knowledge of the language or culture of the island nation, nor did he have training in civil law and government.

One of Knapp's initial actions was the establishment of the infamous press censorship regime. He was also responsible for the decree establishing military provost courts and empowering them with full jurisdiction, including civilian issues.

Knapp's relations with the Dominicans were strained. Angered by their refusal to serve his regime and lacking an appreciation for the local culture, Knapp's attitudes reflected the prevailing attitude of Anglo-Saxon superiority among U.S. military men. He accorded scant consideration to the Dominicans, whom he considered inferior.

Knapp was reassigned when Washington turned its attention to the Dominican Republic after World War I. In spite of his poor relations with the Dominican people, he dealt with a difficult situation in establishing a complete government with an entire range of services with little direction from Washington.

Kenneth J. Grieb

REFERENCES

Bruce J. Calder, *The Impact of Intervention: The Dominican Republic During the U.S. Occupation of 1916–1924* (Univ. of Texas Pr., 1984); Dana G. Munro, *Intervention and Dollar Diplomacy in the Caribbean, 1900–1921* (Princeton Univ. Pr., 1964).

Lake Lanao, Moro Province, The Philippines, Gunboat Operations

During the early U.S. military campaigns against the Moros (Philippine Muslims), a fleet of gunboats was established in 1904 by the United States Army to serve on Lake Lanao, Mindanao Island, the Philippines. Some vessels were built in China specifically for this purpose, but others were ships that had been used by the Spanish and scuttled at the conclusion of the Spanish-Cuban/American War.

The Moros used *vintas* (canoe-like vessels) for commerce and warfare. A fleet of modern gunboats was a significant asset for the United States Army because the vessels interdicted *vinta* transportation and bombarded *cottas* (Moro forts), located near the shores of Lake Lanao.

From the early 17th century to the late 19th century the Spanish made little effort to control the Moros around Lake Lanao. In 1894, the Spanish decided to assert themselves primarily to help protect non-Muslim Filipino settlers on Mindanao. Four gunboats and three iron barges were built at Hong Kong, disassembled, transported to Lake Lanao, and reassembled there. The gunboats resembled the steam launches

common in many countries during the late 19th and early 20th centuries. Although they were relatively open for warships, the upper decks and awnings protected the crews from the elements. Overall, the vessels had a rather festive appearance. The barges were designed for carrying and landing troops. They were well fitted for use as landing barges because even when fully loaded they had a very low draft, only two or three feet.

This modest fleet served the Spanish well, but it was sunk in November 1898 when the Spanish were ordered to leave Mindanao. The existence of the sunken vessels was unknown to the U.S. military until 1904 when an officer learned about the ships from some Moros. U.S. authorities had built or purchased a number of vessels already, some *vintas* and other types. They were useful, but could not compare with steel gunboats.

The first significant vessel provided for U.S. forces at Lake Lanao was a launch that had been attached to the hospital ship *Relief* and was named for its mother ship. The *Relief* had many shortcomings, but managed to stay afloat for three years before being wrecked. A much more substantial vessel was the *Flake*, which was built in Shanghai for the United States Army. The *Flake*

247

mounted a 37-mm automatic gun and a Gatling gun and was crewed by five Filipinos. The gunboat figured importantly in a war with the sultan of Oatu, a conflict that resulted in the destruction of his *cotta*.

Meanwhile, an extensive and difficult salvage operation was undertaken to add the scuttled former Spanish gunboats to the U.S. fleet on Lake Lanao. The *General Almonte, General Blanco,* and *Corcuera* were salvaged between 1904 and 1906, although the *Corcuera* could not be used. The *General Blanco* was in action against dissident Moros as late as the 1930s, but under Filipino rather than direct U.S. control.

Benjamin R. Beede

REFERENCES

Parker Hitt, "Amphibious Infantry: A Fleet on Lake Lanao," *United States Naval Institute Proceedings,* 64 (1938), 234–250; Mamitua Saber, *Battle of Marawi, 1895 and Other Historical Notes,* enl. ed. (Univ. Research Center, Mindanao State Univ., 1986).

Lake Lanao Operations, Moro Province, The Philippines (1902–1903)

The Lake Lanao region of the island of Mindanao in the Philippines is home to a group of Moro (Philippine Muslim) people who call themselves Maranaos (for lake dwellers). In 1900 their number was placed at 80,000 to 100,000, which ranked them as one among the three largest groups of Moro people of Mindanao and Sulu. The Moros, more than the other "non-Christian" tribes, posed a menace to colonial governments. In 1901 the Philippine Commission led by William H. Taft declared that they were a serious threat to U.S. governance, as they had been to Spanish rule for more than 300 years before 1898 (*Reports of the Philippine Commission . . .* , p. 160):

> The Moro tribes of southern Mindanao, the Sulu Archipelago and southern Palawan are the only ones among these non-Christian peoples which could afford any serious menace to public order and to the peace of any important portion of the archipelago . . . . The Moros of the Lake Lanao region have been long reputed to be the fiercest and most uncompromising members of their tribe.

British writer Henry Savage Landor corroborated this view: "The Lanao region is overrun with panditas [chief priests], wise men and medicine men, officials and sayids or priests, who are the chief instigators of trouble" (Landor, p. 307).

To avoid open conflict with the Moros, the U.S. military first secured peace by signing the Bates Treaty with the sultan of Sulu in 1899. During 1900, the United States Army garrisoned Jolo, Sulu, and Parang-Parang, Cotabato, and then slowly entered the Lanao country in 1901 by way of two approaches: from the north, through Iligan and from the South via Malabang. Camp Overton in Iligan was established, complemented by Camp Vicars in Malabang. The following year, 1901, the road connecting Iligan and Marahui in Lake Lanao was constructed. Meanwhile, U.S. authorities were busy laying the groundwork for a massive pacification campaign aimed at the inhospitable Moros. The Philippine Commission was instructed to deal with the "uncivilized tribes" of the Philippines in roughly the same way the U.S. government dealt with Native Americans on the western frontier.

Meanwhile, the fall of Philippine nationalist leader Emilio Aguinaldo y Fama in 1901 and the U.S. proclaimed end of the Philippine War in 1902 did not stop fighting in the Philippines. Oblivious of what occurred in the northern and central islands, the Moros viewed the U.S. presence in Mindanao and Sulu with suspicion. Some Moro chiefs were, in fact, provoked by the occupation of their homeland by U.S. forces. They interpreted U.S. motives as no different from those of the Spanish colonizers; that is, to take away Moro possessions and proselytize the Moros for Christianity. While the Moros did not engage U.S. forces in open warfare, they ambushed soldiers in small parties or stole their weapons. In some instances, they stole U.S. property and constantly sniped at camps. It was this series of overt acts that occasioned an armed confrontation in May 1902 which came to be known as the Battle of Bayang, the first deadly encounter between the Moros and U.S. troops. The battle claimed over 300 Moro lives and scores of killed and wounded among U.S. forces. The punishment inflicted on the Moros did not immediately pay dividends, however. While some Marango *datus* (chiefs) or sultans accepted U.S.

friendship and even cooperated with U.S. authorities, other chiefs continued to defy the white man's proposition for peace and attacked U.S. troops whenever they could.

Shortly after the Battle of Bayang, Frank D. Baldwin, commanding officer, was promoted. His relief was Capt. John J. Pershing, who had made earlier contacts with the Lanao *datus* through Amai Manabilang. At that time, Pershing was assigned in Iligan, mapping out a strategy of his own to penetrate the Laguna. Pershing took command of two squadrons of the 15th Cavalry Regiment, a battalion of infantry, and a battery of mountain guns stationed at Camp Vicars, which was named after Lt. Thomas A. Vicars, a U.S. officer who had fallen in the Battle of Bayang. The U.S. force at Camp Vicars was larger than that usually commanded by a captain, but Pershing was extremely well fitted to campaign against the Moros. Although the Moros were hostile from the start, Pershing nonetheless attempted to write to the *datus* to come to Camp Vicars for peace talks. Acts of violence and theft, however, continued unabated. Between August and September 1902 night attacks were made on Camp Vicars by defiant Moros from nearby Butig and Maciu. At one time, the Moros cut and removed telephone lines for a kilometer, interrupting communications between Camp Vicars and Zamboanga. By September, four soldiers had been killed, and 12 had been wounded in the line of duty (*Report of the Secretary of War, 1902*, p. 264).

By then, Pershing decided it was time to punish the recalcitrant Moros. The first of a series of campaigns around Lake Lanao was the expedition against Sultan Uali of Butig, 18–22 September 1902. The *cotta* (fort) of Sultan Uali was pulverized by Pershing's artillery, killing some of the sultan's *sacopes* (followers). While the sultan eluded arrest or death, his name was never heard again.

The following month, Pershing again led the 15th Cavalry to take adjacent Maciu, whose chiefs, Tawagon and Gandauali, did not acknowledge U.S. friendship and refused to return government property they had stolen. Troops shelled the Moros with mountain guns, pounding several *cottas* to pieces. When the battle smoke cleared, some 40 to 50 Moros, including one of their sultans, were killed (*Report of the Secretary of War, 1902*, p. 264).

In November 1902 Pershing decided to make a tour around Lake Lanao in an effort to win the Moros over to the government. He then sent peace overtures through his *amigos* (friendly chiefs), inviting them to come to Camp Vicars. Writing to all the *datus*, Pershing gave notice that U.S. forces were in the Laguna "not to make war, nor to dispossess" the Moros but to help them in every way. He promised to buy their produce, give them jobs, provide them with medicines, and more. However, he warned the unfriendly *datus* that if they persisted in obstructing the establishment of peace and continued their opposition, they would suffer the consequences. Accompanied by Datu Amai Manabilang, Pershing's march earned the friendship of some *datus*, except the chiefs from the west side of Lake Lanao. There, the sultans of Bacolod, Pualas, and other allied *rancherias* (settlements) remained adamant, or, at worst, defiant.

For his part, the sultan of Bacolod displayed mixed attitudes toward Pershing, perhaps to baffle Pershing, or perhaps because the sultan was uncertain himself. At times, he professed friendship to the U.S. authorities; at other times he challenged them. In his letter of June 1902, he wrote a declaration of war, burning the sides of the letter to show that he was serious. He asked Pershing and his men to return to the coast and to follow Moro customs and the Moro religion or else take the blame for what would happen. "This letter goes (to you) burned in six places to indicate it means war" (Sultan sa Bacolod to Pershing, 17 June 1902, Box 319, Pershing Papers). The following day, however, 18 June 1902, the sultan, astonishingly, wrote a friendly letter. Then, in July 1902 he again wrote Pershing an insulting letter that he "[Pershing] should not live among circumcised Moros . . . . If you stay here we want to fight you this month and in no event do we wish to be your friends for you are marauders and you do not wish to follow our religion and you eat pork." He then urged Pershing to "come and live in Bacolod and the sultan and Panondiongan [the sultan's adviser] will circumcise you" (Sultan sa Bacolod to Pershing, 4 July 1902, Box 319, Pershing Papers).

Feeling insecure, some friendly *datus* began to fear that their status was dwindling and that internal conflict between them and the "bad" Moros was imminent. They allowed Pershing to explore the entire Lake Lanao area to make friends with them or else punish the others. That helped provide some justification for the massive exploration and pacification campaign. By year's end, Pershing had recommended to the department commander that an expedition be sent to the western shore of Lake Lanao to Marahui and then to the east. He felt "that the time had come when we must give up handling these people with gloves" (Pershing Memoirs, p. 274, Box 374, Pershing Papers).

On 3 April 1903 an expedition left Camp Vicars heading toward the western side of Lake Lanao with a clear set of instructions from Gen. Samuel S. Sumner: "If on reaching the vicinity of Bacolod, you find these Moros unfriendly and determined to oppose your progress, you will take the necessary military measures to bring them into subjection" (Sumner to Pershing, 2 April 1903, Box 278, Pershing Papers). The expedition had an impressive force of three troops of cavalry, four companies of infantry, a medical unit, and a field battery of Vickers Maxim guns. Each soldier was authorized to carry 200 rounds of ammunition, and an appropriate supply of ammunition was provided for the mountain guns. Along the way, members of the expedition met only minor resistance, which they quickly disposed of with few casualties. In two days, they reached Bacolod. The troops positioned themselves for a siege of the Bacolod *cotta*, which was regarded as impregnable, eliciting awe even among the Moros. By the afternoon of 8 April 1903 Pershing flashed the green light for the troops to start firing. The Bacolod warriors, outnumbered and outgunned, responded with superb courage. With only their *krises* and *campilans* (bladed weapons for combat) and a few *lantacas* (brass cannons) that threw slugs, they defended themselves mightily in what they considered their indestructible fortress. U.S. troops kept their distance at some 2,000 yards, thereby effectively avoiding Moro firepower and minimizing the possibility of hand-to-hand combat. Their mountain guns eliminated Moros who were no doubt helpless in the face of a militarily superior enemy. In a moment, the artillery rounds hit their marks. The *cotta* was set ablaze, and soon the loud yells of Moro defiance subsided. Bacolod was destroyed. With it perished 60 Moro warriors, including the sultan's advisor and several sympathetic *datus* from Maciu, Taraca,

Pindolonan, and Binidayan, among others. U.S. forces incurred minor casualties, 11 wounded. The heavy losses in lives and property would have been avoided if the Bacolod Moros had surrendered or talked peace. They did not because they had no term for peace. Whatever it amounted to, the fall of Bacolod meant the elimination of any strong opposition to U.S. rule in the Lake Lanao areas.

The following day, 9 April 1903, in the afternoon, the expeditionary force discovered another fortress in nearby Calahui, also a hostile *rancheria*. Like the Bacolod *cottta*, the Calahui fortification received continuous bombardment, giving no opportunity to its warriors to use their sharp *krises*. The Moro fighters in the fort retreated that night, carrying the bodies of their 23 fallen comrades under cover of darkness. When U.S. troops entered the *cotta* with a group of Moro hostages, they saw nothing but an empty and battered fort. In all, the casualties in the Bacolod and related fighting totaled 120 dead, according to conservative estimates of friendly Moros (Pershing Memoirs, Box 374, Pershing Papers).

In May 1903 Pershing's expedition took the other side of Lake Lanao to complete his tour as he had planned. He then marched his troops to Taraca, a densely populated *rancheria* on the eastern shore which also dared to challenge U.S. rule. Taraca was where another formidable "outlaw," Datu Ampuana Gaus, lived and maintained a strong *cotta*. Pershing encountered "a severe opposition" among Datu Gaus's men and fought with many other *datus*. In every case, the troops quashed them with dispatch and with slight U.S. losses. These were but small *cottas* except that of Ampuana Gaus, and there was no Moro force powerful enough to stand in the way of the expedition. Pershing destroyed 10 such Moro forts, including Ampuana Gaus's, killed 115 Moros, and wounded 14 others, captured 52 Moro prisoners and confiscated quantities of rifles and cannons, dealing a heavy loss to the Moros (Pershing to Robert L. Bullard, 6 May 1903, Box 370, Pershing Papers). In the fight with Ampuana Gaus that *datu* was among those who surrendered, only to escape later. He remained at large, pestering the authorities until he died in 1916.

From Taraca the troops proceeded to the village of Datu Amai Manabilang in Madaya, near Marahui and then returned to Camp Vicars via the western side of Lake Lanao. Pershing completed his tour around the Lake Lanao region with flying colors, giving much satisfaction to him and to his superiors.

The last of these military campaigns in the Lake Lanao area occurred in November 1903, under the command of Moro Province Governor Leonard Wood. This campaign was essentially punitive, like the others he had sent to Buldon, Cotabato, and other places in Moroland. However, the expedition was oriented toward a different aim: to teach the Moros some lessons for not renouncing slavery, slave-catching, theft, and other "uncivilized" practices. Not much was accomplished during the hunt, but it nonetheless bore fruit. It helped break the back of Moro resistance around Lake Lanao; for the first time in their history the Moros suffered crushing defeats.

Federico V. Magdalena

REFERENCES

Henry F. Funtecha, *American Military Occupation of the Lake Lanao Region, 1901–1913* (Univ. Research Center, Mindanao State Univ., 1979); Henry Savage Landor, *Gems of the East* (Harper, 1904); John J. Pershing papers, Manuscript Division, Library of Congress; "Report of John J. Pershing, Captain, 15th Cavalry," in *Annual Report of Maj. General George W. Davis, 1903; Report of Gen. Samuel S. Sumner, Brigadier General, Commanding, Department of Mindanao*, Zamboanga, 30 June 1903; *Report of the Secretary of War, 1902* (U.S. Government Printing Office, 1903), vol. 1; *Reports of the Philippine Commission, the Governor and the Heads of the Executive Departments of the Civil Government of the Philippine Islands, 1900–1903* (U.S. Government Printing Office, 1904).

Las Guásimas, Cuba, Battle (1898)

The little battle at Las Guásimas, Cuba, had major significance for the U.S. campaign at Santiago de Cuba. A U.S. victory, it prepared the way for deployment against the Spanish main line of defense, provided a timely boost in morale, and, perhaps most importantly, committed the U.S. force to attack Santiago de Cuba by an interior ground route rather than by a water route in conjunction with the navy. The fighting, which occurred early in the morning of 24 June, lasted about two hours; then Spanish forces withdrew.

Las Guásimas lay on the main route between the coast, where U.S. forces landed first at Daiquirí and later at Siboney, and Santiago de Cuba, the center of Spanish strength in eastern Cuba and the key U.S. military objective early in the island campaign. It was located on a bluff about three miles northwest of Siboney. Beyond it was a well-watered plain, the tiny village of Sevilla, and the road to Santiago de Cuba.

As they debarked, U.S. troops took up positions along the coast. Maj. Gen. Joseph Wheeler, commanding a dismounted cavalry division, quickly pushed his troops forward from Daiquirí, and at midnight on the 23rd one of his brigades, under the command of Gen. Samuel B.M. Young, was assembled at Siboney. Wheeler, who reached the village in the afternoon, learned from Gen. Demetrio Perez-Castillo Duary, a Cuban revolutionary leader with about 800 men, that Spanish forces were at Las Guásimas and Sevilla. He determined to attack.

Early the next day Wheeler divided his command. He sent Young with 464 men, including squadrons of the 1st and 10th Cavalry Regiments (the latter a black unit), and three Hotchkiss revolving cannons along the main road. He ordered Col. Leonard Wood with about 500 men, including two squadrons of the 1st Volunteer Cavalry (the Rough Riders) and two rapid-fire Colt automatic guns, to take a trail about a mile west of the road to Las Guásimas. Both the road and trail, as they ascended steep slopes to a strong Spanish position, passed through a tangled thicket of trees and underbrush.

Gen. Antero Rubín commanded the Spanish forces of about 1,500 men. His immediate superior, Gen. Arsenio Linares Pomba, maintained headquarters some four miles to the rear. Linares, believing U.S. troops would launch their main attack at Aguadores near the mouth of the San Juan River and not wanting Rubín to be cut off, had determined to make no great stand at Las Guásimas, but to remove his troops toward Santiago de Cuba. Accordingly, Linares had ordered Rubín to withdraw his troops with deliberation and caution as Rubín repelled the enemy.

Thus, when the enemy attacked, Rubín's troops met the U.S. force with spirited volleys. The fire was heavy enough that Wheeler asked for reinforcements from Gen. Henry W. Lawton, who commanded a division of infantry at Siboney. Just as the additional troops arrived, however, Rubín sent his men to the rear. In an orderly fashion the Spanish soldiers retreated with their baggage and wounded and started for Santiago de Cuba. U.S. forces, exhausted but jubilant, bivouacked on the battlefield rather than give chase.

Casualties were light. The U.S. force lost one officer and 15 men killed, and 6 officers and 46 men wounded. The Spaniards lost 3 officers and 7 men killed and 18 men wounded.

Although the casualties were light and the fighting brief, the battle was important. It removed the enemy from a strong position close to the beachhead. It dislodged Spanish forces from a strategic gap in the hills through which U.S. troops must pass. It also cleared a route to the open plain about Sevilla, the only good site for a U.S. camp between the coast and the Spanish fortifications at Santiago de Cuba.

The skirmish at Las Guásimas was the first battle of the Spanish-Cuban/American War for the United States Army. Within two hours of its conclusion, the 9th Cavalry (a black unit) and Gen. Adna R. Chaffee's brigade in Lawton's division joined the tired U.S. troops on the battlefield. Shortly after, Wheeler received orders to hold his position, but over the next few days U.S. forces moved forward to encamp near Sevilla, the staging ground for the siege of Santiago de Cuba.

Paul H. Carlson

REFERENCES

Graham A. Cosmas, *An Army for Empire: The United States Army in the Spanish-American War* (Univ. of Missouri Pr., 1971); Frank Freidel, *The Splendid Little War* (Little, Brown, 1958); Matthew Forney Steele, *American Campaigns* (U.S. Infantry Association, 1935), 2 vols.; David F. Trask, *The War With Spain in 1898* (Macmillan, 1981); Joseph Wheeler, *The Santiago Campaign, 1898* (Lamson, Wolffe & Co., 1898).

Latimer, Julian Lane (1868–1939)

From 1925 to 1927 Rear Adm. Julian Lane Latimer was commander of the Special Service Squadron, a collection of five old, slow cruisers, based in Panama for patrolling Central American waters. During Latimer's duty with the squadron, U.S. Marines landed in Nicaragua to begin the second intervention.

Born in Shepherdstown, West Virginia, in 1868, Latimer graduated from the United States Naval Academy in 1890. He served in Cuban waters during the Spanish-Cuban/American War and commanded the battleship *Rhode Island* pa-

trolling the Atlantic coast during World War I. He was made admiral in 1923.

After Gen. Emiliano Chamorro Vargas's *coup d'état* of October 1925, the opposition Liberal party forces raised the banner of counterrevolution on Nicaragua's eastern coast in May 1926. In response to U.S. and British consular requests at Bluefields, and with Washington's approval, Admiral Latimer sent the cruiser *Cleveland* and its marines to occupy the town and to protect the customs house and customs collector, then under U.S. supervision. Chamorro was able to reestablish his authority along the Caribbean coast within a few weeks, but by August Latimer had to send ships to Corinto on the Pacific side and again to Bluefields because of disturbed conditions. As Nicaragua was about to begin a new revolutionary cycle, Latimer and the United States chargé d'affaires, Lawrence Dennis, talked with antagonists to arrange a conference in October at Corinto aboard the *Denver*, another of Latimer's old cruisers. Although the conferees reached no agreement, Chamorro resigned by the end of the month and Adolfo Díaz, a former conservative president, emerged as the new head of state.

The United States extended diplomatic recognition to Díaz's government, but because he was no more acceptable to the Liberals than Chamorro had been, the revolution continued. Latimer responded to pleas for protection from U.S. citizens by creating neutral zones, including one at Puerto Cabezas, where the Liberal claimant to the presidency had established his government. Another zone in which fighting was prohibited was established along Nicaragua's Pacific Railroad from the west coast port of Corinto to Managua. Although neutral zones were created primarily to protect lives and property of U.S. citizens, they also controlled Liberal bases in a manner that favored the Conservative government. When Liberals attempted to collect an export tax on mahogany logs, Latimer instructed U.S.-owned companies to pay taxes only to the government. There were also charges that Latimer had ordered the destruction of ammunition belonging to the Liberals at Puerto Cabezas, and there was criticism, denied by Latimer, that Conservative forces used the railway while the Liberals were excluded.

Admiral Latimer briefed Henry L. Stimson when Stimson arrived in April 1927 as President Calvin Coolidge's special emissary to resolve the

Nicaraguan situation. Latimer understood Stimson's arranged peace to include a threat to disarm forcibly Liberal troops if they did not surrender arms voluntarily. Disarmament went well except for Augusto C. Sandino's small group which at first seemed no great problem. After about a month of waiting, while Sandino appeared increasingly defiant, Latimer on 2 July ordered the marines to begin operations against the rebels, which led to the bloody engagement at Ocotal. Although the U.S. Marine and Nicaraguan national guard offensive into Nueva Segovia Province was successful in occupying towns and defeating Sandinista attacks, Sandino remained free and armed. Shortly before the Battle of Ocotal, Rear Adm. David F. Sellers arrived in Panama to replace Latimer, who had requested to be relieved as commander of the Special Service Squadron.

Latimer received praise as a sea-going diplomat from an observant *New York Times* reporter who wrote that Latimer combined his military duties with "tactful essays" toward settling the Liberal-Conservative dispute. In conversations with President Díaz, presidential claimant Juan B. Sacasa, and Liberal General José María Moncada, Latimer seemed to have both sides' respect for his efforts to achieve peace.

In November 1927 Latimer received command of the Fourth Naval District of Philadelphia. He retired in 1930 and died nine years later.

William Kamman

REFERENCES

Harold Norman Denny, *Dollars for Bullets: The Story of American Rule in Nicaragua* (Dial Pr., 1929); William Kamman, *A Search for Stability: United States Diplomacy Toward Nicaragua, 1925–1933* (Univ. of Notre Dame Pr., 1968); Neill Macaulay, *The Sandino Affair* (Quadrangle, 1967); U.S. Congress, Senate, Committee on Foreign Relations, *Use of the United States Navy in Nicaragua: Hearings on S. Res. 137*, 70th Congress, 1st Session, 11 & 18 Feb. 1928 (U.S. Government Printing Office, 1928).

Lawton, Henry Ware
(1843–1899)

Henry Ware Lawton was noted for his participation in campaigns against Native Americans and his significant roles in the Spanish-Cuban/American War and the Philippine War.

Born in Ohio in 1843, Lawton was raised in Indiana and educated at Fort Wayne Episcopal College. He enlisted in the 9th Indiana Infantry in the Civil War and emerged from that conflict as a lieutenant colonel (and breveted a colonel) and holding the Medal of Honor for his actions in the Battle of Atlanta, 1864. He entered Harvard Law School, but soon returned to the army as a second lieutenant in the 41st Infantry Regiment (Colored). In 1871, he transferred to the 4th Cavalry Regiment and fought in campaigns against Native Americans. Under orders from Gen. Nelson A. Miles, Captain Lawton led a column in pursuit of the Apache band under Geronimo for 1,300 miles through Arizona and Mexico and captured the famous Apache leader. Although he had made colonel only in 1898, he was rapidly promoted to brigadier general and then to major general of volunteers in the Spanish-Cuban/American War. In Cuba, he led the crucial attack on El Caney on the outskirts of Santiago in June 1898, enabling U.S. forces to take that city, and he became one of the highly publicized heroes of the war, following which, he conducted President William McKinley on a tour of Cuba. The latter activity won some very influential connections in Washington for Lawton. He arrived at Manila at the head of two regular army infantry regiments on 18 March 1899, when the Philippine War was only six weeks old.

Lawton and his new commander, Gen. Elwell S. Otis, seemed to dislike each other instantly. Lawton brought unwanted reinforcements, which suggested that Washington was already discounting Otis's optimistic reports that the war in the Philippines was essentially over. At six feet, four inches tall, Lawton towered over Otis, a condition that was even further exaggerated by Lawton's preference for a British-style pith helmet. Their personalities and public images were even further apart. Lawton was a dashing, gallant, and imaginative field general, in sharp contrast to his commander, who was a fussy, overly cautious desk general. In addition, the Manila correspondents seemed to adore Lawton as much as they despised Otis, which meant totally unsolicited panegyrics for the tall, handsome Lawton, while these journalists roasted Otis whenever they could bypass his censor. In essence, Lawton had become a U.S. equivalent to Lord Herbert H. Kitchener, the noted British colonial campaigner.

As a result, Otis kept Lawton cooling his heels in Manila for three weeks before allowing him to lead a force of 1,500, assembled from fragments of various commands, on a lightning strike on Santa Cruz on the southeastern shore of Laguna de Bay. It failed when an amphibious force of marines became mired in shallow water due to faulty Spanish charts, and Lawton became bogged down in swamps and dense jungle that did not appear on Spanish maps. Nevertheless, Otis exploited Lawton's popular image, reporting the strike as a major victory, which gave Lawton a lesson in public relations warfare. Lawton led another strike to the south in Cavite, but the navy landed marines too early for the planned trap to work. Everywhere, Lawton found civilians and white flags, but no soldiers, and he realized that the war could not be won without sufficient U.S. manpower to occupy towns permanently. He made it clear to reporters that many more troops were desperately needed, despite Otis's assertions to the contrary. When Otis turned down an offer from the Macabebes (a Philippine minority group hostile to the dominant Tagalogs) to serve with the United States Army, Capt. Matthew A. Batson turned to Lawton, who used his influential friends in Washington to persuade the War Department to accept the Macabebes. Without even consulting Otis, the War Department ordered him to enlist Macabebes as armed scouts. Otis had to know that Lawton was behind this decision, which only served to widen the breach between the two generals.

As the rains abated in October 1899, Lawton joined Gens. Arthur MacArthur and Loyd Wheaton in Northern Luzon in an attempt to trap Gen. Emilio Aguinaldo y Famy before he reached a mountain refuge. Otis contributed to the failure of this campaign by refusing to allow Lawton to establish advanced supply bases earlier when the swollen rivers would have supported heavily laden boats. As a result, Lawton bogged down when his supply boats grounded, so that his advance was restricted to the pace of carabao-drawn carts and Chinese bearers. In desperation, Lawton launched his chief of cavalry, Gen. Samuel B.M. Young, with very limited supplies; this "flying column" narrowly missed capturing Aguinaldo. An increasing number of editors in the United States suggested that Lawton should replace Otis.

While waiting for Otis to approve his plans for another major campaign in Northern Luzon, Lawton led a "scout-in-force," hardly appropriate for a man of his rank, from Manila during an unseasonably late downpour on 18 December 1899. The next morning he confronted Gen. Licerio Geronimo and 250 Filipino riflemen at San Mateo. His long frame draped in a bright yellow slicker and topped with a white pith helmet offered an inviting target as he paraded upright behind his men firing from sitting, kneeling, and prone positions. He had just returned to the line after carrying a wounded young aide to the rear when he was struck in the heart. The "pride of Indiana" was elevated to the status of a national martyr, as a grateful nation mourned its fallen hero and named towns, schools, streets, and parks after him.

Stuart Creighton Miller

REFERENCES

Stuart Creighton Miller, *"Benevolent Assimilation"*: *The American Conquest of the Philippines, 1899–1903* (Yale Univ. Pr., 1982).

Lee, Fitzhugh (1835–1905)

Fitzhugh Lee served as U.S. consul general in Havana from April 1896 until the outbreak of the Spanish-Cuban/American War. A soldier, politician, and diplomat, he was born in Fairfax County, Virginia, in 1835. His father, a naval officer, was the elder brother of Gen. Robert E. Lee and the second son of Revolutionary War hero Gen. Henry E. (Light Horse Harry) Lee. Following preliminary education in private schools Fitzhugh Lee attended the United States Military Academy at West Point, where he narrowly avoided expulsion for poor scholarship and various pranks. Distinguishing himself only in horsemanship, Lee graduated in 1856 near the bottom of his class. After serving briefly as a cavalry instructor at Carlisle Barracks, Pennsylvania, he served in Texas under Maj. Earl Van Dorn and was seriously wounded in skirmishes with Indians. In 1860 he was named an assistant instructor in the department of tactics at West Point and served there until resigning to serve as a first lieutenant in the regular Confederate army.

Quickly rising to the rank of lieutenant colonel of the 1st Virginia Cavalry under Gen. J.E.B. Stuart, he saw action at Manassas (Bull Run) and the Peninsular Campaign. He was promoted to brigadier general in July 1862 and distinguished himself at Chancellorsville. In September 1863 he was made major general and became the senior cavalry commander in the Army of Northern Virginia following the death of General Stuart.

Lee accepted the results of the Civil War and spoke frequently on the need for reconciliation. His family name and his own personal popularity, combined with skill in campaigning, all contributed to his election as governor of Virginia in 1885. Other than strengthening the Democratic control on state government, his four-year term was without notable achievement. He was defeated in a bid for the nomination to the United States Senate in 1893.

On 13 April 1896, Lee was named consul general to Havana to replace Ramon O. Williams, who, because of his vigorous representations on behalf of U.S. citizens caught up in the civil warfare after 1895, had become "obnoxious to the Spanish authorities in Havana" (Mattox, p. 86). Lee, rotund and gloriously mustachioed, spoke no Spanish, unlike his veteran predecessor who had served in the post for 12 years. In Cuba Lee dressed each day in a white suit and wore a Panama hat. Seldom venturing outside Havana, he lived at the Hotel Inglaterra, which also housed Hearst syndicate reporters Richard Harding Davis, Frederic Remington, and others. Lee did enjoy the complete confidence of President Grover Cleveland, and he dutifully reported extensively on the Cuban political and military situation. Lee also continued his predecessor's active pursuit of numerous welfare and protection cases arising from the increasing turbulence and the reconcentration polling implemented by the Spanish authorities. President William McKinley kept Lee on in Cuba, but also sent a private emissary, William J. Calhoun of Illinois, on a secret mission to report on the Cuban situation.

In January 1898 Lee analyzed the complex political situation in a report to Washington in which he stated that any form of autonomy consisting of continued colonial status had little chance for success. He stated that the revolutionaries wanted independence and that the island's educated elite desired annexation by the United States. By this time the Spanish authorities were objecting to what they considered Lee's "active and open sympathy" for the Cuban revo-

lutionaries, but the Department of State defended Lee, and Spain dropped the issue. However, Lee's correspondence clearly shows him favorably inclined toward the Cubans, anxious for U.S. intervention, and desirous of eventual annexation.

Soon after his arrival in Havana, Lee had suggested that as a "precautionary measure" a warship be stationed at Key West. This proposal was never acted on, but on 24 January 1898, Lee was informed by the Department of State that the USS *Maine* was on its way to Havana because of the disturbances in the city. Despite his earlier recommendation, Lee immediately cabled Washington advising a week's delay to allow a volatile situation to settle down. The *Maine* arrived the next day. A month later Navy Secretary John D. Long wanted to withdraw the warship, but Lee advised Washington on 4 February that the *Maine* should remain in a "position of peaceful control of [the] situation." Eleven days later, in a terse cable of less than 100 words, Lee coolly reported that the great ship had exploded in the harbor. Two officers and 258 of the ship's company of 355 were killed.

As events moved toward war in the weeks following the explosion of the *Maine*, an event Lee attributed to "unknown conspirators," the consul general successfully urged the McKinley administration to delay asking Congress for authority to use military force until after U.S. citizens could depart Havana. Upon his own return to Washington on 12 April 1898, Lee received a hero's welcome. He was commissioned a major general of volunteers on 5 May and assigned the VII Army Corps, designed to be the major combat force for the occupation of Cuba. Although the capture of Santiago de Cuba obviated the need for Lee to participate in any military operations, Lee took his command to Cuba, establishing his headquarters at Camp Columbia outside Havana. In January 1899 Maj. Gen. John R. Brooke appointed him military governor of Havana. From 12 April 1899, until his retirement on 2 March 1901, he held the rank of brigadier general.

While stationed in Cuba Lee believed that the Spaniards in Cuba who owned most of the land and dominated commerce were annexationists but kept their views quiet. To Senator Joseph B. Foraker of Ohio he expressed the view that the United States needed to occupy Cuba "until after this experiment in free government has been tried and failed" (Eggert, p. 484). Gen. Leonard Wood, after assuming command in Cuba on 20 December 1899, consolidated his authority, and Lee, along with other aging military commanders whose actions under Brooke's command were less than harmonious, were removed. In February 1901 he was appointed to the regular army and was briefly in command of the Department of Missouri. He retired permanently on 2 March 1901.

Following his retirement Lee returned to Virginia. A gifted public speaker with a commanding physical presence, Lee was also a facile writer, authoring a biography, *General Lee* (1894), which, though marred by numerous factual errors, served as a standard work on its subject. His address "Chancellorsville" was published in *Southern Historical Society Papers* (December 1879). At the time of his death he was active in planning for the Jamestown Exposition of 1907. Lee had married Ellen Bernard Fowle on 19 April 1871. She and five children survived him.

Michael J. Devine

REFERENCES

Gerald G. Eggert, "Our Man in Havana: Fitzhugh Lee," *Hispanic American Historical Review*, 47 (1967), 463–485; Fitzhugh, Lee, "Cuba and Her Struggle for Freedom," *Fortnightly Review*, 63 (1898), 855–866; Henry E. Mattox, *Twilight of Amateur Diplomacy: The American Foreign Service and Its Senior Officers in the 1890s* (Kent State Univ. Pr., 1989), 86–89; Henry B. Russell, *The Story of Two Wars: An Illustrated History of Our War With Spain and Our War With the Filipinos* (Hartford Pub. Co., 1899); Hugh Thomas, *Cuba: The Pursuit of Freedom* (Harper, 1971).

Lee, Harry (1872–1935)

Brig. Gen. Harry Lee was sent to the Dominican Republic to command the marine brigade in August 1921. His arrival was part of the transition in U.S. policy aimed at withdrawing U.S. forces from the Dominican Republic that was initiated by the administration of President Warren G. Harding. Lee had served in Europe with considerable distinction during World War I, participating in several significant battles and winning the Legion of Merit, the Distinguished Service Medal, and a prestigious French decoration. His selection represented part of the Harding administration's transfer to the island nation of experienced officers who were considered amenable to civilian control. Thus, they were viewed as appropriate instruments for arranging a transfer of power to the Dominicans by improving the administration of the intervention and strengthening ties with the local citizens and political figures. After initially serving under Military Governor Adm. Samuel S. Robison until Robison's recall in 1922, Lee was military governor during the final stages of the transition period and supervised the withdrawal of the marines from the island nation in 1924.

Lee arrived with instructions to reduce hostility between the marines and the local populace, and he took strong measures that achieved considerable success. He issued clear orders regarding the need to treat civilians fairly, directed marines to avoid Dominican political gatherings, and even instructed marines to avoid congregating in large groups when away from their posts. His orders directed respect for local customs. These efforts significantly reduced clashes with the local population, an essential step in promoting the exchanges and cooperation leading to the withdrawal. He also supported offering amnesty to rebels who surrendered and turned in their arms and emphasized the establishment of civil guard groups, both new methods in combating the unrest in the eastern provinces.

During his service in the Dominican Republic Lee had responsibility for the training and expansion of the Guardia Nacional Dominicana and devoted considerable attention to reforms of that organization. Its condition shocked him, and Lee worked diligently to expand recruitment and improve training. He established training facilities at Haina that began the process of providing specific training for the Dominican officers of the Guardia. Convinced that the force was not sufficiently prepared to perform the duties assigned to it, he opposed State Department plans to accelerate training and to withdraw the marine officers from the Guardia, advocating a more gradual transition. His objections were overruled because the State Department's plans reflected the views of the Dominican political leaders.

Lee helped conciliate the Dominicans and, despite his reservations about the implications of rapid withdrawal, he effectively promoted the U.S. plan for withdrawal after becoming military governor. He cultivated friendly relations with Provisional President Juan Vicente Vicini Burgos, enabling the military authorities to work effectively in cooperation with the provisional government. It was Lee who presided over the final implementation steps and the withdrawal of the last marines from the Dominican Republic.

Kenneth J. Grieb

REFERENCES

Bruce J. Calder, *The Impact of Intervention: The Dominican Republic During the U.S. Occupation of 1916–1924* (Univ. of Texas Pr., 1984).

See also Dominican Republic, Occupation (1916–1924); Guardia Nacional Dominicana.

Legation Guard, Beijing (Peking), China

The history of U.S. military involvement in China between 1900 and 1941 begins and ends with the United States Marine Corps's legation guard in Beijing, China. Marines helped defend the legation during the Boxer Uprising in 1900 and were interned with the diplomats there at the beginning of the Pacific War in 1941.

Between 1901 and 1905, the legation was guarded by a company of the United States Army's 9th Infantry Regiment. In 1905, the U.S. minister, William W. Rockhill, replaced the soldiers with marines. This simplified the command structure, making it easier to reinforce the legation guard from the Asiatic Fleet.

The numbers of men assigned to the guard fluctuated, starting at about 100 officers and men in 1905, reaching its height in the 1920s during the Northern Expedition, with a troop strength of more than 500 officers and enlisted men. One unusual feature of legation guard duty was the mounted marine unit—the only instance of "horse marines" in Marine Corps history. Created in 1907 and mounted on Mongolian ponies, it was designed to aid in crowd control, safeguard U.S. lives and property in Beijing, and help the legation keep in touch with U.S. citizens living outside the city. It was disbanded in 1938. After the 15th Infantry Regiment's withdrawal from Tianjin (Tientsin), marines were sent to replace those army troops.

The guard's military duties consisted of field training with rifles, machine guns and light artillery; shooting; dress parades; and athletic contests, both intramural and against teams of other foreign detachments. The legation guard, as well as the other foreign detachments stationed in Beijing, was an adornment of the foreign social scene in the city.

Life was pleasant for botn officers and enlisted men. The former's mess had at least three servants assigned to each officer, while the latter hired coolies to do laundry, clean the barracks and equipment, and cook for them.

The social scene was important for the officers. Brooke Astor, the daughter of the guard's commander (1911–1914), recorded that her parents employed 15 servants and went out, at one point, 36 nights in a row (Astor, pp. 48–128).

The main function of the guard, as of all U.S. military units in China, was to safeguard U.S. lives and property. In case of serious trouble it was expected to engage in token resistance and submit to capture, providing the U.S. government with reasons to protest Chinese actions. It, as well as the other national legation guard contingents, never had the strength to independently resist determined Chinese, and after 1937 determined Japanese, military action.

Lewis Bernstein

REFERENCES

Brooke Astor, *A Patchwork Child* (Harper & Row, 1962), 48–128; "Living with the Marines in Peking, China," *Leatherneck*, 7 (1 Jan. 1924), 2–5; James M. McHugh, "Living Conditions in the Marine Corps: The Marine Detachment, American Legation, Peking, China," *Marine Corps Gazette*, 12 (1927), 110–114; Allan R. Millett, *Semper Fidelis: The History of the United States Marine Corps* (Macmillan, 1980), 212–235; "Peiping's Mounted Marines Disband," *Leatherneck*, 21 (April 1938), 7, 64.

Legation Guard, Managua, Nicaragua (1913–1925)

When the large body of U.S. Marines left Nicaragua after that country's 1912 election, a small force of about 100 marines remained in Managua as a legation guard. Ostensibly, the guard's purpose was to protect the U.S. legation in the Nicaraguan capital, but there was a broader intent, more understood than official, of preserving the peace and stability of the country. The marine presence in Managua was not large, but it and the frequent visits of U.S. warships at Nicaraguan ports were symbols of Washington's ability to concentrate quickly a few thousand troops in that Central American country as it had in 1912, if such revolutionary conditions again prevailed or remnants of the ousted José Santos Zelaya's regime threatened a return.

Most of the legation guard was housed in a portion of the Campo de Marte near downtown Managua about four blocks from the U.S. legation. One visiting naval officer commented after reviewing the arrangement that the guard would have confronted a militarily difficult situation if it had been challenged by a Nicaraguan force because of the distance from the legation and because downtown Managua was dominated by a walled fortress, La Loma, occupied by 300 to 400 Nicaraguan soldiers. When in 1922 a group of dissident Conservatives did seize La Loma, Maj. John Marston, then commanding the legation guard, warned the rebel generals against firing on his camp and Managua generally because it would jeopardize U.S. lives and property. In the face of Marston's warning and the U.S. minister's threat of possible military intervention, the insurgents surrendered the fortress to a marine officer. During the crisis most U.S. residents of the city and many Nicaraguan officials and their families, including the president, took refuge in the Campo de Marte under marine protection. Another example of the legation guard's role in domestic affairs was its leadership and instruction of the resguardo de hacienda, a native revenue force used by the marines for domestic intelligence and counted on as an auxiliary force in case of serious disturbance.

An unintended result of the marine presence for over 12 years was the continuation in office of a succession of Conservative party presidents. Incumbents controlled the election machinery, and opponents had little chance of electoral success. Washington and the legation guard discouraged the revolutionary alternative. At presidential election times—1916, 1920, and 1924—the State Department encouraged free elections by proposing new election codes and supervision of registration and balloting, but did not force these measures when the in-party opposed them. Discussions within the State Department indicate that U.S. officials recognized the legation guard's influence on Nicaraguan elections and that the opposition Liberal party was probably in the majority, but there was the overriding fear that withdrawal of marines would encourage political instability.

Duty for the marines in the legation guard was not easy; it was boring. Managua was small, hot, and dusty. There were some sports—an occasional baseball game with a ship's team at Corinto or perhaps with a Nicaragua team, if officers approved. Free time spent in exploring Managua's diversions sometimes led to incidents, but generally relations were peaceful. There were some serious episodes involving the legation guard. On 9 February 1921 over 20 marines ransacked the offices of *La Tribuna*, a Managuan newspaper that had published statements considered derogatory by the attackers. A general court-martial levied dishonorable discharges and prison terms on the perpetrators, but later the sentences were remitted, and the men were honorably discharged. In December 1921 marines in an assault on Managua police killed three of them. Four of the assailants deserted, and in an attempt to arrest them two more police and one marine were killed. The leaders received dishonorable discharges and prison terms while their accomplices received prison terms. The obvious lack of discipline demonstrated by these cases caused a marine detachment from Haiti to be brought to relieve the entire legation guard in 1922.

These incidents emphasized the need to withdraw the marines as soon after the 1924 Nicaraguan election as possible. To provide for political stability the United States pressed the Nicaraguan government to conduct a free election and to create a nonpartisan national constabulary for preserving peace. Although a new election law was enacted, there was no desire on the part of the Nicaraguan government to have the marines or anyone else supervise its implementation. Nor was there much cooperation on creation of the constabulary until after the election and inauguration of Carlos Solórzano. Even then the new president seemed to believe that delaying legislation for the constabulary would keep the legation guard in Nicaragua and thus protect his administration. Although exasperated by these tactics, the State Department feared that precipitate withdrawal would permit political upheaval. The department still hoped that the marines might start training the constabulary, pending arrival of instructors employed directly by the Nicaraguans. When Calvin B. Carter arrived by the end of June 1925 as chief of the constabulary, the marines prepared to leave. Despite last-minute appeals from Solórzano to delay departure, the marines of the legation guard left on 1 August 1925. During the last few months of the intervention there had been some incidents between marines and civilians but in comparison with those in 1921–1922 they had been relatively minor.

Within a few weeks Nicaragua was in another cycle of political turmoil, and in 1926 marines returned to that troubled Central American country. On 6 January 1927 marines were once more in Managua protecting the legation.

William Kamman

REFERENCES

Harold Norman Denny, *Dollars for Bullets: The Story of American Rule in Nicaragua* (Dial Pr., 1929); William Kamman, *A Search for Stability: United States Diplomacy Toward Nicaragua, 1925–1933* (Univ. of Notre Dame Pr., 1968); Vernon Edgar Megee, "United States Military Intervention in Nicaragua, 1909–1932," M.A. thesis, Univ. of Texas, 1963; Dana G. Munro, *Intervention and Dollar Diplomacy in the Caribbean, 1900–1921* (Princeton Univ. Pr., 1964); Dana G. Munro, *The United States and the Caribbean Republics, 1921–1933* (Princeton Univ. Pr., 1974).

See also Nicaragua, Intervention (1912–1925).

Long, John Davis (1838–1915)

As secretary of the navy before and during the Spanish-Cuban/American War of 1898, John Davis Long prided himself on being a civilian untested and inexperienced in naval affairs. He advocated civilian supremacy in the U.S. military and suggested that a person with good administrative and organizational skills could better ensure the proper balance of civilian control over the military establishment. Although Long came to his office with little to suggest he would be successful, he served as the navy's chief from 1897 to 1902, five years that saw the emergence of the U.S. naval establishment as a leading power in the world.

Long was born near Buckfield, Maine, on 27 October 1838. He spent his youth near his birthplace, never venturing far from home until his departure for Harvard University in 1853. Long compiled an admirable scholastic record, receiving Phi Beta Kappa and other honors as an undergraduate. After graduation, he became headmaster of the academy at Westford, Massachusetts, which convinced him that education was not in his future.

In 1860 he began reading law in a firm in Boston and later attended Harvard Law School, becoming a member of the bar the next year.

After a brief term in private practice, Long entered politics, winning election to the state legislature in 1874. Thus began a 15-year period when Long held successive offices in Massachusetts, eventually taking the governor's chair in 1880. He went on to serve in the United States Congress and established himself as an effective lawmaker and loyal Republican.

Long's service with William McKinley in Congress in the 1890s helped him secure the navy post in McKinley's cabinet, winning confirmation by the Senate on 2 March 1897. McKinley named Theodore Roosevelt to serve under Long as assistant secretary of the navy. Both men had similar backgrounds, and neither could claim any "special aptitude for the Navy Department." The two men failed to find anything else in common. Long was a traditionalist, bound by reason and sound practice while Roosevelt was a firebrand, injecting the Navy Department with energy and impatience for change and activity. Long was careful to confine Roosevelt to duties in which he could be controlled.

Long was committed to a naval buildup as the United States began to expand its powers well beyond its borders, but at the same time he pledged his support of McKinley's commitment to peace and pushed for conservative expenditures for defense. This policy did not provide for preparation for an impending war (which Roosevelt was urging), nor did it provide necessary funding for expansion of the program to build up the navy.

During the first year of his service, Long performed well, since the tasks presented to him resembled other political duties he had performed throughout his career. He handled congressmen, naval officers, and others seeking favors or counsel. He maneuvered through a maze of official and social functions, making speeches and "showing the flag," making sure the navy was well represented in public. His relationship with the press was congenial, despite his conviction that much of the danger of war with Spain was due to irresponsible publishers and writers.

By February 1898 events began to overtake Long, forcing him to deal with crises and to provide McKinley with advice and contingency plans. During this period, Roosevelt continued to push aggressively for war preparation to the point that Long grew frustrated with his assistant's preoccupation.

A letter disparaging McKinley's character written by Spanish Ambassador Enrique Dupuy de Lôme produced an avalanche of public outcry forcing Long to cancel a social engagement with the ambassador. On the heels of the de Lôme fiasco, the battleship *Maine* blew up in Havana harbor in Cuba causing an already delicate situation to escalate to a point where war seemed not only possible but probable. Long was distressed that events had taken a turn for the worst, convinced that the press had blown everything out of proportion.

By the middle of February Long was convinced that without a miracle war was inevitable. During the 10 days following the *Maine* disaster, Long met with congressmen and reporters in hopes that war could be averted. On 26 February 1898 Long left Roosevelt in charge of the department while he took the day off. Roosevelt seized the opportunity to issue a number of orders for war preparations, including the famous telegram sent to Commodore Dewey at Hong Kong, ordering him to keep his ships fully coaled and ready for immediate operations against the Philippines. Roosevelt indicated that Dewey's primary mission was to prevent the Spanish fleet from sailing to intervene in the Cuban theater. Dewey was to then begin offensive operations in the islands. When Long returned, he countermanded most of Roosevelt's orders, but was finally convinced that more readiness was in order.

With Secretary of War Russell A. Alger, Long coordinated plans for coastal defense. In March 1898 Long sent to the president Capt. William T. Sampson's report on the sinking of the *Maine*, fearful that public opinion would force Congress to declare war before McKinley could hope to reach a settlement between the Spanish and the Cuban revolutionaries. April began with a request for a $50 million appropriation from Congress to bring U.S. military forces to readiness. At this point, war seemed imminent, and the cabinet continued to discuss options. It was clear to Long that McKinley would have to ask Congress for a declaration of war against Spain. On 16 April Long agreed to a postponement of the war message because of the difficulty in evacuating U.S. citizens in Cuba. More time was needed. Five days later McKinley requested Congress to declare war on Spain. Long subsequently released statements praising the president for going the distance to give Spain time and an opportunity to accede to U.S. demands for a resolution to the affair—in spite of the fact that Long knew and was a party to the decision to allow more time for evacuation without any expectation of Spanish capitulation.

Long's first year in office was marked by passive leadership, and it was clear that his lack of knowledge of naval affairs limited his ability to lead the Navy Department effectively—forcing him to leave the initiative in the hands of bureau chiefs and other high-ranking admirals afloat. Long contended that admirals who had reached their positions through merit could best advise the civilian leadership where the final authority was vested. He argued that the secretary did not need to have a knowledge of naval affairs, but needed only to be a good administrator and be able to use the expertise available to him. Unfortunately, Long's shortcomings with regard to naval affairs prevented dynamic decision making in areas such as planning, establishing logistical systems for operations, personnel, and the recognition of sound strategy. If in 1898 the United States had gone to war with any nation other than the fading Spanish empire, the consequences would have been disastrous. Germany or Great Britain would not have forgiven the strategic errors or tardy preparations.

With war looming, Long attended a meeting on 20 April with McKinley and the military and civilian leadership of the Navy and War departments. No agreement was reached on operations, but the next day Long promoted Captain Sampson to rear admiral and ordered him to take up blockade duties off Cuba. Sampson was moved over 17 more senior officers to reach this post.

On 25 April Long sent Dewey orders for Asiatic Squadron operations against the Spanish Philippines. The next day Congress passed the declaration of war. Under Long the navy had made little progress in preparing for war. Since 1895 war plans against Spain had undergone periodic study and revision with insufficient commitment to any plan by the department. In 1895 the Naval War College and the Office of Naval Intelligence produced a three-part strategy calling for naval operations against Spain in Europe, the Philippines, and Cuba. The plan called for the taking of Manila in the Philippines and a naval blockade of Cuban ports in the Caribbean, thereby cutting Spain's global logistical support network. If the plan was successful, no army operations would be necessary. In 1896 Long's predecessor, Hilary A. Herbert, convened a board of senior officers, headed by Rear Adm. Francis M. Ramsay, who suggested the army could be introduced in Cuba if the Spanish did not surrender. The Ramsay Board eliminated operations in the Philippines, but added a plan to seize the Canary Islands and operate against the Spanish homeland from bases there.

Long convened his own board in 1897 to review the two previous plans and adopted the original Naval War College plan, advising that operations in the Philippines made more sense than the Canary Islands plan, since the United States could expect to receive military assistance from Filipino resistance elements in taking Manila and other points in the Philippine archipelago. The new plan included combined army-navy operations in the Philippines and in the Cuban theaters. Roosevelt pushed for Long to initiate preparations to ensure that the navy would be ready to execute these plans. What was needed, Roosevelt argued, was a naval general staff to formulate specific plans and to bring the navy to a state of readiness. Long disagreed. He favored using the traditional bureau system in place since 1842 and tested in two wars. Long relied on his bureau chiefs for advice, especially Capt. Arent S. Crowninshield, chief of the Bureau of Navigation. Not until McKinley ordered the blockade of Cuba did Long advise the president to execute the war college plan as amended by the 1897 board. McKinley waited until the 24th to give his assent to the plan—forcing the navy into frenzied activity to acquire ships, men, officers, and at the same time, activate naval operations off North America and in the Far East.

Long purchased a variety of ships, chartered others, and transferred some vessels from the Lighthouse and Revenue Services. Because none of the battleships under construction would be available soon (none were more than 50 percent completed), Long had to rely on the major combat ships already in the fleet.

On 29 April Adm. Pascual Cervera y Topete and the Spanish fleet departed the Cape Verde Islands for North America. Long expected him to attack U.S. targets—perhaps New York City or some other major port city on the Atlantic coastline. Despite advice to the contrary, Long divided the Atlantic Fleet to meet the threat along the U.S. East Coast and to support needed blockade operations in Cuba. He ordered Sampson to

Key West where he was to be responsible for the Cuban blockade and operations against Puerto Rico; Commodore Winfield Scott Schley commanded the "Flying Squadron" and was to protect the coast below Delaware. Commodore John A. Howell in command of the Northern Patrol Squadron was to patrol from the Delaware Capes northward. In dividing the fleet in this manner, Long hoped to destroy Cervera's fleet wherever he chose to strike and at the same time keep Cuba sealed off from the outside world.

In the Far East, Long telegraphed Dewey at Hong Kong that the United States was at war with Spain and ordered the Asiatic Squadron to steam at once to the Philippines. Long ordered Dewey to start offensive operations against the Spanish fleet. The secretary emphasized that Dewey had to either capture or destroy every Spanish vessel. The Spanish fleet under Adm. Patricio Montojo y Pasarón, Long warned, must not be able to relieve the besieged Spaniards in Cuba. Long need not have worried. In a brief, but decisive naval battle in Manila Bay on 1 May 1898, Dewey destroyed the Spanish fleet, leaving nothing afloat and the Spanish in disarray.

Long dismissed a plan to take the naval war to Spain and its commercial trading routes in Europe. He supported a strategy under which the navy would provide the army time to prepare for an invasion of Cuba and then support those land operations ashore. Long viewed any operations against Spain in Europe as a last resort.

When the Spanish fleet was sighted steaming toward Cuba, Long ordered converted ocean liners out to look for the enemy, while Sampson at Key West made ready to steam for Puerto Rico where he was sure Cervera would have to coal. Cervera slipped by the U.S. patrols, and Long received word that the enemy had been sighted at Curaçao. Long ordered Schley, who meanwhile had been ordered to Key West, to sail for Cienfuegos, Cuba, where it was thought Cervera would try to deliver much needed supplies to the hard-pressed Spanish army in Havana. Sampson returned to take command of the overall operation. Later, Sampson ordered Schley to Santiago de Cuba, where Cervera was thought to be. Schley's tardiness in arriving off Santiago threatened to allow the Spanish fleet to escape and gave rise to charges later that Schley was hesitant and reluctant to place his fleet in harm's way. Long ordered Sampson to steam for

Santiago in case Schley had failed to establish the blockade of the harbor. Schley's brilliant service in the Battle of Santiago failed to diminish the ranks of his detractors because many gave Sampson credit for the victory over the Spanish fleet on 3 July 1898.

The Schley-Sampson controversy lingered for years and created for Long the chaos he most sought to avoid. A devotee of order and discipline, Long sought to suppress the intra-service bickering, but advocates of both sides refused to let the issue die. When both officers' promotions to rear admiral were sent to Congress for confirmation, Long hoped that the strife would die a quick death. He ordered officers of the navy not to mention the case, but Schley requested and received a court of inquiry into his conduct during the campaign.

The board was chaired by George Dewey. After three months of deliberations, it issued a majority report condemning Schley for his actions before the Battle at Santiago. Schley appealed to the new president, Theodore Roosevelt, who consulted with Long and refused to overturn the decision. Although the issue was resolved satisfactorily for Long, he never understood the basic error of placing a junior officer over one more senior.

The end of the Spanish-Cuban/American War brought no return to the comfortable days before the Battle of Manila Bay. The navy under Long's leadership assumed the responsibility for some operations in the Philippines as Filipino nationalists sought to win independence amid the Spanish collapse. Blockade and riverine warfare placed heavy demands on the navy's shallow-draft inventory of vessels. Long purchased small boats, refloated wrecked Spanish gunboats, and reassigned gunboats normally stationed on the Yangzi (Yangtze) River to the islands. Long's blockade denied European and Japanese access to trade and influence in the islands, and at the same time, began to squeeze Filipino opposition as the United States sought to acquire the Philippines for itself.

In 1900 the Boxer Uprising brought danger to U.S. lives and property in China as Chinese nationalists sought to drive all foreigners out of the country. Drawing from naval and marine forces in the Philippines, Long contributed to the international expeditionary force that successfully relieved the besieged legations in Peking. Other military and marine forces bound for China from the United States were not needed, and Long redirected them to the Philippines. When the Boxer crisis was over, Long transferred most of the battleships from the Far East to the Atlantic Fleet. The Philippines continued to require large numbers of small vessels and officers to command them, but the number of major combat ships continued to be reduced.

In 1900 vacillating somewhat in his earlier opposition to the idea of a navy general staff, Long established the General Board of the Navy. The board was not a naval general staff, reflecting Long's steadfast determination to keep the power in the hands of the civilian secretary. According to Long's design, the board would have no decision-making authority, but would provide the secretary with counsel and plans. George Dewey was appointed president of the board, bringing to the office his prestige and respect. Dewey served in that capacity until his death in 1917.

Long's service as head of the navy can be described as competent. His tenure coincided with a naval war and a national commitment to a "Big Navy" and expansion overseas—forces that produced a cooperative Congress. His administration ushered in growth and change.

On the negative side, Long failed to grasp the tools needed to mediate political struggles within the uniformed leadership and could not delegate the authority necessary to generate initiative and effective leadership within the department. His preoccupation with civilian supremacy over the military prevented his use of the talent available to him.

As secretary of the navy, Long never enjoyed Theodore Roosevelt's confidence. Roosevelt left the Navy Department to serve in the Rough Riders during the war and in 1900 ran for vice-president on the McKinley ticket. When Vice President Roosevelt became president at McKinley's death, Long's tenure in the department was short-lived. On 1 May 1902 Long resigned his position and returned to private law practice, spending the rest of his life actively engaged in Republican politics and community affairs. He died on 28 August 1915.

Vernon L. Williams

REFERENCES

Paolo E. Coletta, ed., *American Secretaries of the Navy* (U.S. Naval Institute Pr., 1980), vol. 1; John D. Long, *The New American Navy*, 2 vols. (Outlook,

1903); John D. Long, "Reminiscences of My Seventy Years," *Proceedings of the Massachusetts Historical Society*, 42 (1909), 348–358; Margaret Long, ed., *The Journal of John D. Long* (Richard R. Smith, 1956); L.S. Mayo, ed., *America of Yesterday, as Reflected in the Journal of John Davis Long* (Atlantic Monthly Pr., 1923).

See also Naval Operations in the Spanish-Cuban/ American War (1898).

Ludlow, William (1843–1901)

William Ludlow first arrived in Cuba in 1898 during the Spanish-Cuban/American War as a major general of volunteers. He commanded the 1st Brigade of the United States Army's V Corps in the attack on El Caney and the subsequent investment of the city of Santiago de Cuba. On 13 December 1898 Secretary of War Russell A. Alger appointed him military governor of the city of Havana and commander of the military forces in the Department of Havana. Ludlow assumed his duties on 21 December in time to oversee the final withdrawal of the Spanish troops from the city on 1 January 1899.

Ludlow was an 1864 graduate of the United States Military Academy at West Point. He served with distinction as a military engineer in Gen. William T. Sherman's campaigns in the closing months of the Civil War; he later acquired extensive experience in management and improvements of municipal water systems and other municipal services through his postings to Philadelphia and Washington, D.C. Ludlow's broad range of experience served him well in the desperate and chaotic conditions he found in Havana.

The end of the war found Havana packed with refugees, and the withdrawal of the Spanish left the city bereft of the few remaining municipal services and government. Ludlow's report of 30 June 1899 tells a story of poor sanitation, widespread disease, few medical facilities, a break down in social order, and an absence of civil authority. There were few resources or supplies at hand with which to rebuild: the Spanish had stripped their offices bare of all records and anything else they could take.

Relief for refugees and disease required immediate attention. Yellow fever was a particular problem. Ludlow gave the thorough cleaning of houses and streets priority and then turned to paving streets and repairing public buildings. The cause of yellow fever had yet to be established,

but Ludlow's attention to streets and sewers was critical in reducing deaths from a variety of common diseases.

Ludlow used his three regiments of U.S. troops to establish order in the city and the surrounding countryside but at the same time he began to organize Cuban forces to take their place. In January 1899, he turned over the countryside to a 350-man rural guard which soon succeeded in imposing order. For municipal policing, Ludlow organized a 1,000-man force. He recruited both forces from former Cuban army officers and men. Gen. Mario García Menocal accepted the position of chief of police, and Ludlow had no difficulty filling the municipal force. He turned over the new police force to the civilian mayor of Havana on 1 March 1899 and reported that, despite a difficult start, the force soon operated effectively.

Ludlow also organized the municipal civilian government, and the first Cuban administration was sworn in on 14 January 1899. Ludlow noted that he consulted with Cubans before he made appointments to the government and that he gave the municipal government complete liberty to decide local matters.

Early in 1900, Ludlow left Cuba to become president of the Army War College Board.

Jennifer Bailey

REFERENCES

Dictionary of American Biography, s.v. "Ludlow, William"; Department of War, *Annual Report of the War Department for the Fiscal Year Ended June 30, 1899* (U.S. Government Printing Office, 1899).

See also Cuba, Military Government (1898–1902).

Lukban, Vicente (1860–1916)

Vicente Lukban was a major Filipino military leader in the central Philippines during the Philippine War, 1899–1902.

Lukban was born on 11 February 1860, in Labo, Camarines Norte, the Philippines, to Agustin Lukban and Andrea Rilles. After schooling in Labo, he went to Manila and studied law at the Colegio de San Juan de Letran. He returned to Labo, where he became a clerk of the court, then a municipal councilor, and eventually, a justice of the peace.

Lukban left office in 1896, probably because of his disenchantment with the Spanish authorities. He did some farming and trading. During the year, he went to Manila on business, got caught up in the throes of the revolution and was arrested, imprisoned, and tortured. After his release in 1897 he went to Hong Kong, where he joined Emilio Aguinaldo y Famy's junta. While in Hong Kong, Lukban supposedly studied British military tactics and strategy.

When Aguinaldo returned in triumph to the Philippines in 1898, Lukban was with him. He was appointed a colonel in the revolutionary army and sent to coordinate affairs in the Camarines. This was Lukban's home area and he quickly brought the provinces into line. Aguinaldo sent Lukban to pacify the Eastern Visayas, where the situation was in flux and where there was some anti-Aguinaldo sentiment. Lukban, at this point a general, arrived in Catbalogan, Samar, on 31 December 1898.

For the next two years, Lukban was the dominant personality in the Samar-Leyte region, and he became well known to U.S. authorities. Lukban was well educated, had earned respect in the Camarines as an official and businessman, had gained Aguinaldo's confidence in Hong Kong, and had shown in the Camarines department that he knew how to run an operation. He was also a master of planning and supply, came to know the terrain and the people of Samar very well, and was able to carry on an effective guerrilla campaign for two years.

Lukban's troops had scores of skirmishes with U.S. volunteer regiments, as well as with the newly formed Philippine Scouts, and he usually bested them or evaded them. The most famous incident on Samar in this period was the guerrilla assault on Company C, 9th Infantry Regiment, at Balangiga in southern Samar, on 28 September 1901. This surprise raid resulted in 59 U.S. deaths and became a "cause" for U.S. authorities for some time. Lukban was a "notorious bandit and thief" according to New York newspaper accounts. Several historians have investigated the Balangiga incident, but Lukban's role has not been established. It seems likely that because of his standing, authority, and experience Lukban was behind the incident. In later years he never denied his participation.

For several different periods Gen. Ambrosio Móxica was in command on Leyte, but his hesitancy and lack of commitment meant that Lukban frequently had to supply him with arms and ammunition. The reasons for Móxica's failure on Leyte are many, but certainly the locals

resented taking orders from a Tagalog from Cavite. Lukban, although not a local, considered himself a Bikol, not quite so "foreign" in the eyes of Samar residents. Lukban was very aware of local attitudes. On 11 January 1901, he married Paciencia Gonzales of Samar and in a communication to residents of the island, wrote that the marriage further exemplified his devotion to Samar, which should never surrender to U.S. forces.

Lukban's stature in the Philippines was high, even though he had a late start in revolutionary circles. In the issues of the newspaper *Republica Filipina* of 1900 and 1901, emblazoned on the masthead were the names of revolutionary leaders, including Aguinaldo, Miguél Malvar, António Luna, and Vito Belarmino. V. Lukban's name was also included, accompanied by the phrase "I will not be free if my people are enslaved" [translated].

Increasing U.S. military pressure, the capture of Aguinaldo in 1901, and the defeat of most of the revolutionary units put Lukban to flight. His supplies were low, and he was gradually cut off from the local villagers by the vigorous pursuit of U.S. forces. In February 1902, General Lukban and a small party were captured in northern Samar. Lukban was the last effective guerrilla leader at large, and his capture opened a new phase of Philippine-U.S. relations.

After a few years of imprisonment, Lukban took a pledge to the new government, and he eventually became a part of it. In fact, the entire Lukban family made a dramatic shift to the U.S. regime. Lukban's two brothers became national figures: Cayetano Lukban became a judge, and Dr. Justo Lukban, a participant in the revolution, later became mayor of Manila.

Vicente Lukban entered local politics and in 1912 was elected governor of Tayabas Province; he was reelected in 1916. He died at his Manila home on 16 November 1916. His funeral was attended by Speaker of the Philippine House Sergio Osmeña and Senate President Manuel L. Quezon, confirming the high status of Vicente Lukban as a politician and as a dedicated leader of the revolution.

Donald Chaput

REFERENCES

Elias M. Ataviado, *The Philippine Revolution in the Bicol Region* (Manila, 1953); Donald Chaput, "The American Press and General Vicente Lukban,

Hero of Samar," *Leyte-Samar Studies*, 8 (1974), 21–31; Donald Chaput, "Leyte Leadership in the Revolution: The Moxica-Lukban Issue," *Leyte-Samar Studies*, 9 (1975), 3–12; *Manila Times*, 5 & 8 June 1912; 17–18 Nov. 1916; Peter E. Traub, "The Island of Samar and the Capture of Lukban," *Journal of the Military Service Institution of the United States*, 33 (1903), 370–381; Gregorio F. Zaide, *Great Filipinos in History* (Verde Bks., 1970), 264–269.

See also Samar Campaigns, Philippine War; Smith, Jacob Hurd; Visayan Campaigns in the Philippine War; Waller, Littleton Waller Tazewell.

Luna de St. Pedro, Antónío Narciso (1866–1899)

Antónío Narciso Luna de St. Pedro was a leading general on the Filipino side during the Philippine War, 1899–1902.

Luna was born in Binondo, Manila, the Philippines, on 29 October 1866, into a family that was upper middle class rather than *ilustrado* (intellectual). Luna's formative years were filled with success. He worked in a chemistry laboratory, excelled in Spanish, religion, and mathematics, and received a B.A. with high honors in 1882 from the Ateneo de Manila. He entered the University of Santo Tomas as a pharmacy student and won an important literary scientific competition in 1885. He wrote poetry, studied fencing and pistol-shooting, and became accomplished with mandolin, piano, and guitar.

In 1885 Luna went to Spain to continue his studies. He received his licentiate in Barcelona, and in 1890 in Madrid he was awarded a Doctor of Pharmacy degree. He did advanced studies in Paris and carved out a respectable career as author of scientific articles and of a book on pharmacology. He also lectured on scientific subjects and wrote articles, editorials, and polemics for *La Solidaridad*, a periodical established at Barcelona, Spain, in 1889 and issued fortnightly. The purpose of *La Solidaridad* was to advocate reforms in the administration of the Philippines by Spain, and to promote the general welfare of the Filipinos. During his sojourn in Spain, Luna became closely associated with José Rizal y Mercado, one of the most noted Filipino nationalist leaders of the late 19th century.

Luna returned to the Philippines in 1894, having received a commission from the government to study bacteriology and contagious diseases. He became chemist expert at the Municipal Laboratory of Manila.

Meanwhile, the Philippine revolutionary movements were forming, and Rizal suggested to Luna that he help the movement, especially the newly formed Filipino revolutionary society, the Katipunan. Luna was intelligent, widely known, familiar with military subjects, and could provide access to the best homes in Manila. Luna declined, claiming the time was not yet ripe for revolution.

In the crackdown on the Katipunan in August and September 1896, Luna and his brothers were arrested and thrown into the Santiago prison simply on the suspicion that they were involved in the nationalist movement. Governor Ramón Blanco y Erenas, who thought highly of Luna, arranged his escape from the firing squad. In February 1897, Luna was exiled to Spain.

Luna was in Model Prison, Madrid, while turbulent times prevailed in the Philippines: Rizal was executed, and Andres Bonifacio, the power behind the Katipunan movement, was betrayed and murdered by Emilio Aguinaldo y Famy. Subsequent Spanish pressure on Aguinaldo and his revolutionary group caused his surrender, and following the Pact of Biak-na-bato in 1897, Aguinaldo and many of his leaders went into exile in Hong Kong.

Meanwhile, one of Luna's brothers had received a pardon and had gone to Spain, where he appealed to the queen regent for Luna's release. Luna was released but was not permitted to return to the Philippines.

Following the defeat of Spain by the United States in 1898, Luna left Spain for Hong Kong, asked pardon for his previous lukewarm attitude toward the revolution, and offered his services. Felipe Agoncillo, a prominent Filipino attorney and nationalist leader who had had to flee Spanish authorities in the Philippines, recommended him highly to Aguinaldo, who was at this point back in the Philippines.

When Luna returned to the Philippines he was not received with open arms by Aguinaldo and his followers. He had a questionable past and was known for his volatile personality. On the other hand, he was intelligent, a respected medical professional who traveled in the best circles, and was well read in military subjects. Reluctantly, Aguinaldo appointed Luna a brigadier general and under secretary of war in his cabinet.

The U.S. forces in the Philippines under Gen. Ewell S. Otis surrounded Spanish forces in Manila, preempted the ground, and kept the Philippine forces out of the Spanish surrender in August 1898. Luna urged Aguinaldo to act and suggested changes in fortifications, transportation, and other military moves. Aguinaldo hesitated, and the United States assumed control over the Filipinos' destiny. In the subsequent Malolos government established by Aguinaldo's forces, Luna was an elected representative from Ilocos Norte and was appointed to several important committees, but as a "new man," many of his recommendations were disregarded. Meanwhile, the United States pretty much ignored the Malolos activities.

The months of September-November 1898 were a standstill for the revolutionary forces, but Luna was active. He was assistant secretary of war and had been appointed to the faculty of the Universidad Literaria de Filipinas. On 8 September the first issue of *La Independencia* appeared. It was a revolutionary periodical funded by Luna and his brothers; Antónío was its leader and major writer. In October a military academy was established at Malolos at Luna's urging, and he arranged the placement of several Spanish officers on the staff.

On 25 November Luna was appointed supreme chief of the army, a position more important sounding than it was. He still reported to the secretary of war, who in turn reported to Aguinaldo, the general-in-chief.

On 10 December 1898, the Treaty of Paris spelled doom for Philippine independence because the United States was given control of the islands. Luna demanded immediate action—the calling up of more troops, encirclement of Manila, and an attack. Aguinaldo instead fragmented his forces and sent expeditions to the provinces, a good public relations move, but an ill-fated military decision.

Early in January 1899 the Philippine Republic was founded, and Aguinaldo headed the government, with Apolinario Mabini in charge of foreign affairs. On 4 February, hostilities erupted between the United States and Filipino forces, and the battles of the Philippine War began. Luna was nominally in charge of the Manila region, but Aguinaldo kept interfering in military matters.

In a dozen military events in February, Luna prodded, begged, and led troops; argued with Aguinaldo; and did what he could to confuse U.S. plans. Luna's troops were forced out of La Loma, and in the well-known Battle of Caloocan he was also forced to retreat. On 9 February, Luna and Mabini issued a general order to the army detailing how to act, what to do, and where to go. The order was logical and precise, but had little impact because Aguinaldo and his advisers vacillated in accepting its intent.

On 20 February Luna unveiled his plan to attack the U.S. Caloocan garrison. He called for an uprising, with fires, in Manila, and then a vigorous attack on Caloocan from several fronts. Aguinaldo hesitated. The fires were set, and Tondo and Binondo were ablaze, but all the Filipino troops did not participate as planned. One battalion of Kawit troops (four companies) refused to act, claiming they listened only to Aguinaldo. Luna almost shot the commanding officer, but instead he sent the troops to the rear.

In the many actions of February, Luna tried to force decisive actions and personally appeared on the front lines with the troops. He engaged in house-to-house fighting and fired rifle and pistol in the heat of battle. His strategy and personal bravery have been admired by historians. His problem was that his contemporaries ignored his advice. Luna was too stern for undisciplined troops; he had not joined the revolution in its earliest phase; and he was an Ilocano, whereas Aguinaldo and most of his advisors were Tagalogs.

One can imagine Luna's anger a few days after the firestorm in Manila when he learned that the Kawit battalion, which he had disciplined for cowardice and incompetence, had just been created a corps of presidential guards. These Kawit [Cavite] troops were from Aguinaldo's home province.

In the next few months skirmishes with U.S. forces resulted in a series of defeats for the Filipino forces. Aguinaldo and his cabinet, in spite of opposition from Mabini and Luna, opened negotiations with the United States. Mabini was forced out of office, and Luna had to be removed.

On 5 June 1899, at Cabanatuan, Neuva Ecija, General Luna arrived for a meeting with Aguinaldo, but was told that Aguinaldo had left. In charge of the post were the same Kawit troops that Luna had earlier disciplined at Caloocan. Luna and his *aide-de-camp*, Col. Francisco Roman, were assassinated in one of the ugliest incidents in Filipino history. There is no direct evidence of Aguinaldo's participation, but the circumstances suggest his involvement. He wanted Luna removed, a rendezvous had been decided, and the Kawit troops were on hand. With Luna out of the way, negotiations were easier with U.S. diplomats. The U.S. newspaper in Manila, *Freedom*, on 15 June headlined an article "He Died Like a Dog," praising the Filipino action and acknowledging that Luna was "the backbone of the insurrection."

The highlights of Luna's military career occurred in February 1899. There were no major victories. Yet, his strength of character, his understanding of military thinking, and his personal example were beacons of light among a people who had no significant military past. Luna's career gives a glimpse of what could have been if nationalistic rather than provincial policies had prevailed.

Luna's story, though, is part of the Aguinaldo saga. Aguinaldo was, at best, a mediocre military man, with little political vision. Yet, Aguinaldo was what none of the other Filipino leaders were: a survivor. In 1896 Aguinaldo had eliminated a true force for reform when he had Andrés Bonifacio, founder of the Katipunan, assassinated. In 1899, Aguinaldo forced the resignation of his secretary of foreign affairs, Mabini, a man of intellect and of the highest moral standards. By having Luna removed, Aguinaldo left no military voice to protest his arrangements with the United States. All talent was put by the wayside, and Aguinaldo the mediocre held sway.

Mabini wrote: "Luna would have succeeded in enforcing and keeping discipline if Aguinaldo had supported him with all the might of his prestige and authority as president. But the latter began to be jealous, too, on seeing the former making an impression forcibly and gradually by his courage, audacity and military skill" (Mabini, p. 337). Mabini's tragic conclusion: "The Revolution failed because it was badly directed; because its director gained his place, not by meritorious, but by reprehensible acts; because, instead of sustaining the men who were most useful for the country, he rendered them useless by his jealousy" (Mabini, p. 340).

Donald Chaput

REFERENCES

Vivencio R. Jose, *The Rise and Fall of Antonio Luna* (Univ. of the Philippines, 1972); Teodoro M. Kalaw, *The Philippine Revolution* (Vargas Filipiniana Foundation, 1969); Apolinario Mabini, *The Filipinos' Fight for Freedom* (Oriental Commercial Co., 1933/AMS Pr. Inc., 1973); John R.M. Taylor, *The Philippine Insurrection Against the United States* (Lopez Foundation, 1971), 5 vols.

See also Aguinaldo y Famy, Emilio.

Luzon Campaigns, Philippine War

Military operations on Luzon during the Philippine War moved through two distinct phases. Between February and December 1899, U.S. forces defeated the conventional forces of the Philippine Republic and placed garrisons in most of the island's larger towns. This did not, however, impose U.S. authority in the countryside because the Republic's political infrastructure survived these campaigns largely intact. The war's second phase was a protracted guerrilla struggle that began in spring 1900. Although resistance to U.S. rule ended in most areas of the island by summer 1901, the southwestern province of Batangas was not pacified until spring 1902, after exceptionally harsh coercive measures caused widespread civilian suffering.

Until 1892, Spain's hold over the Philippines had never been seriously threatened. In that year a secret society, the Katipunan, began to agitate against Spanish authority and to demand a redistribution of the landholdings of the Catholic Church. Instrumental in the Katipunan's formation were the *ilustrados*, Filipino intellectuals influenced by European liberal and nationalist thought. In 1896 an armed revolt broke out in Cavite Province, south of Manila, and a young man named Emilio Aguinaldo y Famy rose to a commanding position within its ranks. Suppressed with some difficulty, this revolt was still smoldering in April 1898, when the United States and Spain went to war over Spain's repression of a revolution in another of its island possessions, Cuba.

Within days of Commodore George Dewey's 1 May 1898 destruction of Spain's eastern fleet in the naval battle of Manila, President William McKinley ordered the formation of a U.S. expeditionary force to occupy that city and other key ports throughout the archipelago. Because the bulk of the regular army had been concentrated along the Gulf Coast for the invasions of Cuba and Puerto Rico, this force was built around 14 state volunteer regiments that had been mobilized at the Presidio of San Francisco.

The first of these troops did not arrive until late June, and in the interim the forces of the Philippine revolution had risen and laid siege to Manila. Aguinaldo had hoped to present McKinley with a *fait accompli*: a Philippine republic with broad popular support governing from Spain's former colonial capital. While the revolutionary leadership quickly established its authority in the more remote regions of Luzon, it failed to reduce Manila's Spanish garrison. In August, U.S. forces entered the city after negotiating surrender terms with the Spanish commander that excluded the Filipinos from any role in the city's occupation or subsequent administration.

An uneasy truce followed between Filipino troops and U.S. forces, which rapidly deteriorated after the United States announced its intention to annex the islands at the conclusion of the Treaty of Paris on 10 December 1898. Republican forces surrounding Manila at this point faced 11,000 U.S. state troops and three regular army infantry regiments supported by artillery and river gunboats. On 4 February, firing broke out in Santa Mesa, an eastern suburb, and quickly spread along the U.S. outpost line north and south of the Pasig River. By the 10th, Republican forces had been driven away from Manila up the Manila-Dagupan railway toward Malolos, the Republican capital, 25 miles to the north. (The following discussion relies heavily on Sexton.)

Scholars are divided over whether the February fighting resulted from a gradual buildup of tensions or was provoked intentionally by the U.S. commander in the Philippines, Maj. Gen. Elwell S. Otis. In a larger sense, however, the war appears to have been an inevitable consequence of the decision in favor of annexation, together with the strong support the revolution initially received from the most influential elements of Luzon's population.

For the rest of 1899 the Philippine Republic tried to halt the U.S. forces and to retain key towns with a territorially based conventional army. However, on 31 March Malolos fell to a column of state troops commanded by Brig. Gen. Arthur MacArthur, and similar sweeps were made into Cavite Province and to the southeast along the Pasig River to its source, the Laguna de Bay.

The first months of combat revealed several strengths and weaknesses in both the Filipino and U.S. armies. Filipino soldiers needed little logistical support and were individually brave fighters, but collectively they were prone to leave their positions when flanked or brought under artillery fire. Their commanders repeatedly failed to support each other's efforts, and on several occasions they abandoned excellent earthwork defenses, including trenches, prepared well in advance of fighting.

By contrast, U.S. troops were very aggressive and skilled at improvising river crossings under fire. They were, however, overly dependent on resupply by rail or water buffalo carts and were poorly acclimated to the rigors of tropical field duty. MacArthur's division was stopped at San Fernando, beyond Malolos, not by armed resistance but by illness: in mid-May nearly half his men were too sick to march. Brig. Gens. Henry W. Lawton and Loyd Wheaton took columns to the northeast of Manila and again through Cavite, but were slowed by poor roads, extreme heat, and the wariness of Filipino commanders who refused to give battle on unfavorable terms. As the summer monsoon approached, U.S. offensive operations ceased.

On 6 February 1899, during the fighting for Manila, the Senate had ratified the Treaty of Paris. Because the state troops had enlisted only for the war with Spain, a new force was required for the Philippines. On 2 March Congress authorized the regular army, which had neglected its own recruiting since spring 1898, to return to its prewar ceiling of 65,000 men and to raise a new force of 35,000 two-year "United States Volunteers" for Philippine service. By the late summer recruiting was completed for one cavalry and 24 infantry regiments, which began to reach Manila in mid-October.

In November 1899, with the return of drier weather, the U.S. forces launched a three-pronged envelopment campaign in central Luzon that inflicted several thousand casualties on the Republican Army, destroyed its cohesion, and drove its remnants into the island's mountainous north. General Wheaton's division made an amphibious landing at Lingayen Gulf and moved east, while Generals Lawton and Samuel B.M. Young swept north up the western foothills of the Sierra Madre mountains to block possible Republican escape routes. Simultaneously, General MacArthur moved north from San Fernando to distract the main Republican force from the mortal threat developing in its rear.

The United States Army had lightened its marching order since the previous spring and expanded its mounted force, but was still unable to trap the entire Republican Army. U.S. troops did kill or capture several of Aguinaldo's closest subordinates and occupied Luzon's central lowlands and its northwestern coast. Armed resistance to U.S. forces ceased, temporarily, in December 1899.

This marked the end of the first phase of the Philippine War. However, the U.S. success in conventional operations was of little long-term importance because in most provinces the revolution could still rely on the support of a majority of the Filipino people.

The guerrilla war is still not fully understood. Until recently, most U.S. scholars have focused either on the domestic debate over annexation or on the tension within the military between "benevolent" civic action policies and the more clearly coercive measures taken after summer 1901 to break resistance in the last unpacified provinces. However, several recent works have begun to add to the understanding of the difficult and costly second phase of the Philippine War. (The discussion of the second phase is deeply indebted to Linn's work.)

The key fact of the counterguerrilla campaign was its decentralization. Neither Aguinaldo nor MacArthur, General Otis's replacement after May 1900, was able to centrally direct operations: poor communications over long distances and a general ignorance of local conditions forced both men to rely on subordinate district officers to mount efforts tailored to the social, political, and economic realities of their particular regions. Even so, a general chronology for the guerrilla war can be formulated for most areas of Luzon, excepting Batangas Province and portions of adjoining Laguna and Tabayas, the last strongholds of resistance.

From December 1899 through April 1900 most U.S. personnel remained unaware of the extent of the revolution's local political infrastructure, and most revolutionary leaders were content to restrict their activities to recruiting men and procuring supplies, often under the very noses of army garrison commanders. During this initial period three critical factors operated to determine the length of the pacification effort in any given province: (1) the speed with which the army was able to establish its garrison network; (2) the insight and skill of the first U.S. and Filipino commanders in each district; and, most importantly, (3) the support the revolution received from local members of the Filipino landed elite, the *principales*. The army experienced its greatest difficulties in areas it was slow to enter and in which capable revolutionary leaders had strong ties with local landowners to whom the rural population was linked by bonds of agricultural patron-client deference.

As early as 13 November 1899, Aguinaldo had called on local nationalists throughout the archipelago to organize a localized guerrilla effort to be supported by the Republic's cadre of political officers, military recruiters, purchasing agents, and tax collectors. Many of these men were local *principales* who remained in positions of authority under General Orders No. 40 and No. 43, Manila's instructions for the reestablishment of municipal government. Many army district commanders thus unwittingly helped revolutionary officials organize the upcoming guerrilla campaign.

By April 1900 the revolution had created a two-tiered guerrilla organization throughout Luzon. Relatively small forces of well-armed partisans operated from sanctuaries outside populated areas to establish remote storehouses, cut telegraph lines, and ambush small bodies of U.S. troops. Supporting the partisans was a larger pool of part-time Sandahatan militia who pursued their normal occupations in the U.S.-garrisoned towns. Their duties were to gather intelligence on U.S. units, grow food for the partisans, and, if necessary, punish other villagers for cooperating with U.S. officials.

Unlike MacArthur, General Otis never understood the revolution's strength. Fond of describing revolutionaries as *ladrones* (bandits), he devoted most of his energies to army administration and municipal government, which he believed would be sufficient to reconcile the Filipino people to U.S. authority. However, in April 1900, he responded to increased guerrilla pressure by reorganizing his army into geographical departments. In Luzon, 10 military districts were established, six in the North and four in the South. Each new United States Volunteer regiment was assigned pacification duties where possible in a single district. Remaining for long periods of time in small garrisons, the volunteers began the slow but cumulative processes of developing intelligence networks and honing their field skills, including their ability to mount patrols, raids, and ambushes at night and in bad weather.

As the number of clashes with guerrillas escalated in summer and fall 1900, many army district commanders became disenchanted with civic action efforts and began to advocate "sterner" measures. At this stage they generally meant individual registration laws and movement restrictions through the enforcement of pass laws, increased patrolling to destroy guerrilla base camps, and expanded efforts to recruit native police and military auxiliaries from among ethnic and religious minorities hostile to the revolution, such as the Macabebes and a millenarian religious sect known as the Guardia de Honor.

In most areas of Luzon these measures, along with a purge of municipal officials thought to be sympathetic to the revolution, gradually made headway, particularly after the 1900 presidential election in the United States. Revolutionary leaders had overestimated William Jennings Bryan's chances for an electoral victory over President McKinley and the strength of anti-imperialist sentiment among the American people of the United States. McKinley's victory persuaded several provincial revolutionary commanders to surrender the following spring.

However, in the far northwestern provinces of Abra and La Union, and in Batangas, Laguna, and Tabayas in the South, the pacification campaign made little initial headway. This led General MacArthur in December 1900 to impose martial law in Luzon's remaining unsecured provinces. Martial law was administered by army provost courts, which accorded suspects none of the protections of U.S. civil law. MacArthur also began actively to support the Federal party, a group of Filipino *ilustrados* (intellectuals) and merchants who had begun to doubt, in Brian Linn's words, that a revolutionary triumph was "worth the necessary sacrifices" (Linn, p. 168).

MacArthur was also aware that his 25 United States Volunteer regiments would have to be returned to the United States by 1 July 1901, halving his force in the islands. This led him to authorize a wide range of new coercive measures to be applied with increasing severity. The following three lists summarize: (1) ongoing civic action projects intended to attract support from poorer Filipinos; (2) exclusively military elements of the counterguerrilla campaign; and (3) martial law measures carried out from spring 1901 by troops of the regular army, increased to 100,000 men that February. These last actions had a decisive effect, convincing many Filipino

principales that continued support for the revolution would mean the loss of their land, wealth, and social status, and quite possibly, their lives.

"Attractive" civic action projects included the following:

- Health and sanitation improvements;
- Opening of secular public schools;
- Construction of markets and public buildings; and
- Road and bridge building.

Military elements consisted of:

- Gradual expansion of the garrison network, from 53 posts in November 1899 to 502 in March 1901;
- Gradual extension of the all-weather road network for better communications and faster pursuit of guerrillas;
- Gradual improvement in intelligence gathering, using dissident Filipinos and the local clergy;
- Increased and more aggressive patroling, with raids and ambushes coordinated across districts;
- Greater use of Philippine auxiliary troops for scouting and special raids, such as the capture of Filipino leaders; and
- Gradual tightening of naval surveillance of ports and interdiction of coastal supply routes to guerrilla forces.

Coercive measures administered under martial law included the following:

- Cessation of prisoner releases;
- Individual registration and movement restrictions administered through pass regulations;
- Reconstitution of the Spanish corvée for the conscription of civilian labor without payment;
- Use of army provost courts to arrest suspects without indictment, to deport them to Manila or Guam without trial, and to confiscate their property;
- Regulation of food supplies to deny them to guerrillas and to intimidate recalcitrant towns;
- Increased numbers of executions of convicted "terrorists";
- Execution of hostages chosen by lot in retaliation for the deaths of U.S. soldiers;

- Widespread destruction of crops;
- Concentration of civilian populations within selected "secure areas"; and
- Authorization to kill Filipino men on sight outside the "secure areas."

It was the last of these measures—the destruction of crops and the concentration of province populations into small secured areas near U.S. garrisons—that caused the greatest suffering among the Filipino people. Various scholars have estimated that between 130,000 and 600,000 Filipino soldiers and civilians died during the period of guerrilla war and the cholera epidemic of 1902–1903 (Gates, p. 374). The last campaigns also caused much controversy in the United States, along with reports of the "water cure," a violent interrogation technique practiced by U.S. soldiers, sometimes under the direction of their company officers.

Shortly after Emiliano Aguinaldo was captured in April 1901, he issued a statement urging Filipinos to reconcile themselves to U.S. authority. Additional surrenders of revolutionary leaders followed in May and June 1901, ending resistance in central Luzon, Cavite, the Northwest, and finally, in late June, Laguna Province. Only Batangas in Luzon and the southern island of Samar still resisted, and it was there that the full force of the last campaigns were felt.

In July 1901, Gen. Adna R. Chaffee replaced MacArthur as military governor. On 28 September, an attack on Company C of the 9th Infantry Regiment in the town of Balangiga, on the island of Samar, killed 59 U.S. soldiers, the worst single U.S. loss of the war. Chaffee, under pressure to end the fighting from both the War Department and his own subordinate commanders, assigned two separate brigades, the 3rd and 6th under Brig. Gens. J. Franklin Bell and Jacob H. Smith, to end resistance in Batangas and Samar.

Batangas and Samar were subdued through total destruction of crops and livestock and a wide application of the policy of concentration. Smith's campaign began in the aftermath of Balangiga, Bell's in early December 1901, and both ended in the spring of the following year. Samar's Gen. Vicente Lukban was captured in February, and in Batangas Gen. Miguél Malvar surrendered on 16 April. This ended the six-year revolution in the Philippines. On 4 July 1902, during the celebration of an earlier declaration of independence, President Theodore Roosevelt announced the end of the "insurrection" against U.S. authority, and the Philippine War was at an end.

John Scott Reed

REFERENCES

John M. Gates, "War-Related Deaths in the Philippines, 1898–1902," *Pacific Historical Review*, 53 (1983), 367–378; Brian M. Linn, *The U.S. Army and Counterinsurgency in the Philippine War, 1899–1902* (Univ. of North Carolina Pr., 1989); Glenn A. May, *Battle for Batangas: A Philippine Province at War* (Yale Univ. Pr., 1991); Glenn A. May, "Why the United States Won the Philippine-American War, 1899–1902," *Pacific Historical Review*, 52 (1982), 353–377; William T. Sexton, *Soldiers in the Sun: An Adventure in Imperialism* (Military Service Pub. Co., 1939).

See also Philippine War (1899–1902).

M

Macabebe Scouts

The Macabebes are a tribe in Pampanga in central Luzon, the Philippines, and the ancient and hated enemies of the Tagalogs. They served Spain in the first revolution of 1896, which was largely dominated by Tagalogs, as was the second one in 1898. The Macabebes made the Spanish promise to transport them to the Carolines if the first insurrection succeeded. Early in the U.S. phase of the war, they offered their services to Capt. Matthew A. Batson, who relayed the message to Maj. Gen. Elwell S. Otis, the U.S. commander. Otis, however, turned down the offer, "afraid that they would, if armed, turn traitors" (Miller, p. 81), according to Batson. Batson then took the offer to Maj. Gen. Henry W. Lawton, who peddled it among his influential friends in Washington. U.S. imperialists had been very sensitive to advice on how to manage colonies properly by creating "sepoys" to do the fighting. The *London Daily Chronicle* counseled in April 1899 (Miller, p. 82):

> Americans do not seem to understand the game, which is to use one set of natives against the other. This would not be a difficult matter in the Philippines; the suspicion of some tribes against the dominating Tagals could easily be aroused.

Over Otis's protests, the War Department ordered the Macabebes put into service as armed scouts with U.S. officers. Perhaps suspecting Lawton's influence behind this decision, Otis put the recruited Macabebes under Lawton's control. Otis had Batson promoted to major and placed in direct command of these scouts, an outfit that grew to about 5,000 before the war was over. The scouts proved to be fierce fighters but very prone to committing atrocities, particularly against their Tagalog enemies, failing often to distinguish between civilians and armed guerrillas.

Indeed, Filipino complaints to Gen. Arthur MacArthur, who had succeeded Otis in command, about the atrocious behavior of the Macabebe scouts were so numerous that he was forced to order an investigation by Gen. Loyd Wheaton in whose sector they were operating. The investigating officer, Maj. Frank B. McKenna, catalogued numerous atrocities that caused over 300 families to flee Montalban alone. In commenting on McKenna's report Wheaton stated that local troops misbehaved in terms of looting and even murder when not under the direct supervision of their officers. The problem with Wheaton's candid explanation is that it ignored McKenna's subtle implication that their officers tolerated such conduct. Had McKenna seen the private letters Batson wrote to his wife only months before, he would have had to say that these officers encouraged such terroristic tactics (Miller, p. 183):

> I am king of the Macabebes and they are terrors . . . . Word reaches a place that the Macabebes are coming and every Tagalo hunts his hole . . . . The time has come when it is necessary to conduct this warfare with the utmost rigour. "With fire and sword" as it were. But the numerous, self styled, humane societies and poisonous press makes it difficult to follow this policy if reported to the world, so what I wrote to you regarding these matters is not to fall into the hands of newspaper men . . . . At present we are destroying, in this district, everything before us. I have three columns out, and their course is easily traced by the smoke from burning houses . . . . Of course no official report will be made of everything.

Eighty Tagalog-speaking Macabebe scouts volunteered to pose as reinforcements and accompany Gen. Frederick Funston to Emilio Aguinaldo y Famy's remote headquarters. The objective was to capture Aguinaldo, the Philippine president. This was accomplished in an extraordinarily brave and daring maneuver in spring 1901.

Stuart Creighton Miller

REFERENCES

John A. Larkin, *The Pampagans: Colonial Society in a Philippine Province* (Univ. of California Pr., 1972); Stuart Creighton Miller, *"Benevolent Assimilation": The American Conquest of the Philippines, 1899–1903* (Yale Univ. Pr., 1982); Richard F. Welch, *Response to Imperialism: The United States and the Philippine-American War, 1899–1902* (Univ. of North Carolina Pr., 1979).

MacArthur, Arthur (1845–1912)

Arthur MacArthur, one of the most important leaders in the Philippine War (1899–1902), was a lieutenant colonel in the United States Army's adjutant general's office when the Spanish-Cuban/American War erupted in April 1898. He had been in the army for almost 36 years. At age 17, MacArthur joined the 24th Wisconsin Volunteers in 1862 as a first lieutenant. From September 1862 to June 1865, he participated in nearly every major battle in Tennessee and Georgia, including Murfreesboro and Missionary

Ridge, Tennessee and Atlanta, Georgia. For his heroics at the Battle of Missionary Ridge in November 1863, MacArthur received a Medal of Honor. Shortly before his 19th birthday, he was promoted to major and placed in command of the 24th Wisconsin. He was the youngest regimental commander in the Union Army. By the end of the Civil War he was a brevet colonel.

After the Civil War, MacArthur joined the regular army as a lieutenant and then became captain of an infantry company. Because of severe budgetary restraints, the regular army numbered only about 2,800 officers and 28,000 enlisted men. Promotion was slow; for 20 years, MacArthur served as a company commander in small isolated frontier forts from the Dakotas to Arizona. In the entire 20 years, his company never fired a shot at hostile Indians. MacArthur earned a reputation as an excellent trainer of men, as a scholar, and as a lawyer. Promoted to major in 1889, MacArthur transferred to the adjutant general's office. Nine years later, he was a lieutenant colonel, a fairly high rank in the restricted regular army of those years.

A highly trained soldier and administrator, MacArthur was 53 years old in April 1898. A stocky man who weighed about 185 pounds, sported a moustache, and wore glasses, he looked like the famous Theodore Roosevelt. As a professional soldier, MacArthur had spent his life preparing to lead men into battle. He petitioned his friend and mentor, Adj. Gen. Henry C. Corbin, for a field assignment as an infantry commander. Commissioned as a brigadier general of the volunteers on 1 June, he joined Gen. Wesley Merritt in San Francisco where the VIII Army Corps was organizing to be sent to the Philippines.

Placed in command of the Third Expeditionary Force composed of a little over 4,500 men, General MacArthur left San Francisco for the Philippines on 27 June. The transport ships arrived in Manila Bay on 30 July. The U.S. fleet under the command of Adm. George Dewey controlled the bay, but the city itself remained in Spanish hands. Twenty thousand soldiers of the Philippine Republic Army led by Gen. (later president) Emilio Aguinaldo y Famy surrounded the Spanish garrison of 15,000.

The arrival of MacArthur's forces increased the total strength of the U.S. army in the bay to approximately 12,000 men. Brig. Gen. Thomas M. Anderson had arrived on 30 June with 2,386 men and 117 officers and landed at Cavite, 10 miles south of Manila; the Second Expedition under Brig. Gen. Francis V. Greene arrived in Manila on 17 July with 3,500 men and landed two miles north of the city to occupy three-fourths of a mile of trenches near the bay. Aboard the *Newport*, Gen. Wesley Merritt anchored in the bay on 25 July with about 1,000 men. After MacArthur arrived Merritt dubbed MacArthur's forces the 1st Brigade and ordered him to land his men two miles south of the city near Malate. General Merritt remained aboard the *Newport* in overall command of U.S. ground forces.

Despite the monsoon rains, MacArthur began landing the 1st Brigade on 1 August. The brigade included 3,691 men and 139 officers. The landing site was about two miles south of Manila near the districts of Malate and Ermita. Spanish fortifications began at Malate with Fort San Antonio Abad. MacArthur's brigade occupied almost a mile of trenches right on the bay. The Philippine Republican Army continued to occupy over seven miles of the front line as it circled westward, then northward, before Greene's brigade occupied another three-fourths of a mile north of Manila.

While MacArthur landed his brigade, General Merritt opened negotiations with the Spanish commander of Manila, Gov. Gen. Fermín Jáudenes y Alvarez. Merritt suggested that Jáudenes surrender because the Spanish position was untenable. The Spanish governor knew defeat was inevitable, but he refused to surrender. He was certain the Filipinos would torture and execute Spanish prisoners of war. If Merritt agreed to exclude the Filipinos from participating in a battle for the city, Jáudenes assured Merritt that Spanish resistance would be symbolic rather than tenacious.

From 7 August to 12 August, Merritt conferred with his field commanders. Merritt revealed his battle plan. On the morning of 13 August, after an extended naval bombardment of Spanish defenses, MacArthur's 1st Brigade would attack the Spanish positions south of Manila. Simultaneously, General Greene's 2nd Brigade would attack the Spanish positions north of Manila. Although Merritt implied resistance would be light, he did not tell his brigade commanders of his arrangement with Jáudenes. On one point Merritt was perfectly clear: the Filipinos were not to participate in the attack. If necessary, he authorized MacArthur and Greene to

use force to prevent any armed Filipino from entering the city.

On the morning of 13 August 1898, MacArthur mobilized the 1st Brigade south of Manila. In the predawn haze, the troops checked their weapons. The day opened with heavy thunder clouds overhead. There was rain most of the day, which turned the roads into quagmires. At 9:30 a.m., four of Dewey's warships opened fire on the Spanish trenches south of the city. After an hour's bombardment, MacArthur's brigade attacked.

The first Spanish position was Blockhouse No. 14, a fortified house with sandbag emplacements that blocked the road. In heavy force on MacArthur's right flank, throngs of Filipinos jostled and elbowed U.S. troops as they moved forward. The surging mob of Filipinos frightened the Spanish defenders, who opened fire and offered stiff resistance. Two U.S. soldiers were killed, and several were wounded.

Moving to the front, MacArthur examined the Spanish position. Throughout the battle, he was on the front line with Spanish Mauser bullets singing about his head. Rather than expend men by attacking a fortified position, MacArthur ordered his artillery to open fire on the Spanish blockhouse.

The Spanish deserted the position and retreated northward up the Paco Road. As instructed by General Merritt, MacArthur left two battalions at the blockhouse to prevent the Filipinos from following, and with the rest of his brigade he pursued the Spaniards up the road. The Filipinos refused to desist, and many went around the roadblock charging after the U.S. troops. MacArthur ordered them disarmed, but some refused and opened fire on the U.S. soldiers. Throughout the morning, occasional shots were exchanged with the Filipinos who buzzed around the edge of the front line.

MacArthur moved his brigade forward about a mile to the Singalong Crossroads where the Spanish had established another defensive position. After a brief firefight, the Spanish retreated behind the walls of Fort Santiago but fell into the hands of General Greene. Attacking from the north of Manila, Greene's brigade had encountered no opposition and had entered the old city unmolested to accept the surrender of Governor Jáudenes around 11:20 a.m. MacArthur's men were the only ones who engaged in actual fighting. The 1st Brigade suffered several dozen casualties before entering old Manila. MacArthur left detachments at key bridges and street intersections to prevent the Filipinos from following.

Soldiers of the Philippine Republican Army occupied the former blockhouses and surrounded the city. Rumor was rampant that the United States intended to remain and supplant Spain as the new colonial master.

General Merritt placed the city under martial law. The next day, 14 August, he appointed General MacArthur provost marshal with three regiments under his direct command. As provost marshal, MacArthur controlled all public buildings and was in charge of policing the city.

Maj. Gen. Elwell S. Otis arrived on 29 August with the Fourth Expeditionary Force from San Francisco. He brought with him an additional 4,000 men with information that a Fifth Expeditionary Force would follow to bring the total U.S. force to about 20,000 men. Otis, who replaced Merritt as commander of the Philippine Expeditionary forces, reorganized the VIII Army Corps into two divisions, naming Major General Anderson head of the 1st Division and recommending General MacArthur, who had been promoted on 13 August 1898, as the commander of the 2nd Division. Washington agreed, and on 3 September MacArthur was promoted to major general of the volunteers. Otis assigned Anderson's division the area south of the Pasig River and placed MacArthur's division north of the river.

The U.S. defensive line paralleled the old line of Spanish blockhouses occupied at this point by President Emilio Aguinaldo's army. Located about two miles beyond the old city, the front line curved around the city from bay to bay and was about nine miles long. Beyond the blockhouses, Aguinaldo's army dug trenches and built barricades. An estimated 40,000 soldiers of the Philippine army manned the nine-mile line. Less than half of the men had rifles, the rest had only bolos for weapons. Relief units took the weapons and the ground area of those returning to the rear. Without modern artillery to protect his line, Aguinaldo was overextended.

North of the city, General MacArthur placed his forward outposts about 400 yards inside the city line along the various roads that entered Manila from the north and the northeast. The 2nd Division's left flank rested on Manila Bay north of the walled city, swung inland (east) in a rough semicircle to the San Juan River very close to its conjunction with the Pasig River, a distance of about five miles. To cover that distance, MacArthur had 9,177 enlisted men and 362 officers in 11 infantry regiments formed into three brigades plus a number of batteries of light artillery. His primary task was to mold the volunteers of his division into a well-drilled and disciplined force.

As his major line of defense, MacArthur constructed barricades about a half mile from the front line. Each regiment remained concentrated in one camp area with an outpost line manned by one of the 10 companies in a revolving fashion. Recognizing the need for constant surveillance of the enemy, MacArthur drew men from every regiment to form special reconnaissance units to patrol constantly along the Filipino lines and to report the strength of the Filipinos at every location. Telegraph lines connected the regiments to brigade and to division headquarters where MacArthur always kept four regiments in reserve.

In December 1898, President William McKinley decided to annex the islands, and tensions escalated in Manila. General Otis assumed the Filipinos would resist U.S. rule. He expected the greatest resistance to occur north of Manila in the area protected by General MacArthur's 2nd Division. The only railroad in the Philippines ran north up the island of Luzon through the Pampanga plain. The plain encompassed only about one-tenth of the land area of Luzon, but it was the prime source of supply for the Republican Army. The Pampanga plain was the breadbasket of Manila and the most strongly held Republican area. The farmland of the plain was bordered on the east, toward the interior, by the towering ranges of the Benguet Mountains and on the west, near the coast, by the Zambales Mountains.

The long awaited incident occurred on 4 February. Around 8:30 p.m. several Filipinos ventured into no-man's land along a tiny dirt road in front of the 1st Nebraskan picket line. The 1st Nebraska, under the command of Col. John M. Stotsenburg, defended an area near the confluence of the Pasig and San Juan rivers in the interior sector of MacArthur's line. Directly across from the 1st Nebraska was Blockhouse No. 7, commanded by a Filipino officer who enjoyed harassing the U.S. forces. He often sent his men into no man's land, and on several occasions, he tried to establish his pickets within a few yards of the 1st Nebraska's forward outposts. Nearly every night, firing erupted along the line in the Nebraska section. That Saturday evening, two Nebraskan sentries opened fire on several Filipinos in no-man's land. The first volley killed two Filipinos. Yelling obscenities, the rest of the Filipinos quickly retreated to Blockhouse No. 7.

Secure behind their trenches, the Filipinos opened fire on the Nebraskan outpost. The U.S. sentries responded, and the shots alerted the entire Nebraskan regiment. Within minutes after the first shots were fired, the whole Nebraskan line was ablaze as both sides responded to the incident.

Colonel Stotsenburg wired a report back to division headquarters where General MacArthur had just settled down to an after-dinner game of cards with some of his staff officers. A few minutes later, a staff member interrupted the whist game with the wire from the front. Throwing the cards aside, MacArthur ordered all officers to their regiments and wired the brigade commanders to mobilize all their units and to move forward to protect their picket lines. During the previous five months, General Otis, his division commanders, and Admiral Dewey had carefully prepared a battle plan.

In conformity with that plan, at 6:00 a.m. Dewey's warships opened fire. North and south of the city, shells from the heavy naval guns tore gaping holes in the Filipino trenches near the bay. The barrage along the shore signaled MacArthur's land-based artillery to open fire on the interior eastern end of the Filipino trenches in the 1st Nebraska section. Anderson's artillery to the south also began to batter the enemy. MacArthur checked his regiments and placed himself near his artillery. The Utah and Astor batteries used their guns to destroy the blockhouses and trenches along the northeast end of the line. The devastating artillery fire killed hundreds of Filipinos before they fled from their trenches.

At 8:00 a.m. MacArthur ordered Stotsenburg and his Nebraskan regiment to occupy the deserted Filipino trenches. In MacArthur's area, Aguinaldo's army remained strong only in the center. South of the Pasig, General Anderson attacked the enemy in his area, and the battle continued most of the day as his division moved south to San Pedro Macati, extending his line by two miles.

With the right flank captured, MacArthur moved his artillery to the center of the line where the Filipino defenses remained strong. With his artillery in place at approximately noon, MacArthur renewed the offensive. Opening up with a half-hour artillery bombardment to cover his advance, his division moved forward about a quarter of a mile into no-man's land to within 400 yards of the Filipino line. U.S. soldiers boomed away with their heavy Springfields, and the enemy returned fire with its smaller caliber Mausers. Soon, a pall of white smoke blanketed the battle from the black powdered cartridges of the Springfields.

In the first exchange of small arms fire, the U.S. soldier proved to be a vastly superior marksman compared with the Filipino soldier. U.S. accuracy with the rifle became legendary in the Philippines. For a Filipino to rise above the trenches meant almost certain death.

Around 12:30 p.m., MacArthur passed the order down the line to fix bayonets, and the ominous clatter of metal striking metal sounded along the whole front. Using tactics he had advocated while an instructor at Fort Leavenworth, Kansas, MacArthur ordered his division forward by platoons—there would be no grand parade with regiments and brigades forming for an open attack as at Missionary Ridge. Modern weapons made such tactics ridiculous. MacArthur trained his men to use all available cover when attacking, and they brilliantly executed his strategy. A platoon rushed forward about 50 yards, threw themselves prone, and provided covering fire as another platoon rose to rush pass to repeat the maneuver. Although the ground was flat, bamboo growths, wooded spots, and fences sprinkled the 400 yards between the lines. The division advanced by leapfrogging companies, the rear line pelting the tops of the Filipino trenches with deadly accurate fire. Slowly but surely they moved toward the Filipino trenches.

When about 70 yards from the enemy's entrenchments, the buglers sounded the charge. The men yelled and dashed forward to leap to the top of the Filipino trenches. The Filipino line crumbled.

The Filipino fortifications were in shambles; 160 dead Filipinos lined the trenches, most barefoot, and many armed only with bolos or spears. The 2nd Division lost 17 men killed, a 10-to-1 ratio.

Before the bullets ceased, MacArthur, mounted on his favorite grey horse and accompanied by his staff, rode across the battlefield strewn with the dead enemy. Every man in his division stood to cheer. He was their "General," and he inspired pride and confidence in his men. They trusted him, they believed in his ability, and they respected his judgment. Many of the officers, volunteers and regulars alike, considered him the perfect commander, and the fact that he was always right on the front line made them appreciate him even more. A quiet, calm man, MacArthur was methodical in his preparations and always careful with the lives of his men.

After a brief halt to reorganize, General MacArthur's division moved forward four miles to reach the outskirts of Calacoon before General Otis telegraphed an order to halt. MacArthur established a temporary divisional headquarters at La Loma Church near the Calacoon Road. Naturally, he ordered the men to entrench and to be prepared for an attack, for he had not forgotten the lessons of Murfreesboro. Except for a few fusillades that proved false alarms, the whole line was quiet that night, 5 February.

In the two divisions, U.S. casualties amounted to 59 killed and 278 wounded—minor losses by Civil War standards. On the field, U.S. soldiers actually buried 612 Filipinos. They found few wounded and almost no rifles. In wars at that time five men were normally wounded for every man killed. In the Philippines, the figures for Filipino casualties were 15 dead to every wounded.

After a five-day halt to reorganize and resupply, MacArthur renewed the offensive. South of Calacoon, the Filipino trenches were within range of Dewey's heavy naval guns. At 3:00 p.m. on 10 February, Dewey's guns opened fire on the Filipino positions. Thirty minutes later, MacArthur attacked the right flank, and despite stubborn Filipino resistance, quickly captured the position. He then attacked the center. The Filipinos abandoned their trenches, burned the town, and retreated as the sun was setting.

At Calacoon, MacArthur captured the railroad maintenance yard almost intact. The only railroad in the Philippines ran north from Calacoon to Malolos, the temporary Republican capital, then on to Calumpit, San Fernando, Angeles, Tarlac, and Bayambang to Dagupan on the Lingayen Gulf, a distance of about 150 miles. At the Calacoon Railroad maintenance yard,

MacArthur captured 5 railroad engines, 50 passenger coaches, and over 100 freight and flat cars. British manufactured, the trains were smaller than their U.S. counterparts. Possession of this rolling stock, repaired by MacArthur's troops, enabled the division to use the railroad on its future advances. MacArthur used the rolling stock to create his own special armored train.

At sunrise on 25 March MacArthur attacked the Filipino forces north of Calacoon. Using his armored train, the general bombarded the Filipino trenches for a half-hour. The armored train was a rolling powerhouse. The first flat car held three machine guns and a naval six-pounder. The rapid fire pompom gun fired shell after shell atop the enemy trenches while the three machine guns peppered the top of the trenches to prevent any Filipino defender from raising his head. MacArthur ordered his division to attack. The 10,000 men stretched for eight miles on each side of the railroad tracks. Headquarters was the armored train. The infantry moved forward and added to the firepower as Krags and Springfields opened fire on the Filipino line.

In five days, the 2nd Division shoved the Philippine army back 18 miles to the outskirts of Malolos, the Republican capital. During the evening of 30 March MacArthur visited all his regiments to reconnoiter the forward positions of the enemy. Fired on by a Filipino outpost, the bullets missed the general but struck his aide, Maj. Putnam B. Strong, standing less than three feet away. Fortunately, the wound was slight.

During the night, MacArthur formed his division for an attack. At 7:00 a.m. he opened with a 25-minute artillery barrage. After the barrage, MacArthur simultaneously advanced his left flank and center. The advance was not resisted. During the night, Aguinaldo had withdrawn his army. The retreating Filipinos attempted to burn the town, but U.S. troops quenched the fires before any real damage was done. In six days, MacArthur had achieved his objective. After the capture of Malolos on 31 March the northern campaign ended except for a restructuring of the line when MacArthur moved a few miles further north to Angeles City. The onset of the monsoon season curtailed military operations.

In June and July, MacArthur reorganized the 2nd Division. Most of his combat troops belonged to state volunteer regiments whose enlistments had expired. In July and August, inadequately trained federal volunteer regiments replaced the state volunteers. For the next three months, MacArthur drilled his 16 new regiments.

On 8 November, after five months of limited military activity, MacArthur renewed the offensive north of Angeles City. Resistance was light. The Philippine Republican Army provided just enough opposition to make MacArthur deploy his forces for battle. Although they no longer burned towns and villages, the Filipinos burned bridges and destroyed tracks as they retreated north up the railroad line. In four days MacArthur's division advanced 30 miles to capture Tarlac, the second Republican capital.

On 17 November MacArthur left Tarlac with 1,000 handpicked men in a dash north up the railroad. In the next three days the forward column occupied the railroad line all the way to Dagupan on the Lingayen Gulf. MacArthur's advance was so rapid that the retreating Filipinos did not have an opportunity to remove a single rail or destroy a single bridge or culvert. Despite heavy rains, MacArthur's division had moved over 60 miles in 12 days.

Otis assigned the 2nd Division the job of repairing, maintaining, and protecting the railroad line from Dagupan to Manila. Broken up into company units, the 14,000 men and 400 officers of the division's 16 regiments were dispersed to garrison 117 towns and small villages along the 150 miles of railroad track. All regular and systematic tactical operations ceased.

The war had not ended, only the tactics had changed. Aguinaldo dispersed his army to engage in guerrilla war. The Filipinos fired on garrison towns, set booby traps, and attacked patrol parties repairing the railroad and telegraph lines. Although U.S. casualties were small in each of hundreds of rebel attacks, the U.S. dead and wounded mounted. By April 1900, U.S. casualties in the guerrilla war exceeded the dead and wounded sustained in the 1899 fall offensive.

The War Department recalled General Otis to the United States on 5 May 1900 and appointed General MacArthur to command all U.S. forces in the Philippines. Recognizing the political nature of the war, President McKinley named MacArthur military governor of the islands. U.S. troops and other U.S. figures in the Philippines were wild with enthusiasm. Manila was alive with hope as MacArthur moved into Malacañang Palace, the governor's residence. Under his command were 71,727 enlisted men and 2,367 officers scattered in 502 garrisons throughout the archipelago covering almost 150,000 square miles of territory and inhabited by eight million people.

General MacArthur realized that military force alone could not suppress the Filipino revolution. The United States could rule the islands by force, but there would be unending discord, conspiracy, and strife. MacArthur believed it was essential to gain the popular support of the people by instituting dramatic political reforms. As the first step in a good-faith contract with the Filipinos, MacArthur issued a proclamation in June that guaranteed Filipinos all personal liberties held by the people of the United States except for the right to bear arms. Before the law, Filipinos were treated the same as any U.S. citizen. Except for curfew, initially 8:00 p.m. later raised to midnight, and finally dropped entirely, the general refused to impose draconian measures of martial law in Manila. At the order of the War Department, press censorship continued, but MacArthur refused to curtail freedom of speech except to prohibit any speech advocating the violent overthrow of the U.S. government in the Philippines. MacArthur allowed Filipino civic and fraternal groups, even secret societies, to continue their meetings simply on their pledge not to use the meetings to support the war. He encouraged Filipino leaders to speak publicly. He reminded his staff to treat all Filipino visitors with respect, and he encouraged all his officers to form friendships with the local aristocracy.

On 3 June 1900, the day after his 55th birthday, MacArthur's euphoria of high command was dampened. On that hot and blistering summer Sunday, Judge William H. Taft arrived aboard the USS *Hancock* with the Second Philippine Commission. Within days of his arrival, Taft was certain he knew more about the Philippines than MacArthur who had served there for almost two years. It was soon apparent that they disagreed on nearly every aspect of rule in the Philippines.

MacArthur considered the Taft Commission primarily an advisory body on civilian affairs, while Taft considered the commission in charge of civilian affairs. MacArthur informed the commissioners that their powers were extremely limited. The commission had the power to legislate, to control the civilian budget, and to appoint civilian administrators, but no law could be passed or implemented by the commission without the approval of General MacArthur, who was the military governor.

Taft protested. In consultation with Secretary of War Elihu Root, Taft had drafted the commission's instructions, and he was certain MacArthur did not have the power to veto legislation. MacArthur reminded Taft that the Philippines were under martial law, and as military commander and governor, MacArthur held absolute power over both civilian personnel and military personnel. The Philippine Commission could advise him, but the commission could not act without his approval. To MacArthur's credit, he worked with the commissioners and tried to deal with the difficulties caused by inadequate instructions from Washington. When invited to attend commission meetings, MacArthur accepted. In his dealing with the commission he was formal and reserved, but not obstructive.

Commissioner Taft and General MacArthur never agreed on who had final authority. Relations between the two deteriorated throughout the fall of 1900. In public they were friendly, but privately their relations were cold. As the power struggle intensified, Taft attacked MacArthur in devastating letters to Secretary Root, his contact in Washington.

In late November, MacArthur reluctantly concluded that harsher military measures were needed to curtail the guerrilla bands harassing the U.S. garrisons. His lenient humanitarian policies had failed. From June to November, only 5,022 Filipinos had accepted amnesty, a small part of the total force in the field. The guerrilla attacks actually escalated in summer 1900 with U.S. garrisons suffering 344 casualties, 118 killed and 226 wounded. While publicly supporting the U.S. occupation, Filipino town and village officials were in reality loyal to the revolution. This loyalty was almost universal.

Guerrilla warfare demanded harsher measures than MacArthur wished to use, but he realized that the war could be won only by ending town and village support for the guerrillas. The towns furnished them with information, supplies, and sanctuary. Without this support, the guerrillas could not operate. If the army could isolate the guerrillas from local village support, the war would end.

MacArthur initiated a new military campaign in early December. He sent out his 70,000 veteran troops from their garrisons with the goal of cutting the towns off from the guerrillas. His army struck hard against the guerrillas everywhere in the Philippines. Republican soldiers in uniform were treated as prisoners of war, but guerrillas captured out of uniform were sometimes executed. In the next three months, 79 captured guerrillas were hanged for murder.

Simultaneously, the general instituted stricter political controls. He ordered his garrison commanders to maintain close surveillance and to arrest anyone even suspected of aiding the guerrillas. Townspeople were made responsible for their actions in support of the guerrillas. Any Filipino who refused to swear loyalty to the United States was to be considered a rebel who was aiding the enemy. Anyone who aided or assisted any person in active, violent opposition to U.S. rule was to be arrested with fear as no excuse. Suspicion was sufficient reason for arrest, and any who were arrested were not to be released until the end of the war. MacArthur reluctantly adopted a deportation policy for captured rebel leaders. In January 1901, he deported to Guam 38 of the most prominent leaders.

The new military tactics were effective. By January 1901, the army had captured over 2,000 guerrillas. Filipino troops surrendered in dramatically increasing numbers from a 175 monthly average to over 650 in December to about 800 a month in January and February 1901.

The army and Congress showed their approval. On the recommendation of Lt. Gen. Nelson A. Miles and Maj. Gen. Henry C. Corbin, the adjutant general, MacArthur was promoted to major general in the regular army on 5 February 1901. In three short years, he had risen from an obscure lieutenant colonel in the adjutant general's office to the youngest major general in the army.

Yet, the war continued. MacArthur believed the war would not end until Aguinaldo was captured or surrendered. Aguinaldo was the incarnation of the Filipino effort. Since it seemed unlikely that Aguinaldo would surrender, capturing him was the key. MacArthur did not want Aguinaldo killed. The Filipinos had created a legend of invincibility around Aguinaldo, and if he were killed, millions of Filipinos would not believe he was dead, and even those who did would make Aguinaldo a martyr of the revolution much like José Rizal y Mercado in 1896.

MacArthur's primary objective was to capture Aguinaldo alive to dispel the myth of his invincibility and to end the war. Unfortunately, the United States Army had no idea where Aguinaldo was hiding. Because of possible traitors, Aguinaldo took great care in selecting his base camps and allowed only a few of his more important generals to know where he was. He conducted the war through correspondence with his subordinates in various parts of the islands.

In early February 1901, a bit of good fortune fell to U.S. forces. Brig. Gen. Frederick Funston, commander of a brigade at San Isidro in central Luzon, captured Cecilio Segismundo, one of Aguinaldo's messengers. Segismundo revealed that Aguinaldo had his headquarters deep in the jungles and mountains on the northeastern edge of Luzon 20 miles in the interior at the small village of Palanan.

Funston hurried to Manila to report to MacArthur. Funston was one of MacArthur's most devoted officers and had served in the 2nd Division as commander of the 20th Kansas Volunteers. He viewed MacArthur as the best general in the army, and MacArthur treated him as a father treats a favorite son.

MacArthur and Funston worked out an audacious plan to capture Aguinaldo. Palanan could not be approached directly by a large force because Aguinaldo would simply flee into the jungle. Funston suggested a subterfuge. With a small force of 80 Macabebe scouts, indistinguishable from other Filipinos, Funston and four other U.S. officers would take a gunboat from Manila to northeastern Luzon. The sea trip would take from six to 10 days. After a clandestine landing, the Macabebes would pose as reenforcements for Aguinaldo's headquarters while the five U.S. officers posed as prisoners. Funston hoped to penetrate Aguinaldo's headquarters and take the Filipino president alive. Few commanding generals would have approved Funston's reckless plan. The possibility of failure, even disaster, was great. If Funston's deception failed, he and the other U.S. officers would be captured or killed. MacArthur proved as bold as Funston and approved the mission. He accepted the possibility of failure, as well as full responsibility for the mission because he believed that risks were necessary to end the war.

On 6 March, Funston, four other army officers, and the 80 Macabebes boarded the gunboat *Vicksburg* and steamed out of Manila. MacArthur waited anxiously. Three weeks passed without a word from Funston, and the general began to fear that the mission had failed. Around 6:30

a.m. on 28 March a member of MacArthur's staff woke him. Funston had returned and was waiting downstairs. The normally formal MacArthur dashed downstairs in his pajamas. Funston's plan had worked perfectly. He had captured Aguinaldo and his entire headquarters staff.

MacArthur treated the Filipino president with extreme consideration. He quartered Aguinaldo in a spacious villa near Malacañang Palace and allowed his family and friends to visit. The ever-present U.S. guards were as unobtrusive as possible.

After 23 days of negotiations, Aguinaldo agreed to terms with General MacArthur. On 19 April 1901 Aguinaldo swore allegiance to the United States and issued a proclamation requesting his followers to surrender. In return, MacArthur immediately released from prison a thousand captured Filipinos with another thousand in early May and an additional thousand in June.

With Aguinaldo's capture, Washington decided to implement civilian government in the Philippines. The War Department notified MacArthur that his term as military governor would end on 4 July 1901. MacArthur moved rapidly to transfer vast areas of Luzon to civilian control. By June, over half the towns and villages on Luzon were administered by municipal governments appointed by the Taft Commission. U.S. troops were slowly withdrawn, and by June 1901 the Department of the Philippines had only 42,000 men.

On 4 July 1901, in a grand military ceremony in Manila's Cathedral Plaza, MacArthur formally surrendered power to Taft as the new governor and to Maj. Gen. Adna R. Chaffee as the new military commander of the Department of the Philippines. General MacArthur addressed an audience of hundreds of soldiers, thousands of Filipinos, and a few U.S. civilian dignitaries. He praised his officers and men for their hard work, and he proclaimed the Filipinos would now obtain the full benefits of U.S. civilization under civilian control. MacArthur admired and liked the Filipino people. He believed their abilities meant that their future was to become a model of republican government in Asia.

The officers and soldiers of the Department of the Philippines loved and respected their general. An artillery battery stationed in Fort Santiago fired a military salute to their departing commander as he was escorted to the pier by an honor guard down streets lined with soldiers. Each regiment saluted as he passed. At the bay, he boarded a launch to take him to a transport waiting to return him to the United States.

General MacArthur never received appropriate honors for his role in the suppression of the Philippine War and the establishment of civil government in the Philippines. Quiet and reserved, MacArthur refused interviews with reporters and never expressed his emotions in public. He was a formal man, in writing as well as in manners, and he never became the "darling" of the press. The general did not forbid his officers from giving interviews, and the reporters made a number of his subordinates more famous than their commander.

MacArthur was promoted to lieutenant general of the army in 1906, but he was not named chief of staff. Ignored by Washington, he retired on 2 June 1909 at age 64. He is best remembered today as the father of General Douglas MacArthur.

Kenneth Ray Young

REFERENCES

David H. Bain, *Sitting in Darkness: Americans in the Philippines* (Houghton Mifflin, 1984); Frederick Funston, *Memories of Two Wars: Cuban and Philippine Experiences* (Scribner, 1911); John M. Gates, *Schoolbooks and Krags: The United States Army in the Philippines, 1898–1902* (Greenwood Pr., 1973); William T. Sexton, *Soldiers in the Sun: An Adventure in Imperialism* (Military Service Pub. Co., 1939); Leon Wolff, *Little Brown Brother: How the United States Purchased and Pacified the Philippine Islands at the Century's Turn* (Doubleday, 1961).

McCoy, Frank Ross (1874–1954)

Frank Ross McCoy, a career officer in the United States Army, was a military leader in the campaigns against the Philippine Muslims (Moros) and later played other significant diplomatic and military roles during the pre-World War II era of U.S. interventionism.

Less than one year after McCoy graduated from the United States Military Academy at West Point the Spanish-Cuban/American War broke out in April 1898. Transferring to the 10th Cavalry Regiment, McCoy left for Cuba in June. In the Santiago campaign he fought at Las Guásimas on 24 June; on 1 July he received a leg wound during the battle at Kettle Hill, part of the San Juan heights on the outskirts of the city.

This ended McCoy's role in the war. However, while lying wounded on the battlefield he by chance met Leonard Wood, who was to have a major impact on McCoy's career.

After recuperating in the United States, McCoy rejoined his unit and returned to Cuba as part of the occupation forces in April 1899. One year later the military governor of Cuba, General Wood, requested him as his *aide-de-camp*, beginning a friendship that lasted until Wood's death. McCoy soon took control and reorganized the military government's finances, making them efficient and accountable. In June 1901, he was promoted to first lieutenant, and when the occupation ended in May 1902, McCoy remained as Wood's aide.

In early 1903 Wood was appointed the military commander of the Department of Mindanao and governor of Moro Province in the Philippines. Wood again asked McCoy to be his aide, and the two arrived in the Philippines in July. McCoy had a very low opinion of the Moros, viewing them on the same level as Native Indians. He also believed that U.S. rule would enlighten and civilize the Filipinos. By August, McCoy held the rank of captain, and at various times during his tenure in the Philippines, he served as acting secretary and provincial engineer in the Moro Province Legislative Council.

As the intelligence officer of the Department of Mindanao, McCoy often joined campaigns against the Moros. In autumn 1906 he planned and successfully completed a move to defeat the Moro leader Datu Ali. Ali, one of the last of the hostile Moro chieftains, had resisted all attempts to subdue him. Using information gathered from Ali's rivals, McCoy and his small mobile force of 100 U.S. infantry and 10 Philippine Scouts, surprised Ali with a rear attack on 22 October 1905. In a brief battle Ali and 11 Moros died and 50 others were captured, while U.S. forces suffered only one casualty. Both Wood and President Theodore Roosevelt praised McCoy for this action.

On leave in late 1905 McCoy visited Japan and Canton, China, where he gathered intelligence. He returned to Manila early in January 1906 before leaving for the United States in midyear.

During the next 11 years McCoy served in many capacities, including as an aide to William H. Taft while he was the provisional governor of Cuba (1906), an aide to President Roosevelt

(1907–1908), troop commander along the U.S.-Mexican border (1915–1916) during the Mexican Revolution, and military attaché in Mexico City (1917).

Gregory C. Ference

REFERENCES

A.J. Bacevich, *Diplomat in Khaki: Major General Frank Ross McCoy and American Foreign Policy, 1898–1949* (Univ. Pr. of Kansas, 1989); William S. Biddle, *Major General Frank Ross McCoy* (Mifflin County Historical Society, 1956).

See also Ali, Datu.

McKinley, William, and the Spanish-Cuban/American War (1898)

William McKinley was president of the United States during the Spanish-Cuban/American War of 1898. Setting diplomatic and military policy, he led the United States through a popular war that resulted in the nation taking a more prominent position in world affairs.

McKinley had little experience in foreign affairs before becoming president. Born in a modest family in Ohio, he obtained a limited education; served with distinction in the Civil War, attaining the rank of major; and became a lawyer. He never traveled to Europe or to Latin America. Entering Congress as a Republican in 1876, McKinley became chairman of the House Ways and Means Committee. Failing to be reelected in 1890, he won two terms as governor of Ohio. In 1896 he defeated William Jennings Bryan to gain the presidency.

McKinley's political talent lay in his ability to work harmoniously with other men and to communicate well with his constituents. Always courteous, kind, and thoughtful, he listened carefully to others. Guarding his own views, he often achieved his goals indirectly, allowing others to take the credit. Hard-working and congenial, McKinley rapidly moved to the inner circle of congressional leadership and national prominence.

During two decades of public office, McKinley showed an interest in expansionism. He favored developing U.S. foreign markets through reciprocal trade agreements, acquisition of the Hawaiian Islands, and the construction of an Isthmian canal. McKinley also voted to support the construction of a modern navy.

President-elect McKinley's initial effect on foreign and military policy was his choice of cabinet officers. For secretary of state, he picked Senator John Sherman, Republican of Ohio. But Sherman, age 73, was declining physically and mentally, and after a few months the president chose his close friend from Canton, Ohio, Judge William R. Day, to be the assistant secretary of state. Although Day had no previous Washington or diplomatic experience, he was loyal and a trusted advisor. McKinley turned the Cuban problem over to Day. When Sherman resigned as secretary of state at the start of the Spanish-Cuban/American War, McKinley named Day to replace him.

McKinley selected Russell A. Alger to be secretary of war and John D. Long to be secretary of the navy. Alger, a Civil War general, businessman, and governor of Michigan, proved to be a weak administrator. When the war came, he was overwhelmed by the task. Accordingly, McKinley relied on Brig. Gen. Henry C. Corbin. Long, a former governor of Massachusetts, was a more competent administrator; moreover, the navy was better prepared for war.

When McKinley entered the White House, he inherited a critical Cuban problem which had been developing since the Cuban revolution began in February 1895. Organized by José Julián Martí y Perez, the war for independence spread across the island, creating great destruction. Martí died during the first months of the uprising, and leadership devolved on Máximo Gómez y Báez, general of the Cuban army, and Tomás Estrada Palma, chief diplomat of the Cuban Republic and head of the Cuban Junta in New York City. Since the Cuban army was too small and poorly armed to defeat the Spanish, Gómez pursued a campaign of property destruction, aimed at turning the island into an economic desert that Spain would abandon. In carrying out this strategy, Gómez willfully destroyed U.S. investments. In the United States, Estrada Palma directed a successful publicity campaign that rallied the support of the people. Congressional politicians quickly took up the cause of *Cuba Libre*.

Faced by a serious rebellion, Spain sent Gen. Valeriano Weyler y Nicolau to Cuba with 200,000 troops. Weyler sought to crush the rebellion by separating the rural masses from the revolutionaries, thus depriving the revolutionaries of food, arms, and information. He herded

about 400,000 *reconcentrados* (peasants) into fortified towns guarded by Spanish troops. He destroyed rural housing and crops and closed sugar
mills suspected of paying protection money.
Weyler had some success in 1896 in western
Cuba, and Spanish troops killed Antonio Maceo,
one of Cuba's most popular generals. But
Weyler's harsh measures did not end the revolution.

With Gómez and Weyler destroying the
Cuban economy, *reconcentrados* soon faced starvation and disease. During the war, approximately 200,000 civilians died, most during the
latter part of the conflict.

Before McKinley became president, President
Grover Cleveland had wrestled with the prob-
lem. The war destroyed U.S. investments, and
U.S. trade with the island collapsed. Cleveland
offered to mediate an end to the war, and he
urged Madrid to grant Cubans self-government.
When Spain refused, Cleveland warned that if
Madrid was unable to restore peace, the United
States would eventually intervene.

The Republican party supported the Cuban
cause more than the Democratic administration.
Congressional Republicans criticized Cleveland
for failing to side with the Cubans, and in 1896
the Republican platform took a stronger stand
for Cuban independence than the Democrats did.
Although presidential candidate McKinley did
not speak about Cuba during the campaign, he
favored the Cubans more than Cleveland.

After several months in office, McKinley selected Stewart L. Woodford to serve as U.S.
minister to Spain. At the same time the president obtained reliable information on the deplorable and worsening condition of the
reconcentrados. Deeply disturbed, he directed
Woodford to go to Madrid to press the Spanish
government to end the war through political reforms and to offer presidential mediation. But
by the time Woodford entered Spain in September 1897, the Spanish government was already considering reforms.

In August 1897 an anarchist had assassinated
Spanish Prime Minister Antonio Cánovas del
Castillo, which resulted in a change of government. The Conservative party left office in October 1897, and Práxedes Mateo Sagasta headed
the new Liberal party government. A critic of
Cánovas's Cuban policy, Sagasta initiated extensive changes. He was ably assisted by Segismundo
Moret y Prendergast, the new minister of colo-

nies. Sagasta replaced Weyler with Gen. Ramón
Blanco y Erenas and initiated a policy of negotiation and amnesty. Moret drafted a law that
provided local autonomy to Cuba and promised
tariff reforms. Since Sagasta's efforts paralleled
those advocated by Washington, McKinley was
willing to allow the Spanish government time to
implement its program.

But Cuban nationalists flatly rejected autonomy, and some Spaniards resisted it as well.
When Spain launched Cuban self-government
on 12 January 1898, Spanish nationalists on the
island, including some army officers, rioted. The
display of Cuban and Spanish intransigence convinced the McKinley administration that autonomy would not work.

Although the January riots had not been
against the United States, McKinley feared that
deteriorating conditions might threaten U.S.
lives and property. Accordingly, in late January
he sent the battleship *Maine* to Havana harbor.
The Navy Department also augmented the fleet
in southern waters.

Hardly had the *Maine* anchored in Havana
harbor, when the Cuban Junta released a stolen
private letter in which the Spanish minister,
Enrique Dupuy de Lôme, sarcastically criticized
President McKinley. Dupuy de Lôme had
worked closely with the Cleveland administration and was critical of the Republicans. After
McKinley delivered his December State of the
Union address to Congress, Dupuy de Lôme
wrote to a Spanish friend that McKinley was a
political weakling who played to the crowds;
McKinley slandered Spain in order to keep the
support of Republican jingoes. Moreover, Dupuy
de Lôme implied that Madrid's reforms were
designed to woo U.S. support away from Cuban
independence. Published on 9 February in the
New York Journal, the letter set off an emotional
outburst against Spain.

President McKinley moved quickly to settle
the issue. After determining that the letter was
authentic, he demanded that Spain recall its minister and disavow his words. But Dupuy de Lôme
had resigned as soon as the letter appeared in
print. Because the Spanish foreign minister had
accepted Dupuy de Lôme's resignation with regret and commended his diplomatic service,
Woodford insisted that the Spanish government
remove the commendation and explicitly repudiate Dupuy de Lôme's words. The Spanish gov-

ernment capitulated, and Madrid's apology satisfied both Woodford and McKinley.

The next day the *Maine* exploded and sank in Havana harbor. The ship's forward magazines, located under the crew's quarters, ignited, killing 266 sailors. The cause of the disaster was unknown.

Despite the lack of evidence many in the United States suspected that Spain was responsible. Yet, the most likely cause of the explosion was spontaneous combustion in the ship's coal bunkers. President McKinley called on the people of the United States to remain calm. He asked them to suspend judgment until the results of a naval court of inquiry were known. McKinley expected the investigators to find that an accident caused the disaster.

While the naval court of inquiry was deliberating, both the United States and Spain prepared for war. When McKinley learned that Spain was seeking to buy Brazilian warships which were nearing completion in a British dockyard, he asked Congress to appropriate $50 million for defense. In one day Congress unanimously approved the bill, and the navy blocked the Spanish purchases.

Shortly before the naval court completed its investigation, Senator Redfield Proctor, Republican from Vermont, delivered an influential speech on Cuba to the Senate. A conservative and wealthy businessman who had served in an earlier cabinet, Proctor conferred with McKinley before visiting Cuba, and he consulted with him upon his return.

On 17 March the senator described the terrible suffering of the Cuban people. He explained the military stalemate in Cuba and declared his belief that the Cuban people were ready for self-government. He urged the United States to look beyond the tragedy of the *Maine* to the struggle of a million and a half Cubans against a barbaric Spanish government. He defined the grounds for U.S. intervention in terms of humanitarian aid for the *reconcentrados* and justice for the Cuban people.

Proctor's speech caused a sensation. Business conservatives and religious groups rushed to support intervention. Although the White House insisted that McKinley was not behind the speech, it served his diplomatic purpose well. The president did not want to intervene in Cuba because of the *Maine*; if war came, he wanted to take the high ground of humanitarianism.

Two days after Proctor's speech the *Maine* investigators informed McKinley that an external explosion, probably a mine, had detonated the ship's forward magazines. They did not know who had set off the mine.

The president expected the publication of the *Maine* investigation to cause a demand for war. For several days he consulted congressional Republicans and Democrats in an effort to contain the impending crisis and to define a consensus policy. He listened carefully and pleaded for time for a diplomatic solution.

Despite McKinley's efforts to dampen the outburst, release of the *Maine* report on 28 March 1898 caused great emotional excitement. The public demanded immediate intervention in Cuba even if it meant war; and Congress revolted against the president's desire to continue diplomatic efforts. Large numbers of Republican congressmen threatened to join with the Democrats in declaring war on Spain.

Given the public and congressional furor, McKinley had only a few days for negotiations. He asked Spain to make full reparation for the *Maine* and to end the war and suffering in Cuba. If Spain could not do this by 15 April, McKinley told the Spanish that he would ask Congress to take up the issue. It was understood that this meant war.

In reply Madrid denied that it had any responsibility for the *Maine*, but offered to arbitrate the dispute. As for Cuba, Moret suggested a truce on the island during which the Cuban autonomy government could negotiate a settlement with the revolutionaries. Woodford advised McKinley to support a Spanish-Cuban armistice. Once the fighting stopped, he reasoned, it would never resume, and Spain would inevitably leave the island.

Accordingly, McKinley proposed a three-point plan for solving the Cuban problem. First, the Spanish and Cubans would adopt an armistice for six months during which they would negotiate a permanent peace, using McKinley's good offices if needed. Second, Spain would immediately allow all Cuban civilians to return to their homes, and it would cooperate with the United States to provide relief. Third, Woodford should, if possible, get Spain to agree that if there was no durable peace by 1 October, McKinley would arbitrate a solution. Washington expected these proposals to result in Cuban independence.

When Spain rejected McKinley's plan, war seemed inevitable. Sagasta agreed to allow some *reconcentrados* to return to their homes, and he was willing to cooperate with the United States in relief efforts. But Spain's military leaders would accept only a suspension of hostilities if the Cuban rebels requested it. Noting that the new Cuban legislature was scheduled to meet on 4 May, Sagasta proposed that it attempt to negotiate a peace with the revolutionaries. The Spanish did not respond to McKinley's offers of mediation and arbitration. Disappointed, McKinley decided on 1 April to give the Cuban issue to Congress.

But negotiations continued for another 10 days. Europe's Great Powers and Pope Leo XIII urged Spain to prevent a disastrous war. In late March the pope had sent Archbishop John Ireland of St. Paul, Minnesota, to visit McKinley in an effort to restrain the U.S. government. A friend of the president, Ireland supported McKinley's diplomacy. After meeting with the president, Ireland asked the Vatican to pressure Madrid to grant an armistice.

The pope made an appeal to Madrid, and the Great Powers provided their support. When Sagasta's government began to reconsider, McKinley delayed sending his message to Congress. During the interval the diplomatic representatives of the Great Powers called at the White House to request U.S. restraint and met with the Spanish foreign minister to urge an armistice. Their efforts bore fruit. Spain ended reconcentration throughout Cuba, and on 9 April Spanish Queen Regent María Cristina proclaimed a suspension of hostilities in Cuba in order to facilitate peace.

Hopes for peace were soon dashed. The Cuban revolutionaries refused to lay down their arms before achieving independence and the recognition of their government. McKinley was unable to use the queen regent's proclamation to alter the congressional demand for intervention.

On 11 April McKinley turned over the Cuban issue to Congress. In a lengthy message the president reviewed Cuban developments and his futile efforts to bring peace to the island. He did not call, however, for Cuban independence or recognition of the Cuban Republic. Noting that Madrid had just proclaimed a suspension of hostilities, the president asked Congress to take this into account.

Congress was in no mood to delay; it overwhelmingly supported military intervention. Congress was divided, however, over McKinley's opposition to recognizing Cuban independence and the Cuban Republic. McKinley argued that recognition would tie U.S. hands. When U.S. troops entered Cuba, they would be subject to Cuban sovereignty and would fall under the jurisdiction and laws of Gen. Máximo Gómez. Moreover, the McKinley administration did not believe that the Cuban Republic satisfied the legal requirements of sovereignty nor could it be counted on to protect people and property. McKinley wanted a free hand during the war and the ability to ensure a responsible government afterward.

Many congressmen believed McKinley was betraying the Cuban patriots. Nevertheless, the Republican-controlled House passed a resolution that supported McKinley's position; the Senate, however, voted to recognize Cuban independence and the Republic. In addition, Senator Henry M. Teller, Silver Republican from Colorado, offered a resolution which declared that the United States intended to leave the island once peace was restored. McKinley accepted Teller's language, which passed the Senate by voice vote. After a week's debate, Congress adopted a resolution recognizing Cuban independence but not the Cuban Republic. It authorized the president to use armed force, and on 21 April 1898 McKinley ordered a naval blockade of Cuba.

Once the war began President McKinley fully exercised his constitutional power as commander in chief of the armed forces. He adopted the basic strategy of the war and sometimes took part in issuing directives to field commanders. McKinley established the White House as a center of operations by installing telegraphic and telephone facilities that linked him to key offices in Washington and abroad. News poured into the White House 24 hours a day, and maps displayed the movements of ships and men.

As early as 1894 the Navy Department had started planning for war with Spain. By 1898 naval officers advocated a blockade of Cuba, destruction of Spain's fleets, attacks on Spanish colonial positions which were least defended, and disruption of Spanish commerce. Plans for a land assault against Havana, Cuba, were less clear. Since the professional army of 25,000 men was unprepared to attack Havana, it might carry out a limited invasion of the island which would permit furnishing military supplies to the Cuban revolutionaries. Adopting many of these ideas, McKinley favored minimizing U.S. losses while placing maximum pressure on Spain to end the war quickly.

Naval war plans did not cover mobilizing an army. Only days before the fighting began, Congress rejected a bill that McKinley proposed to place the National Guard under regular army control. Guardsmen, Civil War veterans, and volunteers wanted to select their own officers. After war was declared, Congress and McKinley agreed on establishing a volunteer army of 125,000 men and a regular army half that size.

Creating the volunteer army soon became a national scandal. The War Department was unprepared for the task, and Secretary Alger provided little leadership. The flood of volunteers was inadequately housed, clothed, and fed; troops lacked basic military supplies, including modern rifles and ammunition. Soldiers sent to Tampa, Florida, to form an invasion force encountered great confusion. Press criticism focused on Alger, who became a political liability. Gradually conditions improved, but after the war McKinley forced Alger from office and encouraged a thorough reform of the War Department.

As the McKinley administration struggled with army mobilization, the navy won a spectacular victory in Manila Bay in the Philippines. The McKinley administration knew that the Spanish fleet in the Philippines was obsolete. Shortly after the war started, McKinley authorized Commodore George Dewey to attack the Spanish outpost. When the news arrived in Washington that Dewey had annihilated the Spanish fleet, McKinley immediately ordered U.S. troops to the Philippines.

The U.S. victory led to the annexation of the Hawaiian Islands, which McKinley had favored before the Spanish-Cuban/American War. When he had entered office in 1897, he had sent a treaty of annexation to the Senate which it set aside. Dewey's success and the dispatch of U.S. soldiers to the Philippines galvanized interest in acquiring the islands. Besides being a military asset, they would also encourage trade throughout the Far East. On 4 May Senator Francis G. Newlands, Democrat of Nevada, introduced a joint resolution for annexation. Popular support for annexation was strong, but Congress was nearing summer adjournment. McKinley pressed

for an early vote, and on 6 July Congress passed the resolution.

Another result of Dewey's victory was renewed Philippine resistance to Spanish authority. Emilio Aguinaldo y Famy, who had commanded an unsuccessful revolution and had been exiled, received Dewey's assistance to return to the Philippines to resume the rebellion. McKinley warned Dewey, however, to make no political commitments.

But Cuba was the major theater of the war. As U.S. naval officers expected, the Spanish government directed its main fleet, under the command of Adm. Pascual Cervera y Topete, to sail to Cuba to counter the U.S. blockade of the island. While Cervera crossed the Atlantic Ocean, the United States Navy lost track of the fleet. In mid-May Cervera entered the harbor of Santiago de Cuba. The United States Navy blockaded the port, and the McKinley administration devised a plan to destroy the fleet. McKinley ordered Gen. William R. Shafter to land troops east of Santiago de Cuba and to attack the port city.

The battle for Santiago and Cervera's fleet was the most important campaign of the war. By late June Shafter's forces began to move against the city. In a week of fighting U.S. soldiers penetrated the city's outer defenses, but Spanish resistance, directed by Gen. José Toral, was determined, and U.S. casualties were significant. Moreover, tropical diseases, including yellow fever, started to take their toll of U.S. lives. Shafter concluded that he had insufficient troops to take the city by storm, and he considered retreating, but McKinley encouraged him to hold his ground. Meanwhile, the Spanish government ordered Cervera to chance a sea battle, and on 3 July the U.S. fleet destroyed all of Cervera's ships.

Despite the naval victory, Shafter's army remained in difficulty. But Toral's situation was even more bleak. A Spanish relief expedition had failed to break through Cuban forces, and with no hope for additional troops, military supplies, and food, the Spanish position was ultimately hopeless.

Rather than attack Toral, Shafter initiated negotiations for the surrender of the city. McKinley followed the talks closely, stiffening Shafter's demands. Toral offered to surrender the city if Shafter allowed the Spanish troops to leave with their arms and to remain in Cuba to fight. Shafter wanted to accept the offer, but McKinley refused. The president suggested that if the Spanish surrendered the city and their arms, the United States would transport the soldiers back to Spain. Failure to accept these terms would lead to a naval bombardment of the city and an army assault. The Spanish government accepted McKinley's terms.

A week later U.S. forces landed in Puerto Rico. As in Cuba, they debarked at a site distant from the capital. U.S. troops encountered little resistance, but by the end of the war, they had neither defeated the Spanish army nor taken the island's capital.

Late in July the Spanish government sought peace. Spain had suffered two humiliating naval defeats, and its army was on the defensive on all fronts. Nevertheless, Spain still held most of Cuba and all of the important colonial cities, including Havana, Manila, and San Juan. The Spanish wanted a cease-fire to prevent further military defeats, and they hoped to trade their military position in Cuba for the removal of U.S. forces from the Philippines and Puerto Rico.

The McKinley administration had begun to consider peace terms after Dewey's victory. There was wide agreement in Washington that Spain must evacuate Cuba and allow the United States to restore order on the island. Spain must cede Puerto Rico to the United States as compensation for U.S. losses in the Cuban war. Ending Spanish colonialism in the Western Hemisphere was expected to eliminate any future cause for conflict between the United States and Spain. The United States would not ask for a financial indemnity, and it would not assume any of Spain's colonial debts. The McKinley administration also wanted an island in the Marianas, and during the war it captured Guam.

The United States, however, was divided over the future of the Philippines. As the summer passed, the people grew increasingly interested in annexing part or all of the islands. Although McKinley remained silent, it was increasingly apparent from U.S. troop movements that he expected to gain at least Manila. His cabinet was split, with arguments made for taking all, some, or none of the islands. The administration grew increasingly concerned about the Philippine forces.

Sagasta opened negotiations through the French ambassador, Jules M. Cambon, who represented Spanish interests in Washington. On 25 July Cambon began a series of meetings with McKinley in the White House to seek a means for ending the war. The initial Spanish request was for peace in Cuba and a statement of U.S. terms.

McKinley prepared the U.S. response. He rejected an immediate truce, insisting that the war continue until Washington received complete satisfaction. Spain must cede Puerto Rico and Guam and leave Cuba. As for the Philippines, McKinley offered to settle the future of the islands at a peace conference.

The Spanish government attempted to alter the U.S. demands. It wanted to cede Cuba to the United States in order to assure the protection of Spanish citizens and their property from the Cuban troops. It sought to keep Puerto Rico and suggested ceding some other island in its place. It also objected to the undetermined status of the Philippines. When McKinley turned aside all changes, the Spanish government capitulated.

At McKinley's suggestion, Day and Cambon prepared a protocol containing all the U.S. demands. It also included the means of accomplishing Spanish military withdrawal from Cuba and Puerto Rico during the armistice. In a White House ceremony on 12 August, Day and Cambon signed the protocol which ended the fighting. Since there was no telegraphic communication with the Philippines, the news did not reach Manila until after a U.S. assault had taken the city.

The protocol ending the war left several matters unresolved. In addition to the Philippines, there was the status of Spanish citizens in the ceded territories, public debt, state property, legal cases, and future trade. These were relegated to a conference in Paris, where commissioners from both nations would prepare a treaty for ratification.

McKinley carefully chose five commissioners. Heading the delegation was Day, who resigned as secretary of state. Whitelaw Reid, a prominent Republican, owner of the *New York Tribune*, and former ambassador to France, was another member. McKinley added three senators from the Foreign Relations Committee: Cushman K. Davis, Republican of Minnesota; William P. Frye, Republican of Maine; and George Gray, Democrat of Delaware. On the key issue of the Philippines, Reid, Davis, and Frye favored acquisition, Gray opposed it, and McKinley could count on Day to follow his lead.

The U.S. and Spanish commissioners met in Paris on 1 October. Eugenio Montero Ríos, a prominent Liberal senator, led the five-member Spanish commission.

McKinley decided to acquire the Philippines. From the start of the war the president said little about the disposition of the islands. But he expected some benefit from Dewey's victory and sent a large military contingent to the Philippines. During the summer and fall, the president gathered information about the islands. He learned of German and Japanese interest in them, and informants told him that Aguinaldo could not defend the islands against expansionist nations. Moreover, Great Britain urged the United States to acquire the entire archipelago. By the end of the war McKinley considered keeping the island of Luzon which contained Manila. When the Paris Peace Conference convened in October, he advised his commissioners to delay the Philippine issue by taking up other matters.

A U.S. election was approaching. During mid-October the president made a campaign tour through the nation's heartland. He delivered several major addresses, gave dozens of talks, and met with scores of local politicians. Clarifying his position on the Philippines, McKinley argued that the United States entered the war with Spain solely for humanitarian reasons. But the war had brought new responsibilities and opportunities. McKinley noted that the people of the United States opposed returning the islands to Spain, and he asserted that it was not feasible to turn them over to another nation. He concluded, therefore, that the United States should keep them and bring U.S. political and economic benefits to the inhabitants. McKinley called on his fellow citizens to take up their duty and destiny. He then instructed his commissioners to acquire the entire archipelago.

For one month the peace commissioners had marked time discussing the Cuban debt. The U.S. representatives had rebuffed all Spain's attempts to place part of the debt on the United States. They had also rejected Spain's argument that the U.S. military conquest of Manila after the protocol had been signed was illegal. Nevertheless, the commissioners privately acknowledged that Spain's contention had a basis in international law.

As the weeks passed, the U.S. commissioners worried that if the Spanish received nothing, they would refuse to sign any treaty. The Spanish might return to Madrid, thereby allowing a state of war to continue indefinitely. Unofficially, Reid hinted to the Spanish that if they accepted the U.S. refusal of the Cuban debt, the United States might financially compensate Spain in a Philippine settlement. The commissioners later recommended to Washington that the United States pay as much as $20 million for Spanish public improvements in the islands, which they believed would be a sufficient sum of money to satisfy Madrid.

During the final weeks of the conference the U.S. government expressed an interest in acquiring Kusaie, an island in the Spanish-owned Caroline Islands, which might serve as a cable station. The Spanish rejected this proposal. The United States agreed that Spanish citizens in annexed territories would have the right to elect U.S. citizenship. In the Philippines, the United States provided preferential tariff rights to Spanish subjects for 10 years, but it did not extend these to Puerto Rico.

The final treaty provided for Spain's cession of Puerto Rico, Guam, and the Philippines to the United States. Spain gave up sovereignty over Cuba, and it accepted $20 million in compensation.

McKinley still had to steer the Treaty of Paris through the Senate. Although the November 1898 election had increased the Republican membership, a lame-duck Senate would consider the treaty, and in that body Republicans filled only 50 of 90 seats. This was insufficient to provide a two-thirds majority. Moreover, several Republicans disapproved of the treaty. But Democrats and Populists were also divided. At the start of the debate, it appeared that a majority of the Senate favored the treaty, but not two-thirds.

McKinley directed the campaign to win Senate approval. He toured the South, emphasizing to Democrats the new national unity that had come with the successful war. He pressured several reluctant Republicans to support the party. He also used patronage to gain needed votes.

Opponents of the treaty were unable to hold their loose coalition together. William Jennings Bryan advised Democrats to vote for the treaty in order to end the war. On the eve of the Senate vote, fighting broke out between Aguinaldo's forces and U.S. troops. Apparently, this last-minute event did not alter any Senate votes. When votes were finally counted, the senators approved the treaty by one vote more than two-thirds; it was a political triumph for the president.

Thus, President McKinley successfully concluded the most popular war in U.S. history. He had defined the causes of U.S. entry into the war, brought it to an early conclusion, and determined the settlement. In broader terms, McKinley had changed the scope of U.S. foreign relations as the nation entered the 20th century.

John L. Offner

REFERENCES

Lewis L. Gould, *The Spanish-American War and President McKinley* (Univ. of Kansas Pr., 1980); Margaret Leech, *In the Days of McKinley* (Harper, 1959); Ernest R. May, *Imperial Democracy: The Emergence of America as a Great Power* (Harcourt, 1961); John Offner, "The United States and France: Ending the Spanish-American War," 7 (1983), 1–21; David F. Trask, *The War With Spain in 1898* (Macmillan, 1981).

See also Congress and the Spanish-Cuban/American War; Teller Amendment (1898); Turpie-Foraker Amendment (1898).

Magoon, Charles Edward (1861–1920)

Little did Charles Edward Magoon realize in 1899 that his position in the United States War Department would result in his appointment as provisional governor of Cuba in 1906 during the second U.S. intervention. Three factors were responsible for this intervention: the Platt Amendment, the presidency of Tomás Estrada Palma, and Cuban law. During the first intervention (1899–1902) following the Spanish-Cuban/American War, plans and procedures were put in motion to prepare the Cubans for independence and self-government and to clarify Cuba's future relations with the United States. In November 1900, under orders of the U.S. military governor, a convention was convened to frame and adopt a Cuban constitution that would provide the legal foundation for the transfer of government to the Cuban people and to establish a continuing relationship with the United States. Meanwhile, the United States Congress enacted the Platt Amendment to the 1901 army appropriations bill which authorized the president to agree to self-rule for Cuba as soon as the Cubans established a government under a constitution that included the right of the United States to intervene. Consequently, the Platt Amendment became the constitutional law of Cuba and part of the permanent treaty of 1903.

In February 1902, the electoral college met and, without opposition, selected Estrada Palma as the first president of the Republic of Cuba. Estrada Palma attempted to give his nation a nonpartisan administration. For the first few years everything seemed to fall into place, and the United States did not intervene. In fact, President Theodore Roosevelt was pleased with the apparent progress the nation was making in self-government. However, internal forces were at work that would overturn Estrada Palma's ideals of liberty with law and order and would bring about a second intervention. In spite of his nonpartisan position, the Cuban Congress was divided between the Moderate and Liberal factions. This situation prevented the enactment of laws required to make the Cuban Constitution effective. The Moderates wanted to make Estrada Palma a partisan in order to increase their political power through patronage, and Estrada Palma, failing to secure the legislation that he wanted, decided to cast his lot with them. He replaced his cabinet with Moderates, and that faction began to support his administration.

In 1905 Estrada Palma decided to run for a second term and allowed himself to be nominated by the Moderates. In addition, 50 percent of the House and Senate seats were to be selected, and all six provinces were to elect governors. Much was at stake, and the Moderates and the Liberals prepared to do political battle. Estrada Palma and the Moderates controlled the police, the Guardia Rural (Rural Guard), and the municipal alcaldes, and pressure was extended to ensure victory in December 1905. He ousted the Liberal officials in 20 municipalities. In September preliminary elections were held with the aid of the government's Guardia Rural and police, which resulted in fraud and violence. The situation worsened in October when thousands of fictitious names were added to the registration rolls by the election boards controlled by the Moderates. In protest, the Liberals withdrew from the final elections in December. Estrada Palma was unanimously reelected president, and not a single Liberal candidate won an election across the island.

Thwarted at the polls, the Liberals resorted to armed rebellion, and following the December election, discontent became widespread. In April 1906, at the opening of Congress the Liberals remaining in that body presented a resolution to declare the 1905 elections illegal and void. When that failed, they walked out. Discontent among the populace continued throughout the spring and summer and erupted in open rebellion in August 1906. The Liberals wanted the elections of 1905 declared void and the ousted municipal officials and government employees restored, but Estrada Palma refused to compromise. Instead, he issued a decree calling Congress into special session, suspending the Constitution, and ordering the arrest of all Liberal leaders not in custody. This action by Estrada Palma invoked Article III of the Platt Amendment, which provided that the United States could intervene to protect Cuban independence and to maintain a government adequate for the protection of life, property, and individual liberty.

The Moderates preferred intervention to civil war and government by the United States to Liberal control. However, Roosevelt was slow to act until the rebellion had increased to a degree that the Cuban government was no longer able to prevent the destruction of lives and property. Estrada Palma asked for intervention and U.S. troops to protect the capital, and he threatened to resign in order to force intervention unless the Liberals laid down their arms. Roosevelt, hoping to find a solution short of full-scale intervention, dispatched the Taft-Bacon Peace Commission. The commission was soon convinced that the 1905 elections were fraudulent, and it was willing to support compromise proposals of the Liberals, but Estrada Palma refused to compromise for the sake of political expediency. If he could not restore order and avoid civil war, it was only natural for him to resign and turn the government over to the United States.

On 28 September 1906, Estrada Palma convened Congress to submit his resignation and those of the vice president and his cabinet. The Moderate members, in order to avoid responsibility, asked Estrada Palma to reconsider. He refused, and the Moderates in turn refused to attend another meeting to select a new president. Since a quorum could not be obtained, Cuba was without a government. The peace commissioners took charge, and with Roosevelt's approval Secretary of War William H. Taft proclaimed himself provisional governor of Cuba.

From all outward appearances, the second intervention (1906–1909) was to be a civil operation. The Army of Cuban Pacification consisted of 6,000 U.S. troops stationed at some 27 posts around the country. Their major responsibility was to bolster confidence in the provisional government and to assist in keeping law and order. Once order was restored, the troops devoted much of their time to revising maps of Cuba and making topographical surveys of the various provinces. The medical corps provided valuable service in the area of sanitation.

The greater part of Taft's time during his short tenure as governor of Cuba was devoted to disarming the rebels and to discharging the militia. Because Taft was needed in Washington to look after his duties as secretary of war, Roosevelt sent a civilian commissioner, Charles E. Magoon, to administer the government in Cuba. Magoon's background and experience prepared him for the task at hand. He had been a successful lawyer before entering public service as a law officer of the Bureau of Insular Affairs in the War Department. In 1904, the 43-year-old Minnesota native was sent to Panama as general counsel of the Isthmian Canal Commission and soon became a member. This led to his appointment in a dual capacity as minister and governor of Panama. His knowledge of the Spanish colonial legal system and his experience in Panama qualified him for the post of provisional governor of Cuba.

Upon his arrival in Cuba, Magoon made it clear that the United States was administering Cuba for the Cubans. That is, Cuba was to continue to be a sovereign state. As provisional governor he would rule by decree, and his power was limited only by his sound discretion and instructions from Washington. All provisions of the Cuban Constitution and laws that were inconsistent with the power claimed and exercised by the United States under the Platt Amendment were suspended. Magoon was to draw up electoral and municipal laws, to hold fair elections, and to leave as soon as the new government was in place.

It was apparent that it would take time to establish a new government. Meanwhile, Magoon had to govern Cuba. Because the principal cause of the revolution was the interference by the Palma government with the municipalities, the provisional governor proceeded to identify towns where there had been illegal interference by the Moderates, and Liberal governments were reestablished. Another political problem was the demand by the Liberals that they be appointed to governmental positions. A committee of leading Liberals was established to qualify persons to fill the vacancies when they occurred until equality was restored between the Moderates and the Liberals. However, that did not entirely solve the patronage question because the Liberals insisted that every job opening be filled with a member of their group. The problem was made more difficult when the Liberals split into two factions, and each sought favors from Magoon. Later, during the second intervention, a strong moderate party was organized, forcing the Liberals to unite to win the elections of 1908.

In addition to restoring a government, Magoon and his administration had to deal with natural forces and an economic depression. The provisional governor had hardly assumed office when a hurricane swept over the island. Damage to the crops and property was extensive, adding to the woes of a prolonged drought in 1906. The August 1906 revolution had increased the economic dislocation of Cuba by destroying crops and causing foreign and domestic capital to dry up. Then came the Panic of 1907 in the United States, which resulted in a drastic decline in the value of sugar and allied industries. It was in the face of these economic conditions, which continued throughout his administration, that Magoon took charge of Cuba to restore political stability.

There were several issues that had to be considered before the provisional governor could concentrate on his major mission. It was essential that law and order be maintained. Consequently, Magoon ordered that all weapons turned in by the rebels be dumped at sea. The Guardia Rural was reorganized by the United States Army. All political activity was prohibited, and promotion was based only on merit, not influence. As a result, the countryside was pacified, and the Guardia soon regained the confidence and good will of the Cuban people.

Another issue was the many foreign and domestic claims for damages against the government because of the August revolution. They were eventually settled satisfactorily by a claims commission appointed by Magoon. He also carried out Taft's decree that provided for congress to remain in recess until tranquility and public confidence were fully restored. Elections would then be held giving effect to the establishment of the provisional government.

Other issues that Magoon faced were the spread of yellow fever, sanitation, the agricultural economy, and the national deficit. One of the first decrees he issued concerned the need to bring yellow fever under control and to eradicate its source. To expand the sanitation project he issued a decree nationalizing the sanitation service of Cuba. The National Board of Sanitation was created, which appointed officers for each municipality. Another agency that rendered excellent service under the provisional administration was the Advisory Commission of Agriculturalists. The commission was established to make practical suggestions to the government concerning the two principal cash crops—coffee and sugar—during periods of economic stress. When Magoon took office, the national treasury was running a deficit. Fortunately, the estimate of expected revenue proved to be wrong, and for a while the treasury was running a surplus due to increased receipts from various sources and the economy enforced by the provisional governor.

The most important act of the provisional government was the appointment of the Advisory Law Commission. It was composed of nine Cubans and three U.S. citizens, one of whom was Col. Enoch H. Crowder of the United States Army. Crowder who, at that time, was advisor to the acting secretary of state and justice and legal advisor to Magoon, was designated president of the commission. The commission grew out of the plan approved by the peace commissioners for the enactment of four laws requested by the Liberals to correct the political abuses that led to the August revolution and the second intervention of the United States under the Platt Amendment. However, as the commission proceeded to draft the four laws—a municipal law, an electoral law, a law to reorganize the judiciary, and a civil service law—it became obvious that all Cuban law required revision and codification. Cuban law was a mixture of Spanish laws, amended at various times by royal orders and decrees, overlaid with orders and decrees of the U.S. military government, the Cuban Constitution, laws enacted by the Cuban Congress, and the decrees of the provisional governor. The Cuban Congress had failed to pass the necessary legislation to give effect to the Liberal decentralizing constitution of 1902.

Other laws prepared by the commission were the law of the executive power; laws of the armed forces, including provisions relating to military crimes and procedures; and a game law. Several laws drafted were not promulgated by Magoon but were submitted to the newly elected Cuban Congress for consideration. The work of the commission extended beyond writing laws. Acting as an advisory body to Magoon and the executive departments, the commission drafted decrees dealing with a variety of subjects, such as port regulations, education, and tariffs.

Magoon and his administration did not limit their activity to writing laws and holding elections. When he arrived in Cuba the economy was in disarray, agriculture was in ruin, and industry and commerce were damaged. Inflation was rising rapidly, and the margin of profit in sugar production was declining. Lack of money and credit was creating high interest rates, and the working class was suffering from low wages and unemployment. Realizing the relationship between economic prosperity and political stability, Magoon initiated a general program of improvements in transportation, communications, health and sanitation, and public works as well as reforms in custom house regulations, in money and banking, and in primary and higher education.

At the outset, the Roosevelt administration anticipated a brief intervention. However, more time was needed to draft additional laws and to take a census before elections could be scheduled. By spring 1908 much of this work was completed. In May, Magoon issued a proclamation providing for municipal and provincial elections to be held 1 August 1908, and in August he selected 14 November 1908 as the date for the congressional and presidential elections. Cuban politicians had not been waiting for the dates of the elections to be announced. Candidates and Cuban voters were anxious to test the new electoral laws. By mid-1907 a Conservative party was organized to challenge the Liberals and as the elections approached, the new Independent Party of Color emerged.

The elections of 1908 were carried out in accordance with the new laws. Colonel Crowder was in charge of the central election board. Every precaution was taken to guarantee an honest registration list and fair elections. In the municipal and provincial elections all seats were contested. The elections were conducted in an orderly fashion, and the results were accepted by all parties.

Following these elections, both parties began to gear up for the general elections in November. The Conservatives nominated Gen. Mario García Menocal as their presidential candidate, and the Liberals who had won a majority of the votes in the local elections decided to bury their differences and support Gen. José Miguel Gómez. A heated fall campaign ensued. The outcome favored the Liberals. They won a majority of presidential and vice presidential electors in all provinces and won control of the upper and lower houses.

With the successful conclusion of the elections, the promise to restore Cuban self-government was kept. On 28 January 1909, the birthday of José Julían Martí y Perez, one of the major leaders of the Cuban independence movement, the second intervention and Magoon's term as provisional governor of Cuba ended. Even before Magoon left the island, evaluations were being made as to the success or failure of the provisional government. The major complaints centered around the governmental deficit, favoritism with regard to U.S. contractors, discrimination in patronage and awarding of sinecures, excessive granting of pardons, and following policies of compromise.

It is true that Magoon's administration created a significant governmental debt; however, considering all of the necessary expenditures and the condition of the Cuban economy, the financial affairs were well managed. Magoon was accused by his critics of improprieties related to a Cuban bond issue with a U.S. company, but there was no evidence to support the charges. Regarding patronage, the system of appointments did result in some dishonesty and inefficiency, but the responsibility must be shared by Cuban party bosses and national leaders who advised the provisional governor and sought positions for themselves and their friends. Magoon felt it necessary to award sinecures to get the revolutionaries and the undesirables out of the country. There is justification for the criticism that Magoon was too generous with his pardoning power. However, there is no evidence that pardons were sold, and Cuban leaders who recommended clemency must share responsibility along with the United States. After all, Magoon was placed in the difficult position of administering a civil government satisfactory to both the Cubans and Washington, based on Washington's policy of temporization and compromise; passing judgment on his record is very difficult, if not impossible.

Thomas E. Gay, Jr.

REFERENCES

Charles E. Chapman, *A History of the Cuban Republic* (Macmillan, 1927); Russell H. Fitzgibbon, *Cuba and the United States, 1900–1935* (Russell & Russell, 1964); Leland Jenks, *Our Cuban Colony* (Vanguard Pr., 1928); David A. Lockmiller, *Magoon in Cuba: A History of the Second Intervention* (Univ. of North Carolina Pr., 1938); Hugh Thomas, *Cuba, the Pursuit of Freedom* (Harper, 1971).

See also Cuba, Intervention (1906–1909); Public Works in Cuba (1906–1909).

Mahan, Alfred Thayer (1840–1914)

Before the Spanish-Cuban/American War Alfred Thayer Mahan called for a strong navy. The United States Navy was so weak, Mahan charged, that it could be defeated by even the navy of Chile. A small, but growing, group of influential people in the United States listened and responded.

At age 16 Mahan, the son of a professor at the United States Military Academy, received an appointment to the United States Naval Academy at Annapolis. He graduated in 1859, second in his class. During the Civil War the ship to which he was assigned helped blockade the coast of the South.

In 1875 Mahan joined others in calling for a stronger, more modern navy. The United States Navy consisted entirely of ships dating from the Civil War. The first three modern steel ships were authorized by Congress in 1883. By then Commander Mahan was calling privately for a United States Navy second to none.

The same year, he published a small book on naval operations in the Civil War. It established his credentials as a naval historian and led to his appointment to the faculty of the new Naval War College at Newport, Rhode Island. Its founder, Stephen B. Luce, wanted a graduate school for the study of the science of war. Mahan's lectures there became the basis of his most significant work, *The Influence of Sea Power upon History,*

1660–1783, published in 1890. By that time Luce, ordered to sea, had chosen Mahan as his successor as president of the college.

In his first important book, Mahan found principles and lessons in his study of sea history that could be applied to war in the future. His thesis was simple: that international influence and power rested on naval power. Wars in the 17th and 18th centuries were fought to control the seas and trade and to secure the enemy's colonies. Naval power was based on the absence of land enemies, a long coast with good harbors, bases and colonies, and a seagoing population that was materially acquisitive and had an aptitude for commerce. The outstanding example of such a nation was Great Britain. It was a world power because it had the largest and strongest navy. Sea power and world power were synonymous.

How did a book of theory, backed by numerous historical examples, chiefly from before the American Revolution, apply to the United States? The United States, Mahan declared, had to look outward. It needed to join the race for empire or fall behind other nations. Nations rose or fell according to their ability to wage war, especially at sea. The United States had all the prerequisites for becoming a great sea power. What the country needed was colonies and bases in the Caribbean, a large fleet, an extensive foreign trade, a canal in Central America, and markets in China, a country too rich in goods to be dominated by Europe alone.

The book was not a best seller. The ideas were not original. Most of the book was too military for the U.S. public, and many people probably never read beyond the introduction, an essay which he had added at the last moment to make his book more popular. Yet the book was highly influential. Mahan sent complimentary copies to important naval and political leaders in Great Britain and the United States, including Senator Henry Cabot Lodge, soon a major supporter of Mahan and the Naval War College. Theodore Roosevelt enthusiastically reviewed the book in the *Atlantic Monthly*, adding his own call for a large fleet of U.S. battleships and cruisers. The book called attention not only to the author but, more important, to the lack of a substantial United States Navy. It represented a major attack on U.S. isolationism.

The book also called attention to the struggling Naval War College. In 1886 there were only 21 students. Funds were so short that classes had to be held in Mahan's home, his family leaving as the students arrived. Critics within the navy called for a more practical, technical curriculum, forcing Mahan to lobby for congressional support. A Republican Congress authorized the building of a new Naval War College, where Mahan was soon working on a contingency plan in case of war with Spain.

Mahan's book had more immediate impact on the naval powers abroad than on U.S. opinion. The British feted and dined him. They cited his book in Parliament as they argued for a stronger British navy. Cambridge and Oxford awarded Mahan honorary degrees in the same week. Queen Victoria invited him to a dinner in honor of the German Kaiser, who ordered that copies of his book be put on all ships in the German navy. The Japanese, busily building their navy, were also enthusiastic. Copies were distributed to governmental leaders, the officer corps, and military schools.

In 1890 the *Atlantic Monthly* published "The United States Looking Outward," Mahan's first popular article on an expansionist, imperialist theme. The United States, Mahan contended, must look outward, compete vigorously in overseas trade, cooperate (but not ally itself) with Great Britain, find coaling stations abroad, and build a large fleet to defend its national interests in Hawaii, Samoa, and Central America. It was time to abandon its inward-looking isolation and military weakness, time to seek its rightful place as a world power. Doing so would bring the nation security and prosperity.

Article followed article. Mahan's retirement from the navy in 1896 gave him more time for writing. He called for U.S. annexation of Hawaii as necessary for national defense, but the new Democratic president, Grover Cleveland, withdrew the annexation treaty then before Congress. Mahan called repeatedly for a navy ready for war, for overseas bases, and for penetration of the Caribbean area, the United States's proper sphere of influence. U.S. influence there was needed to protect the Central American canal, which in turn would become the key to commercial expansion into the Pacific.

In an article published in December 1897 Mahan pointed out that all other governments followed their national interests in foreign policy. The United States likewise had to promote its own national interests or lose out. The United States would get more and more involved internationally. He wrote of the historical probability and moral necessity of war.

Mahan's influence peaked just before the Spanish-Cuban/American War. Expansionists had never been more active or outspoken. Washington social life was then led by the wives of such senators as Henry Cabot Lodge, in whose home expansionists gathered regularly. Theodore Roosevelt, assistant secretary of the navy, lunched regularly with Lodge. The ideas of Mahan were often discussed. U.S. leaders found the ideas of Mahan exciting and demanded a stronger navy and a U.S. canal. They would soon get both as well as a war with Spain. The Spanish-Cuban/American War transformed Mahan, the military historian, into a successful prophet. It gave the United States a strong navy, an empire with possessions in the Caribbean and Pacific, and an overseas trade which in 1900 boasted $1.4 billion in exports.

Ironically, Mahan did not support intervention in Cuba, not even after the battleship *Maine* exploded. He did not join such interventionists as Lodge and Roosevelt and did not blame Spain for the explosion. He did advise the assistant secretary of the navy on contingency war plans against Spain, but did not expect war to come. Instead, he blithely left the United States with his family for a vacation in Italy.

Once war was declared, Mahan was ordered back to the United States to serve on the Naval War Board. To Mahan the U.S. conflict in the Caribbean was a "just war" as well as a way to get colonies. He applauded the annexation of Hawaii and supported efforts to get coaling stations in Asia.

At first, Mahan was not interested in securing the Philippines. A coaling station there, at least at Subic Bay, would be sufficient. War against the Philippine people, however, persuaded Mahan that the United States had a Christian duty to take all of the Philippines, useful as stepping stones to the vital markets of China.

The Spanish-Cuban/American War gave Mahan numerous opportunities for more articles. Altogether he authored 20 books and 137 articles. He justified the taking of Guam from the Spanish as necessary to protect U.S. interests in China. He pointed out that during the war it had taken the battleship *Oregon* two months to reach the Caribbean from Puget Sound. The canal in Panama was begun a few years later by his friend Roosevelt. Mahan urged President William McKinley to purchase St. Thomas in the Danish West Indies from Denmark before an unfriendly European power got it. McKinley tried to do so, but Congress would not approve the purchase of the Danish Virgin Islands until they seemed threatened in World War I. He supported John Hay's Open Door policy in China, warning the United States of Japan's expansionist aims. He predicted that the European alliance system would lead Europe into war and urged the United States to increase its navy to prevent Great Britain from being defeated by Germany. But the military historian died before he could see such predictions come true.

Mahan was a popularizer of ideas. Because people in positions of power listened and acted and because many in the United States supported his ideas, the United States Navy was the third strongest in the world as the 20th century began, and the United States was recognized as a world power.

Wilson E. Strand

REFERENCES

William E. Livezey, *Mahan on Sea Power* (Univ. of Oklahoma Pr., 1947); Alfred Thayer Mahan, *From Sail to Steam: Recollections of Naval Life* (Harper, 1907); Alfred Thayer Mahan, *The Influence of Sea Power Upon History, 1660–1783* (Little, Brown, 1890); Robert Seager, *Alfred Thayer Mahan: The Man and His Letters* (U.S. Naval Institute Pr., 1977).

See also Naval Operations in the Spanish-Cuban/ American War (1898); Naval War Board (1898).

Maine, **Battleship, Sinking (1898)**

Under President Grover Cleveland (1893–1897), warship calls to Spanish ports had been suspended, and winter exercises of the U.S. North Atlantic Squadron had been held in the cold North Atlantic. Cleveland's objective was to not exacerbate relations with Spain over the latter's attempt to curb the Cuban rebellion that began in 1895, while he sought to have Spain grant Cuba autonomy. Under President William McKinley, however, on 17 January 1898 three large warships (i.e., the second-class battleships *Texas* and *Maine*, and the heavy cruiser *New*

York) and several other ships converged on Key West, Florida, to hold winter exercises under much more favorable conditions in the Bay of Florida. The *Maine* had orders to make for Havana, Cuba, 90 miles away, if Consul General Fitzhugh Lee required its presence. Its captain, Charles D. Sigsbee, hoarded the bituminous coal taken aboard at Newport, Rhode Island, even though it was susceptible to spontaneous combustion, because it was better than the anthracite available in Key West.

On 12 January 1898 mobs, including Spanish army officers, attacked the offices of three Havana newspapers that supported Cuban autonomy. On the 24th, McKinley replied to a request from Lee for help in protecting U.S. lives and property by sending the *Maine*. His clearing the visit with Madrid made it apparent that the ship was being sent merely as a mark of friendship and international courtesy. With quiet restored in Havana, Lee sought to delay the *Maine*'s arrival, but McKinley took a calculated risk that no untoward incident regarding the ship at the hands of either the Spanish or rebellious Cubans would occur. Spain reciprocated by sending a ship to call at U.S. ports.

Sigsbee was given a warm official reception when he reached Havana on the 25th, and Lee was so happy that he wished the *Maine* or an even more powerful ship could be based there permanently. With protective booms out, riflemen patrolling its decks to guard against sabotage, and no health problems (the greatest danger was from yellow fever), Sigsbee noted nothing extraordinary for almost a month while he and his officers—he denied his men liberty—exchanged courtesy visits with Spanish officers. At 9:40 p.m. on 15 February, however, while sitting at his desk in his cabin he was thrown up to the overhead when his ship exploded. Lost were 266 officers and enlisted men.

The *Maine* rested on the bottom with its stern superstructure above water. Its amidships was a mass of tangled wreckage. Nothing in the forward third of it was above water. If it had been destroyed by accident or by its crew, how could Sigsbee explain? Had it been destroyed by deliberate act by treacherous, hostile hands? By Spaniards? By rebellious Cubans? No matter, vengeance was demanded by an aroused U.S. public and an excited Congress. Congress, although dominated in both houses by Republicans, was divided on the issue of going to war with Spain.

While the Navy Department said the cause of the explosion was unknown, and high officials in both Spain and Cuba sent condolences, Sigsbee said that he had no information about the cause of the explosion and asked that public opinion be suspended until an inquiry was made. Rear Adm. Montgomery Sicard, commanding the North Atlantic Squadron, ordered Capt. French E. Chadwick to take his ship, the *New York*, to Key West, where he would be in telegraphic communication with the Navy Department and by cable with Havana. Chadwick carried clothing for the *Maine*'s survivors and forwarded diving equipment. On 19 February Sicard appointed a board of three officers, all from the *New York*, to inquire into the disaster. When the Navy Department overruled him, the board was headed by an ordnance expert, Capt. William Thomas Sampson, commanding the *Iowa*. In addition there were Chadwick, a former chief of the Bureau of Equipment, hence familiar with coal; and William P. Potter, the executive officer of the *New York*. Lt. Cmdr. Adolph Marix, a former executive officer of the *Maine*, hence familiar with its construction, served as judge advocate general. Ens. Wilfred Van Nest Powelson, who had transferred from naval architect duty to the line, was in charge of diving operations. There was also a stenographer. Spain conducted its own investigation, for which the United States provided assistance. After a hasty examination of the ship, a preliminary report by Spanish officials held an internal explosion responsible.

The Sampson board sat for a week beginning 21 February in private sessions in a lighthouse tender in Havana harbor. Four possibilities for the explosion were considered: internal accident, internal deliberate act, external accident, and external deliberate act. Sigsbee and his officers assured the court that proper procedure had been followed in taking the temperatures of the magazines and bunkers, disposing of ashes, and stowing paints. Since the keys to the forward magazine were in Sigsbee's cabin, no one could have entered it. But what external force could have caused the explosion? A mine? For the next two weeks the board interviewed *Maine* survivors in the hospital to which they had been taken in Key West, then returned to Havana harbor.

Under oath, no crewman of the *Maine* said that he had any complaint against any officer or man on their ship on the night of its destruction. Had his ship been destroyed by accident or internal explosion, Sigsbee was responsible but war with Spain could be averted. Had it been destroyed by an external force, however, war was probable. Had a Spaniard destroyed the ship to ensure that war would come? Had a rebellious Cuban done so and hoped that the finger would point to a Spaniard? U.S. ordnance experts and divers reported that an explosion forced the *Maine*'s hull plates inboard and upward; Spanish divers said outboard. In sum, U.S. inquiries pointed to an external force that had exploded the magazines, which had then bent its hull planes outboard. Spaniards disagreed and in addition noted that a geyser of water would have shot up if the explosion had been an external one, there were no dead fish near the wreck, no one had had an opportunity to place a mine near the ship, and it was astonishing that the *Maine*'s magazines had been placed so close to its coal bunkers.

After avidly searching for 23 days for evidence of the cause of the destruction of the *Maine*, the Sampson board concluded unanimously on 21 March that two explosions had occurred; the conclusion naturally fanned the flames for war. Assistant Secretary of the Navy Theodore Roosevelt spoke of "an act of dirty treachery." Fitzhugh Lee thought that perhaps a mine planted near the *Maine* had struck it and exploded its magazines. If so, the most that could be charged against Spain was that it had been negligent in protecting the ship and that Spain should make reparation.

Secretary of the Navy John D. Long, however, cleared Spain of any responsibility.

The report that reached the White House on 25 March exonerated Sigsbee and his officers from fault or negligence, found no evidence of a conspiracy on the part of Spaniards, and found no proof that a mine had ever been laid in Havana harbor. It held no person or persons responsible. When the report was given to Congress and published, however, the U.S. public interpreted it to mean that Spain was guilty of premeditated massacre and destruction. Congress spurned McKinley's invitation to give the report "deliberate consideration" and demanded intervention to free Cuba. When several ordnance experts and Sigsbee told the Senate Foreign Relations Committee that a mine had caused the *Maine*'s explosion, they further stimulated the demand for war.

After hoping to avoid, or at least defer, a war for which his nation was unprepared, on 11 April McKinley delivered a war message to Congress that did not mention the *Maine*. While he disassociated the ship from the Cuban problem and asked that Spain merely do what justice and honor required in the instance, at his request, as a "peace measure," Congress swiftly provided $50 million "for the national defense," and Secretary Long quietly began to prepare his navy for war. Congress approved a war resolution on the 25th, making it retroactive to the 21st, when McKinley had ordered Cuba blockaded.

Almost immediately following the war, Sigsbee reverted to his belief that a mine had exploded the *Maine*'s magazines and held that Spain had been responsible for the safety of visiting ships. He was contradicted by those who mentioned two explosions, one by spontaneous combustion in its coal bunkers, the second in its magazines. The thought was also expressed that Spain, which did not want war, would not have planted a mine. Chadwick had seen Spanish ships in the Battle of Santiago driven ashore in flames. When their magazines exploded, they blew out the sides of their ships but did not drive their bottoms upward. Would not raising and inspecting the wreck provide some answers?

In 1911 Congress appropriated funds to remove the *Maine* from Havana harbor but did not call for an investigation. Cuba gave permission and promised support, but Spain was uninterested. After a cofferdam was erected and much of the wreckage was exposed, a new U.S. board of inspection examined it. What was left of the ship was towed four miles off Cuba's coast and sunk in 600 fathoms of water. Meanwhile, the board placed the area of the explosion much further aft than originally thought and concluded that an explosion had been caused by gasses created by black and brown gunpowder which had then caused the magazines to blow up. No credence was placed in a primary external force such as a mine. Still other investigations led to the proper conclusion about the destruction of the *Maine*; spontaneous combustion in its coal bunkers caused black and brown gunpowder to explode and ignite the nearby six-inch reserve magazine and 10-inch magazine.

Paolo E. Coletta

REFERENCES

French Ensor Chadwick, *The Relations of the United States and Spain: The Spanish-American War* (Scribner, 1911), 2 vols.; Margaret Leech, *In the Days of McKinley* (Harper, 1959); John D. Long, *The New American Navy* (Outlook, 1903), 2 vols.; Hyman G. Rickover, *How the Maine Was Destroyed* (Naval History Division, Department of the Navy, 1976); David F. Trask, *The War With Spain in 1898* (Macmillan, 1981).

See also Sigsbee, Charles Dwight.

Malolos, The Philippines, Battle (1899)

On 21 January 1899, the town of Malolos, 25 miles north of Manila on the island of Luzon, the Philippines, became the first capital of the Philippine Republic. Two weeks later, on 4 February, the Philippine War began. On 31 March Malolos was occupied by U.S. troops and was garrisoned by U.S. forces for the rest of the war. The events leading to the capture of Malolos illustrate the strengths and weaknesses of the U.S. and Filipino military efforts during the 11 months of conventional fighting that ended in December 1899.

Spain first occupied the Philippines in 1565. Its hold over the islands was not seriously threatened until 1892, when a secret society, the Katipunan, began to agitate against Spanish authority and for a redistribution of the landholdings of the Catholic Church. Propagandists for this movement were the *ilustrados*, Filipino intellectuals, influenced by European liberal and nationalist thought.

In 1896 an armed revolt broke out in Cavite Province south of Manila, and a young man named Emilio Aguinaldo y Famy rose to a commanding position within its ranks. Suppressed with difficulty by Spanish forces, the revolt was still smoldering in April 1898 when the United States and Spain went to war over Spain's actions in another of its island possessions, Cuba.

The first U.S. forces in the Philippines were a landing party of sailors and marines that secured the Cavite naval station on 2 May 1898, the day after Commodore George Dewey's destruction of the Spanish fleet in the Battle of Manila Bay. On 4 May, President William McKinley directed the formation of a U.S. expedition to occupy Manila and to strengthen his bargaining position in future peace negotiations with Spain.

Because the bulk of the regular army had been committed to the invasions of Cuba and Puerto Rico, the expedition was formed around 15 state volunteer regiments mobilized at the Presidio of San Francisco. The first of these troops did not arrive in the Philippines until early July, however, and in the interim Filipino revolutionaries had risen and laid siege to Manila's Spanish garrison. Revolutionary leaders had hoped to present the United States with a *fait accompli*: a Philippine Republic with broad popular support governing in the former colonial power's capital. While they quickly established their authority in the more remote areas of the Philippines, at Manila they were frustrated by Spanish resistance. U.S. troops moved into the siege line around the city in late July.

From the first, relations between U.S. officers and Filipino leaders were strained by U.S. doubts that non-Europeans were capable of self-government and Filipino suspicions that the United States would annex the islands. These suspicions were fueled by an agreement reached in August between U.S. and Spanish officials in which Manila's garrison surrendered under terms that excluded Filipinos from any role in the city's occupation or its subsequent government.

While the Filipino army remained in its siege works, the leaders of the Philippine Republic pressed the United States to recognize Philippine independence. However, President McKinley had already decided on annexation, and in December 1898 Spain ceded the islands to the United States under the terms of the Treaty of Paris. When word of the treaty reached Manila, relations between Filipino and U.S. forces rapidly deteriorated. A large Filipino force at this point surrounded Manila, faced by 11,000 U.S. state troops and three regular infantry regiments supported by artillery and river gunboats.

On 4 February 1899, firing broke out between U.S. troops and Filipinos in Santa Mesa, a suburb of Manila, and quickly spread to all sectors of the U.S. outpost line north and south of the Pasig River. By the 10th, the Republican Army had been driven in retreat up the Manila-Dagupan railway toward Malolos.

Scholars are divided over whether the February fighting resulted from a gradual buildup of tensions or was provoked by the army's senior commander in the Philippines, Maj. Gen. Elwell S. Otis. Equally disputed is the timing of McKinley's decision in favor of annexation, as opposed to the option of protectorate status with internal autonomy. In a larger sense, however, the war was a direct result of that decision, which was opposed not only by Filipino revolutionaries but also by the islands' landholding elite, the *principales*. On 6 February the United States Senate ratified the Treaty of Paris, and the United States was committed to a war of uncertain duration.

In the early fighting several state regiments had become disorganized after attacking past their objectives. The need to reassemble these units and later to suppress a rising of the Filipino militia, the Sandahatan, provided Otis with pretexts to wait for reinforcements before taking further action. By late February Manila was secured and by 25 March five more regular infantry regiments had arrived to strengthen a U.S. offensive in Bulacan Province toward Malolos. (The following account is based on Sexton, *Soldiers in the Sun*.)

Malolos's chief vulnerability was its nearness to Manila on Luzon's only north-south railway. U.S. troops were poorly conditioned for tropical campaigning and overly dependent on frequent resupply, so that any move north would have to use the railroad as a primary axis of advance. Thus, the army's chief limitation, its poor mobility across difficult terrain, did not hinder its march on Malolos.

The U.S. advance began on 25 March under Brig. Gen. Arthur MacArthur. From the outset, Filipino leaders in the area failed to cooperate, defending some towns along the railway line while abandoning others. The countryside north of Manila was cut by a number of small rivers running roughly northeast to southwest, each of which could have been exploited as a barrier, had its bridges been destroyed and its northern bank adequately defended. The rivers did not slow the U.S. advance, however. In several cases state volunteers improvised assault crossings under direct fire from Filipino positions, aided by the very low standard of marksmanship prevalent in the Republican Army.

On the morning of 31 March, Malolos was abandoned by Filipino troops and entered by a force of Nebraskans and Kansans led by Frederick Funston, colonel of the 20th Kansas. This victory was not, however, to be immediately exploited. Maj. Gen. Otis believed that his logistical base was still too narrow to support further movement away from Manila, and the monsoon would soon render the limited road network of central Luzon impassable to marching troops and the water buffalo carts used for transportation away from the railroad.

During the monsoon season U.S. forces corrected most of their deficiencies from the spring. Troops became better acclimated, and tactical columns were made more mobile. When fighting resumed in November the field army of the Philippine Republic was decisively defeated and driven into Luzon's mountainous north. In mid-November, Aguinaldo ordered Filipino forces to be restructured into a localized guerrilla force for an extended campaign against the U.S. occupation. The war that began in February 1899 did not finally end until spring 1902, after an increasingly harsh struggle that required over 120,000 U.S. troops and caused over a hundred thousand Filipino deaths from combat, hunger, and disease.

John Scott Reed

REFERENCES

Thomas F. Burdett, "A New Evaluation of General Otis' Leadership in the Philippines," *Military Review*, 55 (1975), 79–87; Frederick Funston, *Memories of Two Wars: Cuban and Philippine Experiences* (Scribner, 1911); Joseph I. Markey, *From Iowa to the Philippines* (Thomas D. Murphy Co., 1900); Lewis O. Saum, "The Western Volunteer and 'The New Empire,'" *Pacific Northwest Quarterly*, 57 (1966), 18–27; William T. Sexton, *Soldiers in the Sun: An Adventure in Imperialism* (Military Service Pub. Co., 1939).

Malvar, Miguél (1865–1911)

Miguél Malvar was the political and military governor of Batangas Province, Luzon, the Philippines, and succeeded Emilio Aguinaldo y Famy as leader of Filipino resistance from 12 April 1901 to 16 April 1902. Despite a prevalent U.S. myth that he was a bandit, Malvar's background, marriage, and financial success made him a member of the Batangas political and social elite. Although he had served as a civic official under the Spanish regime, he formed a guerrilla band during the anti-Spanish uprising of 1896 and joined Aguinaldo in January 1897. After unsuccessfully opposing peace with Spain, he went into exile with Aguinaldo, returning in June 1899 to organize his province's military forces. When U.S. forces occupied Batangas in January 1900, he

quickly dispersed his forces and began a highly effective guerrilla resistance.

Malvar's patriotism, tenacity, and intelligence, coupled with his organizational skills and his popular support, made him the most formidable guerrilla commander of the Philippine War. He selected competent civilian and military subordinates and thus retained far more control of the resistance than did most Filipino partisan leaders. Recognizing that the resistance would not survive without a sustained military presence, he endeavored to demonstrate the guerrillas' ability to strike at any time. Malvar sought less to defeat the United States Army than to convince it that U.S. occupation would require interminable warfare. He avoided pitched battles, launching military attacks only to achieve political or psychological objectives. He actively courted popular support, constantly exhorting the population of Batangas to unite against the United States. Those who collaborated were ruthlessly punished; some were assassinated in the very middle of U.S.-occupied towns. There is some evidence that, unlike most of the Filipino revolutionary leaders, he considered the war for independence a social as well as a political struggle; he promised that all patriots, regardless of social status, would benefit from victory. Until late in the war this mixture of exhortation and terrorism maintained his authority over the population and frustrated United States Army pacification efforts.

After the capture of Aguinaldo, Malvar rejected appeals by both Aguinaldo and many of his own guerrillas to capitulate. On 12 April 1901 he declared that he commanded all guerrillas in southern Luzon, and on 13 July he enlarged his authority to include all military forces in the Philippines. Although by 1901 he had fewer than 1,000 full-time guerrillas, Malvar estimated that with his 3,500 firearms, and an administrative and recruitment organization largely intact, he could continue fighting for another decade. This intransigence eventually prompted the most intense U.S. pacification campaign of the war. Between December 1901 and April 1902, Brig. Gen. J. Franklin Bell concentrated the population of Batangas into protected zones as some 7,500 U.S. troops, and thousands of Filipino volunteers hunted down Malvar's guerrillas. At the cost of much suffering, the revolutionary organization was smashed, and Malvar, his health broken, surrendered on 16 April 1902, effectively ending the Philippine War.

Brian McAllister Linn

REFERENCES

John M. Gates, *Schoolbooks and Krags: The U.S. Army in the Philippines, 1898–1902* (Greenwood Pr., 1973); Brian McAllister Linn, *The U.S. Army and Counterinsurgency in the Philippine War, 1899–1902* (Univ. of North Carolina Pr., 1989); Glenn Anthony May, *A Past Recovered* (New Day, 1987).

See also Luzon Campaigns, Philippine War.

Maneuver Division, United States Army

In 1910 revolution broke out in Mexico against the durable authoritarian regime of Gen. Porfirio Díaz, president from 1877 to 1880 and continuously since 1884. Relations between the United States and Díaz were cordial, and the aging dictator had welcomed U.S. investment in Mexico, which accounted for over half of all foreign investment by 1910. The 1910 revolution had been planned in the United States by Mexican exiles, most notably Francisco I. Madero, and most of the significant fighting was taking place in northern Mexico close to the U.S.-Mexican border. In particular, the town of Ciudad Juárez, Chihuahua—across the international boundary from El Paso, Texas—was a major target for the revolutionaries, who hoped that conquest of the city would help to finance their revolution and to aid in importing military supplies from the United States.

A major rebel attack on Juárez threatened lives and property on the U.S. side because it would be virtually impossible to contain the fighting. With revolutionary activity increasing, rebel forces under the leadership of Pascual Orozco were poised in February 1911 to attack Juárez. While the threatened attack did not occur, it encouraged U.S. officials to take more aggressive action to defend the border area; the result was the formation of the so-called Maneuver Division in March 1911.

The presidential administration of William H. Taft had been following a cautious policy in regard to Mexico, particularly trying to avoid any situation that might lead to military intervention. While the creation of the Maneuver Division was seen by many as a prelude to intervention, Taft's intention in forming it was to avoid intervention by influencing both the Mexican revolutionaries and the federal forces under Díaz to restrain their activities. The official explanation for the creation of the division was that it was to provide "field training" for officers and men. Later, federal officials also said that the division would be used to enforce federal neutrality laws along the border. The organization of the division meant a major redeployment of forces along the border; the total number of troops assigned to the division was about 20,000 men, a figure representing approximately one-fourth of the United States Army. Headquarters for the division were at Fort Sam Houston in San Antonio, Texas.

Taft privately admitted that the creation of the division was, in fact, a pre-positioning of troops for possible intervention in Mexico to protect U.S. lives and property. He still hoped, however, that the presence of the division would be a deterrent to the various Mexican factions, thus helping the United States avoid intervention. Taft also hoped that the creation of the division might silence the domestic critics of his Mexican policy who accused him of inaction.

Despite the formation of the division, there was no change in the orders governing military operations along the border. U.S. forces were still specifically prohibited from crossing the border without prior approval from Washington, regardless of the provocation. A further factor was Taft's personal view that he did not have the authority to send troops across the border without congressional authorization, something Taft was extremely reluctant to seek.

The division failed to have the desired deterrent effect on the Mexican revolutionaries. A rebel attack on Agua Prieta, Sonora, in April 1911 resulted in two persons killed and 11 wounded in the neighboring U.S. town of Douglas, Arizona. The long-expected attack on Juárez occurred in May, with casualties in El Paso of six killed and 15 wounded.

While the division had failed as a deterrent, it was soon dismantled rather than used to intervene in Mexico. The rebel victory at Juárez led to the resignation of Porfirio Díaz in late May 1911, ushering in a brief period of calm along the border. Taft took the opportunity to begin the dismantling of the division in July; in early August the War Department ordered that all units of the division that had not returned to their regular posts be permanently transferred to the United States Army's Department of Texas. The expanded army forces were soon needed as other threats to border security developed.

The Maneuver Division had succeeded in its original officially stated purpose of providing field training for the regular army; it was in fact the largest peacetime army maneuver to that date. It had also demonstrated the growing expense of maintaining border defenses; the division had cost more than $2 million. It also showed how difficult it would be for the United States to influence the internal dynamics of the revolution that shaped Mexico in the decade from 1910 to 1920, a lesson that was also learned by Taft's successor, Woodrow Wilson.

Don M. Coerver

REFERENCES

Don M. Coerver and Linda B. Hall, *Revolution on the Border: The United States and Mexico, 1910–1920* (Univ. of New Mexico Pr., 1988); Don M. Coerver and Linda B. Hall, *Texas and the Mexican Revolution: A Study in State and National Border Policy* (Trinity Univ. Pr., 1984); Robert D. Gregg, *The Influence of Border Troubles on Relations Between the United States and Mexico, 1876–1910* (Johns Hopkins Univ. Pr., 1937); P. Edward Haley, *Revolution and Intervention: The Diplomacy of Taft and Wilson with Mexico, 1910–1917* (MIT Pr., 1970); Michael E. Meyer, *Mexican Rebel: Pascual Orozco and the Mexican Revolution, 1910–1915* (Univ. of Nebraska Pr., 1967).

See also Mexican Border Battles and Skirmishes (1911–1921).

Manila, The Philippines, Battle (1898)

When Emilio Aguinaldo y Famy proclaimed the establishment of the Republic of the Philippines on 12 June 1898, the Spanish still retained control of about 15 square miles of Manila, including Fort Santiago, a 300-year-old medieval fortress. Entrance into the fort was through arched gateways where drawbridges crossed a moat. The old, grey stone walls of the fort were 30 feet high and 10 to 20 feet thick. The walls were capped with parapets and bastions for the obsolete Spanish cannons. Within the walls, government buildings and churches loomed over the harbor and the mouth of the Pasig River. Twenty-five thousand soldiers of the Philippine Republican Army surrounded the Spanish garrison while Adm. George Dewey's Asiatic Squadron controlled Manila Bay. Dewey's naval guns could have easily pounded the fort into oblivion, but Washington wanted the city intact.

About two miles beyond the walls of Fort Santiago, the Spanish occupied a string of 15 blockhouses. Beyond the blockhouses, an ocean of brown nipa huts stretched for miles east, north, and south. With over 300,000 people, Manila encompassed a number of smaller suburbs stretching 10 miles south to Cavite and seven miles north to Caloocan. A few hundred yards beyond the Spanish blockhouses, the Filipino army dug trenches and placed the Spanish under siege. The Filipino trenches began on the bay south of Manila near Malate, curved inland, then curved back to the bay just north of Malabon to encircle the city. From bay to bay, the line covered about nine miles. Along the line, the Spanish and Filipinos engaged in small nightly firefights.

Brig. Gen. Thomas M. Anderson arrived in Manila on 30 June 1898, with the first contingent of U.S. ground forces composed of 2,386 men and 117 officers. Anderson's arrival stimulated a crisis for the new Philippine Republican government. President Aguinaldo wanted diplomatic recognition for his new republic before he allowed Anderson's forces to land. Aguinaldo asked Admiral Dewey and General Anderson to refer to his army as the Republican Army, not the Insurgent Army, and to refer to him as President Aguinaldo rather than General Aguinaldo. The Filipinos were perhaps "insurgents" against Spain, but they were allies of the United States in the war against Spain. Aguinaldo was upset when Dewey and Anderson continued to refer to the Filipinos as "insurgents" and was equally upset when they suggested that the Filipino army be placed under Anderson's command. The Filipinos became suspicious of U.S. intentions and wanted guarantees from the United States that it had no intention of acquiring the Philippines as a colony.

Under the pressure of Dewey's naval guns, the Filipinos allowed Anderson to land his forces at Cavite, 10 miles south of Manila. The landing at Cavite did not threaten the Filipino positions surrounding Manila. Cavite was a narrow peninsula separated from Manila by 10 miles of practically impassable roads and some 10,000 armed Filipinos. It was unlikely that any men at Cavite would participate in any battle for Manila.

On 17 July the Second American Expedition under Brig. Gen. Francis V. Greene arrived with 3,500 men. Reluctantly, Aguinaldo allowed Greene to land his men two miles north of Manila where they encamped at an old peanut farm dubbed Camp Dewey. Greene's men occupied about three-fourths of a mile of trenches near the bay. The monsoon season was in full bloom, and the trenches were full of water. The rain poured down for 24 straight days. Field conditions were harsh as the men's clothes literally rotted, equipment mildewed, and rifles rusted; the men ate, slept, and drilled in the constant drizzle and downpour. They went to bed wet and woke up to put on wet clothes.

Every night, the U.S. soldiers listened to the sounds of war without participating. After dark, the Spanish and the Filipinos played games. Beginning around 10:00 p.m. every evening, a furious exchange of small arms fire occurred and continued at intervals throughout the night. The nightly fusillades did little harm to either side; few men were killed or wounded. Neither side left the cover of their barricades.

On 25 July Maj. Gen. Wesley Merritt, the commander of the U.S. Expeditionary Forces, arrived with an additional 1,000 men. On 30 July Brig. Gen. Arthur MacArthur arrived with an additional 4,650 men and 197 officers to increase U.S. strength to approximately 12,000 men. General Merritt labeled his combined force the 1st Division of the VIII Army Corps, and he expected more divisions to arrive in the next few weeks. General Anderson was made field commander of the First Division, which was divided into two brigades. General MacArthur commanded the 1st Brigade while General Greene commanded the 2nd Brigade.

MacArthur's 4,000-man brigade landed three miles south of Manila and occupied nearly a mile of trenches near the bay. The Republican Army continued to occupy over seven miles of the front line as it circled west, then north, before Greene's brigade occupied three-fourths of a mile north of Manila.

General Merritt ignored Aguinaldo and opened negotiations with the Spanish commander of Manila, Governor General Fermín Jáudenes y Alvarez. Governor Jáudenes knew his garrison was doomed. Cut off from reinforcements, starving, threatened by the guns of Dewey's fleet, and surrounded by hostile forces numbering almost 35,000 men, the Spanish had no chance of winning. The question was not how to win the war in the Philippines, because that was clearly impossible, but rather how to prevent Filipino atrocities while simultaneously appearing gallant in defeat.

General Merritt suggested that the Spanish garrison surrender Manila before a battle was necessary to dislodge it. Impossible, Governor Jáudenes proclaimed. Perhaps a mild confrontation, a staged battle followed by Spanish surrender was possible, but only on one condition—that no Filipinos would be in the attacking forces and that only U.S. personnel would be allowed into Fort Santiago. If U.S. troops joined forces with the Filipino army, the Spanish garrison would fight to the last man. They would never surrender to the Filipinos because Governor Jáudenes was convinced that Aguinaldo would torture and execute every Spaniard in the fort. He was terrified of a bloody massacre. If the U.S. commander agreed that the battle for Manila was an affair only between Spain and the United States, then Jáudenes assured Merritt, Spanish resistance would be nominal.

Merritt accepted Jáudenes's offer and agreed to stage a mock battle to save Spanish military face. From 1 August to 12 August, Merritt conferred with his field commanders. The plan was for General MacArthur to attack the Spanish blockhouses from the south while General Greene engaged in a simultaneous assault from the north. Although Merritt implied resistance would be light, he did not tell his brigade commanders of his arrangement with Jáudenes. He wanted them to act as if they were engaged in a real battle. On one point, however, Merritt was very specific—the Filipinos were not to participate. As Spanish positions were captured, the brigade commanders were to station guards and to establish road blocks to prevent armed Filipinos from flooding into the inner city. Merritt authorized his brigade commanders to use necessary force to prevent indiscriminate killing by armed Filipinos. General Merritt sent Aguinaldo an order to keep his men out of the confrontation.

On the morning of 13 August Merritt implemented his plan. North and south of the city, bugles rasped out reveille at 4:00 a.m. to mobilize the U.S. troops. A fine drizzle descended as the troops checked their weapons in the predawn haze. Around 9:30 a.m. the warships of Dewey's squadron and the division artillery units of the two U.S. brigades opened fire on the Spanish front lines. The assaulting columns lay behind barricades unable to see, but they heard the boom of the heavy naval guns and the scream of shells across their front. The shelling lasted for almost an hour, then silence descended on the battlefield. Around 10:30 a.m. U.S. units attacked. North of Manila, Greene's brigade encountered no Spanish opposition. South of the city, it was a different story. When the naval guns ceased firing around 10:30 a.m., MacArthur's brigade moved forward to attack Blockhouse No. 14. His men were jostled and elbowed by throngs of Filipino Republican soldiers who were in heavy force on his right flank. As the Filipino soldiers surged forward, the frightened Spanish defenders opened fire. In the brief skirmish, two U.S. soldiers were killed and several wounded. Rather than expend men by attacking a fortified position, MacArthur ordered his artillery to open fire on the Spanish blockhouse. The roar of the two Hotchkiss guns was deafening.

The Spanish deserted the position and retreated north up the Paco Road to a second defensive position near Singalong Crossroads. MacArthur dropped off two battalions at the blockhouse to prevent the Republican soldiers from following, and with the rest of his brigade he pursued the Spaniards. The Filipinos refused to desist, and many charged around the blockhouse to follow MacArthur's brigade up the road. MacArthur ordered his rear echelon to stop the Filipinos and to disarm them. A number refused to surrender their weapons, and when the U.S. troops persisted, they fired on MacArthur's men. MacArthur ordered additional road blocks to his rear as the U.S. soldiers returned fire. The skirmish with the Filipinos quickly ended although occasional shots were exchanged throughout the morning. Armed Filipinos buzzed around the edge of the front line, angry at the U.S. attempt to exclude them from the battle and the prize of Manila for which they had worked so hard.

With the Republican soldiers held in check to his rear, MacArthur moved his brigade forward about a mile to the Singalong Crossroads, where the Spanish had established another defensive position. After a brief firefight, the Spanish retreated behind the walls of Fort Santiago into the hands of General Greene. Attacking from the north of Manila, Greene's brigade had encountered no opposition and had entered the old city unmolested to accept the surrender of Governor Jáudenes around 11:20 a.m. MacArthur's men were the only ones who engaged in anything resembling actual fighting. His brigade suffered several dozen casualties in passing through Singalong. Leaving detachments at key bridges and street intersections to prevent armed Filipinos from following, MacArthur's brigade entered Fort Santiago around 1:30 p.m.

By late afternoon, U.S. troops occupied 15 square miles, including the walled city and surrounding suburbs. U.S. outposts were maintained about four hundred yards inside the old line of Spanish blockhouses at this point controlled by soldiers of the Philippine Republican Army. The Republicans were in an ugly mood. As night descended, about 4,000 angry Filipinos massed in Malate just south of the city. They periodically fired on the U.S. outposts and threatened to attack. Fires lit the night sky as angry mobs set aflame sections of the outer city. Because General Merritt feared looting, he ordered the Spanish civil guards, or police, to remain on duty as part of the outer defenses until U.S. troops could relieve them the following morning. The explosive situation was diffused only by a tropical storm that raged most of the night and made movement along the roads almost impossible.

An uneasy truce developed in the following weeks. When the Hong Kong cable was restored around 20 August, one of the ironies of the war was revealed. The battle for Manila occurred one day after a cease-fire had been arranged at the negotiating table.

Kenneth Ray Young

REFERENCES

James H. Blount, *The American Occupation of the Philippines, 1898–1912* (Putnam, 1913); John M. Gates, *Schoolbooks and Krags: The United States Army in the Philippines, 1898–1902* (Greenwood Pr., 1973); Jesse George, *Our Army and Navy in the Orient* (1899); William T. Sexton, *Soldiers in the Sun: An Adventure in Imperialism* (Military Service Pub. Co., 1939); Leon Wolff, *Little Brown Brother: How the United States Purchased and Pacified the Philippine Islands at the Century's Turn* (Doubleday, 1961).

See also Merritt, Wesley.

Manila, The Philippines, Battle (1899)

The Battle of Manila in 1899 marked the start of the Philippine War. The battle itself was atypical in the conflict because of its urban setting and the fact it was fought largely in the open. Thus, U.S. forces in the Philippines demonstrated their overwhelming superiority in waging conventional warfare, while the Filipino army displayed chronic lack of leadership and coordination.

Tension between U.S. forces and Filipinos rose steadily after the fall of Manila in August 1898. Filipino revolutionaries, furious at being denied the fruits of victory over Spain, especially the conquest of Manila, grew apprehensive once it became obvious that the United States intended to annex their country as a colony.

Maj. Gen. Elwell S. Otis, the U.S. commander, rarely left his office, had a low opinion of Filipinos generally, and sent overly optimistic reports to Washington, thereby leading the administration of President William McKinley to underestimate Filipino opposition to U.S. annexation of the Philippines.

Filipino leaders were divided between accepting an accommodation with the United States and resisting it to the bitter end. Some sought to negotiate with Otis in order to delay any U.S. advance. As it happened, such efforts were too late. Meanwhile, Filipino commanders planned to launch a surprise attack on U.S. troops from inside Manila in early 1899. Accordingly, revolutionary agents were smuggled into the city.

Fighting began by accident on the night of 4 February 1899. Several Filipinos approached two U.S. sentries and were shot after failing to obey the order to halt. Shooting began almost immediately in the vicinity, and by dawn fighting had begun in the lines north of Manila.

The outbreak of hostilities caught the Filipino generals by surprise; most of them were away from their units on 4 February. Although they hurried to the fighting, events were rapidly reducing their options for dealing with U.S. forces.

On the morning of 5 February, U.S. troops north of the city went on the offensive and captured the Filipino trenches opposite them. During the next few days, U.S. units advanced, capturing Manila's reservoir and water works along with Filipino strongpoints.

The lines south of Manila were generally quiet on 4 February, but shooting erupted the next day. U.S. units advanced rapidly driving Filipino forces out of towns and fortifications. Within a few days, Filipino forces had been thrown back a considerable distance. Soon afterward, U.S. troops in the southern sector pulled back to a shorter defense line.

The town of Caloocan was the Philippines' main railway terminus and thus the gateway to central Luzon. The United States Army was determined to capture the town and its railway yard. On 10 February a massive assault began against Caloocan, which quickly fell. The fighting was fierce and nearly leveled the town.

Filipino irregular forces attempted to launch an attack in Manila when hostilities began, but were thwarted by alert U.S. troops. On the night of 22 February they rose in the suburbs of Tondo and Binondo, starting several large fires and causing tremendous confusion. The rebellion lasted only a few days and succeeded only in burning several communities to the ground.

By late February, the battle for Manila was largely over. The United States had not been expelled from the Philippines, and the Filipinos realized that capturing Manila would be extremely difficult. With reinforcements arriving at a steady pace, U.S. forces were poised to expand beyond Manila and capture Malolos, the Filipino revolutionary capital. Nonetheless, the United States lacked the manpower at that point to conquer the entire Philippines.

James C. Biedzynski

REFERENCES

James H. Blount, *The American Occupation of the Philippines, 1898–1912* (Putnam, 1912); Stuart Creighton Miller, *"Benevolent Assimilation": The American Conquest of the Philippines, 1899–1903* (Yale Univ. Pr., 1973); William T. Sexton, *Soldiers in the Sun: An Adventure in Imperialism* (Military Service Pub. Co., 1939).

See also Otis, Elwell Stephen.

Manila Bay, The Philippines, Naval Battle (1898)

On the morning of 1 May 1898, Commodore George Dewey guided his small Asiatic Squadron into the still waters of Boca Grande Passage. In the darkness ahead lay the waiting Spanish fleet and the beginning of a journey toward empire for the United States. Few U.S. citizens realized the significance of the event in Manila and what the new age held for optimistic imperialists.

Tension between Spain and the United States had been building in the months leading up to Dewey's departure from the United States for Japan to assume the command of the Asiatic Squadron. Public pressure demanded war with Spain while President William McKinley sought to negotiate a diplomatic solution to the delicate Cuban situation. Dewey arrived in Japan on 3 January 1898 and hoisted his flag aboard the *Olympia*. It was clear to him that war could occur at any time, and he lost no time in making war preparations. Convinced that operations would best be conducted from Hong Kong, he moved the small fleet to the China coast immediately. He explained that it was apparent that if any "emergency" occurred, Hong Kong offered the most favorable station from which to operate against the Philippines.

By the time Dewey and the fleet arrived at Hong Kong, the political situation had worsened. In February the diplomatic incident involving Enrique Dupuy de Lôme, the Spanish ambassador to the United States, had increased public anti-Spanish sentiment, and the sinking of the *Maine* caused increased pressure for war. Assistant Secretary of the Navy Theodore Roosevelt, taking advantage of the absence of his superior, sent a telegram to Dewey ordering him to "keep full of coal. In the event . . . of war . . . , your duty will be to see that the Spanish squadron does not leave the Asiatic coast, and then offensive operations in Philippine Islands" (Trask, p. 81). Dewey wasted no time. He purchased two support vessels, the *Zafiro* and the *Nanshan*. Refusing to rely on logistical support from distant bases, Dewey planned to use the two ships to bring supplies and coal with him during his cruise to the Philippines. Once war was declared, neutrality statutes in British Hong Kong would seal off supply from the China coast. Dewey could depend on no local sources if he needed additional ammunition or coal; he was determined to take it with him.

On 14 February the protected cruiser *Raleigh* arrived at Hong Kong from the European station. In April the fleet was expanded by three ships when the *Baltimore*, *Concord*, and the *Petrel* arrived in China. At this point, the fleet boasted 10 ships in all, including the ancient paddle-wheeler *Monocacy*, which Dewey decided to leave behind. Opposing the Spanish fleet would be four protected cruisers, two gunboats, a revenue cutter, and the two support vessels. While Dewey waited for orders, he instituted a vigorous training and maintenance program. He ordered the hulls cleaned and the peacetime white paint replaced with a coat of battle gray. Wood-paneled interiors were removed to reduce the risk of collateral casualties from flying debris. Ships' crews drilled daily under Dewey's personal direction. Urgently needing intelligence, Dewey sent an agent to Manila to report on the Spanish fleet and coastal fortifications. Another agent was placed into Hong Kong to investigate sources of information and to question travelers arriving in the Chinese city from the Philippines. When word came, Dewey was ready.

On 23 April British authorities in Hong Kong informed Dewey that the United States was at war with Spain and that consistent with British law, all ships of war must be removed from British jurisdiction. It was the first Dewey had heard of war. Complying with the British request, Dewey moved his fleet to Mirs Bay, China, and waited for news from Washington. On 25 April Secretary of the Navy John D. Long cabled Dewey that war had been declared and instructed him to "Proceed at once to the Philippine Islands. Commence operations particularly against the Spanish Fleet . . . must capture vessels or destroy. Use utmost endeavor" (Dewey, p. 195). Long's message indicated that the U.S. strategy was to eliminate the Spanish fleet in the Philippines to prevent support of the Cuban theater by elements from the Philippines. Dewey could let no vessel escape.

Dewey cabled the U.S. consul at Manila, Oscar F. Williams, asking for the location of the Spanish fleet and any news relating to the overall situation in the islands. Williams responded by sailing immediately to Mirs Bay to confer with Dewey. He carried the news that Rear Adm. Patricio Montojo y Pasarón planned to meet the approaching U.S. threat at Subig Bay, north of Manila near Olongapo. On 27 April the U.S. fleet sailed for the Philippines. During the voyage each crew engaged in day and night battle drills, fire fighting, and damage control.

On 30 April Dewey arrived off the coast of Luzon near Bataan and Corregidor. Acting on Williams's intelligence, Dewey ordered the *Boston* and the *Concord* to Subig Bay to establish the location of the Spanish fleet. Unknown to Dewey, Admiral Montojo had rejected the Subig site for fear of being caught by the U.S. ships without adequate maneuvering room. Montojo was convinced that his fleet would be hard-pressed to win in an outright fight with the U.S. fleet. Instead, the Spanish commander selected a position in Manila Bay and placed his ships in an east-west line across Cañacao Bay at Cavite. Montojo counted on the gun emplacements in Manila to support his defensive stand. He had no illusions as to the outcome, carefully placing his vessels in shallow anchorages where his men could escape to land when they were abandoned. When his ships could find no trace of the Spanish fleet, Dewey ordered his fleet into the Boca Grande Passage later that evening. By midnight the small U.S. fleet was underway and meeting little resistance from coastal positions. Rumors had indicated that Manila was a formidable target protected by mines throughout the approach to the city. Dewey rejected the possibility, convinced that the Spanish did not have the technological capability to mine deep water sites successfully. As the U.S. vessels steamed past the gun positions on Corregidor, Dewey set his course for Manila Bay and ordered the small flotilla to reduce speed to four knots. Dewey wanted to time his arrival off the city of Manila to ensure adequate daylight to locate Montojo's ships. He sent the two supply ships and the revenue cutter to an isolated area of the bay where they would be safe from attack and available to the warships when the time came for refueling and resupply.

As day broke across Manila Bay, Dewey arrived off the city's waterfront section. Expecting Montojo to be anchored near Manila, Dewey searched across Manila's waterfront area to the south and then west in search of the elusive enemy. Dewey altered course toward Cavite and soon found the Spanish battle line facing east toward Dewey and the city of Manila. At 5:40 a.m. at a range of 5,000 yards, Dewey turned to the commander of the flagship *Olympia*, Capt. Charles V. Gridley, and said "You may fire when you are ready, Gridley" (Dewey, p. 214). With those words active operations began in the Spanish-Cuban/American War.

The U.S. fleet steamed west across the Spanish line, firing from the port guns and then reversing course, made the run again firing from the starboard guns. Dewey kept up a relentless fire on the beleaguered Spanish crews. In all, Dewey made five passes across the battle line, reducing the Spanish ships to a billowing inferno.

Dewey received word at 7:35 a.m. that his ships were running desperately low on ammunition. He immediately ordered his ships to cease fire and disengage from the Spanish line. The U.S. fleet steamed northeast staying within range of the artillery along the city of Manila waterfront. The Spanish gun positions continued to fire, causing Dewey to send a messenger to the Spanish commander ashore indicating that if the guns continued to fire, he would have no alternative but to shell the city. The gun positions fell silent soon afterward.

During the interim, Dewey took advantage of the lull in the fighting to send his crews to breakfast. They had been at battle stations all night, and Dewey did not know when they would have the opportunity to eat again. Meanwhile, Dewey ordered his captains to a conference where it was determined that the ammunition report was in error and that his vessels were ready to resume the attack. At 11:16 a.m. Dewey ordered the fleet to reengage the Spanish and the fight began anew. The battle for Manila Bay lasted but 74 minutes more. At 12:30 p.m., Dewey ordered a cease-fire. The Spanish fleet lay smoldering, either sunk or burned to the water line. Enemy gun positions were left silenced and deserted as the Spanish sailors and soldiers rushed to the safety of inland areas. Total losses included 370 Spanish sailors killed in the morning's action. Dewey lost one man to heat stroke and none to battle conditions.

As soon as the guns fell silent, Dewey assumed responsibility for consolidating his position in the islands. Without the benefit of orders from Washington, Dewey sent word to the Spanish commander for assurance that forts supporting the city of Manila would not fire on the U.S. ships in the harbor. Additionally, Dewey demanded that all torpedo boats in the Pasig River be turned over to U.S. authorities and that he be given access to the Manila-Hong Kong cable. Dewey suggested that since Manila would soon surrender to overwhelming odds, common sense dictated that both sides benefit from a reasonable course of action. The Spanish commander agreed to the provision regarding the guns, making sure that Dewey had no excuse to fire on the city. On the question of torpedo boats and the cable, he refused to accept Dewey's demands. Dewey promptly ordered the *Zafiro* to drag the entrance to Manila Bay and cut the cable, after which both Dewey's fleet and the Spanish were cut off from direct communications with the outside world. Dewey had the resources to reach Hong Kong by ship and there make use of cable intercourse with Washington. The Spanish sent dispatches overland to Iloilo and then on to Borneo by boat, a slow but effective means of gaining access to cable communications with Spain. Only the United States could hope to send reinforcements. The Spanish could but wait for the inevitable.

The U.S. consul advised Dewey that Filipino forces had "tapped" into the cable line and could read his traffic with Hong Kong, prompting delays in restoring cable service until August after the Spanish surrender of Manila. Historians have suggested in recent years that Dewey used his communication "isolation" as an excuse to operate without the interference from the Navy Department in Washington. Regardless of his motivation or opportunity, Dewey took advantage of his isolation to proceed with his plans independent of his superiors in Washington.

During the first days following the battle, Dewey busied himself with the tasks of blockade and control. On 4 May he reported to Washington that he had taken Cavite, the naval base across the bay from Manila. Dewey cabled that all Spanish positions at Cavite were in his hands and that he could take the city of Manila at any time but did not have the ground forces necessary to hold it.

President McKinley responded to Dewey's success at Manila Bay with a letter to Secretary Long putting to rest all speculation about U.S. intentions in the archipelago. McKinley indicated that the naval victory brought with it an obligation for the United States to protect its investment there. McKinley emphasized his intention to successfully defeat the Spanish and eliminate their rule in the Philippines and then establish an army of occupation that would guarantee law and order for the Filipinos.

Two weeks after the battle Dewey drafted a letter to Secretary Long outlining his plans for operations in the islands. Naval planners in Washington urgently needed logistical requirements for the defeat of the Spanish and the occupation of the islands in the long term. Dewey's assessment included a recommendation for a large ground force to be sent to the Philippines from the United States to consolidate positions in and around Manila and other military installations nearby. He suggested that additional reassignments from army stations in China might be added to the Philippine force.

Dewey sent requests to Washington for reinforcements but had to rely on his original nine ships to initiate operations of containment in the islands. It would be June before the army could reach the Philippines, and Dewey had to establish a blockade against foreign trade, prevent resupply to Spanish positions, and maintain a delicate balance among the Filipino nationalist forces, the Spanish, and his own units. His operations in May and June were limited until other ships arrived in the early summer. In the days after the Battle of Manila Bay, Dewey's operations remained small and his logistical requirements adequate for his diminutive fleet. As the summer progressed, the U.S. deployment represented an expanded commitment to the Philippines. Ahead was victory in the war against Spain and another war with the Filipino nationalists.

For the two naval commanders at Manila Bay, the battle produced momentous consequences. Defeated and without a fleet, Admiral Montojo returned to Spain in disgrace to stand courtmartial. Although he was not held responsible for the inability of his fleet to successfully survive the attack, Montojo's career was effectively at an end.

Congress conferred on Dewey a new grade of "Admiral of the Navy," a four-star rank created just for the occasion. After a few months of further duty in the Philippines, Dewey made a triumphal return to the United States, where he was considered for the presidency in 1900, was the hero for the moment, and assumed his position as the ranking member of the United States Navy. For the next 17 years, Dewey presided over the General Board of the United States Navy, lending to the navy and U.S. foreign policy his knowledge and expertise gained from over 50 years of naval service.

Vernon L. Williams

REFERENCES

George Dewey, *Autobiography of George Dewey: Admiral of the Navy* (Scribner, 1913); Philip Y. Nicholson, "George Dewey and the Transformation of American Foreign Policy," Ph.D. diss., Univ. of

New Mexico, 1971; David F. Trask, *The War With Spain in 1898* (Macmillan, 1981); Vernon L. Williams, "George Dewey: Admiral of the Navy," in James C. Bradford, ed., *Admirals of the New Steel Navy: Makers of the American Naval Traditions, 1880–1930* (U.S. Naval Institute Pr., 1990); Vernon L. Williams, "The U.S. Navy in the Philippine Insurrection and Subsequent Native Unrest, 1898–1906," Ph.D. diss., Texas A&M Univ., 1985.

See also Dewey, George; Montojo y Pasarón, Patricio.

Marine Operations in Cuba (1912)

The 1906 U.S. intervention and its reorganization of the Cuban army improved Cuba's counterinsurgency capability, but failed to address the root causes of revolutionary unrest: grotesque racial, economic, and class inequalities. Thus, armed popular uprisings remained common in Cuba and recurrently threatened destruction of private, especially foreign, properties. While the Cuban army could protect the incumbent government against rebel forces, it could not guarantee the security of foreigners and their investments, a task which increasingly fell on the shoulders of the United States Marine Corps.

By 1912 the political achievements of José Miguel Gómez's Liberal government had exacerbated these underlying tensions. Struggling to enlarge their political constituency, the Liberals supported legislation that discharged socially prominent loyalist government bureaucrats and replaced them with Cuban veterans of the Ejercito Libertador (Cuban Liberation Army); they also politicized the army, threatened to discriminate against foreign (especially U.S.) capital, funded additional public service jobs to alleviate unemployment and expand patronage, and provided profitable state concessions to prominent Liberal party members.

The resulting corruption and prosperity, which disproportionately benefited wealthy white Cubans, alienated Afro-Cubans (composing 30 percent of the population), poor peasants, and workers who together constituted the great majority of Cubans for whom independence was to have meant social justice, political freedom, and racial equality. On 20 May 1912, these conflicts erupted in a new revolutionary threat to Cuban capitalism and to its place in the international political and economic order. Led by Evaristo Estenoz and the Independent Party of Color,

this Afro-Cuban rebellion spread throughout Cuba demanding justice, liberty, and equality for all Cubans. The rebels appealed to the international community and especially to the United States to support their cause, but threatened widespread damage to foreign properties if that support was not forthcoming.

Fearing U.S. intervention under terms of the Platt Amendment, the Gómez government's response was immediate and ruthless, but insufficient either to suppress the uprising or to prevent unilateral U.S. military actions. On 23 May U.S. President William H. Taft, over the objections of Gómez, who feared that a new U.S. invasion would offend Cuban nationalist sensibilities and expand the ranks of the insurrectionists, ordered U.S. forces to intervene. Taft's hasty decision to dispatch marines to Cuba, according to Capt. Clyde H. Metcalf, the Marine Corps's official historian, reflected his administration's fear of the "possibility of a black republic at our door" (Metcalf, p. 325). The Marine Corps's 1st Provisional Regiment was ordered to board the transport *Prairie*, and the *Prairie*, along with the *Nashville* and the *Paducah*, set off for Guantánamo Bay. The 3rd and 4th Divisions of the Atlantic Fleet, a total of nine battleships, were also sent steaming toward Key West. More than 5,000 troops were activated for duty in Cuba.

The marines' responsibility was to protect U.S. investments in Cuba and to support the Liberal government in its effort to quell the Afro-Cuban rebellion. They accomplished their mission by landing men in the vicinity of Santiago de Cuba to protect the Daiquirí Mines and other U.S. properties near Siboney, El Cobre, Puerto Sal, Hermatanas, and El Cuero where they engaged Cuban rebels in combat.

Under the command of Lt. Col. John A. Lejeune, the marines in the Santiago district later occupied Ocana, Firmeza, and the Aguadores Railroad Bridge. Similar operations were undertaken in the districts of Guantánamo and Manzanillo, where the Central Teresa Sugar Company, Spanish-American Iron Company, Cuban Railroad Company, and other U.S. properties requested protection. "The railroad company," according to Metcalf, "later showed its appreciation for the protection afforded by sending in a claim for transportation furnished the marines while acting as guards on the trains" (Metcalf, p. 329).

In effect, these marines guaranteed the safe operation of sugar plantations, mining industries, and transportation facilities essential to the prosperity of U.S. businesses in Cuba. In the process, they freed Cuban army regiments from routine policing functions and permitted a more effective deployment against the revolutionaries. On 26 June Cuban government troops defeated rebel troops at Miraca, near Nipe Bay, and killed Evaristo Estenoz, the principal leader of the revolt. Within a month, Estenoz's second-in-command, Ibonet, suffered military defeat and escaped with his men to the mountains. By 23 July a gradual withdrawal of U.S. marines and naval personnel had been completed.

The revolt had ended, leaving some 3,000 Afro-Cubans dead, but its precipitating social, economic, and political conditions remained essentially undisturbed. A scant five years later, these same conditions once again produced the general lawlessness and threats to foreign property that had prompted the marine invasion in 1912. The scope and duration of the "Sugar Intervention" of 1917, not its method or mission, principally distinguished it from the events of 1912. More significantly, however, successive U.S. military interventions fueled the fires of Cuban nationalism, further discredited Cuban political and economic elites in the eyes of the Cuban people, and contributed to the historical conditions that eventually produced the Cuban Revolution of 1959.

Keith A. Haynes

References

Russell Fitzgibbon, *Cuba and the United States, 1900–1935* (Russell & Russell, 1964); Lester Langley, *The Banana Wars: An Inner History of American Empire, 1900–1914* (Univ. Pr. of Kentucky, 1983); Clyde H. Metcalf, *A History of the United States Marine Corps* (Putnam, 1939); Louis A. Pérez, Jr., *Cuba Under the Platt Amendment, 1902–1934* (Univ. of Pittsburgh Pr., 1986); Louis A. Pérez, Jr., *Cuba and the United States: Ties of Singular Intimacy* (Univ. of Georgia Pr., 1990); Teresita Yglesia Martinez, *El segundo ensavo de republica* (Editorial de Ciencias Sociales, 1980).

Marine Operations in Samoa (1899)

In 1899, the competing colonial ambitions of Germany, the United States, and Great Britain provoked an international crisis in the Samoan Islands. Although all three countries had coveted the island chain since the mid-1800s, in 1889 the colonial powers compromised and established an international commission of representatives from each nation. In August 1898, however, Germany upset this delicate diplomatic balance when it intervened in an internal Samoan power struggle. Both the United States and Great Britain reacted to Germany's attempt to expand its influence in the region by sending warships to the islands in March 1899.

The U.S. intervention in Samoa can be divided into three phases, the first involved the occupation of the Samoan capital of Apia on the island of Upolu. On 11 March, Adm. Albert Kautz, commander of the USS *Philadelphia*, announced that the provisional Samoan government was dissolved. Two days later, the *Philadelphia* and two British warships, the HMS *Porpoise* and HMS *Royalist*, landed troops in Apia harbor. A detachment of marines led by Lt. Constantine M. Perkins fortified the U.S. consulate, while other U.S. and British forces established defensive positions throughout the town and surrounding countryside.

On 15 March the *Philadelphia*, *Royalist*, and *Porpoise* began shelling villages on the outskirts of Apia in response to scattered sniper attacks on the U.S. and British positions. Although the bombardments were generally haphazard and inaccurate (misfired shells hit both the German warship *Falke*, which was anchored in the harbor, and the U.S. consulate, killing marine Pvt. J.E. Mudge), they were sufficient to drive off many of the hostile natives. As the Samoans retreated into the island's hinterland, U.S. and British troops extended their lines across the neck of the Mulinuu Peninsula and set up machine gun posts along the beach to prevent any surprise attack by boat. By 23 March Apia had been secured, and the first phase of U.S. military involvement in Samoa was complete.

The second stage of the U.S. intervention began on 24 March with the arrival of the HMS *Tawanga*, which disembarked additional troops. The reinforcements increased the onshore contingent to 250 men and prompted the U.S. and British officers to begin a series of operations against native strongholds in Upolu's interior. On 31 March Ens. David F. Sellers commanded a cutter from the *Philadelphia* and attacked several native villages west of Apia.

An even larger expedition left the capital on 1 April, proceeding toward a hostile native village near Vailele. The force included 60 marines and sailors from the *Philadelphia* led by Lt. Perkins and navy Lt. Philip V. Lansdale, along with 62 British soldiers and more than one hundred friendly Samoans. After marching several miles inland and encountering little enemy opposition, the column turned back toward the shore, following a road that led through a ravine along the Fugali'i River.

Although the U.S. and British officers had been warned about the possibility of an ambush, a large number of hostile Samoans succeeded in surprising the column as it left the ravine. The Samoans soon surrounded the U.S. and British troops, forcing them back across a swamp to the unprotected shoreline. Several U.S. troops died during the retreat, and Lt. Lansdale was killed on the beach as he attempted to repair a malfunctioning Colt machine gun. There was a total of 13 British and U.S. casualties, and only the arrival of the *Royalist*, which landed reinforcements and began shelling the Samoan positions, prevented a worse disaster.

The debacle ended any further effort to subdue the Samoans by force. U.S. and British forces remained in their fixed positions around Apia. This final stage of the military intervention was marked only by minor incidents. On 12 April a small group of U.S. marines attacked and burned an empty village, but this was the last time the British and U.S. troops left the security of Apia. The fighting ended on 24 April when the Samoans agreed to a cease-fire after the British and U.S. warships promised to stop shelling nearby settlements.

On 13 May the USS *Badger* arrived in Apia, carrying representatives from all three colonial powers. After several months of negotiations, the United States, Great Britain, and Germany agreed to divide the islands into formal spheres of influence. Germany retained Apia and the island of Upolu, while the United States kept the island of Tutuila and the important naval base at Pago Pago. Great Britain renounced its claim to Samoa in return for concessions in other Pacific islands and parts of Africa.

James H. L. Lide

REFERENCES

T.T. Craven, "A Naval Episode of 1899," *United States Naval Institute Proceedings*, 54 (1928), 185–200; Foster Rhea Dulles, *America in the Pacific: A Century of Expansion* (Houghton Mifflin, 1932); D. Michael O'Quinlivan and Bernard C. Nalty, "Ambush in Samoa," *Leatherneck*, 42 (1959), 30–31; Frank H. Rentflow, "Samoan Imbroglio," *Leatherneck*, 19 (1936), 3, 49–50.

Marine Operations in the Philippine War

In the months leading up to 4 February 1899 and the beginning of hostilities between U.S. forces and the Filipino nationalists, assignments of U.S. Marines were limited to shipboard duty. Marines aboard Adm. George Dewey's ships, before and after the Battle of Manila Bay, were used as part of landing parties.

When Dewey arrived off Corregidor in the early morning hours of 1 May 1898 he had aboard his fleet six detachments of marines. These 189 marines were used as landing parties to take the naval base and town of Cavite a few days after the battle for Manila Bay. This action represents the first use of marines in operations in the islands. Throughout the next year Dewey used his shipboard marines for the garrison of Cavite, guard duty, and crowd control in the populated neighborhoods in the Manila area.

When hostilities began in the Philippine War, Dewey cabled Washington and requested a battalion of marines to support naval land operations. The navy responded by forming the 1st Marine Battalion with 260 enlisted men and 16 officers. The 1st Battalion arrived in the Philippines on 23 May 1899, with a second battalion arriving during the next seven months. This was the first time that the United States Marine Corps deployed a regimental-size force, and it represented a change in the role the navy and the Marine Corps would play in U.S. ground operations.

In the first year of operations, the use of marines was limited to traditional guard and support duties. Shortages of marines for these tasks precluded their use in expanded operations. These shortages led to additional marines being assigned to the islands. By June 1900 marine strength had reached two regiments of four battalions with two artillery companies each. Unrest in China with the Boxer Uprising led to further increases in the number of marines in the Far East, and eventually the Philippines. During the Boxer period, however, the number of marines in the Philippines was drastically reduced and their roles were limited.

On 8 October 1899 naval and Marine Corps forces began a significant combined operation with army units to secure the area around Cavite. The action proved to be the first notable Marine Corps action of the Philippine War. While two army columns attacked defenses at Noveleta and Cavite Viejo, 427 marines and the gunboat *Petrel* were assigned to attack the fort at Noveleta. The plan called for the marines to attack the fort in order to produce a diversion for the army assault at Cavite Viejo. Using the *Petrel* for covering fire, the marines encountered heavy opposition as they approached the fort. Hemmed in by a "dense thicket of thorn bushes," the marines initiated a direct assault on the Filipinos' position, forcing the Filipinos to quit their station. Marine losses in their first major engagement were three killed and nine wounded. The action effectively consolidated U.S. control of the area around Manila and the Cavite sector.

During the rest of 1899 and early 1900, the Marine Corps was active in the navy's efforts to bring Luzon under U.S. control. Marine operations usually took the form of patrols into the area surrounding the marine outpost and protection of the local inhabitants while searching for bandits and guerrillas. Many of the Luzon operations consisted of punitive patrols of this sort with related pacification efforts directed at the friendly villagers.

Marines were active in the southern islands as well. Operations were usually small scale and were in reaction to intelligence reports of enemy concentration or activity. In these sweeps, the marines captured a variety of prisoners, often including Spanish priests, merchants, and Filipinos. These raids, using the mobility of the marines and the power of the guns aboard the ships that transported them, provided an effective response to isolated trouble spots.

By 1900 the marines also began to assume many of the garrison duties of the army while at the same time establishing new garrisons of their own throughout the archipelago. Marine officers assumed command of entire districts or islands. In July 1900 the U.S. military governor of the Philippines turned over administrative responsibility for the island of Basilan to the Marine Corps. In Basilan and other similar areas, marine officers collected taxes, regulated trade, supervised Filipino local officials, and directed pacification projects. Command and control was vested with the navy with the marine officer reporting directly to the senior United States Navy officer present, not to the army authorities.

On 4 July 1901 the military occupation government was replaced by a civil government headed by William H. Taft, the civil governor. During the year enemy activity decreased, but was not eliminated. Marines continued antiguerrilla operations, with both successes and catastrophe.

By fall 1901 marines returned from duty in China, and marine strength in the Philippines increased dramatically, the marines being organized as a brigade of two regiments. The 1st Regiment was based at Olongapo at Subig Bay, and the 2nd Regiment was posted to Cavite. During this period the number of outposts occupied by marines increased to 14 stations. At these positions marines faced their greatest challenge.

In late September 1901 a company of the army's 9th Infantry Regiment at Balangiga on Samar was surprised and massacred by Filipino guerrillas. The U.S. response was both swift and severe. Army Brig. Gen. Jacob H. Smith ordered marine commander Littleton W.T. Waller to mount a search-and-destroy mission on Samar.

Early efforts along the coast of Samar yielded little success, so on 6 November Waller moved inland, tracking the Filipinos to a camp on the Sohotón River. Although Waller's marines successfully destroyed the camp and captured most of the Filipino stores, Waller erroneously concluded that the fight effectively ended hostile operations on Samar. The Filipinos, however, continued to attack U.S. outposts on Samar until early 1902.

On 28 December Waller led a small patrol into the interior of southern Samar with the intention of finding a route for a telegraph line to connect outposts on both coasts of Samar. The expedition proved to be a disaster because Waller and his men hazarded the elements without proper equipment and supplies. The party, exhausted by the harsh terrain and suffering from the uncharitable climate, fell victim to the jungle. Waller, with one group of the fittest men, eventually found his way back to the outpost at Basey. It was the middle of January 1902 before an army rescue party found the rest of the survivors. In all, 12 of the patrol were dead.

Beset by fever and exhaustion, Waller charged his native guides with mutinous conduct which he blamed for the deaths of many of his men and ordered 11 Filipinos shot. Army Maj. Gen. Adna R. Chaffee directed that Waller be tried for murder, and in an 18-day trial, Waller was acquitted on the charges by a vote of 11 to 2. The calamitous expedition proved that the guerrillas were not to be found in the interior; instead, they were nearer the coast where they could receive food from the towns and could maintain contact with their families. U.S. policy compelled Filipinos to live in U.S.-controlled towns depriving the rebels of their logistical network. As time went on, it was this policy and not operations in the bush that prompted the decline of the guerrilla resistance.

Vernon L. Williams

See also Samar Campaigns, Philippine War.

REFERENCES

John M. Gates, *Schoolbooks and Krags: The United States Army in the Philippines, 1898–1902* (Greenwood Pr., 1973); Allan R. Millett, *Semper Fidelis: The History of the United States Marine Corps* (Free Pr., 1980); J. Robert Moskin, *The U.S. Marine Corps Story* (McGraw-Hill, 1977); Vernon L. Williams, "The U.S. Navy in the Philippine Insurrection and Subsequent Native Unrest, 1898–1906," Ph.D. diss., Texas A&M Univ., 1985.

Martí y Perez, José Julían (1853–1895)

The political leader of Cuba's struggle for independence, José Julían Martí y Perez, was also an outstanding literary figure, journalist, diplomat, and revolutionary. Born into a military family of the occupying Spanish forces, he was arrested at age 16 and imprisoned for his opposition to Spanish control of the island. Deported to Madrid in 1871 for three years, he continued his political and literary activities. Between 1875 and 1878 he traveled in Latin America (Mexico, Guatemala, and Venezuela), developing a strong appreciation for "Nuestra América" (Our [Latin] America). Returning to Cuba in 1878, Martí entered the political fray once again—and was deported a second time.

Between 1880 and 1895 Martí was based in New York, where he headed the campaign to overthrow Spanish rule in Cuba. During this time

he worked as a journalist, producing scores of articles on life in the United States (his *Escenas Norteamericanas*) for the leading Latin American newspapers of the day. During this time he also published his greatest literary works, including his collections of poetry *Versos Sencillos* and *Versos Libres* and his monthly magazine for the children of Latin America, *La Edad de Oro*. Martí's importance as a literary figure is beyond question. Not only was he the originator of the school of *modernismo* (arguably the first truly Latin American literary movement after centuries of Spanish influence), but his poetry was quite exceptional.

Even more striking, however, was Martí's role as a revolutionary organizer. A tireless politician, he traveled extensively along the eastern seaboard, raising money for the Partido Revolucionario Cubano (Cuban Revolutionary Party), and winning political support for the liberation of Cuba. In 1892 he was elected *delegado* (delegate) of the Partido Revolucionario Cubano and was reelected in subsequent years until 1895. That year he sailed for Cuba, following the beginning of the Cuban War of Independence, and was killed in action at Dos Ríos on 19 May.

As a political leader and thinker, Martí was also exceptional. He used his considerable talents to unite more than two dozen associations of Cuban exiles living in the United States, raising money to purchase armaments for the revolutionary forces. He drew up a series of resolutions (1891) and the *Bases and Secret Statutes of the PRC* (1892), and edited the party's journal *Patria*. These publications laid out clear guidelines for the model revolutionary society to be developed in an independent Cuba. In sum, Martí was the most important political and revolutionary leader in the struggle for Cuban liberty.

Martí's socio-political thought was of an extremely radical nature—as one might expect from someone who had undergone such a dramatic revolutionary trajectory. He had extremely clear (albeit occasionally contradictory) ideas about the kind of socio-political development needed for an independent Cuba, insisting on a revolutionary model in which all would participate. Extremely critical of anything that divided Cubans (and yet rather dogmatic in his insistence that all citizens had to exercise their political rights and undertake their obligations), he struggled to both unite their political objectives and channel them toward a single goal, namely liberation from Spain.

A study of Martí's extensive work (28 hefty volumes in the most complete edition) reveals a great literary figure, an exceptional revolutionary organizer with increasingly radical ideas. It is unfortunate that in death he has become the source of significant political tension between Cubans of opposing ideological persuasions. On one hand, his name is invoked by leaders of the revolutionary government as their political mentor; on the other, exile groups have (literally) taken his name to support their cause against the Castro government. Regardless of the diversity in their opinions, the importance of Martí—as a radical thinker, a literary genius, and a revolutionary—will remain untouched by disputes over the ages.

John M. Kirk

REFERENCES

Christopher Abel and Nissa Torrents, eds., *Jose Marti, Revolutionary Democrat* (Duke Univ. Pr., 1986); Richard Butler Gray, *Jose Marti, Cuban Patriot* (Univ. of Florida Pr., 1962); John M. Kirk, *Jose Marti, Mentor of the Cuban Nation* (Univ. Pr. of Florida, 1983); C. Neale Ronning, *Jose Marti and the Emigre Colony in Key West* (Praeger, 1990); Peter Turton, *Jose Marti, Architect of Cuba's Freedom* (Zed, 1986).

Maynard, Charles Clarkson Martin (1870–1945)

Maj. Gen. Charles Clarkson Martin Maynard was the British commander of the Allied forces at Murmansk, North Russia, from 23 June 1918 to 20 September 1919. Placed in charge of a polyglot army, including an element of the American Expeditionary Force, North Russia, Maynard consolidated Allied control over the Murmansk Railroad Front for a distance of some 600 miles to the south and secured land communications with the much larger Allied forces located around Archangel, 200 miles to the east.

Born in Burma in 1870, Maynard graduated from the Royal Military Academy at Sandhurst in 1890. In 1914, having campaigned with distinction in Burma, Malta, India, and South Africa, the rising young officer entered World War I and served for more than three years in various staff and command positions. In May 1918, having been invalided home from France, Maynard was selected to command the Allied force at

Murmansk under the direction, successively, of Maj. Gen. Frederick C. Poole and Maj. Gen. William Edmund Ironside.

Arriving at Murmansk on 23 June, Maynard took command of a force consisting of at least eight different nationalities and, by early July, secured control of the Murmansk Railroad as far south as Soroka (Belomorsk), some 250 miles from Murmansk. During the winter of 1918–1919, Maynard advanced the front to Segezha, 60 miles south of Soroka, and contended successfully with some very difficult financial and supply problems. In the spring, his troops having been reinforced by two companies of U.S. transportation troops, the aggressive general launched a new offensive that eventually reached all the way to Kiappesel'ga, roughly 550 miles south of Murmansk. In mid-September, having directed a final disengagement operation at Lizhma, Maynard fell sick and was relieved by Brig. Gen. H.C. Jackson, who then supervised the final Allied evacuation of Murmansk on 12 October 1919.

After returning to England, Maynard spent three years in charge of the administration of the postwar Western Command. He retired as a major general in 1925 and died 20 years later.

John W. Long

REFERENCES

A.W. Abbott, "Campaign by Rail: Murmansk to Lake Onega, 1918–1919," *Army Quarterly*, 88 (1964), 236–239; A.W. Abbott, "Combined Operations, 500 Miles in the Interior of Russia," *Army Quarterly*, 89 (1965), 238–243; W.K.M. Leader, "With the Murmansk Expeditionary Force," *Journal of the Royal United Service Institution*, 66 (1921), 662–691; Edward E. MacMorland, "Our First War with the Russians," *Collier's*, 128 (1951), 18–19, 70–73; Major-General Sir C. Maynard, *The Murmansk Venture* (Hodder & Stoughton, 1928).

Mayo, Henry Thomas (1856–1937)

Rear Adm. Henry T. Mayo was the commander of the 5th division of the United States Atlantic Fleet, stationed at Tampico, Mexico, during April 1914, when a minor incident involving the detention of U.S. sailors became a cause of major contention between the United States and Mexico, largely because of the actions of Admiral Mayo. President Woodrow Wilson, who strongly opposed the Mexican government of Gen. Victoriano Huerta and was actively campaigning diplomatically for Huerta's removal from the Mexican presidency, stationed U.S. warships in Mexican waters in large numbers to exert pressure on the Huerta regime.

While many assumed the vessels were present to protect U.S. citizens and their interests in Mexico, Wilson had little concern for protecting individuals he considered avariciously seeking large profits. Instead, Wilson regarded the ships as a reminder of U.S. power and as a means of securing reports on the situation in Mexico. The principal squadrons were stationed at Veracruz and Tampico, Mexico's principal ports.

A career naval officer and 40-year veteran, Mayo had graduated from the United States Naval Academy at Annapolis, Maryland, at age 19, and had risen slowly through the ranks, commanding several naval stations. Secretary of the Navy Josephus Daniels selected Mayo to be his aide for personnel matters in 1913, and later Daniels arranged Mayo's promotion over more senior officers, from the rank of captain to rear admiral. Requesting sea duty, Mayo first completed study at the Naval War College, at Newport, Rhode Island, and then assumed command of the 5th Division in December 1913, at age 57. Thus, he rose rapidly after a slow climb.

Tampico in April 1914 was under siege and crowded with U.S. citizens and other foreigners who had fled from the nearby oil fields at the approach of the rebels. Mayo, who was known as a businesslike, self-assured individual who acted rapidly and without hesitation, went to Tampico fully determined to do everything necessary to protect U.S. citizens, including landing troops if necessary.

The 5th Division consisted of the battleships *Connecticut* and *Minnesota*, each carrying marine detachments; the cruisers *Chester* and *Des Moines*; the *San Francisco*, a mine depot ship, and the gunboat *Dolphin*. Both battleships had a draft too deep to negotiate the sand bar at the mouth of the Pánuco River and, hence, were stationed in the gulf, three miles from the city of Tampico. Only the cruisers and the aging gunboat were able to enter the river and sail to the port itself, forcing Mayo to transfer his flag to the *Dolphin* in order to assure the ability to stay close to the city.

The Tampico incident occurred on 9 April 1914, when the crew of a small boat from Mayo's flagship was detained by Mexican troops as it landed within a military zone to pick up a supply of fuel. Because some of the men were ordered at gunpoint from a boat flying the U.S. flag, Mayo strongly protested to the local Mexican commander, Gen. Ignacio Morelos Zaragoza. The general immediately apologized and ordered the men released. The entire incident lasted less than one hour.

Mayo was not satisfied by the general's apology and demanded further redress. Stressing that the men had been taken down the street to the local commander's office, thus making the act public, and that the men had been removed from a vessel under U.S. sovereignty by virtue of its flying the stars and stripes, Mayo demanded that the Mexican commander hoist the U.S. flag in a prominent location and fire a 21-gun salute within 24 hours. Admiral Mayo acted entirely on his own authority, issuing this demand without consultation with Washington or with other commanders. He considered this action entirely a local matter and did not report the episode until after he had issued his ultimatum, to Rear Adm. Frank F. Fletcher in Veracruz, whose ships constituted the only means of radio contact with Washington.

Mayo's actions shocked U.S. Consul Clarence W. Miller, who believed that the general's verbal apology to Mayo's aide had ended the matter. Indeed, Miller reported that further apologies could have been obtained at the time, but not a salute as subsequently demanded by the admiral. Even Secretary Daniels believed that Mayo had overreacted, but President Wilson and most of the officials of the State Department and the Navy Department concurred with Mayo's actions.

Mayo's demands raised a minor incident to a major crisis, an action that suited the purposes of the Wilson administration. The Mexican commander would not take the steps demanded without instructions from his superior officers, which were not forthcoming. Anticipating that his demands would be rejected, Admiral Mayo prepared plans to seize Tampico. Meanwhile, the troopship *Hancock* arrived in Tampico with 1,000 marines, providing sufficient force to take control of the port. When diplomatic negotiations failed to resolve the crisis, President Wilson dispatched the entire Atlantic Fleet to Mexican waters.

Mayo's plans were superseded by other events because Wilson determined to seize Veracruz instead of Tampico after learning of the impending arrival of a shipment of arms for Huerta. Mayo was suddenly ordered, without any explanation, to pull all his ships out of the river and to sail to Veracruz to aid Fletcher. Mayo was shocked and feared leaving U.S. citizens at Tampico unprotected, but was compelled to withdraw his ships from the river. When Admiral Fletcher later asked for only the cruisers, Mayo was left in an awkward position because he feared that any effort to return the gunboat to the river would be interpreted as a landing operation.

Consequently, Mayo, whose actions escalated the incident to a full-blown crisis, was relegated to the sidelines, helpless even to assist the U.S. community at Tampico. With the landing, the center of attention shifted to Veracruz, and the original incident that sparked the crisis was virtually forgotten. The United States later agreed to rescind its demand for redress as part of the agreements reached at the Niagara Falls Conference, and U.S. citizens at Tampico, left unprotected during the tumultuous days following the landing in Veracruz, were ultimately evacuated by German and British warships, while Mayo's weakened squadron remained helplessly outside the river in the Gulf of Mexico.

Admiral Mayo later served as commander in chief of the Atlantic Fleet during World War I.

Kenneth J. Grieb

REFERENCES

Kenneth J. Grieb, *The United States and Huerta* (Univ. of Nebraska Pr., 1969); Robert E. Quirk, *An Affair of Honor: Woodrow Wilson and the Occupation of Veracruz* (Univ. of Kentucky Pr., 1962).

See also Tampico Incident (1914).

Merchant Marine in the Spanish-Cuban/American War

The U.S. merchant marine played a small role in the Spanish-Cuban/American War and was affected by the war only indirectly.

When the war began, a great Spanish fleet under Adm. Pascual Cervera y Topete was rumored to be steaming toward the United States to attack U.S. shipping and the cities of the East Coast. Marine insurance rates rose sharply, but there was no attack, and no U.S. merchant ships were lost during the entire war. On the other hand, many Spanish merchant vessels were captured by the United States Navy during the brief war, mostly near Cuba.

The tonnage of the U.S. flag merchant marine in 1898 was lower than that of any year since 1839, and U.S. ships carried only 9.3 percent of U.S. foreign commerce. Even the short war with Spain found the U.S. merchant marine inadequate for the vital tasks of coaling the navy, transporting the army, and resupplying U.S. forces, though most forces were operating very close to U.S. shores. The shortage of U.S. flag merchant ships was more acute in the Atlantic than in the Pacific.

The Civil War (1861–1865) had seen a 40-percent reduction in the size of the merchant marine, and a steady, albeit slower, decline continued to the end of the century. Wooden ships were phased out, and steel ships were more expensive to build in the United States, which placed high protective tariffs on iron and steel. U.S. crews were paid higher wages, and the U.S. government would not compete with the high subsidies that European governments gave to their shipping lines. Even when U.S. citizens owned merchant ships, they often registered them in foreign countries to avoid the higher costs of U.S. flag operation. The use of a "flag of convenience," as this practice is called, is still very common among U.S. shipowners.

The shortage of U.S. flag shipping did not seriously harm the war effort because the armed forces were able to charter foreign ships. Neutral nations were not unfriendly to the United States in this conflict, and they sold or leased 136,000 tons of merchant ships to the United States Navy at very high prices. It was, however, embarrassing for the United States, recognized as a major power, in the midst of building a first-class navy and on the threshold of possessing colonies, to depend on foreign ships in fighting a war.

When Commodore George Dewey prepared to leave Hong Kong for Manila, he was obliged to buy coal from a British ship. Impressed by his own dependence, he bought the British collier on the spot. Adm. William T. Sampson's ships, operating on the Cuban coast, had to return to Key West, Florida, to refuel because there were not enough colliers available to bring the coal to the navy. Even when a foreign ship was obtained, its officers and crew refused to take it into a combat zone, and there was a delay until a U.S. crew could be assembled. The ship itself was often badly suited for the purpose for which it was intended.

The U.S. merchant ships that served as transports revealed problems. They were required in peacetime to have U.S. citizens as officers and as a majority of the crew. The foreign members of the crew declined to risk their lives in war and had to be replaced. The civilian captains of merchant ships resisted bringing their ships within range of enemy shore batteries. Though highly skilled in sailing a solitary ship, these merchant captains were embarrassed by their ineptness in the special maneuvers used by convoys.

What the U.S. merchant marine of 1898 lacked in quantity it made up in quality. The navy took over 12 of the finest ocean liners and converted them into warships, manned by the naval reserve. The American Transatlantic Line's *St. Paul*, *St. Louis*, *New York*, and *Paris* were chartered by the navy, which renamed the last two *Harvard* and *Yale*. These four ships were returned to their line after the war. The navy purchased and kept eight somewhat smaller merchant ships from various other lines. These appear in the navy's records as *Yankee*, *Dixie*, *Prairie*, *Yosemite*, *Badger*, *Panther*, *Resolute*, and *Nictheroy*. Most of these ships were involved in serious fighting and were very effective, even though they had smaller guns than naval vessels and lacked the armor and watertight compartments of normal warships.

Advocates of a strong U.S. flag merchant marine argued that the experience of the war with Spain proved the need for government subsidies to keep the merchant fleet larger than was economically necessary in peacetime in order to have it available in wartime. They were not heeded, and the United States felt the effects of continued neglect in World War I. Because of its much greater duration and scope, and because so much Allied shipping was sunk by the enemy, World War I forced the United States to build a large merchant fleet in a hurry and at very high cost.

Allan A. Arnold

Merrimac, **Scuttling of (1898)**

On 29 April 1898, a Spanish fleet of three modern torpedo boat destroyers and four ramshackle armored cruisers sailed from the Cape Verde Islands toward Cuba to await the expected U.S. onslaught during the Spanish-Cuban/American War. The Spanish managed to slip into Santiago harbor, Cuba, undetected by Adm. Winfield Scott Schley's covering force. Once found on 29 May, the Spanish force soon faced Adm. William T. Sampson's main battleship force stationed outside the harbor entrance, which was illuminated at night with searchlights at close range. The Spanish fleet was anchored in the large mushroom-shaped harbor of Santiago de Cuba, where it was protected by the narrow harbor entrance through which the channel wound its tortuous course under dominating cliffs. To enhance the natural obstacles, the Spanish had emplaced heavy artillery and electrically detonated mines. There were not enough mines or modern guns, but Santiago harbor was a formidable military obstacle, and the U.S. commanders were unaware of Spanish weaknesses.

Even before leaving Key West, Admiral Sampson began planning to neutralize Adm. Pascual Cervera y Topete's fleet by bottling it up in Santiago harbor. Selecting the collier *Merrimac*, Sampson ordered Assistant Naval Constructor Richmond P. Hobson to begin planning the operation, a task complicated by the necessity for speed. Hobson, an officer on the battleship *Oregon*, arrived off Santiago early 1 June. Moon and tide conditions dictated that the best available opportunity would be early 2 June when flood tide would coincide with a period of darkness between moonset and daybreak. A shorter period would be available the next morning. Lack of time and resources required that less than ideal means be used to sink the collier. Hobson finally determined to use 10 torpedoes, electrically detonated. Each torpedo consisted of a normal eight-inch charge of 78 pounds of powder. The charges were to be placed along the port side below the waterline and in a position where they would serve to breach the watertight bulkheads.

Because the *Merrimac*'s length was barely sufficient to block the channel, it would be necessary to swing the ship across the channel. But it would also be necessary to approach the entrance at high speed to minimize detection. This meant there was only a short distance available in which to slow, turn, and sink the vessel. Hobson's plan called for the *Merrimac* to approach the channel at full speed, cut off power outside the entrance, and allow the ship's momentum to carry it into the mouth of the harbor. Then "the helm would be put hard aport," and when the ship began to swing, first the bow and then the stern anchors rigged to absorb as much momentum as possible would be released, and the torpedoes fired.

The crew of the *Merrimac* began its journey into history about 1:30 a.m., 3 June 1898. They were all volunteers selected from throughout the fleet. The men stripped to their long underwear, and each wore a life jacket and pistol belt.

Hobson expected to be detected from Morro Castle, the Spanish fort that dominated the harbor entrance. But in the predawn darkness the lumbering collier got within 400 yards of the entrance before it was discovered and fired on by a small picket boat which coolly concentrated its quick-firing guns on the exposed rudder of the *Merrimac*. Other heavier batteries joined in with an indescribable din. The double bottom having already been flooded, the seacocks were opened, and Hobson ordered the first torpedoes detonated. Without waiting for a response, he then ordered the final turn to starboard. The ship failed to respond and plowed blithely straight down the channel at six knots. The steering gear had been shot away in three different places.

Amid the noise of the heavy Spanish fire, which had become general, Hobson ordered the remaining torpedoes fired. Only two torpedoes responded, and these were insufficient to sink the ship quickly enough to lodge it in the narrow part of the channel. The ground tackle proved incapable of stopping the 7,000-ton *Merrimac*, which was moving at six knots, and both anchors tore loose. The ship continued to move with the tide into the inner harbor under increasing Spanish fire. The ship was hit literally hundreds of times, primarily by light, quick-firing weapons. At least 10 remote controlled mines were also detonated, one of which damaged the *Merrimac*. The Spanish fire was so intense that they took heavy casualties from their own cross fire.

Somehow in this incredible gunfire the crew of the *Merrimac* remained untouched save for one cut lip. Crowding in a small circle on deck, they rode the slowly sinking ship to its grave well inside the harbor entrance. It came to rest with just the extreme upperworks above water and offered no real obstacle to navigation. Although banged around by the rush of water as the ship sank, Hobson and his crew were again unhurt and found cover on the surface by clinging to a catamaran, which was tied to the sunken *Merrimac* and which capsized as the larger vessel sank.

For about an hour, the men clung to the bottom of the catamaran in the uncomfortably cold water. Then, in the early daylight, they saw a canvas-covered steam launch approaching them. Hobson swam out to it. He was pulled aboard and to his amazement found himself before Admiral Cervera. The admiral's first words were of praise for the courage of Hobson and his crew ("*valiente, valiente*"), and he treated the U.S. naval personnel with Old World courtesy. At first held by the Spanish navy, *Merrimac*'s crew was later turned over to the Spanish army and held ashore where they learned that their futile efforts had made them instant world celebrities.

Hobson and his crew were later exchanged for Spanish prisoners of war, and each one was awarded the Medal of Honor, although Hobson only received his award in 1933. Hobson used his fame as a springboard to politics and became a national leader in Congress of Prohibition forces and the foremost spokesman of naval expansion for many years.

Walter E. Pittman, Jr.

REFERENCES

Richmond Pearson Hobson, *The Sinking of the "Merrimac": A Personal Narrative of the Adventure in the Harbor of Santiago de Cuba and of the Subsequent Imprisonment of the Survivors* (Century, 1899); Walter E. Pittman, Jr., "Richard P. Hobson and the Sinking of the *Merrimac*," *Alabama Historical Quarterly*, 38 (1976), 101–111; Barton C. Shaw, "The Hobson Craze," *United States Naval Institute Proceedings*, 102 (1976), 54–60.

See also Hobson, Richmond Pearson.

Merritt, Wesley (1834–1910)

Wesley Merritt had a distinguished 45-year career in the military, taking part in the Civil War, the Indian wars, and the Spanish-Cuban/American War. Merritt was born in 1834 in New York City and was the 4th of 11 children born to John Willis and Julia Anne (de Forest) Merritt.

Merritt's father John was a successful New York attorney, who fell on hard financial times after the Panic of 1837. Consequently, he moved his family to southern Illinois, farmed for several years, became editor of the Salem, Illinois, *Advocate* in 1851, and went on to do well in local and state politics. The Merritts were avid Democrats, despised disunionists and hated abolitionists even more.

Merritt came to Salem when he was age 15 and left four years later imbued with his family's political beliefs. He attended the Christian Brothers school and then read law with a Salem judge. At age 19, however, he decided not to practice law, secured an appointment to the United States Military Academy at West Point, and began his course of study on 1 July 1855.

Secretary of War Jefferson Davis had extended the West Point program by one year, and Merritt's class was the only one ever forced to endure a half decade of the academy's strict discipline and training in order to graduate. Also, unlike previous classes, Merritt's colleagues often had heated arguments over political issues arising from growing sectional animosities in the United States. His class began with 121 students, but only 41 graduated in June 1860. Merritt compiled a good, but not outstanding, academic record; he was 22nd in his class.

Merritt was first sent to the famous 2nd Dragoons, then stationed in Utah under the command of Philip St. George Cooke, the most gifted cavalry commander of the ante bellum period. He arrived in November 1860 and, by May 1861 had been promoted to first lieutenant and had been made temporary regimental adjutant and acting assistant adjutant general of the Department of Utah. By then, the Civil War was underway, and his regiment was ordered to Washington, D.C. After it arrived in October 1861, Merritt rose steadily to ever higher ranks, becoming known as a "boy wonder."

Merritt had all the attributes of a fine leader, but so did many others who would never be promoted. He benefited from additional advantages, most of which were more a matter of good luck than careful calculation. First, he drew certain administrative duties on the staffs of various generals, the most important of which was service as *aide-de-camp*. As such, he could demonstrate his bravery and competence in battle in full view of his superiors and represent his commanders on noncombat missions; at the very least, he was always in close contact with his senior officers. Generals tended to mention their aides by name in their combat reports if they had performed well. Moreover, Merritt was almost always attached to units led by generals who participated

in and often won important battles. All this helped to advance his career tremendously.

After the Civil War, some cavalry units were sent to the Southwest to help prevent possible confederate uprisings; Emperor Maximilian's Mexican regime had offered ex-Confederate soldiers a new home. In response, Gen. Philip H. Sheridan sent Merritt, his chief of cavalry, to San Antonio, Texas, with 5,000 men. The presence of this force ended the threat peacefully, and most of the cavalry volunteers were sent home.

Merritt then toured Europe and returned to find that Congress was about to reorganize the regular army. Because the frontier needed increased protection, an August 1866 law tripled the size of the prewar army. However, regular army officers began competing vigorously for their jobs when they learned that half of the available spots were to go to volunteers. For his part, Merritt merely allowed his record and Sheridan to speak for him. Yet, in the end, he was offered only the rank of lieutenant colonel with the 9th Cavalry Regiment, one of two new black regiments. It took Merritt a full decade to secure another promotion.

Merritt served with the 9th from 1867 to 1874 at Fort Davis, Fort Stockton, Fort Clark, and Fort Concho. Most of his time was taken up with arduous administrative duties, difficult construction projects, disciplinary actions, and detailing hundreds of patrols, which seldom managed to locate the phantom-like marauders they pursued. Nevertheless, Merritt worked diligently to improve morale and to train his officers and men. These efforts, combined with his sense of fairness, produced results. The 9th compiled one of the lowest desertion rates in the army, and, later, in New Mexico, it fought with uncommon valor and effectiveness.

Merritt did not stay in Texas continuously during these seven years. In September 1869, he was sent to Leavenworth, Kansas, to serve on a board of officers, headed by Gen. John M. Schofield. Among other things, these leaders were to investigate current tactics, arms, and equipment and recommend changes they thought were necessary. Merritt represented the cavalry and gained the acceptance of Cooke's prewar tactics, with minor alterations, which were used until the end of the Indian wars. Completing this task in January 1867, Merritt secured a leave of absence, sailed to Europe, and in May, married Caroline Warren. The couple returned in September and went to Texas. In early 1875, Merritt was given a new assignment on Sheridan's staff in Chicago.

On the northern plains, many Sioux and Cheyenne were attacking whites because they were angry over broken promises and efforts to locate them on newly created reservations. Meanwhile, Indians who had moved to the reservations encountered constant food shortages, and, as a result, many planned to leave and join war parties. In 1876, the army tried to crush these movements, but Gen. George Crook was forced into a defensive position in Montana's Little Big Horn Mountains, and in June a large portion of the 7th Cavalry was killed.

To help meet this situation, in the summer of 1876, Sheridan promoted Merritt to colonel of the 5th Cavalry. Merritt joined his unit near Fort Laramie, Wyoming, and waited for Crook's orders. He soon learned, however, that some 800 Cheyennes were leaving the Red Cloud Agency in northwest Nebraska to join the warriors in Montana. In response, Merritt marched the 5th Cavalry some 85 miles in 31 hours in order to arrive ahead of the Cheyennes at a place on the trail near War Bonnet Creek. His troops surprised the Indians and drove them back to Red Cloud without suffering a single casualty. The Cheyennes had been amazed by the sudden appearance of the 5th and subsequently decided to stay at the agency, lest the same thing happen again. This encounter kept a large force of Indians out of Montana and was one of the few bright spots for the army during 1876. Merritt's regiment then joined Crook in early August for the 800-mile Little Big Horn and Yellowstone campaign, which ended on 24 October, having accomplished little.

Between 1865 and 1880, Army officers were generally isolated in frontier posts and showed little interest in new military advancements or the future of the regular army as a whole. Merritt transcended this pattern. He read and traveled widely and published articles advocating progressive ideas about the proper role of the army. In addition, in fall 1887, he helped found and became the first president of the United States Cavalry Association, which developed its own journal. A practical thinker, Merritt wanted officers to have a broader education and to learn modern military methods. During his five-year assignment at West Point, he reinstituted a policy of strict discipline, introduced the first world history course offered in 21 years, and inaugurated a graduation ceremony, in part, to help instill pride in the cadets.

In 1883, Sheridan became General of the Army and, by April 1887, finally secured Merritt's promotion to brigadier general. Merritt was given command of the Department of the Missouri, with headquarters at Fort Leavenworth, Kansas. Sherman had started an officers' postgraduate school there, and Merritt pressed to expand the program to help broaden and professionalize the Army's leaders. His major duty in this period came in handling Indian Territory, which is today Oklahoma. On 22 April 1889, two million acres were to be opened to white settlement. Merritt's troops successfully held back thousands of citizens until the opening, and with a minimum of force, later ousted gamblers and bootleggers, prevented hostile political factions from going to war with each other, and protected the Indian lands that remained.

Although he enjoyed his duty at Leavenworth and later at St. Louis, two events saddened Merritt deeply. On 5 August 1888, Sheridan, his good friend and mentor, died. In 1891, his wife became seriously ill with a kidney disease, which took her life two years later.

In June 1891, the new General of the Army, John M. Schofield, transferred Merritt to St. Paul, Minnesota, to command the Department of Dakota. At this point, he had enough time to co-author *Armies of Today* (1893), which compared the contemporary United States Army with its European counterparts. During his career, Merritt wrote nine articles dealing with military history and current problems and advocating the need for a large, modern regular army to protect the United States.

Merritt's department, however, was soon embroiled in the labor-capital conflicts stemming from the 1893 depression. He believed that the regular army, rather than United States marshals or the often unpredictable national guard, provided the best means for quelling riots and preserving domestic peace. In his view, the army was disciplined, professional, and efficient, and, thus, would keep violence to a minimum. This scenario was viable, however, only if the army stayed detached and dispassionate. Officers, for a variety of understandable reasons, however, tended to favor management over unions.

On 25 April 1895, Merritt was promoted to major general and moved to Chicago. He headed the Department of the Missouri, which was Sheridan's former division under a different title, and which encompassed the entire trans-Mississippi West, excluding states along the West Coast.

Within a short time, Merritt was called on to fight in one last conflict. The United States declared war on Spain in April 1898. On 1 May, Commodore George Dewey's squadron destroyed the Spanish fleet in Manila Bay. President William McKinley decided to send Merritt with enough troops to take the city of Manila and perhaps more of the Philippines. In the end, he led about 11,000 enlisted men and officers, including 5,000 professional soldiers, on this 7,000-mile voyage.

For roughly six weeks, as commander of the VIII Corps and the Department of the Pacific, Merritt trained troops, chartered ships, and gathered supplies near San Francisco. With no naval ships available to transport the expedition, he acquired privately owned trading vessels and had their interiors and decks rebuilt to meet his needs. He also slowly collected accurate intelligence, which allowed him to prepare properly for the operation. Merritt was partially successful in obtaining lightweight clothing for his troops and managed to amass livestock, refrigeration units, water distilleries and pumps, artillery, and as many modern Krag rifles and machine guns as possible.

Merritt sent the expedition in three phases, under the command of Brig. Gens. Thomas M. Anderson, Francis V. Greene, and Arthur MacArthur, respectively. On 29 June, Merritt and his staff followed the last detachment on the steamship *Newport*. The campaign to take Cuba was notable for its botched logistics and the disgraceful number of sick and dying men it produced. Merritt's troops, on the other hand, were trained, adequately supplied, and healthy. Moreover, Merritt made sure that supplies were placed in the ships so that they were readily accessible when needed. As a result of his experience and organizational talents, there were no serious problems during the month it took to get to Manila or thereafter.

On 25 July, Merritt met with Dewey, and they prepared to attack the city. The commanders faced a delicate situation. About 12,000 Filipino guerrillas, led by Emilio Aguinaldo y Famy,

had been fighting the Spanish for some two years. They were now besieging Manila, which contained 12,000 Spanish troops and some 300,000 citizens. Aguinaldo expected U.S. forces to back him and his Republican government. Merritt, however, had orders to avoid allying himself with the Filipinos. McKinley wanted the United States to become master of the islands, in order to provide maximum flexibility with respect to their disposition during the peace negotiations. Merritt, therefore, had to persuade the guerrillas to leave so that his forces alone could take the city.

By 1 August, Merritt's men and materiel had been shifted to Camp Dewey, south of Manila. Merritt had sent Greene to discuss the situation with Aguinaldo, and Greene had convinced the unsuspecting leader to move his force away from the city. The Pasig River divided Manila. Spanish troops were south of the river in an old section, encircled by walls, which was, in turn, surrounded by suburbs. Gen. Fermín Jáudenes y Alvarez commanded the Spanish troops. He realized that Dewey's guns could easily pound his garrison into submission, but he had no desire to surrender to the embittered guerrillas.

On 7 August, Jáudenes, Merritt, and Dewey began to negotiate a secret arrangement. Jáudenes pledged to defend only his perimeter and to keep his artillery silent during a U.S. attack. In return, Merritt and Dewey were to keep Aguinaldo's men out of the battle and refrain from hitting the city with artillery fire. Merritt did not tell his officers about the deal, and prepared for all-out combat in case Jáudenes reneged. On the morning of 13 August, Dewey began shelling the Spaniard's outer defensive lines. Merritt's troops then attacked and, within an hour, won the battle, having suffered only 49 casualties. They moved into the city, consolidated their position, and kept out the angry guerrillas. On 14 August, Jáudenes formally surrendered before news arrived that Spain had relinquished Manila a day before the battle occurred. Merritt assumed power as military governor of Manila and persuaded Aguinaldo to accept the new situation. However, within a few months after Merritt left, Aguinaldo's men began fighting U.S. forces; the guerrillas were not defeated until 1902.

Merritt was convinced that he had won a permanent victory in August 1898, and he asked to be replaced. He was ordered to the Paris Peace

Conference to provide information about the Philippine situation. He arrived on 3 October and met with the U.S. delegates, who were eager to hear his views. In his opinion, the Filipinos wanted to be annexed to the United States, and it should keep Manila and the island of Luzon at the very least. In December, he was ordered back to the United States and arrived in New York City that same month, with his reputation enhanced.

Merritt once again commanded the Department of the East, continuing until his mandatory retirement in June 1900. In some ways, this was a disappointing time for him. He would never be named General of the Army. His friends also failed in their persistent attempts to have him promoted to lieutenant general and to have him awarded the Medal of Honor for his performance at Brandy Station. On the other hand, he continued to participate actively in professional organizations, supported major changes in the army's command system, and seldom missed a chance to urge the need for a larger, better prepared regular army.

During retirement, Merritt lived in Washington, D.C. He died on 3 December 1910 and was buried at West Point.

Gerald W. Wolff

REFERENCES

Don E. Alberts, *Brandy Station to Manila Bay: A Biography of General Wesley Merritt* (Presidial Pr., 1980); Barry C. Johnson, *Merritt and the Indian Wars* (Johnson-Taunton Military Pr., 1972); Douglas Merritt, *Revised Merritt Records* (n.p., 1916); Wesley Merritt, "Important Improvements in the Art of War in the Last Twenty Years and Their Probable Effect on Future Military Operations," *Journal of the United States Military Service Institution* 4 (1883), 172–187; Wesley Merritt, Garnet Wolseley, and T. Janier, *The Armies of Today: A Description of the Armies of the Leading Nations at the Present Time* (Harper, 1893).

See also Manila, The Philippines, Battle (1898).

Mexican Border Battles and Skirmishes (1911–1921)

The outbreak of revolution in Mexico in 1910 led to a decade of political upheaval and military activity. Because much of the fighting took place in northern Mexico, the U.S. border states often were drawn into the conflict. In particular, the "twin cities" on the international boundary, such as Brownsville–Matamoros, El Paso–Ciudad Juárez, and Douglas–Agua Prieta, were often involved in military incidents. Control of these border entry points gave the various Mexican factions a port of entry for importing war materials from the United States, a source of revenue from their customs houses, and a psychological lift and public relations tool in trying to extend their control.

Except for the World War I period, U.S. military forces were concentrated on the border in response to the situation in Mexico. This concentration of forces provided only minimal security due to the limited number of troops involved and the extensive border (nearly 2,000 miles) that had to be covered. The operational orders governing the use of troops on the border also restricted their effectiveness. U.S. forces could fire across the border in defense of U.S. lives and property, but they were not authorized to cross the border before 1916 without previous approval from Washington, which was consistently refused.

The early years of the Mexican Revolution brought the potential for a clash between U.S. and Mexican forces on the border but no real conflict. In March 1911, President William H. Taft had ordered the creation of the Maneuver Division, a concentration of U.S. forces at San Antonio, Texas. While considering intervention, Taft was primarily interested in deterring military action by the different Mexican factions that might endanger U.S. lives and property. A rebel attack on the border town of Agua Prieta, Sonora, on 13 April 1911 resulted in two persons killed and 11 wounded in the neighboring U.S. town of Douglas, Arizona. Another rebel attack on the key border city of Ciudad Juárez, Chihuahua, in early May left six killed and 15 wounded in El Paso, Texas. Neither of these incidents provoked a military response from the United States; in fact, the Taft administration repeated its orders that U.S. troops were not to cross the border without prior approval from Washington.

The rebel victory at Ciudad Juárez led to the resignation of Mexico's durable dictator, Porfirio Díaz, and the assumption of the presidency by the nominal rebel leader, Francisco I. Madero. There were numerous rebellions against Madero's regime, many along the U.S.-Mexican border. Despite fears that these rebellions might spill over into the United States, there were no major border conflicts, and U.S. troops did not become involved in the fighting.

In February 1913 a military coup in Mexico City led to the overthrow and assassination of Madero, ushering in a new period in the revolution and posing a new threat to border security. The following month a new president, Woodrow Wilson, took office in the United States; Wilson soon found himself at odds with the new Mexican president, Gen. Victoriano Huerta. New revolts broke out immediately, with northern Mexico a major focus of military activity; the anti-Huerta element, known as the "Constitutionalists," was under the leadership of Venustiano Carranza.

When Constitutionalist forces attacked Nogales, Sonora, on 13 March 1913, stray bullets immediately fell on Nogales, Arizona, which was separated from the combat zone by only one street. U.S. forces responded by setting up a machine gun on a nearby hill and ordering Huerta's forces to stop firing. Huerta's troops meekly complied, laid down their weapons, and crossed over to the U.S. side. The incident at Nogales was one of the few times that revolutionary activity brought a military response on the border from the United States in the 1913–1914 period.

While Wilson was interested in interfering in Mexico to achieve the ouster of Huerta, he was reluctant to intervene militarily. He finally abandoned his noninterventionist policy in April 1914 but not in response to action on the international boundary. Instead, Wilson converted a minor incident at the Mexican oil center of Tampico on the Gulf Coast into an occupation of the key Mexican port of Veracruz. The intervention at Veracruz led to the dispatch of additional troops to the border because U.S. authorities feared possible reprisal attacks. Both the various Mexican factions and the Wilson administration worked to keep the intervention localized while the border region remained remarkably calm.

While the occupation of Veracruz did not bring about the ouster of Huerta as Wilson had hoped, Wilson's partial lifting of the arms embargo to permit the Constitutionalists to acquire arms did contribute to Huerta's overthrow in July 1914. Huerta's resignation, however, led to the bloodiest phase of the Mexican Revolution and to the greatest period of military conflict between the United States and Mexico during

the 1911–1921 period, with Francisco "Pancho" Villa breaking Constitutionalist ranks to contest Carranza for ultimate power. The revolution turned into a civil war, producing major conflict in the border area.

One of the first clashes between the supporters of Carranza and Villa occurred at Naco, Sonora, defended by Carranza's forces. When Villa's forces attacked on 4 October 1914, shells fell on the U.S. side, wounding two soldiers and a civilian. The attack turned into a siege, and on 11 October troops of the U.S. 9th and 10th Cavalry Regiments skirmished with Villista forces that had crossed the border to get a better line of fire. By December 1914, 41 residents of Naco, Arizona, had been injured as a result of stray shells falling on the U.S. side. The impasse was finally resolved not by military action but by a U.S.-mediated armistice in January 1915.

As the crisis at Naco was being resolved, a much more serious threat to border security was developing in Texas. On 24 January 1915 local officials at McAllen, Texas, discovered documents detailing the "Plan of San Diego," a revolutionary scheme supposedly formulated at the south Texas town of San Diego. The plan called for a combination revolution, race war, and separatist movement aimed at liberating the territory lost by Mexico in 1848.

Raids in support of the plan began in July 1915 in the lower Rio Grande Valley. Federal authorities were in a weak position to deal with the situation. Most of the raids were occurring in the Brownsville military district, which included almost 300 miles of the Rio Grande with only 1,100 troops to patrol it. Many of the troops were infantry and of little use in pursuing the highly mobile raiders. U.S. forces were still prohibited from crossing the international boundary, permitting the raiders a privileged sanctuary in northern Mexico where they encountered no opposition from Carranza's forces.

As the raids increased in intensity and frequency, the possibility of a clash between U.S. troops and Carranza's forces increased. There were frequent exchanges of fire across the Rio Grande, sometimes involving U.S. forces and Carranza's troops. There were even charges that Carranza's forces provided covering fire for raiders retreating into Mexico. When the U.S. government extended *de facto* recognition to the Carranza government in October 1915, raids under the plan of San Diego abruptly stopped.

The reduction in tensions over the border situation was short-lived as new problems developed with Villa over U.S. diplomatic recognition of his rival, Carranza. Villa—angered by what he considered his "betrayal" by Wilson—became increasingly anti-United States in his actions, culminating in a raid by Villa's forces on Columbus, New Mexico, on 9 March 1916. The raid resulted in 17 U.S. citizens being killed and prompted an immediate military response by the United States.

Although still prohibited from crossing the international boundary without prior approval from Washington, United States Army troops stationed at Columbus pursued Villa's retreating forces without consulting higher authorities. A cavalry detachment of some 60 men pursued the much larger Villa force of several hundred, fighting 4 separate battles and killing some 75 to 100 raiders. After almost eight hours of pursuit and fighting in Mexico, the U.S. force returned to Columbus.

This brief retaliatory action was the prelude to a much bigger military operation along the border, the "Punitive Expedition" under Gen. John J. Pershing. Pershing and his forces were charged with capturing Villa and dispersing his forces so that they would no longer be a threat to border security. The United States had hoped to receive the cooperation of the Carranza regime in its pursuit of Villa but proceeded anyway when Carranza balked at having U.S. troops operating on Mexican soil.

The Punitive Expedition was handicapped by the fact that it was not really engaging in "hot pursuit" of Villa at all; the first elements of the expedition did not cross into Mexico until 15 March, nearly a week after the attack on Columbus. Pershing's troops also had the difficult task of pursuing Villa's forces while avoiding a clash with Carranza's troops.

As the expedition grew in size and penetrated deeper into northern Mexico, the likelihood of fighting between Pershing's forces and Carranza's troops increased. By early April the expedition comprised almost 7,000 troops and had driven over 300 miles into Mexico. The first clash between U.S. forces and Carranza's troops occurred on 12 April at Parral, Chihuahua, resulting in two U.S. dead and several wounded, with Mexican casualties of approximately 40. Much more serious was the firefight at Carrizal, Chihuahua, on 21 June that left 12 U.S. soldiers dead, 10 wounded, and 24 captured; Mexican casualties were at least 74.

With the expedition essentially stalemated in Chihuahua, there were new threats to peace in other areas of the border region. On 5 May a group of approximately 80 Mexican bandits attacked Glenn Springs, Texas, killing three U.S. soldiers and one civilian, then retreated into Mexico, taking several prisoners. The Wilson administration responded by sending a "second punitive expedition" under Maj. George T. Langhorne after the raiders. Although the raiders freed their U.S. captives and dispersed, Langhorne continued the pursuit, penetrating more than 100 miles into Mexico and remaining in Mexican territory for 10 days.

The Glenn Springs attack also led to a major change in operations orders for U.S. forces on the border. U.S. troops were authorized to follow raiders across the international boundary when in "hot pursuit." A series of raids in June in the lower Rio Grande Valley led to more U.S. incursions into northern Mexico. The presence of large numbers of Carranza's forces in the region made hot pursuit a particularly dangerous policy. On one crossing in the Matamoros area U.S. forces exchanged fire with Carranza's troops, killing two of Carranza's soldiers.

By June both sides seemed to be heading for a larger conflict on the border. In early July, however, both Carranza and Wilson retreated from their positions; the "war crisis" quickly evaporated when the two parties agreed to turn over the problems of the Pershing expedition and border security to a joint commission. Although the joint commission produced no agreement, it did serve as an effective mechanism for reducing clashes along the border. The United States unilaterally withdrew the Pershing expedition in early February 1917. With the United States soon to be involved in World War I and with Carranza consolidating his power, the border became a less volatile region.

U.S. entry into World War I in April 1917 led to a major redeployment of forces for the European war, but defense of the border with Mexico still figured prominently in military planning. Those troops remaining in the United States continued to be concentrated along the border, partially in response to a perceived German involvement in the region. The policy of hot pursuit was continued during the war years although with growing restrictions as to how long (three days) and how far (60 miles) troops could pursue into Mexico.

Raids continued through the war years of 1917–1918, with most taking place along the Rio Grande. Although the raids were smaller and less frequent than those of 1915–1916, casualties were suffered by both sides. In December 1917 near Indio, Texas, a group of bandits on the Mexican side of the river fired on a United States Army patrol, leading to hot pursuit and the killing of 12 of the bandits. A raid near Van Horn, Texas, in March 1918 led to another crossing by U.S. forces which killed 33 bandits and burned their headquarters. These incursions did not lead to clashes with Carrancista forces, although they did produce the predictable diplomatic protests from the Carranza government. In May 1918 the U.S. government placed further restrictions on the hot pursuit policy, limiting it to the rescue of U.S. captives.

The end of World War I meant that the U.S.-Mexican border again became the principal focus of U.S. military interest. The presence of a large U.S. force on the border not only promoted border security, it also gave the U.S. government a tool for exerting pressure on the Carranza administration on a broad range of problems between the two countries.

U.S. forces were also operating under new instructions authorizing them to enter into Mexico in defense of U.S. lives or property. The new instructions received their most important implementation when Pancho Villa's forces attacked Ciudad Juárez on 15 June 1919. The assault caused several casualties in El Paso. After warning the Carranza troops to stay out of the way, a U.S. force of 3,600 men entered Juárez, routing Villa's forces and causing approximately 100 casualties. U.S. troops withdrew on 16 June having suffered two killed and 10 wounded.

As relations deteriorated between the United States and the Carranza administration, U.S. policy involved a military buildup on the border, including the addition of tanks and aircraft, with a border air patrol a regular part of military activity. This new border air patrol led to the last of the "punitive expeditions" of this turbulent decade. Although U.S. aircraft were ordered not to cross the international boundary, fliers often accidentally or deliberately violated the restriction. In August 1919, two fliers disappeared on a routine flight along the Rio Grande, turning up later as captives of Mexican bandits who demanded a ransom for their return. After ransoming one of the fliers, a U.S. officer rescued the second; with both airmen safe, a combination air and cavalry punitive expedition was launched in pursuit of the bandits. The expedition remained in Mexico for almost a week, killing five of the bandits and capturing six others.

This last punitive expedition was a fitting end to a decade of border battles and skirmishes. With new administrations taking office in both Washington and Mexico City, relations between the United States and Mexico improved considerably, and the border never again saw the kind of military activity that had occurred during the revolutionary decade.

Don M. Coerver

REFERENCES

Clarence C. Clendenen, *Blood on the Border: The United States and the Mexican Irregulars* (Macmillan, 1969); Clarence C. Clendenen, *The United States and Pancho Villa: A Study in Unconventional Diplomacy* (Cornell Univ. Pr., 1961); Don M. Coerver and Linda B. Hall, *Texas and the Mexican Revolution: A Study in State and National Border Policy, 1910–1920* (Trinity Univ. Pr., 1984); P. Edward Haley, *Revolution and Intervention: The Diplomacy of Taft and Wilson With Mexico, 1910–1917* (MIT Pr., 1970); Linda B. Hall and Don M. Coerver, *Revolution on the Border: The United States and Mexico, 1910–1920* (Univ. of New Mexico Pr., 1988).

See also list of entries at front of book for Mexican Border Battles and Skirmishes (1911–1921).

Miles, Nelson Appleton (1839–1925)

As commanding general of the United States Army in 1898, Nelson Appleton Miles was one of the key U.S. military leaders during the Spanish-Cuban/American War.

Miles was born on 8 August 1839 to a farming family near Westminster, Massachusetts. His formal education was limited, supplemented by a few night classes in Boston. The Civil War brought him into national history. At the outbreak he was commissioned a second lieutenant in a Massachusetts volunteer regiment. Thereafter, his performance as an officer was heroic and his rise in rank meteoric. He suffered a serious wound in the throat at Fredericksburg, Virginia, and a more serious one in the abdomen at Chancellorsville, Virginia. Although abdominal wounds were often fatal, an unusually strong physique saved his life. On 12 May 1864 he became a brigadier general, and only three months later, a major general by brevet. A participant in most of the important battles in the eastern theater, he missed Gettysburg only because of the Chancellorsville wound.

Because Miles had shown himself to be a talented combat leader, the much-reduced army retained him after the war as a colonel. His marriage to Mary Sherman on 30 June 1868 related directly to his future military career because she was the niece of Senator John Sherman of Ohio and of Gen. William T. Sherman. Miles never let the general forget about him. Driven by ambition, he made continuous requests and complaints in letters which often exasperated the recipient.

Miles continued to show talent as a field commander in the conflicts against Native Americans. He took an active and effective part in the Red River War, 1874–1875, against the Comanche, Kiowa, and Cheyenne. On the Northern Plains he was engaged against the Sioux in the later 1870s and against the Nez Percé. It was to him that chief Joseph surrendered on 5 October 1877.

General George Crook, of whom Miles was often critical, commanded in the Southwest against the Apaches in the 1880s. When Geronimo escaped from Crook after being captured, Crook was transferred, and in 1886 Miles became commander of the Department of Arizona. His command pursued Geronimo across the border into Mexico. The relentless pursuit wore the Apaches down, too, and Geronimo surrendered in September 1886.

Crook received a major general's post that Miles coveted and thought he deserved. When Crook died in 1890, President Benjamin Harrison struggled with some doubts about placing Miles in the vacant place because of his criticism of other officers and his relentless ambition. In the end, he made the appointment. Miles thus commanded the Department of the Missouri when the slaughter at Wounded Knee occurred on 29 December 1890. He was determined to court-martial Col. James W. Forsyth, who was in command in that action, but the War Department suppressed his recommendation and reinstated Forsyth.

In the Civil War as in the later Indian actions, Miles drew maximum performance from his men whom he drove to the limits of their endurance. He himself had uncommon physical stamina and was persistently cheerful. He was, in short, an effective field commander.

In spite of the resentments that his career had produced, Miles became commanding general of the army after Gen. John M. Schofield's death in 1895. That was his post when the United States declared war on Spain in April 1898. The army of 28,000 men was not prepared to fight any enemy but Native Americans. Only a small part of the unpreparedness can be charged to Miles. Because the War Department and the commanding general did not have the resources to supply and train the troops, the task of doing what they could fell to the corps commanders. Miles regarded these corps as administrative, but the commanders expected that they would themselves command their corps in combat.

Miles did not believe that a large force was necessary against Spain; the regular army moderately enlarged, supported by about 60,000 volunteers to serve in the United States, would suffice. The best strategy, he said, would be to send a limited force of regulars to land on the northern coast of Cuba, penetrate inland far enough to establish contact with Cuban forces, provide them with supplies, and then withdraw. He took the Cuban revolutionaries into account more than did the other strategists. Since summer was coming, with hot, sickly weather, he opposed hurrying into Cuba. More than other U.S. decision makers, he feared disease as the deadliest enemy in the island.

After a council meeting, which included Miles, Secretary of War Russell A. Alger on 8 May 1898 ordered the general to take 70,000 volunteers and attack Havana. Miles persuaded the president to give up this thrust. He did not favor attacking the enemy's strongest point and could not assemble 70,000 prepared troops. Next, on 26 May the same council (the president, the secretaries of war and navy, Miles, Adj. Gen. Henry C. Corbin, and Adm. William T. Sampson) decided to attack Cuba as soon as possible via Santiago on the southeastern coast. Although this suited Miles better than the frontal attack, he was really focused on Puerto Rico. If the attack were held up at Santiago, or if epidemics developed, he favored taking the forces to Puerto Rico, conquering it and returning later, at a better season, to Santiago. Even after the Spanish squadron had sortied out from Santiago Bay and been destroyed in the Gulf, he proposed transferring

Maj. Gen. William R. Shafter's army to Puerto Rico.

Secretary Alger and General Miles never got along. Alger joined with the other members of the strategic council to veto most of Miles's recommendations. He was especially scornful of the general's proposal that a force of 15,000 cavalry move overland from east to west on the island to take Havana from the land side. As the months went by, President William McKinley drew away from General Miles as counselor. He had been offended in May after the Santiago campaign plan had been adopted by Miles's letter proposing to scrap that plan and substitute a different one. McKinley wanted a short war and a quick victory and resented proposals not in accord with the accepted strategy. He turned increasingly to Adjutant General Henry C. Corbin for military advice.

Secretary Alger said that he had offered the Cuban command to the commanding general, who had turned it down in order to conduct a campaign in Puerto Rico. Consequently, the Cuban post, which turned out to be the most important assignment, went to Major General Shafter. Shafter headed the V Corps, the spine of the Cuban expeditionary force. The president, the secretary of war, the adjutant general, and Miles all concurred in the selection of Shafter.

Miles recommended that the regulars be concentrated at three Gulf ports, not just one: New Orleans, Mobile, as well as Tampa, Florida. By his order, volunteers gathered at first in state camps, but were later drawn into federal installations. Men and supplies poured into the camps faster than they could be accommodated. This was especially true at Tampa, where the confusion became notorious. Miles, only partially responsible for the tangle, was there to help Shafter untangle it.

Arriving off Santiago, Shafter adopted Miles's recommendation and landed at Daiquirí and Siboney, 16 and 10 miles, respectively, from the city of Santiago. But the commanding general had little influence over what Shafter did once he was ashore. Miles backed Shafter's decision to leave to the navy the problem of entering Santiago Bay and coping with the mines at the entrance.

General Shafter was unwell in both body and mind. The losses at El Caney and San Juan Hill depressed him fearfully while mild malaria and heat prostration sapped his physical strength and, with it, his will. He notified Washington on 3 July that he might have to withdraw from the heights overlooking Santiago and move five miles to a railhead. That same day Alger dispatched General Miles to Santiago with 3,500 men to take command if Shafter was unable to exercise it. The secretary did not make clear who was to determine whether Shafter was fit to command; Miles's role was, therefore, ambiguous.

Miles reached Siboney on 11 July, but kept the troops with him on board ship lest they contract the infections that were weakening Shafter's army. Shafter actually neither withdrew from the heights nor yielded the command. Alger, through channels, urged Shafter to assault and take Santiago, thus shortening the war. The president required unconditional surrender. Shafter, instead of making an assault, resorted to intensifying the blockade, drawing his troops tighter around the city. At the same time he negotiated with the Spanish officials, demanding surrender and threatening bombardment. Miles, present at the negotiations, supported Shafter. Finally, Washington agreed to something less than unconditional surrender; the United States would pay to ship the Spanish troops back to Spain. With this condition, and a few minor ones, the Spanish capitulated on 16 July, surrendering not only the troops in the city, but all those in southeastern Cuba.

At this point, the campaign to subdue Puerto Rico could begin. U.S. forces entered Santiago on 17 July, and on 18 July Miles received his orders to proceed. This was the moment for which the commanding general had been waiting. Because Shafter's men were in no condition to join the new expedition, Miles set out from Guantánamo on 21 July with the men he had kept from going ashore. Before leaving, he burned Siboney from which typhoid and malaria had spread. Thirteen thousand men, most of them volunteers, were converging on Puerto Rico from different ports in the United States. Miles quashed a proposal by naval officers to assault and capture San Juan without army assistance. At the same time, he demanded more assistance from the navy than Admiral Sampson was willing to offer. He appealed to the president, who directed the admiral to enlarge the navy's support.

It was agreed that Miles would land his army at Cape Fajardo, about 30 miles east of San Juan, and operate against the city from there. On 22 July at sea, the general shifted his objective. He saw no need to sustain the losses that would come from assaulting a major city. Accordingly, on 25 July his expedition landed at Guánica on the southwestern coast, as far as possible from Fajardo.

Miles was careful not to alienate the people of Puerto Rico. For that and other reasons, the conquest of the island was swift. The army was in action for 18 days, fighting six engagements. On 12 August the War Department ordered the end of military action because Spain had surrendered. It had never become necessary to attack San Juan. U.S. losses were 3 enlisted men killed, and 4 officers and 36 enlisted men wounded. So great was the urge among citizen soldiers to spend some time in military service that the National Guard forced the administration to accept new units to occupy the island after hostilities had ended.

In the Philippines, Commodore George Dewey destroyed the Spanish squadron in Manila harbor on 1 May. He had no troops to occupy Manila; so Miles recommended on 3 May that 5,000 men be sent at once under the command of Maj. Gen. Wesley Merritt who stood next below him in rank. In July he proposed a total of 15,000 men for the Philippines, but Merritt argued that twice that number would be needed. In fact, by late 1899 there were 120,000 U.S. soldiers in the Philippines. Miles was permitted a very small part in the war in the Far East.

Because of the confusion at Tampa and the heavy casualties in Cuba, together with the diseased condition of the troops returning to the United States, the war with Spain generated severe criticism of the army. In hearings before congressional committees General Miles sharpened the criticism. He condemned the supply departments, especially the commissary, which he accused of issuing canned beef to the troops that was spoiled, indeed "embalmed." His charges gave great offense to the commissary general, Charles P. Eagan, who called Miles a liar during the hearings. They also gave offense to the meat packers. Later investigation revealed that the beef was not rotten or "embalmed," but that it was hard to eat and to keep down.

Miles became a lieutenant general in 1901, but at the same time he was on his way out of the center of military affairs. President Theodore Roosevelt appointed Elihu Root to replace Alger as secretary of war. Root was to handle the legal aspects of empire building. Root also undertook to reform the army. To him and to Roosevelt, General Miles was obsolete. He belonged to the era of Indian fighting which had ended and did not fit into a United States that was a rising international power. They shipped Miles off to the Far East to get him out of the way while the army was reorganized. From the Philippines Miles wrote to protest the harsh methods used by U.S. authorities to force information from natives who were in rebellion. His critique was as unwelcome as his condemnation of the action at Wounded Knee, a decade earlier, and it was suppressed.

Root's reforms eliminated the office of commanding general, whose responsibilities had never been clear. Miles had considered the commanding general the equal of the secretary of war, and he opposed the change with his usual militance. Nonetheless, the change was made. On 8 August 1903, at age 64, he had to retire; the president did not attend the retirement ceremonies.

Mentally and physically, Miles was perfectly sound. In 1917 the United States entered World War I, and Miles, age 77, offered his services. They were not accepted. During his retirement, Miles was not conspicuous in public affairs, but he was recognized as a person of distinction. He died in Washington on 15 May 1925.

Historians have described Miles as pompous, conceited, stubborn, egotistical, and overly ambitious. Some have said that his actions as an officer in the latter part of his service were shaped by his desire to be president. They considered him gullible and politically naive, however. All historians concede that he was a courageous soldier and an outstanding combat leader. He was effective in the Civil War and in the Indian wars. His striving to see justice done to Native Americans and his protests at the treatment of the Filipinos marked him as a troublemaker in some circles. On whatever account, he loved martial display. Miles personified an era that was passing. He had been an exceptionally effective combat officer at a time when command was exercised in person. He did not fit well into the less personal, more systematized new army.

John K. Mahon

REFERENCES

Graham A. Cosmas, *An Army for Empire: The United States Army in the Spanish American War* (Univ. of Missouri Pr., 1971); Virginia W. Johnson, *The Unregimented General: a Biography of Nelson A. Miles* (Houghton Mifflin, 1962); Margaret Leech, *In the Days of McKinley* (Harper, 1959); David F. Trask, *The War With Spain in 1898* (Macmillan, 1981).

See also Corbin, Henry Clark; McKinley, William, and the Spanish-Cuban/American War (1898); Puerto Rico Campaign (1898); War Department in the Spanish-Cuban/American War (1898); War Department Investigating Commission.

Military Cooperation of the United States With the Cuban Revolutionaries (1898)

In April 1898 the United States joined an armed struggle in Cuba that had already been in progress for more than three years. During that period the Spanish army had demonstrated its inability to defeat the Cuban revolutionaries whose estimated numbers in 1898 ranged from 25,000 to 50,000. The U.S. press fondly styled the insurgents as an "army" conducting maneuvers and fighting battles under the skillful direction of its commander, Gen. Máximo Gómez y Báez. In reality the "army" was disorganized and widely dispersed throughout the island. It consisted mainly of roving bands of soldiers led by individual chiefs who assumed the titles of "general" and "colonel." Lacking training and more often armed with machetes than rifles, these men adopted the tactics of guerrilla warfare in which skirmishes and ambushes were preferred to large-scale battles. The insurgents enjoyed their greatest success in the southeastern province of Oriente. Although unable to capture any city or important center of local government, their ability simply to prolong the revolution inflicted continuous and ultimately crippling losses on the Spanish forces.

By its refusal to grant diplomatic recognition to the provisional government formed by the Cuban rebels, the administration of President William McKinley ensured that there would be no formal alliance between U.S. military leaders and the insurgent generals. There was, therefore, no suggestion of the Cubans being directly incorporated within the U.S. forces or command structure. Indeed, uncertainty reigned in Washington as to the exact contribution that the insurgents might make to winning the war. The implicit assumption always was that victory would be secured by the efforts of U.S. military and naval forces. Secretary of War Russell A. Alger was insistent that a substantial force of U.S. troops must be landed in Cuba as quickly as possible, but the army commander, Gen. Nelson A. Miles, believed that a major invasion was not feasible and should be postponed until the late summer. Although he approved the landing of small-scale U.S. raiding parties to harass the Spaniards, Miles remained particularly fearful of the danger posed by yellow fever to U.S. troops unaccustomed to campaigning in the tropics. Miles persuasively argued that the insurgents should assume the major role in land operations, until the United States had recruited and trained an invasion force. In his opinion, the combination of insurgent military pressure and a U.S. naval blockade of the island would bring about Spain's defeat with minimal cost in U.S. lives.

Miles was alone among U.S. political and military leaders in emphasizing the role of the Cuban insurgents. He was especially eager to enter into discussions with Gen. Calixto García, who operated in Oriente and commanded the largest and most successful of the Cuban insurgent forces. On 9 April, almost two weeks before the United States's actually entering the war, Miles had sent Lt. Andrew S. Rowan to establish contact with General García. Rowan eventually located García at Bayamo, Cuba, on 1 May and later in the month returned to the United States accompanied by three of García's senior officers. The delegation met with Alger and Miles in Washington, where they discussed future military cooperation. Maps and information about the disposition of Spanish forces in Oriente were presented. The Cubans also revealed that García currently controlled 3,000 men and was very short of ammunition.

Even before the meeting in Washington with García's representatives, U.S. officials were directing a steady flow of supplies and recruits to the insurgents. The largest expedition was that of Capt. Joseph H. Dorst of the 4th United States Cavalry Regiment, who landed on 26 May at Banes in northeastern Cuba, where he put ashore 400 armed Cubans, 7,500 Springfield rifles, and more than one million rounds of ammunition.

Despite the increased frequency of contact between insurgents and United States Army officers, their relationship remained unofficial and informal. U.S. officers coordinated military operations with individual insurgent leaders and studiously avoided any contact not only with the Cuban provisional government but also with General Gómez, the commander of the Cuban Liberation Army. A perplexed Gómez repeatedly complained of being kept in ignorance of U.S. war plans.

In fact, officials at the War Department in Washington were unilaterally designing a plan to assist Gómez. On 29 April Gen. William R. Shafter was given orders to prepare a detachment of 10,000 regular soldiers for a "reconnaissance in force" on the southern coast of Cuba. Shafter's mission was to march inland and make contact with Gómez. After supplying weapons and ammunition to the insurgents, Shafter was to withdraw. This aspect of the operation was to be completed in a matter of days. Shafter was to avoid engaging the Spaniards in battle; the intention was that Gómez's forces would do the fighting.

Shafter's orders were abruptly canceled on 30 April as a much more ambitious plan emerged which contemplated a direct U.S. attack on Havana, the center of Spanish power in Cuba. Buoyed by news of Commodore George Dewey's victory at Manila Bay, President McKinley agreed on 2 May to a bold scheme which would involve landing up to 50,000 U.S. troops to storm the Cuban capital. But the whole venture was suddenly rendered precarious by reports that the main Spanish naval squadron commanded by Adm. Pascual Cervera y Topete was possibly in the vicinity. It was clear that the threat of the Spanish squadron must be removed before U.S. troops could be put to sea.

By the end of May it was confirmed that Cervera's fleet was anchored in the harbor of Santiago de Cuba. The attack on Havana was abandoned in favor of a joint army and navy operation to capture Santiago and thereby destroy Spain's sole naval striking force in U.S. waters. The switch from Havana to Santiago also made tactical sense because it was the region of the island where the Cuban insurgents would furnish their most substantial and significant assistance to U.S. operations. In fact, the province of Oriente was already effectively cut off from the rest of the island. The insurgents, clearly in the ascendancy, controlled the countryside and had confined the Spaniards to a few fortified cities. In Santiago itself the beleaguered Spanish garrison numbered no more than 12,000 regulars, many of whom were believed to be unfit and sick. General Miles also had information showing that Calixto García had more than 6,000 men in the northern hills overlooking the city. Another 1,000 Cubans were known to be operating close to Guantánamo Bay about 40 miles to the east.

The initial stages of the Santiago campaign involved a good deal of Cuban-U.S. cooperation and military coordination. As General Shafter prepared his expeditionary force at Tampa, General Miles wrote to García informing him of the plan to strike at Santiago and requesting assistance from the insurgents in that region. García received this letter on 6 June and expressed his delight at the prospect of direct U.S. military intervention. His prompt reply stated not only that he would march immediately to support the campaign against Santiago but that he would place himself and his troops under U.S. direction.

The value of insurgent support was quickly demonstrated on 10 June when a Cuban detachment of around 80 men assisted a battalion of marines sent by Adm. William T. Sampson to establish control of Guantánamo Bay. Several skirmishes occurred between the marines and Spanish forces in which Sampson openly praised the Cubans for their assistance.

Meanwhile García undertook the difficult journey from Bayamo across the Sierra Maestra to the coastal village of Aserraderos west of Santiago. On 19 June he visited Sampson on the cruiser *New York*. On the next day General Shafter arrived in the bay and with Sampson made his way to Aserraderos for a two-day conference with García. The main question to answer was where to land the several thousand U.S. troops waiting offshore. On the advice of García, Shafter agreed on Daiquirí, a small port less than 20 miles east of Santiago.

García believed that only a few hundred Spaniards were stationed at Daiquirí and that they could easily be overcome by a combination of shelling from U.S. warships and an insurgent land attack. But García's role extended well beyond simply recommending the most suitable landing site. To confuse the Spanish command in Santiago as to the exact location of the U.S. landing, García instructed 500 of his men to make a diversionary attack west of Santiago at Cabañas Bay. Insurgent forces were also positioned to provide a protective cordon for their disembarking allies. García had already left behind a strong force close to Holguín to cut off the Spanish garrison in that city. Detachments of insurgents were also stationed east at Guantánamo and west close to Manzanillo to intercept any Spanish reinforcements that might be sent to aid Santiago. Moreover, García had brought 4,000 men to Aserraderos. These soldiers would be taken by U.S. ships to the vicinity of Daiquirí where they would link up with the U.S. forces in preparation for the march on Santiago.

The landing of U.S. troops and supplies at Daiquirí began on 22 June. Within a few days around 15,000 U.S. soldiers were put ashore. García was proved correct in that U.S. naval bombardment persuaded the local Spanish garrison to withdraw so that no military resistance was offered to the landing forces. The fact that there was no fighting was a tribute to good planning, effective U.S.-Cuban military cooperation, and the ability of the insurgents to restrict the movement of the Spanish forces.

However, friction soon emerged between U.S. elements and Cubans. At the tactical command level Shafter determined to mount a rapid frontal assault on Santiago. Such tactics were contrary to the desultory guerrilla warfare practiced by the insurgents. Eager to enter into combat with the Spaniards at the first opportunity, U.S. officers soon became contemptuous of the unwillingness of the Cubans to engage in a large-scale battle. The relationship was also fast deteriorating at the personal level, with U.S. soldiers openly accusing the insurgents of showing more interest in rations than in fighting the war.

In contrast to the landing phase, Shafter gave minimal attention to the insurgents in planning his attack on Santiago. He was content to see them remain in the defensive positions they had adopted at the time of the landing at Daiquirí. The U.S. general was also careful to stress that the insurgents were not under his formal command. He considered their services voluntary. In return, they would be provided with rations and supplies. For Cubans who had joined with the U.S. forces at Daiquirí, Shafter directed that they be employed in routine tasks as scouts, messengers, sentries, porters, and trench diggers. García was greatly offended and protested that his men should be regarded as soldiers and not laborers. It was evident that the U.S.-Cuban relationship was not intended to be an equal one.

In effect, the landing of 15,000 U.S. troops had transformed a civil war between Spaniards and Cubans into a war of military conquest by the United States. Despite the fact that more than 1,000 Cubans fought with U.S. troops in the bitter struggle to capture El Caney and San Juan Hill on 1–2 July, insurgents rapidly became a footnote in the Santiago campaign. In the eyes of U.S. soldiers, they were no longer heroes but thieves and cowards. First, there was the belief that a nearby Cuban unit did not fulfill its promise to assist Gen. Joseph Wheeler's attack at Las Guásimas on 23 June. The Cubans explained that the U.S. troops chose to ignore their advice and rushed ahead to engage in what was an extremely risky maneuver. Even more contentious, however, was García's alleged failure to prevent Col. Federico Escario from reinforcing Santiago on 2 July with approximately 3,500 men brought from the garrison at Manzanillo. Shafter considered this proof of Cuban incompetence and lack of fighting spirit. Shafter conveniently ignored the facts that García had a much smaller force than that of Escario and that the Spaniards had to fight all the way to Santiago losing 27 killed and 71 wounded in the process.

The evident U.S. resolve to minimize the Cuban contribution to the capture of Santiago was underlined by Shafter's pointed exclusion of García from both the peace negotiations and the formal ceremonies of surrender that took place on 17 July. The insurgents had actually expected to assume control of the city. Instead, they were informed by Shafter that they would not be allowed to enter the city under arms. The order was ostensibly justified as a measure to prevent possible public disorder and reprisals against the defeated Spanish troops. What most disturbed García, however, was the implication that Santiago was under U.S. military control. The Cuban general retaliated by instructing his forces to withdraw from joint military operations. U.S. soldiers regarded this as simply further proof of Cuban ingratitude.

Quite simply the insurgents were expendable. They were ignored as peace talks were concluded between the U.S. and Spanish governments. In fact, the policy of denying official status to the insurgents and limiting their participation in the war effort was used by the McKinley administration to justify its exclusion of the Cubans from the peace settlement.

In Cuba itself, the new task of the U.S. military authorities was to deal with the insurgent forces. No longer able to forage, the insurgents became increasingly destitute. As such they posed not only a threat to law and order but also a source of potential trouble for U.S. forces. A policy of economic pressure was instituted in which the U.S. authorities declared that rations and jobs would be withheld from Cubans who remained under arms. The insurgents succumbed and were effectively disbanded in November 1898. The United States Army therefore achieved in three months what the Spaniards had failed to do in three years.

Joseph Smith

REFERENCES

Graham A. Cosmas, *An Army for Empire: The United States Army in the Spanish-American War* (Univ. of Missouri Pr., 1971); Philip S. Foner, *The Spanish-Cuban-American War and the Birth of American Imperialism, 1895–1902* (Monthly Review Pr., 1972), 2 vols.; Louis A Pérez, Jr., *Cuba Between Empires, 1878–1902* (Univ. of Pittsburgh Pr., 1983); David F. Trask, *The War With Spain in 1898* (Macmillan, 1981).

See also García, Calixto; Gómez y Báez, Máximo.

Military Government and Civic Action in the Philippines

When U.S. troops first began arriving in the Philippines on 30 June 1898, approximately two months after Commodore George Dewey's decisive naval victory over the Spaniards, their officers were uncertain of their mission. President William McKinley's instructions to Maj. Gen. Wesley Merritt, the commander of the expeditionary force, gave no indication of the president's plans for the future status of the archipelago, and when the army first embarked on the task of military government in the Philippines, following the surrender of Manila on 13 August, the soldiers occupying the city did not know whether their presence in the islands was part of a limited action in the war against Spain or the first step in the establishment of a U.S. colony in Asia.

The problems facing U.S. authorities in Manila were staggering. The forces of the Philippine revolution under Emilio Aguinaldo y Famy had besieged the city since the beginning of June, and behind its walls some 70,000 people were crowded into an area that usually housed about 10,000. Food was scarce, the port was closed, and commerce was at a standstill. The city's schools were also closed, and its churches were filled to capacity with refugees. Spanish officials refused to serve the United States, and the city's governmental machinery was thoroughly disorganized. Some 13,000 disaffected Spanish prisoners within the city and the Filipino revolutionary army on its outskirts were both potential sources of disorder. The rubbish and garbage accumulated during the siege combined with the abnormally large population to create a significant public health hazard.

Fortunately for General Merritt and his subordinates, McKinley's instructions provided excellent guidelines for the conduct of any military government to be established in the Philippines. The president had directed Merritt to respect local customs, laws, and governmental routines as far as possible and to impress on the inhabitants of the islands that the United States Army had not come to make war on the Philippine people but to protect them. Private property was to be strictly respected, and the U.S. occupation was to be as free from severity as possible. In sum, the president had instructed the general to establish as benevolent and liberal a government as was possible given the wartime conditions that McKinley expected would prevail.

Merritt outlined the president's instructions to his troops before the attack on Manila to ensure that they understood them. The day following the attack, he publicly proclaimed the beneficent purpose of the United States and indicated to the Filipinos that as long as they cooperated with the army they would have nothing to fear.

The president's instructions and Merritt's proclamation both bore a striking resemblance to earlier instructions and proclamations issued by the United States in Louisiana, Florida, and Mexico. In the Philippines, however, the U.S. authorities placed greater emphasis on their "civilizing" mission to reconstruct in the U.S. image the territory falling under their control.

The actual burden of developing the U.S. military government soon fell to Maj. Gen. Elwell S. Otis, who took command from Merritt on 29 August. To maintain order in the city Merritt had created a provost guard of three regiments, and by the end of August Otis had organized a superior provost court. By the end of September an inferior branch of the court had been established to try minor offenders, but with Spanish justices refusing to continue in service, civil cases went untried.

Worried by the threat of epidemic, the army created a board of health in which both Filipino and U.S. health professionals worked under the general direction of Maj. Frank S. Bourns, chief surgeon. Board of health inspectors examined markets, slaughterhouses, pharmacies, and other establishments affecting the health of the community. The board also monitored the port against epidemic disease and enforced strict quarantine regulations. When smallpox broke out among the Spanish prisoners in November extensive vaccination averted an epidemic, and constant attention by the board of health and army engineers to the city's water system helped improve the quality of the water and its distribution through the public hydrants.

A general cleansing of the city and the enforcement of existing Spanish laws on municipal sanitation were among the first projects undertaken by the board of health. Patrols of the provost marshal's guard were responsible for enforcing the sanitary regulations, putting U.S. troops often in conflict with the city's inhabitants as long-standing but unsanitary practices were challenged. The result was a noticeable improvement in the cleanliness of the city.

The task of reopening the schools, closed during the siege, fell to Father William D. McKinnon, chaplain of the 1st California Volunteers. When sufficient local teachers could not be found, McKinnon used military personnel. A few months after the U.S. occupation began, some 3,700 pupils were enrolled in 37 schools. In keeping with U.S. practice, the army began reconstruction of the educational system on secular rather than religious lines.

The military government also gave significant attention to the commercial affairs of the city. A revised set of customs duties and tariff regulations retained the Spanish rate scale, but U.S. authorities abolished the head tax and the transportation tax. They retained, with slight modifications, the stamp taxes and the taxes on property, rent, and industrial and commercial operations, while reforming the mechanisms for assessment and collection.

Particularly evident was the army's active program of public works. In addition to the renova-tion of the water system, U.S. authorities repaired street lights and installed new ones. They also repaired or rebuilt many of the city's bridges and made plans for the development of markets and port facilities.

Within weeks of occupying Manila, the U.S. expeditionary force had established a military government characterized by its emphasis on reform. Although when its governmental efforts began the army did not know that its work would soon broaden in scope, it began a variety of programs that created a firm foundation for the development of a reform-oriented colonial government at a later date.

When President McKinley decided to make the Philippines a U.S. colony the army's relations with Aguinaldo's Filipino revolutionaries deteriorated rapidly. General Otis hoped that the reforms implemented by his military government would demonstrate the sincerity of the United States's benevolent intentions and gain Filipino acceptance of U.S. rule, but tensions continued to mount.

When war broke out on 4 February 1899, the work of the military government became more complex. All of the varied tasks of the government, including the improvement of health and sanitation, the development of schools, and the establishment of reformed governmental institutions had to be undertaken throughout the island in the midst of an active military campaign. The outbreak of war also meant that the implementation of any policy calculated to win Filipino acceptance of U.S. rule became both more important and more difficult.

Even after hostilities began, Otis continued to see enlightened government as a more powerful tool of pacification than forceful military operations. Other officers also believed that the war would end quickly if the United States could only make the Filipinos aware of its good intentions. Orders issued by U.S. commanders in the field showed that many officers recognized the connection between their new mission of conquering the Philippines as a colony and the way in which their troops treated its inhabitants.

The basic guidelines for the military government remained the same as those issued by the president when the expeditionary force had embarked. After deciding to take the Philippines as a colony, President McKinley reiterated his initial instructions in a letter to the secretary of war in December 1898, declaring it "the earnest wish and paramount aim of the military administration to win the confidence, respect, and affection of the inhabitants." The policy was to be one of "benevolent assimilation, substituting the mild sway of justice and right for arbitrary rule" (Blount, p. 149).

Throughout 1899, as the army occupied territory outside of Manila, commanders organized public schools and municipal governments. They also implemented public health measures and other civic projects with a reform orientation comparable to those already begun in Manila. Many U.S. officers continued to believe, as they had when hostilities began, that military government could be an effective tool of pacification, although developing its full potential in the midst of a hard fought colonial war would prove difficult.

Maj. Gen. Arthur MacArthur succeeded Otis on 5 May 1900. Like Otis, he hoped to convince Filipinos that a U.S. colonial government would have a sincere interest in their welfare and deal with them justly. MacArthur rejected the recommendations of subordinates who urged him to adopt a highly repressive policy, although he did implement harsher measures against the noncombatant supporters of the revolution to break their link with the guerrillas.

Even during the most frustrating period of the guerrilla war, many officers continued the reform-oriented work of the military government. During the same period, however, other U.S. soldiers engaged in deplorable acts of brutality out of frustration or a belief that the Filipinos could be terrorized into submission.

Although clearly affected by the guerrilla war, the work of the military government continued in the pattern created earlier. One of the primary considerations was the public health of the areas coming under U.S. control. To prevent epidemics in occupied towns, the army used the same general approach developed earlier in Manila, giving attention to improved sanitation, health inspections, vaccination, quarantine, the provision of medical care to the indigent, and the regulation, administration, and reform of key institutions. A drop in mortality accompanied the U.S. effort, providing vivid evidence of at least one potential benefit of the U.S. colonial occupation.

The development of schools was another project that remained high on the U.S. agenda, and one of the first actions undertaken by many

U.S. units occupying municipalities in 1899 was the organization of a local school. The early efforts, however, were rudimentary, given the shortage of local teachers, supplies, and revenue. Seeing the value Filipinos placed on their educational efforts, a number of army officers believed that school development provided the key to pacification, but by early 1900 the army's work in education was too poorly funded and haphazard to have much intrinsic value except as a way of showing the goodwill of the U.S. government.

In the newly conquered areas, army officers soon recognized the need to create capable municipal governments. Although a few officers had organized municipalities early in 1899, the first systematic U.S. effort came in August, when General Otis published General Order No. 43 setting out a plan for the organization of municipal government based on work done north of Manila by Col. William A. Kobbé. Although final authority remained in the hands of U.S. commanding officers and suffrage was limited, the plan provided for the creation of elected town councils with presidents having broad executive and legislative powers.

General Order No. 43 was followed in March 1900 by a new plan for the establishment of local governments set forth in General Order No. 40. As in earlier governments, an elected municipal council and president oversaw both legislative and executive activities. Suffrage remained highly restricted, limited to males age 23 or over who owned property valued at more than 500 pesos (about two hundred and fifty United States dollars), paid over 30 pesos (about fifteen United States dollars) in taxes, had served previously in an elected office, or were literate in English or Spanish. Local army commanders retained supervisory powers under the new plan, and General Order No. 40 explicitly noted that the municipal governments had a tutorial as well as an administrative function. In the field, however, officers tended to develop local governments along whatever pattern appeared to be best suited to the situation, at times deviating entirely from the models set down in General Order Nos. 43 and 40.

When the U.S. occupation increased in scope, so did the army's governmental activities, although the army created only one provincial government, on the island of Negros. There, some of the wealthier inhabitants had drafted a constitution providing for autonomy under U.S.

sovereignty. It was not implemented, but General Otis did organize Negros under General Order No. 30 on 22 July 1899. Col. James F. Smith, promoted to brigadier general, became its military governor.

In the various offices of the military government in Manila greater attention was given to the development of institutions serving the entire colony than to individual provinces. By the end of 1899 U.S. authorities legalized civil marriage and began the development of an insular court system. In April 1900 the military government instituted more far-reaching legal reforms with the revision of the insular criminal code to include U.S. practices and safeguards.

A similar reform took place in the insular internal revenue system. U.S. authorities streamlined it by abolishing a number of taxes. The *cédula* (head tax) that had been abolished in 1899 was reinstated at a nominal fee in 1900, however, because the populace was so accustomed to using the certificate as a means of identification. Although the army thought the Spanish system of taxing commercial enterprises and not land was unjust, it left the solution of that difficult problem to the civil government that would eventually rule the islands.

Other departments of the military government also looked forward to the time when a civil government would be in place. The mining bureau, for example, refused to grant any new concessions, devoting its efforts to the study of the Spanish system, the investigation of pending claims, and the preparation of laws and regulations for later implementation. Similarly the forestry bureau devoted its time to the classification, translation, and revision of regulations. An important result of the army's methodical approach was the discouragement of concession hunters and the protection of existing property interests, Filipino as well as Spanish.

To oversee the army's work in education, a department of public instruction was created in March 1900 under the direction of Capt. Albert Todd, who proceeded to outline a comprehensive plan for a new system, including industrial schools and a normal school. He recommended making English the language of instruction and bringing teachers from the United States to help in the system's development. Five months later over 100,000 pupils were enrolled throughout the islands in some 1,000 schools run by the military government.

Although public works projects in the provinces were not as extensive as those in Manila, the repair and building of roads and bridges took place continuously. The work served a triple purpose: improving logistics, providing local employment, and showing the Filipinos one more example of the assumed benefits of U.S. rule. Some commanders believed that an important reason for joining the guerrillas would be removed if the poorer Filipinos were given additional opportunities for employment.

Although considerable commitment existed among U.S. officers to a program of pacification based on the development of enlightened and humanitarian government, numerous problems were evident in the pacification program. Cultural conflict, for example, was apparent from the earliest period. The enforcement of unfamiliar sanitary regulations alienated many people, as did the tendency of some commanders to attempt to legislate morality. The military government's opposition to cockfighting created a particular problem until commanders saw the wisdom of tolerating such long-standing practices.

The frustrations of guerrilla warfare combined with the naive overconfidence of the United States Army during the 1899–1900 period created a much greater problem. Increasing frustration led to greater severity in the U.S. campaign and diminished the impact of good works. In particular, many U.S. soldiers were distressed by the evidence that some of the Filipinos holding office in the municipal governments organized by the United States Army also served the revolutionaries in shadow governments.

Friction developed between the civil authorities sent by President McKinley to the Philippines to begin the transition from military to civil government. The First Philippine Commission, a fact-finding and advisory body, arrived in 1899 and soon departed to make its recommendations in Washington. If anything, it proved helpful to the military government by reiterating McKinley's policy statements about benevolent government and strengthening contacts between the U.S. government and potential Filipino collaborators. The Second Philippine Commission, headed by William H. Taft, represented the first step in the transition from military to civil government, and jurisdictional conflicts between the two soon developed.

Taft and MacArthur vied with each other for status and power, and smaller versions of their civil-military conflict developed between military and civil officers in the provinces. When the president transferred the insular government to Taft in 1901, Brig. Gen. Adna R. Chaffee replaced MacArthur as military commander.

Despite its problems, the military government proved successful in a number of particulars. It maintained its reform orientation in the midst of a frustrating war, and the historical record of the military government provides a needed corrective to the common stereotype of the army having pacified the Philippines entirely through the use of terror.

In individual cases, the success of a local military government depended on key variables, such as the nature of the situation in the region where it was implemented and the commitment of U.S. authorities in the area to its development. Conditions in the Philippines not only placed great responsibility on individual commanders, but effectively prevented extensive management of either the pacification campaign or local military governments. In military units widely dispersed through the islands, junior officers often found themselves shouldering great responsibilities. In addition to their military duties, they might be expected to supervise the municipal governments and local police, organize schools, collect customs and internal revenues, act as provost judges, and see that the towns were kept clean and orderly.

The commanding general in Manila could do little to ensure that the official policy of benevolent government would be implemented at the lower levels of command. In such a situation the individual on the local scene became all-important. If the U.S. officer in charge was cruel, callous, unthinking, or just too busy to concern himself with the problems of government, he could hinder the pacification effort. Where officers had a real concern for the Filipinos or an understanding of the value of benevolence, however, they engaged in work that furthered pacification even when they were unsupervised or uninformed about the exact nature of official policy. Tremendous variation existed in the degree of commitment and reform activity from unit to unit and place to place.

Despite the problems, the work of the military government contributed to the success of the army's pacification campaign by helping to convince a number of Filipinos that life under U.S. rule could be tolerable, even advantageous. In particular, many members of the Filipino elite looked to the United States for the protection of their lives, property, and wealth from the revolution's rank and file. They shifted their support to the United States as they became convinced that through such action they could achieve the power and prestige that they had held earlier in Aguinaldo's government.

Filipino guerrilla leaders worried about the U.S. "policy of attraction," a term the revolutionaries used to describe such army activities as the establishment of schools, municipal governments, and public works projects. Fearing that the United States might win Filipino acceptance of U.S. rule through such a policy, some guerrilla leaders ordered acts of terrorism against their own people in an attempt to counter it. Terror, however, did not prevent all Filipinos from collaborating with the United States when the reforms implemented in the occupied towns created a positive image of the benefits of colonial rule.

Unfortunately, some U.S. soldiers, both officers and enlisted men, were not convinced of the value of reform-oriented government as a technique of pacification or became disillusioned with it as a result of the frustrations of guerrilla warfare. Their use of more severe measures resulted in a number of well-publicized atrocities, including the torture of prisoners to obtain information, but in general the reform orientation of the army's leaders remained a dominant theme of the Philippine campaign.

To be decisive, however, the actions of the army in the governmental sphere had to be combined with more traditional military activities. Alone, good government was not sufficient to achieve pacification, and in many areas pacification came only after the development of more comprehensive approaches to campaigning that included well-conceived military operations in addition to other, more benign methods. By 1901 the army had developed the proper combination, giving more attention to aggressive military action in the field to track down and harass guerrillas, the increased deployment of U.S. units in municipal garrisons to protect the population, and swift action by military commissions against Filipinos believed to be supporting the guerrillas.

The army's work set the pattern for Taft's civil government and the Philippine Commission, which took administrative control of the insular government in July 1901, and the policies followed by Taft and the commission often represented a continuation of programs initiated by the army in the previous two and a half years. The military government's efforts in public health and public works had been widespread, and the military was also responsible for developing the basis for the insular educational system, code of municipal government, tax structure, and revised legal system.

The lure of civil government provided a powerful incentive to Filipinos who wanted to be free of the restrictions of martial rule, and the reform orientation of the civil authorities helped further conciliation between U.S. authorities and Filipinos in the final months of the war. At times, however, Taft advocated a more repressive policy of pacification than that conceived by MacArthur, and stories of Taft saving his "little brown brothers" from the harshness of military rule are exaggerated. To the extent that Filipinos were won over to the U.S. side by the work of enlightened or shrewd colonial government in the period before 1902, officers of the United States Army deserve as much or more credit for that accomplishment as Taft and the commission.

The work of the military government in the Philippines was similar to that undertaken at the same time by the army in Cuba and Puerto Rico, and the reforms implemented in all three places often mirrored the efforts of reformers calling themselves progressives in many states and cities in the United States. As progressives in uniform, the army officers who directed the military governments in the Philippines and the Caribbean shared a commitment to political, social, and economic reforms with their civilian counterparts in the United States.

The approach to pacification developed by the United States in the Philippines, including the reform of civil institutions, was used in subsequent U.S. interventions in the succeeding decade. The army drew on its Philippine experience during the Cuban intervention of 1906, and the conduct of similar operations by U.S. military forces elsewhere in the Caribbean also resembled the army's work in the Philippines. A more explicit theoretical basis for the approach was seen later, particularly in the "civic action" concept developed in the 1960s and after.

The debate over the degree to which the concept was applied effectively in Vietnam continued long after the Vietnam War, much as the debate over the nature of the army's campaign in the Philippines has endured. Less open to debate is the clear success of the army in pacifying the Philippine colony. Individuals aware of the work done by the military government in the U.S. campaign may logically conclude that it played a significant role in achieving that end.

John Morgan Gates

REFERENCES

James H. Blount, *The American Occupation of the Philippines, 1898–1912* (G.P. Putnam's Sons, 1912), p. 149; John Morgan Gates, *Schoolbooks and Krags: The United States Army in the Philippines, 1898–1902* (Greenwood Pr., 1973); Brian McAllister Linn, *The U.S. Army and Counterinsurgency in the Philippine War, 1899–1902* (Univ. of North Carolina Pr., 1989); Virginia Frances Mulrooney, *No Victory, No Vanquished: United States Military Government in the Philippine Islands, 1898–1901* (Univ. Microfilms International, 1979).

Militia in the Spanish-Cuban/American War

In 1897 the U.S. state militias were reported to contain 106,250 enlisted men, most of them infantry with a scattering of cavalry and artillery. There were 9,376 officers, elected by the men in most states. Five states supported an entire division within their borders; 25 a brigade each; the rest went no higher than regiments. There was a leaven of Civil War veterans among both officers and men. When the militia units, known by then as national guard, offered themselves for federal service, however, it was discovered that 40 percent of the men were virtually untrained, and a surprising number had never fired a military weapon.

The shoulder arm for the regular army was a five-shot repeater, but because the supply was limited, militiamen received a .45-caliber, breech-loading, fixed-cartridge rifle, a reliable weapon, but a single-shot. Because the states had not kept supply and technical staffs in peace time (e.g., quartermaster general) their citizen soldiers were short of all types of equipment. The overall condition of the militia/national guard caused the commanding general of the army, Lt. Gen. Nelson A. Miles, and many other professional soldiers, to believe that it would take as long to put the national guard on a war footing as to organize new units controlled altogether by the War Department. Miles and others strove for the latter type of volunteer force.

A congressman sympathetic to them introduced a bill on 13 March 1898 to establish a volunteer organization apart from the militia system and free of any state control. States rights advocates, proponents of the national guard, mostly from the southern states or from Populist states in the Midwest, defeated it. They argued that to use the army instead of the organized citizen soldiery to fight for the nation was not only poor policy, it was also immoral.

As U.S. indignation grew over the alleged repression carried out by the Spanish government in Cuba, the military high command turned its attention to that island. Its members knew that in case of active U.S. involvement, the navy would have the primary role. The commanding general of the army envisioned a short campaign focused on aiding Cuban forces. A small army of 75,000, mostly regulars, would be sufficient to force a landing, march inland, deliver supplies and other help to the revolutionaries, and leave Cuba. The War Department could take about 60,000 militia/national guard into federal service to function as home guards. This small-scale war concept, with only a defensive role for the national guard, was killed on 23 April 1898.

President William McKinley did not want war, but as the prospect of conflict loomed, trusted advisors told him that he had to opt for war and enlarge the role in military operations for citizen soldiers or bring down the Republican party. McKinley gave in to this pressure and on 23 April called for, not the 60,000 volunteers planned for, but 125,000 instead; on 26 May he called for another 75,000.

The first chance to volunteer went to the units of the national guard, because they were considered the only organizations with some training and military armament. There was a problem because the United States Constitution plainly declared that the militia could be taken into federal service for three defensive missions only: to suppress insurrection, repel invasion, and enforce the laws of the United States. An overseas war was none of these. An added problem was that militia traditionally, and by law in some states, had been confined to use within the national boundaries.

The United States declared war on 25 April 1898, and war fever quickly burned away the handicaps in the way of militia/national guard use. It remained true that guardsmen had to enter the volunteer army as individuals, but a law passed on 19 April permitted the men of a unit to be sworn in en masse, keeping their officers and peacetime organization. To do so, however, they had to be at full wartime strength. Not many of the national guard units were at or even near war strength; so they drew heavily on a huge pool of eager volunteers. Almost all recruits from that pool lacked military training.

Kansas bypassed its militia to get volunteers because the governor hated the guard officers. Most of the other states, however, used the militia system to meet their quotas under the call of 23 April. Some states balked at the quotas assigned and there were individual guardsmen who did not volunteer with their companies because of the obligation to serve two years if necessary. The elite 7th Infantry Regiment of New York declined to volunteer lest it lose its identity under the command of graduates of the United States Military Academy.

Overall, though, the rally to the colors surpassed by 10 times the first six weeks of the Civil War, even though the two-year commitment exceeded by eight times that of the requirement of the first Civil War call. The war became a crusade to rescue a repressed colonial population from the allegedly bloodthirsty Spaniards. Senator George F. Hoar of Massachusetts called it the "most honorable single war in all history." The lust for military glory which had political value, never far below the surface, welled up in men in the United States. Close to 250,000 citizens volunteered to be soldiers in this war. But 25 percent of them could not pass the physical examinations. Those who passed and entered the volunteer army were statistically in their mid-20s, unmarried, native-born, and members of the blue collar population. Some blacks came from states that maintained separate black units in peacetime: Alabama, Illinois, Massachusetts, North Carolina, and Virginia. White officers commanded most of the black units.

The president appointed 1,032 officers for volunteers, 441 of them from the regular army and the rest from civil life. Six percent of them had served in the Civil War; 8 percent were graduates of the United States Military Academy. At the same time, 481 volunteer officers commanded in regular units.

A fact that must be stressed is that when a militia/national guard organization entered federal service, it ceased to be militia, operating under the militia clauses of the Constitution, and became part of the United States Volunteer Army. In all, 233,000 citizen soldiers made this transition, far more than the number needed. The erstwhile guard units retained their officers and a thin cadre of trained militiamen, but most of their men had not trained with them in peacetime. Even diluted by recruits as they were, and no longer militia/national guard, the units thought of themselves as an extension of the community they came from. The community, for its part, followed its unit as long as the war continued. Moreover, neither guardsmen nor the folks at home ever became reconciled to the caste system of the regular army or ever ceased to believe that the citizen soldiers could fight as well or better than the professionals.

The martial enthusiasm and political pressure from state officials and the national guard had created an army too large for the mission. There was on the one hand a small, reasonably efficient expeditionary force, which was manageable, and on the other hand, a volunteer army larger than the War Department could train and supply. The department was not organized to handle both forces efficiently at the same time. Nor could the states supply even their own troops in the volunteer army.

One fateful result was that the volunteers were scattered in camps without enough officers to train them and with poor sanitation. A great many of the surgeons appointed by the states had greater political than medical qualifications. Sickness became epidemic; typhoid fever accounted for 80 percent of deaths from disease. The ratio of killed in combat to killed by sickness was one to 15. Since only about 35,000 volunteers ever reached the combat zone, the rest lay around in camps, subject to infection, bored, and often unruly.

There were naval militias which fared better than the soldiers of the volunteer army. Eighteen states had organized citizen sailors: 10 on the Atlantic coast, two on the Gulf coast, one on the Pacific, and five that bordered either the Great Lakes or Lake Champlain. From these, 4,224 men entered the wartime navy and were assigned individually to ship or shore duty.

Maj. Gen. William R. Shafter, commanding V Corps, made the initial landing in Cuba with 16,058 enlisted men and 819 officers. Five volunteer organizations were with him. The 1st United States Volunteer Cavalry (the Rough Riders) had no connection with the militia/national guard. The other four were the 2nd Massachusetts Infantry Regiment, 863 men; the 33rd and 34th Michigan Infantry Regiments, 958 and 612 men, respectively; and the 71st New York Infantry Regiment, 922 men. These regiments joined the initial invasion force primarily due to political influence at home. Four more national guard regiments arrived in time at least to be part of the besieging force around Santiago. These were the 1st District of Columbia Infantry Regiment, 1st Illinois, 8th Ohio, and 9th Massachusetts. Secretary of War Russell A. Alger saw to it that Michigan was represented, and President McKinley did the same for Ohio. Opinions differ concerning the performance of the guard units. The total of the militia/national guard to serve in Cuba was 7,443.

Miles, commanding general of the army, had advocated strenuously from the beginning for an invasion of Puerto Rico. Finally he received orders to lead an expedition there, and on 25 July 1898 he arrived on the southern coast with about 3,500 men. His numbers rose quickly because U.S. politicians pressed heavily to get units from their constituencies a chance to garner some military glory. In the end his army grew to 16,235 national guardsmen and 3,787 regular troops. Illinois, Pennsylvania, and Wisconsin each contributed two regiments, and Missouri, Massachusetts, Ohio, and Kentucky each contributed one regiment. Most of the regiments had a strength of 1,100 to 1,200 officers and men, but the 1st Kentucky mustered only 614, and the 16th Pennsylvania only 794. Pennsylvania sent three troops of cavalry and three batteries of artillery. New York supplied two troops of cavalry; Illinois, Missouri, and Indiana, one artillery battery each. There was a company of engineers from the District of Columbia and an engineer detachment from Illinois.

Miles's army had six engagements in which three men were killed and 40 wounded. Then, only 18 days after landing, Washington informed the general that a peace protocol had been signed and that there was to be no more combat. The pressure on the government to give militia/national guard soldiers a chance to earn military glory had been intense; with that chance gone, pressure was equally intense to bring the boys home.

John K. Mahon

REFERENCES

French Ensor Chadwick, *The Relations of the United States With Spain: The Spanish-American War* (Scribner, 1911), 2 vols.; Graham A. Cosmas, *An Army for Empire: The United States Army in the Spanish American War* (Univ. of Missouri Pr., 1971); Marvin A. Kreidberg and Merton G. Henry, *History of Military Mobilization in the United States*, Department of the Army Pamphlet No. 20–212 (U.S. Government Printing Office, 1955); Gerald F. Linderman, *The Mirror of War: American Society and the Spanish American War* (Univ. of Michigan Pr., 1974); David F. Trask, *The War With Spain in 1898* (Macmillan, 1981).

The Monroe Doctrine and Its Corollaries

The Monroe Doctrine has been described by diplomatic historians as "the American Doctrine," "the ark of the American covenant," and the "holiest of holies" in U.S. diplomacy. During the late 19th century and the early decades of the 20th century the doctrine and its various interpretations served as the diplomatic umbrella for U.S. military interventions and meddling in the internal affairs of many nations in the Western Hemisphere, especially in the Gulf of Mexico-Caribbean region.

Originally presented by President James Monroe in 1823 as general principles to guide the foreign affairs of the United States, the ideas were primarily those of Monroe's secretary of state, John Quincy Adams. The four major elements of what was only much later called the Monroe Doctrine were as follows:

1. The Western Hemisphere was no longer open to further European colonization.

2. The United States was opposed to any attempt to extend the European system of monarchy to the Americas.

3. The United States would not interfere with existing European colonies in the Americas.

4. The United States would not meddle in the internal affairs of any European country.

The immediate reasons for Monroe's message to Congress were his concerns with Russian interest in the Pacific Northwest and the possibility that Spain might attempt to regain its hegemony over its newly independent colonies in South America.

Monroe's pronouncement was received with contempt by most European powers at that time and never became international law. As U.S. military and economic power increased, however, the Monroe Doctrine took on additional meaning and importance for this country, the Western Hemisphere, and U.S. competitors in the game of empire.

The major corollaries to and interpretations of the doctrine are discussed briefly below.

1848 Polk Corollary. Faced with possible foreign intrigue in the western territories of the United States and concerned about French activity in the Yucatan and in the Caribbean, President James K. Polk expanded the "no transfer" policy that President John Quincy Adams added to the doctrine in 1826. Polk informed Congress that the United States would not consent to the transfer of "dominion and sovereignty" over the Yucatan to any foreign power even if the inhabitants of that peninsula wished it. European nations were thus warned against not only armed intervention in the Americas but against diplomatic intrigues and meddling as well.

1858 Cass Doctrine. As President James Buchanan's secretary of state, Lewis Cass used the doctrine to further impede the grasp of Spain and other European powers in the New World. He announced that the United States would neither permit the establishment of European protectorates in the hemisphere nor countenance any other direct political influences that might lead to the subjugation of any independent Western Hemisphere nation.

1862 Seward Application. Coincident with the Civil War, Napoleon III hoped to create a reborn French empire in the New World using Mexico as the "host" nation. Secretary of State William H. Seward announced the United States's consternation over this encroachment of the French monarchy in Mexico but the United States was unable to take further action for fear of pushing France closer to the Confederacy. When the outcome of the Civil War was no longer in doubt, however, the House of Representatives passed a resolution condemning French intrigue and manipulation in Mexico. Pressured by the possibility of armed intervention by the United States, complications in Europe, and a deteriorating situation in Mexico, Napoleon withdrew his troops in 1867.

1895 Olney Doctrine. A dispute between Great Britain and Venezuela over the British Guiana-Venezuela boundary occasioned another application of the Monroe Doctrine. Great Britain resisted U.S. pressure to bring the dispute to arbitration, and there was fear that it would use force to obtain a favorable settlement. This concern prompted President Grover Cleveland and his secretary of state, Richard Olney, to apply the noncolonization principle of the doctrine. Olney informed the British that the concepts included in the Monroe Doctrine were universally accepted and, because the United States was practically sovereign on the continent, its decisions should be accepted by all. Britain initially refused to accept this rather presumptuous interpretation but, given problems with the Boers and Germany and a desire to protect its western flank, Great Britain eventually submitted the dispute to arbitration in accordance with the U.S. demand.

1904 Roosevelt Corollary. President Theodore Roosevelt's use of the Monroe Doctrine to legitimize the policies of the U.S. government in the Caribbean region is perhaps the best known and most controversial interpretation of the doctrine. During the early years of the 20th century the United States was faced with the possibility of European intervention in a number of Caribbean states for the purpose of collecting debts incurred by often unstable and corrupt governments. Both the inability of the various nations to maintain financial and political stability and the potential for foreign interventions were unacceptable to Roosevelt and others who attempted to apply the yardstick of the U.S. progressive movement to the nations of the Caribbean.

The so-called Venezuelan affair of 1902–1903 was the incident that eventually led to the Roosevelt Corollary. In December 1902 Great Britain, Italy, and Germany sent warships to Venezuela in response to that country's refusal to repay a large bonded debt. Following the sinking of several Venezuelan patrol boats and in view of the possibility that German troops might be put ashore to seize territory, President Roosevelt instructed the European nations to withdraw and to send the dispute to arbitration. Germany was reluctant to accept Roosevelt's demands until the president ordered the U.S.

battle fleet to sea and set a 10-day deadline for withdrawal. Germany withdrew its naval force with little time to spare, and the dispute went to arbitration.

The judgment of the international tribunal was announced in 1904. Venezuela was to pay its debtors, with payment going first to the nations that had engaged in the naval blockade. Roosevelt thought that this decision put a premium on the use of force in the collection of debts and, by doing so, raised the possibility of further interventions.

On 6 December 1904 the president announced that in the event of "chronic wrongdoing" or "impotence" on the part of the nations to the south, the United States would be forced, "however reluctantly," to exercise an "international police power." In a message to the Senate on 15 February 1905, Roosevelt observed that under the Monroe Doctrine, the United States could not sanction any European power's seizure and permanent occupation of the territory of one of the republics to force the payment of debts. He acknowledged that such seizure of territory might be the only way the debt could be collected unless there was interference by the United States. In essence, the United States was going to intervene to prevent intervention.

The Dominican Republic, a nation beset by financial woes and clamoring creditors, was the test case for the Roosevelt Corollary. The U.S. financial intervention in 1905, with a retired United States Army colonel serving as collector of customs, prevented intervention in the Dominican Republic by European creditor nations but that presence ultimately led to the U.S. military occupation of that country from 1916 to 1924.

In its continuing search for security and regional stability, the United States exercised the police power it granted itself in the Roosevelt Corollary through military intervention in nations of the region more than 60 times in the next 30 years. These interventions created a great reservoir of bitterness toward the United States, which is basis for much of the present-day animosity.

1912 Lodge Corollary. In August 1912 the Senate passed a resolution prohibiting acquisition of harbor or naval facilities in the Western Hemisphere by any foreign power. Sponsored by Massachusetts Republican Senator Henry Cabot Lodge, this extension of the Monroe Doctrine was occasioned by the attempt of Japanese business interests to acquire port facilities in lower California. The Lodge Corollary marked the first application of the doctrine to an Asian power.

1923 Hughes Interpretation. Realizing that the seeds sown by the Roosevelt Corollary to the Monroe Doctrine, the Platt Amendment, and heavy-handed economic and military interventions had reaped a harvest of hate and little else, Secretary of State Charles Evans Hughes's reinterpretation of the Monroe Doctrine essentially removed Roosevelt's "big stick" (military intervention) approach from future applications of the doctrine.

1928 Clark Memorandum. Undersecretary of State J. Rueben Clark's memorandum repudiated the Roosevelt Corollary and restricted the application of the Monroe Doctrine as a rationale for U.S. intervention to situations more in keeping with the role of a "good neighbor," such as self-defense.

The Good Neighbor policy, initiated under President Herbert Hoover but more closely identified with President Franklin D. Roosevelt, was really a nonintervention policy. This change in U.S. attitudes was given formal acknowledgement at the Pan-American Conferences of 1933 (Montevideo) and 1936 (Buenos Aires) at which the United States pledged to abstain from intervention.

The United States realized that it could no longer exist in its own version of "splendid isolation." A changing world and the threat posed by fascism and war required collective security, cooperation, and continental solidarity, not a unilateral protectorate system.

Subsequent diplomatic activity by the United States in the Caribbean region was aimed at gaining hemispheric support for the basic concepts of the doctrine, especially the concept of no transfer (i.e., territory held in the Western Hemisphere by an outside power could not be transferred to another outside power). This principle was incorporated in the Declaration of Havana in 1940 and was designed to prevent French and Dutch territories in the New World from coming under German control after the fall of France and the Netherlands during the Nazi spring offensive in 1940.

In its new guise as a hemispheric policy—carefully guided by the United States—the Monroe Doctrine continued to play a role throughout World War II and during the Cold War as well.

Writing in the 1960s, the dean of the Monroe Doctrine scholars, Dexter Perkins, observed that, like it or not, the governments of the New World are likely to be governed by the principles enunciated by James Monroe.

Lawrence H. Douglas

REFERENCES

Howard K. Beale, *Theodore Roosevelt and America's Rise to World Power* (Johns Hopkins Univ. Pr., 1956); Lester Langley, *The United States and the Caribbean in the Twentieth Century* (Univ. of Georgia Pr., 1985); Dana G. Munro, *Intervention and Dollar Diplomacy in the Caribbean, 1900–1921* (Princeton Univ. Pr., 1964); Dexter Perkins, *A History of the Monroe Doctrine* (Little, Brown, 1963); Dexter Perkins, *The Monroe Doctrine, 1867–1907* (Johns Hopkins Univ. Pr., 1937); J. Fred Rippy, *The Caribbean Danger Zone* (Putnam, 1940).

Montojo y Pasarón, Patricio (1839–1917)

Adm. Patricio Montojo y Pasarón commanded the Spanish fleet destroyed by Commodore George Dewey in the Battle of Manila Bay, 1898. Montojo had studied in Cádiz, Spain, and entered the navy in 1852. In 1860 he went to the Philippines to serve under Adm. Castro Méndez Núñez fighting the Moros (Philippine Muslims) of Mindanao. He visited Vietnam, Cochin China, and China, and later served on the frigate *Almansa* at Callao in 1861. Promoted to commander, he became secretary to Méndez Núñez. He later captured a vessel in the Philippines and returned to Spain in 1890. Promoted to rear admiral in 1891, he commanded the Spanish naval forces against Tagalog rebels in the Philippines. In 1897 he was awarded the Grand Cross of Maria Christina.

In the Battle of Manila Bay, on 1 May 1898, Montojo's fleet at Cavite was greatly inferior to Dewey's U.S. squadron. Recognizing his fleet's weakness, Montojo had planned to take his fleet to Subig Bay on 26 April and anchor it behind a line of Mathieson torpedoes (mines), but the torpedoes proving to be highly ineffective and the land batteries nonexistent, he returned to Cavite. His fleet could have remained under the guns of Manila, but he thought the probable shelling would greatly injure the people and town. He rejected fighting at Corregidor near Boca Grande, the main entrance to Manila Bay because at that location the water was very deep and mines not available. He chose to anchor off Cavite in Cañacao Bay—within Manila Bay close to the battery at Sangley Point. He rejected an open sea battle or dispersal which would have forced Dewey to pursue him. He might have stockpiled coal and provisions for dispersal, but rejected this alternative also.

His opponent Dewey's six fighting ships included four protected (armored decks) cruisers: *Olympia, Baltimore, Raleigh, Boston*; the unprotected cruiser *Concord*; and the gunboat *Petrel*; a total of 19,360 (David F. Trask says 19,098 tons), with 53 heavy guns including ten 8-inch breech loaders and 1,611 men. Montojo's squadron had two unprotected cruisers, *Reina Christina* and *Castilla*, the latter a wooden vessel; and five small gunboats, *Don Juan de Austria, Don Antonio de Ulloa, Isla de Cuba, Marqués del Duero*, and *Isla de Luzón*. Two other gunboats, *Velasco* and *General Lezo*, were undergoing repairs. Montojo's fighting ships displaced 12,029 tons (Trask says 11,328 tons) or 62 percent of Dewey's and had 37 heavy guns (69 percent of Dewey's). Only seven were 6.3-inch rifles; most of the rest were muzzle loaders. Secondary armament was 110 guns (81.4 percent) to Dewey's 135 light secondary guns.

Dewey's eight-inch guns outranged the Spanish guns, and his superior armament, relatively free from land battery fire, settled the action. His five fastest vessels were faster than the two fastest Spanish ships. He had 7,330 more tons and significantly more personnel than Montojo. Dewey's squadron could have remained beyond the range of Montojo's and the heavy Spanish guns onshore and used the eight-inch guns to devastate the Spanish squadron. Dewey steamed in for a closer action. Montojo had 167 killed and 214 wounded; 391 casualties. (Trask claims 161 killed and 210 wounded, a total of 371 casualties.) Montojo listed 75 killed and 281 wounded, total 356. Most casualties were on the Spanish flagship, *Reina Cristina*, which lost 130 killed and 80 wounded and which was sunk alongside the *Castilla* and *Don Antonio de Ulloa*. The *Petrel* later fired on the *Don Juan de Austria, Isla de Cuba, Marqués del Duero, Isla de Luzón, Velasco*, and *General Lezo*.

Montojo suffered a severe wound in the action, and his brother Eugenio was also wounded. He had rejected scattering his ships among the Philippines, a tactic that would have been strenuously resisted by the Spanish governor general

of the Philippines who wanted him to concentrate all available naval forces at Manila Bay behind mines and under land batteries. Montojo later declared he did not undertake dispersal because his vessels would have fallen one by one into U.S. hands and because he had no such orders from the Spanish government. Such a plan would have left Manila without naval defense and would have been subject to the governor general's veto. Trask has argued that dispersal of the Spanish ships in the islands would have been the soundest strategy because it "would have delayed their destruction, postponed American success and Madrid might have been spared the political shock that followed the naval battle of Manila" (Trask, p. 71). While dispersal would have denied Dewey a major battle, it would have left his concentrated force supreme. Montojo's squadron had only two vessels displacing more than 1,250 tons with coal capacity exceeding 250 tons. They were little more than coast defense vessels.

In September 1898 Montojo was suspended from further functions as general commander of the Philippines and left in October for Madrid, where he presented himself on 11 November. He was given a court-martial because of the destruction of his squadron, a normal practice for a losing commander. He defended himself by pointing to his squadron's relative weakness in guns, crew, and the need to avoid a bombardment of Manila. His ships were not designed to fight modern war vessels. He had chosen Cavite because Subig Bay was inadequately fortified and asserted the Spanish government had failed to provide adequate reinforcements. Despite a stout defense, he was found guilty, separated from the service, and imprisoned; thus, another admiral was made a scapegoat for his government's inadequate diplomatic, political, and financial support.

Dewey criticized his opponent for attending a reception and not remaining with the squadron the evening before the action; Dewey could not understand why the batteries of Boca Grande had not fired on his squadron as it arrived. Nor did he understand why Montojo had not ordered torpedo attacks from two of his cruisers.

Montojo was also a writer of critical essays, a novela, nautical manuals, technical and literary articles, and studies on terrestrial physics; he also translated James Fenimore Cooper's *The Two Admirals* and contributed to the *Diario de Ma-*

nila, Diario de Cadiz, Revista General de Marina, and other periodicals.

Frederick C. Drake

REFERENCES

French Ensor Chadwick, *The Relations of the United States and Spain: The Spanish American War* (Scribner, 1911); Spain, Ministry of the Marine, *Correspondencia oficial referente a las operaciones navales durante la guerra con los Estados Unidos en 1898* (1899), 17–19, 21, 25, 29–30, 89–90; David F. Trask, *The War With Spain in 1898* (Macmillan, 1981); U.S. Department of the Navy, *Annual Report of the Navy Department for the Year 1898* (U.S. Government Printing Office, 1898).

See also Manila Bay, The Philippines, Naval Battle (1898).

Moore, Dan Taylor (1877–1941)

Dan Taylor Moore, a career United States Army officer, was a highly influential figure in the development of army artillery during the early decades of the 20th century. As a captain in the United States Army Moore established the army's Field Artillery School at Fort Sill, Oklahoma, in June 1911. Until 1907, all U.S. artillery was grouped into a single branch, with its school located at Fort Monroe, Virginia. When the artillery was split into field and coastal branches, the "Cosmolineers" (as coastal gunners were called) stayed at Fort Monroe while the "Redlegs" (field artillery men) had to find a new home. Although only a captain, Moore was sent out to the old cavalry post in the former Indian Territory and given complete authority to establish the facilities and courses of instruction to train company-grade officers, field-grade officers, and noncommissioned officers.

Moore was born in Montgomery, Alabama, on 9 February 1877 into a family with strong military traditions. His great-great-grandfather was Gen. Israel Putnam's adjutant at Bunker Hill, and his great-great-uncle was Aaron Burr. His father, Irish-born Alexander Moore, was Garibaldi's cavalry commander during the wars of Italian unification. His grandfather, Daniel Tyler, for whom he was named, was a Union major general in the Civil War and a significant figure in U.S. artillery development during the early 1830s.

Moore grew up in Hannover, Germany, and was educated in Switzerland. In 1898 he graduated from the prestigious Federal Polytechnic School at Zurich, two classes in front of Albert Einstein. Moore returned to the United States just before the Spanish-Cuban/American War. He was commissioned in the 15th United States Infantry Regiment and served in Cuba between 1899 and 1901. He then transferred to the artillery and served in the Philippines from 1902 to 1903.

From 1904 to 1906 Moore served as a military aide to President Theodore Roosevelt, who was married to Moore's cousin, Edith Crow. The president was an enthusiastic amateur boxer, and used his aide almost daily as a sparring partner.

The early 1900s was a period of radical changes in artillery tactics and technology. The technique of indirect fire (the system that allows gun crews to shoot at targets they cannot actually see) was in its infancy. Only Germany had a completely workable system, and it was a closely guarded secret. With his fluency in German and his training in mathematics and physics, Moore was the obvious candidate for the United States Army to get inside the German Artillery School at Jüterbog. Roosevelt wrote a personal note to Kaiser Wilhelm II asking him to accept his "young cousin" as a student at the school. The Kaiser reluctantly agreed, and Moore became the first non-German to enter the school. Moore attended Jüterbog in late 1909 and early 1910. He gave his hosts the impression of an amiable but not very energetic officer; at the same time he took in every bit of technical detail he could grasp. His roommate at Jüterbog was Franz von Papen, who became German chancellor during the Weimar Republic and later vice chancellor under Hitler.

With the knowledge he brought back from Jüterbog, Moore set up the school at Fort Sill, which trains both army and marine field artillerymen to this day. At first, Moore operated the school on a shoestring. His entire staff consisted of two lieutenants and one sergeant. One of the lieutenants, Ralph McT. Pennell, later became a major general and commanded the school in 1944. The other lieutenant, Leslie J. McNair, became the commander of Army Ground Forces during World War II. He was the principal architect of the expanded United States Army, and the only U.S. four star general ever killed in action.

Moore remained at the school until October 1914. In 1915 he was assigned to the staff of the Army War College, which was then located in

Washington, D.C. For a short period that year his house guest was Franz von Papen, who was then the German military attaché. In an ironic twist of fate, von Papen turned the tables on his old roommate by running a portion of the Washington-based German intelligence operation from Moore's house. Von Papen was later discovered and expelled long before the United States entered the war.

Moore served in France during World War I. Although he commanded a field artillery brigade, he was never promoted to general. In 1919 he returned to the United States, resigned from the active army and took a colonel's commission in the officer reserve corps. He still held his status as a reserve colonel when he died in April 1941. In 1958 the army placed a bronze plaque on his grave site in the National Cemetery at Fort Sam Houston, Texas.

David T. Zabecki

REFERENCES

David T. Zabecki, "Dan T. Moore: Founder of the Field Artillery School," *Field Artillery Journal* (Nov.-Dec. 1981), 58–60.

Moro Campaigns (1902–1913)

The establishment of U.S. sovereignty over the Philippines after they were acquired from Spain at the end of the Spanish-Cuban/American War in 1898 was initially hindered by the Filipino resistance under Gen. Emilio Aguinaldo y Famy and by the uncertainty about Moro (Philippine Muslim) acceptance of U.S. rule. The "Moro problem" involved three major groups resisting foreign domination: the Tausugs of Sulu, the Maguindanaos of Cotabato, and the Maranaos of Lanao. The U.S. approach to the problem was the subtle use of effective diplomacy and military force.

While U.S. forces were occupied with the war against the Filipino revolutionary elements in the Visayan Islands and Luzon in 1899, Brig. Gen. John C. Bates of the United States Volunteers used diplomacy with the Sulu sultanate, resulting in the conclusion of a historic treaty on 20 August 1899 which not only neutralized possible armed conflict with the Sulu Moros, but also laid down in principle the foundation of U.S. sovereignty and rule in the Sulu archipelago. The continued exercise and demonstration of sovereignty by the sultan and *datus* (chiefs)

brought direct conflict with U.S. authority, especially over issues of slavery, armed defiance, and criminality which prompted the unilateral abrogation of the treaty in March 1904 by the United States. This abrogation surprised the sultan and his *datus*, who had been receiving annuities under the treaty. Subsequent armed disturbances were attributed by U.S. authorities to the encouragement of the sultanate. In anticipation of dealing seriously with the Moro issue after the end of the Philippine War in 1902, the Moro Province was organized in 1903 as a political mechanism to coordinate U.S. efforts not only to suppress Moro resistance, but also to encourage the general development of Moroland, especially its economic potential.

To Gen. Leonard Wood, as first Moro Province governor (1903–1906), was entrusted the task of neutralizing Moro resistance in Sulu. Most notable of the disturbances at that time were the uprisings led by Panglima Hassan of Luuk (1903–1905), Datu Andung of Taglibi (1903), Datu Usap of Luuk (1905), Datu Pala of Jolo (1905), and Jikiri of Pata (1907–1909). The bloodiest encounter, perhaps, was the Battle of Bud Daju in 1906 which ended in the massacre of about 600 Moros by what Senator John S. Williams of Mississippi called the "Charge of the Wood Brigade." The other sensational U.S. battle was Bud Bagsak in 1913 after which General John J. Pershing ended his politico-military career in the Philippines as the last military governor of Moro Province.

Except for the incidents of anarchy in the Rio Grande following the pullout of Spanish troops by 1899, the U.S. presence in the area was not challenged until about 1903 when the Ali rebellion broke out. The uprising was the open collective defiance of the Maguindanaos, who followed more or less the rationale of the earlier movement of Datu Uttu of Buayan, who fiercely resisted the Spanish attempt to bring the Rio Grande and Pulangi under control. Datu Ali, Uttu's son, had every reason to continue the legendary exploits of his father when U.S. sovereignty was enforced in the southern Philippines. Lack of support from Datu Piang, his father-in-law, did not deter him from confronting U.S. troops sent to neutralize his rebellion. This co-optation of Datu Piang by U.S. diplomacy weakened the base of Ali's resistance. U.S. military hardware provided the final blow to Ali's struggle.

After the suppression of the Ali rebellion, peace in Cotabato was established, and socioeconomic progress and development were becoming evident. No significant outbreaks disturbed the situation until about 1912 when Datu Alamada rallied about 300 recalcitrant Maguindanaos against U.S. rule. His band roamed around Buldon and Upper Cotabato causing problems for the local leaders who were under pressure to cooperate with the colonial government. In December 1912 a U.S. campaign against Alamada succeeded in getting Datu Ynuk to neutralize the band. With the assistance of Datu Piang, negotiations were conducted, and Governor Edward Dworak finally persuaded Alamada to yield in exchange for his resettlement in a colony in Pikit. Subsequent attempts by Datu Ampatuan of Maganui and Datu Ingkal of Kidapawan to renew armed resistance failed to materialize in 1913. The successful campaign in Cotabato brought peace to Mindanao.

In the Lake Lanao region initial U.S. military efforts were directed against the rampant cattle rustling and horse stealing perpetrated by organized bands. The most serious disturbances occurred in the area between the lake and Malabang on the Illana coast. In April 1900, Datu Udasan of Malabang raided the town of Callalanuan and carried away captives and loot. A detachment of 25 troopers from Parang under Lt. Col. Lloyd M. Brett, aided by Datu Piang's 100 men, was sent to look into the incident. The result was an armed clash between Piang's men and Udasan's followers, two Moro groups traditionally in conflict. The death of Datu Amirul Umbra and 14 of Udasan's men intensified the feud between the Malabang Maranaos and the Maguindanaos. U.S. officials were blamed by the Maranaos for taking sides with the Maguindanaos. The Maranao attacks on a U.S. exploring party in 1902 and the killing of a U.S. soldier in Parang were traced to Maranao resentment for the killing of Datu Umbra and two kinsmen of Datu Dacula, Umbra's father.

U.S. losses from Maranao attacks prompted the initiation of a general military campaign to enforce U.S. sovereignty in the lake region. About 1,200 soldiers were involved in the operation. Col. Frank D. Baldwin, U.S. commandant of Parang, was authorized to bring the Maranaos to submission. Earthen fortifications called *cottas* mounted with *lantacas* (brass cannons) had to be destroyed, resulting in the kill-

ing of several of the Maranao defenders. The attacks of *amucks* (religious enthusiasts who killed non-Muslims), called *juramentados* by the Spaniards in the preceding decade, posed a more serious threat to U.S. troops.

One significant engagement during the lake campaign was the Battle of Bayan, on 2 May 1902, where the sultans of Bayang and Pandapatan; and *datus* of Binidayan, Butig, Bacolod, Maciu, and other lake *rancherias* (settlements) were massed against the U.S. 27th Infantry Regiment and 25th Mountain Battery. The *cottas* were destroyed, and about 400 of the 600 Maranaos were slain, including the sultan of Bayang and the sultan of Pandapatan. Only 10 died and 44 were wounded on the U.S. side. Again, U.S. superior weaponry and Baldwin's policy of "shoot first and then talk peace" resulted in a Maranao capitulation. From this battle on, U.S. campaigns to persuade peaceful acceptance of U.S. sovereignty brought several of the lake *datus* to the first U.S. military post south of the lake, Camp Vicars, to show their submission.

In late 1901, Captain John J. Pershing was assigned to the lake region to assist Baldwin. It was here that the young officer, who a decade later became the last military governor of Moro Province (1909–1913), demonstrated his effective handling of both diplomacy and force against the Moros of the lake. While Colonel Baldwin was operating against the Moros south of the lake, Pershing successfully kept those to the north at bay through peaceful dialogues with the *datus* and sultans. After Baldwin's promotion to brigadier general, Pershing was designated in May 1902 as commander of Camp Vicars, an elevation over his seniors. He began his service with a conciliatory policy toward the Moros of the lake and tried to apply humane treatment to his wards. He personally demonstrated courtesy, respect, and regard for the Moros, especially their leaders, eating, playing, and mixing with them. This type of friendly relation was encouraged between U.S. soldiers and Moros.

Late in the year the *datus* and Moros who remained unreconciled to foreign rule started trouble for Camp Vicars. This led Pershing to initiate a military solution that earned for him the enduring respect of the lake Moros. His devastating blow against Datu Uali of Butig and the sultan of Maciu, two principal opponents of U.S. rule, brought peace to Camp Vicars and the southern region of the lake. Still to be neutralized was the continuing defiance of the west side Moros. On orders of Gen. Samuel S. Sumner, Pershing led another operation to the west on 5 April 1903 with four infantry companies, two field batteries, and three cavalry troops. The stiff resistance from the Moros collapsed, and the final phase of the campaign ended with nine *datus* and 120 of their men slain. On the U.S. side only one was killed and 14 wounded. Seven U.S. soldiers died from cholera during the campaign, however. From the west, the troops moved against Marawi in the north, wiping out resistance along the way. The fall of Marawi left 23 Moros dead. On the way back to Camp Vicars, Pershing's troops destroyed the 50 small *cottas* of Taraca, resulting in the death of 250 Moros and two U.S. soldiers and several wounded. By 1903, the entire lake region had been pacified, and Pershing's military prestige took a great leap forward. He returned to the United States for health reasons and was promoted in 1906 from captain to brigadier general over 862 senior officers.

Samuel K. Tan

REFERENCES

Peter Gowing, *Mandate in Moroland: The American Government of Muslim Filipinos, 1899–1920* (Univ. of the Philippines, 1977); Vic Hurley, *Swish of the Kris: The Story of the Moros* (Dutton, 1936); George William Jornacion, "The Time of Eagles: United States Army Officers and the Pacification of the Philippine Moros, 1899–1913," Ph.D. diss., Univ. of Maine, 1973; Richard K. Kolb, "Campaign in Moroland: A War the World Forgot," *Army*, 33 (Dec. 1883), 50–59; Samuel K. Tan, *Sulu Under American Military Rule, 1899–1913* (Univ. of the Philippines, 1967).

See also list of entries at front of book for Moro Campaigns (1902–1913).

Moro *Cotta*

Mindanao Moros are born fighters. The term "Moro" is a Spanish concoction for the Muslims in the Philippines, after the Moors of Europe with whom the Spanish had fought for several centuries. In the past, their lifestyle centered on conflict and consequently took shape around it. William H. Taft (1902), head of the Philippine Commission and civil governor of the Philippine Islands, described them as "warlike . . . every Moro is armed with a sharp sword or knife, and

fighting is about as normal to him as a peaceful life" (Taft, p. 1018a).

For well over three centuries, the Moros waged a *jihad* (holy war) against the Spanish colonizers, beginning in 1578 and ending in 1898 when Spain withdrew from the Philippines after its defeat by the United States. The Moros also frequently warred among themselves and other neighboring tribes. One *datu* (chief) conducted feuds with another and resorted to physical violence in defense of his honor or territory. When tranquility was disturbed, it was inevitable that the economic and cultural lives of the people were similarly affected. This cultural characteristic among the Moros caught the attention of Gen. Leonard Wood, first governor of the Moro Province (1903–1906), who commented in his 1903 diary that constant conflict held the Moros back.

Bred under conditions of conflict, Moro society came to develop a social structure whose contours were delineated by warfare. Children were socialized early in life for war. The boys underwent rites of passage to test their bravery. Houses were built so as to protect the residents from external attacks. Every established Moro village was fortified by a *cotta* (fort) for defense, the strength of which varied according to the prestige and power of the local chief. In the *cotta*, the warriors and their families stood pat to protect themselves from their enemies. In many ways, the *cotta* symbolized war, or the readiness for it among its builders. Gen. John J. Pershing, last military governor of the Moro Province (1909–1913), remarked that "unlike the American Indian warrior, who usually held his position, the Moro retreats to his fort or *cotta* to make his stand . . . . The Moro *cottas* are the natural product of years or perhaps centuries of internecine warfare and were primarily intended to protect themselves and their property from covetous neighbors" ("Fieldnotes Among the Moros," Pershing Papers).

The *cotta* was a stronghold made of earthen or rock wallings, from 10 to 12 feet high. It was fronted by a tremendous ditch and a high parapet, which was planted thickly with bamboos for natural cover. Each *cotta* was located on high ground to permit a view of the enemy from a distance and to afford a tactical advantage during any attack. Although fortified heavily, the *cotta* also had a secret passage for retreat in case it is overrun by a stronger enemy.

One of the major *cotta* battles in Moroland occurred in Bayang, Lanao, on 2 May 1902 just as U.S. troops occupied Mindanao Island. Over 300 Moro warriors died there. When the smoke of this infamous battle cleared, Gen. Adna R. Chaffee vividly described this Moro fortification as follows (Chaffee to Corbin, Henry C. Corbin papers):

> I should imagine that the Fort of the datto of Pandapatan, the one that was taken by our troops May 2nd was over 100 years old. Its construction is mainly of sod, faced with rock on the outside on two sides. The interior was about 80 feet square, and the bottom of the raised work at the ground is about 20 feet thick for about four feet high; the next layer is about 16 feet wide, four feet high, and the next layer is about six feet thick and four feet high. There were various holes in all of this for serving the lantakas which were laid on the ground and discharged through the holes. The exterior side of the fort was completely hidden by live bamboos so thick that a field mouse could hardly get through it. The tops of these bamboos had been lopped off by the Moros when our troops arrived in the vicinity, leaving a foot or two above the wall. Outside of the walls about 12 feet from the same was a large ditch probably 10 feet deep and 12 feet wide at the top, then a space of undisturbed ground about 10 feet wide. On this ground was driven split bamboo slanting outward very close together, perhaps six or eight inches apart and about three feet high, forming a *chevaux de frise* which a man could find difficult in walking over. Then another ditch about six feet wide and six feet deep. This was the run way around the fort; after this came a cleared space ground about four feet wide and another circle of split bamboo driven into the ground as above mentioned, about eight feet wide. Outside of this were sunk wells about eight feet deep and three feet in diameter and separated apart about three feet. A man could not rise out of one of these walls should he fall into it as the sides were vertical. Immediately outside of this line of walls was another line of split bamboo about 12 feet wide, then a line of oblong wells, three by six feet and six feet deep, separated one from another by about a yard, outside of these was another *chevaux de frise* of split bamboo 20 or 30 feet wide. The Moros outside the fort occupied the second line or ditch, lying upon the four feet of cleared space referred to and firing either through or over the bamboo spikes. There was but one entrance to the fort, at the north west corner. It was in an endeavor to get into

the fort at this point where all our officers were wounded. To defend this entrance, the Moros had a swinging piece of artillery rather uniquely suspended on what I may call a carpenter's saw horse, the horizontal piece being about eight feet from the ground, the cannon (3" calibre) was swung by ropes or bamboo strips from the cross piece attached to the trunnions of the gun. They could revolve it in any direction . . . .

While *cottas* were normally man-made fortifications, some were not. The Moro builders took advantage of natural covers onto which they fashioned their *cottas*. In Sulu, two extinct volcanoes, Bud Daju and Bud Bagsak, were the favorite refuge of Moros from pursuing U.S. troops. In 1906, the Moros revolted against U.S. policies regarding the abolition of slavery and the payment of taxes, resulting in a massacre of hundreds of Moro warriors, including their women and children atop Bud Daju. In 1913 a similar uprising broke out to protest the U.S. government order on disarmament. The Moros fortified and brought supplies to Bud Bagsak where they fought with U.S. troops.

In other districts of the Moro country, *cottas* have become a household term. The name of a place, Cotabato, for example, has its origin from the phrase "*kata watu*," meaning stone fort. Near the mouth of the Pulangui River, perched atop a hill, was a magnificent fort built by the sultan of Maguindanao for purposes of defense against the Spaniards. There, many protracted battles were fought between the Spaniards and the Moros who valiantly defended their homeland. From then on, every stranger would call this land Kuta Wato. But this was not the only *cotta* in the Cotabato district.

Next to Kuta Wato in magnificence was the *cotta* of Datu Ali in Seranaya, one of the largest in the area, which he and hundreds of his followers defended to their deaths against the advancing U.S. troops in 1905. Like the Bayang *cotta*, the Seranaya *cotta* was large and heavily fortified, capable of holding several thousand men and ample food supplies lasting for weeks. It took a series of expeditions to finally destroy this *cotta* and the chief who built it, Datu Ali, the last of the reigning Maguindanao royalty to oppose the U.S. occupation of Moroland.

All these *cottas*, however, proved no match to the mountain batteries that the U.S. troops deployed to bring the Moros to submission. When the U.S. military regime ended in the Moro Province in 1913, the once proud *cottas* stood no more to oppose the succeeding government.

Federico V. Magdalena

REFERENCES

Henry C. Corbin papers, Chaffee to General Henry C. Corbin, 7 May 1902, Box 1, Manuscript Division, Library of Congress; John J. Pershing papers, "Fieldnotes Among the Moros," Box 279, Manuscript Division, Library of Congress; William H. Taft, "People of the Philippines," *Independent*, 54 (1, 8 May 1902), 1099–1104, 1018a–1020.

Moro Province, The Philippines (1903–1913)

The Moro Province was formally organized on 3 September 1903 as an answer to the Moro (Philippine Muslim) problem in the southern Philippines where U.S. sovereignty had to be initially enforced by purely military means. The long history of Moro wars from the beginnings of Spanish rule to the advent of the U.S. presence showed the special and unique character of the Moro problem, requiring a more direct rule, different from the general pattern of governance established in the rest of the Philippines. To Maj. Gen. Leonard Wood, commanding general of the United States Army in Mindanao, was entrusted the task of organizing the province.

The preliminary survey of the Moro areas was undertaken by Wood in August 1903 immediately upon his arrival in Zamboanga, where the capital of the Moro Province was to be established. He first visited Dapitan, Misamis, and Lanao and conferred with local *datus* (chieftains) to get insight into their history, culture, economy, and government. Then stopping briefly at Zamboanga, he proceeded south of Borneo and the Sulu archipelago touching on Sandakan, Bongao, Siasi, and Jolo. He tried to gain some understanding of British and Dutch methods of dealing with their Muslim subjects as well as some knowledge of Tausug and Sama folkways. Finally, he called a meeting of *datus* in Jolo, the center of Moro resistance in Sulu. To them, he delivered the message that the United States desired the friendship of the Moro people but would enforce peace and order against all who defied authority.

With the formal opening of the Legislative Council on 3 September, the Moro Province

began its historic role under General Wood as its first governor. The other members of the Council were Capt. George T. Langhorne, secretary; Fred A. Thompson, treasurer; John E. Springer, attorney; Capt. Charles Keller, engineer; and Najeeb M. Saleeby, superintendent of schools. Only Captain Langhorne served throughout the entire period of the Moro Province. In 1906 General Wood was succeeded by Brig. Gen. Tasker H. Bliss, who served until 1909 when Brig. Gen. John J. Pershing became governor. Pershing was the last military governor of the province when military rule came to an end in 1913. Under the structure of the province, the governor was very powerful, directly responsible only to the governor general and the Philippine Commission in Manila. Consequently, the character of the province reflected the personality of its governor.

The province was further subdivided into five districts, each headed by a district governor. Each district was in turn divided into municipalities, and each municipality into wards. The five districts were Davao, Cotabato, Lanao, Sulu, and Zamboanga. Davao District had five municipalities (Davao, Mati, Cateel, Baganga, and Caraga) and six tribal wards. Cotabato District had two municipalities (Cotabato and Makar) and 18 tribal wards. Under Lanao District were the municipalities of Malabang and Iligan and 13 tribal wards. Sulu District was constituted of the municipalities of Jolo, Siasi, and Cagayan de Sulu and nine tribal wards. Zamboanga District had two municipalities (Zamboanga and Dapitan), five tribal wards, and 56 subdistricts. In addition to the district governor, a secretary and a treasurer constituted the district board which served as the governing entity in the district with power to initiate ordinances, including the designation of local headmen for subdistricts. The headmen were generally chosen from those who already had recognition from their people. In turn, the headmen were to appoint their deputies to take charge of the subdistricts which constituted their wards. The subdistrict deputies assumed the role of local police chiefs who were responsible for the peace and order of their jurisdictions. The organization of the Moro Province was anchored on the participation of the local people but limited to a large extent by the overall authority of U.S. officials.

The establishment of the Moro Province as an administrative mechanism contributed to the political gains of U.S. rule. The democratic participation of the local inhabitants in government opened opportunities for new local leaders otherwise hindered by the monopoly held by the traditional holders of power, especially the *datus*. Consequently, the new colonial system eroded the importance of even the sultanate. This led to the subsequent abrogation of the Bates Treaty in 1904 by a unilateral action of the United States, thus taking from the sultan the U.S. recognition he had enjoyed as a sovereign of Sulu since 1899 by the terms of Bates Treaty.

But the more important achievements of the province were in the social and economic aspects of development. Taxation was gradually enforced and accepted, from the annual *cédula* (head tax) of one peso for native and alien, except U.S. citizens and pagans, to other levies on products. Establishing the tax structure, despite initial opposition from the Moros, resulted in gradually increased revenues for the province. The impressive increases in revenues was the encouragement given by policies and laws that liberalized requirements and allowed much freedom in commerce, trade, and agriculture. Even saloons in Jolo yielded an annual income for the local government. Internal trade, as well as export, was stimulated and boosted by the active participation of the Chinese, particularly in the pearl fisheries of Sulu, agricultural production in the rest of the province, and trade in forest products especially timber. Industrial fairs and exchanges, especially during the Bliss governorship (1906–1909), widened economic participation and encouraged agricultural development. This was partly encouraged by the promotion of small landholdings.

With revenues rising, the provincial government was able to improve social services and public works. The education of the local inhabitants received priority through the establishment of a public school system to replace the military-run schools. Although non-Christian enrollment, especially that of the Moros, was initially a problem due to prevailing fears of parents that their children would become Christians, the remaining years of Governor Wood's rule saw an increase in non-Christian enrollment as well as in others. A U.S. Syrian physician, Dr. Najeeb M. Saleeby, who served as superintendent of schools until 1906, was credited with the successful promotion of education among the Moros. By the end of the province in 1913, the non-Christians,

including the Moros, had learned to value education as a means for social progress. In the area of health, hospitals and dispensaries were established in addition to the medical assistance the military doctors extended to the inhabitants. The impact on both the health values and attitudes of the people was encouraging. More public buildings, wharves, roads, and ports were put up in the province, greatly stimulating commercial and trading activities, as well as the effective enforcement of laws to ensure peace and order in the province. Although the problems of cholera epidemics, armed disturbances, and increased demand for services marked the development of the province, the 10 years of special, direct rule among the non-Christians proved to be a commendable period in U.S. colonial rule.

As a whole, the transition from colonial military rule to civil government in Mindanao and Sulu was hastened by the role of the Moro Province in integrating local, especially non-Christian, participation in the democratic system being pursued in the islands. Perhaps this was the more enduring legacy of the province to the political reorientation of the Moros. Subsequent political events in Mindanao and Sulu which characterized civil government under Frank W. Carpenter owed the Moro Province for the active participation of the Moros in their local affairs as well as for the socioeconomic support of the populace for the new democratic system.

Samuel K. Tan

REFERENCES

Annual Report of the Governor of the Moro Province for the Fiscal Year Ended June 30, 1913 [Brig. Gen. John J. Pershing, Governor] (Mindanao Herald Pub. Co., 1913); Peter G. Gowing, *Mandate in Moroland: The American Government of Muslim Filipinos, 1899–1920* (Univ. of the Philippines, 1977); Samuel K. Tan, *Sulu Under American Military Rule, 1899–1913* (Univ. of the Philippines, 1967).

See also Bliss, Tasker Howard; Moro Campaigns (1902–1913); Pershing, John Joseph; Wood, Leonard.

Motion Pictures in the Spanish-Cuban/American War

The Spanish-Cuban/American War was the first military conflict in history to be captured in motion pictures. Disparaged as a novel gimmick, movies received a new lease on life from the public's enthusiastic reaction to clips of the war.

The sinking of the *Maine* in Havana harbor in February 1898 offered the first opportunity to filmmakers. Shortly after the explosion, Albert E. Smith and J. Stuart Blackton of Vitagraph Pictures set up a small flagpole with a Spanish flag at the top. On film, Blackton's hand reached up and tore the flag down, then he raised the Stars and Stripes. Shown in theaters throughout the upper East coast, the movie was a sensation. Edison Company followed with similar scenes, as well as footage of the sunken *Maine*. Both studios shot the funeral parade and burial of the ship's victims, and audiences reacted with tearful emotion.

After the United States declared war on Spain, Edison, Vitagraph, and Biograph studios shot scenes of soldiers and sailors training, en route for Florida and Cuba, in battle, and returning home. Some were authentic, others obviously staged. Vitagraph perhaps pulled off the biggest coup. At Tampa, Smith and Blackton joined Theodore Roosevelt, always a hound for publicity, and his Rough Riders. They shot the famous "charge up San Juan Hill," actually a slow advance on foot under withering Spanish fire. Circulated widely in the United States, the 30-minute *Fighting With Our Boys in Cuba* did not stop the myth of the Rough Riders' charge on horseback from developing.

Soon returning to New York, the young men falsely told reporters that they also had filmed the Battle of Santiago Bay. Under pressure, Blackton and Smith secretly shot a staged naval battle with toy boats, dashes of gunpowder, and tobacco smoke. The two minute *The Battle of Santiago*, which cost $1.98 to produce, was an early example of special effects. Though crude in the extreme, the film was a raging success.

Even if not always authentic, film brought the ambiance of the war to the public with a vividness unavailable to print and still photographs. In 1899 both Edison and Vitagraph sent cameramen to Africa to cover the Boer War, and newsreels of war and other catastrophes became a staple of early motion pictures in the United States.

Jeffery C. Livingston

REFERENCES

Raymond Fielding, *The American Newsreel, 1911–1967* (Univ. of Oklahoma Pr., 1972), 29–34; Kemp R. Niver, *Motion Pictures from the Library of Congress Paper Print Collection, 1894–1912* (Univ. of California Pr., 1967); Albert E. Smith, *Two Reels and a Crank* (Doubleday, 1952), 51–68, 97, 132.

Moton Commission, Haiti (1930)

On 6 December 1929 U.S. Marines violently suppressed unrest that stemmed partly from a student strike at the Damien state agricultural school in Haiti. The incident led to widespread international condemnation of the occupation of Haiti. President Herbert Hoover, in response, appointed a general commission of inquiry, headed by W. Cameron Forbes, a former Philippine governor. Liberals pressed Hoover to include a representative black, but he instead named a second commission, led by Robert Russa Moton, president of Tuskegee Institute. The Moton Commission was charged specifically with investigating Haitian education. The members, all blacks, were Moton; William T.B. Williams, dean of the College Department, Tuskegee Institute; President Mordecai W. Johnson of Howard University; President Benjamin F. Hubert of Georgia State Industrial College; and Professor G. Lake Imes of Tuskegee, who served as secretary.

Haitian education had been primarily for the elite. It emphasized the classics and preparation for liberal professions and civil service careers. Students so oriented resented physical labor requirements, such as those at Damien. Tuskegee Institute, however, represented a different educational concept. The Alabama college, founded by Booker T. Washington in 1881, stressed manual labor and training. Its curriculum dated from an epoch when political and economic oppression barred most blacks from full civic participation and prestigious occupations. "Industrial education," as advocates termed it, purported to make productive citizens of unschooled rural blacks and rationalized their exclusion from the mainstream. High Commissioner John H. Russell and other U.S. officials believed that industrial education suited Haitian needs, and treaty authorities had endorsed it as early as 1917.

The commissioners arrived in Haiti in June 1930 to a cool reception by Haitians who resented their role and the pedagogy associated with them. The U.S. government did not support them, failing to accord the commission equal status and remuneration with the Forbes group. United States Navy objections to accommodating black passengers, even in an official capacity, temporarily stranded the group in Port-au-Prince following the completion of its work.

The Moton Commission's final report pleased no one. It did not endorse U.S. policies. Drafted in an era when student revolts on black campuses challenged the Tuskegee philosophy, the document reflected a changing consciousness. The educators antagonized Haitians by criticizing the separation of agricultural and industrial education from the standard curriculum and by rebuking the Haitian government for past failures in public education. U.S. liberals also disliked the report because they believed Moton had abetted segregation by leading a separate, all-black commission. Because treaty officials operated only the agricultural schools, they also observed, the commission's general criticisms would fall exclusively on Haitians.

The Moton Commission's problems reflect an important transition in the history of the occupation of Haiti. The rugged imperialism that colored U.S. public opinion concerning Haiti in 1915 had largely dissipated by 1930 and lacked support even from conservative pedagogues forced to respond to new trends at home. When the continued—and increasingly costly—domination of Haiti could no longer be justified, the stage was set for eventual military withdrawal.

Brenda Gayle Plummer

REFERENCES

Brenda Gayle Plummer, "The Afro-American Response to the Occupation of Haiti, 1915–1934," *Phylon*, 43 (1982), 125–143; Hans Schmidt, *The United States Occupation of Haiti, 1915–1934* (Rutgers Univ. Pr., 1971).

See also President's Commission on Conditions in Haiti (1930); Forbes Commission.

Motorized Supply for the Punitive Expedition

When troops of the Mexican bandit-revolutionary Francisco "Pancho" Villa attacked Columbus, New Mexico, in March 1916, the United States responded by sending the Punitive Expedition under Gen. John J. Pershing into Mexico, presenting the army with supply problems that it was not prepared to handle. Logistical planning had been predicated on free use of the Mexican railroads which the government of Mexican President Venustiano Carranza refused to allow. Instead, the expedition had to depend heavily on a hastily devised system of motorized supply.

The United States Army had been purchasing only a few trucks annually, did not have them organized into truck companies, and had no experience in motorized supply. The first two motortruck companies assembled at Columbus—each with 27 trucks—were composed of vehicles brought together from various posts along the border; this early shipment of trucks arrived without their wagon bodies fitted to the truck chassis, causing additional delay.

The army immediately began to purchase new equipment rapidly. By June 1916 the army had purchased almost 600 trucks, most of them assigned to supplying the Punitive Expedition.

Truck manufacturers worked closely with officers of the Quartermaster Corps in developing vehicles for use in Mexico. After the hurried initial purchases of trucks, subsequent truck orders were placed only after field testing with the Punitive Expedition. Fourteen types of trucks made by eight manufacturers were purchased by the army. By far the most popular make was the Jeffery two-ton truck of which 139 were purchased at an average price of about $2,700. This proliferation of models caused major problems with maintenance and spare parts.

The supply trucks required a great deal of support and related equipment. The expedition had 57 motor tank trucks, 10 trucks outfitted as mobile machine shops, and 6 wrecker trucks. The Quartermaster Corps also purchased a dozen trailers at a cost of $8,000, but the trailers proved unsatisfactory for regular motorized supply. The limited repair facilities at Columbus were overwhelmed by the rapid increase in trucks, leading to the establishment of large maintenance depots at El Paso and San Antonio, Texas.

The unprecedented use of motorized supply also posed major personnel problems. Officers for the new truck companies were hastily recruited from other army branches. Mechanics and drivers were both in short supply and often lacked practical experience; under existing regulations, enlisted personnel could qualify as drivers by passing a written examination without any driving experience. Early shipments of trucks included civilian drivers furnished by the manufacturers, causing problems with supervision and discipline.

The motor trucks operated in groups or "trains," traveling over 300 miles into Mexico. Truck company personnel were armed, and a squad of troops was assigned to guard each train.

Roads were poor to begin with, and heavy use caused them to deteriorate rapidly. During the rainy season, much of the route was impassable. Members of the Corps of Engineers, using road machinery specially purchased for the expedition, attempted to keep the roads open, but a shortage of equipment and personnel restricted activities. Despite the problems, truck companies could still average 60 to 90 miles per day.

By June 1916 there were 12 motor truck companies using over 300 trucks involved in direct supply of the Punitive Expedition. Another six motor truck companies were in operation along the Mexican border. With the limitations on rail supply, motorized supply became crucial to the maintenance of the expedition in northern Mexico.

The expedition's experience with motorized supply had a profound influence on later army practices. The expedition clearly demonstrated the need for more trucks and illustrated the personnel problems associated with motorized supply. The multiplicity of truck models emphasized the need to develop a standard army truck, a process that was well advanced when the United States entered World War I in April 1917. With the army truck fleet expanding from some 600 trucks in June 1916 to over 82,000 trucks by June 1918, the Punitive Expedition's experiment with motorized supply became a crucial prelude to the demands of World War I.

Don M. Coerver

REFERENCES

Clarence C. Clendenen, *Blood on the Border: The United States Army and the Mexican Irregulars* (Macmillan, 1969); Jeff Jore, "Pershing's Mission in Mexico: Logistics and Preparation for the War in Europe," *Military Affairs*, 52 (1988), 117–121; Frank Tompkins, *Chasing Villa: The Story Behind the Story of Pershing's Expedition Into Mexico* (Military Service Pub. Co., 1934); Frank E. Vandiver, *Black Jack: The Life and Times of John J. Pershing* (Texas A&M Univ. Pr., 1977), 2 vols., U.S. War Department, *Annual Reports*, 1916, 1917 (U.S. Government Printing Office, 1916, 1917).

Murmansk Railroad Front, North Russia (1919)

The Murmansk Railroad Front constituted the westernmost line of advance of the forces that participated in the U.S. intervention in North Russia, 1918–1919. Located along the course of the railroad that proceeded due south from Murmansk on the Kola Inlet of the Barents Sea, the front provided direct access to the key city of Petrograd, located approximately 900 miles to the south and west. At the same time, the railroad also served as a vital communications and supply link between ice-free Murmansk and the Allied forces engaged in intervention at Archangel, some 200 miles to the east.

Although Allied intervention at Murmansk began as early as March 1918, direct U.S. engagement in the area did not begin until early 1919 when President Woodrow Wilson consented to a British request for the dispatch to the region of a contingent of transportation troops to bolster the Allied forces of British Maj. Gen. Charles C.M. Maynard. Recruited in France, these troops consisted of the 167th (Operations) and 168th (Maintenance) Companies of the United States Army's Transportation Corps, which were soon reorganized as the North Russia Transportation Corps of the American Expeditionary Force, North Russia. Totaling 720 officers and men, these units sailed from England in three groups and arrived at Murmansk between 25 March and 17 April 1919.

Having detached an element of the 168th for service at Murmansk, the rest of the U.S. troops headed south some 300 miles to Soroka (Belomorsk) on the White Sea, where they immediately took over the maintenance and operation of the railroad from that point to the front, then located at Urosozero, about 90 miles to the south. While most of the troops were detailed to undertake the care and maintenance of the railroad, two units of the 168th were detached for active service with the forces of General Maynard, who had just initiated an offensive intended to advance the front some 25 miles southward to the northern shore of Lake Onega. Of these detachments, the first, aggregating about 65 officers and men, manned an armed flatcar and participated at once in the successful capture of Masel'ga, incurring the only two fatalities suffered by the Transportation Corps in North Russia. Following the victory at Masel'ga, the flatcar detachment also took part in the successful seizure of Medvezh'ia Gora, on the northern shore of Lake Onega, where it then constructed a two-mile spur to the lakefront for the purpose of adding two 50-foot U.S. motor launches to the local Allied flotilla.

For its part, the other operational component of the 168th consisted of an armored train staffed by 20 officers and men and equipped with 4-Vickers naval guns and 22 sandbagged machine guns. Created in May, this formidable unit ranged up and down the roadbed supporting the infantry in a number of engagements, including the victorious Battle of Kiappesel'ga in early July, which marked the high-water mark of the military engagement on the Murmansk Front.

On 12 July U.S. forces on the railroad handed over responsibility to the local North Russian forces of Gen. V.S. Skobel'tysn and withdrew to Murmansk, from which they were then evacuated as the last U.S. land forces to leave North Russia on 28 July 1919. In September, the Allies staged a final disengagement operation on the railroad that advanced the front all the way to Lizhma, about 600 miles south of Murmansk. The Murmansk Railroad Front remained operative until 23 March 1920, the very last day of the anti-Bolshevik struggle in the Russian North.

John W. Long

REFERENCES

A.W. Abbott, "Campaign by Rail: Murmansk to Lake Onega, 1918–1919," *Army Quarterly*, 88 (1964), 236–239; Dennis Gordon, *Quartered in Hell: The Story of the American North Russian Expeditionary Force, 1918–1919* (GOS, 1982); W.K.M. Leader, "With the Murmansk Expeditionary Force," *Journal of the Royal United Service Institution*, 66 (1921), 662–691; Edward E. MacMorland, "American Railroading in North Russia," *Military Engineer*, 21 (1929), 416–426; C. Maynard, *The Murmansk Venture* (Hodder & Stoughton, 1928).

N

Naco, Mexico, Battle (1914–1915)

The Battle of Naco, 1914–1915, was the longest sustained battle of the Mexican Revolution, lasting 119 days from start to finish. Occurring at the tiny binational hamlet of Naco, Arizona-Naco, Sonora, on the Arizona-Sonora border, just seven miles southwest of Bisbee, Arizona, the conflict directly and indirectly engaged many of the major figures of the Mexican Revolution and politically and strategically affected its outcome.

Grounded in internecine rivalry between revolutionary forces allied with Gen. Francisco "Pancho" Villa and those associated with the Constitutionalist faction of Venustiano Carranza and Álvaro Obregón, the battle was precipitated by Governor José María Maytorena's decision to challenge Constitutionalist forces under the command of Plutarco Elías Calles for control of the state of Sonora in fall 1914. Maytorena's contingent of Yaqui troops first engaged Calles's forces at Santa Barbara Ranch, southeast of the border twin city of Nogales, Arizona, forcing Calles to withdraw by rail to Naco, Sonora. At Naco, the Constitutionalists dug in, backs to the border. The Maytorenistas laid siege to the town but were unable to overrun Calles's defenses.

Thus began an extended siege lasting nearly four months.

The protracted siege and repeated assaults by Maytorena's forces on the Mexican village incurred numerous casualties and significant property damage in the adjoining U.S. community of Naco, Arizona. U.S. officials also feared potential violations of federal neutrality laws. In December 1914, President Woodrow Wilson sent troops from Fort Sill, Oklahoma, and Texas City, Texas, under the command of Gen. Tasker H. Bliss to reinforce federal forces at Fort Huachuca, Arizona, in protecting U.S. interests. He also sent United States Army Chief of Staff Hugh L. Scott to seek a brokered solution to the conflict. Scott accomplished this in a series of meetings with Villa and Governor Maytorena during January 1915, culminating in the Treaty of Naco, 12 January 1915.

The Battle of Naco was politically significant for two reasons. First and foremost, it overlapped the important Convention of Aguascalientes, which attempted to reconcile critical differences among contending factions in the Mexican Revolution. The ongoing hostilities at Naco during the formal cease-fire associated with the debates at Aguascalientes dramatized factional divisions and contributed to the convention's failure.

Maytorena's negotiated withdrawal at Naco also gave Constitutionalist leaders a strategic reprieve, strengthening their position in the revolutionary struggle in which they eventually triumphed.

Militarily, the Battle of Naco is notable as one of the first battles on the North American mainland to use the technologies of modern warfare, including defensive trenches, barbed wire, and electronically detonated minefields. In this respect it prefigured subsequent engagements during the Mexican Revolution.

Stephen P. Mumme

REFERENCES

Susan M. Deeds, "Jose Maria Maytorena and the Mexican Revolution in Sonora," *Arizona and the West*, 18 (1976), 21–40, 125–148; Linda B. Hall, "The Mexican Revolution and the Crisis in Naco, 1914–1915," *Journal of the West*, 16 (1977), 27–35; Stephen P. Mumme, "The Battle of Naco, Factionalism and Conflict in Sonora, 1914–1915," *Arizona and the West*, 21 (1979), 157–186.

Nanjing (Nanking) Incident, China (1927)

The Nanjing incident of 24–25 March 1927 was one of the most controversial events of the Guomindang's (Kuomintang's) Northern Expedition (1926–1928): its military conquest of warlord China. Before the expedition, which was motivated by Chinese nationalism, Sino-foreign relations focused on Chinese nationalism and revision of the unequal treaties with the Treaty Powers. After it, the question of whether the Treaty Powers would collaborate in armed intervention to safeguard the lives and property of their nationals (after the fashion of 1900 to suppress the Boxers) temporarily overshadowed these issues.

The incident brought the simmering antagonism between the Guomindang (GMD) and foreigners to the boiling point. The Northern Expedition began in July 1926 as the GMD's National Revolutionary Army (NRA) advanced into Hunan from Guangdong (Kwangtung).

By early March 1927, it had conquered most of South China and the middle Yangzi (Yangtze) Valley and was poised to strike at the urban centers of the lower Yangzi, Nanjing, and Shanghai. In Shanghai, the center of foreign influence in China, workers under the direction of radical trade unions opened the gates of the city to the NRA.

At the same time, the Shanghai Municipal Council (the foreign concessions' government) requested U.S., Japanese, and Dutch forces be landed to maintain order. The warlord troops either surrendered to the foreign contingents or retreated north.

The NRA, cooperating with the unions, occupied the city (except for the concessions) and maintained order. Though the situation remained tense, there were no serious clashes between Chinese and foreign troops in Shanghai.

The same was not true in Nanjing. As it became obvious that Nanjing would either fall to or be besieged by the NRA, many foreign nationals (women and children) were evacuated before the conflict reached the city.

On 23 March 1927 defeated warlord troops retreated through the city. As the day wore on, their discipline dissolved and approximately 10,000 were stranded as transportation arrangements broke down. That night looting and sporadic gunfire occurred throughout Nanjing.

NRA contingents entered the next morning and began to capture Northern warlord soldiers who had not escaped the city. Shortly after arriving in Nanjing, shells from NRA artillery killed a Japanese naval officer while the U.S. vice president of Nanjing University, Dr. John E. Williams, was shot to death by uniformed NRA soldiers. Foreign-owned businesses were looted and foreigners threatened. It was rumored that the British and Japanese consuls were killed and that mobs were attacking the British legation.

Refugees from the British and U.S. legations retreated to buildings owned by Socony-Vacuum Corporation (Standard Oil and Caltex) on Socony Hill. This location was a prominent landmark and one mile closer to the river and the protection of U.S., British, and Japanese warships than the U.S. and British legations. The foreigners sought refuge in the house of the Socony manager, Earle T. Hobart. It was soon surrounded by NRA soldiers and looters. Negotiations between the foreigners and the soldiers went on through the late morning and into the afternoon.

At 3:38 p.m., the U.S. consul requested that U.S. warships open fire on the hill to drive off the soldiers. Between 3:38 and 3:45 p.m., the USS *Preston*, USS *Noa*, and HMS *Emerald* fired approximately 110 rounds of shrapnel and high explosives on Socony Hill, routing the Chinese soldiers. The shelling also halted sniping along the Nanjing Bund and a sortie by GMD gunboats against territory held by warlord troops. The refugees were then able to retreat undisturbed down the hill to the refuge of the British and U.S. warships.

Contemporaries disagreed over what had transpired. The local GMD Chinese commander reported that Dr. Williams was shot to death by retreating warlord soldiers and that before he could restore order, rebels and bandits plundered foreign property and set fire to houses. British and U.S. warships then fired on the city. NRA soldiers, assuming that the foreign troops were assisting warlord forces, began to fire back. The general, who perceived what had happened, then ordered a cease-fire. He reported this to the Chinese foreign minister, who conveyed this story to the British and U.S. authorities. Similar conclusions were reached by several other Chinese and foreign eyewitnesses. Evidence was assembled to show that the retreating Northern warlord soldiery was responsible for the attacks (Isaacs, p. 145).

This view ran counter to the official reports of the U.S., British, and Japanese consuls in Nanjing. The U.S. consul, John K. Davis, had no doubts that the outrages were committed by NRA soldiers acting under orders.

The staff of the British consulate reached the same conclusion. The consul general, Bertram Giles, was wounded, two other Britons killed, and the consulate completely looted. The Chinese soldiers did not cease their actions until fired on by the British and U.S. warships. The British eyewitnesses all believed their attackers were members of the NRA because the warlord soldiers had evacuated the area around the British consulate on 23 March.

The Japanese consul, Morioka Shohei, reached the same conclusion, since the warlord soldiers disappeared from the vicinity of the Japanese consulate at about the same time. The soldiers began to loot the consulate at about 7:00 a.m. and wounded the consul. Several hours later an NRA officer restored order.

In the immediate aftermath of the incident, the Chinese commander, Zheng Jian (Cheng Chien), apologized for the incident and requested the naval bombardment cease. This message was answered with three demands: (1) protection and escort of all foreigners to the riverbank, (2) protection of all foreign-owned property and (3) Zheng's personal arrangement for the safeguarding of the foreigners.

In the end, no ultimata were sent to the Chinese government, and no military action was taken. Instead, the United States, Great Britain, Japan, Italy, and France presented notes to the Chinese stressing their willingness to take appropriate measures to ensure compliance with their demands.

Comparing all the reports, it appears that the Nanjing incident was the work of undisciplined elements of the NRA. Their superiors immediately disowned responsibility for these acts. The official GMD interpretation of the event is that the entire affair was sponsored and organized by the Chinese Communist radical elements of the NRA. It is likely that this lie was initially dreamed up to shield the NRA command structure from the consequences of its troops' indiscipline.

Lewis Bernstein

REFERENCES

Dorothy Borg, *American Policy and the Chinese Revolution, 1925–1928* (American Institute of Pacific Relations, 1947); Bernard D. Cole, *Gunboats and Marines: The United States Navy in China, 1925–1928* (Univ. of Delaware Pr., 1983); Glenn Howell, "Operations of the United States Navy on the Yangtze River— September, 1926, to June, 1927," *United States Naval Institute Proceedings*, 54 (1928), 273–286; Harold R. Isaacs, *The Tragedy of the Chinese Revolution* (Stanford Univ. Pr., 1961); Donald A. Jordan, *The Northern Expedition: China's National Revolution of 1926–1928* (Univ. Pr. of Hawaii, 1976); Roy C. Smith, Jr., "Nanking, March 24, 1927," *United States Naval Institute Proceedings*, 54 (1928), 1–21.

National Guard Black Militia in the Spanish-Cuban/American War

See Militia in the Spanish-Cuban/American War.

National Guard Mobilization (1916–1917)

The 1916–1917 mobilization of the National Guard in the United States for Mexican border service was a significant event in the development of the National Guard and its relations with the regular army. It had little impact, however, on the dispute with Mexico that arose after the raid of Francisco "Pancho" Villa on Columbus, New Mexico, in March 1916.

From their beginning in the early colonial period, the state militias consisted of white male citizens who volunteered for service. The Militia Act of 1792 left training, organization, and equipment decisions to the discretion of each state. As a result, the state militias were usually poorly trained and equipped, and their officers were chosen primarily for their political accomplishments not their military skills. By the mid-19th century the militias had become largely social clubs, with members meeting four times a year for parties masquerading as training sessions. During the Civil War the federal and state governments called out many state militia units but quickly found them unreliable and began to recruit men in new organizations.

Limited changes for the better began to occur as the result of strikes in the late 19th century which often required use of the militia to maintain order. The states reformed their militias, which became known as the National Guard, to provide themselves with a kind of state police force. There was little progress in improving training, equipment, or leadership skills, however. The lack of improvement was glaringly exposed during the Spanish-Cuban/American War and the Philippine War. Some units refused to enlist en masse, others had little equipment, while the vast majority required extensive training in order to meet the requirements of wartime duty.

There were two views on how to deal with this problem. Most regular army officers wanted to abandon the National Guard as a reserve force and replace it with a federally controlled reserve, such as that proposed in Secretary of War Lindley M. Garrison's 1915 Continental Army plan. Most state guard officers desired to improve the National Guard by bringing it into closer contact with the federal government and upgrading its training and equipment. Because of their political maneuvering, the state approach became law.

Between 1903 and 1916 several statutes defined the status of the National Guard and its relationship to the federal government. Under this legislation, the guard was made the nation's second line of defense, with the federal government helping to define its structure and training procedures. In 1908 Congress gave the federal government more authority to use the National Guard outside the United States. Four years later, the attorney general issued an opinion questioning this authority. In June 1916 Congress again legislated on the matter, allowing the National Guard to serve outside the United States if deemed necessary by the federal government.

The new National Guard was called into duty in 1916 as the situation along the Mexican border deteriorated. On 9 May 1916, two months after Pancho Villa's raid, the National Guards of Arizona, New Mexico, and Texas were called up and sent to the border. In Oklahoma a group of ex-Confederates volunteered but were not accepted because the federal government thought that additional forces did not appear necessary. Nevertheless, problems continued to mount. There were raids by Mexicans on Glenn Springs and Boquillas, Texas. Livestock was stolen, and some U.S. camps were attacked. It became quickly apparent that the small number of guardsmen on the border was inadequate to defend the international boundary, especially in the event of a full-scale war with Mexico.

Such a war appeared probable in June 1916. On 16 June 1916 Gen. Jacinto B. Trevino, who commanded the Carranzist forces of Mexican President Venustiano Carranza, informed Gen. John J. Pershing, commander of the Punitive Expedition, that U.S. forces should not attempt to go any direction but north. The U.S. government had sent the Punitive Expedition into Mexico to capture Villa as a result of the raid by Villista forces on Columbus, New Mexico, in March. At the same time, elements of the 3rd Cavalry had crossed the border at Brownsville, Texas, after another group of Mexican raiders. Mexican authorities responded to this incident by ordering that U.S. troops crossing the border be shot. As tension mounted and war appeared possible, President Woodrow Wilson mobilized the rest of the National Guard.

The recently enacted National Defense Act of 1916 gave the president the authority to call out the National Guard in time of emergency. In this circumstance, the guard would come under federal authority. On 18 June 1916 Wilson exercised this authority. The call-up applied to all states except Arizona, New Mexico, and Texas, where the guard had been called up earlier, and Nevada, which did not have a National Guard. The units were ordered to protect the border with Mexico. The expectation was that units would assemble at their armories, concentrate at a central location in each state, and then move to the border.

Shortly after, Congress approved the president's action. It passed a joint resolution authorizing the president, under the National Defense Act of 1916, to call troops into federal service. It also authorized one million dollars to support the dependents of guardsmen on active duty. In addition, Congress gave the president the authority to pay up to $50 per month for families with no other source of income. This move illustrated one result of the new relationship between the National Guard and the federal government.

The state units were tremendously enthusiastic about service along the border and felt it their duty to go to the nation's defense. In Tennessee, for example, National Guard units doubled in size and reached their authorized strength after the president's call. Problems did occur, however. In Oklahoma, there was a delay in calling the men up because the state could not find a good site for the central rendezvous. Some criticized the Oklahoma authorities for seeming to be opposed to the call-up. In Alabama some women volunteered as nurses to accompany the troops but were not accepted.

Similarly, in several states blacks offered to join but were not allowed to enlist. For example, in Alabama and Oklahoma they tried to join their states' understrength white units. Each state insisted on maintaining segregation, however, and the federal government would not authorize the organization of another unit. Segregation continued in the National Guard until after World War II.

Misunderstandings arose about the oath of allegiance that the new legislation required. The guardsmen had to take an oath to serve three years in the National Guard and three years in the federal reserve. Some thought this meant they would have to serve three years in the regular army, which they did not want to do. Not until the army clarified that the oath meant serving only three years in the reserve, did many men take the oath. A few who refused to serve outside their state were discharged. An even smaller number of men did not report for duty, and some of them were prosecuted.

After the units were assembled and the oath had been taken, more problems emerged. The mobilization was only slightly more organized than the one in 1898. First the states and then the federal authorities gave the men physical examinations. In Wisconsin 25 percent of the men failed the tests and had to be sent home. Many of the units did not have proper equipment. Regiments that began to move to the border in late June were assemblies of men, largely

untrained and poorly equipped but greatly enthusiastic about the adventure of defending their country against attack by Mexicans.

The trip to the border for the more than 112,000 guardsmen was not smooth going: trains broke down; and food service by railroads unprepared to feed so many was irregular and scanty. In addition, the hot weather, especially as they approached the border, foreshadowed the next phase of their service.

Initially the guardsmen were concentrated at camps near San Antonio, Brownsville, and El Paso, Texas; and Douglas, Arizona, before being dispersed to smaller facilities. There were many problems with their living conditions. Like their Spanish-Cuban/American War predecessors, they sweltered in their wool uniforms. Their camps were usually simple collections of tents which they tried to improve in as many ingenious ways as they could. The Tennessee National Guardsmen stationed at Eagle Pass, Texas, for example, reinforced their tents with wood, added electric lights and, as winter drew near, stoves. Food was often a real challenge because cooking was not well organized, and the supply system was rudimentary. Some New York National Guardsmen resolved this problem by buying tortillas and other Mexican specialties from local vendors. Their enthusiasm for this food soon waned when they saw how it was prepared.

Regular officers had long believed that the guard units needed a great deal of training to be an effective reserve force and quickly recognized the training possibilities in having thousands of National Guardsmen under their authority. In this situation, they saw an opportunity and took advantage of it. The units were assigned long practice marches, often staged early in the morning to avoid the heat. In addition to company and regimental exercises, the army joined regiments from several states in larger maneuver units. Several Kansas regiments became part of the 12th Division, which gathered in San Antonio.

For many of the troops such activities were senseless. The summertime threat posed by Mexican raids and the Carrizal battle quickly evaporated. Boredom began to spread, and enthusiasm for their assignment declined. Conditions were primitive, and the temperature extremes were punishing. Disease also became a problem; some men in the Alabama units contracted pneumonia, while other state units had outbreaks of measles, which were contained through regimental quarantine. Nevertheless, the sickness rate in the National Guard units was 1.8 percent, somewhat below the 2 percent for the regular army regiments in the same area.

The officers used various activities to make up for the lack of action. The Young Men's Christian Association set up movie houses. State units competed in baseball and football. Many regimental bands put on concerts. During Christmas they decorated mesquite trees and gave gifts to the local children. The guardsmen also indulged in more traditional soldierly activities, including drinking and visiting prostitutes. Some evangelists visited the camps to persuade the men to avoid these evils; they were but moderately successful.

Many guardsmen were on the border during the 1916 national elections, but few states had provisions for absentee voting. More troublesome was the issue of money. Neither the state governments nor the national government was prepared to pay the National Guardsmen for a long time. The average private received $15 a month; a sergeant, $45. Many tried to help their dependents by sending some of this money home, but it was inadequate. In addition, as service on the border continued into the fall, the soldiers began to worry about their civilian jobs being given to someone else. Finally, the federal government began addressing some of these concerns. The June 1916 appropriation of funds was supplemented with an additional $10 million for dependents, largely through the efforts of Senator Robert M. LaFollette of Wisconsin. In addition, in fall 1916 the army allowed the states to send home some of the married men.

Fall also marked the beginning of the end of the mobilization. In November and December 1916 some units were ordered home. As the border garrisons shrank, the remaining troops became even more despondent. Finally, on 15 February 1917, the government announced the demobilization of the National Guard, and by early March 1917 the last state regiments were on their way home.

Many evaluated the success or failure of the National Guard mobilization. United States Army Chief of Staff Gen. Hugh L. Scott, an opponent of the National Guard as a major reserve force, believed that the militia system had shown itself a "failure," that the training period of the guard was too short to develop effective units, and that the state units were normally too far below strength to be effective. The head of the army's Militia Bureau argued that the guardsmen wanted to learn, but were so little prepared that they could not use their time along the border effectively. While the guardsmen had time for training, they lacked the basic skills of soldiers and also lacked sufficient, experienced leaders who could guide and supervise their training. Others criticized the chaos of mobilization and the states' lack of plans and proper equipment. They also argued that the border experience suggested that universal military training, rather than training the National Guard, would more effectively create a reserve force.

Some reviewed the performance of the state units sympathetically. Secretary of War Newton D. Baker praised the National Guard and the way it met its challenges of adjusting to full-time military service and living under field conditions. Given the political significance of the National Guard, it is hardly surprising that Baker avoided sharp criticism of its civilian soldiers. Others defended the National Guard indirectly by pointing out that the War Department had neither adequately planned for the National Guard mobilization nor effectively used the guard to patrol the border.

A more realistic view is that the mobilization was a good practice for World War I, which began in April 1917 for the United States. Most of the problems exposed during the 1916 mobilization were addressed before the troops left for France in 1917. In addition, the earlier mobilization created a cadre of somewhat better trained men, most of whom joined to fight the Germans. Life on the border helped train them and teach them what military life is like. It was also clear that some improvements had been made in the organization and training of the National Guard, but that much more needed to be done. On the other hand, the guardsmen seemed to have had little impact on the Mexican situation. In summary, the National Guard mobilization of 1916 was more significant as an indicator of the progress of the National Guard reforms and as having had an impact on World War I than as a deterrent against further Mexican raids across the international border.

Marvin E. Fletcher

REFERENCES

Clarence C. Clendenen, *Blood on the Border: The United States Army and the Mexican Irregulars* (Macmillan,

1969); John P. Finnegan, "Preparedness in Wisconsin: The National Guard and the Mexican Border Incident," *Wisconsin Magazine of History*, 47 (1964), 199–213; Donald E. Houston, "The Oklahoma National Guard on the Mexican Border, 1916," *Chronicles of Oklahoma*, 53 (1975), 447–462; H.E. Sterkx, "Unlikely Conquistadors: Alabamians and the Mexican Border Crisis of 1916," *Alabama Review*, 24 (1971), 163–181; Margaret R. Wolfe, "The Border Service of the Tennessee National Guard, 1916–1917: A Study in Romantic Inclinations, Military Realities, and Predictable Disillusionment," *Tennessee Historical Quarterly*, 32 (1973), 374–388.

Naval Operations at Samoa (1899)

The decision to send United States Navy vessels to Samoa in 1899 was the climax of a longstanding colonial dispute. During the last decades of the 19th century, the imperialist ambitions of the United States, Great Britain, and Germany had led to several confrontations over the islands. A serious clash between U.S. and German warships in 1889 had persuaded the three powers to establish an international commission for Samoa composed of representatives from each country. This compromise proved to be only a temporary solution because the Samoan International Commission collapsed during a Samoan civil war which began in August 1898. Both the United States and Great Britain reacted with force after Germany began supporting one side in the internal Samoan conflict.

The U.S. naval vessels that participated in the 1899 Samoan intervention had a major military impact on the fighting and played a pivotal political role in the settlement that followed. The first U.S. ship sent to Samoa during the period of civil unrest was the cruiser *Philadelphia*, commanded by Rear Adm. Albert Kautz. On 6 March, when the *Philadelphia* arrived at the Samoan capital of Apia, on the island of Upolu, two British warships, the HMS *Porpoise* and HMS *Royalist*, and the German corvette *Falke* were already anchored in the harbor.

Kautz's instructions were to protect U.S. interests in the islands and to act in accordance with the majority opinion of the Samoan International Commission. He carried out the first part of his mission by using the *Philadelphia* to shelter U.S. citizens during the worst of the fighting in the weeks that followed; he completed the

second by cooperating with British forces to defeat the native followers of Mataafa, the German-supported Samoan chieftain.

On 11 March, Kautz ordered the provisional government of Chief Mataafa and his German allies dissolved. The order was enforced by a mixed landing force of British and U.S. marines sent to occupy key points in the Samoan capital. Four days later, the *Philadelphia*, *Royalist*, and *Porpoise* began shelling villages in response to scattered attacks on British and U.S. lines. As Mataafa's supporters retreated into the Samoan hinterland, British and U.S. forces advanced to occupy the entire port.

The role of U.S. naval forces essentially ended once the British and U.S. marines had secured Apia. While the *Philadelphia* landed additional troops and continued shore bombardments, British and U.S. forces were unable to move far beyond the outskirts of Apia itself. Even the arrival of the HMS *Tawanga* on 24 March did not end the military stalemate. On 1 April, an attempt to subdue a native stronghold in the island's interior failed after Samoan tribesmen ambushed the column of British and U.S. troops, killing several U.S. naval officers.

On 13 May, the USS *Badger* arrived in Apia, carrying representatives from all three colonial powers. The ensuing negotiations formally divided Samoa into spheres of influence. Although Germany retained control of Apia and the islands of Savai'i and Upolu, the United States received the island of Tutuila with its important naval base at Pago Pago. The British renounced their claim to the islands altogether in return for concessions on their claims to other Pacific islands and parts of Africa.

James H.L. Lide

REFERENCES

T.T. Craven, "A Naval Episode of 1899," *United States Naval Institute Proceedings*, 54 (1928), 185–200; Foster Rhea Dulles, *America in the Pacific: A Century of Expansion* (Houghton Mifflin, 1932), chap. 8; Frank H. Rentflow, "Samoan Imbroglio," *Leatherneck*, 19 (1936), 3, 49–50.

Naval Operations in the Philippine Islands (1898–1903)

The victory under Commodore George Dewey at the Battle of Manila Bay on 1 May 1898 signaled the beginning of U.S. naval operations in the Philippine Islands. In the period that followed, the navy and marines engaged in a campaign that included traditional blockade assignments, as well as numerous land operations. The United States sought first to end Spanish rule on the islands, and after 4 February 1899, to eliminate Filipino opposition to the U.S. annexation of the Philippines.

Prior to 1898 the Asiatic Squadron consisted of a few ships and one flag officer and remained isolated from the mainstream of U.S. policy. Despite its involvement in several significant naval actions in the decades before the war with Spain, the Atlantic and Caribbean areas continued as the focus in the naval strategy of the United States. European powers, notably Germany and Great Britain, posed the primary threat to the United States in the minds of United States Navy war planners. Yet while the European menace lingered, the acquisition of the Philippines produced innumerable possibilities for the emerging U.S. empire. The navy rapidly assumed responsibility for the protection of U.S. interests in the Pacific forcing dramatic increases in naval assets there. Expansion into the Pacific thus marked a watershed in U.S. naval policy and was reflected by changes in command structure, ship assignments and deployment, and the tasks assigned to the navy in the Philippines.

Command and fleet organizations during early operations in the Philippines changed rapidly to reflect the new responsibilities assigned to the navy. Between 1898 and 1900 one flag officer commanded the station. By 1900 the fleet was divided under two flag officers, and after July 1903 the Asiatic Station was organized into several fleet configurations under three admirals. Various organizational schemes emerged during that period as the navy increased its deployment of ships in the area. By 1903 the Asiatic Fleet was further reorganized into a battleship squadron (with an accompanying gunboat division), a cruiser squadron, and a Philippine squadron to accommodate the navy's expanding responsibilities.

Perhaps the single most important indication of the growth of U.S. power in the Far East was the deployment of ships to the Asiatic Station after 1898. While the majority of major combat ships, battleships and cruisers, remained in the Atlantic commands even after 1898, a significant increase in the numbers of these vessels on the Asiatic Squadron occurred between 1899 and 1902. The numbers of all other types of vessels, especially gunboats, remained at high levels during this same period. Subjugation of the Philippines, the Boxer Uprising, and the U.S. commitment to the Open Door Policy for China contributed to these increases. The characteristics of U.S. naval power in Asiatic waters clearly demonstrated that shallow-draft vessels played an important role in the Philippines and in China where geographic features rendered battleships and cruisers less useful than gunboats. Controlling vast waterways, showing the flag, and protecting U.S. citizens and property mandated that the Asiatic Fleet expand its coastal and river forces.

After destroying the Spanish fleet at Manila Bay and while waiting for army and marine forces from the United States, Dewey placed the Philippines under naval blockade. The blockade involved three stages designed to establish control over neutral shipping in the islands and to undertake operations against the Spanish and later against the Filipinos. During the first stage, from the Battle of Manila Bay on 1 May 1898 until the fall of Manila in August, naval forces maintained a rigid blockade to cut the Spanish off from outside assistance. Dewey cabled Washington at one point that "strict blockade continues. The neutral vessels are not allowed to enter." During the first stage, all ports remained closed, and trade between the Philippines and the outside world came to a standstill.

The second stage commenced with the surrender of Manila and Dewey's decision to open that port city to trade. During this phase major coast ports were opened to international commerce as they came under U.S. aegis. After the close of hostilities with the Spanish, growing Filipino dissatisfaction with U.S. peace negotiations, particularly the increasing prospect of continued U.S. rule, prompted the navy to restrict inter-island trade that supported Filipino military units. Despite United States-Filipino tensions, however, from 14 August 1898 to 26 December 1899, six ports were opened to international trade.

After 27 December 1899 inter-island ports were opened at a rapid rate, marking the beginning of the third stage, with U.S. control of the region continuing to be the criterion for opening ports to trade. Despite the outbreak of the Philippine War in February 1899 the army commander reported that 51 ports had been opened during the first four months of 1900.

The Battle of Manila Bay also triggered other naval actions in the Philippines, establishing a pattern of deployment and mission assignment. The navy and marines began a period of operation that went well beyond traditional blockade duties. Following Dewey's victory at Manila Bay, naval forces participated in operations designed to take possession of shore facilities and to suppress opposition to U.S. control. Combined army and navy operations on shore varied in scope and the size of forces committed. Often the navy merely supported army land operations, but occasionally the availability of naval personnel and firepower allowed it to contribute substantively to ground operations.

One of the principal problems facing U.S. forces in the archipelago was the expiration of the enlistments of volunteers sent to the Philippines during the Spanish-Cuban/American War. Existing law mandated that these troops be discharged, making it necessary for President William McKinley to look to the regular army for men. Unfortunately, overly optimistic assessments by the army commander in the Philippines convinced McKinley that the regular army could secure the islands, but the force was ill-prepared in numbers, training, and logistics to accomplish U.S. objectives in the Philippines. For the first two years of operations the delay in recognizing the need for new volunteer regiments left the navy as a major instrument of U.S. power outside Manila. During these years the navy augmented its assets in the islands, straining its limited resources while waiting for the army to provide troops in sufficient numbers to begin land operations to secure the island group. Naval participation in early Philippine land operations can be arranged into four categories: artillery support of army, navy, and marine actions; transport of army forces to target areas; conjunct operations involving the army, navy, and marines; and independent navy and marine operations.

From the beginning of army operations in the islands, the navy provided artillery support from vessels. The first instance occurred during the siege of Manila in August 1898. Firing from ships anchored in Manila Bay, the navy laid down a barrage effectively supporting army units. A few months later the navy again provided fire support for the expedition to Iloilo that helped provoke a broader war with the Filipinos. Geographically the Philippines presented unique and difficult demands as U.S. forces moved inland on Luzon and to the South through the islands. The navy's ability to maneuver in shallow rivers and other waterways provided artillery for army and navy operations, often far from established bases and shore commands. While navy participation usually was limited to a single vessel, this type of naval operation was perhaps the most common and the most influential (other than blockade operations) on the overall outcome of the Philippine War.

Land mobility proved difficult for all U.S. forces in the Philippines. Use of naval vessels to provide inter- and intra-island transportation proved to be a priority assignment for the navy. The dense jungle terrain coupled with the few roads and long rainy seasons, caused the army to depend heavily upon the navy to move troops and to provide logistical support. These difficult conditions, moreover, prompted the army to develop its own steamer fleet. That fleet never became self-sufficient, however, leaving the navy to provide "most of the logistical support for the American campaign."

A third type of operation saw navy and marine personnel directly involved in army land campaigns or fighting in concert with the army. Before 1900 naval units on shore were composed primarily of men from ships' companies, thereby limiting the nature and size of the navy's shore operations. By 1900 marine strength reached levels that allowed the navy's role to increase significantly.

The most important role played by naval forces was that of conducting land operations when it acted alone, a naval officer wielded command, or the navy contributed most of the personnel involved. Independent naval operations expanded beyond historical norms as the navy deployed more and more ships and increased its manpower commitment in the islands. Vessels offshore often supported naval sorties or campaigns along the coast and against inland targets accessible only through shallow rivers or other waterways. While similar in nature to naval support of army operations, these campaigns or missions involved the use of naval personnel alone and came under navy command. Navy shore operations sought to establish new marine bases, ensure stability in areas beyond the army's reach, and provide coaling and other facilities for naval vessels functioning at the fringe of U.S. control in the Philippines. The navy thereby increased its ability to wage aggressive and independent warfare. Beginning with the Battle of Manila Bay and ending with the conclusion of the Philippine War, the navy's contribution was significant in securing U.S. objectives in the Philippines.

Vernon L. Williams

REFERENCES

Vernon L. Williams, "George Dewey: Admiral of the Navy," in James C. Bradford, ed., *Admirals of the New Steel Navy: Makers of the American Naval Traditions, 1880–1930* (U.S. Naval Institute Pr., 1990); Vernon L. Williams, "Naval Service in the Age of Empire," in James C. Bradford, ed., *Crucible of Empire: America and the War With Spain* (U.S. Naval Institute Pr., 1990); Vernon L. Williams, "The U.S. Navy in the Philippine Insurrection and Subsequent Native Unrest 1898–1906," Ph.D. diss., Texas A&M Univ., 1985.

Naval Operations in the Puerto Rico Campaign (1898)

The United States Navy played an important role in the U.S. invasion of Puerto Rico and carried out a bombardment of San Juan even before that invasion.

While searching for Adm. Pasqual Cervera y Topete's squadron, Adm. William T. Sampson took his squadron—consisting of the *New York*, *Iowa*, *Indiana*, and two monitors *Terror* and *Amphitrite*—to Puerto Rico. Although he learned Cervera's ships were not in the harbor, Sampson ordered a bombardment of San Juan, the capital of Puerto Rico, at 5:15 a.m. on 12 May 1898 and ended it after three hours with one killed and several wounded on the *New York* and many civilians killed and wounded in the town.

Later, although the main campaigns had been won at Manila and Santiago de Cuba, an expedition under command of Gen. Nelson A. Miles was sent to the Spanish island colony. The battleship *Massachusetts* as flagship (commanded by Capt. Francis J. Higginson); the auxiliary cruiser *Dixie*; the armed yacht *Gloucester*; and the armed steamships *Yale*, *Columbia*, and *Macon* carrying 3,415 infantry with two companies of engineers and one of signal corps escorted nine transports which spearheaded the invasion on 21 July 1898. Two other contingents of troops joined the invasion: 3,600 left from Charleston, South Caro-

lina, and 2,900 from Tampa, Florida, with 4,000 more preparing to leave Newport News, Virginia.

The force steamed at night along the northern coast of Haiti, and the navy understood the invasion was planned to land at Fajardo, southeast of San Juan. General Miles kept his plans secret and changed them en route to the island, landing at a different port, Guánica, at the opposite end of Puerto Rico from San Juan. Higginson protested, and although the navy appeared off San Juan, the town was left relatively unmolested. On 25 July the *Gloucester* preceded the main force, and 28 men under Lt. Harry P. Huse landed in the harbor of Guánica, in the southwestern corner of the island, under cover of the ship's three and six pounder guns. The party captured 10 lighters later used to land 2,000 troops. The *Massachusetts*, carrying 1,100 New York volunteer cavalry with 1,100 horses, ran onto a reef and, with disabled ventilating fans, was stuck for 24 hours. The between decks were crowded, the air putrid, and eyewitnesses remembered the scene as equivalent to breathing sewer gas. The navy finally oversaw the disembarkation of General Miles's army at Guánica and Ponce, 20 miles to the east, and also captured Fajardo. Miles acknowledged, "I was very ably and cordially assisted by the navy, which rendered invaluable aid in disembarking troops and supplies from the transports, using their steam launches to tow the lighters loaded with men and animals from the transports to the shore" (Chadwick, vol. 2, p. 291). He later blocked a naval attack on San Juan. The campaign became a succession of marches overland as the troops worked their way toward the capital. Most troops embarked for home 30 days after it began. The cartoonist Finley Peter Dunne sardonically jibed that it had been a moonlight picnic, yet casualties were kept to a minimum, and Miles achieved success against rapidly diminishing Spanish forces by the time hostilities ended on 12–13 August 1898.

Frederick C. Drake

REFERENCES

French Ensor Chadwick, *The Relations of the United States and Spain: The Spanish-American War* (Scribner, 1911), 2 vols.; Frank Freidel, *The Splendid Little War* (Little, Brown, 1958), chap. 14, 261–278; John D. Long, *The New American Navy* (Outlook, 1903), 2 vols.; Charles Oscar Paullin, "The Navy in the Spanish-American War, 1898,"

United States Naval Institute Proceedings, 40 (1914), 419–420; David F. Trask, *The War With Spain in 1898* (Macmillan, 1981), 336–368.

See also Puerto Rico Campaign (1898).

Naval Operations in the Spanish-Cuban/American War

The Spanish-Cuban/American War was pre-eminently a naval war. Military operations for the capture of Cuba, Puerto Rico, and the Philippines could not have occurred without control of the sea by the United States Navy. That the war erupted was due to a naval incident, the explosion of the U.S. battleship *Maine* in the harbor of Havana, Cuba, on 15 February 1898. Naval operations in the war proved the efficacy of the new U.S. steel navy—its technology, its strategic concepts, and its fighting men. Naval power also swept away the decrepit Spanish fleets and with them, Spanish colonies in the Caribbean and the Far East. U.S. aspirations for glory and empire rode on the wakes of famous warships with names like the *Olympia, Oregon, New York*, and *Brooklyn*. Naval heroes such as George Dewey, William T. Sampson, Winfield Scott Schley, and Richmond P. Hobson became household words across the United States. Naval operations marked the coming of age of the United States Navy, and the success of the fleet led to postwar naval appropriations eventually designed to produce a "navy second to none."

Naval operations leading to the war began tragically with the explosion aboard the USS *Maine*; 251 officers and enlisted men of the ship perished or were injured, and the incident inflamed already tempestuous relations between the United States and Spain. A naval court of inquiry blamed the disaster on a submarine mine—traceable, said everyone, to Spanish treachery. Naval preparations went forward as diplomats wrangled with supplies of ammunition and coal stockpiled, warships recalled from foreign stations, and the battleship *Oregon* ordered around South America from the Pacific for service in Atlantic waters. Congress appropriated $50 million for national defense, and Spain, too, took precautions to prepare its widely dispersed squadrons for hostilities. Secretary of the Navy John D. Long ordered imposition of a naval blockade on Cuban ports, and the United States declared war on 25 April 1898, following Spanish rejection of U.S. demands for immediate Cuban independence.

Although the U.S. fleet outclassed its Spanish foe in every regard, excepting numbers, U.S. civilian and military leaders feared that they faced a superior European power. Panicky citizens up and down the East Coast imagined Spanish squadrons sweeping across the Atlantic and laying tributes on their ports and major coastal cities. The United States Navy responded by splitting the major components of the North Atlantic Squadron between Cuban blockade and U.S. coastal defense duties, to the detriment of both missions. Meanwhile, in Far Eastern waters, with guidance from Assistant Secretary of the Navy Theodore Roosevelt, Commodore George Dewey prepared his Asiatic Squadron for a lightning strike from Hong Kong upon the exposed Spanish flotilla in Manila Bay in the Philippines. Proclaiming stridently to his flagship commander, "You may fire when you are ready, Gridley" (Trask, p. 102), Dewey aboard the *Olympia* led the seven warships into Manila Bay at dawn on 1 May 1898 and won a remarkable, if one-sided victory over the Spanish. Adm. Patricio Montojo y Pasarón lost every one of his obsolete and outgunned vessels to point-blank U.S. gunfire while Dewey lost one man (to heat exhaustion) and no ships.

Dewey's squadron then supervised a blockade of Manila until arrival of army troops and their occupation of the Philippines later in the summer. Mop-up naval support operations against the remaining Spaniards ashore eventually merged with a prolonged and bloody counterinsurgency war following the end of the war with Spain. The navy also confronted a German squadron which appeared in an effort to assume sovereignty over the islands in the wake of Spanish defeat. Dewey's small flotilla of protected cruisers was reinforced by the *Charleston* as well as slow-moving monitors *Monterey* and *Monadnock* whose heavy guns could provide fire support for army operations ashore.

Confusion and inefficiency attended U.S. efforts in the Atlantic for coping with possible Spanish naval activity. Commodore Winfield Scott Schley commanding a "Flying Squadron" of armored warships, Rear Admiral William T. Sampson, his commanding officer with the main North Atlantic Squadron, and a special Northern Patrol Squadron under Commodore John A. Howell all managed to deter Spanish raids on the U.S. East and Gulf coasts. They failed, however, to prevent the principal Spanish fleet from slipping through the blockade and taking refuge in the harbor at Santiago, Cuba.

Adm. Pascual Cervera y Topete with seven warships departed the Cape Verde Islands bound for the Caribbean on 29 April 1898. Eluding detection by U.S. warships that had been sent to Puerto Rico under the false impression that the Spanish would make port there, Cervera slipped into Santiago and avoided Schley's unsuccessful search along Cuba's southern coast in May. On 3 June 1898, after the whereabouts of the Spanish fleet was discovered, Assistant Naval Constructor Richmond P. Hobson and a volunteer crew unsuccessfully tried to block the harbor entrance by scuttling the collier *Merrimac*. United States Marines landed at Guantánamo Bay, Cuba, a week later, followed on 22 June by army debarkation at Daiquirí designed to attack the Spanish fleet. Then, at 9:35 a.m. on 3 July 1898, Cervera's fleet issued from the harbor in a daring attempt to gain freedom.

The U.S. naval response once again proved fumbling and controversial. Sampson had just departed in his flagship, the armored cruiser *New York*, to confer with army leaders down the coast. Schley swung his ship, the *Brooklyn*, sharply away from the onrushing enemy and across the bow of the battleship *Texas*, narrowly avoiding collision. U.S. confusion eventually subsided, and superior speed and gunfire annihilated the enemy squadron. By 1:20 p.m., the last Spanish warship, the cruiser *Cristóbal Colón*, had been beached, disabled and ablaze. Every other ship had been destroyed in succession while almost 300 Spaniards lost their lives at the cost of only one U.S. sailor killed. As at Manila Bay, U.S. naval power at Santiago had proven ultimately awesome in battle.

Schley later requested a board of inquiry and became the focus of feuding among the naval officer corps. Lost in the internal service strife were the glorious victories as well as successful performance of the navy in smaller skirmishes that formed part of the Cuban blockade effort. Sharp firefights had also ensued between U.S. warships and Spanish land and naval contingents at Cárdenas, Cienfuegos, Guantánamo, Manzanillo, Nipe, and Port Mariel, Cuba. Small Spanish craft were destroyed or salvaged for U.S. use, a large number of merchant prizes taken,

and commerce interdicted before the blockade of Cuba was lifted on 14 August 1898.

The Spanish government gathered a squadron for dispatch to the Philippines via the Mediterranean, the Suez Canal, and across the Indian Ocean. It never arrived, however. U.S. naval intelligence discerned the move, and a counter force was organized for operations in Spanish home waters, thus causing the Spanish monarch to recall the rickety flotilla of Adm. Manuel de la Cámara y Libermoore to Cádiz, Spain. An armistice was signed between the two countries on 12 August 1898. The formal treaty of peace in December relieved Spain of Cuba, while the United States received the Philippines and the islands of Guam and Puerto Rico for $20 million. The naval campaigns had been brief and strikingly effective. They laid the groundwork for naval expansion during the Progressive Era during which the navy ultimately equaled and later surpassed the pride of European squadrons. Late 20th-century U.S. global supremacy could be traced directly to the spectacular rise of U.S. naval power in the war against Spain.

B. Franklin Cooling

REFERENCES

French Ensor Chadwick, *The Relations of the United States and Spain: The Spanish-American War* (Scribner, 1911), 2 vols.; John D. Long, *The New American Navy* (Outlook, 1903), 2 vols.; David F. Trask, *The War With Spain in 1898* (Macmillan Co., 1981); Richard S. West, *Admirals of American Empire: The Combined Story of George Dewey, Alfred Thayer Mahan, Winfield Scott Schley, and William Thomas Sampson* (Bobbs-Merrill, 1948).

See also list of entries at front of book for Spanish-Cuban/American War—Naval Operations.

Naval Operations off Cuba (1912)

The U.S. naval forces were called on to play a critical role in the 1912 military intervention in Cuba. Their mission was to protect foreign, especially U.S., properties on the island, to defeat the Afro-Cuban revolution led by Evaristo Estenoz, to support the Liberal government of José Miguel Gómez, and to induce Gomez's administration to be more sympathetic to the demands of U.S. businesses. These naval operations were also aimed to intimidate the Gómez administration, assist the deployment of marines to landing bases throughout the island, and provide a measure of deterrence to guerrillas.

In late May, the United States Navy prepared to transport more than 5,000 troops to Cuba. The *Prairie* picked up approximately 800 marines at the Philadelphia Navy Yard and brought them to Guantánamo Bay. Meanwhile, U.S. naval forces in the Caribbean were redeployed: the *Nashville* was diverted from its station at Santo Domingo in the Dominican Republic, and the *Paducah* was ordered to sail from Santa Cruz, Cuba, to Guantánamo. Moreover, nine battleships from the 3rd and 4th Divisions of the Atlantic Fleet were directed to embark marine detachments and set sail for Key West, Florida, where they were to await further orders.

On 9 June, over the persistent objections of President Gómez and notwithstanding his government's immediate deployment of 3,000 Cuban soldiers to defeat the Afro-Cuban revolutionists, President William H. Taft ordered two warships to Havana. The apparent objective was to induce the Gómez government to support the unilateral U.S. military actions and to be more responsive to the interests of U.S. businessmen who claimed that it discriminated against them in favor of Cuban and other foreign (especially British) investors.

Once in Cuba, U.S. marines relied on the navy to transport them to specific staging areas, from which they deployed their forces to protect the properties of U.S. companies. For example, the commandant of the naval station in Guantánamo, in response to the U.S.-owned Daiquirí Mine Company's requests for protection, ordered the *Paducah* to transport Company A of the 1st Marine Regiment to Santiago Bay, where it landed troops at El Cobre, Puerto Sal, Hermatanas, and Siboney. After the landings, the *Paducah* remained anchored in the bay to lend necessary artillery and medical support.

Often, the navy was expected to provide a deterrent force against Cuban guerrilla attacks. Thus, in early June, after Cuban guerrillas had burned the town of Sagua la Grande, the Spanish-American Iron Company requested naval protection of its $8 million investment at Nipe Bay. The *Nashville* and the *Paducah* were immediately dispatched, only to discover that the Cuban threat had been greatly exaggerated. Nonetheless, to deter any future Cuban attack, 54 sailors under the command of Lt. Earl P. Finney landed on 10 June "and proceeded by rail to

Woodfred to guard some mines, the Spanish-American Iron Company, and other American property" (Metcalf, p. 328). Meanwhile, additional reinforcements were brought on the *Eagle*. There were no reported enemy engagements with the guerrillas.

By the middle of July, the Cuban army, with the assistance of the United States, had effectively suppressed the rebellion and the secretary of the navy ordered a gradual withdrawal of its forces. Between 12 July and 23 July, troops stationed throughout Oriente Province were evacuated to Guantánamo Bay, from where they returned to the United States aboard the *Cyclops*, *Lebanon*, and *Prairie*. New orders to intervene came when these soldiers and marines were mobilized for similar duties in Veracruz, Mexico, in 1914. Thereafter, until 1934, naval and marine detachments saw steady action throughout the Caribbean Basin, from Panama and Nicaragua to Haiti and the Dominican Republic.

Keith A. Haynes

REFERENCES

Russell F. Fitzgibbon, *Cuba and the United States, 1900–1935* (Russell & Russell, 1964); Clyde H. Metcalf, *A History of the United States Marine Corps* (Putnam, 1939); Louis A. Pérez, Jr., *Cuba Under the Platt Amendment, 1902–1934* (Univ. of Pittsburgh Pr., 1986); Teresita Yglesia Martinez, *El segundo ensavo de republica* (Editorial de Ciencias Sociales, 1980).

See also Cuba, Intervention (1912); Marine Operations in Cuba (1912).

Naval Operations off North Russia (1918–1919)

The U.S. naval operations in North Russia were conducted in conjunction with U.S. intervention in North Russia, 1918–1919. With minor exceptions, the operations did not entail active hostilities but were confined to the provision of supply, support, and administrative services at the ports of Murmansk and Archangel and other locations in and around the White Sea.

U.S. naval activity in North Russia began on 24 May 1918 with the arrival at Murmansk of the USS *Olympia*, the once famous flagship of Adm. George Dewey. Though ordered by President Woodrow Wilson not to participate in active operations in the North, some 51 of the

Olympia's crewmen were at once employed in the occupation of Archangel, an operation carried out on 2 August under the leadership of British Maj. Gen. Frederick C. Poole, the original Allied commander in chief in North Russia. Of these sailors, some 25 then took part in the inland pursuit of the enemy on what soon became known as the Vologda Railroad Front. At the same time, another party of approximately the same size participated in the initial operations on the so-called Northern Dvina River Front, while contributing also to the formation of the collateral Seletskoe Column of the Vologda Railroad Front. Following these early operations, the *Olympia* crewmen returned to their ship, which then proceeded to the peaceful patrolling of northern waters until its final withdrawal from the region on 13 November.

On 24 October, Rear Adm. Newton A. McCully arrived at Murmansk to take charge of U.S. naval forces in North Russia. In fact, until mid-February 1919, no such forces actually existed in the region. At that point, however, prompted by the recent initiation of a Bolshevik offensive all across the Archangel front, McCully requested the dispatch of naval reinforcements to the North at the earliest possible opportunity. In early April the troopships *Chester* and *Galveston* arrived at Murmansk bearing members of the American North Russia Transportation Corps, who had been sent for service on the Murmansk Railroad Front. In mid-May, the naval reinforcements requested by Admiral McCully began to arrive in the North in the form of the cruisers *Des Moines*, *Sacramento*, and *Yankton*, as well as submarine chasers Nos. 95, 256, and 354 and the so-called Eagle boats Nos. 1, 2, and 3.

On 29 May two U.S. motor launches, manned by officers and crew from the recently arrived reinforcements, joined the Allied flotilla on Lake Onega on the Murmansk Railroad Front. Although their activities were apparently routine and uneventful, these vessels remained in active service on the lake until as late as 9 July. Beginning in early July, U.S. naval operations in the North were gradually scaled down in close coordination with the ending of all U.S. military activities in the region. On 13 July, Admiral McCully left Murmansk on board the *Sacramento*. The last U.S. vessel in northern waters, the *Des Moines*, departed Archangel on 2 September 1919. As finally recorded, the total casualties in-

curred as the result of U.S. naval operations in North Russia consisted of three sailors slightly wounded.

John W. Long

REFERENCES

Henry P. Beers, *U.S. Naval Forces in Northern Russia (Archangel and Murmansk), 1918–1919* (Navy Department Ref. Pub. No. 5, 1943); Dennis Gordon, *Quartered in Hell: The Story of the American North Russian Expeditionary Force, 1918–1919* (Gos, 1982); Chester V. Jackson, "Mission to Murmansk," *United States Naval Institute Proceedings*, 95 (1969), 82–89; Henry Newbolt, *A History of the Great War*, vol. 5.: *Naval Operations* (Longmans, 1931); Kemp Tolley, "Our Russian War of 1918–1919," *United States Naval Institute Proceedings*, 95 (1969), 58–72.

Naval Operations off Siberia (1918–1922)

Political conditions in Siberia deteriorated in the aftermath of the Bolshevik coup of November 1917, and vast amounts of Allied supplies at Vladivostok presented a tempting target. To forestall their unauthorized and undesired use by the Bolsheviks, including their possible transfer to Germany as a result of the Brest-Litovsk Treaty (March 1918), Allied naval forces exerted a substantial political role in monitoring the situation in Vladivostok and keeping a friendly government in the city. Naval officers also became involved in policy decisions in the Russian Civil War in Siberia.

U.S. warships periodically called at Vladivostok, beginning in November 1917. These included the *Brooklyn*, flagship of the U.S. Asiatic Fleet. Such visits continued throughout 1918 and after. Adm. Austin M. Knight, commander of the U.S. Asiatic Fleet, frequently consulted and negotiated with his British, French, and Japanese naval counterparts at Vladivostok. This was especially the case in the six-month period between March and September 1918, when Knight virtually administered U.S. policy in the area.

Major problems confronting the naval commands included the seizure of the Vladivostok government by Czech troops in June 1918. Knight on several occasions exceeded his authority in adopting policies later overturned by Washington. These included U.S. policy toward Japanese troops landing in Siberia and U.S. aid for Czech forces.

President Woodrow Wilson later agreed to send U.S. soldiers to Siberia, and the first major contingent arrived in September 1918. Gen. William S. Graves arrived in Vladivostok on 1 September and took effective shore command of U.S. operations from Admiral Knight. Knight left Vladivostok in October 1918, being replaced by Adm. William L. Rodgers.

Rodgers and other U.S. leaders worried about the formidable Japanese army deployed in Siberia as well as the sizable Japanese naval forces off the coast. Rodgers recommended in March 1919 the expansion of U.S. naval forces in the western Pacific and warned Washington in July that the Japanese intended to carve out a sphere of influence in East Asia unless U.S. and Allied efforts contained such efforts.

With the departure of U.S. ground forces in spring 1920, the only U.S. presence in the region was the United States Navy. Adm. Albert Gleaves succeeded Rodgers as commander of the Asiatic Fleet in early 1920, as the Russian Civil War was ending. One U.S. ship remained in the Vladivostok area until the departure of all Japanese troops in October 1922. This naval vessel, the *Sacramento*, sailed from Vladivostok in November 1922, closing a small chapter in U.S. naval history.

In retrospect, the United States Navy could do little to influence conditions in Siberia, and naval commanders became more concerned about the presence of the Japanese than the resolution of the turmoil of the Russian Civil War. Nonetheless, relations between the Japanese and U.S. naval commanders in the region (notably Admirals Knight and Kanji Kato) were consistently courteous with few serious differences or problems.

Taylor Stults

REFERENCES

William R. Braisted, *The United States Navy in the Pacific, 1909–1922* (Univ. of Texas Pr., 1971); William S. Graves, *America's Siberian Adventure, 1918–1920* (Cape & Smith, 1931); George F. Kennan, *Soviet-American Relations, 1917–1920: Russia Leaves the War* (Princeton Univ. Pr., 1956); George F. Kennan, *Soviet-American Relations, 1917–1920: The Decision to Intervene* (Princeton Univ. Pr., 1956); James W. Morley, *The Japanese Thrust into Siberia, 1918* (Columbia Univ. Pr., 1957).

Naval Operations Relating to Panama (1903)

When the Colombian Senate on 12 August 1903 rejected an isthmian canal treaty with the United States, not only did it encourage Panamanian dissidents to consider revolution but it also persuaded U.S. president Theodore Roosevelt to consider such a revolution as desirable. As president, Roosevelt felt that his earlier diplomatic negotiations with Colombia had been both generous and just. Convinced that no nation other than the United States should build a canal at Panama, he fumed over what he perceived to be the lack of cooperation on the part of the Colombian government.

By mid-October, Roosevelt believed that a revolution on the isthmus was likely. He instructed the United States Department of the Navy, therefore, to be prepared to move ships toward Panama if a revolution on the isthmus occurred. The Navy Department acted with dispatch. On 15 October, the Pacific Squadron at San Francisco under Rear Adm. Henry Glass received unexpected orders to conduct a naval exercise toward Acapulco, Mexico, beginning "about" 22 October. On 19 October, Glass received additional orders to have the *Boston* sail toward San Juan del Sur, Nicaragua, so that it reached that port by at least 1 November. The *Boston* began its journey south on 21 October.

Not only Pacific units of the U.S. fleet were alerted to move south. On 19 October, the cruiser *Dixie* embarked a battalion of marines at Philadelphia and sailed for Guantánamo, Cuba. The cruiser *Atlanta* at Boston also received orders to head for Cuba on the 19th. Five days later, on 24 October, the *Nashville*, a gunboat, received orders to proceed to Kingston, Jamaica, where it would be only 30 hours steaming from Colón, Panama.

Therefore, within 10 days of Roosevelt's instructions, the United States Department of the Navy had begun placing naval units within easy steaming of the Pacific and Gulf coasts of Panama. By late October and early November, Washington began concentrating forces even closer to Panama. On 29 October, the Navy Department ordered the *Dixie* to Kingston. On 1 November, similar orders were given to *Atlanta*. On 30 October, the *Nashville*, already at Kingston, received orders to sail to Colón.

Fearing the arrival of Colombian forces on the isthmus could jeopardize a revolution, the Roosevelt administration moved into high gear on 2 November when it ordered the *Boston*, the rest of the Pacific Squadron, and the *Dixie* to sail to Panama "with all possible dispatch." The commanding officers of the *Boston*, *Nashville*, and *Dixie*—the three vessels expected to arrive first at Panama—also received cables warning them that Colombian forces were approaching the isthmus and that they were to prevent their landing "if, in your judgment, the landing would precipitate a conflict" (*Foreign Relations of the United States, 1903*, p. 247).

Ironically, despite the naval movements of mid- and late October, only one U.S. vessel was in a position to reach Panama quickly. On 2 November, the *Boston*, experiencing engine trouble, had not yet reached San Juan del Sur, Nicaragua, let alone Panama. Glass's squadron, which had arrived at Acapulco on 31 October, experienced problems refueling which delayed its departure for Panama until 4 November. At Kingston, the *Dixie* had also experienced problems refueling. Consequently, it was unable to sail immediately to Colón upon receiving orders from Washington.

Only the *Nashville* was in a position to act. It had arrived at Colón at 5:30 p.m. on 2 November. However, Comdr. John Hubbard initially failed to receive the cable advising him to stop Colombian forces from landing. He did not receive that message until 10:30 a.m. the next day. Unfortunately for Hubbard and Washington, at 8:30 that same morning, approximately 450–500 Colombian soldiers had disembarked at Colón. With the proper leadership, those soldiers greatly endangered the anticipated Panamanian revolution.

Panamanian dissidents, not yet in open revolution, quickly reacted to the military threat on 3 November. They lured the highest ranking Colombian officers from Colón across the isthmus to Panama City with assurances that their men would be transported later in the day. Having successfully isolated the officers from their men, the Panamanian conspirators arrested the generals.

Shortly after 10:30 a.m., Hubbard, having finally received his orders, rushed to the Panamanian railroad office to ensure that the remaining Colombian soldiers at Colón would not be transported across the isthmus to Panama City. He discovered that the general superintendent of the railroad, James S. Shaler, had already decided not to transport the Colombian soldiers. When, at approximately 6:00 p.m., Hubbard learned of the formal declaration of independence at Panama City, he again met with Shaler and informed him that no military forces, either insurgent or Colombian, would be allowed to use the isthmian railroad.

By 11:00 a.m. on 4 November, Col. Eliseo Torres, temporarily commanding the Colombian forces at Colón, had learned of the declaration of independence at Panama City, the arrest of his commanding officers, and Hubbard's closure of the Panamanian railroad to military forces. By 12:30 p.m., he threatened to use force against the city of Colón and U.S. citizens residing there unless his commanding officers were freed by 2:00 p.m. Responding to that threat, Hubbard met with the U.S. consul, vice consul, and Shaler at 1:00 p.m. By 1:30 p.m., Hubbard had landed 42 men under the command of Lt. Comdr. Horace M. Witzel to protect U.S. citizens. Hubbard then used his gunboat to patrol the Colón waterfront. While the *Nashville*'s patrols were uneventful, Witzel, his men, and the U.S. citizens they were there to protect were soon surrounded by Torres and his men. Torres, uncertain of what to do, requested a temporary "truce." If Hubbard would reembark Witzel's contingent, Torres would not use force against Colón or U.S. citizens. By 6:00 p.m., Hubbard agreed, and the crisis at Colón eased. Witzel and his men returned to the *Nashville*; U.S. citizens returned to their homes.

After a peaceful night, Hubbard relanded his forces the next morning and resumed patrolling the waterfront. Torres, still separated from his commanding officers and facing a revolutionary government, a hostile U.S. naval presence augmented by the arrival of *Dixie* that evening, and an inability to use the Panamanian railroad to transport his men to Panama City, finally agreed to depart. The newly established Panamanian revolutionary government provided U.S. $8,000 to Torres to book passage to Colombia for his soldiers and equipment on the steamer *Orinoco*. When the steamer sailed with Torres and his men at 7:35 p.m. on 5 November 1903, the only real Colombian military threat to the revolution ended.

Because nature had created an almost impenetrable barrier between Panama and Colombia, a barrier through which no army could march, a Colombian land invasion of Panama was impractical. While Colombia, in theory, could have attempted a naval assault, that too was impractical. Colombia's largest warship was no match for even the oldest and slowest U.S. cruiser, let alone additional units of the Caribbean or Pacific squadrons of the United States.

So long as U.S. warships remained at Panama, Colombia had no feasible method of regaining control of its own territory. That prospect pleased President Roosevelt. The revolution had been successful, Colombian military forces had been neutralized, and on 18 November 1903 diplomats of the United States and Panama signed a treaty guaranteeing Washington perpetual use and control over a 10-mile-wide corridor extending the entire width of the isthmus and through which a canal would be constructed. The United States Navy, representing the power and prestige of the Roosevelt administration, subsequently ensured that Colombia would not jeopardize either the independence of Panama or the isthmian treaty.

Richard L. Lael
© 1990 all rights reserved.

REFERENCES

Eduardo Lemaitre Román, *Panamá y su Separación de Colombia* (Banco Popular, 1972); David McCullough, *The Path Between the Seas* (Simon & Schuster, 1977); John Nikol and Francis X. Holbrook, "Naval Operations in the Panama Revolution, 1903," *American Neptune*, 37 (1977), 253–261; Richard Turk, "The United States Navy and the 'Taking' of Panama, 1901–1903," *Military Affairs*, 38 (1974), 92–96; U.S. Department of State, *Papers Relating to the Foreign Relations of the United States, 1903* (U.S. Government Printing Office, 1904).

Naval War Board (1898)

On the eve of the war with Spain in 1898 Secretary of the Navy John D. Long asked Theodore Roosevelt, the assistant secretary, and three top naval officers to form a naval war board. Long recognized the Navy Department's requirement for a single administrative body to prepare war plans and direct naval strategy. These critical tasks demanded expertise in naval affairs that no single bureau or office could offer. Informally organized in March 1898, the Naval War Board (also known as the Strategy Board) met without the benefit of written orders, specific authority, or a prescribed agenda to consider most of the important issues and decisions confronting the navy in 1898, exercising profound influence on, if not absolute authority over, the conduct of U.S. naval operations.

The informal structure of the Naval War Board precludes a precise accounting of all members. The original board included Roosevelt, as president of the board, and officers best able to offer expert counsel: Capt. Arent S. Crowninshield, chief of the Bureau of Navigation; Capt. Albert S. Barker, of the secretary's office; and Comdr. Richardson Clover, chief intelligence officer, from the Office of Naval Intelligence. When war came in the third week of April, Roosevelt resigned his civilian post to join the army. Barker, too, departed for other duties. To fill these vacancies, Long made Rear Adm. Montgomery Sicard, late commander in chief of the North Atlantic Squadron, president of the board and called Capt. Alfred Thayer Mahan back to active duty on the board. In early May, when Mahan reported, the board consisted of Sicard and Crowninshield. Before his arrival, Mahan said, "other officers also were at times present, officially yet informally, and afterwards dropped out, with equal informality" (Mahan, p. 627). An army officer even reported as a "member." The triumvirate of Sicard, Crowninshield, and Mahan, however, composed the Naval War Board for the greater part of the war.

Roosevelt refused to confine the board's business to strategy. In his role as president of the board, he led the effort to organize the department for war and outfit the fleet for sea. Roosevelt's competence to make judgments on naval matters was well known, in particular to Long, who complained about him. A pacifist by some accounts, the secretary, in Roosevelt's opinion, required an occasional prod to act on the navy's preparations for war. After the *Maine* exploded in mid-February, these arrangements went forward with amazing speed, owing to the individual industry and initiative of Roosevelt, who approved locations for coastal signal stations, involved himself in scheduling refits for the battleships, and urged Long to send elements of the fleet to sea for drill and exercise.

When war erupted, the Naval War Board advised the department to concentrate on the enemy's poorly defended and far-flung colonial outposts. This strategy followed a basic war plan developed by *ad hoc* study groups and the Naval War College over the previous 16 months. As a result, the navy initiated a blockade of Cuba, with secondary action around Puerto Rico. In the western Pacific, Commodore George Dewey, in command of the Asiatic Squadron, was directed to attack the Spanish squadron at Manila. To collect information on Spain's resources, conditions, and ship movements, the board organized a modest intelligence operation in Europe.

The Naval War Board dominated the crucial interaction of command, control, and communication during active naval operations. Modern telegraphic systems, the board demonstrated, modified traditional relationships between central governments and commanders. Mahan, who conceded the potential for an intrusive higher body to stifle individual initiative, acknowledged: "Telegrams can always outrun vessels." (Mahan, p. 632) Having a central and fixed position, the board remained in continuous communication with the larger and rapidly changing strategic situation because it obtained and processed information in greater amounts and at faster rates than local commanders. "As regards [naval] movements," Mahan remarked, "most, if not all, were in accordance with the advice of the Board." (Mahan, p. 634)

Mahan made no effort to hide his contempt for the Naval War Board. He understood that the secretary, as the appointed civilian chief, must exercise singular responsibility for the conduct of the Navy Department. "But with the varied and onerous duties resting upon him," Mahan pointed out to his superior, "it [became] inevitable that, in such highly technical matters as the conduct of war, he must depend largely upon the technical familiarity with the subject that only seamen, and military seamen, can possess." (Mahan, p. 552) Thus, on 10 May 1898, his second day on the board, Mahan wrote a letter to Long, recommending the board's abolition. In his view, as the secretary's principal advisors, the board wielded significant, although "irresponsible," influence over the operational commanders in chief, given its lack of authority. Instead of advice by committee, Mahan suggested that one officer, assisted by a staff of experts, offer official advice to the secretary and accept responsibility for its results. In spite of the unfolding drama of events, Mahan received a perfunctory interview

from Long, who voiced a highly favorable view of the board's performance.

With the end of hostilities in August, the board completed its work. Except for the tardy dispatch of two monitors to reinforce Dewey, the Naval War Board, said Mahan, committed no serious oversights. Long said that it made no errors. The board's very existence and recognized success accelerated the movement to create a permanent organization to deal with strategic planning. As a result, in 1900, Long established the General Board of the Navy.

Richard A. Russell

References

Robert Greenhalgh Albion, *Makers of Naval Policy, 1798–1947*, edited by Rowena Reed (U.S. Naval Institute Pr., 1980); Alfred Thayer Mahan, "The Work of the Naval War Board of 1898," in Robert Seager II and Doris D. Maguire, eds., *Letters and Papers of Alfred Thayer Mahan*, vol. III, *1902–1914* (U.S. Naval Institute Pr., 1975), 627–643; Charles Oscar Paullin, "A Half Century of Naval Administration in America, 1861–1911," *United States Naval Institute Proceedings*, 40 (1914), 111–128.

Niagara Falls Conference (1914)

After U.S. troops landed at Veracruz, Mexico, in April 1914, the representatives of Argentina, Brazil, and Chile in Washington, D.C., offered to mediate the resulting dispute between the United States and Mexico. The sessions took place in Niagara Falls, Ontario, Canada, a neutral location, from 20 May through 1 July 1914 and became known as the Niagara Falls Conference. In Latin America, it is often referred to as the ABC Mediation Conference. The mediators were the Brazilian ambassador, Dr. Dominico da Gama; the Argentine minister, Dr. Rómulo S. Naón; and the Chilean minister, Eduardo Suárez Mujïca. Da Gama served as chairman because of the seniority conferred by his ambassadorial rank.

The mediators wished to confine the agenda to the U.S.-Mexican dispute, viewing the purpose of the sessions to be to deal with an international conflict. The administration of President Woodrow Wilson, however, insisted on including Mexican internal affairs, seeking to use the conference to force the removal of the government of Gen. Victoriano Huerta. The United States had refused to recognize the Huerta regime. The landing at Veracruz was designed to promote his fall through preventing an arms shipment from reaching his army, which was resisting the Mexican revolutionary forces. While the Wilson administration was willing to seize the port, its objective was limited. There was no plan to move farther. Mexicans saw the situation differently, fearing that the landing was the precursor of a full-scale invasion. Huerta sought to invoke patriotism to gain new support as the defender of the Mexican nation and to embarrass the Constitutionalist revolutionaries, who also opposed the U.S. landing but refused to accept the armistice proposed by the mediators.

Reflecting President Wilson's unwillingness to recognize the Huerta regime, delegates from the United States were selected and officially designated "Special Commissioners of the President of the United States near the Mediators." This implied that the conference really involved only the two Mexican factions, with the United States as an observer, speaking only to the ABC mediators. Such a position violated the terms of the original offer of mediation. The U.S. delegates had no clear powers and were restricted to relying on telephone instructions from Secretary of State William Jennings Bryan. Because of Wilson's insistence that the Huerta government lacked legality, the U.S. representatives were individuals with legal rather than diplomatic expertise: Associate Supreme Court Justice Joseph R. Lamar and the former solicitor of the Department of Justice, Frederick W. Lehman.

A protracted dispute resulted regarding the agenda and who would be represented at Niagara Falls, producing a situation in which the various delegations never gathered around the same table and failed to agree even on the purpose and composition of the conclave. The Wilson administration insisted that the Carranza revolutionaries be full participants and that the talks reach agreement on the composition of an interim regime to end the civil war in Mexico. Although U.S. efforts resulted in sessions dealing with both the internal and external disputes, Constitutionalist leader Venustiano Carranza rejected even the call for an armistice, preferring to continue the civil war in which his forces were clearly gaining the ascendancy. The constitutionalist representatives steadfastly refused to negotiate with or to meet with representatives of Huerta, who stayed in nearby Buffalo, New York, never actually attending the formal sessions. To complete the circle, the mediators refused to admit the constitutionalist representatives to the formal sessions, contending that only the U.S. and the Mexican governments were participants and proposing that the constitutionalist delegates confer separately with the mediators. Hence only one delegation, that of Huerta's Mexican government, was formally accredited to the conference as a full participant. The Constitutionalists for their part conferred only with the United States and made it clear that they supported Huerta's demand for immediate U.S. withdrawal from Veracruz. They resolutely refused to talk with Huerta's representatives, insisting that compromise was impossible and that the only acceptable solution was for Huerta to resign and hand over power to Carranza. The Huerta delegates just as steadfastly refused to consider this possibility.

The resulting negotiations were protracted and limited in scope, offering scant prospects for success because no two of the participants agreed either on the purpose of or participants in the conclave. With the rebel withdrawal from the conference, the U.S. representatives in effect argued the revolutionary constitutionalist cause, pressing Huerta to resign, despite the fact that the constitutionalists made it clear that they would not accept a provisional regime, but demanded a complete surrender of power to them.

Huerta at first sought to limit the agenda to the withdrawal of U.S. troops and the consequences of the occupation of Veracruz. Indeed, he agreed to send representatives only at the urging of the British minister in Mexico City. The Mexican delegates were prestigious personages not associated with the Huerta regime. The delegation consisted of an expert on international law, Emilio Rabasa, as well as Agustín Rodríguez and Luis Elguero, who were important in Catholic circles. Elguero had also been prominent in the Díaz regime. As the talks continued, Huerta offered to resign the presidency in favor of a compromise candidate if the United States would pledge to support the resulting government against the Carrancistas. Both the United States and the Constitutionalists rejected this proposal.

The protocols resulting from the conference settled little and had no effect on the civil war, which continued unabated throughout the negotiations. All parties sought to promote their political ends and to allow the real issues to be settled on the battlefield. Agreements were limited to the Huerta regime's abandonment of its demands for reparations and for simultaneous salutes to both flags, and a U.S. pledge not to claim an indemnity or "any other international satisfaction," thereby rescinding the U.S. demand that the Mexican government salute the U.S. flag. The protocols stated vaguely that the composition of the provisional government would be decided in negotiations between the two Mexican factions, which would clearly never take place.

The mediators considered the conference a success in averting further conflict or a full-scale war between the United States and the Mexican government, because the talks provided each party with a pretext for avoiding provocation of the other during the early days of the occupation and in effect forced both sides into fixed positions. While U.S. troops began planning to withdraw from Veracruz a few months later, their withdrawal resulted from the fall of the Huerta regime rather than the Niagara Falls Conference. Indeed, an acrimonious dispute with the Constitutionalists followed because they refused to make any pledges or to provide any guarantees regarding their subsequent conduct. U.S. troops finally withdrew from Veracruz without an accord because of the crisis resulting from World War I.

Kenneth J. Grieb

REFERENCES

Kenneth J. Grieb, *The United States and Huerta* (Univ. of Nebraska Pr., 1969); Kenneth J. Grieb, "The ABC Mediation Conference at Niagara Falls, Ontario in 1914," *Niagara Frontier*, 16 (1969), 42–54; Berta Ulloa, *La Revolución intervenida: Relaciones diplomáticas entre México y Estrados Unidos* (El Colegio de Mexico, 1971).

Nicaragua, Intervention (1912–1925)

The U.S. intervention in Nicaragua in 1912 was a natural development of Washington's policies of the early 20th century. The Roosevelt Corollary to the Monroe Doctrine establishing a police role for the United States in the Western Hemisphere, the Platt Amendment and subsequent treaty with Cuba providing for intervention in the island republic, and construction of the Panama Canal creating a vital link between the Atlantic and Pacific coasts confirmed an already important U.S. presence in the Caribbean. In the view of progressive leaders such as Theodore Roosevelt, William H. Taft, Philander C. Knox, and even Woodrow Wilson and William Jennings Bryan, who supported peace and stability and the protection of lives and property, there was little in the politics, economics, and finance of the area that was not of interest to the United States.

Nicaragua, scene of William Walker's filibustering activities in the 1850s and possible site of an isthmian canal, once again attracted U.S. attention in the early 20th century during the presidency of José Santos Zelaya (1893–1909). Zelaya seemed the source of many Central American disturbances and often granted and canceled business concessions regardless of contractual arrangements. In Washington's view he was despotic, a violator of personal and property rights. Largely because of his activities in neighboring countries and the unsettled situation in Central America, the United States and Mexico sponsored a Central American conference in Washington in 1907. The treaties emerging from the conference were intended to discourage revolution and war and provide for judicial settlement of international disputes. Despite these arrangements, Central America remained troubled, and Zelaya frequently seemed in the center of the problems. Events leading to Zelaya's downfall and eventually to U.S. intervention began in October 1909, when an anti-Zelaya revolt erupted on Nicaragua's eastern coast. Officials in the State Department were sympathetic to the rebel movement, but there has been no evidence that Washington planned or instigated the revolt. After the revolution was underway, Zelaya ordered the execution of two captured U.S. citizens, Lee Roy Cannon and Leonard Groce, who had been aiding the rebels. The State Department angrily denounced what it termed the murder of U.S. citizens and broke diplomatic relations with the Nicaraguan government. U.S. policy was still presumably one of neutrality, but harsh public criticism by the United States of Zelaya aided the revolutionaries. Faced with an increasingly futile situation, Zelaya deposited the presidency with fellow Liberal party member José Madriz. The State Department viewed the change as a continuation of Zelayaism and maintained nonrecognition of the Nicaraguan regime.

Nonetheless, the new president vigorously fought the revolutionaries and was on the point of success at the eastern coast town of Bluefields in 1910. When the government covered the town on the land side and prepared to blockade and bombard it from the sea, U.S. marines under Maj. Smedley D. Butler occupied Bluefields, established a neutral zone, and forbade an armed attack while the warships *Dubuque* and *Paducah* prevented the blockade and bombardment. These acts were done in the name of protecting U.S. lives and property, but also had the effect of weakening government forces. After failure at Bluefields and faced with continued U.S. hostility and a resurgent revolutionary spirit, Madriz surrendered the presidency to the insurgents on 20 August 1910.

There followed a confused and unstable period in Nicaraguan politics during which Thomas C. Dawson, the State Department's special representative, tried to arrange Nicaragua's political and financial affairs. The political arrangement placing Juan J. Estrada in the presidency and Adolfo Díaz in the vice presidency was weak in the face of the stronger and more popular leaders, such as Luis Mena and Emiliano Chamorro Vargas. After a dispute with Mena, his minister of war, Estrada abandoned the presidency, leaving Adolfo Díaz to confront Mena's presidential ambitions and Washington's program of financial reforms, which included a U.S.-controlled collector of customs. Mena convinced a compliant legislature to elect him to the presidency for the term beginning 1 January 1913, despite the Dawson Agreement's plan for a popular election. In July 1912, Mena sought to strengthen his position by bringing loyal troops into Managua; Díaz countered by putting Emiliano Chamorro in charge of government forces. After a short conflict on the afternoon of 29 July, the U.S. minister, George T. Weitzel, at Díaz's request, arranged a truce and an agreement by Mena to resign as minister of war. That night Mena cut Managua's electric power. Under cover of darkness he departed the city with his army and the city police controlled by his brother.

Despite Weitzel's belief that Mena did not intend serious resistance, the Nicaraguan situation worsened. Mena proceeded to Masaya and Granada and seized portions of the U.S.-owned railroad and the steamers on Lake Nicaragua while working with former Liberal supporters of Zelaya to present formidable opposition to the government. An uprising at the Liberal-controlled city of León on the only railroad between Managua and the Pacific port city of Corinto threatened to isolate the capital. Already, telegraph lines into Managua had been cut, leading the minister to request naval vessels at San Juan del Sur and Corinto on the Pacific and Bluefields on the Atlantic to enable transmission of messages by wireless.

Growing insurgency led Weitzel to remind the Nicaraguan government of its responsibility to protect U.S. lives and property. The Díaz regime responded with a request that the United States use its forces to protect all inhabitants of the republic. Weitzel then turned to Capt. Warren J. Terhune, commanding officer of the USS *Annapolis* at Corinto. Terhune, thinking that U.S. citizens and other foreigners in danger might appropriately retreat to Corinto and that investors presumably considered similar risks when making their investments, was extremely reluctant to send a large force to Managua, but did dispatch about 100 men following the minister's urgent appeal. The marines arrived at Managua early in the morning of 4 August 1912, and almost immediately Weitzel recommended sending more marines from Panama to Corinto. The force in Managua was described as a legation guard, and U.S. officials denied that the United States was intervening. Alvey A. Adee, the second assistant secretary of state, asserted there was no intention to intervene but that the United States had an imprescriptible right to protect the legation and the nation's interests whether they were in Managua, Bluefields, or anywhere else.

The arrival of the marines in Managua seemed to have a quieting effect. Nonetheless, the *Tacoma* was sent from Guantánamo, Cuba, to Bluefields, and a few days later when General Mena's forces seized part of the railroad near León, temporarily cutting off the capital by rail, the *Justin* with 350 marines under Major Butler was ordered to Corinto from Panama. The outlook worsened when Gen. Benjamin F. Zeledon, Zelaya's former minister of war who was at this point cooperating with Mena, notified Weitzel that he intended to bombard Managua. At 6:00 a.m. on 11 August the shelling began and continued for four days. In response to Weitzel's alarming reports concerning the danger to U.S. lives and property and the possibility U.S. troops might be necessary to reestablish order, the *Justin*'s marines were sent to Managua, and the *Denver* was ordered to Corinto.

Meanwhile, Nicaraguan government troops had held their positions around the capital and forced the rebels to withdraw toward Masaya and Granada southeast of the city. Despite this success there was little indication that the government could stop the revolution. On 18 August a Liberal force annihilated 500 government troops at León, and the situation at Corinto and San Juan del Sur appeared to worsen. Particularly worrisome was the railroad between Corinto and Managua via revolutionary-dominated León. The safety and well-being of the U.S. legation and the U.S.-backed Nicaraguan government seemed to hinge on keeping the railroad free of obstruction.

In the face of these mounting difficulties, Adee requested a greater navy presence in Nicaragua. The Department of the Navy ordered the armored cruiser *California*, the flagship of the Pacific Squadron, to proceed from San Diego to Corinto where Adm. William H.H. Southerland was to survey the Nicaraguan situation. Before Southerland arrived in Nicaragua, President William H. Taft, fearing a delay in securing enough marines to protect U.S. citizens and comparing the situation to the Boxer Uprising, ordered the 10th Infantry Regiment to Nicaragua. When the secretary of war advised the president to send marines rather than the army because of international opinion and Taft learned that sufficient marines were available, he rescinded his order.

Meanwhile, the Nicaraguan situation deteriorated. The government was unable to restore order; a small group of U.S. troops going from Managua to Corinto faced a hostile mob at León and was forced to abandon its train, and hike most of the way back to the capital; and rebels threatened the port of Corinto, encouraging foreign women and children to spend nights aboard U.S. warships while a small landing party and U.S. civilian volunteers patrolled the city.

Officials in the State Department at this point believed the issue in Nicaragua was more than a question of protection, but one of prestige which, if left unattended, would give rise to a succession of contentions and further occasions for threats and possible interventions. The State Department thought that "if the United States did its duty promptly, thoroughly and impressively in Nicaragua, it would strengthen our hand and lighten our task, not only in Nicaragua . . . but throughout Central America and the Caribbean and would even have some moral effect in Mexico" (Scholes and Scholes, pp. 65–66).

For about a month after arriving in Nicaragua, Admiral Southerland believed the U.S. policy should be to protect U.S. nationals and maintain neutrality between the Nicaraguan government and the rebels. This approach ran counter to the desires of the Nicaraguan government and U.S. diplomats. After strong objections to the State Department and President Taft from the Nicaraguan government and the U.S. legation, it was changed.

After securing the Pacific ports of Corinto and San Juan del Sur and stopping filibustering parties through the Gulf of Fonseca, Southerland concentrated on control of the railroad, first to Managua and from there to Granada. In early September Major Butler with 75 marines made extensive repairs to the tracks and bridges while 300 bluejackets were stationed near León, 125 at Chinandega, and squads of 20 at the important bridges. When Col. Joseph H. Pendleton took a force of several hundred from Corinto to the capital he decided to occupy that section of León through which the trains had to pass. At the same time U.S. forces took possession of all railroad rolling stock in León.

With the rail line from Corinto to Managua relatively under U.S. control by 12 May, attention was turned to the line from the capital to Masaya and Granada. Three days later Major Butler began the task of securing this part of the railroad and protecting U.S. lives and property in Granada, where General Mena had his headquarters. The other rebel concentration, under Gen. Zeledon, was at Masaya, about halfway between the capital and Granada. On the eastern outskirts of Masaya, Butler's force confronted gunfire from Zeledon's men at a place called the Barranca, a high sloping hill which had been divided by excavation for the railroad. The higher of the resulting two hills was called Coyotepe, and the lower was known as the Barranca. The hills commanded the railroad from both directions and in Central America were considered impregnable. After prolonged discussions over four days between the U.S. commanders and the revolutionaries and a threatening clash between the two sides, Zeledon allowed Butler's train to proceed. Because of nightfall and possible impediments along the way, Butler's force remained in Masaya for the night. During the stay, there was some firing on the train, which the marines returned. Three marines were slightly wounded. Zeledon apologized and disavowed the action, and the next morning Butler proceeded toward Granada, entering the town early in the morning of 22 September. Almost immediately he was reinforced by the 1st Battalion of marines under Colonel Pendleton. They provided for the recovery and protection of U.S. property and the distribution of Red Cross supplies. They also opened discussions with the revolutionary commander, Luis Mena, who was sick and confined to his bed. Admiral Southerland participated in these discussions and agreed to accept Mena's surrender and that of his 700 men at midnight on 24 September. Gen. Luis Mena and his son were exiled to Panama, and his 700 troops were paroled.

The remaining obstacle to control of the railroad and to ending the revolution was Zeledon's continuing occupation of the Barranca, despite a siege by Nicaraguan government troops. On the morning of 27 September 1912, Nicaraguan government forces began to bombard the Barranca, which lasted until 1 October. At that time the Nicaraguan government tried unsuccessfully to negotiate Zeledon's surrender. After Admiral Southerland decided that government troops would not take the Barranca by bombardment and would not attempt to take it by assault because of anticipated heavy losses, he ordered preparations for U.S. forces to take the positions. On the morning of 3 October the marines opened fire on the Barranca and continued it throughout the day. There was no rebel response. At daybreak of the next morning, Colonel Pendleton led an assault on Coyotepe, and within 37 minutes the hill was captured. The Barranca had been evacuated because of the previous day's bombardment. Four marines were killed and five wounded in the attack. Of the 550 rebels on the two hills, the U.S. command reported 40 killed, 18 seriously wounded, and 14 captured. Many of the rebels fled into the town of Masaya where government troops, after severe fighting, killed or captured most of them. Zeledon had left the Barranca the day before and had escaped from Masaya before or about the time of the U.S. attack. He later died from wounds inflicted by a government force that intercepted his fleeing party.

After completing operations in Masaya, Southerland ordered occupation of all of León to stop harassment of the U.S.-controlled railroad. There was some resistance, leading to 3 U.S. deaths, 3 U.S. wounded, and about 50 rebels killed. Thereafter, peaceful conditions gradually returned to Nicaragua, and Admiral Southerland reported on 23 October that if it were not for Nicaraguan elections in early November he would not hesitate to withdraw much of the U.S. force. The marines and bluejackets maintained order during the elections, and afterward the force that at one time numbered a little over 2,300, not counting men on ships in Nicaraguan waters, was gradually withdrawn. A force of about 100 marines remained in Managua as a legation guard until 1925. Historian and diplomat Dana G. Munro has noted that the 1912 intervention in Nicaragua marked the first time that U.S. forces had actually fought to suppress a revolution in the Caribbean area.

William Kamman

REFERENCES

Isaac Joslin Cox, *Nicaragua and the United States, 1909–1927* (World Peace Foundation Pamphlets, 1927); Harold Norman Denny, *Dollars for Bullets: The Story of American Rule in Nicaragua* (Dial Pr., 1929); Robert Debs Heinl, Jr., *Soldiers of the Sea: The United States Marine Corps, 1775–1962* (U.S. Naval Institute Pr., 1962); Clyde H. Metcalf, *A History of the United States Marine Corps* (Putnam, 1939); Dana G. Munro, *Intervention and Dollar Diplomacy in the Caribbean, 1900–1921* (Princeton Univ. Pr., 1964); Walter V. Scholes and Marie V. Scholes, *The Foreign Policies of the Taft Administration* (Univ. of Missouri Pr., 1970).

See also list of entries at front of book for Nicaragua, Intervention (1912–1925).

Nicaragua, Intervention (1927–1933)

Not long after 13 years of intervention ended with marine departure from Nicaragua in 1925, circumstances leading to a second long intervention began. Emiliano Chamorro Vargas, popular Conservative party leader, led a successful *coup d'état* against the coalition government of Carlos Solórzano (Conservative party) and Juan Bautista Sacasa (Liberal party) brought to office by the 1924 election. Knowing that Washington supported the Central American treaties of 1907 and 1923, which sought to discourage revolution by refusing diplomatic recognition to governments reaching power by other than constitutional means, Chamorro tried to convince the State Department that his path to power was legitimate.

Vice President Sacasa fled the country in fear of his life, and when he refused to return to answer charges of conspiracy brought by a Chamorro-controlled Congress, the office was declared vacant. Chamorro then pressured President Solórzano to resign, allowing a congressionally picked first designate to assume the presidency in the absence of a vice president. Emiliano Chamorro was the first designate and became president in March 1926. The United States refused to recognize him and undertook to force him out of office. Meanwhile, Sacasa, claiming the presidency, visited Washington where State Department officials, who did not favor a new revolution, refused to place him back in Managua. Nonetheless, a Liberal force landed on and took control of much of the sparsely inhabited eastern coast of Nicaragua in May 1926. In the process, the Liberals occupied a Nicaraguan-owned but U.S.-managed national bank and took the Bluefields customs house presided over by a U.S. citizen. After a request from the U.S. consul at Bluefields, the light cruiser *Cleveland* arrived and marines, temporarily occupying the town, declared it a neutral zone. Although Chamorro apparently reestablished his authority along the eastern coast by the end of May, this was the beginning of extended Liberal attempts to undo the *coup d'état*, and U.S. Marines landed again at Bluefields in August.

Fearing the political instability and bloodshed of civil war, the United States sponsored a conference of opposing sides at Corinto in October on board the cruiser *Denver*. After the conference adjourned without success, mounting pressure forced Chamorro's resignation, and the Nicaraguan Congress, after a substantial attempt to restore the government the way it was elected in 1924, eventually selected Adolfo Díaz to serve through the 1928 election. The United States recognized the Díaz presidency, but within two weeks Sacasa established a rival government at Puerto Cabezas on the eastern coast which was recognized by Mexico. Because these political-diplomatic events complicated any settlement, and as suggestions of Bolshevism moving south

from Mexico floated around Washington, the Liberal revolution spread, Díaz called for U.S. aid. Responding in December 1926 and early 1927 to perceived threats to U.S. lives and property and to fears of Mexican and Bolshevik meddling in Nicaragua, marines began landing at eastern coast towns, including Puerto Cabezas, and returned to Corinto and Managua. Supposedly neutral, they nonetheless helped Díaz. Still, rebel activity increased and greater U.S. involvement seemed imminent. To forestall this, President Calvin Coolidge sent his special representative, Henry L. Stimson, to stop the fighting through negotiation. Stimson persuaded Liberal Gen. José María Moncada to recommend that the Liberal soldiers accept his offer of U.S.-supervised elections in 1928 and the creation of a nonpartisan national guard in return for turning in their arms. If they refused, there was an ill-disguised threat that marines would disarm them. All of the Liberal officers complied except Augusto C. Sandino and a handful of followers who retreated into the jungles and mountains of northern Nicaragua to carry on an extended struggle against U.S. intervention and the Nicaraguan government which he charged was under Washington's control.

Sandino's action did not overly concern the United States, which within a short while began reducing the marine contingent in Nicaragua. Then, on 16 July 1927, Sandinistas attacked a group of 87 marines and Nicaraguan national guardsmen at Ocotal. The arrival of five bombing and strafing planes changed what might have been a Sandino victory into defeat. Ocotal was a lesson for Sandino about direct frontal attacks and air power. In the future he relied on more classic guerrilla techniques which engaged up to 5,000 U.S. Marines and sailors for over five years. The United States with its technological superiority was able to protect the government and the major towns in the western part of the country; supervise the elections of 1928, 1930, and 1932; and create and train a national guard, but it was not able to capture Sandino or stop his hit-and-run tactics and in the end was not willing to guarantee the safety of lives and property of U.S. citizens in the interior of the nation. Faced with the cost of the Nicaragua intervention during troubled economic times; with growing criticism from Latin America, congress, and elsewhere; with the inability to reach a complete military victory; with growing disillusionment about intervention; and with the belief that the United States had fulfilled the promises about elections and a national guard, Hoover and Stimson decided to withdraw the marines. Withdrawal of the last 910 marines and sailors came on 2 January 1933. The Nicaraguan imbroglio convinced many U.S. leaders that such use of the marines was too heavy-handed and contributed to the growing mood for the nonintervention of the Good Neighbor policy. Another long-term result of the intervention was the rise of Anastasio Somoza García who, as head of the U.S.-created national guard, seized power in Nicaragua and established a dynasty that continued through his sons until 1979.

William Kamman

REFERENCES

Lejeune Cummins, *Quijote on a Burro: Sandino and the Marines, A Study in the Formulation of Foreign Policy* (La Impresora Azteca, 1958); Robert Debs Heinl, Jr., *Soldiers of the Sea: The United States Marine Corps, 1775–1962* (U.S. Naval Institute Pr., 1962); William Kamman, *A Search for Stability: United States Diplomacy Toward Nicaragua, 1925–1933* (Univ. of Notre Dame Pr., 1968); Neill Macaulay, *The Sandino Affair* (Quadrangle, 1967); Clyde H. Metcalf, *A History of the United States Marine Corps* (Putnam, 1939); Dana G. Munro, *The United States and the Caribbean Republics, 1921–1933* (Princeton Univ. Pr., 1974).

See also list of entries at front of book for Nicaragua, Intervention (1927–1933).

North Atlantic Squadron, United States Navy (1898)

By 15 April 1898, the United States Navy had deployed two major forces in the Atlantic. The North Atlantic Squadron, which was stationed at Key West, Florida, under the command of Capt. William T. Sampson, was built around the battleships *Iowa* and *Massachusetts* and the armored cruiser *New York*. Its assignment was to blockade Cuba and also to operate against any Spanish naval units that entered the Caribbean. Another force of two battleships and three cruisers under Commodore Winfield S. Schley, identified as the "Flying Squadron," was to protect the East Coast of the United States and, if possible, reinforce Sampson before a major fleet engagement.

By the time Sampson left Key West on 22 April for his blockading assignment, he had been promoted to rear admiral and given command of all U.S. naval forces in the North Atlantic, including Schley's. Within a few weeks he had organized a blockade that closed most of Cuba's ports. On 4 May, learning that a Spanish squadron under Adm. Pascual Cervera y Topete was on its way to Cuba, Sampson moved east toward Puerto Rico to intercept it, taking his battleships and cruisers with him. On 19 May he arrived at San Juan and bombarded the port, but Cervera was not there; instead, on that same day, Cervera had arrived in the harbor at Santiago de Cuba. Cervera's action, which ended any threat he could make to the U.S. East Coast or to the blockade, gave the United States Navy an opportunity to concentrate its ships, but the Spanish fleet was not located for 10 days. Meanwhile, Sampson ordered Schley to blockade Cienfuegos on Cuba's southern coast, while he positioned the North Atlantic Squadron where it could threaten Havana, protect the blockade or the Atlantic Coast, or move against Cervera when he was located. When Sampson learned that Cervera was in Santiago harbor, he ordered Schley to blockade him there, but Schley, who was extremely dilatory, did not arrive at his station until 28 May.

On 1 June Sampson arrived off Santiago with his squadron, which included the battleship *Oregon* having just completed its storied passage around South America from the West Coast. The combined U.S. forces, which now included four battleships and two armored cruisers, were far superior to Cervera's squadron, which had only four armored cruisers and two destroyers. By trapping Cervera, Sampson provided the key to U.S. victory over Spain because his forces controlled the Caribbean, and U.S. troops could proceed without danger to land in Cuba. Despite his advantage, Sampson hesitated to risk challenging the harbor's defenses and instead waited for U.S. land forces to reduce them. On 3 July, Cervera, realizing that U.S. troops had gained control of the heights overlooking Santiago, and under orders, made a break for the open sea. U.S. naval forces easily dispatched his ships in the ensuing engagement, sealing the fate of Spanish Cuba.

On 21 June 1898, the Navy Department had reorganized its commands, eliminating the Flying Squadron and redesignating the North Atlantic Squadron as the North Atlantic Fleet, which was divided into the First and Second North Atlantic Squadrons.

Richard H. Abbott

REFERENCES

Paolo E. Coletta, *French Ensor Chadwick: Scholarly Warrior* (Univ. Pr. of America, 1980); David F. Trask, *The War With Spain in 1898* (Macmillan, 1981).

See also Sampson, William Thomas.

North Russia, Intervention (1918–1919)

The U.S. intervention in North Russia was a policy formulated by President Woodrow Wilson during the first half of 1918 at the urgent insistence of Britain, France, and Italy, his chief World War I Allies. Motivated by the Allies' deep concern about the impact on their ongoing war effort of the aftermath of the Russian Revolution of 1917, intervention was conceived by the president as a strictly limited operation but soon became enmeshed in Allied military strategy and the unfolding Russian Civil War with consequences that far exceeded the modest intentions of the United States. As a result, from its inception in mid-1918 to its final termination in July 1919, U.S. intervention in the North was characterized by confusion, controversy, and disaffection.

Following the Bolshevik Revolution of November 1917 and subsequent prompt initiation of peace talks between the new Soviet government and the Central Powers, the Entente nations became convinced that some kind of Allied intervention in Russia was essential to their continued vigorous prosecution of the war. Accordingly, as early as December, the Allies began to search for ways to reexert their influence in Russia with the ultimate aim of somehow bringing about the reconstitution of the Eastern Front.

Among the most convenient points of Allied access to Russia were Archangel and Murmansk, the two chief seaports of the European North. In fact, in early March 1918, using an alleged German threat from neighboring Finland, the British engineered the occupation of Murmansk by a small contingent of Royal Marines. Thereupon, with the successful conclusion of peace between Russia and Germany at Brest-Litovsk, the British War Office promptly began discussions that soon resulted in the dispatch to Murmansk of a small military mission, whose avowed purpose was to prepare the way for full-scale Allied intervention in the North.

Having initiated intervention, however, the British at once became conscious of their own critical inability to provide the personnel necessary to carry it out. To meet this need for more men, the War Office first proposed to divert to the North at least a part of the so-called Czechoslovak Legion, a pro-Allied force formed in Russia during the war and then en route out of the country via the Trans-Siberian Railway. Though approved by the Allied Supreme War Council on 2 May, the prospective addition of the Czechs did not fully satisfy the British, who felt that still more troops were needed in the North. In these circumstances, Allied attention was increasingly drawn to the United States, which alone among the Western powers possessed the available reserves to implement the proposed intervention.

From the outset, the Allied campaign to convince Washington to participate in intervention encountered the stubborn resistance of President Woodrow Wilson, who was determined not to interfere in Russia's internal affairs. In the end, however, nearly six months of relentless Allied supplication in addition to persistent pleas on behalf of the embattled Czech Legion (which was never able to reach the North) were at last sufficient to force the president's hand. Thus, on 1 June, Wilson reluctantly agreed to send to Murmansk a small contingent of U.S. troops providing that such a diversion was approved by Allied Supreme Commander Gen. Ferdinand Foch. This concession was immediately seized on by the Allied-dominated Supreme War Council which, on 3 June, produced Joint Note No. 31 calling formally for the dispatch of up to six battalions of Allied infantry to the North in order to retain Murmansk and, if possible, to occupy Archangel. At the same time, it was decided to place the expedition under the command of British Maj. Gen. Frederick C. Poole, who was already at Murmansk.

Throughout June, in spite of its agreement to Joint Note No. 31, the United States continued to resist the idea of armed intervention in Russia. In response, in early July, the Supreme War Council returned to the issue of intervention, both in the North and in the Far East. Thus, on 2 July, the council decided on a Siberian intervention. On the next day, a similar decision was reached regarding North Russia, to which the United States was requested to send three battalions of infantry together with appropriate auxiliary support. In acceding to this request, however, President Wilson, on 17 July, issued a famous *aide-mémoire* which, while rejecting "in principle" the idea of armed intervention in Russia, nevertheless yielded to "the judgment of the Supreme [War] Council" and agreed to the employment of U.S. troops in Russia in order "to help the Czecho-Slovaks" and, more equivocally, "to steady any efforts at self-government or self-defense in which the Russians themselves may be willing to accept assistance." In effect, it was the ambiguous nature of this directive that led to much of the subsequent confusion surrounding U.S. intervention in the North.

On 30 July, Gen. John J. Pershing detached from his command in France the requested U.S. troops for service in North Russia. As selected by Pershing, these forces, comprising some 4,487 officers and men under the overall command of Col. George E. Stewart, became the nucleus of the future American Expeditionary Force, North Russia (AEFNR). Prepared in England, the U.S. force set sail for North Russia on 27 August.

Even before the embarkation of the AEFNR, however, developments in the North had taken a turn sharply at odds with U.S. expectations. This situation was largely attributable to the activities of British Major-General Poole, the recently appointed Allied commander in the North. A fervent interventionist, Poole had at once begun the implementation of an extremely ambitious plan of operations in the region which amounted, in effect, to the virtual invasion of central Russia with a projected army of 5,000 Allied troops supplemented by an expected 100,000 anti-Bolshevik Russian volunteers. On 2 August, as the first stage of this plan, Poole carried out the occupation of Archangel, using for this purpose a small task force of a few warships and some 1,500 Allied troops. Thereupon, despite the paucity of his reserves, the British chief launched an energetic offensive to the south with targets deep in the interior as his ultimate objectives.

In these circumstances, the arrival of the AEFNR at Archangel on 4 September was greeted with enthusiasm by General Poole, who immediately ordered almost two-thirds of its complement to take up positions on the fighting fronts. Though opposed by Colonel Stewart,

these orders, which were in direct violation of President Wilson's *aide-mémoire*, were fully supported by U.S. Ambassador David R. Francis. As a result, within a few days of their arrival in the North, U.S. troops were heavily engaged in numerous small-scale combats with units of the fledgling 6th Red Army. When this misuse of U.S. soldiers in the North at last came to the attention of Washington, the reaction was swift and unequivocal. On 26 September, the United States circulated a general memorandum addressed to all the major Allied governments which bluntly demanded that "all military effort in northern Russia be given up except the guarding of the ports and as much of the country round about them as may develop threatening conditions." Despite its categorical tone, there is no evidence that this directive had any effect on the military situation in the North, where U.S. troops continued to function as the majority of combat forces in the region.

In early September, as if their military misuse was not a sufficient violation of the president's wishes, U.S. troops in the North were also drawn into the trammels of local Russian domestic politics in the wake of an unsuccessful *coup d'état* in Archangel. So sharp was Washington's reaction to this development that General Poole was relieved of his command in mid-October and replaced by a new Allied chief, Maj. Gen. William Edmund Ironside. Although the new commander immediately adopted a far less aggressive strategy than his predecessor, he could do nothing to clarify the ambiguous status of his U.S. troops, who were by then engaged in sporadic clashes with the enemy on five widely dispersed fronts spread over a vast territory extending some 150–200 miles south of Archangel.

At that point, the total anomaly of U.S. intervention in the North was laid bare by the sudden termination of World War I. In these circumstances, which effectively negated virtually all of the original justifications for an Allied presence in the region, President Wilson desired to withdraw U.S. forces from the North "by the first boat." At length, however, he was prevailed upon to leave his troops in place in the region until their disposition could receive inter-Allied considerations at the impending Paris Peace Conference. When, however, the peace talks began in January 1919, it soon became apparent that the Allies were unable to reach any mutual agreement with regard to intervention in Russia. On the contrary, in spite of at least two U.S. efforts to resolve the problem, Britain and France remained adamantly opposed to any outcome that left the Bolsheviks in power in Russia.

Finally, in early February, frustrated by the Allies' prolonged inability to achieve unanimity on the Russian problem and confronted, on one hand, by a determined enemy offensive in the North and, on the other, by a rapidly mounting tide of domestic opposition to any further intervention in Russia, President Wilson at last decided on the unilateral evacuation of the North. Thus, on February 18, responding to a British plea for the dispatch of two additional companies of U.S. troops to bolster the Allied forces of British Maj. Gen. Charles C.M. Maynard on the Murmansk Railroad Front, the president announced his agreement but only on strict condition that all U.S. and Allied troops would be withdrawn from the North "at the earliest possible moment that weather conditions will permit in the spring." As it turned out, this vague and rather presumptuous statement was the only formal announcement of its intention to withdraw from North Russia ever issued by the U.S. government. Nevertheless, so far as President Wilson was concerned, the decision was final.

In mid-April, having been briefed personally by the president, Brig. Gen. Wilds P. Richardson arrived at Archangel to take charge of the U.S. evacuation from the North. Within weeks, the new commander began a phased withdrawal of U.S. troops from the fighting fronts to bases in and around Archangel. Beginning in early June, all of the U.S. forces at Archangel, followed by those more recently arrived units at Murmansk, were gradually shipped out of the North. As a result, by 28 July 1919, U.S. intervention in North Russia, which from the outset had developed far beyond its planners' modest intentions, came formally to an end.

John W. Long

REFERENCES

E.M. Halliday, *The Ignorant Armies: The Anglo-American Archangel Expedition, 1918–1919* (Harper, 1958); George F. Kennan, *Soviet-American Relations, 1917–1920: The Decision to Intervene* (Princeton Univ. Pr., 1958); John W. Long, "American Intervention in Russia: The North Russian Expedition, 1918–1919," *Diplomatic History*, 6 (1982), 45–67; Benjamin D. Rhodes, *The Anglo-American Winter War With Russia, 1918–1919: A Diplomatic and Military Tragicomedy* (Greenwood Pr., 1988); Leonid I.

Strakhovsky, *Intervention at Archangel: The Story of Allied Intervention and Russian Counter-Revolution in North Russia, 1918–1920* (Princeton Univ. Pr., 1944); Leonid I. Strakhovsky, *The Origins of American Intervention in North Russia (1918)* (Princeton Univ. Pr., 1937).

See also list of entries at front of book for North Russia, Intervention (1918–1919).

Northern Dvina River Front, North Russia (1918–1919)

The Northern Dvina River Front constituted one of the main lines of advance of the forces that participated in the U.S. intervention in North Russia, 1918–1919. Established along the course of the Northern Dvina River, which extends southeastward some 500 miles from the city of Archangel on the Dvina Gulf of the White Sea, the front had as its chief objectives the capture of the cities of Kotlas, 400 miles into the interior, and Viatka (Kirov), some 250 miles farther southeast, where, it was planned, Allied forces would link up with Czechoslovak and anti-Bolshevik Russian troops advancing westward from Siberia.

Established simultaneously with the occupation of Archangel on 2 August 1918, the Northern Dvina Front was created by British Maj. Gen. Frederick C. Poole, the initial Allied commander in chief in the North, whose preapproved plan of operations conceived this front as one of the primary avenues of Allied advance in the region. Based originally on a so-called C Force consisting of some 400 British, French, Russian, and Polish troops and three river steamers, the front advanced without opposition and, by 11 August, reached Bereznik, about 150 miles upstream at the junction of the Northern Dvina and Vaga rivers. At that point, however, unexpected resistance was suddenly encountered from a small fleet of Bolshevik gunboats which successfully held up any further Allied movement until 31 August, when the arrival of reinforcements in the form of three companies of British troops, two improvised gunboats, and the Royal Navy monitor M25 at last permitted the Allies to resume their offensive up the river.

On 11 September, the first U.S. troops arrived on the Dvina Front in the guise of the 1st Battalion (four companies) of the 339th Infantry Regiment, which collectively comprised almost one-third of the so-called American Expeditionary Force, North Russia. On 15 September, having moved up from Bereznik, the battalion was divided at Ust'-Vaga with Company A directed to reinforce the newly formed Vaga River Front, located to the south, while the rest of the troops continued up the Northern Dvina to Chamova, where they arrived on 17 September. On 19 and 20 September, Companies B, C, and D of the 339th took part in the difficult but successful capture of Sel'tso, on the left bank of the river, where, on 27 September, an Allied line was established opposite Borok, on the right bank, almost 200 miles upriver from Archangel.

On 2 October, all of the U.S. troops on the Northern Dvina were transferred to the Vaga Front from which, however, Companies B and D had at once to return owing to the crisis caused by the withdrawal to Archangel of the British monitor M25. This action, which was apparently prompted by concern about the imminent freezing of the river, exposed the Allies to the unhindered bombardment of Bolshevik gunboats, whose range of fire greatly exceeded that of any available Allied artillery. In these circumstances, a number of enemy attacks during the first half of October compelled the Allies to withdraw to a new line at Kurgomen', on the right bank, and Tulgas, on the left, some 20 miles to the rear.

On 11 November, following a series of attacks and counterattacks in late October, the Bolsheviks launched an overwhelming assault against the Allied garrison at Tulgas, which consisted of Companies B and D of the 339th together with a small detachment of British troops and two batteries of recently arrived Canadian artillery, about 400 men in all. In the ensuing so-called Battle of Armistice Day, Allied and U.S. forces engaged in a fierce, seesaw struggle with some 2,500 attacking Bolsheviks, which exacted a heavy toll of casualties on both sides. After four days, however, a desperate Allied bayonet charge, together with a sharp drop in temperature, which compelled the retirement of the enemy's superior riverine artillery, finally caused the Bolsheviks to break off the attack.

By the time of the battle at Tulgas, General Poole's offensive strategy on the Dvina had been replaced by the essentially defensive approach of his successor, British Maj. Gen. William Edmund Ironside. For their part, by contrast, the Bolsheviks in early 1919 mounted a strong counteroffensive throughout the North as a part of which Tulgas was subjected to further deter-

mined, but unsuccessful, enemy assaults in both January and February. Following these attacks, U.S. activity on the Dvina was confined to frequent, often dangerous patrols including one in early March in which a small contingent of soldiers from Company B was virtually annihilated near Zastrov'ia, about eight miles south of Tulgas. Finally, beginning in early April, U.S. troops on the Dvina began gradually to be replaced by elements of the newly organized North Russian Army. On 25 April, however, one of these units, having taken over at Tulgas, mutinied and deserted. In these circumstances, U.S. troops were required to return and recapture the town on 18 May. In the wake of this incident, they resumed their piecemeal evacuation of the Dvina, which was finally completed on 6 June.

Following the departure of U.S. forces, the Northern Dvina Front was the scene of a final, dramatic disengagement operation conducted by a brigade of British volunteer troops that had arrived in Archangel in June. Carried out in August, this operation achieved a point of penetration on the river that extended just beyond the Sel'tso-Borok line of 1918 and successfully covered the Allied evacuation of Archangel that occurred in September. Handed over to Russian troops, the Dvina Front existed until the last days of the anti-Bolshevik North in early 1920.

John W. Long

REFERENCES

Edward Altham, "The Dvina Campaign," *Journal of the Royal United Service Institution*, 68 (1923), 228–253; A Chronicler [John Cudahy], *Archangel: The American War With Russia* (A.C. McClurg & Co., 1924); Dennis Gordon, *Quartered in Hell: The Story of the American North Russian Expeditionary Force, 1918–1919* (GOS, 1982); E.M. Halliday, *The Ignorant Armies: The Anglo-American Archangel Expedition, 1918–1919* (Harper, 1958); Joel Moore, Harry Mead, and Lewis Jahns, *The History of the American Expedition Fighting the Bolsheviki* (Polar Bear, 1920).

Nurses in the Spanish-Cuban/American War

The Spanish-Cuban/American War created many opportunities for trained nurses to prove their worth—from caring for those wounded in battle to, more often, aiding soldiers who fell victim to the various epidemics that swept through the army. Their performance in the face of these challenges raised the prestige of female nurses both with the armed forces and with the public and went a long way toward dispelling the notion that women could not work effectively in army field hospitals.

Conditions in army hospitals during the first months of the Spanish-Cuban/American War were demoralizing for all concerned. Tropical fevers in Cuba and Puerto Rico and typhoid fever at home pushed hospital populations over their limits and strained the already tight supply situation. The men of the Hospital Corps, who took on all of the nursing duties, were swamped, as the deteriorating condition of many patients graphically demonstrated.

The need for better nursing quickly became apparent. Journalists reported on the sorry conditions found in medical facilities, and civilians who visited army bases were appalled at what they saw in the hospitals. Because the need was so visible, the work of female nurses provided by the American Red Cross and the Daughters of the American Revolution (DAR) came to be even more appreciated than it would have been otherwise.

At each step of the path toward acceptance, female nurses, particularly Red Cross nurses, had to overcome entrenched opposition. Initially, Surgeon General George M. Sternberg resisted aid from the American Red Cross, nursing or otherwise, for fear that the group would act independently of the Medical Department and that the public would take the acceptance of Red Cross aid as a sign that the army could not take care of its own. But from the beginning the Surgeon General needed to employ more nurses, and so he accepted the help of Dr. Anita Newcomb McGee, a prominent physician, who offered to recommend nursing applicants through the Hospital Corps Committee of the DAR. The nurses recommended by the DAR would then be put under army contract, whereas American Red Cross nurses were often expected to retain a Red Cross identity.

Until September 1898, the DAR committee was the principal agency for procuring nurses for the war. Of the approximately 1,500 nurses who served under army contract during the war, over 1,000 were DAR-recommended.

American Red Cross nurses, in addition to serving in stateside hospitals after Sternberg softened his stance and decided to accept Red Cross aid, provided relief through an expedition to Cuba aboard the relief ship *State of Texas*. The ship would have gone to Cuba but was long delayed by the U.S. blockade. Nurses from the ship established a fever hospital in June 1898 and assisted army field hospitals in Cuba, despite some initial local resistance from more traditional doctors to the idea of women working in the field.

High-level opposition to female nurses working in the field hospitals rather than just base hospitals was finally overcome when Surgeon General Sternberg allowed women nurses to help the overworked staff at Chickamauga Park field hospital in Georgia overcome a raging typhoid fever epidemic. Similarly, at Camp Wikoff on Long Island, New York, the chief surgeon agreed to accept the aid of women nurses in fighting tropical fevers afflicting quarantined troops who had recently returned from Cuba.

A postscript to the work of female nurses in the Spanish-Cuban/American War came shortly after the war ended. The congressional committee investigating the conduct of the war lauded the work of female nurses during the war and concluded that the Medical Department should create a permanent reserve corps of trained women nurses—which in 1901 became the Army Nurse Corps.

Eric R. Emch

REFERENCES

Lavinia Dock and others, *History of American Red Cross Nursing* (Macmillan, 1922); Foster Rhea Dulles, *The American Red Cross: A History* (Harper, 1950); Portia Kernodle, *The Red Cross Nurse in Action, 1882–1948* (Harper, 1949).

See also American National Red Cross; Barton, Clara, in the Spanish-Cuban/American War.

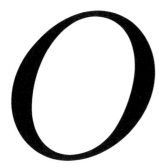

Obregón, Álvaro (1880–1928)

Among the revolutionary leaders who ousted Mexican dictator Victoriano Huerta in 1914, Álvaro Obregón has been overshadowed by the popular image of Francisco "Pancho" Villa. Erstwhile allies during the Huerta era, Villa and Obregón became enemies when Villa turned against the Constitutionalist leader, Venustiano Carranza in 1914. As Carranza's military leader, General Obregón was responsible for bringing Carranza to power in 1914–1915 by defeating Villa, most notably at the Battle of Celaya. Obregón accomplished this feat through a combination of superior strategy and modern tactics. In 1920 Obregón was elected president of Mexico. He is generally credited with consolidating many of the social and political changes brought about by the Mexican Revolution.

At the time of the Columbus, New Mexico raid in March 1916 by Villa's troops President Carranza, having gained power through most of Mexico, was striving to reduce the autonomy and influence of his military chieftains, including General Obregón. For his part, Obregón, whose support for Carranza was derived from the exigencies of the political and military situation, was working to secure a power base among the political elite as well as the agrarian and labor movements.

Ironically, it was Villa and his attack on Columbus that made it possible for Obregón to regain political power. In view of the possibility of U.S. intervention, Carranza considered it essential to demonstrate his ability to keep order in Mexico and especially to stop Villista depredations in the border region. Thus, on 13 March 1916, only four days after the attack on Columbus, New Mexico, which resulted in the U.S. Punitive Expedition led by Gen. John J. Pershing, Carranza named Obregón to be his secretary of war.

Obregón's direct involvement in the Punitive Expedition episode resulted from the first serious clash of Mexican and U.S. forces at Parral on 12 April 1916. Obregón indirectly informed the U.S. State Department that lack of communication between Mexican and U.S. military commanders may have been responsible for the incident. Secretary of State Robert Lansing took the hint and proposed a formal meeting between Obregón and Gen. Hugh L. Scott, the United States Army's chief of staff. Carranza agreed, and on 24 April Obregón departed in secrecy for Ciudad Juárez on the border.

The flexibility of the military negotiators was constrained by instructions from their respective superiors. Thus, an impasse occurred when Obregón called for the immediate withdrawal of U.S. forces, while Scott and Maj. Gen. Frederick Funston requested cooperation from Mexican forces and the use of the Mexican railroad for supplies. Into this atmosphere swirled rumors and reports of impending conflict. Scott and Funston were warned by Washington to look after their personal safety.

Obregón had been unable to show any flexibility at the initial meeting, which was held in public. When mutual friends suggested that it would be useful for Obregón and Scott to meet privately, the Mexican general asked the president of a mining company for use of his room at the Paso del Norte Hotel in El Paso for just that purpose. For 12 hours Scott, Funston, and Obregón met and finally emerged with a tentative agreement. The agreement called for the gradual removal of Pershing's troops and the intensification of Mexican efforts to eradicate the Villista menace from the border.

The U.S. acknowledgement that Obregón's army was competent to deal with any remaining Villista threat constituted a major victory for Obregón. To limit Obregón's political advantage and appear to be tougher on the United States, Carranza insisted on removal of a clause that might permit U.S. withdrawal to be delayed. Scott and Funston refused to accept the change.

Obregón and Scott met again, but no official agreement was ever signed. Their meetings served a useful purpose, however. The conferences between them were a symbol that Mexico and the United States were seeking a peaceful solution to the differences between the two countries.

Anthony K. Knopp

REFERENCES

Clarence C. Clendenen, *The United States and Pancho Villa: A Study in Unconventional Diplomacy* (Cornell Univ. Pr., 1961); Mark T. Gilderhus, *Diplomacy and Revolution: U.S.-Mexican Relations Under Wilson and Carranza* (Univ. of Arizona Pr., 1977); Linda B. Hall, *Álvaro Obregón: Power and Revolution in Mexico, 1911–1920* (Texas A&M Univ. Pr., 1981); Linda B. Hall and Don M. Coerver, *Revolution on the Border: The United States and Mexico, 1910–1920* (Univ. of New Mexico Pr., 1988); Hugh L. Scott, *Some Memories of a Soldier* (Century, 1928).

See also American-Mexican Joint Commission (1916); Scott, Hugh Lenox.

Ocotal, Nicaragua, Battle (1927)

The Battle of Ocotal was the first important engagement between U.S. marines and the Sandinistas. It was the first engagement in which the Nicaraguan national guard participated; it included the first organized dive-bombing attack, and one historian suggests it may have been the first low-altitude attack launched in support of ground troops. After the Battle of Ocotal, the Sandinistas decided that pitched battles against the marines were a mistake and developed guerrilla tactics more suitable in countering their enemy's technological superiority.

After presidential envoy Henry L. Stimson's mission to Nicaragua ended the Liberal revolution to unseat Nicaraguan president Adolfo Díaz, the U.S. Marines had the task of disarming the contending forces. A small group of Liberals under Augusto C. Sandino refused to disarm and moved northward into the mountainous terrain of Nicaragua's Nueva Segovia Department along the Honduran border. To establish control over Nueva Segovia, U.S. Marines and members of the newly reformed Nicaraguan national guard also moved into the northern province. A garrison of 39 marines under Capt. Gilbert D. Hatfield, supplemented by about 50 national guardsmen, was stationed at Ocotal, the departmental capital. As the marines and their *guardia* allies settled in, Hatfield and Sandino exchanged a series of communications in which the marine captain called on the Nicaraguan general to surrender and in which Sandino boastfully and graphically refused.

The Battle of Ocotal began in the early morning of 16 July 1927, after Sandino's troops had infiltrated the town during the night. A sentry discovered the attackers and immediately the Sandinistas opened a general fire with rifles and machine guns on the marine and *guardia* quarters. The defenders beat back three headlong rushes before the attackers retreated; they had taken heavy casualties, including the death of one of their leaders, Rufo Marín. Despite the confusion and the lure of looting, the Sandinistas re-formed to resume heavy firing until around 8:00 a.m., when Sandino sent a messenger promising no harm to Hatfield and his men if they surrendered. When the offer was refused, the fighting continued as the Sandinistas inched closer to attain more accurate sniper fire but they avoided an all-out assault.

The defenders' precarious situation was relieved when two patrol planes discovered their plight. One plane landed on the recently built landing strip; it was only barely able to take off under fire while the second plane began strafing the attackers. After expending their ammunition, the planes returned to Managua to report the battle. A five-plane formation led by Maj. Ross E. Rowell returned to Ocotal with four bombs for each plane and 600 rounds of ammunition for each of the planes' two machine guns. After locating the enemy, each aircraft, in column, dived down, fired the fixed machine gun, dropped a bomb, and then used the observer's gun as the plane pulled away. The procedure was repeated until all of the bombs were dropped and the attackers were routed. The marines had one killed and one wounded in the battle; the national guard had three wounded; estimates of Sandinista losses ranged from 50 to 300.

Reports of the battle, including extensive use of aviation and hundreds of Sandinista attackers, alarmed Washington and brought Sandino to the front pages. Nonetheless, by August 1927, the situation in northern Nicaragua seemed to be quieting and some marines were withdrawn. The withdrawal reflected an underestimation of Sandino and his followers. In a few months there was an expansion of the war and the U.S. intervention.

William Kamman

REFERENCES

E.H. Brainard, "Marine Corps Aviation," *Marine Corps Gazette*, 13 (1925), 25–36; William Kamman, *A Search for Stability: United States Diplomacy Toward Nicaragua, 1925–1933* (Univ. of Notre Dame Pr., 1968); Neill Macaulay, *The Sandino Affair* (Quadrangle, 1967); Peter B. Mersky, *U.S. Marine Corps Aviation, 1912 to the Present* (Nautical & Aviation, 1983); Bernard C. Nalty, *The United States Marines in Nicaragua*, rev. ed., Marine Corps Historical Reference Series No. 21 (Historical Branch, G-3 Division Headquarters, U.S. Marine Corps, 1962).

Ojos Azules, Mexico, Battle (1916)

After an attack on Columbus, New Mexico, by forces of Mexican revolutionary leader Francisco "Pancho" Villa in March 1916, the United States dispatched a Punitive Expedition of U.S. troops into Mexico to disperse Villa's troops.

The U.S. intelligence reports of 4 May 1916 indicated that approximately 200 Villistas under Julio Acosta, Cruz Domínguez, and Antonio Ángel were camped at Ojos Azules Ranch, 45 miles south of the San Antonio de los Arenales, Mexico, base camp. These Villistas had just defeated a Carrancista force (Mexican government troops) under Major López, who was requesting U.S. aid in protecting the nearby town of Cusihuiriachic. Under orders from Gen. John J. Pershing, Maj. Robert L. Howze hastily assembled six troops of 11th Cavalry, a machine gun troop, a pack train loaded with three days of rations, and 20 Apache scouts, who would fan out as an advance guard for the main column. The force totaled approximately 320 men. Upon reaching Major López's position, Howze found that the Carrancista commander was no longer willing to cooperate in the pursuit, nor was he willing to provide guides for the column. After hiring a U.S. doctor and a Mexican doctor at Cusihuiriachic to lead him to the ranch, Howze continued the night march in an effort to achieve total surprise the next morning. Exactly a month earlier he had been forced to give up a pursuit of Francisco "Pancho" Villa himself due to a lack of Apache scouts to follow the trail, but now Howze sensed that the trap was closing with the aid of the Apaches and the two civilian guides.

Following a rapid movement through the windless, cold night, the combined formation prepared to attack at sunrise on 5 May, by first sending the scouts on a flanking movement to take the high ground behind the ranch buildings and thus cutting off the natural avenue of escape. A direct frontal assault on the three fortress-like adobe structures and several outbuildings made sense only if the element of surprise could be achieved because heavily armed marksmen firing down from the rooftops could command the complete field of fire while simultaneously concealing themselves. Howze ordered one cavalry troop to attack the ranch buildings along a direct line while receiving covering fire from the machine guns. The remaining five troops were to attack to the left and right of the buildings as they tried to panic the Villistas by enveloping them in a pincer-like movement.

The well-conceived plan unraveled because of delays in positioning the soldiers. Immediately upon the crackling of rifle shots from inside the fortress, Lt. James A. Shannon rushed his Apaches forward to gain the high ground, but his men took cover and began firing from an ineffective distance of 900 yards. Two other troops found their way blocked by a barbed wire fence, and the main advance waited a bit too long for a bugle signal. Despite all of the problems associated with the charge, pure courage and spontaneity carried the day as scouts and soldiers alike resumed the attack. The main part of the battle was over within 20 minutes, and the results were clearly one-sided. While 61 Villistas were killed and approximately 70 captured, none of the U.S. soldiers were even wounded despite the closeness of much of the fighting. Furthermore, Howze was able to rescue a Carrancista lieutenant and three of his soldiers who had been taken captive in a recent battle with the Villistas, and who had been marked for a firing squad.

As military events go, the cavalry fight at Ojos Azules was of little tactical consequence except for raising the morale of U.S. soldiers. Yet Pershing wired Gen. Frederick Funston, commander of the Southern Military Department, that it was "a brilliant piece of work," and it did prove to be the most one-sided victory of the entire campaign. Although Julio Acosta escaped, he was never able to muster a guerrilla band of more than 20 men after that. Perhaps 1st Sgt. Eskehnadestah of the Apache scouts best summarized the U.S. view of the battle with his exclamation, "Huli! Damfine fight."

Michael L. Tate

REFERENCES

Herbert Molloy Mason, Jr., *The Great Pursuit* (Random, 1970); James A. Shannon, "With the Apache Scouts in Mexico," *Journal of the United States Cavalry Association*, 27 (1917), 539–557; Frank Tompkins, *Chasing Villa: The Story Behind the Story of Pershing's Expedition into Mexico* (Military Service Pub. Co., 1935); S.M. Williams, "The Cavalry Fight at Ojos Azules," *Journal of the United States Cavalry Association*, 27 (1917), 405–408.

Olympia

Named for the capital of the state of Washington, the cruiser *Olympia* was laid down by the Union Iron Works of San Francisco on 17 June 1891, and launched 17 months later. It was commissioned 5 February 1895, and classed as a protected cruiser (armor on turrets and around the main gun sponsons plus protective armor at the water line). Its dimensions included a 344-foot length, 53-foot beam, a normal draft of 21 feet, 6 inches, and a displacement of 5,870 tons. Its armament comprised four eight-inch guns in turrets, 10 five-inch broadside guns, 14 six-pounders and six one-pounders, and some machine guns. Powered by six "Scotch" boilers, a balanced pair of triple expansion engines of 9,000 horsepower each, it had a coal capacity of 1,200 tons. It was capable of exceeding 21 knots speed, and its complement was 34 officers and 454 enlisted men including the marine guard.

Designated the flagship of the Asiatic Squadron, *Olympia* cruised the Far East for three years before the onset of the Spanish-Cuban/American War, proudly "showing the flag," its hull painted white and its upper works painted buff in the normal peacetime scheme of the period. Then, under command of Capt. Charles V. Gridley, and flying the flag of Commodore George Dewey, it led the fleet in the Battle of Manila Bay on 1 May 1898, which destroyed Spain's Asian fleet in a battle pivotal to the history of the Far East and the world. Later, the *Olympia* took part in the blockade and capture of Manila and the early stages of the subsequent Philippine War, before returning in triumph to victory celebrations in the United States in 1899.

The *Olympia*'s subsequent career was anticlimactic. As flagship of the Caribbean Division of the North Atlantic Squadron and as a midshipman's cruise and barracks ship, its armament changed and its role was modified over the years. It served as flagship for the North Russia expedition at the end of World War I, and its final moment of glory came in 1921 as it bore the remains of the Unknown Soldier home from France for interment in Arlington National Cemetery. Finally decommissioned at Philadelphia on 9 December 1922, today, it remains the Navy's oldest steel ship still afloat as a shrine at Penn's Landing, Philadelphia, and is maintained by the private Cruiser Olympia Association.

B. Franklin Cooling

REFERENCES

Dictionary of American Naval Fighting Ships (U.S. Government Printing Office, 1981), vol. 5, 152–153.

See also Dewey, George; Manila Bay, The Philippines, Naval Battle (1898).

Onega River Front, North Russia (1918–1919)

The Onega River Front represented the western flank of the forces that participated in the U.S. intervention in North Russia, 1918–1919. Situated on the lower reaches of the Onega River, which empties into the Onega Gulf of the White Sea some 75 miles west of Archangel, the front was formed in September 1918 to provide lateral support to the Vologda Railroad Front and, especially, to protect the vital winter supply route between Archangel and Murmansk.

The Onega Front originated as early as 31 July 1918 when a mixed Allied force, including a small party of sailors from the cruiser *Olympia*, seized the port of Onega, at the mouth of the river, as a prelude to the occupation of Archangel on 2 August. On 16 September, the garrison at Onega was reinforced by the arrival of two platoons of Company H of the 339th Infantry Regiment, an element of the American Expeditionary Force, North Russia, which had debarked at Archangel 11 days earlier.

Between 18 and 21 September, the full complement of Company H, together with a small detachment of anti-Bolshevik Russians, moved some 40 miles upriver to Chekuevo, a crucial communications center on the route between Archangel, Murmansk, and the Vologda Railroad. On 24 September, this force repulsed a strong enemy counterattack following which, on 1 October, a further advance was made to Kaska, another 10 miles upstream. The advance to Kaska was soon nullified by the failure of a corollary Allied attack on the Vologda Railroad Front. On 31 December, U.S. forces advanced to, and then retreated from, Prilutskoe, 60 miles upriver at the deepest point of penetration ever achieved on the Onega Front.

During the first 10 weeks of 1919, U.S. troops on the Onega Front were engaged in frequent, essentially peaceful patrolling aimed at keeping open the line of communications between Chekuevo and the Vologda Railroad Front. Beginning in mid-March, however, Company H—joined by Company M and a large contingent of Russian, British, and French troops—played a critical role in turning back a major Soviet counteroffensive at Bol'shie Ozerki, located on the main route between Chekuevo and the railroad. Following the Battle of Bol'shie Ozerki, Company H and its allies returned to patrol duties

until the final U.S. withdrawal from Onega on 5 June 1919.

John W. Long

REFERENCES

A Chronicler [John Cudahy], *Archangel: The American War With Russia* (A.C. McClurg & Co., 1924); Dennis Gordon, *Quartered in Hell: The Story of the American North Russian Expeditionary Force, 1918–1919* (GOS, 1982); E.M. Halliday, *The Ignorant Armies: The Anglo-American Archangel Expedition, 1918–1919* (Harper, 1958); Joel R. Moore, "The North Russian Expedition: The 85th Division's Participation," *Infantry Journal*, 29 (1926), 1–21; Joel Moore, Harry Mead, and Lewis Jahns, *The History of the American Expedition Fighting the Bolsheviki* (Polar Bear, 1920).

Oregon

The USS *Oregon* captured the public's imagination during an epic voyage at the beginning of the Spanish-Cuban/American War. Launched in 1893 and commissioned in 1896, the *Oregon* was the most heavily armed warship in the world in 1898, carrying four 13-inch guns. Its crew consisted of 30 officers and over 400 men.

Following the sinking of the *Maine* in February 1898, the Navy Department ordered the *Oregon*, then in San Francisco loading munitions, to Callao, Peru, to await instructions. Under Capt. Charles E. Clark, it weighed anchor on 17 March 1898. At Callao orders came to sail to Key West, Florida, and reinforce the U.S. fleet. During the next two and one-half months the U.S. public followed newspaper reports of the ship's progress. Clergy offered prayers from the pulpit for its safety.

The vessel safely navigated the hazardous Strait of Magellan. With war imminent, Clark had the ship painted dull grey and began battle drills. Concern grew that Spanish warships lay in ambush, but no engagement occurred. On 26 May the *Oregon* dropped anchor at Key West after a record run of 68 days and 14,706.7 nautical miles from its home base, Bremerton, Washington.

The *Oregon* sailed to Cuba as part of the blockading squadron. At the Battle of Santiago, Cuba, on 3 July 1898, the *Oregon* demonstrated its fighting qualities. It destroyed three Spanish warships and chased down the Spanish flagship *Cristóbal Colón*, forcing it to surrender.

Following the Spanish-Cuban/American War, the *Oregon*'s voyage furnished arguments for proponents of a two-ocean navy. It also dramatically showed the need for an interocean canal, which would have cut the *Oregon*'s voyage in half.

The *Oregon* soon became obsolete, although it served in the Philippine War and World War I. During World War II, it was a munitions barge at Guam. Later efforts to restore and preserve the old ship failed. In 1956 it was sold to a Japanese firm, which broke it up for scrap.

Richard H. Bradford

REFERENCES

Richard H. Bradford, "And *Oregon* Rushed Home," *American Neptune*, 36 (1976), 257–265; Charles E. Clark, *My Fifty Years in the Navy* (Little, Brown, 1917); Edward W. Eberle, "The *Oregon*'s Great Voyage," *Century Magazine*, 58 (1899), 912–924; Ralph E. Shaffer, "The Race of the *Oregon*," *Oregon Historical Quarterly*, 76 (1975), 269–298; Sanford Sternlicht, *McKinley's Bulldog: The Battleship Oregon* (Nelson-Hall, 1977).

Ortez y Guillén, Miguel Angel (1895?–1931)

Miguel Angel Ortez y Guillén, who used the *nom de guerre* Gen. Gregorio Ferrera, was one of Nicaraguan nationalist Augusto C. Sandino's most active leaders. Born in Ocotal, Nicaragua, around 1895, he was very popular with his men and had the respect of his marine and national guard opponents because of his courage and willingness to fight. He had a reputation among the marines for operating constantly and continually seeking contact with marine and *guardia* patrols.

When Sandino went to Mexico for a year in 1929–1930 and other Sandinista generals left for Honduras, Ortez remained active in the field. There were times when he seemed to be acting independently of Sandino's leadership, but by June 1930 the young lieutenant recognized Sandino's authority. Among Ortez's notable achievements were a successful attack against an empty pack mule train guarded by marines at Bromaderos on 27 February 1928; an ambush of a *guardia* patrol at Ojoche on 28 June 1930 during which the marine commander was wounded and an ambush of 10 marines in Achuapa on New Year's Eve, 1930, during which eight marines were killed and two wounded. The latter

engagement encouraged renewed demands in the United States for ending the intervention. Ortez was mortally wounded in a guerrilla attack on the national guard barracks at Palacaguina on 15 May 1931 when he was hit by a rifle grenade.

William Kamman

REFERENCES

Robert Edgar Conrad, ed. and trans., *Sandino: The Testimony of a Nicaraguan Patriot, 1921–1934*, compiled and edited by Sergio Ramirez (Princeton Univ. Pr., 1990); Neill Macaulay, *The Sandino Affair* (Quadrangle, 1967); Julian C. Smith and others, *A Review of the Organization and Operations of the Guardia Nacional de Nicaragua* (n.p., n.d.).

See also Achuapa, Nicaragua, Battle (1930).

Otis, Elwell Stephen (1838–1909)

Gen. Elwell S. Otis was a highly controversial commander of United States Army forces during roughly half of the Philippine War, 1899–1902.

Born in Rochester, New York, in 1838, Otis was a graduate of the local university and of Harvard Law School in 1861. He joined the 22nd Infantry Regiment during the Civil War, emerging a lieutenant colonel with a Purple Heart. He continued with the same regiment through various Native American campaigns until he was made a major general of volunteers in the Spanish-Cuban/American War. He was sent to the Philippines to relieve Gen. Wesley Merritt in command of all U.S. troops there on 29 August 1898. He inherited a very unusual situation in that U.S. forces held only Manila. They were surrounded by a line of siege mounted by their erstwhile *de facto* allies against Spain, the Filipino nationalists. Their leader, Gen. Emilio Aguinaldo y Famy, justified this aggressive stance by the fact that he had been excluded from the peace negotiations in Paris and that Manila could be returned to Spain, in which case he had to be in position to attack the city.

Otis was also the U.S. chief diplomat as well as military leader, and as such he provided Washington with very misleading assessments of Aguinaldo and his government, which he perceived to be little more than "a band of looters." He also launched a diplomatic offensive that was anything but diplomatic. Designed to humiliate the nationalists, it ranged from petty refusals to return salutes from "an armed mob" to threats of force if they did not retreat from redoubts that he quite arbitrarily decreed to be within the city's municipal borders. In one case, his predecessor, General Merritt, had agreed that the position was outside the city. Aguinaldo protested, but to no avail. Otis also began a surveillance of Filipino positions in the guise of "recreational activities" and reacted with outraged innocence when Aguinaldo banished to Manila U.S. soldiers caught photographing and measuring his fortifications.

When the Spanish garrison at Iloilo on the island of Panay, some 300 miles south of Manila, offered to surrender to U.S. forces in December 1898, Otis readied a task force under Gen. Marcus P. Miller, but Adm. George Dewey refused to provide transportation until Washington gave authorization for this move. The War Department gave such authorization, but with the stipulation that the transfer of power must be carried out peacefully, or not at all. By the time Miller arrived the Spaniards had departed, and he was greeted by the mayor, who refused to allow him to land without permission from Aguinaldo's government. Both Miller and Otis wanted to land and take the city by force, but the more cautious Dewey vetoed that. Instead, Otis ordered Miller to stay at anchor "until something happened" (Miller, p. 60).

Over the next few weeks, Otis appears to have made sure that "something" did happen, but before this he carefully prepared for that event. He ordered his officers out of dress whites and into "fighting Khaki" and placed his army on full alert. He moved the Utah battery up to a more favorable position and coaxed Dewey to move his warships closer to shore on the flanks of Aguinaldo's semicircular line around the city. On 2 February 1899, he discharged all Filipinos in his employ. That day he tested the waters by ordering sentries posted at a much disputed position from which he had earlier forced the Filipinos to retreat. When this was done in the past, an angry Filipino officer would respond by posting his own sentry at that spot. This time a Filipino lieutenant called Col. John M. Stotsenburg, commanding the Nebraska volunteers, "a son of a bitch," and Stotsenburg ordered him arrested if he could be caught. February 4 was an ideal evening to start the war because the senior Filipino officers were at a celebration in Malolos, Aguinaldo's capital some 30 miles north of Manila, so Otis posted no sentries at this position

on the 3rd. The next day he not only ordered sentries posted again, but this time with instructions to shoot any intruders. His provocation paid off that evening when four unarmed, and possibly drunk, Filipinos ignored U.S. commands to halt, even mocking sentries with their own shouts of "halto" and were gunned down by Nebraska troops.

Wild firing commenced from both sides and continued until 2:00 a.m. There were no significant casualties on either side, so the entire incident could have been dismissed as an unfortunate accident. Clearly, Otis wanted this war, which he appears to have provoked so skillfully; the record extant indicates that he did this without prodding, consultation, or permission from Washington. As soon as the first light silhouetted the Filipino positions on the 5th, Dewey's gunners, joined by land batteries, opened up a devastating barrage on the sleeping Filipinos. They continued it for several hours, until the bugles sounded charge, sending the "boys in blue" off with fixed bayonets. It was such a rout that Otis refused even to entertain peace proposals from Aguinaldo. His emissaries were informed by Otis's aide that they "lacked proper credentials" or that an audience with Otis could be construed as "recognition of their so called political organization." The only possible basis for peace was "complete submission" to U.S. rule, they were curtly advised. When Aguinaldo tried to sweeten his proposal by offering to release some of his U.S. prisoners, Otis refused to recognize them as prisoners of war. They were instead "merely stragglers from within our lines captured by robbers," he declared (Miller, p. 76).

Over the next 16 months of his command, Otis seemed more interested in winning favorable headlines than battles, continually wiring dispatches describing "crushing blows" and "final moments" that were duly parroted in the nation's press. He constantly assured the War Department that final victory was at hand and that he needed no more troops to complete a mopping-up operation. The reality was that his army, heavily equipped for more conventional battle, rarely caught up with its lightly clad enemy who moved more rapidly on bare feet over familiar terrain. Otis never went into the field to observe the reality of the situation. Unable to delegate the slightest authority, he sat from morning to night shuffling mountains of paper on his desk. Even before the war began, Edward

W. Harden, who had been sent to the islands by President William McKinley to assess the commercial potential of the Philippines, wrote that Otis was "too weak a man for the important office he fills and exhibits his incompetency by struggling with little matters of detail to the detriment of matters of graver importance" (Miller, pp. 82–83). The Papal delegate to the Philippines described Otis as "of about the right mental caliber to command a one-company post in Arizona" (Miller, p. 46). Nevertheless, Otis does seem to have anticipated the style of military leadership appropriate to societies with extensive and sophisticated mass media, in which impressions back home seem as crucial as realities on the battleground and in which effective public relations officers are as important as good field commanders.

Such a style earned Otis the near universal contempt of those serving under him. Gen. Henry W. Lawton openly contradicted him, and Colonel Stotsenburg, commanding the Nebraska volunteers, and Gen. Irving Hale of the Colorado regiment, engaged in shouting matches with Otis in front of their men. Once, Otis threatened Hale with "official action," whereupon the latter charged him with "cowardice." After the volunteers in the state regiments were repatriated and discharged during summer 1899, they had a field day with reporters at the expense of this "desk general." The commander of the Astor Battery declared that his men would have reenlisted except for "the blundering despotism and incompetence of Otis" (Miller, p. 80). Three volunteer generals gave press conferences or wrote articles condemning his leadership, even before they became civilians. They openly blamed him for provoking the war and then prolonging it by being an unimaginative and incompetent leader. Headlines proclaimed "No Friend For Otis Among the Volunteers"; "Soldiers Call Otis A 'Foolish Old Woman'"; "The True Situation in the Philippines Is Said to be Much Worse Than Official Reports Indicate." One reporter concluded that the overriding sentiment of these veterans was "Damn Otis and damn the Filipinos" (Miller, p. 87).

Otis had protected his vision of the war by strictly censoring the dispatches that correspondents could wire from the cable terminal at Manila. Reporters could bypass his censor by mailing reports to Hong Kong's terminal; they not only risked delay, but also the general's wrath in doing this. Finally, the correspondents rebelled, mailing a collective statement to their editors, complaining that censorship was designed more to protect the ineptness of Otis than to keep military information from the enemy. In bizarre fashion, Otis denied that there was any censorship, and in almost the same breath, announced the appointment of a new censor. He also closed a Spanish language newspaper in Manila and indicted the U.S. editor of an English language one for "sedition" when he published a letter Otis did not like. He deported two British reporters for similar reasons and even declared that Harden, the president's emissary, to be "not acceptable here in any capacity" (Miller, p. 82), after he dared to criticize the general.

The private letters of soldiers were not subjected to censorship, and when some describing U.S. atrocities fell into the hands of anti-imperialist editors, they were widely published. The War Department would order Otis to investigate, but his idea of an investigation was simply to send a copy of the offending letter to the writer's commanding officer, who had little trouble wringing a retraction from the soldier. When a genuine investigation did take place, producing damaging evidence that prisoners and enemy wounded were murdered under orders, Otis ignored the results.

The worst consequence of Otis's deception and sublime optimism was that he was very short of troops by June 1899, as the state volunteers, who made up to half of his 30,000 men, prepared to return to San Francisco. He had insisted to the War Department that these volunteers wanted to stay and would reenlist. Realizing that he, too, had been hoodwinked by the general's sublime optimism, the secretary of war set about to raise new national volunteer regiments to replace the state ones, over the protests of Otis. Indeed, a new secretary of war, Elihu Root, quickly learned to ignore the general's assessments and recommendations and to foist reinforcements on him. The nation seemed amazed to learn that after all of the "stunning victories" proclaimed by Otis, the army actually controlled very little territory outside of Manila, as the first rainy season began. Oblivious to all this, Otis continued to report more "crushing blows," until one editor suggested that "the general does not even have enough sense to come in out of the rain" (Miller, p. 79).

By the end of 1899, the Filipinos began to resort exclusively to guerrilla warfare, a mode of combat that escalated the number of atrocities committed by both sides. Reports of brutal and lawless U.S. retaliation for Filipino atrocities began to appear in the press, enhanced by some leaders, such as Col. Jacob H. Smith and Gen. Frederick Funston making self-incriminating statements to reporters about murdering prisoners to deter guerrilla activity. With Aguinaldo effectively isolated in a mountain refuge in Isabela Province, local Filipino commanders were more autonomous, making decisions based on immediate conditions, which made the resistance more effective. On top of this, Otis continually bickered with his own commanders, some of whom had contradicted his rosy assessments to reporters by insisting that many more soldiers would be needed to pacify the islands. Some field commanders openly defied Otis and did so with impunity if they achieved success. Otis seemed immensely jealous of General Lawton and his adoring press, and he virtually hated Gen. Samuel B.M. Young, while they made no secret of their contempt for him.

By spring 1900, rumors were rampant in the press that Otis would have to be sacked or replaced by a more competent commander. Finally, in April it was announced that Otis, at his own request, would soon be relieved by Gen. Arthur MacArthur. After 21 months in command, and "with the end of the war," the general had "earned a rest," it was announced. The opposition press hooted that the "opinion of the country is, that he ought to have taken it [the "rest"] before he went to the Philippines," and that "MacArthur may not do better, but the country will be glad that 'Otis is over,' if the war isn't" (Miller, p. 99).

On the eve of his departure from the Philippines, Otis told a flabbergasted reporter: "I have held that opinion for some time that the thing [i.e., the war] is entirely over. I cannot see where it is possible for the guerrillas to effect any reorganization, concentrate any force or accomplish anything serious" (Miller, p. 100). The very day before this announcement a U.S. company had fallen into a trap and lost 19 men before fighting its way out. Their captain observed that the ambush was well-planned and executed. With McKinley's bid for reelection only months away, however, it was essential to convince the U.S. public that Otis had won the war. Thus, Otis strutted down the gangplank in San Francisco on 3 June 1900 to a huge honor guard and an army band playing "See the Conquering Hero Comes." Almost immediately, he again informed reporters on hand to greet him that the war was over. Critical editors pointed out that one of MacArthur's first acts as commander was to request more men, up to 100,000. Nevertheless, Otis was feted everywhere on a slow trip across the nation until he reached Washington, where all doubts about his "victory" and military competency were washed away in a sea of toasts and the thunderous applause a jointly convened Congress afforded him in its standing ovation. The president personally thanked him for his "splendid military achievement in the Philippines" (Miller, p. 101). Finally, Rochester, his city of birth, capped this, greeting him with a city decked out in flags and bunting and a parade several miles long.

The opposition press was not so cooperative, reporting such events under such headlines as "The Incorrigible Otis," or "Otis in Wonderland" and "Otis Through a Looking Glass." Some editorials printed speculations about the general's sanity because during Otis's triumphant journey the news of more successful ambushes and of the escalating war on Mindanao dominated the front pages. But Otis seemed impervious to the press, or to reality. He was given command of the Department of Great Lakes and waited in Chicago for a higher award which never came. He retired in 1902, quietly exchanging his sword for a pen with which to defend his "victory" in magazines and to attack anti-imperialists simultaneously for prolonging the struggle. Otis died in 1909.

Stuart Creighton Miller

REFERENCES

Thomas F. Burdett, "A New Evaluation of General Otis' Leadership in the Philippines," *Military Review*, 55 (Jan. 1975), 79–87; Stuart Creighton Miller, *"Benevolent Assimilation": The American Conquest of the Philippines, 1899–1903* (Yale Univ. Pr., 1982).

P

Pacification

"Pacification" was a term used more by the army than by the marines or the navy during the period examined in this volume. Between 1861 and 1898 the army received a good deal of experience with pacification; that is, noncombat assignments involving interaction with and services to the civilian population. During the Civil War the army had to deal with economic and social problems, such as assisting loyalists in the Southern states and providing aid to escaped slaves. After the Civil War the army operated the Freedmen's Bureau, supervised elections, and helped reestablish federal institutions in the South.

During the Western campaigns against Native Americans the army did much more than simply patrol and, as needed, fight on the plains and in the mountains. It fed Native Americans and settlers on occasion, encouraged economic development, especially by supporting the building of railroads; and provided much support for reservations and their agencies. For many years military leaders insisted that the army should assume responsibility for the Native American population. From time to time, legislation did permit the appointment of army officers as agents on reservations.

The experiences of the Civil War, Reconstruction, and the Western campaigns probably gave army officers the impression that civilian government was often corrupt and inefficient and that the army could do better than civilian agencies in coping with many economic, political, and social problems. Therefore, the army seems to have tackled the challenges presented by pacification in the Philippines and Cuba with considerable self-confidence and much ingenuity.

In both countries, the army was fully in control for some time. Schools, hygiene, economic development, and, indeed, all aspects of life were of concern to the army. Soldiers assumed varied duties. Some army officers, notably medical officers, such as Walter Reed, won considerable fame for their achievements in what would today be termed "nation-building" in Cuba and the Philippines. When civilian officials came to the Philippines they seem to have been less than welcome, just as Bureau of Indian Affairs officials had once been unpopular with the army.

Despite the achievements in the Philippines, there was concern in the army about the heavy fighting that occurred and the large loss of life among the Philippine people. Therefore, attitudes changed within the officer corps between 1902 and 1906 when Cuba was re-occupied. Based on extensive research, Allan R. Millett believes that there was a revulsion against the violence against civilians that occurred during the Philippine War. He believes that new views among the army elite helped make the second occupation of Cuba very different from the Philippine War.

The army attempted one more major intervention before World War I: the occupation of Veracruz, Mexico, in 1914. Once again, a Latin American city was cleaned and "reformed," but with more limited results than in Havana and other cities. After 1914, the army did conduct some limited pacification activities along the U.S. border with Mexico, but its incursion into Mexico in 1916–1917 did not involve pacification programs. It was primarily a large-scale patrol action to deter Mexican irregulars from crossing the border.

There was, in effect, a gradual retreat from pacification activities by the army before World War I. The navy and marines pacified Haiti, the Dominican Republic, and Nicaragua. Particularly in Haiti and the Dominican Republic the navy and marine corps undertook significant programs in economic and social development.

The amount of theoretical literature on pacification was relatively limited at the time. An important, but largely ignored, article by Robert L. Bullard in 1910 surveyed army pacification from Reconstruction onward. Somewhat surprisingly, the *Small Wars Manual, 1940*, which reflected what the marines had learned in the Caribbean countries they occupied, said little about pacification except for the supervision of peaceful elections.

During and after World War II all of the services were significantly involved in relief operations of various kinds. Gradually, as the conflict between the United States and the Soviet bloc grew sharper, there was more interest within the U.S. armed services and civilian branches of the federal government, such as the State Department, in what became known as "civic action" (i.e., all types of nonmilitary programs managed or supported by the United States and Allied armed forces in Third World countries). In undertaking such responsibilities the U.S.

armed forces were following patterns already long established by the army, navy, and marine corps.

Benjamin R. Beede

REFERENCES

Robert L. Bullard, "Military Pacification," *Journal of the Military Institution of the United States*, 46 (Jan.-Feb. 1910), 1–24; Henry C. Davis, "Indoctrination of Latin-American Service," *Marine Corps Gazette*, 5 (June 1920), 154–161; Allan R. Millett, *The Politics of Intervention: The Military Occupation of 1906–1909* (Ohio State Univ. Pr., 1968).

See also entries beginning with the phrase "Civic Action."

Panama, Intervention (1903)

Addressing an audience at the University of California in March 1911, former President Theodore Roosevelt, reflecting on his actions as president in 1903, proudly boasted, "I took the Canal Zone" (Lael, p. 73). Such an assertion did not mean that he had officially plotted with Panamanian dissidents to overthrow the Colombian government's control of its northern state in fall 1903. It did signify, however, that while Panamanian revolutionaries had declared independence from Colombia for themselves, the timing of their declaration and the success of their movement hinged in large part on decisions reached by Roosevelt in Washington.

Not until the conclusion of his meeting with Roosevelt and his meetings with officials in the United States Department of State, did Philippe Jean Bunau-Varilla, for example, alert the Panamanian revolutionaries that the president would assist them once they declared independence. Indeed, in a private letter to one of his advisors the day following that meeting, Roosevelt revealed that he would be "delighted" if Panama declared its independence. While he had not conveyed that message officially to Bunau-Varilla, that had been Bunau-Varilla's conclusion as well.

Anticipating the possibility of a revolution on the isthmus, Roosevelt in mid-October directed the United States Navy Department to send U.S. naval forces toward Panama. On 3 November 1903, hours before the revolution began, the *Nashville*, anchored at Colón, Panama, was ordered to prevent the landing of Colombian forces in what was still at that time Colombian territory. On 4 and 5 November, the officers and men of the *Nashville* were instrumental in neutralizing the 450–500 Colombian soldiers at Colón. Within 72 hours of Panama's declaration of independence, Washington recognized the newly created isthmian government. Within 15 days of the beginning of the revolution, the United States and Panama signed a diplomatic agreement guaranteeing Panama's independence and securing for the United States perpetual use and control over a 10-mile corridor through which a canal would be constructed.

Had U.S. naval forces not been positioned on both coasts of Panama, the Colombian government of José Marroquín would have probably had little difficulty in suppressing the rebellion. That government had, after all, only one year earlier successfully suppressed a three-year civil war involving far more revolutionaries than those rebelling on the isthmus in 1903. By using the United States Navy to deny Colombia access to its own state, Roosevelt, therefore, assured Panama's independence.

The Bogotá government recognized this reality. By late November 1903, Colombian diplomat Rafael Reyes arrived in Washington to seek a resolution to the Panama crisis. While he claimed that the United States had taken Panama by "bloodless conquest—but by conquest, nevertheless," he sought an amicable solution to the isthmian crisis (Lael, p. 27). President Roosevelt promptly rejected Reyes' assertion that Washington had taken Panama by conquest. He firmly believed that Colombia's reluctance in the first 10 months of 1903 to grant the United States the right to construct a canal at Panama blocked "a mandate from civilization." Since, by recognizing Panama's independence, his administration could fulfill that mandate and launch construction of an isthmian canal, Roosevelt argued that he had acted correctly in guaranteeing Panamanian independence and in preventing Colombian forces from suppressing the insurrection.

While Roosevelt had not officially "taken" the canal zone, his intervention to assist the Panamanian revolutionaries on 3 November 1903 ensured that Colombia's sovereignty over its northernmost state had been lost forever. It also ensured that the United States could soon begin construction of an interoceanic canal at Panama.

Richard L. Lael
© 1990 All rights reserved.

REFERENCES

Gustave Anguizola, *Philippe Bunau-Varilla* (Nelson Hall, 1980); Philippe Bunau-Varilla, *Panama: The Creation, Destruction and Resurrection* (Constable, 1913); Richard L. Lael, *Arrogant Diplomacy: U.S. Policy Toward Colombia, 1903–1922* (Scholarly Resources, 1987); David McCullough, *The Path Between the Seas* (Simon & Schuster, 1977).

See also list of entries at front of book for Panama, Intervention (1903).

Panama Revolution (1903)

In October 1899, frustrated and angered over their loss of power in 1885 and the subsequent Conservative governments' successful efforts to strengthen the power of the central government at the expense of the heretofore highly autonomous Colombian states, Colombian Liberals revolted against the Bogotá government. Not until November 1902, with the surrender of the last of the great Liberal armies, did the three years of death and destruction during the subsequent civil war end. Colombia in November 1902 faced an initially bleak future. Not only did it need to reunify a divided populace, but it also had to do so with an empty national treasury, an unsound currency, and a weak, war-torn economy.

Events in Washington in summer 1902 posed an additional burden on the government of José Marroquín in Bogotá. Using power granted him by Congress during the summer, President Theodore Roosevelt eagerly pressed Bogotá for a treaty authorizing the United States to construct an interoceanic canal through Colombia's isthmian territory. While both Roosevelt and Marroquín favored a canal at Panama, neither agreed on the precise terms to be incorporated in an isthmian canal treaty.

Complicating matters, Chargé Tomás Herrán, under pressure from the Roosevelt administration and fearful that failure to act might lead Washington simply to seize Panama, signed the Hay-Herrán Treaty on 22 January 1903. That treaty granted Washington the right to construct a canal at Panama, authorized payment to Colombia of $10 million plus a $250,000 annuity, and transferred judicial control in the canal zone to the United States. Given poor communication with Marroquín, Chargé Herrán learned only on the 24th, two days after signing the treaty, that he was to sign no treaty without first consulting Bogotá.

Under the constitutions of both nations, a treaty negotiated and signed by the executive was not binding until it had been ratified by the appropriate legislative branch. In Washington, ratification by the United States Senate posed no problem. In Bogotá, however, the Colombian Senate unanimously rejected the treaty on 12 August, despite a threat from U.S. Secretary of State John Hay that "if Colombia should now reject the treaty or unduly delay its ratification, the friendly understanding between the two countries would be so seriously compromised that action might be taken by Congress next winter which every friend of Colombia might regret" (Lael, p. 8).

Despite that threat, the United States undertook no "action" until the Colombian Congress adjourned on 31 October without changing its position on the treaty. Roosevelt was clearly angry. In a letter to Hay in August, he referred to the Bogotá officials as that "lot of jack rabbits." By October, he wanted a canal. He wanted it now. And he wanted it at Panama.

When, in June 1902, the United States Congress originally authorized Roosevelt to negotiate a treaty for an isthmian canal at Panama, it had stipulated that if treaty negotiations with Colombia failed, the president was to negotiate with Nicaraguan and Costa Rican officials for an isthmian route through Nicaragua. Originally recommended in 1901 by the Walker Commission, a group of respected U.S. engineers, as the preferable isthmian site, the Nicaraguan route became second choice of the United States Congress in summer 1902 when it appeared construction and acquisition of a canal at Panama would be slightly less expensive.

Angered by Bogotá's initial reluctance and eventual refusal to ratify the Hay-Herrán Treaty, resentful that the central government now exercised powers which prior to 1885 would have been under the control of Panamanian leaders, and fearful that the United States would abandon the Panama route altogether in favor of a canal through Nicaragua, Panamanian leaders discussed the possibility of revolution during summer 1903. Fewer than two dozen men, led by Manuel Amador Guerrero, José Agustín Arango, and Carlos Constantino Arosemena, began discussing the possibility of revolution in late July and early August 1903. Traditionally distrustful of central authority and nurtured in an era of political and military resistance to

Bogotá's control which had culminated in civil war, these men proved receptive when in late summer, two of the most influential Washington lobbyists for the Panama route, William Nelson Cromwell and Philippe Jean Bunau-Varilla, urged secession.

On 26 August, two weeks after the Colombian Senate had rejected the Hay-Herrán Treaty, Amador sailed to New York to ascertain the degree of United States' support for a revolution. Bunau-Varilla, following private talks with officials in the United States State Department and with President Roosevelt, met Amador in New York on 13 October and promised to provide $100,000 to finance the revolution. When Amador sailed for Panama on the 19th, he not only had assurances of financial support but also Bunau-Varilla's assurances that the uprising would be protected by the United States within 48 hours of its initiation. While neither the United States State Department nor the president had made a formal pact with Bunau-Varilla, the astute Frenchman correctly surmised that the administration would aid the Panamanian revolutionaries.

Amador arrived in Panama on 27 October. Still uncertain of U.S. support, he and fellow revolutionaries moved cautiously. The arrival of the *Nashville* at Colón on 3 November convinced them that Bunau-Varilla's assurances of U.S. aid were valid. At this point, even the unexpected arrival of 450–500 Colombian soldiers on 3 November did not weaken their resolve to declare independence. They merely lured the highest ranking officers of that force to Panama City, located on the other side of the isthmus, where they arrested them. In a bloodless coup, they then declared Panama's independence of Colombia. Within three days, the United States had extended diplomatic recognition to the revolutionary government, and within 15 days it had guaranteed the independence of the newly formed nation of Panama. The revolutionary leaders, with the critical aid of the United States, had successfully achieved independence from Colombia.

Richard L. Lael
© *1990 All rights reserved.*

REFERENCES

Charles Bergquist, *Coffee and Conflict in Colombia, 1886–1910* (Duke Univ. Pr., 1978); Rubén Carles, *Reminiscencias de los Primeros Años de la República de Panamá, 1903–1912* (La Estrella de Panamá, 1968);

Richard L. Lael, *Arrogant Diplomacy: U.S. Policy Toward Colombia, 1903–1922* (Scholarly Resources, 1987); Eduardo Lemaitre Román, *Panamá y su Separación de Colombia* (Banco Popular, 1972); David McCullough, *The Path Between the Seas* (Simon & Schuster, 1977).

See also Panama, Intervention (1903).

Panay Incident, China (1937)

A flotilla of six river gunboats was constructed for the United States Navy Department in Shanghai's Jiangnan (Kiangnan) Shipyard in 1927–1928 to replace the obsolete ships of the Yangzi (Yangtze) Patrol. All were relatively shallow-draft vessels; the *Panay* was 191 feet long, with a draft of seven feet, equipped with quadruple screws and triple rudders, designed to negotiate the river's rapids and safeguard U.S. interests in Central and West China. Given its relatively deep draft, it could serve only in West China above the Yangzi rapids at Yizhang (Ichang) between May and October.

Panay was lightly armed for a warship, with two three-inch guns (one fore, one aft) and eight .30-caliber machine guns. It was expected to police the area, protecting U.S. lives and property from Chinese bandits and regional militarists.

Although much of the antiforeign danger from bandits and warlords had passed from the lower and central parts of the river by the time the *Panay* was commissioned, the writ of the Guomindang (Kuomintang) government did not run far on the upper river. Nevertheless, the Chinese government saw the gunboats as an imperialist remnant and was determined to do away with them.

Imperialism, however, was not quite ended in China. Beginning in 1931, Japan, faced with economic discrimination in the midst of world depression, embarked on a series of campaigns designed to subdivide China into several friendly client states. This struggle, which began with the Manchurian Incident, culminated, in 1937, in what the Chinese call the Second Sino-Japanese War and what the Japanese refer to as the China Incident.

The *Panay* incident and crisis is part of the initial stage of this conflict, which widened until it became part of World War II in December 1941. The *Panay*'s sinking occurred in the context of the Japanese Army's campaign to seize the Chinese capital, Nanjing (Nanking), in July–December 1937.

As fighting neared the city in November, the U.S. ambassador and most of the embassy staff were evacuated to the new Chinese capital at Hankou (Hankow). Four members of the staff remained in Nanjing to carry on the embassy's remaining official business, staying until the last possible moment. *Panay* was assigned to relay diplomatic messages and evacuate U.S. personnel when it became necessary.

Japanese attacks forced the evacuation of the remaining embassy personnel on 7 December 1937. The Japanese requested that all foreign nationals evacuate Nanjing on 8 December. The *Panay* was moved to a safer anchorage several miles from the city and remained there, waiting for other U.S. citizens who might shelter in it.

On 11 December Japanese shells fell near the gunboat's new anchorage. The following day, 12 December, the *Panay* set off upriver to escape the shelling, accompanied by three Standard Oil Company barges. Later that morning the convoy was stopped by a Japanese army unit. After ascertaining the gunboat's neutral status and the reason for its trip, the convoy was allowed to pass. At 11:00 a.m., the convoy anchored 28 miles from Nanjing, and the *Panay* radioed the Shanghai consulate its position and requested it to inform the Japanese.

The gunboat was clearly marked as a U.S. ship, flying its largest colors and painting them on its awnings to be visible from the air. The weather was clear and visibility was excellent. At 1:30 p.m. Japanese planes began to attack the *Panay*. Two bombs struck the ship, wounding the commanding officer and several others. The ship was also strafed. By 1:58 p.m. the ship was sinking. The captain gave the order to abandon ship at 2:00 p.m. The ship was finally evacuated at 3:00 p.m., and it rolled over and sank bow first at 3:54 p.m. As the ship was abandoned, Japanese planes continued to make bombing and strafing attacks. The oil barges were also attacked and sunk. Three men were killed, and a number were wounded. The surviving crews were rescued on the following day and reached Shanghai on 17 December.

The uproar surrounding the gunboat's sinking was intense and short-lived. In response to the U.S. protest, Japan offered regrets and compensation and took steps to prevent a repetition of the incident. In Tokyo, Japanese people stopped at the embassy, expressed their personal condolences, signed a memorial book, and contributed money to aid the survivors. The Japanese Navy started an investigation to determine culpability and offered to pay compensation, collected from officers and men, to the survivors. With the navy's admission of guilt, the government's indemnity payment, the official expression of regret, and the promise to punish the guilty, the incident passed into history.

Neither the United States nor Japan wished the incident to bring about a war between the two countries. Japanese compliance with U.S. wishes, U.S. isolationist sentiment, as well as U.S. military weakness, precluded the government's taking any strong action.

Lewis Bernstein

REFERENCES

Dorothy Borg, *The United States and the Far East Crisis of 1933–1938: From the Manchurian Incident Through the Initial Stage of the Undeclared Sino-Japanese War* (Harvard Univ. Pr., 1964), especially 486–518; Manny T. Koginos, *The Panay Incident: Prelude to War* (Purdue Univ. Pr., 1967); Masatake Okumiya, "How the *Panay* Was Sunk," *United States Naval Institute Proceedings*, 79 (1953), 587–596; Hamilton Darby Perry, *The Panay Incident: Prelude to Pearl Harbor* (Macmillan, 1969); Harlan J. Swanson, "The *Panay* Incident: Prelude to Pearl Harbor," *United States Naval Institute Proceedings*, 93 (1967), 26–37.

Parral, Mexico, Battle (1916)

The Battle of Parral, Chihuahua, Mexico, was fought between troops loyal to Constitutionalist leader Venustiano Carranza and the citizens of the town on the one hand and a column of about 100 men of the 13th Cavalry led by Maj. Frank Tompkins of the United States Army on the other. During the month that the Punitive Expedition had been in Mexico, resentment had been growing among the civilian population and within the Constitutionalist forces, despite the expedition's intended purpose of pursuing their own enemy, Francisco "Pancho" Villa. According to Tompkins's report, an officer from the Parral garrison had visited his camp on 11 April 1916 and invited him and his men to enter the city. The next day at about 11:00 a.m., Tompkins proceeded into Parral, where he was received cordially by town authorities, both civil and military. The U.S. column of troops then began to

pull away from the city because they were attracting increasingly negative attention. Although they were accompanied by one of the Mexican officers, they were attacked near the edge of town by civilians and Mexican troops, who threw rocks, jeered, shouted "Viva Villa!," and even fired on the U.S. troops. As Tompkins's troops moved farther from the town, they were pursued by a mob of irate civilians, troops, and an agitator whom Tompkins thought might be German, judging by his appearance.

Although Tompkins quickly took up a defensive position north of the railroad, he was soon flanked by Mexican troops and forced to withdraw. According to Gen. John J. Pershing's initial report, about 300 Constitutionalist troops were involved in the pursuit. The U.S. soldiers returned fire, and approximately 40 Mexicans were killed. U.S. losses amounted to two killed and six wounded, including Tompkins.

According to the Mexican account, presented to the U.S. Secretary of State the next day, the mayor of Parral, José de la Luz Herrera, had warned Tompkins immediately upon entry into the town that his entry was inadvisable, given the Mexican resentment of the presence of U.S. troops on Mexican soil. The military and civilian leaders of the town tried to restrain the populace, but according to them, one individual fired his rifle, setting off the battle that followed. The Mexican authorities went on to urge that the U.S. troops refrain from occupying towns in order to prevent further incidents, and again insisted, as they had been doing since the day the expedition entered Mexico, that U.S. troops be withdrawn immediately to the U.S. side of the border. The Mexicans added that they were eager for good relations with the United States and wished to prevent any further problems. A note sent from President Carranza reiterated the necessity for withdrawal, indicating that Mexican Secretary of War Álvaro Obregón had sent orders for the fighting to stop, but that they were proving difficult to enforce as a result of the excitement of the people of the town.

Pershing's own belief, relayed in a message to Gen. Frederick Funston, commander of the Southern Department of the Army in San Antonio, Texas, was that although some of the Constitutionalist military leaders had made sincere efforts to help capture Villa, Carranza had maintained an obstructionist attitude. He indignantly pointed to the example of the refusal by Carranza to permit U.S. troops to use Mexican railroads to facilitate their movements. He noted that as his men had moved farther south into Mexico, resentment and hostility among the populace had become more marked; and he indicated that Mexican government troops were approaching his own lines of communication, a movement he regarded with great concern and suspicion. He even accused the Mexican government of carrying out a premeditated attack at Parral.

Given the gravity of the tensions generated by the incident, both sides found it useful to negotiate to relieve the situation. The suggestions for talks came from Secretary of State Robert Lansing, and Carranza quickly acquiesced. The Parral incident led directly to talks between U.S. Army Chief of Staff Hugh L. Scott and Mexican Secretary of War Obregón in El Paso, during late April and early May 1916. Unfortunately, no agreement could be reached because Mexico demanded immediate withdrawal of the Punitive Expedition.

Linda B. Hall

REFERENCES

Clarence C. Clendenen, *The United States and Pancho Villa: A Study in Unconventional Diplomacy* (Cornell Univ. Pr., 1961); Linda B. Hall and Don M. Coerver, *Revolution on the Border: The United States and Mexico, 1910–1920* (Univ. of New Mexico Pr., 1988); Frank Tompkins, *Chasing Villa: The Story Behind the Story of Pershing's Expedition into Mexico* (Military Service Pub. Co., 1934).

Patton, George Smith, Jr., in the Mexican Punitive Expedition

George Smith Patton, Jr. was turned down in his initial effort to take part in the Mexican Punitive Expedition. Undaunted, he bypassed channels and made a direct appeal to expedition commander Gen. John J. Pershing, who selected him as a special aide-de-camp. The staff duties were not heroic enough for Patton who, after a month, was reassigned to a field command with H Troop of the 11th Cavalry. On 14 May 1916, while searching for Villistas at San Miguelito Ranch, he killed three gunmen, most notably Gen. Julio Cárdenas, a prominent leader of Villista armies. From this single event, Patton became an overnight celebrity in the U.S. press, and he gained respect among his superiors. Pershing, who affectionately dubbed Patton "the Bandit," pro-

moted him to 1st lieutenant, and they became lifelong friends. Patton reveled in the glory of "the kill," but his Mexican service was interrupted temporarily during October when he was badly burned by an exploding kerosene lantern. Following treatment at Columbus, New Mexico, he took recuperative leave in California with his family, but returned to the Punitive Expedition a month later and served until its recall from Mexico in February 1917.

Michael L. Tate

REFERENCES

Martin Blumenson, *The Patton Papers, 1885–1940*, I (Houghton Mifflin, 1972); Herbert Molloy Manson, Jr., *The Great Pursuit* (Random, 1970); George S. Patton, "Cavalry Work of the Punitive Expedition," *Journal of the United States Cavalry Association*, 27 (1917), 426–433; Donald Smythe, *Guerrilla Warrior: The Early Life of John J. Pershing* (Scribner, 1973); Vernon L. Williams, "Lt. George S. Patton, Jr. and the American Army . . . ," *Military History of Texas and the Southwest*, 17 (1982), 1–76.

Peace Commission (1898)

Following the arrangement of an armistice in the Spanish-Cuban/American War on 12 August 1898 President William McKinley appointed a five-member peace commission to negotiate a treaty with Spain. The U.S. terms had already been set out in the 30 July peace protocol authored by Secretary of State William R. Day. The terms of the protocol demanded of Spain the complete surrender of Cuba, cession of Puerto Rico and one of the islands of the Marianas, and the U.S. occupation of Manila pending final disposition of the Philippines. Day resigned from the cabinet effective 16 September to accept the president's appointment to head the commission in negotiations, which began in Paris on 1 October.

The commission included three members of the Senate Foreign Relations Committee: Republicans Cushman K. Davis of Minnesota, chairman of the committee, and William P. Frye of Maine, and conservative Democrat George Gray of Delaware. Whitelaw Reid, the powerful owner and publisher of the *New York Tribune* and former United States ambassador to France, whose editorials and private correspondence had supported McKinley's war policies and encouraged overseas acquisitions, completed the commission. Edward D. White, an associate justice of the United States Supreme Court, had accepted an appointment but withdrew and was replaced by Gray. In making his appointments the president recognized the need for Senate approval of any treaty and knowingly appointed a commission of individuals with differing views. All except Gray favored some acquisition of territories in the Pacific, although Day believed that a coaling station in the Philippines would be sufficient. Davis and Frye wanted all or more of the Philippines, and Reid believed that the United States had a duty to occupy the islands. All except Gray met with the president to discuss their instructions before their departure for France.

At an introductory breakfast arranged by their French hosts, the Spanish minister to France, Fernando de Léon y Castillo, told Reid that, while the United States had enjoyed a great victory, it must remember that "victory will be dimmed by any lack of magnanimity to a fallen foe" (Coletta, p. 138). As the negotiations proceeded it became apparent to both sides that the defeated Spanish were negotiating only for some remnant of national dignity.

Initial discussions on the surrender of Cuba and the cession of Cuba and Guam went smoothly, but Spanish resistance arose over the question of the Cuban debt. On 24 October Day asked his Spanish counterparts directly if they intended to reject any articles related to Cuba and Puerto Rico unless they included provisions for debt assumption by the United States and/or an independent Cuba. Two days later, after Spanish Ambassador Castillo had a private meeting with Reid in which Reid made it clear that negotiations could rupture if Spain did not accept the U.S. positions, the Spanish commissioners relented.

Meanwhile, the U.S. commissioners discussed the Philippines among themselves, with Davis and Reid maintaining that all the islands be taken and Gray continuing his opposition to any territorial acquisition in the Pacific. Day and Frye took middle positions. On 25 October the commissioners, still not in agreement among themselves, cabled three letters to Secretary of State John Hay. Reid, Davis, and Frye cautioned that any division of the islands would be a "moral, political and commercial mistake." Day, citing existing instructions, suggested taking only Luzon, and Gray argued against taking the islands "in whole or in part" and reminded Hay that the president had stated that the United

States had no territorial ambitions when the war began. On the 28th Hay cabled Day with the president's position. McKinley believed it was his duty to accept the entire archipelago, and with the backing of the entire cabinet, was delegating to the commissioners the responsibility for drafting the articles and forcing the Spanish to accept them. Knowing that the Spanish commissioners would not agree to give up the islands for nothing, Day, acting on advice from Frye, determined to offer $20 million for the Philippines. He communicated this to the Spanish commissioners on 21 November, and they responded by asking for time to consult with Madrid. Ultimately, the Spanish officials realized that they had no choice but to accede.

By 9 December all documents were in their final form. John Bassett Moore, a State Department official and an expert on international law, drafted most of the articles for the U.S. commissioners. Papers were signed on 10 December, and the U.S. commissioners departed on the 16th. They arrived in New York on the 24th and traveled immediately to Washington.

During the negotiations Reid played a key role. He was the only U.S. commissioner with overseas experience, and his three years in Paris and his service as a delegate to Queen Victoria's Golden Jubilee in 1897 had provided him with numerous foreign contacts. Furthermore, the *New York Tribune* bureau in Paris kept him well informed of foreign attitudes and concerns regarding the negotiations. While none of the U.S. commissioners spoke Spanish, Reid did know French and could communicate directly in that language with three of his counterparts. Day provided the tact and diplomacy expected of the head of the commission and received praise from his fellow commissioners for his negotiating skills. Gray, a minority of one in opposition to the acquisition of the Philippines, frequently failed to attend meetings and had little impact on the negotiations.

The commissioners were never wanting for comfort or entertainment during their service. They sailed to Paris on 17 September aboard the luxurious Cunard liner *Campania* with 15 secretaries and assistants. All commissioners were accompanied by their wives. The Reids' party included their daughter, her governess, and three servants. Théophile Delcassé, the French foreign minister, arranged for meeting facilities in the ornate Salle des Conférences at the French

Foreign Office on the Quai d' Orsay. At formal sessions, usually held at 2:00 p.m., the hosts provided a buffet with cold dishes, wines, and cigars. In the evenings, the French hosted dinners, plays, operas, and even an excursion to the horse tracks for commissioners from both nations.

Michael J. Devine

REFERENCES

Duncan Bingham, *Whitelaw Reed, Journalist, Politician, Diplomat* (Univ. of Georgia Pr., 1975); Paolo E. Coletta, "McKinley, the Peace Negotiators and the Acquisition of the Philippines," *Pacific Historical Review*, 30 (1961), 341–350; Paolo E. Coletta, "The Peace Negotiations and the Treaty of Paris," in Paolo E. Coletta, ed., *Threshold to American Internationalism: Essays on the Foreign Policy of William McKinley* (Exposition Pr., 1970); Charles E. Hill, *Leading American Treaties* (Macmillan, 1924); Whitelaw Reed, *Making Peace With Spain: The Diary of Whitelaw Reed, September-December, 1898*, edited by W. Wayne Morgan (Univ. of Texas Pr., 1965).

See also Treaty of Paris (1898).

Pensions and Other Benefits for Veterans of the Spanish-Cuban/American War and Other Conflicts

The Spanish-Cuban/American War terminated the period when pensions formed the basic benefit for veterans. In future conflicts, a very different pattern of benefits was provided, including educational grants. Benefits for veterans of the Spanish-Cuban/American War, the Philippine War, and the Boxer Uprising deserve attention because as Table 4 demonstrates dramatically the cost of veterans' benefits of the 1898–1902 era vastly outweighed the other costs of the conflict.

Pensions for Spanish-Cuban/American War veterans began in 1920 when a statute gave payments to veterans at or over the age of 62 who had served at least 90 days or who were incapable of performing manual labor. Military and naval personnel who had been in the Boxer Rebellion or the Philippine War were included. Although the period of service was not stipulated, it was presumably between 21 April 1898, and 4 July 1902, which had been established in a 1918 statute giving pensions to widows of these three conflicts.

Pension levels were increased in 1926 and in 1930. The 1930 legislation also constructed a two-tier system for pensions. Veterans with 90 days or more service were treated more favorably than a new class of veterans which was created by the legislation. This class consisted of veterans with more than 70 days but less than 90 days of service.

Virtually the entire system of Spanish-Cuban/American War pensions was disrupted by an economy bill in 1933 which transferred sweeping powers to the President who could revise pension eligibility and levels of benefits. Such powers were to be exercised through the issuance of administrative regulations. These regulations limited rates or curtailed pensions. The earlier system of pensions was fully restored in 1934 and 1935.

Costs of United States wars versus pension expenditures from the Revolutionary War through the Spanish-Cuban/American War

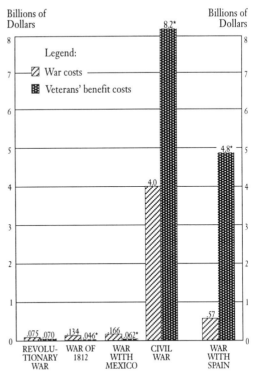

* Partly estimated

From U.S. President's Commission on Veterans' Pensions Report: *Findings and Recommendations* (1956): 111.

Service pensions for those with 90 days or more service, as opposed to disability pensions for men unable to perform manual labor, were established by legislation in 1938. Numerous clarifications in the law were necessary. In 1940, for example, a statute stated that the "continuous active service" required could have begun in the Spanish-Cuban/American War and proceeded into the time period of either the Boxer Uprising or the Philippine War.

Despite the apparent simplicity of the situation of the veterans of 1898–1902 a considerable number of congressional hearings were held, and quite a few statutes were passed further defining the entitlements of these veterans. Efforts to expand benefits fell into several categories. Veteran organizations made quite successful efforts to liberalize benefits for persons generally acknowledged as veterans. The United Spanish War Veterans consistently argued that veterans of 1898–1902 should be treated like the veterans of the Civil War, and, essentially, they were successful in reaching this goal. It was generally assumed that those who enlisted or were commissioned in 1898 expected the same benefits as the Civil War veterans in due course. Over the years, moreover, there were a number of changes in pension rates to meet increases in the cost of living.

For Civil War veterans a distinction had been made between "invalid or disability pensions" and "service pensions." In 1862, legislation had given pensions to men disabled as a result of military service. In 1890, a system of pensions based solely on one's having had military service in the Civil War or having a disability of any kind was established. The 1862 legislation had also provided pensions for widows, a veteran's children under a particular age, or a veteran's mother. In 1864, amending legislation gave pensions for partial disabilities arising from military service. The 1862 statute was made permanent and thus applied to the veterans of 1898–1902. Pensions awarded under the 1862 statute were often called "general law pensions."

Little or no controversy existed over the awarding of pensions to soldiers and sailors who served in the Philippines from 11 April 1899, when Spain formally ceded the Philippines to the United States, and 4 July 1902, when Governor William H. Taft proclaimed the end of the Philippine War. These men and women, along with men who served in the Boxer Upris-ing, were given the same status as veterans of the Spanish-Cuban/American War in terms of benefits. Some Veterans Administration rulings were necessary from time to time to define the eligibility of individuals. A soldier who served as a hospital corpsman aboard a transport going between the United States and Philippines between 13 November 1900 and 21 May 1901, for example, was given benefits because he could have been ordered ashore and into a combat area. The widow of a contract surgeon, a civilian, was given a pension when her husband died in 1933 of wounds sustained during the Philippine War. However, a nurse was denied benefits even though she served in the Philippine War. In that case, the disease that attacked her had emerged after her service and could not be shown as a result of the war.

A very different official view was taken of men who had served in the Philippines after 4 July 1902. Civil government had been established on that date for all of the Philippines except Moro Province. Scattered and sometimes heavy fighting continued in many areas of the islands for years. Troops were consistently called out to deal with guerrillas every year from 1903 through 1907. Meanwhile, sporadic but serious fighting continued in the Moro Province until late 1913. The violence that occurred after 1913 was usually contained by the paramilitary Philippine Constabulary.

Veterans of the fighting in the Philippines from the second half of 1902 onward were not eligible for pensions and had to show service-connected physical disabilities to receive governmental benefits. The only concession made by the federal government was to allow service in the Moro Province up to 15 July 1903 to count as war service. The Veterans Administration and, ultimately, Presidents Franklin D. Roosevelt and Harry Truman, insisted that service in the Philippines after 4 July 1902, was comparable to the "expeditions" undertaken by the armed forces, especially the marines, in other geographical areas and did not merit special consideration.

Philippine veterans and their supporters countered that this service was simply a continuation of the Philippine War and charged that it was illogical to use an arbitrary date to deprive soldiers and sailors of needed benefits. Therefore, they tried repeatedly to persuade Congress to pass a law that would extend the termination date of the Philippine War to 31 December 1913. Numerous hearings were held on the matter.

The closest the proposed legislation came to passage was in 1944 when Franklin D. Roosevelt vetoed a bill that had passed both houses. The nub of his argument in the veto message was that:

> This measure would grant special benefits to a particular group and exclude other members of the Regular Military and Naval Establishments who similarly have been called upon, on numerous occasions, to engage in similar military operations in times of peace. I believe that it is sound in principle to abide by the official beginning and ending dates of wars in providing benefits, heretofore described, and feel that extension of the period of the Philippine Insurrection, beyond that established in conformity with recognized legal precedents, would constitute sufficient deviation from that principle to invite further exceptions for additional groups with service in military occupations, expeditions, or campaigns other than during a period of war. [U.S., Congress, House, *House Document 804*, 78th Congress, 2nd Session (8 Dec. 1944)]

The problem for the Veterans Administration was that if the date of the termination of the war was changed, particularly in the dealings with countries like the Philippines, it would bump into the proclamations that had been issued, and legal actions that had been taken which had been based upon the termination date of the war.

Although concern was publicly expressed about the possibility that veterans of other "peace time" campaigns would apply for pensions if such legislation were passed, one may surmise that broader political considerations led the executive branch to oppose extending the date of the Philippine War. For many decades the fiction had been maintained that the Philippine War had ended neatly on 4 July 1902. Legislation extending the duration of that conflict by more than a decade would clearly suggest that reapprochment between the United States and the Filipinos was less rapid than had been officially recognized. The 1930s and 1940s were another period of delicate relations between the United States and the Philippines. During these years the decision on Philippine self-government began to be implemented, culminating in independence for the Philippines on 4 July 1946.

Focusing attention on the earlier bloody conflict might have damaged United States-Philippine relations, sully the memory of the United States-Philippine cooperation during World War II, and, possibly, damage changes for the retention of United States military, naval, and air bases in the Philippines after independence. This is merely speculation, but it seemed plausible.

The Philippine veterans learned from Roosevelt's veto message and tried somewhat different tactics through the late 1940s and the 1950s to have legislation passed that would recognize military and naval service in the Philippines between 4 July 1902 and 31 December 1913, but without success.

Veterans of other "small wars" did not seem to fare well with the Veterans Administration. When wartime pension rates were requested by the families of two marine sergeants (lieutenants in the Guardia Nacional de Nicaragua) who were killed in mutinies, the Administrator of Veterans Affairs made the following decision:

> Clearly neither of the occurrences resulting in the deaths of the two marines were incidents of or directly connected with the military operations for the purpose of accomplishing the ends of the expedition or occupation. The marines were doing mere police-duty, in an attempt to maintain discipline in the ranks of their respective commands.

Therefore, pensions at only the peacetime rates could be conferred.

Controversies over marines and navy and Coast Guard personnel were relatively few. By far, most campaigns for benefits were waged by army veterans and civilians who aspired to veteran status because of their roles in support of the army, especially in the Spanish-Cuban/American War and in the Philippines campaigns, but also in Siberia. The hearings related to claims for veterans benefits constitute a valuable source of information about military and naval life in the period from 1898 into the 1920s, although they must be used with some care because virtually all of the witnesses were representatives of interest groups or were government officials with specific policy agendas.

Benjamin R. Beede

REFERENCES

William H. Glasson, *Federal Military Pensions in the United States*, ed. by David Kinley (New York:

Oxford Univ. Pr., 1918); U.S., Congress, *The Historical Development of Veterans' Benefits in the United States: A Report on Veterans' Benefits in the United States by the President's Commission on Veterans' Pensions*, Staff Report No. 1, House Committee Report No. 244, 84th Congress, 2nd Session, 1956, 105; U.S., Veterans Administration, *Decisions of the Administrator of Veterans Affairs Veterans Administration, Volume I. March 1, 1931 to June 30, 1946* (U.S. Government Printing Office, n.d.).

Péralte, Charlemagne Masséna (1886–1919)

Charlemagne Masséna Péralte was a leading Haitian guerrilla leader who fought against U.S. occupation forces until marines killed him in 1919.

Often depicted as a primitive guerrilla chief, Charlemagne Masséna Péralte was actually an educated, well-dressed member of a respected family in the town of Hinche, Haiti. A devout Roman Catholic as a youth, he attended the College of St. Louis de Gonzague in Port-au-Prince from 1900 to 1904. He took part in an unsuccessful uprising against President Pierre Nord Alexis in 1908 and later served as military commander of the districts of Léogane and Port-de-Paix. In 1915 he resigned from the army to cultivate his land in Hinche about the time that Dr. Rosalvo Bobo was raising a rebel force in northern Haiti to challenge the government that Vilbrun Guillaume Sam had installed in Port-au-Prince. On 27 July Sam's massacre of political prisoners and his own brutal murder in the streets of the capital provoked a U.S. intervention. Adm. William B. Caperton proceeded to install President Philippe Sudre Dartiguenave in flagrant disregard of the popular preference for Dr. Bobo. Bobo, exiled to Kingston, Jamaica, kept his cause alive in the months that followed by staying in contact with Péralte and other opponents of Dartiguenave.

Early in 1918 a provost court convicted Péralte of attempting to steal a $12,000 payroll from gendarmerie headquarters at Hinche and sentenced him to five year's hard labor in Cap Haïtien. On 3 September 1918 he escaped to the mountains behind Plaine-du-Nord and began rallying *Cacos* (Haitian peasants) loyal to Bobo and Oreste Zamor, another northern leader. His army grew rapidly because peasant resentment over U.S. abuse of the *corvée* (labor conscription) was widespread. While mounting a traditional rebellion from the north and the Artibonite to overthrow Dartiguenave and make way for Bobo, Péralte also proclaimed a war to drive the U.S. invaders "into the sea and free Haiti."

Péralte carried out lightning attacks against isolated outposts manned by small detachments of gendarmerie, and soon much of the North was under his control. By 6 October 1919 when he boldly raided Port-au-Prince, he was at the height of his power. Calling himself general-in-chief of the revolution, he had appointed a cabinet and commissioned generals. Three thousand *Cacos* were under his immediate command; 2,000–3,000 more were led by Benoît Batraville, and there was another thousand in scattered bands led by minor chiefs. In addition, several thousand peasants not under arms were prepared to fight for him if needed. These part-time *Cacos* and their wives, who as market women circulated everywhere, formed an efficient intelligence network throughout the island.

Since the peasants believed that Péralte was invincible, the marines realized that only his death would end the rebellion. They devised an elaborate assassination plot that depended on the treachery of one of his generals, Jean-Baptiste Conzé, and the personal bravery of the gendarmerie commanders of Grand Riviére, Capt. Hermann H. Hanneken and Lt. William R. Button. Late in October Conzé informed Hanneken that Péralte was encamped with 1,200 men near Cap Haïtien. On 30 October Hanneken and Button, who spoke fluent creole, disguised themselves as *Cacos*, eluded the sentries, and reached the rebel hideout. Thinking that the newcomers were messengers, Péralte allowed them to approach, whereupon Hanneken shot him twice through the heart while Button emptied his automatic rifle into his guards. The next morning they brought the body back to Cap Haïtien, where it was identified by Abbé Le P. Pocro, Péralte's friend and confessor.

To convince the Haitians that Péralte was dead, the marines stripped the clothes from his corpse. They tied the corpse to a door and leaned a flagpole bearing his *Caco* banner beside it. They photographed this tableau and then dropped thousands of prints all over the island from airplanes. The grisly picture, which suggested Christ crucified, heightened Péralte's reputation as a martyr, but the news of his death demoralized his followers. The *Caco* movement in the north collapsed as many prominent chiefs surrendered. Those still in rebellion chose Batraville as supreme head and transferred their activities to Mirebalais farther south. After Batraville was killed in battle on 19 May 1920, peace was restored throughout the island.

In death as in life Péralte remained a powerful symbol of Haitian resistance to the U.S. occupation. The marines buried his body in concrete at Post Chabert between Cap Haïtien and Port Liberté to prevent necromancy, but after the U.S. withdrawal, he was reburied with a state funeral at the Cap. Writing in 1935 the mulatto author François Dalencour praised Péralte for "saving the national honor," and a painting entitled "Crucifixion of Charlemagne Péralte for Liberty" completed by the Haitian artist Philomé Obin in 1946 is regarded as his masterpiece.

Jane M. Rausch

REFERENCES

H. P. Davis, *Black Democracy*, rev. ed. (Biblo & Tannen, 1967); Roger Gaillard, *Charlemagne Péralte: le caco* (Imprimerie Le Natal, 1982); Robert Debs Heinl, Jr., and Nancy Gordon Heinl, *Written in Blood: The Story of the Haitian People, 1492–1971* (Houghton Mifflin, 1978); James H. McCrocklin, *Garde d'Haiti, 1915–1934* (U.S. Naval Institute Pr., 1956); David Nicholls, *From Dessalines to Duvalier: Race, Colour and National Independence in Haiti* (Cambridge Univ. Pr., 1979).

See also Caco Campaigns, Haiti (1918–1920); Hanneken, Herman Henry.

Pershing, John Joseph
(1860–1948)

John J. Pershing, best known as the commander of the American Expeditionary Force in World War I, made a notable record as a soldier and quasi-diplomat during the Moro campaigns in the Philippines and the Punitive Expedition against Mexican revolutionary troops in 1916–1917.

Pershing accepted appointment to the United States Military Academy to get an education. Several times in his long life, he came close to leaving the army, but he never did so. Pershing, who was from Missouri, graduated in 1886, at age 26 and was 33rd in a class of 70. Assigned to the cavalry, he spent from 1886 to 1891 in the frontier army. He was with the 6th Cavalry Regiment on the fringes of the fighting centered around the ghost dance movement, but was not at the Wounded Knee battle in 1890. During these five years, he dealt with Native Americans and developed respect for them and many aspects of their culture.

Lieutenant Pershing became professor of military science at the University of Nebraska on 1 October 1891. He not only vitalized the cadet corps there, but made contacts which were useful to him throughout his life. Some of his acquaintances were Charles G. Dawes, George D. Meiklejohn, Charles E. Magoon, and the chancellor of the university, James H. Canfield. His ambition never flagged; he did not hesitate to ask help from his friends, but he also helped them.

On 1 October 1895, Pershing joined the 10th Cavalry, which with other regiments, all black, was at Fort Assiniboine in Montana. In 1897 he joined the staff of the United States Military Academy, where, in contrast to the University of Nebraska, he became very unpopular with the cadets.

Pershing went to Cuba in 1898 as quartermaster of the 10th Cavalry. On 1 July he went up Kettle Hill with the regiment. His baptism of fire brought from him the statement that only fighting could fulfill a soldier. He returned to the United States debilitated by malaria. Years later, he suggested in private correspondence that Theodore Roosevelt had squeezed far more public acclaim from his action with the Rough Riders than his contribution deserved.

In the west and in Cuba, Pershing had served on the outer edges of the growing U.S. empire. He believed that the United States had to fulfill a mission to civilize peoples it considered uncivilized; he scorned anti-imperialists. At the same time, having served with black troops and against Native Americans and Cubans, he had developed a deeper appreciation for other races and nationalities than was common among U.S. soldiers, or for that matter, among U.S. civilian leaders.

The next segment of empire where the action would be interesting was the newly acquired Philippines. Earlier, Pershing had worked to get his Nebraska friend George D. Meiklejohn placed as assistant secretary of war. Meiklejohn continued to be essential to Pershing's career. He had the lieutenant ordered to the islands as adjutant general for the Southern District of Moro Province, consisting of Mindanao and Jolo.

Pershing arrived in the capital, Zamboanga, in January 1900.

There were 211,000 Christians and 400,000 Muslims in Mindanao. This was the heart of Moro country; the Moros were Muslims who believed that the surest way to enter heaven was to kill a Christian. They practiced bigamy, held slaves, and were steadily hostile to being governed by intruding white men. Pershing, discounting their non-Christian characteristics, not only got along well with the Moros, he liked them. He could squat hour after hour with them, the position in which they conferred and could match them cigarette for cigarette. At five feet, nine inches tall, he towered over the Moros, but never patronized them. They respected his erect carriage and obvious physical strength, so that many chiefs trusted him.

Others, however, murdered, forced captured foes to be slaves, and destroyed property. Pershing had an unusual aversion to taking human life of all sorts, but reluctantly decided that he had to open military action against some recalcitrant chiefs. To get to their strongholds taxed men and animals to their limits. Trails were often like tunnels through cogon grass, 20 feet high and with cutting edges. Beyond the grass were jungles that closed behind a column hacking its way through. Every minute the flanks were open to attack through the thicket by Moros swinging *krises* (sharp bolo knives) and *campilans* (two-handed, double-edged, straight-bladed swords). Serving under Brig. Gen. William A. Kobbé, Pershing was effectively introduced into Moro-style guerrilla warfare in December 1900.

At his own request Pershing was sent on 1 November 1901 to Iligan, one of the remotest posts. He believed that attempts to enforce order on hostile Moros would have to originate there. Brig. Gen. George W. Davis, commander of the district, recognized by this time that Pershing knew more about the Moros and felt more sympathy for their culture than any other officer under his command. Accordingly, he assigned two troops of cavalry and three companies of infantry to the captain and sent him toward Moro strongholds to negotiate from strength, with force to be used only as a last resort. Pershing, still a captain at age 41, in this expedition commanded enough troops to merit the rank of colonel. There were many conferences and no fights. At length one of the chiefs invited him to visit his stronghold. No such invitation had ever been extended before. Pershing accepted, and although advised against it, he went with one interpreter, one servant, and no weapons.

At the other end of Lake Lanao from where Pershing had been operating, there was fighting. In one action 50 U.S. troops were killed or wounded. This confrontation was unacceptable to Maj. Gen. Adna R. Chaffee, commanding in the Philippines. Col. Frank D. Baldwin, more inclined to fight than to parlay, commanded in Mindanao. Because Pershing seemed to accept the Moros as human beings, Chaffee put him in charge of Moro affairs in Mindanao. Colonel Baldwin could do nothing relative to the Moros without consulting Captain Pershing. Such command reversal was difficult for all parties, but it held. The captain sought Moro goodwill by buying supplies and horses from them and hiring them as laborers. He went unarmed to visit any chief who invited him.

In spite of the effort to resolve problems without fighting, some Moros continued to kill and to plunder. Thus, on 2 April 1903 Pershing was ordered to move along the western shore of Lake Lanao, fighting where he could not pass peacefully. He had 500 men, infantry and cavalry, 340 animals, two mountain guns, and two 3.5-inch field mortars, once again an oversized command for a captain. Supply boats sailed parallel to the march. There was even a correspondent from a London newspaper. A fort called Bacolod had to be reduced. It was protected by the steep banks of the lake, but Pershing worked his men and howitzers, by the utmost exertion, to elevations higher than the fort. His line, anchored at each end by the lake, closed off the land side. Throughout the night, during a tropical downpour drenching men and horses, the Muslims in the works rang gongs and screamed. But in the morning three chiefs under a white flag offered to surrender if they could keep their arms. Like Ulysses S. Grant at Fort Donelson in the Civil War, Pershing insisted on unconditional surrender. Firing resumed.

The mountain howitzers chewed away a side of the fort; the Moros had no cannon equal to firing counterbattery. For a time mortars lobbed shells inside the walls; then Pershing ordered an assault. The first wave of attackers threw brush into a wide, deep moat, thatched it with bamboo, crossed over this obstacle and moved onward to scale the walls. They then fought hand-to-hand, their Krags and bayonets against *krises* and *campilans*, overcoming the defenders in 30 minutes. Only three soldiers were wounded. They had killed perhaps 60 Moros, including the sultan of Bacolod. Pershing ordered the fort burned and moved northward. This description of the Battle of Bacolod, 8 April 1903, provides a sample of Captain Pershing's style of warfare against the Moros when at last he was obliged to use force.

By summer 1903, after three and one-half years in the Philippines, Captain Pershing was worn out and quite unwell. He had demonstrated to the succession of commanding officers that he worked hard and was effective, especially with the Moros. At age 43, he was still a captain and on the permanent list was still a first lieutenant. On 26 June 1903 he started for the United States with three months' leave. He looked back at the Mindanao Department with affection and stated his intention to return. Once in the United States he found that he had become a hero. His accomplishments both peaceful and military had been publicized by the press. Even this early, officials in the War Department talked of making him a brigadier general.

Pershing's new assignments were in Washington, D.C., on the recently created General Staff and then at the War College. At a social event at Christmas time 1903 he met Frances Warren. They were drawn to each other, but Pershing slowed the courtship. He was sensitive about the difference in their ages: he was 44 and she 23. He knew, too, that he could not support her in the style to which she was accustomed because she was the daughter of Francis Warren, a very wealthy Wyoming rancher. Warren was also a senator from Wyoming and chairman of the Senate Committee on Military Affairs. After a year, however, Pershing went to the Warren ranch at Christmas 1904 and asked the senator for permission to marry his daughter. The marriage took place on 26 January 1905, set early so that Frances could travel to Japan where her husband was to accompany the Japanese Army as an observer in the war against Russia.

A ranking Republican, Senator Francis Warren pressed for the promotion of his son-in-law through Secretary of War William H. Taft. In September 1906, Theodore Roosevelt nominated Pershing to be a brigadier general. Senator Warren steered the nomination through the Senate, which confirmed the promotion on 10 December 1906. There was bitterness among the 257 captains, 364 majors, 131 lieutenant colonels, and 110 colonels over whom Pershing was jumped. Certain objectors tried to prevent his promotion. Nonetheless, Pershing became one of only 22 general officers, 15 of them brigadier generals.

On 11 November 1909, Pershing returned to Zamboanga as military commander and civil governor of Mindanao and Jolo. His hope was, as before, to live peacefully with the Moros. Unfortunately, the hatred between Muslims and Christians was too great. Because of continued outrages, he decided to disarm the Moros. The governor general of the Philippines granted permission, and on 8 September 1911, Pershing issued an executive order requiring the Moros to surrender all weapons by 1 December.

The level of violence in Jolo climbed upward until some resident U.S. citizens wondered if the general would ever defend them. Moro disregard of the weapons order caused Pershing to move against the center of the opposition, a fort called Bud Daju, built atop the crater of a tall extinct volcano. Five years earlier in March 1906, Gen. Leonard Wood had assaulted the same strongpoint, killing 600 Moros, including women and children; Pershing was much more careful with Moro life. Late in December 1911, he cut off all access to and all exit from the fort. Those in the garrison surrendered with their weapons; there was no loss of life.

Pershing returned to Zamboanga and removed some troops from Jolo. Violence continued on that island, and even W. Cameron Forbes, governor general and a strong supporter of Pershing, began to hint that the general had let disorder continue too long. Pershing knew that once more the time had come to use force, but he kept his intentions to himself. Ostentatiously, he boarded a vessel which sailed northward, but when well out to sea the ship reversed direction and headed for the island of Jolo. Pershing landed there in secret, assembled 1,200 men stationed on Jolo, most of them Moro scouts, and moved toward a fort on Mount Bagsak where the hostiles were centered. It sat on heights protected by vertical walls of rock.

On 11 June 1913 Pershing's force appeared before Bud Bagsak, without the Moros realizing it was approaching. By hard labor the soldiers worked two mountain howitzers to a point at which they could direct plunging fire into the fort. It killed the principal chief. Pershing could tell from the clanging gongs and the screaming on 13 June that the Moros were preparing to sally. In their brightest clothes they came on the run, howling. "They've gotten themselves," Pershing said, "all dressed up to die." From behind a small earthwork the soldiers mowed them down.

Two days after this carnage, the general ordered an assault on the fort. The soldiers scaled the rock walls, entered the fort, and battled the Moros hand-to-hand. In a short time the fight was over. It was Pershing's severest up to that point in his life. Slaughter of this magnitude violated Pershing's philosophy of handling the Moros, but it did break their military power on Jolo. No other general in the army had advanced as far as he in fair dealing with other peoples or in the ability to defeat them in their own guerrilla-style warfare. None had had more experience on the fringes of empire. Six months after the Battle of Bud Bagsak to the day, on 15 December 1913, General Pershing left the Philippines.

Pershing's next assignment was to command a brigade with headquarters at the Presidio in San Francisco. He arrived there on 13 January 1914, and three months later was sent to the Mexican border to establish a regular border patrol. At El Paso, Texas, word reached him that Frances and his daughters had been killed on 27 August 1915 by smoke inhalation when their house at the Presidio burned. His son Warren, age 6, survived. Near collapse for a time, the general suffered silently and for therapy intensified his soldiering. His sister, May, took care of Warren and kept house.

Francisco "Pancho" Villa, a Mexican caudillo, raided Columbus, New Mexico, on 9 March 1916 with 485 men, killing 18 and wounding eight U.S. personnel. Woodrow Wilson's administration demanded permission to pursue Villa into Mexico from the Carranza government, which it had recognized.

Maj. Gen. Frederick Funston commanded the United States Army's Southern Department. Five years younger than Pershing, Funston wanted to lead the Punitive Expedition, but the administration put Pershing in command. On 15 March 1916 Pershing led his column across the border from El Paso. He controlled 10,000 men, his largest command up to that time, but

took with him only the 7th, 10th, 11th, and 13th Cavalry Regiments, the 16th Regiment of Infantry, and two batteries of the 6th Artillery. The internal combustion engine had entered the army: the expedition included eight airplanes, JN-2, known as "Jennies" and trucks and passenger cars. Chief of Staff Hugh L. Scott had, without authority from Congress, invested $450,000 in trucks.

The aircraft were supposed to be able to locate Villa in the vast territory of Chihuahua, but they did not have enough power to climb over some of the foothills. Within six weeks all eight were out of commission. Someone leaked their failure to a New York newspaper, which annoyed Pershing, who had forbidden reporting any unfavorable information. This news did prompt Congress to appropriate $500,000 for better planes.

Two railroads ran south out of Cuidad Juárez, forming an oval that was at its widest 75 miles, but the U.S. force did not have the use of those lines. Supply had to be by truck. In the rough terrain, somewhere in that oval, Villa was expected to be. The general formed four detachments to search that area. They operated separately, unable to keep in touch with each other or with headquarters. The first combat came when Col. George A. Dodd, with the 7th Cavalry, engaged 500 Mexican soldiers about 250 miles south of the border at Guerrero. Four U.S. cavalrymen were wounded. Villa received a severe wound in one leg, but he escaped, carried in a wagon.

Although there were no clashes with the Carrancista forces, it became apparent that the Carranza government did not want the U.S. expedition to penetrate deep into Mexico. Civilians, too, were unfriendly, obviously aiding Villa and his men. Pershing insisted to the news media that Mexicans welcomed U.S. forces, and he would not permit the opposite point of view to be published.

At Parral, 350 miles south of the border, on 12 April 1916 a crowd turned on the 13th Cavalry which had to fight its way out of the town with a loss of two killed and six wounded. This stopped the U.S. advance from moving deeper into Mexico. Frustrated, Pershing wanted Funston to recommend to the Wilson administration that the Punitive Expedition conquer the entire state of Chihuahua. To intimates the general expressed disgust with what he referred to as a policy of quasi-intervention. He believed that Mexico would be better off if the United States took it over.

Pershing hired a Dodge touring car from a Mormon settler in order to stay closer to his detachments. Since he had eased the news censorship, several carloads of reporters strung along after the Dodge. On 6 May Maj. Robert L. Howze with the 11th Cavalry surprised the Villistas at Ojos Azules, almost capturing Villa. As before, the *caudillo* escaped, still in pain from the leg wound. His original band was broken up, however, and most of the effective leaders dispersed.

On 9 May 1916 Pershing was ordered to move back toward the border. When the main body was about 125 miles south of Ciudad, Juárez, Pershing directed Capt. Charles T. Boyd to take two companies of the 11th Cavalry and reconnoiter to Villa Ahumada to see if there was a large concentration of Mexican troops there. Boyd was ordered to avoid a fight. At Carrizal, a few miles short of Ahumada, a force of Carrancistas blocked his way. Determined to reach his objective, he tried to fight his way through the town. Boyd and one lieutenant were killed, with a total loss of 12 killed, 10 wounded, and 24 taken prisoner. This action on 21 June 1916 was the costliest of the Punitive Expedition. Moreover it was against government, not Villista, forces. News of it in the United States for a time somewhat jolted public confidence in the general.

Although this was the last fight of the Punitive Expedition, the Wilson administration kept the troops in Mexico, while it negotiated with Carranza. Pershing established a model camp, 75 miles south of El Paso, supplying it from Columbus, New Mexico, with 22 truck companies, each with 25 trucks. With inactivity, the men grew bored. Pershing instituted a firm training program and to cut the ever increasing cases of venereal disease, he even licensed prostitution supervised by army surgeons. On 31 August the situation was stabilized enough for him to take a week's leave in Columbus.

Finally, Pershing received orders to withdraw the expedition from Mexico. His force recrossed the border on 5 February 1917. Service in Mexico had taxed men, horses, and equipment to the limit. But before the expedition left Mexico, Villa assailed the border again. His original band was shattered, however. Later, Secretary of War Newton D. Baker said that they were glad not to

have captured the *caudillo*. What would they have done with him? Pershing, in contrast, considered the episode a disgrace to U.S. arms. He would have captured Villa if it had required conquering all of Mexico.

Only two weeks after Pershing's return to the United States, Maj. Gen. Funston died, and Pershing took his place. Two months later the United States entered the war in Europe. Whatever the Mexican Punitive Expedition may have accomplished, it had made Pershing the best known general in the army. Because he had followed orders, even when he plainly disapproved of them, and because his career was uniformly distinguished, President Wilson selected him to command the American Expeditionary Force (AEF).

At its maximum strength the AEF contained more than two million soldiers. It exceeded by 200 times Pershing's biggest previous command. Its mission, too, was different from those he had led on the fringes of empire, in guerrilla-style combat. Nevertheless, he received a complete delegation of authority to handle the AEF. The general jealously guarded all efforts to dilute his authority. His instructions included the following directive: "The forces of the United States are a separate and distinct component of the combined forces, the identity of which must be preserved" (Vandiver, vol. II, p. 695). Pershing fiercely adhered to this order, never permitting his troops to become replacements for shattered Allied units. As a result, on 4 July 1918 he was able to constitute the 1st United States Army to fight alongside the other armies.

Because of Pershing's firmly-held views, premier Georges Clemenceau of France attempted more than once to have him removed from the command. One was extending training periods so long that the Allies feared the war would be lost before U.S. troops were ready. Another was restoring mobility to the battlefield, getting out of the trenches. A third was his stress on the importance of individual marksmanship. Also he organized divisions of 27,000 men, twice the size of others. In the end, the AEF shaped by General Pershing was critical in defeating Germany.

John K. Mahon

REFERENCES

Richard O'Connor, *Black Jack Pershing* (Doubleday, 1961); Donald Smythe, *Guerrilla Warrior: The Early Life of John J. Pershing* (Scribner, 1973); Wayne Wray Thompson, "Governors of the Moro

Province: Wood, Bliss, and Pershing in the Southern Philippines, 1903–1913," Ph.D. diss., Univ. of California at San Diego, 1975; Robert S. Thomas and Inez V. Allen, *The Mexican Punitive Expedition Under Brigadier General John J. Pershing United States Army, 1916–1917* (War Histories Division, Office of the Chief of Military History, Department of the Army, 1954); Frank E. Vandiver, *Black Jack: The Life and Times of John J. Pershing* (Texas A&M Pr., 1977).

See also list of entries at the front of the book for Moro Campaigns (1902–1913); Punitive Expedition, Mexico (1916–1917).

Philippine Constabulary

The Philippine Constabulary was the paramilitary police force of the colonial government of the Philippines. It was established to aid in the preservation of peace, law, and order throughout the archipelago during the latter stages of the Philippine War of 1899–1902. While the constabulary was organized, equipped, and uniformed in a manner similar to the U.S. Army Philippine Scouts, constables were policemen and not combat soldiers (*Annual Report of the Philippine Commission, 1901*, pp. 79–80).

Martial law in the Philippines was formally ended on 4 July 1901, even though scattered nationalist and outlaw bands continued to resist U.S. colonial rule. When martial law was lifted, the responsibility for the day-to-day conduct of civil affairs was transferred from the United States Army to the U.S.-controlled Philippine Commission. The eight-member commission, under Governor General William H. Taft, deemed it imperative the United States's law enforcement and military role in the Philippines be decreased because "it is politically most important that Filipinos should suppress Filipino disturbances and arrest Filipino outlaws" (*Annual Report of the Philippine Commission, 1900–1903*, p. 182). As a result, on 18 July 1901, by Act No. 175, the commission established the Philippine Constabulary to act as the law enforcement arm of the civilian government. The constabulary was placed within the government's Department of the Interior and was considered equal in status to all other bureaus. It received its orders from the governor general, through the chief of constables, and was under the sole control of the Philippine Commission.

The constabulary was recruited primarily from among the rural peasant tribes and was open to any male citizen of the Philippines who had declared his allegiance to the United States and was between the ages of 18 and 25. All potential constables had to be able-bodied, free from disease, of good moral character and habits, of average intelligence, and capable of demonstrating literacy in Spanish or English (*Manual for the Philippine Constabulary*, Art. 15, Sec. 146). Initially, Filipinos served only as enlisted men and noncommissioned officers. Recruits were enlisted for two and later three-year tours and could retire with a pension after 20 years of service (*Manual for the Philippine Constabulary*, Art. 20, Secs. 385–386). They were armed, equipped, and clothed in a fashion similar to U.S. Army Philippine Scouts, except that constabulary uniforms had distinctive red collar flashes. Each constable received a clothing allowance in addition to his monthly pay, as well as a daily ration allowance that could be dispersed in cash, in kind, or both (*Manual for the Philippine Constabulary*, Art. 16, Secs. 210–261; Art. 21, Secs. 439–475; Art. 24, Sec. 594). Constables were paid monthly from Philippine government funds, but at a rate lower than that paid to Philippine Scouts (*Manual for the Philippine Constabulary*, Art. 24, Sec. 687; Elliott, p. 173).

Constabulary units were raised and permanently stationed in the province of recruitment, unlike the indigenous police forces raised by Great Britain and Spain in their colonial empires (Farinas, pp. 80–81; *A Compilation of Acts of the Philippine Commission*, pp. 409–508). The Philippine Commission believed that indigenous police units could generate greater respect and cooperation among local peasants who knew them. This deliberate policy ensured a higher degree of peasant loyalty, stability, and cooperation than if constables had been drawn from a single class or ethnic source. The enlisted ranks of the constabulary eventually represented a cross-section of the rural tribes of the Philippines, and every major ethnic group had members serving in one or more units by 1913.

The constabulary was commanded by a chief of constables with the temporary rank of brigadier general, and four assistant chiefs, each with the temporary rank of colonel. All were regular U.S. Army officers. The chief constable drew up new regulations and policies for operations, developed examination and inspection boards to oversee police recruitment and implementation of reforms, and designed uniforms. Henry T.

Allen, Harry H. Bandholtz, and David J. Baker, Jr., were among the U.S. Army officers who served as chief of constables during the early history of the force (Elliott, pp. 168, 173–174; *Manual for the Philippine Constabulary*, Art. 8, Secs. 42–44).

Individual units were commanded by field- and company-grade officers of the United States Army on detached service, who retained their commissions in the regular army and received a higher temporary rank in the constabulary. Rank and precedence for officers and noncommissioned officers were similar to those of the United States Army. By the end of 1901, about 1,000 U.S. Army officers had been procured for constabulary service. Initially, all officers were U.S. citizens and throughout the history of the force, they filled the majority of leadership positions. After 1908, new constabulary officers were recruited directly from U.S. colleges and military schools (in the case of U.S. citizens) or were nominated by various officials of the commission government following a competitive examination (in the case of Filipinos). Once selected as an officer candidate, each man received three weeks of training at the Philippine Constabulary Academy at Banguio. About 60 students were in attendance in 1922, for example, and received their instruction from U.S. Army and constabulary officers. Upon completion of training, graduates were commissioned as 3rd lieutenants and were attached to a constabulary company for further field training (Elliott, p. 176).

The Philippines were divided into four constabulary districts in 1901, each under an assistant chief of constables. At the outset constables were formed into 150-man companies with one company being assigned to each province (Forbes, pp. 204–205). These companies were designated by their numbers only (i.e., Philippine Constabulary, 50th Company or 51st Company). Because constables were supposed to operate in small numbers against rebel or outlaw bands, the company was the primary constabulary unit, and most actions before the end of the commission government normally involved patrols of 20 men or less. No organizations of battalion or regimental size ever existed (*Manual for the Philippine Constabulary*, Art. 21, Sec. 416; Elliott, p. 175). The number of Philippine Constables grew from 2,417 at its inception in 1901, to a peak of 8,800 men in 1905. By 1913 the number of constables fell to 4,600 due to the

success of government pacification programs (Forbes, p. 227).

The members of the Philippine Constabulary were first and foremost peace officers, and they were empowered to prevent and suppress brigandage, unlawful assemblies, riots, insurrections, and other breaches of the peace and violations of law. They executed arrest warrants or, when the occasion arose, made arrests on reasonable suspicion without warrants for breaches of the peace and violations of the law (*Manual for the Philippine Constabulary*, Art. 1, Secs. 1, 2). Although the constabulary was the main police force available to the Philippine government, the jurisdiction of the constabulary did not extend to any areas under martial law in the Philippines or to municipalities where local police units existed, unless their aid had been requested by a military commander or local police official (*Manual for the Philippine Constabulary*, Art. 37, Secs. 1269–1272). After 1912, however, the constabulary was given the task of reforming the notoriously inefficient and corrupt municipal forces of the Philippines, a task that had been delayed because of the necessity for constables to track down bandits and anti-government forces (Elliott, pp. 180–181). In addition to these duties, constables routinely guarded jails, patrolled highways and villages, enforced quarantines, and regulated the possession of firearms by civilians. On special occasions, when high-ranking civil and military officials passed through a village containing a constabulary garrison, constables served as an honor escort (*Manual for the Philippine Constabulary*, Art. 18, Sec. 336; Art. 21, Sec. 425).

The main duty of the constabulary was to patrol the countryside in three- to five-man squads, keeping in touch with the people, preventing and detecting crime, enforcing the laws, and obtaining information as to general rural conditions. These patrols were instructed that when not in actual pursuit of bandits, they were to travel main routes and spend some hours with the peasants in each barrio of importance and one or more nights in important towns.

While constables often served alongside U.S. Army Philippine Scouts and regular soldiers during the final stages of the Philippine War, their primary adversaries were the groups formed after 1901 who were labeled *ladrones-politicos* (anti-U.S. bandits who still harassed governmental forces), or *ladrones-fanaticos* (members of peasant religious sects who resisted U.S. rule for sectarian reasons) (*Annual Report of the Philippine Commission, 1903*, pp. 79–134; Asprey, p. 196; Sturtevant, p. 119). When a large-scale bandit group was reported as operational in a particular region, constables were told that its suppression must take precedence over all their other duties. All units received detailed tactical instructions for use against bandit gangs and were told that it was essential to know both their enemy and its environment thoroughly. Local peasants, the *Philippine Constabulary Manual* read, could aid in gathering this intelligence. When a bandit camp was located, constables were encouraged to attack vigorously and without delay, preferably at daybreak or during rainy weather when bandits were least active and least prepared. Bandits, constables were reminded, were loathe to leave their own province or locality, and experience showed that bandits seldom, if ever, remained for long in one place. While operating under such conditions imposed hardships on constables, unit leaders were informed that these tactics had the greatest chance of success (*Manual for the Philippine Constabulary*, Art. 23, Secs. 502, 528–533).

Between their inception and the end of World War I, constables performed nearly constant service in all regions of the Philippines. Service medals and ribbons were authorized for veterans of operations, which included the following actions:

- Between March 1902 and July 1904, in Luzon in the provinces of Bataan, Batangas (*see* May), Bulacan, Cavite, Laguna, Rizal, Isabela, and Cagayan against Faustino Guillermo and Lucio San Miguel and other outlaw leaders and their followers;
- Between June 1901 and September 1906, in Batangas, Cavite, Laguna, and Rizal provinces, against Macario Sakay, Cornelio Felizardo, Lucio De Vega, Leon Villafuerte, Julian Montalan, and their followers;
- Between December 1901 and July 1910, in Bulacan, Bataan, Nueva Ecija, Pampanga, and Tarlac provinces, against Felipe Salvador and his followers;
- Between June and September 1903, in the provinces of Albay, Ambos Camarines, and Sorsogon, against Simeon Ola and his followers;
- Between February 1904 and June 1911, in the Visayan Islands, in the provinces of Samar, against organized *pulahan* forces under "Papa" Pablo, Pedro de la Cruz, Enrique Dagujob, Otoy (Isidro Pompar) and other leaders;
- Between January 1902 and November 1907, in the islands of Cebu, Negros, and Panay, against Quintin and Anatalio Tabal, "Papa" Isio, and other outlaw chiefs and their bands;
- Between March 1903 and April 1904, in Mindanao-Sulu Campaigns in the province of Surigao in the Adriano Concepcion operations;
- Between May 1905 and May 1906, in the Jolo group, against the outlaw Pala and other hostile leaders and their followers;
- Between July 1906 and June 1908, in Cotabato, Lanao, and Zamboanga, against Sultan Sa-Dimabara, Sultan Dilumbayan, Sultan Uali-Ulama, Nuval Hakim, Ampuan Agaus, and other Moro chiefs and their followers;
- Between May 1914 and July 1917, in Cotabato and Lanao provinces in the Pidatan Operations;
- Between November 1914 and May 1917, in the Sulu pacification campaign; and
- Between July and November 1918, in the Sulu group against Sampang and Jauni. (*Manual for the Philippine Constabulary*, Art. 19, Sec. 380; Linn, p. 117).

Despite the widespread service of the Philippine Constabulary after mid-1901, the force had an inauspicious start and numerous early civilian and military critics. U.S. military authorities in the Philippines were especially slow to recognize the value of constables and regarded them as little more than amateur native policemen who could not possibly be of any assistance to U.S. Army Philippine Scouts or regular forces. According to one officer, the army looked with disfavor on the constabulary, with attitudes varying "from scoffing to resentment, particularly when large numbers of Scout companies were detailed from the Army to augment the commands of constabulary officers" (Forbes, p. 216). Another officer observed that constables were a police force paid from insular funds and not comparable to the Philippine Scouts (Franklin, p. 45).

Scouts were highly disciplined and loyal forces, which the constables, after a mutiny of 22 constables in Davao in 1909, could not claim. This altercation over harsh treatment by U.S. officers resulted in one U.S. officer being killed and the disbanding of the constabulary unit involved. The Philippine Commission, however, termed the mutiny an incident of no general significance, which was caused by poor leadership and "natural racial animosities" (*Annual Report of the Philippine Commission, 1909*, pp. 42, 137; Forbes, p. 235). Nonetheless, U.S. Army skepticism of the constabulary remained, and soldiers usually avoided serving with or under constabulary units and commanders.

As a symbol of U.S. colonial authority, the constabulary often ran afoul of other Filipinos and by its mere presence at times created small civil wars in many rural and urban areas of the islands. Indeed, the Philippine Commission admitted that it took years to establish a proper policy and role for the constabulary and that at first there were constant friction and suspicion between constables and local civil officials, as well with peasants in the countryside (*Annual Report of the Philippine Commission to the Secretary of War, 1907*, vol. 3, 251). After the first several years, however, prominent merchants, property owners, and other educated Filipinos came to see the constabulary as a force capable of creating and maintaining law, order, and stability throughout the Philippines. Such favorable feelings were not as widespread among peasant populations in the countryside who often had no more sophisticated concerns than seeking to avoid forced labor, tax increases, and constabulary inquisitiveness (Sturtevant, p. 121).

There is little doubt that the Philippine Constabulary successfully fulfilled the missions developed for it by the Philippine Commission. In helping to establish order throughout the archipelago, thereby allowing the U.S. military to curtail its large commitment, the constabulary was very effective. The Philippine Commission reported in 1902 that since civil government was established the previous year and since the formation of the Philippine Constabulary, "not a single shot has been fired by an American soldier in the preservation of peace and order" throughout the islands, nor had any requests been made for regular troops to suppress any disturbance (*Annual Reports of the Philippine Commis-*sion, *1900–1903*, p. 312). Following the Philippine War intensive efforts were made to improve constabulary discipline and quality, and constables gradually won over many peasants through the practice of impartial justice and law enforcement and by limiting petty thievery and crime. Often war-weary peasants, who were also tired of lawlessness, accepted the constabulary as the lesser of many evils. The commission succeeded in teaching peasants that the constabulary was not a military force, but a police force organized to assist in a sympathetic way Filipino local officers in the work of suppressing disorder and lawlessness (*Annual Report of the Philippine Commission*, vol. 3, p. 251). In its annual report for 1907, the Philippine Commission reported that relations between the Philippine Constabulary and civil officials and people of the provinces and municipalities were highly satisfactory. Constables had gained the confidence, trust, and goodwill of the people, without employing extreme or extraordinary measures (*Report of the Executive Secretary of the Philippine Commission, 1907*, vol. 1, p. 237).

Constables gained praise from U.S. civil officials, especially Governor General Taft. He was gratified to learn that past constabulary abuses had ended and that constables were performing efficiently in a spirit of cooperation with provincial and municipal authorities. Any continued criticisms of the constabulary, Taft felt, were "very grossly exaggerated, deliberate misrepresentations by persons whose sympathy and profit are with the ladrones, and who do not welcome the presence of the Constabulary on any ground" (Elliott, pp. 174, 218).

The role played by the constabulary allowed the rapid pacification of the Philippines and furthered the interests of the U.S. Philippine Commission (Asprey, p. 196; Hall, pp. 808–809). Constables supplied a permanent U.S. presence in unstable provinces and ensured tranquility through persuasion or, when necessary, by force. This insular police force ensured that areas secured by military force would remain loyal, or failing that, peaceful. It further ensured that nationalist or religious rebellions would be quickly reported, contained, and neutralized by Filipinos.

Clayton D. Laurie

REFERENCES

Robert Asprey, *War in the Shadows: The Guerrilla in History* (Doubleday, 1975); George Yarrington Coats, "The Philippine Constabulary: 1901–1917," Ph.D. diss., Ohio State Univ., 1968; Charles B. Elliott, *The Philippines to the End of the Commission Government: A Study in Tropical Democracy* (Bobbs-Merrill, 1917); Rod. J. Farinas, *The Philippine Constabulary* (The Constable, 1976); W. Cameron Forbes, *The Philippine Islands* (Houghton Mifflin Co., 1928); Charles W. Franklin, *The History of the Philippine Scouts, 1898–1936* (Army War College, 1936); Daniel E.G. Hall, *A History of Southeast Asia*, 4th ed. (St. Martin's Pr., 1981); Vic Hurley, *Jungle Patrol: The Story of the Philippine Constabulary* (E. Dutton, 1938); Brian McAlister Linn, *The U.S. Army and Counterinsurgency in the Philippine War, 1899–1902* (Univ. of North Carolina Pr., 1989); Glenn A. May, *The Battle for Batangas: A Philippine Province at War* (Yale Univ. Pr., 1991); Philippine Constabulary, *Manual for the Philippine Constabulary* (Bureau of Printing, 1922); Richard W. Smith, "Philippine Constabulary," *Military Review*, 48 (May 1968), 73–80; David R. Sturtevant, *Popular Uprisings in the Philippines, 1840–1940* (Cornell Univ. Pr., 1976); Heath Twichell, Jr., *Allen: The Biography of an Army Officer, 1859–1930* (Rutgers Univ. Pr., 1974); U.S. Philippine Commission, *A Compilation of Acts of the Philippine Commission* (Bureau of Public Printing, 1908); U.S. Philippine Commission, *Annual Report of the Philippine Commission, 1901* (U.S. Government Printing Office, 1901); U.S. Philippine Commission, *Annual Report of the Philippine Commission, 1903*; U.S. Philippine Commission, *Annual Report of the Philippine Commission, 1909* (Government Printing Office, 1909); U.S. Philippine Commission, *Annual Report of the Philippine Commission to the Secretary of War, 1907* (Government Printing Office, 1907); U.S. Philippine Commission, *Annual Reports of the Philippine Commission, 1900–1903* (U.S. Government Printing Office, 1903); U.S. Philippine Commission, *Report of the Executive Secretary of the Philippine Commission, 1907* (Government Printing Office, 1907).

Philippine Constabulary Manual

On 18 July 1901, by Act. No. 175, the Philippine Commission established the paramilitary Philippine Constabulary as the law enforcement arm of the U.S. colonial government. The constabulary existed within the Department of the Interior and was equal in status to all other civilian bureaus. It received its overall orders from the U.S. governor general, through the chief of constables, and was under the sole control of the Philippine Commission.

To guide the operations of the force, and to acquaint new U.S. constabulary officers with the force and the country they served, the chief of constables, usually a high-ranking U.S. Army officer on detached service, created a book of regulations known as the *Manual for the Philippine Constabulary*. Once approved by both the governor general and the secretary of the interior, it became the sole doctrine of the constabulary. The manual has gone through many editions with only minor changes. The edition used for this article is the *Manual for the Philippine Constabulary* published in Manila by the government Bureau of Printing in 1922.

The 1922 version was typical of the series. It had a soft, maroon-colored cover, was 408 pages in length, and fit in a uniform tunic pocket. Its table of contents listed 37 general articles or regulations, the text itself, an index, and appendices of laws and miscellaneous regulations. The manual was similar in format to the *Regulations of the Army of the United States* and was patterned after the army's basic field manual.

The 1922 version of the *Manual for the Philippine Constabulary* was extraordinarily comprehensive. Articles 1 through 4 dealt with various aspects of constabulary organization, describing the various regional divisions and staff positions and duties of top constabulary officials. Articles 5 through 14 dealt with the duties and responsibilities of constabulary unit commanders (who were almost always U.S. Army officers), and with the chain of command, promotion system, rank and precedence, and matters of leave. Articles 15 through 17 addressed topics concerning the enlisted ranks, such as uniforms, furloughs, discharges, and pensions, discipline requirements, enlistments and reenlistments, honorary and ceremonial functions, and medals and decorations. Articles 24 through 28 dealt with the duties and organization of the various constabulary support branches, such as the Medical, Quartermaster, Transportation, and Intelligence divisions, and the Constabulary Academy and band. The remaining sections dealt with miscellaneous topics, including instruction, company administration, records, reports and returns, and general provisions governing the force.

Considering that the constabulary was in constant action from its inception through the end of the commission government, it is surprising that only 34 pages of the manual were devoted to tactics. There, under an article entitled "Patrols and Escorts," was a host of common sense, "how to," information that was familiar to the Filipinos who made up the enlisted ranks of the force, but which was invaluable, as was the rest of the manual, to U.S. constabulary officers, most of whom were unfamiliar with the Philippines and its people.

Clayton D. Laurie

Philippine Revolution (1896–1899)

The Philippine Revolution, the first revolution against Western colonial rule in Asia, was directed against Spain, which had colonized the Philippines since 1565. The revolution against Spain had two phases: the first was from the declaration of defiance against Spanish rule on 23 August 1896 to the conclusion of a truce in December 1897, and the second was from the return from exile in Hong Kong of revolutionary leader Emilio Aguinaldo y Famy to the outbreak of the Philippine War in February 1899.

After over three centuries of Spanish colonial rule characterized by unenlightened government, outright exploitation of the *Indios* (i.e., the indigenous population of *Filipinas*), half-hearted attempts at reform, and on the part of the governed, countless sporadic and isolated revolts and other forms of resistance, the Philippine Revolution exploded on 23 August 1896 in the event that is commemorated as the "Cry of Pugadlawin." Located in the outskirts of Manila, there assembled on that day members of a secret revolutionary society known as the Katipunan (Katass-taasan Kagalang-galang na Katipunana nang manga Anak nang Bayan, meaning Highest and Most Respectable Society of the sons of the People) led by its founder, Andrés Bonifacio. The revolutionaries tore up their *cedulas* (identification receipts issued for payment of taxes) as a symbol of their determination to take up arms against Spain.

The seeds of revolution were, in fact, sown earlier in the 19th century when Spain's enforced isolation of the Philippines was shattered. The most important event which possibly made the revolution inevitable was that of 17 February 1872, when three Filipino priests, leaders in the movement for the secularization (in effect, nationalization) of Philippine parishes, were executed publicly by garrote for their supposed complicity in a military mutiny at a Cavite arsenal on 20 January 1872. By linking them with the mutiny, the Spanish administration, with the instigation of Spanish friars, found a convenient way of doing away with the troublesome priests, considered by the Spanish as *filibusteros* (anyone who showed any radical tendencies).

The first manifestation of the Philippine nationalism followed in the decades of the 1880s and 1890s as a reform or propaganda movement conducted both in Spain and in the Philippines for the purpose of publicizing Philippine conditions in the hope that desired changes in the social, political, and economic life of the Filipinos would come about through peaceful means. This propaganda movement failed to secure its desired reforms, such as the expulsion of the friars and their replacement by Filipino secular priests and equality before the law between Spaniards and Filipinos, largely because the Spanish friars used their power and money to thwart the activities of the Filipino *ilustrados* (educated Filipinos) who led the movement.

The revolutionary society Katipunan was established on 7 July 1892 by Filipinos who had given up hope that the Spanish government would administer the affairs of *Filipinas* in the interests of its subjects with justice and dignity. A secret association patterned after Freemasonry and the Liga Filipina (a mutual aid society founded by the *ilustrado* José Rizal y Mercado, also in July 1892), the Katipunan recruited members in the suburbs of Manila and in the provinces of Central Luzon. By the time of the outbreak of the revolution in August 1896, membership had soared to about 30,000, including some women. The revolution erupted prematurely on 23 August because of the untimely discovery by a Spanish friar on 1 August of the existence of the revolutionary society. The immediate cause of the outbreak of the revolution was the institution of a reign of terror by the Spanish authorities in an attempt to frighten the population into submission. Hundreds suspected of joining the Katipunan and revolution were arrested and jailed; prominent Filipinos were shipped to exile in the Caroline Islands or the Spanish penal colony in Africa; and still others were executed, including Rizal, who was shot by musketry on 30 December 1896. The revolution spread from Manila and Cavite to Laguna, Batangas, Bulacan, Pampanga, Tarlac, and Nueva Ecija, and the eight rays in the Philippine flag today represent the first eight provinces to revolt against Spain.

Andrés Bonifacio led the revolution in its early stages, although he did not excel on the battlefield. Internal rivalry led to the division of the ranks within the Katipunan, and with the elimination of Bonifacio in May 1897, leadership of the revolution fell to another Katipunan member from Cavite, Emilio Aguinaldo y Famy, who had distinguished himself on the battlefield in Cavite, at that time the heartland of the revolution.

The first phase of the revolution ended inconclusively with both Filipino and Spanish forces unable to pursue hostilities to a successful conclusion. Consequently, between 18 November and 15 December 1897 a truce was concluded between the two sides which resulted in a temporary cessation of hostilities. Aguinaldo agreed to go into temporary exile in Hong Kong after the Spanish government compensated him and his revolutionary junta with 400,000 pesos (about $200,000). The truce failed because both sides entered the agreement in bad faith. Neither side was willing to abandon hostilities, but each was biding time and resources to resume the armed conflict.

The second phase of the revolution began after Aguinaldo returned to the Philippines from Hong Kong on 19 May 1898 on board a U.S. ship from Commodore George Dewey's fleet, which on 1 May 1898 had defeated Spanish naval forces in the Battle of Manila Bay. The United States had declared war on Spain in April 1898 because of Spain's refusal to grant independence to Cuba and Dewey was sent to Manila to destroy the Spanish fleet there. The initial Filipino enthusiasm for U.S. support of the revolution against Spain turned increasingly sour as the Filipino revolutionaries became convinced that the United States was preparing to take over sovereignty of the Philippines from Spain. Thus, while the Filipino revolutionaries succeeded in ending Spanish rule in the Philippines, they had to contend with the U.S. occupation of the Philippines.

By the time Filipino and U.S. forces faced each other in battle after 4 February 1899, the Filipino revolutionaries had declared Philippine independence on 12 June 1898, had convened a revolutionary constitutional congress to draft a constitution for a Philippine Republic, and had inaugurated the First Philippine Republic at Maloḷos on 23 January 1899.

Bernardita Reyes Churchill

REFERENCES

Pedro S. de Achútegui and Miguel A. Bernad, *Aguinaldo and the Revolution of 1896: A Documentary History* (Ateneo de Manila, 1972); Renato Constantino, *A History of the Philippines From the Spanish Colonization to the Second World War* (Monthly Review Pr., 1975); O.D. Corpuz, *The Roots of the Filipino Nation* (Aklahi Foundation, 1989), 2 vols.; John R.M. Taylor, *The Philippine Insurrection Against the United States: A Compilation of Documents With Notes and Introduction* (Eugenio Lopez Foundation, 1971), 5 vols.

Philippine Revolutionary Government

The Philippine Revolutionary Government refers to the first Philippine Republic, inaugurated at Malolos, Bulacan Province, north of Manila, on 23 January 1899. This was, however, not the first revolutionary government that the Filipinos attempted to establish after the outbreak of the revolution against Spain.

The Philippine Revolution was initiated by a secret revolutionary society called the *Katipunan* that was founded in July 1892 by Andrés Bonifacio. The revolution broke out in open hostilities against Spanish authorities in August 1896. By March 1897 the revolution had developed beyond the confines of the *Katipunan*, and revolutionaries from Cavite Province, south of Manila, in the heartland of the Revolution, decided at the Tejeros Convention to replace the *Katipunan* organization with a revolutionary government. Emilio Aguinaldo y Famy, an active member of the *Katipunan* from Cavite, was elected president of the revolutionary government that was to be established and thereby replaced Bonifacio as the foremost leader of the Philippine Revolution. A spirited campaign by the Spaniards against the Filipino revolutionaries drove Aguinaldo and his forces to Bulacan Province. There, a short-lived Biak-na-bato Republic was established in June 1897, and a constitution was adopted in November 1897. A military stalemate between Spanish and Filipino forces resulted in a truce in December 1897; and so the Biak-na-bato Republic was of very short duration.

After the outbreak of the Spanish-Cuban/American War in April 1898 and the defeat of the Spanish fleet by Adm. George Dewey in the Battle of Manila Bay on 1 May 1898, the Revolution against Spain resumed with the return of Aguinaldo from voluntary exile in Hong Kong where he had been staying in accord with a truce proclaimed in December 1897. Aguinaldo's task as leader of the Revolution was to set up a government that it was hoped would take over after the Spaniards were driven from the Philippines. He had hoped for U.S. cooperation in this enterprise, and he was encouraged initially by the seemingly sympathetic U.S. response to Filipino revolutionary actions against the Spaniards. On 25 May 1898 Aguinaldo established a dictatorial government, which was replaced by a revolutionary government on 23 June 1898. On 12 June 1898 Philippine independence was proclaimed at Kawit, Cavite, but that event had no official U.S. representation. Local governments were organized in areas under revolutionary control. Even while Filipino-U.S. relations became increasingly tense as the United States determined to take over positions in Manila and elsewhere in the archipelago, Aguinaldo proceeded to organize his government.

A revolutionary constitutional congress was convened in Malolos on 15 September 1898 to draft a constitution for a Philippine Republic. The constitution was promulgated on 21 January 1899, and the First Philippine Republic was proclaimed on 23 January 1899. The Malolos Republic was a republican and parliamentary government dominated by an educated elite of *ilustrados* (intellectuals). The Republic undertook several activities to make its deals and aspirations known to the world. It founded an official organ, *El Heraldo de la Revolucion* (subsequently known as the *Gaceta de Filipinas*); it opened schools, including the Universidad Literaria de Filipinas; and it created diplomatic missions abroad—in the United States, Japan, Great Britain, France, and Australia—to seek recognition of Philippine independence.

The republic established at Malolos did not survive because of the U.S. victory in the Philippine War, 1899–1902. Less than two weeks after the Malolos Republic was inaugurated, armed hostilities broke out between the Filipino revolutionaries and U.S. military forces in the Phil-

ippines, marking the beginning of the Philippine War. In the face of U.S. military superiority and disunity in the ranks of the Filipino leaders (conservative *ilustrados* in the Malolos Republic, eager for U.S. protection in exchange for internal autonomy, abandoned the revolution), Aguinaldo ordered his troops to shift to guerrilla warfare beginning in November 1899, and a brutal series of counterinsurgency campaigns ensued. Aguinaldo retreated from one provincial capital to another as the U.S. military pursued him. Finally, on 24 March 1901, Aguinaldo was captured in the mountain regions of Palanan, Isabela Province, and on 2 April 1901, he took his oath of allegiance to the United States. On 19 April 1901 he appealed to all Filipinos to accept the sovereignty of the United States. The existence of the revolutionary government came to an end officially when on 4 July 1901 U.S. military government ceased to exist in the Philippines.

Bernardita Reyes Churchill

REFERENCES

Teodoro A. Agoncillo, *The Revolt of the Masses, The Story of Bonifacio and the Katipunan* (Univ. of the Philippines Pr., 1956); Teodoro A. Agoncillo, *Malolos, The Crisis of the Republic* (Univ. of the Philippines Pr., 1960).

The Philippine Scouts

Philippine Scouts were combat units of the United States Army consisting of Filipinos recruited to fight troops commanded by Emilio Aguinaldo y Famy and other anti-U.S. groups in the years following the Philippine War (1899–1902). Scout units existed within the United States Army until 1947. The term "scout" in reference to these units is a misnomer dating from the days of the earliest use of Filipino soldiers by U.S. forces. After 1901 these troops were never organized or intended exclusively for scouting purposes, but were in fact similar in all ways to other combat units of the United States Army (Franklin, p. 39).

Philippine Scout units were originally created to aid U.S. Army troops in the Philippines, both volunteers and regulars, who had no experience in fighting irregular forces or with colonial rule (Asprey, vol. 1, p. 187). The jungle guerrilla warfare encountered by U.S. Army forces in the Philippines after February 1899 was strange and frustrating. Most U.S. soldiers lacked any knowledge of Filipino races, cultures, languages, and religions and were completely ignorant of Philippine geography. They were frustrated by the war, found the climate disagreeable, and resented the Filipino people for their seeming lack of support against enemy forces. Rumors of atrocities committed on captured rebels meant to "settle the score" were an indication of the growing U.S. frustration (Woolard, pp. 53–54).

Many military leaders soon realized that the answer to U.S. pacification difficulties could be found in the Filipinos themselves. Despite signs of increasing resistance to colonial rule throughout the islands, it was discovered that numerous groups of potential martial value were willing to cooperate with U.S. forces. One such group were the Macabebes from the region surrounding the village of the same name in Pampanga Province, Luzon. Due to past affiliations with the Spanish military, the Macabebes were unsympathetic to Aguinaldo and were despised by other Filipinos, especially Tagalogs. In early 1899 the Macabebes came to the attention of Lt. Matthew A. Batson, 4th Cavalry, who had difficulty maneuvering his troopers over the many waterways in Northern Luzon. Batson hired Macabebes as boatmen and guides and found them so useful in these tasks, and as scouts and interpreters, that he suggested through his superiors that Maj. Gen. Henry W. Lawton enlist Macabebes in the United States Army (Woolard, pp. 3–10; Tabaniag, pp. 8–9; Cruz, p. 102). Lawton agreed, and despite the initial misgivings of Maj. Gen. Elwell S. Otis, commander of the United States Army forces in the Philippines, and Secretary of War Elihu Root (Elliott, pp. 170–171), the first unit of Macabebe Scouts was organized on 10 September 1899 (*Report of Major General E.S. Otis, U.S.A., Commanding Division of the Philippines, 1 September 1899–5 May 1900*, Special Order no. 112, pp. 13–14; Cruz, pp. 105–106).

The Macabebes performed well in Pampanga Province. They inspired fear in the native population, guided U.S. troops, and harassed outlaw and rebel bands. The propensity of Macabebes to rob and abuse Tagalogs and to treat captives cruelly, however, caused General Otis to move slowly in employing Macabebes more fully. Nonetheless, their service in Luzon demonstrated their usefulness and led to the creation of four more Macabebe companies of 100 men

each (Woolard, pp. 12–43 passim; Franklin, p. 7).

The concept of using indigenous peoples against one another to further imperial rule was already popular among Europeans and was adopted by U.S. authorities (Ward, pp. 793–805). Batson's original Macabebe units were reorganized in late May 1900, and further units of Macabebes, and later Tagalogs, and Ilocanos, in numbers of 120 each, were formed as the Philippine Squadron of Cavalry, United States Army. Although they lacked specific legal standing within the army, their reputation as loyal and excellent fighters soon spread. By late 1900, both Congress and the Philippine Commission, on the advice of military officers, unanimously decided that large numbers of native troops should be raised for pacification purposes and to allow the discharge of U.S. volunteer units (*Annual Report of the Philippine Commission, 1901*, p. 77).

Proponents cited numerous advantages for using indigenous troops. Filipino units could replace U.S. troops in rural outposts; U.S. soldiers were not well suited, or trained, for guerrilla warfare; Filipinos were acquainted with native languages and habits; the cost of using Filipinos was cheaper than the cost of using white troops; and the enlistment of Filipinos would inspire others to cooperate with U.S. authorities against the guerrillas (*Annual Report of the Philippine Commission, 1901*, pp. 79–80; *Annual Report of the Philippine Commission, 1900–1903*, p. 181; Schirmer, p. 227). Loyalty and reliability were concerns, but the commission believed this was guaranteed by "judicious selection and discipline." Spain held the islands before 1896 with only 5,000 regulars, relying on loyal Filipino forces until the end, even though they were abused by their officers and were poorly paid, housed, fed, and equipped. Great Britain's example in using Indian sepoys throughout the British Empire was also repeatedly cited (Ward, pp. 800–801; *Annual Report of the Philippine Commission, 1901*, pp. 80–81). The commission concluded that the organization of indigenous regiments was timely and could have been initiated at least a year before (*Annual Report of the Philippine Commission, 1901*, pp. 80–81).

The favorable findings of U.S. leaders in the Philippines were read avidly by Secretary of War Root. He proposed to Congress that Filipinos be enlisted on a large scale for military service and, on 2 February 1901, Congress authorized the president to enlist Philippine natives for service in the army. These "Scouts" were to be organized in squadrons or battalions, not to exceed a total of 12,000 men (*Annual Report of the War Department, 1904*, p. 17; Schirmer, p. 277). They were to be paid by the United States Treasury like U.S. regulars. Between 1899 and September 1901 privates received $15.60 per month and sergeant majors $30 monthly. In addition, they received $3 per month clothing allowance, and a $0.13 daily food ration (*General Orders and Circulars*, General Order no. 25). After September 1901 Scout pay was halved to avoid a massive economic dislocation of the Philippine economy. Neither the pay rates of U.S. scout officers nor the scout clothing and ration allowances were reduced. To the gratification of the War Department the retrenchments had no effect on scout enlistments or morale, and the average Filipino scout at this point cost one-half that of his U.S. counterpart, about $500 annually (*Annual Report of the Philippine Commission, 1901*, p. 78; Tabaniag, p. 11; Cruz, p. 131; Forbes, vol. 1, p. 200; Woolard, pp. 59, 156–159; Blount, p. 600). The total cost of the entire scout force between 1903–1914 was just over $11 million (Miller, pp. 81–82; Elliott, p. 524).

Scout uniforms, rations, and equipment were similar to those of U.S. Army officers and enlisted men. In keeping with the practices of other colonial armies, however, scouts received outdated weapons, initially .45-caliber U.S. Springfield carbines, models 1873 to 1878, which fired black powder cartridges. These were later replaced by .30-caliber model 1903 Springfield rifles (Woolard, pp. 131–132; Franklin, p. 13).

The 1901 act of Congress initiated full-scale recruitment of Filipinos. Originally, scouts were enlisted according to their ethnic background or geographic region and, except in Mindanao, served outside the province of their recruitment. It was soon discovered that many ethnic groups were traditional enemies of other groups within their home regions. Taking advantage of traditional enmities, the army deployed scouts in the same areas where they were raised. As the war diminished in intensity, scouts from different ethnic groups were placed in the same unit to prevent further intensification of ethnic rivalries and animosities. This experiment proved unsuccessful, and new Scout battalions were homogenous ethnic units (*Roster of Troops Serving in the Division of the Philippines, Maj. Gen. George W.*

Davis, U.S.A., Commanding, p. 6; Cruz, pp. 130–131; Franklin, Table B-1; Woolard, pp. 72, 237–238). Each scout was required to take an oath to "obey and abide by all such laws, orders, and regulations," as stated by the articles of war. Each man was enlisted for three years (*General Orders and Circulars*, General Order no. 25; Franklin, p. 9; Woolard, pp. 55–57).

The United States Army intended the Philippine Scouts to be a counterinsurgency force capable of successfully penetrating the countryside in small numbers and defeating anti-U.S. groups on their own terms. Units larger than company-size were seen as impractical for these purposes, and Scout units were initially organized only as companies. As the war ended and the conventional military role of the Scouts increased, they were reorganized into battalions, then regiments and, by 1922, a full tactical division (Woolard, p. 256). In total, prior to 1917, the United States Army enlisted 11 companies of Macabebes, 13 of Ilocanos, 4 of Tagalogs, 2 of Bikols, and 16 of Visayans. Later recruiters enlisted Filipinos from Bohol, Panay, Leyte, Negros, and Cebu. By mid-1901, 5,500 Filipinos had joined the Philippine Scouts, and enlistments peaked at nearly 8,000 men in 100 companies in 1916. The Philippine Scouts never reached their authorized strength of 12,000 men (Elliott, p. 172; Chaput, p. 5; Franklin, pp. 66–85, for all Scout units, 1899–1935).

Scouts companies were always commanded by U.S. Army officers, either regulars or volunteers, holding the ranks of 1st and 2nd lieutenant. Filipinos noncommissioned officers were selected by commanders from the ranks. After 1914, Filipinos were admitted to the United States Military Academy for training as officers of Philippine Scouts, but as late as 1934 only 17 had taken advantage of this opportunity. Officers applying for scout duty had to have two years of military service and be between ages 21 and 30, single, physically fit, and of good moral character. Candidates had to agree to volunteer for at least four years of scout duty (*Roster of Troops*, p. 61; Tabaniag, p. 13; *Appointment of Second Lieutenants in the Philippine Scouts*, p. 7; Woolard, pp. 63–64). Competent U.S. officers were believed to be the key to the success of the entire program because Filipinos were thought to be capable fighters if they were properly paid, fed, disciplined, and led (*Annual Report of the Philip-*

pine Commission, 1903, p. 46; Graff, p. 121; Ward, pp. 793–798 passim, 804).

The scouts rendered extensive service during the Philippine War between 1899 and 1902. Thirty-four scout companies served alongside U.S. Army units in the Military Department of Luzon, 13 in the Department of the Visayas, and three companies in Mindanao Department. Scouts fought guerrilla forces in the battles of Santiago, Zaragoza, and Carmen in Central Luzon and on the islands of Negros, Samar, and Leyte. Scouts rarely operated independently of U.S. units in large numbers until the latter stages of the war and frequently performed noncombat functions (e.g., garrison and occupation duty, and construction of roads, bridges, and telegraph lines).

The two most notable scout achievements of the Philippine War occurred in February and March 1901 when a Macabebe unit under Gen. Frederick Funston captured rebel leader Emilio Aguinaldo, and a company of Leyte Scouts captured Vincente Lukban, the major leader in Leyte and Samar. The captures of these men were a major setback to the Filipino bid for independence and signaled the beginning of the end of the war (Chaput, pp. 5–9; Tabaniag, p. 24; for Aguinaldo's capture see Funston, p. 396).

Following the war, U.S. and Filipino units increased their operations against various anti-U.S. peasant revolts inspired by religious leaders. In the period 1902–1914 scouts were involved in over 28 major engagements and thousands of lesser actions, suffering over 1,000 casualties from all causes. They saw action in Luzon, Paragua, Jolo, Bantayan, Samar, Mindanao, and Laguna (Franklin, p. 49) and battled such groups as the Pulahanes, the Moros, the Colorados, Cazadores, Babailanes, Santo Niño, Soldaros Militantes de la Igelsia, Dios-Dios, Cruz-Cruz, and Anting-Anting. Most of these revolts were short-lived, but others, like those led by Macario Sakay and Artemio Ricarte, lasted for years and required the assistance of white troops of the United States Army to quell (Salamanca, pp. 178–181; Sturtevant, p. 119). Operations in 1905 alone involved 3,500 scouts and 11,000 other U.S. troops and resulted in the capture of 9,155 rebels and the deaths of 25,000 more (Forbes, pp. 205–206).

The Moros of Mindanao continued to resist U.S. rule despite the large number of scouts in the region, and the United States Army was forced to intervene on a massive scale in 1906. White U.S. forces stayed until 1913 when the scouts could again hold the province alone. Pacification of the entire archipelago was completed by this time, except for sporadic outbreaks which were suppressed by scout units. By 1917 only one U.S. Army garrison was located south of Manila with all remaining posts being manned by scouts. At no time between 1899 and 1947 did Philippine Scouts serve in combat beyond the territorial confines of the Philippine archipelago.

Under U.S. officers Filipinos performed well. According to the reports of the Philippine Commission, the War Department, and U.S. Army officers, they "uniformly performed faithful and effective service" and "were ready to follow, or precede their officers into any danger, blindly and without question" (*Annual Reports of the Philippine Commission, 1900–1903*, p. 182; Farinas, p. 181; Ward, pp. 798–799). Desertion rates were lower than those of white troops (7.26 percent for whites in 1926, for example, compared to .08 for scouts), and scout service was popular in most regions (*Annual Reports of the Philippine Commission, 1900–1903*, p. 182; *Report of Major General E.S. Otis*, p. 365; Graff, p. 121). Although never considered the equal of U.S. soldiers, scouts were considered adept at "ferreting out insurgents and criminals," and in understanding local motives and methods (Chaput, p. 6). Scout discipline was described as good, and the scouts proved themselves to be effective and loyal. They were deemed instrumental in maintaining peace and order and were thought capable of defending the islands (with U.S. support) against all enemies (Elliott, p. 171). Several officers stated that the scouts were the "best soldiers in the islands today." They were more amenable to discipline than white troops, were content to serve in rural outposts, and complained less and worked harder. They shot well, were less prone to contract tropical diseases than white troops, and were able to outmarch both infantry and cavalry (Elliott, p. 171). Generals Arthur MacArthur, Funston, Lawton, and Frank D. Baldwin praised the scouts as "the finest body of native troops in existence" who "as an auxiliary force to our regulars . . . [were] unexcelled" (*Report of Major General E.S. Otis*, pp. 13–14; *Annual Report of the War Department, 1900*, p. 266; Tabaniag, p. 20; Franklin, pp. 50–54). The Philippine Commission concluded that "the service of native troops has conclusively shown the wisdom of their creation (*Annual Report of the Philippine Commission, 1904*, p. 21).

The scouts did have numerous critics who cited the general lawlessness and brutalities that characterized their units, especially the Macabebes (*American Imperialism*, pp. 64–134 passim). Major General Otis reported that most scouts considered looting and torture part of their normal duties and that Filipinos feared the approach of the native scouts, be they Macabebe, Tagalog, or Visayan (*Report of Major General E.S. Otis*, pp. 14, 365). General Funston confessed that many scouts lacked a great deal of intelligence (Blount, pp. 403-404), while an officer who had served with both scout and Philippine Constabulary forces considered them "outfits of doubtful loyalty," which were inadequate for maintenance of public order (Funston, pp. 399). U.S. anti-imperialists were certain of the immorality of recruiting Filipinos, whom they considered innocent people uninitiated in the brutalities of modern warfare (Esty, p. 11).

The greatest hatred for the scouts was harbored by Aguinaldo and the guerrillas who controlled large portions of the islands when U.S. forces first arrived. Collaborators, especially those in the scouts, were dealt with harshly, usually being shot on sight (*Annual Report of the Philippine Commission, 1901*, p. 17). Aguinaldo declared in January 1901 that hiring Filipinos to fight Filipinos in contravention of the International Treaty of Geneva only sowed the seeds of future civil war, which would further devastate a poor and ravaged nation after the war (Kalaw, p. 273). Nonetheless, the Philippine Scouts were an integral part of the U.S. colonial government in the Philippines and served U.S. interests well for nearly 50 years.

Clayton D. Laurie

REFERENCES

Robert Asprey, *War in the Shadows: The Guerrilla In History*, 2 vols. (Doubleday, 1975); James H. Blount, *The American Occupation of the Philippines, 1898–1912* (Putnam, 1912); Donald Chaput, "The Founding of the Leyte Scouts," *Leyte-Samar Studies*, 9 (Feb. 1975); Romeo Cruz, "Filipino Collaboration With the Americans, 1899–1902," M.A. thesis, University of the Philippines, 1956; Charles B. Elliott, *The Philippines to the End of the Commission Government: A Study in Tropical Democracy* (Bobbs-Merrill, 1917); Thomas B. Esty, *Views of the American Press on the Philippines* (Esty & Esty, 1899); Rod J. Farinas, *The Philippine Constabulary* (Constable, 1976); W. Cameron Forbes, *The Philippine Islands* (Houghton Mifflin, 1928); Charles H. Franklin, *History of the Philippine Scouts: 1899-1934* (Army War College, 1935); Frederick Funston, *Memories of Two Wars: Cuban and Philippine Experiences* (Scribner's, 1911); Henry F. Graff, *American Imperialism and the Philippine Insurrection* (Little, Brown, 1969); Theodore M. Kalaw, *The Philippine Revolution*, reprint ed. (J.B. Vargas Filipina Foundation, 1969); Stuart Creighton Miller, *"Benevolent Assimilation": The American Conquest of the Philippines, 1899–1903* (Yale Univ. Pr., 1982); Bonifacio S. Salamanca, *The Filipino Reaction to American Rule, 1901–1913* (Shoe String Pr., 1968); Daniel Schirmer, *Republic or Empire, American Resistance to the Philippine War* (Schenkman, 1972); David R. Sturtevant, *Popular Uprisings in the Philippines, 1840–1940* (Cornell Univ. Pr., 1976); Antonio Tabaniag, "The Pre-War Philippine Scouts," *Journal of East Asia Studies* 9 (April 1960); Heath Twichell, Jr., *Allen: The Biography of an Army Officer, 1859–1930* (Rutgers Univ. Pr., 1974); U.S. Army, Philippines Division, *Appointment of Second Lieutenants in the Philippine Scouts* (U.S. Government Printing Office, 1917); U.S. Army, Philippines Division, *General Orders and Circulars, 7 April 1900* (Headquarters, Department of the Pacific & 8th Army Corps, Headquarters, Division of the Pacific, 1900); U.S. Army, Philippines Division, *Roster of Troops Serving in the Division of the Philippines, Maj. Gen. George W. Davis, U.S.A., Commanding* (Bureau of Public Printing, 1902); U.S. Philippine Commission, *Annual Report of the Philippine Commission, 1901* (Government Printing Office, 1901); U.S. Philippine Commission, *Annual Report of the Philippine Commission, 1904*; U.S. Philippine Commission, *Annual Reports of the Philippine Commission, 1900–1903* (Government Printing Office, 1904); U.S. War Department, *Annual Report of the War Department, 1900* (Government Printing Office, 1900); U.S. War Department, *Annual Report of the War Department, 1904*; U.S. War Department, *Report of Major General E.S. Otis, U.S.A., Commanding Division of the Philippines, 1 September 1899–5 May 1900* (U.S. Government Printing Office, 1900); J.W. Ward, "The Use of Native Troops in Our Possessions," *Journal of the Military Service Institution of the United States*, 31 (1902), 793–805; James Richard Woolard, "The Philippine Scouts: The Development of America's Colonial Army," Ph.D. diss., Ohio State Univ., 1975.

See also Philippine Constabulary.

Philippine War (1899–1902)

The U.S. war with the Philippines had its roots in the war against Spain at the close of the 19th century. The removal of Spain from the Philippines provided the opportunity for Filipino nationalist forces to project their power into the political vacuum that was created. However, much to their chagrin, the United States quickly stepped into the breech, supplanted the Spanish and prevented Filipino forces from extending their control into Manila and much of the Philippine archipelago. For the United States, the Spanish-Cuban/American War in 1898 was a watershed in U.S. politico-military policy. While most earlier U.S. politico-military efforts focused primarily on domestic issues and extension of the federal government (e.g., continental expansion and the Civil War), the war with Spain propelled the United States into the external world and marked its entrance onto the world stage. This was reinforced by the occupation of the Philippines, making the United States a colonial power. At the same time, the involvement in the Philippines also plunged the United States into a conflict with Filipino nationalist forces and later with the Moros (Philippine Muslims). While the war with Spain was short-lived, the wars with the Filipinos and the Moros were more challenging and complex, characterized by conventional and unconventional operations and involving operations throughout the archipelago.

When Commodore George Dewey's naval squadron entered Manila Bay and for all practical purposes ended Spanish control of the Philippines, few in the United States envisioned a long U.S. presence. Nonetheless, President William McKinley ordered the dispatch of a U.S. expeditionary force to complete the destruction of Spanish power and bring order to the islands. Part of the mission of the expeditionary force was to provide a political education to the Filipinos regarding the benefits of democracy and U.S.-style political system. The landing of U.S. forces and their efforts to prevent the Filipino forces from entering Manila signaled the start of the U.S.-Philippine conflict that was to last until 1902. For most, U.S. military operations in the Philippines were highlighted by the campaign against the forces led by Emilio Aguinaldo y Famy with the end coming officially in 1902.

However, a more accurate view is that the U.S. military engaged in three types of conflicts during the period. The first was against Spanish regular forces, which was almost bloodless and marked primarily by naval warfare. The second was against the Filipino nationalist forces seeking independence from the United States. And third was the longer conflict against the Moros in the southern Philippines. During the campaign against Filipino national forces, the U.S. military initially engaged in a conventional-type war as the Filipinos used conventional tactics. In a later phase, the war became unconventional as Filipino forces shifted to unconventional tactics and guerrilla warfare. The third conflict was primarily a protracted conflict against the Moros which lasted until the beginning of World War I. Interestingly, the legacy of the Moro conflict in the early 20th century is reflected today in the Philippines in the Moro Liberation Army's struggles against the government in Manila. The main focus here is on the Philippine War, with particular attention on the unconventional phase.

The conflict against regular Spanish forces was fought by a mix of U.S. Army regulars, state militia, and volunteers. This was relatively bloodless with the Spanish ground forces putting up token resistance before surrendering to U.S. forces. The outcome was decided, not necessarily by the ground forces, but by U.S. naval action in Manila Bay. Commodore Dewey's squadron had handily defeated the Spanish naval forces in a short engagement. With the surrender of Spanish troops, the U.S. military faced the Philippine nationalist forces. During the first months of the latter conflict, President McKinley ordered the mustering out of about 100,000 volunteers, with the regiments in the Philippines remaining until 1899, ending the first period of operations.

Military operations against the Philippine nationalist forces were undertaken by U.S. Army regulars and volunteers. This war can be divided into periods with each reflecting a particular type of conflict: "the conventional war in 1899; the unconventional (guerrilla) war under Emilio Aguinaldo until 1901; and the fragmented unconventional (guerrilla) war in the post-Aguinaldo period until 1902" (Sarkesian, p. 168).

The Battle of Manila set the stage for the type of warfare that would be fought against the Philippine army during the first period. United States forces prevented Filipino forces from entering Manila during the peace negotiations with Spanish forces. Angered by the U.S. insistence that Filipino forces not enter Manila, the Filipino revolutionary government ordered preparations to engage U.S. forces. Eventually, Aguinaldo and his primary commander, Gen. António Luna created an army of 80,000. Further, the rudiments of a central government were established. Military operations were triggered when a patrol from the Filipino forces challenged a U.S. guard post on the outskirts of Manila. Seeing this as a challenge to all U.S. forces, the VIII Army Corps under Gen. Elwell S. Otis initiated operations against the Filipino forces. Within a short time, U.S. forces engaged the 40,000-member Filipino army around Manila.

At this time U.S. forces consisted of both volunteers and regulars. Immediately following the Battle of Manila, the Aguinaldo forces withdrew and tried to operate against U.S. forces in a series of conventional battles characterized by trench warfare and attempts by the Filipinos to hold specific locations. The effort to maintain centrally controlled conventional forces was based on Aguinaldo's attempt to develop an effective central government. "[H]e realized that only a well-armed and well-disciplined force, completely under the command of the central government, could suppress challenges from other provincial leaders" (Linn, p. 13). But his attempt to develop a conventional army, yet retain some of the flexibility of a guerrilla army, proved disastrous.

U.S. forces consistently routed the Filipino forces, particularly when artillery and naval gunfire were used against the Filipinos. In trying to stop U.S. forces from advancing beyond Manila toward their proclaimed capital of Malolos, the Filipinos constructed a "Hindenberg line of entrenchments between Caloocan and Malolos, and positioned about 16,000 Filipino insurgents to block any American advance" (Wolff, p. 240). A U.S. force of approximately 11,000 regulars and volunteers supported by artillery captured Malolos after a series of sharp skirmishes. "The description of the capture of the city reads like a standard operation of conventional forces in a built-up area" (Sarkesian, p. 169).

By the time the Filipino forces had retreated to Malolos, it had become clear that they could not stand up to U.S. forces in conventional battle. Subsequently, a series of lesser battles confirmed this, and Aguinaldo retreated to a mountain stronghold in northeastern Luzon. It was here that Aguinaldo announced to his forces that it was time to change tactics and shift to guerrilla

war. The Philippine Army was disbanded and dispersed to the hills where elements formed the nucleus of various guerrilla units to continue the campaign against U.S. forces. Thus, by November 1899, the conventional war had been lost by the Filipinos, and the second period (unconventional war) began.

The unconventional period was more difficult for U.S. forces. While the number of casualties is not necessarily a definitive sign of the nature of the war, it does support the difficulty facing U.S. forces in engaging the Filipino guerrilla armies. The character of unconventional conflict—ambushes, raids, and close-in fighting—doubled the number of U.S. casualties. "The Americans were not fighting a uniformed army. They were fighting determined groups of men who tilled the fields by day and stalked outposts by night. The new type of warfare was infinitely more dangerous" (Sexton, p. 238).

U.S. forces responded by engaging in what is today called search-and-destroy operations. U.S. troops would strike in an area thought to contain revolutionary forces, attempt to kill or capture them, disrupt their operations and sources of support, then return to Manila. No attempt was made to hold territory. As was the case decades later during the Vietnam War, the revolutionary forces would return to the area vacated by U.S. forces. In sum, Filipinos learned that regardless of the effectiveness of U.S. forces in the area, they would eventually withdraw and the Filipino forces could return. The reports of such operations emanating from General Otis's headquarters were highly optimistic and painted a picture of military success. The fact was that after every operation, the Filipino revolutionary forces reestablished themselves in the very area the United States Army claimed to have cleared. Shortly after, another U.S. strike was needed in the same area. The similarities with the initial years of U.S. operations in Vietnam are clear.

General Otis's military training in conventional conflict robbed him of the temperament to deal with unconventional conflicts. Indeed, he refused to accept the notion that Filipino revolutionary forces were struggling to "free" their homeland. His references were primarily to bandits operating in the hinterlands. But these optimistic reports were increasingly challenged by the realities of the conflict and raised serious questions in Washington regarding Otis's competence. Interestingly, some of the serious questions were raised by newsmen visiting the Philippines. Later, Otis asked to be relieved and was replaced by Gen. Arthur MacArthur followed by Adna R. Chaffee, and later by Gen. Robert H. Hall, during which time a civilian administration was established under William H. Taft. It was shortly before Otis left the Philippines that the United States Army shifted its tactics and operations.

The organizational structure was changed "from that of a divisional tactical organization to that of a territorial occupational system of organization" (Baclagon, p. 123). Also, the area of operations was divided into four departments: Northern Luzon, Southern Luzon, Visayas, and Mindanao. Otis was appointed military governor in Manila controlling the four departments. Equally important, the United States Army shifted its tactics and operational guidelines after the assumption of command by General MacArthur.

Taking over from Otis, MacArthur put into place an amnesty program and attempted to establish measures designed to attract the support of Filipinos to U.S. efforts. This established the groundwork for the eventual success against the Filipino nationalist forces.

MacArthur initiated a pacification policy intended at isolating guerrilla units from the Filipino population. In addition to preventing the guerrilla forces from drawing food and recruits, the effort was aimed at breaking the psychological links between guerrilla units and villages. Again, there are clear similarities to efforts in Vietnam in the 1960s. Further, the pacification policy combined with zones of protection took the initiative from the revolutionary forces.

In every instance when the Army stormed and destroyed a village, it promptly rebuilt it, reopened its market, hacked out new roads, and set up a school. It was an effective military policy. "Benevolent pacification" and "beneficient administration" were key words in McKinley's vocabulary, and the emphasis of the army was always on reform rather than control" (Goldhurst, p. 101).

At the same time, the United States Army engaged in search-and-destroy operations. Revolutionary forces in the zone of operations of various U.S. units would be sought out and destroyed, while "peaceful" Filipinos reaped the rewards of compliance. In these zones, U.S. forces placed the population in controlled areas.

There, food and other benefits were provided, while outside these areas food was confiscated. Further, Filipinos caught outside these areas without justification were presumed to be members of the Filipino forces and were killed or imprisoned.

The pacification policy involved the establishment of an indigenous government in towns captured by U.S. forces, allowing local Filipinos to govern themselves. But the Filipino revolutionary forces established their own administrative structure throughout the Philippines, which in many areas was recognized by Filipinos as the "real" government. The Filipino forces tried to ensure compliance by threatening and killing those who directly cooperated with the United States. A similar pattern appeared in the Vietnam conflict in the 1960s and 1970s.

But the tide began to turn in 1900. By that time, U.S. military forces reached a peak strength of 70,000, most of them consisting of veterans of Philippine campaigns. Moreover, MacArthur's pacification policy was beginning to take hold. At this point, the policy included support of political parties, the organization of local governments, and development of a variety of social and economic projects. Beginning in 1901 "the American military placed continual pressure on the revolutionaries on military, social, and economic fronts" (Linn, p. 25). At the same time, some Filipinos felt that their future and well-being rested with U.S. success. Filipino auxiliaries were organized and protected their villages and towns against Filipino guerrilla forces, freeing U.S. forces to undertake operations against Filipino revolutionary forces. With the carrot, MacArthur also used the "stick," instituting a rigorous program of confiscating the land holdings of revolutionaries and of closely monitoring the activities of relatives of revolutionaries. Many were arrested and deported. It did not take long for many major actors in the revolutionary movement to realize that continued support of the Filipino forces would lead to their own loss of power and prestige and could result in imprisonment (Linn, pp. 24–25).

In combination with the U.S. strategy, two events occurred that sealed the fate of the Filipino forces. Emilio Aguinaldo was captured by Col. Frederick Funston and a band of scouts in March 1901. Earlier, the commander of Philippine forces in Cavite Province surrendered with almost all of his men and weapons. What was particularly important was that both leaders called for the end of Filipino resistance and acceptance of U.S. sovereignty over the islands.

Following the capture of Aguinaldo, central direction of Filipino forces was totally destroyed—not that there was a great deal of central direction before his capture. What followed was considerable fragmentation of the Filipino effort with guerrilla warfare being undertaken on the initiative of local commanders with little if any coordination with other commanders. This consisted primarily of hit-and-run raids and ambushes. But as one account from the Philippine perspective notes, "guerrilla resistance had become a nightmare of American troops. Being incessantly booed and fired upon from cover, was, if anything, more nerve-racking than out-and-out fighting" (Constantino, p. 293). At the same time, U.S. Army commanders in the various departments and provinces applied their own experience and understanding of the local area to develop tactics suited to the particularly area. Whether such local initiatives were undertaken as a deliberate strategy or simply a reaction by local U.S. commanders is not clear. But in any case, this flexibility and adaptability proved to be increasingly successful against the now fragmented Filipino effort (Linn, *U.S. Army and Counterinsurgency in the Philippine War*).

By 1902 the conflict had taken on harshness reflecting the character of unconventional conflicts. U.S. troops reacted with a vengeance upon learning of the massacre of U.S. soldiers at Balangiga in September 1901. The subsequent U.S. operation under the command of Brig. Gen. Jacob H. Smith provoked so much controversy in the United States that it led to a congressional investigation (Sarkesian, p. 176). Again, certain parallels can be detected with military operations in Vietnam decades later. By summer 1902, Filipino resistance had virtually ceased. "So the insurrection faded away in the manner of all such struggles, a minor sequel to a comic-opera war, lost in the clamor and shuffle of greater events; and the United States found herself in possession of an Asian archipelago as a gift, which under other circumstances, might well have been spurned" (Wolff, p. 363).

But no sooner had this conflict faded than another began. The conflict against the Moros was to prove exasperating and protracted. Even though it did not receive a lot of attention in the United States because of its sporadic nature and

later because of the unfolding events in Europe, it continued to challenge U.S. politico-military policy and strategy in unconventional conflicts. Perhaps more important in the long run, it was to be a proving ground for John J. Pershing and his future involvement in the pursuit of Francisco "Pancho" Villa and in World War I.

The Philippine War revealed the tendency of U.S. military forces to respond to such conflicts in an *ad hoc* fashion ignoring "lessons learned" from the past. Although the U.S. military had a long history of engaging in unconventional conflicts dating back to the Revolutionary War, little, if any of this institutional experience was reflected in response to the unconventional periods of the war. Indeed, it was only by trial-and-error at the operational unit level in the latter part of the Philippine War that successful tactics were adopted. Further, it became clear that military means alone could not determine the outcome of the war. This should have become part of U.S. military institutional memory and incorporated into U.S. politico-military strategy. But these "lessons" were soon forgotten. The conclusions of Russell F. Weigley in his analysis of U.S. military operations against the Seminole Indians in the pre-Civil War era is particularly appropriate here.

> A historical pattern was beginning to work itself out: occasionally the American Army has had to wage guerrilla war, but guerrilla war is so incongruous to the natural methods and habits of a stable and well-to-do society that the American Army has tended to regard it as abnormal and to forget about it whenever possible. Each new experience with irregular warfare has required, then, that appropriate techniques be learned all over (Weigley, p. 161).

Nowhere was this more true than in the U.S. involvement in Vietnam, particularly the initial phases. All of the earlier lessons had to be learned over again with reactions from the people of the United States and later from U.S. political leaders reminiscent of reactions against the harshness of the war and U.S. tactics in the Philippine War. Indeed, it can be argued that the legacy of this earlier war surfaced in the public reaction to the Vietnam War during the late 1960s and early 1970s. Ignoring the lessons of the Philippine War in both military and political terms, a domestic environment was fashioned that induced a number of people in the United States to turn their wrath on the most visible manifestations of the United States in Vietnam—the U.S. military. In the long run, it was the U.S. foot soldier who paid the highest price and endured more than a decade of approbation from the U.S. public. A black marble memorial in Washington and parades honoring service in Vietnam a decade after the war cannot grasp the depth of the price paid by those who served, nor exorcise the "guilt" rooted in the U.S. psyche for virtually abandoning their military at the time of greatest need.

Sam C. Sarkesian

REFERENCES

Uldarico S. Baclagon, *Philippine Campaigns* (Graphic House, 1952); Renato Constantino and Letizia R. Constantino, *A History of the Philippines: From Spanish Colonization to the Second World War* (Monthly Review Pr., 1975); Richard Goldhurst, *Pipe, Clay, and Drill: John J. Pershing; The Classic American Soldier* (Reader's Digest Pr., 1977); Brian McAllister Linn, *The U.S. Army and Counterinsurgency in the Philippine War, 1899–1902* (Univ. of North Carolina Pr., 1989); Sam C. Sarkesian, *America's Forgotten Wars: The Counterrevolutionary Past and Lessons for the Future* (Greenwood Pr., 1984); William T. Sexton, *Soldiers in the Sun: An Adventure in Imperialism* (Military Service Pub. Co., 1939); Russell F. Weigley, *History of the United States Army* (Macmillan, 1967); Leon Wolff, *Little Brown Brother: How the United States Purchased and Pacified the Philippine Islands at the Century's Turn* (Doubleday, 1961).

See also list of entries at front of book for Philippine War (1899–1902).

Pilar, Gregorio Hilario del (1875–1899)

Filipino writers, with justification, have glorified the heroic martyrdom of Gregorio Hilario del Pilar at Tirad Pass in the Philippine War, 1899–1902. The "boy general" hailed from a Bulacan Province family of revolutionaries. Brother Pio served the Philippine Republic as a major general, while uncle Marcelo propagandized revolutionary doctrine.

As a youth, Gregorio embraced the cause of Filipino independence. He disseminated propaganda critical of Spain and, on one occasion, exchanged religious pamphlets for political leaflets in a Malolos chapel that a Spanish clergyman unknowingly gave out to the congregation. By late 1896, the 21-year-old graduate of Ateneo de Manila University became a Katipunan member and fought the Spanish in his native province, where he was wounded at Kakaron. There, he was also later commissioned a lieutenant.

In 1897, del Pilar arrived at Emilio Aguinaldo y Famy's refuge in Bulacan, asking permission to attack the Spaniards at Paombong. The foray, successful in the capture of booty, brought the young officer to Aguinaldo's attention and gained him promotion to lieutenant colonel. Together, they were exiled to Hong Kong and returned to the Philippines via Singapore in 1898. By the time of their meeting with Rear Adm. George Dewey on the *Olympia*, del Pilar had become Aguinaldo's trusted confidant. Given command of Bulacan and Nueva Ecija Provinces, he readily defeated the Spanish in both provinces and was quickly promoted to brigadier general.

As U.S. reinforcements poured into the Manila area, del Pilar, acting as Aguinaldo's emissary, offered proposals to avoid war with the United States. The Filipino sought amity with U.S. forces under conditions that would also satisfy the Philippine Republic's self-respect. Gen. Elwell S. Otis insolently told del Pilar "complete submission" was necessary.

When hostilities began and U.S. troops advanced on Malolos, del Pilar engaged them northwest of Manila as President Aguinaldo fled the republic's capital and moved to San Isidro, Neuva Ecija. At Quingua (present-day Plaridel), in April 1899, he inflicted a rout and losses on U.S. cavalry. Among the U.S. dead was Col. John M. Stotsenburg. But afterward, outnumbered and outmaneuvered along the Bagbag River, he failed to hold the line protecting an approach to Calumpit.

Meanwhile, del Pilar demonstrated his brutal side. When quarreling between Aguinaldo and Gen. António Narciso Luna resulted in the latter's assassination, the young general supervised the cruel punishment of Luna's assistants. Ironically, one of those tortured was the father of a girl del Pilar had wooed.

Otis, hoping to exploit the turmoil within revolutionary ranks, designed a trap for Aguinaldo. He ordered Gen. Loyd Wheaton to Pangasinan Province's Lingayen Gulf, site of Gen. Douglas MacArthur's later return to Luzon in World War II, while he sent Gen. Arthur MacArthur, Douglas's father, in northward pursuit of the Filipino leader. Del Pilar guarded Aguinaldo's rear defenses as U.S. troops chased him through Tarlac, Nueva Vizcaya, and

Pangasinan provinces. To ensure the fleeing president's escape, del Pilar stopped to fight a delaying action. He chose to deploy at Tirad Pass in Ilocos Sur. Over 14,000 feet high and providing a vista of the countryside, its thread-like path could accommodate only single-file access. The young general's 60 soldiers prepared defensive positions along the pass's slopes, which commanded the view beneath, and waited for the advancing enemy.

On 2 December 1899 Maj. Peyton C. March, freed by General Wheaton to run down Aguinaldo, encountered del Pilar at Tirad Pass. Unable either to see the concealed Filipinos or to force their trenches, the 300 U.S. soldiers, aided by an Igorot guide, scaled the summit and outflanked the defenders. In a short time, the Filipinos were overwhelmed and del Pilar, who had a shoulder wound, was shot when he tried to escape.

Del Pilar's corpse, which was plundered by souvenir hunters, remained unburied for 48 hours. Eventually, its odor caused local people to overlay it with soil. Before the battle, del Pilar had penned his own epigram in sentiments reminiscent of the martyred Nathan Hale: "What I do is done for my beloved country. No sacrifice can be too great."

Rodney J. Ross

REFERENCES

David Haward Bain, *Sitting in Darkness: Americans in the Philippines* (Houghton Mifflin, 1984); Nick Joaquin, *A Question of Heroes: Essays in Criticism on the Key Figures of Philippine History* (National Book Store, 1981); Teodoro M. Kalaw, *An Acceptable Holocaust: Life and Death of a Boy-General* (National Historical Commission, 1974); Teodoro M. Kalaw, *Gregorio H. Del Pilar: El Heroe de Tirad* (Bureau of Printing, 1930); James A. LeRoy, *The Americans in the Philippines* (Houghton Mifflin, 1914), 2 vols.

Pilar, Pio del
(1860 or 1865–1931)

Maj. Gen. Pio del Pilar played political and military roles in the Philippine Revolution. Aside from a wavering political allegiance, he commanded a Filipino force at the siege of Manila and gained notoriety for his hatred of the United States and his treatment of Filipinos disloyal to the cause.

An early revolutionary enthusiast, del Pilar sketched one of many flags used by the Katipunan. His design featured a triangle of equal sides with a *K* in each corner and a rising sun ascending behind a mount in the center. The three *K*'s symbolized Katass-tassan Kagalang-galang na Katipunan nang manga Anak nang Bayan, or Katipunan (Highest and Most Respectable Society of the Sons of the People). This was an important Filipino nationalist organization.

When the Cavite-based rebellion against Spain split in 1897 between Emilio Aguinaldo y Famy's Magdaló group and Andrés Bonifacio's Magdiwang faction, del Pilar supported the latter and signed an agreement at Naic, creating an independent government apart from Aguinaldo's at Tejeros. The document assigned command of military forces to del Pilar. After President Aguinaldo's faction apprehended Bonifacio, the revolutionary Council of War convicted him of treason and ordered his execution. Del Pilar, once more loyal to the president, urged the death sentence and successfully argued against any commutation. He later served as a member of the Philippine National Assembly, which met at Malolos in fall 1898 and ordained the Constitution.

In early June 1898, General del Pilar led Filipinos surrounding Spanish forces in the second zone of four about Manila. He held San Pedro Macati and neighboring areas southeast of the city. After a triumphant drive northward into Sampaloc, his troops forced enemy defenders to retreat from the Colgante Bridge to the Bridge of Spain, and, consequently, shortened the perimeter of the besieged Spaniards.

During the Spanish-Cuban/American War, del Pilar warned repeatedly of foreign threats. On 10 August 1898 he wired Aguinaldo an alarm about a rumored German invasion of the Philippines. Four days later, he began preparing defenses against a possible U.S. attack and communicated to Aguinaldo: "Most urgent. Ask send general to arrange avoid conflict which is probable." In desperation, del Pilar and Lt. Gen. Mariano Trías even considered collaboration with Spain as a means of forestalling U.S. intervention.

While in command of revolutionaries deployed parallel to the Pasig river north of Manila, del Pilar expressed a readiness to battle U.S. forces and bargained with the Spaniards to entice their surrender to him instead of the United States Army. In an effort to force a capitulation at Santa Ana, he cautioned the Spanish commander about a pending U.S. assault and, asserting Aguinaldo's authorization, pressured the Spaniard to yield. Apparently, Aguinaldo was aware of del Pilar's dickering with the Santa Ana commander and granted tacit approval to his field officer's initiative.

General del Pilar clung to the Paco and Pandacan suburbs of Manila despite Aguinaldo's ordering revolutionary troops to evacuate that city. He built fortifications, harassed city residents, and provoked U.S. authorities. His soldiers crossed into U.S. territory after dark, committing acts of thievery and abduction and causing disorder in the vicinity of Maj. Gen. Elwell S. Otis's billet. Most provocatively, del Pilar prevented a U.S. division commander from traveling through Filipino lines via the Pasig River.

Forced out of his Manila positions by the U.S. offensive at the beginning of the Philippine War in early 1899, del Pilar retreated eastward across the Pasig, still posing a threat to the city's rear. Maj. Gen. Henry W. Lawton attacked and dispersed del Pilar's demoralized troops, who subsequently resorted to guerrilla warfare in the Mariquina Valley and punished inhabitants suspected of disloyalty to the revolution. Lawton campaigned again in June to chase the depredator out of the valley and into the Morong Peninsula, which extends into Laguna de Bay. Del Pilar remained in his mountain hideaway east of Manila until falling into U.S. hands and being exiled to Guam after 1900.

Rodney J. Ross

REFERENCES

Teodoro A. Agoncillo and Milagros C. Guerrero, *History of the Filipino People*, 6th ed. (R.P. Garcia Pub. Co., 1983); Teodoro M. Kalaw, *The Philippine Revolution* (Vargas Filipiniana Foundation, 1969); James A. LeRoy, *The Americans in the Philippines* (Houghton Mifflin, 1914), 2 vols.; William T. Sexton, *Soldiers in the Sun: An Adventure in Imperialism* (Military Service Pub. Co., 1939); Leon Wolff, *Little Brown Brother: How the United States Purchased and Pacified the Philippine Islands at the Century's Turn* (Doubleday, 1961).

Pinega River Front, North Russia (1918–1919)

The Pinega River Front was the easternmost flank of the forces that engaged in the U.S. intervention in North Russia, 1918–1919. Located on a major tributary of the Northern Dvina River, the front was formed in August and September 1918 to protect the left flank of the Allied invasion forces on the Northern Dvina River Front and, if possible, to establish contact with Czechoslovak and anti-Bolshevik Russian units believed to be approaching the North from western Siberia.

Manned originally by anti-Bolshevik Russians, the Pinega River Front was reinforced in mid-October by two platoons of Company G of the 339th United States Infantry Regiment, an element of the American Expeditionary Force, North Russia. Headquartered at Pinega, some 50 miles above the Pinega River's confluence with the Northern Dvina, their action on the front during October and November was confined to patrols and light skirmishes extending southward down the river from Pinega. On 4 December, however, a mixed detachment of U.S. and Russian troops was confronted by a Red Army battalion at Karpogory, some 50 miles downstream from Pinega. Following a brief clash, the Allies withdrew to Pinega, where they were soon reinforced by Company M of the 339th, which had been rushed eastward from the Vologda Railroad Front.

In January and February 1919, Pinega was subjected to several attacks as part of a Bolshevik counteroffensive all across the northern front. Following the failure of these assaults, the front reverted to a condition of occasional light skirmishing. In early March, Company M returned to the Vologda Railroad Front and, in May, the last U.S. troops at Pinega were withdrawn to Archangel. The Pinega River Front remained in existence until the final collapse of the North in early 1920.

John W. Long

REFERENCES

A Chronicler [John Cudahy], *Archangel: The American War With Russia* (A.C. McClurg & Co., 1924); Dennis Gordon, *Quartered in Hell: The Story of the American North Russian Expeditionary Force, 1918–1919* (Gos, 1982); Joel R. Moore, *'M' Company, 339th Infantry in North Russia* (Central City Book Bindery, 1920); Joel Moore, Harry Mead, and Lewis Jahns, *The History of the American Expedition Fighting the Bolsheviki* (Polar Bear, 1920).

Plan of San Diego, Texas (1915)

While periodic bandit raids had occurred along the international boundary dividing the

United States and Mexico since the beginning of the Mexican Revolution in 1910, it was not until the discovery of the Plan of San Diego, Texas, on 24 January 1915, that the raids assumed a larger political context. On that day, McAllen, Texas, law enforcement officers arrested Basilio Ramos, Jr., a known supporter of former Mexican President Victoriano Huerta. A search of the prisoner revealed a copy of the Plan of San Diego, which had been drafted by nine Huerta partisans in the jail at Monterrey, Mexico, but which carried the name of a South Texas town.

The revolutionary document called for Mexican people on both sides of the border to rise up in a war of national liberation and seize the southwestern lands extending from Texas to California, territories that had been seized by the "imperialistic United States" during the Mexican War of 1846–1848. This coordinated uprising, to begin on 20 February 1915, ordered that every Anglo-American male over age 16 would be put to death and all property seized in the name of the supreme Revolutionary Congress. Further evidence of the racial orientation of this uprising was found in the plan's restrictive membership—only persons of "the Latin, the Negro, or the Japanese race." While Hispanics would reclaim the southwestern United States, six additional states would be reserved for blacks, and Native Americans were promised their ancestral territories. The plan was sadly lacking on the details of how such an overlapping pattern of land ownership could be achieved. A revised version of the document added the revolutionary concept of a "laboring proletariat" of the Latin, African, and Oriental peoples, plus an emphatic directive that all cultivated land was to be equally distributed in the form of agricultural communes.

Even after copies of the plan turned up in Laredo and other South Texas towns, authorities paid little attention to the document, which seemed too preposterous to be taken seriously. The McAllen judge who heard Ramos's case set a low bond which facilitated Ramos's release and escape into Mexico.

The seriousness of the situation became evident during a series of July and August attacks throughout the Rio Grande Valley. Events escalated as a large raiding party under Aniceto Pizaña destroyed the Fresnos Pump Canal station near Harlingen on 2 September and killed several workers. Within three weeks, additional depredations occurred near Brownsville, San Benito, Ojo de Agua, and Progreso, as well as the wrecking of a train at Tandy's station on 18 October, resulting in the deaths of three civilians and a soldier. Gen. Frederick Funston, commander of the Southern Military Department, was faced with the impossible task of guarding a 1,745-mile border from Texas to California with only 20,000 troops and with no capability for taking the offensive because of the lack of U.S. troops and the large distances involved.

It soon became evident to army intelligence officers and members of the State Department that these bloody events were traceable to higher authorities than a few hundred frustrated Huertistas. Clearly, the powerful Carrancista commander at Matamoros, Gen. Emiliano Nafarrete, was actively supporting the raiders. Even the Carrancista-controlled newspaper at Matamoros, *El Democratica Diario Constitucionalista*, publicly urged Mexicans to unite in a war to liberate Texas. Intelligence gatherers also found a direct German link to the recent events through monetary payments by German consul Johann Bouchard, commercial attaché Heinrich Albert, and minister to Mexico, Count Heinrich von Eckhardt. More threatening was the revelation that President Venustiano Carranza was cooperating with the plotters and providing them with limited covert aid. All the elements for a major border crisis existed.

Yet, in the midst of crisis, promoters of the Plan of San Diego found themselves isolated and on the defensive. Increased U.S. military activity in South Texas took its toll on the raiders, as did the unwillingness of Mexicans on both sides of the Rio Grande to support such an unpromising venture. With the discovery of their duplicity, German agents also distanced themselves from the other conspirators. The deciding factor was President Carranza who evidenced a spirit of cooperation toward the United States after his government received *de facto* recognition from Washington on 19 October 1915.

Brief though it had been, the hysteria and violence surrounding the Plan of San Diego had exacted a heavy price along the Rio Grande frontier. Twenty-seven raids resulted in the deaths of 33 U.S. citizens, the wounding of 24 others, the destruction of thousands of dollars of property, and the disruption of normal economic activity for four months. The raiders officially had lost 31 men killed, 11 wounded, and 22 captured. The chief casualties, however, were innocent civilians, mostly Mexican victims of vengeful and racist vigilante groups. Perhaps as many as 300 civilians died, according to General Funston.

Michael L. Tate

REFERENCES

Don M. Coerver and Linda B. Hall, *Texas and the Mexican Revolution: A Study in State and National Border Policy, 1910–1920* (Trinity Univ. Pr., 1984); Allen Gerlach, "Conditions along the Border—1915: The Plan de San Diego," *New Mexico Historical Review*, 43 (1968), 195–212; Charles H. Harris, III, and Louis R. Sadler, "The Plan of San Diego and the Mexican-United States War Crisis of 1916: A Reexamination," *Hispanic American Historical Review*, 58 (1978), 381–408; Friedrich Katz, *The Secret War in Mexico: Europe, The United States and the Mexican Revolution* (Univ. of Chicago Pr., 1981); James A. Sandos, "The Plan of San Diego: War and Diplomacy on the Texas Border," *Arizona and the West*, 14 (1972), 5–24.

The Platt Amendment and Cuba (1901–1934)

The rapid and complete victory by the United States over the forces of the tired and overextended Spanish empire in 1898 signaled the arrival of a new and powerful player to the game of empire. The Spanish-Cuban/American War left no doubt that the United States was the preeminent power in the Caribbean area.

The United States, in fulfilling its role as the "first new nation," generally rejected the European approach to empire building—the acquisition of colonies—and instead attempted to gain economic and political hegemony in the Caribbean region by establishing a system of protectorates. The island of Cuba was to be the laboratory for U.S. policies in the Caribbean, and the Platt Amendment was the initial experiment.

The expansionists—U.S. leaders who wanted to annex Cuba—were dismayed when that island was placed off limits by Senator Henry M. Teller's amendment to the resolutions favoring intervention in Cuba's struggle for independence from Spain in 1898. Disavowing any intention by the United States to retain permanent sovereignty or control over the island, the Teller Amendment declared that self-government by the Cubans would begin as soon as the island was pacified. Those eager to colonize Cuba were

even more put out when it appeared that the administration of President William McKinley was not going to seek some way of circumventing the promise of eventual Cuban independence.

In mid-December 1899 Gen. Leonard Wood was appointed military governor of Cuba, replacing the well-intentioned but politically inept Gen. John R. Brooke. Wood began a series of progressive political, social, and health-related reforms in an attempt to improve conditions. No amount of "good works" would guarantee that the United States's vital strategic and economic interests in the island and in the Caribbean would be protected by a new Cuban government, however.

Even as the Cuban constitutional convention began its deliberations under Wood's supervision in early November 1900, Secretary of War Elihu Root, Wood, and others sought some way of further defining the special relationship between Cuba and the United States in a way that would provide the desired guarantee. The Platt Amendment was to provide that safeguard.

Introduced by Senator Orville H. Platt of Connecticut as an amendment to the army appropriation bill passed by Congress in 1901, the Platt Amendment was essentially the work of Root and incorporated provisions that he had unsuccessfully submitted to Cuban lawmakers for inclusion in the new Cuban Constitution.

The rejection of Root's suggestions paved the way for a continued U.S. military presence in Cuba to maintain a stable government. This "foot-in-the-door" approach kept the annexation fire glowing while a search for a permanent solution continued. It was at Root's request that Platt offered the same provisions as an amendment to the appropriation bill.

Root and Wood, as well as the leading expansionist of 1898 and now president, Theodore Roosevelt, thought that the Platt Amendment was the first step in the annexation of Cuba. The amendment stipulated that control of the island would be returned to the Cuban people as soon as they included the following items in their constitution:

1. Cuba would not enter into an agreement or treaty with a foreign power that would threaten its independence or permit a foreign military presence on the island.

2. Cuba would not contract any debt beyond its normal ability to repay.

3. Cuba was to acknowledge the right of the United States to intervene to preserve Cuban independence; to maintain a government stable enough to protect life, property, and individual liberty; and/or to discharge the obligations it had assumed under the Treaty of Paris that had ended the Spanish-Cuban/American War.

4. Cuba was to ratify all acts of the United States during the military occupation.

5. Cuba would agree to the execution of the sanitary arrangements (projects to eradicate disease and improve the general health of the population) already undertaken by the United States.

6. Title to the Isle of Pines (U.S. colonists had settled there when it was thought to belong to the United States) was to be determined at some point in the future.

7. The United States was to have the right to purchase or lease naval stations.

8. These provisions were to be included in a permanent treaty with the United States.

It was clear to both Cubans and U.S. authorities that acceptance of these provisions would give the United States a virtual protectorate over Cuba. Cuban opposition to the most nettlesome articles (the right of intervention and the lease of naval stations) was eventually overcome once it became clear that the withdrawal of U.S. forces from the island was dependent on their acceptance.

The provisions of the Platt Amendment were included in a treaty of "general relations" between the United States and Cuba (22 May 1903) and in an addendum to the Cuban Constitution. Similar provisions were also included in U.S. agreements with Nicaragua and Haiti; the Platt Amendment served as a model for the extension of the U.S. protectorate system in the Caribbean area.

The United States exercised its right to intervene in Cuba under the Platt Amendment on several occasions, most notably in 1906–1909 when it established a provisional government following the fractious second Cuban national election.

The Platt Amendment was a product of a time and of a governmental mentality that thought that intervention or meddling in the internal affairs of Cuba and other Caribbean nations was the only way to obtain stability in the United States's "backyard." Within two decades, however, both the interpretation of the amendment and the times had changed. As secretary of state (1905–1909), Root himself thought that Section III of the Platt Amendment (the right to intervene) should be used only in the most unusual circumstances. His successor, Philander C. Knox (1909–1913), favored a "policy of prevention" under the amendment that sought to avoid intervention by giving advice (including "meddling"), so that military action by the United States would not be necessary.

By the early 1920s world events and the changes brought by the passage of time had outdistanced the original intention of the amendment. There was little danger of a foreign power challenging U.S. dominance in the area. The United States felt secure behind its ocean moats, had a navy well on its way to being second to none, and had a system of strategically located bases. Both the Department of State and U.S. administrations wanted to avoid intervention, which was at this point seen as being much more difficult and costly than it was worth.

In fact, the legal right to intervene in Cuba as set forth in Section III of the Platt Amendment became somewhat of an embarrassment to the United States. As the United States moved forward with the policies of the "Good Neighbor," a premium was placed on order in Cuba even if it meant dealing with a politician of questionable ethics in the person of President Gerado Machado y Morales. Machado's alleged illegal "adjustments" to the Cuban Constitution in 1927–1928 and other excesses brought demands for intervention from both Cubans and U.S. citizens, but no action was taken. The "big stick" of a few years earlier, though not completely abandoned, had definitely lost favor.

One of the unclarified points of the Platt Amendment from its inception was whose life, liberty, and property was to be protected through intervention. Clearly, the U.S. government's intention was to protect U.S. and other foreign interests and not those of Cubans.

In somewhat of a paradox, the Platt Amendment became a pillar of strength for a dictator. As long as President Machado maintained stability, that is, avoided chaos, the United States would not intervene. The last thing the U.S. government wanted was chaos because that condition would call for intervention under the amendment.

Secretary of State Henry L. Stimson (1929–1933) adhered strictly to the Root interpretation of the Platt Amendment; that is, no intervention in the internal affairs of Cuba, thereby effectively nullifying the amendment in practice. The threat of U.S. intervention posed by the Platt Amendment had not, however, completely outlived its usefulness.

Sumner Welles was appointed U.S. ambassador to Cuba in May 1933. With the quiet approval of the new secretary of state, Cordell Hull (1933–1944), and President Franklin D. Roosevelt, Welles presented a five-point plan to Machado which demanded that Machado take an extended leave of absence. Welles, exercising what amounted to almost a free hand in dealing with Cuba, indicated to Machado that the United States wanted to avoid carrying out its obligations under the Platt Amendment, but would intervene if the plan was rejected. Machado, realizing that he had lost virtually all support in Cuba, accepted a slightly revised version of the original plan and left the country on 12 August 1933.

Welles's "advice" to Machado signaled a departure from the Root interpretation of the Platt Amendment favored by the previous secretary of state. Was the threat to intervene a bluff? Fortunately, President Machado decided against playing the game to the end.

The pressures of the Great Depression, continuing Cuban dissatisfaction with its protectorate status, and the desire of President Roosevelt to liquidate the protectorate system and become a "good neighbor" brought about both the demise of the Platt Amendment and a radical change in the Cuban-U.S. relationship. In 1934 the United States and Cuba signed a treaty of "general relations" which abrogated the Platt Amendment, abolished the protectorate, but permitted the United States to retain the naval station at Guantánamo Bay.

The Platt Amendment served as the United States's stamp of empire in the early years of this century, but by 1934, it was a vestige of a bygone era in the history of the United States that most in this country preferred to forget.

Lawrence H. Douglas

REFERENCES

Lester D. Langley, *The United States and the Caribbean in the Twentieth Century* (Univ. of Georgia Pr., 1985); Louis A. Pérez, Jr., *Cuba Under the Platt Amendment, 1902–1934* (Univ. of Pittsburgh Pr., 1986); Louis A. Pérez, Jr., *Intervention, Revolution, and Politics in Cuba, 1913–1921* (Univ. of Pittsburgh Pr., 1978); Bryce Wood, *The Making of the Good Neighbor Policy* (Norton, 1961).

Poole, Frederick Cuthbert (1869–1936)

Maj. Gen. Frederick Cuthbert Poole was the British commander in chief of the Allied forces in North Russia, including the American Expeditionary Force, North Russia, from 24 May to 14 October 1918. An ardent supporter of the policy of Allied military intervention in Russia, Poole was largely responsible for its initiation, conduct, and ultimate failure in the Russian North.

Born in Great Britain in 1869, Poole joined the Royal Artillery at age 20 and served with distinction in campaigns in India, South Africa, and Somaliland. Prematurely retired in February 1914, the veteran gunner was soon recalled to active duty in World War I, rising rapidly to the rank of colonel. In early 1917, Poole was appointed chief of the British Artillery Mission to the Russian Army, which was an element of War Minister Lord Alfred Milner's famous Russia Supply Committee.

Returning to Britain after the overthrow of tsarism, Poole became a leading proponent of the policy of Allied military intervention in Russia. Because of this attitude, the persistent general was soon selected to head a small military mission to Murmansk to investigate the prospects for Allied intervention in North Russia. In this situation, when the Allied Supreme War Council finally decided to intervene in the North on 3 July, Poole was the logical choice to assume its command. At once, encouraged by the possibility of effecting a junction with the rebellious Czechoslovak Legion in western Siberia, the ebullient Poole devised a grandiose scheme calling for the virtual invasion of central European Russia with a projected army of 5,000 Allied troops supplemented by an expected volunteer contingent of some 100,000 anti-Bolshevik Russians.

On 2 August, as the first step in his plan, Poole carried out the occupation of Archangel, using for this purpose a small force of just under 1,500 Allied troops. Thereupon, in spite of the scarcity of his reserves, the dauntless general launched a vigorous offensive to the south which, however, soon fell well short of its objectives deep in the Russian interior. In addition to the failure of his military plans, Poole also became enmeshed in the trammels of local North Russian politics. In fact, it was this entanglement that finally led, on 14 October, to his replacement as Allied commander in the North by British Maj. Gen. William Edmund Ironside.

Returning to London, Poole was at once dispatched as British military liaison to the Volunteer Army of Gen. Anton I. Denikin in South Russia. Recalled from that assignment in early 1919, Poole left the army in 1920. Having made several unsuccessful campaigns for Parliament in the early 1920s, the old soldier died in retirement in 1936.

John W. Long

REFERENCES

Field Marshal Lord Ironside, *Archangel, 1918–1910* (Constable, 1953); E.M. Halliday, *The Ignorant Armies: The Anglo-American Archangel Expedition, 1918–1919* (Harper, 1958); Major-General Sir C. Maynard, *The Murmansk Venture* (Hodder & Stoughton, 1928); Benjamin D. Rhodes, *The Anglo-American Winter War With Russia, 1918–1919: A Diplomatic and Military Tragicomedy* (Greenwood Pr., 1988).

Port-au-Prince, Haiti, Battles (1919, 1920)

The *Caco* Rebellion of 1918–1920 was largely contained within the northern and central hinterlands of Haiti, but on two occasions, its leaders, Charlemagne Masséna Péralte and Benoît Batraville, brought the fighting to the streets of the capital. The first battle occurred when Péralte had reached the peak of his power and was encamped with 300 *Cacos* (Haitian peasant guerrillas) in the hills behind Cabaret, 15 miles north of Port-au-Prince. At 4:00 a.m. on 7 October 1919 Péralte sent 200 men into the capital—some by way of Portail St. Joseph and the rest via Portail Léogane. Armed with swords, machetes, and pikes, they surprised the marines and gendarmes, but the latter reacted quickly and with their superior automatic weapons chased the *Cacos* out of the city before they could do much damage.

As the rebels regrouped, Péralte sent a letter to the British chargé d'affaires dated 7 October stating that he was "at the doors of the capital with his troops," but that he did not wish to strike the city with all his might because of the danger to its Haitian and foreign residents. He called on the chargé to consult with the diplomatic corps, presumably for the purpose of surrendering Haiti to him, but he received no answer. Instead, on 8 October Lt. Kemp C. Christian with 12 gendarmes attacked Péralte's camp, killing 30 *Cacos* and dispersing the rest. One group fled toward Pont Beudet and Croix-des-Bouquets. Coming upon a house occupied by three Haitian engineers in the service of the Department of Public Works, the fleeing *cacos* murdered the three men and their housekeeper and set the building afire before escaping to the mountains.

While the first "battle" of Port-au-Prince produced few casualties, it brought home to the government of Philippe Sudre Dartiguenave and the U.S. Marines the gravity of the *Caco* revolt. Soon after, letters were discovered that had been written to Péralte by persons living in the capital disclosing valuable military information. The minister of the interior demanded that large numbers of troops be stationed at every approach to the city, but eventually backed down when the brigade commander assured him that the best strategy was to continue to rely on small reconnaissance patrols. Finally, the battle reinforced U.S. determination to assassinate Péralte, an action carried out by Capt. Hermann H. Hanneken on 30 October 1919.

After Péralte's death, leadership of the rebellion fell to Batraville, Péralte's second-in-command. Batraville was in communication with Dr. Rosalvo Bobo, exiled rival of Dartiguenave. With 2,500 *Cacos* concentrated southeast of Mirebalais, he still posed a serious threat to the occupation government. At 4:00 a.m. on 15 January 1920, Batraville attacked Port-au-Prince for the second time. With flags flying and conch horns blowing, 300 *Cacos* entered the city. Wearing stolen gendarmerie uniforms, one column came by way of the waterfront while two others marched farther inland and advanced around Bellair Hill by the radio station. This time the marines and gendarmes were prepared, having been warned the night before by a startled citizen who heard the rebels approaching. When they opened fire with Browning automatic rifles and machine guns, the *Cacos* broke ranks and rushing into buildings, sniped back from windows and around corners. They set fire to some houses in the Bellair section, and the light from this conflagration lit up the surrounding country. Despite their fierce fighting, the marines forced the *Cacos* out of the city by daybreak, leaving 66 dead and many more wounded or captured, including one of the leaders of the attack, Solomon Janvier, a Port-au-Prince resident. The survivors fled to Plaine du Cul de Sac and from there back to their hideouts around Mirebalais.

The defeat was a major setback for Batraville, who saw most of his supporters surrender to U.S. forces in the following weeks, but reports of the battle in the U.S. press revived public criticism of the occupation. In an election year, Republicans were eager to exploit any issue that might embarrass the administration of President Woodrow Wilson, and responding to protests by the National Association for the Advancement of Colored People, presidential candidate Warren G. Harding roundly denounced Wilson's handling of the *Caco* Rebellion in Haiti.

Jane M. Rausch

REFERENCES

H.P. Davis, *Black Democracy*, rev. ed. (Biblio & Tannen, 1967); Roger Gaillard, *Charlemagne Péralte: le caco* (Imprimerie Le Natal, 1982); Robert Debs Heinl, Jr., and Nancy Gordon Heinl, *Written in Blood: The Story of the Haitian People, 1492–1971* (Houghton Mifflin, 1978); James H. McCrocklin, *Garde d'Haiti, 1915–1934* (U.S. Naval Institute Pr., 1956); "When Insomnia and a few Marines Saved Port-au-Prince," *Literary Digest*, 64 (1920), 56–58.

See also Péralte, Charlemagne Masséna.

President's Commission on Conditions in Haiti (1930); Forbes Commission

In December 1929 violence erupted in southern Haiti. It started with a student strike at the Central School of Agriculture at Damien. Many students from bourgeois backgrounds perceived their role as future administrators and agronomists rather than as cultivators, and they refused to do manual work. They instead hired peasants to perform the agricultural chores needed to meet the practical requirements of their courses. School authorities wanted students to acquire practical experience and tried to discourage this practice by withholding part of the scholarships of those who engaged in it. Most of the students then went on strike on 31 October. Law and

medical students joined them in a nationwide expression of solidarity.

Customs employees in Port-au-Prince meanwhile took offense at the firing of a colleague and walked off their jobs on 4 December. Spontaneous strikes ensued, and angry crowds threatened violence in the capital. The government declared martial law and sent the Garde d'Haiti to stem disorders.

Peasant protest accompanied the disaffection expressed by urban elements. Rural discontent centered on taxes and a new coffee standardization law which increased the cost of production of this critical commodity. Agrarian dissatisfaction combined with student opposition and civil service displeasure to create a volatile situation. When 1,500 peasants marched to Aux Cayes on 6 December to protest rural conditions, a unit of 20 U.S. Marines fired on them, killing a number of Haitians.

Popular unrest during this time of depression had direct economic causes, but occupation authorities persisted in attributing it to nationalist agitators. Officials tried to minimize the Cayes incident's import, but it made front-page news in the United States. Public opinion no longer supported imperialist interventions in republics in the Western Hemisphere. Thoughtful citizens recognized that the occupation's human cost outweighed the dubious advantages of police control and tepid reforms.

President Herbert Hoover, under pressure from occupation critics, appointed a five-member commission of inquiry, chaired by former Philippines governor W. Cameron Forbes. Its formal name was the President's Commission for the Study and Review of Conditions in the Republic of Haiti. Forbes had governed the Philippines, and Washington officials viewed him as experienced in colonial affairs. Other Forbes Commission members were Henry P. Fletcher, a diplomat and veteran of the Spanish-Cuban/American War; newsman James Kerney, appointed to represent the Democratic perspective; Elie Vezina, a francophone Catholic layman; and William Allen White, a noted anti-imperialist editor. Hoover also named a second commission (the Moton Commission), composed of conservative black college administrators, to investigate Haitian education. The Forbes Commission, budgeted at $50,000, arrived in Haiti on 28 February 1930. For two weeks, it conducted hearings in Port-au-Prince and in the provinces. The commissioners left Haiti on 16

March and submitted their report to President Hoover on 26 March 1930.

The Forbes Commission had little direct contact with the Haitian government while conducting its investigation. It approached President Louis Borno only through the mediation of High Commissioner John H. Russell. It nevertheless took Borno's side against the high-handedness with which Russell and other functionaries treated him. The commission retained some sympathies for the client government, but it did not believe that Haitian nationalist opposition to the occupation had deep popular roots. Forbes thought that Haitians distrusted the native governing class, from which U.S. rule protected them. The Forbes Commission consequently did not recommend immediate withdrawal of U.S. troops. Federal control, the commissioners believed, should continue until the Haitian-U.S. treaty expired in 1936. They did, however, reproach the treaty regime for its failure to send officials of high quality to Haiti. Acting as a representative of a Republican administration, Forbes placed the blame for this on former Democratic President Woodrow Wilson. The commission praised High Commissioner Russell and President Borno for performing their duties competently, but concluded that the occupation had been ill-advised from the beginning.

The Forbes Commission called for significant reforms in the protectorate's operations. A significant shortcoming, from its standpoint, was the failure of treaty officials to train Haitians for self-government and for technical service. Policies that were simultaneously paternalistic and technocratic could not provide the indigenous leadership that a prosperous and stable Haiti required for the future. The commissioners were not optimistic that Haitians could create a sound government, but they believed that political unrest in Haiti would continue until self-rule was restored. It advocated abolishing the High Commission, reinstating normal parliamentary and presidential government, and resuming conventional diplomatic relations between the United States and Haiti. These recommendations synchronized well with Hoover's new approach to Latin American affairs. Worldwide economic depression made costly protectorates untenable. The United States decided to pursue a policy of normal relations. Washington upgraded its diplomatic representative in Port-au-Prince to ambassador. It also replaced U.S. Marines with U.S.-trained native troops. Haiti, as the Dominican Republic and Nicaragua, was henceforth to police itself.

Brenda Gayle Plummer

REFERENCES

Dana G. Munro, *The United States and the Caribbean Republic, 1921–1933* (Princeton Univ. Pr., 1974); *Report of the [U.S.] President's Commission for the Study and Review of Conditions in the Republic of Haiti* (U.S. Government Printing Office, 1930); Hans Schmidt, *The United States Occupation of Haiti, 1915–1934* (Rutgers Univ. Pr., 1971); Robert M. Spector, *W. Cameron Forbes and the Hoover Commission to Haiti (1930)* (Univ. Pr. of America, 1985).

See also Cayes, Haiti, Riot (1929); Moton Commission, Haiti (1930).

Press Censorship in the Spanish-Cuban/American War

In late February 1895, the second revolt by Cubans against Spain was inaugurated. In contrast to an earlier conflict 1868–1878, this one was island-wide, and all of Cuba supported the revolutionaries. The Spanish immediately tightened the reins on news and information leaving the island. All news was censored to minimize the importance of the uprising and to give the impression that Spain had matters well in control.

Despite the restrictions, journalists covering the conflict were resourceful in getting copy to U.S. editors. The most important means for evading the censors were dispatch boats. These vessels, owned or hired out by the newspapers, met reporters secretly at various points along the coast of the island to get their reports or sometimes to take the reporters to Key West, Florida, where they telegraphed their reports to their newsrooms. Reporters also used the cable stations at Môle Saint-Nicholas, Haiti, and Jamaica to evade Spanish censorship.

At first, reporters were given passes allowing them to move freely within Spanish-held territory. They used these passes to get by sentries and cross the lines over into Cuban revolutionary areas. As public opinion in the United States began to rally against Spain, reporters, with a few exceptions, were confined to Havana and forbidden to accompany either the Spanish army or the Cubans. Eventually, the Spanish commander, Gen. Valeriano Weyler y Nicolau, began to arrest and deport errant journalists.

In April 1898, the United States entered the war and immediately censors set up headquarters. The navy occupied the cable office at Key West, Florida. In New York, the United States Army Signal Corps put a censor in each office of its six cable companies. Reporters and editors both complained that U.S. censorship was worse than that of Spain.

Besides the offices in New York, the Signal Corps took the land lines of Florida, the French cable on the south coast of Cuba, the British cables in Puerto Rico and Santiago de Cuba, and, in time, the Cuban submarine cables at Santiago de Cuba. Censorship was entrusted to the respective superintendents, who worked under the direction of an officer from the corps.

Although reporters believed restrictions were severe, the censorship in this conflict was not oppressive. All coded messages to the West Indies, and Spain and its holdings were barred. Any messages involving troop movements or military matters likewise were forbidden. The newspapers were scrutinized daily by officers to determine whether any information that might aid the enemy had been printed. Any reporters who violated censorship rules were in jeopardy of losing their press credentials. However, 2nd Lt. Grant Squires, who worked in the New York cable offices, claimed that there was more interference with commercial messages than with press interests.

As in World War II, navy restrictions were more severe than those of the army. All personnel were forbidden to have any conversation with the press corps. Although journalists were not restricted in their movements, news of fleet movements out of Key West in pursuit of Spanish naval vessels recently departed from Cape Verde was strictly forbidden. Among naval officers, Adm. George Dewey maintained very good relations with the press, despite the censorship restrictions. This was largely because, when appealed to, he often allowed information to be cabled that his own censor had refused.

Two other elements worked, in effect, to censor news reporters. First, they were restricted to 100 words over cable. Although cost was a factor from the point of view of the dailies, some blamed the situation on the Washington authorities, who gave credentials to everyone who asked

for them. In consequence the numbers of reporters using the cable swelled.

A second factor was the censorship of Clara Barton. Any journalist covering the work of the Red Cross—important news, given the outbreak of sickness among the troops—was required to submit all letters and news copy to her. According to George Kennan, who worked for *Outlook* magazine, any news unfavorable to Barton did not leave the Red Cross ship *State of Texas*.

Because of the speedy transmission of news via cable both the Spanish and the U.S. forces imposed censorship on the press. Although Spanish censorship was severe, reporters were able to evade it. U.S. military censorship irritated correspondents. However, they were not able to circumvent it. Nevertheless, many reporters who later covered World War I conceded that, put in historical perspective, the censorship during the Spanish-Cuban/American War was mild.

Mary S. Mander

REFERENCES

Ray Stannard Baker, "How the News of the War Is Reported," *McClure's Magazine*, 11 (1898), 491–495; Arthur Brisbane, "The Modern Newspaper in War Time," *Cosmopolitan*, 25 (1898), 541–557; Charles Brown, *The Correspondent's War: Journalists in the Spanish American War* (Scribner, 1967); Mary S. Mander, "Pen and Sword: Problems Reporting the Spanish American War," *Journalism History*, 9 (1982), 2–9, 28; George Bronson Rea, *Facts and Fakes about Cuba* (George Munro's Sons, 1897); Grant Squires, "Experiences of a War Censor," *Atlantic Monthly*, 83 (1899), 425–432.

See also Public Opinion and the Spanish-Cuban/American War.

Prisoners of War, Spanish, in the Spanish-Cuban/American War

Almost 26,000 Spanish soldiers and sailors were taken prisoner by U.S. military forces in Cuba as a result of the Spanish-Cuban/American War. All but a handful were captured in land and sea engagements at Santiago de Cuba.

Naval prisoners of war (POWs) numbered 1,774, consisting of the crews of the entire Spanish fleet that was defeated at the Battle of Santiago harbor, 3 July 1898. Seventy-nine officers, including Adm. Pascual Cervera y Topete, who headed the fleet, and 14 sailors were housed at Annapolis, Maryland. Twenty officers and 1,661 enlisted men were incarcerated at Seaveys Island, Portsmouth, New Hampshire, along with a small contingent of Spanish soldiers captured in skirmishes outside Santiago City.

Officers and enlisted men enjoyed lenient conditions in both places. Six Spanish sailors were killed in a disturbance on the USS *Harvard* while en route to New Hampshire, but once in camp there were no discipline problems. The Spaniards arrived at Portsmouth in poor health, typically underfed, and often dressed in rags. Many believed they would be shot or subjected to hard labor, but discovered otherwise. The cooler climate helped to cure malaria contracted in Cuba. Clothing was sufficient, housing adequate, leisure time ample, and in terms of quantity and quality, camp food better than that served on Spanish ships.

Given parole, officers at Annapolis were free during the day to wander about the city without supervision. At least once, Admiral Cervera, who became something of a celebrity during his stay in the United States, traveled without escort to visit his men at Portsmouth. All officers and sailors were repatriated early in September 1898.

Over 23,700 Spanish soldiers in Cuba became POWs following the land siege of Santiago. With regard to them, a unique U.S. commitment was made. The administration of President William McKinley at first planned to detain Spanish army POWs at Galveston, Texas, but projected expenses and logistics appeared formidable. Secretary of War Russell A. Alger ordered Gen. William R. Shafter, during negotiations for the enemy's surrender in early July 1898, to promise that Spanish combatants would be shipped home directly from Cuba at U.S. expense. Alger reasoned that the proposal would simplify matters for the United States at a cost just slightly higher than imprisonment in Galveston. He also believed it would have a beneficial impact on Spanish and world opinion, would lower the morale of Spanish troops elsewhere in Cuba, and might end the war before yellow fever overtook American forces.

The Spanish accepted the offer, and the United States Army took 12,000 POWs at Santiago. Soon, about 12,000 more soldiers in the surrounding countryside gave themselves up, attracted by the prospect of returning home quickly.

The U.S. offer was generous but repatriation proved complicated and controversial. In the heat of July and August, the United States Army faced the task of feeding and housing multitudes of prisoners, while at the same time assuming civil control of Cuba. Tropical disease struck thousands of soldiers on both sides, and the army stockaded prisoners in camps away from U.S. troops as much as possible to curb the spread of yellow fever.

In late July the army opened bidding on transport of the prisoners to private shippers. Angering many in the United States, the job went to a Spanish line, Compania Transatlantica, which had brought many of the soldiers to Cuba under contract to the Spanish government. At a cost of $20 per enlisted man and $55 for each officer, the line shipped out 22,864 soldiers at a total sum of $513,860. The task was completed in mid-September 1898. Cuban volunteers and permanent Spanish residents of Cuba remained on the island.

United by white racism and Western cultural bias against the Cubans, Spanish and U.S. soldiers socialized heavily before repatriation. Their fraternization received wide and favorable publicity in the United States, and it helped set off a rapid reversal of U.S. attitudes toward wartime ally and former enemy. Labeled a short time before as depraved butchers, Spanish fighting men were being lauded as gallant and heroic in the United States.

A public letter from Spanish POWs written upon their departure contrasted the bravery of U.S. soldiers with the alleged cowardice and savagery of Cubans. The letter warned that the Cubans, "the descendants of the Congo and of Guinea mingled with the blood of unscrupulous Spaniards and of traitors and adventurers" (Alger, pp. 280–281), would not be able to govern themselves. Many whites in the United States agreed, and they used the letter and the hobnobbing between jailers and jailed to justify the protectorate status enforced upon newly "liberated" Cuba.

Jeffery C. Livingston

REFERENCES

Russell A. Alger, *The Spanish-American War* (Harper, 1901), 276–281; William Dean Howells, "Our Spanish Prisoners at Portsmouth," *Harper's Weekly*, 42 (1898), 826–827; George C. Lewis and John Mcwha, *History of Prisoner of War Utilization by the*

United States Army, 1776–1945, facsimile ed. (Center of Military History, U.S. Army, 1982), 43–46; U.S. Department of Navy, Bureau of Navigation, *Appendix to the Report of the Chief of the Bureau of Navigation for 1898: The Spanish American War* (U.S. Government Printing Office, 1898), 701–702; U.S. Department of War, Adjutant-General's Office, *Correspondence Relating to the War with Spain* (U.S. Government Printing Office, 1902), 2 vols.

Prisoners of War, United States, in the Spanish-Cuban/American War

Unlike the conflicts in Korea and Vietnam, the issue of U.S. prisoners of war (POWs) was a minor one in the Spanish-Cuban/American War. When contrasted with the thousands of Spanish captured by the U.S. forces, the number of U.S. POWs was infinitesimal.

Early in the war, two U.S. correspondents, Hayden Jones and Charles Thrall of the New York *World*, were arrested and charged with espionage by the Spanish. Within days the United States Navy secured their release through an exchange of prisoners.

The only other U.S. POWs on record in the Spanish-Cuban/American War became national heroes. On 3 June 1898 Lt. Richmond P. Hobson, a naval construction officer, was captured along with seven other men while on a mission to sink a ship, the collier *Merrimac*, in order to bottle up the Spanish fleet at Santiago harbor. After failing in their mission, the Spanish captured and incarcerated Hobson and his crew for a few days at Morro Castle, a fort overlooking the harbor. The military and newspapers in the United States charged that Adm. Pascual Cervera y Topete deliberately exposed Hobson, at this point a national celebrity, and his men to U.S. naval bombardment of Morro Castle. The press vilified Cervera, citing the move as evidence of innate "Spanish savagery" and called for retaliating by placing enemy POWs in the line of fire (*New York Times*).

Hobson and compatriots were soon moved to a barracks compound within the city of Santiago. Though the Spanish had a reputation for handling captured Cuban revolutionaries with extreme cruelty, it was quickly evident that they treated the U.S. sailors well, and tempers in the United States cooled down. The British consul at Santiago, Frederick W. Ramsden, kept a so-licitous eye on the prisoners and channeled reports on their condition back to their country. Two men fell ill with malaria, but recovered. The group was exchanged for Spanish POWs on 6 July 1898, just five weeks after capture.

The peace treaty officially ending the war called for an exchange of POWs by both sides. The provision was in a sense moot because by the war's conclusion the Spanish held no U.S. prisoners.

Jeffery C. Livingston

REFERENCES

Elbert J. Benton, *International Law and Diplomacy of the Spanish-American War* (Johns Hopkins Univ. Pr., 1908), 155, 158–160; Richmond P. Hobson, *The Sinking of the "Merrimac"* (original ed., Century Co., 1899; reprint ed. with introduction and notes by Richard W. Turk, U.S. Naval Institute Pr., 1987); *New York Times*, 11, 18, 19 June 1898.

Public Opinion and the Haiti Occupation

The examination of U.S. public opinion and the Haitian intervention of 1915–1934 can be divided into three parts corresponding to the major events that characterize the intervention. During the first period, 1915 to 1922, the United States invaded Haiti and established a military occupation. It created a Haitian government by coercion, formulated a bilateral treaty, and forced Haiti to sign it. Finally, U.S. Marines conducted guerrilla campaigns against peasant insurgents. The second phase, 1920 to 1928, began when Washington, prompted by extensive North American criticism of the methods used to pacify and govern Haiti, created the High Commission in Haiti as a substitute for direct military rule. The last period, 1929 to 1934, begins with the gradual withdrawal of U.S. forces and direct political control, provoked by demonstrations and popular violence in 1929. It includes "Haitianization," or the substitution of indigenous political and military control for foreign, and the restoration of normal diplomatic relations. U.S. public opinion varied over time and in synchronization with events taking place in Haiti. Because survey data on attitudes toward the occupation do not exist, public opinion is defined here as mass organization activity, statements and activities of mass leaders, and editorial policy.

Racist stereotypes and ethnocentrism dominated U.S. perceptions of the Caribbean republics in 1915. Writers widely attributed the poverty and backwardness of these underdeveloped countries to inherited factors. Caribbean political instability seemed to substantiate social Darwinist claims that superior European civilization would permanently dominate African, Native American, and mixed race populations and perhaps drive them to extinction. Critics especially scored Haiti, a black nation, for political disorder, voodoo, and inadequate acculturation to Western standards. When the marines first landed on Haitian shores, most observers applauded the invasion as salutary. Black commentators in the United States shared this opinion. Many regarded Haiti as an embarrassment to those who argued for racial equality because its experience seemed to demonstrate the failure of black self-government. Booker T. Washington depicted Haiti as a living example of the consequences of miseducation.

In 1915 and again in 1918 fighting erupted in Haiti as peasants rose against the foreign invaders. The U.S. Marines engaged them in bloody counterinsurgency campaigns. The fighting attracted such yellow journalists as Harry A. Franck, whose 1920 book on the West Indies illustrates how U.S. authorities made light of casualties endured by the Haitian peasantry. Few established newspapers questioned the war against the so-called *Cacos* (Haitian peasant guerrillas). The public widely believed that only U.S. application of the Monroe Doctrine could ensure that the great power rivalries of World War I would not spill over into the Caribbean region.

The liberal anti-imperialist press did oppose U.S. forays into colonialism and took note of Haitian resistance. The *Nation* objected to U.S. policies in Haiti and detailed abuses. In 1920 it opened its pages to Haitian nationalists who brought their case before the liberal public. This campaign marks the beginning of the 1920–1928 era, when reports of arbitrary justice, racial discrimination, physical brutality, and assassination in Haiti drew the attention of such groups as the National Association for the Advancement of Colored People and the Women's International League for Peace and Freedom.

The Republican party, hoping to regain the White House, also appropriated the Haitian issue in 1920. Pressure from sophisticated organizations that could mobilize public opinion and influence election results led the United States Senate to initiate an investigation in 1921. Aside from direct political motives, anti-occupation agitation reflected a changed political climate and altered sentiments. Pacifist, internationalist, and isolationist views became more prevalent after World War I and made the occupation less palatable to a larger segment of the public. Shifting attitudes toward race also played a part. New social science theories about race challenged past sociobiological interpretations and questioned public policies based on such perspectives. The 1920s also witnessed a widespread cultural and political revival among blacks who, after Booker T. Washington's death, became more appreciative of Haitian history and culture and less accommodating in their approach to race relations. Black organizations called for Haiti's liberation.

An increasingly unfavorable press and criticism from both the right and left led the State Department to reorganize the protectorate and give it the semblance of civilian government. U.S. officials relied more heavily on native police forces and made every effort to keep Haiti out of the news. Censorship and surveillance of Haitian dissidents and U.S. visitors made it difficult for occupation critics to challenge the status quo in any terms other than general ones.

After a relatively long quiescence in the mid-1920s, Haitian unrest became manifest again as students and customs employees went on strike in late 1929. In a separate incident, U.S. Marines fired on a group of peasants who were protesting deteriorating agricultural conditions and killed a number of Haitians. The resulting international outcry indicated that the occupation was no longer acceptable to the public. When the third phase, 1929 to 1934, began, the United States had governed Haiti for 15 years, but foreign control had accomplished little. Public opinion had changed substantially since the marines landed in 1915. Those in the United States who wanted an end to the occupation were responding to the same conditions that spurred Haitian protest—the economic dislocations of the Great Depression. Protectorates had become more expensive to maintain, especially if no one could point to obvious improvements in, or advantages to, the host country. These colonial arrangements also belied the United States's democratic heritage. Following the recommendations of two commissions of inquiry, the administration of

President Herbert Hoover began a program of gradual withdrawal from Haiti and normalization of relations.

In retrospect, public opinion played a significant role in setting limits to the abuses of power, especially military power, in Haiti. It failed, however, to prevent the establishment of the treaty regime or to abolish it once it had consolidated. Ultimately, a reorientation in Latin American policy, due in great measure to depression-era conditions rather than public opinion, caused policy makers to terminate the occupation.

Brenda Gayle Plummer

REFERENCES

John W. Blassingame, "The Press and American Intervention in Haiti and the Dominican Republic, 1904–1920," *Caribbean Studies*, 9 (1969), 27–43; Harry A. Franck, *Roaming Through the West Indies* (Century, 1920); James Weldon Johnson, *Along This Way: The Autobiography of James Weldon Johnson* (Knopf, 1933); Brenda Gayle Plummer, "The Afro-American Response to the Occupation of Haiti, 1915–1934," *Phylon*, 43 (1982), 125–143; Hans Schmidt, *The United States Occupation of Haiti, 1915–1934* (Rutgers Univ. Pr., 1971).

See also Cayes, Haiti, Riot (1929); President's Commission on Conditions in Haiti (1930); Forbes Commission.

Public Opinion and the Intervention in the Dominican Republic

While public opinion in the United States was initially indifferent to the military intervention in the Dominican Republic, the Dominican opposition was able to stimulate a considerable outcry which played a significant role in the U.S. decision to withdraw from the island nation. Initially, U.S. attitudes reflected a belief in the Monroe Doctrine, the prevailing attitude of Anglo-Saxon superiority, and a scant regard for the Caribbean island nations.

The refusal of the Dominican elite to cooperate with the intervention, compelling U.S. authorities to assume full powers, played a major role. President Francisco Henríquez y Carvajal refused to work with the conquerors, choosing to go into exile, and no member of the Dominican elite could be found to serve in a provisional government under the occupation authorities. As a result, U.S. officers were compelled to hold all posts, including cabinet positions, a fact which sharply differentiated U.S. actions in the Dominican Republic from those in Haiti. This established a firm basis for a propaganda campaign employing nationalist rhetoric.

The Dominican political elite launched an extensive effort to undermine the intervention. Recognizing that they could not hope to defeat the North American colossus militarily, they perceived that they could cause it considerable embarrassment politically and internationally. Working tirelessly, several political groups sent envoys to the United States, Europe, and Latin America, spreading propaganda, giving press interviews, and presenting their case before governments, and skillfully keeping the matter in the news. Henríquez y Carvajal visited the United States shortly after the intervention, and continued to travel throughout Europe and Latin America. At the conclusion of World War I, the effort was intensified, with the Dominicans even sending a delegate to the Versailles Peace Conference, contending that their nation should be included in the category of oppressed nationalities, much to the embarrassment of U.S. President Woodrow Wilson.

In the United States, the propaganda campaign was spearheaded by the Haiti-Santo Domingo Independence Society, using the name by which U.S. figures commonly referred to their nation. The group proved skillful in keeping both nations in the news, particularly in using the columns of the *Nation* and *Current History*, which bristled with news of U.S. oppression and atrocities, written in the muckraking tradition. Numerous visiting Dominican dignitaries furnished interviews, and their speeches to various groups were widely reported. Dominican propaganda was equally effective in Europe and Latin America, stimulating press outcries in numerous countries. In Latin America, Dominican envoys skillfully employed nationalistic themes to present the intervention as the precursor of further military actions by the northern colossus and hence as a threat to the entire hemisphere.

Warren G. Harding criticized the Wilsonian interventions during the 1920 presidential campaign, thus placing the issue in the political arena. Drawing on the isolationist reaction to Wilson's commitment of U.S. power abroad, Harding declared in a speech on 28 August 1920, that the Wilsonian interventions in Latin America had "made enemies of those who should be our friends." Recognizing the domestic desire to reduce commitments abroad and cut military expenses, Harding criticized the "repeated acts of unwarranted interference in the domestic affairs of the little Republics of the Western Hemisphere." Dominicans welcomed this statement as a virtual commitment to withdrawal.

The Dominican effort also involved extensive lobbying and political action. The former U.S. minister to the Dominican Republic, Horace G. Knowles, was hired to represent the Dominican interests in Washington. Billing himself as the "legal counsel of the deposed constitutional government" and using his extensive contacts in Washington, Knowles played skillfully on the isolationism prevalent in the United States Senate in reaction to Wilson's postwar plans. Knowles worked tirelessly to provide a constant stream of memos to government officials and senators; he also wrote numerous articles for the press. He arranged and coordinated the visits of several Dominican envoys to the United States. Samuel Gompers and the American Federation of Labor also strongly supported the campaign, assisting efforts of the AFL's labor affiliates in the Dominican Republic while passing resolutions calling for an end to the intervention.

This campaign was a primary factor in the establishment of a subcommittee of the Senate Foreign Relations Committee to investigate the occupation of both Haiti and the Dominican Republic. The committee hearings during 1921 and 1922 provided a major propaganda vehicle. The committee's investigations and visits to both island nations kept the occupations at the center of the political stage. The committee's conclusions contributed to the prevailing view that while prolonged occupation of Haiti would prove necessary, the Dominican occupation was temporary and need not continue.

The propaganda campaign launched by the Dominican exiles and the changing attitudes of the U.S. public played key roles in the initiation and conduct of the negotiations necessary to arrange for the withdrawal of U.S. troops from the Dominican Republic. The actions of the Harding administration reflected a recognition of these public attitudes at home.

Kenneth J. Grieb

REFERENCES

Bruce J. Calder, *The Impact of Intervention: The Dominican Republic During the U.S. Occupation of 1916–1924*

(Univ. of Texas Pr., 1984); Kenneth J. Grieb, *The Latin American Policy of Warren G. Harding* (Texas Christian Univ. Pr., 1976); Kenneth J. Grieb, "Warren G. Harding and the Dominican Republic U.S. Withdrawal, 1921–1923," *Journal of Inter-American Studies*, 11 (1969), 425–440; Melvin M. Knight, *The Americans in Santo Domingo* (Vanguard Press, 1928).

See also Select Committee on Haiti and Santo Domingo.

Public Opinion and the Nicaragua Intervention

The U.S. intervention in Nicaragua beginning in 1926 and 1927 and the resulting guerrilla war with Augusto C. Sandino aroused strong feelings in the United States and elsewhere. Through the supervised Nicaraguan election of 1928, the policy of President Calvin Coolidge as formed by the Stimson agreement seemed to have support of majority opinion at home, but as the guerrilla war continued and the Great Depression descended, support eroded and policy changed. The Stimson agreement of 1927 provided for U.S. supervision of the election, an end to fighting between the Nicaraguan political parties, and disarmament. A nonpartisan constabulary was also to be established. There are no precise measurements of public opinion on the Nicaraguan issue, but views reported in the press and freely expressed in Congress allow indications of the country's mood, or at least that of the individuals who might have influenced policy. Frequently, debate on Nicaragua was coupled with discussion of Mexico because the Coolidge administration saw what it termed Mexican radicalism (Secretary of State Frank B. Kellogg suggested communism) moving south to Central America. Such charges brought a mixed reaction in the United States and a generally hostile, sarcastic response in Europe and Latin America. Despite the adverse comment, Stokeley W. Morgan of the State Department's Latin American Division thought it important not to allow propaganda, criticism, and appeals to the Senate over the head of the secretary of state to change U.S. policy.

In Congress, in the press, and among the public generally, debate on Nicaragua rose and fell depending on the heat or quiescence of events in that Central American country. Much, but not all, of congressional debate was along party lines. Critics questioned presidential authority to send marines into Nicaragua and suggested that support of the Adolfo Díaz government deprived Nicaraguans of self-determination. One Democrat referred to Secretary Kellogg's fear of Bolshevism as absurd. In response to the administration's major argument of protecting U.S. lives and property, there were questions and doubts about what dangers existed. Critics were hesitant to condemn protection of lives but expressed reservations about protection of property. The Democratic party platform in 1928, while abhorring conquest and imperialism, desired the protection of U.S. lives and rights.

Supporters of the administration's position referred to a possible Nicaraguan canal, the Monroe Doctrine, and continuation of a long-term relationship of friendship and helpfulness. Republican William E. Borah, chairman of the Senate Foreign Relations Committee, had reservations about the intervention at the start, but after Stimson's agreement with Nicaraguan political parties he accepted the commitment as binding. There were attempts in Congress to restrict the use of appropriations for actions in Nicaragua, but these failed until 1932. By that time the restriction had little effect.

Foreign newspapers were generally critical; they spoke of the easy slope to the hill of imperialism; others noted U.S. hypocrisy in international politics. Reportedly some European opinion found sly pleasure in that the United States would have to remain silent if European powers took analogous steps. Latin American newspapers condemned U.S. policy as a reflection of the U.S. local oligarchy combining with U.S. capitalists to sell out South and Central America. In the United States, editorial opinion reflected political leanings. Commenting on the Stimson agreement, Democratic newspapers referred to peace in the form of a hawk and noted U.S. determination to have its own way in the domestic affairs of these little states; the Republican *New York Herald-Tribune*, on the other hand, approved this natural and successful application of friendly guardianship. After Sandino began his resistance, the anti-intervention press asserted that Washington's imperialistic policy was bound sooner or later to lead to bloodshed, while more friendly newspapers believed withdrawal of marines would lead to a more disastrous situation in Nicaragua. Many newspapers supported the Coolidge administration because they felt the nation should finish the job it had started in Nicaragua. By 1931 and 1932 as the administra-

tion of President Herbert Hoover reduced the marine presence in Nicaragua and refused to alter policy in the face of resurgent Sandinista attacks endangering foreign lives and property, there was general editorial support for ending interventions, but there were some cautionary remarks about abandoning the policy of protecting U.S. citizens abroad. Among the editors opposing the intervention were William Allen White, Oswald Garrison Villard, and Herbert Croly. Villard's periodical the *Nation* published a series of friendly articles on the enigmatic Sandino based on personal interviews by Carlton Beals in the jungles of Nicaragua.

Academic views as reported in the newspapers seemed more to oppose than support the Nicaraguan affair. Scholars, such as Clarence H. Haring, John H. Latane, Charles W. Hackett, and Thomas Moon, questioned U.S. policy, but Jeremiah W. Jenks was supportive. Other college faculty and presidents joined editors and politicians to form the National Citizen's Committee on Relations with Latin America to oppose the intervention. Various men of religion bemoaned the lack of peace, but the leadership of the Knights of Columbus, focusing on Mexico where President Plutarco E. Calles and the Catholic Church were at loggerheads, saw the menace of communism of that country extending southward into Central America and thus seemed to support Secretary Kellogg's similar fears.

The political left at home and abroad opposed Washington's Nicaraguan policy. The Sixth World Congress of the Communist International (Comintern) meeting in Moscow in 1928 sent words of encouragement to Sandino. In the United States the All-America Anti-Imperialist League held rallies sometimes featuring General Sandino's half-brother Socrates Sandino. That organization sold pro-Sandino stamps, marched, and picketed to support the Nicaraguan guerrilla leader.

Although numerous reports of individual and organizational views on the intervention exist, overall opinion in the country is difficult to fathom. Adverse opinion did not force President Coolidge to abandon Stimson's commitments, and it did not seem to play an important role in the 1928 U.S. presidential election. As the guerrilla war continued, there was recognition in the Coolidge administration and that of his successor that the situation was unsatisfactory. Hoover and Secretary of State Henry L. Stimson, besieged by an unwanted military campaign and a worsening economic crisis, wanted to remove the marines, and there seemed little doubt that most citizens supported their efforts.

William Kamman

REFERENCES

For a selection of views on public opinion and the second Nicaraguan intervention consult the *Literary Digest*, *Congressional Record*, and such newspapers as *The New York Times* and its convenient index.

Public Opinion and the Philippine War

In the absence of allegedly more precise measurements, such as public opinion polls, one has to rely on elections, crowd behavior, the leadership of particular groups, and editorial opinion to gauge rather roughly U.S. public opinion during the Philippine War. The U.S. presidential incumbent, William McKinley, won reelection handsomely in 1900, having left campaigning pretty much to his youthful, bumptious vice presidential candidate, Theodore Roosevelt. Both proponents of imperialism and opponents of the war, the anti-imperialists, viewed this election as a showdown, a virtual political Armageddon, to decide once and for all if the United States was to continue on its new course of empire. How much the election reflected a mandate on this issue is problematic. Prosperity had returned during McKinley's first term, and "a full dinner pail" may have had as much to do with the outcome as anything else, along with the advantage usually enjoyed by an incumbent. In addition, the Democratic candidate, William Jennings Bryan, added the controversial issue of free coinage of silver to his platform and represented to many the more narrow regional interests of populism and Protestant fundamentalism with its own pietistic "imperialism." The strict Sabbath laws and prohibition pushed by Bryan's followers more than their candidate may have alienated many German-American and Catholic voters who might have voted against the war.

Although Bryan declared in the beginning of his campaign that "imperialism" was "the paramount issue," he said less and less about it as the campaign wore on (Miller, p. 137). Governor Roosevelt was so sure of popular support for the war that he was not about to let the Democrats

off the hook, keeping the issue to the fore in rather demagogic fashion. It was an era of intense nationalism and unabashed, sentimental patriotism which Roosevelt exploited to the hilt. He seized on a comment by Governor William Amos Poynter of Nebraska in a speech in support of Bryan's candidacy in which Poynter asked his audience if it wanted a swollen federal budget to support more "idlers" and "hirelings" in an expanded army. Roosevelt put these words into Bryan's mouth, and bellowed (Miller, p. 141):

> I fought next to these "hirelings!" I saw them . . . shed their blood for the honor of the flag . . . and the reward is that these men should be sneered at as "hirelings" and "idlers." Colonel [Charles M.] Stotsenburg, General [Henry W.] Lawton no longer walk about in idleness . . . . They have found rest where their comrades from 1861 to 1865 who gave their lives have found their rest. Woe to the country that has lost its capacity to appreciate the sacrifice of the gallant souls who do and dare and die for its honor and glory.

It was only a short *a priori* step to blame "the Bryanites" for the war and its continuance by giving the enemy false hopes. It was noted that Philippine nationalist leader Emilio Aguinaldo y Famy favored Bryan's election and that Bryan was toasted in *"insurrecto"* circles. Thus, Roosevelt was able to meld war critics, silverites, Populists, and Democrats together, painting this coalition as "irresponsible, anarchistic and treasonable" (Miller p. 137).

The Anti-Imperialist League that led the opposition to the war seemed low in numbers, but high in quality. Its leaders read like a combination of *Who's Who in America* and the *Social Register* with patrician names, university presidents, and leading professors, along with the most prominent members of the Protestant clergy.

This was equally true of the leading apologists for the war, however, who could match their opponents in erudition, degrees, and pedigrees. The major difference between the two groups was that of age. The former averaged 15 years older than the latter, not quite a generation, but sufficiently great for Roosevelt to characterize the critics as "men of a bygone age having to deal with facts of the present" (Miller, p. 117).

This "generation gap" was mirrored in the larger population. The critics of imperialism tried to claim that universities were solidly behind them, a claim that seemed to be enhanced by editorial attacks on the professoriate in the imperialist press, urging the trustees to fire these "sympathizers with a public enemy" (Miller, p. 116). If the petitions to end the war and grant independence to the Filipinos that emanated from universities are any gauge, it does not appear that many professors took this position. One from Harvard University bore only 17 signatures out of 496 professors, instructors, and administrators, in spite of the anti-imperialist sentiment of the university's president, Charles W. Eliot. One from Chicago garnered only 36 signatures out of 130 professors and many more lower ranking teachers. Some universities featured public lectures against the war, particularly the University of Michigan, whose president, James Burrill Angell, strongly opposed the war. There is no solid evidence indicating how well attended they were, or if the audience was mostly students or older alumni and "townies." Professor Charles Eliot Norton was rudely hissed at by students when he publicly criticized the war at one such meeting, while the University of Chicago's Professor J. Lawrence Laughlin was threatened with violence by students when he called Old Glory "an emblem of tyranny and butchery" (Miller, p. 109). Former congressman Charles A. Towne angered students at the University of Michigan when he declared that the country had fallen "within a single year . . . from the moral leadership of mankind into the common brigandage of the robber nations of the world" (Miller, p. 109). On the other hand, Roosevelt was given wildly enthusiastic receptions at campuses across the nation, including the University of Chicago, allegedly a bastion of anti-imperialism, during his 1900 campaign.

It would appear that youth in general favored the war and imperialism, perceiving it as United States's new "frontier," since historian Frederick Jackson Turner had noted that the old one that had had such a significant role in U.S. history was over, ending an important era in U.S. history. The next generation would have to look overseas for expanding opportunities. In addition, there was a stress on swashbuckling adventure, the very staple of children's books at the time. Nowhere is this better reflected than in the "gung ho" spirit of the U.S. volunteers who fought the war. There was no problem raising new regiments, and about 10 percent of the state volunteers reenlisted in the new national regiments in 1899 for another tour of combat. Few seemed to sense any real danger in the war, although 4,200 soldiers perished during it. The Filipinos were notoriously poor marksmen; so the popular belief was that if they aimed at you, you were safe. The assurance that one soldier gave to his parents, "I hardly think I was born to be killed by a nigger," reflected a widespread belief in their invulnerability (Miller, p. 67). While they were sentimental patriots, as their songs indicated, they did not perceive the war to be a solemn obligation as much as a wonderful, crazy, violent, and altogether fulfilling adventure, one that would provide them with some good war stories for future winter evenings back on the farm. In a way, the war in the Philippines reenacted the wars of the old frontier fought against Native Americans by their fathers and grandfathers.

Perhaps nowhere is this adventurism and revival of the old frontier spirit more revealed than in the wild adulation afforded Gen. Frederick Funston, the leading hero of the war, upon his return from the Philippines. More than anyone else, he personified the reckless, swashbuckling, bumptious, and lawless frontier spirit and captured the imagination of the crowds that so idolized him. He basked in headlines and fawning editorials, as earlier escapades of his youth were either invented, or grossly exaggerated, to create a legend of endless derring-do, raw courage, perseverance, and a contempt for legal restrictions. The fact that Funston was the leading *bête noire* of the anti-imperialists seems only to have enhanced his heroic stature among his admirers.

There certainly was no shortage of anti-imperialist editors, although it is impossible to ascertain their number relative to their counterparts who supported the war and imperialism. Overwhelmingly, the critics were Democrats, with important exceptions. The editor of the *Call* in San Francisco was an anti-imperialist Republican, while the Democratic newspaper chain of William Randolph Hearst strongly supported the war. In New York City, the *Times*, *Sun*, and *Tribune* fervently favored imperialism, while the *Journal*, *Evening Post*, and *World* just as adamantly opposed it and the war. The *Herald* waffled on these issues over the course of the war.

Surprisingly, it is just as difficult to assess accurately the position of organized labor on these issues. While Samuel Gompers was a vice president of the Anti-Imperialist League, and such labor stalwarts as Henry Demarest Lloyd and George E. McNeil did stump for Bryan in 1900, most local labor councils followed Gomper's policy of not endorsing candidates. In Cleveland, the American Federation of Labor refused to allow Bryan to address its members, while in Chicago, it agreed to hear him only if Indianapolis and San Francisco defied tradition to endorse William McKinley for reelection. Some politicians associated with organized labor proved to be embarrassing, such as Ohio's Silver Democrat John J. Lentz, who called the president "a murderer," and former governor of Illinois, John P. Altgeld, who interrupted his anti-war speeches to lead cheers for Aguinaldo and the Filipino nationalists.

Even more surprising is the endorsement of McKinley only weeks before the election of 1900 by the Roman Catholic hierarchy, then closely associated with organized labor. Returning from the Vatican, Archbishop John Ireland declared that the safety of the Church and the protection of its properties in the Philippines were best served by U.S. rule and that Rome recognized this. Bishop John J. Keane followed Ireland officially carrying the Pope's *ex cathedra* blessings for the U.S. conquest of the Philippines, adding: "On this subject, His Holiness is very firm" (Miller, p. 138). Cardinal James Gibbons added his endorsement, while Archbishop Placide L. Chappelle even denounced the anti-imperialists as being "devoid of the conception of national honor," and insisting that "to retire under fire is unAmerican" (Miller, p. 138). Of course, as with labor, it is impossible to know how much the pronouncements of leaders really represented, or affected, the rank and file. There were also dissenters, such as the editor of the Catholic *Monitor* in San Francisco, who wrote that "there are many millions of American citizens whose sentiments do not concur with those of His Holiness in that matter" (Miller, p. 139).

McKinley's success in winning the endorsement of the Roman Catholic Church for his Philippine policy was due to his compromise on the friar question. Initially, the imperialists criticized the friars as much as did the Filipino nationalists as a product of Catholic corruption. Indeed, like his strong Protestant supporters, particularly the missionary establishment, McKinley had talked of "Christianizing" the Filipinos, which essentially meant liberating them from the decadence of Roman Catholicism. Since the rebel Aglipyan Church of native priests was inextricably woven into the Philippine Revolution and converting the natives to Protestantism was unrealistic, at least in the short run, McKinley did an about face on this issue, much to the chagrin of many of his Protestant supporters. He made Archbishop Chappelle his unofficial advisor on the Philippines, or as the press dubbed him, "the President's agent to rehabilitate the friars" (Miller, p. 139). The Vatican, in turn, made Father William D. McKinnon, chaplain to the 1st California Volunteer Regiment, the bishop of Manila to complete the rapprochement.

The nature of the anti-imperialist leadership probably helped to alienate workers and Catholics. Many were aging "mugwumps," with an elitist bias against mass democracy and the leveling effects of egalitarianism. It was "ignorance" and an "appeal to savage instincts" that elected McKinley, who enjoyed the support of "the fighting mob hysteria" of "common men," alienating "the better elements," they opined (Miller, p. 120). To Charles Francis Adams, all this was inevitable as the nation sank into "a European and especially a Celtic proletariat of the Atlantic coast, an African proletariat on the shores of the gulf, and a Chinese proletariat on the Pacific" (Miller, p. 120). This elitism also was expressed in a rather cavalier attitude toward poverty and working conditions. Most were committed to Adam Smith and *laissez-faire* economics. They were opposed to labor unions as much as they were to trusts and imperialism, warning against fatuous interventions to alleviate such "natural" conditions as poverty and inequality, which could only reproduce the bread and circuses that had once destroyed the Roman republic. Their anti-war polemics, for which they claimed such a wide, and obviously inflated, readership, tended to be too intellectual, even pedantic, to have much mass appeal, at best. At worst, they could only have repulsed workers, immigrants, Catholics, and the urban poor.

It would appear then that public opinion largely supported the United States's imperialistic venture, and subsequent war of conquest in the Philippines, with an important and influential minority dissent. Perhaps nowhere is this contention better supported than by the presidential election of 1904. Although the war in the Philippines was declared to be over, *ipse dixit*, by President Roosevelt in his Independence Day address in 1902, it had dragged on for several more years, albeit at a greatly reduced scale and fought increasingly on one side by Filipinos serving the United States, often led by former officers in Aguinaldo's army. The election followed Roosevelt's "scandalous grab of real estate in Panama," as the anti-imperialists labeled it (Miller, p. 262). The Democrats nominated a more genuine anti-imperialist than Bryan, if also rather obscure, this time in Judge Alton B. Parker of Esopus, New York, to run against the ebullient incumbent. Taking his cue from McKinley's reelection bid four years earlier, Roosevelt sat out the campaign at Sagamore Hill, his summer home at Oyster Bay on Long Island's north shore. He considered the anti-imperialists the "Achilles heel of the Democracy" (Miller, p. 262), so any messages emanating from the incumbent featured these "virtuous neurotics," whom he called "professional goo goos" who "bleed for the Filipino" (Miller, p. 262). Roosevelt's contempt was amply justified because he won a landslide victory with almost no effort.

Stuart Creighton Miller

REFERENCES

Thomas A. Bailey, "Was the Election of 1900 a Mandate on Imperialism?" *Mississippi Valley Historical Review*, 24 (1937), 43–52; Willard B. Gatewood, *Black Americans and the White Man's Burden, 1898–1903* (Univ. of Illinois Pr., 1975); Stuart Creighton Miller, *"Benevolent Assimilation: The American Conquest of the Philippines, 1899–1903* (Yale Univ. Pr., 1982); E. Berkeley Tompkins, *Anti-Imperialism in the United States: The Great Debate, 1890–1920* (Univ. of Pennsylvania Pr., 1970); Richard E. Welch, Jr., *Response to Imperialism: The United States and the Philippine-American War, 1898–1902* (Univ. of North Carolina Pr., 1979).

See also Atrocities in the Philippine War.

Public Opinion and the Punitive Expedition

"Villa is coming! Pancho Villa is coming!" Many times during the Mexican Revolution which began in 1910 the people of the U.S.-Mexican border region thrilled to reports and rumors of the approach of the forces of Gen. Francisco "Pancho" Villa, whose stronghold was the border state of Chihuahua. The fascination Villa held for U.S. southwesterners, however, was similar to that provided by a coiled rattlesnake—the Mexican bandit/hero merited atten-

tion not only because of his charisma but also because of the threat of death and destruction he posed for border communities. To the larger public in the United States, Villa seemed to offer the solution to the Mexican governmental problem after his defeat of President Victoriano Huerta's federal forces in late 1913. The attitude of most people in the United States toward Villa remained favorable through 1914 and much of 1915, although this attitude was far from unanimous.

Public opinion of this era was assessed both then and later primarily through summaries of newspaper editorial comment, especially those provided by the *Literary Digest* and *Current Opinion*. As Villa met defeat at the hands of his former allies in April 1915, editorial opinion indicated a shift away from support for Villa's faction. When President Woodrow Wilson recognized the government of Villa's adversary, Venustiano Carranza, and provided some support, Villa struck at U.S. citizens and their property in Mexico. Apparently Villa had lost any concern for public opinion because he openly denounced the United States. Rumors and reports of Villista depredations appeared almost daily in San Antonio and El Paso, Texas, newspapers.

The murder of 12 engineers from the United States at Santa Ysabel, Mexico, by a Villista band provoked a strong public outcry for U.S. intervention and widespread condemnation of Villa. In El Paso the sight of the bodies being returned caused a major riot as soldiers and civilians attacked Mexicans. It required troops from Fort Bliss, Texas, to halt the riot and prevent a posse bent on vengeance from entering Mexico.

U.S. outrage over Villista actions exploded when word of the attack on Columbus, New Mexico, on 9 March 1916 was received. Citing national honor, newspapers across the country demanded punishment for the criminals who had invaded U.S. territory to kill peaceful citizens. U.S. towns on or near the border appealed for military protection, and their elected representatives demanded it. Newspapers expressed impatience over delay in sending U.S. forces into Mexico to punish a "bandit" from an "inferior" nation.

In an election year Republicans were eager to exploit the crisis to the detriment of a Democratic president. At the time of the Santa Ysabel murders, former President Theodore Roosevelt placed the blame on the weakness of administration policies. In the furor after the Columbus raid Roosevelt was joined by Senators Henry Cabot Lodge and Albert B. Fall in accusing President Wilson of inviting such actions by failing to act during previous provocations. Republican newspapers strongly endorsed the pronouncements of their leaders, but journalists and politicians from the Southwest called for more than retribution. The *El Paso Times* recommended a military occupation of Mexico, a concept endorsed by Texas Governor James Edward Ferguson. William Randolph Hearst insisted on a complete annexation of Mexico.

Hearst's great journalistic rival, Joseph Pulitzer, directed his verbal fire at Villa personally, asserting that only Villa's death could atone for his crimes. Considering the earlier public fascination with Villa, it was not surprising that the "bandit chief" became the focus of public vengeance. President Wilson contributed to this attitude when he told the press that Gen. John J. Pershing had been ordered to "get Villa." The press transformed Wilson's announcement into a pledge that Villa would be taken "dead or alive." In the eyes of the U.S. public Pershing's Punitive Expedition was regarded as a failure because it failed to catch Villa, despite considerable success in defeating and dispersing his guerrilla bands.

As Pershing's troops moved deeper into Mexico and then stalled with no apparent success, press reports and comments diminished, only to jump to life when U.S. and Mexican forces clashed at Carrizal. Congressmen of both parties demanded a stronger policy, and these views had support within the administration itself. The Republican national convention of 1916 denounced Wilson for failing to protect U.S. lives and property. Wilson could have taken the country to war in June 1916, had he so desired, with popular support. Publication of the official report on the Carrizal clash showing U.S. forces at fault provided the opportunity for the American Union Against Militarism, a pacifist group, to turn public opinion around through advertisements in newspapers. The president received enough public support to enable him to resist the pressure for war.

Wilson could avoid war, but public attitudes opposed withdrawal of U.S. forces without completing their mission. Only after he was securely reelected could the president quietly withdraw the troops as attention turned to events in Eu-

rope. If public opinion was not responsible for Pershing's expedition, it was undoubtedly the major factor in its duration.

Anthony K. Knopp

REFERENCES

Clarence C. Clendenen, *The United States and Pancho Villa: A Study in Unconventional Diplomacy* (Cornell Univ. Pr., 1961); Mark T. Gilderhus, *Diplomacy and Revolution: U.S.-Mexican Relations Under Wilson and Carranza* (Univ. of Arizona Pr., 1977); J. Ralph Randolph, "Border Reaction to the Villa Raids," *West Texas Historical Association Year Book*, 49 (1973), 3–15; Paul J. Vanderwood and Frank Samponaro, *Border Fury: A Picture Postcard Record of Mexico's Revolution and U.S. War Preparedness, 1910–1917* (Univ. of New Mexico Pr., 1988); Leon Wolff, "Black Jack's Mexican Goose Chase," *American Heritage*, 13 (1962), 22–27, 100–106.

Public Opinion and the Siberian Intervention

The Russian Revolution in March 1917 established a new moderate government and a Russian republic to replace the Romanov dynasty. The United States was the first nation to recognize the new democratic government. Eight months later V.I. Lenin's Bolsheviks overthrew the government in a coup and began the consolidation of power across the entire nation, a process lasting from late 1917 into 1920 in the Russian Civil War.

Concern at this excessive and violent behavior by the undemocratic regime soon led to vocal U.S. public opinion opposing the Bolsheviks and a call for efforts to suppress Lenin's government in order to restore democratic institutions. Complicating this situation was the Russian surrender to Germany during World War I (Treaty of Brest-Litovsk, March 1918) which gave the Germans the opportunity for shifting military forces to the Western Front and the possibility of obtaining Allied military supplies sent to the Russian government for wartime use. Many of these supplies were located in Siberian depots, especially at the seaport of Vladivostok.

The United States and its wartime Allies agreed in 1918 to send troops to Siberia to prevent these materials from falling into Bolshevik or German hands and to provide direct or indirect aid to the White forces fighting the Bolsheviks. The bulk of U.S. forces landed at Vladivostok beginning in September 1918, and

U.S. public opinion initially supported this undertaking as a justifiable and necessary step related to the ultimate victory in the European war against Germany and its allies. Some editorial comment raised the more fundamental issue of whether Russians were capable of self-government, and if the United States should become involved in a situation which might have no outcome that would accord with its democratic values and objectives.

This division in opinion became even more pronounced after the German surrender in November 1918, after which the Russian Civil War increased in intensity and ferocity. White and Red forces often used the same violent and destructive tactics, which caused opinion shapers in the United States to speculate whether it made any difference which side won. President Woodrow Wilson's views on Russian democracy rang hollow as the turmoil and tragedy of the civil war continued without abatement.

As public opinion became more vocal in opposing the involvement in Russia in a kind of "a plague on both your houses" approach, the presence of approximately 7,000 U.S. troops in remote Siberia halfway around the world intensified the criticism of the president's policy of intervention. People wanted the troops home following the Armistice, not placed in remote areas of North Russia (Archangel and Murmansk) or even more isolated Siberian areas. Although the forces involved were ordered to avoid confrontation, fighting did kill and wound U.S. troops. This further increased the desire to "bring the boys home."

During 1919 public opinion focused on the immediate postwar questions of jobs and domestic conditions, rather than on overseas ventures. Even political issues related to Russia had a domestic effect, with the public expressing growing concern about real or alleged subversion within the United States. Public opinion grew hostile to radicals in the United States who were often identified as communist sympathizers. The creation of the Communist Party of the United States in 1919 increased the tense atmosphere. Government investigations and accusations during the year culminated in the infamous efforts of Attorney General A. Mitchell Palmer to round up the subversives and send many of them to Russia by ship. The "Red Scare" continued into 1920.

Advocates of the U.S. military presence in Russia, including Siberia, did exist, and they reiterated their message of support for the intervention policy. A notable advocate was George Kennan, the most informed and famous of U.S. specialists on Russia. Kennan favored the intervention in 1918 and continued to express and publish his views calling for a more energetic involvement to swing the tide against the Bolsheviks. Other supporters saw the economic potential of trade, commerce, and investment in Siberian markets, which implicitly required the presence of U.S. forces to protect their interests in Siberia.

By 1920, the Russian intervention had neither overthrown the Bolsheviks nor seemed to have any substantial positive effect on either Russia or the United States. Government officials, including Secretary of War Newton D. Baker, concluded the best policy was to end the Russian enterprise. Wilson's serious illness in the latter part of 1919 (and continuing to the end of his term in early 1921) removed a leader whose voice might have been able to persuade the people of the United States of the need to continue the Russian intervention. Even he had been dubious about the initial intervention in 1918. Both U.S. public opinion and congressional opinion were turning inward. The election of 1920 further emphasized this tendency, so far as international activity was concerned.

The last U.S. military forces departed from Vladivostok 12 April 1920, ending the U.S. intervention in Siberia.

Taylor Stults

REFERENCES

Thomas A. Bailey, *America Faces Russia: Russian-American Relations From Early Times to Our Day* (Peter Smith, 1964); Peter G. Filene, *American Views of Soviet Russia, 1917–1965* (Dorsey Pr., 1968); Peter G. Filene, *Americans and the Soviet Experiment, 1917–1933* (Harvard Univ. Pr., 1967); Frederick F. Travis, *George Kennan and the American-Russian Relationship, 1865–1924* (Ohio Univ. Pr., 1990); William A. Williams, *American-Russian Relations, 1781–1947* (Rinehart, 1952).

Public Opinion and the Spanish-Cuban/American War

The term "public opinion" came into popular usage during the French Revolution when Louis XVI's finance minister remarked that public opinion governed the behavior of investors in the Paris market. Although there is no consensus on what constitutes public opinion, it can be generally defined as aggregate opinion on an issue of public interest that is thought to influence government policy.

The measurement of opinions based on polls came into prominence following the 1936 U.S. presidential elections in which both George Gallup and Elmo Roper correctly predicted the outcome based on the sample survey method. This method spread rapidly thereafter, was modified and refined as a result of the failure to predict the outcome of the election in 1948, and came into widespread usage by 1965. Thus, in speaking of public opinion regarding events before 1936, one must remember that neither the government institutions nor the instruments for data-gathering had evolved into sophisticated storehouses or tools capable of tapping into, or even responding to, public sentiment.

When William McKinley assumed the presidency of the United States, few issues were conceived of as national in import. Even fewer issues affected public opinion as a matter of foreign policy. Problems were experienced and solved at the local level. No government institution was equipped to handle the popular demand for national action in 1898. A vacuum between popular will and the government opened. That vacuum was filled by the press.

Communications media disseminate ideas on which public opinion is based. Some historians have given credence to the notion that the newspapers in the United States played an important role in bringing about the war with Spain. The popular press was an ardent supporter of intervention in favor of Cuban revolutionaries. Its influence can be found in the degree to which members of Congress referred to or read aloud newspaper reports in debates on resolutions concerning the Cuban uprising. These references had the added effect of making larger city newspaper fare available to smaller city papers because they were published in the *Congressional Record*.

Newspapers printed banner headlines indicating the latest in a series of "crimes" the Spanish had committed against Cubans. Editorially they emphasized that the presence of Spain in Cuba violated U.S. economic interests in the Caribbean and was contrary to the United States's "manifest destiny." Yet, the press alone

cannot account for the tidal wave of public opinion in favor of intervention after the battleship *Maine* exploded in Havana harbor in February 1898.

A second factor in building public support for intervention in Cuba was the Cuban Junta. The Junta, largely staffed by Cuban-born naturalized citizens of the United States, was appointed by the Constituent Assembly of the revolutionary government. Its headquarters was in New York City. Concurrently, the Constituent Assembly set up a Cuban Legation in Washington, D.C., to carry on diplomatic relations with other countries.

The methods used by the Cuban Junta demonstrate its sophisticated knowledge and understanding of the art of persuasion. It organized and oversaw the work of the Cuban League, which had chapters in most of the larger cities across the United States. The league raised many millions of dollars for its cause at public speeches, and the fairs and carnivals it sponsored.

The Cuban Junta also organized sympathy meetings, usually held at very opportune moments, such as just before Congress convened. These meetings were addressed by important local personages who often noted the similarity between the Cuban cause of their time and the American Revolution.

Besides these meetings, stage plays were written and performed. The newspaper *La Patria* was published, detailing revolutionary victories and Spanish incompetence. These accounts likewise found their way into papers in the nation's heartland. Pamphlets supporting *Cuba Libre* were widely disseminated.

The Cuban Junta also was instrumental in pointing out to Republicans the political implications of President Grover Cleveland's policy of neutrality. In this way, the issue entered into domestic politics—although once Republicans gained office they hedged on intervention in Spain's relationship to Cuba.

This all changed when the *Maine* blew up. The explosion was likely the result of an accident, but a tidal wave of public clamoring for intervention washed over all sentiments to the contrary. Over 250,000 men responded to President McKinley's call for volunteers.

The Spanish-Cuban/American War was celebrated in the United States as a great success. It closed the 19th century, leaving behind institutions unused to responding to crisis at a national level. Along with World War I and the Gulf War of 1991, it was one of the most popular wars in U.S. history.

Mary S. Mander

REFERENCES

George Auxier, "Middlewestern Newspapers and the Spanish American War, 1895–1898," *Mississippi Valley Historical Review*, 26 (1940), 545; George Auxier, "The Propaganda Activities of the Cuban *Junta* in Precipitating the Spanish American War, 1895–1898," *Hispanic American Historical Review*, 19 (1939), 286–305; Gerald Linderman, *The Mirror of War: American Society and the Spanish-American War* (Univ. of Michigan Pr., 1974); David F. Trask, *The War With Spain in 1898* (Macmillan, 1981); Marcus Wilkerson, *Public Opinion and the Spanish American War* (Louisiana State Univ. Pr., 1932).

Public Works in Cuba (1906–1909)

Extensive public projects were undertaken by the United States during its second occupation of Cuba (1906–1909) in order to stabilize economic conditions, and ultimately, the political situation, in Cuba.

On 13 October 1906 Charles E. Magoon replaced Secretary of War William H. Taft as the U.S. provisional governor of Cuba after a decision of President Theodore Roosevelt to use armed intervention in Cuba. Although Magoon's most important objective was to initiate legal reforms, he quickly decided on other objectives as well. Early on, he saw the need to improve economic conditions, to reduce the high cost of transportation, and to remedy the absence of roads and harbor facilities (Millett, pp. 191–192, 196).

A particularly pressing problem was the dearth of good roads. Cuba had only 610 kilometers of improved roads, whereas nearby Jamaica, one-fifth the size of Cuba, had approximately 10,000 kilometers. Generally, the Cuban roads were cart trails which were difficult to traverse in dry weather and almost impossible during the rainy season. Traveling the trails were carretas (two-wheeled carts), which often became mired in mud holes. When fully loaded, at most they could make 20 kilometers per day (Millett, p. 205; Lockmiller (1938), pp. 99–100; Patrick, p. 263).

The lack of good roads (as well as bridges) hindered the transportation of sugar and tobacco.

Recognizing this, and also in an attempt to promote political stability, in April 1907 the provisional government adopted a program for the building or improvement of 2,304 kilometers of roads at a cost of $13 million. Assisting in this endeavor was the 2nd Battalion of Engineers from the United States Army of Cuban Pacification along with engineers who came from the United States. By September 1908 Magoon's administration was responsible for the construction of 570 kilometers of new roads in addition to the repair of 200 kilometers of existing roads (Lockmiller (1938), p. 101).

On the whole, the results were positive. By providing employment to hundreds of people during the dead season, the provisional government helped to defuse social unrest in the short term. The costs of transporting sugar and tobacco in the affected areas were substantially decreased, and the isolation of the Cuban people was diminished. By the time that Magoon departed from Cuba in 1909, road mileage had been increased 125 percent over that which existed in October 1906. Magoon considered the construction of roads in Cuba his greatest achievement (Lockmiller (1938), pp. 102–103; Millett, p. 206).

In addition to the building of roads, the provisional government carried out other public works initiatives. Harbors and rivers were widened and deepened, and several new lighthouses were constructed. Improvements were made in Havana harbor, and the street railway system of Havana was extended. Magoon reorganized the post office, and 32 new telegraph offices were established. Government telegraph lines also were increased substantially. State buildings, sanitation works, and drainage systems were constructed or repaired (Lockmiller (1938), pp. 104–110; Millett, pp. 262–263).

Meanwhile, the provisional government coped effectively with yellow fever, which had been suppressed during the first U.S. military occupation, 1899–1902. However, the disease recurred in Havana in October 1905 and subsequently spread to other parts of the island. Partly because of a concern over the health of tourists, government officials, and 6,000 U.S. soldiers dispersed throughout Cuba, Magoon's administration became involved in vigorous measures to eradicate it. Under the leadership of Dr. Carlos J. Finlay, chief of the National Board of Sanitation; Maj. Jefferson R. Kean, advisor to the Department of Sanitation; and others, yellow fever was virtually eliminated in Cuba by 1909 (Lockmiller (1938), pp. 113–114).

In connection with his concern for improving the economy, Magoon was sympathetic to the need for Cuban agricultural development and diversification. Around the time that he became provisional governor, agriculture was suffering partly because of the revolution and a drought. Magoon's administration responded to the deterioration of the agricultural economy by providing various kinds of assistance: rural roads and bridges were built; diversified crops were encouraged; and scientific farming was promoted. However, such problems as seasonal agricultural unemployment, low wages, and absentee ownership were not addressed; thus, no fundamental changes were made in Cuban agriculture (Lockmiller (1937), pp. 182–183, 188; Millett, p. 202).

The public works activities of the provisional government had their shortcomings. In 1906 Magoon inherited a surplus in the Cuban treasury of $26 million; when he left office in 1909, there was less than $3 million, along with debts of almost $12 million. The impoverished state of the treasury arose primarily out of the cost of public works. Magoon also contracted out public works to U.S. firms and arranged payment by issuing bonds on the provisional government for $16.5 million. Some projects were not completed when the occupation ended. In Magoon's defense, some projects were already under way when he took office. In addition, there were occurrences that diminished government revenues over which Magoon had no control, such as the Panic of 1907 in the United States and a bad harvest in Cuba because of the drought (Healy, pp. 212–213; Langley, p. 45).

In spite of these shortcomings in the public works sphere, it is clear that one dimension, the construction of roads, was a significant reform although it alone could not totally change the economic situation for the better. More than $11 million was spent on roads; the results were that during the Magoon era almost as many miles were built in Cuba as had been constructed in the preceding two centuries (Thomas, pp. 492–493).

Dale W. Peterson

REFERENCES

David Healy, *Drive to Hegemony: The United States in the Caribbean, 1898–1917* (Univ. of Wisconsin Pr., 1988), pp. 212–213; Lester D. Langley, *The Banana Wars: United States Interventions in the Caribbean* (Dorsey Pr., 1988), p. 45; David A. Lockmiller, "Agriculture in Cuba During the Second United States Intervention, 1906–1909," *Agricultural History*, 15 (1937), 181–188; David A. Lockmiller, *Magoon in Cuba: A History of the Second Intervention* (Univ. of North Carolina Pr., 1938); Allen R. Millett, *The Politics of Intervention: The Military Occupation of Cuba, 1906-1909* (Ohio State Univ. Pr., 1968); Mason M. Patrick, "Notes on Road Building in Cuba," *Professional Memoirs*, 2 (1910), 263–284; Hugh Thomas, *Cuba: The Pursuit of Freedom* (Harper & Row, 1971), pp. 492–493.

Puerto Rico Campaign (1898)

The U.S. plans formulated in 1896 for a war against Spain envisioned a naval conflict aimed at destroying the Spanish navy and blockading Cuba. The project of a land attack on Puerto Rico did not surface until 4 April 1898, when a joint army-navy board suggested it as a means of depriving the Spanish navy of a fleet base in the Caribbean in the impending hostilities. Seizure of the island would also provide the United States with a base ideally suited for protecting the approaches to the projected isthmian canal. From the outset, Nelson A. Miles, commanding general of the United States Army, strongly supported an assault on Puerto Rico in conjunction with an attack on eastern Cuba in preference to a direct assault on Havana. On 26 May the decision was made, and preparations for a landing in Puerto Rico were begun.

Spanish forces in Puerto Rico at the beginning of the Spanish-Cuban/American War numbered over 17,000: 8,233 Spanish troops supplemented by 9,107 Puerto Rican volunteers. The first priority of the United States was raising troops for the Cuban expedition, and it was not until 18 June that President William McKinley, Secretary of War Russell A. Alger, and General Miles agreed on a Puerto Rican assault force of 34,000 men: 12,000 to come from IV Corps at Tampa, Florida; 16,000 volunteers from I Corps at Chickamauga Park, Georgia; and 6,000 from II Corps in northern Virginia. Miles was named commander of the expedition on 26 June.

After the fall of Santiago de Cuba on 17 July the U.S. government became anxious to seize Puerto Rico before any armistice or cessation of hostilities, so as to be able to lay a strong claim to the island in peace negotiations. Accordingly, Miles sailed from Santiago on 21 July with nine transports carrying 3,300 troops. They were accompanied by the battleship *Massachusetts*, three armed steamers, and two smaller warships. The rest of the troops for the assault were embarking at Tampa, Florida; Charleston, South Carolina, and Newport News, Virginia. As his landing force neared its original objective, Fajardo on the eastern coast, Miles decided to land instead near Ponce on the southern coast. In part, this decision was made in the expectation that fewer Spanish troops would be encountered in the neighborhood of Ponce; in part, this approach was made because Miles was intent on seizing Puerto Rico without the navy bombarding San Juan and taking credit for the victory.

Early in the morning of 25 July the expedition landed at Guánica, a deep and sheltered harbor in the southeastern corner of the island. The Spanish offered only token resistance, and the railroad and road to Ponce were seized after minor skirmishes on the following day. On the 27th the brigade from Charleston arrived. Naval reconnaissance having revealed that the port of Ponce was neither defended nor mined, this brigade attacked Ponce from the sea on the 28th and linked up with troops sent from Guánica by land. The Spanish withdrew up the military road to San Juan. The capture of Ponce was greeted enthusiastically by the inhabitants, and it was soon evident that, despite the recent installation of an autonomous government, the Puerto Rican population was overwhelmingly favorable to the U.S. invasion. The Puerto Rican volunteers deserted the Spanish colors en masse, halving the Spanish forces, and many of them sought to join U.S. forces. Puerto Rican public officials entertained U.S. commanders, and many individuals supplied labor and materiel to the invaders.

Having secured the area and provided himself a base with two excellent harbors to assure the flow of troops, supplies, and rearward communication, Miles set about building his force to 17,000. As he planned his campaign, it was evident that he had learned much from logistical fiascoes in Cuba. Landings of men, horses, and goods were carried out efficiently, and local commodities were purchased as necessary. Miles wanted to dislodge the Spaniards blocking the military road at Aibonito and do so with a mini-

mum of bloodletting as a preparation for investing San Juan. Because the Spaniards had good positions in a mountain barrier running east-west across the island, Miles designed a campaign built on two pincer attacks, one directed against Arecibo, the other against Aibonito. He sent an assault column under Gen. Theodore Schwan to flank the mountains to the west via Mayagüez and Aguadilla and take Arecibo on the northern coast. Another column, under Gen. Guy V. Henry, was to march from Ponce over the mountains via Adjuntas and Utuado, rendezvous with Schwan at Arecibo and march eastward with him to Bayamón and threaten San Juan. Another force that had landed at Arroyo under Maj. Gen. John R. Brooke and had moved on Guayama, was directed to attack Cayey and cut the military road at Aibonito. A fourth column under Maj. Gen. James H. Wilson was to march up the military road from Ponce, join Brooke at Aibonito and together with him move on Aguas Buenas near Bayamón. These columns could thus find it possible to support one another and outflank enemy resistance as necessary.

The offensive got under way 9 August and met only weak resistance from the Spanish. Apart from a skirmish at Coamo that cost the United States Army 6 wounded and the Spanish 6 killed and about 40 wounded, and smaller skirmishes at Guayama, at Las Marias near Mayagüez, and outside Adjuntas, the campaign was almost without incident. When word arrived on 13 August that an armistice had been signed, the United States controlled Puerto Rico, and the remaining Spanish forces were retreating on San Juan. Despite Miles's efforts to minimize the role of the navy in the course of which he had gone so far as getting President McKinley to order Adm. William T. Sampson not to bombard San Juan, the navy had earned its share of the triumph by capturing Fajardo.

A month after they had landed, most of the U.S. troops were on their way home. The campaign had gone so easily and quickly that it was not taken very seriously in the United States. Miles's hopes for glory had been in vain. Had he planned and executed less competently and shed more of his troops' blood, he might have cut a more heroic figure in the popular press.

Joseph M. McCarthy

REFERENCES

Graham A. Cosmas, *An Army for Empire: The U.S. Army in the Spanish-American War* (Univ. of Missouri Pr., 1971); Frank Freidel, *The Splendid Little War* (Little, Brown, 1958); Virginia W. Johnson, *The Unregimented General: A Biography of Nelson A. Miles* (Houghton Mifflin, 1962); Nelson A. Miles, *Serving the Republic: Memories of the Civil and Military Life of Nelson A. Miles, Lieutenant-General United States Army* (Scribner, 1911); Angel Rivero, *Cronica de la guerra Hispanoamericana en Puerto Rico* (Editorial Edil, 1972).

Puller, Lewis Burwell (1898–1971)

Lewis Burwell (Chesty) Puller, who achieved fame in World War II and in the Korean War, became one of the most decorated marines. He served in Nicaragua early in his military career, during which time he led a Nicaraguan national guard patrol and demonstrated a tough, courageous attitude toward training and combat and a good understanding of guerrilla warfare.

Puller was born in West Point, Virginia, on 26 June 1898. After attending local schools, he went to the Virginia Military Institute for about a year. In 1918 he enlisted in the United States Marine Corps, but the war ended before he was shipped to France. Although he attended officers' training school and was commissioned a second lieutenant, he was mustered out in the postwar reduction of the Marine Corps. He returned to the marines as a corporal and served in Haiti as an officer in the U.S.-trained Haitian constabulary from 1919 to 1924. Returning to the United States in 1924, he was commissioned a second lieutenant in the Marine Corps and served in various posts in the United States and Hawaii. In 1928 he began his first tour of duty in Nicaragua, returned to the United States in 1931 to attend the Army Infantry School at Fort Benning, Georgia, and then went back to Nicaragua for a second tour in 1932 and 1933.

When Puller first arrived in Nicaragua in 1928, he had assignments in Managua and Corinto, and was promoted to first lieutenant in the Marine Corps in October 1929. His chance to participate in the antiguerrilla campaign against the Nicaraguan rebel leader Augusto C. Sandino came with the arrival of Col. Douglas C. McDougal as commander of the Nicaraguan National Guard. Puller was promoted to captain in the guard and assigned to lead Company M, a mobile patrol based in Jinotega but operating mostly in the field. Puller quickly learned the hazards of patrolling in the jungles and mountains of northern Nicaragua, not dissimilar to his experience in Haiti fighting the *Cacos* (Haitian peasant guerrillas).

Under Puller's leadership Company M became one of the most effective guerrilla-fighting units. Maj. Julian C. Smith, a veteran of the second intervention and coauthor of a study of the organization and operation of the Nicaraguan national guard, noted that one unique and important feature of Company M was its mobility. Its mission was offensive, not defensive, and it moved widely and was away from its base for weeks at a time. Puller did not favor the use of horses because they slowed a patrol's pace and required too much attention; he found pack mules more acceptable.

Normally Company M had a complement of 30 men and two officers. Puller's second-in-command was Lt. William A. Lee. Puller was strong on drill and discipline and helped to instill high confidence and morale in his men. Both friend and foe recognized the patrol's abilities and dubbed Puller "*El Tigre*" for his aggressiveness. There were atrocity stories about Puller and his men and, as Neill Macaulay has written, he was a worthy opponent of a savage foe, but the charges were often absurd. Perhaps an indication of the guerrillas' fear of and respect for him was the reward Sandino placed on Puller's head.

At the time of the Managua earthquake in 1931, Puller volunteered to help bury the dead and distribute supplies. His last effort at pacification in Nicaragua was to command a successful engagement ensuring a peaceful dedication of the León-El Sauce railroad by President José María Moncada. For this achievement, a grateful Moncada promoted Captain Puller to major in the Guardia Nacional de Nicaragua. During his service in Nicaragua, he received two Navy Crosses. Puller was one of several marine officers whose experience in Nicaragua proved beneficial in later World War II assignments.

After leaving Nicaragua in 1933, Puller served in posts in the United States and the Far East. During World War II he was in the Pacific and participated in the Guadalcanal campaign and the assault on Peleliu. During the Korean War he was involved in the Inchon landing and the Chosin Reservoir campaign. He was promoted to brigadier general in 1951, to major general in

1953, and to lieutenant general when he retired in 1955; he died on 11 October 1971.

William Kamman

REFERENCES

Burke Davis, *Marine! The Life of Lt. Gen. Lewis B. (Chesty) Puller, USMC (Ret.)* (Little, Brown, 1962); Neill Macaulay, *The Sandino Affair* (Quadrangle, 1967); J. Robert Moskin, *The U.S. Marine Corps Story* (McGraw-Hill, 1977); Lewis B. Puller, Jr., *Fortunate Son* (Grove Weidenfeld, 1991); Julian C. Smith and others, *A Review of the Organization and Operations of the Guardia Nacional de Nicaragua* (n.p., n.d.).

Punitive Expedition, Mexico (1916–1917)

The Mexican Revolution of 1910 ushered in a bloody period as claimants to power fought to gain control of Mexico following the overthrow of Porfirio Díaz. Over the period 1910–1916 the revolutionary struggle led to the loss of U.S. lives in Mexico and U.S. property taken, damaged, or stolen. Border incidents rose dramatically, triggering protests to Washington by U.S. citizens living close to the border. At the same time, President Woodrow Wilson was convinced that the United States had an important role in shaping Mexico's political system. This conviction was based on the view that democracy was the only just and fair system of government. Gen. Victoriano Huerta had taken power in Mexico in 1913 following the assassination of President Francisco I. Madero. But before his government would be recognized by the United States, President Wilson demanded that fair elections be held in which Huerta would not be a candidate. General Huerta refused, prompting President Wilson to undertake a campaign to rid Mexico of Huerta.

The occupation of Veracruz, Mexico, political pressure by the United States, and arms sales to Huerta's opponents eventually led to Huerta's resignation. In the struggle that followed, the Constitutionalists led by Venustiano Carranza, the former governor of the state of Coahuila, occupied Mexico City. Carranza declared himself the "First Chief." However, Emiliano Zapata in the South and Francisco "Pancho" Villa in the North challenged his rule, and the revolution continued.

Wilson turned his attention to Villa as a viable successor to Carranza. A native of the soil and having the support of many peasants, Villa controlled the state of Chihuahua, adjacent to Texas. By 1914 he appeared to be a powerful figure, with an estimated 40,000 well-armed men with artillery and adequate supplies, much of it from U.S. mining interests.

Relations between Villa and the United States appeared good in 1914. However, after Carrancista forces defeated Villa, limited his forces to Chihuahua, and pushed Zapata further south, President Wilson became convinced that Carranza was the wave of the future. An arms embargo was placed on Villa's forces. What seemed to infuriate Villa was the fact that U.S. forces under Gen. John J. Pershing coordinated defense lines along the Texas-Mexican border with Carrancista forces. Another defeat was inflicted on Villa when he tried to take Agua Prieta, a Mexican suburb of Douglas, Arizona. Villa was humiliated. Blaming the United States, Villa's forces raided Columbus, New Mexico, in revenge. This set the stage for the Punitive Expedition into Mexico in 1916.

U.S. forces reacted quickly by entering the state of Chihuahua. Pershing, in command of U.S. forces numbering about 10,000, organized his forces into two columns. The east column included one cavalry squadron, two infantry regiments, an artillery battalion plus one battery, and one aero squadron of eight aircraft. The west column included two cavalry squadrons (less two troops) and one battery of field artillery.

Three battles marked critical periods of the Punitive Expedition. The first occurred at Guerrero, where U.S. and Villista forces met in battle for the first time. In preliminary actions, Villista forces attacked Carrancista troops in several locations. Villa defeated the government forces except in one battle during which not only were the Villista forces repulsed, but Villa was wounded and taken by his men to Guerrero. It was at Guerrero that the battle occurred that affected the course of the Punitive Expedition. It marked the end of Villa's threat to the United States for some time. The critical problem after this fight was relations between the United States and Mexico and their armed forces (Atkin, p. 280).

The action began when a detachment from the west column learned of Villa's presence in Guerrero. Villa was able to depart before the battle began. As the column formed for the attack, Villa's forces scattered and dispersed in various directions, many heading for the mountains and safety. Even so, 30 Villistas were killed and only four U.S. soldiers were wounded. In the aftermath, Villista forces scattered throughout the state of Chihuahua, making them more difficult to find and bring to battle.

Later, another battle occurred in the area around Parral, 200 miles into Mexico, that led to a change in the relations between U.S. and Carrancista forces. Earlier, Carrancista and U.S. forces had cooperated, more or less, in the pursuit of Villa. But the presence of U.S. troops so deep in Mexico triggered a Mexican nationalistic reaction. The Carranza government told Pershing and his men to leave Mexico. This set the stage for the battle in Parral.

One detachment of U.S. troops under Maj. Frank Tompkins moved into the outskirts of Parral in search of Villa and his forces. The U.S. soldiers were prevented from entering the town and were attacked by Carrancista forces supported by the townspeople. The detachment conducted an orderly retreat, taking defensive positions at Santa Cruz del Sur. It held off more than 600 Carrancista troops, while losing 40 killed. As a consequence of this battle, Pershing became convinced of the futility of chasing Villa across the countryside. It was also clear that the Carranza-Villa armies had formed an alliance against the U.S. forces. In an effort to stabilize the relations between U.S. and Carrancista forces and to set the stage for a more fully coordinated effort against Villa, Pershing established five military districts. Each was commanded by a regimental cavalry commander with the mission of clearing his area of Villista forces.

The third battle, at Carrizal, ultimately led to the withdrawal of the Punitive Expedition from Mexico. Two troops of U.S. cavalry commanded by Capt. Charles T. Boyd were on reconnaissance and attempted to pass through Carrizal. The passage was prevented by the Mexican commander, supported by 200 Carrancistas in entrenched positions. The U.S. troops attacked and were repulsed with heavy casualties, including 24 captured. A relief column from the 11th Cavalry rounded up the survivors. This was the worst defeat suffered by the U.S. forces. The battle was the last action of the Punitive Expedition. U.S. forces withdrew as the war in Europe began to seriously affect U.S. interests.

Throughout the expedition, U.S. forces numbered about 10,000 regulars and suffered 500–600 casualties. The Villista forces numbered between 450–800. Even with this disparity in numbers, Villa was not captured and was able to regroup after the withdrawal of the U.S. forces from Mexico. Although the Punitive Expedition provided experience for many officers who were to command U.S. forces in World War I, the lessons learned in unconventional conflict were quickly lost. U.S. leaders were to try to learn the same lessons 50 years later (O'Connor, p. 122).

Sam C. Sarkesian

REFERENCES

Ronald Atkin, *Revolution! Mexico, 1910–1920* (John Day, 1970); Haldeen Braddy, *Pershing's Mission in Mexico* (Texas Western Pr., 1966); Clarence C. Clendenen, *Blood on the Border: The United States Army and the Mexican Irregulars* (Macmillan, 1966); Richard O'Connor, *Black Jack Pershing* (Doubleday, 1961); Sam C. Sarkesian, *America's Forgotten Wars; The Counterrevolutionary Past and Lessons for the Future* (Greenwood Pr., 1984); Donald Smythe, *Guerrilla Warrior, The Early Life of John J. Pershing* (Scribner, 1973).

See also list of entries at front of book for Punitive Expedition, Mexico (1916–1917).

Q-R

Quilalí, Nicaragua, Siege (1927–1928)

In December 1927, the U.S. Marine command in Nicaragua decided to launch a ground offensive against nationalist leader Augusto C. Sandino's headquarters at El Chipote. This decision came after air attacks failed to dislodge the Sandinistas who were well dug in and protected by heavy woods. Two strong marine and Nicaraguan national guard columns totaling about 175 men were selected for the task. The first patrol, under Capt. Richard Livingston, left Jinotega for Quilalí, the rendezvous point, on 19 December; the second, under national guard 1st Lt. Merton A. Richal, left Telpaneca for Quilalí. On 30 December as Livingston's patrol neared Quilalí from the south on a narrow path bordered by a steep slope to the right and the Jícaro River to the left, the Sandinistas ambushed the patrol. After 80 minutes of heavy fighting, the rebels withdrew. Five marines were killed and 23, including Livingston, were wounded; two national guardsmen were killed, and two were wounded.

On the same day, guerrillas also attacked Richal's column but withdrew after a short engagement in which one marine was wounded. On New Year's Day Richal's patrol faced a more serious attack about six miles northwest of Quilalí near Las Cruces Hill. National guard 1st Lt. Thomas G. Bruce was killed by the first volley of enemy fire, and the men composing the point fell back in disarray. Using a stokes mortar and 37-mm gun, the patrol counterattacked. Lieutenant Richal was seriously wounded, but Sgt. Edward G. Brown led the successful taking of Las Cruces Hill. Relief came from a platoon of Livingston's column in Quilalí and from planes strafing enemy positions. The next day the combined patrols reached their destination without further fighting.

The two columns, at this point under siege in Quilalí, had been badly hit—eight killed, 31 wounded, more than half of them seriously. They needed medicine, supplies, and an experienced commander to replace the wounded Livingston; the casualties needed to be evacuated. Because the town had no landing strip, tools were airdropped so that one could be constructed. In a day's time the marines and national guardsmen razed a number of buildings along the town's main street and constructed a short landing field ending at a deep ravine. First Lt. Christian F. Schilt volunteered to fly his Vought 02U-1 Corsair, with oversize wheels, into Quilalí. After the first landing was aborted Schilt decided to drop the plane from an altitude of about 10 feet and have marines grab the wings to slow down his craft. Despite the difficulties and enemy fire, Schilt completed 10 trips between 6–8 January 1928. He delivered 1,400 pounds of medicine and supplies and a new troop commander. He evacuated 18 wounded men in the first use of a plane as an ambulance by U.S. forces in warfare. For his heroism, Lieutenant Schilt received the Medal of Honor. The reinvigorated marine and national guard columns were able to leave Quilalí on 10 January for San Albino.

William Kamman

REFERENCES

Edwin H. Brainard, "Marine Corps Aviation," *Marine Corps Gazette*, 13 (1928); 25–36; Neill Macaulay, *The Sandino Affair* (Quadrangle, 1967); Peter B. Mersky, *U.S. Marine Corps Aviation, 1912 to the Present* (Nautical & Aviation, 1983); Robert Lee Sherrod, *History of Marine Corps Aviation in World War II* (Combat Forces Pr., 1952); Julian C. Smith and others, *A Review of the Organization and Operations of the Guardia Nacional de Nicaragua* (n.p., n.d.).

Railroad: Manila to Dagupan During the Philippine War

When hostilities erupted between the United States Army occupying Manila and the Philippine Republican Army surrounding the city on 4 February 1899, both sides recognized the importance of the only railroad line in the Philippines. Built and owned by a British firm, the railroad ran northward through the Pampanga plain of central Luzon from the Manila suburb of Caloocan to Malolos, the temporary Republican capital, through Calumpit, San Fernando, Angeles, Tarlac, and Bayambang to Dagupan on the Lingayen Gulf, a distance of about 150 miles. The principle farming area on Luzon stretched northward along the railroad. Although less than one-tenth of the total land area of Luzon, the Pampanga plain was the breadbasket of the island and strongly held by the Philippine Republican Army. Thirty to 50 miles wide, the plain was bordered on the east, toward the interior, by the towering ranges of the Benguet Mountains and on the west, near the coast, by the Zambales Mountains.

The best supply line in central Luzon was the railroad, and its capture, with bridges intact and with as much rolling stock as possible, was the major objective of U.S. forces in 1899. To conduct military operations away from its base in Manila, the United States Army needed the railroad to transport supplies; the Philippine Republican Army depended on the railroad for supplies from the fertile farming communities located along the 150 miles of track.

On 10 February Maj. Gen. Arthur MacArthur, commander of the 2nd Division, attacked Caloocan five miles north of Manila and captured the railroad maintenance plant with a considerable amount of rolling stock, including 5 railroad engines, 50 passenger coaches, and over 100 freight and flat cars. British-manufactured, the trains were smaller than their U.S. counterparts. Possession of this rolling stock, repaired by MacArthur's troops, enabled the 2nd Division to use the railroad on its future advances. MacArthur created his own special armored train consisting of four cars, the first and last being flat cars, while the other two were box cars. MacArthur mounted a rapid-fire, six-pound naval gun and three machine guns on the first flat car. The other three cars carried supplies. When the division took the offensive, the armored train became MacArthur's field command post and provided sleeping quarters for the general and his staff.

At sunrise on 25 March MacArthur attacked the Filipino forces north of Caloocan. Using the armored train, the general bombarded the Filipino trenches for 30 minutes. The first flat car was a rolling powerhouse with its three machine guns and naval six pounder, a rapid-fire pompom gun. As the train neared the trenches, the naval gun fired shell after shell atop the enemy trenches while the three machine guns peppered the top of the trenches to prevent any Filipino defender from raising his head. The infantry moved forward and added to the firepower as Krag and Springfield rifles fired on the Filipino line. The 10,000 men of the division stretched for eight miles on each side of the railroad tracks.

The Filipino army retreated, unbolting railroad tracks and destroying bridges as they withdrew north to Malolos. Because they failed to heat and bend the rails, MacArthur's men quickly repaired the damage to the tracks. Destroyed bridges were more difficult to repair because of the absence of good timber, but MacArthur used newly captured rolling stock to reconstruct his battle train on the far side of streams and rivers.

If no locomotive was available, Chinese coolies pulled the train up the track to the next battle line. As soon as bridges were repaired, or a new engine captured, MacArthur rehooked his train and continued the offensive. The speed of his movements often surprised the Filipino leadership which retreated north, abandoning Malolos (31 March) and San Fernando (5 May). MacArthur's final offensive was delayed by army reorganization and by the monsoon rains in June.

On 8 November MacArthur resumed his offensive from San Fernando north up the railroad. Resistance was light. Retreating north up the railroad, the Filipino army did not attempt to hold any position, but instead provided just enough opposition to make MacArthur deploy his forces for battle. In six days, MacArthur's division advanced 30 miles. On 12 November he captured Tarlac, the second Republican capital. On 17 November MacArthur left Tarlac with 1,000 handpicked men in a mad dash north up the railroad. In the next three days, the forward column occupied the railroad line all the way to Dagupan. MacArthur's advance was so rapid that the retreating Filipinos did not have an opportunity to remove a single rail or destroy a single bridge or culvert.

MacArthur's division at this point controlled the railroad from Manila to Dagupan. The 16 regiments, including 14,000 enlisted men and 400 officers, were divided into company units and dispersed to garrison 117 towns and small villages along the railroad line. Filipino guerrillas harassed the garrisons and small work parties repairing destroyed bridges, tracks, and telegraph lines. A favorite guerrilla tactic was to excavate a hole under the railroad tracks so that the tracks would collapse and wreck the train when a heavy locomotive passed. To limit the damage, locomotives were placed in the rear of the trains rather than in the forward positions.

In April 1900, the railroad line was returned to its British owners, although U.S. garrisons continued to maintain security against guerrilla harassment for the next two years.

Kenneth Ray Young

REFERENCES

Frederick Funston, *Memories of Two Wars: Cuba and Philippine Experiences* (Scribner, 1911); William T. Sexton, *Soldiers in the Sun: An Adventure in Imperialism* (Military Service Pub. Co., 1939).

Railways and the Punitive Expedition

When the Punitive Expedition commanded by Gen. John J. Pershing crossed into Mexico in March 1916, United States Army logistical planning was based on extensive use of the Mexican railway system. The United States believed that the Mexican government of President Venustiano Carranza would cooperate with the expedition in ridding Carranza of his longtime rival, Francisco "Pancho" Villa. The United States had earlier permitted Carranza to use U.S. railways to transport his troops, a concession that was most significant in the victory of Carranza's forces over Villa at Agua Prieta, Sonora, in November 1915.

U.S. forces were interested in using the Mexican Central Railway running south from Ciudad Juárez to Chihuahua City and the Northwestern Railway running southwest from Juárez. The use of these two lines would bring most of the expedition's units within reasonable distance of rail supply. U.S. political and military leaders expected Carranza's officials to expedite and protect U.S. rail shipments.

In the early days of the expedition, the confused situation permitted the generally unrestricted use of the railways envisioned by army planners. Efforts to extract formal cooperation from the Carranza government, however, soon unraveled in the diplomatic wrangling over the presence of the Punitive Expedition in Mexico. Carranza was worried both about the intentions of the United States during the intervention and the public relations problem of aiding the expedition by permitting free use of Mexican railways. The result was a working arrangement that the United States reluctantly accepted. Supplies for the expedition could be shipped by Mexican railways as regular commercial freight, but had to be consigned to civilians who acted as intermediaries for the United States Army. The Carranza government agreed to expedite shipments, but refused to furnish them protection; there was also a specific prohibition on the shipment of ammunition by rail.

This working arrangement was maintained despite worsening relations between the Mexican government and the U.S. government. In November 1916 an agreement was reached permitting the direct shipment of supplies from El Paso to expedition headquarters at Colonia

Dublán, Chihuahua. This latest agreement represented the type of arrangement that U.S. officials had expected from the beginning. It came far too late, however, to assist the operations of the Punitive Expedition, which began its withdrawal within two months.

U.S. officials suspected that the Carranza administration's position on the use of railways was designed to hasten the expedition's departure. Problems with the use of railways had the unintended benefit of forcing a rapid improvement in motorized supply, which became crucial to the logistics of the expedition. While restrictions on the use of Mexican railways hampered the expedition's activities, other operational problems and diplomatic restraints were equally important in influencing the expedition's outcome.

Don M. Coerver

REFERENCES

Clarence C. Clendenen, *Blood on the Border: The United States Army and the Mexican Irregulars* (Macmillan, 1969); Linda B. Hall and Don M. Coerver, *Revolution on the Border: The United States and Mexico, 1910–1920* (Univ. of New Mexico Pr., 1988); Jeff Jore, "Pershing's Mission in Mexico: Logistics and Preparation for the War in Europe," *Military Affairs*, 52 (1988), 117–121; U.S. Department of State, *Foreign Relations of the United States, 1916* (U.S. Government Printing Office, 1925); Frank E. Vandiver, *Black Jack: The Life and Times of John J. Pershing* (Texas A&M Univ. Pr., 1977), 2 vols.

See also Motorized Supply for the Punitive Expedition.

Railways in the Spanish-Cuban/American War

Most historians agree that, although the rails at first were thought to have little commercial application and would play only a limited role in the economy, the United States was shaped by its transportation system. The rails encouraged the shift from a rural to an urban society; expanded the scope of businesses from local to regional and, finally, to a national market; altered the relationship between producers and consumers; and played a key role in the shift from a *laissez-faire* economy to regulatory capitalism.

Although a full-grown national system of rails was not achieved until the 20th century, by the time of the Spanish-Cuban/American War in 1898 about three-quarters of the total number of rail miles had been laid. In addition, railroads had adopted standardized time (1883) and a uniform track gauge (1886). Trains also had the convenience of both heating (1881) and lighting (1887). Despite the greater ease of travel, rail passage in the 1890s was still fairly dangerous and fraught with problems.

In the South, in particular, where the military disembarkation point for Cuba was located, the roads were troubled with a chronic shortage of labor. The history of railroads in the South indicates that the Southerners' dislike of mechanical pursuits left much of the operation of its trains to Northerners. Even after the Civil War, the scarcity of skilled labor persisted. Many elements contributed to this problem. Wages, for example, for unskilled labor in the North were $1.50–$1.75 per day, while in the South they were $.80–$1.00 per day.

More importantly, by the onset of the war with Spain, nationwide standardized equipment had brought about a need for greater efficiency and control of trains. In response, the railroad companies began a modern system of corporate management. No other business, except perhaps the telegraph, required so many, so varied, and so intricate short-term operating decisions. The sheer size of some roads led a group of companies to decentralize management to regions. At the top was a small group of executives coordinating and appraising several autonomous but interlocking systems. Nevertheless, as rail systems were entering a period of consolidation rather than expansion, management problems were still not fully resolved and played an important role in the poor organization of the U.S. military supply system.

Since their inception, rails have had an enormous impact on the conduct of the war. They made conscription possible in the sense that they transported thousands of troops to the battlefield. Eliminating long marches, the rails enabled the troops to arrive at the front fresh and ready for battle. They also allowed for the quick evacuation of the wounded from the front and their immediate replacement with healthy soldiers. Along with the telegraph, the railroads transformed war from remote campaigns waged by nations with small professional armies to the business of the entire national population.

The rails created problems in combat, as well as resolved them. The primary problem was the organization and transport of supplies. Many hard lessons centering on organizing and operating adequate supply lines were learned in military campaigns. In the United States, the first opportunity for the military to learn of the drawbacks of the rail was during the Civil War. However, due to problems related above, transport of supplies remained a thorny problem for military officers in the conflict with Spain at the end of the century.

The breakdown of military organization in the Spanish-Cuban/American War cannot be ascribed solely to inadequate rail systems. For one thing, neither the military nor Congress had ever formulated a policy for military organization. As historian Richard Goldhurst observed, it was nobody's business to see whether there were adequate terminals to handle supply trains at Tampa, Florida. In the 19th century, generals presided over geographic divisions with little interdivisional communication. Oversight of military matters was had by 10 bureaus in Washington, each operating as a small autonomous kingdom.

Thus, when John J. Pershing, quartermaster in charge of supplies for the 10th Cavalry, arrived in the South to take up his duties he was met with chaos. He found, for example, only one chute to load 300 horses on the train. It took the troops two days to traverse 675 miles. Most of Pershing's time was spent in stamping out fires caused by sparks from the engines.

As troops jammed Florida, troop trains as far north as Gainesville waited for clearance to proceed to Tampa. A single track was provided to move both troops and supplies from Tampa to Port Tampa for loading on ships. Furthermore, freight cars arrived without bills of lading. This meant that quartermasters had to go from car to car to find what they needed. More often what they found was that freight cars had been loaded with little thought to organization. For example, the harnesses for the artillery caissons were loaded in the same cars as naval supplies.

In summary, the rails contributed to the organizational breakdown of the military in the Spanish-Cuban/American War. The national rail system was burdened by problems of inefficiency, labor shortages, and safety. The most serious drawback of the rails in the conflict was the lack of organization in the loading and transport of supplies from points north to Tampa.

Mary S. Mander

REFERENCES

Alfred Chandler, comp. and ed., *The Railroads: The Nation's first Big Business* (Johns Hopkins Univ. Pr., 1965); Robert William Fogel, *Railroads and Economic Growth: Essays in Econometric History* (Johns Hopkins Univ. Pr., 1964); Richard Goldhurst, *Pipe Clay and Drill: John J. Pershing: The Classic American Soldier* (Reader's Digest Pr., 1977); Walter Licht, *Working for the Railroad* (Princeton Univ. Pr., 1983); John F. Stover, *American Railroads* (Univ. of Chicago Pr., 1961).

Reed, Walter (1851–1902)

Walter Reed, an army physician, led the U.S. effort to eradicate yellow fever in Cuba during the U.S. occupation 1899–1902.

Reed was born on 13 September 1851, in Gloucester County, Virginia, to the Reverend Lemuel and Pharaba Reed. After serving small Methodist churches in North Carolina and Western Virginia, Rev. Lemuel Reed requested and received an assignment in 1865 to Charlottesville, where Walter entered the University of Virginia at age 15. At age 17, Reed entered medical school and received his medical degree in 1869. He began further training at Bellevue Hospital in New York that same year and also became assistant physician at Infants' or Nursery Hospital at Randalls' Island. Bellevue withheld the M.D. degree until Reed reached age 21.

After a residency in orthopedics at Brooklyn City Hospital and service on the Brooklyn Board of Health, Reed entered the Army Medical Corps as a first lieutenant in 1875 and began duty at Willets Point, New York. In April 1876, he married Emilie Lawrence, whom he had known from childhood and began married life by traveling to a new post in Yuma, Arizona. Reed served in various posts in the West and was promoted to captain in 1880.

Because he was unable to keep abreast of the numerous medical advances taking place, Reed successfully requested leave to pursue additional training in pathology and bacteriology at Johns Hopkins Medical School. In 1891 he was assigned to posts in Montana and Minnesota. At the end of 1893, he was assigned to Washington, D.C., as curator of the Army Medical Museum and professor of clinical and sanitary microscopy in the newly created Army Medical School. He also served on the staff of Columbia Medical School as professor of pathology and bacteriology and conducted research on various diseases, including smallpox, rabies, malaria, and typhoid fever.

By the outbreak of the Spanish-Cuban/American War, Reed had become familiar with the latest research on yellow fever as a result of working with Surgeon General George M. Sternberg, an authority on the disease. Because of the many deaths from typhoid fever during the war, a typhoid fever board, later called a commission, was appointed with Reed as the chair to investigate the causes of the outbreak in army camps along the Atlantic seaboard. In 1899 Surgeon General Sternberg appointed Reed chairman of a board to investigate the acute infectious diseases prevalent in Cuba. Shortly, it became the Yellow Fever Commission, or Reed Commission. The commission's use of human volunteers resulted in scientific proof of the mosquito method of transmission of yellow fever as first suggested by Dr. Carlos J. Finlay of Cuba. Reed received international recognition for this work. In 1901 Reed returned to Washington, from Cuba, where he remained until his death 23 November 1902. In 1906 Congress honored Reed by naming the new Army Hospital and Medical Center outside Washington in his memory.

Robert D. Talbott

REFERENCES

William B. Bean, *Walter Reed: A Biography* (Univ. of Virginia Pr., 1982); Edward F. Dolan, Jr., *Vanquishing Yellow Fever, Walter Reed* (Encyclopaedia Britannica, 1964); William Crawford Gorgas, *Sanitation in Panama* (Appleton, 1915); A. Kelly, *Walter Reed: A Biography* (Univ. of Virginia Pr., 1982).

See also Reed Commission.

Reed Commission

On 23 May 1900, Surgeon General George M. Sternberg requested an order establishing a board of medical officers which would meet in Cuba to investigate the infectious diseases prevalent there, especially yellow fever. By the end of the month the War Department approved the request.

The board, later called the Yellow Fever Commission or Reed Commission, was composed of Maj. Walter Reed and contract surgeons James Carroll, Arístides Agramonte, and Jesse W. Lazear. Dr. Reed had previously served on the Typhoid Board and had studied yellow fever. Drs. Reed and Carroll arrived at Columbia Barracks in Cuba on 25 June, and the board began its investigations.

Just before the establishment of the Reed Commission, yellow fever had appeared at 20 General Lee Street in Quemados located beside Columbia Barracks, about eight miles from Havana. Both Havana and Quemados had been disinfected and cleaned up. Quemados was a health resort where people from Havana retired to avoid the heat and diseases of the city. Such an unexpected outbreak of yellow fever in a location thought to be safe provided the Reed Commission with readily available yellow fever patients for its work.

Reed decided that the most important activity should be the immediate investigation of the widely accepted theory that had not yet been disproved, the Sanarelli theory that credited the *bacillus icteroides* as the causative agent. As a result of performing autopsies and blood cultures on several patients in different stages of the disease and with varying degrees of severity, the Sanarelli theory was disproved.

Another theory that had not yet been investigated was that of Dr. Carlos J. Finlay, a Cuban who had been advancing the mosquito theory for several years. Members of the board visited Finlay and returned with several mosquito larvae and eggs. Lazear took charge of mosquito culture; Carroll studied intestinal flora; and Agramonte was placed in charge of the laboratory as well as of autopsies and pathological work. Hospital steward John Neate was transferred from Washington, at Reed's request, to serve as noncommissioned officer in charge of the laboratory. In addition to the routine bacteriological work, he raised and cared for the mosquitoes used by the board.

To test the mosquito theory, the members of the board, except Agramonte, an immune, volunteered to be human subjects. Gen. Leonard Wood, a doctor and governor general of Cuba, and Surgeon General Sternberg had approved the use of volunteer human subjects, a decision later severely criticized.

Toward the end of August, Carroll and Pvt. William E. Dean became infected with yellow fever as a result of being bitten by one of the infected mosquitoes. Both recovered. A short while later Lazear also contracted yellow fever as the result of the bite of an infected mosquito and died on 25 September.

Major Reed decided to announce the preliminary results in a paper delivered to the American Public Health Association meeting in Indianapolis, Indiana, on 14 October 1900. The paper was published in the *Philadelphia Medical Journal* on 22 October. Few doctors accepted the preliminary findings, and some researchers rejected them.

Because the human subjects had not been isolated during the experiment, it was necessary to repeat it under controlled circumstances. An isolation camp named Camp Lazear was established in November 1900, near Columbia Barracks. Two mosquito-proof wooden buildings were constructed. In one building, experiments with infected clothing, bedding, and other articles were conducted. Three nonimmune volunteers, a doctor and two privates in the hospital corps, were exposed to the soiled clothing and bedding of yellow fever patients for 20 days. They were kept in strict quarantine for the 20-day period. None of the volunteers developed the disease.

In December the experiment was repeated with two additional nonimmune volunteers. During this 20-day experiment, the volunteers wore the soiled clothing and slept on the soiled bedding of yellow fever patients. These two men did not contract yellow fever either.

At the same time other volunteers, who had been quarantined for two weeks before the December experiment started, were being bitten by infected mosquitoes. Of the 12 volunteers bitten, 10 developed yellow fever. Two of the 10 had previously participated in the experiment with infected articles without contracting the disease. The fact that no resident of Camp Lazear contracted yellow fever except those purposely bitten by infected mosquitoes or injected with infected blood, in spite of the fact that everyone at the camp lived under the same conditions, provided corroborating evidence for the theory.

More experiments in December 1900 and January 1901 with bites of infected mosquitoes and injections of contaminated blood proved that a patient cannot infect a mosquito after the third day of the disease and that the mosquito cannot transmit the disease until 12 days after biting a yellow fever victim.

The board's report was read at the meeting of the Pan-American Medical Congress in Havana on 6 February 1901. Because of the thoroughness of the experiments, the report was accepted, and the *stegomyia fasciata mosquito*, now named *aëdeo aegypti*, was acknowledged as the carrier of yellow fever.

Robert D. Talbott

REFERENCES

William B. Bean, *Walter Reed: A Biography* (Univ. of Virginia Pr., 1982); William Crawford Gorgas, *Sanitation in Panama* (Appleton, 1915); Walter Reed, *Recent Researches Concerning the Etiology, Propagation, and Prevention of Yellow Fever by the U.S. Army Commission*, Senate Doc. No. 118, 57th Congress, 2nd Session, 9–23; Albert E. Truby, *Memoir of Walter Reed: The Yellow Fever Episode* (Paul B. Hoeber, 1943).

See also Reed, Walter.

Reilly, Henry Joseph
(c. 1840–1900)

Henry J. Reilly was the best U.S. artillery battery commander between the Civil War and World War I. Born in Ireland in the early 1840s, Reilly spent the first years of the Civil War in the United States Navy, serving on a Union gunboat on the Mississippi River. In September 1864 he enlisted in the 5th United States Artillery and spent the rest of his life in that regiment.

By March 1866 Reilly held the rank of sergeant; in December, he received a direct commission to second lieutenant. Because promotion in the United States Army in the late 19th century was very slow and based strictly on seniority within each regiment, Reilly did not reach the rank of captain until 1894. He commanded batteries of the 5th Artillery in Cuba during the Spanish-Cuban/American War and during the fighting in the Philippines.

Reilly's Light Battery F habitually supported the 14th United States Infantry and was considered the best firing unit in the Philippines. Reilly hand-picked his three battery officers and trained them and the unit to his own exacting standards. Reilly's three lieutenants all became general officers, and their names constitute a "Who's Who" of U.S. artillery commanders of World War I.

During the Boxer Uprising in China (1899–1901) Reilly's battery was the only U.S. artillery unit in the Allied relief column that lifted the siege of the legation compound at Beijing. Reilly, still a captain after 34 years of commissioned service, was close to age 60 at the time. His battery supported the 14th Infantry when it passed through a stalled Russian attack against the Boxer siege force. After the Allies entered the legation compound, the Chinese withdrew behind the inner walls of the Imperial City, and the Allies continued the attack. Reilly supported the attack by moving four of his three-inch guns to the top of a wall that commanded the Shunchun Gate. Standing in an exposed position he directed his unit's fire.

Reilly's remaining two guns, under 1st Lt. Charles P. Summerall, accompanied the attacking infantry. In the face of concentrated Chinese fire, Summerall calmly walked up to the city gate and marked an "X" in chalk where he wanted his gunners to hit. The U.S. guns blasted the gate open, and Summerall did the same thing to the next gate. Reilly's battery performed magnificently; but as the battle came to an end, its commander was hit by a bullet that had ricocheted off masonry. Reilly died on 15 August 1900.

David T. Zabecki

REFERENCES

Fairfax D. Downey, *The Sound of the Guns: The Story of American Artillery From the Ancient and Honorable Company to the Atomic Cannon and Guided Missile* (McKay & Co., 1956); William H. Powell, *List of Officers of the Army of the United States from 1779 to 1900* (L.R. Hamersly & Co., 1900).

Remington, Frederic (1861–1909)

Frederic Remington covered events in Cuba and the Spanish-Cuban/American War as a war correspondent and illustrator. One of the most famous artists of the western United States, the illustrator, painter, sculptor, and author was born in Canton, New York, on 4 October 1861. His father, Seth Pierre Remington, a cavalry officer in the Civil War, moved the family to Ogdensburg, New York, where he published the *Ogdensburg Journal* and became influential in politics. Remington admired his father and was fascinated by stories of the Civil War and the military. As a youth he constantly sketched soldiers in the margins of his school notebooks. Remington attended Yale University where he studied fine arts and played football. At age 19, he made a trip to the West working as a cowboy, scout, and rancher. Upon his return, he studied

at the Art Student's League in New York. Aided by his late father's acquaintances, he secured a job in Albany, New York, but he had decided on a career of traveling and illustrating. In the 1880s he worked as an illustrator for *Harper's Weekly* and *Outing Magazine*. Fascinated by men of action, horses, and scenes of combat, he traveled through Germany, Russia (from which he was expelled), and North Africa. On a trip to the West he met Theodore Roosevelt, and in 1889 *Century Magazine* published a series of articles by Roosevelt with Remington's illustrations (later published as *Ranch Life and the Hunting Trail*). In 1891 Remington was elected an associate of the National Academy of Design.

Remington's first Cuban illustration, "The Flag of Cuba—Insurgent Cavalry Drawn up for a Charge," was drawn from a photograph and appeared March 1896 as the frontispiece in *Harper's Weekly*. He had yet to visit Cuba, but the opportunity came when he was commissioned by William Randolph Hearst's *New York Journal* to go to Cuba to illustrate and report on the war with correspondent Richard Harding Davis. Attempts to sail from Key West, Florida, in a small boat to avoid a Spanish blockade of Cuban ports proved unsuccessful—and nearly fatal. Eventually, the two booked passage on a commercial steamer, the *Olivette*, and arrived in Havana without any difficulty. They even had a formal interview with Capt.-Gen. Valeriano Weyler y Nicolau, which had been arranged by U.S. Consul General Fitzhugh Lee. Remington was disappointed by the lack of action and repulsed by the poverty and suffering brought by Spanish policies. He returned after a few weeks of drawing Spanish troops who were riding on emaciated ponies and scenes of soldiers executing rebels. Supposedly, before leaving Cuba, he cabled Hearst stating: "Everything is quiet. There is no trouble here. There will be no war." Hearst is said to have replied, "Please remain. You furnish the pictures. I'll furnish the war."

On 13 February the *Journal* published a Remington illustration with a sensational account of the search of Cuban women on the *Olivette* as it was departing Cuba for the United States. The article reported that Cuban women were stripped of their clothing and searched for messages from Cuban revolutionaries. Remington depicts several male officials leering over a naked woman. In actuality, women officials searched women passengers, but the artist had no way of knowing this because he was in New York City when the incident took place. The illustration is artistically noteworthy because it is one of the artist's few drawings featuring a woman.

After the explosion of the *Maine* in 1898, Remington began illustrating military training exercises for *Harper's Magazine*. On contract for both *Harper's* and the *Journal*, he spent seven days on the battleship *Iowa* off the Cuban coast, viewed training exercises and encampments in Tampa and Key West, Florida. Then he produced a remarkable number of sketches and paintings depicting naval maneuvers and camping life, as well as portraits of naval commanders, war correspondents, and cavalry officers. His accounts of the long voyage to Cuba with U.S. forces, the landing at Daiquirí, and the campaign of the Rough Riders were recorded in vivid prose and depicted in exquisite illustrations showing heroic fighting. Remington's published accounts of combat, in particular "With the Fifth Corps," published in *Harper's Monthly* (November 1898), are considered among the best written on the war and did much to advance the ambitions of his friend Theodore Roosevelt. In February 1899 Remington returned to Cuba as a special correspondent for *Collier's Weekly* to provide a series of personally illustrated articles entitled "The United States Army in Cuba."

Tall, handsome, and athletic, though portly in his later years, Remington married Eva Adele Caten of Gloversville, New York, in 1883, and her family supported them until his career was established. Throughout his adult life he maintained an elaborately equipped studio and library in New Rochelle, New York, where he resided until just six months before his death on 26 December 1909 at his new home and studio in Ridgefield, Connecticut.

Michael J. Devine

REFERENCES

Douglas Allen, *Frederic Remington and the Spanish-American War* (Crown, 1971); Royal Cortissoz, *American Artists* (Scribner, 1923), 225–243; Augustus Thomas, "Recollections of Frederic Remington," *Century Magazine*, 86 (1913), 354–361; Ben M. Vorpahl, "A Splendid Little War; Frederic Remington's Reaction to the Cuban Crisis as Revealed Through His Letters to Owen Wister," *American West*, 9 (1972), 28–35.

Richardson, Wilds Preston (1861–1929)

Brig. Gen. Wilds Preston Richardson was the commander of the American Expeditionary Force, North Russia (AEFNR) from 9 April to 5 August 1919. Briefed personally by President Woodrow Wilson, Richardson successfully extricated U.S. military forces from their controversial involvement in the intervention in North Russia, 1918–1919.

Born in Texas in 1861, Richardson graduated from the United States Military Academy at West Point in 1884 and then spent more than 30 years in a variety of command and technical posts, mostly in Alaska. Promoted brigadier general in early 1917, Richardson was commanding the 55th Infantry Brigade in France when, on 10 March 1919, he received orders from AEF commander Gen. John J. Pershing to take command of the AEFNR. Summoned to the headquarters of the U.S. peace delegation in Paris, Richardson was charged personally by President Wilson with supervising the U.S. evacuation from the icebound North as soon as possible after the opening of navigation.

Arriving at Archangel on 17 April, Richardson immediately replaced Col. George E. Stewart as commander of the AEFNR and took prompt steps to bolster sagging U.S. morale in the North. On 3 June, Richardson began the expeditious withdrawal of all U.S. military forces from Archangel, a process fully completed in just 24 days. In July, the energetic commander accomplished a similar evacuation of U.S. troops from Murmansk following which, on 5 August 1919, AEFNR headquarters in the North were officially discontinued.

On returning to the United States, Richardson reverted to his peacetime rank of colonel and retired from the army in 1920. Much esteemed by his military colleagues, Richardson died in 1929 and was buried at West Point.

John W. Long

REFERENCES

Dictionary of American Biography, s.v. "Richardson, Wilds Preston"; Wilds P. Richardson, "America's War in North Russia," *Current History*, 13 (Feb. 1921), 287–294.

See also Stewart, George Evans.

Rizal y Mercado, José (1861–1896)

José Rizal y Mercado was the first national figure to emerge in the Philippines. His position within Philippine nationalism has always been highly ambiguous. Although a strident advocate of reform, Rizal stopped short of advocating complete separation from Spain. Instead, he sought elite-led efforts to improve the Philippines through education and various internal improvements. One contemporary observed that Rizal's experiences were formed in libraries; he knew little of real life. Saving the Philippines from its misfortunes became his obsession. Rizal believed he held his country's salvation in his hands and was frequently oblivious to the great risks to his personal safety that his mission entailed.

Rizal, a highly gifted man, accomplished much during his short life of 35 years. He became a physician, artist, sculptor, writer, poet, scientist, linguist, historian, and social activist. Rizal was born in Calamba, Laguna, on 19 June 1861. His parents were affluent and well educated by the standards of the day. From an early age, Rizal was fascinated with books and knowledge encompassing all subjects. In 1872, he was sent to Manila to study at the Ateneo Municipal. After graduating in 1877, he studied medicine at the University of Santo Tomas.

In 1882, Rizal sailed for Europe to further his medical studies. His first sojourn abroad made a profound impression on him. Rizal continued his medical studies and received his lincentiate in medicine in 1884. He attempted to organize the tiny Filipino student community in Spain to fight for reform in the Philippines, but met with limited success.

Disillusioned by repression at Spanish universities, Rizal journeyed to France and Germany. Travel and study in these two countries greatly expanded his intellectual development. He began an extensive correspondence with Professor Ferdinand Blumentritt of Leitmeritz, Austria-Hungary. Over time, the two men became soul mates in their quest for Philippine reforms.

In 1887, Rizal published *Noli Me Tangere*, his first novel, which exposed social injustices in the Philippines under Spanish colonial rule. The book's impact on the Philippines was immediate, and it was later banned by the authorities. Nonetheless, it gained Rizal considerable notoriety. Against his friends' advice, he returned

home later that year, and in 1888, the colonial government strongly requested that he depart.

Rizal returned to Europe via Japan and the United States. In Great Britain, he copied and annotated Antonio de Morga's *Sucesos de las Islas Filipinas* to prove that the Filipinos were highly civilized prior to the Spaniards' arrival. The work was published in early 1890. Rizal also contributed articles to *La Solidariadad*, a Filipino periodical, published in Spain, devoted to encouraging reforms.

Most of Rizal's energies were devoted to *El Filibusterismo*, his second novel. Published in 1891, the work was a continuation of the *Noli* and explored the possibility of revolution if sweeping reforms were not granted. Meanwhile, disputes arose between Rizal and fellow Filipino reformers in Spain. Later that year, he moved to Hong Kong, where he joined his family, who had fled from Spanish persecution.

Rizal returned to the Philippines in 1892 to organize La Liga Filipina, which had the aim of fostering peaceful reforms. The colonial government responded by banishing him to Dapitan on the northern coast of Mindanao, where he languished for four years. Blumentritt urged him to petition to be sent to Cuba as a surgeon in the Spanish army.

While Rizal was in exile, more radical Filipinos led by Andrés Bonifacio formed the Katipunan, a secret society which strove for complete Philippine independence and forcible expulsion of the Spaniards. The Katipunan's leadership used Rizal as a rallying symbol without his knowledge or consent. When the Spaniards learned of the society's existence, they assumed Rizal was its mastermind.

In 1896, Bonifacio sent Dr. Pío Valenzuela to Dapitan to seek Rizal's advice on the impending revolt. Rizal strongly argued against revolution or violence, which angered the Katipunan leadership. Soon after, the colonial government suddenly granted Rizal's request for Cuban service. Rizal left for Europe shortly after the Revolution of 1896 erupted and was arrested for treason at the Suez Canal and jailed in Spain. He was later transported to Manila for trial. Rizal was tried in December 1896, found guilty, and sentenced to death by firing squad.

Rizal's final days have been shrouded in controversy. The Spaniards claimed he renounced Freemasonry and returned to the Catholic Church. Documents supporting this claim surfaced in 1935, but considerable doubt exists concerning their authenticity. Rizal was also said to have denounced the revolution then raging in the Philippines against Spanish rule. The night before his execution, he wrote *Mi Ultimo Adios*, which was a farewell poem to his country. There has also been controversy as to whether Rizal married Josephine Bracken shortly before the execution. Rizal was executed on 30 December 1896 at the Luneta.

Rizal's death destroyed most of what remained of goodwill between Spaniards and Filipinos. Once the United States gained control of the Philippines, the United States attempted to elevate Rizal to the role of a model Filipino. This policy has created a great deal of controversy. In recent decades, Filipino views of Rizal have fluctuated between hero worship and denunciation. Despite distortions of the historical record by Spaniards, U.S. commentators, and Filipinos, his importance to Philippine history cannot be disputed.

James C. Biedzynski

REFERENCES

Austin Coates, *Rizal: Philippine Nationalist and Martyr* (Oxford Univ. Pr., 1968); Leon Ma. Guerrerro, *The First Filipino* (National Hero's Commission, 1963); Rafael Palma, *Pride of the Malay Race* (Prentice-Hall, 1949); Carlos Quirino, *The Great Malayan* (Philippine Education Co., 1940); José Rizal, *Political and Historical Writings* (National Historical Commission, 1972).

See also Philippine Revolution (1896–1899).

Robison, Samuel Shelburne (1867–1952)

The administration of President Warren G. Harding selected Rear Adm. Samuel S. Robison for the post of military governor of the Dominican Republic as one of its initial appointments to that island nation during the U.S. occupation. Robison served from June 1921 through September 1922, a crucial period during which arrangements were completed for the withdrawal of the U.S. administration and occupation force.

Robison's appointment resulted from a full review of U.S. policy toward the Dominican Republic, and it reflected a commitment by the new administration to change this policy. Harding reestablished the primacy of the State Department over Dominican policy; henceforth,

the military governor was to be detailed to the State Department and to take his orders from it rather than from the Navy Department. This was an important shift because the State and Navy departments differed sharply on policy toward the island nation. The State Department was committed to ending the occupation as soon as practicable. The shift also resulted from the prevailing ill will between the military occupation authorities and the local populace.

The Harding administration conducted a careful evaluation before filling the post. The administration wanted a "civilian minded" officer who would be amenable to taking directions from the State Department because the new governor would play a crucial role in the preparations and evaluations necessary to implement the withdrawal to which Harding was committed. Admiral Robison, commander of the Boston Navy Yard before being sent to the Dominican Republic, was considered appropriate for this role; his arrival was intended to symbolize a change in U.S. policy.

Shortly after he arrived in the Dominican Republic in June 1921, Robison issued the proclamation containing the so-called Harding plan for withdrawal, in accordance with his instructions from the Harding administration. Although the plan proved unacceptable to the local populace, it was a significant shift in U.S. policy and launched a series of negotiations in which the United States was committed to withdrawal.

Even though Robison followed his initial instructions, he proved unsuited to the role of negotiator, becoming disenchanted with the Dominican objections and the protracted discussions. He came to differ with the State Department negotiators and became convinced that a prolonged occupation would be necessary. He was consistently overruled and was withdrawn after the installation of the provisional president.

Robison was discouraged by the continued Dominican demands for control of the Guardia Nacional Dominicana (the Dominican constabulary), having been alarmed by its condition and lack of training after his arrival. On this issue he clashed with diplomatic representatives, who recognized that conceding control of the constabulary to the provisional government was essential to secure any withdrawal agreement. President Harding overruled Robison's objections. Robison now issued proclamations reflecting the decisions of the Harding administration as influenced by the State Department's chief representative in the Dominican Republic, Sumner Welles, and establishing the basis for the various elections conducted as preliminary steps toward withdrawal.

Because of the deadlock and the protracted negotiations with the Dominicans, Robison's military government had to contract a foreign loan to keep the Dominican government afloat during the difficult post-World War I depression. The 1922 loan of $6.7 million in 5.5 percent, 20-year bonds was smaller than Robison felt necessary, but larger than the Dominicans wanted and thus represented a compromise between the two positions. The Dominicans initially objected strongly to the loan, but later accepted it, thus removing an obstacle to the withdrawal negotiations.

Kenneth J. Grieb

REFERENCES

Bruce J. Calder, *The Impact of Intervention: The Dominican Republic During the U.S. Occupation of 1916–1924* (Univ. of Texas Pr., 1984); Kenneth J. Grieb, "Warren G. Harding and the Dominican Republic U.S. Withdrawal, 1921–1923," *Journal of Inter-American Studies*, 11 (1969), 425–440; Dana G. Munro, *The United States and the Caribbean Republics, 1921–1933* (Princeton Univ. Pr., 1974).

Round Robin, Cuba (1898)

The round robin written by U.S. military and medical leaders in Cuba detailed a growing alarm over the appearance of malaria and yellow fever among U.S. soldiers in Cuba during the Spanish-Cuban/American War. It produced a firestorm of controversy and caused the War Department to alter its plans for bringing the troops home.

During the last two weeks of July 1898, following the Spanish surrender of Santiago de Cuba, a growing number of U.S. soldiers became ill from malaria or yellow fever. Initially, there had been little concern because officers believed that by moving the camps to high ground they could shake off the illnesses. Severe logistical problems prevented the removal, and the diseases spread. By 1 August some 4,000 troops had fallen sick. Worried, Gen. William R. Shafter informed his staff that to save hundreds of lives, he planned to recommend that all men he could spare be returned home at once.

His subordinates concurred and drafted a tough letter in which they urged immediate withdrawal. Joseph Wheeler, Leonard Wood, Theodore Roosevelt, and eight others signed it.

The round robin appeared on the front pages of some U.S. newspapers. Its impact was dramatic and led to a public demand for an explanation. President William McKinley and Secretary of War Russell A. Alger, who were delaying removal of troops until a reception point was ready, considered the letter a criticism of their leadership. Some newspapermen interpreted the letter as a criticism of General Shafter, and they blamed him for the medical difficulties. In response, McKinley and Alger, rather than shipping additional medical aid to Cuba and taking other appropriate steps, ordered Shafter to begin quickly the removal of soldiers from the island.

The letter was a mistake. It should not have been sent while diplomatic negotiations with Spain over the general course of the war were being held. It may not have saved lives, as intended, but it angered McKinley and embarrassed the country, laying bare its inability to hold territory won in Cuba.

Paul H. Carlson

REFERENCES

Paul H. Carlson, *"Pecos Bill:" A Military Biography of William R. Shafter* (Texas A&M Univ. Pr., 1989); Graham A. Cosmas, *An Army for Empire: The United States Army in the Spanish-American War* (Univ. of Missouri Pr., 1971); Margaret Leech, *In the Days of McKinley* (Harper, 1959); John D. Miley, *In Cuba With Shafter* (Scribner, 1899); David F. Trask, *The War With Spain in 1898* (Macmillan, 1981).

Rowan, Andrew Summers (1857–1943)

Andrew Summers Rowan, a career United States Army officer, made an initial contact with Cuban forces during the Spanish-Cuban/American War.

Rowan was born on 23 April 1857, in Gap Mills, Virginia (now West Virginia). He graduated from the United States Military Academy in 1881.

As war with Spain neared in 1898, First Lieutenant Rowan was sent on a secret mission to contact the Cuban insurgent leader, Gen. Calixto

García. After sailing from Jamaica to Cuba in a small open boat, Rowan made his way across country to García's camp at Bayamo. He successfully returned to Washington with a delegation of Cuban rebels. Rowan's mission subsequently became famous as a result of the appearance of Elbert H. Hubbard's story, "A Message to García," which used the episode to preach the importance of following orders regardless of obstacles.

During the war with Spain, Rowan served in Cuba and Puerto Rico. From 1899 to 1902 he participated in the Philippine War. He died in San Francisco, 10 January 1943.

Gerald W. McFarland

REFERENCES

Elbert H. Hubbard, *A Message to Garcia and Other Essays* (Thomas Y. Crowell, 1924); New York Times, 12 Jan. 1943.

Russell, John Henry (1872–1947)

Maj. Gen. John H. Russell, a career marine and 16th commandant of the United States Marine Corps, was the leading U.S. proconsul in Haiti. He was born on 14 November 1872 at Mare Island, California. The son of Rear Adm. John H. Russell, he received little encouragement from his father when he expressed an interest in going to the United States Naval Academy. Thus, at age 14 he obtained a meeting with President Grover Cleveland in quest of the nomination. When the president informed him of his reluctance to make further appointments because previous nominees had not performed well at the academy, Russell promised Cleveland that he would succeed. Russell reported to the Naval Academy in 1888, completed his studies there in 1892, and served two years at sea before being commissioned a second lieutenant in the Marine Corps in 1894. In a service where promotion was based on seniority and vacancies, Russell advanced to first lieutenant in 1898, captain in 1899, major in 1906, lieutenant colonel in 1916, and colonel in 1917. While serving in Haiti, he was promoted to brigadier general in 1922. On 1 March 1934, he became the major general commandant of the Marine Corps, with his permanent promotion to major general occurring on 7 March 1935 with a date of rank of 1 September 1933. On 1 December 1936 he retired with over

four decades of active service. Shortly after, he accepted an invitation to write a military commentary column for the *San Diego Union*. Russell died on 6 March 1947, and his last column appeared the day after his death. Russell married Mabel Howard on 11 June 1901, and they had one daughter, Mrs. Vincent (Brooke) Astor.

Russell could be called "the statesman commandant" because of his long service in Haiti, much of it in a diplomatic capacity, and his ability to work within the naval establishment and the Washington political arena. Between 11 February 1922 and 12 November 1930 he served in Haiti as high commissioner with the rank of ambassador extraordinary. This came after two tours as commanding officer of the 1st Marine Brigade. As a young officer, Russell had a normal career pattern for an officer of the "Old Corps." He alternated between sea duty (*Massachusetts*, *Yosemite*, and *Oregon*), barracks tours (many short postings, plus assignments of a year or longer in Washington, D.C.; Portsmouth, New Hampshire; Annapolis, Maryland; and Honolulu, Hawaii), and expeditionary duty (Guam, Panama, China, Mexico, the Dominican Republic, and Haiti).

Russell missed service in France during World War I, despite his requests for duty there, and remained in the Caribbean. In 1917 he commanded the 3rd and 4th Marine regiments in the Dominican Republic until promoted to colonel and detached to command the 1st Marine Brigade in Haiti between 28 November 1917 and 7 December 1918. At the special request of the State Department, he returned to Haiti as brigade commander between 1 October 1919, and 11 February 1922, until appointed U.S. high commissioner there. Thus, between 1917 and 1930, Russell served mostly in Haiti in military and diplomatic capacities. In 1929 and 1930 when the office of commandant became vacant, the State Department supported him for the position; in the 1920s it had advocated his advancement in the corps and for other significant assignments. But Russell had little backing within the Marine Corps because of his many years away from that service. Hence, the office went to Wendell C. Neville and Ben H. Fuller, respectively. In 1934, however, he became the 16th commandant of the Marine Corps.

Within the evolution of the Marine Corps from a service with traditional missions and a colonial infantry force to a modern institution with an amphibious warfare capability, Russell was a most important figure. He believed the traditional missions of ships' guards, security of naval bases, and expeditionary forces in "small wars" were not in the corps nor the nation's interests. Beginning with his studies on the defense of advanced naval bases while at the Naval War College in Newport, Rhode Island, between 1908–1910, to his service with the Naval Intelligence Division between 1913–1917, to his famous 1916 article in the *Marine Corps Gazette* titled "A Plea for a Mission and Doctrine," Russell advocated a new mission and capability for the Marine Corps. In 1933, as assistant commandant, he obtained Marine Corps and navy approval for the creation of the Fleet Marine Force (which is still a vital element of the nation's naval forces). This newly institutionalized permanent force became a component of the United States Fleet, under the operational control of its commander in chief. As assistant commandant and later commandant, Russell ordered the Marine Corps schools to develop doctrine for amphibious operations and supported their efforts to accomplish this task. To ensure the leadership for his changing corps, Russell in 1934 persuaded Congress to change the promotion laws affecting Marine Corps officers from a system based on seniority and vacancy to board selection based on merit.

All Russell could do was lay a foundation for the future. In an era affected by the Great Depression and isolationist sentiment, his Marine Corps had limited manpower and financial assets. Although the commitments in Central America and the Caribbean had ended, service in China and traditional duties with the navy diverted manpower from the Fleet Marine Force. Thus, marine detachments remained aboard the navy's battleships, carriers, and cruisers, and each new vessel commissioned further consumed his limited personnel, as did the many marine barracks at naval stations at home and abroad. It was his successor, Thomas Holcomb, who continued the rapid evolution of the corps begun by Russell and prepared it for a possible future war in the Pacific.

Although described by his peers as a "Washington Marine," General Russell also had extensive service in overseas operations, including the Veracruz expedition in 1914, duty in the Canal Zone in 1907–1908 shortly after Panamanian independence, and other Caribbean duty. He also served in China and saw naval combat in the Spanish-Cuban/American War. But he is most associated with Haiti, and his long years there were full of short-term successes amid continual turmoil. Despite the restoration of order in the countryside by his marines through the suppression of the *Caco* Rebellion and the efforts made in civic works, internal unrest continued. The marine presence was a political issue in the United States and aroused partisan opposition in Haiti. Contributing to this were actions by marines: excessive use of force by some individuals and unenlightened policies by a few commanders. This resulted in newspaper, Marine Corps, Department of the Navy, and congressional investigations. Through it all, Russell remained in service in Haiti.

Further unrest arose in 1929 and a disturbance in Cayes ended with over 50 Haitian casualties when heavily outnumbered marines fired, without orders, on a crowd of over 1,500 people. This incident produced yet another investigation (the Forbes Commission in 1930), which eventually contributed to Russell's withdrawal in 1930 and the removal of all the marines in 1934. Despite this, in recognition of his long, continuous, and arduous service in Haiti, both the U.S. and Haitian governments decorated him (the Navy Cross, 1918; the Haitian Medaille Militaire, 1920; and the Distinguished Service Medal for duty in Haiti between 11 February 1922 and 12 November 1930).

Upon his return to the United States, Russell resumed his Marine Corps career, serving in San Diego, California; Quantico, Virginia; and, finally, Washington, D.C., as the deputy to and then senior officer of the Marine Corps.

General Russell, as the chief U.S. official in Haiti and twice 1st Marine Brigade commander there, bore the responsibility for what occurred in the country, both the praise and the criticism. One reference work with a Haitian orientation (Roland I. Perusse, *Historical Dictionary of Haiti*) described Russell in the following mixed terms: "He ruled Haiti as virtual dictator in collaboration with Haitian President Luis [sic] Borno . . . He was not very sophisticated in the art of government, but he was firm, honest and a born disciplinarian" (Perusse, p. 90). Of course, the later commandant had a different perspective, which is reflected in his unpublished account of the U.S. presence in Haiti: he described it as "one of the most outstanding acts of international humanitarianism in world history," while also acknowledging that "fifteen or twenty years is too brief a period for a thorough going national reformation." He continued: "We stayed to help Haiti lift herself out of disease, poverty, ignorance, and political anarchy. For nineteen years America has labored to bring this hemisphere's most turbulent and backward republic into step with modern civilization. All this the United States has done with no important material advantage to herself, truly an act of international humanitarianism." (Russell, pp. 1, 2, 8)

Russell was an officer who entered and served in a Marine Corps with traditional roles and missions. But while excelling in them, he had the vision to see the reforms and changes needed in the institution. Ironically, despite the nature of his departure from Haiti, it was this departure that enabled him to assume offices and pursue policies that helped shape the Marine Corps for decades and helped prepare it for a major Pacific war which he foresaw over three decades before it began. Although Russell spent a large part of his career in Haiti, most of his years as a general officer there, and his unpublished writings are about his service in that country, in reality his policies as commandant were his most important and enduring legacy to Corps and country. Successes in Haiti were limited and transient, but his achievements as commandant are still influencing the Marine Corps at the end of the 20th century; that is, the Fleet Marine Force, amphibious doctrine and the ability to implement it, and an officer advancement system through selection board based on merit, although the laws governing promotions have changed.

Donald F. Bittner

REFERENCES

Robert Debs Heinl, Jr., and Nancy Gordon Heinl, *Written in Blood: The Story of the Haitian People, 1492–1971* (Houghton Mifflin, 1978); Allan R. Millett, *Semper Fidelis: A History of the United States Marine Corps* (Macmillan, 1980); Roland I. Perusse, *Historical Dictionary of Haiti* (Scarecrow Pr., 1977); John H. Russell, "A Marine Looks Back on Haiti," unpublished history (Marine Corps Historical Center, Washington, D.C., n.d.); Hans Schmidt, *The American Occupation of Haiti, 1915–1934* (Rutgers Univ. Pr., 1971).

Russell, William Worthington (1859–1944)

William Worthington Russell served as U.S. minister in the Dominican Republic throughout the U.S. occupation of that nation, 1916–1924. A diplomat with considerable experience in Latin America, Russell had held the post of minister to Colombia and Venezuela and had previously served in the Dominican Republic from 1910 to 1913. The occupation occurred during his second tour as minister in that nation, when he resided in Santo Domingo from October 1915 to September 1925.

Russell continued at his post after the landing of troops to help the United States substantiate its contention that the occupation was temporary; in reality, he represented the United States before a government headed by a U.S. admiral appointed from Washington. This left Russell in a secondary position without clear powers because inevitably he was superseded by the military governor. He actually functioned as an advisor to the various military governors during the occupation.

While his presence served to emphasize the fact that the Dominican Republic was not considered a colony, Russell was an advocate of military occupation. During the initial stages of the occupation, he was involved in the effort to prevent the Dominican Congress from convening to elect a provisional president. Although Russell advocated continued negotiations with the Dominicans at some difficult times, he proved intransigent and often recommended an extended occupation. As a result he was effectively bypassed because the principal negotiations were conducted at times by the military governors, and ultimately by a special presidential envoy, Sumner Welles, the chief of the State Department's Latin American Division. Welles was more attuned to the objectives of the new administration of President Warren G. Harding, which was firmly committed to arranging a withdrawal. Russell later served as U.S. minister to Siam.

Kenneth J. Grieb

REFERENCES

Bruce J. Calder, *The Impact of Intervention: The Dominican Republic during the U.S. Occupation of 1916–1924* (Univ. of Texas Pr., 1984); Kenneth J. Grieb, *The Latin American Policy of Warren G. Harding* (Texas

Christian Univ. Pr., 1976); Dana G. Munro, *Intervention and Dollar Diplomacy in the Caribbean, 1900–1921* (Princeton Univ. Pr., 1964).

Russian Railway Advisory Mission

In the aftermath of the Russian Revolution and the creation of the provisional government in early 1917, the United States offered to provide assistance to strengthen the infrastructure of the Russian economy to assist the war effort. The importance of the Trans-Siberian Railway, and its deteriorating condition, led to the U.S. suggestion that a group of railroad experts be sent to study the rail network and make proposals for its improvement. This included the purchase of U.S. railroad equipment to meet Russia's needs.

A positive Russian governmental response in early April 1917 led to the creation of a Russian Railway Advisory Mission in May, under the chairmanship of John F. Stevens, a prominent and reputable railway administrator. Other members included George Gibbs (previously with the Pennsylvania Railroad), John E. Greiner (of the Baltimore and Ohio Railroad), William L. Darling (a civil engineer), and Henry Miller (of the Wabash Railroad). President Woodrow Wilson appointed the mission, which left by ship for Vladivostok on 14 May 1917 on the *Empress of India*. Besides the official members, others associated with the mission were Edward P. Shannon (secretary), Eugene C. Stevens (clerk), Leslie R. Fellows and C.A. Decker (stenographers). Henry J. Horn joined the mission later. Two U.S. citizens in Russia served as primary interpreters: F.A. Golder and Eugene Prince.

The party arrived in Vladivostok in June 1917 and traveled by rail to Petrograd, arriving on 12 June. Consultations with the Russian Ministry of Ways and Communication were followed by on-site review of railroad conditions. Chairman Stevens became ill and was hospitalized for several weeks, and Miller served as acting chairman during that period. Following the Russian cabinet change in July and the appointment of Alexander F. Kerensky as the new prime minister, the mission made its recommendations, which the government accepted with satisfaction.

Stevens was in Moscow in early November 1917 at the time of the Bolshevik coup there,

after which he returned to Vladivostok in December. Horn remained in Petrograd where he had a liaison office in the Ministry of Ways and Communication. The other members, their review tasks completed, returned to the United States before the end of the year. Stevens remained in Russia for several more years, working with Allied governments on Siberian railroad issues.

Implementing the proposals of the mission required the creation of a group of U.S. technical specialists who would work in Russia on the rail system. This was the Russian Railway Service Corps, created in September 1917 and placed under the immediate direction of George H. Emerson. The group arrived in Siberia in March 1918.

The work of the Russian Railway Advisory Mission was completed by the end of 1917, and with the Bolshevik coup in the capital and the start of the Russian civil war, the committee was dissolved.

Taylor Stults

REFERENCES

Dictionary of American Biography, s.v. "Stevens, John Frank"; David R. Francis, *Russia From the American Embassy, April 1916–November 1918* (Scribner, 1921); George F. Kennan, *Soviet-American Relations, 1917–1920: Russia Leaves the War* (Princeton Univ. Pr., 1956); George F. Kennan, *Soviet-American Relations, 1917–1920: The Decision to Intervene* (Princeton Univ. Pr., 1958); U.S. Department of State, *Foreign Relations of the United States, Russia, 1918* (U.S. Government Printing Office, 1931–1932), 3 vols.

See also Russian Railway Service Corps; Stevens, John Frank.

Russian Railway Service Corps

The demands of World War I overwhelmed Russia's economic structure, the failure of which had helped bring down the czarist regime. The provisional government, which had come to power in March 1917, faced the same problems. Transportation was especially crucial. The provisional government would be undermined unless Russian railways were improved sufficiently to provide adequate distribution of food and materials. To stave off this threat, President Woodrow Wilson sent the United States Railway Advisory Mission to Russia to evaluate the rail system and make recommendations for greater efficiency. The mission, headed by a prominent railroad man, John F. Stevens, landed in Vladivostok on 31 May 1917 and began an inspection tour lasting seven weeks.

In addition to suffering from huge shortages of locomotives and freight cars, the mission found that Russian railways were badly organized and managed. The Stevens group therefore advised Washington to provide Russia with technical expertise as well as new equipment. This led to the formation of the Russian Railway Service Corps headed by Col. George H. Emerson, former general manager of a large U.S. railroad. The corps, under the overall direction of Stevens, numbered about 350 railroad men who were given army commissions at pay higher than their rank called for. Organized into teams by specialty, each team was assigned to a specific rail operation in order to teach their Russian counterparts modern methods.

The corps ran into trouble from the start. Dispatched from San Francisco two weeks after the Bolshevik revolution of 7 November 1917, it arrived at Vladivostok at a time when the city was rent with factional strife, and the port was about to freeze over. Stevens, already there, decided the corps could accomplish nothing under the circumstances. He had the corps rerouted to Japan (he went along with it) where it stayed until March 1918. At that time the first contingent, numbering 110 men, was sent to assist the operations of the Chinese Eastern Railway, which connected with the Trans-Siberian Railway. Other groups were sent during the following weeks.

How much the corps accomplished is impossible to calculate. Language barriers and often unreliable interpreters hampered the flow of information. Also, many Russian railway employees were reluctant to change the ways in which they were used to doing things. After the military intervention began during summer 1918, the rail lines became a focus of struggle among the participating nations. The Japanese, in order to undermine the corps' influence, opened their own training program to which they sent Russian railroad employees. The Inter-Allied Railway Agreement was hammered out in January 1919, but the Japanese repeatedly violated it. Chronically short of funds, the Railway Corps suffered from low morale and high turnover. It was evacuated with U.S. troops in April 1920.

Robert James Maddox

REFERENCES

George F. Kennan, *Soviet-American Relations, 1917–1920: The Decision to Intervene* (Princeton Univ. Pr., 1958); Betty Miller Unterberger, *America's Siberian Expedition, 1918–1920: A Study of National Policy* (Duke Univ. Pr., 1956); John Albert White, *The Siberian Intervention* (Princeton Univ. Pr., 1950).

See also Emerson, George Henry; Russian Railway Advisory Mission.

S

Sagasta, Práxedes Mateo (1825–1903)

Práxedes Mateo Sagasta, prime minister of Spain during the Spanish-Cuban/American War of 1898, was his country's leading politician. Seventy-three years old in 1898, he had had a distinguished political career.

Sagasta was born in 1825 in Torrecilla, Spain, of middle-class parents. He studied engineering, but in his youth turned to politics. He opposed the reactionary Spanish monarch, Isabella II, favoring liberal reforms. Repressed by the regime, Sagasta became a revolutionary, and was jailed and exiled. While in France, he edited a revolutionary journal and continued plotting against the monarchy.

During the post-Isabella years, Sagasta took part in governing Spain. He held several Spanish cabinet positions, including that of foreign minister. In 1875, he was prime minister when the Spanish Republic was overthrown and Isabella's son, Alfonso XII, assumed the throne.

Sagasta cooperated with the reestablished monarchy. He accepted the constitution of 1876, formed the Liberal party, and during the following decades served repeatedly as prime minister. He helped to bring many changes to Spain, including universal manhood suffrage. But most of his energy was directed toward ensuring the cohesion of liberal politicians in the Cortes and cabinet.

When the Cuban revolt began in 1895, Sagasta relinquished power to Antonio Cánovas del Castillo, who had better relations with the army generals. Initially, Sagasta supported Cánovas's policy of using military means to suppress the Cuban revolution. After two years, however, Sagasta began to criticize the war effort. He called attention to failed military campaigns, the large loss of life, and an empty treasury. He argued that even if Spanish arms succeeded, Cuban hostility toward Spain would remain. Sagasta called for ending harsh military campaigns and substituting political reforms, such as local autonomy and liberalized trade.

Cánovas was assassinated on 8 August 1897, and after his death the Spanish queen regent, María Cristina, changed the cabinet in order to seek a political solution to the Cuban war. Having persuaded some army generals to support insular autonomy, she asked Sagasta in October 1897 to head the government.

Sagasta brought Segismundo Moret y Prendergast into the cabinet as colonial minister, and together they attempted to end the war. Sagasta removed General Valeriano Weyler y

477

Nicolau from command in Cuba, replacing him with Ramón Blanco y Erenas, who favored a negotiated peace. The prime minister sharply curtailed the transportation of Spanish troops to Cuba. Moret drafted an autonomy decree, and on 1 January 1898 the Spanish government extended home rule to the island. Moret also sought to initiate trade negotiations with the United States. A trade treaty was expected to promote Cuban sugar exports and open the island to greater U.S. imports. Talks were about to start when the de Lôme letter and *Maine* disaster stymied this effort.

Having set in motion these new policies, Sagasta and Moret looked for assistance from the United States. They wanted the U.S. government to prevent shipments of men and munitions to Cuba, and they asked Washington to close down the Cuban Junta in New York City. Moreover, Sagasta wanted the administration of President William McKinley to provide time for Cuban reforms to take effect.

As a result of the *Maine* explosion in February 1895, U.S. pressure for intervention in Cuba grew rapidly. Threatened by a U.S. war, Moret proposed a temporary cease-fire on the island. Sagasta maneuvered his government and the Spanish army leadership into accepting it, and on 9 April 1898 the queen regent proclaimed a suspension of hostilities. But the Cuban revolutionaries immediately rejected such a suspension, so that the McKinley administration was unable to use it to cool the congressional ardor for intervention.

When the war began, Sagasta reformed his cabinet, dropping Moret who was the leading exponent of peace and bringing in several talented administrators who were expected to improve Spain's military performance. Sagasta wanted a quick war. He hoped to bloody the U.S. fleet even if Spain lost Cuba to U.S. arms. He approved sending the Spanish fleet to the Caribbean to defend Cuba and Puerto Rico, rather than taking a defensive position in Spanish home waters.

The war was a disaster for Spain. Its fleets were sunk in Manila Bay, and the United States successfully landed an army on Cuba and took the city of Santiago de Cuba. With little hope of checking U.S. advances and believing that an early peace might save Puerto Rico and the Philippines, Sagasta obtained the approval of Spain's military leaders to negotiate a settlement.

U.S. peace terms came as a blow to Spain. Sagasta expected to cede Cuba and Guam to the United States, but he hoped in return to obtain up to $200 million to cover Cuba's prewar debts. He reluctantly gave up Puerto Rico, and after months of negotiation, Madrid agreed to relinquish the Philippines for $20 million. Shortly after the peace treaty was ratified, Sagasta's cabinet fell as a result of the disastrous outcome of the Spanish-Cuban/American War.

John L. Offner

REFERENCES

Juan del Nido y Segalerva, *Historia política y parliamentaria del Excmo. Sr. Práxedes Mateo Sagasta* (Congreso de los diputados, 1915); Natalio Rivas Santiago, *Sagasta: conspirador-tribuno-gobernante* (Editorial Purcalla, 1946); Alvaro Romanones, *Sagasta, o el político* (Espasa-Calpe, 1930); Carlos Serrano, *Final del imperio: España, 1895–1898* (Siglo veintiuno, 1984); José Varela Ortega, *Los amigos políticos partidos, elecciones y caciquismo en la restauración, 1875–1900* (Alianza editorial, 1977).

Samar Campaigns, Philippine War

Samar is the easternmost island of the Visayan group in the Philippines. The Visayan Islands are the middle islands between Luzon and the Sulu group inhabited by Moros (Philippine Muslims). They include Leyte, Bohol, Cebu, Negros, Panay, and Masbate. Samar is by far the most rugged of the group, hilly except for the narrow coastal plain. According to a 1901 census, most of its then unmapped 5,000 square miles of jungle-covered terrain was inhabited by 222,690 Samarenos. It can receive up to 170 inches of rainfall in one year. Maj. Littleton W.T. Waller, who commanded U.S. Marines on Samar, called it "an evil-looking humpbacked island" (Schott, p. 4). The Spanish had their hands full controlling its population, and it was rumored that they even outlawed table knives on the island. The first U.S. troops to arrive in 1900 were elements of the 1st United States Infantry; they were greeted by charging Pulahane bolomen, who believed their *ante ante* (talismans) made them impervious to rifle fire. Some got past the deadly fusillade to slash U.S. soldiers before dropping dead, giving the Samarenos a particularly fierce and treacherous reputation among U.S. troops.

Elements of the 9th Infantry Regiment, fresh from fighting in the Boxer Uprising in China, arrived on Samar in late summer 1901. The *presidente* (mayor) of Balangiga, a town of about 200 nipa huts and the usual solid monuments to Spanish rule—church, convent, and town hall—had requested the presence of U.S. troops to protect the Samarenos from Moro raids. Had army intelligence prepared properly, it would have been suspicious because such raids had practically ceased in the middle of the 19th century. Mayor Pedro Abayan was, in fact, working for Gen. Vicente Lukban, son of a prominent Luzon family, who had arrived much earlier with 100 riflemen to make himself governor of the island under Emilio Aguinaldo y Famy's government. Abayan warmly greeted Capt. Thomas W. Connell, whose Company C occupied Balangiga on the southwestern coast.

Connell was a graduate of the United States Military Academy at West Point and a devout Irish Catholic with a puritanical streak which irritated both his men and the Filipinos. He set about to clean up the town physically and morally. He pressed work gangs to clean up their own garbage at gunpoint and then accepted Abayan's offer to use men from the environs to work off back taxes. Soon 100 of Lukban's best bolomen were inside Balangiga on work details. Connell forbade his men from fraternizing with women or attending the cockfights. When several women claimed they had been raped by his soldiers, he decreed that lewd glances or touching a woman would be equivalent to rape. Connell also took his diplomatic role seriously, outlawing the use of such terms as "gugu" or "nigger." To foster a more peaceful atmosphere, he banned the carrying of firearms except while on sentry duty or at official functions. All this was reported to Lukban.

A mail boat stopped by the town in the late Saturday afternoon of 26 September 1901, bringing news of President William McKinley's recent assassination. Connell ordered the flag to be flown at half mast and black arm bands to be sewn on to all uniforms. He planned a special formation for the next morning followed by a memorial mass. The local priest seemed to have vanished, and Connell retired early to get up early to prepare the ceremonies. All that night women arrived carrying small coffins of child victims of a cholera epidemic in the interior. A suspicious sentry ordered a coffin to be opened,

only to find a child's body. Had he lifted that, he would have discovered concealed weapons. He also noted that the women were too heavily dressed for such heat, but he was not going to risk the captain's wrath by taking a closer look, which would have revealed that they were men.

Most of the soldiers were up early that sultry Sunday morning, loitering around the mess hall while the cooks prepared breakfast. The local police chief chatted with a sentry and then seized his rifle and shot him. Lukban's men rushed the other unarmed U.S. soldiers, and several, disguised as women lounging near the convent, rushed in to murder the officers in their beds. Connell leaped out a window with a sidearm, but was cut down before he could use it. Some soldiers improvised weapons out of baseball bats, canned goods, and scalding water to fight their way with heavy losses to the arsenal. They formed a defensive formation and reached native vessels on the shore to sail to Basey, garrisoned by Company G. In the end, 59 of their comrades had been killed or succumbed to wounds en route or in Basey. Only six were unscathed and returned to Balangiga with the avenging force from Company G, raking the shoreline with gatlings on the way. They interrupted a funeral for 250 Filipinos who had been killed. Anyone around was killed, and the Filipino cadavers were burned when the U.S. soldiers discovered that the bodies of their slain comrades had been horribly mutilated.

Perhaps no single event in the Philippine War shocked the United States as much. The order for revenge and complete pacification of Samar emanated from the new commander in chief, President Theodore Roosevelt. Gen. Adna R. Chaffee handpicked Brig. Gen. Jacob H. Smith, a celebrated Indian fighter well known for his draconian methods in the Philippines, for the job. Smith made his headquarters at Tacloban on nearby Leyte, just across the narrow Strait of San Juanico from Basey. He accepted the offer of a battalion of marines from the navy to help pacify Samar. They were stationed in Basey and in Balangiga under Major Waller.

Smith gave Waller rather bizarre orders: "I want no prisoners. I wish you to kill and burn, the more you kill and burn the better it will please me. I want all persons killed who are capable of bearing arms in actual hostilities against the United States" (Miller, p. 220). When Waller asked Smith the limit of age to respect, he was told age 10. Waller, however, chose not to follow such orders literally and informed his men that they were not to make war on children. Smith also sent Waller handwritten orders from his headquarters across the straight "to kill and burn" (Miller, p. 220), to make Samar "a howling wilderness" (Miller, p. 222).

Waller soon located Lukban's headquarters on the Sohotón cliffs along the swollen Cadacan River in the interior. Warned that it was impregnable, Waller carefully planned a combined land and amphibious assault to take the fortress; 30 defenders were killed without the loss of a single marine. It was a sensational victory, ballyhooed in official reports and in the press back home. Smith compared these "gallant marines" to "those barefooted Americans at Valley Forge" (Miller, p. 221) in his press release.

Waller planned another invasion of the interior, starting from the army base at Lanang on the eastern coast after reaching it by water. The army commander tried to dissuade Waller from this undertaking, since the rivers were running very swiftly and he could supply his party with only four days of rations. Marines rarely take advice from soldiers, and Waller pushed on with his plans to cross the island from east to west, encountering a supply base established in Lukban's captured fortress. The weather worsened, and the terrain was even steeper than he had anticipated. The jungle proved almost impregnable, and leeches kept up a steady assault on his men. Since he was forced to halve rations, and then halve them again, his force grew weaker and weaker, slowing the pace. He made the fatal decision of splitting the contingent in two, sending the weaker ones back to Lanang under the command of Capt. David D. Porter while his own group pressed on.

The Filipino bearers grew increasingly uncooperative as the marines grew weaker. They refused to help build rafts for those returning to Lanang and feigned ignorance about what was edible in the jungle. When Waller's group discovered a clearing planted with yams, Waller sent a trusted Filipino guide to turn the other men headed for Lanang around to join him. "Victor" returned with the unlikely story that "insurgent" activity prevented his getting through. That night Waller discovered his bolo missing. He arrested Victor at gunpoint after he stole Waller's bolo.

Meanwhile, Porter's command fared much worse during its retreat to Lanang. David D. Porter had to leave more starving marines behind while he and the others pushed on to Lanang. An army rescue team found nine of them dead, and another had run into the jungle insane, never to be seen again. Many of the bearers had deserted, but those who had remained returned voluntarily to Lanang. When Porter heard that these bearers stood by while a weakened Lt. Alexander S. Williams was attacked by one of them before he fled, he had them all arrested and sent to Basey in chains.

Racked with fever, Waller made it back to Basey where he collapsed in bed for days. In his absence, Lt. John H.A. Day had discovered a conspiracy to reenact the Balangiga massacre in Basey. Day convened a court-martial and had the mayor executed and the padre imprisoned for life. Day asked a delirious Waller for permission to execute the 10 bearers arrested by Porter and received it. He had them shot down immediately in the public square to avenge the 10 dead marines, and ordered that their bodies be left there to serve as an example. Under cover of darkness, however, some brave Samarenos buried the victims that evening. Upon his recovery, Waller reported all this to Smith, who passed it on to Chaffee, and from whom it went to the War Department, from which it was leaked to the anti-imperialist press. Editors had a field day at Waller's expense, grossly exaggerating what had occurred on Samar. The story that the bearers had been shot in stages over several days while their screams of pain pierced the night was repeated so often it became "fact" in the minds of the war's critics.

Serving in a rival force, Waller must have seemed an ideal scapegoat to Secretary of War Elihu Root, who ordered him court-martialed. Waller remained loyal to Smith and wanted to justify his actions under General Order No. 100 from the Civil War, which provided for sanctions against guerrillas and the civilian populations that tolerated or actively aided them, without mentioning Smith's strange orders to him. Smith, however, testified that Waller had acted on his own in executing the bearers illegally. This flagrant betrayal ended Waller's self-imposed silence, resulting in his acquittal and forcing Root to order a court-martial for Smith, who was convicted.

The dapper Waller was as honorable a soldier who ever wore the marine green, and his shabby treatment in this case probably added to the marine legend of the Samar battalion. For many years, marines of whatever rank stood at attention when a veteran of Samar entered a room.

Stuart Creighton Miller

REFERENCES

Richard S.V.D. Arens, "The Early Pulahan Movement in Samar and Leyte," *Journal of History*, 7 (1959), 303–317; Stuart Creighton Miller, *"Benevolent Assimilation": The American Conquest of the Philippines, 1899–1903* (Yale Univ. Pr., 1982); Joseph L. Schott, *The Ordeal of Samar* (Bobbs-Merrill, 1964); James O. Taylor, *The Massacre of Balangiga* (n.p., 1931); Richard P. Weinert, "The Massacre at Balangiga," *American History Illustrated* (1966), 5–11, 37–40.

See also Smith, Jacob Hurd; Visayan Campaigns in the Philippine War; Waller, Littleton Waller Tazewell.

Samoa, Intervention (1899)

The 1899 U.S. naval intervention in Samoa was rooted in the complex relationship between Samoan internal politics and the international rivalry among Germany, Great Britain, and the United States. The islands' native inhabitants lived in a tribal society ruled by a ceremonial king, the *tafa'ifa*. Because each King was chosen by a consensus of village chieftains, the islands' early history is crowded with intermittent warfare as each contender for the throne struggled to dominate a majority of villages and clans. During the middle and late 1800s, Germany, Great Britain, and the United States took advantage of Samoa's chaotic internal politics to assume control over large parts of the island chain.

While the competing Great Powers coveted Samoa for a variety of economic, political, and diplomatic reasons, the islands were especially valued as an important source of copra and coconuts and as a base for additional expansion of territory and influence in the South Pacific. Composed of three main islands, Upolu, Savaili, and Tutuila, the Samoan archipelago occupies a strategic point in the heart of the South Pacific, roughly 2,000 miles south of Hawaii and 2,000 miles northeast of Australia and New Zealand. By 1880 the United States, Great Britain, and Germany had all extended their influence in the area, seizing the archipelago's most important harbors and constructing naval stations and trading posts.

International rivalry over the Samoan Islands provoked several Great Power conflicts during the latter part of the 19th century. The worst of these confrontations occurred in March 1889, when German and U.S. warships clashed in the German-controlled port of Apia on Upolu. War was prevented only by the arrival of a hurricane, which sank most of the naval vessels involved. Three months later, Great Britain, the United States, and Germany reached a settlement at the Conference of Berlin, which established a joint commission for Samoa composed of representatives from each country.

This compromise lasted less than a decade. The immediate cause of the unrest in Samoa in 1899, and the U.S. intervention that followed, was the death of the reigning Samoan monarch in August of the previous year. The Samoan International Commission collapsed during the subsequent civil war because Germany aided one contender for the throne, Chief Mataafa, while Great Britain and the United States supported another, Chief Malietoa Tanu. Although the German-backed candidate eventually defeated his rival, Great Britain and the United States moved to prevent an expansion of German influence in the islands by landing men at the Samoan capital of Apia on 13 March 1899. Chief Malietoa Tanu was crowned king on 23 March, because Great Britain, Germany, and the United States established a commission that accepted a recommendation from the Samoa chief justice that he was the rightful king. British and U.S. forces continued to fight with Samoan tribesmen supporting Chief Mataafa during the next six weeks, while warships from both countries periodically shelled Samoan villages.

On 13 May a U.S. ship carrying U.S., British, and German officials arrived to settle the conflict. After several months of negotiation, the three colonial powers signed a treaty on 2 December 1899, which formally divided Samoa into spheres of interest. It was an agreement that ostensibly satisfied all of the involved nations. Germany gained outright control of the islands of Savaili and Upolu; the United States retained the island of Tutuila with its important naval base at Pago Pago; and Great Britain received a favorable settlement in its claims to other Pacific islands and parts of Africa.

James H.L. Lide

REFERENCES

T.T. Craven, "A Naval Episode of 1899," *United States Naval Institute Proceedings*, 54 (1928), 185–200; Foster Rhea Dulles, *America in the Pacific: A Century of Expansion* (Houghton Mifflin, 1932), chap. 8; Paul M. Kennedy, *The Samoan Tangle: A Study in Anglo-German-American Relations, 1878–1900* (Barnes & Noble, 1974), chap. 4; George Herbert Ryden, *The Foreign Policy of the United States in Relation to Samoa* (Yale Univ. Pr., 1933), chap. 15.

See also Marine Operations in Samoa (1898); Naval Operations at Samoa (1899).

Sampson, William Thomas (1840–1902)

Throughout a 36-year naval career prior to the start of the Spanish-Cuban/American War in 1898, William Thomas Sampson made his mark as a technologist and administrator. When war loomed with Spain, Sampson's professional demeanor, thorough knowledge of technology, and creditable service made him one of the navy's top officers in line for a primary combat assignment. The war of 1898 gave him the opportunity to round out his record with command of a fleet.

As a cadet at the United States Naval Academy at Annapolis, Maryland, Sampson went against the stereotype. He was one of seven children in a Scots Irish working-class family; his father was a day laborer. Most cadets in Annapolis classes came from middle-class or upper middle-class backgrounds. In Sampson's case, however, his outstanding academic work at local schools in his home town of Palmyra, New York, brought him to the attention of the district's member of Congress, who nominated him to Annapolis. There, he led his class for three out of four years, graduating number one of 27 cadets in 1861.

For two years of the Civil War Sampson held staff positions at the Naval Academy (temporarily relocated to Newport, Rhode Island), but he also served at sea. He was promoted to lieutenant in July 1862. His ship-board assignments sent him on patrols down the Potomac River and through the Gulf of Mexico, as well as on blockade duty off the South Carolina coast. In one of those assignments he served with Master Winfield Scott Schley, United States Naval Academy class of 1860. Later, Schley was Sampson's most important subordinate in the Spanish-Cuban/American War.

Sampson's post-Civil War assignments allowed him to demonstrate his abilities in administration and technology. Orders first put him in the steam frigate *Colorado* on the European Station (1865–1867), but after that, Sampson, by then a lieutenant commander, returned to the Naval Academy. He taught courses in the Department of Natural Philosophy and later became head of the department, which changed its name to "Physics and Chemistry," Sampson's best subjects as an undergraduate. On two other occasions he served on U.S. warships on the European Station and again administered the Department of Physics and Chemistry at Annapolis (1874–1879). He was promoted to commander in 1874. He also conducted laboratory experiments, wrote reports, and went on scientific expeditions while supervising and encouraging the experiments of other naval officers.

Consolidating his administrative reputation, Sampson was assistant superintendent of the Naval Observatory in Washington, (1882–1884), which updated charts and navigational aids. He held the office of inspector of ordnance at the Torpedo Station, Newport, Rhode Island (1884–1886), conducting numerous tests on explosives, mines, and detonators.

Sampson also sat on the eight-member Endicott Board, chaired by Secretary of War William C. Endicott. This board reevaluated U.S. coastal defenses. Sampson added a detailed appendix, entitled "Floating Batteries," to the board's report, which was issued in 1885.

Meanwhile, in 1884 Sampson had joined with Rear Adm. Stephen B. Luce to urge the foundation of a naval war college. The purpose of the college, which had been requested before by other officers, would be to provide postgraduate training and education for officers in naval warfare and scientific subjects. The establishment of the United States Naval War College at Newport, Rhode Island, in 1885 led to significant improvements in naval professionalism.

Adding to his personal prestige, Sampson served as superintendent of the naval academy (1886–1890) and was promoted to captain in 1889. He took several steps leading to reforms. Among them were reducing hazing among cadets, replacing outdated equipment, expanding the library, and confirming new regulations for cadet hygiene. Sampson's most lasting reform came when he instituted the "aptitude for the service grade"—an evaluation of each cadet to determine his fitness as a naval officer. This grade has been in continuous use since Sampson's superintendency.

Leaving the academy in 1890, Sampson gained a prize appointment: command of the new protected cruiser *San Francisco*, then being built in California. Two years later he moved to the District of Columbia, successively holding the positions of inspector of ordnance and then chief of the Bureau of Ordnance (1893–1897). In these roles Sampson supervised construction of the naval gun foundry; received or rejected gunpowder from the most important U.S. powder-making firms, such as Dupont; approved new gun turret designs for U.S. warships; and accepted only the highest quality shipbuilding steel produced under contract by the nation's best manufacturers.

In Washington Sampson came into contact with top political leaders, including Secretary of the Navy Hilary A. Herbert. This contact and his seniority led in 1897 to command of another new ship, the 11,000-ton battleship *Iowa*.

Unfortunately for Sampson, he could not enjoy the *Iowa* to the fullest: the earliest indications of declining health manifested themselves. As reported after the Spanish-Cuban/American War, he had begun to experience severe headaches and widely spaced bouts of aphasia, which meant that he had difficulty in speaking coherently (*Army and Navy Journal*, p. 544). On most days Sampson appeared to be in good health, but when his illness was acute he could not even attend to routine duties, much less command a ship. He may have been suffering from early stages of Alzheimer's disease, or it may have been some form of dementia. Whatever the malady, it began to worsen during 1898.

Remarkable as it appears today, in the late 19th century the U.S. military services held no routine medical examinations for their officers. Thus, by carefully monitoring his health, Sampson could remain on active duty, obtain promotion, and take on greater responsibility.

In contrast to Sampson's case, Maj. Gen. William R. Shafter, soon to lead the United States Army's V Corps in Cuba, suffered from unconcealed health problems, including gout, shortness of breath, obesity, and vertigo. Yet President William McKinley still appointed the 63-year old Shafter to command an overseas expeditionary force. The examples of Sampson and Shafter indicated the necessity of reforms, such

as medical tests and adequate retirement benefits for service personnel, which encourage infirm officers to step down.

During 1897 the attention of many in the United States, especially politicians, journalists, and reformers, turned to the revolution in the Spanish colony of Cuba. Relations between the United States and Spain grew strained as McKinley sought to end the war and gain independence for Cuba. To support his policy, in February 1898 the president ordered the battleship *Maine* to Havana. On 15 February the *Maine* exploded, killing more than 200 U.S. servicemen. Some in the United States suspected Spanish foul play, and the president quickly sent a team of experts to investigate. Sampson led the team and chaired a court of inquiry in Havana. He concluded the explosion that destroyed the *Maine* had been caused by an unknown external source. Sampson's well-regarded technological expertise lent credence to his finding, although there was no conclusive proof for it, then or later. Thus, suspicions of Spanish culpability and cries of "Remember the *Maine*" helped push the United States toward war.

Only a few days after the court of inquiry issued its report, Sampson was ordered to take charge of the United States Navy's North Atlantic Squadron. The assignment was recognized as the most important seagoing command in the navy. The next month, on 21 April, he was promoted to acting rear admiral, boosting him over a dozen other officers who were his seniors. One of those was Commodore Winfield Scott Schley, who was assigned to command the separate Flying Squadron to guard the East Coast of the United States. Sampson's career as a technologist had not reduced his appetite or competence to be a squadron commander.

President McKinley soon announced that the navy would blockade Cuba to prevent Spanish reinforcements and supplies from reaching the island. Sampson set up a patrol off of Havana, then bombarded San Juan, Puerto Rico, and planned to provide convoy protection for the transports of General Shafter's V Corps, staging out of Tampa, Florida. After Sampson was unable to intercept the Spanish squadron moving into the Caribbean, the blockade became his primary task. Of course, he anticipated the possibility of a showdown between his ships (redesignated the North Atlantic Fleet on 21 June) and the Spanish under Adm. Pasqual Cervera y Topete.

Meanwhile, Secretary of the Navy John D. Long directed Schley's Flying Squadron to Cuban waters. Schley's ships departed Key West, Florida, on 19 May. During the next several days the commodore made his way along the southern coast of Cuba, at times appearing indecisive about his course of action. Receiving information from Secretary Long that the Spanish squadron was in port at Santiago de Cuba, Sampson directed Schley to steam there and blockade the harbor. Schley dallied off Cienfugos, Cuba, confusing his ships' captains by this inactivity. Long and Sampson were losing patience with Schley, who finally reached Santiago on 28 May. By that time Long decided that Sampson should proceed from Key West, Florida, to Santiago, Cuba, where he arrived on 1 June. Schley's actions at that stage of the campaign later contributed to the Sampson-Schley controversy.

Sampson applied himself to the professional challenge of the blockade. Naturally, he calculated how to use new technology, such as large searchlights, which sailors aimed on the channel mouth after nightfall. Incorporating Schley's Flying Squadron into the North Atlantic Fleet on 21 June gave Sampson a vast superiority of ships, guns, and men over Admiral Cervera's modest six-ship squadron. Three of them either had missing or inoperable main battery guns, thus significantly reducing the ships' firepower. Moreover, all of the Spanish ships needed to be overhauled, and some Spanish shells and powder were of low quality.

Usually five or six U.S. ships were coaling or resupplying at a base the United States had established at Guantánamo, Cuba, leaving 10 or 11 warships blockading Santiago. Sampson picked the location of each vessel in the blockade arc and issued standing orders to move toward the channel if the Spanish sortied. Most U.S. naval officers commended Sampson for laying out a technically perfect blockade.

During 22–24 June some of Sampson's ships covered the unopposed landing of Shafter's V Corps at Daiquirí and Siboney on Cuba's southern coast. The secretaries of the War and Navy departments, conveying the orders of President McKinley, directed the two commanders to cooperate in every way to ensure success of the campaign.

Unfortunately, Sampson and Shafter found much to disagree about, including where to land troops and when or how naval landing forces and naval gunfire might work with army units to destroy or capture Spanish gun emplacements near the mouth of the Santiago channel. Sampson and most naval officers feared that the loss of U.S. ships to shore batteries or undersea mines would hurt U.S. national morale and appear to bring the strengths of the opposing fleets closer together.

Despite admonitions to cooperate, neither commander evinced much inclination to plan or carry out joint operations, beyond the landings at Daiquirí and Siboney. Although Sampson sent his chief of staff, Capt. French E. Chadwick, to confer with General Shafter, no joint staff was formed to solve tactical problems or to write operations orders. Moreover, the poor health of both senior officers discouraged them from traveling back and forth to conferences.

At the same time the U.S. high command did not appoint a unified leader for the Santiago campaign. By the mid-20th century, naming a single commander to take charge of a campaign became standard procedure; even then, interservice cooperation was sometimes sporadic and difficult to achieve. These difficulties indicated other reforms needed in the U.S. armed forces.

For a month Sampson monitored the blockade. William A.M. Goode, an Associated Press reporter on the admiral's flagship *New York*, noted that from time to time Sampson was ill. In those instances Captain French E. Chadwick acted in his place. After days of putting off meetings with Shafter (he later said that a headache had laid him low), Sampson agreed to confer at the general's headquarters.

The commanders' conference was set for the morning of 3 July. Two days earlier the army had attacked Santiago's outlying defensive works. The ground combat at San Juan Heights and elsewhere on 1 July seemed to threaten the city of Santiago seriously as well as its harbor and the Spanish ships in it. Therefore, rather than rely on their army's defenses to repel more attacks, the Spanish authorities ordered Cervera's squadron to risk a breakout.

When the Spanish ships came out of the channel (at about 9:25 a.m. on 3 July), Sampson and the *New York* had steamed nine miles east, leaving Schley in *de facto* command. As usual, several U.S. ships were being resupplied at Guantánamo, but the rest of the North Atlantic Fleet shifted from blockade to offensive action. Schley's cruiser, the *Brooklyn*, appeared to pass dangerously close to the U.S. battleship *Texas*, but the two ships missed one another and set out in pursuit of Cervera, who did not offer squadron action and instead turned toward the Gulf of Mexico in an effort to escape.

Sampson and the *New York* came about to join the chase but, except for firing on one Spanish ship already dead in the water, the admiral played no direct role in the battle. The ships of Sampson's fleet each operated on their own—a captain's fight rather than a coordinated battle, although some officers later claimed that Sampson's tight blockading dispositions had been one of the keys to victory. U.S. ships outgunned the Spanish but it still took almost four hours to overtake and sink or cripple the enemy squadron. The Spanish lost six ships and suffered 474 casualties, including 323 killed, with hundreds of other sailors and officers made prisoner. By contrast, the United States lost one killed and took no serious damage to any of its 10 ships involved.

If Sampson had been onshore with General Shafter all of the praise for the naval victory off Santiago would have gone to Schley. However, Sampson's proximity to the fighting complicated matters. As the *New York* drew near the *Brooklyn*, Sampson and Schley exchanged messages that created animosity rather than solidified goodwill in the aftermath of victory. Furthermore, in telegrams to the president, Sampson failed to mention that Schley was the senior officer present during the battle or to thank Shafter and the army for posing the threat to Santiago that prompted Cervera to sortie.

Sampson was hailed in newspaper editorials and congressional speeches as the victor of Santiago, and the battle confirmed U.S. naval supremacy over the Spanish. Santiago complemented Commodore George Dewey's victory at Manila Bay (on 1 May) and combined to change European perceptions of the United States's military potential.

However, the battle also perpetuated sour relations between Sampson and Shafter and created an internecine fight between the admiral and Schley over credit for the victory.

Sending messages back and forth, Sampson and Shafter again argued over plans for joint operations to attack the channel gun emplace-

ments. No ground attack was made, but the navy did shell Spanish shore positions. It is debatable whether attacks on the shore batteries were needed. Nevertheless, the disagreement heightened ill will between the army and the navy. In addition, when Santiago formally surrendered on 16 July, Shafter declined to invite a naval officer to be present and later insisted that the army take control of all Spanish vessels in the harbor. Sampson, naturally, wanted the captured ships to go to the navy. In a fit of pique, Shafter reminded the admiral that the army had not claimed any credit for capturing Cervera, implying that the navy should not claim credit for the surrender of the city or the ships located there. The poor health of both men prevented holding face-to-face meetings that might have ameliorated the interservice squabbles.

The Sampson-Schley controversy over credit for the naval victory was fought out in newspapers, magazines, books, the halls of Congress, and in ships' wardrooms for years to come. Sampson's health declined steadily during the three years following the battle. For the most part, he left his defense to friendly editors, politicians, and naval officers. Each claimant had well-known supporters. Alfred Thayer Mahan endorsed Sampson; George Dewey favored Schley; Secretary Long awarded plaudits to Sampson.

The report of an official court of inquiry issued in December 1901 criticized Schley's actions during the campaign. Sampson had been too ill to testify to the court. He died on 6 May 1902 in Washington, D.C.

Trying to put the controversy to rest, President Theodore Roosevelt directed that military officers cease voicing public opinions about the Battle of Santiago. The Sampson-Schley controversy continued nevertheless and divided the navy's officer corps into "Sampsonites" and "Schleyites"—a long-lasting negative legacy of a great U.S. victory.

Joseph G. Dawson, III

REFERENCES

Army and Navy Journal, 7 February 1903; French E. Chadwick, *The Relations of the United States and Spain: The Spanish-American War* (Scribner, 1911), 2 vols.; Joseph G. Dawson, III, "William T. Sampson: Progressive Technologist as Naval Commander," in James C. Bradford, ed., *Admirals of the New Steel Navy* (U.S. Naval Institute Pr., 1990), 149–179; Louis J. Gulliver, "Sampson and

Shafter at Santiago," *United States Naval Institute Proceedings*, 65 (1939), 799–806; David F. Trask, *The War With Spain in 1898* (Macmillan, 1981); Richard S. West, *Admirals of the American Empire* (Bobbs-Merrill, 1948).

See also North Atlantic Squadron, United States Navy (1898); Santiago, Cuba, Naval Battle (1898); Schley, Winfield Scott.

Sandino, Augusto Calderón (later Augusto César Sandino) (1895–1934)

The U.S. interventions in Nicaragua evoked feelings of nationalism among the people of that Central American country. These feelings produced little overt opposition to the first intervention (1912–1913) after its early weeks, but the second (1927–1933) faced continuing resistance under the leadership of Augusto Calderón (later César) Sandino, a strong nationalist and talented guerrilla fighter. Sandino's war against the marines and against Washington's program of free elections and a nonpartisan national guard eventually convinced the U.S. government that marine interventions were too costly in money and goodwill. This conclusion led to marine withdrawal and the renunciation of armed interventions under the Good Neighbor policy.

Sandino was born in the village of Niquinohomo, West of Granada, probably on 18 May 1895 but other dates appear in various interviews with Sandino. His parents were Gregorio Sandino, a small prosperous landowner, and Margarita Calderón, a poor worker on one of Gregorio's farms. According to Sandino the early years were a struggle for him and his unmarried mother, who had been abandoned by his father. During these miserable times, Sandino later told the Nicaraguan writer José N. Román, he thought about the tragedies of life, the lives of the poor, his misery and powerlessness. He related how he observed the relative well-being of his half brother, Sócrates, and then by chance confronted his father with questions about his parentage and why he was not treated like Sócrates. As a result he went to live with his father; his mother had already gone to live in Granada. Sandino attended the village school and also received training at the Instituto de Oriente in Granada. While still in his teens he worked for his father, eventually left home to work as a mechanic's assistant, and returned in 1919 to woo a childhood sweetheart. Before they could be married Sandino was forced to flee for shooting a prominent citizen during a fight. He went to Honduras, then Guatemala, and finally Mexico, where he worked for the U.S.-owned Huasteca Petroleum Company in Tampico.

Revolutionary Mexico greatly influenced Sandino. Whether Sandino's thought, developed during these years, went beyond ardent nationalism is a matter of scholarly debate. Some would argue the lack of a well-developed ideology, but philosopher Donald C. Hodges sees a complex set of beliefs embracing selections from Mexican Freemasonry and spiritualism, anarchism, theosophy, populism, and communism. Sandino was eclectic, sometimes inconsistent, and, whenever it suited his purpose, misleading and ambiguous. Despite the eclecticism, Hodges concludes coherence and originality existed in Sandino's beliefs. For Sandino's critics, his head was full of an unassimilated jumble of ideas. Whatever composed his philosophical foundation, it seems clear that those years abroad piqued his nationalism. He believed that the other people of Central America and Mexico detested Nicaraguans for failing to confront United States's influence in their country. Concluding that he should struggle against U.S. power, he returned to Nicaragua.

Meanwhile in Nicaragua, a revolutionary movement had broken out against the Conservative government of Emiliano Chamorro Vargas who through a *coup d'etat* had ousted the coalition government of President Carlos Solórzano (Conservative party) and Vice President Juan B. Sacasa (Liberal party) in 1925. Because Solórzano had actually resigned while Sacasa had fled without resigning, the Liberals claimed that the vice president was entitled to the presidency. Early efforts of the Liberals to remove Chamorro through revolution had failed, but by August, 1926, their efforts resumed with Mexican assistance. Facing mounting opposition at home and the refusal of Washington to recognize his regime, Chamorro stepped aside for Adolfo Díaz, who received U.S. diplomatic recognition. The Liberals, however, refused to accept Díaz, and two weeks after his inauguration Sacasa returned to the eastern coast of Nicaragua to establish a rival government and to carry on the counter-revolution. As fighting intensified, U.S. Marines landed to protect U.S. lives and property.

Sandino had returned to Nicaragua after the early futile efforts to oust Chamorro. He went to work for the U.S.-owned San Albino gold mine in northern Nicaragua where he told fellow workers about exploitation by capitalists and large foreign companies and about working conditions in other countries, including medical services, schools, and unions. He gradually gained popularity and trust among the workers and in November 1926 began his war against the Conservative government of Nicaragua. He and a small group of men acquired arms and attacked 200 of Chamorro's soldiers quartered at the village of Jícaro. Although the attack failed, Sandino disdained discouragement and decided to acquire more arms from the insurgent government (Constitutionalists) of Juan B. Sacasa at Puerto Cabezas. Sacasa and his secretary of war and field commander, Gen. José María Moncada, were not inclined to share limited war supplies with Sandino, a man whom Moncada distrusted for his seemingly radical ideas. Nonetheless, in the confused situation caused by the landing of marines and establishment of a neutral zone, Sandino was able to acquire rifles and ammunition. He became a full participant in Sacasa's cause to oust Díaz (Chamorro's successor), but relations between Sandino and Moncada were limited and full of distrust. As fighting increased and the revolutionaries advanced toward Managua, President Calvin Coolidge sent Henry L. Stimson to Nicaragua to resolve the conflict. He met with Moncada at Tipitapa in May 1927, and the two men finally agreed on retention of Díaz, a general disarmament, and U.S.-supervised elections in 1928. Moncada then consulted the other Liberal generals who, except for Sandino, agreed to the terms. Sandino believed that Moncada had sold out, but he hid his feelings temporarily to avoid possible detention. He withdrew to northern Nicaragua to organize opposition to the U.S. intervention and its Nicaraguan supporters. During the move north, Sandino married Blanca Arauz, a young girl whom he had met earlier when she had served him as a telegraph operator in San Rafael del Norte.

At first his departure did not alarm the U.S. military, but by the end of June 1927, he was plundering U.S. and European-owned property, and in July he attacked a marine and Nicaraguan national guard detachment at Ocotal. But for the timely arrival of five bombing and strafing planes, Sandino might have won the battle. As it was, he had to retire because he underestimated the fighting capacity of the marines and lacked experience with military aviation. This encounter was the first of many to engage the marines and Nicaraguan national guardsmen until 1933 and bring Sandino to world attention. Over the months he developed his guerrilla tactics: taking advantage of the mountainous jungle terrain, using cover to avoid detection from the air, moving in small groups, living off the land, hitting and running, and using surprise and terror. These were the tactics that prevented his army's defeat. At the same time he was not able to prevent the relatively free, even if harassed, movement of marines and Nicaraguan national guardsmen about the country. In the end he had more determination and staying power than the U.S. government and the people of the United States, who eventually questioned the wisdom of the intervention.

After the Battle of Ocotal, Sandino remained an enigma for the United States, and because of the relative tranquility in Nicaragua, Washington thought pacification was near. In fall 1927 and early 1928, however, Sandino's reemergence belied those thoughts and brought additional marines to Nicaragua. There followed a protracted conflict that lasted until early 1933. Over these years the role of the marines was gradually confined to the larger towns, to training the Nicaraguan national guard, and to providing officers for its units.

In June 1929, Sandino arrived in Mexico where he hoped to get military support and perhaps add luster to his movement. Military aid was not forthcoming, but after several months of waiting in Mérida he was allowed to visit President Emilio Portes Gil in Mexico City. He returned to Mérida for a few months and then left to rejoin his guerrilla forces. During his visit to Mexico Sandino broke with his communist supporters. The communists had organized the Hands Off Nicaragua Committee in Mexico to tout Sandino's cause, the Sixth World Congress of the Communist International in Moscow recognized his heroic struggle, and the El Salvadoran communist Agustín Farabundo Martí was a close advisor, but essentially the relationship between the communists and Sandino was one of convenience. The communists were critical of his departure from Nicaragua and even accused him of accepting a bribe to do it. Sandino countered that he had come to Mexico because there had been so little help from the communists. Years later after the marines had departed Nicaragua and Sandino had made peace with the Nicaraguan government, the communists again criticized him for defining his struggle as only against the intervention.

After Sandino returned to Nicaragua in May 1930, there was a gradual increase in guerrilla activity in north central and eastern Nicaragua. In one encounter with the national guard a few weeks after his return, Sandino was wounded; after that he took little or no part in attacks. Nonetheless his generals continued their forays. One such offensive toward the eastern coast in April 1931 brought requests from U.S. citizens for protection, but by this time the Hoover administration was well along in its policy of reducing U.S. forces in Nicaragua and was hesitant to reengage large numbers of troops. In fact, Secretary of State Henry L. Stimson was contemplating complete withdrawal shortly after supervision of the 1932 Nicaraguan elections. Although Sandinista activities were worrisome, they did not upset the timetable for U.S. withdrawal in early 1933.

Sandino remained defiant while U.S. Marines were in his country. The disastrous Managua earthquake of 31 March 1931 saddened him, and he paired this injustice of fate with the injustice at the hands of the military occupation. Sandino also contemplated the 1932 election and considered an arrangement to end his opposition if the Liberals won; he did not believe it would be possible with a Conservative victory. After the Liberal candidate Juan B. Sacasa won the election and was inaugurated, Sandino, on 2 February 1933, concluded a peace agreement with the government, providing for the disarmament and amnesty of his followers. He was allowed a force of 100 men, who were permitted to keep their arms temporarily and who would establish farms in a zone of uncultivated territory in northern Nicaragua.

For the next several months Sandino and his men exchanged denunciations with the U.S.-created national guard and its leader Anastasio Somoza García. Sandino believed that the national guard was unconstitutional and a threat to the Nicaraguan government, while Somoza believed that the arrangement with Sandino had created a state within a state and that the former guerrilla chief was a block to his political ambi-

tions. On 21 February 1934, about a year after the original agreement, Sandino was again in the capital to discuss the next steps in the peace arrangement. That evening after dinner with President Sacasa and while Sandino was returning to his residence, he and two of his aides were taken from their car to a landing field on the outskirts of Managua and shot by national guard troops. Within a few weeks, the national guard had destroyed or scattered his remaining followers.

Sandino, the hero of the Segovias, attracted much attention and sympathy from those who despised the U.S. intervention. In death his influence reemerged, particularly in Latin America. He came to personify heroic struggle against foreign aggression and to inspire those who wanted to overthrow oppressive governments, such as Nicaragua's Somoza dynasty. In Nicaragua his name, his ideas, and even some of his veterans were resurrected and mixed with a Marxist influence in the Sandinista Front of National Liberation, which in 1979 was victorious over the national guard and its leader, the son of the man who had ordered his killing.

William Kamman

References

Robert Edgar Conrad, ed. and trans., *Sandino: The Testimony of a Nicaraguan Patriot, 1921–1934*, compiled and edited by Sergio Ramirez (Princeton Univ. Pr., 1990); Lejeune Cummins, *Quijote on a Burro: Sandino and the Marines, A Study in the Formulation of Foreign Policy* (La Impresora Azteca, 1958); Donald C. Hodges, *Intellectual Foundations of the Nicaraguan Revolution* (Univ. of Texas Pr., 1986); William Kamman, *A Search for Stability: United States Diplomacy Toward Nicaragua, 1925–1933* (Univ. of Notre Dame Pr., 1968); Neill Macaulay, *The Sandino Affair* (Quadrangle, 1967).

See also list of entries at front of book for Nicaragua, Intervention (1927–1933).

San Juan Hill, Cuba, Battle (1898)

The Battle of San Juan Hill is the better known of two separate but related fights between U.S. and Spanish forces near the city of Santiago de Cuba on 1 July 1898 during the Spanish-Cuban/American War. Many misconceptions have grown up around the attacks on El Caney and San Juan Heights. Neither U.S. victory in these battles was immediately decisive because the garrison of Santiago did not surrender until 16 days later, after protracted negotiations. Lt. Col. Theodore Roosevelt did not seize the San Juan Heights alone at the head of his 1st Volunteer Cavalry, the "Rough Riders," but was one of several officers who led improvised assaults on their own initiative without orders. It was no easy success: 140 officers and men were killed and 940 wounded taking a position that was in fact being abandoned by its defenders.

President William McKinley's reputation as a war leader has risen in recent histories of the Spanish-Cuban/American War. He is now portrayed as having successfully directed the political and military efforts of the United States toward a single objective: the neutralization of Spanish military power in the Caribbean. He consistently favored the least costly method of implementing that objective, choosing the isolated southeastern coast of Cuba and its port city of Santiago as the primary theater for U.S. ground operations rather than the island's populous and better defended northern coastline.

However, even this more limited aim was almost beyond the reach of the contemporary U.S. military. The 25 infantry and 10 cavalry regiments of the regular army had not tactically combined in brigades, much less divisions and corps, since 1865. Nor was the extensive administrative and logistical organization of the Civil War army anything more than a distant memory. Neither was a single organization responsible for coordinating a military effort outside the continental United States, nor was any effective planning accomplished for operations in the Caribbean between the *Maine* crisis of mid-February 1898 and the outbreak of hostilities in late April.

This meant that the purchase of essential equipment, supplies, and foodstuffs; the hiring of sea-going transportation; and even the loading of individual cargo ships were severely mismanaged throughout the Cuban expedition. The U.S. war effort in the Caribbean was thus marked by an operational and logistical muddle redeemed only by the efficiency of the navy, the courage and tactical skill of its individual soldiers, and a series of egregious Spanish military blunders.

U.S. historians have long ignored the relationship between the Cuban War of Independence of the 1890s and the Spanish-Cuban/American War of 1898. The military consequences of the earlier struggle were profound:

by the time U.S. forces landed near Santiago, Cuban forces had inflicted thousands of casualties on Spain's occupation army and driven it into a pattern of dispersed, static local garrisons unable to cooperate against an invasion and effectively isolated from the island's major food-producing centers. By July 1898, near-starvation, combined with a range of endemic tropical diseases, had reduced the Spanish army in Cuba to a state of offensive impotence.

The Spanish commander of Cuba's eastern garrison, Gen. Arsenio Linares Pomba, had also violated the maxim that to defend everything is to defend nothing: rejecting a concentration of strength at the most likely U.S. objective he placed only 10,500 of his total force of 33,000 in the defenses of Santiago de Cuba and deployed even those troops without adequately guarding the most likely avenues of approach to the city. Thus, only a small fraction of Linares's force would be able to resist an enemy offensive massed at a single point of attack.

However, the U.S. commander, Maj. Gen. William R. Shafter of the United States Army's V Corps, largely negated this advantage by sending his 17,000 men against two separate objectives on 1 July, thereby reducing the margin of superiority needed to overpower an entrenched enemy equipped with modern, high-velocity, magazine-fed rifles. Shafter was also deficient in field artillery, the arm traditionally used to "soften up" defensive positions before an assault. This weakness was partially remedied on 1 July by a well-handed battery of rapid-fire Gatling guns, the first significant use of such weapons by the United States Army.

By 23 June 1898, U.S. troops occupied the small ports of Daiquirí and Siboney east of Santiago. Although troops came ashore quickly, supplies accumulated with agonizing slowness: on 1 July V Corps had no more than a three-day reserve supply of ammunition, food, and animal fodder. A skirmish on 24 June at Las Guásimas, eight miles from Santiago, confirmed General Shafter in his decision to move overland and attack Santiago at the northern end of its harbor rather than call on the navy to land him in an amphibious assault on its entrance, a decision that remains controversial to this day. Neither course of action was without risks; the overland route involved an approach march through unmapped country known to harbor malaria and yellow fever, while a large seaborne assault was without recent precedent and would have required a level of staff coordination probably beyond the abilities of either service.

By 30 June, plans had been finalized for an attack on two fortified outposts in advance of the main defenses of Santiago. One division, commanded by Brig. Gen. Henry W. Lawton, was to reduce a blockhouse position at El Caney, northeast of the city, and then march three miles to take position on the right flank of two other divisions for an attack on two adjacent strongpoints at San Juan Hill and Kettle Hill.

However, on 1 July this plan went seriously awry. Preattack reconnaissance had been negligible: the strength of the defense at El Caney had been underestimated and the terrain between the U.S. camp and the San Juan Heights remained a mystery. Officers in charge of the lead battalions lost their way in a dense jungle along the San Juan River, and these forces suffered under a plunging fire from Spanish positions they could not locate. Lawton became too heavily engaged at El Caney and failed to support the main effort at the San Juan Heights. Worse yet, troops moving to attack the Heights lost their unit integrity, crossed each other's path, and were unable to find clear protected ground to deploy for their final assault. Suddenly emerging from the jungle directly under their objective, they immediately began to receive heavy fire and take serious casualties.

At this point, a number of battalion and company commanders made simultaneous decisions to charge the works on San Juan Hill and Kettle Hill immediately, and their men followed them. They were supported by a critical eight minutes of rapid fire from three U.S. Gatling guns located on high ground a mile to their rear. The Gatlings' commander, 1st Lt. John H. "Machine Gun" Parker, later argued that his guns had effectively suppressed the Spanish fire just as U.S. troops began their assent of the Heights. Just as important, however, were the initiative of individual U.S. infantrymen and dismounted cavalry troopers and the local Spanish commander's decision to obey orders he had recently received to abandon the Heights and pull back into the main defenses of Santiago. By late afternoon both El Caney and the San Juan Heights were securely in U.S. hands.

On the morning of 2 July V Corps was exhausted and dispirited; only later would its victory be mythologized into a devil-may-care adventure. U.S. commanders at all levels were impressed by the brief but fierce Spanish resistance and shocked by the large number of U.S. casualties sustained. Malaria and yellow fever quickly began to deplete the ranks of U.S. regiments already thinned by Spanish rifle fire, quickly depriving V Corps of its combat effectiveness. The naval battle at Santiago on 3 July, which permanently severed Cuba from Spain, combined with mounting hunger and disease within the city itself, brought about a local capitulation on 17 July and, by mid-August, a general surrender of all Spanish forces in Cuba.

John Scott Reed

REFERENCES

Graham A. Cosmas, *An Army for Empire: The United States Army and the Spanish-American War* (Univ. of Missouri Pr., 1971); Graham A. Cosmas, "San Juan Hill and El Caney, 1–2 July 1898," in Charles E. Heller and William A. Stofft, eds., *America's First Battles, 1776–1965* (Univ. Pr. of Kansas, 1986); Jack C. Dierks, *A Leap to Arms: The Cuban Campaign of 1898* (Lippincott, 1970); Frank Freidel, *The Splendid Little War* (Little, Brown, 1958); David F. Trask, *The War With Spain in 1898* (Macmillan, 1981).

See also El Caney, Cuba, Battle (1898).

Santiago, Cuba, Naval Battle (1898)

A Spanish fleet under Vice Adm. Pascual Cervera y Topete was sent to the West Indies after Spain's declaration of war on the United States. On the evening of 19 May 1898 it entered the harbor of Santiago, Cuba. Cervera chose Santiago because from his point of view it was a less dangerous anchorage than Puerto Rico or the Cuban ports of Havana and Cienfuegos. A Cuban telegraph operator in Havana sent a secret message to Key West, Florida, notifying U.S. authorities of the arrival of Cervera's fleet. That message was forwarded to the Navy Department in Washington, but it was not considered reliable information. It was not until 26 May that the Flying Squadron under Commodore Winfield Scott Schley arrived off Santiago, and it was two days later before the presence of Cervera's fleet was confirmed. Schley instituted a blockade of the port on 29 May, and a day later Rear Adm. William T. Sampson arrived with the North Atlantic Fleet and assumed command. Sampson attempted to prevent the escape of the

Spanish squadron by sinking the collier *Merrimac* at the entrance to the harbor, but the *Merrimac* drifted out of place and only narrowed the passageway. Once the Spanish fleet was blockaded, the United States Army was able to land an expeditionary force at Daiquirí on 22–23 June which advanced on Santiago. The day after the U.S. landings the Spanish minister of marine authorized Cervera to depart from Santiago, but the admiral sought to avoid doing so because of the condition of his ships and the strength of the forces that were awaiting him.

Cervera had expected to find coal and supplies at Santiago but was disappointed. He held a series of councils of war with his captains over whether it would be better to attempt to escape from the harbor or to remain there and be captured when the city fell. Cervera and his officers had decided against a sortie, but his force had been placed under the control of Governor General Ramón Blanco y Erenas, and that officer ordered the admiral to leave as soon as possible. Accordingly, Cervera issued orders on the evening of 2 July for the squadron to leave the next morning.

At sunset on 2 July, the officer of the deck in the U.S. battleship *Iowa* called to the attention of Capt. Robley D. Evans the six columns of smoke near the harbor entrance and expressed the belief that it indicated a movement of the Spanish squadron. Captain Evans thought that the smoke simply indicated another of Spanish ship movement in the harbor, and he attached no special significance to it. Evans told the officer that since the *Iowa* had the duty of shining a search light into the harbor that night, the ship would have a good chance to attack any Spanish ship that emerged. A signal quartermaster in the *Iowa* had also seen the smoke, and on his own initiative he broke out the flag for signal 250, "Enemy ships coming out," and tied it to the halliards so that it would be ready to hoist if needed.

On Sunday morning, 3 July, Cervera's chief of staff studied the channel and the U.S. ships. He noted that the blockading squadron was not as strong as it usually was. The battleship *Massachusetts*, the cruisers *New Orleans* and *Newark*, and the converted tender *Suwanee* had gone to Guantánamo for coal. This was also the morning that Admiral Sampson planned to meet with Maj. Gen. William R. Shafter, the army commander, to discuss strategy. So Sampson's flagship, the cruiser *New York*, hoisted the signal "Disregard the motions of the commander in chief," and accompanied by the armed yacht *Hist* and the torpedo boat *Ericsson*, it steamed east toward Siboney. Sampson's departure left Schley in command of the blockading squadron, but the admiral had not told him of the planned conference and the resulting weakening of the force. Schley's ship, the cruiser *Brooklyn*, was lying farther out than usual that morning, thus creating a gap at the western end of the semicircular blockade. Since the *Brooklyn* was the fastest of the U.S. ships, Cervera planned to ram it with his flagship, the cruiser *Infanta María Teresa*, with the hope of disabling it and allowing the other Spanish ships to escape. They planned to steam west to Cienfuegos. The other U.S. ships were arranged in a rough semicircle from east to west that consisted of the converted yacht *Gloucester*; the battleships *Indiana*, *Oregon*, *Iowa*, *Texas*, the *Brooklyn*; and the converted yacht *Vixen*. A straight line between the *Gloucester* and the *Vixen* would reach eight miles. In the U.S. ships the crews were assembling on deck in their white uniforms for inspection, followed by the reading of the Articles of War and divine services. At 9:35 a.m. the Spanish ships were observed coming out of the harbor. The *Infanta María Teresa* was in the lead followed by the cruisers *Vizcaya*, *Cristóbal Colón*, and *Almirante Oquendo*, and the torpedo-boat destroyers *Plutón* and *Furor*. The *Iowa* fired an alarm gun and raised signal 250 while its crew rushed to their battle stations. Next the *Oregon* fired a six-pound gun, sounded a siren, and hoisted signal 250. The *Texas* and the *Brooklyn* also raised this same signal.

As the word spread through the blockading squadron, crews sprang into action. Within two minutes the *Iowa* was ready and moved toward the mouth of the harbor. That Sunday morning the fires in many of the U.S. ships had been banked, and engines were uncoupled. Once every hour the engines were turned over to maintain their stations in deep water. At this point, with the Spaniards emerging, every ship had to move as quickly as it could with what power was available. In the *Indiana* there were light fires in all of the boilers but little steam could be produced at first. Moreover, growths on its hull prevented it from attaining more than 10.5 knots. The *Oregon*'s bottom was fairly clean, and it was the practice on the ship to keep the fires going under all the boilers. Before the battle this had necessitated frequent recoaling, but on the day of the battle it was ready. The *Brooklyn* had two of its four engines uncoupled. There was steam in three of its double-ended boilers but the fires had not been fully spread. Two other double-ended boilers did not have enough water, and sea water had to be used in an emergency. Two single-ended boilers were full of water but were not ready to use. Thus, throughout most of the squadron there was a rush to get fires going and to produce as much steam as possible in the shortest time.

In the *Brooklyn*, Schley had earlier built a wooden platform around the outside of the armored conning tower in the forward part of the ship. This platform not only gave him an excellent view of the battle, but it also kept him in touch with Capt. Francis A. Cook, the commander of the *Brooklyn*. When the movement of the Spanish ships was reported, Schley rushed to his platform with his binoculars in hand. The Spanish ships were concentrating their fire on the *Brooklyn*, and the *Infanta María Teresa* and the *Vizcaya* were heading straight for it. Schley told Cook that the two leading Spanish cruisers were going to try to ram the *Brooklyn*. He also ordered that word be sent to the men below decks to prepare for ramming. As the *Teresa* narrowed the gap between itself and the *Brooklyn* it was coming under intense fire from its target as well as from other U.S. ships. Cervera then abandoned the attempt to ram and concentrated on escaping if he could. The *Teresa* suddenly turned westward and in so doing left a small gap between it and the *Vizcaya*, which continued to advance toward the *Brooklyn*. Spanish shore batteries were also firing on the U.S. ships. Suddenly the *Vizcaya* also turned to the east. In the *Brooklyn*, Captain Cook ordered the ship to be turned rapidly and continuously to port, so that it swung around a little more than half of its tactical diameter.

Those in the squadron who observed the turn were puzzled by it. Why had the *Brooklyn* moved away from the advancing *Vizcaya*? Had the ship been badly damaged? Years later, when asked about this controversial "loop," Schley said that if the ship had turned to starboard it would have placed it in a dangerous position for a broadside torpedo attack. He did not think that the *Brooklyn* should be sacrificed early in the battle. Other considerations were to avoid the cross-fire of the U.S. battleships, and most of all to allow the

Brooklyn to continue to fight. Later, the captain of the *Texas* claimed that the unexpected move of the *Brooklyn* forced him to back his engines in order to avoid a collision. Schley disputed this and said that the *Texas* was never nearer than 500 to 600 yards and that there was no danger of a collision with the *Brooklyn*.

When the turn was completed, the *Teresa* was ahead on the Brooklyn's starboard bow. The guns of the *Brooklyn* were directed at the *Teresa* and the *Vizcaya*. By this time the battle was becoming very intense. Schley ordered that the men serving below deck be kept informed of the progress of the battle. Every few minutes a report was made through the voice tube that produced cheers down below. The *Teresa* was disabled by the concentration of U.S. firepower and headed for the beach. It ran aground on a small beach west of Punta Cabrera. The time was 10:35 a.m., or only an hour after the flagship had emerged from the channel at Santiago.

While the *Brooklyn* was concerned with the *Vizcaya*, the *Oregon* turned its attention to the *Almirante Oquendo*, the fourth Spanish ship to emerge from the harbor. Indeed, it was struck repeatedly by waiting U.S. ships before it had cleared the harbor entrance. Once out it had to run the gauntlet of fire from most of the squadron. Guns from the *Oregon* fired from a range of about 2,000 yards, while the *Texas* shot from 2,500, the *Iowa* from 3,000, and the *Indiana* from 5,500 yards. The *Brooklyn* sent an occasional shot toward it. But at a range of 1,400 yards the *Iowa* was in the position to do the most damage and it poured its entire battery into the Spanish ship. Meanwhile, the *Oregon* moved to within 900 yards and subjected the *Oquendo* to an intense fire. Within 12 minutes the *Oquendo* was on fire, and it headed for the shore. The *Oregon* came abeam of the Spanish ship and continued to batter it. The *Oquendo* ran ashore about two miles west of the *Teresa*. It struck its flag at 10:40 a.m.

Next the attention of the large U.S. ships turned to the *Vizcaya*. The *Brooklyn* had been engaging it at a range of about 2,500 yards. At this point, *Texas* fired from 6,000 yards and the *Iowa* from 8,000. The *Oregon* shot from about 3,000 yards while it advanced. Through a cloud of smoke some 400 to 500 yards off the starboard quarter of the *Brooklyn*, Schley saw the approach of the *Oregon*. In the *Brooklyn* the signals "close up" and "follow the flag" were hoisted. The *Oregon* replied, and the signal was repeated to other ships. The *Vizcaya* was afire and scenes on board it were appalling. The *Oregon*'s thirteen- and six-inch guns destroyed the upper works of the *Vizcaya*. It was too much. The *Vizcaya* turned and reached the shore at a place that was 15 miles from Santiago. It struck its flag at 11:15 a.m.

Meanwhile, the *Furor* and *Plutón* had emerged from Santiago harbor. They supposedly had tarried inside in order to raise the steam pressure in their boilers. If so, the delay cost them whatever support the cruisers would have supplied. The *Furor*, in the lead, at first planned to go eastward, but seeing the *Gloucester* approaching from that direction, it changed direction and headed west. The *Plutón* followed. As the ships emerged from the harbor entrance they came under fire from the smaller guns of the *Indiana*, *Iowa*, *Oregon*, and *Texas*, all of whose gunners were shooting from extreme ranges. When the *Indiana* hoisted the signal: "The enemy's torpedo boats are coming out," Lt. Cmdr. Richard Wainwright in the *Gloucester* misread it as "gunboats close in," and accordingly moved his ship across the line of fire of the *Indiana*. Fortunately, the ship was not hit, but in this exposed position a shell from the *Iowa* narrowly missed the *Gloucester*'s bow. Moving at a 17-knot speed, the *Gloucester* began to fire at the destroyers from a range of 2,500 yards with its two six-pound and one three-pound guns. The Spanish replied with four 14-pound guns, four six-pounders, and four Maxim machine guns.

Repeatedly struck by shells and leaking badly, the *Plutón* headed for the shore. As it was nearing the land, it was struck amidships by a 13-inch shell from the *Indiana*, which exploded the forward boilers and killed all but two men in the engine room and stokeholds; the ship was unmanageable and nearly torn in two. It ran upon the rocks, tore open its bow, rebounded and sank. Some of its crew were drowned when they jumped overboard to avoid the U.S. fire; others escaped ashore. The rest were rescued from the water by the men of the *Gloucester*. Those men also went to the aid of the Spanish sailors from the *Teresa* and the *Oquendo* despite the risks posed by exploding ammunition, magazines, and boilers. Admiral Cervera, who had escaped from the *Teresa* and made it to the shore, surrendered to a boat from the *Gloucester*. Cervera was taken to that ship where he was received with great kindness by the U.S. officers.

The *Furor* also met a dreadful fate. Its boilers and forced draft mechanism were disabled early in the battle. Later, the engine was damaged, and a projectile struck the after shell room and exploded the ammunition stored there. Portions of a dead body were tangled in the steering gear and the *Furor* circled wildly and with a heavy list. The white flag of surrender was displayed. Soon after the survivors were removed, the *Furor* was shaken by a series of explosions and sank about five miles west of the entrance to the harbor of Santiago. Both *Furor* and *Plutón* were destroyed about 10:30 a.m.

Meanwhile, the beginning of the battle had been observed in the flagship *New York*, and about 9:40 a.m. Sampson turned back from Siboney and headed west. By the time Sampson arrived off Santiago, the *Teresa*, *Oquendo*, and *Vizcaya* had been eliminated. The *New York* fired three four-inch shells at the *Furor*. These were the only shots fired by that ship during the battle. When the flagship came within signal distance of the *Indiana* and *Iowa*, Sampson ordered those ships to resume their stations on the blockade. The *New York* pressed on, hoping to join the fight with the remaining Spanish ship, the *Cristóbal Colón*.

When the *Colón* emerged from the harbor it came under attack by guns from the *Iowa* at a range of 2,800 yards and from the *Texas* and *Oregon* a little farther out. The *Indiana* fired from 3,000 yards, yet the *Colón* suffered little damage. This was due in part to its armor and its lack of wooden deck fittings. It could sail at speeds of up to 14.5 knots and was thus faster than the U.S. ships, but it lacked its 10-inch guns. Speed had kept the *Colón* ahead of its pursuers as long as it was burning good quality coal. When it had to use the inferior grade of fuel that was available at Santiago, however, it began to lose speed. The *Brooklyn* sheered off and tried to head off the *Colón* at a distant headland. At a range of 9,500 yards the *Oregon* began to fire its forward 13-inch guns. The sixth shot landed just ahead of the *Colón*. Its captain decided not to waste the lives of his men in a hopeless battle, and he ordered the *Colón* turned toward the shore. Observing this change in direction, the men in the *Oregon* cheered. At 1:12 p.m. a 13-inch shell exploded under the stern of the *Colón*. It struck its colors and about 1:15 p.m. its bugler sounded cease-fire. When it reached the shore about 50 miles west of Santiago the Spanish sailors opened the sea cocks and began to disable the guns.

At the time of the surrender of the *Colón*, the *Brooklyn* and the *Oregon* were closest to it. The *Brooklyn* signaled "cease firing; the enemy has surrendered," and Captain Cook went in a boat to accept the formal capitulation. A prize crew from the *Brooklyn* and *Oregon* went on board the *Colón* and tried unsuccessfully to save the Spanish ship. The Spanish prisoners were rounded up and preparations were made to transfer them to a U.S. ship.

The approach of the *New York* was observed in the *Brooklyn*, and a signal was hoisted: "We have gained a great victory; details will be communicated." This signal was flying about a half hour before it was answered from the *New York* by the order: "Report your casualties." Schley responded with the message that one man had been killed and two wounded. It was a remarkable record for the squadron, but no note of congratulation was forthcoming from Admiral Sampson. The *Brooklyn* displayed another signal: "This is a great day for our country!" which the *New York* simply acknowledged with an answering pennant.

At 2:23 p.m. the *New York* moved into a position between the *Brooklyn* and the *Colón*. Captain Cook was returning to the *Brooklyn* when he was ordered to the *New York* to make a report. He did so, and when he returned to his ship, Schley went to the flagship to make his own report of the battle. While in the *New York*, a report was received of a Spanish battleship on the coast. Sampson ordered the *Brooklyn* and the *Oregon* to investigate the sighting, but for some reason only the *Brooklyn* went. The ship in question proved to be Austrian, and it flew a flag that resembled that of Spain, which had resulted in the misidentification.

It was later established that the Battle of Santiago had cost Spain 323 dead. In addition, one officer died of a heart attack after his ship surrendered, and another officer died on the beach. About 150 Spaniards made it back to Santiago and others escaped detection. The officers and men who were taken prisoner totaled 1,720.

In the U.S. squadron, the *Brooklyn* fired the most shells, followed by the *Oregon* and the *Indiana*, but the percentage of hits for most of the guns was below 3 percent. Only the eight-inch guns achieved a hit ratio of 3.1 percent. Spanish gunnery was also poor. The *Brooklyn* was struck 20 times by solid shot and more often by fragments and machine gun fire, but one six-pound shell that struck at the waterline did not penetrate. Two one-pound shells hit the chart house. The *Iowa* was hit 11 times, two of which were potentially serious. One six-inch shell hit the hull two or three feet above the waterline but did not explode. Another entered the ship five feet above the waterline, exploded, started a small fire, but did no serious damage. The *Texas* was hit several times but sustained no significant damage. A shell that struck its funnel sent fragments down on the chart house soon after the captain had left the bridge. The *Indiana* was hit twice but the damage was minor.

The Battle of Santiago eliminated the only Spanish naval force in the Caribbean and thus gave the United States a complete freedom of action in that area. It also resulted in a further tightening of the blockade of Cuba. In Spain the defeat halted the deployment of a naval squadron to the Philippines.

After the battle one of Sampson's officers sent a message to Washington in his name that proclaimed that the victory was a Fourth of July present to the nation. Because no mention was made of the fact that Schley was technically in operational command during the battle, it began a long controversy between the partisans of Sampson and Schley over who should be given the credit for the victory.

Harold D. Langley

REFERENCES

French E. Chadwick, *The Relations of the United States and Spain: The Spanish-American War* (Scribner's, 1911), 2 vols.; George E. Graham, *Schley and Santiago. An Historical Account of the Blockade and Final Destruction of the Spanish Fleet under the Command of Adm. Cervera, 3 July 1898* (W.B. Conkey Co., 1902); L.J. Gulliver, "Sampson and Shafter at Santiago," *United States Naval Institute Proceedings*, 65 (1939), 799–806; William T. Sampson, "Atlantic Fleet in the Spanish War," *Century Magazine* 57, new series (1899) 886–913; David F. Trask, *The War With Spain in 1898* (Macmillan, 1981).

See also Sampson, William Thomas; Schley, Winfield Scott; Santiago Campaign, Cuba (1898).

Santiago Campaign, Cuba (1898)

Because the fate of Cuba depended on whether the United States or Spain controlled the Caribbean Sea, the location of Spanish warships there governed military strategy during the Spanish-Cuban/American War. No significant Spanish naval presence was in those waters in April 1898, but the United States administration knew that Adm. Pascual Cervera y Topete was coming from Spain in command of a substantial squadron. Uncertain where the Spaniards would find a harbor, the United States navy scurried around the Caribbean looking for his ships.

As for Cervera, even before he left the Cape Verde Islands for the Caribbean in April, he believed his squadron was doomed. The Spanish admiral entered the Bay of Santiago de Cuba undetected by the U.S. navy with four armored cruisers and four torpedo boats in tow on 19 May. As late as 23 May Commodore Winfield S. Schley believed Cervera to be at Cienfuegos. It was not until 28 May that Schley arrived off Santiago and established a blockade. Soon, Rear Adm. William T. Sampson, commanding in the Caribbean, arrived. He established an arc of 11 ships, the ends of the arc two miles offshore and eight miles apart, with the apex of the arc six miles out to sea. All night, every night, searchlights on the U.S. ships illuminated the mouth of the harbor.

Cervera's presence focused the attention of President William McKinley's administration on Santiago. On 31 May Maj. Gen. William R. Shafter was directed to load the troops collected at Tampa, Florida, and to sail for Santiago. Shafter could debark at points of his own choosing after which his orders read: "Move onto the high ground and bluffs overlooking the harbor or [move] into the interior, as shall best enable you to capture or destroy the garrison there and cover the navy as it sends its men in small boats to remove torpedoes, or, with the aid of the navy, capture or destroy the Spanish fleet" (Sargent, vol. 1, p. 121).

On 3 June U.S. naval officer Richmond P. Hobson and seven sailors took the *Merrimac*, an old collier, into the neck of the harbor to sink it where it would block passage in or out. The *Merrimac* at once came under heavy fire; one shot disabled the rudder; so that Hobson could not steer the ship into the narrows. Instead, it sank in deep water, not blocking the passage, and Hobson and the crew were captured.

Admiral Sampson asked Shafter to attack and capture the forts at the mouth of Santiago harbor to permit the navy to remove the mines in the neck of the harbor. Armored vessels, Sampson said, were too precious to be risked against the forts and the mines. Shafter, however, insisted that getting at the Spanish fleet was the navy's responsibility. The forts crowned bluffs close to 250 feet above the water line with no paths and with a tangle of undergrowth on the steep slopes. Defenders would inflict too many casualties on U.S. troops. Very sharply he wrote to the admiral, "I am at a loss to see why the navy cannot work under a destructive fire as well as the Army." With surprising restraint Sampson replied, "If it is your earnest desire that we should force our entrance, I will at once prepare to undertake it . . . our position and yours would be made more difficult if . . . we fail in our attempt" (Trask, p. 253). He knew that the power of ships' guns should exceed that of the forts by three times. The navy, therefore, did not attempt to enter the harbor until peace had been arranged.

Shafter chose to land two of his three divisions at Daiquirí over a sharp coral shore in a heavy surf. Men and supplies went in from the transports in strings of ship's boats towed by navy steam launches. Horses and mules had to be thrown overboard to swim ashore; 30 did not make it, and two men drowned. Except for the heavy surf there was no opposition from the Spanish forces to the landing, and by evening on 22 June there were close to 17,000 men and some supplies ashore. One of the three divisions of V Corps waded ashore at Siboney, nine miles closer to Santiago.

There were 200,000 Spanish troops in Cuba, and 36,582 of them in the Santiago area, but Gen. Arsenio Linares Pomba chose to scatter his force in six locations within 50 miles of Santiago. He never concentrated them. Shafter's army, at first poorly organized and supplied, was very vulnerable; it was saved by the enemy's incompetence. Shafter intended to hold his troops in place until they were fully organized and supplied; he stayed aboard ship to be sure that materiel reached the shore as needed. While he was afloat, Maj. Gen. Joseph Wheeler, a former Confederate general, pushed his cavalry division forward and brought on an action at Las

Guásimas on 23 June which spoiled Shafter's timing. Wheeler engaged approximately 1,000 men to oppose about 1,500 placed there by the Spanish. Wheeler lost 16 men killed and 49 wounded without achieving any significant military goal.

To attack the garrison at Santiago, U.S. forces had to gain the hills to the east and northeast of the city. A rail line ran along the coast, turning north at Agudores, then to the shores of Santiago Bay. Determining that he could not use this, Shafter elected to go northwest on a narrow trail through jungle vegetation. Because he had learned of a reinforcement of 8,000 men for the Santiago garrison, he decided to begin operations on 1 July. The narrow trail was soon congested by the traffic of a few wagons and six-pack trains plus soldiers on foot. Shafter, sick with light malaria and overcome by the heat (he weighed 300 pounds), attempted to command from a hill four miles east of Santiago. He sent 6,653 men to take El Caney, assuming that this could be accomplished in a couple of hours after which this detachment could join the main body of troops for an attack on Kettle Hill and San Juan Hill. It took all day to overrun El Caney even though it was held by only 500 men, and the attackers were late in joining the other attack, late and worn out. By evening of 1 July, the United States Army had gained its objectives, but at heavy cost: 81 killed, 360 wounded at El Caney; 142 killed and 1,014 wounded at San Juan Hill, close to 10 percent of the men engaged. Shafter's army at this point looked down on the city and a garrison entrenched in front of it behind rolls of barbed wire. The armies exchanged fire throughout 2 July. U.S. troops squatted in narrow trenches, first broiled by tropical sun, then drenched by torrential rains. They had little to eat because although there was plenty at Siboney, no way existed to get it to the firing line. They were also very short of needed rest.

The initiative shifted to Gen. Ramón Blanco y Erenas who commanded all the Spanish forces, land and water, in Cuba as well as serving as governor general. He began to urge Cervera to leave Santiago Bay. The admiral replied, "the sortie will entail the certain loss of the squadron and majority of its crews. I shall never take this step on my own account, but if your excellency so orders I shall carry it out" (Chadwick, vol. 2, p. 118). Blanco insisted that Cervera overestimated the dangers of a sortie, adding that the honor of Spain depended on the squadron. Finally on 1 July he gave a positive order to depart. Cervera prepared on 2 July to make the sortie the next day. It took 12 hours to get up the necessary steam. The lives certain to be lost, he said, were sacrificed on the "altars of vanity." He waited for daylight because the searchlights illuminating the harbor's mouth eliminated the advantage of darkness.

On the morning of 3 July, four U.S. ships had left the blockade to take on coal elsewhere, and the flagship had headed eastward carrying Admiral Sampson to meet with General Shafter, a meeting that the president had ordered to take place. Five armored vessels were still on station when at 9:30 a.m. a U.S. sailor observed the Spanish cruiser *Infanta María Teresa* steaming toward the open sea from the harbor's mouth. After traveling four and one-half miles from their position in front of the city, the Spanish vessels bore down the narrow neck, about 450 feet wide, in single file, 800 yards apart moving at about 10 knots an hour. They came under concentrated fire, which sank or drove the ships to the beach. The last to remain in action, the *Cristóbal Colón*, beached 56 miles west of Santiago. As Cervera had foreseen, Spanish losses were fearsome: of 2,150 men, 323 were killed, 151 wounded, and 1,782 taken prisoner. One U.S. sailor was killed and one wounded. U.S. crews abandoned destruction and turned to rescuing Spanish sailors from burning ships and from the sea.

At the sound of the guns, Admiral Sampson reversed course and sped toward the battle, but the action was finished by the time he arrived. Nevertheless, in his report he took credit for the astounding victory, heightening the antagonism that had existed between him and Admiral Schley, who had been in command during the battle.

While the battle at sea went on, the campaign on land reached a low point. The losses at El Caney and San Juan Hill, coupled with his own wretched health, had drained Shafter's desire to fight. On 3 July, before he learned of the destruction of the Spanish fleet, he cabled the War Department that he might have to retreat from his location and draw back five miles to the rail head at Aguadores. This was unacceptable to the president and his advisors, who required a quick victory. They dispatched Gen. Nelson A. Miles to Santiago with 3,500 troops to take over if Shafter continued to be unable to drive ahead. On 4 July, learning of the naval triumph, and being somewhat rested, Shafter informed the

War Department that he would hold his position. The reply was: "when you are strong enough to destroy the enemy and take Santiago . . . you do it" (Chadwick, vol. 2, p. 216).

The general made no assault, but chose instead to tighten the blockade of the besieged city. The capture of El Caney had given him control of the town's water supply. Although 3,500 Spanish reinforcements had entered the city on 3 July on a road from the west that the Cubans failed to close, the addition only further strained the dwindling supplies available. Bit by bit the U.S. lines extended until they closed off all access to Santiago by land or water. Shafter demanded unconditional surrender, threatening bombardment by naval guns if it was refused. Those guns had lightly shelled the town on 31 May from five miles off shore. On 6 June and again on 14 June they had heavily bombarded the forts at the harbor's mouth, without inducing surrender. Shafter deferred shelling, scheduled for 5 July, in order to let civilians escape. About 20,000 of them fled to El Caney where the U.S. commissary did its best to subsist them. General Miles arrived on 8 July and joined Shafter in negotiating with the Spanish officials, but Shafter remained in command.

Even though the Spaniards recognized that their situation was hopeless, they refused to surrender unless they could march out with colors flying, bearing their weapons, thereby saving martial honor, to Holguín, 50 miles inland. The U.S. administration ordered Shafter to accept nothing less than unconditional surrender. Naval guns carried out a persuasive bombardment on 10 July and continued the following day. They fired the last shot of the Cuban campaign on 11 July 1898.

The U.S. government finally agreed that the Spanish soldiers might march out with their arms, stacking them to be turned over to the victors. In addition, it agreed to ship all men who had come from Spain back to their country at U.S. expense. In return, Spanish authorities contracted to help clear the mouth of the harbor of mines. Under these terms, the surrender occurred on 16 July. It included not only the troops in Santiago, but all those in the province, approximately 12,000 of whom were outside the Santiago area and the reach of the United States Army. U.S. troops entered the city of Santiago on 17 July. From 9 August through 18 September, 22,864 Spaniards returned to Spain in vessels contracted for the work and paid for by the United States.

In the two weeks during which Shafter had negotiated a bloodless surrender, only four U.S. soldiers had been killed and 14 wounded. But in the same period, around 15 a day had been dying from malaria and dysentery. On 2 August Shafter wrote to the War Department that about 75 percent of his men had malaria and that the army was too weak from disease to operate any longer in the island. Moreover, yellow fever had appeared and would become an epidemic. He asked that V Corps be returned to the mainland at once. His general officers concurred in this and wrote a letter to him giving the grisly details of their commands. Their letter ("the round robin") got into the hands of the press, and on 4 August appeared as front-page news. This gave the U.S. public its first view of the wretched plight of the army in Cuba. It induced outrage and indignation. The War Department responded instantly by designating 5,000 acres on Long Island, New York, as the receiving area for the returning soldiers. The first shiploads left Santiago on 7 August and others followed as fast as transports could be secured for them. The reception center could not be made ready that rapidly, and the sick men landed with inadequate facilities to take care of them.

From 28 May when Admiral Schley arrived to blockade Santiago bay, until the capitulation on 16 August, eleven and one-half weeks had passed. That was the time span of the Santiago campaign. Many commentators, civilian and military, have since pilloried the U.S. commanders for their errors in Cuba. Those errors flowed from a total unreadiness to wage a campaign anywhere against any enemy, coupled with the shortcomings of a War Department that was out of date and an army that was not organized on modern lines. They stemmed, too, from the determination of the McKinley administration to win fast. The failings of the Spanish commanders contributed as much as any factor to ensure U.S. success in Cuba. If they had handled their military resources with even moderate skill, they might have repelled Shafter's advance and greatly prolonged the entire war. As it was, they did nothing to oppose the landing of the U.S. expeditionary force, even though the place chosen to go ashore favored the defense. Although Spanish troops exceeded by twice the numbers that Shafter landed, they were scattered in small detachments. Shafter did not know it, but there were probably no more than 6,000 men before him in the trenches at Santiago. The Spanish lacked artillery, but the commanders neglected to land guns from Cervera's ships to defend the city, even though the crews were put ashore to man the defenses. Undue reverence for pride and honor cost Spain dearly, witness Governor General Blanco's order to Cervera to sortie from the bay although the admiral knew for certain that complying with this order would entail the destruction of his fleet. Spanish blunders gave the McKinley administration the quick military and political victory in Cuba that it needed.

John K. Mahon

REFERENCES

French E. Chadwick, *The Relations of the United States and Spain: The Spanish-American War* (Scribner, 1911), 2 vols.; Graham A. Cosmas, *An Army for Empire: The United States Army in the Spanish American War* (Univ. of Missouri Pr., 1971); Margaret Leech, *In the Days of McKinley* (Harper, 1959); Herbert H. Sargent, *The Campaign of Santiago de Cuba* (A.C. McClurg & Co., 1907, 1914), 3 vols.; David F. Trask, *The War With Spain in 1898* (Macmillan, 1981).

See also El Caney, Cuba, Battle (1898); García, Calixto; Gómez y Báez, Maximo; Las Guásimas, Cuba, Battle (1898); Military Cooperation of the United States With the Cuban Revolutionaries (1898); San Juan Hill, Cuba, Battle (1898); Santiago, Cuba, Naval Battle (1898); Shafter, William Rufus.

Schley, Winfield Scott (1839–1911)

Admiral Winfield Scott Schley had immediate command of U.S. naval forces during the naval battle off Santiago, Cuba, on 3 July 1898, the largest naval engagement of the Spanish-Cuban/American War. He was easily the most controversial naval officer of that war owing to questions that arose over his performance before and after the Santiago battle and the problem of whom to credit the total victory of the U.S. fleet, Schley or his superior officer, William T. Sampson.

Born at Richfields, Frederick County, Maryland, on 9 October 1839, the son of John Thomas and Georgianna Virginia (McClure), Schley was named for Gen. Winfield Scott, a hero of the War of 1812, a friend of his father and a presidential candidate. John Thomas Schley was

educated for the law, but preferred the life of a gentleman farmer. The family was proud of its relatives who had served in the American Revolution and the War of 1812, and as a boy Winfield was filled with thoughts that one day he would serve in some patriotic cause.

After he had completed his secondary education in Frederick, Maryland, Schley expected to enter the United States Military Academy at West Point with the assistance of his mentor and namesake, General Scott. But when the time came for such action, Scott was without influence as a result of disagreements with the secretary of war. Schley had resigned himself to a career in business when his congressman secured him an appointment to the United States Naval Academy. He began there as an acting midshipman in September 1856.

Schley stood out from many of his classmates because at age 19 he was older, self-confident, athletic, and a natural leader. Men and women admired him, but there were those among his colleagues who were jealous and resentful of his attainments. He applied himself to his studies sufficiently, so that in 1860 he graduated number 18 in a class of 25.

After graduation he made a cruise in the frigate *Niagara* to Japan to return members of that country's first diplomatic mission to the United States. During that voyage Schley showed himself to be a resourceful officer and one who was liked by his men. When the ship returned to the United States, the Civil War had begun, and President Abraham Lincoln had declared a blockade of the Southern confederacy. The *Niagara* was sent to a blockading station off Charleston, South Carolina. When the ship *General Parkhill* tried to escape the blockade and was captured, it was sent to Philadelphia as a prize under the command of Schley. After delivering the ship, Schley was granted a leave of absence to visit his family. In summer 1861 he was promoted to the rank of master and ordered to the frigate *Potomac*, which had been assigned to the Gulf Blockading Squadron under Flag Officer David G. Farragut.

Promoted to lieutenant, Schley was ordered to the steam gunboat *Winona*, then off Mobile, Alabama. Later, while on patrol duty on the Mississippi River, he became the acting commander of the steam sloop *Monongahela* when its captain was wounded. In the course of an attack on one of the citadel defenses of Port Hudson, Farragut hoisted a signal for the

Monongahela to withdraw from the action, but because of smoke and a lack of wind Schley could not read it. When the citadel was silenced he reported to Farragut, who censured him for disobeying orders. Schley explained the circumstances and noted that his orders were to destroy the citadel. Farragut then invited him into his cabin. There, Farragut said that Schley had been reprimanded for what appeared to be a disregard for orders, but he commended him for carrying out what he believed to be his duty. This exchange reinforced in Schley the belief that success depended on the responsible judgment of an officer on the spot. If circumstances made it necessary to disregard orders to achieve success for his country, then disobedience was a virtue.

Transferred to the sloop *Richmond* as its executive officer, Schley participated in at least 20 engagements with Confederate batteries along the Mississippi River. Damage to the ship as a result of these actions made it necessary for the *Richmond* to go to New York City for repairs. During the repair work Schley was granted a leave which he used to hurry to Annapolis and to marry Annie Rebecca Franklin, to whom he had been engaged for two years.

The end of the Civil War brought a reduction in the size of the navy and in the opportunities available to its officers. For Schley the years of peace led to his being promoted to lieutenant commander in July 1866 and ordered to the Naval Academy.

In 1869 Schley became the executive officer of the steam sloop *Benicia*. The *Benicia* arrived in China to become a part of the Asiatic Squadron under Adm. John Rodgers, which attempted to open diplomatic relations with Korea. When Rodgers' men entered a restricted area on the Salee River to do some surveying, the Korean forts fired on them. Interpreting this as an insult to the flag and failing to receive an apology for the act, Rodgers sent a landing force ashore to capture the forts. During the assault on the main fort, Schley was slightly wounded in the left arm by a spear. The *Benicia* returned to the United States in August 1872, and Schley was sent to the Naval Academy as the head of the Department of Modern Languages.

At the academy he also joined with other officers to establish in 1873 the United States Naval Institute, a private, nonprofit, professional organization devoted to advancing the profes-

sional, literary, and scientific knowledge of the navy through lectures and which published a periodical that would be a forum for discussions, proposals, and criticisms. It was during this period that Schley was promoted to commander in June 1874.

Ordered to command the screw steamer *Essex*, Schley made a cruise to Mexico, Africa, and South America between 1876 and 1879. This was followed by duty as a member of the Lighthouse Board under Commander George Dewey, a classmate.

Amid his lighthouse duties, Schley became interested in the newspaper accounts of the departure of a polar expedition under army Lt. Adolphus W. Greely. Rising public concern about the safety of this group led President Chester A. Arthur to appeal to Congress, and that body authorized the sending of a navy rescue expedition composed of volunteers. Schley was offered the command of the expedition, and he departed from New York in the *Thetis*, 21 April 1884. On 22 June, one ship reached Cape Sabine where it found Greely and five other survivors of his expedition. Schley believed that if he had been delayed another 24 hours, Greely and all of his men would have perished. Their rescue thrilled the United States and made Schley a nationally known figure. It was the high point of his professional career.

Returning to New York, Schley and his men were thanked by President Arthur for their efforts. Arthur told Schley that he could become the new chief of the Bureau of Equipment and Recruiting in Washington.

An interest in keeping abreast of the new technology led Schley to apply for the command of the cruiser *Baltimore* even before its keel was laid. By the time it was completed in 1889, Schley had been promoted to captain and had secured the command. While the ship was in Europe, an uprising took place in Chile which caused the administration of President Benjamin Harrison some concern because of U.S. interests in that country. At Schley's suggestion, the *Baltimore* was ordered to Valparaiso where it became the flagship of Rear Adm. William Penn McCan, the commander of the South Atlantic Squadron. U.S.-Chilean relations had become more tense as the result of unneutral acts by the United States minister to Chile and by the shipment of arms purchased abroad to the rebels. The attempts by the U.S. naval commander to determine what portions of the country were under the control of the insurgent forces were regarded by them as intelligence-gathering for the government in power. Furthermore, the *Baltimore* was ordered to land Chilean refugees in neutral territory. All of these actions made the *Baltimore* the symbol of U.S. involvement in Chilean affairs. Adding to that feeling was the landing of sailors and marines to protect the U.S. consulate when Valparaiso fell to the rebel forces.

When order appeared to be restored in Valparaiso, Schley asked the local *intendente* if there would be any objection to his granting shore leave to his men. That official replied that there was no reason why U.S. sailors could not enjoy the same privileges as those of other nations. So, on the afternoon of 16 October 1891 Schley granted liberty to 115 sailors. En route to the shore the men in the liberty boat passed near a Chilean warship and were the recipients of hostile gestures. On shore, a few civilians told the sailors not to be out at night, and some checked into hotels. About 8:00 p.m. Schley received a report from a merchant captain that U.S. sailors were being attacked in the city. One had been killed and others wounded. Schley appointed a three-man court of inquiry to ascertain the facts and to make a report.

The court established the fact that trouble began in a saloon when a Chilean spat in the face of a U.S. sailor. A brawl followed in which two U.S. sailors were killed, 17 were wounded, and others were beaten and imprisoned. Foreign witnesses and the Chilean Sisters of Charity who treated the wounded in a hospital agreed that the sailors were not drunk.

By the time the court had made its report, the *Baltimore* had been relieved of its duties and was sent to San Francisco. At the Mare Island Navy Yard a second court of inquiry on the incident was held on the orders of Secretary of the Navy Benjamin F. Tracy. The findings of this court were in agreement with the earlier one.

In February 1898 Schley was promoted to commodore. Shortly after this, the battleship *Maine* blew up in the harbor of Havana, Cuba, and the public and some members of Congress clamored for war. Congress declared war on Spain on 25 April, effective four days earlier.

Public concern over the possibility that Spanish warships might raid the coastal cities of the United States led the navy to create the Flying Squadron, which was to guard the Atlantic coast-line. To command this squadron, Schley was chosen over at least a dozen admirals and senior commodores. His selection was apparently due to Assistant Secretary of the Navy Theodore Roosevelt. The action created feelings of envy and jealousy among some naval officers. Schley's flagship was the cruiser *Brooklyn*, and the squadron was based at Hampton Roads, Virginia. Acting Adm. William T. Sampson, the commander of the North Atlantic Squadron, asked Secretary of the Navy John D. Long to clarify the relationship between his force and Schley's, but Long declined to do so, resulting in a series of confusing orders and movements.

When war was declared Sampson placed northern Cuba under blockade. But upon hearing that a Spanish squadron under Adm. Pascual Cervera y Topete was en route to the West Indies, Sampson moved his force to Puerto Rico where he hoped to intercept the enemy. Instead, Cervera went to Martinique in search of coal. A report that Cervera was at Martinique led the Navy Department to order Schley's squadron to Key West, Florida. When he arrived, Schley was ordered to blockade Havana. Before he could do so, Sampson arrived at Key West, conferred with Schley and sent him to the Cuban port of Cienfuegos to search for Cervera. When he reached Cienfuegos Schley believed that Cervera was in that port; he did not learn otherwise until 24 May. Four days earlier the Navy Department received a report that Cervera was in Santiago de Cuba, and it ordered Schley to take his force to blockade that port. Schley's squadron was increased by the addition of the battleship *Iowa*, the unprotected cruiser *Marblehead*, the converted yachts *Vixen* and *Eagle*, and the collier *Merrimac*. Schley's squadron arrived off Santiago the day after he received his orders.

Already in position off Santiago was the auxiliary cruiser *St. Paul*, whose captain told Schley that Cervera's squadron was not in the harbor. A Cuban harbor pilot said the same thing. Schley began to wonder if he was the victim of a ruse. By this time some of his ships needed fuel, but in the case of the *Marblehead* and the battleship *Texas* their projecting sponsons made them difficult to coal in high seas. Reasoning that if the Spanish ships had not yet reached Cuba, Schley believed they would need several days in port to refit before emerging again. Once they were in port a tight blockade would be necessary. Therefore, the time to get the ships coaled was before the Spanish arrived or before they could exit. Schley, therefore, notified the Navy Department that he was proceeding to Key West to recoal. Believing that Cervera was already in Santiago, the Navy Department and President McKinley expressed great anxiety over Schley's departure. Sampson was also concerned and headed for Santiago. While en route there the weather moderated, his ships were coaled at sea, and the squadron was back before Santiago on the night of 28–29 May. The next day Schley saw a Spanish cruiser inside the harbor, and Cuban revolutionaries confirmed that all of Cervera's squadron was there. Using his three largest ships, Schley investigated the strength of the forts at the mouth of the harbor and engaged in a long-range shelling of a Spanish cruiser.

Sampson arrived on the scene with his force on 1 June and Schley's squadron was placed under his command. The new commander imposed his own version of a blockade of the port, attempted to block the harbor entrance by sinking the collier *Merrimac* in the channel, and conducted a bombardment of enemy installations. On 20 June the U.S. army landed in Cuba and advanced toward Santiago. To prevent Cervera from attempting a night escape, Sampson used the searchlights on his ships to illuminate the harbor entrance. Cervera was ordered to depart with his force, and he made preparations to do so.

On Sunday 3 July, Sampson left the blockading force, sailing in his flagship *New York*, and steamed eastward for a meeting with the army commander. This left Schley in command of the blockading force. The Spanish noted that on this morning the blockade was weaker due to the departure of the *New York* accompanied by a torpedo boat and an armed yacht. In addition, a battleship, two cruisers, and a converted tender had gone to Guantánamo for coal. The *Brooklyn* was the fastest and most powerful ship then on blockade, and this Sunday morning it was anchored farther out than usual, creating a gap in the western end of the semicircular blockade. Cervera thought that if his flagship, *Infanta María Teresa*, could ram and disable the *Brooklyn*, the Spanish ships would have a chance to escape.

At 9:35 a.m. the *Teresa* was observed coming out of the harbor followed by the other Spanish ships. Signals were hoisted, and the officers and men in the U.S. ships rushed to their battle stations. With binoculars in hand, Schley rushed to the semicircular wooden platform he had had built around the ship's conning tower. The Spanish ships came out of the harbor at eight- to 10-minute intervals. Led by the *Teresa* they concentrated their fire on the *Brooklyn*. The Spanish ships came under heavy fire from the U.S. vessels. Intending to ram, the *Teresa* headed for the *Brooklyn*, but the hits it was taking led Cervera to turn the ship suddenly westward. Under orders from the ship's captain, and with Schley's approval, the *Brooklyn* made a rapid and continuous turn to port, or a little more than half of its tactical diameter. When it was completed, the *Teresa* was ahead on the *Brooklyn's* starboard bow. Behind the *Teresa* was the cruiser *Vizcaya*, which also tried to ram, but it now turned westward as well. The major ships of the U.S. force chased the larger Spanish ships in a running fight. The rest of the blockading squadron turned its attention and firepower on the cruiser *Almirante Oquendo* and the destroyers *Furor* and *Plutón* as they emerged from the harbor. Battered by the guns of its pursuers, the *Teresa* was disabled and headed for the beach. The same fate overtook the *Vizcaya* and the *Cristóbal Colón*. The last Spanish ship struck its colors at 1:15 p.m., and Schley ordered a cease-fire.

Meanwhile, the sounds of guns had led Sampson to return to the scene of action, but by the time he arrived the battle was over. When the *New York* was within signal distance Schley sent a message to Sampson reporting the victory. No word of congratulation was received, only a request for the casualties. Schley reported that one man had been killed, and two were wounded. It was subsequently established that the Spanish had lost 323 men. Later that afternoon, one of Sampson's officers sent a message to Washington in his name reporting the victory and making no mention of the fact that Schley was in command. In their coverage of the battle, most of the newspapers gave credit to Schley for the victory. This set the stage for a controversy between the supporters of Sampson and those of Schley over who was the victor, and it led to bitterness and division in the navy and among the civilian population. The relationship between the two officers was courteous and correct.

Schley was promoted to rear admiral on 3 March 1899, and he served as a member of the Puerto Rican Commission and on various boards. His popularity led to invitations and public appearances where he received loving cups, special medals, and other awards. In November 1899 Schley was given the command of the South Atlantic Squadron.

While he was away, a history book was published that dealt with the Battle of Santiago and subjected Schley to abuse and defamation for his part in it. This book was adopted as a text at the Naval Academy, and Schley felt that he had no choice but to request a court of inquiry into his conduct in the war. Adm. George Dewey was appointed the president of the court which began its work at the Washington Navy Yard on 12 September 1901. A number of navy men of all ranks were summoned as witnesses, but only testimony directly related to Schley was admitted. The court ruled that Sampson's conduct was not under review, and, as it turned out, he was too ill to testify. After considering the 14 questions it was asked to answer, the court criticized Schley's actions off Cuba before 1 June, but in the battle itself he was considered self-possessed and encouraged his men to fight bravely. Admiral Dewey, the president of the court, filed a minority opinion in which he dissented from some of the findings. He concluded that Schley was in absolute command and entitled to credit for the victory. Schley's lawyers called attention to the shortcomings of the inquiry and appealed to President Theodore Roosevelt to reverse the findings. After reviewing the evidence and talking to the surviving captains about the battle, Roosevelt narrowed the criticism of Schley. The failure to get the verdict reversed hurt Schley deeply.

Schley retired from the navy on 9 October 1901. In 1909 he began to show signs of failing health. While walking to his son's office in New York City on 2 October 1911 he collapsed and was taken to a hospital, where he died. After a funeral with full military honors, including the participation of a representative of the president and the brigade of midshipmen from the Naval Academy, Schley was buried in Arlington National Cemetery.

Harold D. Langley

REFERENCES

George Edward Graham, *Schley and Santiago* (W.B. Conkey Co., 1902); Winfield Scott Schley, *Forty-Five Years Under the Flag* (D. Appleton, 1904); Winfield Scott Schley, *Record of Proceedings of a Court of Inquiry in the Case of Rear-Admiral Winfield S. Schley, U.S. Navy* (U.S. Government Printing Office, 1902); David F. Trask, *The War With Spain in 1898* (Macmillan, 1981); Richard S. West, *Admirals of American Empire* (Bobbs-Merrill, 1948).

See also Flying Squadron, United States Navy (1898); Sampson, William Thomas; Santiago, Cuba, Naval Battle (1898).

Scott, Hugh Lenox (1853–1934)

Hugh Lenox Scott was an officer in the United States Army who played a major role in peace-making on the U.S. border with Mexico in 1916. Scott was born at Danville, Kentucky, on 22 September 1853 to Rev. William McKendry Scott and Mary Elizabeth (Hodge) Scott. He graduated from the United States Military Academy at West Point in 1876, and then served for two years with the 7th Cavalry in the Sioux, Nez Percé, Camp Robinson, and Cheyenne expeditions. In total, he spent more than 20 years on the Native American frontier, becoming knowledgeable in the customs, languages, and history of the Plains Indians. From 1899 to 1902, he served as adjutant general in Cuba under Gen. William Ludlow and later under Gen. Leonard Wood. His politico-military duties continued in the Philippines when he became governor of the Sulu archipelago and commander of Post Jolo. Between 1906 and 1910, he served as superintendent of West Point. His reputation for skill as a negotiator and his deep knowledge of Native American ways led to his being called into service regularly to solve problems with various tribes, including the Navajo and Mexican Kickapoos (1908), the Hopi (1911), the Apache (1912), the Navajo again (1914), and the Piaute (1915).

From 1912 until 1917, in addition to his other duties, Scott was deeply involved in events on the U.S.-Mexican border. In 1912, he commanded the 3rd Cavalry in Texas, stationed in San Antonio, but he soon left that post to take command of the 2nd Cavalry Brigade and Patrol with responsibility for the length of the line from Fabens, Texas, to California. He took up his post at El Paso, and it was at this time (1913–1914) that he first met Mexican revolutionary leader Francisco "Pancho" Villa, with whom he was to establish cordial relations that lasted for some time. Scott himself attributed this good relationship to his habit of using "truthful, direct, forceful statements" in his dealings with Villa. It is reported that about this time Scott gave Villa a pamphlet on the ways in which civilized nations made war, although his own later comments about Villa's practices indicated that it had had little effect. He also communicated regularly with Álvaro Obregón, a revolutionary leader who controlled the state of Sonora. These friendships led to his taking a major role in negotiations on border problems during the Mexican Revolution. An early instance of his activities in this area occurred in late 1914, when he discussed with Villa the problems that factional fighting on the border at Naco, Sonora, was causing as a result of bullets and artillery rounds being fired across the line and causing civilian casualties on the Arizona side.

Meanwhile, Scott had become chief of staff of the army on 17 November 1914, and he was serving in this capacity when Villa attacked Columbus, New Mexico, early on the morning of 9 March 1916. Therefore, he took a major role in the ensuing Punitive Expedition which was ordered into Mexico to pursue the retreating Mexican forces. Scott was in constant communication with both John J. Pershing, the commander of the expedition, and with Gen. Frederick Funston, the Southern Department commander stationed at San Antonio. From the beginning of the march of forces into Mexico, both Scott and Pershing were aware that the difficulties of catching Villa were significant and revealed their doubts in their personal correspondence. When U.S. troops were attacked by Mexican civilians and then by Constitutionalist army troops at Parral, Chihuahua, on 12 April 1916, Scott was called on to negotiate with Venustiano Carranza's government to reach an agreement on the movements of Pershing's men.

Scott's acquaintance Gen. Álvaro Obregón was the negotiator on the Mexican side, but unfortunately the two men had brought mutually exclusive instructions to their meetings. Obregón was authorized only to obtain the withdrawal of U.S. forces from Mexican soil, whereas Scott was instructed to deal only with military questions and leave the issue of withdrawal to diplomatic channels. As the meetings proceeded, Scott was given further instructions to offer a retrenchment of U.S. forces to a position nearer the border—a relocation that Scott had already proposed to President Woodrow Wilson and that Wilson had accepted—and to indicate that a complete withdrawal would take place as soon as the area was secured against further Villista attacks. Although Obregón and Scott were able to reach an agreement on 2 May that provided for the gradual withdrawal of the expedition to begin immediately, with Mexican forces moving into position to prevent any further incursions by Mexican dissidents into U.S. territory, it was never acceptable to President Carranza. Moreover, an additional raid took place across the border into Glenn Springs and Boquillas, Texas, on 5 May, making it clear that the Mexican government forces were still insufficient to control the area. Consequently, U.S. forces remained in Mexico without an agreement between the two governments.

As a result, the situation on the border remained extremely tense, and in mid-June, Scott ordered the Army War College to draw up new plans for the invasion of Mexico in the event that some new incident might lead to full-scale war between the two countries. On 18 June the mobilization of the national guard units of 44 states was ordered by Wilson; the Texas, Arizona, and New Mexico contingents had already been called up and Nevada did not have a force. When a clash occurred at Carrizal between Carrancista and U.S. troops on 21 June, Scott notified Funston that he was sending the new militia units south as quickly as possible. War was averted, however, when Carranza quickly ordered the return to the United States of the prisoners taken by the Mexican army. Scott remained extremely pessimistic about the prospects for real control of the border by Mexican troops, but by September he was acknowledging in communications with Pershing that the expedition no longer had any military role. He indicated, however, that it did have a function as a source of pressure on the Mexican government. By the time the expedition was withdrawn in February 1917, Scott's attention had turned strongly to the European situation. There is considerable evidence that Scott looked on the expedition and the presence of national guard troops on the border as an opportunity for training personnel for the European struggle to come.

Scott was replaced as chief of staff in September 1917, but remained on active duty until 12 May 1919. He commanded the 78th division of the army at Camp Dix, New Jersey, in 1918–1919. After retiring from the army, he served as a member of the Board of Indian Commissioners and later as chair of the New Jersey State Highway Commission. He also wrote an autobiography and numerous studies of the Plains Indians.

Linda B. Hall

REFERENCES

Clarence C. Clendenen, *Blood on the Border* (Macmillan, 1969); Clarence C. Clendenen, *The United States and Pancho Villa: A Study in Unconventional Diplomacy* (Cornell Univ. Pr., 1961); Don M. Coerver and Linda B. Hall, *Revolution on the Border: The United States and Mexico, 1910–1920* (Univ. of New Mexico, 1988); Don M. Coerver and Linda B. Hall, *Texas and the Mexican Revolution: A Study in State and National Border Policy* (Trinity Univ. Pr., 1984); Hugh L. Scott, *Some Memories of a Soldier* (Century, 1928).

See also American-Mexican Joint Commission (1916); Obregón, Álvaro.

Select Committee on Haiti and Santo Domingo

The U.S. occupation of Haiti and the Dominican Republic during the administration of President Woodrow Wilson created considerable controversy and dispute in the United States, eventually resulting in a Senate investigation. The controversy was sufficient to render the occupation an issue during the 1920 election campaign, when Democratic officials of the Wilson administration boasted of their roles, and Republican candidate Warren G. Harding pledged to restrain U.S. actions in both of the island nations. While the controversy began over whether the occupations were necessary and over the expenses incurred, it eventually focused on the length of the occupations, the conditions of withdrawal, and the effect of the military landings on U.S. relations with all of Latin America.

There was opposition to the occupation from the start, stimulated by the muckraking press and fostered by the exiled Dominican government. The so-called Haiti-Santo Domingo Independence Society kept the issue before the public, using the pages of such publications as *The Nation* and *Current History*, and aided by visits by former members of the Dominican government and by the Haitian *Union Patriotique*. In addition to the press, the debate was fueled by isolationist senators who opposed U.S. imperialism, such as Senators William E. Borah (Republican, Idaho) and William H. King (Democrat, Utah). A lively debate resulted, in large part reflecting the dispute regarding the future role of the

United States abroad that followed World War I and the Versailles treaty, as well as an effort to reduce expensive commitments abroad.

On 19 July 1921 the United States Senate adopted Resolution 112, establishing a subcommittee of the Senate Foreign Relations Committee, referred to as the Senate Select Committee on Haiti and Santo Domingo. The committee consisted of Senators Joseph Medill McCormick (Republican, Illinois) Chairman, Tasker L. Oddie (Republican, Nevada), Atlee Pomerene (Democrat, Ohio), and Andrieus A. Jones (Democrat, New Mexico). Its hearings lasted throughout the rest of 1921 and the first half of 1922 and included a visit to both Haiti and the Dominican Republic during December 1921. The committee held open sessions in both Santo Domingo and Port-au-Prince.

The Senate Committee played an important role in the evolution of U.S. policy toward the island nations. Senator McCormick was particularly influential through correspondence with President Harding. The committee was instrumental in convincing the administration to overrule the initial recommendations of the State and Navy departments and to appoint Col. John H. Russell high commissioner in Haiti instead of the original nominee, Gen. Smedley D. Butler. This action avoided a potential mistake because Butler was disliked in Haiti, reflecting his role in disbanding the Haitian Congress shortly after the occupation began. The appointment of Russell facilitated negotiations and improved the U.S. image in the island nation and throughout Latin America. Senator McCormick also played a role through advice to the president in facilitating the establishment and later broadening of the Comision de Representantes of Dominican leaders, with whom presidential representative Sumner Welles negotiated the terms of the U.S. withdrawal from that nation.

The Senate committee was instrumental in promoting a conciliatory approach, and in the decision that early withdrawal from the Dominican Republic could be arranged, but that the occupation of Haiti for a longer period would be necessary. The unanimous recommendation of the committee regarding the prospects for withdrawal and the length of occupation necessary greatly facilitated and supported the Harding administration's conclusions, and its efforts to promote a rapid withdrawal from the Dominican Republic. The Senate Select Committee was consequently helpful in silencing the criticism of the isolationists and also influential in supporting the views of the administration. Its impact on the appointment of representatives and officials in the island republics served to promote the selection of individuals favoring a conciliatory approach and negotiation with the local political elites.

Kenneth J. Grieb

REFERENCES

Kenneth J. Grieb, *The Latin American Policy of Warren G. Harding* (Texas Christian Univ. Pr., 1976); U.S. Congress, Senate, Committee on Foreign Relations, *Inquiry Into the Occupation and Administration of Haiti and Santo Domingo: Hearings Before a Select Committee on Haiti and Santo Domingo*, U.S. Senate, 67th Congress, 1–2 Session (U.S. Government Printing Office, 1922).

Sellers, David Foote (1874–1949)

Rear Adm. David Foote Sellers succeeded Rear Adm. Julian L. Latimer as commander of the Special Service Squadron patrolling Central American waters in July 1927. During his tenure, which lasted until 1929, Augusto C. Sandino's guerrilla war against the Nicaraguan government and the interventionist marines broke into full fury and eventually brought a U.S. force of 5,000 men to subdue Sandino and his followers.

Born in Austin, Texas, on 4 February 1874, Sellers was an 1894 United States Naval Academy graduate. He served in the Spanish-Cuban/American War, the Samoan campaign in 1899, and the Philippine War; during World War I he was commander of the battleship *Wisconsin* and the transport *Agamemnon*.

As Special Service Squadron commander, Seller's major problem was the Nicaraguan conflict. Shortly after Sellers assumed his command, Sandino attacked U.S. Marines at Ocotal and became internationally known. Although the guerrilla chief suffered several defeats in encounters with marines and Nicaraguan national guardsmen, he maintained a core of armed support and honed his skills for a long-term challenge to the U.S. intervention. In January 1928, Sellers appealed to Sandino to avoid unnecessary sacrifice of lives, but Sandino demanded the departure of foreign troops, a choice not acceptable to Washington because of the Stimson agreement of 1927 which promised supervised elections and which was to have brought an end to fighting in Nicaragua. Fearful that the unsettled conditions would not allow free elections, Secretary of State Frank B. Kellogg and army Gen. Frank R. McCoy, head of the electoral commission, were critical of the military situation. In turn, Sellers and Gen. Logan Feland, commander of the 2nd Marine Brigade in Nicaragua, were not happy with McCoy's criticism of marine operations and with McCoy's direct orders to the Nicaraguan national guard. Sellers defended Feland and discussed the issues with McCoy. Although their differences were glossed over, divisions remained. Hints of army aviators and officers joining U.S. forces in Nicaragua brought opposition from Sellers, Feland, and Adm. Charles F. Hughes, chief of naval operations. When McCoy left Nicaragua after the 1928 election Sellers was greatly relieved.

After the inauguration of José María Moncada as president of Nicaragua in 1929, there developed a split between the chief of the *guardia*, Gen. Elias R. Beadle (lieutenant colonel, United States Marine Corps), supported by the U.S. legation, and Feland who encouraged Moncada to place the national guard under the marine command and to create an armed force, other than the *guardia*, to fight the Sandinistas. In this dispute Sellers supported Feland. Sellers also seemed to support Moncada's efforts to amend Washington-supported legislation governing the national guard. The State Department thought the changes would allow greater politicization of the guard; Sellers thought they were trivial and would have little effect on the nonpartisan nature of the force.

Because of the Feland-Beadle dispute, and upon recommendation of U.S. Minister Charles C. Eberhardt, both officers were transferred. When Sellers opposed the reassignment of Feland, Eberhardt accused him of undercutting the State Department's efforts in Nicaragua, a charge angrily denied by Sellers. Later that year Sellers was replaced by Rear Adm. Edward H. Campbell and Eberhardt by Matthew E. Hanna.

Sellers was superintendent of the Naval Academy from 1934 to 1938. He retired in March 1938 and died on 27 January 1949.

William Kamman

REFERENCES

William Kamman, *A Search for Stability: United States Diplomacy Toward Nicaragua, 1925–1933* (Univ. of

Notre Dame Pr., 1968); Neill Macaulay, *The Sandino Affair* (Quadrangle, 1967); Richard Millett, *Guardians of the Dynasty: A History of the U.S. Created Guardia Nacional de Nicaragua and the Somoza Family* (Orbis, 1977).

Seymour Column, China (1900)

The Seymour Column, or Seymour Expedition, was the first Allied attempt to succor the legations at Beijing (Peking), China, during the Boxer Uprising. Under the command of British Adm. Edward H. Seymour, the column consisted of approximately 2,100 officers and enlisted men from the warships anchored off Dagu (Taku). The column suffered more than 300 casualties during its advance and its final retreat, and its mission was aborted. Its failure to reach Beijing was not only a disappointment to the Allied commanders, it also invalidated a long-held assumption foreigners had about the Chinese army: that a small body of well-equipped and well-disciplined foreign troops could cross China without meeting effective resistance. In fairness to Admiral Seymour, it must be acknowledged that he was a naval officer with little experience or knowledge of land warfare. Furthermore, as the leader of a multinational force, he held his position as a result of seniority, not of command.

The column left Tianjin (Tientsin) for Beijing on 10 June with provisions for only three days because Seymour expected the column to be in the capital that evening. The troops traveled by train; Seymour's plan was to repair the track destroyed by the Boxers as the column moved toward Beijing. Damage to the railway was more extensive than anticipated and between 10 June and 13 June, the column advanced only half way to the capital. On 13 June, Seymour stopped at Langfang, 40 miles from Beijing, and sent a train back to Tianjin for more supplies. When the train returned two days later, he learned that the rail line to Tianjin had been cut after a certain point, and that he was surrounded by Chinese troops and Boxers. He then decided to return to Tianjin by rail, repairing the rails during the retreat and fighting Chinese forces until a passage could be opened and the rails repaired.

On 19 June, the column reached the town of Yangzun (Yangtsun) and discovered the bridge across the river was too damaged to support the weight of the train. Abandoning the train and all the heavy equipment, the column commandeered river junks and floated down the river to Tianjin.

The drought in North China, however, had caused the river level to drop, and the boats continually ran aground. In addition, the column was constantly harassed by both Boxers and Imperial troops.

On 23 June, three miles from Tianjin, the column seized the Xigu (Hsi-ku) Arsenal, with its supply of food, water, and ammunition. That same day, regular Imperial soldiers tried to retake the arsenal, but were repulsed by the resupplied column. Appeals for relief were sent to Tianjin, and it arrived three days later. The defeated column returned to Tianjin after destroying the arsenal. In the face of large Chinese forces and his column's need for more food and ammunition, Seymour had to give the order to fall back.

Lewis Bernstein

REFERENCES

A. Henry Savage Landor, *China and the Allies* (Scribner, 1901), 2 vols.; Edward H. Seymour, *My Naval Career and Travels* (Smith, Elder & Co., 1911); Arthur H. Smith, *China in Convulsion* (Fleming H. Revell Co., 1901), 2 vols.; J.K. Taussig, "Experiences During the Boxer Rebellion," *United States Naval Institute Proceedings*, 53 (1927), 403–420; Daniel W. Wurtsbaugh, "The Seymour Relief Expedition," *United States Naval Institute Proceedings*, 28 (1902), 207–219.

Shafter, William Rufus (1835–1906)

Gen. William R. Shafter commanded U.S. land forces in the Santiago, Cuba, campaign during the Spanish-Cuban/American War.

Shafter was born on 16 October 1835 in Kalamazoo, Michigan. He went to school, then taught school, and worked on his father's farm. He did not enter the history of the nation until the Civil War began. At that time he enrolled as a first lieutenant in the 7th Michigan Volunteer Infantry Regiment. He distinguished himself at the Battle of Fair Oaks on 31 May 1863, taking his company away from bridge construction to oppose Confederates charging across an open field. Thirty-three years later, 12 June 1895, he received the Medal of Honor for this day's performance.

Shafter had risen to the grade of lieutenant colonel when the battle of Thompson's Station took place on 5 March 1863. His regiment, the 19th Michigan, and three others, opposed by

Gen. Earl S. Van Dorn's entire army of 15,000 men, were surrounded and obliged to surrender. Conditions of imprisonment were harsh in transit to and at Libby Prison, Richmond, Virginia. His stay was short, however; Shafter was returned to duty at Annapolis, Maryland, on 8 May 1863.

Shafter commanded the 19th Michigan until 19 April 1864 when as colonel he received command of the 17th United States Colored troops. Col. Thomas J. Morgan, commanding the brigade at the Battle of Nashville, 15 and 16 December 1864 reported that the 17th Colored was "an excellent regiment . . . under a brave and gallant officer."

In the scaled-down post-Civil War army, Shafter, with the grade of lieutenant colonel, continued to command black troops, this time the 24th Infantry Regiment. He led them in the arid, hot Staked Plains and other harsh areas of Texas. Known in those campaigns as "Pecos Bill," coarse, profane, and a harsh disciplinarian, he established himself as an effective leader. He was so heavy that his bulk would have immobilized other men in the stern desert conditions.

In 1877 and 1878 Shafter operated against Native Americans who went back and forth across the Mexican-U.S. border whenever they chose. Part of the time the U.S. government believed that Mexico permitted U.S. forces to pursue raiders into Mexico, and most of the time U.S. forces acted as if permission had been granted. Shafter displayed remarkable ability to lead nonwhite troops, not only black infantry and black cavalry, but also Seminole scouts. Some of the below-the-border actions were skillful military operations, but questionable diplomatically.

In May 1897, Shafter became a brigadier general, and one year later, as the threat of war with Spain loomed, he was advanced to major general of volunteers. The secretary of war, Russell A. Alger; the commanding general of the army, Nelson A. Miles; and the adjutant general, Henry C. Corbin, agreed that Shafter should command the V Corps, which was to be the expeditionary force to fight Spain in Cuba. He was age 53, had never commanded large forces, and weighed 300 pounds.

On 29 April, Secretary Alger ordered Shafter to assemble 6,000 regulars, land them on the southern coast of Cuba, penetrate inland far enough to supply the Cubans, aid them briefly, and then withdraw. He rescinded the order the next day, but followed it with others giving numbers of men to employ and places on the coast of Cuba to land them, all different. All the while, men and equipment were pouring into Tampa, Florida, creating chaos. No one knew what should go first down the single railroad track to the port, or where to find it after it had arrived.

Finally, an order of 7 June directed Shafter to take at least 10,000 men and depart at once for Santiago de Cuba, on the southeastern tip of Cuba. Working around the clock, the general and his staff cleared up the Tampa tangle sufficiently to have 32 transports loaded on 8 June. About to sail, they were halted by word from the navy that because of a Spanish squadron it was too dangerous. Not until 14 June did the convoy get under way. By 20 June the convoy was off the coast near Santiago. The expedition lacked sufficient engineers, medical personnel, reconnaissance units, and equipment. For lack of transport space Shafter had left behind three volunteer regiments, a brigade of artillery, and horses for the cavalry.

Shafter's orders permitted him to land in the Santiago area at any place of his own choosing: Occupy "the high ground and bluffs overlooking the harbor or [move] into the interior, as shall best enable you to capture or destroy the garrison there, and cover the navy as it sends its men in small boats to remove torpedoes, or, with the aid of the navy, capture or destroy the Spanish fleet" (Sargent, vol. 1, p. 121). Adm. William T. Sampson urged Shafter to assault the two forts at the mouth of the harbor, but the general refused this mission as too hazardous. He considered penetrating the harbor to be the duty of the navy. Instead, he chose to land at two points; Daiquirí, 16 miles east of the city of Santiago, and Siboney, nine miles away. There was no harbor at Daiquirí, where the water was turbulent. The navy supervised the landing. By 22 June about 6,000 men were ashore with some supplies, at a loss of two men and 50 horses and mules drowned. Had Spanish forces opposed the landings, losses could have been heavy.

There were too few lighters to shuttle between ship and shore; thus, it took days to get all the equipment on land. The transports offshore continued to function as storehouses. What was landed was often wasted because of a lack of army know-how. Shafter did not intend to start his attack until all supplies and men were ashore and organized. He stayed aboard ship to send in materiel according to need. Brig. Gen. Joseph Wheeler, a former Confederate major general of cavalry, temporarily commanded on land. Wheeler, naturally aggressive and eager to gather honor, brought on a premature, nasty fight at Las Guásimas on 24 June. Shafter managed to stop him from a farther advance at Sevilla, a few miles beyond Las Guásimas. Wheeler's battle upset Shafter's timing, but he made the best of it by stating the fight gave him more room to arrange his army ashore.

Shafter had other reasons to move faster than he had intended. Scouts told him that Santiago would soon receive heavy reinforcement. Then, too, there was the threat of tropical disease. The general had studied British Adm. Edward Vernon's attack on Santiago in 1741, which had been defeated by malaria and yellow fever. He changed his plans and set 1 July as the date to capture the high ground northeast of the city. To do this he split his force, sending three-sevenths of it under Brig. Gen. Henry W. Lawton to capture El Caney, a fortified position about five miles northeast of the city. He assumed that El Caney would be captured in less than an hour and that Lawton's troops would then travel three miles southwestward to augment the line under Brig. Gen. Jacob F. Kent, and Brig. Gen. Joseph Wheeler to capture the twin high points: San Juan Hill and Kettle Hill. Shafter himself, prostrated by the heat, gout, and a touch of malaria, attempted to direct the battle from a hill several miles distant. The two sections of the split army did not, in fact, mesh well, and the units fought as they had been trained, separately and not as parts of a cohesive force. By nightfall, the united army reached the hills three-quarters of a mile from the outworks of Santiago, at a cost of 223 killed and 1,374 wounded. At daylight on 2 July, the armies resumed firing and kept it up all day.

The U.S. troops were low in spirit. They had had little to eat for two days. There were provisions aplenty on the ships at anchor, but not enough lighters to bring them in. The men had done without sleep and were obliged to squat in narrow trenches under a broiling sun, alternating with pouring rain. Their condition affected Shafter as did the heavy losses and his own ill health. Drained of aggressiveness, on 3 July he telegraphed the War Department that he might have to withdraw from his position overlooking Santiago. Dismayed by this proposal, Alger dispatched General Miles to Santiago with added troops.

Shafter's war council opposed withdrawal; so, feeling somewhat more optimistic, he decided to remain where he was and so notified the administration. The president wanted him to finish the war by storming Santiago. The Santiago garrison, Shafter believed, was about equal to his army in numbers, and it was dug in behind wire entanglements. He had no intention of storming the place, especially after 3 July when the Spanish squadron left the harbor and was destroyed in the Caribbean by United States naval forces.

The hills that the U.S. force had won were within range of the navy's 13-inch guns, but it did not occur to Shafter to ask for their fire, nor to the admiral to offer it. Nor did Shafter use the 1,000 marines who had been landed at Guantánamo. His previous experience had not conditioned him to cooperate with naval forces.

Instead of storming Santiago, the general besieged it. The capture of El Caney had given the United States Army control over the water supply of the city while access to supplies from inland and from the Caribbean were effectively blockaded. At the same time Shafter began time-consuming negotiations with Spanish authorities on capitulation. The administration instructed him to accept nothing less than unconditional surrender, so he sent demands, with deadlines attached, on those terms. He threatened bombardment by the navy's guns if his demands were rejected, but he allowed time for civilians to leave the city. Around 20,000 of them did so, trudging the five miles to El Caney where the United States Army Commissary Department did its best to feed them. By this time about 40,000 hungry people looked to that commissary for their food. When the Spaniards let one deadline pass, the navy bombarded the city on 10 and 11 July, doing little damage. The Spanish officials recognized the hopelessness of their situation, but military honor stood in the way of conceding unconditional surrender. To save their honor, they asked to be allowed to march out and to Holguín, carrying their weapons. Shafter, joined on 11 July by Miles, rejected this request.

Finally, the Spaniards surrendered under condition that the United States would pay to ship Spanish troops back to Spain. They included in the surrender the armed personnel of the Cuban Southeastern Division. That division had 12,000 soldiers who had not taken part in the fight and whom the U.S. force would not have been able to capture. Shafter had kept the naval officers out of the negotiations and did not permit them to sign the documents of capitulation on 17 July 1898.

The 15-day interval between the battles of 1 July and the capitulation on 16 July enabled Shafter to arrange a creditable surrender. It saved lives that would have been lost in storming Santiago, but lost lives to disease. Fifteen U.S. soldiers were dying each day from malaria and dysentery, and a few from yellow fever. Shafter informed Alger that the army should be removed from Cuba at once. The generals of his brigades agreed and wrote a more vivid account of the weakened condition of the soldiers. Their letter (the "round robin") to Shafter was picked up by the press and made headline news all over the nation. This was the first knowledge the public had had of the ravages of disease in the army in Cuba. Widespread indignation welled up. The administration then arranged to buy 5,000 acres on Long Island, New York, to receive the returning troops. The first convoys left Santiago on 7 August.

Opinion in the United States was hypercritical of the way the war had been run. Press correspondents had been everywhere with the army and had reported events in great detail. Shafter had been unfriendly to correspondents, but, although they lampooned him for his bulk and his succumbing to the heat, they did not pillory him. Theodore Roosevelt, however, had sent the word home that Shafter had proved to be criminally incompetent. Still, Shafter was less criticized in the hearings on the conduct of the war than the administration was.

When the war was over Shafter became commander of the Department of California. He retired as a brigadier general on 16 October 1899, but remained in command as major general of volunteers until 30 June 1901. That same day he was retired as a major general. He died in Bakersfield, California, on 13 November 1906.

One historian has written that Shafter was saved from the consequences of his mistakes by the ineptitude of the Spanish commanders. He did concentrate 86 percent of his available force at the crucial point, Santiago de Cuba, whereas his opponent brought together only 13 percent of his. Shafter achieved dominance over the entire eastern portion of Cuba at a human cost of

243 killed in action and 1,445 wounded. In spite of this achievement historians have given Shafter low marks. There seems to be no doubt that he was coarse, profane, and a harsh disciplinarian or that he was gruff, blunt, honest, and free of political ambition. He had never commanded large numbers of men before 1898, but he had been an effective regimental commander during the Civil War and a significant leader in the post-Civil War actions against Native Americans in the West. By the late 19th century Shafter was a typical field officer in a military system that was obsolete. This affected how he has been judged.

John K. Mahon

REFERENCES

Paul H. Carlson, *"Pecos Bill," A Military Biography* (Texas A&M Univ. Pr., 1989); French Ensor Chadwick, *The Relations of the United States and Spain: The Spanish-American War* (Scribner, 1911), 2 vols.; Graham A. Cosmas, *An Army for Empire: The United States Army in the Spanish American War* (Univ. of Missouri Pr., 1971); Margaret Leech, *In the Days of McKinley* (Harper, 1959); Herbert H. Sargent, *The Campaign of Santiago de Cuba* (A.C. McClurg & Co., 1907, 1914), 3 vols.; David F. Trask, *The War With Spain in 1898* (Macmillan, 1981).

See also Santiago Campaign, Cuba (1898).

Siberian Intervention (1918–1920)

In August 1918, during the last months of World War I, two understrength United States Army infantry regiments were sent from the Philippines to the Siberian port city of Vladivostok. Later augmented by reinforcements from California, some detachments remained in Vladivostok while others were sent far into the interior to guard the Trans-Siberian Railway. These units remained in Siberia until April 1920, at which time they were evacuated to avoid being overrun by advancing Communist armies. The Siberian intervention has been the subject of controversy among historians ever since.

Russia had suffered grievously during the war. Hideous losses in the field and shortages of necessities at home had produced two revolutions in 1917. The first had toppled the tsarist government and brought into nominal power a provisional government of moderates. They in turn were overthrown by the Communists led by V.I. Lenin. The Communists assumed power in most of the major cities, but a brutal civil war ensued as various "White" factions (so named because they opposed the "Reds") established themselves in outlying areas. To buy time, the Communists in March 1918 signed a peace treaty with Germany that closed down the Eastern Front. This raised the possibility that Germany might be able to transfer enough divisions to achieve victory on the Western Front.

The British and French, fearing defeat in the West, began clamoring for intervention in Siberia. They hoped to unseat the Communists and to install a government that would resume the war. The Japanese, less interested in the conflict with Germany than in carving out a sphere of influence in mineral-rich Siberia, also advocated sending military forces. President Woodrow Wilson stoutly opposed such schemes for several months. He regarded as foolish the idea that troops landing on the Pacific coast of Russia could make their way thousands of miles overland to influence events in the West. Besides, he thought, foreign intervention might well strengthen the Communists by allowing them to appear as defenders of Russian sovereignty. He had no sympathy whatever for Japanese ambitions.

Events in May and June 1918 altered Wilson's position. The Czechoslovakian Legion, composed of men who had volunteered to fight on the Russian front in return for Allied pledges of independence for Czechoslovakia from Austria-Hungary after the war, had negotiated an agreement with the Communists for passage eastward along the Trans-Siberian Railway to Vladivostok for evacuation. Local clashes between the legion and Communists escalated into a mini-war along the railroad. Viewing the beleaguered Czechs and Slovaks as "cousins" of the Russians, Wilson thought that intervening to help loyal allies would negate charges of violating Russian sovereignty. He agreed to a joint U.S.-Japanese expedition, accompanied by smaller detachments from the other Allies.

Wilson's ultimate goals have been debated. The most common view is that he suspected Japanese motives and acted to prevent them from intervening unilaterally in Siberia (they eventually enlarged their forces to almost 10 times the size of the U.S. contingent and stayed until 1922, when they were pried out by diplomatic pressure). Others have seen that aspect as subsidiary to his larger purpose of overthrowing the Communists: not by direct military means, as the British and French advocated, but by supporting and nourishing "White" governments in hopes they would grow powerful enough to do the job. The rail line U.S. troops guarded, after all, became a pipeline to the anti-Communist government located at Omsk, to which the United States provided large amounts of military equipment and supplies of all kinds. If that was his intention, the operation failed because none of the "White" governments attracted sufficient popular support. Whatever the truth, it is certain that the intervention helped confirm then and later Communist fear of "capitalist encirclement."

Robert James Maddox

REFERENCES

William S. Graves, *America's Siberian Adventure, 1918–1920* (Cape & Smith, 1931); Robert James Maddox, *The Unknown War With Russia: Wilson's Siberian Intervention* (Presidio Pr., 1977); Betty Miller Unterberger, *America's Siberian Expedition, 1918–1920: A Study of National Policy* (Duke Univ. Pr., 1956); John Albert White, *The Siberian Intervention* (Princeton Univ. Pr., 1950).

See also list of entries at front of book for Siberian Intervention (1918–1920).

Sigsbee, Charles Dwight (1845–1923)

Charles Dwight Sigsbee was commanding officer of the battleship *Maine* when it blew up in Havana harbor on 15 February 1898 with the loss of 266 lives.

Born in Albany, New York, in 1845, Sigsbee attended the United States Naval Academy from 1859 to 1863 and saw action during the Civil War on blockade duty and at the Battle of Mobile Bay, and in attacks on Fort Fisher. Sigsbee avoided the career frustrations that confronted most naval officers in the tiny post-Civil War United States Navy by immersing himself in coastal survey and hydrographic duty. He made a complete deep-water survey of the Gulf of Mexico, invented deep-sea sounding instruments, and served as chief hydrographer between 1893–1897. He earned the reputation during his years of exploration as a clever and courageous sea captain but also appeared somewhat indifferent to the latest developments in steam engineering, machinery, and ordnance aboard the new armored warships of the U.S. fleet. In April 1897, the navy gave Sigsbee command of one of those new armored warships, the *Maine*.

Sigsbee took precautions to guard the *Maine* from external attack when he anchored in tense Havana harbor in January 1898. However, he made no special effort to check alarms in the ship's coal bins, which were filled with a volatile quick-burning coal brought on board for the emergency cruise to Cuba, or to closely inspect the ship's machinery. Years later Adm. Hyman G. Rickover determined in a study of the *Maine*'s sinking that Sigsbee's record of commanding dirty, sloppy ships may have contributed to an internal explosion in a forward coal bunker. At the time, Sigsbee and several naval investigative boards insisted that a floating Spanish mine had caused an external explosion that destroyed the *Maine*. A rabid public and yellow press anxious to blame Spain for the tragedy accepted this external sabotage view.

The *Maine* explosion did not injure Sigsbee's subsequent career. He commanded the auxiliary cruiser *St. Paul* during the Spanish-Cuban/American War and captured several Spanish ships. After the war, Sigsbee headed the Office of Naval Intelligence, where he cooperated with the Naval War College, and General Board of the Navy to form an early version of an office of naval operations. Sigsbee later commanded the *Texas* and several squadrons before retiring in 1907. He died in New York City in 1923 and was buried as a naval hero in Arlington National Cemetery.

Jeffery M. Dorwart
© 1992 All rights reserved.

References

Jeffery M. Dorwart, *The Office of Naval Intelligence: The Birth of America's First Intelligence Agency, 1865–1918* (U.S. Naval Institute Pr., 1979); Hyman G. Rickover, *How the Battleship "Maine" was Destroyed* (Naval History Division, U.S. Department of the Navy, 1976); Charles D. Sigsbee, *Deep-Sea Sounding and Dredging* (United States Coast and Geodetic Survey) (U.S. Government Printing Office, 1880); Charles D. Sigsbee, *The "Maine": An Account of Her Destruction in Havana Harbor* (Century, 1899).

Small Wars

The term "small wars" originated in the development of light infantry doctrine in the 18th century and was first used in various treatises on that subject in the late 1700s. These include Col. de la Roche Aymon's *Essay sur la petite guerre* (1770) and Georg Wilhelm von Valentini's *Abhandlungen ueber den kleinen Krieg* (1799). Maj. Karl von Clausewitz also devoted his first year (1810) as an instructor at the Prussian war academy to the subject of Kleiner Krieg (Laqueur, pp. 104, 110). The earliest use of the expression in English seems to have been Charles E. Callwell's *Small Wars: Their Principles and Practice*, which first appeared in Great Britain in 1896 and in subsequent editions in 1899 and 1906. The United States Marine Corps began publishing articles on the subject in 1921 and formally adopted the term in 1935 for its first official manual, *Small Wars Operations* (later reissued as the *Small Wars Manual, 1940*).

Most analysts found the term both slippery and inadequate, in much the same way that current national security specialists bemoan the shortcomings of "low intensity conflict." Callwell described small wars as "somewhat difficult to define," and marine Lt. Col. Harold H. Utley echoed his British counterpart's belief that the phrase was used "in default of a better one." Despite the connotations of size, the doctrine was unrelated to the scope, intensity, or duration of the conflict. The official United States Marine Corps definition did little to eliminate the ambiguity (*Small Wars Manual, 1940*, p. 1-1):

> Small wars are operations undertaken under executive authority, wherein military force is combined with diplomatic pressure in the internal or external affairs of another state whose government is unstable, inadequate, or unsatisfactory for the preservation of life and of such interests as are determined by the foreign policy of our nation.

However, Callwell, Utley, and the *Manual* agreed that the essence of small wars was combat between the regular forces of a modern state and the irregular forces of a lesser opponent. Almost by definition, this conflict would occur on the enemy's territory. The marine theoretician, Utley, added two caveats: only a portion of the local inhabitants would be hostile to the intervening power, and no formal state of war would exist between the parties. While these additional elements never made it into the *Manual*, its doctrinal prescriptions seem to recognize their importance.

Utley's early writings also followed Callwell in defining three types of small wars. A nation might undertake such a war as a punitive measure, to conquer new territory, or to suppress revolution and lawlessness. Of these rationales, the third dominated most U.S. interventions during the early part of the 20th century, although the Indian wars and the Philippine campaign contained elements of both conquest and counterinsurgency. Punitive operations tended to be so inconsequential that they received little attention in the literature.

There was a significant difference between British and U.S. campaigns to suppress revolution because Britain was for the most part operating within its empire and in support of its own local civil administrations. The British army acted when the colonial government and police could no longer maintain order. U.S. campaigns, on the other hand, usually occurred in countries that might be protectorates but that were not in any formal sense part of the United States. This often resulted in a complex triangular relationship between the local government, the United States State Department, and the U.S. military.

The development of doctrine for small wars was haphazard until very late. Captain Callwell published his first edition as a private venture, and it was largely ignored by the British military until the Boer War revealed shortcomings in its ability to fight a well-organized enemy using guerrilla tactics. Callwell's third edition of 1906 met with greater interest, perhaps because he was then a colonel, but it was still not an official document.

Despite extensive U.S. experience in small wars against Native Americans, the United States Army and Marine Corps entered the Philippine campaign, beginning in 1899, without any formal doctrine for such contingencies. This may have been due to a lack of professionalism or to the focus of a newly rising professionalism on more conventional types of conflict. After World War I, an increasingly rigorous emphasis on formal training and education gave rise to greater interest in written doctrine in this previously ignored field. Articles on the theory of small wars began to appear in the *Marine Corps Gazette* in 1921 and remained a staple of that journal for the next two decades. The culmination of this interest was the publication of the Corps' *Small Wars Operations* in 1935 and its revision as the *Small Wars Manual* in 1940.

The United States Army, which played the lead role in the Philippine campaign, seemed to have forfeited the small wars mission to the marines in the years after World War I. A few articles appeared in *Infantry Journal* (at least one by a marine officer), but the army never developed any service doctrine. Moreover, it never engaged in small war campaigns after World War I. Part of this may have been due to an army focus on preparation for conventional wars against likely enemies, such as Germany and Japan. The infantry and cavalry were also in the process of absorbing the tank and developing armored doctrine, while the fledgling air corps concerned itself with spreading the gospel of air power theory.

Another important factor in the interservice transfer of responsibilities was probably the nature of deployments between the world wars. Most of the army was garrisoned in the continental United States and far from potential trouble spots. Those few units located overseas were dedicated to the defense of vital interests, such as the Panama Canal, and were thus unavailable for rapid deployment.

The navy, and by extension the marines on sea duty, always seemed to be in the vicinity of likely problems. Unlike the army, the Marine Corps often had as much as two-thirds of its manpower deployed overseas. In 1917 the U.S. consul in Cuba called for intervention and received a marine landing party within three days. In 1927 the marines met an emergency in China with a provisional battalion of 20 officers and 455 men scraped together from the Asiatic Fleet and various western Pacific naval bases. The small size of most crises and the rapid response capability of the navy and marines allowed these services to monopolize the small wars spectrum of conflict.

Utley's original articles made an additional argument for the heavy reliance on marine forces in small wars. He felt that use of the army connoted a much more serious national commitment which belied the limited goals of a small war. Marines and sailors, on the other hand, presaged no such commitment of national resolve or prestige and could therefore be used without concern for international political sensitivities. The *Manual* seemed to agree when it noted that "Marines have been referred to as State Department troops" (*Small Wars Manual, 1940*, pp. 1–7).

In the early years of the 20th century the British and U.S. militaries seemed to hold identical ideas about strategy for small wars. Callwell noted that conventional objectives of military action were often irrelevant in this realm. The enemy rarely had an army that could be destroyed in a Clausewitzian fashion, nor was the fall of its capital likely to bring resistance to an end. The British theorist therefore recommended that operations should focus on the enemy's will and capability to fight. If one could destroy the livelihood of one's opponents or strike fear into their hearts, then there would be an incentive for them to lay down their arms.

In essence, Callwell advocated a scorched-earth policy as the best means to win a small war. If one destroyed the villages, trampled the fields, and drove off the livestock, the enemy would have no choice but to surrender. Alternatively, the enemy would be forced to fight to defend these assets, in which case the conventional force would finally be able to bring its superior firepower and discipline to bear in a stand-up battle. If the latter occurred, Callwell noted that a classic military victory that gained control of the battlefield was insufficient. The true objective was to inflict casualties in order to prevent the irregular force from melting away to fight another day. In this respect, he seemed to foreshadow the body-count fixation of a much later war, the U.S. involvement in Vietnam.

Callwell's heavy reliance on punitive methods of war was largely conditioned by his attitude regarding the "lower races," which he felt were most effectively impressed by force. U.S. forces initially seemed to agree with Callwell's ideas. The various army campaigns against Native Americans were often ruthless, and brutal reprisals occurred in the Philippines. The Samar campaign of 1901 probably marked the apogee of this strategy, as demonstrated by army Brig. Gen. Jacob H. Smith's orders to marine Maj. Littleton W.T. Waller: that no prisoners be taken. Such activities were not part of a formal military policy, of course, and many U.S. commanders pressed civic action campaigns in their sectors. But atrocities took place precisely because there was no doctrine to guide forces in the field.

Marine Corps practices eventually diverged from those of Smith and Callwell. This may have been at least partly due to government inquiries and bad publicity stemming from Waller's operation on Samar and from a subsequent series of investigations into marine actions during the Haitian revolt of 1918–1920. Accusations of indiscriminate killing led to public outcry and unprecedented government interest in the conduct of small wars.

The concern over public opinion was highlighted in all of the early marine writings on small wars. Most authors mentioned, often more than once, the need to limit force because of domestic and foreign opinion. E. H. Ellis commented explicitly on the problem (Ellis, p. 1):

> Somebody rises up and yells in print: "Marines are down in Jungleland!—and killed a man in war!—and we didn't know anything about it!" Presto! and the people mill around like liaison officers in a World War and inaugurate such a campaign of investigation, castigation and restoration that the Hired Hessians are forced to do the job over again.

The negative publicity only contributed to a positive trend which had already been present in previous U.S. campaigns. As noted earlier, many army and marine officers in the Philippines had rejected Callwell's ideas and used civic action programs to attract opponents to their cause. Similar instances occurred in other early 20th-century small wars.

Because the marines could no longer compel surrender by fear, they soon adopted the alternative, a more benign strategy based on diplomacy and politics. The point of the campaign would be to convince the population to support a lawful government.

As a consequence, the *Manual* devoted considerable space to topics such as psychology, the role of the State Department, the military-civil relationship, military government, and the supervision of elections. More important, many commanders in the later interventions strove mightily to implement the policy. In the second Nicaraguan campaign, 1927–1933, for instance, marine pilots generally refrained from attacking opposition forces in populated areas, while commanders on the ground treated civilians as potential allies rather than as enemies. The marines also emphasized the rapid buildup of constabularies as a means to limit or to avoid the use of U.S. arms against the local citizens. There were undoubtedly instances of excessive use of force, but these were the exception rather than the rule.

New strategy was not the only factor bringing changes to small war tactics; advances in technology had a substantial impact, too. Aviation, beginning with the use of aircraft in Haiti and the Dominican Republic, came to play a major role in counterinsurgency operations. Marine pilots developed divebombing in order to improve the accuracy of aerial firepower, and ground commanders soon relied heavily on it because the rough terrain of most Central American nations rendered impractical the use of artillery.

Planes had a marked effect on logistics, as well. Aerial evacuation improved the odds for marine wounded and freed units to continue with their missions. In some instances entire units were transported by air to new operational areas. The most important contribution was in the area of resupply, however. Airdropped food and equipment revolutionized marine patrolling tactics because commanders could then move deep into remote areas without fear of losing contact with vital logistic lines. Merritt A. Edson made particular use of this feature in his Coco River patrols and was thus able to put the nationalist and guerrilla fighter Augusto C. Sandino on the run in what had formerly been a safe haven in Nicaragua's central highlands. Fewer marines were also needed to guard static posts along rivers and trails because these routes were now less important.

Communications made several major strides. Radio proved vital in maintaining contact between static outposts and the central reserves, and in some cases it allowed reaction forces to respond to pleas for aid from remote garrisons under siege. The development of mobile radio sets was slow, however. Edson's detachment built a "portable" radio from spare parts on board the *Denver*, but it weighed 125 pounds and had to be broken into two parts for transport by mule. Cumbersome batteries were another limitation for the patrols, and they frequently broadcast for only brief periods each day.

The most common means of communication in Nicaragua was the air-delivered message. Planes dropped notes to patrols to pass on orders from higher headquarters or findings from air reconnaissance. Ground units communicated with aircraft through brightly colored panels or used a unique method to pass on written messages. Two marines in a clearing held up poles with a string running between the tops and the message tied to it. The planes swept low between the poles, hooked the string, and gathered in the attached document. The advent of aviation radios in the 1930s vastly improved the system.

Despite their importance, new technologies did not ease the life of the average infantryman. The tactical mainstay of small wars was still the foot patrol in what was often rather inhospitable countryside. During most of the campaigns in Central America and the Caribbean small detachments of squad or platoon strength marched day after day through jungles, over hills, and across streams in search of their guerrilla opponents. Roads were generally nonexistent; so they followed rough trails or cut their own as they went. In a few cases, notably the Coco River patrols of the second Nicaraguan campaign, marine units operated from native boats.

Because conventional military superiority quickly pushed opposing forces into remote areas, marine patrols necessarily operated in sparsely inhabited regions where food and other supplies were not readily available. U.S. units quickly learned to use mule trains to carry heavy equipment like radios and machine guns, as well as extra rations for extended operations. Aerial resupply efforts never fully replaced beasts of burden because of inherent limitations due to bad weather, load capacity, and the small number of available aircraft. Air delivery was also still a primitive art; goods were air-dropped from tree-top level without parachutes and generally suffered from the impact. The tactical and logistic challenges of small wars meant that most soldiers still developed sore feet, ate poor rations, and moved at the same slow pace that had governed earlier generations of infantry.

Although there was an apparent contradiction between the marine emphasis before World War II on small wars and the large-scale conventional conflict that ensued, the corps gained a great deal from its counterinsurgency activities in the prewar period. The development of close air support doctrine proved to be extremely important in an island campaign that limited the usefulness of artillery. Extensive operations against wily guerrillas also prepared marines for the infiltration tactics of the Japanese.

The most important dividend of the small wars was neither technological nor tactical. It was combat experience that proved most valuable to the generation of young officers and sergeants who had missed World War I. Such marine legends as Merritt A. "Red Mike" Edson and Lewis B. "Chesty" Puller received their baptism of fire in the jungles of Central America and went on to lead the corps to victory in the bloody and bitter Pacific campaign. They were better prepared for war than their army counterparts, most of whom had had no combat experience.

Success in the more conventional conflict of World War II may have undermined, perversely, the capacity of the Marine Corps to perform in future small wars. Until recently, it was accepted that the *Small Wars Manual* disappeared in the 1940s and played no role in the development of doctrine for the Vietnam War. This is not entirely accurate because the *Manual* was used as a reference tool by those who drafted new doctrine for counterinsurgency warfare in the early 1960s. It was also mentioned frequently in various military and private publications of that time.

Nevertheless, modern writers ignored most of the strategic, operational, and tactical precepts in the early document. The relevant 1962 Marine Corps manual noted that counterinsurgency involved "paramilitary, political, economic, psychological, and civic actions," but then dwelt exclusively with military force. It is no surprise, then, that U.S. forces in Vietnam waged a campaign of firepower and attrition that would have been more familiar to Callwell than to Utley. The U.S. military had become too imbued with conventional ideas of conflict to adjust to the small wars familiar to earlier marines.

Jon T. Hoffman

REFERENCES

C.E. Callwell, *Small Wars: Their Principles and Practice* (Harrison & Sons, 1906); E.H. Ellis, "Bush Brigades," *Marine Corps Gazette*, 6 (1921), 1–15; Samuel M. Harrington, "The Strategy and Tactics of Small Wars," part 1, *Marine Corps Gazette*, 6 (1921), 474–491; part 2, 7 (1922), 84–93; Walter Laqueur, *Guerrilla* (Little, Brown, 1976); U.S. Marine Corps, *Small Wars Manual, 1940* (U.S. Government Printing Office, 1940); Harold H. Utley, "An Introduction to the Tactics and Techniques of Small Wars," *Marine Corps Gazette*, part 1, 16 (May 1931), 50–53; part 2, 18 (Aug. 1933), 44–48; part 3, 18 (Nov. 1933), 43–46.

See also Pacification; *Small Wars Manual.*

Small Wars Manual

The United States Marine Corps published its first volume on small wars doctrine in 1935 under the title *Small Wars Operations*. This official work apparently grew out of an earlier unofficial effort by Maj. Harold H. Utley. He had written a lengthy manuscript entitled "The Tactics and Techniques of Small Wars" and had published parts of it in the *Marine Corps Gazette* beginning in May 1931.

The project gained official sanction under the leadership of Brig. Gen. Randolph C. Berkeley, who was then head of the Marine Corps Schools in Quantico, Virginia, where Utley was an instructor. At that time General Berkeley was playing a similar role in codifying marine amphibious doctrine in *Tentative Manual for Landing Operations*, which appeared in print in 1934. In 1928, as chief of staff of the 2nd Brigade in Nicaragua, he had also headed an unfinished effort to gather the lessons of that intervention into a pamphlet for the use of future marine expeditionary forces.

The Marine Corps delegated four officers to revise *Small Wars Operations* in 1939 and published the result in 1940 as the *Small Wars Manual, 1940*. The new work was considerably changed from its predecessor, particularly in terms of small-unit tactics. All members of the board had experience in small wars, but only Maj. Merritt A. Edson had served in an infantry unit in direct contact with the enemy. He had led the Coco River patrol in 14 months of operations against Nicaraguan nationalist leader Augusto C. Sandino during 1928–1929. His commanding officer in Nicaragua at that time had been Major Utley.

The evidence of Edson's influence on the revision is overwhelming. The chapters on river operations, patrol bases, and ambushes were drawn directly from his experiences in Nicaragua. Many of the tactics advocated in the *Manual* were Edson trademarks that had been considered heresies by other marine commanders. Some passages were taken verbatim from the major's earlier writings, both published and private. As a result, the small-unit tactical doctrine in the *Manual* is almost exclusively Edson's thinking.

The *Small Wars Manual* went well beyond tactics, however, and included a heavy emphasis on the political nature of foreign interventions. It even noted that "this feature has been so marked in past operations, that Marines have been referred to as State Department Troops" (*Small Wars Manual, 1940*, pp. 1–7). Several chapters dealt with the general characteristics of small wars, the operation of military governments, and the supervision of elections.

The *Manual* divided small wars into five phases, although it noted that conflicts would not always follow this pattern. The first phase consists of growing military involvement in a country as troops are added to reverse a deteriorating situation. These initial formations, generally marine detachments and sailors, act to control vital areas such as the capital and seaports.

In the next stage, expeditionary forces seize the offensive and concurrently begin to organize native police and military units. The third phase consists of ensuring a strong national government, continuing the offensive, and beginning the employment of local troops.

When rebellious forces are subdued, marine units assume a reserve role, and elements of the national police and army take on increasing responsibility for security of the state. In the final phase, U.S. forces are withdrawn when local authorities demonstrate their ability to control the country.

The authors of the *Manual* clearly understood the special considerations governing counterinsurgency campaigns. The work noted that "strategy must be adapted to the character of the people encountered" and that the cause of the war may sometimes be "of an economical, political, or social nature and not a military problem" (*Small Wars Manual, 1940*, pp. 1–8, 1–9). Therefore, only a concerted plan of military, political, and diplomatic efforts could bring the war to a successful conclusion.

The *Small Wars Manual* had a short life because it was shunted out of sight by the World War II emphasis on large-scale amphibious assaults, and it was not revived after that conflict. It was used sparingly as a reference in the development of doctrine for the Vietnam War, but in the process most of its special insights into guerrilla war fell by the wayside. As a result of the renewed interest in counterinsurgency warfare in the late 1980s, the Corps rescued the *Manual* from the museums to use as a teaching tool in the Quantico schools where it originated half a century earlier.

Jon T. Hoffman

REFERENCES

Jon T. Hoffman, "Back to the Future," *Marine Corps Gazette*, 75 (1991), 32–34; Ronald Schaffer, "The 140 Small Wars Manual and the 'Lessons of History,'" *Military Affairs*, 36 (1972), 46–51; U.S. Marine Corps, *Small Wars Manual, 1940* (U.S. Government Printing Office, 1940); Harold H. Utley, "An Introduction to the Tactics and Techniques of Small Wars," *Marine Corps Gazette*, part 1, 16 (May 1931), 50–53; part 2, 18 (Aug. 1933), 44–48; part 3, 18 (Nov. 1922), 43–46.

Smith, Jacob Hurd (1840–1918)

Jacob Hurd Smith, a career United States Army officer, earned considerable notoriety because of the severity of the campaign he waged against Filipino nationalists on the island of Samar in 1901.

Smith was born in Kentucky in 1840 and enlisted in the Union Army at age 21, being commissioned a second lieutenant one year later. He was disabled at Shiloh, Tennessee, and carried a Minié ball in his hip for the rest of his life. He also carried a scar from a saber cut received at Barboursville, West Virginia, and was shot once again many years later at El Caney in Cuba. After the incident at Shiloh, he sat out the rest of the Civil War as a recruiting officer in Louisville, Kentucky. It was there he committed the first of a number of shady financial deals that plagued his career. Apparently, he speculated with money provided for bounties to entice blacks to enlist, increasing his worth in this manner from $4,000 to $40,000 in three years. Revelations of this operation cost him an appointment as judge advocate in 1869, after he had been given a regular commission following the war.

Like most regular officers, Smith spent his postbellum years in the West fighting Native Americans. Allegedly, he was nicknamed "Hell Roaring Jake" because his booming voice could be heard over others on the battlefield and seemed so out of proportion to his short, slight stature. Others claimed that it was bestowed upon him because he so loudly heaped dreadful invective on his subordinates. He slowly climbed the ranks, entering the Spanish-Cuban/American War as a major; reaching the Philippines as a colonel, he commanded the 12th Infantry Regiment. More scandals produced guilty verdicts by two court-martials in 1885 and 1886. The reviewing authority of the first one thought the court's sentence too lenient, and when it was discovered that he had perjured himself, a second court ordered him cashiered from the army. Only the intervention of President Grover Cleveland saved Smith's career by commuting that sentence to a reprimand. In 1891, Smith was accused of using soldiers as his personal house servants, but nothing came of this.

Interestingly, an 1867 efficiency report hinted at Smith's major weakness when it criticized him for being excessively "garrulous." He was recklessly outspoken to news correspondents in the Philippines, informing them as early as 1899, before the guerrilla phase of the war began, that he no longer respected flags of truce and that he had ordered his regiment to shoot all Filipino combatants on the spot. This earned him front-page headlines back home, such as "Colonel Smith of 12th Orders All Insurgents Shot At Hand" (Miller, p. 95), and considerable criticism from anti-imperialists. He also constructed jails out of railroad tracks torn up by the retreating Filipinos into which he crammed up to 50 suspects for months at a time in cages 15 feet by 30 feet by 6 feet high, with no toilet facilities. He was so proud of this "cattle pen," that he posed in front of one for a photograph that was published in the *Manila News*. He seemed even prouder of the grim statistics on the death rate in these cages. He contributed an article to the *Critic* in Manila, attributing the Balangiga massacre to U.S. "officers who love 'little brown brother'" (Miller, p. 238). As one Boston editor lamented at the time of Smith's court-martial in 1902, "It seems that General Smith's method of carrying on civilized warfare was well developed . . . long before he was sent to wreak vengeance on Samar" (Miller, p. 238).

It would appear that Gen. Adna R. Chaffee selected and promoted Smith in 1901 to command the 6th Separate Brigade that was to pacify Samar and Leyte precisely because he was such a hard-liner. Ultimately, Chaffee's commander in chief, President Theodore Roosevelt, must bear the responsibility for setting this tone, when he ordered Chaffee to adopt, "in no unmistakable terms," "the most stern measures to pacify Samar" (Miller, p. 206). Smith's orders to a marine battalion on loan to him carried out this spirit of revenge for the Balangiga massacre: "I want no prisoners. I wish you to kill and burn, the more you kill and burn, the better it will please me. I want all persons killed who are ca-

pable of bearing arms in actual hostilities against the United States" (Miller, p. 220). The marine commander, Maj. Littleton W.T. Waller, asked "to know the limit of age to respect" (Miller, p. 220), and Smith told him that boys 10 years and older were capable of bearing arms. Later, Smith penned an unsigned note in his headquarters on Leyte across the narrow strait from Samar, informing Waller that "the interior of Samar must be made a howling wilderness" (Miller, p. 222).

Waller did not take such orders literally and told his officers that they were not to make war on children. In reality, the Samar campaign was not that draconian, certainly far less bloody than the campaigns on Panay, where Gen. Robert P. Hughes burned a path 60 miles wide from one end of the island to the other, or in Batangas on Luzon, where as many as 11,000 died in Gen. J. Franklin Bell's concentration camps alone and where indiscriminate burning was widespread. Waller was selected as a convenient scapegoat in 1902, when U.S. atrocities had received considerable attention in the nation's anti-imperialist press. Probably the fact that he came from the rival Navy Department made him an even more attractive scapegoat to Secretary of War Elihu Root. Waller's crime was that he had ordered the execution of 10 native bearers, who did act somewhat treacherously during a march across Samar that cost the marines 10 fatalities. In contrast to Hughes's and Bell's policies, or to earlier reprisals ordered by Gens. Loyd Wheaton and Frederick Funston, Waller's action was child's play.

In the end, Smith proved to be his own worst enemy. Waller, always honorable, tried to protect Smith by justifying Smith's action on the basis of General Order No. 100, issued during the Civil War. This order included instructions of retaliating for guerrilla activities behind the fighting lines. Only when Smith betrayed Waller on the witness stand in an attempt to save his own career did Waller reveal the bizarre orders that he had received from Smith. This resulted in Waller's acquittal and left the chagrined Secretary Root with no alternative but to order Smith court-martialed. At the same time, Root declared that Smith's orders had never been intended to be taken literally, whereupon Smith informed reporters that they were and that his tactics were the only ones that were effective against "savages." Root then concocted a scheme to have Smith declared "temporarily insane," but this backfired when two of the three medical officers Chaffee had appointed to a board for this purpose refused to go along with the ruse.

Ironically, General Wheaton, who had ordered the first awesomely bloody mass reprisal in the war, presided over the court that found Smith guilty of "conduct to the prejudice of good order and military discipline," sentencing him "to be admonished by the reviewing authority" (Miller, p. 238). Root, in his endorsement pleaded "extenuating circumstances," recommending a light sentence in view of the "conditions of warfare with cruel and barbarous savages" (Miller, p. 255). Roosevelt concurred, noting "the well nigh intolerable provocation" on Samar, and the general "cruelty, treachery and total disregard of the rules of civilized warfare" by Filipinos, adding that he, Roosevelt, personally approved of the "sternest measures necessary" (Miller, p. 255). It seems reasonable to infer that Smith's major transgression in the president's eyes was his "loose and violent talk" (Miller, p. 255). Roosevelt made this clear in private comments. By way of illustration, he wrote to a friend (Miller, p. 255):

> Inspector General [Joseph Cabell] Breckinridge happened to mention quite casually to me with no idea that he was saying anything in Smith's disfavor, that when he met him and asked what he was doing, he responded "shooting niggers." Breckinridge thought this was a joke. I did not.

Roosevelt retired Smith with no additional punishment, ending his 40-year career in the army.

Soldiers lined the dock in San Francisco on 1 August 1902 to cheer General Smith as he came ashore after more than three years of combat in the Philippines. Smith granted one interview with reporters, blaming his troubles on Maj. Cornelius Gardener (who publicized General Bell's indiscriminate burning in Batangas), and the "meddlesome" officer in Washington (Lt. Gen. Nelson A. Miles), who leaked Gardener's report to enhance his own political ambition, which aroused public opinion by distorting conditions in the Philippines and created the need for a national scapegoat. Smith's medical officer added (Miller, p. 256):

> It makes me sick to see what has been said about him [Smith]. If people knew what a thieving, treacherous, worthless bunch of scoundrels those Filipinos are, they would

think differently than they do now. You can't treat them the way you do civilized folks. I do not believe that there are half a dozen men in the U.S. Army that don't think Smith is all right.

Both Smith and his medical officer were quite correct. Almost to a man, the army supported Smith, felt that his court-martial and conviction were a national betrayal, and believed that Smith was, indeed, a national scapegoat. Other ranking officers should have followed him to the dock, but having sacrificed Smith, the president and the nation seemed eager to sweep the whole nasty business under the rug and forget it.

Stuart Creighton Miller

REFERENCES

David L. Fritz, "Before the 'Howling Wilderness': The Military Career of Jacob Hurd Smith, 1862–1902," *Military Affairs*, 34 (Dec. 1979), 186–190; Stuart Creighton Miller, *"Benevolent Assimilation": The American Conquest of the Philippines, 1899–1903* (Yale Univ. Pr., 1982); Joseph L. Schott, *The Ordeal of Samar* (Bobbs-Merrill, 1964).

See also Atrocities in the Philippine War; Samar Campaigns, Philippine War; Waller, Littleton Waller Tazewell.

Snowden, Thomas (1857–1930)

Rear Adm. Thomas Snowden became military governor of the Dominican Republic and commander of the United States Navy's Atlantic Cruiser Squadron stationed in the Caribbean in February 1919, serving until June 1921. A distinguished officer nearing the end of his career and entering what was to be his final command, Snowden took over after Rear Adm. Harry S. Knapp had established the structure of the military government. Known as a rigid disciplinarian, Snowden was poorly prepared for the details of governance.

Shortly after his arrival, Snowden was directed to constitute the Junta Consultiva, a commission of prominent Dominican political leaders, to propose needed reforms. The commission demanded an end to restrictions on the populace and sought the withdrawal of U.S. forces. Snowden rejected these proposals, disbanded the commission, and became firmly opposed to consulting with the Dominicans. The incident strengthened his belief that continued occupation was necessary.

Snowden had little respect for the Dominicans, and, save for this initial effort directed by Washington, he failed to consult them about the future of their nation. His manner and policies were abrasive, aggravating the already strained relations between the military occupation forces and the local citizens. He regarded the rebels as simply "bandits" and reflected the racial stereotypes and attitudes of the era, acting in accordance with the prevailing perspective of Anglo-Saxon superiority. Snowden was firmly convinced that the Dominicans were incapable of effectively governing their nation and advocated continuing the occupation indefinitely. He persisted in the belief that the majority of the local population favored continued U.S. occupation, in spite of the protests against the intervention.

During his tenure, Snowden issued decrees tightening press censorship and broadening regulations to bar all criticism of the military government, the intervention, and the United States, as well as prohibiting any "incitement" of protest or unrest or advocacy of "Bolshevism." This resulted in several protests and the arrest of several prominent Dominican journalists. In December 1920 Snowden issued new decrees broadening the sedition laws to prevent any criticism, although the State Department soon ordered these revoked. It was Snowden who issued the new land laws, which were designed by a board whose members were all U.S. citizens.

While his actions provoked considerable controversy, Snowden played a significant role in completing the steps begun by Knapp in regularizing the occupation. He devoted considerable effort to establishing specific programs and long-term plans for the island nation, a task facilitated by his conviction that the occupation should continue. His decrees continued the process of law codification and of centralization of power in the hands of the national government in the capital.

The new administration of President Warren G. Harding replaced Snowden soon after taking office because the administration was committed to arranging a withdrawal from the island nation. That task required an individual more amenable to State Department direction, more acceptable to Dominicans, and more "civilian minded."

Kenneth J. Grieb

REFERENCES

Bruce J. Calder, *The Impact of Intervention: The Dominican Republic during the U.S. Occupation of 1916–1924* (Univ. of Texas Pr., 1984); Kenneth J. Grieb, "Warren G. Harding and the Dominican Republic U.S. Withdrawal, 1921–1923," *Journal of Inter-American Studies*, 11 (1969), 425–440; Lester D. Langley, *The Banana Wars: An Inner History of the American Empire, 1900–1934* (Univ. of Kentucky Pr., 1983).

Somoza García, Anastasio (1896–1956)

Anastasio Somoza García emerged from the second marine intervention in Nicaragua as chief of the U.S.-trained Nicaragua *guardia nacional*. Using the national guard as a power base, Somoza established a dynasty that ruled that Central American nation for over four decades.

Somoza was born at San Marcos, Nicaragua, in 1896, one of four children of Anastasio Somoza Reyes and Julia García. His father was a farmer of modest means whose livelihood depended on the annual coffee crop. With financial aid from a relative, young Anastasio studied at a business school in Philadelphia, where he met Salvadora Debayle of an old and distinguished Nicaraguan family. Despite her family's opposition they were married in 1919. Somoza held a series of jobs, none too successfully, and at one time was a sanitary inspector for the Rockefeller Foundation Sanitation Mission.

During the Liberal revolution against Emiliano Chamorro Vargas and Adolfo Díaz in 1926–1927, Somoza supported Juan B. Sacasa, his wife's uncle, and when Henry L. Stimson went to Nicaragua as President Calvin Coolidge's representative to stop the fighting, Somoza, having excellent English, acted as interpreter during the Tipitapa conferences when Stimson negotiated a peace settlement between Nicaragua's warring political factions. That agreement, in turn, eventually brought the United States into conflict with Augusto C. Sandino. Somoza impressed the emissary as a likeable young Liberal whose attitude was more favorable than almost any other. Somoza's service attracted the attention of José María Moncada, who became president after the 1928 election. Under the new administration Somoza held various positions, including consul in Costa Rica and under-secretary of foreign affairs.

In 1932 as the marines prepared for withdrawal from Nicaragua and marine officers in the *guardia nacional* were replaced by Nicaraguans, Somoza was appointed to command that force when Calvin B. Matthews, its last marine director, left in early January 1933. Somoza had the support of Moncada, President-elect Juan B. Sacasa, Matthews, and Matthew E. Hanna, the U.S. minister in Managua. Hanna said of him: "I look upon him as the best man in the country for the position. I know no one who will labor as intelligently and conscientiously to maintain the non-partisan character of the Guardia, or will be as efficient in all matters connected with the administration and command of the Force" (Kamman, p. 210). Somoza impressed most U.S. officials in Nicaragua.

As director of the *guardia nacional*, Somoza prepared a power base to succeed to the presidency after Sacasa. Augusto C. Sandino was an obstacle, but he was removed on 21 February 1934 when members of the national guard with Somoza's approval abducted and killed him while he was in Managua negotiating with the president. In 1936 when Somoza believed that Sacasa and other politicians were trying to block his presidential candidacy, he forced the president and vice president out of office, controlled an interim administration, and arranged his own election beginning in 1937.

Washington recognized the new regime, and Somoza considered himself a special friend of the United States and President Franklin D. Roosevelt, whom he visited at the White House in 1939. Somoza always retained leadership of the *guardia* but did relinquish the presidential office, if not the power, in 1947. He resumed the presidency in 1950, retaining it until his assassination in 1956. His two sons, Luis and Anastasio Somoza Debayle, maintained the family rule until 1979 when the Sandinista Front of National Liberation forced the latter's departure from office and country.

William Kamman

REFERENCES

Bernard Diederich, *Somoza and the Legacy of U.S. Involvement in Central America* (Dutton, 1981); William Kamman, *A Search for Stability: United States Diplomacy Toward Nicaragua, 1925–1933* (Univ. of Notre Dame Pr., 1968); Neill Macaulay, *The Sandino Affair* (Quadrangle, 1967); John D. Martz, *Central America: The Crisis and the Challenge* (Univ. of North Carolina Pr., 1959); Ralph Lee Woodward, Jr., *Central America: A Nation Divided* (Oxford Univ. Pr., 1976).

Spanish-Cuban/American War

In April 1898, the United States declared war on Spain, proclaiming a selfless motive: to end Spanish colonial control over Cuba. Although the conflict lasted only a few months, it greatly expanded U.S. influence in the Caribbean and in the Far East, with consequences that few anticipated even though some U.S. citizens had for years been urging their leaders to assume a more aggressive and expansive role in world affairs. The expansionist and imperialist philosophy these people popularized definitely helped legitimate the broader diplomatic decisions and agreements that resulted from U.S. participation in what had begun as an internal struggle in Cuba itself.

Spain held sway over Cuba for 400 years, although periodic stirrings of resentment and actual rebellion had occurred. The most serious rebellion had erupted in 1868; the insurgency continued for a decade before the Spanish government promised to introduce several reforms, including an end to slavery. Critics complained that many promises were broken, and the persistence of poor economic conditions left many Cubans dissatisfied.

Some of the rebels who had fought for full independence from Spain migrated to the United States after 1878. There, they continued their anti-Spanish activities even after becoming naturalized U.S. citizens. Their hopes for a renewed rebellion suffered a setback in 1890 when the United States Congress drafted the McKinley Tariff Act which canceled the tariff on sugar. With the door to the vast U.S. market for its primary export wide open, the Cuban economy prospered enormously. U.S. investment money flowed to the island to buy plantations and finance milling and shipping operations. This heady prosperity faded quickly when depression crippled the United States beginning in 1893 and, in the next year, the Wilson Gorman Tariff Act reimposed a tariff on sugar imports. The return of hard times rekindled revolutionary sentiments among Cuban peasants and the exiled veterans of the earlier conflict.

Leaving behind a political organization, the Cuban Junta in New York City, José Julián Martí y Perez led the first wave of exiles back to Cuba in 1895. Martí became one of the rebellion's first martyrs, and the fight continued with greater intensity after his death. The rebels used guerrilla tactics which proved most effective in the eastern portion of the island. From remote camps, they staged hit-and-run attacks on Spanish property, burning sugar fields and buildings with the aim of destroying the economic value of the colony to Spain.

Spanish authorities responded with increasingly repressive countermeasures, the most notorious of which was the *reconcentrado* policy. Governor General Valeriano Weyler y Nicolau ordered substantial segments of the civilian population into fortified camps or villages. The Spanish army then treated any person found outside the concentration areas as a rebel or a rebel sympathizer. Unfortunately, disease and malnutrition plagued the camps, and thousands of peasants accustomed to living in less crowded conditions died.

Public opinion in the United States swung behind the rebel cause. The junta in New York issued stirring accounts of noble warriors fighting for traditional U.S. ideals, such as independence and human rights. The group's literature depicted Spaniards as inhuman torturers. The U.S. press often republished slanted reports about the activities of "Butcher" Weyler without attempting to establish their accuracy. The U.S. newspapers that did send reporters to Cuba were no less partisan. Locked in a titanic circulation war, both William Randolph Hearst's *New York Journal* and Joseph Pulitzer's New York *World* recognized the popularity of Cuban atrocity stories. Both publishers altered or sensationalized their reports to raise public interest and sales.

For some time the U.S. government remained much more restrained than the U.S. public. Both Democratic President Grover Cleveland and his Republican successor, William McKinley, would have preferred that the crisis fade away. To encourage that outcome, Cleveland urged Spain to introduce reforms and thereby undermine support for the rebellion. By the time of McKinley's inauguration in March 1897, U.S. sympathy for the rebels had grown so strong that the new president recognized that he must demand Spanish concessions for the revolutionaries. But, having seen military action in the Civil War and having no desire to participate in another conflict, McKinley devoted his efforts in his first year in office to promoting a peaceful resolution of the problems in Cuba.

McKinley showed particular interest in an autonomy scheme the Spanish developed in 1897. Its advertised objective was to give the Cuban people control of their internal political affairs while keeping the island as a dominion within the Spanish Empire. The autonomy proposals satisfied no one. The rebels remained committed to nothing short of full independence; Spanish troops rioted at the prospect of even a partial capitulation by Madrid. Fearing that the rioting might endanger U.S. citizens and their property, the U.S. consul general in Havana, Fitzhugh Lee, requested that the United States Navy send a ship to protect U.S. interests. Because the rioting ended long before the *Maine*, a second-class battleship, dropped anchor in Havana harbor in late January 1898, the government in Washington portrayed its mission as a goodwill visit.

Two calm weeks passed before the *New York Journal* published a stolen document prepared by Minister Enrique Dupuy de Lôme, the highest ranking Spanish diplomatic representative in the United States. Writing privately to a friend in Cuba, de Lôme had described President McKinley as "weak and a bidder for the admiration of the crowd, besides being a would-be politician who tries to leave a door open behind himself while keeping on good terms with the jingoes of his party" (Trask, p. 28). These same "jingoes," militant Republicans itching for war, had leveled much harsher criticisms at McKinley and his apparent indecisiveness, but they now objected strenuously to a foreigner—especially a Spaniard—making unflattering comments about their president. Moreover, the letter revealed that de Lôme was deliberately using stalling tactics, hoping to prevent increased U.S. involvement in the Cuban situation.

Public outcry over the de Lôme letter had hardly subsided when a massive explosion racked the *Maine* in Havana harbor on the evening of 15 February 1898. More than 260 officers and men lost their lives when the ship burned and settled to the bottom of the harbor. The members of a contemporary naval board of inquiry attributed the tragedy to an external explosive device. A more recent analysis blames it on spontaneous combustion of coal in the ship's improperly maintained bunkers adjacent to explosive shells and gunpowder.

The true cause of the explosion was irrelevant to its immediate consequences. Assistant Secretary of the Navy Theodore Roosevelt wrote privately that it had resulted from "dirty treachery" on the part of Spaniards, and many shared his desire to avenge the U.S. sailors' deaths. The *Maine* tragedy supplied a dramatic rationalization for implementing an already widespread enthusiasm for expansion, and "Remember the *Maine*" became a popular rallying cry.

President McKinley had meanwhile concluded that he would accept no political solution short of full independence for the island. In late March 1898 he sent an ultimatum demanding that Spain institute a cease-fire and begin negotiations that would lead to Cuba's independence. While the government in Madrid did announce a suspension of hostilities, it did not yet seem willing to relinquish its colony. Taking Spain's actions as a rejection of his demands, McKinley requested that Congress allow him to use the U.S. armed forces.

Congress had some difficulty defining the objectives for military action. Some members hoped it would lead to the annexation of Cuba as a U.S. colony; others urged immediate recognition of the junta's revolutionary provisional government. Yet neither the revolutionaries, who had hoped to win their struggle on their own terms without direct U.S. intervention, nor the president, who did not wish to have his hands tied by restrictive legislation, was eager for a formal alliance. It fell to Colorado Senator Henry M. Teller to develop a formula most U.S. citizens could accept. His amendment to the resolution authorizing U.S. intervention stated that the purpose of the U.S. action was to ensure the independence of the island from Spanish rule. It specifically denied any U.S. intention of annexing Cuba. The congressional action carefully avoided recognizing any faction as the island's legitimate government, however, leaving the status of the revolutionaries and the political structure of a free Cuba to be determined only after a Spanish surrender.

The war resolution won approval on 25 April 1898 and the United States celebrated news of a dramatic naval victory just one week later. Surprisingly, it occurred in the Philippines, halfway around the globe from Cuba. Although Assistant Secretary of the Navy Roosevelt took considerable credit for arranging the action, suggestions for protecting the West coast of the United States by neutralizing Spanish naval power in the Pacific had figured in Navy Department planning as early as 1895. Roosevelt's primary contribution was making sure that George Dewey was given command of the Asiatic Squadron just before the conflict began.

Commodore Dewey's small fleet left the China coast immediately after news of the U.S. declaration of war was telegraphed around the world. Both the Chinese government and British officials in Hong Kong declared neutrality in the Spanish-Cuban/American conflict, leaving Dewey with no friendly port in the region. His squadron stole quietly past Spanish shore batteries at night and arrived in Manila Bay at dawn on 1 May 1898. There, his gunners raked an anchored Spanish fleet, sinking or burning most of it in a brief skirmish that left just eight U.S. crew members wounded and one dead of heat exhaustion. When the Spanish admiral surrendered his devastated command, Dewey faced the dilemma of what to do next. His relatively small force could not mount a substantial land invasion. Hastily promoted to the rank of admiral, Dewey had to settle in and await the arrival of troop transports carrying reinforcements from San Francisco.

While the navy won international acclaim for its definitive victory in Manila Bay, it exhibited embarrassing incompetence in the Caribbean. U.S. ships blockaded Havana and Cienfuegos on Cuba's northern coast, but Adm. Pascual Cervera y Topete managed to assemble a rickety fleet in Spain, sail it across the Atlantic and slip it undetected into Santiago harbor. Once Cervera's force had been located, the United States tardily extended its blockade to Cuba's southern coast as well.

Political pressure meanwhile mounted at home to ensure that the army would see action. Prominent politicians, such as William Jennings Bryan and Theodore Roosevelt, rushed to organize volunteer regiments similar to those that had appeared in the Civil War. The excitable head of an unprepared War Department, Russell A. Alger, had scarcely enough equipment to supply the relatively small regular army units that constituted the bulk of the expeditionary force assembling at Tampa, Florida. There, chaos reigned as soldiers fought over the limited supplies of weapons and clothing the department managed to send down on the single-track railroad that supplied the camp.

On 14 June 1898, 17,000 troops, including the men of four volunteer regiments, boarded crowded ships for a six-day voyage to southern Cuba. A detachment of 600 marines made the first U.S. assault, landing at Guantánamo Bay and establishing the foundations for a future U.S. naval base. When the main body of troops splashed ashore further west, they encountered little resistance. After landing their inadequate supplies, U.S. troops headed west toward Santiago. They ran into determined opposition at two outlying villages, El Caney and Las Guásimas, before arriving at the base of the hills that encircled the city's eastern flank. On 1 July Lt. Col. Theodore Roosevelt's Rough Rider volunteer regiment and two black regular army regiments boldly charged up Kettle Hill. Other units routed Spanish defenders on nearby San Juan Hill. U.S. lines soon spread around the city, allowing gunners to train their cannons on the ships in the harbor.

Spanish Admiral Cervera was ordered to escape from the besieged city. On 3 July, his ships steamed out through the narrow harbor mouth and headed west along the coast. The blockading U.S. fleet easily picked them off one by one. The Spanish suffered hundreds of casualties but only one U.S. sailor was killed in this second one-sided naval engagement of the war.

The United States Army's siege of Santiago was far weaker than it appeared. Most of the soldiers were ill, suffering from diarrhea and fever. Gen. William R. Shafter wisely paused to negotiate a peaceful surrender of the city, which took place on 17 July. Meanwhile, Gen. Nelson A. Miles led several shiploads of fresh troops on a sweep of Puerto Rico, Spain's other major colony in the Caribbean. As its authority in the region disintegrated, the Spanish government urgently pressed the United States for a ceasefire.

The Spanish haste was fueled in part by a desire to prevent further United States moves in the Philippines. Some U.S. ships called at Guam in the Mariana Islands and effortlessly took control of that Spanish outpost. By late July, 15,000 U.S. troops, most of them in volunteer units, had landed in the Philippines and were encamped south of Manila. Gen. Wesley Merritt negotiated an agreement in which the outnumbered Spanish defenders of Manila agreed to put up only token resistance. Emilio Aguinaldo y Famy, the leader of a large Filipino army hostile to Spanish control, was left out of these discussions. He and his followers were determined to play a leading role in any transfer of power, causing the 13 August takeover to involve more casualties and destruction on all sides than had been anticipated as U.S., Spanish, and Filipino soldiers clashed in various locations.

Just a few hours after U.S. forces had completed their occupation of Manila, news reached them that the United States and Spain had signed a worldwide armistice the previous day. The U.S. involvement in the conflict had lasted a scant 14 weeks and inflicted just 379 combat-related deaths on the U.S. side. Except for the fact that nearly eight times as many men lost their lives to disease as to combat, it could be hailed as an efficient and effective military action. Indeed, the war's consequences were far broader than the fighting would seem to have justified.

The fate of the former Spanish possessions the war had touched was decided at bilateral peace negotiations in Paris that began in October 1898. The Spaniards entered the talks ready to concede the loss of both Puerto Rico and Cuba and to grant the United States authority over Guam. The Philippines remained a sticking point. U.S. troops occupied only Manila and its immediate environs, giving the Spanish hope that U.S. forces would withdraw if McKinley was assured of obtaining his objectives in the Caribbean.

A number of factors weighed against any U.S. retreat. Both Germany and Great Britain had sent large fleets to observe U.S. activities in the Philippines. If the United States pulled out, one or both of these European powers seemed poised to move into the power vacuum Dewey's lightning victory had created. Besides, a sense of its imperialist mission had risen to a peak in the United States by fall 1898, and people were confident that they could best administer and "civilize" the Filipinos. Moreover, the archipelago's location made it a potential entrepôt for what many anticipated would be a greatly expanded U.S. trade with China.

President McKinley delayed announcing a decision until he had sampled public opinion during a campaign swing in October. He also consulted the five members of his peace commission in Paris and Secretary of State John M. Hay in Washington before concluding that the United States must control the Philippines. The Spanish agreed only after the U.S. commissioners offered substantial financial compensation. Concluded on 10 December 1898, the Treaty of Paris assigned to the United States outright control of the Philippines, Puerto Rico, and Guam; freed Cuba of all Spanish authority; and stipulated that the United States would pay $20 million to Spain.

Even before the treaty was signed, determined opposition to its provisions arose in the United States. A hastily formed Anti-Imperialist League counted among its members ex-presidents Benjamin Harrison and Grover Cleveland, industrialist Andrew Carnegie, and author Mark Twain. Anticolonial rallies, speeches, and articles flooded the nation, urging the people of the United States to maintain their traditional commitments to isolationism and self-determination.

This publicity barrage threatened to derail the administration's policies when some of the senators expected to vote for the treaty appeared to waver. But, on 6 February 1899 the Senate supported President McKinley's approach, approving the treaty 57 to 27, just one vote more than the required two-thirds majority.

Some people in the United States saw the Filipinos themselves as responsible for that outcome. Two days earlier, firing had broken out between units of the U.S. occupation force and Aguinaldo's Filipino army. The conflict thus begun ravaged the islands for more than three years. More than 4,000 U.S. troops were killed before the Filipino leader was captured, breaking the back of his resistance movement. Strict military censorship kept news of the conflict to a minimum in the United States. As a result, this protracted war, marked by atrocities on both sides, received less attention in the United States than the much shorter and less damaging conflict with Spain.

The persistent and bloody struggle in the Philippines did little to dampen U.S. enthusiasm and relief at the outcome of the conflict with Spain. People gloried in their exhilarating victories over decrepit Spanish fleets. These victories earned the United States Navy and, by extension, the nation as a whole, respect among the world's great powers, and they encouraged an expanded naval buildup during succeeding years.

The Spanish-Cuban/American War altered international relationships around the world. The United States suddenly emerged as a major political factor in the drive to keep the doors open for all foreign commerce with China. The U.S. outpost in the Philippines failed, however, to expand significantly U.S. trade in the Far East. Postwar U.S. influence in the Caribbean did expand dramatically. The nature of the relationship with an independent Cuba, the location and construction of a canal through the Isthmus of Panama, the attitude of U.S. investors and statesmen to political instability in Central and South America—these and many other issues would have to be addressed in the new century.

The complexities and burdens inherent in this broadening of international relationships, combined with the disappointing consequences of U.S. efforts to expand trade, led to a rapid waning of U.S. enthusiasm for imperialism. The war with Spain had been a heady experience, stirring patriotism and stimulating expansionism. But, in a sense, it acted as a safety valve as well, releasing much of the pent-up pressure for an expanded and adventuresome foreign policy that had built up in the 1880s and 1890s.

John M. Dobson

REFERENCES

Graham A. Cosmas, *An Army for Empire: The United States Army in the Spanish-American War* (Univ. of Missouri Pr., 1971); Walter Millis, *The Martial Spirit: A Study of Our War With Spain* (Literary Guild, 1931); H. Wayne Morgan, *America's Road to Empire: The War With Spain and Overseas Empire* (Wiley, 1965); G.J.A. O'Toole, *The Spanish War: An American Epic, 1898* (Norton, 1984); David F. Trask, *The War With Spain in 1898* (Macmillan, 1981).

See also list of entries at front of book for Spanish-Cuban/American War.

Special Service Squadron, United States Navy

The United States Navy's Special Service Squadron was established in September 1920. Nicknamed the "Central American Banana Fleet," it was the embodiment of U.S. naval diplomacy in the Caribbean area between the two world wars. As such, its brief 20-year history revealed the limitations and contradictions of U.S. Caribbean policy during this period; that is, the maintenance of an informal U.S. empire through a combination of gunboat diplomacy, good neighborliness, and, increasingly, a reliance on indigenous military strongmen.

In the aftermath of World War I, the Caribbean region, never known for its political stability, experienced a wave of political unrest and revolutionary violence. As had been the pattern for decades, instances of political violence in the Caribbean generated the almost automatic response of sending one or more U.S. warships to the area until the situation calmed. The navy's fleet structure was ill-suited, however, to respond to the increased demands for gunboat diplomacy in 1919 and 1920, especially because no single force was responsible for patrolling the greater Caribbean area. Several naval officers, most notably Rear Adm. William B. Caperton and Capt. Charles S. Freeman, voiced their opinion that a special naval unit, created specifically for Latin American service, needed to be formed to put curbs on the State Department's practice of raiding the fleet during crises in Caribbean republics; such a fleet could also help foster goodwill for the United States in the region by showing the flag.

Believing that their own interests would be served by the formation of a Latin American naval patrol, the Navy and State departments agreed to establish the Special Service Squadron in 1920 after a few months of negotiation and intradepartmental study. From the navy's perspective, the existence of the squadron would place limits on the State Department's tendency to increase the numbers of warships assigned to diplomatic duty. The State Department was happy to have a small naval force at its disposal to respond to crises in Latin America.

Assigned eight vessels initially (mostly old cruisers and gunboats), the squadron was composed generally of five vessels throughout the 1920s and as few as three throughout the 1930s. During particularly acute political crises, the navy expanded the squadron by attaching fleet units to it.

The Special Service Squadron was charged with two primary missions: gunboat diplomacy and showing the flag. For most of the squadron's history, the mission of gunboat diplomacy overshadowed that of goodwill cruising. During the peak years of gunboat diplomacy (1920–1934), the State Department requested that squadron vessels respond to political unrest and revolutionary violence 51 times. Most of these episodes were relatively trivial, but collectively they formed a pattern of coercive naval diplomacy. Political unrest or sometimes merely the rumor

of trouble would prompt nervous U.S. field diplomats or consular officials to request a naval presence to calm the situation. In the vast majority of cases, the State Department deemed the request justifiable and forwarded it to the Navy Department, which ordered the squadron commander to send a vessel or vessels to the area. Generally, a brief stay was sufficient to produce at least a cosmetic change in the local political environment, and the warship(s) could leave the area after a week or so. Occasionally, more extended stays were necessary, and in a few instances (for example, Honduras in 1925 and Nicaragua in 1926) sailors and/or marines landed ashore to set up temporary neutral zones, where U.S. and other foreign nationals could seek safety.

On two occasions, the political turmoil was sufficiently serious to lead to prolonged naval operations (Nicaragua 1926–1933 and Cuba 1933–1935), during which the scope of the squadron's activities as well as its size increased dramatically. The policing of Cuban waters in 1933–1935 proved to be the climax of the Special Service Squadron's gunboat diplomacy mission. Thereafter, the unit's other mission, goodwill cruising, took precedence. Gunboat diplomacy became more and more irrelevant to the Caribbean situation as the U.S. consciously attempted to shed its interventionist image, and its Latin American policy became more and more associated with the "good neighbor approach." Also, as the 1930s progressed, military strongmen emerged in several Caribbean republics (for example, Leonidas Rafael Trujillo in the Dominican Republic, Anastasio Somoza Garcia in Nicaragua, Jorge Ubico in Guatemala, and Fulgenico Batista y Zaldívar in Cuba) and removed many of the outward signs of political instability. This enabled the navy to shift its concern away from chronically unstable political conditions in the Caribbean toward the more potent threat of fascist aggression in Latin America. The practice of anchoring aging warships in tropical harbors to discourage revolutionary activities appeared almost quaint by 1940, when Catalina patrol bombers and modern destroyers anxiously searched the Caribbean for Nazi surface and subsurface raiders.

The Special Service Squadron's other mission of goodwill cruising remained secondary until after the Cuban crisis of 1933–1935. From the outset, the squadron commander and the navy chafed under State Department restrictions on where and when the squadron could conduct its routine cruises. The State Department considered such cruises as having diplomatic importance and expected the squadron to clear any visits to Latin American ports with its Latin American Affairs Division. Initially, the navy resisted this as an unwarranted intrusion on its freedom to employ its vessels in peacetime. But by spring 1922, the navy conceded virtual operational control of the Special Service Squadron to the State Department

From 1926 to 1935, the squadron's involvements in the Nicaraguan intervention and the Cuban crisis resulted in almost no goodwill cruising. But from 1935 to 1939, the mission of showing the flag received primary attention. During this time, squadron vessels visited nearly all of the major Caribbean ports, and the unit performed its goodwill mission smartly. Illustrative of the importance of goodwill cruising to the squadron, two new gunboats specifically designed for this duty joined the squadron in 1937 and 1938.

The revival of goodwill cruising was short-lived, however. As the construction of U.S. warships expanded in the late 1930s in response to an increasingly troubled international climate, the navy frequently sent newly commissioned men of war on shakedown cruises to the Latin American ports, making the squadron's routine goodwill cruises somewhat superfluous. Then with the outbreak of war in Europe and the creation of the U.S. Neutrality Patrol, the squadron was charged with the task of guarding the Panama Canal and policing the Caribbean. Its original missions were supplanted by neutrality patrolling and related duties, so that the Special Service Squadron lost its *raison d'être*. The navy abolished the unit in September 1940 and reassigned most of its warships to the 15th Naval District, headquartered in the Panama Canal Zone.

The Special Service Squadron was relatively effective as an instrument of U.S. foreign policy during a time when gunboat diplomacy was the standard U.S. response to Caribbean political turmoil. While the squadron's activities did nothing to address the factors underlying the chronic political turmoil in the Caribbean—nor realistically could they have—they were effective on a short-term basis in deterring violence. But when U.S. policies became less outwardly coercive,

when dictators removed some of the manifestations of political unrest, and when international events forced the navy to refocus its activities, the Special Service Squadron became a relic of an earlier era of naval diplomacy.

Donald A. Yerxa

REFERENCES

Robert Blake, "Campaigning Around the Caribbean," *Marine Corps Gazette*, 22 (1938), 7–11; Richard Millett, "The State Department's Navy: A History of the Special Service Squadron," *American Neptune*, 35 (1975), 118–138; Gordon F. Oglivie, "Remember the Rochester," *United States Naval Institute Proceedings*, 97 (1971), 68–70; Donald A. Yerxa, "The Special Service Squadron and the Caribbean Region, 1920–1940: A Case Study in Naval Diplomacy," *Naval War College Review*, 39 (1986), 60–72.

Spooner Amendment (1902)

The Spooner Amendment authorized negotiations leading to a Panamanian route for a U.S.-built isthmian canal. It modified legislation (the Hepburn Bill) calling for a canal through Nicaragua. Republican Senator John C. Spooner of Wisconsin introduced the amendment in January 1902 with the support of the Roosevelt administration.

The amendment authorized President Theodore Roosevelt to pay up to $40 million for the rights and property of the French company which had abandoned an earlier attempt to build a canal in Panama and to acquire from Columbia a canal zone at least six miles wide in Panama, then a Columbian province. If negotiations with Columbia failed, the president was to proceed with the Nicaraguan route.

Adoption of the Spooner Amendment resulted from a prodigious lobbying effort because it altered the Hepburn Bill, which had won House approval by a margin of 308 to 2. Spooner was merely a spokesman for a tenacious group of pro-Panamanian lobbyists, including Philippe Jean Bunau-Varilla, who sought to salvage part of the French investment; New York lawyer William Nelson Cromwell; and Senator Mark A. Hanna of Ohio, Republican National Committee chairman.

Democratic Senator John T. Morgan of Alabama, proponent of the Nicaraguan route and chairman of the Committee on Interoceanic Canals, guided the original Hepburn Bill through his committee, but Hanna and three supporters wrote a minority report backing the amendment. The amendment narrowly passed its crucial Senate test on 19 June 1902; a shift of five votes would have meant the canal would have been built in Nicaragua. Republican domination assured passage in the House, and the President signed the Spooner Amendment into law on 28 June 1902.

Andrew J. Dunar

REFERENCES

Lawrence O. Ealy, *Yanqui Politics and the Isthmian Canal* (Pennsylvania State Univ. Pr., 1971), 48–56; Willis Fletcher Johnson, *Four Centuries of the Panama Canal* (Holt, 1906), 125–129; 400–404 [text of the amendment]; Walter LaFeber, *The Panama Canal: The Crisis in Historical Perspective* (Oxford Univ. Pr., 1989), 17; David McCullough, *The Path Between the Seas: The Creation of the Panama Canal, 1870–1914* (Simon & Schuster, 1977), 260, 269, 324, 328–329, 406; Dana G. Munro, *Intervention and Dollar Diplomacy in the Caribbean, 1900–1921* (Princeton Univ. Pr., 1964), 41–44.

State of Texas

State of Texas, a chartered relief ship, was the main vehicle for battlefield relief provided by the American Red Cross during the Spanish-Cuban/American War. The ship sailed for Havana on 23 April 1898, but was held in port at Key West and Tampa, Florida, for two months because Rear Adm. William T. Sampson refused to let it through the blockade of Cuba for fear its supplies would fall into Spanish hands.

When the *State of Texas* arrived in Cuba, its original mission of aiding Cuban refugees (it was chartered before the war started) was put aside temporarily, and the 23 Red Cross workers aboard, including doctors and nurses, found themselves primarily aiding U.S. military forces. Red Cross workers helped in Cuban and U.S. military hospitals in the town of Siboney and established a special Red Cross fever hospital. Later, the workers from the ship distributed food and clothing to the starving population in Santiago de Cuba.

True to her nature, American Red Cross founder and director Clara Barton traveled to Cuba aboard the *State of Texas* and personally directed Red Cross relief near the battlefield. In a letter she wrote from Key West to a friend, she described the *State of Texas* as well-suited for Red Cross needs.

Eric R. Emch

REFERENCES

Lavinia Dock and others, *History of American Red Cross Nursing* (Macmillan, 1922); Foster Rhea Dulles, *The American Red Cross: A History* (Harper, 1950); Portia Kernodle, *The Red Cross Nurse in Action, 1881–1948* (Harper, 1949).

See also American National Red Cross; Barton, Clara, in the Spanish-Cuban/American War.

Stevens, John Frank (1853–1943)

John Frank Stevens, a U.S. railroad expert, assisted in restoring the Russian railway transportation system during the Russian Revolution and the Russian Civil War. Born 25 April 1853, Stevens gained experience in building U.S. railroads moving westward in the late 19th century. He also oversaw the construction of the Panama Canal in 1906.

In May 1917 Stevens was appointed chairman of the Russian Railway Advisory Mission to study the needs of the Russian transportation system, with the goal of improving those facilities to assist the Russian war effort in World War I. The immediate need was to increase the movement of Allied supplies from Vladivostok across Siberia to European Russia. Stevens and his associates reached Vladivostok in June 1917 and traveled to Petrograd to coordinate the project with officials of the provisional government. Illness, leading to hospitalization, hampered his efforts. Afterward he surveyed the problems of the railroad system in the industrial Donets region. He was in Moscow at the time of the Bolshevik coup in November 1917. From there he returned to Harbin, Manchuria, and Vladivostok.

Stevens's primary task was to supervise the repair and efficiency of the Siberian railroad system, and this occupied his tenure in Russia from late 1917 until he left in 1923. An important component of his work was the Russian Railway Service Corps, which arrived in the region in early 1918. This group of U.S. personnel, directed by George H. Emerson, concentrated its work primarily on the Chinese Eastern Railway linking Vladivostok with other systems in central and western Siberia. Stevens faced many obstacles in his task: growth of Bolshevik efforts to take power in Siberia, the rise of independent factions and armies, lack of cooperation from Russian and Chinese railroad officials, the turmoil and even conflict arising from the presence of Czech military forces in Siberia, as well as the poor mechanical condition of railroad equipment and limited repair facilities in the region. He also differed with U.S. Ambassador David R. Francis on priorities and policies. Several times he threatened to resign but was convinced by his superiors in Washington to remain. The introduction of Allied forces into Siberia (1918–1920), especially large numbers of Japanese troops, further complicated his task and the work of his U.S. railroad personnel. Stevens was named the first chairman of the Inter-Allied Advisory Technical Commission of Railway Experts, formed in January 1919, and he continued in that capacity striving to improve the Russian railway system during the civil war.

While some improvement was made, the Siberian railroad effort never fully achieved the goals Stevens sought. After returning to the United States, he continued his association with the railroad industry. Stevens died on 2 June 1943.

Taylor Stults

REFERENCES

Dictionary of American Biography, s.v. "Stevens, John Frank"; David R. Francis, *Russia From the American Embassy, April 1916–November 1918* (Scribner, 1921); George F. Kennan, *Soviet-American Relations, 1917–1920: Russia Leaves the War* (Princeton Univ. Pr., 1956); George F. Kennan, *Soviet-American Relations, 1917–1920: The Decision to Intervene* (Princeton Univ. Pr., 1958); Betty Miller Unterberger, *America's Siberian Expedition, 1918–1920: A Study of National Policy* (Duke Univ. Pr., 1956); U.S. Department of State, *Foreign Relations of the United States, Russia 1918–1920* (U.S. Government Printing Office, 1931–1932, 1936), 3 vols.

See also Russian Railway Advisory Mission.

Stewart, George Evans (1872–1946)

Col. George Evans Stewart was the commander of the American Expeditionary Force, North Russia (AEFNR), from 4 September 1918 to 9 April 1919. Placed in a thoroughly untenable position, Stewart found that his leadership in North Russia was subject to harsh criticism both during and after the fact and had the effect of destroying a hitherto promising military career.

Born in Australia in 1872, Stewart came to the United States in 1890 intending to pursue a career in architecture. In 1896, however, apparently discouraged about the prospects in his chosen field, Stewart enlisted as a private in the United States Army. Three years later, having decided on a military career, he applied for and received a commission as a second lieutenant. Attached to the 19th Infantry Regiment, Stewart at once became part of the U.S. effort in the Philippine War (1899–1902) and, in his first combat, was awarded the Medal of Honor, the nation's highest military decoration, for conspicuous bravery under fire. On detached duty after the Philippine War, he spent two years in the Quartermaster Department and two more as commander of a military outpost in Alaska. With the United States's entry into World War I, Stewart rose rapidly to major in 1917 and colonel in early 1918. On 2 July 1918, the recently promoted colonel assumed command of the 339th Infantry Regiment which, when it was selected for duty in North Russia, immediately transformed him into the commander of the AEFNR.

From the outset of his tenure in the North, Stewart was plagued by vague and contradictory instructions. For reasons unknown, he was not at once entrusted with a copy of President Woodrow Wilson's authoritative *aide-mémoire* of 17 July, which sharply restricted U.S. military action in Russia. Instead, he was confronted by orders from his immediate superior, British Maj. Gen. Frederick C. Poole, to send his troops directly to the fighting fronts; contradictory directives from AEF headquarters in France ordering his subordination to Allied command except in matters of "internal administration" were of little assistance to the puzzled colonel. Nor in this confusing situation was Stewart able to get assistance from Ambassador David R. Francis, the highest ranking U.S. political official in the North; Francis, in fact, encouraged him to obey the commands of General Poole. In these circumstances, on 26 September and 5 October, Stewart was shocked to receive, respectively, a State Department directive and a copy of President Wilson's *aide-mémoire* both of which ordered him, in effect, not to permit the use of U.S. forces in the North for other than purely defensive purposes. Since, by this time, his troops were already heavily engaged on virtually every front south of Archangel, the hapless U.S. commander found himself in a dilemma from which he was thereafter never able to escape.

Unfortunately, Colonel Stewart's situation was not improved by subsequent events. Thus, in mid-October, when General Poole, who was largely responsible for the original misuse of U.S. troops in the North, was at last replaced as Allied commander by Maj. Gen. William Edmund Ironside, Stewart was requested to take command of the Allied forces on the Vologda Railroad Front. Given his recent instructions from Washington, the U.S. chief, to the intense irritation of his new commander, could do nothing but decline. The end of World War I in early November also failed to resolve Stewart's difficulties. On 14 November, hoping to use the Armistice as a way out of his dilemma, Stewart sent a plaintive cable to London requesting the immediate withdrawal of his troops from the North. In response, on 3 December, he was informed that his forces would remain on duty in North Russia until their status could be clarified at the impending Paris Peace Conference. In these circumstances, Stewart had no alternative but to retire to his headquarters in Archangel while avoiding insofar as possible any direct observation of the continued misuse of his troops in the field. This pattern, which lasted until the end of his command, brought about the breakdown of Stewart's health and the all but unanimous denunciation of Stewart by his subordinates, both officers and men, who accused him of being indifferent to their essential needs and welfare.

On 9 April 1919, Colonel Stewart was finally succeeded as commander of the AEFNR by Brig. Gen. Wilds P. Richardson, who had been sent personally by President Wilson to take charge of U.S. evacuation from North Russia. Although the new commander found groundless most of the charges leveled against Stewart, the unfortunate Stewart was never publicly exonerated nor in any way commended for his difficult service in the North.

Following his return from Russia, Stewart remained on active duty for 12 years. During this time he occupied a series of undistinguished posts and was periodically subjected to the largely undeserved criticism of his former North Russia subordinates. Retired in 1931, the unlucky colonel, notwithstanding his status as a winner of the nation's highest military honor, lived out his days in virtual obscurity. He died in 1946.

John W. Long

REFERENCES

Dennis Gordon, *Quartered in Hell: The Story of the American North Russian Expeditionary Force, 1918–1919* (GOS, 1982); E.M. Halliday, *The Ignorant Armies: The Anglo-American Archangel Expedition, 1918–1919* (Harper, 1958); Joel Moore, Harry Mead, and Lewis Jahns, *The History of the American Expedition Fighting the Bolsheviki* (Polar Bear, 1920); Benjamin D. Rhodes, *The Anglo-American Winter War With Russia, 1918–1919: A Diplomatic and Military Tragicomedy* (Greenwood Pr., 1988); U.S. Department of the Army, *The Medal of Honor of the United States Army* (U.S. Government Printing Office, 1948).

See also Poole, Frederick Cuthbert.

Stimson Mission to Nicaragua (1927)

In March 1927, President Calvin Coolidge requested that Henry L. Stimson, New York lawyer, one-time unsuccessful Republican candidate for governor of New York, and former secretary of war, go to Nicaragua to settle a revolution headed by Liberal Juan B. Sacasa and his military commander José María Moncada against the government of Adolfo Díaz. Washington feared that continued fighting might topple the government recognized by the United States, increase Mexican influence in Central America, and lead to United States participation in the fighting. Arriving in Managua in April, Stimson made clear in talks with Liberal and Conservative party leaders that Díaz should remain as president until the next election (1928), but Washington would encourage the president to bring Liberals back into national political life from which they had been ousted by an earlier (1925) revolution that had brought Emiliano Chamorro and then Díaz to power. After talking with Díaz and representatives of Sacasa, Stimson met General Moncada on 4 May at Tipitapa, a small village not far from Managua. Moncada was agreeable to most of Stimson's proposals but objected to the retention of Díaz. Stimson was insistent but indicated that the United States would supervise the 1928 Nicaraguan election, and, if the Liberal party was the majority party as asserted by Liberals, they would have the opportunity to gain control. Furthermore, Stimson noted that he was authorized to state that there would be forcible disarmament of those unwilling to lay down arms. Not wanting to fight the United States, Moncada agreed to recommend that his troops yield. Moncada requested and Stimson provided a letter outlining the U.S. proposal: (1) President Díaz would remain in office for the remainder of his term; (2) the United States would supervise the 1928 election; (3) United States troops would accept custody of the arms of those willing to lay them down, including those of the government, and disarm forcibly those who would not do so. According to Stimson, the latter phrase was aimed at the "bandit fringe" to indicate the earnestness of the U.S. commitment. In a second letter a week later Stimson noted that U.S. officers would train and command a nonpartisan national constabulary for Nicaragua to ensure free elections and protect duly elected governments. President Díaz had accepted all of these provisions earlier. The following day Moncada and all of his promi-

nent chiefs except Augusto C. Sandino agreed to lay down their arms. Disarmament proceeded quickly. The Nicaraguan government paid $10 for every rifle and machine gun surrendered to the United States Marines. Meanwhile Sandino retreated to northern Nicaragua and in July opened a guerrilla campaign against the government and American forces. Stimson's commitment for U.S. personnel to supervise the 1928 election was kept and continued in 1930 and 1932. U.S. personnel also organized and trained a national guard. Its nonpartisan character was more hope than fact and became the vehicle for its commander, Anastasio Somoza, to seize power after U.S. forces withdrew in 1933.

William Kamman

REFERENCES

William Kamman, *A Search for Stability: United States Diplomacy Toward Nicaragua, 1925–1933* (Univ. of Notre Dame Pr., 1968); Jose Maria Moncada, *Estados Unidos en Nicaragua* (Tipografía Ateneas, 1942); Henry L. Stimson, *American Policy in Nicaragua* (Charles Scribner's Sons, 1927).

T

Taft, William Howard (1857–1930)

William Howard Taft arrived in Manila, the Philippines, aboard the USS *Hancock* with the Second Philippine Commission on 3 June 1900. Appointed on 6 February 1900, by President William McKinley, the primary mission of the Second Philippine Commission (also called Taft Commission) was to begin implementation of civil government in the Philippines. Taft was the chairman of the commission that included Luke E. Wright, usually called General Wright, a Democrat and former attorney general of Tennessee; Dean C. Worcester, a zoologist from the University of Michigan, who was the only member of the commission who had ever been in the Philippines; Henry C. Ide of Vermont, former chief justice of the U.S. court in Samoa; and Bernard Moses, a professor of history at the University of California and a writer of note on the Spanish colonies in America. The commissioners were politicians or scholars, not military men, and the U.S. soldiers in Manila immediately nicknamed them the "fat men" because their average weight was 227 pounds. Taft, the fattest of them all, was massively overweight and traveled with his own bathtub because hotels did not have tubs large enough to accommodate him. His only exercise was an occasional game of golf.

When President McKinley appointed Taft chairman of the Second Philippine Commission, even Taft would not have predicted that he would eventually become president of the United States. Born in Cincinnati, Ohio, on 15 September 1857, Taft attended Yale University and graduated second in his class in June 1878. After returning to Cincinnati, Ohio, he studied law and was admitted to the Ohio Bar in 1880. In March 1887, he became an associate judge of the Superior Court of Cincinnati. In February 1890, President Benjamin Harrison appointed him solicitor general; two years later, Taft accepted an appointment to the U.S. Court of Appeals for the Sixth Circuit. His appointment as chairman of the Second Philippine Commission on 6 February 1900 came as a surprise and was based not on displayed ability but on his friendship with Elihu Root, the new secretary of war. Taft knew absolutely nothing about the Philippines. The war in the Philippines was a political liability for the McKinley administration, and with the elections of 1900 looming on the horizon, it was a political issue haunting the Republicans. It was absolutely essential that the Republicans convince the U.S. public that the war was over in the Philippines. A monumental effort was mounted to convert this fiction into a reality for the electorate. The Second Philippine Commission was appointed with political instructions to proclaim that only a small group of hot-headed Filipinos remained in the field. The official line espoused by the McKinley administration was that the remaining guerrillas were mere *ladrones* (bandits), who were no threat to U.S. rule—their capture was not likely to be either hard or dangerous.

When Judge Taft arrived in Manila in June 1900, the Filipinos had been engaged in open warfare against U.S. rule for 17 months. Seventy thousand U.S. soldiers under the command of Maj. Gen. Arthur MacArthur were stationed in 501 villages throughout the islands to maintain the peace. Although the United States Army had achieved dramatic military successes in the campaigns of 1899, the Philippine Republican Army had not been destroyed but had simply dispersed, with the soldiers returning to their various home provinces to engage in guerrilla warfare. There were two categories of guerrillas. One consisted of about 25,000 full-time fighters who maintained base camps in the jungles and mountains throughout the islands, with the highest concentration on the island of Luzon. Operating in scattered bands of 15 to 200 men, the guerrillas came down from the mountains to raid and to obtain food and supplies from the towns. The second group consisted of thousands of part-time guerrillas who lived in small barrios within the U.S. lines and were absorbed in a dense mass of sympathetic people who spoke dialects of which few white men, and no U.S. citizens, had any knowledge. Most U.S. soldiers believed the majority of Filipinos were either part of the guerrilla forces or at least supported the revolution.

Filipino troops could not protect territory, nor could they afford to engage in any more set-piece battles. As a rule, the Filipinos allowed the United States Army to take any town it wished. Whenever U.S. forces captured a town, they set up a local government, but the underground government of the revolutionists was the true government. Often the U.S.-selected mayor and police chief were local leaders of the revolutionaries. Secret committees were formed in all the barrios and towns to obtain contributions and to maintain the loyalty of the masses. The towns

gathered information and supplies for the roving bands in the field. While publicly supporting the U.S. occupation, Filipino town and village officials were in reality loyal to the revolution. This loyalty was almost universal.

Refusing to engage in pitched battles, the guerrillas harassed small U.S. detachments repairing railroad and telegraph lines. Signal parties, railroad work parties, and supply wagons were favorite targets in well-planned hit-and-run attacks. Railroad tracks and bridges were destroyed. When chased, the guerrillas merged with the local village population that clearly supported them. From December 1899 to June 1900, hundreds of skirmishes occurred between the U.S. garrisons and the guerrillas. In over 700 engagements, 199 U.S. personnel were killed and 744 wounded. Although no systematic records of Filipino casualties were kept, Filipino losses were estimated at 3,227 killed, 694 wounded, and 2,864 captured. The number reported killed was probably too high while the number of wounded was probably too low.

Within days of his arrival, Taft was absolutely certain he knew more about the Philippines than General MacArthur, who had been serving there for almost two years. To Taft's irritation, MacArthur refused to gloss over the war and publicly rejected Washington's interpretation. For excellent political reasons, Taft wanted to implement civil government as rapidly as possible to support the myth that the conflict was over and that the Filipino people welcomed U.S. rule. MacArthur asserted that the majority of Filipinos were loyal to the revolution and wanted independence, not U.S. colonization. Taft wrote Secretary Root that MacArthur was too pessimistic in his view of the situation. Even if the majority of Filipinos had desired independence, Taft believed it would be inappropriate for the United States to leave the islands because the vast majority of Filipinos were nothing but grown-up children who would need training for 50 or 100 years. The United States had an obligation to remain and teach its "little brown brothers" the principles of liberty and democracy.

Army officers and enlisted men resented the Taft Commission for engaging in politics for home consumption. An officer on MacArthur's staff later wrote that Taft's position that Filipino guerrillas were mere bandits was a rock-bottom falsehood. The soldiers ridiculed Taft for referring to the Filipinos as "little brown brothers." One soldier wrote home that the commissioners should have been forced to join the army for six months as privates to personally see if the Filipinos were little brown brothers in favor of U.S. rule.

On 1 September 1900, the Taft Commission became the legislative body with control of the civil budget. As chairman of the commission with veto powers, Taft considered himself the acting civil governor of the islands. Although MacArthur remained the military governor, his authority was to be restricted to execution of laws passed by the commission. Taft quickly discovered that MacArthur disagreed. MacArthur considered the Taft Commission primarily an advisory body on civilian affairs. He refused to surrender any executive or military power. He informed Taft that the commission's powers were extremely limited; it had the power to legislate, to control the civilian budget, and to appoint civilian administrators, but no law could be passed or implemented by the commission without the approval of MacArthur, the military governor.

Taft protested. In consultation with Secretary of War Root before leaving Washington, Taft had drafted the commission's instructions, and he was certain MacArthur did not have the power to veto legislation. MacArthur reminded Taft the Philippines were under martial law, and as military commander and governor, MacArthur held absolute power over both civilian personnel and military personnel. The Taft Commission could advise him, but it could not act without his approval.

Taft fumed over MacArthur's interpretation of the powers of the commission, and they never agreed on who had final authority. Taft wrote Root that MacArthur's attitude toward the commission made it very difficult. Relations between Taft and MacArthur deteriorated through September and October 1900. Publicly they were friendly, but privately their relations were cold.

As the power struggle intensified, Taft attacked MacArthur in devastating letters to Root and President McKinley. One of the great letter writers of his time, or any time, Taft was a hoarder who saved copies for posterity. Residing in the Taft Papers in the Library of Congress, these letters have served for generations as the prime source on the conflict between Taft and MacArthur. Taft's weekly letters to Root

describing conditions in the islands often ran 15 to 25 typed pages. The letters were packed with interesting details and gossip about people Taft met. The details were fascinating, and his character studies delightfully entertaining. On careful reading, his style was subtlely malicious. Taft was harsh in his evaluation of the U.S. military and every U.S. general in the Philippines. He divided army officers into two categories: a very small group that was sympathetic to the commission; and the majority that believed in pacification by the sword. He portrayed MacArthur as an obstinate military martinet who was a pompous stickler for military details from uniforms to forms in triplicate and who was unwilling to cooperate and work with civilians. Taft observed that Gen. Samuel B.M. Young, commander of the Department of Northern Luzon, was a good fighter but poorly suited for the transition from a state of war to a state of peace. Taft described Gen. J. Franklin Bell, the provost marshall of Manila, as a poorly trained administrator of civil affairs, and he considered Gen. John C. Bates a dangerous reactionary.

Surprisingly, Taft also complained that MacArthur's political policies were too liberal. Taft advocated curtailment of personal liberties, such as freedom of speech, press, and assembly, and the implementation of stronger military measures, including the execution of any Filipino captured with fire arms, confiscation of the property of all known guerrilla leaders, concentration camps for suspected guerrillas, and deportation of all captured guerrilla leaders. Pressured by Washington, MacArthur reluctantly accepted Taft's advice. In December 1900, harsher measures were implemented to curtail the guerrilla bands harassing U.S. garrisons. Guerrillas were divided into two categories: those constantly in the field and the part-time guerrilla farmer. Republican soldiers in uniform were treated as prisoners of war, but the guerrilla captured out of uniform could be executed. In the next three months, 79 captured guerrillas were hanged for murder. MacArthur ordered his garrison commanders to maintain close surveillance and to arrest anyone even suspected of aiding the guerrillas. The war could be won only by terminating town and village support for the guerrillas. Townspeople were made responsible for their actions in support of the guerrillas. Anyone who aided or assisted any person in active, violent opposition to U.S. rule would be arrested with fear as no excuse. Any Filipino who refused to swear loyalty to the United States was to be considered a rebel who was aiding the enemy. Suspicion was sufficient reason for arrest, and any who were arrested were not to be released until the end of the war. MacArthur's army simultaneously struck hard against the guerrillas everywhere in the Philippines.

When the new political and military policies proved effective, Taft claimed the credit. Popular support for the revolution began to collapse. U.S. support in small garrison towns increased, and the army had less difficulty obtaining guides, agents, and informants in the villages. In December 1900 and January 1901 about 2,000 guerrillas were captured. Guerrillas surrendered in dramatically increasing numbers from a 175 monthly average to over 650 in December 1900 to about 800 a month in January and February 1901. Captured leaders were deported to Guam.

In areas where guerrilla attacks ceased, martial law was lifted, and the Taft Commission assumed civil powers. Municipal governments were established, taxes collected, and roads built. Taft encouraged the wealthy, well-educated Filipinos to form political parties, and elections were scheduled in peaceful areas, although the franchise was extremely limited.

In late March, good fortune came to the U.S. forces when Brig. Gen. Frederick Funston captured Emilio Aguinaldo y Famy, president of the Philippine Republic. Aguinaldo's capture was the most momentous event of the war. Taft suggested that Aguinaldo be shot or at least deported to Guam. MacArthur had a better idea. He persuaded Aguinaldo to issue a proclamation declaring an end to the war and requesting all his followers lay down their arms. Aguinaldo's capture and proclamation meant the end of the conflict. Although some Filipinos branded Aguinaldo a traitor, many others responded to his call to surrender. From all over the Philippines reports of guerrillas surrendering poured into MacArthur's headquarters. Over 13,000 rebels swore allegiance to the United States in April and May 1901, surrendering almost 7,500 firearms. Guerrilla activity had dropped dramatically.

With the end of active rebellion on Luzon, Taft recommended the immediate recall of MacArthur and the establishment of civil government in the islands. Washington agreed and in early April notified MacArthur that his term

as military governor would end on 4 July 1901, when Taft would become the first civil governor of the islands. In meetings with the commission, MacArthur offered to assist in a smooth transition of power, but Taft, knowing he was soon to be governor, was not in a compromising mood. Relations between MacArthur and Taft reached a low point. Despite Taft's attitude, MacArthur moved rapidly to turn over vast areas of Luzon to civilian control. By June, over half the towns and villages on Luzon were administered by municipal governments appointed by the Taft Commission.

On 4 July 1901, in a grand military ceremony in the Cathedral Plaza facing the Ayuntamiento, the government building in downtown Manila, MacArthur formally surrendered power. Maj. Gen. Adna R. Chaffee became the new military commander of the Department of the Philippines while Taft became the governor of the islands. Taft and his wife moved into Malacañang Palace, and within days, Taft asserted his new power. He moved the military out of Ayuntamiento and replaced it with his civilian administrators, most of whom were detached military officers. He informed General Chaffee that all military personnel in the Philippines were subject to the orders of the civilian administrators. To Taft's disgust, Chaffee objected and questioned Taft's authority to command military officers in a war zone. More than half of the islands were still under martial law. On Leyte and Samar, the war dragged on and required the continued presence of a large contingent of U.S. troops. In areas still under martial law, Chaffee believed that he, not Taft, was in control. Even the president could not appoint a civilian to command troops in a war zone. Chaffee presented the same constitutional arguments that MacArthur had used in September 1900.

Taft exploded—he had heard the arguments before and wrote a 13-page legal rebuttal. When his legal brief did not convince Chaffee, Taft complained to Washington. Maj. Gen. Henry C. Corbin was sent to Manila to deliver verbal orders to Chaffee. To circumvent Chaffee, Taft created the Philippine Constabulary. Armed and organized into nine companies, the constabulary was directly under Taft's control. He asserted that loyal Filipinos could suppress bandit activity more effectively than the United States Army.

Governor Taft's program was undercut on 29 September 1901, when Company C of the 9th Infantry Regiment suffered a devastating defeat at Balangiga on the island of Samar. Of the 90 men in Company C, 59 were killed and 23 wounded. There was an uproar in Manila, and Chaffee ordered a harsh policy of suppression. In October and November a reign of terror descended on Samar, Leyte, and Southern Luzon as the United States Army responded to the Balangiga massacre. Taft also implemented harsher civilian policies to punish any rebels or opponents to the U.S. regime. The commission passed a series of sedition acts that curtailed freedom of the press, freedom of speech, and freedom of assembly. Surprisingly, in the United States the Balangiga massacre aroused little comment because another major story dominated the news. Earlier in September, President McKinley had been assassinated, and the nation was still in mourning.

When the United States Senate formed a committee to investigate U.S. policy in the Philippines, President Theodore Roosevelt decided to recall Governor Taft from Manila to testify. Taft left Manila on 24 December 1901 and arrived in Washington in late January 1902. He had several conferences at the White House with President Roosevelt and Secretary Root on the Philippine situation. The three men became so close they began to refer to themselves as the "Three Musketeers." Taft testified before the Senate in February 1902 and presented the standard Republican party view that the Filipinos were incapable of self-government and that most Filipinos welcomed U.S. rule. The war was over, and only a few bandits remained in the field.

After his Senate testimony, Taft went to Rome to negotiate the sale of church land in the Philippines. He did not arrive in Manila again until August 1902. For the next 15 months, Taft worked to improve municipal governments, establish schools, reform the currency, and stabilize the taxation system. In the United States, Republicans portrayed him as the savior of the Philippines, depicting him as a man who cared deeply for the Filipino people, who would lead the islands to economic prosperity, and who would educate the Filipinos in the meaning of democracy, liberty, and justice. His administration laid claim to establishing municipal governments throughout the islands, to expanding the educational system through the importation of thousands of U.S. teachers, and to the establishment of the Philippine Constabulary. Less applaudable were the results of Taft's economic policies. Although land reform was implemented, the result was the creation of large plantations growing tropical products for export to the United States. Because Congress restricted U.S. citizens' purchase of land in the Philippines, Taft supported the Filipino aristocracy in obtaining large tracts of land to grow export products. U.S. business investment concentrated on transportation, banking, and processing mills to support the export market. An alliance developed between the U.S. leaders and the Filipino aristocracy that led to political reforms, but these reforms, such as the right to vote, were restricted to the aristocracy.

By late 1903, many in the United States believed that Taft's successes in the Philippines demonstrated his executive ability. He was presidential material. In December 1903, Taft accepted the position of secretary of war and resigned as governor of the Philippines. He left Manila on 23 December 1903 and arrived in Washington on 31 January 1904. As secretary of war, Taft was involved in other areas besides the Philippines, but he knew his reputation was based on the image that he had provided enlightened civil government to the Philippines. To maintain that image, he visited the Philippines twice in the next four years. In August 1905 and again in August 1907, Taft traveled to Manila with dozens of senators, congressmen, and reporters. The political junkets drew newspaper attention to Taft's executive abilities and contributed to his nomination and election as president in 1908. Ever since, Taft's name has been linked to enlightened colonialism in the Philippines.

Kenneth Ray Young

REFERENCES

Rowland T. Berthoff, "Taft and MacArthur," *World Politics*, 5 (1953), 196–213; Ralph E. Minger, "Taft, MacArthur and the Establishment," *Ohio Historical Quarterly*, 70 (1961), 308–331; Henry F. Pringle, *Life & Times of William Howard Taft* (Little, Brown, 1939); Peter W. Stanley, *A Nation in the Making* (Harvard Univ. Pr., 1974); Taft, Mrs. William Howard, *Recollection of Full Years* (Dodd, Mead, 1914); Dean C. Worcester, *The Philippines: Past and Present* (Macmillan, 1914).

See also MacArthur, Arthur.

Tampico Incident (1914)

The Tampico incident in Mexico was a minor misunderstanding which became the basis of a U.S. military intervention in Mexico during April 1914. At that time Mexico was torn by civil war between the revolutionary forces loyal to Gen. Venustiano Carranza and forces of the government of Gen. Victoriano Huerta. U.S. President Woodrow Wilson opposed the Huerta government, denying it diplomatic recognition, and relations were tense.

Tampico, Mexico, was under siege by the revolutionary forces. With combat on its outskirts, the city was jammed with refugees, including many U.S. citizens and other foreigners, who had fled the nearby oil fields that had fallen under rebel control. U.S. warships were stationed off both Tampico and Veracruz to establish a presence and to protect U.S. citizens. The city itself was located on the Pánuco River, 10 miles from the Gulf of Mexico. A sandbar at the mouth of the river prevented large ships from entering, restricting traffic at the bustling oil port to medium-sized vessels.

On 9 April 1914, a whaleboat from the gunboat *Dolphin*, flagship of Rear Adm. Henry T. Mayo at Tampico, landed at a dock in a military zone to pick up fuel. The sailors were intercepted while loading their cargo at the dock by a detachment of Tamaulipas state guard troops, who took the men into custody declaring that they were in a military zone without authorization. Some of the sailors were ordered from the whaleboat at gunpoint by the Mexican troops, in spite of the fact that the small craft prominently flew the U.S. flag. The men were escorted a short distance to the headquarters of the sector commander, Col. Ramon H. Hinojosa, who ordered them returned. They were detained, however, at the dock until he received clearance for their release from the commander of the Tampico Garrison, Gen. Ignacio Morelos Zaragoza. When Admiral Mayo sent an aide and U.S. Consul Clarence W. Miller to protest, the general readily apologized, noting that the Mexicans involved were state rather than federal troops. He immediately ordered the release of the U.S. sailors, who returned to their ship within an hour of their original departure.

Focusing on the fact that some of the sailors had been removed at gunpoint from a boat flying the U.S. flag, Admiral Mayo, acting on his own and without seeking instructions, demanded the arrest of the officers involved and a formal salute to the U.S. flag by the Mexicans. This action escalated the minor incident into a major diplomatic crisis because the Mexican commander could not take such an action without orders. President Wilson supported these demands and used them as an opportunity to bring further pressure on Huerta. Wilson later cited this incident with several other minor episodes, such as delayed telegrams and the mistaken accosting of a U.S. sailor by a Mexican soldier, to contend that the Mexican government had established a "pattern" of hostility toward the United States.

A week of negotiations led to a diplomatic stalemate, with Huerta refusing to order the salute, and the United States insisting. Huerta did offer a simultaneous salute by both countries, which the United States rejected. Both sides invoked national honor, and Wilson sent the entire Atlantic Fleet to Mexican waters to enforce the demand.

At the time, most observers assumed that any U.S. military action would occur at Tampico, site of the incident. Action in Tampico would have been rendered difficult by the inability of large ships to approach the shore, with only the gunboat and cruisers able to enter the river, the cruisers only with difficulty.

During the diplomatic maneuvering, however, the Wilson administration changed its objective, using the incident as a pretext for a landing in Veracruz on 21 April in an effort to intercept a shipment of arms and ammunition consigned to the Huerta government. The ships were withdrawn from Tampico, leaving the U.S. residents without protection, and the original incident was all but forgotten. Indeed, virtually the only subsequent reference to the event occurred at the Niagara Falls Conference, convened by the representatives of Argentina, Brazil, and Chile to prevent the U.S.-Mexican crisis from escalating into a more extensive clash. While that conference focused on the issue of the control of and withdrawal from Veracruz, the United States did agree in the resulting protocols not to demand any further satisfaction, thus laying the demand for a salute to the flag to rest.

U.S. citizens in Tampico were forgotten during the crisis and resulting action and were outraged at their lack of protection. While the naval forces were originally sent at least in part to protect U.S. citizens, the ships at Tampico were withdrawn from the river and rushed to Veracruz, leaving U.S. citizens exposed during the resulting Mexican reaction to the Veracruz landing. The ships that remained off Tampico were unable to help the citizens left ashore, since any effort to return to the river would have been interpreted as a landing maneuver. Eventually, they were evacuated by British and German warships remaining in Tampico, placed aboard transports, and taken to Galveston, Texas. They were not informed that they were being evacuated to the United States, but instead believed they were leaving temporarily only to allow a landing. As a result, they were effectively forced to abandon all their personal property and belongings when they were transported out of Mexico. These individuals, believing that their citizenship entitled them to protection by the U.S. government, felt betrayed.

Kenneth J. Grieb

REFERENCES

Kenneth J. Grieb, *The United States and Huerta* (Univ. of Nebraska Pr., 1969); Robert E. Quirk, *An Affair of Honor: Woodrow Wilson and the Occupation of Veracruz* (Univ. of Kentucky Pr., 1962).

See also Mayo, Henry Thomas; Veracruz, Mexico, Battle (1914); Veracruz, Mexico, Occupation (1914).

Taylor, John R.M., *The Philippine Insurrection Against the United States*

John Rogers Meigs Taylor's *The Philippine Insurrection Against the United States* was an unusual by-product of the Philippine War. U.S. forces captured several tons of Filipino revolutionary documents during the conflict. Known as the Philippine Insurgent Records (PIR), they were shipped to Washington. In 1902, Capt. Taylor was detailed to the newly created Bureau of Insular Affairs (BIA) to prepare a history of the war based on this material. After four years of labor he produced a multivolume narrative along with translations of hundreds of documents.

Taylor's narrative presented a very different picture of the Philippine Revolution than was the case elsewhere. He chronicled the numerous atrocities and abuses committed by Filipino revolutionaries against their own people and provided a highly critical assessment of Philippine

President Emilio Aguinaldo y Famy and other Filipino leaders.

In 1906, the history was ready for publication and required only Secretary of War William H. Taft's approval. Taft read only a portion of Taylor's narrative before he became displeased with what he read. After the war ended, many of the Filipino leaders who had committed abuses acquired posts within the colonial government. Taft and the BIA feared the Filipino reaction to Taylor's history. Accordingly, the history was suppressed, and Taylor was returned to his regiment.

Taylor was determined that his work be published and attempted to secure its release during the following 30 years. The War Department was uneasy about its ramifications and repeatedly refused to do so. Dean C. Worcester, a former Philippine government official, obtained a copy of Taylor's galley proofs and used them in his *The Philippines Past And Present*, published in 1914. Worcester distorted Taylor's narrative, presenting the Filipino revolutionaries in a sinister light. Taylor and the BIA were furious at Worcester, but Taylor's history remained censored. Several individuals in the Philippines and the United States requested access to the history, and most were rebuffed. Taylor made his final plea for publication in 1936, but as late as 1939, the War Department still refused to release the history.

During the 1950s and 1960s, several historians gained access to the history at the United States National Archives. In 1957, the PIR were returned to the Philippines. Ironically, the Eugenio Lopez foundation published Taylor's history in the Philippines in 1971.

The War Department thus withheld a substantial portion of the documentary record pertaining to the Philippine Revolution and Philippine War for nearly four decades. It deemed maintaining cordial Philippine-U.S. relations as being more important than permitting complete public access to the historical record.

James C. Biedzynski

REFERENCES

John T. Farrell, "An Abandoned Approach to Philippine History: John R.M. Taylor and the Philippine Insurrection Records," *Catholic Historical Review*, 39 (1954), 385–407; John M. Gates, "The Official Historian and the Well-Placed Critic: James A. Le Roy's Assessment of John R.M. Taylor's *The*

Philippine Insurrection Against the United States," *Public Historian*, 7 (1985), 57–67; John R.M. Taylor, *The Philippine Insurrection Against the United States* (U.S. Government Printing Office, 1906) (U.S. National Archives, Record Groups 94 & 350, microcopy 719, roll 9); *The Philippine Insurrection Against the United States* (Eugenio Lopez Foundation, 1971), 5 vols.

Teller Amendment (1898)

When President William McKinley asked Congress for authority to intervene in Cuba in 1898, Congress manifested little disagreement over intervention, but argued at length over the status of Cuba. McKinley's message ignored the Cuban revolutionaries, producing concerns that he intended annexation. A proposal to recognize the revolutionary government passed in the Senate, but failed in the House of Representatives on a nearly straight party vote, with only three Republicans in favor.

Horatio S. Rubens, a representative of the Cuban Junta, later claimed to have convinced Senator Henry M. Teller to introduce an amendment resolving: "That the United States disclaims any disposition or intention to exercise sovereignty, jurisdiction, or control over said island except for the pacification thereof, and asserts its determination when that is accomplished to leave the government and control of the island to its people." Passed on a voice vote, the amendment became the fourth section of the resolution authorizing intervention.

Teller had served in the Senate from Colorado since 1876, except for a brief period as secretary of the Department of the Interior. A Republican, he bolted his party over the silver issue, supported William Jennings Bryan for president in 1896, and won election to a fourth Senate term as a Silver Republican. An erstwhile expansionist, he came to share other silverites' support for the Cuban revolutionaries. Colorado had recently begun to raise significant amounts of sugar beets; therefore, Teller had an additional reason to oppose the annexation of Cuba, a major sugar-producing country. Some researchers have suggested that some members of Congress supported the amendment from racist motives, and others have suggested that Cuban Junta bonds played a role in generating support.

Robert W. Cherny

REFERENCES

Elmer Ellis, *Henry Moore Teller: Defender of the West* (Caxton Printers, 1941); Philip S. Foner, *The Spanish-Cuban-American War and the Birth of American Imperialism, 1895–1902* (Monthly Review Pr., 1972), vol. 1; Horatio S. Rubens, *Liberty: The Story of Cuba* (Warren & Putnam, 1932).

Telpaneca, Nicaragua, Battle (1927)

As U.S. Marines and Nicaraguan national guardsmen sought in the summer and fall of 1927 to reestablish government control over the Department of Nueva Segovia in northern Nicaragua they had frequent encounters with nationalist guerrillas under the command of Augusto C. Sandino. The first important engagement had come in July 1927 at Ocotal, where marine planes had been instrumental in repelling Sandino's attack. Additional defeats followed at San Fernando and Santa Clara. The guerrillas retired to their mountain redoubt, El Chipote, to consider their next moves.

After a quiet August and the formal organization of Sandino's followers as the Army in Defense of the National Sovereignty of Nicaragua, the guerrillas renewed hostilities on 19 September at the town of Telpaneca on the Coco River. Between 140 and 200 Sandinistas attacked the garrison of 20 marines and 25 *guardia* troops commanded by marine 1st Lt. Herbert S. Keimling (captain in the national guard). Under cover of heavy fog the Sandinistas infiltrated the town and were not discovered until a dynamite bomb exploded in the rear of the marine quarters. The attackers fired machine guns, Thompson submachine guns, and rifles, threw dynamite bombs and hand grenades, and carried machetes. They were almost at the doors and windows of the barracks before the defenders were alerted. Despite the surprise, the marines and national guardsmen held firm, firing their rifles rapidly and using a Lewis machine gun for traversing fire across the plaza in front of the quarters. Lieutenant Keimling reported later that after the first 15 minutes his men had settled down and shot like veterans; they demonstrated excellent fire control and discipline. In the same report he noted that several of the attackers fired by commands and "did some pretty good shooting." At one point in the midst of battle, guerrillas threw two dynamite bombs through the roof at the rear of the *guardia* quarters; both were thrown out but one wounded the hand of a national guardsman. A marine then cleared the rear area of attackers.

The fog began to rise around 2:30 a.m., and by 3:00 a.m. the Sandinistas were beginning to remove their dead and wounded. By 5:00 a.m. they had withdrawn. Casualties included two marines killed and one national guardsman wounded; there were estimates of 25 to 50 Sandinistas killed and many wounded. The renewal of guerrilla activity at Telpaneca indicated that the rumors of a Sandino base at El Chipote were correct.

William Kamman

REFERENCES

"Combat Operations in Nicaragua," *Marine Corps Gazette*, 14 (1929), 16–30; Neill Macaulay, *The Sandino Affair* (Quadrangle, 1967); Bernard C. Nalty, *The United States Marines in Nicaragua*, rev. ed., Marine Corps Historical References Series, No. 21 (Historical Branch, G-3 Division, Headquarters, U.S. Marine Corps, 1962).

Tianjin (Tientsin), China, Battle and Siege (1900)

The siege of the foreign concessions and the battle for the walled city of Tianjin (Tientsin), China, lasted one month, 15 June–14 July 1900, during the Boxer Uprising. The ferocity of the fighting was so great that at its end, approximately two-thirds of both the foreign concessions and the walled city were destroyed.

From early spring 1900, foreign residents of the Tianjin concessions were conscious of the Boxer danger, actually more than were their official representatives. In early March, it was argued that "[i]f official disbelief possessed some magic power to avert evil it refuses to recognize, we should be enjoying a foretaste of the millennium" (*Peking and Tientsin Times*, p. 2). It was not until late May that the first troops designated to protect the concessions arrived.

These reinforcements led to complacency among the foreign population, even though their servants warned them "to go while there is still time" (Dix, p. 20). Even the most pessimistic assumed "the Imperial army would protect them, if matters came to a head" (Dix, p. 20). It was not until the second week of June that they realized that without sufficient reinforcements they would be overwhelmed because "the rebels are sure to pour over the fences and walls and mass in the streets to such an extent that the troops here would have to be greatly divided up to cover so large a territory" (*The Boxer Rising*, p. 10).

The siege was characterized by the Chinese artillery's constant and effective shelling and constant sniping. The sniping proved to be particularly demoralizing because the concessions' broad streets emptied into the riverfront, and the land opposite was filled with villages and salt piles (property of the government's salt monopoly), and of course, snipers.

The solution was to erect a barricade "of bales of wool, more than a mile long, and two bales high, along the Bund" (Rasmussen, p. 121). Besides wool, the crates and bales that came out of the warehouses contained camel hair, rice, hides, beans, peanuts, wheat, sugar, condensed milk, soap and other "sorts of suitably packed merchandise" (Rasmussen, p. 121; Hoover, p. 49). The labor was provided by Chinese refugees from Tianjin and the surrounding areas. At first seen "as a menace and a nuisance" by most of the foreigners, "it was not long before it was perceived that without their help the necessary labor simply could not have been performed" (Smith, p. 445).

Initially, foreign morale was high: "As regards the Boxers we have no fear, and of Imperial troops not much. Indeed we aspire to have the honor of pricking this monstrous Boxer bubble" (McLeish, p. 3). Others were not as sanguine. Herbert Hoover recorded that the fight at the concessions "was not altogether a fight between soldiers. It was a group of civilian men, women and children fighting for very life . . . with their eyes open to a form of death that everyone knew but did not mention" (Hoover, p. 52).

Between 15 June and 19 June, the defenders of the concessions had been subjected to murderous bombardment and fought two pitched battles with the Chinese army: one to destroy the artillery and troops at the military college across the river from the British concession and the other to maintain control over the railway station. Although the Chinese were dislodged from the college and the railway station, the concessions were isolated because the railway line to Tanggu was cut. The Russian commander summed up the new foreign feeling when he said, "The Chinese are fighting well and more skillfully [sic] than ever before" (McLeish, p. 6).

Fires started in both the concessions and the walled city on 18 June, which raged out of control and were quenched only by an afternoon rainstorm.

The thought that most oppressed the foreigners was that the outside world thought them dead and, therefore, was in no great hurry to reach them. By 19 June they were certain the Dagu (Taku) forts were in friendly hands but that no relief expedition was being organized because they were all assumed to be dead; there had been no communication with the outside world since 10 June.

On 19 June three Cossacks and James Watts, an Englishman, volunteered to ride to Dagu to tell the Allied forces that foreigners were still alive at Tianjin. After a night's journey lasting 10 hours (it normally took three hours to cover the 30 miles), lit "only by the glare of burning villages fired by the Boxers" (Rasmussen, p. 154), they reached Tanggu on 20 June.

Watts left the next day for Tianjin with a relief column. His journey to the coast was rapid when compared to the column's trip back to Tianjin. It took three and one-half days to cover the same 30 miles. Facing more opposition, it took two attempts to reach the concessions.

However, the "relief of the Tianjin concessions" was not an end but merely a means to one. The garrison was reinforced, but was still not strong enough to assault the walled city. The Chinese army and its Boxer auxiliaries were intact and occupied the surrounding territory. Neither the Chinese nor the Allies made any attempt to stop each other from receiving reinforcements. However, the Allies found that it was becoming more difficult to dislodge the Chinese from their positions around the walled city.

Over the next three weeks, the Allies attacked and held various Chinese positions around the concessions to enable them to prepare an assault on the city. They were hampered by a lack of men, supplies, and a logistical log jam at Dagu. There were simply not enough barges and tugs available to move supplies upriver to the concessions.

Part of the problem was the result of the brutality of the Allied advance. The country between the railroad right of way and the river, from Dagu to Tianjin was "a track of graves and desolation . . . . [T]here were no signs of human life, . . . a palpable breath of blasting desolation passed over the land." The landscape was littered with "tenantless houses, often roofless, frequently with charred walls, empty doors and windows, that gave them a skull-like appearance" (Lynch, pp. 19–20).

After the first Allied reinforcements arrived, the spectre of immediate defeat vanished. However, the battle for Tianjin was not yet over. The Allies had to integrate reinforcements into the garrison, keep the supply line between Tianjin and the sea open, evacuate as many noncombatants (foreign and Chinese) from the concessions as possible, prevent the Chinese from storming the settlements and various strategic points in and around the concessions to prepare for an assault on the city.

The Chinese were not passive observers. Over the next three weeks, they launched attacks against the concessions in an attempt to seize them and to forestall the inevitable Allied attempt to storm Tianjin.

Life in the concessions and the walled city went on much as it had before the reinforcements arrived. The siege was not raised, although it was more difficult for the Chinese army to mount attacks. The Allies had neither the numbers nor the artillery to assault the walled city. In fact, "there is still no security for life in Tientsin; . . . a feeling of anxiety and uncertainty prevails. All indications are that additions of both Boxers and Imperial soldiers are daily being brought into the native city" (Ricalton, pp. 199–200).

There were four more engagements fought before the Allies mounted their assault. Two were Allied defensive actions; two were Chinese offensives.

The first was an Allied attack on the Eastern Arsenal on 27 June (after the rescue of the Seymour Column from the Xigu [Hsi-ku] Arsenal). It was designed to make access to the concessions easier for expected reinforcements. The second was a Chinese attack on the railway station, 3–5 July. Its objective was to destroy the Allied troops defending it and to prevent reinforcements from reaching Tianjin easily by rail. The third action was the Allied attack on the Western Arsenal and the race track, 6–9 July. This was designed to eliminate a Chinese artillery redoubt and to provide the Allies with a start line for their assault. The fourth action was the final Chinese attack on the railway station. It was designed to destroy the foreign defenders, to make reinforcing the concessions by rail difficult, if not impossible, and to turn an Allied flank thereby forcing the Allied commanders to contemplate a retreat to the sea.

The Allies faced logistical and manpower problems that seemed to doom prospects for an assault on Tianjin. By 12 July approximately 8,000 foreign troops were in the concessions and were effectively kept under cover by Chinese artillery bombardment. The city was defended by approximately 20,000 Chinese, including a foreign-trained division and Boxer auxiliaries.

There was also a marked disparity between Chinese and foreign artillery strength. The former had approximately 60 guns of various calibers concentrated in the northwestern part of the city and in the area of the viceroy's *yamen* (outside the walls) and the Lutai (Lu-t'ai) Canal. They also had smaller pieces that could be mounted on the walls.

To face them and to provide support for the assault, the Allies had 58 light artillery pieces, of insufficient weight to blast breaches in the wall, and nine machine guns. Artillery was a constant problem for the Allies.

The other obstacles facing the Allies were the city wall and the terrain surrounding it. The wall was 25 feet high, "a height which make scaling impossible," constructed with "a facing of three feet of masonry backed by about 30 feet of solid earth" at its base. At its top, the wall was between 10 and 15 feet thick and "the facing extends above the earth backing about 6 feet pierced with loopholes and embrasures." The city was surrounded by "an unfordable moat, and fronting that are marshes that have various depths at various points" (Leonard, p. 53).

There were rice paddies in front of the marshes; the shell holes in them were between six inches and eight feet deep. The plain looked smooth and level; flooding hid the holes. It was also "interspersed with ditches and low embankments and . . . grave mounds" (Daggett, p. 28).

Despite these obstacles, the Allied commanders "decided that the Walled City must be taken even though the number of troops at hand . . . was insufficient" (Leonard, p. 51). The assault on the walled city consisted of two separate infantry attacks.

In one, a feint, a Russian force reinforced by French and German contingents was to attack from the east, cross the Lutai Canal and seize the artillery batteries, and then assault the city's eastern gate. In the main attacks, the Japanese were supposed to assault the southern gate and force their way into the city while British, French, and U.S. contingents aided them by attacking the south wall.

In the southern attack, the only way on "entirely solid ground over which the wall can be approached is a roadway running from the west arsenal to the south gate" (Leonard, p. 53). The causeway was narrow, "not more than thirty feet in width. The troops advancing along it were consequently unable to extend, and were obliged to proceed in close order," coming under rifle fire as well as "intermittent shell and shrapnel fire" (Thomson, pp. 70–71). The main assault on the walled city was to be across swampy, shelterless, inadequately reconnoitered ground, made by troops with a vague plan of action, no common language of command, and inadequate artillery support against a well-protected, well-armed, and numerically superior foe.

The attack began at approximately 3:00 a.m. on 13 July, when Allied artillery began to bombard the city walls. The Western Arsenal was the starting line for the assault, with the objective, the city's south gate, approximately one mile away. In the original plan, the French were on the right, the Japanese, British, and Austrians in the center, with U.S. troops on the left, screened by Japanese cavalry (*Reports on Military Operations in South Africa and China*, p. 549).

The assault proper on the south gate began at dawn. As the troops advanced from the arsenal, and they "came within the enemy's range they were met by a well-directed fire from the south wall" (Thomson, p. 13). The Japanese began the advance, followed by the British and U.S. troops. The marines, advancing at the head of the U.S. contingent, advanced "by rushes of 50 to 75 yards, and then lying down to recover our breath and open fire" (Leonard, p. 52). They were able to advance until they "reached a position about seven hundred yards from the wall and 'dug in' in one of the shallow trenches. The Chinese held us there the remainder of the day" (Bevan, p. 65).

Two battalions of the U.S. 9th Infantry Regiment followed the marines. Because they received no instructions from the British commander of the column, instead of turning left and following the marines, they turned right "and were gradually worked into the hottest corner of the fight" (Rasmussen, p. 209). By turning the wrong way, the regiment's commander exposed his force to direct fire from the entire south wall and to enfilading fire from the ruins of the houses between the wall and the French concession. The troops took cover in ditches and behind grave mounds but were sheltered only from the direct fire, not from the enfilading fire.

At about the same time, the Japanese and French advanced along the causeway to within 900 yards of the south gate and took "welcome though precarious shelter" in a cluster of ruined Chinese houses where they remained for the rest of the day (Thomson, pp. 64–65). They lacked sufficient men and ammunition to press the assault.

All this happened by 9:30 a.m. Fighting was stalemated for the rest of the day. The Chinese made no attacks while the Allies were pinned down in their positions. It was impossible to resupply the troops with food, water, and ammunition, so the various contingents had to rely on their own resources to care for their casualties.

An Allied war council met late in the afternoon and initially favored withdrawing all troops to the arsenal under cover of darkness. The commander, Gen. Yasumasa Fukushima, opposed this and proposed that British and U.S. forces be withdrawn from their positions after dark and that the center be reinforced and that Japanese combat engineers blow a breach in the wall or the south gate just before dawn. The council agreed to this course of action (Davis, p. 865).

As the British and U.S. troops retreated and reformed, the Japanese advanced. Shortly after 3:00 a.m., "on 14 July, the South Gate was blown up" (Landon, vol. 1, p. 187). The destruction of the gate, combined with the Russian-led assault to the east and north, panicked and demoralized the Chinese defenders, and they retreated out of the city through the north gate. The Allied force then entered and occupied the walled city.

The siege of the foreign concessions and the Battle of Tianjin was over. During this month of fighting, the Chinese gave the Allies a bloody nose. The tenacity and skill of the Chinese resistance caused the Allies to reassess the ease with which they thought they could rescue the foreigners in the Beijing legations. The direct result of the battle was that the Allied relief expedition rested, reinforced, and resupplied itself for three weeks after the battle before advancing on Beijing.

Lewis Bernstein

REFERENCES

Arthur Allison Stuart Barnes, *On Active Service With the Chinese Regiment: A Record of the Operation of the First Chinese Regiment in North China, March to October, 1900*, 2d ed., rev. and enl. (Grant Richards, 1902); James Bevan, "From Filipinos to Boxers in 1900," *Leatherneck*, 18 (1935) 5–7, 65–66; *The Boxer Rising: A History of the Boxer Trouble in China Reprinted from the Shanghai Mercury* (Shanghai Mercury, 1900/Paragon, 1967); Aaron S. Daggett, *America in the China Relief Expedition: An Account of the Brilliant Part Taken by United States Troops in the Memorable Campaign in the Summer of 1900 for the Relief of the Besieged Legations in Peking, China* (Hudson-Kimberley, 1903); Oscar King Davis, "The Looting of Tientsin," *Harper's Weekly*, 44 (1900) 865; C.C. Dix, *The World's Navies in the Boxer Rebellion* (Digby, Long & Co., 1905); Herbert Hoover, *The Memoirs of Herbert Hoover, Vol. 1: The Years of Adventure, 1874–1920* (Macmillan, 1952); A. Henry Savage Landon, *China and the Allies* (Scribner, 1901-1902), 2 vols.; Henry Leonard, "The Visit of the Allies to China in 1900), *Journal of the Military Service Institution of the United States*, 29 (July 1901) 40–55; George Lynch, *The War of the Civilizations* (Longmans, 1901) 19–20; William McLeish, *Tientsin Besieged and After the Siege: From the 15th of June to the 16th of July 1900* (North-China Herald, 1900); *Peking and Tientsin Times*, 3 March 1902); Otto D. Rasmussen, *Tientsin: An Illustrated Outline History* (Tientsin Pr., 1925); James Ricalton, *China Through the Stereoscope: A Journey at the Time of the Boxer Uprising* (Underwood, 1901); Arthur H. Smith, *China in Convulsion* (Revell, 1901); Henry Crauford Thomson, *China and the Powers: A Narrative of the Outbreak of 1900* (Longman, 1902); U.S. War Department, Adjutant General's Office, *Reports on Military Operations in South Africa and China* (U.S. Government Printing Office, 1901).

Tinio, Manuel (1877–1924)

Manuel Tinio was a native of Nueva Ecija Province, the Philippines. He is best remembered as "the soul of the Insurrection [the Philippine War] in the Ilocano provinces." When a schoolboy of age 16 he prodigiously demonstrated leadership qualities with classmates who were soon to become revolutionary officers, and he showed rebellious behavior by knocking a Spaniard from his bicycle. To elude retribution, Tinio fled to his home in Aliaga, became a member of the nationalist Katipunan, and served under Gen. Mariano Llanera in the early fighting against the Spanish. By 1897 he followed Gen. Emilio Aguinaldo y Famy into Hong Kong exile as a brigadier general.

Despite his youth and lack of formal military training, Tinio's appearance alongside Aguinaldo and Gen. António Narciso Luna as a ranking *principal* (member of the oligarchy) gave the Philippine Republic at Malolos a strong class consciousness. As a provincial notable and landowner, he exercised considerable political and economic influence in Nueva Ecija with the aid of his older brother Col. Casmirio Tinio, nephew of Capt. Pascual, and cousin Lt. Julio Tinio.

After the Battle of Manila Bay, 1 May 1898, Tinio accompanied Aguinaldo in his return from exile and, supported by brother Casmirio, initiated assaults on Spanish strongholds to liberate his native province. Nueva Ecija, located in the northeastern corner of Luzon's central plain and 50 miles north of Manila, had a population exceeding 130,000 and an expanse of about 2,040 square miles. Its Rio Grande de la Pampanga river system produced rice and sugar, making the province with its many Tagalog inhabitants a significant feature of the Philippine economy. San Isidro fell to the Tinio brothers, and Nueva Ecija declared independence by July 1898. The province remained under the Philippine Republic for less than a year; nevertheless after U.S. forces seized Malolos in early 1899, San Isidro and Cabanatuan were briefly the regime's capitals.

In August 1898 General Tinio, then age 22, advanced northwestward and took La Union Province's coastal city of San Fernando in the Ilocos. Situated on Luzon's northwestern side from Lingayen Gulf northward to the Babuyan Channel, the provinces' Ilocano population of 531,000, including Tagalog and Chinese elements, centered on coastal La Union, Ilocos Sur, and Ilocos Norte as well as the Lepanto and Abra provinces' Abra River Valley. With ample popular support, Tinio defeated tottering Spanish forces in 30 days and made the Ilocano region subject to Malolos authority. The young general so impressed the natives of one Ilocos Notre *pueblo* (town), that they adopted his surname as their own.

Tinio commanded Philippine Republic forces in the Ilocano provinces when, after the outbreak of the Philippine War, a U.S. force under Gen. Samuel B.M. Young marched into La Union Province in November 1899. Unable to stop U.S. troops, he disengaged from San Fernando, retreated to Tagudin, Ilocos Sur, and moved northward to prepare a defense of the Abra Valley at Tangadan Pass, Abra Province.

Following U.S.-administered defeats at Vigan, Ilocos Sur, and Tangadan Pass, Tinio withdrew into the highlands of Ilocos Norte and resorted to guerrilla warfare in a conflict lasting 18 months. Within the U.S. military-designated First District, Department of Northern Luzon, an underground resistance comparable to the National Liberation Front in South Vietnam during the Vietnam War linked the U.S.-established local administrations and guerrilla units; thus, many town officials secretly worked with the guerrillas. The revolutionaries' authority permeated La Union Province. Through taxation and manipulation of records, municipal governments supported guerrilla bands, many of which camped near towns. Tinio brazenly resided in and around La Union's municipalities and regularly contacted their officials.

Tinio alternated politically between intimidation and appeasement in order to persuade wavering villagers in the Ilocano provinces not to aid U.S.-appointed governments. He also engaged U.S. forces. In late 1900 his guerrillas imposed a severe defeat on the United States Army at Cusucus in Ilocos Sur. Earlier that year, he had mismatched Filipino guerrillas with superior U.S. weaponry. Hundreds died in an uneven fight similar to the Tet battles of 1968 in Vietnam.

By spring 1901, Tinio and the Philippine Republic had lost the campaign for the Ilocos. In addition to the military strength of the United States, there was animosity among the revolutionaries. The Tagalog-speaking Tinio from Nueva Ecija quarreled with Father Gregorio Aglipay, an excommunicated priest in control of Ilocos Norte. Personality conflicts and language differences combined with supply problems and a popular inclination to surrender. Tinio, his zone commanders, and their forces capitulated on 30 April.

Tinio took the Oath of Allegiance to the United States and supported the U.S.-established commission government. As governor of Nueva Ecija, he urged the building of roads and, after becoming director of labor, he managed to reduce work stoppages. Tinio won recognition from Governor General W. Cameron Forbes as "one of the ablest of Filipinos," which would also be an appropriate accolade for his role in the Philippine War.

Rodney J. Ross

REFERENCES

Brian McAllister Linn, *The U.S. Army and Counterinsurgency in the Philippine War, 1899–1902* (Univ. of North Carolina Pr., 1989); Joaquin Natividad, "General Tinio and his Glorious Campaign," *Philippine Free Press*, 7 Aug. 1948; William Henry Scott, *Ilocano Responses to American Aggression, 1900–1901* (New Day, 1986); Manuel Tinio, "General Tinio Reports," *Ilocos Review*, 16 (1984): 142–155; Willis B. Wilcox, *Through Luzon on Highways and Byways* (Franklin, 1901).

Treaty of 1915: United States–Haiti

The Treaty of 1915, agreed to in principle on 29 November 1915 and ratified on 3 May 1916 by the United States Senate, established Haiti as a protectorate of the United States. On 17 August 1915, three weeks after U.S. Marines landed at Port-au-Prince, Haiti, to restore order, the U.S. Chargé R. Beale Davis, Jr. paid a formal call on the newly elected Haitian president, Philippe Sudre Dartiguenave, bringing a draft of the treaty that the United States expected to be accepted "without modification." Although the Chamber of Deputies approved the treaty in early October, there was strong resistance from members of the Haitian Senate and of Dartiguenave's cabinet, which objected in particular to the proposed financial advisor. In November Adm. William B. Caperton was instructed to tell the Haitians that the United States would retain control whether or not the treaty was ratified and that "those offering opposition" could not expect favorable treatment (Heinl, p. 424). Such threats were impressive in view of the existing martial law, and the Haitian Senate approved the treaty by a substantial majority.

The key provisions of the treaty were as follows: (1) the establishment of a customs receivership under U.S. control; (2) the appointment of a U.S. financial advisor to assist in the settlement of the foreign debt and in other financial and commercial matters; (3) the organization of a Haitian constabulary under the command of U.S. officers; (4) the disarming of all revolutionary forces; and (5) a guarantee on the part of Haiti to cede no territory to any nation but the United States. All points involving discretion were left to the United States. The treaty was to remain in force for 10 years and could be renewed for another 10 years if its objectives had not been satisfactorily accomplished. On 28 March 1917 an agreement was reached to extend it for an additional 10 years or to 1936, although the legality of the extension was questionable because it was approved by neither the Haitian Congress nor the United States Senate.

The Treaty of 1915 was a high-water mark of its kind among U.S. treaties either proposed or concluded in the Caribbean, yet its shortcomings were soon apparent. The document did not expressly recognize the presence and status of U.S. occupation forces. Public education, the courts, and judiciary were not made subject to U.S. advice or control. The result was a system that had neither the virtues of a treaty regime based on true agreement nor those of a clear-cut military administration, such as that established in the Dominican Republic, but only the bad features of both. Moreover, Haitians deeply resented the arrangement, accusing the United States of deliberately usurping the power of their civil government, failing to give sufficient financial aid, and backing the autocratic methods of Presidents Dartiguenave and Louis Borno while preventing the formulation of a more liberal constitution. Despite these liabilities, the treaty remained in effect until the dismantling of the occupation in 1934.

Jane M. Rausch

REFERENCES

Robert Debs Heinl, Jr., and Nancy Gordon Heinl, *Written in Blood: The Story of the Haitian People, 1492–1971* (Houghton Mifflin, 1978); Lester D. Langley, *The United States and the Caribbean in the Twentieth Century*, rev. ed. (Univ. of Georgia Pr., 1985); Dana G. Munro, *The United States and the Caribbean Republics, 1921–1933* (Princeton Univ. Pr., 1964); Graham H. Stuart and James L. Tigner, *Latin America and the United States*, 6th ed. (Prentice Hall, 1975).

See also Caperton, William Banks; Dartiguenave, Philippe Sudre.

Treaty of Paris (1898)

The Treaty of Paris of 1898 concluded the Spanish-Cuban/American War. The treaty disposed of many of Spain's colonies—Cuba, Puerto Rico, Guam, and the Philippines—and provided a financial and commercial settlement.

Negotiations occurred in two phases, the first during August 1898 in Washington, and the second from October to December in Paris. The Washington talks resulted in a protocol that provided for a cease-fire, the withdrawal of Spanish troops from Cuba and Puerto Rico, and the end of Spanish sovereignty in Cuba, Puerto Rico, and one island in the Ladrones (Mariana Islands). In Paris, negotiations centered on the Cuban debt and the fate of the Philippines. In the end Spain ceded the Philippines to the United States for $20 million.

The Washington protocol defined much of the settlement for Cuba, Puerto Rico, and Guam. From the start of the war with the United States, Spain realized that it would lose Cuba. But the Spanish government did not want to turn the island over to the Cuban revolutionaries, fearing that they would take reprisals on Spanish citizens and property. Rather, Spain preferred ceding the island to the United States, believing that the U.S. government would protect Spanish interests. In addition Spain wanted up to $200 million to pay for Cuba's debts which were pledged to the island's customs receipts.

Washington shared Madrid's concern about Cuban self-rule. During the rebellion, the revolutionaries had willfully destroyed U.S. property. Moreover, the administration of President William McKinley did not believe that the Cuban people, after 400 years of Spanish rule, were prepared to direct their own affairs. Chronic mismanagement in Cuba would adversely affect U.S. investments and commerce.

Neither the U.S. government nor the Cuban revolutionaries wanted to assume Cuba's debts. Therefore, the protocol simply directed Spain to relinquish sovereignty over Cuba. Because the U.S. government did not acquire sovereignty, it refused to accept responsibility for Cuba's debts.

Puerto Rico also formed part of the protocol. Because there was no colonial rebellion in Puerto Rico, the Spanish government expected to retain the island. For the United States, Puerto Rico commanded one of the strategic entries into the Caribbean Sea. Moreover, the McKinley administration believed that if Spain kept Puerto Rico, at some future time there would be a rebellion on the island which would inevitably involve the United States. During the war, U.S. troops occupied part of Puerto Rico, and at the end of the war the United States insisted that Spain cede the island as a war indemnity.

The Washington agreement also specified that Spain relinquish an island in the Ladrones. During the war, U.S. armed forces took Guam,

and the Treaty of Paris later acknowledged United States possession of the island.

With an August cease-fire in place, both countries prepared for the final peace talks in Paris. Each nation sent a delegation of five commissioners. President McKinley selected Secretary of State William R. Day to head the U.S. team. Day resigned from the State Department to take the new assignment. McKinley also appointed to the committee three senators, all members of the Senate Foreign Relations Committee: Cushman K. Davis, committee chairman and Republican from Minnesota; William P. Frye, Republican from Maine; and George Gray, Democrat from Delaware. His fifth choice was Whitelaw Reid, Republican publisher and editor of the *New York Tribune*, and former minister to France. John Bassett Moore, a legal scholar and assistant to Day, served as secretary of the delegation.

The Spanish commission was led by Eugenio Montero Ríos, president of the Spanish Senate. Buenaventura de Abarzuza also represented the Senate. José de Garnica y Diaz was a member of the Cortés and a justice of the Spanish Supreme Court. Gen. Rafael Cerero brought military representation to the delegation, and Wenceslao Ramírez de Villa-Urrutia, Spain's ambassador to Belgium, added diplomatic experience. All the Spanish commissioners were members of the Liberal party. The secretary of the delegation was Emilio de Ojeda, an experienced diplomat.

The Paris negotiations focused on the U.S. decision to acquire the Philippines and Spain's desire to obtain a financial settlement. The issue of the Philippines was complicated by the way the fighting ended at Manila. At the start of the war, the United States Navy destroyed the Spanish fleet in Manila Bay, and three months later the U.S. army occupied a beachhead on the outskirts of Manila. Spain still held the capital, although Filipino revolutionaries controlled much of the interior of Luzon island. At the time of the cease-fire, the diplomats agreed that the future of the archipelago would be decided in Paris. Before the news of the cease-fire reached Manila, however, the United States Army captured the city by assault; at the same time it refused to allow Filipino troops to take part in the surrender and policing of Manila.

The U.S. public believed that the last-minute military victory amounted to a conquest of the colony and that, therefore, Washington could dispose of the islands as it wished. The Spanish objected, citing international law which held that military action after a cease-fire was without effect. Spain argued that Manila should be returned together with governing responsibilities for all of the islands. U.S. diplomats outwardly maintained the right of conquest, but they understood that their legal position was shaky. The Filipino revolutionaries were angered that they were excluded from the Paris negotiations on the status of the islands.

At the time the fighting stopped, the U.S. government was not yet prepared to discuss the future of the Philippines. With an election less than three months away, politicians scrutinized public opinion.

Most people in the United States had been thrilled by U.S. military successes. The public overwhelmingly opposed turning back the islands to Spain, considering both the Spanish and Filipinos unfit to rule. Most U.S. citizens believed the United States could bring better government to the islands as well as develop expanded trade in the Far East. They were reluctant to allow another power, such as Germany or Japan, to acquire the archipelago. Yet many in the United States resisted the idea of colonial rule. Some strongly held that colonialism was unconstitutional and undemocratic. During several months of national discussion, public opinion moved in the direction of annexation.

President McKinley approached the Philippine issue cautiously. Early in the war he leaned toward acquiring a commercial port and a naval station; Manila was the logical city. To defend Manila, however, it appeared necessary to control all of Luzon. When the war ended, McKinley was not ready to decide. He wanted more information about the islands and a clearer expression of the will of the people of the United States. In September, on the eve of the Paris Peace Conference, the president explained to his commissioners that he wanted Manila, Luzon, and commercial rights throughout the archipelago. He opposed paying any financial settlement.

The U.S. commissioners reflected the indecision over the Philippines. Davis, Frye, and Reid advocated keeping all the islands. Gray opposed expansionism. Day was wary of expansion, although willing to support the president.

For Spain, more was at stake in Paris than many of its colonial possessions. Shocked from suffering one military disaster after another, the government feared public disorder and even the overthrow of the monarchy. Madrid believed that some diplomatic success might revive Spanish spirits and win support for the government. Yet, the Spanish negotiating position was extremely weak. Its navy sunk and credit exhausted, it could not resume the war.

The Spanish government sought the support of the European powers. It wanted to arbitrate disputed issues in an effort to involve the Europeans in a settlement. The Spanish wooed Germany by indicating an interest in selling some of the larger Caroline Islands.

The Spanish government also attempted to delay a settlement. It hoped the November elections in the United States would change the U.S. political situation. With elections over, McKinley might prove less demanding.

On 1 October the U.S. and Spanish commissioners began the Paris negotiations. The first weeks largely concerned Spain's efforts to get the United States to assume Cuba's debts. Disregarding Washington's refusal in August, Spain continued to press this issue. The U.S. delegates, calculating the total Cuban and Philippine debt as high as $600 million, refused to accept any obligation and insisted that the protocol language serve as the basis for the treaty.

Having turned away all Spain's arguments, the U.S. delegates worried that if the Spanish received nothing, they would leave Paris and there would be no peace treaty. In a private conversation with the Spanish, Reid suggested that if the United States got its way over Cuba, then Madrid might receive some financial consideration in a Philippine settlement.

During October the U.S. negotiators gathered information about the Philippines. Testimony suggested that it would be extremely difficult to divide the islands and that acquisition of Luzon led logically to annexation of the entire archipelago. Unable to reach a consensus, the commissioners forwarded their individual recommendations to President McKinley with the request that he provide additional instructions.

At the same time, President McKinley was sounding public opinion. Only weeks before the November election, the president made a tour through the Midwest, during which he talked to many local politicians and delivered several major speeches. He spoke of tradition as well as of duty and destiny, and he listened carefully. By the end of the trip, the president was convinced that the people of the United States supported acquisition of all the Philippines. He instructed the U.S. commissioners to demand the entire archipelago and also authorized purchase of one of the Caroline Islands, preferably Kusaie, for a cable station.

Rejecting the U.S. claim that the United States had conquered the Philippines, the Spanish commissioners insisted that if Spain ceded the islands, it should receive a substantial financial payment. Rather than sign an ignominious treaty, they threatened to return to Madrid. Therefore, the U.S. commissioners recommended paying Spain for its peacetime improvements in the islands, and McKinley authorized as much as $20 million. Disappointed by the amount, Madrid reluctantly accepted the exchange.

With the Philippine agreement at hand, the commissioners quickly settled several other items. The United States agreed to pay for the return of Spanish prisoners of war and to assume the war-time claims of U.S. citizens against Spain. Native Spaniards would have the option to retain their citizenship or to become U.S. citizens. They also agreed to allow Spanish merchandise to enter the Philippines for 10 years on the same terms as those for merchandise of the United States. The U.S. negotiations rejected Spain's request for similar commercial arrangements for Puerto Rico and Cuba, and Spain turned down the U.S. proposal to buy Kusaie.

Signed in Paris on 10 December 1898, the treaty was submitted in January to the United States Senate for approval. Since Senate passage required a two-thirds vote of its 90 members, the 50 Republican senators were insufficient to approve it. Moreover, several Republicans opposed the treaty, and eventually two voted against it. Thus, the treaty needed Democratic and Populist support.

The Senate debate lasted for one month. Senator George G. Vest, Democrat of Missouri, and Senator Arthur P. Gorman, Democrat of Maryland, took a prominent part in attempting to defeat the treaty. Vest declared that the United States Constitution did not provide the authority to govern colonies; moreover, ruling people without their consent violated the precepts of democracy. Gorman attempted to link the treaty battle to his presidential ambitions for 1900. Davis and other expansionist senators countered that it was the sovereign right of every nation to acquire territory and that the United States could do so without extending the guaranties of the United States Constitution to subject peoples.

The debate revealed that less than two-thirds of the senators favored the treaty, but several wavered in their opposition. McKinley used senators to support national unity and used patronage to obtain votes. As Republicans fell in line behind the president, Democrats remained divided. The Democratic party's leader, William Jennings Bryan, advised them to vote for the treaty in order to end the existing state of war, and then Congress could vote to give the islands independence. On the eve of the balloting, fighting broke out between Filipino and U.S. troops, but this last-minute shock apparently did little to change votes.

When on 6 February 1899 the votes were counted, the treaty passed 57 to 27, one vote more than required. The Senate then narrowly defeated a proposal for Philippine independence. The House of Representatives easily passed an appropriation of $20 million for Spain, and President McKinley ratified the treaty on 11 April 1899.

John L. Offner

REFERENCES

Paolo E. Coletta, "The Peace Negotiations and the Treaty of Paris," in Paolo E. Coletta, ed., *Threshold to American Internationalism* (Exposition Pr., 1970); Lewis L. Gould, *The Spanish-American War and President McKinley* (Univ. Pr. of Kansas, 1982); Eugenio Montero Ríos, *El Tratado de Paris* (R. Velasco, 1904); Whitelaw Reid, *Making Peace With Spain: The Diary of Whitelaw Reid, September-December, 1898*, edited by H. Wayne Morgan (Univ. of Texas Pr., 1965); David F. Trask, *The War With Spain in 1898* (Macmillan, 1981).

See also Day, William Rufus; Peace Commission (1898).

Turpie-Foraker Amendment (1898)

By early April 1898, President William McKinley had concluded that war with Spain was inevitable. He had found the Spanish response of 31 March to a recent U.S. proposal that Spain modify its policies in Cuba and, if need be, accept arbitration that would include the possibility of independence for Cuba, so "disappointing" that he had reached "the end of his effort" to resolve the Cuban problem peacefully. He continued diplomatic exchanges for another

10 days but focused his attention on securing the safety of U.S. citizens in Cuba and on preparations for war.

McKinley's opponents in Congress threatened these efforts and posed a serious challenge to his power. The opposition included Populists; Democrats; members of McKinley's own party, the Silver Republicans, who were at odds with him over domestic financial policy; and Senator Joseph B. Foraker of Ohio, a rival of the president and of the other Ohio senator, McKinley's friend Mark A. Hanna. The opponents aimed to influence the conduct of relations with Spain by immediate intervention on behalf of the Cubans and to assert congressional prerogatives against what they considered undue presidential power. In short, they aimed to take charge of the nation's foreign policy. The issue they chose was the immediate recognition of Cuban independence. This demand eventually took the form of the Turpie-Foraker Amendment. The resulting battle over the proposal was intense. Its outcome not only secured McKinley's authority but also laid the basis for the powers of the modern presidency in foreign affairs and on the issue of war.

McKinley's opponents first tried to seize the initiative in late March 1898 with a series of resolutions calling for the recognition of Cuban independence. The administration's response was that recognition was unwarranted because there was nothing to recognize. The majority of Republican members supported Speaker Thomas B. Reed's ruling against such a plan in the House of Representatives. Republican leaders also announced that the president soon would address Congress on Cuba.

McKinley delivered his message on 11 April. Historians have traditionally called it a "war message," but this is not an accurate description. After stating that he meant to help the suffering Cubans, McKinley implied that force would be used, but did not then insist on armed intervention. Setting the pattern for 20th-century presidents, he asked Congress for broad authority, including the power to do whatever was necessary to halt the fighting in Cuba and to use U.S. military forces as required. Finally, he argued vigorously and at length against recognizing Cuban independence on the ground that such a step would be premature and would limit the freedom of action of the United States.

McKinley's opponent in the election of 1896, William Jennings Bryan, urged congressional Democrats to unite on the issue of recognizing Cuban independence. They did so, and the question of immediate recognition of Cuban independence was important in the ensuing debate. The specific Cuban question became intertwined with the larger issue of who should determine foreign policy and war. The political struggle over such authority in April 1898 was the first of a series of battles during the following century—notably in the Korean, Vietnam, and Gulf wars. Its results helped establish the pattern of presidential leadership.

On 13 April Democrats in the House of Representatives introduced a resolution recognizing the independence of a republic of Cuba and directing the president "to employ immediately the land and naval forces of the United States" (Holbo, p. 1326). This resolution would have repudiated McKinley's policy and put Congress in charge. A sharp debate ensued before Republicans defeated this resolution by a largely party line vote of 190 to 150. The House then authorized by a vote of 325 to 19 to grant the authority McKinley had requested (Holbo, p. 1326):

> Resolved, that the President is hereby authorized and directed to intervene at once to stop the war in Cuba, to the end and with the purpose of securing permanent peace and order there and establishing by the free action of the people thereof a stable and independent government of their own in the island of Cuba; and the President is hereby authorized and empowered to use the land and naval forces of the United States to execute the purpose of this resolution.

Meanwhile, the Senate Foreign Relations Committee reported a stronger but still acceptable resolution, stating that "the people" of Cuba "are, and of right ought to be free and independent" (Holbo, p. 1327), demanding that Spain relinquish its authority, and directing and empowering the president to use U.S. military forces as necessary. McKinley had seen and commented on this version.

Democratic Senator David Turpie of Indiana, however, introduced a minority report, really devised by the jingoistic Foraker, stating that "the government of the United States hereby recognizes the Republic of Cuba as the true and lawful government of that island" (Holbo, p. 1328). Foraker, an expansionist, believed that the amendment would facilitate the ultimate acquisition of Cuba by the United States.

The president did not approve the Turpie-Foraker Amendment, but the Senate voted for it on 16 April by 51 to 37. Twenty-nine Democrats voted for the amendment, along with 11 Republicans (mostly jingoes) who broke ranks and 11 Populists and Silver Republicans. The minority included 32 Republicans, led by staunch supporters of McKinley and a number of conservative members who still hoped to avoid war with Spain.

During floor debate in the Senate, a clause was added disclaiming any intention by the United States "to exercise jurisdiction or control" over Cuba (the Teller Amendment) (Holbo, p. 1330). All efforts to salvage the House resolution were defeated. The president's supporters complained to no avail that an effort was underway to "take from the Executive his constitutional power" (Holbo, p. 1330). Indeed, it appeared that the House of Representatives might adopt the Senate resolution.

The two houses remained at impasse for an entire week, leaving the nation's policy toward Spain in limbo. The president and his supporters moved systematically to regain control of the situation. McKinley consulted key lieutenants in the House. Cabinet members and congressional leaders, headed by Speaker Reed, made clear that the president could not approve the Turpie-Foraker Amendment because it infringed his prerogatives in conducting foreign policy and because recognition of Cuba was unwarranted. Aided by prominent newspapers, they also warned that McKinley would veto the Senate resolution. He was prepared to do precisely that.

Republican leaders and prominent senators lobbied vigorously among the Republican representatives, especially from the crucial midwestern states. Not taking any chances, the administration also blocked further debate, added a conciliatory phrase that the people of Cuba "ought to be" free and independent, and carried the vote in the House a second time by a margin of 178 to 156.

The House vote was the turning point, but debate continued in the Senate for 14 hours. Intense lobbying and floor discussion gradually weakened the opposition, and bolting Republican senators returned to the fold. Foraker stated, "We yield for the sake of harmony." On 19 April, approaching exhaustion, the Senate passed the resolution that McKinley wanted by a vote of 42 to 35, while the concurring House vote was a ringing 311 to 6.

The final version was not a war resolution or declaration of war but rather authorized the president to use U.S. military forces to ensure that Spain relinquished its authority and government and withdrew its military forces from Cuba and vicinity. Except for the addition of the modified so-called Teller Amendment, the measure was virtually identical to the original resolution reported by the Senate Foreign Relations Committee and was approved by McKinley.

Foraker and others claimed lamely that Congress had limited the president's power in foreign affairs, but Foraker privately later expressed regret at the outcome. The president, the cabinet, and their supporters in Congress voiced satisfaction.

The outcome of the battle over the Turpie-Foraker Amendment ensured the McKinley administration that it could conduct foreign policy as it chose to do, carefully and systematically. The *New York Herald* announced correctly that the result represented the death of "the doctrine of yellow diplomacy." The longer term result was, as the Springfield *Republican* observed keenly at the time, that "presidential power significantly increased." McKinley's defeat of the Turpie-Foraker Amendment assured his leadership and made him the first modern president in the area of foreign affairs.

Paul S. Holbo

REFERENCES

Lewis L. Gould, *The Spanish-American War and President McKinley* (Univ. Pr. of Kansas, 1980, 1981); David F. Healy, *The United States in Cuba, 1898–1902: Generals, Politicians, and the Search for Policy* (Univ. of Wisconsin Pr., 1963); Paul S. Holbo, "Presidential Leadership in Foreign Affairs: William McKinley and the Turpie-Foraker Amendment," *American Historical Review*, 72 (1967), 1321–1335.

Unión Nacional Dominicana

The Unión Nacional Dominicana was formed in February 1920 by ultranationalists to protest U.S. policy at the height of the confrontation and strained relations between the military occupation authorities and the Dominican populace. It sought the immediate restoration of Dominican sovereignty, termination of the occupation, and the withdrawal of all U.S. forces from the nation. It also focused on discouraging any collaboration by Dominicans with the invaders.

The organization represented primarily the members of the middle class and the elite, who were the trained and educated members of the society. Since its members paid dues, it raised substantial funds to assist the propaganda campaign in the United States and other nations, thus increasing pressure for an end to the occupation. Internally, it promoted several protests and strikes in opposition to the occupation, in particular organizing the Semana Patriótica of May 1920. These week-long events included demonstrations in the nation's principal cities. The protests led to the arrest and trial of several individuals, in particular of journalists, thereby focusing attention on the abuses of the occupation regime and its censorship.

The Unión Nacional Dominicana continued to be effective through 1922 and strongly assisted the efforts of the Haiti-Santo Domingo Independence Society and former Provisional President Francisco Henríquez y Carvajal. The movement consisted of strong nationalists promoting a rigid and unyielding stance, which unfortunately served to alarm occupation officials and convince them of the need for harsh measures. The group was later superseded by the moderate political leaders, who recognized that withdrawal would require negotiations with the United States.

Kenneth J. Grieb

REFERENCES

Bruce J. Calder, *The Impact of Intervention: The Dominican Republic During the U.S. Occupation of 1916–1924* (Univ. of Texas Pr., 1984).

See also Public Opinion and the Intervention in the Dominican Republic.

Union Patriotique, Haiti

The Union Patriotique, a protest organization composed of upper- and middle-class urban Haitians, was founded in August 1915. This group, unlike the Haitian peasant guerrilla forces that opposed the U.S. occupation by force of arms, based its strategy on working within the guidelines of the constitution prescribed by treaty authorities. Founder Georges Sylvain, a Haitian statesman, later consulted extensively with James W. Johnson, secretary of the National Association for the Advancement of Colored People (NAACP), whom the NAACP had sent to Haiti to investigate occupation conditions. Sylvain then patterned the Union Patriotique after the NAACP as a body devoted to protest, reform, and lobbying rather than insurgency. Trepidations about U.S. racism and its potential impact on occupied Haiti as well as specifically nationalist concerns played a key role in the decision to model the new organization on a racial defense group. Other prominent members of the Union Patriotique included Pierre Hudicourt, Joseph Jolibois *fils*, Jean Price Mars, Antoine Pierre-Paul, Pauléus Sannon, Percéval Thoby, and Sténio Joseph Vincent.

The Union Patriotique peaked in influence in the early 1920s with an estimated membership of 16,000. It maintained support networks among U.S. liberals and used these to communicate information about the occupation in the United States. In 1920, the liberal journal *Nation*, for example, published a four-part series on the military protectorate. These articles, detailing abusive and peremptory behavior on the part of U.S. authorities, sparked a United States Senate investigation of the treaty regime. The committee, chaired by Republican Senator Joseph Medill McCormick, met from August 1921 to June 1922.

The organization sent delegates to Washington in 1921 to petition the president of the United States and Congress. Representatives appealed for withdrawal of U.S. troops, termination of martial law, and the revival of the Haitian legislature, armed forces, and police, all of which had been indefinitely suspended by U.S. military authorities, and abrogation of the 1915 Haitian-U.S. convention. When the Senate committee investigating the occupation opened hearings in Port-au-Prince on 30 November 1921, Union Patriotique representatives testified against treaty regime policies and practices.

Its emphasis on protest rather than insurgency, combined with curbs on civil liberties imposed by occupation authorities, limited the effectiveness of the Union Patriotique. It survived the death of its founder in 1925 and continued to the end of the occupation. The organization served to some extent as a political club uniting Haitian nationalists during and after the phased withdrawal of U.S. authority beginning in 1930. It also supplied some of the first postoccupation national leadership.

Brenda Gayle Plummer

REFERENCES

Amsterdam News, 19 Jan. 1930; James Weldon Johnson, *Along This Way: The Autobiography of James Weldon Johnson* (Knopf, 1933); Hans Schmidt, *The United States Occupation of Haiti, 1915–1934* (Rutgers Univ. Pr., 1971); Georges Sylvain, *Dix années du lutte pour la liberté: 1915–25* (H. Deschamps, 1925).

See also Public Opinion and the Haiti Occupation.

United States Volunteers in the Cuban Revolt (1895–1898)

The Cuban Junta had little success recruiting native-born U.S. citizens for service with the Cuban army during the Cuban War of Independence, 1895–1898. Hundreds of Cuban-born, naturalized U.S. citizens returned to their home island to support the uprising, and contemporary U.S. newspapers gave the impression that scores of Anglos also flocked to join the revolution. The actual number was around 30.

Of varied backgrounds, most of the *expedicionarios* appear to have come from the East and Midwest. The best-known were college educated and belonged to middle- and upper-class families. One, Winchester Dana Osgood, had been a star football player at Cornell University and the University of Pennsylvania. Three were medical doctors. Stewart S. Janney and Osmun Latrobe, Jr. were wealthy society men from Baltimore. Frederick Funston, the most famous volunteer and later a hero in the Philippine War, was the son of a Kansas congressman.

Idealistic sympathy for the cause of Cuban independence motivated the volunteers. Funston compared the group to Baron Frederick von Steuben and the Marquis de Lafayette, liberal European aristocrats who fought with the revolutionaries in the American Revolutionary War. Funston was also inspired by Rudyard Kipling's theme of caucasian military glory in tropical climes. Stories in the *New York Times* indicate that people in the United States generally regarded the men as heroes and that the U.S. government did little to stop them from going to Cuba.

The volunteers were smuggled onto the island individually and in small groups. Upon arrival, nearly all seem to have been commissioned as officers. Their assignments varied but most served in artillery under Gen. Máximo Gómez y Báez and Calixto García. Since few Cubans had artillery experience, U.S. personnel proved valuable, especially in battles at Victoria de las Tunas and Guáimaro.

Unlike many other white U.S. citizens, the volunteers came to admire Cuban bravery and guerrilla prowess. Funston suggests in his memoirs, however, that by late 1897, though still supported by the *expedicionarios*, the war had lost its luster. The U.S. volunteers shared severe hardships—inadequate medical care, poor diet, shoddy clothing and equipment, and tropical disease—with their Cuban comrades. The Spanish captured a few, imprisoned them briefly, then expelled them to the United States. At least four, including Osgood, were killed in action. Several sustained serious wounds; Funston was wounded three times, once almost fatally. Also suffering from malaria and typhoid, he returned to the United States in early 1898 weighing less than 100 pounds.

It is uncertain if any volunteers remained with the Cuban revolutionaries after U.S. military intervention in April 1898. Five eventually joined the U.S. armed forces. Two *expedicionarios*, Walter M. Jones and Arthur Potter, resided in Cuba after the Spanish-Cuban/American War ended.

Jeffery C. Livingston

REFERENCES

Thomas W. Crouch, *A Yankee Guerrillero: Frederick Funston and the Cuban Insurrection, 1896–1897* (Memphis State Univ. Pr., 1975); Emory W. Fenn, "Ten Months With the Cuban Insurgents," *Century Magazine* 56 (1898), 302–307; Frederick Funston, *Memories of Two Wars: Cuban and Philippine Experiences* (Scribner, 1914); *New York Times*, 16, 21 May 1898; Horatio S. Rubens, *Liberty: The Story of Cuba* (Brewer, Warren, & Putnam, 1932; rpt. ed., AMS Pr., 1970), 303–305.

United States Volunteers in the Spanish-Cuban/American War and the Philippine War (1898–1902)

During the Spanish-Cuban/American War, 1898–1901 and the Philippine War the regular establishment of the United States Army was reinforced by two separate groups of volunteers. In spring 1898, 200,000 men in 140 state-sponsored regiments were mobilized for the war with Spain. During summer 1899, 35,000 recruits enlisted in 25 federally organized regiments for pacification duty in the Philippines. Although the war in the Caribbean was fought mainly with regular regiments, 47,000 volunteers served in the Philippines between July 1898 and June 1901, fighting during the conventional and guerrilla phases of the Philippine War.

In April 1898, the regular army contained 25 infantry, 10 cavalry, and 7 artillery regiments: too small a force to both guard the Atlantic Coast and operate against Cuba and Puerto Rico. President William McKinley endorsed a plan that would have called on the regulars to absorb 60,000 "federal volunteers" for offensive operations while mobilizing smaller numbers of state national guardsmen for costal defense. That plan was defeated in Congress by guard supporters who demanded a larger offensive role for state troops. In a subsequent compromise McKinley called for 200,000 state volunteers, a number designed to accept all prewar guardsmen willing to enlist.

In August 1898, at the peak of the mobilization, 216,000 volunteers were on the rolls, including 16,500 in 15 federal volunteer units. Ten of these were "immune" regiments, containing men believed to be resistant to tropical diseases. Four immune units, the 7th through 10th Infantry Regiments, were black regiments, and several thousand additional black volunteers served in state regiments from Alabama, Illinois, Massachusetts, North Carolina, Ohio, and Virginia.

In addition to Theodore Roosevelt's "Rough Riders" (the 1st United States Volunteer Cavalry), at least four volunteer regiments fought in the Santiago campaign: the 71st New York, 2nd Massachusetts, and the 33rd and 34th Michigan Infantries. A number of state regiments served in Puerto Rico, and 30 garrisoned Cuba until June 1899, in company with most of the immune regiments. However, the entire force of

216,000 was far too large to employ usefully in the Caribbean, and over two-thirds of the state volunteers were discharged directly from their training camps in the southern United States, where their deaths from disease far exceeded the combined combat casualties of the regular and volunteer forces in Cuba and Puerto Rico.

Spanish-Cuban/American War volunteers also served in the Far East. On 4 May 1898, President McKinley ordered the occupation of key points in the Philippines following Commodore George Dewey's destruction of Spain's Asiatic Fleet in the naval battle at Manila. However, nearly all of the regular army's infantry regiments were being concentrated in Gulf Coast ports for operations in the Caribbean. The Philippine Expedition was thus built around 15 state regiments mobilized at the Presidio of San Francisco; the last of these regiments reached Manila by November 1898.

Ostensibly sent to the Philippines to fight the forces of a European colonial power, these volunteers soon found themselves squared off against the anticolonial army of the newly declared Filipino republic. In August 1898 U.S. forces occupied the Spanish citadel in Manila after negotiating surrender terms with its garrison that barred Filipinos from any immediate role in the city's occupation or civil administration.

While the Filipino army remained in its siege works around Manila, its leaders asked the United States to recognize Philippine independence. McKinley had decided to annex the islands, however, and in December 1898 Spain ceded them to the United States under the terms of the Treaty of Paris. When word of the treaty reached the islands, relations between Filipino and U.S. troops rapidly deteriorated. Fighting broke out in Manila on 4 February 1899 and continued over the next 11 months, with the state regiments taking a leading role in the initial campaign between February and June of that year.

In a second field campaign in November 1899 the conventionally organized Filipino army was thoroughly defeated, causing its leadership to fall back on a guerrilla strategy to resist further the U.S. occupation. That challenge required both a new U.S. approach to pacification and a new force to implement it. The state volunteers' enlistments had technically expired in February 1899 with the Senate's ratification of the Treaty

of Paris, and fewer than 1,400 were willing to stay on in the islands. The state regiments were thus returned to the United States in the order they had arrived, their men having served longer than any other Spanish-Cuban/American War volunteers. The 15 state regiments that served in the Philippines were the 1st California, 1st Colorado, 1st Idaho, 51st Iowa, 20th Kansas, 13th Minnesota, 1st Montana, 1st Nebraska, 1st North Dakota, 2nd Oregon, 10th Pennsylvania, 1st South Dakota, 1st Tennessee, 1st Washington, and 1st Wyoming Infantries. California, Utah, and Wyoming also provided artillery batteries, and Nevada sent a cavalry troop.

On 2 March 1899 Congress acted to create a pacification force for the Philippines. Although the army had requested a minimum strength of 100,000 to meet its commitments in both hemispheres, strong elements in Congress opposed any permanent expansion of the regular establishment. After a political compromise was reached between the Republican administration and its Democratic opposition, the regulars were allowed an increase to 65,000 officers and enlisted men, and a second force of 35,000 two-year volunteers was authorized specifically for Philippine service: the United States Volunteers (USVs). The War Department, not the states, organized these troops, which had important consequences both for their composition and their performance in the field.

Throughout the 19th century, there was general agreement throughout the United States that the regular army should be kept as small as possible, both for reasons of economy and because many citizens feared that a large professional military would threaten democratic political institutions. There was less agreement, however, on the best method of reinforcing a small regular army in time of war. Supporters of the "militia tradition," including the National Guard Association and several influential Civil War veterans in Congress, advocated the guard as an appropriately democratic national reserve force. They argued that in any future war the various states should be called on to provide not untrained individual recruits, but fully organized guard regiments led by their peacetime officers.

The regular army, however, had studied the universal conscription armies then being formed in Europe and concluded that the most efficient solution would be an "expansible army" of regular regiments maintained at two-thirds strength during peacetime. Additional personnel would be carried on the strength of each regiment to quickly train "federal volunteers" for its third battalion within weeks of a declaration of war. An additional pool of reserve junior officers could be trained in leadership programs at land-grant colleges supervised by regular army officers.

At issue in this debate were two sensitive political questions. Should the National Guard, the nation's locally controlled militia, be superseded by another reserve force for use outside the United States? If so, who would control the appointment of officers in this force, the president or the state governors? The legislation that created the Volunteer Army of 1898 was a defeat for the regular army and a victory for the advocates of the militia tradition of decentralized military institutions. The act that created the USVs, however, provided for a temporary armed force that closely resembled the regulars' preference for a national reserve.

In the broadest sense, both volunteer forces, the state troops and the USVs, were drawn from the same population: native and foreign-born working- and middle-class men; a majority of them were between the ages of 21 and 25. However, while the state volunteer had typically served in a National Guard company drawn from a single locality, the USVs were recruited from larger multistate areas, a clear departure from the community-based recruiting of the Civil and Spanish-Cuban/American wars.

The training given National Guard units in different states had varied widely during the 1890s. Most guard regiments were understrength before the outbreak of war in 1898, and in several states large numbers of guardsmen declined to enter federal service. Thus, several hundred new recruits without previous military training were needed to bring many state regiments up to full strength. This meant that the regiments would perform quite unevenly in combat. While most of the western state regiments fought well in the Philippines, at least one eastern unit in Cuba disintegrated when first fired on. In contrast, USV units were trained to a standard that equaled or exceeded contemporary regular regiments, which had been depleted by combat and disease losses during the Santiago campaign and were as a consequence full of raw recruits and seriously understrength in company-grade officers. Roughly 65 percent of the USV enlisted force had served in the Volunteer Army of 1898,

where they had already learned the rudiments of close and extended order infantry drill, route marching, rifle marksmanship, and field sanitation. This enabled them to quickly learn more difficult small-unit patrolling skills in the Philippines.

As part of the legislative compromise that created the first volunteer force, the regular army conceded officer selection to state governors, who usually confirmed their peacetime National Guard appointments. However, many higher ranking National Guard officers had been promoted more for their links to the political party occupying the statehouse rather than for purely military considerations. Many guard companies elected their captains and lieutenants, a practice the regulars were certain destroyed discipline. A few state regimental commanders, such as Frederick Funston and John M. Stotsenburg, were very aggressive leaders, but others, older and less active, failed to display a high level of physical stamina and professional competence.

In 1899, satisfied by its recent participation in the Spanish-Cuban/American War, the guard lobby showed little interest in the formation of the USVs. This freed the War Department from political considerations in selecting its regimental and company officers. Each USV regiment contained five field-grade officers: one colonel, one lieutenant colonel, and majors to command three four-company battalions. Almost without exception these were relatively junior regular officers, majors, captains, and lieutenants, temporarily holding higher ranking volunteer commissions. The company officers also had recent experience as ex-state volunteers who had met rigorous selection board criteria or as regular enlisted men rewarded for outstanding service during the Cuban campaign.

A four-month delay in the formation of the USVs was caused by overly optimistic reporting from the army's commander in the Philippines, Maj. Gen. Elwell S. Otis, who had believed his existing force of state troops and regulars could end Filipino resistance by mid-1899. However, he seriously underestimated the Philippine Revolution's popular support and ability to organize continued guerrilla resistance in the countryside. By September 1899, when the situation had clarified, President McKinley authorized the formation of one cavalry and 24 infantry regiments to be numbered in sequence with existing regular army formations.

The first 20 regiments formed in the United States were authorized in two groups of 10 on 5 July and 10 August 1899. The 26th through 35th Infantry Regiments were recruited, trained, and deployed to the Philippines between 10 July and 28 November 1899, and the 38th through 47th Infantry Regiments between 24 August 1899 and 25 January 1900. Two regiments, the 48th and 49th, were black units in which black soldiers and company-grade officers served under white battalion and regimental commanders, marking the army's first systematic use of black officers. Three additional regiments, the 36th and 37th Infantry Regiments and the 11th Cavalry, were raised in the Philippines around a core of ex-state volunteers supplemented by recruits from the United States.

Four USV infantry regiments—the 33rd, 34th, 36th, and 37th—took part in the final conventional campaign of 1899. The remaining regiments were in place by the time the guerrilla war had begun in earnest. Because no more large-scale field campaigns were anticipated, the army in the Philippines had been restructured from a tactical brigade organization into four geographical departments containing 18 pacification districts, many of which would be commanded by USV regimental commanders. Where possible, each regiment was garrisoned in a single district, with its battalions and companies divided among smaller subdistricts and "circuits" of posts. Serving for long periods of time in specific local areas, the USVs began a slow but cumulative process of building intelligence networks and training themselves to carry out long-distance reconnaissance patrols and raids, which they generally called "hikes," against *cuartels* (guerrilla base-camps).

In May 1900 Maj. Gen. Arthur MacArthur replaced Otis as military governor of the Philippines. MacArthur had an intuitive understanding of guerrilla war and was able to achieve the pacification of most of the archipelago during his 14-month tenure, and the USVs were his first-line troops. In October 1900, five of his USV regiments were stationed outside Luzon: one each on the central islands of Leyte, Cebu, and Panay in the Department of the Visayas; and two in the far south of the archipelago in the Department of Mindanao and Jolo. The remaining 20 were divided between Northern and Southern Luzon. Because their enlistments were to expire by law on 1 July 1901, the USVs were

relieved after the dry weather campaign season of 1900–1901 by regiments of the expanded 100,000-man regular army congress had authorized in February of that year.

Between June 1898 and June 1901, 108,800 officers and enlisted men served in the Philippines: 60,933 regulars, 11,138 state volunteers, and 36,729 USVs. However, many regulars did not arrive on the islands until 1901, and throughout 1899 and 1900 a majority of regular regiments in the Philippines were either assigned to the provost guard of Manila or were stationed in central Luzon. The USVs were thus a majority of the army's field force during the first year of the guerrilla war in the archipelago's most difficult areas: northwestern and southeastern Luzon, the Bicol "hemp provinces," the Visayan Islands of Leyte and Samar, and northern Mindanao.

The USVs lost 315 officers and enlisted men killed in action or died of wounds: nine-tenths of one percent of the total force. One thousand thirty-six died of disease and 27 were lost to a combination of suicides, accidents, drownings, and "assassinations," for a total of 1,078 deaths, or 3.8 percent of the 25 regiments' total personnel. The state volunteers suffered a larger proportion of combat deaths in the higher-intensity campaigns of 1899: 230, or 2.1 percent of their strength.

Individual U.S. Volunteers made contributions to the army long after their regiments were disbanded. A substantial number of enlisted men joined the regulars and served as late as World War I. One such soldier was Samuel H. Cornew, originally a state volunteer in a California volunteer artillery battery who later enlisted in the 36th Regiment. In October 1918, he earned the Silver Star for gallantry in the Meuse-Argonne Campaign while serving in the 1st Division's 28th Infantry Regiment. Approximately a third of the USV's first and second lieutenants were commissioned in the regular army after passing competitive examinations given in 1901.

USV regiments were a training ground for several of the army's most successful World War I combat leaders. A number of former USV battalion and regimental commanders served in critical positions in the American Expeditionary Force of 1917–1918. Robert L. Bullard, colonel of the 39th Regiment, led the 1st Division, the 3rd Corps, and finally the 2nd Army in the 1918 offensives. Henry T. Allen, a major in the 43rd USVs, commanded the 90th Division and later the VIII Corps, while Peyton C. March, a major in the 33rd Regiment, served as the American Expeditionary Forces' chief of artillery.

The United States fought its next two wars with forces much larger than the 250,000 volunteers it mobilized for the Spanish-Cuban/American and Philippine wars. However, the army's ability to mobilize millions of draftees and select competent nonprofessional officers to lead them during 1917–1918 and 1941–1945 was due in no small measure to the institutional and individual experience it had gained between 1898 and 1901 with the state and federal volunteers. Equally important, however less well-remembered, was the central role the USVs had played in the U.S. war in Asia. Largely forgotten by both soldiers and scholars until after the failed counterinsurgency campaigns of the 1960s, the war in the Philippines and the men who fought it are now beginning to receive a much closer examination.

John Scott Reed

REFERENCES

Graham A. Cosmas, *An Army for Empire: The United States Army in the Spanish-American War* (Univ. of Missouri Pr., 1971); Brian McAllister Linn, *The U.S. Army and Counterinsurgency in the Philippine War, 1899–1902* (Univ. of North Carolina Pr., 1989); Clarence Linninger, *The Best War at the Time* (Robert Speller, 1964); Allan R. Millett, *The General: Robert L. Bullard and Officership in the United States Army, 1881–1925* (Greenwood Pr., 1975); William T. Sexton, *Soldiers in the Sun: An Adventure in Imperialism* (Military Service Pub. Co., 1939).

See also Black Volunteer Troops in the Spanish-Cuban/American War and the Philippine War (1898–1902).

Utley, Harold Hickox (1885–1951)

Harold Hickox Utley played a major role in the United States Marine Corps's development of the *Small Wars Manual*. His experience in the field consisted of duty with the Cuban occupation force in 1908, service in Haiti during 1915–1917 and 1919–1921, and participation in the Nicaraguan campaign in 1928–1929. Upon his return from Nicaragua, he was assigned to the Field Officers Course at Quantico, Virginia, as an instructor and later as director.

At Quantico, Major Utley began a private effort to codify the doctrine and historical lessons of minor conflicts. He sent letters to marine officers who had participated in campaigns of this nature and asked them for accounts of their experiences. He conducted extensive research into existing works and adopted the commonly used term "small wars" from these earlier efforts.

Utley published the first three chapters of his "Tactics and Techniques of Small Wars" in issues of the *Marine Corps Gazette* (the Corps's professional journal) beginning in May 1931. His endeavor attracted the attention of senior officers, including the new commander of marine schools, Brig. Gen. Randolph C. Berkeley. This interest eventually led to official sanctioning of the project and to the publication of *Small Wars Operations* in 1935.

This initial version bore the marks of Utley's handiwork. There is the same heavy reliance on historical examples found in "Tactics and Techniques," and several of the situations described were drawn directly from Utley's personal experiences. However, Utley was not the sole author of the final version because he had been transferred from Quantico in June 1933.

There is much evidence to suggest that Utley acquired many of his ideas about small wars from Capt. Merritt A. Edson, one of his Nicaraguan subordinates. The major had little experience at the tactical level because his rank kept him far from the action in both Haiti and Nicaragua. As commander of the Eastern Area in the latter campaign, Utley maintained a voluminous personal correspondence on operational matters with the aggressive captain who conducted most of all combat actions in his domain. During his tour at Quantico, Utley continued to communicate with Edson on the small wars project and even submitted parts of his manuscript for Edson's review.

Jon T. Hoffman

REFERENCES

Jon T. Hoffman, "Back to the Future," *Marine Corps Gazette*, 75 (1991), 32–34; Jon T. Hoffman, "Yesterday's Doctrine," to be published in the *Marine Corps Gazette*; Harold H. Utley, "An Introduction to the Tactics and Techniques of Small Wars," *Marine Corps Gazette*, part 1, 16 (May 1931), 50–53; part 2, 18 (Aug. 1933), 44–48; part 3, 18 (Nov. 1933), 43–46.

Vaga River Front, North Russia (1918–1919)

The Vaga River Front represented the southernmost line of advance of the forces that took part in U.S. intervention in North Russia, 1918–1919. Established along the course of the Vaga River, which flows directly northward into the Northern Dvina River some 150 miles above its confluence with the White Sea, the front was originally created in an effort to outflank the retreating Bolsheviks on the Northern Dvina River Front, but later became vital to the security of the Allied right flank on the river. In addition, the Vaga Front also played an important role in establishing closer contact with the left flank of the Vologda Railroad Front, some 75 miles to the west.

The Vaga River Front was originated on 15 September 1918 when a mixed Allied force including Company A of the 339th United States Infantry, an element of the American Expeditionary Force, North Russia, together with several units of anti-Bolshevik Russians, was sent some 50 miles upriver to Shenkursk, then the second largest city in North Russia. After its arrival on 17 September, this force was soon joined by Company C of the 339th, a platoon of the 310th Engineers, a battery of Canadian field artillery, and a British command staff which quickly established Shenkursk as Allied headquarters on the Vaga. For its part, Company A, together with a small unit of Russian auxiliaries, soon resumed its progress upstream and, by early October, reached Ust' Puya, more than 220 miles upriver from Archangel at the farthest point of advance ever attained by any Allied force in the North. At that juncture, having encountered some desultory resistance, U.S. troops and their Allies withdrew some 15 miles downriver to a small cluster of villages called collectively Ust' Padenga, where a defensive line was established well in advance of that of any other Allied position in North Russia.

After a quiet November, signs of increased enemy activity in the area began to multiply and, in December, several Allied attacks, including two mounted by U.S. forces, were repulsed at Kodema, 30 miles east of Shenkursk. Beginning in mid-January 1919, the Bolsheviks suddenly launched a massive assault in the area with the objective of eliminating the entire Vaga Front. This attack, the first of a series of Soviet counteroffensives during winter 1918–1919, began on 19 January and struck initially at Ust' Padenga, where the roughly 200 men of Company A and its Allies were suddenly set upon by an attacking force of over 1,300 Bolsheviks. Suffering heavy casualties (the foremost platoon of Company A lost 40 of its complement of 47 men), the Allies fought valiantly but after four days were finally compelled to fall back on Shenkursk, 15 miles to the rear. At once, however, heavily outnumbered and invested from three directions, the Allied garrison at Shenkursk had also to evacuate, this time under cover of darkness. Arriving at Shegovary, some 25 miles downriver, the Allies found the position untenable owing to recent attacks by Soviet partisans. On 26 January, they finally consolidated a new defensive line at Vystavka, a full 50 miles to the rear of their original line at Ust' Padenga.

During February, as a part of their continuing effort to eradicate the Vaga Front, the Bolsheviks subjected Vystavka and its neighboring villages, which were garrisoned by a mixed force of U.S., Canadian, Russian, and other troops, to heavy bombardment. Following this action, a number of enemy assaults in early March forced a further Allied withdrawal to Kitsa, another five miles downstream. At this point the Bolsheviks abruptly broke off their Vaga offensive apparently in order to consolidate their forces for a new attack on the Vologda Railroad Front. Beginning in mid-April, U.S. troops were gradually withdrawn from the Vaga which, by early June, was fully in the hands of newly arrived British reinforcements. Although the Vaga Front existed until the last days of the anti-Bolshevik North in early 1920, it never again achieved a point of penetration even close to that of the original U.S. advance of October 1918.

John W. Long

REFERENCES

E.M. Halliday, *The Ignorant Armies: The Anglo-American Archangel Expedition, 1918–1919* (Harper, 1958); Joel Moore, Harry Mead, and Lewis Jahns, *The History of the American Expedition Fighting the Bolsheviki* (Polar Bear, 1920); Gordon W. Smith, "Waging War in 'Frozen Hell,'" *Current History*, 32 (1930), 69–70; Daniel H. Steele, "Bushwhacking Before Kitza," *American Legion Weekly* 4 (11 Aug. 1922), 7, 28–29; Daniel H. Steele, "The Defense of Ust Padenga," *American Legion Weekly* 4 (20 Oct. 1922), 7–8, 24–25; Daniel H. Steele, "The Evacuation of Shenkursk, *American Legion Weekly* 5 (30 Nov. 1923), 11–12, 24; Dorothea York, *The Romance of Company "A"* (McIntyre Printing Co., 1923).

The Vatican and the Spanish-Cuban/American War

The prospect of war between the United States and Spain in spring 1898 alarmed the Vatican. Averse to any recourse to arms, Pope Leo XIII and his secretary of state, Cardinal Mariano Rampolla, were especially concerned that a disastrous conflict would undermine the domestic stability of Catholic, monarchical Spain. The failure of the powers to respond to Madrid's appeal for diplomatic support forced the Vatican to act.

On 27 March Cardinal Rampolla instructed John Ireland, the archbishop of St. Paul and a prelate with contacts at the highest levels of the administration of U.S. President William McKinley, to go to Washington to work for a peaceful resolution of the dispute. Ireland reached the capital after Madrid had returned an unsatisfactory reply to McKinley's demand for an immediate cessation of hostilities in Cuba, as well as for negotiations, under U.S. auspices, between the Spanish authorities and the revolutionaries. In his first meeting with Ireland the president repeated these terms but impressed the archbishop with his commitment to peace. Ireland informed the Vatican that, while the war party in Congress was strong, McKinley desired peace but needed "help to attain it." An armistice would help the president reduce tensions.

For reasons of national honor Spain was reluctant to request an armistice, but reports from Madrid indicated that the queen regent, María Christina, would accept a request from the pope. On 3 April Pope Leo asked María Christina to grant an armistice. The Spanish government promptly announced that it would suspend hostilities to satisfy the Holy Father, who had been acting at the urgent petition of the U.S. president. This announcement caused great consternation in Washington, especially in the White House where McKinley, furious at the suggestion that he had approached the pope as a humble petitioner, denied that he had sought papal mediation. The president's reaction, in turn, caused Madrid to reconsider its decision.

The armistice had fallen victim to a misunderstanding. Before the pope's appeal to the queen, Cardinal Rampolla had discussed the armistice with the Spanish ambassador to the Vatican. The cardinal had noted Ireland's report that McKinley desired peace but needed help. The ambassador understood the cardinal to say that the president had solicited the assistance of the pope when in fact the president had apparently meant that a concession from Spain would be helpful. In Madrid, authorities concluded from their ambassador's report that McKinley had requested papal mediation.

Despite the imbroglio, the Vatican continued to seek an armistice as the best hope for a peaceful settlement. The queen informed the pope that her cabinet would suspend hostilities if the United States withdrew its naval units from Cuban waters. Believing that mutual concessions would ease the political difficulties of the "peace parties" in both countries, Rampolla urged Ireland to seek the removal of the U.S. fleet. When Ireland (who was engaged in a frenetic round of meetings with U.S. officials, the representatives of the Great Powers, and the Spanish minister, whom he alternately cajoled and threatened) reported that McKinley would not withdraw the fleet for fear of irritating Congress, Rampolla instructed him to settle for assurances that the ships would be recalled after the proclamation of an armistice. With Spain the cardinal secretary of state forcefully reiterated the importance of an immediate armistice to defuse the crisis, and he enlisted the aid of other powers, in particular France, in support of the Vatican.

Spain's proclamation of an armistice on 9 April seemed to vindicate the Vatican's efforts. Ireland reported that the news made an excellent impression in Washington and that peace was assured. The subsequent descent into war, thus, came as no little disappointment for the Vatican, which had been led by Ireland to believe that an armistice would help McKinley overcome the war fever in Congress and the nation. In fact, the armistice which had been the centerpiece of papal diplomacy had no impact on a president reluctant to lead and a Congress eager to fight.

David Alvarez

REFERENCES

Luigi Bruti Liberati, *La Santa Sede e le origini dell'impero americano: la guerra del 1898* (Edizione UNICOPLI, 1984); Marvin R. O'Connell, *John Ireland and the American Catholic Church* (Minnesota Historical Society, 1988); John Offner, "Washington Mission: Archbishop Ireland on the Eve of the Spanish-American War," *Catholic Historical Review*, 73 (1987), 562–575.

Veracruz, Mexico, Battle (1914)

The Battle of Veracruz, Mexico, followed the Tampico incident, in which some U.S. naval personnel were temporarily arrested, and the resulting diplomatic impasse. U.S. troops landed at Veracruz in April 1914, resulting in a limited and confused clash and the subsequent occupation. The administration of President Woodrow Wilson and the regime of Gen. Victoriano Huerta had been at odds almost from the moment the two men assumed office early in 1913, with the United States refusing diplomatic recognition and seeking to oust Huerta by methods short of military action. Mexico was torn by a civil war which was part of the great Mexican Revolution, with forces led by Gen. Venustiano Carranza challenging the Huerta government as heirs of the ousted regime of Francisco I. Madero and charging Huerta with responsibility for the assassination of the former president, whom Huerta overthrew in the coup. While the government remained in control of the central heartland of the nation, including the capital and Veracruz and Tampico, the principal ports, rebels gradually gained the ascendancy in the North. Both the revolutionaries and the government devoted considerable efforts to securing arms and ammunition supplies, hoping to gain the ascendancy on the battlefield.

The Wilson administration seized a minor incident at Tampico, along with several other minor annoyances, as a pretext for a limited intervention through seizing the nation's principal port, Veracruz, an ill- and hastily conceived action designed to prevent the landing of a shipment of arms consigned to the Huerta government. In the process, the incident at Tampico, which furnished the pretext, was all but forgotten.

While all observers expected Tampico to be the focus of any U.S. military action, Wilson ordered the seizure of Veracruz when he learned of the impending arrival in Veracruz of the German vessel *Ypiranga*, which was due to arrive on 21 April carrying machine guns and ammunition. Despite possessing only limited forces and with only a few hours warning, Rear Adm. Frank F. Fletcher planned and launched a landing. The instructions called for seizing only the customs house and dock, where three trains awaited the landing of the arms. Civilians in Washington assumed that only the harbor need be seized and that no resistance would be offered, ignoring the difficulty of such an action in the midst of a city and naively assuming that the Mexicans would welcome U.S. forces as liberators from the dictatorship of Huerta. In this they were sadly mistaken, misjudging the Mexican nationalistic and patriotic reaction to what Huerta dubbed "The Second North American Invasion."

U.S. naval forces came ashore at 11:20 a.m. on 21 April 1914, with the initial landing party consisting only of 787 men, principally the 502 marines stationed on the warships and a company of bluejackets. Only the gunboat *Prairie* was inside the breakwater because the other two ships at Fletcher's disposal, the battleships *Utah* and *Florida*, were too large to enter the harbor and were anchored in the gulf nearby. This situation greatly complicated the landing. The initial landing parties came ashore by small boat, under the command of Capt. William R. Rush of the *Florida*. The limited force and its poor tactics would have made the landing difficult if U.S. forces had encountered organized resistance at the waterfront. The Mexican commander, Gen. Gustavo Maass, had only 1,000 troops in two regiments at his disposal because the garrison had been thinned to provide reinforcements at the northern front and in besieged Tampico. Maass rejected the pledge by U.S. Consul William W. Canada that U.S. forces would occupy only the port area, stating that his orders did not allow him to surrender the national territory. He rushed to prepare defenses despite his surprise and the fact that the landing parties were already embarked in small boats at the time of his conversation with the consul. Maass sent only small units to the port to offer token resistance, while positioning most of his troops in more secure defensive positions within the city.

U.S. forces landed and occupied the docks and the adjoining facilities, such as the railroad terminal and cable station, without incident, although they failed to capture the trains awaiting the arms shipment, which fled inland when the landing began. As the troops moved toward the customs house they were fired on at 11:57 a.m. by a small unit of Mexican troops and civilians numbering about 100, who had rushed to the harbor to resist the landing. Mexican resistance was limited because General Maass was ordered to withdraw his troops a few miles inland, and hence never fully committed the main body of his troops. After initial resistance by a small part of a Mexican army regiment, skirmishing resulted

from unorganized sniper fire from small detachments of troops, and in particular from civilians and prisoners armed by the general. Organized opposition by the main Mexican garrison would have produced higher casualties because U.S. personnel came ashore in disarray and moved in large bodies in rank order, offering excellent targets. The invaders overreacted to the resistance, firing wildly and in some cases at each other. The confusion, inexperience, and lack of discipline resulted in extensive Mexican civilian casualties. U.S. forces suffered four killed and 20 wounded during the initial day's combat, during which they secured the original limited objectives in the port area.

Once combat began, the seizure of the entire city became necessary, in spite of the original limited objectives. Late that evening and during the night the *San Francisco* and *Chester* arrived from Tampico. Throughout the night the ships of the Atlantic Fleet, under the command of Vice Adm. Charles J. Badger, which President Wilson had earlier sent to Mexican waters, entered the harbor. Arriving singly as they rushed to reach the port at top speed, each landed the ship's company of marines and hastily formed detachments of bluejackets from the ships crews. By the early morning the transport *Hancock* arrived from Tampico with a detachment of 1,000 marines commanded by Col. John A. Lejeune. Admiral Fletcher remained in charge of the landing throughout the combat.

By the morning of 22 April, the U.S. force ashore had reached 3,000 men. Because virtually all Mexican officials had fled the port, there was no one with authority to order an end to the fighting. U.S. units fanned out into the city in the early morning, proceeding house-to-house to search for snipers. While these tactics proved effective, reflecting the presence of marines with experience in combat in the Philippines, they also enraged the local populace due to the violations of homes which proved necessary. Resistance by a handful of cadets at the naval school resulted in shelling and destruction of the buildings by the guns of the warships.

By 11:00 a.m. on 22 April Veracruz was completely in U.S. hands. U.S. forces had suffered 19 dead and 47 wounded. While Mexican casualties could not be accurately determined, due to the burning of bodies, at least 200 died defending the city; the casualties were overwhelmingly civilian.

Because U.S. forces made no effort to proceed inland from the port, except for securing the water pumping station, they never engaged the main Mexican forces, which had withdrawn to Tejeria, 10 miles inland, to establish a defensive line in the mountain passes.

Eventually, an army infantry brigade under the command of Gen. Frederick Funston was ordered to Veracruz to replace the original landing parties, arriving on 27 April.

Kenneth J. Grieb

REFERENCES

Kenneth J. Grieb, *The United States and Huerta* (Univ. of Nebraska Pr., 1969); Robert E. Quirk, *An Affair of Honor: Woodrow Wilson and the Occupation of Veracruz* (Univ. of Kentucky Pr., 1962).

See also Huerta, Victoriano; Tampico Incident (1914); Veracruz, Mexico, Occupation (1914).

Veracruz, Mexico, Occupation (1914)

The U.S. occupation of Veracruz, Mexico, lasted seven months, from the landing of troops on 21 April 1914 through 23 November 1914. The landing was launched without advance planning, and the occupation evolved haphazardly.

Veracruz was placed under military administration, with Gen. Frederick Funston, commander of the United States Army's 5th Brigade, assuming control. Amid friction between the navy and the army, the marines from the original landing force were detached from the fleet and placed under Funston's command. The occupation force numbered 7,150 troops. Local officials refused to cooperate because Mexican laws, reflecting past foreign interventions, provided severe penalties to anyone cooperating with or accepting employment with a foreign occupation force. Consequently, virtually all administrative services were carried out by U.S. military personnel. Even justice was administered through military provost courts.

Although the United States decided to withdraw during September, after the collapse of the regime of Gen. Victoriano Huerta which the administration of President Woodrow Wilson had opposed, considerable time was consumed making appropriate arrangements due to the refusal of revolutionary leader Gen. Venustiano Carranza to negotiate with the occupiers. Despite Wilson's sympathy for Carranza, the Mexican revolutionary leader invoked patriotism and condemned the landing just as Huerta had done. Carranza refused to provide any guarantees for local citizens who had paid taxes to or done business with the occupation authorities. At length, while still refusing to negotiate, Carranza proclaimed a general amnesty for any residents of Veracruz involved in the administration of the occupation.

U.S. troops withdrew from Veracruz on 9 November 1914 and the city immediately became the headquarters of Carranza, at this time engaged in a conflict with his former allies after the revolutionaries split. The fact that the United States turned the port over to Carranza proved to be a key factor in his ultimate triumph.

Kenneth J. Grieb

REFERENCES

Kenneth J. Grieb, *The United States and Huerta* (Univ. of Nebraska Pr., 1969); Robert E. Quirk, *An Affair of Honor: Woodrow Wilson and the Occupation of Veracruz* (Univ. of Kentucky Pr., 1962); Berta Ulloa, *La Revolución intervenida: Relaciones diplomáticas entre México y Estados Unidos* (El Colegio de Mexico, 1971).

See also Civic Action at Veracruz, Mexico (1914); Huerta, Victoriano; Tampico Incident (1914); Veracruz, Mexico, Battle (1914).

Vesuvius

The *Vesuvius* was a dynamite gun cruiser that saw active service in the Spanish-Cuban/American War. Built by the William Cramp and Sons Ship and Engine Building Company of Philadelphia, it measured 252 feet, 4 inches in length and had a beam of 26 feet, 5 inches. Its maximum speed was 21 knots, but during the Spanish-Cuban/American War its sea speed was 17 knots. What made the *Vesuvius* unique was its main armament which the Cramp Company subcontracted to the Pneumatic Dynamite Gun Company of New York. The main battery consisted of three 15-inch pneumatic guns mounted forward side by side. These had a fixed elevation of 18 degrees. Compressed air was used to fire shells made of a desensitized blasting gelatin composed of nitrocellulose and nitroglycerine. The shells came in four sizes and varied in force from 100 to 500 pounds of explosive. They could be fired at a rate of about one a minute. Depending on the amount of compressed air admitted to the firing chamber, the shells could range from 200 yards to one and a half miles. The ship also carried three 3-pound rapid-fire guns.

Launched on 28 April 1888, *Vesuvius* was commissioned on 2 June 1890 at the Philadelphia Navy Yard. It then joined the North Atlantic Squadron at New York on 1 October 1890. While attached to the squadron the ship operated off the East Coast of the United States and conducted gunnery practice. These tests showed that the ship had two main deficiencies. The first was that the range of its battery was too short and the second was that to use the guns the ship itself had to be aimed at the target. At best, aiming was crude and inaccurate. In April 1895, the ship was decommissioned, underwent major repairs, and reentered the service on 12 January 1897. Despite improvements, the major problems with its guns remained. The ship operated off the East Coast of the United States until the war crisis with Spain led to a decision to assemble the North Atlantic Squadron in Florida waters. The *Vesuvius* arrived off Key West on 13 May 1898 and remained there until 28 May when it was sent to Cuba to participate in the blockade of a portion of that island. While on duty there the ship served as a dispatch boat to carry messages from Cuba to Florida. It was also a part of the scouting force in the Yucatan Channel when Adm. William T. Sampson was searching for the Spanish squadron under the command of Adm. Pascual Cervera y Topete. The *Vesuvius* joined Sampson's squadron off Santiago on 13 June and was used to shell Spanish positions. This and subsequent bombardments later in the month made holes in the ground and tore up trees but did no damage to the fortifications. Sampson reported that the shellings had a "great effect." They may have had a psychological effect because the shells came in without warning and without noise.

When the war ended the *Vesuvius* was ordered to Boston, where it was taken out of active service on 16 September 1898. It remained at Boston until 1904, when it was converted to a torpedo testing vessel. This involved the removal of the pneumatic guns and replacing them with three 18-inch and one 21-inch torpedo tubes. Thus transformed, the ship was recommissioned on 21 June 1905 and was used at the Naval Torpedo Station at Newport, Rhode Island, for torpedo experiments until it was again decommis-

sioned in 1907 for repairs. Recommissioned again in 1910, it remained at Newport where it occasionally served as the station ship until 1921, when it was finally decommissioned and sold for scrap the following year.

Harold D. Langley

REFERENCES

Dictionary of American Naval Fighting Ships (U.S. Government Printing Office, 1981), vol. 7, 499–500.

Villa, Francisco "Pancho" (1878–1923)

Francisco "Pancho" Villa, born Doroteo Arango on 5 June 1878, in the state of Durango, Mexico, became the avenging angel of the Mexican Revolution. He rode down to valleys from the *sierra de Chihuahua* (hills of Chihuahua). His name brought terror to the wealthy of northern Mexico who had exploited the lower classes and held Chihuahua in thrall during the long reign of Porfirio Díaz, president of Mexico (1876–1911).

Preceded by a fearsome reputation as cattle rustler, bandit, occasional operator of a butcher shop which he supplied with rustled cattle, womanizer, scourge of the wealthy, and friend of the oppressed, Villa provided the necessary charisma to carry him and the Anti-Reelectionist movement that supported Francisco I. Madero in 1910 and 1911 during the early stages of the Mexican Revolution. In large measure Villa suffered from an incredible inferiority complex. His constant struggle to attain respectability in the eyes of upper- and middle-class figures accounted in part for his decision to join forces with Abraham González and Madero.

The respect that Madero and González showed Villa nearly deified them in Villa's eyes. Never had educated people, wealthy people, treated him respectfully. Now these two men, neither of whom looked like he could handle a weapon with much competence, treated Pancho as an equal. A peasant could now talk to a member of the upper classes.

Villa began his career with the Anti-Reelectionists as a captain under Cástulo Herrera in October 1910. It soon became apparent that the real power lay in Villa's charismatic appeal to the rank and file. His innate ability to lead men brought recruits to the movement to overthrow the octogenarian Porfirio Díaz.

The initial skirmishes undertaken by Madero's rag-tag, almost *guerrilla*, forces proved inconclusive. The forces that joined the revolutionaries had to furnish their own weapons and horses because supplies were so limited. Thus, this revolt in the North was not a mere peasant rebellion. Ownership of a weapon and a horse implied some means although these might be limited.

Even early in the Maderista revolution, Villa relied on terror. Between 1894 and his appearance on the revolutionary stage in 1910, he was one of the most feared bandits in northern Mexico. U.S. pulp novelists lionized him, and his myth grew throughout Mexico. He used the "good press" to advantage. In March 1911, for example, at Pilar de Conchos he sought to intimidate the federal commander into surrender. He sent him a missive that read, in part (Machado, pp. 21–22):

> [I]f you ignore this order, we shall make use of our weapons. In that case you shall be responsible before history and the nation for fratricide, and you shall be judged militarily. If caprice blinds you, come out to the field of honor; but we do not wish, for highly patriotic reasons, that the war should be effected where there are families.

Although the rebels did not win decisive victories, they did prove an irritant to the *federales*. Maderistas controlled the northern rail lines and the telegraph system and had the capacity to bottle up any information that might get to Mexico City.

It was not until early May 1911, that Madero's troops under the overall leadership of Pascual Orozco began a concerted assault on Ciudad Juárez, Mexico's largest port of entry that bordered El Paso, Texas. Madero had been reluctant to order the attack on Juárez, but Orozco and Villa neatly arranged for the *federales* to fire the first shot. The rebels responded, and the fight for Juárez was launched on 8 May. The battle lasted 8–10 May.

Orozco and Villa squeezed the federal forces into the garrison as more rebels gained control of the city. The capture of a border city resulted in the collapse of the old regime.

Villa, however, had been hoodwinked by Orozco, who wanted to arrest Madero for his reluctance to lay siege to Juárez and to execute

the federal commander Juan J. Navarro. Villa had initially agreed. When he discovered the truth, however, he shamefully resigned his commission and begged Madero's forgiveness. He returned to San Andrés, and there married María Luz Corral on 29 May 1911. With Madero in power and Villa ensconced in San Andrés running a butcher shop, events seemed peaceful.

Orozco, discontented because he did not receive sufficient recognition for his services, however, grumbled and complained about his lot. Madero asked Villa to act as his ears in Chihuahua and report to Mexico City anything untoward.

The Orozco problem continued unabated. By the end of February 1912 Orozco rebelled against Madero. Villa again joined the active military, this time as a general of irregular forces attached to the federal División del Norte. Unfortunately, Villa came under titular command of Victoriano Huerta, a regular army commander with a penchant for imported cognac and a thorough dislike of Villa. To Huerta, Villa was an uncouth peasant who thought of himself as a general. Villa, always difficult to command, ultimately refused orders to return a horse, an Arabian mare, that he had confiscated. In June, Huerta had Villa seized for insubordination and summarily ordered that he be sent to the firing squad. A tearful Villa asked that he be processed according to military justice, not the summary decision of that "drunken Aztec." Last-minute intervention by President Madero at the behest of Raúl and Emilio Madero, the president's brothers, saved Villa's life. He was taken to Mexico City and imprisoned. From there, he escaped in late December and fled to the United States, ultimately watching Mexican developments from El Paso, Texas.

Momentous events occurred in February 1913. Huerta overthrew Madero on 18 February and Madero was assassinated on the 22nd. Abraham González, at this time governor of Chihuahua, sent money to Villa so that he could return to Mexico. In addition, Villa's brother, Hipólito, also provided some cash. The news of Madero's assassination followed by that of González galvanized Villa into action. He began to collect arms and men, and in early March, he and eight followers crossed the border into Mexico. The time for revolutionary vengeance had come.

For the next two years, Villa's personality and his string of successes dominated the revolutionary scene. While at the end of March he titularly subscribed to Carranza's *Plan de Guadelupe*, which established a Constitutionalist movement against the Huerta regime, he reserved independent action for himself. He began to gather more men, and his force took on the trappings of a real army rather than loosely grouped guerrilla bands. He supplied himself by stealing cattle from the vast estates of Luis Terrazas, selling the cattle across the border for gold, and then buying arms and ammunition and smuggling these back into Mexico because the United States refused to lift an arms embargo imposed in March 1912.

By June, Villista forces began to squeeze federal positions in Chihuahua. Villa and his forces accumulated money and supplies, and the revolutionary División del Norte began to move against entrenched federal positions. Throughout the summer Villa had some successes. By mid-fall, he saw a prime target in Torreón, Coahuila, a major railroad nexus and the center of cotton growing in Mexico. On 1 October 1913, Villa threw his forces at Torreón and began to sack Spanish-owned enterprises.

The Spaniards almost universally supported Huerta, and Villa vengefully seized Spanish goods and held some Spaniards for ransom. Once settled in Torreón, Villa began to make plans for a move against Chihuahua City.

Villa's initial attack on Chihuahua City beginning on 5 November 1913 failed. He had not amassed a sufficient number of men for a concerted siege. Yet, as he retreated northward he found a perfect solution: cut Chihuahua off from any communication with the border. In a lightning strike, Villa grabbed a southbound train heading for Chihuahua, threw the train in reverse, stopped at various stations along the way to send telegrams while posing as the federal commander, and entered Ciudad Juárez, which he and his troops took virtually without a shot. By controlling Juárez, Villa was able to choke off a major source of supply for the *federales* who continued to hold Chihuahua City.

Then, Villa began to move southward once again. On 25 November 1913 at Tierra Blanca, he defeated Orozco's forces. Federal troops and many of Chihuahua's wealthy citizens began to flee for the United States. By 8 December Villa occupied Chihuahua City and began a program of confiscation for the benefit of the revolution.

He especially targeted Luis Terrazas, his far-flung family, and his political allies. From Chihuahua, Villa prepared to retake Torreón and to secure his hold on the state of Chihuahua by taking Ojinaga, across the border from Presidio, Texas.

Villa, the uncultured revolutionary, attempted to govern the state of Chihuahua in the name of constitutionalism while at the same time giving attention to military matters. He had reestablished civil government (under a military man) in Ciudad Juárez. He began to impose a statewide government on Chihuahua while occupying that city. He also faced problems with finances.

Fiscal measures soon met resolution when Villa kidnapped and held hostage the son of Luis Terrazas. Luis, Jr., had remained behind while the rest of the family fled. Villa held him, demanding money, cattle, and goods from the Terrazas family to assure the safety of the younger Terrazas. Terrazas was the gosling with the golden egg; Villa had no intention of hurting him. When reports reached the U.S. representative to Villa, George C. Carothers, that Terrazas had been tortured, Villa promised to punish the perpetrators, stating as a caveat, however, that Terrazas had been tortured only "a little."

During this period of late 1913 and early 1914, Villa rode high in the esteem of the United States. He seemed more willing than the stiff-necked Carranza to listen to President Woodrow Wilson's admonitions. While Villa had no qualms about exploiting the rich, there was rarely any question about his personal honesty. Nevertheless, his treatment of foreigners, especially those who supported Huerta as did the Spaniards, cast him in a sort of barbarous role in the eyes of the puritanical Wilson. What severely damaged Villa did not involve a U.S. citizen but rather a Scotsman named William S. Benton.

Benton, still a British citizen, had resided in Mexico for a number of years, married a Mexican woman, owned a mid-sized *hacienda*, and was considered strong-willed and irascible. When Villistas seized some of his cattle for the good of the revolution, Benton, in a rage, went to Juárez to remonstrate with Villa on 17 February 1914. Apparently, Benton drew a pistol on Villa, and the Scotsman was killed by Rodolfo Fierro, Villa's most able, and demonstrably sociopathic, triggerman. Benton's death triggered an international incident. Demands were made for the body and assurances that Benton had received a fair military trial. Villa ordered that papers be falsified to satisfy the *gringos*. Villa even ordered that the corpse be shot so that it seemed that Benton had been killed by a firing squad. The Benton problem did not receive resolution, and Villa's stock in the eyes of the Wilson administration plummeted.

The split between Villa and Carranza was also exacerbated by the Benton affair.

For the next year (1914–1915) Villa dominated the Mexican Revolution. He successfully retook Torreón at the end of March and early April. He prepared to push southward, but was discouraged by Carranza who feared the popular appeal that Villa had and tried to keep Villa confined to Chihuahua. When the time came to take Zacatecas, Carranza ordered that Villa relinquish control of some men for the task. Villa refused. Carranza demanded. Villa resigned. Maclovio Herrera, one of Villa's staff, sent Carranza a telegram stating: "Sir, you are a son-of-bitch!" The telegram was stopped by Felipe Angeles, Villa's artillery commander and generally acknowledged as one of the finest professional soldiers of the revolution. Angeles was able to strike a deal between Villa and Carranza, and Villa personally commanded the forces that took Zacatecas at the end of July.

In foreign affairs, Villa continued to court the United States. He supported Wilson's invasion of Veracruz because it would help rid Mexico of Huerta. Carranza was enraged because he viewed the invasion as a violation of Mexican sovereignty. Villa also went out of his way to protect U.S. property in areas under his control.

Yet, summer 1914 proved to be Villa's ultimate undoing. The growing split between Villa and Carranza forced revolutionary generals to take sides. Álvaro Obregón sided with Carranza after the Convention of Aguascalientes forced the issue in October. Carranza retreated to Veracruz and the convention existed at the pleasure of Villa. Villa then moved toward Mexico City and was joined there by Emiliano Zapata in early December. They conferred and agreed that Carranza was certainly a common enemy. However, the putative military alliance between the two never materialized.

Once the Carrancistas reoccupied Mexico City in late January and early February 1915, Villa began to fight defensive actions. Between April and June 1915, in four separate battles around Celaya and León, Guanajuato, the División del Norte was devastated. Villa, refusing to wait for Angeles to show up with the artillery, used cavalry charges against barbed wire entanglements and machine gun emplacements; soon the attack was smashed. Obregón, commanding Carranza's forces, knew that Villa would become impatient and merely waited. Obregón was aware of the value of such tactics by observing what was going on in Europe in this first year of World War I. From June onward, Villa remained on the defensive, reduced to exercising influence in the rural areas of Chihuahua and Durango. Yet, he was still an influence. He continued to control Juárez, though sporadically, and thus dictated the flow of goods into Mexico through its largest port of entry. Wilson had not yet recognized either faction. Villa continued to court the *gringos*.

Yet, it was merely a matter of time before Wilson had to act. Ultimately, on 19 October 1915, he extended *de facto* recognition to Venustiano Carranza. Villa was enraged and blamed Wilson for the devastating loss he suffered at Agua Prieta in early November. Wilson had allowed Carranza to move troops through the United States to reenforce Constitutionalists under Plutarco Elías Calles at Agua Prieta. Villa vowed vengeance on the *gringos*.

For a few days in early March 1916, it seemed that Villa and his men were active around Palomas, Chihuahua, across from Columbus, New Mexico. Cattle were being gathered, and there was a general movement of the remnants of Villa's army. Suddenly, in the early hours of 9 March 1916, Villistas struck across the border into Columbus. U.S. troops there dispersed the Villistas, but not before the Mexicans had torched a substantial part of the town and killed a number of civilians. Pursuit by the United States Army into Mexico presaged a larger retaliation.

By 16 March 1916 Gen. John J. Pershing moved into Mexico upon orders from President Wilson. Wilson had informed Pershing that he was to destroy, capture, or disperse the Villistas. For nine months Pershing's two columns attempted to lay hands on Villa. The only two major military engagements that they had fought were against Carrancistas who had orders to fight the *gringos* if they continued to penetrate Mexico. Villa, himself, had been wounded in a skirmish at Guerrero, Mexico, and he took a long convalescence in the Chihuahua foothills, protected by peasants and former comrades.

For the next four years, Villa continued to plague the Carranza government. The lack of representation for Chihuahua at the Constitutional Convention at Querétaro in late December 1916 and early 1917 clearly indicated that Villa still had a strong grip on northern Mexico. Attempts to assassinate him had failed, even some that were reputedly sponsored by the United States. Villa engaged in bravado and depredations against the *gringos* who had betrayed him. His agents were all over El Paso and northern Mexico recruiting men and acquiring supplies. In late 1916, the U.S. consul in Durango even alleged that Villistas had organized the local prostitutes who charged soldiers bullets for their carnal services. Villa, the lover, had the ladies on his side.

There was a last clash between Villa's men and U.S. troops at Ciudad Juárez in 1919. Villa was tired. The death in late November 1919 of Felipe Angeles, his beloved artillery commander, at the hands of Carranza galvanized Villa into action again. Vengefully he struck; the fire burned for only a short time, however. By April 1920, elements in Sonora declared against Carranza. Villa offered his services to Adolfo de la Huerta. De la Huerta asked Villa to negotiate a peace first.

With some success and after some attempts at deceit by the government, Villa came to terms with a government headed by Interim President de la Huerta. Carranza had died on the road to Veracruz, fleeing with the national treasury in his saddlebags and packsaddles.

As compensation for his peace with the government, Villa received the Hacienda de Canutillo south of Parral, Chihuahua, in the state of Durango. He was allowed to keep 50 men as bodyguards who were paid by the federal treasury. His other men were either incorporated into the regular army at their current ranks or were granted land in and around Canutillo.

Villa, it has been alleged, sold out to the government for a nice piece of real estate and some emoluments. He still engendered fear in the government of Álvaro Obregón. Villa constantly sought the spotlight. He granted newspaper interviews. In one, he declared that he might run for the governorship of Durango. Secretly, Villa smuggled arms and ammunition into Canutillo,

just in case. He vowed to support Adolfo de la Huerta if de la Huerta sought the presidency.

But Plutarco Elías Calles, the interior minister, was the official candidate so designated in 1923. Villa loathed Calles, a man of singular military incompetence in the view of the army. There always existed the possibility that Villa might run amok once again. In all probability, his assassination on 20 July 1923 was arranged by Calles.

What did Villa contribute to the Mexican Revolution? In strictly military terms, he turned a collection of *guerrilleros* into a well-disciplined military machine that at one point allegedly numbered 60,000 men. In addition, he introduced modern military medicine to the revolutionary forces. Control of the railroads allowed him to do this. He hired the best physicians, usually from the United States, and provided them with the resources to build on railroad cars what were in essence military hospitals similar to mobile surgical hospitals in the United States Army. The incidence of postbattle death as a result of battle trauma dropped dramatically in the División del Norte. Other revolutionary groups soon took the lesson and also established hospital cars.

Yet, Villa remained a guerrilla fighter. He proved to be most effective using rapid strikes. He prefaced many of these with exercises in mental terrorism. His many articulated threats to the Spaniards of Chihuahua and Torreón kept this group off balance and kept them from supporting the Huertistas. Villa had never read Mikhail Bakunin, the noted Russian anarchist, but he instinctively knew when terrorist tactics might be useful.

Ideologically, Villa did not have an articulated ideology as did Emiliano Zapata. Instead, Villa reflected the pragmatism of northern Mexico. His seizure of the Terrazas lands in December 1913 clearly showed some of that practical streak. While the lands would be used to create agricultural *colonies*, some of those lands were reserved for the widows and orphans of men who had fallen in battle under Villa's leadership.

In one respect, Villa proved to be like many other revolutionaries. He often wanted to effect social change through draconian measures. When he gained control of Juárez in late 1913, for example, Villa, the nondrinker, closed the saloons, whorehouses, and casinos because these robbed the poor of their meager pesos. His advisors, however, soon procured changes because the revenues generated by these carnal enterprises supplied much-needed revenue to the revolutionary cause.

Villa's biggest failing, in fact, was his inability to deal with sophisticated politicians like Carranza and his coterie. Roberto Blanco Moheno put it best when he wrote that "the tragedy of the Mexican Revolution is [that] neither Villa, the armed might, nor Zapata, the saving ideology, were capable of vanquishing their inferiority complexes before the 'perfumados'" (Machado, p. 180).

Tragedy ended Villa. His impact on the revolution was monumental. He inspired love and hate, fear and adulation, respect and disgust. In equal numbers, however, Villa came to represent the very best that Mexico could produce in its leaders: fearless and a complete *macho*, unswerving in the pursuit of his ideals. Villa, the Centaur of the North, stamped his personality on the revolution and ultimately forced the leaders to recognize that here was a true man.

Manuel A. Machado, Jr.

REFERENCES

Francisco Almada, *La Revolución en el Estado de Chihuahua* (Biblioteca del Instituto de Estudios Históricos de la Revolución Mexicana, 1964), 2 vols.; Roberto Blanco Moheno, *Pancho Villa, Que es su padre?* (Editorial Diana, 1968); Clarence C. Clendenen, *The United States and Pancho Villa: A Study in Unconventional Diplomacy* (Cornell Univ. Pr., 1961); Marte R. Gómez, *La Reforma Agraria en las Filas Villistas—Años 1913–1915 y 1920* (Biblioteca del Instituto de Estudios Históricos de La Revolución Mexicana, 1966); Manuel A. Machado, Jr., *Centaur of the North: Francisco Villa, the Mexican Revolution, and Northern Mexico* (Eakin, 1988).

See also list of entries at front of book for Ciudad Juárez, Mexico, Battle (1919); Punitive Expedition, Mexico (1916–1917).

Visayan Campaigns, Philippine War

Between 1896 and 1897, the Philippine Revolution was confined to Luzon. In spring 1898, it reached the Visayas when revolutionaries rose in revolt on Cebu. During summer 1898 Spanish control over the Visayas crumbled, until the Spanish retained only a few seaports.

Initially, Visayan leaders were wary of accepting Luzon's leadership, fearing they might be exchanging one overlord for another. For a time, there was sentiment in favor of creating a separate country comprising the Visayan Islands. In late 1898, a Visayan confederation was organized on Panay. This government shortly gave way to the Malolos Republic based on Luzon. Meanwhile, Negros's leaders declared their island to be an independent country.

After the Philippine War began in February 1899, small U.S. detachments landed at Cebu City, Bacolod, and Iloilo, establishing the first footholds in the Visayas. Manpower shortages, however, prevented them from extending their control. On Negros, local leaders welcomed U.S. forces. On the other islands, however, Filipino revolutionaries attempted to contain U.S. troops.

Filipino forces were hampered by the insular nature of the Visayas, which greatly hindered supply and communication. In addition, shortages of rifles and artillery compounded the revolutionaries' problems. Because nationalist leader Emilio Aguinaldo y Famy's forces on Luzon were largely unable to render assistance, Filipino leaders in the central Philippines were left to their own devices.

By fall 1899 U.S. garrisons were sufficiently reenforced to go on the offensive. Army units fanned out from their footholds, defeating conventional Filipino forces. In early 1900, U.S. troops landed on the islands of Bohol, Leyte, and Samar. At the time, many U.S. commanders assumed the conflict was nearing an end, and the army could rapidly consolidate its control over the Visayas. Such optimism, however, was short-lived.

After suffering defeats at the hands of U.S. troops, most Filipino forces switched to guerrilla warfare. U.S. commanders found ending resistance a nearly impossible task as guerrilla and civilian became indistinguishable. Guerrilla bands threatened and killed Filipinos who aided the United States or participated in U.S.-sponsored municipal governments. U.S. units burned the houses of Filipinos suspected of assisting the guerrillas. Most Visayans found themselves caught in the middle between U.S. and Filipino forces. On Cebu, several towns formed their own self-defense forces to protect themselves.

The United States Army attempted to wear down the guerrillas; Aguinaldo's capture in March 1901 and the collapse of most resistance on Luzon hastened the revolution's demise in the Visayas. Gen. Ambrosio Móxica, commander of Filipino forces on Leyte, surrendered in May 1901, while Arcadio Maxilom, who led the guerrillas on Cebu, capitulated in October. By spring 1902, resistance had ceased except for millenarian movements which persisted for several more years.

The revolution's last stand in the Visayas occurred on the island of Samar. Gen. Vicente Lukban commanded a skilled defense which used guerrilla tactics, terror, and the island's rugged terrain. After a U.S. garrison was massacred in Balangiga in September 1901, army units swarmed over the island. Frequently out of control, they destroyed considerable life and property. Lukban was captured in a daring raid in February 1902, effectively ending the war in the Visayas.

James C. Biedzynski

REFERENCES

Richard S.V.D. Arens, "The Early Pulahan Movement in Samar and Leyte," *Journal of History*, 7 (1959), 303–371; Stuart Creighton Miller, *"Benevolent Assimilation": The American Conquest of the Philippines, 1899–1903* (Yale Univ. Pr., 1982); William T. Sexton, *Soldiers in the Sun: An Adventure in Imperialism* (Military Service Pub. Co., 1939).

See also Samar Campaigns, Philippine War.

Vologda Railroad Front, North Russia (1918–1919)

The Vologda Railroad Front represented one of the main lines of advance of the forces that engaged in the U.S. intervention in North Russia, 1918–1919. Established along the route of the railroad that ran in a direct line from Archangel, on the Dvina Gulf of the White Sea, to the key railway junction of Vologda, some 425 miles to the south, the front had as its chief objective to link the Allies and Czechoslovak and anti-Bolshevik Russian forces advancing from Siberia against either Petrograd to the west, and/or Moscow, to the south.

Founded on 3 August 1918, the day after the occupation of Archangel, the Vologda Railroad Front was created as one of the chief avenues of Allied advance in the North in accord with the plan of Maj. Gen. Frederick C. Poole, the initial Allied commander in chief in the region. Manned originally by an "A" Force consisting of French, British, Polish, and Russian troops as well as a small party of sailors from the USS *Olympia*, the

Vologda Railroad Front advanced rapidly to Obozerskaia, some 75 miles south of Archangel, where Allied headquarters were established on 5 September. Meanwhile, in mid-August, a collateral front was created on the so-called Siskoe-Plesetskaia highway, a forest road that proceeded on a southwesterly diagonal from Siskoe, on the Northern Dvina River 100 miles south of Archangel, to Plesetskaia, a major station on the railroad some 50 miles south of Obozerskaia. Staffed originally by an Allied contingent designated as "B" Force, this front, which was later called the Seletskoe Column, was vital to the security of both the left flank of the railroad and the right wing of the Northern Dvina River Front.

On 6 September, the Vologda Railroad was substantially reinforced by the arrival at Obozerskaia of the 3rd Battalion of the 339th United States Infantry Regiment, a major component of the American Expeditionary Force, North Russia. Though relatively untrained, the battalion was ordered into action almost immediately with Companies I and M participating in a generally unsuccessful offensive down the railroad on 28–29 September, while Companies K and L, having been sent to the Seletskoe Column, engaged in an equally fruitless operation against Kodysh, about midway down the road to Plesetskaia, on 27 September.

In mid-October, notwithstanding September's disappointments, the Allied command decided to undertake new offensives on both the railroad and the Seletskoe fronts. The results of these operations, while better than those achieved earlier, were still meager. Thus, on the railroad, an offensive that again featured Companies I and M of the 339th, as well as some French and British forces, advanced the front to a point about 20 miles south of Obozerskaia. Though nearly 100 miles from Archangel, this line was still less than one-quarter of the way to General Poole's ultimate objective at Vologda. Meanwhile, on the Seletskoe front, the 339th's Companies K and L, with Canadian and British support, succeeded in occupying Kodysh on 13 October, only to suffer its surrender later in the month in the face of superior enemy artillery fire.

Simultaneously with the October attacks, the offensive-minded General Poole was replaced as Allied commander in the North by a new commanding officer, British Maj. Gen. William Edmund Ironside. Shocked by what he perceived as the Allies' overextension and lack of proper organization, Ironside immediately ordered a general tightening up of Allied positions in the North with emphasis on the consolidation of an impregnable defense. In response, Allied engineers promptly constructed a chain of log blockhouses and surrounding barbed wire entanglements on all the main fronts in the North in preparation for what Ironside confidently expected would be an essentially inactive winter campaign.

In late December, in spite of his overall intention to remain on the defensive, Ironside decided to undertake a modest offensive on the Vologda Railroad Front. Conceived as a purely tactical operation to improve the Allies' defensive position along the railbed, Ironside's plan called for a converging attack against Plesetskaia, located about 30 miles down the line at the southwestern terminus of the overland road from Siskoe. Carried out between 29 December 1918 and 1 January 1919, this operation was a near total disaster. First, owing to the failure of a specially prepared French snowshoe detachment as well as some murderously effective Bolshevik artillery fire, the attack on the railroad never even got under way. Meanwhile, on the Seletskoe front, Companies E, K, and L of the 399th supported by a section of Canadian field artillery, successfully recaptured Kodysh but were unable to advance any farther due to the drunkenness of the British officer in command and the refusal to fight of a locally recruited Russian regiment. Following this fiasco, U.S. forces were gradually transferred from the Seletskoe Column to the main Vologda Railroad Front, never to return.

Beginning in mid-January 1919, to the general surprise of the Allies, the Bolshevik 6th Red Army launched a series of counteroffensives all across the Archangel front. Of these attacks, the last and most determined sought to bring about a decisive breakthrough on the Vologda Railroad Front. Thus, on 17 March, a force of 2,500 Bolsheviks suddenly attacked and destroyed the small French and Russian garrison at Bol'shie Ozerki, a village located some 15 miles west of the railroad on the main route to Onega and the West. By this action, which was accompanied by a simultaneous attack on the railroad, the Bolsheviks intended to cut off Allied contact with Murmansk and clear the way for a final assault on Archangel itself. Sensing at once the danger posed for the Allies by this strategy, Ironside

immediately threw all available forces into the defense and recapture of Bol'shie Ozerki. On 25 March, having failed to retake the town by storm, Ironside ordered it leveled by artillery fire. Thereupon, on 1 and 2 April, using U.S. and Allied troops both east and west of the town, the Allies successfully contained two determined enemy efforts to break out of Bol'shie Ozerki. As a result, having suffered casualties amounting to nearly 50 percent of their forces, the defeated Bolsheviks retreated southward on 5 April.

The battle at Bol'shie Ozerki was the last significant U.S. engagement of the North Russian campaign. During the rest of April and May U.S. forces on the railroad gradually turned over their positions to representatives of the newly organized North Russian Army of Gen. Eugene K. Miller. Ironically, following the final Allied evacuation of the North in late September, these troops, whose abilities had often been questioned by the Allies, staged a spectacular offensive that advanced the Vologda Railroad Front to Plesetskaia, whose capture had consistently eluded the Allies during their tenure in the North. As a result of this success, the Vologda Railroad Front remained one of the last bastions of northern anti-Bolshevism right up to the final collapse of the region in February 1920.

John W. Long

REFERENCES

Dennis Gordon, *Quartered in Hell: The Story of the American North Russian Expeditionary Force, 1918–1919* (GOS, 1982); E.M. Halliday, *The Ignorant Armies: The Anglo-American Archangel Expedition, 1918–1919* (Harper, 1958); Joel R. Moore, *'M' Company, 339th Infantry in North Russia* (Central City Book Bindery, 1929); Joel Moore, Harry Mead, and Lewis Jahns, *The History of the American Expedition Fighting the Bolsheviki* (Polar Bear, 1920); Ernest Reed, "The Story of the A.E.F. in North Russia," *Current History*, 32 (1930), 64–69.

Voluntario Force, Nicaragua (1929)

After the inauguration in Nicaragua of José María Moncada in January 1929, the new president proposed creation of a *voluntario* force to aid in suppressing nationalist leader Augusto C. Sandino and his followers in northern Nicaragua. Moncada argued that such a force would allow his country to assume greater responsibility for checking "banditry" in the North and permit the U.S. Marines to reduce active field operations. He recognized accomplishments of the nonpartisan, marine-led Guardia Nacional de Nicaragua but believed it would require two years to reach peak efficiency. Meanwhile, he thought, the *voluntarios* could, at relatively low cost, carry on the fight without the constraints that were on the marines or the Guardia, especially if martial law was established in the departments where the Sandinistas were active. Gen. Logan Feland, commander of the 2nd Marine Brigade in Nicaragua, supported Moncada's proposal, but the U.S. minister, Charles C. Eberhardt, and the chief of the national guard, Lt. Col. Ellias R. Beadle, opposed it. Eberhardt and Beadle believed the *voluntario* proposal indicated a lack of presidential support for the Guardia and was an attempt to create a partisan military force loyal to Moncada, undercutting the Henry L. Stimson agreement of 1927.

After a compromise in which the Guardia would have some control over financing and training, two groups of *voluntarios* were created with about 90 men each. Gen. Augusto Caldera and Gen. Juan Escamilla commanded the groups, which were to operate in conjunction with marine patrols. Lt. Herman H. Hanneken, commanding one of the patrols, described Escamilla as a Mexican adventurer and the *voluntarios* as a motley group with little military training.

In the field, beginning in January, there was little control over the *voluntarios*, and their conduct under martial law was fraught with danger. They had few contacts with the rebels, but caused panic among civilians and an international incident by violating the Honduran border. When the marines turned Manuel María Girón Ruano, a captured Sandinista general, over to Escamilla who had him executed after a questionable courtmartial, uneasiness in the State Department and even among the marine command in northern Nicaragua began to rise. Increased pressure from Washington and within Nicaragua influenced Moncada to disband the *voluntarios*, which was completed by August 1929. Later, in 1931, a similar force of *auxiliares* was recruited for temporary service to aid the Guardia in fighting a rebel thrust into west central Nicaragua.

William Kamman

REFERENCES

Herman H. Hanneken, "A Discussion of the Voluntario Troops in Nicaragua," *Marine Corps Gazette*, 26 (1942), 120, 247–248, 250–254, 256, 260, 262, 264, 266; Neill Macaulay, *The Sandino Affair* (Quadrangle, 1967); Vernon Edgar Megee, "The United States Military Intervention in Nicaragua, 1909–1932," M.A. thesis, Univ. of Texas, 1963; Richard Millett, *Guardians of the Dynasty: A History of the U.S. Created Guardia Nacional de Nicaragua and the Somoza Family* (Orbis, 1977); Bernard C. Nalty, *The United States Marines in Nicaragua*, rev. ed. (Historical Branch, G-3 Division, Headquarters, U.S. Marine Corps, 1962).

See also Guardia Nacional de Nicaragua.

Waller, Littleton Waller Tazewell (1857–1926)

Littleton Waller Tazewell Waller, a career marine officer, gained notoriety when he was accused of atrocities on the Island of Samar during the Philippine War. His court-martial received considerable attention in the United States.

Born in Virginia in 1857, Waller was commissioned a second lieutenant in the United States Marine Corps in 1880. Two years later, he saw action in Egypt during the rebellion of Arabi Pasha against the khedive, landing at Alexandria with a detachment of 63 marines. He later fought at San Juan, Puerto Rico, and at Santiago de Cuba, where he was awarded a special medal for "meritorious conduct" during the Spanish-Cuban/American War. He moved on to Cavite on Luzon in the Philippines before being sent to China during the Boxer Uprising in 1900, where he was again cited for "eminent and conspicuous conduct in battles" (Schott, p. 69) at Tianjin (Tientsin) and brevetted a lieutenant colonel. His reputation among his fellow officers and his men was such that he was considered a very likely future commandant. He returned to Cavite with the 1st Brigade to guard a lighthouse and naval stores. In the wake of the Balangiga massacre in 1901, Adm. Frederick Rodgers offered 300 marines for duty on Samar. Gen. Jacob H. Smith accepted the offer, and a battalion under Waller's command immediately got underway to occupy Basey and Balangiga, relieving the army troops stationed there. In doing this, Waller was temporarily detached from the 1st Brigade and placed under control of the army.

Waller was given strong verbal orders by Smith: "I want no prisoners. I wish you to kill and burn, the more you kill and burn the better it will please me. I want all persons killed who are capable of bearing arms in actual hostilities against the United States" (Miller, p. 220). Waller asked "to know the limit of age to respect, sir," only to be told by Smith, "ten years." Surprised, he asked for verification, and Smith reiterated this (Miller, p. 220). Although Waller's orders to his commanders were harsh enough, he did stipulate to his officers that the marines were "not making war on women and children" (Miller, p. 220).

After completing a census in Basey and vicinity, Waller decreed that the natives who did not come to Basey and register would be treated as "armed insurrectos" (Schott, p. 77). He initiated aggressive patrol outside of Basey, encountering some opposition, although leeches, a "weeping eczema" (Schott, p. 113) that was temporarily blinding, and the heavy rains and mud, as the rainy season began, were the chief adversaries the marines faced. All food caches and planted areas were destroyed. Whenever evidence of guerrilla activity was discovered in outlying barrios, they were burned to the ground. When relics or personal effects of the Balangiga massacre were discovered, everyone in sight was gunned down to avenge their late comrades, the murdered men of the 9th United States Infantry.

Finally, one patrol discovered the enemy headquarters in the Sohotón Mountains. Waller planned a combined amphibious and land assault to take this redoubt. While his contingent proceeded up the Cadacan River that passed under the fort on a raft with a three-inch gun and in bancas and barotos paddled by Samarenos, Capt. Hiram I. Bearss left Balangiga with his company to rendezvous with the company from Basey commanded by Capt. David D. Porter. This last contingent stormed the Sohotón cliffs from its land side. Waller's initial probes had tipped his hand, however, and Gen. Vicente Lukban had lined the cliffs along the river approach with hanging cages filled with rocks to make an amphibious assault impossible. Meanwhile, Porter and Bearss stormed the fort, putting the defenders to rout after killing 30 of them with no marine casualties. General Smith signaled Waller congratulations, even comparing Waller's marines to those "barefooted Americans at Valley Forge" (Miller, p. 221). The terse signal of Admiral Rodgers was more in keeping with the spirit of the corps: "Well Done, Marines!" (Miller, p. 221). Headlines back home were ecstatic, and the legend of "the Samar Battalion" in Marine Corps lore was born.

It was clear to Waller that he had won only a battle and not the war for Samar or even for his assigned southern end of the island. His patrols continually ran into enemy activity and some fierce fire fights. Two Filipinos captured in one engagement revealed a plot to reenact the Balangiga massacre in Basey. Several officials who were implicated confessed and documentary evidence exposed others, all of whom had sworn allegiance to the United States. Under Smith's orders, Waller would have been justified to "punishing treachery summarily with death" (Schott, p. 261) in this case. Instead, he placed them in

Basey's jail under marine guard. He also issued a warning that in the event of such an attack, he would immediately burn every house in Basey. Meanwhile, Smith sent an unsigned handwritten message to Waller that "the interior of Samar must be made a howling wilderness" (Schott, p. 98).

In the interest of stringing telephone lines across the interior to establish communication links between army garrisons on the eastern coast with those of the marines on the western littoral, Waller decided to scout the interior, crossing it from Lanang to Basey, about 40 miles away as the crow flies. Army officers at Lanang tried to dissuade Waller from undertaking this march and could not provide him with all the rations he needed for 50 men and approximately 30 Filipino bearers. Nevertheless, on 28 December 1901, Waller started out in clear weather, but soon both it and the terrain worsened, making progress slow and increasingly torturous. Rations had to be cut continually, and his men grew progressively weaker. Although twice the age of the others, Waller seemed in much better shape. He made the fateful decision to split the group and press on with the strongest, ordering Porter to build rafts and float back with the rest on the Lanang River. The bearers became increasingly uncooperative and cut wood they knew would not float. Bearss and one man pushed on after Waller to report their predicament. They found his party just as Waller had stumbled onto a clearing planted with food and as the sun finally came out. Waller immediately sent out his trusted guide, Victor, to turn Porter around. Victor reported back that he was unable to get through because of guerrilla activity. That night Victor was caught stealing the major's bolo. Sure that Porter would know enough to follow him, Waller pressed on to Basey, and even though he was feverish, he personally set out with fresh men in search of Porter.

Meanwhile, Porter again divided his group, pressing on to Lanang, where an army rescue force set out for the others. When they reached them, 10 had already died or disappeared; nine remaining bearers followed the surviving marines back to Lanang. There, Lt. Alexander S. Williams told Porter of being attacked with a bolo while these bearers stood by and did nothing. They were arrested and taken by boat to Basey, where Waller had returned in a delirious state, racked by fever. In this state, he gave Lt.

John H.A. Day permission to execute the bearers, plus Victor. Day added an eleventh Filipino whom he had accused of conspiracy.

Waller's battalion was relieved by the army. He returned to Cavite a hero, only to face a court-martial ordered by Maj. Gen. Adna R. Chaffee, U.S. military commander in the Philippines. Waller must have seemed the ideal scapegoat to Secretary of War Elihu Root, coming from the rival Navy Department. Initially, Waller tried to protect Smith, but when Smith was called to the stand, only to betray Waller, the major then revealed and documented the bizarre orders he had received from Smith. Waller was acquitted, but not before he was tried and convicted in the anti-imperialist press as "the Butcher of Samar." The episode also cost him the post of commandant. As the senior colonel, and the most respected officer in the corps, he was the obvious choice in 1910. Instead, the appointment went to Col. William P. Biddle, who as a member of Waller's court-martial pushed for his rival's conviction to enhance his own career. When General Biddle retired in 1914, Waller was again passed over for the post. Upon Waller's retirement in 1920, he was promoted to major general. He died six years later. The legendary Gen. Smedley D. Butler, who had served under Waller in China and the Philippines as a young officer, declared: "The doctor reported he had a stroke. What he really died of was a broken heart" (Schott, p. 284). Certainly, General Waller deserved better treatment from a country he had served so well.

Stuart Creighton Miller

REFERENCES

Stuart Creighton Miller, *"Benevolent Assimilation": The American Conquest of the Philippines, 1899–1903* (Yale Univ. Pr., 1982); Joseph L. Schott, *The Ordeal of Samar* (Bobbs-Merrill, 1964).

See also Atrocities in the Philippine War; Samar Campaigns, Philippine War; Smith, Jacob Hurd.

War Correspondents at Veracruz, Mexico (1914)

The civil war in Mexico and the U.S.-Mexican conflict between the presidential administrations of Woodrow Wilson and Victoriano Huerta attracted considerable press attention and were thoroughly enmeshed in domestic partisan political debate well before the U.S. landing at Veracruz in April 1914. Given the proximity of and easy access to Mexico, reporters were constantly visiting all camps and factions, observing the battles and military campaigns, and interviewing their leaders. Regular reports appeared in all major U.S. newspapers.

The occupation of Veracruz attracted additional coverage and well-known reporters because most of the press assumed the landing marked the start of full-scale intervention and fully expected the troops to move on to Mexico City. In the days immediately following the initial landing, reporters for 25 newspapers, representing most major U.S. papers as well as both the Associated Press and the United Press, rushed to Veracruz to report on the "military campaign." Also on the scene were magazine commentators, such as Arthur Ruhl of *Colliers* and Frederick Palmer of *Everybody's Magazine*. The journalists included such well-known writers as Richard Harding Davis and Jack London. Many quickly became bored with the routine events and penned emotional and imaginative, and often inaccurate, pieces reflecting their impatience to press on with a major military campaign. Despite their flamboyance, they were unable to proceed beyond the port because the occupation caused a complete break in communications between that city and the capital. Those wishing to enter the Mexican heartland were required to enter by other routes.

Because there were no formal procedures or pool systems, each reporter chose his own themes and sought information from all sources. Official news releases were limited.

Initially, the Veracruz occupation was covered extensively. It rapidly faded from view as it became apparent that it was not the beginning of a larger military campaign. With combat occurring elsewhere in Mexico, the press and public had more exciting events to follow and quickly lost interest in the boring daily routine of administering a city.

Kenneth J. Grieb

REFERENCES

Kenneth J. Grieb, *The United States and Huerta* (Univ. of Nebraska Pr., 1969); Robert E. Quirk, *An Affair of Honor: Woodrow Wilson and the Occupation of Veracruz* (Univ. of Kentucky Pr., 1962).

War Correspondents in the Philippine War

With the rise of cheap, mass-circulation daily newspapers in the 19th century, war correspondents began to influence the conduct of warfare. Battles, it seems, were fought as much in the headlines as on the field. Military leaders sometimes carried out maneuvers more to impress correspondents on hand than the enemy. Occasionally, they engaged in histrionics of little military value to garner personal publicity which often paid off in medals and more rapid promotions. Most generals, even the modest Henry W. Lawton, had a favorite correspondent or two who were taken on their campaigns to tout their deeds in headlines. Official press releases from headquarters were little more than public relations statements to exaggerate victories and enemy losses and to convince the people of the United States via the press that the war being conducted was both victorious and glorious. The war in the Philippines was no exception.

Of course, a commander had to control correspondents to maintain an "appropriate" view of the war, particularly when that view became increasingly divorced from reality. Control methods ranged from personal manipulation of reporters to strict censorship of their dispatches. Even before the war began in the Philippines, Gen. Elwell S. Otis instituted such controls. Because there was only one cable terminal at Manila, he, or his censor, was able to veto any news deemed unfavorable to Otis personally or to the army in general. Because mail was not censored, the correspondents could mail uncensored dispatches to their editors or to the cable terminal at Hong Kong. The Hong Kong route not only meant delay in transmission, but also risked the wrath of Otis if the contents displeased him. Two English reporters who had dared use this means to dispatch critical assessments of Otis and his diplomatic, or undiplomatic, relations with the Filipino nationalists were quickly deported.

Almost from the beginning, Otis had trouble with Robert M. Collins of the Associated Press, who complained to his editor about censorship. Otis denied any censorship, insisting that all correspondents were free to cable "established facts." There were, however, "troublemakers," such as Collins, who tried to send "numerous baseless rumors [which] circulate here tending to excite the outside world" (Miller, p. 83). What Collins tried to report was that the Filipino nationalist Gen. Emilio Aguinaldo y Famy was not "a looter," as Otis had reported to Washington, but a popular and effective leader who had defeated the Spanish throughout the islands with no help from the United States. After publicly denying the existence of censorship, Otis wired the War Department paradoxically, that "all correspondents here satisfied with present censors" (Miller, p. 83).

Once warfare broke out with the nationalists, censorship seemed more legitimate as a means of denying the enemy military intelligence, although it quickly became apparent that it was designed more to cover up U.S. mistakes than to maintain security. Thus, correspondents were not even allowed to report that the U.S. Marines took Iloilo on the island of Panay a full three hours before the army could even land its seasick troops. One correspondent bootlegged a report via the Hong Kong terminal that contrary to the official report that U.S. troops had been enthusiastically welcomed on Negros, they were met with fierce resistance and that the fighting still continued on that island. Editorial eyebrows were lifted over this. Was Otis trying to deny Aguinaldo knowledge of the situation on Negros? Surely, he knew this, mused one editor. More correspondents followed suit, challenging Otis's fictional reports via Hong Kong. Otis demanded that Washington outlaw the use of that terminal, which was, he declared, the source of all the "detrimental reports alarming the country" (Miller, p. 83). Because Hong Kong belonged to the British, it is not clear how he thought Washington could do this.

Finally, the correspondents collectively rebelled in July 1899. Even the general's "favorites," to whom he gave private interviews containing some intelligence that more often than not turned out to be pure fiction, signed a "round robin" to their editors, reporting that the general's "ultra-optimistic view is shared by no one in the islands. Even his leading generals disagree with him" (Miller, p. 84), and complaining that "Otis compelled us to participate in this misrepresentation by excising or altering uncontroverted statement of fact." Collins followed with a long personal account of how "every fight became a glorious American victory, even though every one in the army knew it to have been substantially a failure," and correspondents "were drilled into writing, quite mechanically, wholly ridiculous estimates of the number of Filipinos killed" (Miller, pp. 84–85).

Otis first tried to wean his "favorites" away from the others, but they refused to meet with him alone. He then threatened them with court-martials for "espionage." After publicly denying that there was a censor, he publicly announced his appointment of a new one and escalated the censorship. Correspondents were not allowed to use the word "ambush" or to mention defective ammunition after one reporter revealed that half of the howitzer shells failed to explode on impact. He simply closed down the local Spanish-language *La Democracia*, and indicted Edward F. O'Brien, a former Minnesota volunteer, who had stayed behind as a civilian to edit *Freedom*, an English-language paper to serve the growing U.S. community in Manila, for "sedition." O'Brien's "crime" was that he had published a letter depicting Gen. Frederick Funston's anti-Catholic bigotry in desecrating a church with a mock mass in stolen ecclesiastical garb to amuse his Kansas soldiers from the "Bible belt." Otis had not even checked the validity of that report.

The censorship continued under the successors to Otis, but in much less stringent forms. At least, there were no more complaints from correspondents.

Stuart Creighton Miller

REFERENCES

Donald Chaput, "The American Press and General Vincent Lukban, Hero of Samar," *Leyte-Samar Studies* 8 (1974), 21–32; Stuart Creighton Miller, *"Benevolent Assimilation": The American Conquest of the Philippines, 1899–1903* (Yale Univ. Pr., 1982); Richard E. Welch, "The Philippine Insurrection and the American Press," *Historian* 36 (1973), 34–51.

See also Public Opinion and the Philippine War.

War Correspondents in the Spanish-Cuban/American War

Traditionally, the press in the Spanish-Cuban/American War has been labeled jingoistic and sensational. The newspapers are thought to have failed to meet the criteria for objective reportage. Although arguably one of the best sources for gaining an understanding of the perceptual world of 1899, or of how reporters construed the world they lived in and wrote about, the press until the last decade has been judged by a platonic division between the ideal and the real. This assumes that the history of journalism is independent of newspapers. More recently, scholarship has sought to correct this situation by placing war correspondents at the end of the 19th century in the context of sensibility of their times.

Journalists who covered the Spanish-Cuban/American War lived in a moral universe that passed away with the onset of World War I. It was a universe in which the grit and resolution of the individual still counted. Any social evil operating in the world was thought to result from the failure of the individual to act as he or she should. The keynote ideal was integrity, personal character, comprising moral uprightness and honorable dealings with others. The country was emerging from two decades of economic depression, industrial violence, and the closing of the western frontier. The people of the United States believed that character with a capital "C" was being thrown to the dogs. Consequently, men and women sought to reaffirm the ideals felt to be on the wane. Journalists were no exception.

There were two kinds of reporters in this war: professional journalists (for example, Sylvester Scovel, George Bronson Rea, and James Creelman) and literary stars (for example, Richard Harding Davis and Stephen Crane). Both valued accurate reporting of the facts. However, unlike today's reporters, these reporters believed that truth of correspondence (what actually happened in the field) was important only insofar as it related to truth of significance. That is, reporters believed that everyday events or facts could be understood properly only when their underlying moral significance was demonstrated. Consequently, the reports then appearing in newspapers contain material that today appears to be editorializing.

In keeping with the moral universe the reporters inhabited, the war with Spain presented difficulties to journalists, hardships that allowed the individual to demonstrate his or her mettle. It was not unusual for reporters to participate in as well as report on the skirmishes of battle. They thought theirs was a journalism that acted as well as reported.

From the beginning of the Cuban uprising against Spain, correspondents were faced with communication problems difficult enough to turn back the hardiest among them. Passing undetected through Spanish lines of defense, making their way through the dense jungle to revolutionary camps, and setting up reliable lines of communication from the revolutionaries to dispatch boats carrying their reports to neutral telegraph stations—all these required enormous personal strength and determination.

The conflict against Spain gave correspondents plenty of opportunity to exercise the virtues of self-reliance, devotion to duty, perseverance, and honorable conduct. Supply and communications problems caused more headaches for this generation of war correspondents than any other, with the possible exception of the generation covering the Vietnam War.

The U.S. Commissary was poorly organized and inefficient during the Cuban campaign. Reporters had permission to draw rations if they paid for them, but they were often turned away on the theory that there was barely enough to feed the troops. Some reporters left Tampa Bay, Florida, with their own supplies, but those working for smaller dailies and weeklies had neither the means nor the foresight to take food to Cuba.

Eventually, the army issued rations to the press only at Siboney. Those who had to rely on the army for their food stationed themselves in the rear and wrote their stories based on hearsay rather than on eyewitness accounts of battle. These stories were by and large attacked by the public as fabrications and despised by other reporters, who valued firsthand accounts of battles and who believed in the importance of "getting the facts."

In addition to supply and communications problems, reporters also had to weather difficult times with the U.S. military forces once the United States entered the conflict. At this point in history, the military had not developed any sense of "press relations." Some commanders, for example, Adm. George Dewey in the Philippine campaign, had good rapport with journalists. However, there was a general strain in relations between the press and the military in Cuba. In particular, Gen. William R. Shafter, the leader of the invading armies, got a poor press. He was fighting a war under impossible conditions, with outdated and insufficient equipment in a climate that was decimating his troops. He had little time or patience for journalists.

Even the Rough Riders, who emerged from this conflict with mythical status, did not evade the critical eye of members of the press.

Theodore Roosevelt, for example, was faulted by Richard Harding Davis for fraternizing with enlisted men. Likewise, Jimmy Hare, who was a photographer in this war, thought the Rough Riders were merely exhibitionists.

The reporters in Cuba are best understood in the context of their moral universe. They often participated in the battles they covered, but this reflects more their values than a departure from "objective" reporting. Reporting on the conflict presented supply and communications problems requiring grit, resolution, and devotion to duty, both moral and occupational. While some stories were based on hearsay, most were eyewitness accounts.

Mary S. Mander

REFERENCES

Charles Brown, *The Correspondent's War* (Scribner, 1967); Edwin Emery and Michael Emery, *The Press and America*, 6th ed. (Prentice Hall, 1988); Gerald Linderman, *The Mirror of War: American Society and the Spanish American War* (Univ. of Michigan Pr., 1974); Mary S. Mander, "Pen and Sword: Problems in Reporting the Spanish American War," *Journalism History* 9 (Spring 1982), 2–9, 23; David F. Trask, *The War With Spain in 1898* (Macmillan, 1981).

See also Crane, Stephen; Creelman, James; Davis, Richard Harding; Kennan, George; Press Censorship in the Spanish-Cuban/American War; Public Opinion in the Spanish-Cuban/American War; Remington, Frederic.

War Department in the Spanish-Cuban/American War (1898)

In early 1898, the United States War Department consisted of 10 staff agencies: the Adjutant General's and Judge-Advocate General's offices; the Inspector General, Quartermaster's, Subsistence, Medical, Ordnance, and Pay Bureaus; the Signal Corps; and the Corps of Engineers. Years of bitter controversy between secretaries of war and commanding generals over control of the army had combined with effective political lobbying by many bureau chiefs to give these offices virtual autonomy. Only the adjutant general and the inspector general took their orders from the commanding general; officers in the other bureaus, answerable to Congress and the secretary of war, had grown distant from their brethren in line positions. Bitter public sparring, years of slow promotion, and controversies about whether the campaigns against Native Americans should be considered "legitimate" experience widened the intra-service gap.

President William McKinley's selection of Russell A. Alger, Michigan politician and former Civil War colonel of cavalry, as secretary of war had done little to energize the War Department. Though conscientious, Alger was an inefficient administrator, poorly prepared for the challenges of mobilization and intercontinental war. Maj. Gen. Nelson A. Miles, commanding general of the army since 1895, was a proven battlefield leader, but his contentious personality, unwillingness to make substantial reforms in the institution that had propelled him to fame and fortune, and scorn for the proverbial "school-book soldier," suggested that he, too, would be hard-pressed by events. Further, the army lacked any institution to conduct strategic planning. Although the Military Information Division had been created in 1885, inadequate funding and staffing had limited its effectiveness. If war did come, most officers assumed that tactical expertise, recent modernization of weaponry, and physical bravery would overwhelm the enemy.

As the nation edged closer to war against Spain, belated efforts were made to increase army preparedness. In early March 1898 Congress passed a special $50 million military appropriations act. The navy received 60 percent of the money, however, and McKinley, fearful of upsetting any final chances for peace, ordered the army to confine itself to defensive measures. Coastal defense thus secured the lion's share of the army money, with the remainder dispersed among the Medical, Quartermaster, and Signal bureaus.

Fearful that Spanish raiders might assail the U.S. coastline, Miles welcomed the decision to bolster defenses. The appropriation had done little to improve the War Department's offensive capability. Even when assuming, as did most contemporaries, that the army would take the lead if war came, the regular army of less than 30,000 was incapable of undertaking effective offensive operations. To remedy the problem, Adj. Gen. Henry C. Corbin and Secretary Alger, working closely with John A.T. Hull, chairman of the House Committee on Military Affairs, proposed to increase regular forces to 104,000. Military officials projected a supplementary force of about 50,000 volunteers. Southern Democrats,

Populists, and advocates of state militias and the National Guard combined to block the regular expansion. Caving in to political pressures just four days before Congress declared war on Spain, President McKinley stunned his military advisors by raising his call for volunteers to 125,000. Only then did Congress consent to raise the statutory limit on regular enlisted personnel to 61,000.

Mobilization on this scale overwhelmed the War Department bureaus. Raising the men was relatively easy: clothing, feeding, housing, equipping, and training them was entirely another matter. Years of budgetary parsimony had precluded effective stockpiling of weapons or uniforms. The much-vaunted state militias were woefully unprepared. Plans to keep the recruits in their home states for 30 days, thus giving the army time to select and prepare main encampments, quickly went afoul. Alger's bungling performance at cabinet meetings, combined with the chaos at the Adjutant General's Office, which had been besieged by office-seekers, inspired little confidence among capital observers.

As the bureaus struggled to cope with the new demands, the army belatedly began mapping its strategy. Commanding general Miles believed a summer invasion of Cuba would be premature, citing the potential ravages of yellow fever and the strength of the Spanish garrison, estimated at 80,000 men and 200 artillery pieces. Miles instead recommended an attack on Puerto Rico. After taking that island, he argued, the army should allow the naval blockade to weaken the enemy and the cooler autumn weather to reduce the chances of disease before striking Cuba.

But McKinley had his doubts about the blustery Miles. Recognizing that Alger could not be depended on for sound military advice, the president had invited retired Gen. John M. Schofield to Washington in March. Schofield seemed unable to master the current situation, and the president soon shunted him aside in favor of Adjutant General Corbin as his most trusted military advisor. McKinley also remodeled a second-floor White House office into a war room replete with maps, 15 telephone lines, and 20 telegraph wires. Fearful that the U.S. public might lose interest in a long, drawn-out war, he demanded an early invasion of Cuba.

Commodore George Dewey's annihilation of the Spanish Pacific Fleet at Manila Bay, though opening a new range of strategic and imperial options, further muddled the army's response to an overseas war. Rather than limit offensives to Spanish possessions in the Caribbean, argued McKinley, the army must send an expeditionary force to the Philippines and exploit the victory. Thus, the War Department, already overburdened by the larger than anticipated call for volunteers, was assigned a new military objective of immense administrative and logistical complexity.

Inexperienced in dealing with numbers of the magnitude of 1898 and accustomed to the slower pace of the recent past, staff officers struggled to streamline outmoded bureaucratic rules and procedures. The Quartermaster and Ordnance departments scrambled to contract for and purchase materials for the expanded army, but maddening production delays often forced them to settle for substandard goods. Shortages in smokeless powder and modern Krag-Jörgensen rifles were particularly noticeable at the war's outset, and the volunteer units (with the notable exception of the Rough Riders) were issued the older .45-caliber Springfield single-shot breechloaders. Deficient summer uniforms compounded the soldiers' miseries.

Early plans had envisioned main camps at Chickamauga National Park, Georgia; New Orleans; Mobile, Alabama; and Tampa, Florida. To meet further needs, the army organized additional sites at San Francisco; San Antonio, Texas; and Washington, D.C., to supplement its original encampments. The troops were organized into separate corps of 30,000 infantrymen. Although later necessary for controlling troops in Cuba and the Philippines, the new military corps exacerbated shortages in experienced generals and staff officers in the domestic camps. Inadequate preparations, especially in terms of sanitation, rendered the War Department an easy target for news-hungry journalists. Although some exaggeration occurred, most of the unfavorable stories had much basis in fact.

In accord with McKinley's insistence on a quick Cuban strike, on 24 April Alger, Miles, and Corbin met to select a commander for the invasion force. In a controversial decision, they picked William R. Shafter, an aging Indian-fighter and Civil War veteran whose painful gout and 300-pound weight hardly suited him for summertime campaigning in the tropics. Shafter nonetheless went to Tampa, where the Cuban invasion force was being assembled. Early plans

having estimated that 5,000 men would undertake initial operations, the decision to quadruple the force at Tampa caught staff officers unprepared. A single rail line fed the port complex; logisticians poured in men and materiels without bothering to coordinate the supplies with their intended units. The incredible chaos once again reflected poorly on the entire War Department.

"The whole thing is beyond me," wrote one journalist of the appalling conditions at Tampa. "It is the most awful picnic that ever happened, you wouldn't credit the mistakes that are made" (Davis, pp. 246–247). Alger's anxious telegrams offered no help, and the arrival of commanding general Miles did little to ease the organizational morass. Strenuous if often inefficient efforts finally paid off, however, and 17,000 men were packed aboard overloaded transports, the last of which sailed on 14 June.

Difficulties, many of them attributable to poor administration and planning, continued to beset the Cuban expedition. The 22 June landing at Daiquirí went fairly well, but chronic shortages in specialized landing lighters and transports plagued Shafter's efforts for the rest of the summer. Rivalries between Shafter and Adm. William T. Sampson made planning awkward. Only by limiting troops in Cuba to bare essentials could the campaign even be continued. Rain, primitive roads, and fierce Spanish resistance at El Caney and San Juan Hill nearly led Shafter, dispirited by heavy losses and personally suffering from malaria, to call off his attack against Santiago. But the Spanish were in even worse condition; isolated from their homeland by the defeat of their Caribbean squadron and badly stung by heavy casualties of their own, they surrendered in mid-July.

The War Department had meanwhile learned from its early confusion. At San Francisco, the Philippines expeditionary forces, under the experienced administrative hand of Wesley Merritt, had departed without the chaos associated with Tampa. Miles's long-awaited strike against Puerto Rico, though once again cursed by poor relations with the navy, escaped most of the problems that had marred Shafter's Cuban campaign. Improvisation, expansion of government production facilities, and more expeditious dealings with private contractors had in the end mobilized, equipped, transported, and supplied enough men to launch three offensives. Adjutant General

Corbin, acting as McKinley's *de facto* chief of staff, won high marks for his administrative skills and his determination to give field commanders as much freedom of action as political and diplomatic considerations allowed.

By focusing their energies on the troops in the field, War Department officials had made victory possible. Spain and the United States declared a cessation of hostilities on 12 August. But the emphasis on solving immediate military problems and lax enforcement of regulations by the Inspector General Department left the army vulnerable to new crises in later summer 1898. In July, dysentery, malaria, and yellow fever swept through the force in Cuba. The Medical Department had neither the trained personnel nor the distribution system capable of meeting the epidemics. Shafter's officers composed a "round robin" which predicted impending disaster. Publication of this letter created yet another sensation, and in early August the administration began shipping Shafter's veterans back to Camp Wikoff, New York, long before that site on Long Island was prepared to receive them.

The crisis was not limited to the Cuban expeditionary force. To ensure that the expeditionary forces were combat-ready, the army had stripped units that remained in the United States of their best-trained, best-equipped personnel. But of the 200,000-plus volunteers called out in the spring, only some 35,000 had been sent overseas or even included in units assigned to overseas duty when the armistice was signed. Shortages of trained officers, particularly in staff and medical departments, became critical among the remaining volunteers. By midsummer, as typhoid swept through the camps (90 percent of all volunteer regiments reported cases of typhoid), morale and discipline had disintegrated. The situation at Camps Alger (near Washington, D.C.) and Thomas (at Chickamauga) seemed particularly embarrassing.

Finally awakened to the crisis, the War Department acted quickly and decisively. New commanders were assigned to help restore order, and officials continued to slice through unnecessary red tape. Massive redeployments shifted the largest commands to healthier camps where sanitation facilities were accorded closer inspection. But to a public already horrified by the chaotic mobilization effort, the almost comic assemblage at Tampa, the unprepared reception center at Camp Wikoff, and the specter of yellow fever,

malaria, and typhoid rampaging almost unchecked through the army, the War Department seemed a proper target for outrage. A total of 281 soldiers had died in combat; sickness and disease claimed nearly 10 times this number.

General Miles did nothing to assuage public confidence in late August when he leveled a series of sensational attacks against the War Department. Complaining that his plans to strike Puerto Rico had been leaked to the press, he blasted Secretary Alger for having circumvented proper military lines of authority and ignoring his recommendations which might have alleviated the spread of disease among troops on Cuba.

A furious Alger sought retribution against Miles, but President McKinley recognized that the public and the press demanded an official inquiry into the department's handling of the war. Although many of his original choices declined to serve, a nine-member commission headed by Gen. Grenville M. Dodge had been assembled by September 1898. Its hearings failed to produce much excitement until December, when Miles declared that unfit canned beef had been sent to the Caribbean. Further, an unhealthy chemical process had "embalmed" at least 327 tons of refrigerated meat.

In his own testimony the following month, Commissary General Charles P. Eagan accused Miles of having fabricated the entire episode and offered to "force the lie back down his throat covered with the contents of a camp latrine" (Ranson, p. 91). The sensational episode only reinforced the image of a War Department in shambles. Eagan was forced from active duty for conduct unbecoming an officer, but the Dodge commission refuted Miles's charges. As for the War Department, its report found many errors of procedure and administration, but little evidence of outright corruption. A court of inquiry was assembled to investigate the beef question; finding the commanding general's charges groundless, it also censured him for having failed to go through proper channels.

Although some journalists asserted that the two boards had merely done President McKinley's bidding, the Republican administration emerged from the inquiries the clear winner. The War Department's conduct of the war did not become a crucial issue in either the congressional elections of 1898 or the presidential contest of 1900. Even Alger might have escaped the backlash; only when the secretary allied himself with anti-administration elements did McKinley force his resignation from the War Department in mid-1899. To fill the position, the president selected Elihu Root, whose legal and administrative abilities seemed ideally suited to the needs of the new U.S. empire.

Root also inherited a new United States Army. With nearly 100,000 regulars occupying stations thousands of miles apart, the army, although including a number of veterans of the Indian-fighting constabulary and coastal defense force of years past, was forever changed. The War Department had done much to adapt to the new circumstances; in organizing an occupation force and colonial government in Cuba, its performance after early summer 1898 differed markedly from the moribund organization that emergency mobilization had once paralyzed.

Some of the early problems were beyond the War Department's control. Repeated changes in strategy and number of troops forced many improvisations. To have handled these variations would have required either strong central direction or close cooperation between line and staff officers. The army enjoyed neither of these advantages. Alger, Miles, the bureau chiefs, and corps commanders all dabbled in every phase of the mobilization process, often issuing contradictory orders and counterorders. Insufficient staff and a general unwillingness to delegate authority left high-ranking officials awash in petty details. Line officers, scornful of their brethren in the bureaus, failed to consider logistics when planning and undertaking their campaigns.

Secretary Alger and his bureau chiefs had labored manfully to overcome these obstacles. Upon the war's conclusion, Alger had been satisfied with a return to older procedures in the War Department. His replacement, Elihu Root, recognized that the old system was hardly adequate to administer, occupy, and defend the nation's overseas possessions. Even after Congress had passed Root's reforms, the conservative retinue of the old army mounted a powerful counteroffensive which took years to overcome. Such changes had been made possible only by the oft-embarrassing incidents of the war against Spain.

Robert Wooster

REFERENCES

Graham A. Cosmas, *An Army for Empire: The United States Army in the Spanish-American War* (Univ. of Missouri Pr., 1971); Charles Belmont Davis, *Adventures and Letters of Richard Harding Davis* (Scribner, 1917); Lewis L. Gould, *The Spanish-American War and President McKinley* (Univ. Pr. of Kansas, 1982); Edward Ranson, "The Investigation of the War Department, 1898–1899," *Historian*, 34 (1971), 78–99; David F. Trask, *The War With Spain in 1898* (Macmillan, 1981).

See also Alger, Russell Alexander; Corbin, Henry Clark; Miles, Nelson Appleton; War Department Investigating Commission.

War Department Investigating Commission

In contrast to its actions in 20th-century wars, the United States War Department paid scant attention in 1898 to managing the news and keeping the public informed of its activities. Officials were fully absorbed by the enormous logistical problem of creating an expeditionary fighting force from virtually nothing. The task was achieved, and the resulting military success was extremely gratifying. However, joy turned to shock and bewilderment in August 1898 when the publication in the press of a "round robin" sensationally revealed that the army of U.S. heroes in Cuba was on the point of complete disintegration. The daily press avidly reported gruesome stories of thousands of U.S. troops who were suffering from hunger, disease, and official neglect not only in Cuba but also throughout the volunteer camps in the United States.

Especially scandalous was the painful spectacle during August 1898 of the return of soldiers from Cuba to the hastily constructed rest camp at Montauk Point on Long Island, New York. Civilian visitors were able to see for themselves the inadequate provision of housing, food, and medical facilities. Long-held but concealed suspicions of incompetency and corruption in the War Department burst into the open. Blame for the appalling state of affairs was increasingly personalized and fastened upon Secretary of War Russell A. Alger. In popular speech the word "Algerism" was used as a term of abuse to denote maladministration and insensitivity.

Despite the intense criticism directed at the secretary of war, President William McKinley appeared reluctant either to repudiate Alger or to request his resignation. The president could not ignore the growing public demand for an investigation of the War Department, however.

Indeed, Republican leaders advised McKinley that presidential inaction could only be to the advantage of the Democrats in the midterm elections scheduled for November. Moreover, there was the distinct possibility that the new Congress might take the initiative and launch its own inquiry. The whole question acquired additional urgency on 7 September when Gen. Nelson A. Miles returned to New York from Puerto Rico and repeated allegations, which he had previously made overseas, that the War Department had consistently demonstrated a callous neglect for the welfare of the army.

To avoid the impression that the administration was being forced to act against its will or had anything to hide, Alger wrote to McKinley on 8 September asking for the appointment of a special presidential commission to investigate the War Department's conduct of the war. McKinley invited a number of prominent people to serve and secured nine acceptances by the end of September 1898. The designated chairman was Gen. Grenville M. Dodge, Civil War veteran and railroad builder. Six more active or retired officers agreed to serve: Gen. John M. Wilson, chief of engineers; Gen. James A. Beaver, former governor of Pennsylvania; Gen. Alexander McD. McCook, who had retired from the army in 1896; Col. James A. Sexton, a Chicago businessman who had only recently been elected commander of the Grand Army of the Republic; Col. Charles Denby, former minister to Chile and China; and Capt. Evan P. Howell, a former Confederate and former editor of the *Atlanta Constitution*. In addition, there were two civilians: Dr. Phineas S. Connor, a professor of surgery; and Urban A. Woodbury, former governor of Vermont. Richard C. Weightman, a journalist from the *Washington Post*, was appointed secretary.

The commissioners possessed considerable experience and impressive credentials, but a number of them were also known to be sympathetic to the War Department. Indeed, Dodge was a personal friend of Alger. Consequently, criticism emerged that McKinley had created an "Alger Relief Commission" with the calculated purpose of "whitewashing" the secretary and the War Department. Democrats also suspected an ulterior political motive and accused the president of trying to influence the result of the November midterm elections by his removal of a troublesome issue from public debate.

Whatever its potential shortcomings, the formation of the commission alleviated public anxieties. The commissioners journeyed to Washington and received their instructions from President McKinley in a meeting at the White House on 24 September. The president was most concerned about finding out whether there was any truth to the charges that the War Department had criminally neglected the welfare of the soldiers. He urged the commission to undertake a thorough and systematic examination of the work of the Commissary, Quartermaster, and Medical bureaus. If any failings due to incompetency or maladministration were discovered, the officials responsible must be identified. But the commission was not to be regarded as a legal court of inquiry. Although no constraints or limits were to be placed on the investigation, the commission would not have the power to compel witnesses to attend or to force them to make statements under oath.

Officially described as "The United States Commission Appointed by the President to Investigate the Conduct of the War Department in the War with Spain," and more popularly referred to as "the Dodge Commission," the commission began its proceedings on 26 September 1898 and continued until 9 February 1899. Sessions were open to the public and held in the Lemon Building in Washington. A total of 595 witnesses were called. Further testimony was collected by subcommittees in visits to 12 states around the nation. In addition, the commission requested and duly received the submission of a considerable amount of relevant written material.

The commissioners disregarded material relating to military policy and strategy, preferring to concentrate on technical matters, such as clerical administration, housing and transportation of troops, and provision of medical facilities. As the weeks passed, a mass of statistical information was written into the record, but no sensational revelations of gross incompetence or corruption in high places were forthcoming. Despite being granted immunity from prosecution, military witnesses showed an understandable reluctance to criticize higher-ranking officers or government officials. Especially disappointing for critics of the War Department was the testimony of Gen. Joseph Wheeler whose combative reputation was belied by his diplomatic statements that the War Department had struggled to do its best for the soldiers and was not directly to blame for the initial difficulties faced by the troops at Montauk Point.

In fact, before the commission came into session, the War Department had taken remedial action to improve conditions in all the military camps. Consequently, what had been headline news in August was relegated to the back pages in October. McKinley's strategy was further vindicated by the results of the midterm elections in November. Republicans were relieved that their party's electoral losses were not as bad as had been feared. Indeed, the Dodge Commission seemed on the point of being forgotten until the dramatic intervention of General Miles on 21 December 1898. The commanding general of the army appeared before the commission and reiterated his old criticisms of the War Department's conduct of the war. But he also added new and extremely damaging charges relating to the purchase of large stocks of canned roast beef and its inclusion among the soldiers' rations. According to information he had received, Miles believed that the meat had been treated with chemicals. He also declared that soldiers had suffered considerable sickness after eating what he described as "embalmed beef."

Commissary General Charles P. Eagan was personally incensed by Miles's accusations and demanded the right to reply. What began as a vigorous defense of commissary arrangements was overshadowed by his scathing and intemperate denunciation of Miles. Considerable sympathy existed for Eagan, but the manner of his rebuttal was regarded as ill-advised and as conduct unbecoming an officer. The result was Eagan's court-martial and conviction. Meanwhile, Miles's reference to "embalmed beef" had so aroused public alarm that the Dodge Commission found it necessary to concentrate its investigation on the "beef controversy." The final report of the commission stated that canned roast beef was an acceptable ration though it was also considered an unsuitable food for the tropics. Miles's charges were held to lack substantiation, and the general was rebuked for withholding his suspicions from the proper authorities. A similar conclusion was reached by the separate military court of inquiry appointed by McKinley on 9 February 1899 and which presented its findings to the president on 29 April.

The preliminary report of the Dodge Commission was received by McKinley on 9 February 1899. In its final published form it comprised eight large volumes representing testimony which spanned 109 days of inquiry. On the central question of maladministration by the War Department, the commission found no evidence of corruption or criminal incompetence. The report noted certain deficiencies in the mustering and transportation of troops and in the provision of housing and medical facilities. The commissioners acknowledged, however, that the lack of military preparedness in 1898 was not the fault of the War Department but the result of the historic aversion of the United States to maintaining a large standing army during peacetime. It was to the credit of War Department officials that in such short time, they had mobilized huge numbers of men in preparation for overseas campaigns. The commissioners adopted an ambiguous attitude toward the secretary of war. While the final report noticeably avoided reprimanding Alger by name, an unmistakable note of criticism was contained in the report's concluding statement that "there was lacking in the general administration of the War Department during the continuance of the war with Spain that complete grasp of the situation which was essential to the highest efficiency and discipline of the Army" (*Report of the Commission . . . to Investigate the Conduct of the War Department . . .* , p. 12).

Although the press and public did not deny that the Dodge Commission had performed a thorough investigation, some disquiet was expressed at what was held to be a "whitewashing" of Alger. Proudly and stubbornly, Alger let it be known that he felt personally maligned by the report's concluding statement. His defiance of criticism could not continue indefinitely, however, and he was compelled for political reasons to resign his office in August 1899. By contrast, McKinley appeared beyond reproach. His creation of a special presidential inquiry had initially deflected and eventually dissipated the public outcry aroused by the sensational revelations of August 1898. The Dodge Commission proved to be more than just a successful political maneuver. The material contained in its voluminous report proved invaluable to the new secretary of war, Elihu Root, and greatly facilitated his implementation of an extensive program of reform and reorganization of the War Department.

Joseph Smith

REFERENCES

Russell A. Alger, *The Spanish-American War* (Harper, 1901); Graham A. Cosmas, *An Army for Empire: The United States Army in the Spanish-American War* (Univ. of Missouri Pr., 1971); Edward Ranson, "The Investigation of the War Department, 1898–99," *Historian*, 34 (1971), 78–99; Jasper B. Reid, Jr., "Russell A. Alger as Secretary of War," *Michigan History*, 43 (1959), 225–239; *Report of the Commission Appointed by the [U.S.] President to Investigate the Conduct of the War Department in the War With Spain*, 56th Congress, 1st Session, Senate Doc. No. 221 (U.S. Government Printing Office, 1900), 8 vols.

See also Alger, Russell Alexander; Corbin, Henry Clark; Miles, Nelson Appleton; War Department in the Spanish-Cuban/American War (1898).

War Finance in the Spanish-Cuban/American War

The conflict of summer 1898, the "splendid little war," was a showcase of war financing for the United States. It was a splendid little financing performance by all actors involved: the investing public, the borrowing government, and the political decision makers.

Throughout the 1890s, the U.S. economy experienced repeated bouts of severe recessions and financial crises. In 1897, as war approached, economic activity was in an upswing, and the federal budget registered a small deficit of $18 million, or about 5 percent of total spending. On 9 March 1898, in anticipation of the start of the fighting, President William McKinley secured from Congress the allocation of $50 million for military expenditures. This legislation became known as the "Fifty-Million-Dollar Bill." The actual cost of the war was far greater, and the financing mechanisms were much more complex.

It is remarkable that estimates of the actual direct cost of the war fall within a fairly narrow range of $250 million to $300 million. However, indirect costs, such as pension claims and interest payments, probably added several hundred million dollars to the war bill over subsequent years. To provide some perspective, the estimated direct cost of about $300 million represented 75 percent of total federal receipts in 1898 and 50 percent of total spending in 1899. Millionaires offered great sums to assist with war preparations. For example, William Randolph Hearst volunteered to finance a cavalry regiment

(but was turned down by the army), while John Jacob Astor offered a battery of artillery. In early 1898, only about $25 million from surplus funds was available for immediate use in prosecuting the war. Thus, to finance the war monies had to be raised through taxation and/or borrowing.

At the time, however, two main sources of government receipts (customs duties and the income tax) were virtually incapable of additional yields. The Dingley Tariff, adopted in July 1897 after a long and bitter controversy, was unlikely to be altered by Congress before its first anniversary. For most imported goods, raising tariff rates would have reduced the revenue obtained. To lower the tariff would have defeated its protectionist purpose, a key policy of the McKinley administration. In 1895 the United States Supreme Court had declared the current income tax law to be unconstitutional. In any case, an income tax generates revenue rather slowly, whereas the immediate need was to accumulate war funds as quickly as possible. Thus, in practical terms, the choice of war financing was narrowed to excise taxes and/or borrowing.

The political debate in Washington over war financing mirrored the economic policy controversies of that era between the agrarian-silverite and the gold standard factions struggling for predominance in the country. In Congress, House members from the industrialized North proposed to finance the war by floating loans and increasing excise (or "internal revenue") taxes. Representatives from the agricultural southern and western states countered with proposals for an income tax on high incomes and the issuance of new silver coins and greenbacks. In the end, a compromise was reached that increased the rates of several existing excise taxes and reimposed some of the taxes levied during the Civil War.

The war revenue bill of 1898, among other provisions, doubled the tax rate on beer and tobacco, imposed license taxes on bankers and brokers, and levied amusement taxes on admissions to theaters, circuses, bowling alleys, and billiard rooms. It also placed stamp taxes on legal documents, cosmetics, drugs, chewing gum, and playing cards; imposed a transfer tax on stocks and bonds; and levied an inheritance tax on estates over $10,000 (with some exceptions). The bill, as amended in the Senate and finally adopted in June 1898, was estimated to yield $150 million in additional revenue per year.

Because tax receipts only flow periodically over time into government coffers, however, it was clear that the Treasury Department would be unable to meet war expenditures without borrowing substantial sums. After much discussion, Congress authorized the maximum borrowing, at the discretion of the administration, of $100 million in short-term Treasury notes and $400 million in long-term (10 to 20 years) bonds. An unusual feature of this financing effort was that both Congress and the president favored the experiment of attracting large numbers of small lenders. The long-term bonds were issued in denominations as low as $20, subscriptions were received by mail, every bid under $500 was immediately accepted, and no submission over $4,500 was allowed. Over one-half of the entire issue was taken by 230,000 small subscribers. In all, over 320,000 persons offered to participate in the June 1898 loan, and the total amount tendered was an astonishing $1.4 billion. However, only $200 million was placed. This "popular loan" became the precursor of the massive marketing of war bonds in World War I.

In sum, to meet the expenditures of the brief campaign of summer 1898, the U.S. government assembled a massive bulwark of financial resources. The total direct costs of the war were covered mainly by the $200 million loan described above. But Washington had available for use, if needed, over $1 billion in loan offers. By 1899 tax revenues were $160 million higher than before the war, in large measure due to the wartime excise taxes and the rise in economic activity prompted by the hostilities.

In fact, in 1900 the federal budget registered a surplus of about $80 million, and for the first time in six years part of the national debt was retired. According to Carl C. Plehn: "For the first time in our history the credit of the country was so used that it grew stronger rather than weaker from its use" (Plehn, p. 419). Lewis H. Kimmel concluded: "The economic and financial impact of the war was extremely light, and no significant inflationary pressured developed" (pp. 81–82).

For Spain, the intervention of the United States on the side of the Cuban revolutionaries was but a brief episode at the end of a long struggle to preserve the last remnants of its empire in the Western Hemisphere. Cuban patri-ots had already waged the Ten Years War from 1868 to 1878. Later attempts to secure increased autonomy under the Spanish flag came to nothing. Consequently, the Cuban War of Independence was unleashed in February 1895 under the leadership of José Juláan Martí y Perez, Antonio Maceo, and Máximo Gómez y Báez.

By summer 1898, Spain had strained its economy to finance military operations against Cuban and Filipino revolutionaries. In 1897–1898 more than one-fourth of the Spanish budget was allocated to war expenditures (both army and navy). In confronting the United States, Spanish naval authorities failed to make needed repairs to ships, restore crews to full strength, and provide complete batteries for all armored vessels. It is the majority view among historians that in 1898 Spain was simply unable to pull together sufficient resources to put strong forces on the battlefield against the United States.

In the formal sense of war financing through taxation and borrowing, there is no Cuban side to be related. Rather, the Cuban patriots, whose revolutionary government was never officially recognized by Washington, collected monetary and in-kind contributions for the war effort from cigar workers in Tampa, Florida, and sympathizers in New York and other cities. However, one novel, if unrealized, scheme merits attention. In early 1898, the Cuban revolutionary government in exile offered to purchase the independence of the island from Spain for $200 million. The plan called for the United States to issue bonds to be financed by claims on future customs receipts of the Republic of Cuba. This was the road not taken: the Cuban war financing strategy that never was.

From the U.S. perspective, however, the financing of the war of 1898 was a successful undertaking and a vast improvement over the financing of any U.S. war up to the end of the 19th century.

Sergio G. Roca

REFERENCES

Lewis H. Kimmel, *Federal Budget and Fiscal Policy, 1789–1958* (Brookings Institution, 1959); Carl C. Plehn, "Finances of the United States in the Spanish War," *The University Chronicle* (Univ. of California Pr., 1898), vol. 1; Paul Studenski and Herman E. Krooss, *Financial History of the United States* (McGraw-Hill, 1963).

War Planning Against Mexico

In November 1910, a moderately reformist movement led by Francisco I. Madero and other wealthy provincial elites in Mexico called for armed popular revolt against the government of Porfirio Díaz. Their goal was to rescue the nation from political corruption and short-sighted economic policies that aggravated regional and class conflicts in Mexico. Their most immediate objective was to stabilize existing property and labor relations. Asked to comment on this movement, Díaz is said to have remarked that Madero "has unleashed a tiger. Now let us see if he can control it."

By 1913, however, it had become clear that neither Madero nor Gen. Victoriano Huerta, who overthrew Madero that year, could control the social movement which had been unleashed in 1910. Landless peasants and exploited workers became armed revolutionaries attacking *haciendas*, railroads, mines, and oil fields—the very properties that enriched their owners even as they impoverished the lower classes.

For U.S. policy makers and wealthy businessmen who had substantial investments in Mexico, the Mexican Revolution threatened the growing strategic, economic, and ideological domination of Mexico by the United States. Moreover, many of President Woodrow Wilson's cabinet officers, trusted political advisors, and prominent Democratic party officials had significant personal investments in Mexican properties. Drawing on its recent experience in suppressing anticapitalist and anti-imperialist insurrections among Native Americans, Cubans, Filipinos, and Nicaraguans, the U.S. foreign policy-making establishment immediately began planning for war with Mexico.

Although publicly denouncing the bloody February 1913 coup against Madero, the Wilson administration initially supported Huerta's government by exempting it from the general arms embargo declared by President William H. Taft. Wilson apparently believed that these arms purchases would assist the Huerta government to crush its opposition, stabilize social relations, and promote U.S. investments. But by September Huerta, even with covert U.S. assistance, had failed to defeat his regime's enemies. Moreover, his government, following the example of Porfirian diplomacy, increasingly sought to expand its authority by playing upon imperial rivalries and favoring the investments of countries other than the United States. This, combined with Venustiano Carranza's August intercession against Gen. Lucio Blanco's attempt to redistribute properties in Tamaulipas, tended to increase the U.S. government's confidence in Carranza's Constitutionalist faction even as it undermined support for Huerta.

No longer content to manipulate Mexican events covertly, either through political intrigues, arms embargoes, arms sales, or U.S. army maneuvers on the border, the Wilson administration began developing contingency plans for war with Mexico in November 1913. At a cabinet meeting in early January 1914, the Wilson administration officially embraced a policy of armed intervention in Mexico.

The invasion, planned in the offices of Secretary of War Lindley M. Garrison and Secretary of the Navy Josephus Daniels, essentially recreated the 1847 war plan so successfully executed by Gen. Winfield Scott. It called for simultaneous naval operations off the Gulf coast at Veracruz and the transfer of army troops, munitions, and logistical supplies to Galveston, Texas, which would serve as headquarters for the land assault. Gen. Leonard Wood ordered the activation of the 2nd Division, "composed of ten regiments of infantry assigned to three brigades (Fourth, Fifth, and Sixth), the Sixth Cavalry, the Fourth Field Artillery, an engineer battalion, a signal corps company, an ambulance company, a field hospital, and assorted headquarters and service troops" (Millett, p. 252).

It was generally understood that the 11,000 officers and men included in the 2nd Division would not be sufficient to secure a full-scale occupation of Mexico, which would require "an army of several hundred thousand men and millions of dollars in military spending" (Millett, p. 252). But U.S. objectives in 1914 did not include territorial acquisition; they were limited to basic counterinsurgency; that is, the stabilization of social and political systems that protect and promote private enterprise. Reorganization of the military force structure and the creation of a new "mobile army" was aimed to achieve these goals. Mexico offered the first opportunity to test their effectiveness. The plans were ready to be implemented; only a pretext to intervene was required.

Before January 1914, frequent border clashes between Mexican revolutionaries and Texas Rangers or provocations engineered by navy ships loaded with marines and anchored in Mexican harbors might easily have served as a *casus belli*. The Wilson administration had not yet decided on the military option, however. After that decision was made, excuses to intervene abounded. Informed that two ships, the *Ypiranga* and the *Monterey*, laden with German arms and Colt machine guns destined for Huerta, were en route to Veracruz, Wilson chose to create an international crisis out of an otherwise insignificant incident in Tampico. Within months, U.S. troops occupied Veracruz at the cost of 500 Mexican casualties and decisively tipped the military balance of power among the various revolutionary factions in favor of the more moderate Constitutionalists led by Carranza. The intervention was a triumph for counterinsurgency planning.

Keith A. Haynes

REFERENCES

Guy Renfro Donnell, "United States Intervention in Mexico, 1914," Ph.D. diss., University of Texas, 1951; Allan R. Millett, *The General: Robert L. Bullard and Officership in the United States Army* (Greenwood Pr., 1975).

Watson, John Crittenden (1842–1923)

John Crittenden Watson, a career officer of the United States Navy, commanded the Eastern Squadron during the Spanish-Cuban/American War in 1898.

Watson was accepted as a midshipman on 16 June 1860 and saw extensive duty during the Civil War at Forts Jackson and St. Philip; Chalemette and Vicksburg Batteries; Port Hudson; Grand Gulf, Mississippi; and Mobile Bay. For 33 years thereafter he alternated duty afloat and ashore: the Mediterranean Squadron (1865–1869), the Asiatic Station (1870–1871), New York and Mare Island Navy Yards (1873–1877), and the Pacific Station (1886–1887, 1890–1892). He then served with the North Atlantic Squadron during the Spanish-Cuban/American War from June to September 1898.

U.S. forces defeated one Spanish squadron in Manila Bay on 1 May 1898 and a second off Santiago de Cuba on 3 July. However, a third squadron, commanded by Adm. Manuel de la Cámara y Libermoore, left Cádiz, Spain, on 16 June via the Mediterranean and Suez Canal to relieve the Spanish garrison in the Philippines. The Navy Department in Washington countered by forming from the North Atlantic Squadron an Eastern Squadron that would strike Spain's coasts and then proceed to the Philippines. It leaked the information in the hope that it would result in Cámara's recall. Commodore Watson assumed command of the new squadron on 7 July. With Cámara's fleet being recalled from Port Said, Egypt, to Spain on 6 July and Spain sending out peace feelers on 22 July, the Eastern Squadron—"the fleet that never was"—was no longer needed.

Watson's last important billets were as commandant of the Mare Island Navy Yard (1898–1899) and commander in chief, Naval Forces, Asiatic Station (1899–1900).

Paolo E. Coletta

REFERENCES

French Ensor Chadwick, *The Relations of the United States and Spain: The Spanish-American War* (Scribner, 1911), 2 vols.; William B. Cogar, *Dictionary of Admirals of the U.S. Navy, Volume I: 1862–1900* (U.S. Naval Institute Pr., 1989), 203–204; Margaret Leech, *In the Days of McKinley* (Harper, 1959); John D. Long, *The New American Navy* (Outlook, 1903), 2 vols.; David F. Trask, *The War With Spain in 1898* (Macmillan, 1981).

See also Eastern Squadron, United States Navy (1898).

Welles, Sumner (1892–1961)

Sumner Welles played an important role in the negotiations for the U.S. withdrawal from the Dominican Republic under the administration of President Warren G. Harding, serving as the key conduit during the lengthy talks regarding the details of the withdrawal arrangement and the transition period.

Welles was a young New York aristocrat who, after graduating from the Groton School and Harvard University, joined the Foreign Service in 1915, becoming one of the State Department's most important Latin American specialists. He served in Japan and Argentina, before returning to Washington as chief of the Latin American Division of the State Department. In this post he participated in the initial 1922 talks between Secretary of State Charles Evans Hughes and Francisco J. Peynado regarding the administration's second plan for a military withdrawal to end the occupation. Welles proved highly adept at dealing with the Dominicans, reflecting his understanding and appreciation of Latin culture and the political realities of the Caribbean region.

After the initial agreement was announced, Welles was sent to Santo Domingo as special commissioner and "personal representative" of President Harding to conduct the final negotiations and oversee implementation of the plan. His appointment was designed to assure that the senior U.S. official in the Dominican Republic reflected the views of Harding and the State Department and was committed to the successful implementation of the accord. His understanding of Latin America, knowledge of Spanish, and skillful diplomacy proved essential.

The military governor, the navy, and even the U.S. minister in the Dominican Republic opposed parts of the withdrawal plan, and Welles's task was both to negotiate with the Dominican political leaders and to assure that the U.S. officials did not impede progress. His arrival greatly improved contacts between U.S. officials on the island nation and the local political leaders, who had previously been ignored by arrogant and high-handed U.S. officials convinced of their own righteousness, and who paid scant attention to local opinion. Welles arrived fully committed to successful implementation of the withdrawal plan. He recognized that the support of local moderates, political leaders, and members of the elite was essential to a successful termination of the U.S. occupation.

Welles initially toured the island nation's principal cities to measure public opinion and to emphasize the new U.S. concern for local viewpoints, while building support for the agreement. The envoy then settled into a routine of almost daily negotiations with the Dominican political leaders in Santo Domingo.

Welles convened a commission composed of the heads of all major political parties, Peynado, and Archbishop Adolfo A. Nouel, thus involving all the participants in the Washington negotiations. Upon Welles's recommendation, this Comisión de Representantes was empowered to elect the new provisional president. Only a single party chief, Federico Henríquez y Carvajal, brother of the former provisional president, refused to participate, though his party eventually joined the talks. Welles sat with the commission in all its sessions. On 2 October 1922, the commission began the transition by electing Juan Bautista Vicini Burgos provisional president. This decision assured that a wealthy member of the elite who had no link to any of the nation's political parties would supervise the transition.

The daily commission sessions reviewed and debated all the details of the entire accord, dealing with the myriad of sensitive steps necessary to implementing the withdrawal plan. Its agreements fleshed out the details regarding timetables, identified the laws to be endorsed, established procedures, defined the powers of the provisional government, and clarified the command and control of the Guardia Nacional Dominicana. Welles had the tact and understanding to conduct these sensitive negotiations, recognizing when compromise was essential. His patience and his willingness to debate all issues with the Dominicans made possible a full review of the plan. In the process he committed the Dominicans to its implementation, even though the sessions modified only a few details and added only minor clarifications to the initial plan. While the changes were limited, they were essential to successful implementation of the plan. The procedure provided due respect to Dominican nationalism, thus assuring party and public support.

Welles's function included serving as an intermediary between local occupation officials and the Dominican political leaders. The military governor, Adm. Samuel S. Robison, viewing the matter purely from a military viewpoint, objected to many provisions of the arrangement. He was particularly opposed to withdrawing U.S. officers from the Guardia and turning command of it over to the Dominican provisional government. He frequently disagreed with Welles regarding this matter and other specific steps in the arrangement. In all cases Welles favored compromise and recognized the need for the Dominicans to maintain political control and to protect their public standing. Robison appealed to the Navy Department, which supported his stand, while the State Department consistently supported Welles. With a dispute between cabinet officers, the ultimate decision fell to the president. Harding supported Welles in all cases, reflecting his commitment to arranging a withdrawal.

Hence, Welles proved to be the key instrument in ending the U.S. occupation of the Dominican Republic. Admiral Robison was withdrawn shortly after the provisional president assumed office, while Welles stayed on to oversee the transition. Welles was withdrawn in 1924 by President Calvin Coolidge. Before returning to the State Department under Franklin D. Roosevelt, Welles wrote a two-volume history of the Dominican Republic entitled, *Naboth's Vineyard: The Dominican Republic, 1844–1924,* published in 1928. The work demonstrated his interest in and understanding of the nation and the context of Dominican politics.

Welles continued on to a distinguished career in the Foreign Service, serving as ambassador to Cuba, and as both assistant secretary of state for Latin American affairs and undersecretary of state, the State Department's second ranking position, during the administration of his friend, Franklin D. Roosevelt. Reflecting his actions in promoting withdrawal from the Dominican Republic, Welles served as an important architect and implementer of Roosevelt's Good Neighbor policy.

Kenneth J. Grieb

REFERENCES

Irwin F. Gellman, *Good Neighbor Diplomacy: United States Policies in Latin America, 1933–1945* (Johns Hopkins Univ. Pr., 1979); Kenneth J. Grieb, *The Latin American Policy of Warren G. Harding* (Texas Christian Univ. Pr., 1976); Kenneth J. Grieb, "Warren G. Harding and the Dominican Republic U.S. Withdrawal, 1921–1923," *Journal of Inter-American Studies,* 11 (1969), 425–440; Dana G. Munro, *The United States and the Caribbean Republics, 1921–1933* (Princeton Univ. Pr., 1974).

West Coast Expeditionary Force (3rd Marine Brigade), United States Marine Corps (1927–1929)

The deployment of the West Coast Expeditionary Force to protect U.S. lives in China was the result of the success of the Guomindang's (Kuomintang) Northern Expedition. Launched in the wake of Chinese nationalist leader Sun Yat-sen's death, the Northern Expedition was designed to unify the entire country under Guomindang (GMD) rule and to oppose foreign imperialism. It was supposed to be the military conquest of warlord China by the National Revolutionary Army (NRA).

The NRA began in July 1926 from the GMD's revolutionary base in Canton and drove north into Hunan. It then moved north and east into Hubei (Hupeh) and Jiangxi (Kiangsi). At the same time, a second column advanced north along a coastal route, engaging warlord forces in Fujian (Fukien) and Zhejiang (Chekiang). By late 1926, the GMD was in control of most of China south of the Yangzi (Yangtze). Revolutionary forces were poised to seize the Wuhan cities (Hankou [Hankow], Wuchang, Hanyang) in central China and were approaching Shanghai.

The Northern Expedition was motivated by a Chinese nationalism that was unalterably opposed to foreign territorial concessions and privilege. In the first quarter of 1927, the NRA was advancing on the center of foreign influence and power in China, Shanghai. By February, the antiforeign incidents occurring in the wake of the Northern Expedition, sponsored by the GMD, panicked the concessionaires and their governments.

The most violent episode occurred in Hankow in January. A mob overran the British concession, and bloodshed was avoided only by surrendering part of British authority over the concession. Over the next several weeks, foreigners residing in the Yangzi Valley were evacuated to Shanghai, where they spread tales and rumors of antiforeign incidents and atrocities.

Most foreigners compared the Northern Expedition to the Boxer Uprising (1899–1901). The Treaty Powers' initial inclination was to meet it the same way, with armed force. In February and March 1927, an international force of approximately 10,000 men assembled in Shanghai to defend the International Settlement. In an emergency, sailors and marines from the warships anchored in the river could be used to reinforce the garrison.

The International Settlement was the hub of foreign influence and power in China. It was founded as part of the settlement of the First Opium War in 1842. Because of its exterritorial status, it, and all of the other foreign concessions in China, constituted a state within a state (outside Chinese legal jurisdiction). By the 1920s, the settlement had a population of 1 million, living on 5,500 acres; one-third of the municipality's population was living on approximately half of its land area. To all external appearances, the International Settlement looked like a modern Western city.

The International Settlement had long been a haven for Chinese revolutionaries. Antidynastic groups used it to operate outside the jurisdiction of the Chinese government in the first decade of the century, and although the concession authorities did not favor revolution they had enough trouble keeping track of foreign criminals to prevent them from concerning themselves with Chinese politics. However, as the NRA drew closer to Shanghai, the police cooperated with the city's warlord government to suppress GMD activities.

The role of Shanghai as the center of foreign economic and cultural power in China precluded a peaceful foreign withdrawal from the city. It was against this background of privilege, revolution, and politics that the marine expeditionary force was deployed.

Although the West Coast Expeditionary Force eventually consisted of three infantry regiments (4th, 6th and 12th U.S. Marines), one artillery battalion, a tank platoon, an engineer company, three squadrons of aircraft, and the appropriate staff organization, it was deployed piecemeal. The first contingent, the 4th Marines, arrived at Shanghai in late February 1927. Given the uncertainties surrounding U.S. China policy, they did not land until 21 March.

On that day, the Shanghai Municipal Council, dominated by British, Japanese, and U.S. interests, declared a settlementwide state of emergency. Workers' militias, led by GMD and communist cadres, began an armed insurrection against the warlord troops occupying Shanghai. The fighting lasted until 23 March, when the NRA reached the city, and tension persisted until the middle of April. At that time, the 4th Marines provided internal security patrols for the settlement (in late spring and summer, their mobile patrols took part in its perimeter defense).

The long anticipated antiforeign outbreak occurred at Nanjing (Nanking) the next day, 24 March. This is known as the Nanjing Incident: foreign warships fired on Chinese troops, pillaging parts of the city, to protect foreign lives. These actions aroused the U.S. public's enthusiasm for armed intervention in China. The rest of the expeditionary force sailed for China at the beginning of April. By this time, the GMD purge of the communists, its conciliatory attitude toward the Treaty Powers, and the large numbers of foreign troops in Shanghai lessened the threat of an antiforeign outbreak.

The point of conflict shifted from the lower Yangzi to North China. Leaving the 4th Marines in Shanghai (they were not withdrawn until November 1941), the bulk of the 3rd Brigade

and its commander, Gen. Smedley D. Butler, were sent to the Beijing (Peking)-Tianjin (Tientsin) corridor in June 1927. Joining the United States 15th Infantry (stationed in Tianjin since 1912) and the legation guard, the number of U.S. troops in North China rose to more than 5,000 officers and enlisted men. There was a total of approximately 16,000 foreign troops in the area.

Butler's mission was to protect U.S. lives by discouraging other powers from intervening, which he accomplished through noncooperation with such efforts, and by maintaining good relations with the Chinese military and civilian authorities. It was complicated because the expeditionary force was independent of the legation guard and the 15th Infantry, which were in North China under the terms of the Boxer Protocols (1901) and were bound to cooperate with other national contingents in the defense of the Beijing legations and the Tianjin concessions. The expeditionary force was not bound by this agreement.

Butler informed the other national commanders his troops would not cooperate in the defense of the Tianjin concessions nor would they help guard the Tianjin-Beijing railroad. Over the next 18 months, Butler and his troops supported the U.S. neutrality policy by their presence in North China.

The major military test for the expeditionary force came in June 1928, when, with the 15th Infantry, it placed itself between retreating northern troops and the NRA. Its task was to prevent the retreating warlord armies from occupying Tianjin and Beijing. Chinese troops were dealt with by persuasion and bluff rather than by force. A sliding payment scale for surrendered rifles, pistols, ammunition, and swords was established, along with the promise of a free, hot meal. These benefits were publicized by leaflets written in Chinese and dropped from patrolling aircraft flying reconnaissance missions. Potentially violent situations were thus defused.

The main problem U.S. commanders in China faced at this time was not hostile military action, but maintaining troop morale and combating boredom. In both Shanghai and Tianjin these problems were overcome by a rigorous schedule of military exercises and athletic and social events. In Tianjin, the exercises concentrated on deploying the expeditionary force to reach Beijing by road in order to supervise the evacuation of foreign civilians from the city. To this end, the Beijing-Tianjin highway was strengthened to support heavy trucks and tanks, and exercises emphasizing cooperation between armor, artillery, infantry, and air support were held regularly. In the first six months of 1929, the mission of the North China contingent was broadened to include civic action projects, such as bridge- and road-building as well as canal and waterway repair.

The West Coast Expeditionary Force was the largest combined arms unit the United States deployed overseas in the interwar period. The U.S. operations (military support for diplomacy) contrasted favorably with British and Japanese actions during the same period. U.S. marines, sailors, and soldiers acted as unofficial envoys attempting to defuse violent Chinese anti-imperialist sentiments with diplomacy and tact. The main focus of the expeditionary force's operations was not combat, but mediation between the United States and China, a characteristic of retreating imperial power. China was becoming important as a potential ally/client against Japanese ambition.

Lewis Bernstein

REFERENCES

Dorothy Borg, *American Policy and the Chinese Revolution, 1925–1928* (American Institute of Pacific Relations, 1947); Bernard D. Cole, *Gunboats and Marines: The United States Navy in China, 1925–1928* (Univ. of Delaware Pr., 1983); Donald A. Jordan, *The Northern Expedition: China's National Revolution of 1926–1928* (Univ. Pr. of Hawaii, 1976); Louis Morton, "Army and Marines on the China Station: A Study in Military and Political Rivalry," *Pacific Historical Review*, 29 (1960), 51–73; Hans Schmidt, *Maverick Marine: General Smedley D. Butler and the Contradictions of American Military History* (Univ. Pr. of Kentucky, 1987).

See also Air Operations in China (1927–1928).

Weyler y Nicolau, Valeriano, Marques de Tenerife (1839–1930)

Valeriano Weyler y Nicolau, a career Spanish military officer, tried to suppress the Cuban independence movement in the 1890s through harsh measures, but succeeded only in further arousing public opinion in the United States against Spanish policies in Cuba.

Weyler was born on 17 September 1839 in Palma de Majorca. He was of Prussian descent and entered the military at age 16, attending the Infantry College of Toledo. He next attended the staff college as a lieutenant and graduated at the head of his class in 1861. Two years later Captain Weyler was sent to Cuba and was soon included in the expedition to the Dominican Republic during Spain's reannexation of that country. His able service was recognized with the Cross of San Fernando with laurels.

Between 1868 and 1872, Weyler was stationed in Cuba to participate in the suppression of the Ten Years War and was recognized as a brilliant military officer. In 1872, he returned to Spain as brigadier general and fought against the Carlista rebels. In Spain, as in all of his previous assignments, Weyler used harsh methods to quell insurgency and earned a reputation as an effective but brutal soldier.

Weyler was rewarded by promotion to general of division and with the title of Marques de Tenerife. He was also elected senator. Between 1878 and 1883, he was governor general of the Canary Islands and in 1883 governor general of the Balearic Islands.

In 1888 General Weyler was appointed governor general of the Philippines, where he led the effort to suppress native uprisings in the Caroline Islands, Mindanao, and other provinces. He returned to Spain in 1892 and became commander of the 6th Army Corps, directing the effort to pacify the Basque provinces and Navarre. He then became captain general at Barcelona until January 1896, continuing to be a harsh but effective suppressor of dissent anarchists and socialists in that city.

When Arsenio Martínez de Campos failed to pacify Cuba with his more liberal policies, conservative Prime Minister Antonio Cánovas del Castillo appointed Weyler captain general of Cuba in January 1896, in response to the new tactics adopted by the Cuban revolutionaries. The Cubans knew that time was on their side. They could defeat the Spanish by not losing the war; they did not have to win. If Spain could not protect the property and privileges of the planters, it would not be able to maintain sovereignty. The Cuban revolutionaries began a campaign in rural Cuba to destroy property, production, and peace.

Weyler arrived in Cuba in early 1896 with 50,000 new troops, bringing the Spanish forces to 200,000. He knew that the guerrillas must be denied support by the rural population who supplied them with food, supplies, intelligence, and medicines. In the fall General Weyler issued a series of decrees ordering the rural population to evacuate the countryside and to move into designated fortified towns. Army commanders escorted the rural people into the designated towns and laid waste the countryside, destroying everything capable of sustaining life. Houses, food reserves, fields were set ablaze, and all livestock not driven into fortified towns was slaughtered.

The peasants were crowded into reconcentration camps, an estimated 300,000 young and old, all noncombatants. The resettlement camps were hastily constructed and poorly supplied. No attention was given to health and sanitation. The towns were unable to provide the needs of the resettled peasants, and the Spanish army assumed no responsibility. Diseases and starvation took a high toll. Civilian detainees died by the tens of thousands. Weyler earned the name *El Carnicero* (The Butcher). His policy aroused a storm of protest abroad, especially in the United States, and led to a demand for his recall. The Spanish government led by the Liberal Práxedes M. Sagasta responded to world public opinion by recalling Weyler in October 1897, even though he was achieving success in the struggle against the rebels.

In Spain, Weyler's reputation as a strong and ambitious soldier made him a prominent figure in the political and constitutional troubles during the opening years of the 20th century. In 1900 he became governor general of Madrid and contributed to several ministerial crises. In 1901, 1905, and 1906 he served as minister of war. In 1909 he was again governor general of Barcelona and quelled the disturbances without violence at the time of the controversial execution of the Socialist Francisco Ferrer Guardia.

From 1921 to 1923 Weyler was army commander in chief. He was promoted to field marshal and retained his rank after participating in the unsuccessful plot in 1926 against the Miguel Primo de Rivera regime. Weyler died in Madrid in 1930 with his reputation as a severe and unyielding military man intact.

Robert D. Talbott

REFERENCES

Thomas W. Crouch, *A Yankee Guerrillero: Frederick Funston and the Cuban Insurrection, 1896–1897* (Memphis State Univ. Pr., 1975); Philip S. Foner, *The Spanish-Cuban-American War and the Birth of American Imperialism, 1895–1902* (Monthly Review Pr., 1972), 2 vols.; Louis A. Pérez, Jr., *Cuba Between Empires, 1898–1902* (Univ. of Pittsburgh Pr., 1983).

Wheaton, Loyd (1838–1918)

Loyd Wheaton was a soldier of courage and ability who, like others, experienced an eclipse of his reputation as a result of the frustrations of the Philippine War. A Michigan veteran of the Civil War, Wheaton fought in a number of western battles, rose to the rank of colonel, and won the Medal of Honor for conspicuous bravery during the assault on Fort Blakely, Alabama, in 1865.

After the end of the Civil War Wheaton continued his service in the infantry, soldiered on the western frontier, and was commissioned a brigadier general of volunteers during the Spanish-Cuban/American War. After the war with Spain ended, Wheaton was ordered to the Philippines with two regiments to assist in the suppression of the Filipino nationalists led by Emilio Aguinaldo y Famy. Arriving in Manila on 23 February 1899, Wheaton was assigned a role in an offensive planned by two U.S. commanders, Maj. Gen. Elwell S. Otis and Maj. Gen. Arthur MacArthur. The objective was Aguinaldo's capital at Malolos, about 30 miles from Manila, which, if taken, Otis believed, would result in the end of the war.

As an initial step, Wheaton was sent in early March with a brigade to clear the Pasig River line from Manila to Laguna de Bay, a large lake only a few miles from Manila Bay. Seizing several key towns, Wheaton displayed the boldness that normally characterized his maneuvers and cut Aguinaldo's army into separate portions north and south of the river and the lake. With this success, and with the arrival at Manila of Brig. Gen. Henry W. Lawton's two regiments, MacArthur could confidently undertake his march northward on Malolos.

The U.S. forces were divided into two divisions, the first to be commanded by General Lawton and the second by General MacArthur. The offensive began on 21 March. Wheaton's brigade, attached to MacArthur's division, served with distinction in the sharp fighting, seizing several railroad bridges. Malolos fell in late March, but Filipino attacks continued in the rear of U.S. forces. Wheaton used the opportunity to display his mettle. During a Filipino attack near Guiguintó on 10–12 April Wheaton and his men counterattacked with such enthusiasm and success that General MacArthur specifically called attention to Wheaton's "splendid warlike ferocity" (Leroy, p. 36).

As Aguinaldo retreated northward, a plan was developed by General Otis to crush the enemy completely. Wheaton was to have a critical role, probably earned by his aggressiveness that summer in taking towns on Luzon, such as Dasmarinas and Imus. A three-pronged attack was to be aimed at Aguinaldo's army in autumn as it withdrew into Northern Luzon. Generals MacArthur and Lawton, in separate columns, would push the Filipinos north toward Dagupan on Lingayen Gulf. There, Aguinaldo would be cut off by a third force, commanded by Wheaton, which was to sail from Manila and, with naval support, land on the Lingayen shore at San Fabian and move south to link up with MacArthur at Dagupan. Caught in the trap thus formed by U.S. forces, numbering no less than 35,000 men, Aguinaldo and his army would either surrender or die. Despite poor security, the plan proceeded very well. Both MacArthur and Lawton generally achieved their missions. Wheaton was not so fortunate.

The U.S. offensive began in the South on 12 October. On 6 November Wheaton left Manila in naval transports with 2,500 men of the 13th Regular and 33rd Volunteer Infantry Regiments. On 7 November the transports rendezvoused with naval gunboats in the Gulf. After the navy shelled Filipino entrenchments at San Fabian, U.S. troops headed ashore in two columns of small boats. The enemy withdrew toward Dagupan, however, abandoning San Fabian to Wheaton. Patrols went out shortly, but Wheaton did not immediately set out for Dagupan, and it was not until 11 November that U.S. troops reached San Jacinto, just six miles from the landing zone. A bloody encounter followed in which the 33rd Infantry killed 134 Filipinos.

It was a critical moment in the campaign and, as it occurred, in General Wheaton's career. Had he driven on into Dagupan, or even occupied the nearby town of Rosario in force, Wheaton may well have accomplished one of the major objectives of the campaign: the capture of Aguinaldo. Unaccountably, he did not. Instead, he returned to San Fabian, sending only a small reconnaissance force to Rosario. Perhaps he understood his orders to restrict him to holding the coastal road and preventing a Filipino escape northward. Whatever his reason, Wheaton fumbled a golden opportunity. Even as Wheaton's men moved about the outskirts of Rosario, Aguinaldo was concealed in the home of the local police chief. Shortly after, on 15 November the Filipino leader escaped to Pozorrubio and from there made his way into the jungles and mountains of Isabela Province. There, he launched the guerrilla war that bled the Philippines until 1902. Just a few hours after Aguinaldo left Pozorrubio, Lawton's cavalry occupied the town and made contact with Wheaton's forces.

On 16 November Wheaton moved into Pozorrubio and captured the rebel foreign minister and Aguinaldo's mother and son, but the main prize was lost. Among others, General Lawton understood how much had been forfeited and drafted a bitter complaint to Otis.

Dagupan was at last occupied on 26 November, but well before then the three U.S. columns had converged. Thus, a remarkable campaign closed with the virtual destruction of the regular Filipino army. Undoubtedly, Otis's plan had been a sound one, and, except for Wheaton's hesitation at Dagupan, it had been well executed. Had all its objectives been obtained, the Philippine War may have ended much sooner than it did, and many lives could have been saved.

In 1901 Wheaton was made commander of the Department of Northern Luzon. He fought the guerrillas with determination, imitating their methods of burning villages and visiting reprisals on the population that supported the enemy. He was not, however, alone in conducting this kind of war.

On 30 March 1901 Wheaton attained the rank of major general; on 15 July 1902 he retired from the service. His last years were passed in Chicago. Wheaton died on 17 September 1918, a soldier whose single significant failure cast a lasting shadow over a bright career.

C. David Rice

REFERENCES

James H. Blount, *The American Occupation of the Philippines, 1898–1912* (Putnam, 1912), 234–239;

James A. Leroy, *The Americans in the Philippines* (Houghton Mifflin, 1914), vol. 2, 30–41, 128–133, 138–139, 224; Gregorio F. Taide, *The Philippine Revolution* (Modern Bk. Co., 1954), 326–331; U.S. War Department, *Report of the War Department, 1900* (U.S. Government Printing Office, 1901), vol. 1, pt. 6, 528–561; Richard E. Welch, Jr., *Responses to Imperialism: The United States and the Philippine-American War, 1899–1902* (Univ. of North Carolina Pr., 1979), 26–36.

Wheeler, Joseph (1836–1906)

"Fighting Joe" Wheeler, a Southern cavalry leader in the Civil War, was a lawyer, merchant, farmer, statesman, and writer. In the Spanish-Cuban/American War he became a national hero during the skirmish at Las Guásimas, Cuba, the first significant land battle of the conflict fought by the army, and he played a colorful, if not prominent, role in the campaign before Santiago de Cuba.

Wheeler was born 10 September 1836, in Augusta, Georgia, to parents who had moved there from New England. He received only a sporadic education, but in 1854 won appointment to the United States Military Academy. After graduating four years later, he served two years in the United States Army, including a brief stint against Native Americans in New Mexico. When the South seceded from the United States in 1861, Wheeler resigned from the army to join the Confederacy.

In Confederate service Wheeler moved quickly through the ranks, earning a reputation as a disciplinarian and a leader. In July 1862, he succeeded to the command of the cavalry of the Army of Mississippi, and rose successively to brigadier general, major general, and, although only 28 years old, lieutenant general. He fought at Shiloh, Murfreesboro, Chickamauga, and elsewhere, but he gained lasting fame for his opposition to Union Gen. William T. Sherman in Georgia.

After the Civil War Wheeler engaged in a number of activities. He was a merchant in New Orleans briefly and then a cotton grower, lawyer, and politician in Alabama. He won election to the United States Congress and served continuously from 1885 to 1900. Perhaps his most important public service was his constant effort to reintegrate the Confederacy into the country. Married in 1866, he and his wife, Daniella (Jones) Sherrod, had seven children.

When the Spanish-Cuban/American War started in 1898, President William McKinley appointed Wheeler a major general of volunteer forces, an action designed to help reunite the North and South. Wheeler, then age 62, commanded a dismounted cavalry division in the V Army Corps, the unit assigned to Cuba.

During his brief three and one-half weeks in Cuba, Wheeler was active. Upon debarkation at Daiquirí, on the island's southeastern coast, he was to station his troops in the rear to protect the beachhead. Instead, he ordered his men to take the road to Siboney, a coastal village where landing operations would also occur. At Siboney, he learned that Spanish forces were holding a strategic point, Las Guásimas, about three miles away and inland along the road to Santiago de Cuba.

Wheeler determined to attack. Dividing his command, he sent some 460 men, including units of the black 10th Cavalry, with three Hotchkiss revolving cannons along the main road. He ordered a detachment of the colorful Rough Riders, about 500 men, to take a wooded and tangled trail, about a mile west of the road. They were to meet at Las Guásimas. The subsequent battle, fought early on the morning of 24 June, was a significant victory for the U.S. forces because it boosted U.S. morale, removed any threat to landing operations, and opened a land route to Santiago de Cuba, the center of Spanish strength in the area.

When U.S. troops moved inland, Wheeler, as well as dozens of others, became ill, suffering from such tropical diseases as yellow fever and malaria. Despite his illness, Wheeler participated in the battle of San Juan Hill and gave his commander, Gen. William R. Shafter, advice and support during the subsequent siege of Santiago de Cuba. He took part in the surrender negotiations, and in mid-July he was one of the U.S. representatives at the formal surrender ceremonies.

After the war Wheeler commanded Camp Wikoff, a convalescent and demobilization center, at Montauk Point on Long Island, New York. Situated amid rolling sand dunes on the island's eastern end, the camp aided men in recovering from tropical fevers and wounds suffered in Cuba. Because the camp was not ready when he and the first troops arrived in August, Wheeler worked desperately hard to organize the place, even to overseeing the digging of additional water wells and the building of medical facilities.

With the war over, Wheeler found himself in demand at celebrations around the country—"Peace Jubilees," they were called. He attended several, including one in Atlanta with President McKinley and General Shafter. He also led a brigade of troops to the Philippines, but he soon returned to the United States. Commissioned a brigadier general in the regular army in June 1900, Wheeler just a few months later on his 64th birthday retired from the army. He died 25 January 1906, in Brooklyn, New York, and was buried in Arlington National Cemetery.

Wheeler's military career was marked by aggressiveness, determination, and reliability. Beloved by his men and appreciated by his superiors, his nickname was well earned. He was an excitable soldier and an enthusiastic Southerner; when the Spaniards retired at Las Guásimas, he may have yelled: "We got the damn Yankees on the run!" Wheeler wrote several books, including *Cavalry Tactics* (1863), a textbook; *The Santiago Campaign* (1898), a sketch of his Spanish-Cuban/American War experiences; and with his wife *American Ancestors of the Children of Joseph and Daniella Wheeler* (n.d.).

Paul H. Carlson

REFERENCES

John Percy Dyer, *"Fighting Joe" Wheeler* (Louisiana State Univ. Pr., 1941); Margaret Leech, *In the Days of McKinley* (Harper, 1959); G.J.A. O'Toole, *The Spanish War: An American Epic—1898* (Norton, 1984); David F. Trask, *The War With Spain in 1898* (Macmillan, 1981); Joseph Wheeler, *The Santiago Campaign, 1898* (Lamson, Wolffe & Co., 1898).

See also Las Guásimas, Cuba, Battle (1898).

Wilson, James Harrison
(1837–1925)

James Harrison Wilson commanded the China Relief Expedition, sent by the United States to assist in quelling the Boxer Uprising of 1900–1901.

Born in 1837 in southern Illinois, Wilson entered the United States Military Academy at West Point in 1855 and was commissioned a second lieutenant in the topographical engineers in 1860. He was stationed on the West Coast until summer 1861 when he was ordered east.

Wilson had a brilliant Civil War career, rising from second lieutenant to major general. He spent most of the war as a staff officer, serving in early Union operations in the East and on Gen. Ulysses S. Grant's staff in the West (1861–1863).

In April 1864, Wilson received his first field command, the 3rd Cavalry Division of the Army of the Potomac under Gen. Philip H. Sheridan. Wilson had much to learn about the actual handling of troops and made mistakes during the Wilderness and Spotsylvania campaigns. However, he was a rapid learner who never made the same mistake twice and served Sheridan well in the Shenandoah Valley campaign that fall. In September 1864, he was transferred to Gen. William T. Sherman's command at the latter's request.

In March 1865 he led an offensive through Georgia and Alabama. His mounted corps of more than 14,000 soldiers destroyed supplies, railroads, and factories and defeated Gen. Nathan B. Forrest's army at Selma, Alabama, on 2 April 1865.

Peace found Wilson in central Georgia as a military governor. He supervised the liberation of Andersonville Prison in South Carolina, and his troops captured the fleeing Confederate President Jefferson Davis on 10 May. On the heels of this coup, Wilson was made a major general; he was age 27. He remained a military governor until July, when his command was disbanded.

Wilson stayed in the army until the end of 1870, but peacetime routine and a reduction in rank and pay from wartime caused him to resign his commission. He was married and had a growing family to support.

Between 1871 and 1883, Wilson worked to build, promote, and manage railways in the Mississippi Valley, New York, and New England.

Wilson spent most of the next 15 years as a world traveler and man of letters, writing about his travels, his war experiences, and the famous people he knew. He also helped reorganize public utility companies, successfully traded in the stock market, and was a partner in unsuccessful attempts to start munitions companies (Longacre, p. 318).

In 1898, at age 60, Wilson volunteered his services at the beginning of the Spanish-Cuban/American War. He was given command of the VI Corps, but that unit was never organized. Instead, he went to Puerto Rico as a brigade commander under Gen. Nelson A. Miles. The Puerto Rico invasion was a secondary part of the war and shortly after the U.S. landing, the war ended. Later that year, Wilson was made the military governor of Matanzas, Cuba. He stayed in that post until he was asked to go to China as second-in-command of the American China Relief Expedition.

Wilson was chosen to go to China because of his experience in China in 1885–1886 investigating opportunities for railroad development. He went reluctantly, but was still eager to display his military talents. Unfortunately, Wilson landed in Tianjin (Tientsin) two weeks after the relief of Beijing (Peking).

In the weeks after he arrived in China, the Allies sent three large punitive expeditions to pacify the surrounding countryside, punish localities that harbored Boxers, and eliminate the Boxer units that remained in the capital area. Wilson commanded the third of these expeditions, which set out from Beijing on the afternoon of 16 September.

It was an Anglo-Indian-U.S. force consisting of U.S. artillery; two battalions of the 9th and 14th Infantry Regiments; a troop of the 6th Cavalry Regiment; a Royal Welch Fusiliers battalion; and two battalions of Baluchis, Sikhs, and Pathans; approximately 2,000 officers and men. Its mission was to disperse the last sizeable concentration of Boxers known to be near the capital, at Badazhou (Patachow, also known as the Eight Pagodas).

The force surrounded the temple area and attacked. The plan was executed with little difficulty. There were no Allied casualties, while nine Boxers died and several Chinese civilians were wounded. Although Wilson had no desire to destroy any of the temples, which he had visited 15 years before and which he considered a cultural treasure, the British had other ideas. Wilson offered to withdraw and let the British take whatever action they might wish, but before the U.S. contingent withdrew, the British blew up one of the pagodas. Ironically, Wilson was blamed for this vandalism, but he ultimately cleared his name.

Over the next few weeks, Wilson led smaller expeditions, but found no Boxers. In fact, he was dismayed by the condition of the countryside along the Allied line of march, comparing it unfavorably to central Georgia at the end of the Civil War. Outside the Allied line of march he found only conditions of harmony and industry (Wilson, vol. 2, pp. 521–535).

Wilson left China in December 1900, and by a special act of Congress retired as a brigadier general in the regular army. In 1902, he was a U.S. representative to the coronation of King Edward VII; in 1915 he was advanced on the retired list to major general in the regular army, a rank he had held in the volunteers twice before in 1865 and 1898. He died in 1925.

As a Civil War general, Wilson was in the mold of Forrest, Sherman, and Sheridan. He believed in prosecuting military operations vigorously, and he thought the days of cavalry as a shock arm were finished. He contended that cavalry should be employed as mounted infantry who used horses as a means of transportation and fought dismounted using rapid-fire weapons, supported by mobile artillery, like 20th-century mechanized infantry. Despite his leadership of the China Relief Expedition and his tactical innovations during the Civil War, he remains a comparatively unknown figure in U.S. military history.

Lewis Bernstein

REFERENCES

James P. Jones, *Yankee Blitzkrieg: Wilson's Raid Through Alabama and Georgia* (Univ. of Georgia Pr., 1976); Edward G. Longacre, *From Union Stars to Top Hat: A Biography of the Extraordinary General James Harrison Wilson* (Stackpole, 1972); Edward G. Longacre, "General James Harrison Wilson," *Delaware History*, 16 (1975), 298–322; James Harrison Wilson, *China . . . Together With an Account of the Boxer War*, 3rd enl. ed. (D. Appleton, 1901); James Harrison Wilson, *Under the Old Flag: Recollections of Military Operations in the War for the Union, the Spanish War, the Boxer Rebellion, etc.* (Appleton, 1912), 2 vols.

Wirkus, Faustin E. (1897–1945)

Faustin E. Wirkus, a career marine, achieved distinction and much public notice because of his governance of a portion of Haiti during the U.S. occupation (1915–1934).

Born in Pittston, Pennsylvania, in 1897, Wirkus joined the marines in 1915 to escape from life in the coal mines. He was sent to Haiti in August 1915, but after accidentally breaking his arm, he spent much of his first four years in Haitian and U.S. hospitals. Wirkus reenlisted in April 1919 and returned to Haiti as a second lieutenant in the Gendarmerie d'Haiti. Assigned to Perodin to fight *Cacos* (Haitian peasant guerrillas), he learned to speak creole fluently. Fascinated by Haitian customs and culture, he became convinced that he could improve the life of the peasants if he were given control of a district where the natives were not openly rebellious but merely unhappy.

His opportunity came in 1925 when he was appointed subdistrict commander of La Gonâve, an island separated from Port-au-Prince by 42 miles of Caribbean Sea. Made responsible for the well-being and good conduct of its 10,000 inhabitants, Wirkus was the only white man on the island. He soon discovered that most of the natives were organized in Congo agricultural societies loyal to a local queen called Ti Meminne. By recognizing her authority and working with her, Wirkus proved an unusually effective ruler. He built a landing field and improved the wharf at the island capital, Anse-a-Galets, rationalized the tax collection, protected small landholders from encroachment by their neighbors, and helped the peasants to develop better breeds of hogs and varieties of melons. For their part, the Haitians, impressed by his genuine concern for them and by the coincidence that his first name was identical to that of Faustin Élie Soulougue, king of Haiti from 1848 to 1858, arranged a special voodoo ceremony in the mountains and crowned Wirkus king of La Gonâve.

Wirkus received much publicity in Haiti and the United States after journalist William B. Seabrook visited him on La Gonaïve and recounted his adventures in a widely read book, *The Magic Island*, published in 1929. Americans were fascinated by the story of "The White King of La Gonave," but Haitian President Louis Borno regarded the lieutenant's "kingship" as a threat and arranged for his transfer to another post. In 1931 Wirkus left the marines to devote himself to lecturing and selling securities for a Wall Street firm. His own book about his experiences, ghost-written with Taney Dudley, was published in the same year. It was dedicated "to thousands of men, women and children who have written me for information about La Gonâve, its people and my life on the island." In 1939, he reenlisted in the marines. Wirkus died in 1945 after a long illness.

Jane M. Rausch

REFERENCES

James H. McCrocklin, *Garde d'Haiti, 1915–1934* (U.S. Naval Institute Pr., 1956); William B. Seabrook, *The Magic Island* (Harcourt, 1929); Faustin E. Wirkus and Taney Dudley, *The White King of La Gonave* (Doubleday, 1931).

Wise, Frederic May (1877–1940)

Frederic May Wise, a marine career officer, personifies the "Old Corps" of traditional naval service missions and "small wars" involvement in the first three decades of the 20th century. This was the period before the United States Marine Corps evolved into a fourth co-equal service specializing in amphibious warfare. Born on 6 October 1877 in New York City, Wise served as a commissioned officer between 1899 and 1926. He commanded marine detachments on three ships (the battleships *Oregon* and *Georgia* and the armored cruiser *Tennessee*) before World War I and served numerous tours at marine barracks, including those in Boston, New York, Annapolis, Philadelphia, and Washington, D.C. During World War I, he served in France between 1917–1919, initially commanding the 2nd Battalion, 5th Marines; later, he served in the United States Army's 4th Infantry Division, commanding the 59th Infantry Regiment and later the 8th Infantry Brigade. In World War I, he participated in most of the major battles of the American Expeditionary Force, including Belleau Wood, the Aisne-Marne (Soissons) Offensive, the St. Mihiel Offensive, and the Meuse-Argonne Offensive, plus the occupation of the Mosel Valley.

It is in his "small wars" service that Wise reflects a new, but short-lived, commitment of the Marine Corps to expeditionary duty during the period of U.S. expansion overseas. He served and fought in the Philippines (1899–1901 and 1904–1905), China during the Boxer Uprising (1900), Puerto Rico (1902–1903), Cuba (1907–1909 and parts of 1910, 1911, and 1912), Mexico (Veracruz, 1914), the Dominican Republic (1916), and Haiti (1915–1916 and 1919–1921). During his second tour in Haiti, Wise commanded the U.S. raised, supported, and led Gendarmerie d'Haiti between 19 July 1919 and 22 February 1921; this force, manned by Haitians but officered by U.S. Marines, was a constabulary and not an army; it was charged with the suppression of rebellion in the countryside and generally the maintenance of law and order. It was also backed by the 1st Provisional Marine Brigade stationed in Haiti. During his tour in Haiti, Wise was commended by various marine and naval commanders, and indirectly by the Mayo Court of Inquiry on Gendarmerie d'Haiti abuses. The president of Haiti also awarded him the Haitian Medaille Militaire in 1920 and commended him when he left the island in 1921. Also, upon his departure, the Haitian *Le Nouvelliste*, a daily, anti-occupation newspaper, wrote on 28 February 1921, that "General Wise was one of the few American officers who considered that the respect due to Haitians was one of the duties of his office . . . he is one of the rare officers who has been able to realize the height and delicacy of his position and who has never treated Haiti as a conquered territory."

Wise retired from the Marine Corps as a colonel because of ill-health on 19 January 1926. Because of his commendation for performance of duty in combat in World War I, on 16 January 1936 he was promoted to brigadier general. He died on 24 July 1940. General Wise was awarded the Distinguished Service Medal (United States Navy for Belleau Wood, and United States Army for the Argonne), and the French Legion of Honour and *Croix de Guerre* (with Palm) for his World War I service. He was also commended for his actions during the San Francisco earthquake and for his service in China, the Philippines, Mexico, the Dominican Republic, and Haiti (including, in 1916, by the citizens of a town reluctant to see him transferred), plus the Marine Corps and army for his commands during World War I. After retirement, Wise published a highly personalized memoir, *A Marine Tells It to You.*

Donald F. Bittner

REFERENCES

Robert Debs Heinl, Jr., and Nancy Gordon Heinl, *Written in Blood: The Story of the Haitian People, 1492–1971* (Houghton Mifflin, 1978), 453, 456; Hans Schmidt, *The United States Occupation of Haiti, 1915–1934* (Rutgers Univ. Pr., 1971), 103, 106; Frederick M. Wise and Meigs O. Frost, *A Marine Tells It to You* (J.H. Sears & Co., 1929; reprinted by Marine Corps Assoc., 1981).

Wood, Leonard (1860–1927)

Leonard Wood, military governor, chief of staff, was a controversial and innovative leader in the United States Army from the turn of the century into the 1920s. He was born on 9 October 1860. Leonard grew up in the village of Pocasset, on Buzzard's Bay in Massachusetts, where his father practiced as a physician after arduous service in the Civil War. Those who knew him said he was quiet, adventurous, studious, with perseverance, endurance, and a steady, calm way, marked by occasional bursts of temper and a chuckling sense of humor.

In 1880, his father died and Wood entered Harvard Medical School to take up his father's profession. He delayed taking his degree to gain experience as a house-officer in the Boston City Hospital. There, he ran afoul of Dr. G.H.M. Rowe, the manager, whose petty rules Wood violated. There were many small operations a duty doctor could perform without waiting hours to find a senior physician, and Wood sometimes acted without delay. Several of these instances, combined with a refusal to take admonitions seriously, led to his dismissal. Undeterred, Wood tried private practice in Boston, but inactivity led him to a fateful decision which reflected his strong spirit of adventure. In 1885, he joined the army medical corps, placing second in a group of 59 on the examinations. Since there was no vacancy for a military doctor, he went to Arizona as a contract surgeon.

Wood was posted immediately to Fort Huachuca, Arizona, under Brig. Gen. George Crook and volunteered for service against Geronimo and the Apaches who were on the warpath. He came under the immediate command of Capt. Henry W. Lawton, and Wood showed his appetite for action and responsibility. Wood not only acted as the unit medical officer, but also assumed command of a refractory detachment as Lawton's troop chased Geronimo hundreds of miles into Mexico before capturing the wily chief. For his exploits in combat and as a voluntary hostage, Wood received the Medal of Honor.

In 1886, Wood accepted a commission in the army medical corps and began a period of routine duty in San Francisco and Atlanta. In 1890, he married Louise Condit-Smith, a ward of Supreme Court Justice Stephen Field. He was promoted captain and assistant surgeon in 1891. In this period he became known as a very studious officer and magnificent athlete.

In 1895, Wood was transferred to Washington, D.C. and began to expand his political contacts. He became physician to President and Mrs. William McKinley and met Theodore Roosevelt. Wood and Roosevelt became fast friends and talked over the issues of the day as they boxed, hiked, and rode horseback. When the Spanish-Cuban/American War broke out, the two men formed the 1st United States Volunteer Cavalry Regiment, known as the Rough Riders, composed of college men, cowboys, and others eager for a fight. With Roosevelt's flair for publicity and Wood's organizational ability, the outfit finessed its way aboard rail transport and ships at Tampa, Florida. Wood led the regiment into combat at Las Guásimas, Cuba, 24 June 1898 and succeeded to command a brigade at the San Juan Hill battle a week later, where Theodore Roosevelt led the Rough Riders. Wood earned a growing reputation for his leadership in the assault, where he demonstrated exemplary calm under fire in rallying troops.

Gen. William R. Shafter considered Lawton and Wood the two most capable officers in his command and appointed Wood military governor of the city of Santiago de Cuba. At this point Wood was also promoted to brigadier general of volunteers. As he began to clean up the refuse of Santiago, he joined with other officers in a "round robin," protesting the deplorable condition of the army, decimated by tainted supplies, malaria, and yellow fever. The War Department sent reinforcements and appointed Wood governor of Santiago Province in October 1898.

Wood put Cubans to work cleaning and building roads, streets, bridges, and docks, paying them first with rations and then with checks. Tons of refuse were burned, and thousands of buildings cleaned by squads of workers fighting the dreaded yellow fever. He canvassed the countryside, urging villagers to give what little they could to their municipality so he could provide them with a mayor, policeman, doctor, and some sanitation. He distributed supplies throughout the interior, made merchants keep their prices down, and encouraged farmers to resume cultivation. He solved the brigandage problem by forming the better Cuban soldiers into a rural guard. He appointed capable Cubans to office and gave the inhabitants of Oriente Province a

bill of rights copied from the first 10 amendments to the United States Constitution.

Two examples indicate how Wood stood out among other leaders at this time. Gen. John R. Brooke, military governor of Cuba, wanted to use Santiago revenues for general distribution from Havana. Wood preferred them in Oriente, so Brooke accused him of loose financial methods. Wood demanded a court of inquiry, and Brooke backed down. Also, more than 40 newspaper articles from around the country as well as numerous personal letters to Wood praised him for rejecting a $30,000-a-year job in business and for staying in Cuba to perform humane, reform work. Furthermore, he kept Roosevelt informed about Cuban affairs, and the New Yorker began to recommend Wood for Brooke's post.

In December 1899, after interviewing Gens. William Ludlow, Fitzhugh Lee, and James H. Wilson, Secretary of War Elihu Root and President McKinley selected Wood because they thought he had the necessary tact and forcefulness to get along with the volatile Cubans and would follow presidential policy. McKinley had forced out Russell A. Alger, his inept secretary of war, and appointed Root, who became the architect of his colonial policy of responsible trusteeship. He sacked Brooke because of scandals and mismanagement in Cuba.

Under Wood, the military government of Cuba was reformist. His imagination, drive, and integrity helped prepare Cuba for nationhood. The courts were made more effective and independent of politics. Three thousand schools were built or renovated, and the University of Havana was rejuvenated with new facilities and curricula. A public works program gave people jobs and improved the island's infrastructure with roads, bridges, sewer and water systems, railroads, telegraphs, hospitals, and asylums. Yellow fever was conquered with research Wood financed. The first free elections in Cuba, held in 1900, placed mayors and city councils in office. He prevented U.S. citizens and other foreigners from exploiting Cuba and urged development of the Cuban economy through private sector exports of sugar and tobacco. The tariff provided virtually all of the government revenue.

In fall 1900, an election was held for delegates to a convention that was to frame a constitution and relations with the United States. Wood left them alone as they drafted a constitution, but intervened when they delayed the matter of future relations. Root countered with the Platt Amendment allowing future U.S. intervention, which Wood delivered as an ultimatum in June 1901: accept it or the occupation would continue. The Cubans reluctantly agreed and the military government left Cuba on 20 May 1902, leaving over $1.7 million in the treasury and a newly elected president and congress.

After a tour of Europe and visits with Kaiser Wilhelm II of Germany and German and British military officers, Wood returned with a belief in the necessity for military preparedness. He became military governor of Moro Province in the Philippines. He made his base in Zamboanga and traveled almost constantly, persuading chieftains to accept U.S. rule. When they did not, he used force, such as in the Lake Lanao expedition of 1903, and the Bud Daju battle of 1906, where 600 Moro men, women, and children died, and the assault force suffered 18 killed, 52 wounded, and a barrage of criticism from opponents in the United States. The outbreaks resulted from tribal conflicts over robbery, murder, and slavery as well as from opposition to U.S. impositions. The U.S. approach was not to emulate the British, who let potentates rule princely domains. Wood undercut the *datus* (chiefs) in their *cottas* (forts) by establishing the Moro Council composed of a U.S. engineer, superintendent of schools, attorney, and secretary. Laws came forth installing civil courts, taxes, town councils, schools, and trade promotion. While Wood had not redistributed land in Cuba, he did provide Moro families with title to 40 acres apiece. That the United States was proceeding with reforms persuaded most Filipinos to cooperate. The U.S. government believed that any early U.S. departure would mean war between the Moros and the Filipinos and intervention by Japan or Germany.

Wood had survived a major political battle in 1901 when he was promoted brigadier in the regular army. In 1903, he was promoted to major general after another terrific attack mounted by his enemies. That he was considered at all was due to his meritorious record and to the staunch political support of President Roosevelt and Secretary Root.

In 1906, Wood was assigned as commander of the Philippine Division of the army. He gave the troops realistic drills and exercises and as a result of reading, travel, and discussions with officials in Japan and in the British colonies, per-

ceived Japanese aggression as more serious than Russian or any other in East Asia. In a debate over defense of the Philippines, he argued fortifications should be at Manila, not Subic Bay. When the army and navy war colleges assumed the Philippines could not be defended, Wood argued for a strong fleet in the Pacific and a defense of the Philippines. He was a true disciple of Alfred T. Mahan, the sea power theorist and a believer in U.S. commercial and strategic influence in East Asia.

Wood's appointment in 1908 to command the Eastern Division with headquarters at Governors Island, New York, afforded Wood access again to the center of power in the United States. He also had to face a growing medical problem if he wanted to become chief of staff of the army. In Cuba, he had punctured his skull when he stood suddenly at his desk which had been moved under a heavy lantern. As years went by, he noticed his left arm and leg were becoming numb. After surgery on the bone in 1905 failed to work, he tried to live with the affliction. Then in 1910 he asked Dr. Henry Cushing to perform a relatively new operation removing a tumor pressing on the motor portion of his brain. For a few years he again enjoyed robust health, but by 1917 the limp again appeared.

Wood was appointed army chief of staff due to political favoritism and his representation of the new professional management trend in the army. Those who opposed him were generally the old line Civil War-Indian War officers. Another criticism arose as well from disciples of Gen. Emory Upton, who argued for a professional, West Point-dominated, nonpolitical officer corps. Because Wood was not a West Pointer and used his political connections, he faced a host of political and military opponents.

He had support from Henry L. Stimson, William H. Taft's secretary of war. Through a long battle with Adj. Gen. Fred C. Ainsworth, Wood managed to take some of the power away from the army bureaus and to increase the influence of the chief of staff. He also advocated greater concentration of troops in the United States and the training of a civilian reserve. In 1914 he was reassigned to the Department of the East, and he became an advocate of military preparedness. He supervised the Plattsburg, New York, summer camps where college men could take some basic training. He also gave hundreds of speeches urging military preparations, including universal military training, claiming that lack of training would mean unnecessary deaths in the war to come. As a speaker, the stocky general with the baritone voice and New England accent came across as a man of great sincerity and upright character.

President Woodrow Wilson and Secretary of War Lindley M. Garrison came to believe that Wood was becoming insubordinate in his advocacy of more military preparedness than the Wilson administration was willing to endorse and tried to admonish him. When the nation did go to war in 1917, they passed over Wood and appointed Gen. John J. Pershing commander of the American Expeditionary Force. When Wood said he would accept a division or a command in Italy, Pershing and the president refused. Instead, he languished in the Midwest, training divisions at Camp Funston, Kansas. Wood had exceeded the boundaries of propriety in his association with Republican Party leaders, and Wilson wanted no general to campaign for president in the election of 1920.

In the unsettled scene of 1919–1920, Wood emerged as a national leader, assuming the mantle of Roosevelt who died in 1919. Wood opposed joining the League of Nations, advocated charitable aid for war-torn Europe, urged the occupation of Germany, and a continued alliance with Britain and France. He won notoriety for the use of troops to prevent violence during strikes in Gary, Indiana, and Omaha, Nebraska, where he sided with neither management nor labor. As early as 1916, he began to think about the presidency, and he ran hard for the Republican nomination in 1920. He had many of the old Bull Moose progressives behind him as well as many moneyed Republicans, many who liked the Americanism and stability he espoused in the season of the Red Scare. He made a poor choice of managers in John T. King and William C. Proctor, mistakenly campaigned in uniform, and was outmaneuvered by groups at the Chicago convention who wanted a man they could control. Wood, Frank Lowden, and Hiram W. Johnson fell before the election of Warren G. Harding.

Harding asked Wood to assume the civil governorship of the Philippines, partly to exile the powerful general, mostly because the difficult situation there required an experienced proconsul. After an inspection trip with W. Cameron Forbes, a former governor, Wood decided to remain in the Philippines rather than accept the presidency of the University of Pennsylvania. Wood and the Republicans had not changed their attitude in 20 years: the Filipinos were not ready for self-government. Under Wilson and Governor Francis B. Harrison, the Filipinos had been given more government powers. Wood believed the Filipino government was corrupt and determined to reconstitute the power of the civil governor under the Organic Act of 1916 *vis-à-vis* the legislature. He clashed with Sergio Osmeña and Manuel L. Quezon over the issues of the governing power, economic development, and independence. When Quezon and Osmeña tried to bring about a cabinet fusion with the legislature, Wood replied that under separation of powers, the cabinet reported to the governor. The Council of State resigned in protest, and Wood governed through the bureau chiefs. The Filipinos were afraid of foreign exploitation and stalled Wood's plan for larger land leases and investments. When the Board of Control refused to end the state-run enterprises, such as the national bank, Wood dissolved the Board of Control and appointed capable managers to end nepotism and rescue the islands' credit rating.

Because of the standoff with Quezon and Osmeña, Wood traveled the islands, developing better practices for schools, public health, livestock disease prevention, the leper colony, and independent courts. He was supported by the Filipino bureau chiefs and aided by his small staff of military officers, men loyal to him, and experienced in colonial affairs. In response to the Filipino call for independence that Quezon and Osmeña championed, Wood paternalistically promised only increased autonomy as a reward for clean government. He vetoed a resolution for a plebiscite on independence and opposed a bill in the United States Congress for Filipino freedom. Wood wanted to retain the Philippines for commercial reasons (to promote U.S. trade with the Far East) and strategic reasons (military and naval bases to deter Japan). In his administration Wood received the solid backing of President Calvin Coolidge.

By 1927, his health began to deteriorate. He weighed over 200 pounds; his left side was numb; his head ached; and he had been through two hernia operations and an automobile accident. He returned home for surgery on the brain tumor, and when Dr. Cushing could not stop the hemorrhaging, he died. As thousands observed his funeral, Wood was buried with full military honors at Arlington National Cemetery with other fallen Rough Riders.

Of the two books on Wood's life, Hermann Hagedorn's is favorable, and Jack Lane's is critical. This essay relies on them both and steers a middle course slightly to Wood's side.

In his favor, Wood was very innovative and farsighted in the military sphere. He foresaw the need for an active military reserve in keeping with democratic traditions at home and alliances to keep the peace abroad. He inspired many young people to lives of service, and many achieved notable careers, such as Gen. Frank R. McCoy. At the same time, ambition and adversity made him stubborn and self-righteous. A team player with Root and Roosevelt, he seemed insubordinate to Garrison and Wilson. Hagedorn deems him a progressive of the Roosevelt stripe; Lane concludes Wood became a conservative by 1920. No one knows if Wood as president would have supported progressive goals regarding social welfare and antitrust. He certainly believed in a strong private sector. He also believed in an active executive and fair play. His record in Cuba and the Philippines indicates that if he preferred to work with moderates and men of means, he also helped the underdog and the disadvantaged. While he did make racist remarks, he had more respect for the majority of Cubans and Filipinos than his critics allow. In 1934, under the Democrats, the U.S. government abrogated the Platt Amendment with Cuba and passed the Tydings-McDuffie Act, which promised Philippine independence in 12 years and immediate autonomy in domestic affairs, effecting a withdrawal from the forward position Wood helped create overseas.

James H. Hitchman

REFERENCES

Hermann Hagedorn, *Leonard Wood: A Biography* (Harper, 1931), 2 vols.; James H. Hitchman, *Leonard Wood and Cuban Independence, 1898–1902* (Nijhoff, 1971); Jack C. Lane, *Armed Progressive: General Leonard Wood* (Presidio Pr., 1978); Wayne Wray Thompson, "Governors of the Moro Province: Wood, Bliss, and Pershing in the Southern Philippines, 1903–1913," Ph.D. diss., Univ. of California at San Diego, 1975; Leonard Wood, "Military Government of Cuba," *Annals of the American Academy of Political and Social Science*, 21 (1903), 153–182.

See also Bud Daju, Moro Province, The Philippines, Battle (1906); Cuba, Military Government (1898–1902); Moro Province, The Philippines (1903–1913).

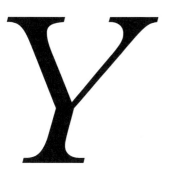

Yangzi (Yangtze) Patrol, China, United States Navy

For many years, the United States Navy maintained gunboats on Chinese rivers to protect U.S.-owned ships from attacks by bandits and Chinese troops. The gunboats were designated as the Yangzi (Yangtze) Patrol.

The Yangzi River is the dividing line between north and south China and one of the country's primary commercial arteries, knitting the two regions together. It is 3,200 miles long and is navigable for much of this distance. Oceangoing ships as large as 10,000 tons can travel 630 miles upriver to Hankou (Hankow) in the spring and summer. Smaller ships can travel another 1,000 miles to Suifu.

The river is usually divided into three regions: upper, middle, and lower: three of China's nine geographic regions. The core of the Upper Yangzi is the Red Basin of Sichuan (Szechwan), drained by the Min and Jiang (Kiang) rivers. The major treaty port and the focus of U.S. concern was Chongqing (Chungking). This city was the final destination on the river for U.S. gunboats. The Middle Yangzi includes the catchment basins of four major rivers: the Han, Gan (Kan), Xiang (Hsiang), and Yuan. The treaty ports of Changsha and Hankou and Lake Dongting (Tung-t'ing) are located there. Hankou, one of the Wuhan cities, served as the headquarters of Yangzi Patrol's depot ship after 1921. The Lower Yangzi includes the basins of the rivers flowing into Hangzhou (Hangchow) Bay; the fertile and wealthy Jiangnan region (Zhejiang [Chekiang] and Anhui [Anhwei]), incorporating the treaty ports of Hangzhou, Suzhou (Soochow), Nanjing (Nanking), and Shanghai.

Depending on the season and the part of the river, water levels on the river can vary widely. At Chongqing, the seasonal variation can be as much as 100 feet, while at Hankou the variation may be half as great. Water levels in the gorges above Yizhang (Ichang) can rise 50 feet in a single night, turning them into foaming whitewater cataracts and making traffic impossible.

The United States Navy has deployed ships in East Asian waters since the 1830s. The first U.S. warship on the Yangzi was the *Susquehanna*, which traveled from Shanghai to Wuhu in June 1854. In April 1874 the *Ashuelot* made a three-month, 1,000-mile cruise from Shanghai to Yizhang, just below the river's gorges.

Despite this early activity, and although foreign warships were a common sight on the river,

U.S. gunboats did not become common on the Yangzi until the 20th century. It was not until 1903, after the U.S. acquisition of the Philippines in the Spanish-Cuban/American War and the Boxer Uprising, that the United States Navy had suitable ships for river patrol. The patrol's purpose was to promote U.S. commerce and protect the lives and property of U.S. citizens. It sailed under the authority of "most favored nation" terms of the Treaty of Tianjin [Tientsin] (1858) and the Sino-Austro-Hungarian Treaty (1869), which gave "ships of war, coming for no hostile purpose, or being in pursuit of pirates, . . . liberty to visit all ports" (Carlson, p. 1546).

Although the patrol began in the 1850s and regular Yangzi cruising began in 1903, it was neither named nor formed as a separate entity until December 1919. It was not until 1921 that three of the patrol's ships had their home port shifted from Manila to Shanghai. It served under the name Yangzi Patrol until disbanded and withdrawn to the Philippines in December 1941. For most of its life, the patrol witnessed civil war and the rebirth of Chinese nationalism. Its ships and men were bystanders, witnesses, and participants in the Northern Expedition and the Nanjing incident, the Second Sino-Japanese War, the Rape of Nanjing, and the *Panay* incident.

The ships of the patrol were usually castoffs and leftovers. They generally consisted of vessels deemed unsuitable for service anywhere else in the world. In the late 19th century, they were refitted Civil War gunboats and monitors, which were usually unable to travel on the upper river. Between 1903 and the late 1920s, they were trophies from the conquest of the Philippines or obsolete ships from other squadrons. Those obtained from Spain have been described as relics and had difficulty negotiating the river's rapids. With the resurgence of antiforeign activity as well as civil war, both the commanders of the patrol and U.S. business interests in the Yangzi valley began to lobby for the creation of a modern, shallow draft gunboat squadron.

In 1925 Congress authorized the construction of a new gunboat flotilla. Contracts were let and construction was begun the following year. The ships were constructed and entered service in 1927–1928. By that time, part of the rationale for U.S. gunboats in China had disappeared. The Guomindang's [Kuomintang] victories and the success of the Northern Expedition, despite the Nanjing incident and the seizure of the British concession at Hankou, brought a modicum of peace and order to the lower Yangzi. The new ships were needed on the middle and upper parts of the river. The new squadron was built at the Jiangnan Shipyard (Shanghai). The six new ships were named *Guam, Tutuila, Oahu, Panay, Luzon,* and *Mindanao.* All were relatively shallow draft vessels, but all could operate year round on the upper Yangzi only with difficulty: the last three because they were too long and drew too much water, the first three because of an insufficient number of rudders (three instead of four). None of them were considered seaworthy enough to travel to the main naval base at Cavite in the Philippines for refitting and repair. This was done at Shanghai.

Much of the time, the ships of the patrol cruised on the river showing the flag at the various treaty ports and negotiating with the various regional militarists governing China during this period. Most of the material written about the "river rats" concentrates on the exotic political and navigational situations and on shipboard living conditions.

Although living conditions were pleasant, even luxurious, naval officers regarded China service as a backwater, which would not help them climb the greasy pole of promotion. The navy's most promising people were seldom sent to the Yangzi Patrol, even though duty could be interesting and challenging, involving diplomatic as well as military functions. To compensate for this, living conditions were higher than those enjoyed by naval personnel on other stations. Officers and their dependents had access to a colonial way of life, replete with servants, numerous parties while in port, as well as cheap food, liquor, and housing. For example, the exchange rate in 1919 was U.S.$1=Mex.$1.11; by 1921, the exchange rate was U.S.$0.83= Mex.$1.00; in the mid-1920s, it was U.S.$1.00= Mex.$3.50. Haig & Haig scotch was Mex.$12.00 a case, while Gordon's Gin was Mex.$3.00 a case. The exchange rate fluctuated, but the levels of magnitude remained approximately the same. The cost for a houseful of servants, No. 1 boy (head servant), cook, gardener, and housekeeper was about Mex.$21 a month. Food was correspondingly cheap.

Despite the pleasant living conditions, the sailors and ships of the patrol frequently engaged in nasty little armed actions with river pirates, bandits, and warlord soldiers. They were responsible for safeguarding U.S. lives and property, both of missionaries and businessmen. These actions consisted of convoying Standard Oil Company barges, firefights with local bandits along the upper river, and carrying ransom to free U.S. citizens kidnapped by local militarists or bandits.

The patrol's focus, along with U.S. foreign policy, began to change after the start of Japanese imperialist expansion in 1931. The beginning of full-scale war between China and Japan in 1937 meant that the patrol was frequently caught in the Sino-Japanese crossfire. This was the fate of *Panay* sunk by Japanese bombers in December 1937, in the campaign that led to the Japanese capture and Rape of Nanjing. The second Sino-Japanese War, or the China Incident, meant the effective end of the patrol. By 1941, one ship, *Tutuila*, was sent to Chongqing (the crew was evacuated in January 1942); the *Panay* was sunk; and the *Wake*, formerly named *Guam*, was captured at Shanghai.

Three ships—the *Mindanao, Oahu*, and *Luzon*—made the ocean voyage to the Philippines, where they were sunk in May 1942. In 1943, the unequal treaties with China were abrogated and the *raison d'être* for the Yangzi Patrol disappeared. Perhaps anticipating this, the *Tutuila* was transferred to the Chinese Navy in March 1942.

Lewis Bernstein

REFERENCES

Dorothy Borg, *American Policy and the Chinese Revolution, 1925–1928* (American Institute of Pacific Relations, 1947); William R. Braisted, *The United States Navy in the Pacific, 1897–1909* (Univ. of Texas Pr., 1958); William R. Braisted, *The United States Navy in the Pacific, 1909–1922* (Univ. of Texas Pr., 1971); Evans F. Carlson, "Legal Bases for Use of Foreign Armed Forces in China," *United States Naval Institute Proceedings*, 62 (1936) 1544–1556; Bernard D. Cole, *Gunboats and Marines: The United States Navy in China, 1925–1928* (Univ. of Delaware Pr., 1983); Dennis L. Noble, *The Eagle and the Dragon: The United States Military in China, 1901–1937* (Greenwood Pr., 1990); Kemp Tolley, *Yangtze Patrol: The U.S. Navy in China* (U.S. Naval Institute Pr., 1971).

See also Nanjing (Nanking) Incident (1927); *Panay* Incident, China (1937).

Young, Samuel Baldwin Marks (1840–1924)

Samuel Baldwin Marks Young, an imposing soldier over six feet tall and weighing 250 pounds, came to the Philippines after serving in the Civil War, the Indian Wars, and the Cuban campaign in 1898. He had quickly moved in rank from private to brevet brigadier general during the Civil War, later served as a captain of cavalry for two decades, and eventually received a colonelcy at age 57.

Hot-tempered and outspoken, Brigadier General Young defied superiors and expressed unorthodox views. He disobeyed Maj. Gen. Elwell S. Otis in 1900 by candidly telling newspapers of manpower shortages on Luzon in the Philippines and the resulting difficulties of stationing troops in occupied areas. Before leaving for the Philippines, he had indiscreetly written a very unfavorable appraisal of Otis for the War Department, which, unaccountably, handed it over to Otis. In the report, Young acknowledged Otis's political talents, but criticized his unaggressive military performance. Sufficient forces commanded by Maj. Gen. Henry W. Lawton, he claimed, might win the Philippine War in a month.

Disagreement turned into intense animosity after Young's landing in the islands. A harsh reprimand by an angry Otis preceded his assignment from volunteer to regular units. The consequent loss of a senior position blocked his elevation to major general. He naturally assumed that some in the army were scheming to undermine his professional standing.

Young's paranoiac and sour temperament affected his views. Known as a hard-liner, such as Gens. Loyd Wheaton and Frederick Funston and Col. Jacob H. Smith, he favored applying severe tactics when fighting Orientals, much the same as those used against Native Americans in the West. Young admired the countries of Europe for using techniques required to "inspire rebellious Asiatics, individual and collectively, with a greater fear of the reigning government than they had of the rebels." (Linn, pp. 53–54) Applauding Lord Herbert H. Kitchener's South African campaign, he recommended that publications on French colonial wars fought in Indochina and Algeria be made mandatory assignments for West Point cadets.

The imperious Young racially stereotyped Filipinos. He spoke for many in the United States

Army by maintaining "the Filipino is happiest when most unhappy. He is born that way. He revels in wrongs and can't get along without them." (Miller, p. 162) Willing to fight a war of imperialism, Young demeaned revolutionaries as *ladrones* (bandits), and insisted "that by keeping up a constant hunt after these murderers, thieves and robbers, the country can be cleared of them within two months." (Scott, pp. 26–27)

Young's interpretation of the techniques of Europeans when pacifying unruly Asians included complete power for the army and no mercy for the rebels. In addition to muzzling newsmen, he advocated reprisals for assassins, capital punishment for espionage agents, deportation of guerrillas, and seizure of the property of the revolution's supporters. He believed that relocating the population under army authority would weaken guerrilla resistance, a policy similar to Spain's in Cuba and, later, the United States's in South Vietnam.

General Young gained renown during the chase after Philippine President Emilio Aguinaldo y Famy in late 1899. After the November debarkation of additional troops, Otis began a triple-winged attack against Filipino forces, north of Manila. With Maj. Gen. Arthur MacArthur diverting the enemy in central Luzon, Lawton drove northeastward and blocked the president's withdrawal to the Sierra Madre Mountains. As Aguinaldo's army retreated northward, Brigadier General Wheaton's arrival at Lingayen Gulf would threaten it with entrapment.

Detached by Lawton and unbeknownst to the cautious Otis, Young's "flying column" raced through hostile countryside to the coast in a jaunt reminiscent of Union Gen. William T. Sherman's march through Georgia during the Civil War. The energetic brigadier general, with artillery, cavalry, and infantry, drove through Nueva Ecija Province and advanced northwestward to a rendezvous with Wheaton. Separated from superiors and supplies, his 1,100 troops fought their way into San Jose and then moved to within 20 miles of Dagupan in Pangasinan Province.

Young's zealous pursuit of the elusive Aguinaldo ended in failure. Despite the aid of Macabebe scouts and the seizure of the president's son, moneys, printing press, and secretary of foreign affairs, his inability to get Wheaton's cooperation and deception by a Ta-galog tracker prevented the snare from closing at Pozorrubio. The frustrated Young remarked: "The only reason that the guide who had led us to Manaoag instead of Pozorrubio was not shot was because he could not be found." (Wolff, p. 283)

In six weeks General Young's spearhead ranged 120 miles across the central Luzon plain to Dagupan's outskirts. A final but futile advance north along the western littoral to trap Aguinaldo with Wheaton's support resulted in the president's escape to the mountains and the exhaustion of Young's force. "My forces are much depleted and worn out," he tersely commented. "Aguinaldo has been playing hide and seek. One day in the mountains, the next . . . on the coast road." (Wolff, p. 285)

While Young's adjutant, Lt. Col. James Parker, landed with a small party from the *Oregon* and moved into Vigan, Ilocos Sur, Young, farther inland, engaged the forces of Nueva Ecija's Gen. Manuel Tinio at Tangadan Pass in Abra Province. Young's troops outflanked the Filipino's defenses, took the ground overlooking their position, and in a decisive attack caused them to retreat. Tinio fled into the highlands of Ilocos Norte as pursuing U.S. forces seized his command headquarters and baggage train. Despite Young's encirclement of him at Solsona, the Filipino evaded his grasp in disguise.

After occupying Vigan and obtaining fresh troops, Young invaded Ilocos Norte Province, coming ashore from points south to north at Laoag, Pasuquín, and Bangued, respectively. Next, his horsemen rode northward out of Vigan and demolished Filipino entrenchments at Sinait, south of Ilocos Norte, as well as moving across the border at Badoc. The 30-day campaign in the Ilocos provinces persuaded the general that Ilocanos wanted peace whereas the Tagalog outsiders promoted disorder.

Five days before Christmas 1899, Otis entrusted Young with command of the recently established District of North-Western Luzon. He gave the district commander various infantry and cavalry units that were later reinforced. With a complement of 4,000, Young received orders to create civil governments and, more precisely, to set up the municipalities according to General Order No. 43, which called for the army to install town administrations, each comprising a mayor, town council, and police force.

Young, moreover, subsequently divided the District of North-Western Luzon into several provincial commands with army governors in charge of civil and military affairs. Even when the district's designation changed to First District, Department of Northern Luzon, in an April 1900 restructuring, the fundamental organization remained the same.

As the Philippine Republican Army resorted to guerrilla warfare, Young initiated military measures to restore order. He accelerated the garrisoning of towns, as reinforcements permitted, and widely dispersed U.S. troops who became involved in small-scale engagements with the resistance. His frustration with telegraph sabotage resulted in Filipinos's houses being torched and in instructions to "shoot anyone you believe to be in any way connected with destruction of telegraph." (Scott, p. 31) Such orders and tactics alarmed some in Manila and resulted in a stern rebuke from General Wheaton.

In spite of his being an advocate of harsh pacification measures, Young proved to be an impressive and able district chief. His administration purged the unqualified and employed the talents of competent subordinates. Capt. John G. Ballance, chief assistant and advisor to the military governor, synchronized local government in the District of North-Western Luzon. Acting as chief of staff and trusted associate, he oversaw intelligence operations and harmonized the carrying out of Young's commands.

Young actually implemented policies unlike those he advocated in his correspondence. Notwithstanding misgivings about Filipino traits and unhappy with the policies of benevolence, he developed warm ties with the district's upper class and clergy. During his tenure, he improved farming, urged the limited arming of faithful Filipinos, and argued for publicly financed schooling.

Young expressed a particular concern for municipal government and educational change in his district. Local administrations were swiftly formed with the populace assigned such tasks as bandit control and self-defense. The army of occupation founded schools in *pueblos* (towns), and regularly informed the district commander about their operation. Young desired authorization to employ U.S. fighting men to teach the English language and planned, at public expense, the creation of two schools in every municipality, each with the necessary staff, construction stock, and provisions.

Unanticipated difficulties hampered the general's civic affairs program. General Order No. 43 proposed that revenue be raised from manufacturing and commerce in a region devoted to farming. Shifting the burden to *pueblos* provided insufficient moneys because of a limited tax base. Problems originating from misunderstandings, cultural differences, and incompetence plagued relations between Filipinos and U.S. personnel and contributed to the subversion of local administration.

Young's good works failed to pacify the Ilocano provinces. With guerrillas and bandits operating in the countryside, he enrolled Filipino spies and clergy as well as La Union Province's controversial Guardia de Honor religious sect led by Crispulo Patajo, although he refused to establish a provincial police force. At the time of his recall and replacement by Brig. Gen. J. Franklin Bell in February 1901, the Ilocos continued to be rebellious.

Brought out of the Philippines because of his immoderate views and William H. Taft's antipathy, Young was appointed army chief of staff by President Theodore Roosevelt, an admirer of the cavalryman, in 1903. Young served that post until his retirement 12 months later.

Rodney J. Ross

REFERENCES

James A. LeRoy, *The Americans in the Philippines* (Houghton Mifflin, 1914), 2 vols.; Brian McAllister Linn, *The U.S. Army and Counterinsurgency in the Philippine War, 1899–1902* (Univ. of North Carolina Pr., 1989); Stuart Creighton Miller, *"Benevolent Assimilation": The American Conquest of the Philippines, 1899–1903* (Yale Univ. Pr., 1982); William Henry Scott, *Ilocano Responses to American Aggression, 1900–1901* (New Day, 1986); Juan Villamor, *Inédita Crónica de la Guerra americano-filipina en el Norte de Luzón 1898–1901* (Imprenta J. Fajardo, 1924–1926); Leon Wolff, *Little Brown Brother: How the United States Purchased and Pacified the Philippines at the Century's Turn* (Doubleday, 1961).

Ypiranga Affair

The *Ypiranga* was a German freighter owned by the Hamburg-American Steamship Line. The ship became famous when it attempted to land a cargo of arms at Veracruz in April 1914, leading to the United States's seizure of the port. While the Tampico incident provided the justification for the action, the U.S. invasion was actually designed specifically to prevent the landing of the cargo of arms.

The administration of President Woodrow Wilson had long opposed the government of Mexican President Victoriano Huerta, which was engaged in a protracted civil war with the forces of the Mexican Revolution. Both the Huerta regime and the Mexican revolutionaries devoted considerable efforts to obtaining arms and ammunition, and the outcome of their efforts to procure weapons and supplies exerted a considerable impact on the conflict. While officially neutral, the United States turned a blind eye to deliveries of arms across the border to the rebels, who were based in Northern Mexico. The Mexican government turned mainly to Europe for its supplies to circumvent U.S. efforts to interdict arms shipments.

During the crisis following the Tampico incident, U.S. officials learned, on 18 April 1914, that the *Ypiranga* was scheduled to land at Veracruz on 21 April bearing a cargo of 200 machine guns and 15 million rounds of ammunition for the Huerta government. Indeed, the Huerta regime had moved three trains to the Veracruz railroad station at the docks to rush the weapons to the capital. The Wilson administration feared that these arms would enable Huerta to turn the tide of battle or at least prolong his hold on the capital. This information convinced Wilson to order the seizure of Veracruz rather than a landing at Tampico. With only one day's warning and having only a small force, Rear Adm. Frank F. Fletcher seized the port.

The landing did not end the *Ypiranga* affair. The *Ypiranga* arrived off Veracruz at 1:30 p.m. on 21 April, a few hours after the U.S. forces landed and at the height of the combat. The battleship *Utah*, stationed outside the breakwater, sent an officer aboard to inform the captain of the *Ypiranga* that he would be allowed to anchor in the harbor but would not be permitted to leave port or unload the arms. Ironically, the bills of lading showed that the weapons and munitions had been purchased in New York, but shipped via Hamburg to escape U.S. surveillance.

Detention of the *Ypiranga* resulted in another dispute with Germany. In the absence of a formal declaration of war, the United States did not have the right to detain the ship under international law. Thus, Secretary of State William Jennings Bryan was compelled to apologize to the German ambassador, explaining that the admiral had exceeded his orders and that the ship would be allowed to depart from the port. The ship was allowed to land its other cargo, but the captain refused to turn the arms over to the U.S. forces occupying Veracruz, stating that he would return them to Germany.

Even the occupation of Veracruz did not prevent delivery of the arms. After taking on additional cargo, the *Ypiranga* left Veracruz on 3 May, sailing to Tampico and Mobile, Alabama, taking on and landing cargo and passengers at each point. On 27 May the *Ypiranga* landed at Puerto Mexico, south of Veracruz, which was still under the control of the Huertista forces. There, it landed the cargo of arms, which was promptly taken by rail to Mexico City. Thus, the arms were ultimately delivered to Huerta in spite of the U.S. seizure of Veracruz. The month's delay in delivery, however, reduced the effect of the shipment because the rebel advance had continued. Huerta was ultimately forced to flee into exile in July 1914.

Kenneth J. Grieb

REFERENCES

Kenneth J. Grieb, *The United States and Huerta* (Univ. of Nebraska Pr., 1969); Robert E. Quirk, *An Affair of Honor: Woodrow Wilson and the Occupation of Veracruz* (Univ. of Kentucky Pr., 1962).

See also Tampico Incident (1914); Veracruz, Mexico, Occupation (1914).

Appendices

Appendix A

Maps

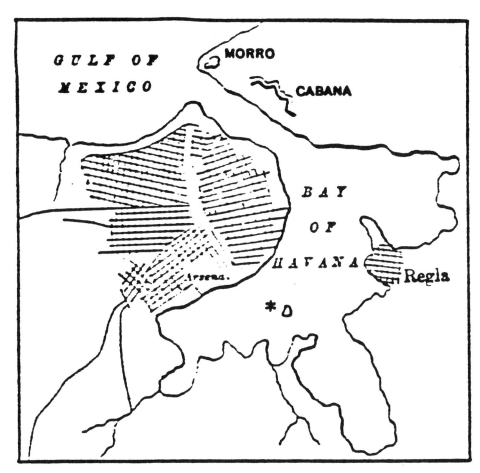

City and Bay of Havana. *Indicates Position of the *Maine* when Destroyed.
Source: Edgar Stanton Maclay, *A History of the United States Navy from 1775 to 1902* (New York: D. Appleton and Company, 1902), III, p. 52.

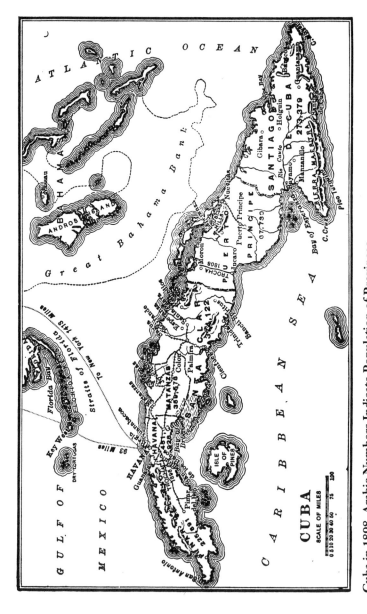

Cuba in 1898. Arabic Numbers Indicate Population of Provinces.

Source: Henry B. Russell, *The Story of Two Wars: An Illustrated History of Our War with Spain and Our War with the Filipinos* (Hartford, Connecticut: The Hartford Publishing Company, 1899), p. 112.

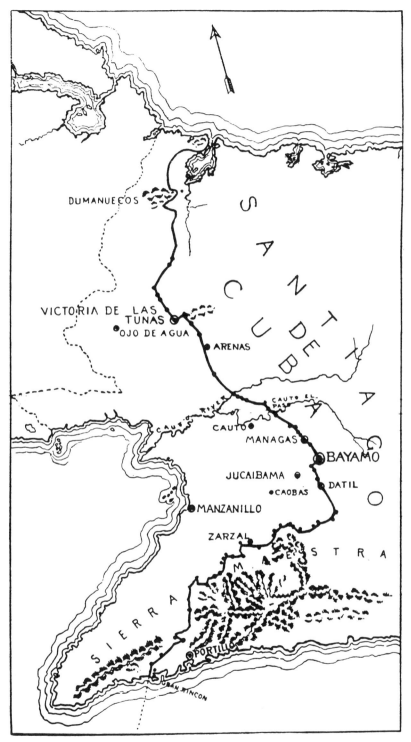

Lieutenant Andrew S. Rowan's Route across Cuba While Carrying the Celebrated "Message to Garcia."
Source: "Lieutant-Colonel Rowan's Exploit: The American Delegate's Visit to Garcia." *Harper's Weekly* 43 (July 2, 1898): 643.

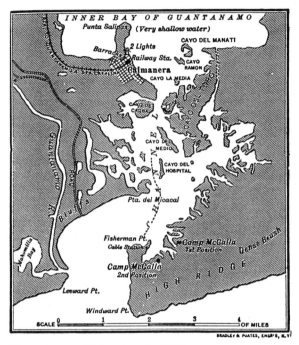

Guantánamo, Cuba, Area in 1898.
Source: Henry B. Russell, *The Story of Two Wars: An Illustrated History of Our War with Spain and Our War with the Filipinos* (Hartford, Connecticut: The Hartford Publishing Company, 1899), p. 449.

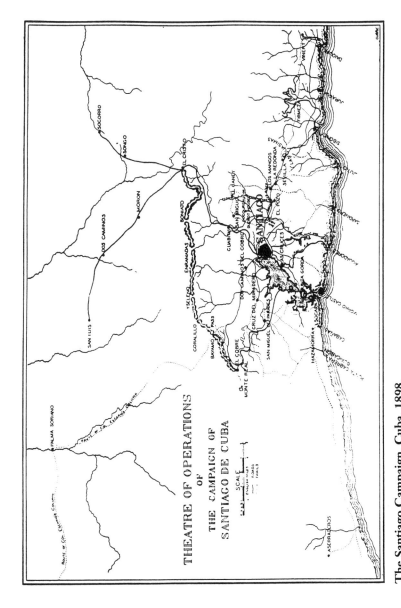

The Santiago Campaign, Cuba, 1898.
Source: Herbert H. Sargent, *The Campaign of Santiago de Cuba* (Chicago: A.C. McClurg & Co., 1914), II, p. 52.

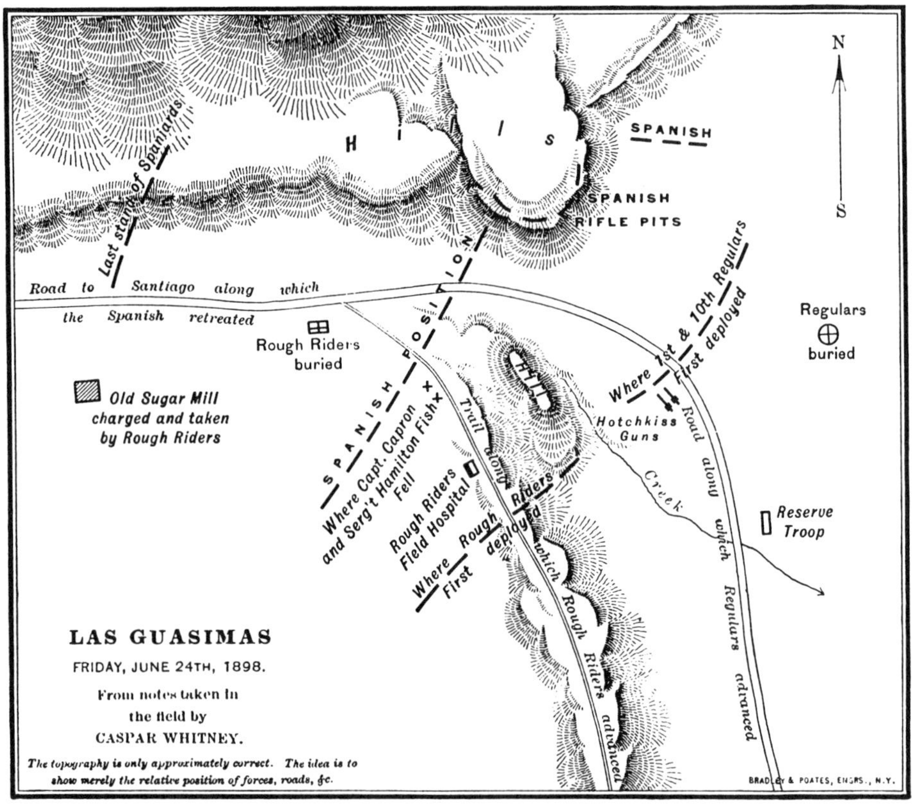
N
S
SPANISH
SPANISH
RIFLE PITS
H I L L S
Last stand of Spaniards
SPANISH POSITION
Road to Santiago along which the Spanish retreated
Rough Riders buried
Old Sugar Mill charged and taken by Rough Riders
Where Capt. Capron and Serg't Hamilton Fish Fell
Rough Riders Field Hospital
Where Rough Riders First deployed
Trail along which Rough Riders advanced
HILL
Where 1st & 10th Regulars first deployed
Hotchkiss Guns
Road along which Regulars advanced
Creek
Regulars buried
Reserve Troop
LAS GUASIMAS
FRIDAY, JUNE 24TH, 1898.
From notes taken in the field by CASPAR WHITNEY.
The topography is only approximately correct. The idea is to show merely the relative position of forces, roads, &c.

The Battle of Las Guásimas, Cuba, 1898.
Source: *Harper's Pictorial History of the War with Spain* (New York: Harper & Brothers Publishers, 1899), II, p. 329.

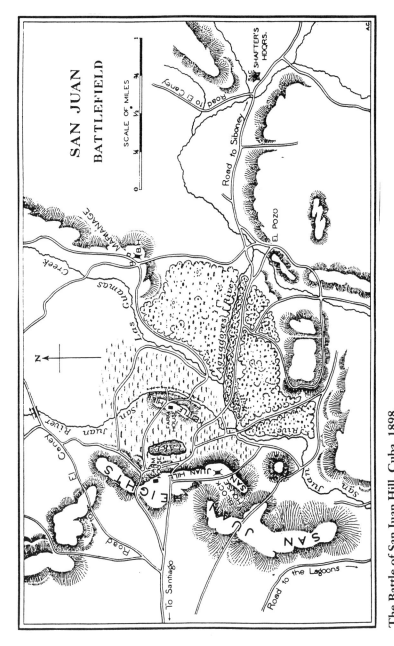

The Battle of San Juan Hill, Cuba, 1898.
Source: Herbert H. Sargent, *The Campaign of Santiago de Cuba* (Chicago: A.C. McClurg & Co., 1914), II, p. 94.

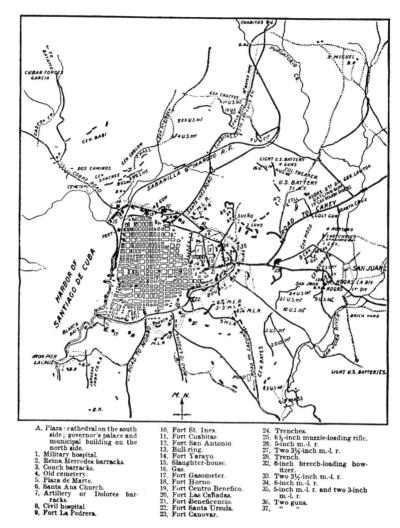

A, Plaza: cathedral on the south side; governor's palace and municipal building on the north side.	10, Fort St. Ines.	24, Trenches.
	11, Fort Cuabitas.	25, 6½-inch muzzle-loading rifle.
	12, Fort San Antonio.	26, 5-inch m.-l. r.
	13, Bull-ring.	27, Two 3½-inch m.-l. r.
1, Military hospital.	14, Fort Yarayo.	28, Trench.
2, Reina Mercedes barracks.	15, Slaughter-house.	32, 6-inch breech-loading howitzer.
3, Conch barracks.	16, Gas.	
4, Old cemetery.	17, Fort Gasometer.	33, Two 3½-inch m.-l. r.
5, Plaza de Marte.	18, Fort Horno.	34, 6-inch m.-l. r.
6, Santa Ana Church.	19, Fort Centro Benefico.	35, 5-inch m.-l. r. and two 3-inch m.-l. r.
7, Artillery or Dolores barracks.	20, Fort Las Cañadas.	
	21, Fort Beneficencio.	36, Two guns.
8, Civil hospital.	22, Fort Santa Ursula.	37, " "
9, Fort La Pedrera.	23, Fort Canovar.	

Military Positions in the Last Days of the Siege of Santiago, Cuba, 1898.

Source: Richard Pearson Hobson, *The Sinking of the "Merrimac"* (New York: The Century Co., 1899), p. 283.

Portion of Eastern Cuba Surrendered as Part of the Santiago Capitulation, 1898.
Source: Henry B. Russell, *The Story of Two Wars: An Illustrated History of Our War with Spain and Our War with the Filipinos* (Hartford, Connecticut: The Hartford Publishing Company, 1899), p. 533.

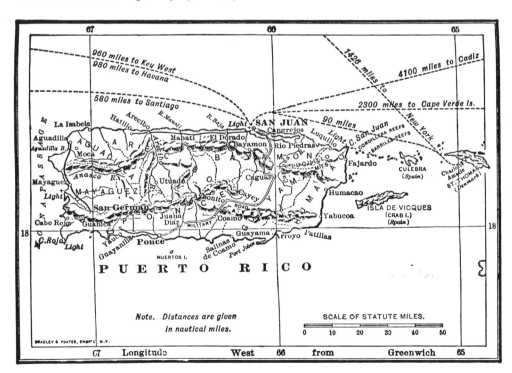

Puerto Rico in 1898. Distances to Other Points Are Shown.
Source: Henry B. Russell, *The Story of Two Wars: An Illustrated History of Our War with Spain and Our War with the Filipinos* (Hartford, Connecticut: The Hartford Publishing Company, 1899), p. 541.

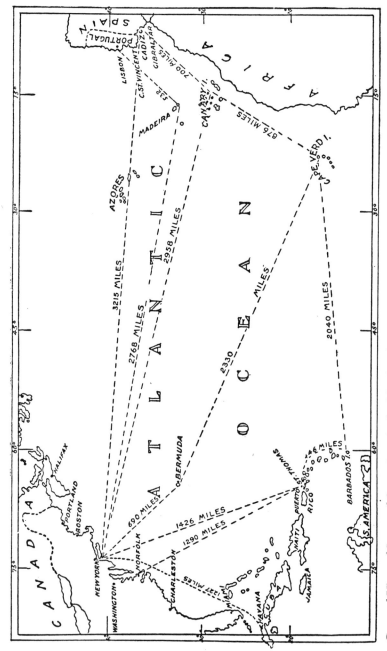

General View of Scene of Operations in the North Atlantic During the Spanish-Cuban/American War of 1898.
Source: Edgar Stanton Maclay, *A History of the United States Navy from 1775 to 1902* (New York: D. Appleton and Company, 1902), III, p. 254.

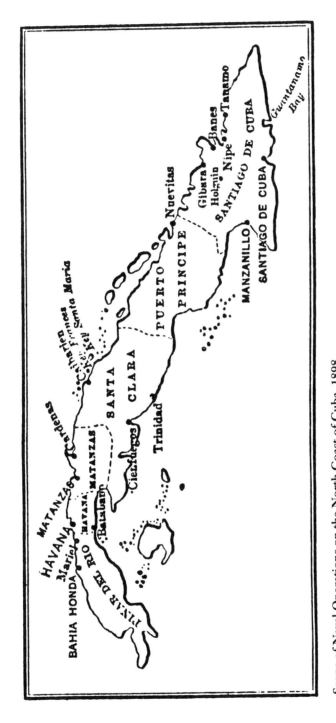

Scene of Naval Operations on the North Coast of Cuba, 1898.
Source: Edgar Stanton Maclay, *A History of the United States Navy from 1775 to 1902* (New York: D. Appleton and Company, 1902), III, p. 240.

Course of the Oregon _____

Course of the Marietta ___.__.__.__.

Voyage of the Battleship *Oregon*, 1898.
Source: Edgar Stanton Maclay, *A History of the United States Navy from 1775 to 1902* (New York: D. Appleton and Company, 1902), III, p. 76.

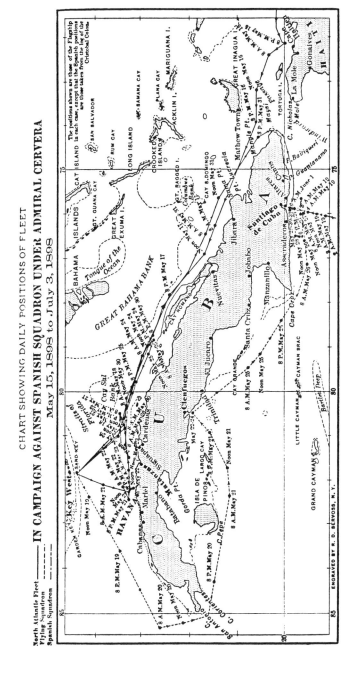

United States Naval Operations against the Spanish Fleet in the West Indies, 1898.
Source: W.A.M. Goode, *With Sampson Through the War* (New York: Doubleday & McClure Co., 1899), p. 80.

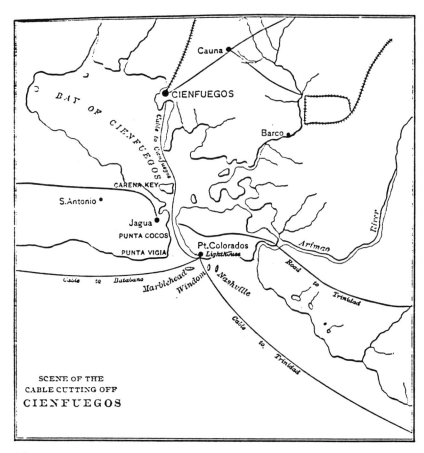

The Attack on the Spanish Cables at Cienfuegos, Cuba, by the U.S. Navy, 1898.

Source: Edgar Stanton Maclay, *A History of the United States Navy from 1775 to 1902* (New York: D. Appleton and Company, 1902), III, p. 121.

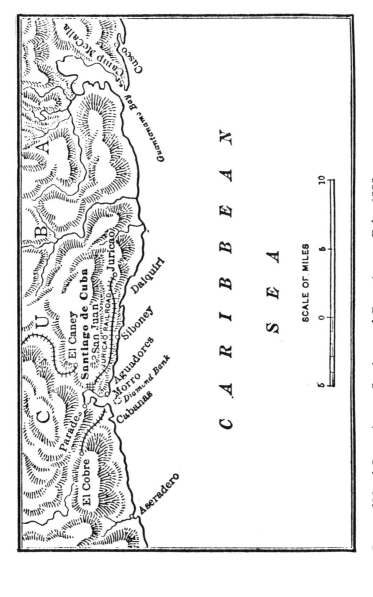

Scene of Naval Operations at Santiago and Guantánamo, Cuba, 1898.
Source: Edgar Stanton Maclay, *A History of the United States Navy from 1775 to 1902* (New York: D. Appleton and Company, 1902), III, p. 340.

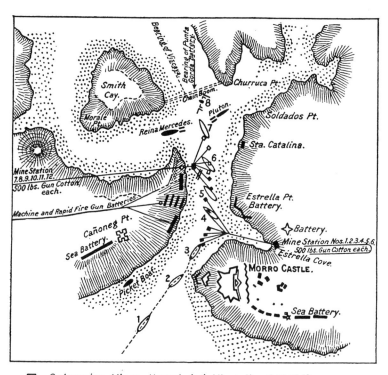

Submarine Mines, Unexploded Mines, Nos. 9, 10, 11, 12.
   "   "   fired at Vessel, Nos. 1, 2, 3, 4, 5, 6, 7, 8.
   "   "   that struck Vessel, No. 5.
   Automatic Torpedoes fired by "Reina Mercedes" and "Pluton".

The Scuttling of the U.S. Navy Collier *Merrimac* at the Entrance to Santiago Harbor, a Spanish View.

Source: Severo Gomez Nunez, "The Spanish-American War: Blockades and Coast Defense" in U.S. Navy, Office of Naval Intelligence, *Notes on the Spanish-American War* (Washington, D.C.: Government Printing Office, 1900), p. 79.

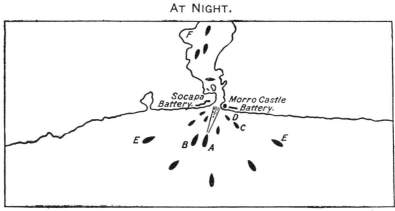

A *Battleship with searchlight.*
B *Supporting battleship ready to open fire
in case of appearance of enemy.*
C *Three small cruisers as pickets.*

D *Three steam-launch pickets.*
E *Blockade outer line.*
F *Spanish ships.*

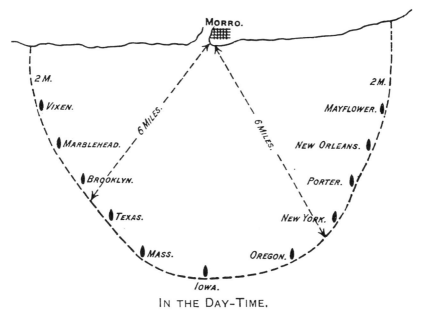

IN THE DAY-TIME.

The U.S. Naval Blockade of Santiago, Cuba, 1898.
Source: Severo Gomez Nunez, "The Spanish-American War. Blockades and
Coast Defense" in U.S. Navy, Office of Naval Intelligence, *Notes on the Spanish-
American War* (Washington, D.C.: Government Printing Office, 1900), p. 77.

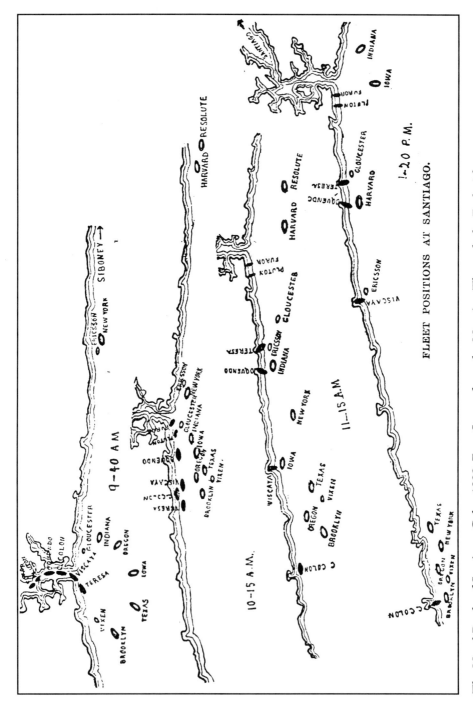

The Naval Battle of Santiago, Cuba, 1898. Four Stages from the Morning Through the Early Afternoon.
Source: Henry F. Keenan, *The Conflict with Spain: A History of the War* (Philadelphia: P.W. Ziegler and Co., 1898), p. 204.

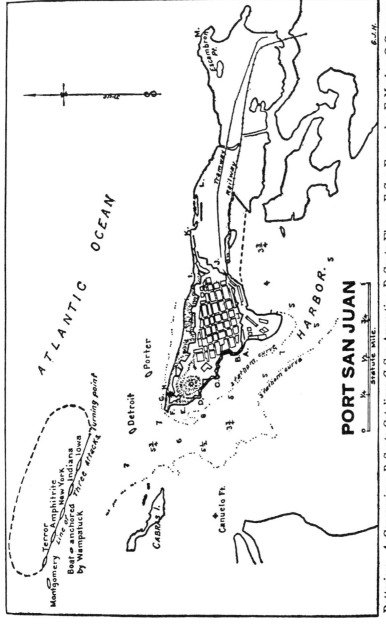

PORT SAN JUAN

ATLANTIC OCEAN

HARBOR.

CABRAS I.

Terror
Montgomery Amphitrite
Line of New York
Boat anchored Indiana Iowa
by Wampatuck Three attacks Turning point

O Detroit
O Porter

Canuelo Ft.

0 ¼ ½ ¾ statute mile.

Batteries: *A,* Concepcion; *B,* Santa Catalina; *C,* San Augustin; *D,* Santa Elena; *E,* San Fernando; *F,* Macho; *G,* Carmen; *H,* San Antonio; *I,* San Cristóbal; *J,* San Carlos; *K,* Santa Teresa; *L,* Princesa; *M,* Escambron.

San Juan, Puerto Rico, in 1898. Illustrating United States Navy Ship Movements.
Source: French Ensor Chadwick, *The Relations of the United States with Spain: The Spanish-American War* (New York: Charles Scribner's Sons, 1911), I, p. 231.

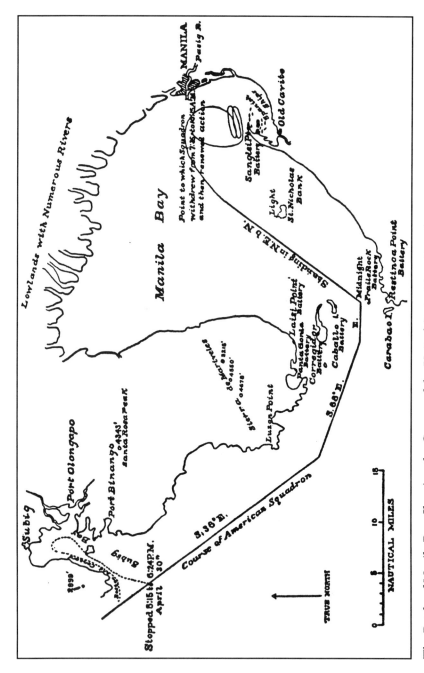

The Battle of Manila Bay. Showing the Course of the United States Navy Squadron.
Source: French Ensor Chadwick, *The Relations of the United States with Spain: The Spanish–American War* (New York: Charles Scribner's Sons, 1911), I, p. 159.

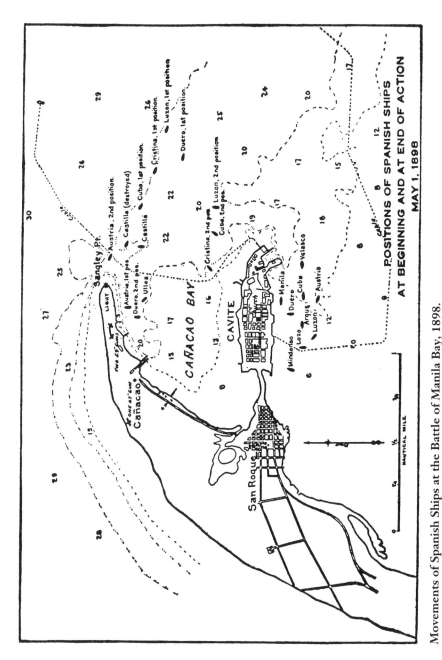

Movements of Spanish Ships at the Battle of Manila Bay, 1898.
Source: French Ensor Chadwick, *The Relations of the United States and Spain: The Spanish–American War* (New York: Charles
Scribner's Sons, 1911), I, p. 189

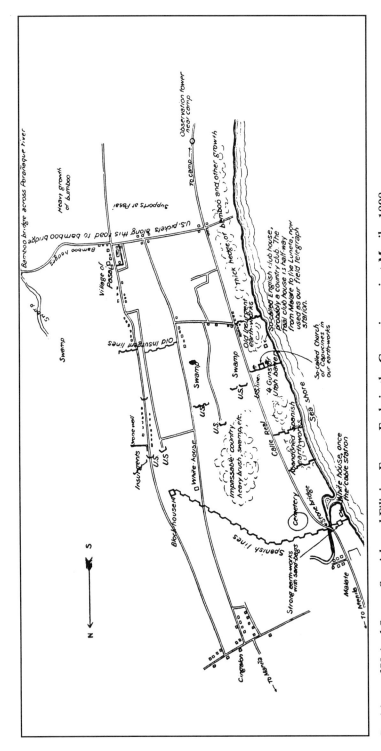

Positions of United States, Spanish, and Filipino Forces Early in the Campaign against Manila, 1898.
Source: *Harper's Pictorial History of the War with Spain* (New York: Harper & Brothers Publishers, 1899), II, p. 410.

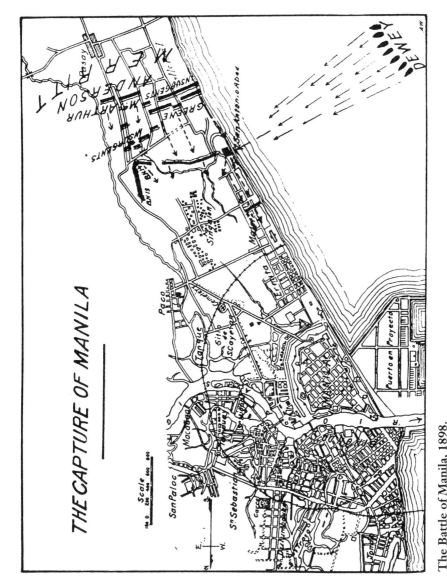

The Battle of Manila, 1898.
Source: Matthew Forney Steele, *American Campaigns* (Washington, D.C.: Byron S. Adams, 1909), II, p. 309.

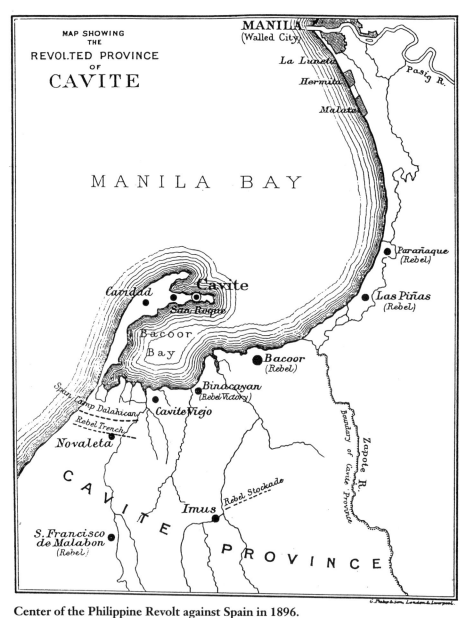

Center of the Philippine Revolt against Spain in 1896.
Source: John Foreman, *The Philippine Islands* (New York: Charles Scribner's Sons, 1899), p. 521.

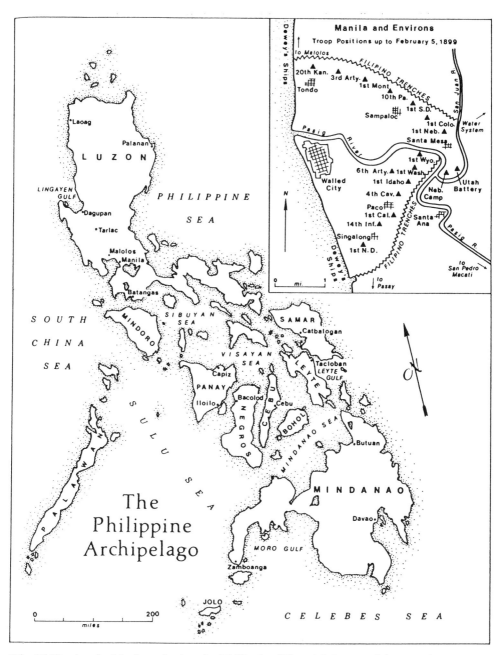

The Philippine Archipelago during the Philippine War with Insert of the Manila Area in 1899.

Source: Stuart Creighton Miller, *"Benevolent Assimiliation": The American Conquest of the Philippines, 1899–1903* (New Haven: Yale University Press, c. 1982), p. 45. Reprinted by permission of Yale University Press.

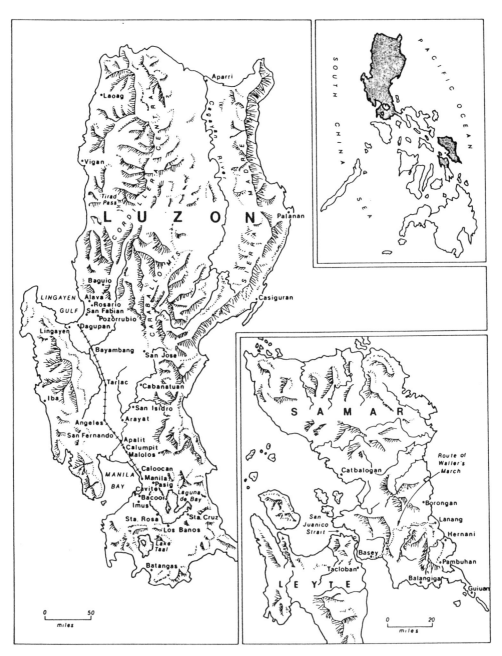

Luzon, Samar, and Leyte Islands, The Philippines, during the Philippine War.
Source: Stuart Creighton Miller, *"Benevolent Assimiliation": The American Conquest of the Philippines, 1899–1903* (New Haven: Yale University Press, c. 1982), p. 223. Reprinted by permission of Yale University Press.

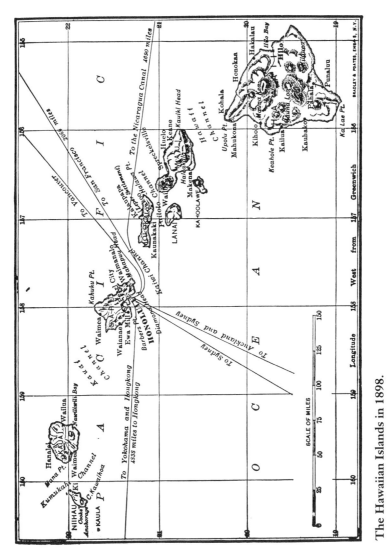

The Hawaiian Islands in 1898.

Source: Henry B. Russell, *The Story of Two Wars: An Illustrated History of Our War with Spain and Our War with the Filipinos* (Hartford, Connecticut: The Hartford Publishing Company, 1899), p. 547.

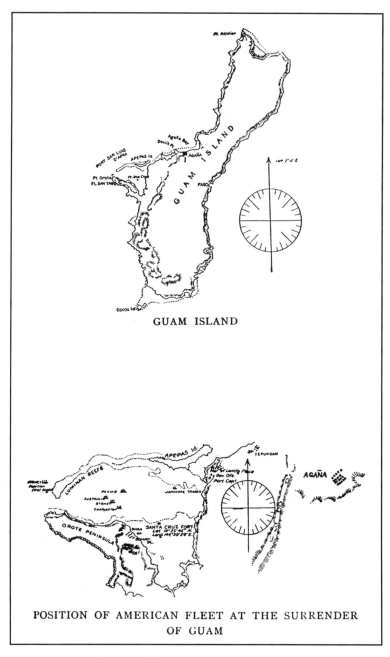

GUAM ISLAND

POSITION OF AMERICAN FLEET AT THE SURRENDER
OF GUAM

Guam in 1898 (above) and the U.S. Navy Seizure of the Island (below).
Source: *Harper's Pictorial History of the War with Spain* (New York: Harper &
Brothers Publishers, 1899), II, p. 275.

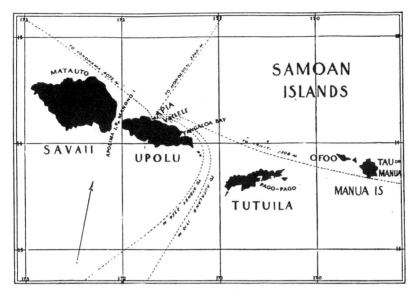

The Samoan Islands in 1899.
Source: Hugh H. Lusk, "Tutuila—Our Share of the Samoan Islands," *Harper's Weekly* 43 (December 2, 1899): 1214.

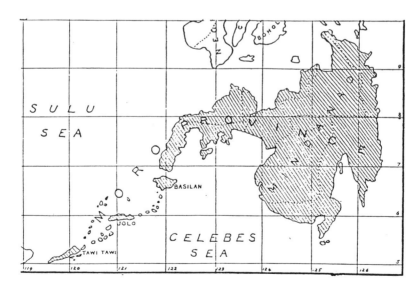

Moro Province, The Philippine Islands.
Source: James H. Blount, *The American Occupation of the Philippines 1898–1912* (New York: G.P. Putnam's Sons, 1912), taken from map on p. 228.

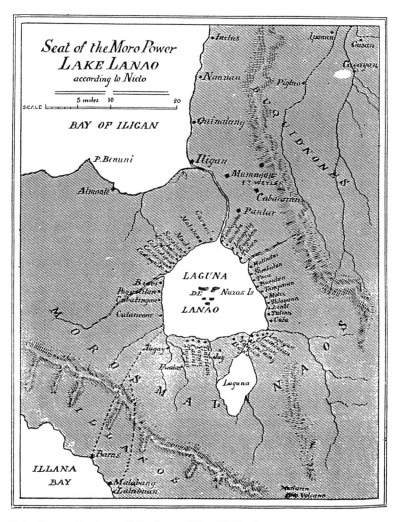

Lake Lanao Region of Mindanao, The Philippines.
Source: Frederic H. Sawyer, *The Inhabitants of the Philippines* (New York: Charles Scribner's Sons, 1900), facing p. 377.

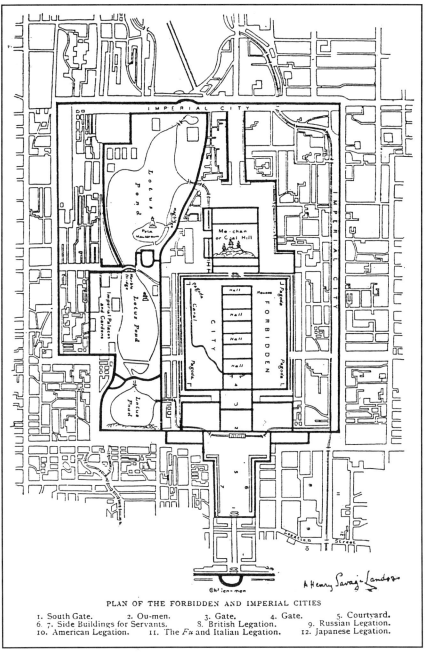

PLAN OF THE FORBIDDEN AND IMPERIAL CITIES

1. South Gate.   2. Ou-men.   3. Gate.   4. Gate.   5. Courtyard.
6. 7. Side Buildings for Servants.   8. British Legation.   9. Russian Legation.
10. American Legation.   11. The *Fu* and Italian Legation.   12. Japanese Legation.

Detailed Plan of Beijing (Peking), China in 1900. Showing the Foreign Legations.

Source: A. Henry Savage Landor, *China and the Allies* (New York: Charles Scribner's Sons, 1901), II, p. 355.

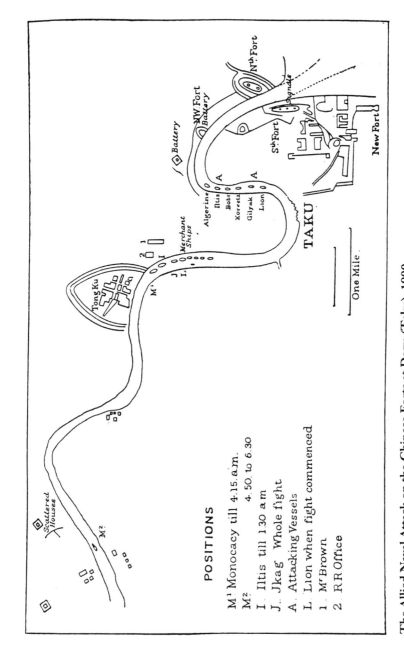

The Allied Naval Attack on the Chinese Forts at Dagu (Taku), 1900.
Source: A. Henry Savage Landor, *China and the Allies* (New York: Charles Scribner's Sons, 1901), I, p. 123.

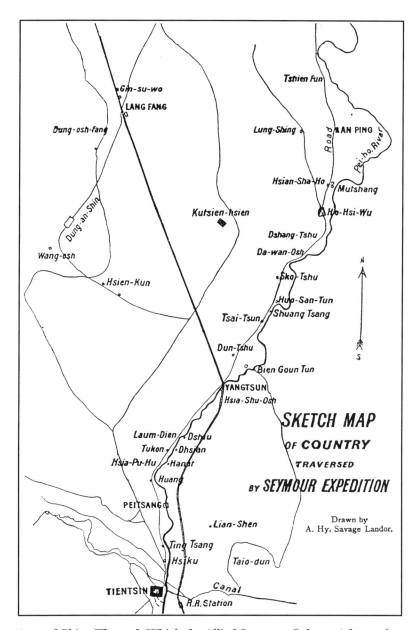

Area of China Through Which the Allied Seymour Column Advanced in the Summer of 1900.
Source: A. Henry Savage Landor, *China and the Allies* (New York: Charles Scribner's Sons, 1901), I, p. 89.

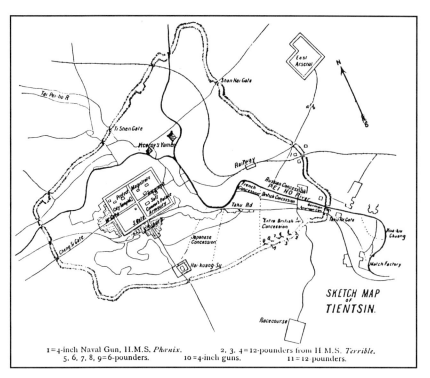

Tianjin (Tiensin), China and Surrounding Country in 1900, Showing the Chinese City and Foreign Concessions.
Source: A. Henry Savage Landor, *China and the Allies* (New York: Charles Scribner's Sons, 1901), I, p. 135.

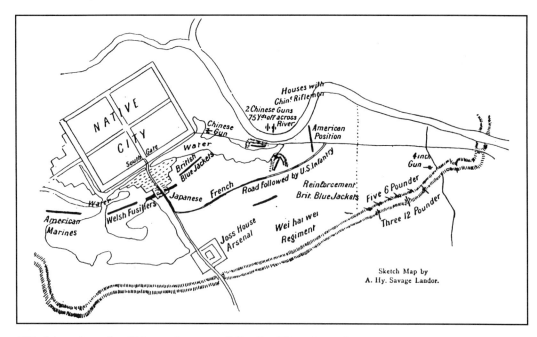

Allied Attack on the Chinese Quarter of Tianjin (Tientsin), China, 1900.
Source: A. Henry Savage Landor, *China and the Allies* (New York: Charles Scribner's Sons, 1901), I, p. 183.

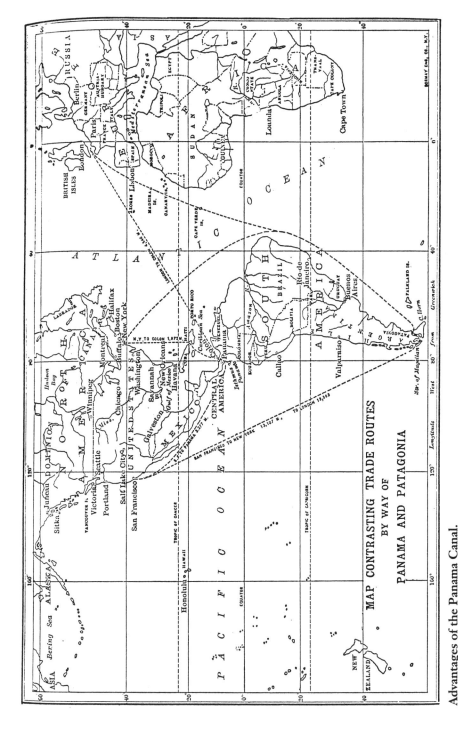

Advantages of the Panama Canal.
Source: Willis Fletcher Johnson, *Four Centuries of the Panama Canal* (New York: Henry Holt and Company, 1906), p. 385.

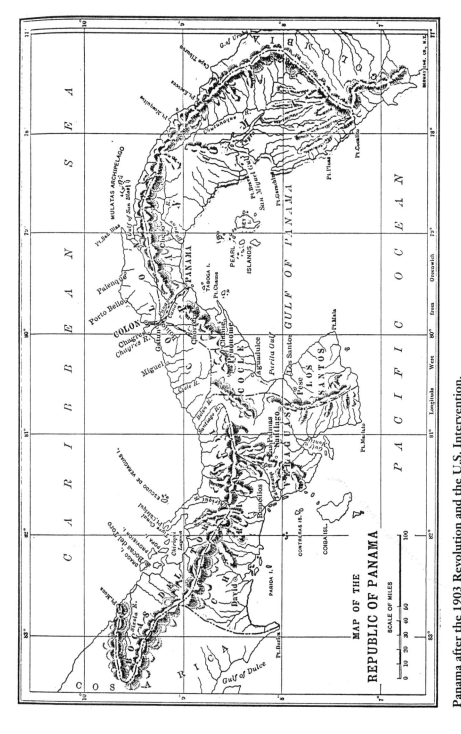

Panama after the 1903 Revolution and the U.S. Intervention.

Source: Willis Fletcher Johnson, *Four Centuries of the Panama Canal* (New York: Henry Holt and Company, 1906), p. 216.

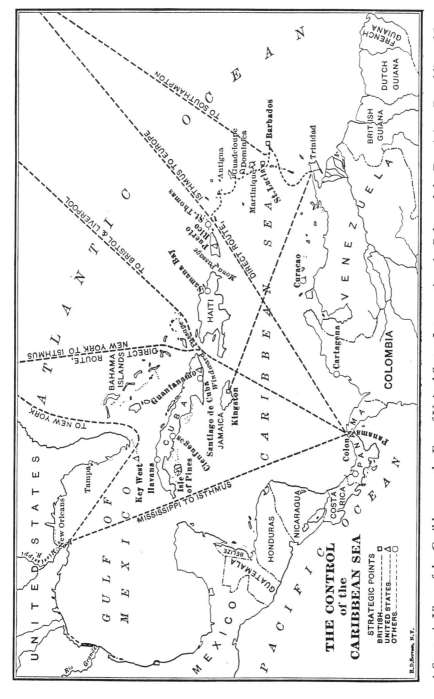

A Strategic View of the Caribbean on the Eve of United States Interventions in Cuba and the Dominican Republic and Later in Haiti and Nicaragua. The Map Is in Error in Ignoring the Dominican Republic.

Source: Archibald R. Colquhoun, *Greater America* (New York: Harper & Brothers Publishers, 1904), p. 190.

Mexico at the Time of the U.S. Occupation of Veracruz.
Source: David N. Buckner, *A Brief History of the 10th Marines* (Washington, D.C.: History and Museums Division, Headquarters, U.S. Marine Corps, 1981), p. 2.

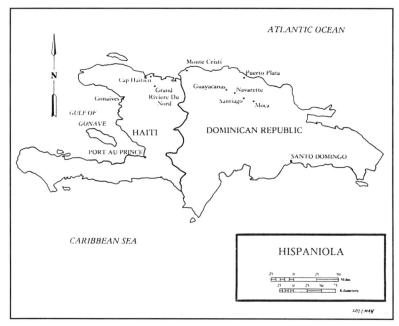

Haiti and the Dominican Republic during the U.S. Interventions. Emphasis Is on the Dominican Republic.
Source: David N. Buckner, *A Brief History of the 10th Marines* (Washington, D.C.: History and Museums Division, Headquarters, U.S. Marine Corps, 1981), p. 11.

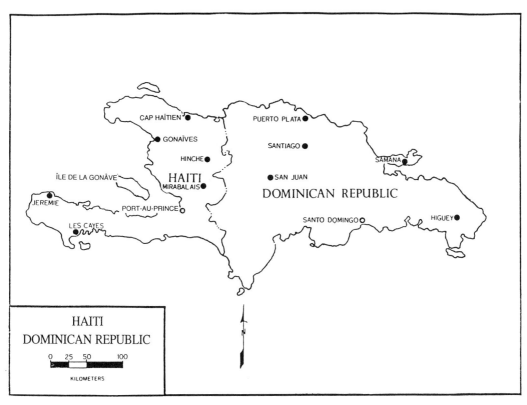

Haiti and the Dominican Republic during the U.S. Interventions. Emphasis Is on Haiti.
Source: James S. Santelli, *A Brief History of the 8th Marines* (Washington, D.C.: History and Museums Division, Headquarters, U.S. Marine Corps, 1976), p. 4.

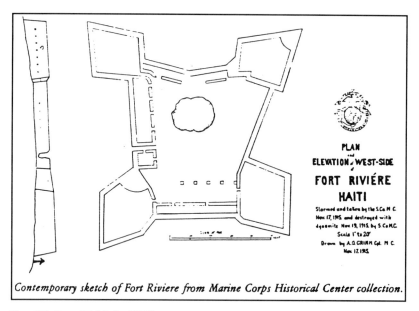

Contemporary sketch of Fort Riviere from Marine Corps Historical Center collection.

Fort Rivière, Haiti, in 1915.
Source: David N. Buckner, *A Brief History of the 10th Marines* (Washington, D.C.: Headquarters, U.S. Marine Corps, History and Museums Division, 1981), p. 10.

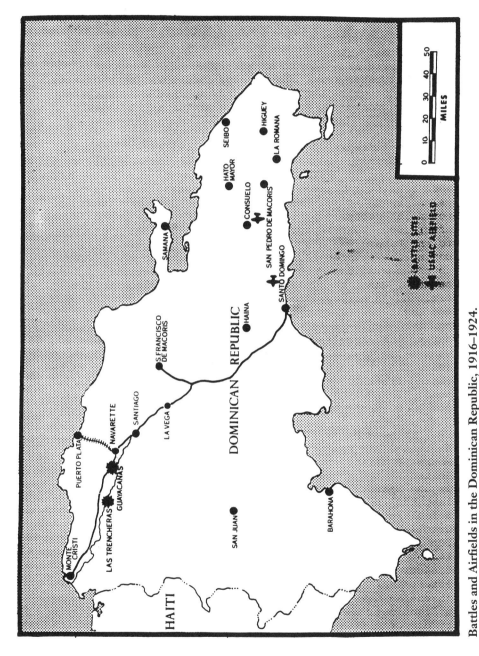

Battles and Airfields in the Dominican Republic, 1916–1924.

Source: Stephen M. Fuller and Graham A. Cosmas, *Marines in the Dominican Republic 1916–1924* (Washington, D.C.: History and Museums Division, Headquarters, U.S. Marine Corps, 1974), p. 4.

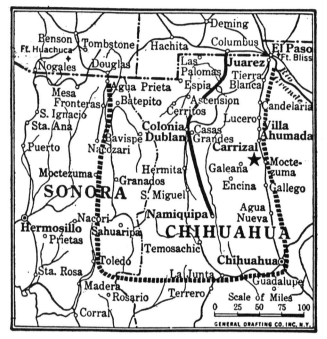

Northern Central Mexico in 1916. The Heavy Line
Represents Carranza Troops Around the Area Held by the
Punitive Expedition, Including the Cities of Colonia Dublán
and Namiquipa.

Source: "Our Task in Mexico," *Literary Digest* 53 (July 1,
1916): 2.

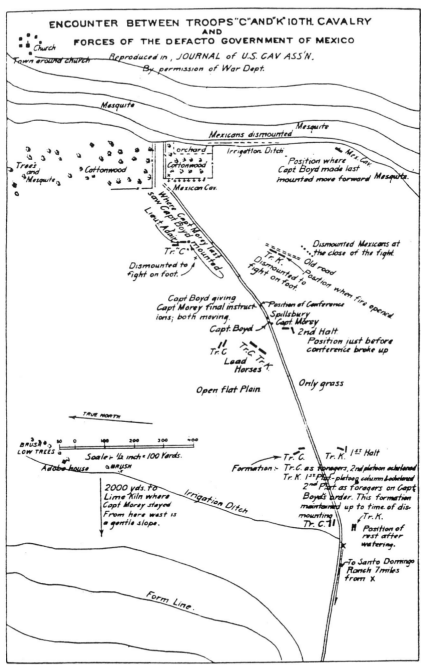

Detailed Chart of the Battle Between U.S. and Mexican Troops at Carrizal, Mexico, 1917.
Source: Lewis S. Morey, "The Cavalry Fight at Carrizal," *Cavalry Journal* 27 (January 1917): 453.

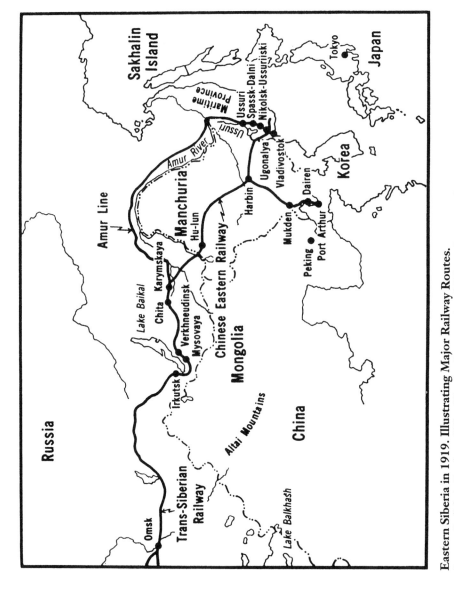

Eastern Siberia in 1919. Illustrating Major Railway Routes.
Source: Judith A. Luckett, "The Siberian Intervention: Military Support of Foreign Policy," *Military Review* 54 (April 1984): 57.

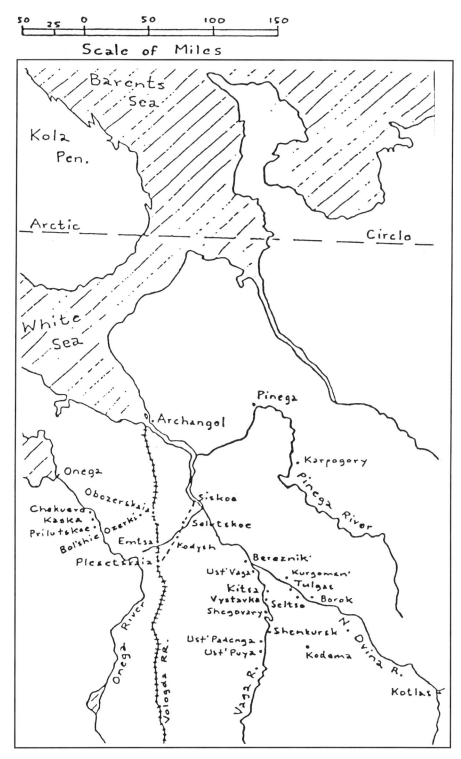

The Archangel Fronts, North Russia, 1918–1919.

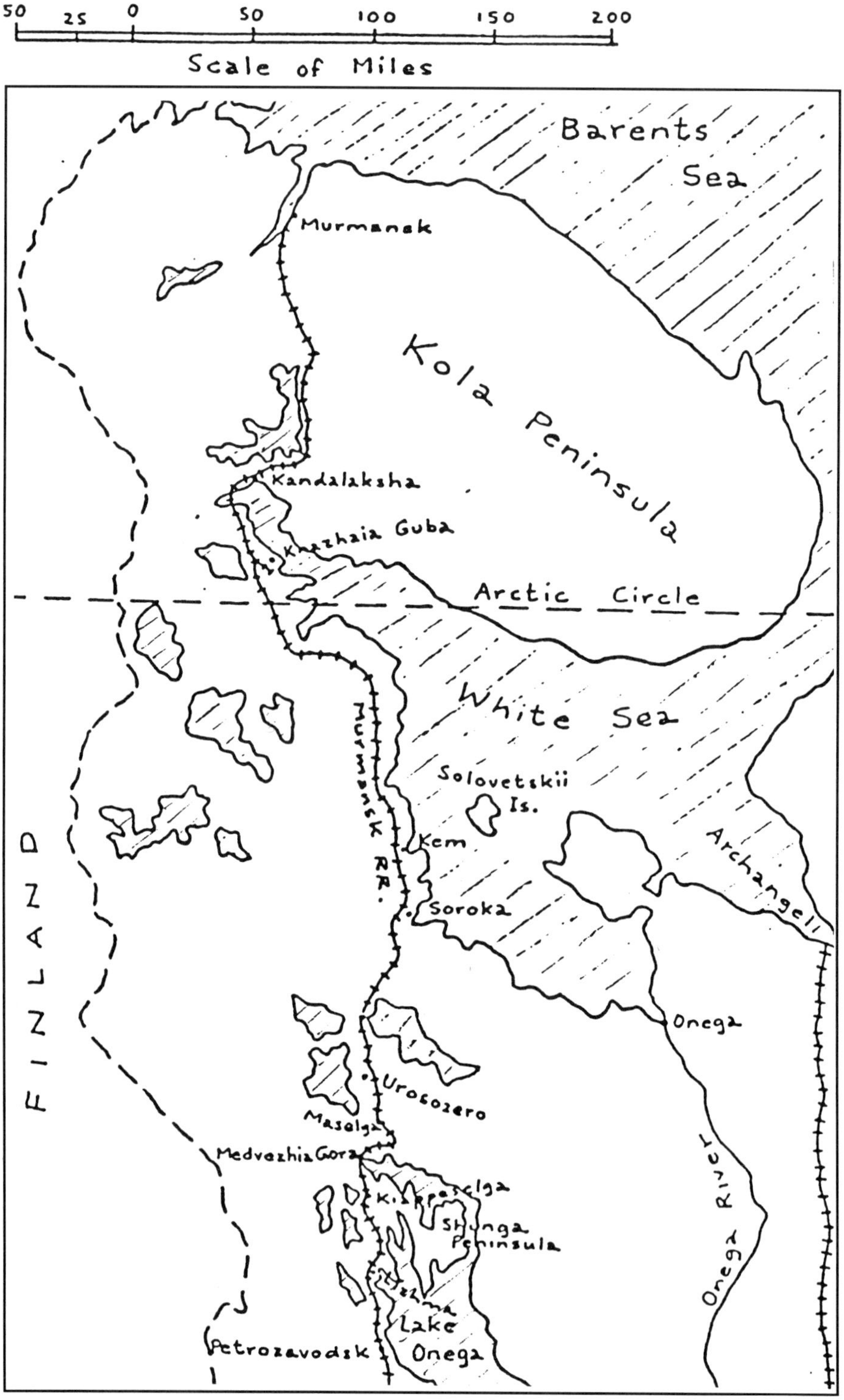
50 25 0 50 100 150 200
Scale of Miles
Barents Sea
Murmansk
Kola Peninsula
Kandalaksha
Arctic Circle
White Sea
Murmansk RR.
Solovetskii Is.
Kem
Soroka
Archangel
Onega
FINLAND
Urosozero
Maselga
Medvezhia Gora
Shunga Peninsula
Lake Onega
Petrozavodsk
Onega River

The Murmansk Front, North Russia, 1918–1919.

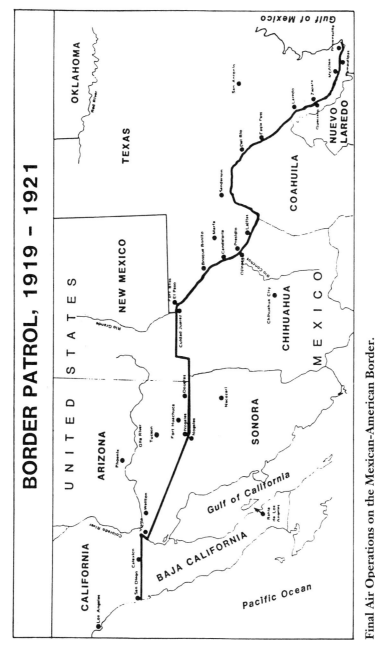

Final Air Operations on the Mexican-American Border.
Source: Maurer Maurer, *Aviation in the U.S. Army, 1919–1939* (Washington, D.C.: United States Air Force, Office of Air Force History, 1987), following p. 100.

Appendix B

Lists of Conflicts in Which U.S. Forces Were
Involved and Lists of U.S. Military Organizations
and Ships That Participated

Contents

SOURCE

U.S., Congress, House, Committee on Invalid Pensions, *Mexican Border Service, Hearings on H.R.
1653 and H.R. 2073 Bills to Extend Pension Benefits to Veterans Who Served During 1916 and
1917 on the Mexican Border, and to Their Dependents*, 79th Congress, 1st Session (U.S. Government Printing Office, 1945).

Wars, Military Expeditions, Occupations, Campaigns, and Other Disturbances, Except Domestic Troubles, in Which the United States Army Has Participated Since 1859, as Furnished by the War Department

36. Military incidents which fall within the purview of the World War Veterans' Act, 1924, as amended, have been included: these incidents do not include engagements in which the United States Navy or the Marine Corps solely participated. The list is necessarily incomplete. In order to determine definitely whether the service claimed by the applicant entitles him to benefits under the legislation, any case in which there is doubt should be referred to the War Department for such pertinent information as may be secured.

1860: Pah-Ute expedition, California, April 12 to July 9, 1860.

1860: Kiowa and Comanche expedition, Indian Territory, May 8 to October 11, 1860.

1860: Carson Valley expedition, Utah, May 14 to July 15, 1860.

1860: Attack on and murder of emigrants by Bannock Indians at Salmon Fork, Snake River, Idaho, September 13, 1860.

1860–61: Navajo expedition, New Mexico, September 12, 1860, to February 24, 1861.

1861–90: Apache Indian War and troubles in Arizona and New Mexico.

1861–66: Civil War, April 15, 1861, to August 20, 1866. Actual hostilities commenced April 12, 1861: ceased May 26, 1865.

1862: Indian massacres at New Ulm and vicinity, Minnesota, August 17 to 23, 1862.

1862–67: Sioux Indian War in Minnesota and Dakota.

1863–69: War against the Cheyenne, Arapaho, Kiowa, and Comanche Indians in Kansas, Nebraska, Colorado, and Indian Territory.

1865–68: Indian war in southern Oregon and Idaho, and northern California and Nevada.

1867–81: Campaign against Lipan, Kiowa, Kickapoo, and Comanche Indians and Mexican border disturbances.

1868–69: Canadian River expedition, New Mexico, November 5, 1868, to February 13, 1869.

1871: Yellowstone expedition, August 28 to October 25, 1871.

1872: Yellowstone expedition, Dakota, July 26 to October 15, 1872.

1872–73: Modoc campaign, November 28, 1872, to June 1, 1873.

1873: Yellowstone expedition, Dakota, June 4 to October 4, 1873.

1874–75: Campaign against Kiowa, Cheyenne, and Comanche Indians in Indian Territory, August 1, 1874, to February 16, 1875.

1874: Sioux expedition, Wyoming and Nebraska, February 13 to August 19, 1874.

1874: Black Hills expedition, Dakota, June 20 to August 30, 1874.

1874: Big Horn expedition, Wyoming, August 13 to October 10, 1874.

1875: Expedition against Indians in eastern Nevada, September 7 to 27, 1875.

1876: Sioux expedition, Dakota, May 17 to September 26, 1876.

1876: Powder River expedition, Wyoming, November 1 to December 31, 1876.

1876–77: Big Horn and Yellowstone expeditions, Wyoming and Montana, February 17, 1876, to June 13, 1877.

1876–79: War with Northern Cheyenne and Sioux Indians in Indian Territory, Kansas, Wyoming, Dakota, Nebraska, and Montana.

1877: Nez Perce campaign, June 14 to October 5, 1877.

1878: Bannock and Piute campaign, May 30 to September 4, 1878.

1878: Ute expedition, Colorado, April 3 to September 9, 1878.

1879: Snake or Sheepeater Indian troubles, Idaho, August to October 1879.

1879–80: Ute Indian campaign in Colorado and Utah, September 21, 1879, to November 8, 1880.

1890–91: Sioux Indian disturbances in South Dakota, November 1890 to January 1891.

1892–96: Troubles with renegade Apache Indians, under Kidd and Massai, in Arizona and Mexican border.

1895: Bannock Indian troubles, July and August 1895.

1898: Chippewa Indian disturbances at Leech Lake, Minn., October 1898.

1898–99: War with Spain, April 21, 1898, to April 11, 1899. Actual hostilities ceased on August 13, 1898, pursuant to the terms of a protocol signed on the previous day. Including hostilities in (a) Cuba, May 11 to July 17, 1898; (b) Porto Rico, July 24 to August 13, 1898; (c) Philippine Islands, June 30, 1898, to April 11, 1899.

1898–1902: Cuban occupation. July 18. 1898. to May 20. 1902.

1898: Porto Rican occupation, August 14 to December 10. 1898.

1899–1902: Philippine Insurrection, April 11. 1899. to July 4, 1902, in all parts of the Philippine archipelago. except in the Moro Province.

1900–1901: China Relief Expedition, June 20, 1900, to May 12, 1901.

1902–3: Philippine Insurrection in the Moro Province ended July 15, 1903.

1903–5: Philippine Islands, encounters with hostile Filipinos in which battle deaths occurred among the United States Army personnel.

1905: Porto Rico, encounters with hostile Porto Ricans in which battle deaths occurred among the United States Army personnel.

1906–7: Philippine Islands, encounters with hostile Filipinos in which battle deaths occurred among the United States Army personnel.

1906–9: Cuban pacification, September 29, 1906. to April 1, 1909.

1909–13: Philippine Islands, encounters in which battle deaths occurred among the United States Army personnel.

1914: Philippine Islands, battle deaths occurred among the personnel of the Philippine Scouts.

1914: Vera Cruz. Mexico. April 24 to November 26. 1914.

1915–19: Mexican border service, including: (a) Raid on Columbus, N. Mex., March 8–9, 1916: (b) punitive expedition. March 15, 1916. to February 5, 1917; (c) the Parral incident, April 12, 1916: (d) raid on Glen Springs, Tex., May 5, 1916: (e) raid on San Ygnacio. Tex., June 15. 1916: (f) the Carrizal incident, June 21, 1916: (g) bandit raids across Mexican border. May 5, June 15, and July 31, 1916: (h) raid near Fort Hancock. Tex.. July 31. 1916: (i) engagement near Buena Vista. Mexico, December 1, 1917: (j) engagement in San Bernardino Canon. Mexico. December 26, 1917: (k) engagement near La Grulla. Tex.. January 8 and 9, 1918: (l) engagement at Pilares. Mexico. on or about March 28, 1918; (m) engagement at Nogales. Ariz., August 27, 1918: (n) engagement near El Paso, Tex.. and Juarez. Mexico. June 15–16, 1919.

1917–21: World War, April 6, 1917, to July 2, 1921. Actual hostilities ceased November 11, 1918.

WARS ENGAGED IN BY THE UNITED STATES SINCE 1897

37. The following list of wars engaged in by the United States since 1897 was taken from an article released by the War Department under date of April 10, 1920 (corrected June 1939).

	Began	Ended
Spanish-American War	Apr. 21. 1898	Apr. 11. 1899
Philippine Insurrection	Apr. 11. 1899	July 4. 1902 [1]
Boxer Rebellion	June 20. 1900	May 12. 1901
Cuban pacification	Oct. 6. 1906	Apr. 1. 1909
Vera Cruz expedition	Apr. 21. 1914	Nov. 26. 1914
Punitive expedition into Mexico	Mar. 15. 1916	Feb. 5. 1917
World War	Apr. 6, 1917	July 2, 1921

[1] With the exception of hostilities in the Moro Province, which terminated June 15, 1903.

THE MILITARY ORGANIZATIONS OF THE UNITED STATES WHICH TOOK ACTIVE PART IN THE HOSTILITIES DURING THE PHILIPPINE INSURRECTION AND BOXER REBELLION

38. Volunteer organizations which served in the Philippine Insurrection:

Organization	Mustered in—	Mustered out—	Left United States—	Arrived in United States—
California:				
Volunteer Infantry: First Regiment.	May 6, 1898	Sept. 21, 1899	May 25, 1898	Aug. 24, 1899.
Artillery:				
Field and Staff	May 9, 1898	do	Oct. 19, 1898	Do.
Battery A	do	do	do	Do.
Battery D	do	do	Oct. 17, 1898	Do.
Colorado: First Regiment	May 1, 1898	June 8. 1899	June 15, 1898	Aug. 16, 1899.
Idaho: First Regiment	May 7, 1898	Sept. 25, 1899	June 27, 1898	Aug. 29, 1899.
Iowa: Fifty-first Regiment	May 30, 1898	Nov. 2. 1899	Nov. 3. 1898	Oct. 22, 1899.
Kansas: Twentieth Regiment	May 9, 1898	Oct. 3. 1899	Oct. 27, 1898	Oct. 10, 1899.

Organization	Mustered in—	Mustered out—	Left United States—	Arrived in United States—
Minnesota: Thirteenth Regiment.	May 7, 1898	Oct. 3, 1899	June 27, 1898	Sept. 7, 1899.
Montana: First Regiment	May 5, 1898	Oct. 17, 1899	July 18, 1898	Sept. 22, 1899.
Nebraska: First Regiment	May 9, 1898	Aug. 23, 1899	June 15, 1898	July 29, 1899.
Nevada: First Troop Cavalry	June 8, 1898	Nov. 15, 1899	Nov. 6, 1898	Nov. 5, 1899.
North Dakota: First Regiment	May 13, 1898	Sept. 25, 1899	June 28, 1898	Aug. 29, 1899.
Oregon: Second Regiment	May 7–15, 1898	Aug. 7, 1899	May 25, 1898	July 12, 1899.
Pennsylvania: Tenth Regiment	May 11, 1898	Aug. 22, 1899	June 15, 1898	Aug. 1, 1899.
South Dakota: First Regiment	May 12, 1898	Oct. 5, 1899	July 23, 1898	Sept. 7, 1899.
Tennessee: First Regiment	May 19, 1898	Nov. 23, 1899	Oct. 30, 1898	Nov. 11, 1899.
Utah:				
Field and staff	May 9, 1898	Aug. 16, 1899	June 15, 1898	July 31, 1899.
Battery A	___do	___do	___do	Do.
Battery B	___do	___do	___do	Do.
Washington: First Regiment	May 6, 1898	Nov. 1, 1899	Oct. 19, 1898	Oct. 9, 1899.
Wyoming:				
First Regiment	May 7, 1898	Sept. 23, 1899	June 27, 1898	Aug. 29, 1899.
Light Battery (Artillery)	June 16, 1898	___do	Nov. 8, 1898	Do.
Eleventh United States Volunteer Cavalry.	Aug. 12, 1899	Mar. 13, 1901	(Org. in P. I.)	Mar. 1, 1901.
Twenty-sixth United States Volunteer Infantry.	July 26, 1899	May 13, 1901	Sept. 25, 1899	Apr. 20, 1901.
Twenty-seventh United States Volunteer Infantry.	July and August, 1899.	Apr. 1, 1901	Sept. 21, 1899	Mar. 13, 1901.
Twenty-eighth United States Volunteer Infantry.	July 1899	May 1, 1901	Oct. 26, 1899	Apr. 14, 1901.
Twenty-ninth U. S. Volunteer Infantry.	August 1899	May 10, 1901	Oct. 5, 1899	Apr. 19, 1901.
Thirtieth U. S. Volunteer Infantry.	July 1899	Apr. 3, 1901	Sept. 23, 1899	Mar. 12, 1901.
Thirty-first U. S. Volunteer Infantry.	July 3, 1899	June 18, 1901	Oct. 25, 1899 Oct. 28, 1899.	June 9, 1901.
Thirty-second U. S. Volunteer Infantry.	July 1899	May 8, 1901	Sept. 30, 1899	Apr. 19, 1901.
Thirty-third U. S. Volunteer Infantry.	July and August 1899.	Apr. 17, 1901	___do	Mar. 29, 1901.
Thirty-fourth U. S. Volunteer Infantry.	August 1899	___do	Sept. 8, 1899	Do.
Thirty-fifth U. S. Volunteer Infantry.	July 1899	May 2, 1901	Oct. 4, 1899	Apr. 14–18, 1901.
Thirty-sixth U. S. Volunteer Infantry.	___do	Mar. 16, 1901	(Org. in Philippine Islands.)	Mar. 2, 1901.
Thirty-seventh U. S. Volunteer Infantry.	___do	Feb. 20, 1901	___do	Feb. 6, 1901.
Thirty-eighth U. S. Volunteer Infantry.	August 1899	June 30, 1901	Nov. 21, 1899	June 25, 1901.
Thirty-ninth U. S. Volunteer Infantry.	September 1899	May 6, 1901	Nov. 3, 1899	Apr. 17, 1901.
Fortieth U. S. Volunteer Infantry.	October 1899	June 24, 1901	Nov. 24, 1899	June 17, 1901.
Forty-first U. S. Volunteer Infantry.	___do	July 1, 1901	Nov. 20, 1899	June 26, 1901.
Forty-second U. S. Volunteer Infantry.	September 1899	June 27, 1901	Nov. 30, 1899	June 21, 1901.
Forty-third U. S. Volunteer Infantry.	November 1899	July 1, 1901	Nov. 16, 1899	June 27, 1901.
Forty-fourth U. S. Volunteer Infantry.	October 1899	June 30, 1901	Nov. 20, 1899	June 25, 1901.
Forty-fifth U. S. Volunteer Infantry	September and October 1899.	June 3, 1901	Nov. 16, 1899	May 17, 1901.
Forty-sixth U. S. Volunteer Infantry.	October 1899	May 31, 1901	Nov. 14, 1899	Do.
Forty-seventh U. S. Volunteer Infantry.	September 1899	July 1, 1901	Nov. 4, 1899	June 26, 1901.
Forty-eighth U. S. Volunteer Infantry.	___do	June 30, 1901	Dec. 21, 1899	June 24, 1901.
Forty-ninth U. S. Volunteer Infantry.	October 1899	___do	Dec. 2, 1899 Dec. 6, 1899	June 26, 1901 June 24, 1901

Squadron Philippine Cavalry was organized in the Philippines.
39. Regular Army organizations engaged in the Philippine Insurrection.

Organization	Left United States—	Arrived in United States—
ENGINEERS		
Company A	June 26, 1898	Aug. 29, 1901
Company B	July 5, 1899	Dec. 26, 1901
Company C	July 24, 1900	Dec. 24, 1901
Company D	(1)	Dec. 26, 1901
Company E	June 17, 1901	Dec. 24, 1903
Company F	do	Do.
Company G	do	July 22, 1903
Company H	do	Do.
FIRST CAVALRY		
Headquarters	July 22, 1900	June 15, 1903
Troop A	July 21, 1900	Sept. 30, 1903
Troops B, C, and D	do	Do.
Troop I	July 22, 1900	June 15, 1903
Troop K	July 19, 1900	Do.
Troop L	June 9, 1900	Do.
Troop M	July 24, 1900	June 16, 1903
THIRD CAVALRY		
Headquarters (less band)	Aug. 9, 1899	June 20, 1902
Band	July 24, 1900	Do.
Troop A	Aug. 7, 1899	Aug. 2, 1902
Troop B	July 24, 1900	Do.
Troop C	Aug. 9, 1899	Do.
Troop D	Aug. 7, 1899	Do.
Troops E and F	Aug. 9, 1899	May 24, 1902
Troop G	July 24, 1900	June 30, 1902
Troop H	July 23, 1900	Do.
Troop I	do	Aug. 24, 1902
Troop K	Aug. 8, 1899	Do.
Troop L	Aug. 9, 1899	Do.
Troop M	Aug. 7, 1899	Do.
FOURTH CAVALRY		
Headquarters	June 28, 1899	Sept. 11, 1901
Troop A	May 24, 1899	Do.
Troop B	June 28, 1899	Sept. 29, 1901
Troop C	July 15, 1898	Sept. 11, 1901
Troop D	June 23, 1899	Do.
Troop E	June 4, 1898	Sept. 9, 1901
Troop F	May 22, 1899	Do.
Troop G	June 14, 1898	Do.
Troop H	June 23, 1899	Do.
Troops I, K, and L	July 15, 1898	Sept. 11, 1901
Troop M	June 28, 1899	Do.
FIFTH CAVALRY		
Headquarters	Mar. 10, 1901	July 29, 1903
Troops A and B	Mar. 8, 1901	Oct. 19, 1903
Troop C	Mar. 4, 1901	Do.
Troop D	Mar. 8, 1901	Do.
Troops I and K	Mar. 10, 1901	July 20, 1903
Troop L	do	July 19, 1903
Troop M	do	July 20, 1903
SIXTH CAVALRY		
Headquarters	June 21, 1900	May 9, 1903
Troop A	do	Do.
Troop B	do	May 10, 1903
Troop C	June 22, 1900	May 9, 1903
Troop D	do	May 10, 1903
Troop E	Mar. 22, 1901	Oct. 28, 1903
Troops F and G	Mar. 25, 1901	Do.
Troop H	Mar. 22, 1901	Do.
Troop I	June 20, 1900	Aug. 21, 1903
Troop K	June 21, 1900	Do.
Troop L	June 20, 1900	Do.
Troop M	June 21, 1900	Do.

Organization	Left United States—	Arrived in United States—
NINTH CAVALRY		
Headquarters	July 28, 1900	Oct. 25, 1902
Troops A and B	do	Nov. 8, 1902
Troop C	July 23, 1900	Do.
Troop D	July 29, 1900	Do.
Troop E	do	Nov. 10, 1902
Troops F and G	do	Oct. 25, 1902
Troop H	July 22, 1900	Do.
Troop I	Apr. 4, 1901	Oct. 31, 1902
Troop K	do	Oct. 13, 1902
Troops L and M	Apr. 2, 1901	Do.
TENTH CAVALRY		
Troop E	Mar. 26, 1901	Aug. 17, 1902
Troop F	Apr. 9, 1901	Aug. 24, 1902
Troops G and H	do	Aug. 18, 1902
ELEVENTH CAVALRY		
Headquarters	Jan. 20, 1902	Apr. 24, 1904
Troops A, B, C, and D	Dec. 7, 1901	Do.
Troops E, F, G, and H	Dec. 4, 1901	Do.
Troops I and K	Jan. 20, 1902	Do.
Troops L and M	do	Apr. 25, 1904
FIFTEENTH CAVALRY		
Headquarters	Dec. 16, 1901	Dec. 20, 1903
Troops A and B	Mar. 18, 1901	Do.
Troops C and D	Apr. 1, 1901	Do.
Troops E and F	Nov. 25, 1901	Do.
Troop G	Mar. 25, 1901	Do.
Troops H, I, K, L, and M	Dec. 16, 1901	Do.
First Battery, Field Artillery	Apr. 4, 1899	July 16, 1901
Eighth Battery, Field Artillery	Apr. 2, 1899	Aug. 4, 1901
Tenth Battery, Field Artillery	Apr. 3, 1899	July 9, 1901
Twelfth Battery, Field Artillery	June 20, 1898	Sept. 28, 1901
Thirteenth Battery, Field Artillery	do	Sept. 29, 1901
Fourteenth Battery, Field Artillery	Aug. 11, 1900	Apr. 14, 1903
Fifteenth Battery, Field Artillery	Aug. 10, 1900	Apr. 15, 1903
Twenty-fifth Battery, Field Artillery	(2)	Aug. 18, 1903
Astor Battery	June 9, 1898	Jan. 22, 1899
Twenty-fifth Coast Artillery Corps	June 19, 1900	July 20, 1903
Twenty-seventh Coast Artillery Corps	July 25, 1900	Apr. 3, 1903
Twenty-ninth Coast Artillery Corps	Apr. 28, 1898	July 25, 1901
Thirtieth Coast Artillery Corps	June 29, 1898	July 24, 1901
Thirty-first Coast Artillery Corps	July 23, 1898	Apr. 17, 1903
Thirty-second Coast Artillery Corps	June 11, 1898	July 26, 1901
Thirty-third Coast Artillery Corps	June 6, 1898	Do.
Thirty-sixth Coast Artillery Corps	July 29, 1898	Apr. 17, 1903
Sixtieth Coast Artillery Corps	Nov. 29, 1899	Nov. 1, 1901

1 Organized in Philippine Islands June 7, 1901.
2 Organized in Philippine Islands Sept. 26, 1901.

Organization	Left United States—	Arrived in United States—	Organization	Left United States—	Arrived in United States—
FIFTEENTH CAVAL-RY—continued			**EIGHTH INFANTRY**		
Sixty-first Coast Artillery Corps	Apr. 12, 1899	Oct. 28, 1901	Headquarters	Sept. 6, 1900	Sept. 18, 1902
Sixty-second Coast Artillery Corps	Apr. 11, 1899	Nov. 4, 1901	Companies E, F, G, and H	....do......	Do.
Sixty-third Coast Artillery Corps	Apr. 12, 1899	Nov. 5, 1901	Company I	Aug. 15, 1900	Sept. 22, 1902
Sixty-fourth Coast Artillery Corps	....do....	Do.	Companies K and L	......do........	Sept. 18, 1902
Sixty-fifth Coast Artillery Corps	....do......	Nov. 8, 1901	Company M	....do........	Sept. 22, 1902
Sixty-eighth Coast Artillery Corps	Apr. 11, 1899	Nov. 7, 1901	**NINTH INFANTRY**		
Sixty-ninth Coast Artillery Corps	....do.........	June 25, 1900	Headquarters	Mar. 17, 1899	July 3, 1902
Seventieth Coast Artillery Corps	Nov. 29, 1899	Oct. 28, 1901	Company A	....do......	July 2, 1902
Seventy-first Coast Artillery Corps	Apr. 12, 1899	Do.	Company B	....do......	Nov. 8, 1905
Headquarters Sixth Artillery	....do.........	(¹)	Companies C and D	......do........	July 2, 1902
			Companies E, F, G, and H	....do......	July 3, 1902
FIRST INFANTRY			Company I	....do......	June 22, 1902
Headquarters	Aug. 14, 1900	May 12, 1903	Companies K, L, and M	......do........	July 3, 1902
Companies A and B	Aug. 13, 1900	May 13, 1903			
Companies C and D	Aug. 14, 1900	Do.	**TENTH INFANTRY**		
Companies E, F, G, and H	Aug. 25, 1900	May 12, 1903	Headquarters	Mar. 5, 1902	Sept. 18, 1903
Company I	Apr. 9, 1901	Do.	Companies A, B, C, and D	Feb. 17, 1901	Do.
Companies K and L	Mar. 26, 1901	Do.	Companies E, F, G, and H	Mar. 5, 1902	Do.
Company M	Apr. 9, 1901	Do.	Companies I, K, L, and M	......do........	Do.
SECOND INFANTRY			**ELEVENTH INFANTRY**		
Headquarters	Aug. 20, 1900	June 16, 1903	Headquarters	Mar. 26, 1901	Mar. 24, 1904
Companies A, B, C, and D	Apr. 10, 1902	June 17, 1903	Company A, B, C, and D	Apr. 9, 1901	Do.
Companies E, F, G, and H	Aug. 14, 1900	June 16, 1903	Company E, F, G, and H	Apr. 8, 1902	Apr. 7, 1904
Companies I, K, L, and M	Aug. 20, 1900	June 17, 1903	Company I	Mar. 26, 1901	May 2, 1904
			Company K	......do........	Mar. 26, 1904
THIRD INFANTRY			Company L	......do........	Apr. 7, 1904
Headquarters	Jan. 30, 1899	Apr. 29, 1902	Company M	......do........	May 2, 1904
Companies A, B, C, and D	....do.........	Do.	**TWELFTH INFANTRY**		
Companies E, F, G, and H	....do.........	Apr. 15, 1902	Headquarters	Feb. 11, 1899	May 9, 1902
Companies I, K, L, and M	....do.........	Apr. 29, 1902	Company A, B, C, and D	......do........	Do.
			Company E and F	......do........	May 15, 1902
FOURTH INFANTRY			Company G and H	......do........	May 16, 1902
Headquarters	Jan. 15, 1899	Feb. 5, 1902	Company I, K, L, and M	......do........	May 8, 1902
Companies A, B, C, and D	....do.........	Do.	**THIRTEENTH INFANTRY**		
Companies E, F, G, H, I, K, L, and M	......do.........	Feb. 6, 1902	Headquarters	Apr. 20, 1899	July 20, 1902
			Company A, B, C, D, E, F, G, H, I	......do........	July 19, 1902
FIFTH INFANTRY			Company K	......do........	July 20, 1902
Headquarters	Aug. 20, 1900	Sept. 13, 1903	Company L	......do........	July 19, 1902
Companies A, B, C, and D	....do.........	Do.	Company M	......do........	July 20, 1902
Companies E, F, G, and H	Mar. 26, 1901	Nov. 22, 1903	**FOURTEENTH INFANTRY**		
Companies I, K, L, and M	Aug. 10, 1900	Sept. 13, 1903	Headquarters	May 18, 1898	Aug. 30, 1901
			Company A	......do........	May 12, 1900
SIXTH INFANTRY			Company B	June 21, 1899	May 11, 1900
Entire regiment	May 17, 1899	July 2, 1902	Company C and D	May 7, 1898	Do.
			Company E and F	......do........	Aug. 3, 1901
SEVENTH INFANTRY			Company G	Aug. 4, 1898	Do.
Company C	Mar. 22, 1901	July 8, 1902	Company H	June 24, 1899	Do.
Company D	Mar. 20, 1901	Do.	Company I, K, L, and M	Aug. 4, 1898	Do.
Company H	Mar. 21, 1901	Do.	**FIFTEENTH INFANTRY**		
Company M	Mar. 20, 1901	Do.	Headquarters	July 10, 1900	Sept. 25, 1902
			Company A, B, C, and D	......do........	Sept. 22, 1902
			Company E and F	Feb. 8, 1902	Sept. 15, 1902
			Company G and H	......do........	Sept. 2, 1902
			Company I, K, L, and M	July 24, 1900	Sept. 25, 1902

¹ Lost identity in reorganization of Artillery February 1901.

77484—45——6

Organization	Left United States—	Arrived in United States—	Organization	Left United States—	Arrived in United States—
SIXTEENTH INFANTRY			**TWENTY-SECOND INFANTRY**		
Headquarters	May 24, 1899	July 21, 1902	Headquarters	Jan. 27, 1899	Mar. 11, 1902
Company A	....do......	July 28, 1902	Company A	....do......	Mar. 8, 1902
Company B	....do......	Aug. 28, 1902	Company B and C	....do......	Mar. 9, 1902
Company C and D	....do......	July 28, 1902	Company D	....do......	Mar. 8, 1902
Company E and F	....do......	July 21, 1902	Company E, F, G,		
Company G and H	....do......	Aug. 28, 1902	H, I, K, L, and M	....do......	Mar. 11, 1902
Company I, K, and					
L	....do......	July 21, 1902	**TWENTY-THIRD INFANTRY**		
Company M	....do......	Aug. 28, 1902			
			Headquarters	June 27, 1898	Dec. 3, 1901
SEVENTEENTH INFANTRY			Company A	Oct. 17, 1898	Dec. 4, 1901
			Company B	June 27, 1898	Do.
Headquarters	Feb. 14, 1899	Apr. 7, 1902	Company C	....do......	Dec. 5, 1901
Company A	....do......	Aug. 1, 1902	Company D	June 14, 1898	Do.
Company B	Jan. 15, 1899	Apr. 12, 1902	Company E, F, and		
Company C	Feb. 14, 1899	Aug. 1, 1902	H	....do......	Dec. 3, 1901 [4]
Company D	Jan. 30, 1899	Do.	Company G	June 27, 1898	Dec. 4, 1901
Company E and F	Feb. 14, 1899	Apr. 7, 1902	Company I	Oct. 17, 1898	Aug. 8, 1900
Company G	Jan. 15, 1899	Do.	Company K	....do......	Aug. 9, 1900
Company H	Jan. 30, 1899	Do.	Company L	June 27, 1898	Aug. 8, 1900
Company I	Jan. 15, 1899	Apr. 12, 1902	Company M	Oct. 17, 1898	Aug. 9, 1900
Company K	Jan. 30, 1899	Apr. 11, 1902			
Company L	....do......	Aug. 1, 1902	**TWENTY-FOURTH INFANTRY**		
Company M	Jan. 15, 1899	Apr. 11, 1902			
			Headquarters	July 14, 1899	Aug. 16, 1902
EIGHTEENTH INFANTRY			Company A	June 29, 1899	Do.
			Company B	Sept. 16, 1900	Do.
Headquarters	June 27, 1898	Oct. 21, 1901	Company C	May 24, 1899	Aug. 8, 1902
Company A	June 14, 1898	July 13, 1900	Company D	Sept. 20, 1900	Do.
Company B	....do......	July 17, 1900	Company E	June 22, 1899	Aug. 16, 1902
Company C and D	June 27, 1898	July 13, 1900	Company F	June 30, 1899	Do.
Company E	June 14, 1898	Oct. 21, 1901	Company G	June 22, 1899	Do.
Company F	June 27, 1898	Do.	Company H	June 24, 1899	Do.
Company G	June 14, 1898	Do.	Company I	June 22, 1899	Do.
Company H	June 27, 1898	Do.	Company K	June 26, 1899	Aug. 8, 1902
Company I	Aug. 21, 1898	Oct. 27, 1901	Company M	Sept. 16, 1900	Do.
Company K, L, and					
M	....do......	Oct. 19, 1901	**TWENTY-FIFTH INFANTRY**		
NINETEENTH INFANTRY			Headquarters	June 27, 1899	Aug. 17, 1902
			Company A	Sept. 21, 1900	Do.
Headquarters	July 17, 1899	June 22, 1902	Company B	June 20, 1899	Do.
Company A	July 20, 1899	Do.	Company C and D	Sept. 20, 1900	Do.
Company B	July 17, 1899	Do.	Company E	June 21, 1899	Aug. 27, 1902
Company C	July 20, 1899	Do.	Company F	June 24, 1899	Do.
Company D	July 17, 1899	Do.	Company G	Sept. 22, 1900	Sept. 18, 1902
Company E	July 20, 1899	Do.	Company H	June 20, 1899	Aug. 27, 1902
Company F, G, H,			Company I, K, L,		
I, and K	July 17, 1899	Do.	and M	June 27, 1899	Do.
Company L	July 20, 1899	Do.			
Company M	July 17, 1899	Do.	**TWENTY-SIXTH INFANTRY**		
TWENTIETH INFANTRY			Headquarters	July 8, 1901	Aug. 18, 1903
			Company A, B, C,		
Headquarters	Jan. 21, 1899	Mar. 23, 1902	and D	Feb. 16, 1901	Do.
Company A and B	....do......	Do.	Company E	(5)	Aug. 19, 1903
Company C	....do......	Mar. 31, 1902	Company F	July 4, 1901	Do.
Company D	....do......	Mar. 23, 1902	Company G	(5)	Sept. 2, 1903
Company E, F, G,			Company H	(5)	Aug. 28, 1903
and H	....do......	Apr. 9, 1902	Company I, K, and		
Company I, K, L,			L	Feb. 16, 1901	Sept. 4, 1903
and M	....do......	Mar. 23, 1902	Company M	....do......	Aug. 26, 1903
TWENTY-FIRST INFANTRY			**TWENTY-SEVENTH INFANTRY**		
Headquarters	Apr. 10, 1899	June 16, 1902			
Company A	....do......	June 15, 1902	Headquarters	Dec. 7, 1901	Feb. 24, 1904
Company B and C	....do......	June 16, 1902	Company A, B, C,		
Company D	....do......	June 26, 1902	and D	Dec. 8, 1901	Do.
Company E, F, G,			Company E, F, G,		
and H	....do......	June 16, 1902	and H	Jan. 20, 1902	Do.
Company I, K, L,			Company I, K, L,		
and M	....do......	June 18, 1902	and M	Dec. 4, 1901	Do.

[4] Company H, Dec. 4, 1901.
[5] Organized in Philippine Islands, July 1, 1901.

Organization	Left United States—	Arrived in United States—	Organization	Left United States—	Arrived in United States—
TWENTY-EIGHTH INFANTRY			**TWENTY-NINTH INFANTRY—con.**		
Headquarters	Nov. 12, 1901	Jan. 14, 1904	Company I	Feb. 20, 1901	May 23, 1904
Company A, B, C, and D	do	Do.	Company K	do	May 31, 1904
Company E	Nov. 13, 1901	Do.	Company L	do	May 25, 1904
Company F and G	Nov. 14, 1901	Do.	Company M	do	May 31, 1904
Company H	Nov. 15, 1901	Jan. 15, 1904	**THIRTIETH INFANTRY**		
Company I, K, L, and M	Nov. 12, 1901	Do.	Headquarters	(6)	Dec. 27, 1903
TWENTY-NINTH INFANTRY			Company A, B, C, and D	Apr. 16, 1901	Do.
			Company E and F	Mar. 15, 1901	Do.
Headquarters	Feb. 20, 1901	May 25, 1904	Company G and H	do	Dec. 26, 1903
Company A, B, C, and D	Feb. 22, 1901	May 23, 1904	Company I	(7)	Dec. 28, 1903
Company E, F, G, and H	Feb. 20, 1901	May 25, 1904	Company K and L	(8)	Do.
			Company M	(9)	Do.

6 Organized in Philippine Islands, June 3, 1901.
7 Organized in Philippine Islands, July 22, 1901.
8 Organized in Philippine Islands, Aug. 19, 1901.
9 Organized in Philippine Islands, July 28, 1901.

40. Regular Army regiments engaged in the Boxer Rebellion, in China, May 1900 to May 1901.

Organization	Left	Date	Remarks
Sixth Cavalry: Headquarters and Troops A, B, C, D, I, K, L, and M.	San Francisco, Calif	July 1, 1900	Remained in the Philippines after May 1901.
Third Artillery: Batteries A, D, I, and O.	do	July 29, 1900	Do.
Fifth Artillery: Battery F (became 10th Battery Field Artillery in February 1901).	Philippine Islands	July 15, 1900	Do.
Ninth Infantry: Entire regiment	do	June 27, 1900	Headquarters and all companies except B, remained in Philippine Islands after May 1901. Company B remained in China as United States legation guard at Peiping.
Fourteenth Infantry: Headquarters and Companies E, F, G, H, I, K, L, and M.	do	July 15, 1900	Remained in the Philippines after May 1901.
Fifteenth Infantry: Headquarters and Companies A, B, C, and D.	San Francisco, Calif	July 17, 1900	Do.

In addition to the troops mentioned above several detachments were sent to China, but the exact dates they left their stations and returned thereto are not shown.

WARS, MILITARY OCCUPATIONS, AND EXPEDITIONS ENGAGED IN BY THE UNITED STATES NAVY AND MARINE CORPS SINCE 1832, AS FURNISHED BY THE NAVY DEPARTMENT

41. As it is manifestly impracticable to secure from the Navy Department a complete and exact list of all minor landings and engagements on foreign soil, any individual application for hospitalization concerning which the Veterans' Administration is in doubt should be referred to that Department for research.

1832, February 7: For making a murderous attack on American merchantmen, the 44-gun frigate *Potomac* landed a large force of men in Sumatra and attacked the town of Qualla Battoo, killing a large number of the natives and destroying their forts.

1838, December 20: Qualla Battoo again bombarded, for repetition of outrages; this time by the corvet *John Adams*.

1840. July 12: U. S. S. *Vincennes* and *Peacock* landed sailors and marines on Feejee Island, Subig Bay.   Later in month Lieutenant Underwood landed party from *Flying Fish* at Malolo of Feejee group—two officers killed.   Landing party from squadron under command of Lieutenant Commander Ringgold consisting of 70 officers and men to avenge death of Lieutenant Underwood and Midshipman Henry.

1841, June: At Drummond Island, Lieutenant Commander Hudson landed 80 sailors and marines from U. S. S. *Peacock* to avenge the murder of one of the crew.

1846, April 24: War between United States and Mexico declared.   May 30, 1848, peace made.

1846, May 8: Five hundred sailors and marines landed from U. S. S. *Raritan* and *Potomac* at Brazas, Santiago, to protect our depot at Point Isabel.

1846, May 18: Two hundred sailors and marines from *Cumberland* and *Potomac* landed at Barita on the Rio Grande.

1855, August 4: U. S. S. *Powhatan* and English sloop *Rattler* in action against fleet of piratical junks.

1856, January 26: Indian War, Seattle, Wash.   *Decatur* involved.

1856, November 20 (November 16, China): Because the Chinese forts wantonly fired on the *Portsmouth* while protecting American lives and property at Canton, a large force of sailors and marines was landed and, after a two days' fight the Chinese were defeated.   The following vessels were involved: *Portsmouth, San Jacinto, Levant,* until November 22, 1856.

1858, January: Detachment of marines at Montevideo for protection of foreign residents.

1858, October 6: Forty sailors and marines landed at Waya, Feejee Islands, to avenge murder of two American citizens.

1859, June 25: China.   Captain Tatnall made his famous dash to the assistance of the British and French who were sorely pressed in their attack on the Peiho forts, North China.

1859, August: U. S. S. *Mississippi* landed portion of crew in Shanghai for protection of American interests.

1859, October 17: (Harpers Ferry); John Brown's raid.   Lieutenant Colonel Lee arrived with a company of marines.

1860, March 3: Fifty sailors and marines from U. S. S. *Marion* landed at Kisembo, Africa, to protect American interests; reembarked next day.

1860, September 27: Sailors and marines landed from U. S. S. *St. Mary* at Panama to protect American interests.

1861, April 15–1865, April 9: Civil War.   (All persons enlisted in the Navy during any of this period.)

1867, January: (For treatment of crew of the American trading schooner *General Sherman,* by Coreans, September 1866.)

1868: *Wachusett,* January 1867; *Shenandoah,* April 1868; *Colorado, Benicia, Monocacy,* and *Palos.*   Six hundred and sixty-four men landed on June 11, 1871.

1868, February 7: Fifty seamen and marines landed at Montevideo; withdrawn same day and landed again on the 19th to remain until the 26th.

1868, February 8: Joint landing from naval forces in Asiatic made at Nagasaki for protection of American interests during civil war in Japan.

1868, February 7–19: Fifty sailors and marines landed at Montevideo to protect American interests.

1867, April: Island of Formosa.   *Ashulot, Hartford,* and *Wyoming* landed and drove the savages into the interior and burned their huts June 13, 1867.   (For destroying crew of *Ashulot*).

1868, November 24: Naval forces landed at Hiago, Japan, to protect American residents.   United States minister ordered out and accompanied the attack on Japanese.   Commander J. B. Creighton, commanding naval forces.

1870, June 17: A boat expedition from the *Mohican* cut out the piratical steamer *Forward,* formerly a British gunboat, which had been operating on the coast of Mexico, and burned *Forward* under gallant fire.

1871: Carried the fort by a storm.   Sailed away on July 3, 1871.

1873, May 7: Two hundred officers and men landed at Panama.

1873, September 24: Three hundred and ninety officers and men landed at Panama.

1874, February 13: One hundred and fifty men landed from *Tuscarora* and *Portsmouth* at Honolulu.

1885, April 11: Revolution in Panama.   *Tennessee.*

1885, April 15: Commander McCalla with a force of sailors and marines took possession of the Isthmus to protect American interests.   Panama was occupied

1889, March 15: Harbor of Apia. Samoa. To protect American interests during German efforts to interfere in the affairs of the natives. *Trenton, Vandalla,* and *Nispic* involved.

1891, October 16: *Baltimore's* sailors attacked at Valparaiso, Chile. *Boston* and *Yorktown* demanded reparation, which was finally granted.

1891, May: U. S. S. *Kearsarge* landed.

1893, January 16: U. S. S. *Boston* lands party at Honolulu.

1894: Marines on Navassa Islands.

1894, July 24: U. S. S. *Baltimore* landed forces at Seoul.

1895, December 4: U. S. S. *Baltimore* lands force of 45 men at Chefoo, China.

1895, March 8: Sailors and marines numbering 60. landed from U. S. S. *Atlanta* at Boca del Toro to protect consulate. Reembarking the 9th.

1898, May 3: Marine company from U. S. S. *Baltimore* was landed at Cavite, P. I., to take charge of Spanish navy yard. Marines from *Olympia. Baltimore, Boston. Raleigh, Concord,* and *Petrel* garrisoned navy yard and station at Cavite until May 1899.

1899, April 1: Sixty officers and men landed from U. S. S. *Philadelphia* at Vailele, Samoa.

1916 to 1924, September 17: Dominican Republic occupied by marines from May 5, 1916, to September 17, 1924.

1921, August 30: Expedition to Panama on the occasion of the boundary dispute between Costa Rica and Panama. A battalion of marines sailed to Balboa, C. Z., arriving August 30, 1921, on the *Pennsylvania*. (Marine and naval officers and marines and enlisted men—Secretary of Navy report, 1922.)

1924, January 20: One officer and 75 men from Cavite on destroyers in Hong Kong and Canton.

1924, February 28: U. S. S. *Denver* landed the American consulate guard at La Ceiba. Honduras.

1924, February 29: U. S. S. *Denver* landed 35 additional men at La Ceiba, guarding the neutral area. Picked up by *Billingsley* March 4, 1924, and proceeded with the landing force to Puerto Cortez. (Contest over the presidency.)

1924, March 4: *Billingsley* landed at Tela, Honduras. 3 officers and 46 men to protect lives and property there. Probably *Billingsley* sent a landing force ashore to establish neutral zone and enforce it.

1924, March 6: One officer and 40 men left Guantanamo Bay for Puerto Cortez. Landing force of *Denver* withdrawn March 6, 1924. Landing force withdrawn March 14, 1924.

1924, March 17: Landing force from *Milwaukee* landed 9 officers and 167 men at Tegucigalpa, Honduras, March 19.

1924, January 13 to February 15: "Colorum" rebellion against authority of the Governor General of the Philippines. Commander in Chief Asiatic Fleet landed a force of marines on the *Sacramento* and drove the insurrectionists from the town. Controversy between Moros and local Philippine officials. Thirty-eighth destroyer division November 28. to December 8, 1924. (1924 or 1925) Bombing operations in Mindanao near Lake Lanao, to assist in quelling Moro uprising.

1924, August to 1925. February: Assisted in protecting American lives and property at ports in China during the various wars between rival Chinese factions extending from the latter part of August to early February.

1924, August: During the latter part of August war broke out around Shanghai for the control of that city. The normal routine of the Asiatic Fleet, with the exception of a few destroyers of the Forty-fifth Division and two mine layers who assisted in the "Round the world flight" was almost continuously interrupted by the various wars in China between rival Chinese factions. The following vessels arrived in Shanghai to take command of the American naval forces: *Isabel*: 3 destroyers of the Thirty-eighth Division, on August 30; 3 more of the Thirty-eighth Division and 3 of the Forty-fifth Division on September 2. The remaining destroyers of the destroyer squadron and the mine detachment, except those under repairs at Cavite, were distributed at ports up the Yangtze River, at Tsingtao, and Chefoo. *Huron,* Shanghai September 12: *Black Hawk,* September 29; *Asheville,* October 1. Landing forces were ashore in Shanghai from some of the destroyers, the *Huron, Asheville,* and 100 extra marines sent from Cavite. Landing forces all withdrawn on October 23 and 24. After landing forces were withdrawn from Shanghai, the *Huron* sailed for Taku Bar and transferred her marine detachment of 75 men plus 50 additional marines to Peking. Others came on 2 destroyers to Tangku on October 31; the *Asheville* arrived at Tientsin on November 1. One destroyer arrived at Tangku November 4 and transferred 50 marines to Peking. Other vessels: 2 destroyers at Tangku; *Huron* and 2 mine layers,

2 destroyers at Chefoo: several destroyers and *Sacramento* at Tsingtao, the *Asheville* at Tientsin: the *Black Hawk* at Shanghai. Conditions quieted down the latter part of November.

1924, August 29: Marine detachment of *Huron* embarked on three destroyers for Shanghai and formed part of landing force on shore organized from other United States vessels present. Withdrawn October 23.

1924, September 23: A provisional company of 2 officers and 100 enlisted men was organized at Cavite and landed at Shanghai.

1924, September 10: Consulate guard of 3 officers and 108 enlisted men landed at La Ceiba with orders to proceed to Masapan and guard American consulate. Masapan declared a neutral zone and denied the combatants entrance thereto. Withdrawn September 15. U. S. S. *Rochester*.

1924, October 23: Marine detachment of *Huron* and one platoon of provisional company from Cavite landed at Taku Bar and transferred to Peking.

1924, October 31: Remaining platoon of Cavite provisional company embarked and subsequently landed at Tientsin.

1924, November 10: One officer and 73 enlisted men joined *Huron* then at Chefoo and new marine detachment was organized.

1925, January 3: *Sacramento* reinforced by Thirty-eighth Destroyer Division later, and Yangtze patrol, sent landing forces ashore at different times. February 9, withdrawn.

1925, January 17: Another provisional company was organized at Cavite consisting of 2 officers and 105 enlisted, embarked on 3 destroyers and submarine landed at Shanghai.

1925, January 21: Thirty-five enlisted men embarked on a destroyer at Cavite, and submarine landed at Shanghai to augment forces already there.

1925, February 12: Marine provisional units were withdrawn from Tientsin and Shanghai to ships and returned to Olongapo. (Disbanded.)

1925, March-April: *Sacramento* or *Asheville* at Foochow practically all the time in connection with a student boycott.

1925, April (latter part): Landing force from *Denver* landed at La Ceiba.

1925, May 30: Trouble broke out again at Shanghai. Three ships of Forty-third Division retained at Shanghai: *Hart* and *Stewart* sent on the 3d of June with marines from the *Huron*, followed the next day by the remaining destroyers of the Forty-third Division. *Sacramento* June 3; *Jason* with 125 marines that were landed. Thirty-ninth Division sent to Shanghai June 19.

1925, June: Assisted in protecting American lives and property at various ports in China during the antiforeign strikes and boycott in the month of June.

1925, June 3: *Huron* detachment of marines embarked on 2 destroyers and landed at Shanghai as part of the United States naval landing force from vessels present. A provisional company of 3 officers and 125 enlisted organized at Cavite and submarine landed at Shanghai, forming part of United States naval landing force on shore.

1925, June 17: One hundred and eighty enlisted embarked on the United States Army transport *Thomas* at San Francisco as replacements to keep station over authorized strength during present emergency.

1925, June 27: A provisional company of 3 officers and 100 enlisted organized at Guam for further transfer to Cavite via United States Army transport *Thomas*.

1925, September: Outbreak in Nicaragua: *Denver* ordered to Corinto, *Tulsa* to Bluefields and other east coast ports during September.

REPORT OF COMMANDER IN CHIEF ASIATIC FLEET OCT. 4, 1925, TO JUNE 30, 1926

Date of arrival	Date of departure	Name of vessel	Place	Remarks
May 7, 1926		*Huron, General Alava, Villanolos. Penguin, Elcano. Monocacy, Isabel. Pegeon. Palos.*	Woosung	Outbreak in China over possession of Chung King.
Spring, 1926		Thirty-ninth Destroyer Division.		Emergency patrol duty on account of civil wars in China.
Oct. 30, 1925	June 10, 1926	*Asheville* (marines)		2 officers and 75 men, landed with United States Army forces in China.

REPORT OF COMMANDER SPECIAL SERVICE AUG. 11, 1926

Date of arrival	Date of departure	Name of vessel	Place	Remarks
May 7, 1926	June 6, 1926	*Cleveland* (marines)		Landed a landing force consisting of 216 officers and men at Blue-
June 17, 1926		*Tulsa* (marines)		fields, Nicaragua. Landing force
Aug. 27, 1926	Oct. 27, 1925	*Galveston*		of 150 marines was landed at
Oct. 10, 1926	Oct. 27, 1925	*Denver* (bluejackets and marines)		Bluefields, Nicaragua. Landing
Dec. 1, 1926		do		force of U. S. S. *Denver* relieved that of *Rochester*.
Dec. 23, 1926		*Cleveland* and *Denver* (bluejackets and marines).		173 officers and men landed at Puerto Cabezas and established a neutral zone in that place for the purpose of protecting Ameri- can and foreign lives and prop- erty.
Do		*Rochester* (bluejackets and marines).		158 officers and marines from *Rochester* landed at Cabezas and established a neutral zone.
1926		*Denver*, *Tulsa*, and *Cleveland*.	Nicaragua	Political upheaval in Nicaragua.

REPORT OF SECRETARY OF THE NAVY AUGUST, SEPTEMBER, AND OCTOBER, 1926

August, Sep- tember, October, 1926.		*Tulsa, Rochester, Gal- veston, Denver*, and 2 destroyers.		Revolutionary outbreak in Nica- ragua in August. Naval vessels and marines required. First brigade of the Marine Corps continued to remain in Haiti and maintain complete order and tranquillity throughout Haiti. All units are now in Port au Prince or Cape Haitien.

VESSELS PARTICIPATING IN THE SPANISH, CHINA, NICARAGUAN, HAITIAN, PHILIP- PINE, AND DOMINICAN CAMPAIGNS, AND CUBAN PACIFICATION, SINCE THE YEAR 1897, AS FURNISHED BY THE NAVY DEPARTMENT

42. List of vessels participating in the various campaigns.

SPANISH CAMPAIGN

Name	From—	To—	Name	From—	To—
Abarenda	June 7, 1898	June 26, 1898	Ericsson	Apr. 21, 1898	Aug. 12, 1898
Accomac	Apr. 21, 1898	Aug. 12, 1898	Fern	do	Do.
Alexander	June 19, 1898	June 30, 1898	Fish Hawk	July 24, 1898	Do.
Amphitrite	Apr. 21, 1898	Aug. 12, 1898	Foote	Apr. 21, 1898	Do.
Annapolis	Apr. 25, 1898	Do.	Frolic	July 31, 1898	Do.
Apache	Aug. 4, 1898	Do.	Gloucester	June 3, 1898	Aug. 12, 1898
Armeria	June 4, 1898	June 23, 1898	Gwin	July 8, 1898	Do.
Do	July 26, 1898	Aug. 12, 1898	Hamilton	May 1, 1898	Do.
Badger	July 1, 1898	Do.	Hannibal	June 25, 1898	July 13, 1898
Baltimore	Apr. 21, 1898	Aug. 16, 1898	Do	July 30, 1898	Aug. 12, 1898
Bancroft	May 9, 1898	Aug. 12, 1898	Harvard	May 11, 1898	June 2, 1898
Brooklyn	May 18, 1898	Do.	Do	July 1, 1898	July 10, 1898
Boston	Apr. 21, 1898	Aug. 16, 1898	Hawk	Apr. 23, 1898	Aug. 12, 1898
Brutus	July 23, 1898	Do.	Hector	June 30, 1898	July 24, 1898
Buccaneer	Aug. 6, 1898	Aug. 12, 1898	Helena	Apr. 21, 1898	Aug. 12, 1898
Caesar	June 6, 1898	July 7, 1898	Hist	June 25, 1898	Do.
Calumet	July 21, 1898	Aug. 12, 1898	Hornet	Apr. 23, 1898	Do.
Castine	Apr. 21, 1898	Do.	Hudson	May 5, 1898	Aug. 6, 1898
Celtic	June 18, 1898	July 30, 1898	Indiana	Apr. 21, 1898	Aug. 12, 1898
Charleston	June 20, 1898	Aug. 16, 1898	Iowa	do	Do.
Cheyenne	Aug. 3, 1898	Aug. 12, 1898	Justin	June 2, 1898	July 2, 1898
Cincinnati	Apr. 21, 1898	May 30, 1898	Lancaster	May 31, 1898	Aug. 12, 1898
Do	July 15, 1898	Aug. 12, 1898	Lebanon	May 28, 1898	Do.
City of Pekin	June 20, 1898	July 30, 1898	Leonidas	June 11, 1898	July 8, 1898
Columbia	June 30, 1898	Aug. 12, 1898	Do	July 30, 1898	Aug. 12, 1898
Concord	Apr. 21, 1898	Aug. 16, 1898	Leyden	Apr. 21, 1898	Do.
Cushing	do	Aug. 12, 1898	Machias	do	Do.
Detroit	do	Do.	Manning	May 7, 1898	Do.
Dixie	June 18, 1898	Do.	Mangrove	Apr. 21, 1898	Do.
Dolphin	Apr. 21, 1898	June 29, 1898	Maple	May 15, 1898	Do.
Dorothea	June 30, 1898	Aug. 12, 1898	Marblehead	Apr. 21, 1898	Do.
Dupont	Apr. 21, 1898	Aug. 3, 1898	Marietta	June 4, 1898	Do.
Eagle	Apr. 23, 1898	Aug. 12, 1898	Massachusetts	May 18, 1898	Do.

SPANISH CAMPAIGN—Continued

Name	from—	To—	Name	From—	To—
Massasoit	July 21, 1898	Aug. 12, 1898	Solace	June 13, 1898	July 12, 1898
Mayflower	Apr. 21, 1898	Do.	Do	Aug. 6, 1898	Aug. 12, 1898
McCulloch	...do	Aug. 16, 1898	Southery	July 3, 1898	July 30, 1898
McKee	July 25, 1898	Aug. 12, 1898	Sterling	May 19, 1898	June 27, 1898
McLane	...do	Do.	Stranger	July 21, 1898	Aug. 12, 1898
Merrimac	May 4, 1898	June 4, 1898	St. Louis	May 10, 1898	May 23, 1898
Maintonomoh	May 5, 1898	Aug. 12, 1898	Do	June 2, 1898	July 5, 1898
Minneapolis	May 17, 1898	June 6, 1898	Do	July 31, 1898	Aug. 10, 1898
Monadnock	Aug. 3, 1898	Aug. 16, 1898	St. Paul	May 17, 1898	May 29, 1898
Monterey	July 23, 1898	Do.	Do	June 12, 1898	June 28, 1898
Montgomery	Apr. 21, 1898	Aug. 12, 1898	Do	July 10, 1898	July 18, 1898
Morrill	May 1, 1898	Do.	Do	Aug. 1, 1898	Aug. 11, 1898
Morris	July 12, 1898	Do.	Supply	May 14, 1898	June 11, 1898
Nanshan	Apr. 21, 1898	Aug. 16, 1898	Do	July 27, 1898	Aug. 12, 1898
Nashville	...do	Aug. 12, 1898	Suwanee	May 14, 1898	Do.
Nero	Aug. 3, 1898	Aug. 16, 1898	Sylvia	Aug. 2, 1898	Do.
New Orleans	May 21, 1898	Aug. 12, 1898	Tacoma	July 31, 1898	Aug. 4, 1898
Newark	June 25, 1898	Do.	Tecumseh	Apr. 23, 1898	Aug. 12, 1898
Newport	Apr. 21, 1898	July 14, 1898	Terror	Apr. 21, 1898	Do.
Do	July 31, 1898	Aug. 12, 1898	Texas	May 18, 1898	Do.
New York	Apr. 21, 1898	Do.	Talbot	July 10, 1898	Do.
Niagara	May 3, 1898	May 21, 1898	Topeka	July 5, 1898	Do.
Do	June 10, 1898	Aug. 12, 1898	Uncas	Apr. 29, 1898	Do.
Olympia	Apr. 21, 1898	Aug. 16, 1898	Vesuvius	May 13, 1898	Do.
Oneida	June 2, 1898	Aug. 12, 1898	Vicksburg	May 1, 1898	Do.
Oregon	May 26, 1898	Do.	Viking	July 21, 1898	Do.
Osceola	Apr. 27, 1898	Do.	Vixen	May 11, 1898	Do.
Panther	Apr. 29, 1898	Do.	Vulcan	July 1, 1898	Do.
Passaic	June 14, 1898	June 23, 1898	Waban	Aug. 3, 1898	Do.
Peoria	June 21, 1898	Do.	Wasp	May 1, 1898	Do.
Petrel	Apr. 21, 1898	Aug. 16, 1898	Windom	May 4, 1898	Do.
Piscataqua	July 21, 1898	Aug. 12, 1898	Wilmington	Apr. 21, 1898	Do.
Pomrey	June 6, 1898	Do.	Winslow	...do	Do.
Porter	Apr. 21, 1898	July 14, 1898	Wompatuck	Apr. 28, 1898	Do.
Prairie	July 1, 1898	Aug. 12, 1898	Woodbury	May 8, 1898	Do.
Princeton	July 27, 1898	Do.	Yale	May 6, 1898	May 29, 1898
Potomac	July 16, 1898	Aug. 6, 1898	Do	June 27, 1898	July 26, 1898
Puritan	Apr. 21, 1898	Do.	Yankee	June 3, 1898	July 3, 1898
Raleigh	...do	Aug. 16, 1898	Do	July 21, 1898	Aug. 12, 1898
Resolute	June 4, 1898	July 8, 1898	Yankton	June 25, 1898	Do.
Do	July 24, 1898	Aug. 12, 1898	Yosemite	June 2, 1898	July 18, 1898
Rodgers	May 9, 1898	Do.	Zafiro	Apr. 21, 1898	Aug. 16, 1898
San Francisco	July 1, 1898	Do.	Officers and men on duty at Key West, Fla.: (See report)	...do	Aug. 12, 1898
Saturn	May 31, 1898	May 31, 1898	Officers and men on duty at Cavite. P. I.: (See report)	May 1, 1898	Aug. 16, 1898
Do	July 28, 1898	Aug. 12, 1898			
Scindia	June 12, 1898	June 26, 1898			
Scorpion	May 18, 1898	Aug. 12, 1898			
Siren	July 25, 1898	Do.			
Solace	May 11, 1898	June 1, 1898			

CHINA CAMPAIGN

Name	From	To	Name	From	To
Brooklyn	July 7, 1900	Oct. 12, 1900	Newark	May 27, 1900	July 22, 1900
Buffalo	Aug. 3, 1900	Aug. 6, 1900	Solace	June 18, 1900	July 29, 1900
Iris	June 29, 1900	July 24, 1900	Wheeling	Apr. 5, 1900	May 1, 1900
Monocacy	June 14, 1900	May 27, 1900	Yorktown	June 15, 1900	Sept. 10, 1900
Nashville	June 18, 1900	Sept. 7, 1900	Zafiro	July 10, 1900	Oct. 11, 1900
New Orleans	Sept. 14, 1900	May 27, 1901			

PHILIPPINE CAMPAIGN

Name	From—	To—	Name	From—	To—
Albany	Nov. 22, 1900	Dec. 26, 1900	Bennington	Feb. 22, 1899	July 5, 1899
Do	Feb. 20, 1901	July 3, 1901	Do	July 15, 1899	Apr. 2, 1900
Albay	May 21, 1899	Mar. 5, 1900	Do	May 27, 1900	Jan. 3, 1901
Do	Sept. 12, 1900	Oct. 6, 1900	Buffalo	Feb. 4, 1899	Mar. 23, 1899
Do	Nov. 19, 1901	July 4, 1902	Do	Aug. 14, 1900	Aug. 21, 1900
Do	Sept. 17, 1902	Nov. 20, 1902	Do	Feb. 26, 1901	Mar. 8, 1901
Do	Jan. 31, 1903	June 30, 1903	Do	Mar. 25, 1901	Apr. 4, 1901
Annapolis	Apr. 24, 1900	Aug. 1, 1903	Brooklyn	Dec. 16, 1899	Mar. 28, 1900
Do	Feb. 10, 1903	Feb. 20, 1903	Do	May 28, 1900	June 26, 1900
Do	Mar. 22, 1903	Apr. 11, 1903	Do	Nov. 3, 1900	Jan. 31, 1901
Arayat	Aug. 10, 1900	July 4, 1902	Do	Feb. 27, 1901	Apr. 10, 1901
Arethusa	Dec. 5, 1900	Do.	Do	Aug. 7, 1901	Sept. 26, 1901
Basco	June 2, 1899	Do.	Do	Feb. 13, 1902	Feb. 28, 1902
Baltimore	Feb. 4, 1899	Apr. 5, 1900	Boston	Feb. 4, 1899	June 8, 1899
Barry	May 6, 1905	May 11, 1905	Calamianes	Aug. 4, 1899	Mar. 1, 1900

PHILIPPINE CAMPAIGN—Continued

Name	From—	To—	Name	From—	To—
Calamianes	Apr. 23, 1900	Aug. 10. 1900	Newark	Dec. 22, 1900	Mar. 2, 1901
Do	Oct. 6. 1900	June 6. 1901	New Orleans	Dec. 21. 1899	Feb. 19, 1900
Do	Jan. 27, 1902	July 4. 1902	Do	May 22, 1900	Aug. 15, 1900
Callao	Feb. 4, 1899	Feb. 21. 1901	New York	May 20, 1901	June 25, 1901
Castine	Apr. 21. 1899	Jan. 18. 1900	Do	Aug. 27, 1901	Mar. 13, 1902
Do	Sept. 19. 1900	June 23. 1901	Nashville	Dec. 31, 1899	June 8, 1900
Celtic	Mar. 30. 1899	May 20. 1899	Do	Feb. 2, 1901	June 22, 1901
Do	Sept. 9. 1899	Nov. 22. 1899	Olympia	Feb. 4, 1899	May 20, 1899
Do	Feb. 22. 1900	May 8. 1900	Oregon	Mar. 18, 1899	Oct. 7, 1899
Do	July 19. 1900	Dec. 10. 1900	Do	Nov. 8, 1899	Feb. 13, 1900
Do	Apr. 3. 1901	June 4. 1901	Pampanga	June 8, 1899	Sept. 29, 1900
Do	Sept. 1. 1901	Oct. 5. 1901	Do	Dec. 15, 1900	June 18, 1902
Do	Jan. 11. 1902	Feb. 18. 1902	Do	Mar. 2, 1906	Mar. 10, 1906
Do	June 18. 1902	July 4. 1902	Do	Mar. 11, 1904	Apr. 12, 1904
Charleston	Feb. 4. 1899	Nov. 2. 1899	Do	May 4, 1904	May 11, 1904
Chauncey	May 6. 1905	May 11. 1905	Do	May 30, 1904	July 9, 1904
Concord	Feb. 4. 1899	Mar. 17. 1900	Do	July 30, 1904	Dec. 2, 1904
Do	May 27. 1900	Feb. 18. 1901	Do	Aug. 16, 1906	Sept. 15 1906
Culgoa	Feb. 4. 1899	Jan. 13. 1900	Panay	June 2. 1899	July 4, 1902
Do	Apr. 22. 1900	June 16. 1900	Paragua	May 22. 1899	Do.
Do	Nov. 1. 1900	Feb. 9. 1901	Do	Nov. 2. 1904	Nov. 29, 1904
Do	May 20. 1901	July 23. 1901	Do	Mar. 15, 1905	Apr. 2, 1905
Don Juan de Austria	Nov. 28. 1900	July 25. 1901	Do	Apr. 23. 1905	May 30, 1905
Do	Sept. 3. 1901	May 22. 1902	Petrel	Feb. 4. 1899	Aug. 17. 1899
Do	Aug. 28. 1902	Aug. 16. 1902	Do	Jan. 13. 1900	June 12. 1901
Do	Feb. 8. 1903	Apr. 12. 1903	Piscataqua	Apr. 24. 1901	July 4. 1902
Frolic	Apr. 24. 1901	July 4. 1902	Princeton	Apr. 16. 1899	Aug. 8. 1899
Do	Jan. 31. 1903	July 15. 1903	Do	Oct. 15. 1899	June 26. 1900
Do	Oct. 9. 1905	Nov. 12. 1905	Do	Dec. 4. 1900	Oct. 26. 1901
Gardoqui	June 2. 1899	Apr. 23. 1900	Do	Dec. 31. 1901	July 20. 1902
Do	Sept. 26. 1900	Oct. 3. 1900	Do	Feb. 9. 1903	Apr. 5. 1903
Do	Nov. 30. 1900	Feb. 15. 1902	Quiros	Mar. 14. 1900	Aug. 2. 1902
Do	Oct. 1. 1904	Dec. 31. 1904	Do	Aug. 31. 1902	Nov. 25, 1902
Glacier	July 15. 1899	Aug. 4. 1899	Do	Jan. 30. 1903	May 3. 1903
Do	Sept. 4. 1899	Mar. 2. 1900	Do	June 29. 1903	July 15. 1903
Do	May 27. 1900	Aug. 12. 1900	Rainbow	Apr. 3. 1902	July 4. 1902
Do	Jan. 6. 1901	Apr. 16. 1901	Do	Nov. 28. 1904	Dec. 4. 1904
Do	July 12. 1901	Aug. 12. 1901	Samar	May 26. 1899	Oct. 10. 1901
Do	Nov. 7. 1901	Dec. 2. 1901	Do	June 19. 1902	Nov. 29. 1902
Do	Mar. 30. 1902	May 8. 1902	Do	Jan. 31. 1903	Feb. 8. 1904
General Alava	Mar. 9. 1900	July 4. 1902	Do	Mar. 22. 1904	Aug. 5. 1904
Helena	Feb. 19. 1899	Oct. 9. 1900	Solace	Dec. 11. 1900	Dec. 22, 1900
Isla de Cuba	May 19. 1900	Mar. 11. 1902	Do	Jan. 15. 1901	Jan. 24. 1901
Do	June 23. 1902	July 4. 1902	Do	May 27. 1901	June 12. 1901
Do	July 21. 1902	Aug. 3. 1902	Do	July 19. 1901	July 28. 1901
Do	Sept. 2. 1902	Oct. 17. 1902	Do	Dec. 20. 1901	Dec. 31. 1901
Do	Apr. 21. 1903	May 9. 1903	Do	Jan. 18. 1902	Jan. 25. 1902
Do	June 20. 1903	July 15. 1903	Urdaneta	June 22. 1899	Sept. 17. 1900
Isla de Luzon	Mar. 31. 1900	Jan. 12. 1901	Do	May 12. 1900	Sept. 26. 1900
Do	May 25. 1901	July 4. 1902	Do	Oct. 3. 1900	July 4. 1902
Iris	Mar. 18. 1899	Nov. 16. 1899	Vicksburg	Feb. 2. 1901	Nov. 13. 1901
Do	Dec. 14. 1899	Jan. 16. 1900	Do	June 2. 1902	July 4. 1902
Do	May 31. 1900	June 21. 1900	Villalobos	Mar. 5. 1900	Do.
Iris	Aug. 1. 1900	Apr. 27. 1901	Wilmington	Jan. 20. 1901	May 10. 1901
Do	July 18. 1901	July 4. 1902	Wompatuck	Apr. 24. 1901	July 4. 1902
Kentucky	Feb. 3. 1901	Feb. 9. 1901	Wheeling	Apr. 14. 1899	Jan. 13. 1900
Do	Apr. 9. 1901	May 29. 1901	Do	Mar. 10. 1900	Mar. 21. 1900
Do	June 28. 1901	Aug. 29. 1901	Yorktown	Feb. 23. 1899	July 12. 1899
Do	Mar. 10. 1902	Apr. 8. 1902	Do	Aug. 3. 1899	Apr. 8. 1900
Leyte	Mar. 19. 1900	Sept. 12. 1900	Do	Sept. 17. 1900	May 23. 1901
Do	Sept. 29. 1900	Jan. 27. 1902	Do	Sept. 11. 1900	Sept. 28. 1901
Manila	Feb. 4. 1899	Apr. 15. 1902	Do	Nov. 17. 1901	Apr. 15. 1902
Manileno	May 26. 1899	Oct. 31. 1900	Yosemite	July 18. 1899	Aug. 1. 1899
Marietta	Jan. 3. 1900	Sept. 22. 1900	Do	June 14. 1900	June 30. 1900
Do	Nov. 30. 1900	June 3. 1901	Do	Aug. 7. 1900	Aug. 12. 1900
Mariveles	June 17. 1899	Mar. 14. 1900	Zafiro	Feb. 4. 1899	June 10. 1899
Do	Aug. 16. 1900	Aug. 22. 1900	Do	July 6. 1899	Aug. 4. 1899
Do	May 1. 1901	July 4. 1902	Do	Aug. 20. 1899	Oct. 13. 1899
Mindoro	June 11. 1899	Apr. 23. 1900	Do	Nov. 3. 1899	Nov. 10. 1899
Do	Oct. 31. 1900	Sept. 26. 1901	Do	Nov. 27. 1899	Mar. 21. 1900
Do	Aug. 31. 1904	Dec. 31. 1904	Do	June 3. 1900	June 21. 1900
Monadnock	Feb. 4. 1899	Jan. 1. 1900	Do	Oct. 20. 1900	Aug. 27. 1901
Do	Apr. 3. 1900	Oct. 27. 1900	Do	Oct. 11. 1901	Feb. 15. 1902
Monterey	Feb. 4. 1899	Apr. 6. 1900	Officers and men on duty at—		
Manshan	...do	Aug. 8. 1900	Cavite. P. I.	Feb. 4. 1899	July 4. 1902
Do	Sept. 11. 1900	Jan. 27. 1901	Olongapo. P. I.	...do	Do.
Do	Mar. 28. 1901	July 8. 1901	Pollok. P. I.	...do	June 3. 1904
Do	Oct. 8. 1901	Feb. 4. 1902	Isabella de Basilan, P. I.	...do	July 15. 1903
Newark	Nov. 25. 1899	Mar. 20. 1900			
Do	Apr. 3. 1900	Apr. 7. 1900			
Do	Aug. 18. 1900	Nov. 30. 1900			

DOMINICAN CAMPAIGN—MAY 5 TO DEC. 4, 1916

Name	From—	To—	Name	From—	To—
Celtic	July 6, 1916		Memphis	July 24, 1916	July 25, 1916
Do	July 23, 1916		Do	July 31, 1916	
Do	Aug. 18, 1916		Do	Aug. 18, 1916	Aug. 29, 1916
Do	Sept. 1, 1916	Sept. 2, 1916	Machias	Nov. 24, 1916	Nov. 25, 1916
Castine	May 5, 1916	June 27, 1916	Neptune	June 15, 1916	June 25, 1916
Do	July 15, 1916	Aug. 5, 1916	Do	July 2, 1916	July 3, 1916
Do	Aug. 17, 1916	Aug. 22, 1916	Do	July 9, 1916	July 11, 1916
Do	Aug. 26, 1916		Do	Oct. 14, 1916	
Do	Aug. 28, 1916	Sept. 9, 1916	Olympia	Nov. 20, 1916	Dec. 4, 1916
Do	Sept. 12, 1916	Sept. 19, 1916	Potomac	Aug. 28, 1916	Sept. 1, 1916
Do	Sept. 25, 1916	Oct. 10, 1916	Do	Sept. 26, 1916	
Do	Oct. 12, 1916	Oct. 15, 1916	Prairie	May 5, 1916	May 27, 1916
Do	Oct. 17, 1916	Oct. 25, 1916	Do	Sept. 1, 1916	Sept. 10, 1916
Culgoa	May 10, 1916	May 28, 1916	Do	Sept. 12, 1916	Oct. 15, 1916
Do	June 7, 1916	June 9, 1916	Do	Oct. 16, 1916	Oct. 17, 1916
Do	Oct. 8, 1916		Do	Oct. 26, 1916	Nov. 8, 1916
Do	Oct. 23, 1916		Salem	Sept. 7, 1916	Sept. 8, 1916
Dixie	Sept. 6, 1916	Sept. 8, 1916	Do	Sept. 29, 1916	Sept. 30, 1916
Do	Sept. 16, 1916	Sept. 18, 1916	Panther	May 22, 1916	May 25, 1916
Hancock	June 18, 1916	June 19, 1916	Dolphin	May 12, 1916	May 22, 1916
Do	Sept. 12, 1916	Sept. 30, 1916	Hector	May 9, 1916	June 3, 1916
Do	Nov. 7, 1916	Nov. 11, 1916	Kentucky	June 11, 1916	June 12, 1916
Do	Nov. 20, 1916	Nov. 22, 1916	Solace	Aug. 27, 1916	
Memphis	May 27, 1916	June 6, 1916	Do	Sept. 1, 1916	Sept. 2, 1916
Do	June 7, 1916	July 16, 1916			

CUBAN PACIFICATION

Name	From—	To—	Name	From—	To—
Alabama	Feb. 11, 1907	Feb. 16, 1907	Marietta	Jan. 18, 1907	Jan. 21, 1907
Brooklyn	Oct. 7, 1906	Nov. 1, 1906	Do	Feb. 7, 1907	Feb. 7, 1907
Celtic	Sept. 28, 1906	Jan. 15, 1907	Do	Mar. 18, 1908	Mar. 25, 1908
Cleveland	Sept. 21, 1906	Jan. 13, 1907	Do	Apr. 15, 1908	Apr. 16, 1908
Columbia	Oct. 20, 1906	Apr. 17, 1907	Do	May 27, 1908	June 9, 1908
Denver	Sept. 12, 1906	Oct. 2, 1906	Do	June 30, 1908	July 11, 1908
Des Moines	Sept. 15, 1906	Jan. 25, 1907	Minneapolis	Sept. 22, 1906	Oct. 22, 1906
Dixie	Sept. 12, 1906	Sept. 21, 1906	Newark	do	Nov. 9, 1906
Do	Jan. 7, 1907	Aug. 18, 1907	New Jersey	Sept. 21, 1906	Oct. 13, 1906
Dubuque	May 18, 1907	May 19, 1907	Paducah	Sept. 12, 1906	Apr. 1, 1909
Illinois	Feb. 11, 1907	Feb. 16, 1907	Prairie	Oct. 6, 1906	Nov. 21, 1906
Indiana	Sept. 30, 1906	Oct. 8, 1906	Do	Jan. 29, 1907	May 16, 1907
Do	Feb. 11, 1907	Feb. 16, 1907	Do	Dec. 25, 1908	Dec. 31, 1908
Iowa	do	Do	Do	Jan. 17, 1909	Jan. 23, 1909
Kentucky	Sept. 30, 1906	Oct. 9, 1906	Tacoma	Sept. 11, 1906	Feb. 26, 1907
Louisiana	Sept. 21, 1906	Oct. 13, 1906	Texas	Oct. 9, 1906	Oct. 30, 1906
Do	Dec. 25, 1906	Dec. 29, 1906	Virginia	Sept. 21, 1906	Oct. 13, 1906
Marietta	Sept. 14, 1906	Oct. 9, 1906			

NICARAGUAN CAMPAIGN FROM JULY 29, 1912, TO NOV. 14, 1912

CALIFORNIA, COLORADO, DENVER, TACOMA, ANNAPOLIS, CLEVELAND, GLACIER

HAITI CAMPAIGN—FROM JULY 9, 1915, TO DEC. 6, 1915

Name	From—	To—	Name	From—	To—
Washington	July 9, 1915	Dec. 6, 1915	Sacramento	Sept. 9, 1915	Dec. 6, 1915
Tennessee	Aug. 15, 1915	Aug. 18, 1915	Culgoa	Sept. 6, 1915	Oct. 8, 1915
Do	Aug. 31, 1915	Sept. 3, 1915	Celtic	Oct. 28, 1915	Nov. 9, 1915
Marietta	do	Sept. 19, 1915	Do	Nov. 28, 1915	Dec. 6, 1915
Do	Dec. 2, 1915	Dec. 6, 1915	Eagle	July 9, 1915	Nov. 2, 1915
Castine	Aug. 4, 1915	Do	Connecticut	Aug. 4, 1915	Dec. 2, 1915
Prairie	Nov. 7, 1915	Do	Solace	Aug. 9, 1915	Sept. 24, 1915
Osceola	Aug. 8, 1915	Nov. 2, 1915	Patuxent	Nov. 1, 1915	Dec. 6, 1915
Nashville	July 9, 1915	Dec. 6, 1915			

LANDING PARTIES

U. S. S. Dixie	Jan. 6, 1903: Marines landed at Colon.	U. S. S. Prairie	June 5 to July 24, 1912: Marines near Guantanamo, Cuba.
U. S. S. Nashville	Nov. 5, 1903: Landing party at Colon.	U. S. S. Paducah	June 6 to July 24, 1912: Landing party at El Cobre, Cuba.
U. S. S. Prairie	Nov. 14, 1903: Marines landed at La Boca, Panama.	Do	June 6 to July 24, 1912: Landing party at Elcuero, Cuba.
U. S. S. Boston	Dec. —, 1903: Landing party at Darien.	U. S. S. Eagle	June 6 to July 24, 1912: Landing party at Siboney, Cuba.
U. S. S. Wyoming	Dec. —, 1903: Landing party at Darien.	U. S. S. Nashville	June 10 to July 24, 1912: Landing party at Woodfred, Cuba.
U. S. S. Newport	Nov. 30, 1905: Landing party at Santa Barbara de Samana, D. R.		
U. S. S. Tacoma	Feb. 1, 1911: Landing party at San Pedre, Honduras.		

678

NAVAL VESSELS PARTICIPATING IN EXPEDITIONS TO CHINA AND NICARAGUA DURING THE YEAR 1928

43. Vessels that were actively engaged in the expeditions to China and Nicaragua during the year 1928, with the beginning and ending dates of the periods during which each of the vessels participated, as furnished by the Navy Department:

CHINA

Vessel	Port of arrival	Date of arrival	Port of departure	Date of departure
Pittsburgh	Hong Kong	Mar. 23	Shanghai	Nov. 26.
Sacramento	Amoy	June 5, 1927	Hong Kong	Jan. 28.
Do	Hong Kong	Feb. 18	Pagoda Anchorage	Sept. 10.
Do	do	Oct. 2	Hong Kong	Dec. 5.
Trenton	Chefoo	June 6	Chefoo	July 8.
Do	do	July 27	Shanghai	Oct. 29.
Memphis	do	June 4	Tsingtao	July 13.
Do	Tsingtao	July 25	Shanghai	Oct. 29.
Milwaukee	Shanghai	July 29	do	Do.
Isabel [1]				
Luzon [2]				
Monocacy [1]				
Oahu [3]				
Palos [1]				
Helena [1]				
Penguin [4]				
Mindanao [5]				
Tutuila [6]				
Panay [7]				
Asheville	Hong Kong	July 30, 1927	Hong Kong	Mar. 6.
Do	do	Mar. 21	do	Oct. 5.
Do	do	Oct. 26 [8]		
Pampanga [9]				
Guam [1]				
Black Hawk	Hong Kong	Mar. 23	Amoy	Apr. 7.
Do	Chinwangtao	Apr. 30	Chefoo	Sept. 18.
Paul Jones	Hon Kong	Mar. 23	Woosung	Oct. 29.
Parrott	Woosung	May 29	do	Do
Edsall	Swatow	Mar. 23	Amoy	July 14.
Do	Shanghai	Sept. 29	Woosung	Oct. 29.
Macleish	Swatow	Mar. 23	Shanghai	Oct. 11.
Simpson	do	do	Woosung	Oct. 29.
Bulmer	do	do	Chefoo	June 5.
Do	Shanghai	July 27	Woosung	Oct. 29.
McCormick	Swatow	Mar. 23	Woosung	Do.
Stewart	Woosung	Mar. 10, 1927	Shanghai	Jan. 13.
Do	Foochow	Mar. 23	Alacrity Bay	Apr. 13.
Do	Shanghai	June 15	Woosung	Oct. 29.
Pope	Shanghai	May 3, 1927	Shanghai	Jan. 13.
Do	Amoy	Mar. 31	Tsingtao	June 26.
Do	Shanghai	Sept. 9	Woosung	Oct. 29.
Peary	Foochow	Mar. 23	do	Do.
Pillsbury	Shanghai	Mar. 28, 1927	Shanghai	Jan. 13.
Do	Foochow	Mar. 23	Woosung	Oct. 29.
J. D. Ford	Woosung	Nov. 30, 1927	Shanghai	Jan. 10.
Do	Foochow	Mar. 23	Hong Kong	Sept. 23.
Truxtun	Shanghai	May 16, 1927	Shanghai	Jan. 13.
Do	Chinwangtao	Apr. 29	do	Aug. 7.
Do	Shanghai	Sept. 29	Woosung	Oct. 29.
Hulbert	do	Jan. 7	Shanghai	May 28.
Do	Hong Kong	July 16	do	Oct. 29.
Noa	do	Jan. 5	do	Oct. 26.
W. B. Preston	Shanghai	Jan. 7	do	June 26.
Do	do	July 24	do	Oct. 29.
Preble	do	Feb. 5	Swatow	Feb. 26.
Do	do	Apr. 4	Shanghai	Oct. 29.
Sicard	do	Jan. 7	Amoy	July 14.
Do	do	Sept. 8	Shanghai	Oct. 29.
Pruitt	do	Jan. 7	do	Aug. 28.
Do	do	Oct. 14	do	Oct. 29.
Canopus	do	May 15	Amoy	Sept. 21.
Beaver	Hong Kong	Mar. 23	do	Sept. 20.
Pigeon [10]				

[1] China during entire year.
[2] Commissioned at Shanghai June 1 and operated in Chinese waters remainder of year.
[3] Commissioned at Shanghai Oct. 22 and operated in Chinese waters remainder of year.
[4] Operated in Chinese waters until Oct. 15.
[5] Commissioned at Shanghai July 10 and operated in Chinese waters remainder of year.
[6] Commissioned at Shanghai Mar. 2 and operated in Chinese waters remainder of year.
[7] Commissioned at Shanghai Sept. 10 and operated in Chinese waters remainder of year.
[8] China remainder of year.
[9] Operated in China until Nov. 9, date of decommissioning.
[10] Operated in Chinese waters until Sept. 28.

CHINA—Continued

Vessel	Port of arrival	Date of arrival	Port of departure	Date of departure
Rizal	Hong Kong	Apr. 23	Shanghai	Oct. 30.
Henderson	Shanghai	Feb. 16	Hong Kong	Apr. 4.
Do	do	Aug. 5	Shanghai	Oct. 3.
Chaumont	Hong Kong	Oct. 12, 1927	Hong Kong	Jan. 15.
Do	Shanghai	Apr. 15	do	July 22.
Do	Hong Kong	Nov. 14	Shanghai	Nov. 28.
Hart	do	Apr. 23	do	Oct. 29.
Finch	Chefoo	May 3	do	Dec. 12.
Bittern	Hong Kong	May 6	Chefoo	Sept. 18.
Jason	Chefoo	May 19	Hong Kong	Oct. 11.
Heron	Shanghai	June 19	Shanghai	Oct. 9.
Avocet	Chefoo	May 2	do	Oct. 16.
Pecos	Hong Kong	Oct. 9, 1927	do	Mar. 3.
Do	Chefoo	May 2	Chefoo	Sept. 18.
General Alava [1]				
S-30, 31, 32, 33, 34, 35	Hong Kong	Mar. 23	Amoy	Sept. 20.
S-36	Tsingtao	June 15	do	Sept. 21.
S-37, 38, 39, 40, 41, 42	Shanghai	May 15	do	Do.

NICARAGUA

Vessel	Port of arrival	Date of arrival	Port of departure	Date of departure
Rochester	Corinto	Jan. 7	Corinto	Feb. 1.
Do	do	Feb. 16	do	Mar. 15.
Do	do	Mar. 24	do	Apr. 7.
Do	do	May 28	do	May 31.
Do	Puerto Cabezas	June 27	Bluefields	June 30.
Do	Corinto	July 8	do	July 18.
Do	do	Aug. 21	do	Aug. 25.
Do	do	Sept. 22	do	Sept. 27.
Do	do	Oct. 19	do	Nov. 27.
Do	do	Dec. 31	do	Jan. 7, 1929
Cleveland	do	Mar. 24	do	Apr. 24.
Do	Puerto Cabezas	Apr. 29	Puerto Cabezas	Apr. 29.
Do	Bluefields	May 15	Bluefields	June 14.
Do	do	July 11	do	July 11.
Do	Puerto Cabezas	July 23	do	July 26.
Do	Bluefields	July 31	do	Aug. 8.
Do	Corinto	Aug. 25	Corinto	Sept. 22.
Do	Bluefields	Oct. 4	Bluefields	Oct. 15.
Do	do	Oct. 20	do	Oct. 20.
Do	Puerto Cabezas	Nov. 3	do	Nov. 8.
Do	do	Nov. 19	do	Nov. 20.
Denver	do	Dec. 30, 1927	do	Jan. 12.
Do	Bluefields	Jan. 21	Puerto Cabezas	Jan. 22.
Do	do	Jan. 29	do	Feb. 19.
Do	Corinto	Mar. 5	Corinto	Mar. 23.
Do	Puerto Cabezas	Apr. 9	Bluefields	May 15.
Do	Corinto	June 17	Corinto	July 22.
Do	Bluefields	Aug. 8	Puerto Cabezas	Aug. 12.
Do	Puerto Cabezas	Aug. 25	do	Aug. 27.
Do	Bluefields	Dec. 6	do	Dec. 20.
Galveston	Corinto	Jan. 8	Corinto	Jan. 23.
Do	Bluefields	Feb. 26	Puerto Cabezas	Mar. 31.
Do	do	Apr. 4	Bluefields	Apr. 11.
Do	Puerto Cabezas	Apr. 30	Puerto Cabezas	Apr. 30.
Do	Corinto	May 15	Corinto	June 18.
Do	do	Sept. 26	do	Oct. 19.
Do	Bluefields	Nov. 2	Bluefields	Nov. 15.
Do	do	Nov. 18	Puerto Cabezas	Nov. 20.
Do	Puerto Cabezas	Nov. 30	Bluefields	Dec. 3.
Tulsa	Corinto	Jan. 6	Corinto	Feb. 16.
Do	Puerto Cabezas	Mar. 10	Puerto Cabezas	Mar. 10.
Do	Bluefields	June 14	do	July 2.
Do	Puerto Cabezas	July 7	Bluefields	July 11.
Do	Corinto	July 21	Corinto	July 25.
Do	do	Aug. 7	do	Aug. 21.
Do	Bluefields	Aug. 31	Puerto Cabezas	Sept. 16.
Do	Puerto Cabezas	Sept. 28	Bluefields	Oct. 4.
Do	Corinto	Nov. 18	Corinto	Dec. 9.
Ramapo	do	Mar. 25	do	Mar. 26.
Do	do	May 27	do	May 27.
Salinas	do	Jan. 26	do	Jan. 27.
Do	do	Feb. 18	do	Feb. 18.
Do	do	June 25	do	June 25.
Nitro	do	Jan. 16	do	Jan. 17.
Do	do	Jan. 22	do	Jan. 22.
Do	Puerto Cabezas	May 3	Puerto Cabezas	May 3.
Do	Corinto	May 10	Corinto	May 10.
Do	do	July 6	do	July 6.

[1] China during entire year.

NICARAGUA—Continued

Vessel	Port of arrival	Date of arrival	Port of departure	Date of departure
Nitro	Corinto	Aug. 29	Corinto	Aug. 29.
Do	do	Oct. 3	do	Oct. 3.
Do	do	Nov. 7	do	Nov. 7.
Sapelo	do	Jan. 18	do	Jan. 19.
Do	do	Mar. 15	do	Mar. 15.
Do	do	Apr. 6	do	Apr. 6.
Do	do	May 18	do	May 18.
Do	do	June 9	do	June 9.
Do	do	Oct. 18	do	Oct. 18.
Do	do	Nov. 9	do	Nov. 9.
Sirius	do	Mar. 23	do	Mar. 23.
Do	do	May 22	do	May 22.
Do	do	Aug. 22	do	Aug. 23.
Do	do	Oct. 20	do	Oct. 20.
Do	do	Dec. 28	do	Dec. 29.
Bridge	do	Mar. 30	do	Mar. 30.
Do	Puerto Cabezas	May 28	Bluefields	May 29.
Do	Corinto	June 2	Corinto	June 3.
Do	Puerto Cabezas	July 1	Bluefields	July 3.
Vega	Corinto	Feb. 4	Corinto	Feb. 5.
Do	do	June 13	do	June 13.
Do	do	Sept. 24	do	Sept. 24.
Do	do	Nov. 24	do	Nov. 24.
Texas	do	June 14	do	June 14.
Medusa	do	July 14	do	July 15.
Neches	do	July 19	do	July 19.
Do	do	Aug. 10	do	Aug. 10.
Marblehead	do	July 12	do	July 12.
Cincinnati	do	do	do	Do.
Richmond	do	do	do	Do.
Kanawha	do	Jan. 22	do	Jan. 22.
Do	do	Nov. 24	do	Nov. 24.
Milwaukee	do	Jan. 15	do	Jan. 15.
Oglala	do	Jan. 18	do	Jan. 21.
Do	do	Mar. 31	do	Apr. 2.
Trenton	do	Jan. 15	do	Jan. 15.

VESSELS OF THE REVENUE CUTTER SERVICE (COAST GUARD) PLACED UNDER THE SECRETARY OF THE NAVY TO COOPERATE WITH THE NAVY DURING THE SPANISH-AMERICAN WAR, TOGETHER WITH THE DATES OF THE EXECUTIVE ORDERS DIRECTING SUCH COOPERATION

44. Executive order dated March 24, 1898, included the following-named vessels: *Gresham, Windom, Hamilton, Hudson, Calumet, Woodbury, Morrill, Guthrie, Manning.*

By an arrangement between the Secretary of the Navy and the Secretary of the Treasury the *Guthrie* was not required to comply with this order. This order also included two vessels known as *Algonquin* and *Onondaga*, in course of construction at Cleveland, Ohio, but not ready to be placed in commission. They were brought around through the Canal and lakes to the Atlantic coast but before being in condition for active service the war had been brought to a close.

Executive order dated April 4, 1898: *McCulloch.*

Executive order dated April 9, 1898: "Cutters now in the North Pacific." This included: *Perry, Grant, Rush, Corwin.*

Executive order dated April 12, 1898: *McLane.*

Executive order dated April 29, 1898, effective as of April 8: *Colfax,*[1] *Boutwell.*[1]

The above-named vessels were returned to the Treasury Department by Executive orders as follows:

Executive order dated August 15, 1898: *Perry, Grant, Rush, Corwin.*

Executive order dated August 17, 1898: *Gresham, Windom, Hamilton, Algonquin, Hudson, Calumet, Woodbury, Onondaga, Morrill, Manning, Guthrie.*

Executive order dated August 25, 1898: *McLane.*

Executive order dated October 29, 1898: *McCulloch.*

The Secretary of the Navy in transmitting the order to the *McCulloch* fixed November 2 as the date on which it should be considered as becoming effective. There were no revenue cutters (Coast Guard) placed under the jurisdiction of the Secretary of the Navy during the Philippine Insurrection or Boxer Rebellion.

---

[1] No reference is made to these vessels in subsequent Executive orders.

NAVAL FORCES MOBILIZED FOR PARTICIPATION IN PHILIPPINE INSURRECTION AND BOXER REBELLION

45. The Navy Department advised that during the Philippine Insurrection and the outbreak of the Boxer Rebellion the entire Asiatic Fleet was mobilized, in the sense that all ships were prepared for active participation in whatever quarter their services would be needed.

In both instances the United States vessels were used as dispatch boats, to receive refugees, to cooperate with the Army, and to patrol the coasts in protection of American and foreign citizens.

The following vessels performed the duty prescribed above:

Boxer Rebellion.—U. S. S. *Newark*, landing party; U. S. S. *Don Juan de Austria*, stood by; U. S. S. *Monadnock*, stood by; U. S. S. *Monocacy*, landing party; U. S. S. *Nashville*, landing party; U. S. S. *Yorktown*, stood by; U. S. S. *Oregon*, landing party; U. S. S. *Wheeling*, stood by; U. S. S. *Helena*, stood by.

Philippine Insurrection.—U. S. S. *Brooklyn*, U. S. S. *Basco*, U. S. S. *Bennington*, U. S. S. *Castine*, U. S. S. *Celtic* (supply ship), U. S. S. *Concord*, U. S. S. *Helena*, U. S. S. *Culgoa* (supply ship), U. S. S. *General Alava* (dispatches), U. S. S. *Glacier* (supply ship), U. S. S. *Guardoqui*, U. S. S. *Iris* (collier), U. S. S. *Isla de Cuba*, U. S. S. *Isla de Luzon*, U. S. S. *Leyte*, U. S. S. *Manila*, U. S. S. *Charleston*, U. S. S. *Monadnock*, U. S. S. *Manileno*, U. S. S. *Marietta*, U. S. S. *Mindoro* (dispatch boat), U. S. S. *Monterey*, U. S. S. *Nashville*, U. S. S. *Oregon*, U. S. S. *Pampanga*, U. S. S. *Paragua*, U. S. S. *Petrel*, U. S. S. *Princeton*, U. S. S. *Quiros*, U. S. S. *Samar*, U. S. S. *Villalobos*, U. S. S. *Olympia*.

VESSELS WHICH PARTICIPATED IN, OR WERE PREPARED FOR ACTIVE PARTICIPATION IN CONNECTION WITH, THE OCCUPATION OF VERA CRUZ AND THE DATES BETWEEN WHICH THESE RESPECTIVE VESSELS WERE ENGAGED

[Extracted from the Bureau of Navigation Manual, pt. A, ch. 1]

46. List of the vessels participating:

Name	From—	To—	Name	From—	To—
Albany	Apr. 22, 1914	Nov. 23, 1914	Cummings	Apr. 29, 1914	May 18, 1914
Do	July 4, 1916	July 23, 1916	Do	June 9, 1914	June 12, 1914
Do	Nov. 25, 1916	Dec. 2, 1916	Cyclops	June 6, 1914	Aug. 4, 1914
Ammen	Apr. 22, 1914	May 5, 1914	Delaware	July 8, 1914	Oct. 9, 1914
Do	May 9, 1914	May 27, 1914	Denver	July 7, 1914	July 8, 1914
Annapolis	Apr. 21, 1914	Oct. 3, 1914	Do	Aug. 13, 1914	Aug. 24, 1914
Do	July 4, 1916	Sept. 18, 1916	Do	Apr. 4, 1916	June 29, 1916
Do	Nov. 11, 1916	Nov. 15, 1916	Do	July 15, 1916	Sept. 14, 1916
Do	Nov. 19, 1916	Feb. 7, 1916	Do	Dec. 16, 1916	Feb. 7, 1917
Arethusa	Apr. 30, 1914	May 2, 1914	Des Moines	May 14, 1914	June 19, 1914
Do	June 2, 1914	June 7, 1914	Do	July 19, 1914	Aug. 21, 1914
Arkansas	Apr. 22, 1914	Sept. 30, 1914	Do	Aug. 27, 1914	Oct. 15, 1914
Do	May 25, 1916	June 1, 1916	Dixie	Apr. 23, 1914	Apr. 24, 1914
Balch	Apr. 28, 1914	May 3, 1914	Do	May 2, 1914	May 27, 1914
Beale	Apr. 22, 1914	May 27, 1914	Do	June 25, 1916	June 27, 1916
Birmingham	do	May 25, 1914	Do	July 13, 1916	Aug. 28, 1916
Brutus	June 13, 1914	Aug. 3, 1914	Dolphin	Apr. 21, 1914	June 20, 1914
Do	July 6, 1916	Aug. 17, 1916	Do	July 2, 1916	July 8, 1916
Buffalo	Nov. 14, 1914	Nov. 26, 1914	Drayton	Apr. 22, 1914	May 4, 1914
Do	Mar. 28, 1916	Mar. 29, 1916	Eagle	May 3, 1914	Aug. 15, 1914
Do	June 22, 1916	June 30, 1916	Florida	Apr. 21, 1914	July 13, 1914
Do	Aug. 31, 1916	Feb. 7, 1917	Flusser	Apr. 28, 1914	Apr. 29, 1914
Burrows	Apr. 22, 1914	May 15, 1914	Do	July 2, 1916	July 9, 1916
Do	May 20, 1914	May 27, 1914	Fanning	Apr. 22, 1914	May 27, 1914
California	Apr. 21, 1914	June 24, 1914	Georgia	May 1, 1914	Aug. 1, 1914
Do	July 16, 1914	Aug. 18, 1914	Glacier	Apr. 21, 1914	Apr. 25, 1914
Cassin	Apr. 29, 1914	June 14, 1914	Do	July 10, 1914	Aug. 6, 1914
Chattanooga	Apr. 21, 1914	June 8, 1914	Do	Aug. 27, 1914	Sept. 28, 1914
Do	July 6, 1914	Nov. 26, 1914	Do	Mar. 29, 1916	Apr. 12, 1916
Do	Mar. 14, 1916	Apr. 13, 1916	Do	June 16, 1916	June 30, 1916
Do	Apr. 30, 1916	Aug. 31, 1916	Do	July 1, 1916	July 7, 1916
Do	Dec. 11, 1916	Dec. 16, 1916	Do	Aug. 1, 1916	Aug. 17, 1916
Celtic	Apr. 25, 1914	May 5, 1914	Do	Oct. 2, 1916	Oct. 30, 1916
Do	July 5, 1914	July 13, 1914	Do	Dec. 12, 1916	Dec. 20, 1916
Do	Sept. 4, 1914	Oct. 12, 1914	Hancock	Apr. 21, 1914	July 14, 1914
Chester	Apr. 21, 1914	June 8, 1914	Do	Apr. 15, 1916	June 25, 1916
Cheyenne	May 15, 1914	May 16, 1914	Do	June 30, 1916	Sept. 30, 1916
Cleveland	May 1, 1914	Oct. 27, 1914	Henley	Apr. 22, 1914	May 2, 1914
Do	Mar. 18, 1914	Nov. 20, 1916	Do	May 8, 1914	May 22, 1914
Colorado	June 24, 1916	Aug. 14, 1916	Hopkins	May 6, 1914	June 20, 1914
Connecticut	Apr. 21, 1914	July 2, 1914	Do	July 6, 1914	Aug. 27, 1914
Culgoa	May 13, 1914	May 28, 1914	Do	June 20, 1916	June 24, 1916
Do	July 19, 1914	Aug. 13, 1914	Do	July 3, 1916	Aug. 22, 1916

Name	From—	To—	Name	From—	To—
Hull	May 2, 1914	Aug. 11, 1914	Paulding	Apr. 22, 1914	May 27, 1914
Do	June 24, 1916	June 21, 1916	Pittsburgh	June 23, 1916	Oct. 4, 1916
Illinois	Oct. 13, 1916	Feb. 7, 1917	Preble	May 2, 1914	Aug. 16, 1914
Iris	Apr. 29, 1914	May 20, 1914	Do	Apr. 19, 1916	Apr. 20, 1916
Do	June 4, 1914	June 12, 1914	Do	July 18, 1916	Aug. 22, 1916
Jenkins	Apr. 22, 1914	May 10, 1914	Proteus	June 30, 1914	July 1, 1914
Do	May 14, 1914	June 14, 1914	Prairie	Apr. 21, 1914	May 26, 1914
Joett	Apr. 22, 1914	May 25, 1914	Do	June 18, 1914	June 28, 1914
Do	May 31, 1914	June 12, 1914	Raleigh	Apr. 21, 1914	June 2, 1914
Jupiter	Apr. 27, 1914	July 9, 1914	Do	July 11, 1914	Aug. 10, 1914
Do	Apr. 6, 1916	Apr. 23, 1916	Do	Oct. 23, 1914	Nov. 26, 1914
Kansas	July 14, 1914	Oct. 29, 1914	Do	Mar. 27, 1916	Mar. 29, 1916
Kentucky	Mar. 23, 1916	June 2, 1916	Do	Aug. 2, 1916	Oct. 21, 1916
Lawrence	May 2, 1914	Aug. 27, 1914	Reid	Apr. 28, 1914	Apr. 30, 1914
Do	Apr. 25, 1914	June 2, 1914	Do	June 26, 1916	June 28, 1916
Lebanon	do	Sept. 1, 1914	Rhode Island	Oct. 8, 1914	Nov. 26, 1914
Louisiana	Apr. 22, 1914	May 29, 1914	Sacramento	May 20, 1914	July 13, 1914
Machias	May 15, 1914	June 14, 1914	Do	Dec. 16, 1916	Feb. 7, 1917
Do	Mar. 14, 1916	June 23, 1916	Salem	May 5, 1914	Sept. 19, 1914
Marietta	do	June 27, 1916	Do	June 25, 1916	Aug. 30, 1916
Maryland	Apr. 28, 1914	Sept. 19, 1914	San Diego	July 10, 1914	Sept. 19, 1914
Do	June 28, 1916	Nov. 28, 1916	Do	Nov. 24, 1914	Nov. 26, 1914
Michigan	Apr. 22, 1914	May 29, 1914	Do	June 22, 1916	July 18, 1916
Do	Oct. 11, 1914	Nov. 26, 1914	Do	Oct. 26, 1916	Aug. 19, 1916
Minnesota	Apr. 21, 1914	May 29, 1914	San Francisco	Apr. 21, 1914	June 13, 1914
Do	July 29, 1914	Aug. 7, 1914	Do	July 6, 1914	July 17, 1914
Do	Oct. 11, 1914	Nov. 26, 1914	Saturn	Apr. 23, 1914	May 20, 1914
Milwaukee	June 25, 1916	Aug. 22, 1916	Do	June 7, 1914	June 15, 1914
Montana	Apr. 28, 1914	May 3, 1914	Saturn	July 22, 1914	Aug. 8, 1914
Mississippi (old)	Apr. 24, 1914	June 12, 1914	Do	Sept. 23, 1914	Nov. 26, 1914
Nanshan	Aug. 8, 1914	Sept. 6, 1914	Do	Oct. 12, 1916	Dec. 14, 1916
Do	Oct. 1, 1914	Oct. 24, 1914	Do	Jan. 13, 1917	Jan. 16, 1917
Do	July 1, 1916	July 11, 1916	Solace	Apr. 26, 1914	May 5, 1914
Do	Oct. 2, 1916	Oct. 19, 1916	Do	June 24, 1914	Oct. 30, 1914
Do	Dec. 11, 1916	Dec. 13, 1916	Sonoma	Apr. 22, 1914	Sept. 5, 1914
Nebraska	May 1, 1914	June 21, 1914	South Carolina	Apr. 21, 1914	May 31, 1914
Do	June 1, 1916	Oct. 13, 1916	South Dakota	July 1, 1914	July 2, 1914
New Hampshire	Apr. 21, 1914	June 21, 1914	Do	May 29, 1916	Aug. 1, 1916
New Jersey	Apr. 22, 1914	Aug. 13, 1914	Stewart	Apr. 25, 1914	Aug. 16, 1914
New Orleans	Apr. 21, 1914	Sept. 9, 1914	Do	June 30, 1916	Aug. 22, 1916
Do	Nov. 26, 1914	Dec. 6, 1914	Tacoma	May 4, 1914	July 27, 1914
Do	Nov. 25, 1916	Dec. 15, 1916	Do	Jan. 11, 1917	Feb. 7, 1917
Do	Dec. 27, 1916	Feb. 7, 1917	Texas	May 26, 1914	Aug. 8, 1914
Nashville	Apr. 23, 1914	July 16, 1914	Do	Oct. 9, 1914	Nov. 4, 1914
Do	July 18, 1916	Feb. 7, 1917	Trippe	Apr. 22, 1914	May 25, 1914
Neptune	Aug. 25, 1916	Sept. 3, 1916	Truxton	Apr. 25, 1914	July 13, 1914
Do	Oct. 25, 1916	Nov. 1, 1916	Do	June 24, 1916	Aug. 27, 1916
Nereus	Apr. 29, 1914	May 13, 1914	Utah	Apr. 21, 1914	June 15, 1914
Do	May 30, 1914	June 8, 1914	Vermont	do	Oct. 22, 1914
Do	Oct. 21, 1914	Nov. 30, 1914	Vestal	May 2, 1914	Sept. 20, 1914
Do	Oct. 29, 1916	Oct. 30, 1916	Vicksburg	May 15, 1914	May 16, 1914
Do	Feb. 6, 1917	Feb. 7, 1917	Virginia	May 1, 1914	Aug. 13, 1914
Nero	May 19, 1914	June 20, 1914	Do	Sept. 7, 1914	Oct. 11, 1914
Do	July 16, 1914	Aug. 7, 1914	Vulcan	Apr. 22, 1914	June 9, 1914
Do	Oct. 29, 1914	Nov. 26, 1914	Do	July 7, 1914	July 28, 1914
Do	July 14, 1916	July 20, 1916	Washington	June 14, 1914	June 27, 1914
Do	Jan. 15, 1917	Jan. 20, 1917	Warrington	Apr. 22, 1914	May 2, 1914
New York	May 4, 1914	Sept. 5, 1914	Do	May 14, 1914	May 27, 1914
Do	Sept. 14, 1914	Sept. 17, 1914	West Virginia	May 9, 1914	July 3, 1914
North Dakota	Apr. 25, 1914	Oct. 8, 1914	Do	Sept. 9, 1914	Nov. 26, 1914
Do	July 4, 1916	Aug. 10, 1916	Do	Oct. 9, 1916	Nov. 8, 1916
Ontario	Apr. 22, 1914	July 5, 1914	Wheeling	Apr. 25, 1914	June 30, 1914
Do	July 11, 1914	July 26, 1914	Do	Mar. 27, 1916	June 29, 1916
Orion	Apr. 22, 1914	July 4, 1914	Do	July 1, 1916	Dec. 16, 1916
Do	July 29, 1914	Sept. 2, 1914	Whipple	Apr. 25, 1914	July 13, 1914
Ozark	May 15, 1914	May 25, 1914	Do	Mar. 17, 1916	Apr. 21, 1916
Patuxent	Apr. 23, 1914	Oct. 8, 1914	Do	June 26, 1916	July 31, 1916
Paul Jones	Apr. 25, 1914	Apr. 28, 1914	Do	Aug. 14, 1916	Aug. 21, 1916
Do	July 18, 1916	Aug. 22, 1916	Wyoming	May 18, 1914	Sept. 7, 1914
Do	Dec. 1, 1916	Jan. 29, 1917	Yankton	Apr. 25, 1914	May 1, 1914
Perry	Apr. 25, 1914	Aug. 16, 1914	Do	May 9, 1914	Sept. 7, 1914
Petrel	Oct. 10, 1914	Nov. 14, 1914	Yorktown	Apr. 21, 1914	June 16, 1914
Do	Nov. 18, 1914	Nov. 26, 1914	Do	Sept. 9, 1914	Nov. 26, 1914
Patterson	Apr. 22, 1914	May 26, 1914	Do	Mar. 14, 1916	Nov. 21, 1916
Paducah	May 14, 1914	June 17, 1914	Do	Jan. 18, 1917	Jan. 20, 1917
Patapsco	Apr. 23, 1914	Sept. 9, 1914			

Wars, Military Occupations, and Expeditions Engaged in by the Marine Corps from the year 1860 to 1927, Together With the Units Taking Part, as Furnished from the Headquarters, United States Marine Corps, and Deemed Necessary at This Time by the Commandant of the Marine Corps

(Also see paragraph 41)

47. List of the wars, military occupations, and expeditions:

1860, March 3. Kisembo, Africa: Marines from the *Marion* ashore to protect American interests and property.

1860, September 27 to October 7. Panama: Marines from the *St. Mary's* landed during an insurrection to protect American interests.

1861, April 15, to 1865, April 9. Civil War: All members of the Marine Corps engaged.

1867, June 13. Island of Formosa: Marines from the *Hartford* and *Wyoming* on shore in the island of Formosa. Punitive expedition against savages.

1870, June 17. Boca Teacapon, Mexico: Marines from the *Mohican* engaged in destroying the *Forward*, a piratical craft bearing the San Salvador flag.

1871, June 10 and 11. Corea: Marines from the *Alaska*, *Benicia*, and *Colorado* ashore capturing forts on the Salee River.

1873, May 7 to 22 and September 24 to October 8. Panama: May 7 to 22, marines from the *Pensacola* and *Tuscarora* ashore to protect American interests. September 24 to October 8, marines from *Pensacola* and *Benicia* ashore to protect American interests.

1874, February 12 to 20. Hawaiian Islands: Marines from the *Tuscarora* and *Portsmouth* ashore at Honolulu.

1882, June 10 to August 29. Egypt, Alexandria: Marines from the *Lancaster*, *Nipsic*, and *Quinnebaug* on duty ashore.

1885, January 18. Panama, Colon: Marines from the *Alliance* landed to protect American interests and property.

1885, March 31 to May 22. Panama, United States of Colombia: Expeditionary force of marines ashore in the State of Panama, April 11 to May 22; Marines from the *Galena* ashore from March 31.

1888, June 19 to 30. Corea: Marines from the *Essex* ashore at Seoul.

1888, November 12 to 1889, March 20. Samoa: Marines of the *Nipsic* ashore at Apia.

1889, July 30 to 31. Hawaiian Islands: Marines of the *Adams* ashore at Honolulu.

1890, July 30. Argentina: Marines of the *Tallpoosa* ashore at Buenos Aires.

1891, August 28 to 30. Chile, Valparaiso: Marines of the *Baltimore* and *San Francisco* ashore protecting American consulate.

1893, January 16. Hawaiian Islands, Honolulu: Marines from the *Boston* ashore protecting American lives and property during the revolution.

1894, 1895, and 1896. Corea: During the Japanese-Chinese War, marines of the *Baltimore*, *Concord*, *Charleston*, and *Detroit*, at various times, served as an American Legation guard at Seoul from July 24, 1894, to June 19, 1895; marines of the *Yorktown* from July 24 to November 30, 1895; and marines of the *Machias* from November 29, 1895, to April 3, 1896.

1895, March 1 to 18. China: Marines from the *Yorktown* ashore at Chefoo.

1895, March 8 to 9. United States of Colombia, Bocas del Toro: Marines landed from the *Atlanta* to protect American interests.

Spanish-American War (April 21 to December 10, 1898).—All units of the Marine Corps engaged in the war during this period.

Cuba, expeditionary service (December 16, 1898, to August 19, 1899).—The marine detachment from the U. S. S. *Resolute* ashore in Havana, Cuba.

Philippines, expeditionary service and Philippine Insurrection (February 4, 1899, to December 31, 1904).—The First Battalion, United States Marines, composed of Companies A, B, C, and D, was organized at Cavite, P. I., April 21, 1899, from the marine detachments of the following vessels: U. S. S. *Boston*, U. S. S. *Charleston*, U. S. S. *Helena*, U. S. S. *Monterey*, U. S. S. *Olympia*, and U. S. S. *Oregon*. The Second Battalion, composed of Companies A, B, C, and D, landed in Cavite, P. I., in September 1899. October 1, 1899, the First Brigade, United States Marines, was organized at Cavite, P. I., composed of the following units: First Battalion, Companies A, B, C, and D; Second Battalion, Companies A, D, C, D, E, F, G, and H; Third Battalion, Companies A, B, C, and D. In January 1900, the First Regiment was organized in Cavite, P. I., and was composed of the following units: Field and Staff, Companies A, B, C, D, E, F, G, and H. The First Brigade was later reorganized as follows: Brigade Field and Staff, First

Regiment, Headquarters Company, Companies A, B, C, D, and E; Second Regiment, Headquarters Company, Companies A, B, C, D, E, and F.

The marine detachments of naval vessels stationed in Philippine waters at any time during the above-stated period were also held to be engaged in the insurrection or on expeditionary duty as the case may be.

A list of naval vessels so stationed is given in enclosure A, under the heading "Philippine Campaign Badge."

Samoan Islands, expeditionary service (March 14 to May 18, 1899).—Marines from the U. S. S. *Philadelphia* landed and were engaged in fighting the natives.

Chinese Campaign, Boxer War (May 24, 1900, to May 27, 1901).—The following units served in China during the Boxer uprising: First Regiment, field and staff; First Battalion, Companies A, B, C, D, E, F, H, and K; Second Battalion, Companies G and I: Third Battalion, Companies A, B, C, and D; Fourth Battalion, Companies E, F, and G; Fifth Battalion, Companies A, B, C, and D; Sixth Battalion, Company A.

Also marine detachments of the following-named vessels during the periods stated: *Brooklyn*, July 7 to October 12, 1900; *Buffalo*, August 3 to 6, 1900; *Monocacy*, June 14, 1900, to May 27, 1901; *Nashville*, June 18 to September 7, 1900; *New Orleans*, September 14, 1900, to May 27, 1901; *Newark*, May 27 to July 22, 1900; *Solace*, June 18 to July 29, 1900; *Wheeling*, April 5 to May 1, 1900; *Yorktown*, June 15 to September 10, 1900.

United States of Colombia, expeditionary service (November 11 to December 4, 1901).—Marines from *Machias, Marietta, Iowa, Concord*, and *Ranger* landed in the State of Panama at various times within this period.

April 17 to April 19, 1902: Detachment of marines from the *Machias* ashore at Boca del Toro.

September 23 to November 18, 1902: Marine Battalion on board the U. S. S. *Panther*, composed of field and staff, Companies A, B, C, and D landed at Colon, Panama, United States of Colombia.

Honduras, expeditionary service (March 21 to April 16, 1903).—The following ships in Honduran waters carried marine guards: U. S. S. *Marietta*, U. S. S. *Olympia*, U. S. S. *Panther*, U. S. S. *Raleigh*, and the U. S. S. *San Francisco*. A Marine Battalion, composed of a Headquarters Company, Companies A, B, and C, was stationed aboard the U. S. S. *Panther*. The detachments from the U. S. S. *Marietta* and the U. S. S. *Olympia* landed March 23, 1903, to guard the American consulate. Marines landed from *Panther* at Truxillo and Ceiba while those of the *Olympia* were ashore at Puerto Cortez from March 24 to 26.

Dominican Republic, expeditionary service (April 1 to April 19, 1903).—Marine detachment from the U. S. S. *Atlanta* landed at Santo Domingo City, Dominican Republic, to guard the American consulate.

Syria, expeditionary service (September 8 to 13, and October 10 to 17, 1903).—Marines of *Brooklyn* and *San Francisco* ashore at different times at Beirut.

United States of Colombia and Republic of Panama (November 4, 1903, to February 26, 1904).—The following units were on duty in Panama during this period:

First Provisional Brigade, Brigade Headquarters.

First Regiment, Regimental Field and Staff: First Battalion, Battalion Field and Staff: Companies A, B, C, D. Second Battalion, Battalion Field and Staff; Companies E, F, G.

Second Regiment, Regimental Field and Staff: First Battalion, Battalion Field and Staff: Companies A, B, C. Second Battalion, Battalion Field and Staff: Companies D, E, F, G.

Marine detachment from the U. S. S. *Nashville* landed at Colón, Panama, United States of Colombia, November 4, 1903.

Abyssinia, expeditionary (November 21, 1903, to January 18, 1904).—Marines from the *San Francisco, Brooklyn*, and *Machias* arrived at Djibouti on board the latter-named vessel, and accompanied an American diplomatic commission from Djibouti, French Somaliland, Africa, to Abyssinia and return.

Corea, expeditionary (January 5, 1904, to November 11, 1905).—Company F, Second Regiment, Philippine Brigade, United States Marines, from marine barracks, Cavite, P. I., embarked on board the U. S. S. *Zafiro* the latter part of December 1903, and sailed for Seoul, Corea. Remained on board the U. S. S. *Zafiro* until the 5th of January 1904, when they landed and established a legation guard with headquarters in the Electric Building. April 23, 1904, the company was transferred to marine barracks, Olongapo, P. I., leaving 25 enlisted men behind as a legation guard. November 11, 1905, this detachment was transferred to Olongapo, P. I.

Dominican Republic (February 25 to February 27, 1904).—Marines of *Yankee* ashore at Santo Domingo City at request of American consul general. A revolution was in progress at the time.

Russia (December 1905, to January 1, 1907).—Embassy guard at St. Petersburg.

Cuban pacification (September 12, 1906, to April 1, 1909).—Headquarters First Expeditionary Battalion on board U. S. S. *Newark*. Headquarters Second Expeditionary Battalion on board U. S. S. *Minneapolis*. Headquarters Third Expeditionary Battalion on board U. S. S. *Newark*. Headquarters Fourth Expeditionary Battalion on board the U. S. S. *Prairie*. Headquarters Fifth Expeditionary Battalion on board U.S.S. *Texas*.

The First Expeditionary Brigade organized at Camp Columbia, Habana, Cuba, in October 1906, composed of First Regiment, headquarters, Companies A, B, C, D, E, F, and M: Second Regiment, headquarters, Companies A, B, C, D, and M. November 1, 1906, the First Brigade was disbanded and all units were organized into the First Provisional Regiment and attached to the Army of Cuban Pacification. The First Provisional Regiment was composed of the Regimental Headquarters Company, Companies A, B, C, D, E, F, G, H, I, K, L, and M.

Honduras, expeditionary (April 28 to June 8, 1907).—The marine detachment from the U. S. S. *Paducah* was ashore at Laguna, Honduras, for the protection of American interests from April 28 to May 23, 1907, and ashore at Choloma, Honduras, from May 24 to June 8, 1907, protecting American interests.

Nicaragua, expeditionary (May 30 to September 4, 1910).—Companies A and C, from the marine battalion, Camp Elliott, Empire, Republic of Panama, embarked on board the U. S. S. *Dubuque* and disembarked at Bluefields, Nicaragua, on May 31, 1910. Stationed there until the 5th of September when they embarked on board the U. S. S. *Tacoma* and returned to Camp Elliott, Empire, Republic of Panama. Companies B and D, on expeditionary duty at Bluefields, Nicaragua, via the U. S. S. *Prairie* from June 8 to 12, 1910.

China, expeditionary (October 10, 1911, to January 19, 1914).—Field and staff, Companies C and D, of the First Regiment and Companies B and E of the Second Regiment from the Philippines served on board the U. S. S. *Rainbow*. These detachments served both afloat and ashore at different places in China during the above-mentioned period. There was a marine guard at the American Legation, Peking, China, during this period.

Cuba (May 28 to August 5, 1912).—In May 1912, the First Provisional Brigade was organized for service in Cuba. The brigade was composed of the following units: Brigade field and staff. First Regiment: field and staff. Companies A, B, C, D, E, F, G, and H: Second Regiment: field and staff, Companies A, B, C, D, E, F, G, H, I, and K. The First Regiment landed at Deer Point, Guantanamo Bay, Cuba. The Second Regiment was stationed aboard the following ships: Company A, on the U. S. S. *Minnesota;* Company B, U. S. S. *Missouri;* Company C, U. S. S. *Ohio;* Company D, U. S. S. *Mississippi;* Company E, on the U. S. S. *Rhode Island;* Company F, U. S. S. *Washington;* Company G, U. S. S. *Georgia;* Company H, U. S. S. *Washington;* Company I, U. S. S. *New Jersey;* Company K, U. S. S. *Nebraska;* and the field and staff on the U. S. S. *Washington*. Companies A, B, C, and D served ashore at various places during the above period.

Nicaragua (August 28 to November 2, 1912).—The marine detachments from the following ships served ashore at various times during the above period: U. S. S. *California,* U. S. S. *Denver,* U. S. S. *Tacoma,* U. S. S. *Cleveland,* and the U. S. S. *Colorado*. The First Provisional Regiment, composed of regimental field and staff, Companies A, B, C, D, E, F, and G. The regiment with the exception of field and staff, Companies E, F, and G, embarked on board the U. S. S. *Buffalo* November 21, 1912. The battalion left behind remained in Nicaragua until the American Legation guard was established January 9, 1913, when they were withdrawn. The legation guard is still stationed at Managua, Nicaragua. (The First Provisional Regiment landed at Corinto, Nicaragua, on September 4, 1912, from the U. S. S. *Colorado*.)

Haiti (January 29 to February 9, 1914).—Marine detachment ashore from the U. S. S. *South Carolina* at Port-au-Prince, Republic of Haiti, during the above period.

Mexican campaign (April 21 to November 23, 1914).—The following units of the Marine Corps served in Mexico, or in Mexican waters aboard ship, during the occupation of Mexico. The First Brigade of United States Marines; field and staff:

First Regiment—Headquarters Detachment, Second Company, Third Company, Fourth Company, Fifth Company, Sixth Company, Seventh Company, Nineteenth Company, Twenty-fourth Company.

Second Regiment—Headquarters Detachment, field and staff, Second Battalion, field and staff, Third Battalion, Eighth Company, Tenth Company, Fourteenth Company, Fifteenth Company, Sixteenth Company, Seventeenth Company, Eighteenth Company.

Third Regiment—Field and staff, Eleventh Company, Twelfth Company, Twentieth Company, Twenty-first Company, Twenty-second Company, Twenty-third Company.

Fourth Regiment—Field and staff, Twenty-fifth Company, Twenty-sixth Company, Twenty-seventh Company, Twenty-eighth Company, Thirty-first Company, Thirty-second Company, Thirty-fourth Company, Thirty-fifth Company, Thirty-sixth Company.

Artillery battalion—Field and staff, First Company, Ninth Company, Thirteenth Company.

April 21 to November 23, 1914: The following ships with marine guards were in Mexican waters during the above-mentioned period: U. S. S. *Delaware*, U. S. S. *California*, U. S. S. *Denver*, U. S. S. *Des Moines*, U. S. S. *Maryland*, U. S. S. *New York*, U. S. S. *North Dakota*, U. S. S. *Texas*, U. S. S. *Virginia*, U. S. S. *West Virginia*, U. S. S. *Wyoming*, and the U. S. S. *Rhode Island*. The Marine detachments from the following ships were landed during the occupation of Vera Cruz, Mexico: U. S. S. *Arkansas*, U. S. S. *Florida*, U. S. S. *Minnesota*, U. S. S. *Louisiana*, U. S. S. *Kansas*, U. S. S. *New Hampshire*, U. S. S. *New Jersey*, U. S. S. *South Carolina*, U. S. S. *Utah*, and U. S. S. *Vermont*. The field and staff, Forty-fourth Company, Forty-fifth Company, and Forty-sixth Company of the marine battalion, special-service squadron, served aboard the U. S. S. *New York*. The Forty-third Company of the marine battalion served aboard the U. S. S. *Salem* and U. S. S. *Chester*. The Seventh Company, First Regiment, served aboard the U. S. S. *Connecticut*.

Mexico (April 21, 1914, to February 7, 1917).—The following-named vessels of the Navy having marine detachments on board were on expeditionary duty in Mexican waters at various times between the above dates. The period during which each vessel was in Mexican waters is shown below:

U. S. S. *Buffalo*, November 14 to 26, 1914, March 28 to 29, 1916, June 22 to 30, 1916, August 31, 1916, to February 7, 1917: U. S. S. *Dolphin*, April 21 to June 20, 1914, July 2 to 8, 1916: U. S. S. *Georgia*, May 1 to August 1, 1914: U. S. S. *Illinois*, October 13, 1916, to February 7, 1917: U. S. S. *Kentucky*, March 23 to June 2, 1916: U. S. S. *Machias*, May 15 to June 14, 1914, March 14 to June 28, 1916: U. S. S. *Marietta*, March 14 to June 27, 1916: U. S. S. *Michigan*, April 22 to May 29, 1914, October 11 to November 26, 1914: U. S. S. *Montana*, April 28 to May 3, 1914: U. S. S. *Nebraska*, May 1 to June 21, 1914, June 1 to October 13, 1916: U. S. S. *Pittsburgh*, June 23 to October 4, 1916: U. S. S. *Prairie*, April 21 to May 26, June 18 to 28, 1914: U. S. S. *San Diego*, July 10 to September 19, November 4 to 26, 1914, June 22 to July 18, August 6 to August 19, 1916: U. S. S. *Washington*, June 14 to 27, 1914: U. S. S. *Yorktown*, April 21 to June 16, September 9 to November 26, 1914, March 14 to November 21, 1916, January 18 to 20, 1917.

Dominican Republic (August 15 to October 30, 1914).—The U. S. S. *Washington* with a detachment of the Forty-sixth Company of the Fifth Regiment aboard was in Dominican waters during the above period. The detachment was stationed ashore at Santo Domingo City, Dominican Republic, from October 1, 1914.

Haiti (October 31 to November 14, 1914, and December 13 to December 17, 1914).—Headquarters field and staff, the Thirty-seventh Company, Forty-fourth Company, Forty-fifth Company, Forty-sixth Company, Forty-seventh Company, and the Forty-eighth Company, of the Fifth Regiment stationed aboard the U. S. S. *Hancock* in Haitian waters during the above period.

Dominican Republic (November 26 to December 11, 1914).—The Headquarters field and staff and the Thirty-seventh Company, Forty-fourth Company, Forty-fifth Company, Forty-sixth Company, Forty-seventh Company, and the Forty-eighth Company, of the Fifth Regiment were stationed aboard the U. S. S. *Hancock* in Dominican waters during the above period.

Haitian campaign and occupation (July 9, 1915, to present day).—The following units of the Marine Corps participated in the campaign and occupation of Haiti during the above-mentioned period: Constabulary detachment; field and staff, First Brigade; field and staff, First Regiment; field and staff, Second Regiment; field and staff, Third Detachment; field and staff, artillery battalion; brigade headquarters, detachment; depot detachment; Brigade Signal Company; motor transport unit; Motor Transport Unit No. 1; Motor Transport Unit No. 2; Flight E, Flight G, Flight H, headquarters detachment Observation Squadron No. 2; Division No. 1, Observation Squadron No. 2; Headquarters Company Second Regiment; Supply Company, Second Regiment; Headquarters Company, Eighth Regiment; Supply Company, Eighth Regiment; Headquarters and Fifty-seventh

Company, First Brigade, Headquarters and Sixty-second Company; Second Regiment; Headquarters and One Hundredth Company Eighth Regiment. Also the following companies: First Company, Artillery Battalion; Third Company (signal) First Regiment; Fourth Company, First Regiment; Fifth Company, First Regiment; Sixth Company, First Regiment; Twenty-third Company, First Regiment; Twenty-fourth Company, Guantanamo Bay, Cuba; Thirty-sixth Company, First Brigade; Fifty-first Company, U. S. S. *Vermont*; Fifty-third Company, Second Regiment; Seventh Company, Second Regiment; Ninth Company, Artillery Battalion; Eleventh Company, First Regiment; Twelfth Company, U. S. S. *Washington;* Thirteenth Company, Artillery Battalion; Fifteenth Company, Second Regiment; Sixteenth Company, Second Regiment; Seventeenth Company, Second Regiment; Nineteenth Company, First Regiment; Twentieth Company, Second Regiment; Twenty-second Company, First Regiment; Fifty-fourth Company, Second Regiment; Fifty-seventh Company, First Brigade; Sixty-second Company, First Brigade; Sixty-third Company, Eighth Regiment; Sixty-fourth Company, Second Regiment; Sixty-fifth Company, Eighth Regiment; One Hundredth Company, Eighth Regiment; One hundred and forty-eighth Company, Eighth Regiment; One hundred and fifty-third Company, Second Regiment; One hundred and ninety-sixth Company, Eighth Regiment; One Hundred and Ninety-seventh Company, Second Regiment.

Dominican Republic campaign and occupation (May 5, 1916, to September 16 1924.)—The following units of the Marine Corps participated in the campaign and occupation of the Dominican Republic during the above-mentioned period: Headquarters detachment, Second Brigade; depot detachment, Second Brigade; Service Company, Second Brigade; policia Nacional detachment, Department of the North; Policia Nacional detachment, Department of the South; field and staff, artillery battalion; field and staff, First Regiment; field and staff, Second Regiment; field and staff, Third Regiment; field and staff, Fourth Regiment; aide, military governor; Headquarters Company, First Regiment; Headquarters Company, Third Regiment; Headquarters Company, Fourth Regiment; Headquarters Company, Fifteenth Regiment; Service Company, First Regiment; Service Company, Fourth Regiment; Howitzer Company, First Regiment; Howitzer Company, Fourth Regiment; Division 1, squadron D, MAF; Headquarters, Observation Squadron No. 1; Division No. 1, Observation Squadron No. 1; and the following-numbered companies: First Company, Fourth Company, Fifth Company, Sixth Company, Eighth Company, Ninth Company, Tenth Company, Twelfth Company, Thirteenth Company, Fourteenth Company, Eighteenth Company, Twenty-first Company, Twenty-fourth Company, Twenty-fifth Company, Twenty-sixth Company, Twenty-seventh Company, Twenty-eighth Company, Twenty-ninth Company, Thirty-first Company, Thirty-second Company, Thirty-third Company, Forty-fourth Company, Forty-fifth Company, Forty-seventh Company, Forty-eighth Company, Fiftieth Company, Fifty-second Company, Sixty-ninth Company, Seventieth Company, One Hundred and Thirteenth Company, One Hundred and Fourteenth Company, One Hundred and Fifteenth Company, One Hundred and Eightieth Company, One Hundred and Eighty-first Company, One Hundred and Eighty-second Company, One Hundred and Eighty-third Company, One Hundred and Eighty-fourth Company, One Hundred and Eighty-fifth Company, One Hundred and Eighty-sixth Company, One Hundred and Eighty-seventh Company, and Two hundred and Tenth Company.

The marine detachments from the following ships served ashore at different places during the above period: U. S. S. *Castine*, U. S. S. *Dolphin*, U. S. S. *Louisiana*, U. S. S. *Memphis*, U. S. S. *New Jersey*, U. S. S. *Prairie*, and the U. S. S. *Rhode Island*.   The detachments from the U. S. S. *Louisiana*, U. S. S. *New Jersey*, and the U. S. S. *Rhode Island* were later designated the Forty-seventh Company, Forty-fifth Company, and the Eighteenth Company, respectively.   The detachment of the U. S. S. *Memphis* was later transferred to the U. S. S. *Olympia*.

Cuba, expeditionary service (February 26 to April 5, 1917).—Marines from Guantanamo Bay (Cuba) Naval Station on expeditionary duty at Guantanamo City, Cuba, and other adjacent points in Cuba.

China (September 9, 1924, to March 1, 1925).—A marine detachment has continued on duty at the American Legation, Peking, China, up to the present date. Expeditionary forces of marines and marines from the following vessels ashore at various times at Shanghai, Tientsin, Peking, Tungchou, etc., and serving as international train guards, etc.: *Huron, Asheville, Sacramento, Smith-Thompson, Tracy, Borie, Pecos, Pillsbury, Steward, Black Hawk, Preble, Barker, Whipple,* and *Edwards.*

Philippine Islands (January 23, 1924).—Marines from the *Sacramento* engaged in capturing the town of Socorro, Bucas Grande Island, occupied by rebel forces.

China (June 5 to July 29, 1925).—Marines from the *Huron* ashore at Shanghai.

Haiti (1925, 1926, and 1927).—Military occupation of Haiti by First Brigade of Marines continuous to the present date.

Nicaragua (1925).—American Legation guard at Managua continuously from date of last report, January 14, 1925, until August 3, 1925, when it was withdrawn.

Expeditionary forces in China (1927).—Marines from the *Pittsburgh* were ashore March 25 and 31, 1927, and marines from the *Sacramento*, March 24 to April 18, 1927. The following-named expeditionary units landed in China on the dates specified and are still there: Third Brigade, Fourth Regiment, March 21, 1927; provisional battalion, March 21, 1927; Sixth Regiment, May 2, 1927; aviation VF Squadron 3, May 9, 1927; Tenth Regiment, Fifth Company Engineers, and Light Tank Platoon, June 6, 1927.

All of the above-named expeditionary units (exclusive of the ships' detachments) are now combined in one command called the Third Brigade.

Expeditionary forces in Nicaragua (1927).—January 1: Marine detachments from *Cleveland, Denver,* and *Rochester,* ashore: January 5: Marine detachment from *Galveston,* ashore: February 21: Marine detachments from *Arkansas, Florida,* and *Texas,* ashore, and detachments from *Florida* and *Texas* later joined the Fifth Regiment: March 4: Marine detachment from *Tulsa,* ashore. The following-named expeditionary forces landed on the dates specified. January 10: Second Battalion of the Fifth Regiment: February 26: Provincial Company, from San Diego, Calif.; February 27: Observation Squadron No. 1: March 9: Fifth Regiment; May 19: Eleventh Regiment: May 21: Observation Squadron No. 4.

Observation Squadron No. 1, consisting of 3 officers and 66 enlisted men, was returned to the United States in June 1927, and about 38 officers and 1,100 enlisted men of the Fifth and Eleventh Regiments were returned to the United States in July 1927. The balance of the expeditionary force remaining at the present time consists of the Second Brigade and the officers and enlisted men serving with the Guardia Nacional of Nicaragua.

LIST OF WARS, MILITARY OCCUPATIONS, AND MILITARY EXPEDITIONS ENGAGED IN BY THE MARINE CORPS

48. From August 9, 1927, to October 30, 1929.

China—expeditionary service.—Continuous since date of last report, August 9, 1927, to October 30, 1929.

Third Brigade, consisting of: Brigade Headquarters (disbanded January 19, 1929); Brigade Service Company (disbanded October 12, 1928); Fifth Company Engineers (transferred to San Diego, Calif., January 19, 1929); Light Tank Platoon (transferred to San Diego, Calif., October 3, 1929); and Provisional Military Police Company (organized October 10, 1927; disbanded August 6, 1928).

Provisional regiment, composed of: Second Battalion, Fourth Regiment; Headquarters Company, Tenth Company; Twenty-ninth Machine Gun and Howitzer Company; Thirty-first Company; Thirty-second Company; Third Battalion, Sixth Regiment: Headquarters Company; Fifteenth Machine Gun Company; Eighty-second Company; Eighty-third Company; Eighty-fourth Company.

Provisional regiment disbanded October 4, 1927, by change of designation to Twelfth Regiment.

Fourth Regiment, composed of: Headquarters Company; Service Company; First Battalion, Headquarters Company; Twenty-fifth Company; Twenty-sixth Company; Twenty-eighth Machine Gun and Howitzer Company; Third Battalion, Headquarters Company; Nineteenth Company; Twenty-first Company; Twenty-second Company; Twenty-fourth Company.

The Fourth Regiment, as shown above, is at present at Shanghai, China, with the expeditionary forces.

Sixth Regiment, composed of: Headquarters Company; Service Company; First Battalion, Headquarters Company; Seventy-third Company; Seventy-fourth Company; Seventy-fifth Company; Seventy-sixth Company; Second Battalion, Headquarters Company; Seventy-eighth Company; Eightieth Company (joined composite battalion November 22, 1928, for transfer to San Diego, Calif., and transferred same date); Eighty-first Machine Gun and Howitzer Company.

The First Battalion of the Twelfth Regiment, composed of: Headquarters Company, Fifteenth Machine Gun Company, Eighty-second Company, Eighty-third Company, Eighty-fourth Company, on April 22, 1928, joined the Sixth Regiment and the designation was changed to Third Battalion, Sixth Regiment. September

15, 1928, the Third Battalion, Sixth Regiment, joined the composite regiment for transfer to San Diego, Calif., and was transferred September 29, 1928. The Sixth Regiment was transferred to San Diego, Calif., January 19, 1929.

Tenth Regiment, composed of: First Battalion, Headquarters Battery, Service Battery, First Battery, Sixth Battery (joined composite battalion, November 21, 1928, for transfer to San Diego, Calif., and transferred November 22, 1928), Thirteenth Battery. The Tenth Regiment joined the composite regiment September 15, 1928, for transfer to San Diego, Calif., and was transferred September 19, 1928. First Separate Battalion organized April 22, 1928, disbanded July 11, 1928, composed of the following companies: Headquarters Company (disbanded May 8, 1928), Twenty-ninth Machine Gun and Howitzer Company, Thirty-first Company.

Twelfth Regiment: Organized October 4, 1927; disbanded April 22, 1928; the following companies were attached: Headquarters Company, Service Company (organized October 24, 1927); First Battalion (designation changed to Third Battalion, Sixth Regiment, April 23, 1928), Headquarters Company: Fifteenth Machine Gun Company; Eighty-second Company: Eighty-third Company; Eighty-fourth Company; Second Battalion (designation changed to First Separate Battalion, April 22, 1928), Headquarters Company: Tenth Company (disbanded December 21, 1927); Twenty-ninth Machine Gun and Howitzer Company; Thirty-first Company; Thirty-second Company (disbanded December 21, 1927).

Aircraft Squadrons: Composed of the following: Headquarters detachment (disbanded September 29, 1928), Fighting Plane Squadron No. 10 (designation changed to Fighting Plane Squadron 6-M, July 1, 1928); Observation Squadron No. 10 (joined Composite Battalion, November 21, 1928, for transfer to San Diego, Calif., and transferred November 22, 1928); Expeditionary Duty Detachment, VS 1-M (disbanded January 31, 1928); Fighting Plane Squadron 6-M (joined Composite Regiment September 15, 1928, for transfer to San Diego, Calif., and transferred September 19, 1928).

The Marine detachment, American Legation, Peking, China, has continued on duty at that station up to this date.

Haiti—Occupation.—Continuous since date of last report, August 9, 1927, to October 30, 1929.

First Brigade: Brigade headquarters, constabulary detachment, brigade depot detachment, brigade Signal Company, brigade Motor Transport Company.

Second Regiment: Headquarters Company, Thirty-sixth Company, Fifty-third Company (machine gun), Fifty-fourth Company, Sixty-fourth Company; Second Battalion, Headquarters detachment, Sixty-third Company; Observation Squadron 9-M, Headquarters Company, Division 1.

First Battalion, Eleventh Regiment, composed of: Headquarters Company, Second Company, Fourteenth Company, Forty-sixth Company (joined August 31, 1927, from Nicaragua and was disbanded September 6, 1927).

Nicaragua—Expeditionary service.—Continuous since date of last report, August 9, 1927, to October 30, 1929.

Second Brigade: Brigade headquarters (organized January 15, 1928), constabulary detachment (designation changed to Nicaraguan National Guard detachment, December 13, 1928).

Fifth Regiment: Headquarters Company; Service Company; Fifty-first Company (August 10, 1929, to Second Battalion, Fifth Regiment); First Battalion, Headquarters Company, Seventeenth Company; Twenty-third Company, Forty-ninth Company; Sixty-sixth Company (disbanded August 10, 1929); Second Battalion, Headquarters Company (organized April 1, 1928, disbanded January 4, 1929, reorganized February 14, 1929); Eighteenth Company (organized March 25, 1928, disbanded January 5, 1929); Forty-third Company (organized March 25, 1928, disbanded January 4, 1929, reorganized August 10, 1929); Forty-eighth Company (organized March 25, 1928, disbanded January 4, 1929); Seventy-seventh Company (organized March 25, 1928, disbanded January 5, 1929, reorganized August 10, 1929); Third Battalion, Headquarters Company; Eighth Company; Sixteenth Company; Twentieth Company; Forty-fifth Company (disbanded August 10, 1929).

The following organizations are at present attached to expeditionary forces in Nicaragua, except those marked transferred:

Second Brigade: Brigade headquarters; Nicaraguan National Guard detachment.

Fifth Regiment: Headquarters Company; Service Company; First Battalion, Headquarters Company; Seventeenth Company; Twenty-third Company; Forty-ninth Company; Second Battalion, Headquarters Company; Forty-third Company; Fifty-first Company; Seventy-seventh Company; Third Battalion, Headquarters Company; Eighth Company; Sixteenth Company; Twentieth Company.

Eleventh Regiment: Headquarters Company (joined January 19, 1928, transferred to Quantico, Va., August 20, 1929); Service Company (joined January 19, 1928, transferred to Quantico, Va., August 20, 1929); First Battalion (The First Battalion, less the Forty-seventh Company, was transferred to Port-au-Prince, Haiti, August 24, 1927, and rejoined the Second Brigade January 15, 1928, transferred to Quantico, Va., August 29, 1929), Headquarters Company; Second Machine Gun Company; Forty-sixth Company; Forty-seventh Company; Second Battalion (joined January 16, 1928, transferred to Quantico, Va., August 20, 1929), Headquarters Company; Fiftieth Company; Fifty-second Company; Fifty-fifth Company; Fifty-seventh Company; Third Battalion (joined March 31, 1928, disbanded June 15, 1929), Headquarters Company; Fifty-eighth Company; Fifty-ninth Company; Sixtieth Company; Sixty-first Machine Gun and Howitzer Company; Aircraft squadrons—Headquarters detachment, Service Company 3-M (organized March 1, 1929); Observation Squadron (VO) 6-M (joined February 16, 1928); Observation Squadron (VO) 7-M.

Marine detachments from the following-named ships served on shore on expeditionary duty in Nicaragua during the periods stated below: U. S. S. *Arizona*, July 15, 1928, to January 24, 1929; U. S. S. *California*, July 15, 1928, to January 24, 1929; U. S. S. *Cleveland*, September 23 to 26, 1927, and April 1, 1928, to March 17, 1929; U. S. S. *Colorado*, July 14, 1928, to January 24, 1929; U. S. S. *Denver*, February 19, 1928, to April 11, 1929; U. S. S. *Galveston*, January 9 to 23, 1928, and April 30, 1928, to April 11, 1929; U. S. S. *Idaho*, July 6, 1928, to January 24, 1929; U. S. S. *Maryland*, July 14, 1928, to November 24, 1928; U. S. S. *Mississippi*, July 14, 1928, to January 24, 1929; U. S. S. *New Mexico*, July 6, 1928, to January 24, 1929; U. S. S. *New York*, July 14, 1928, to January 24, 1929; U. S. S. *Pennsylvania*, July 6, 1928, to January 24, 1929; U. S. S. *Procyon*, July 14, 1928, to January 24, 1929; U. S. S. *Rochester*, January 7, 1928, to February 10, 1929; U. S. S. *Tennessee*, July 14, 1928, to January 24, 1929; U. S. S. *Texas*, June 14, 1928, to January 24, 1929; U. S. S. *Tulsa*, January 7, 1928, to February 8, 1928, and March 10, 1928, to April 12, 1929; U. S. S. *West Virginia*, July 14, 1928, to January 24, 1929.

49. United States Marine Corps expeditionary forces in China, Haiti, Nicaragua, and Siberia from October 30, 1929, to August 31, 1939.

China.—Expeditionary service:

Fourth Marines, Shanghai, China: Headquarters and Headquarters Company; Service Company; Motor Transport Company; First Battalion, Headquarters and Headquarters Company; Company A (25th), Company B (26th), Company C (27th) (disbanded December 17, 1934, reorganized August 20, 1937, disbanded May 5, 1938), Company D (28th); Second Battalion, Headquarters and Headquarters Company; Company E (organized September 18, 1932), Company F (organized September 18, 1932), Company G (organized September 18, 1932, disbanded December 17, 1934, reorganized August 26, 1937, disbanded May 18, 1938), Company H (organized September 18, 1932); Third Battalion, Headquarters and Headquarters Company (disbanded December 9, 1934); Company I (19th) (disbanded December 19, 1934), Company K (21st) (disbanded December 19, 1934), Company L (22nd) (disbanded December 19, 1934), Company M (24th) (disbanded December 19, 1934).

The Marine detachment, American Legation, Peiping, China, has continued on duty at that station up to this date, and consists of the following: Headquarters detachment, Thirty-eighth Company, Thirty-ninth Company, and Sixty-second Company.

Ships' detachments ashore in Shanghai, China:

U. S. S. *Augusta*, August 16, 1937, to September 18, 1937; small detachment ashore October 29–31, 1937; U. S. S. *Houston*, February 5, 1932, to April 28, 1932; U. S. S. *Sacramento*, August 13, 1937, to March 14, 1938; U. S. S. *Tulsa*, October 23, 1937, to June 6, 1938.

Haiti.—Occupation:

First Brigade, Port-au-Prince, Haiti: Brigade Headquarters and Headquarters Company (disbanded August 15, 1934); Constabulary Detachment (disbanded July 31, 1934); Brigade Motor Transport Company (disbanded August 15, 1934); Brigade Depot Detachment (disbanded January 1, 1933); Brigade Signal Company (disbanded August 15, 1934).

Second Regiment: Headquarters and Headquarters Company (disbanded August 15, 1934); Thirty-sixth Company (disbanded January 1, 1933); Fifty-third Machine Gun Company (Company D) First Battalion, transferred to States July

26, 1934; Fifty-fourth Company (disbanded January 1, 1933); Sixty-fourth Company (Company A) First Battalion (transferred to States July 26, 1934); Second Battalion, Headquarters and Headquarters Company (disbanded January 1, 1933); Company B (63rd) (disbanded August 8, 1934); First Battalion, second regiment, Headquarters and Headquarters Company (organized January 1, 1933, disbanded August 15, 1933); Observation Squadron 9–M, Headquarters Squadron, (transferred to States August 15, 1934, Division One transferred to States, August 15, 1934); Constabulary detachment.

Nicaragua—Expeditionary service:

Second Brigade: Brigade Headquarters and Headquarters Company (disbanded June 4, 1930); Nicaraguan National Guard Detachment (disbanded January 2, 1933); Electoral Detachment (organized July 2, 1930, disbanded November 15, 1930); Nicaraguan Electoral Detachment (organized July 18, 1932, disbanded November 30, 1932); Second Provisional Company, August 15, 1930, to November 13, 1930.

Fifth Regiment: Headquarters and Headquarters Company (disbanded April 12, 1930); Service Company (disbanded April 12, 1930); East Coast Casual Company, April 12–22, 1930, in Nicaragua: First Battalion—Headquarters and Headquarters Company, disbanded January 2, 1933: Company A (17th) (disbanded January 2, 1933); Company D (23rd) (disbanded January 2, 1933); Company B (49th) (disbanded January 2, 1933): Sixty-sixth Company (organized April 12, 1930, disbanded May 1, 1931): Second Battalion—Headquarters and Headquarters Company (disbanded April 12, 1930): Forty-third Company (attached to 1st Battalion, 5th Regiment April 12, 1930, disbanded May 5, 1931); Fifty-first Company (attached to 1st Battalion, 5th Regiment April 12, 1930, disbanded April 30, 1931); Seventy-seventh Company (disbanded April 12, 1930); Third Battalion—Headquarters and Headquarters Company (disbanded April 12, 1930): Eighth Company (disbanded April 12, 1930): Sixteenth Company (disbanded April 12, 1930): Twentieth Company (attached to 1st Battalion, 5th Regiment April 12, 1930, disbanded May 15, 1930): Aircraft Squadrons—Headquarters detachment transferred to States January 2, 1933: Service Company 3–M, transferred to the States January 2, 1933: Utility Squadron 6–M, transferred to States January 2, 1933: Observation Squadron 7–M, transferred to States January 2, 1933: Nicaraguan National Guard detachment.

Ships' detachments ashore in Nicaragua:

U. S. S. *Denver*, September 6, 1930, to November 6, 1930; U. S. S. *Memphis*, July 21, 1932, to November 28, 1932; U. S. S. *Overton*, July 15, 1932, to November 28, 1932; U. S. S. *Rochester*, September 6, 1930, to November 6, 1930; U. S. S. *Sturtevant*, July 12, 1932, to November 28, 1932.

Siberia.—Expeditionary service:

Detachment of Marines stationed at United States naval radio station, Russian Island, Vladivostok, Siberia, from February 16, 1920, to November 19, 1922. Detachments from the Marine detachments of the below-named ships were ashore in Siberia on the following dates: U. S. S. *Albany*, June 21–July 5, 1919; July 3–25, 1919: July 17–25, 1919; December 20, 1919, to March 6, 1920; January 17–March 6, 1920; U. S. S. *Brooklyn*, November 18–19, 1919, detached duty aboard U. S. S. *New Orleans* on landing party; U. S. S. *New Orleans*, Ashore at naval radio station, Russian Island, Siberia, July 25–28, 1919; July 27–August 1, 1919; August 30–31, 1919; September 22 to October 31, 1919; Ashore at Tetuhe Bay, Siberia, July 30 to August 1, 1919; Detached duty, Intelligence Office, Vladivostok, Siberia, September 25 to October 31, 1919; U. S. S. *South Dakota*, January 31 to February 1, 1920, on patrol duty in the City of Vladivostok, Siberia.

50. List of United States Navy vessels that are shown or appear to have left the continental United States for Cuba, Guam, or Puerto Rico between August 12, 1898, and July 4, 1902. Bureau of Navigation reports 1899, 1900, 1901, and 1902.

Name of vessels and stations	Date of arrival	Date of departure	Remarks
Alliance:			
Newport, R. I.		Feb. 28, 1899	
Santiago and other points in Cuba	Apr. 21, 1899	May 11, 1899	
Annapolis:			
Tompkinsville, N. Y.		Oct. 27, 1898	
San Juan, P. R.	Feb. 3, 1899	Feb. 15, 1899	
Guantanamo and other points in Cuba	Mar. 24, 1899	Apr. 3, 1899	

Name of vessels and stations	Date of arrival	Date of departure	Remarks
Arethusa:			
League Island, Pa		Dec. 16, 1898	
Habana, Cuba	Dec. 25, 1898	Jan. 14, 1899	
Brooklyn:			
Hampton Roads, Va		Dec. 15, 1898	
Habana and other points in Cuba and Puerto Rico.	Dec. 19, 1898	Apr. 26, 1899	
Brutus:			
Mare Island, Calif		Apr. 2, 1899	
San Luis d'Apra and other points in Guam	Feb. 8, 1900	Mar. 28, 1901	
Caesar:			
San Juan and other points in Puerto Rico	Oct. 23, 1899	Feb. 26, 1900	
Castine:			
Boston, Mass		Dec. 18, 1898	
Habana, Cuba	Dec. 26, 1898	Jan. 5, 1899	
San Juan, P. R	Jan. 11, 1899	Jan. 15, 1899	
Chicago:			
New York, N. Y		Feb. 6, 1899	
Habana, Cuba	Feb. 23, 1899	Mar. 9, 1899	
Hampton Roads, Va		Mar. 13, 1899	
Habana and other points in Cuba	Mar. 17, 1899	Mar. 24, 1899	
Cincinnati:			
San Juan, P. R		Oct. 4, 1898	
Guantanamo and other points in Cuba	Oct. 11, 1898	Jan. 4, 1899	
Detroit:			
Boston, Mass		Jan. 2, 1899	
Santiago and other points in Cuba	Jan. 8, 1899	Feb. 7, 1899	
New Orleans, La		Feb. 22, 1899	
Cienfuegos and other points in Cuba	Mar. 13, 1899	Mar. 25, 1899	
Dolphin:			
Key West, Fla		Mar. 18, 1900	
Habana and other points in Cuba; also in Puerto Rico.	Mar. 18, 1900	May 15, 1900	
Key West, Fla		Mar. 20, 1902	
Habana and other points in Cuba	Mar. 21, 1902	Mar. 31, 1902	Tour of inspection of coaling stations in West Indies, with the Chief of Bureau of Equipment.
Eagle:			
Hampton Roads, Va		Jan. 20, 1899	
Guantanamo and other points in Cuba	Jan. 26, 1899	July 14, 1899	Inspection preliminary to a survey.
Norfolk, Va		Nov. 5, 1899	
Nuevitas and other points in Cuba	Nov. 11, 1899	June 21, 1900	Survey duty.
Key West, Fla		Jan. 27, 1901	
Habana, Cuba	Jan. 28, 1901	Apr. 1, 1901	Surveying work in vicinity of Cape San Antonio, Cuba.
Key West, Fla		Oct. 30, 1901	
Cienfuegos and other points in Cuba	Nov. 2, 1901	Apr. 21, 1902	Surveying harbor, Cienfuegos, Cuba.
Essex:			
Norfolk, Va		Jan. 3, 1899	
Santiago and other points in Cuba	Apr. 10, 1899	Apr. 27, 1899	
Newport, R. I		July 13, 1899	
San Juan, P. R	Feb. 17, 1900	Feb. 25, 1900	Training service.
Guantanamo Bay and other points in Cuba	Mar. 1, 1900	Mar. 22, 1900	Do.
Glacier:			
Guantanamo Bay and other points in Cuba	Sept. 15, 1898	Dec. 17, 1898	
San Juan, P. R	Dec. 20, 1898	Jan. 3, 1899	
Hannibal:			
Lamberts Point, Va		Aug. 22, 1901	
San Juan and other points in Puerto Rico	Aug. 31, 1901	June 12, 1902	
Hist: Santiago and other points in Cuba	Oct. 27, 1898	Jan. 12, 1899	
Indiana:			
Tompkinsville, N. Y		Feb. 16, 1899	
Habana and other points in Cuba	Mar. 1, 1899	Mar. 25, 1899	
San Juan, P. R	Apr. 25, 1899	Apr. 26, 1899	
Lebanon:			
Lamberts Point, Va		Dec. 17, 1898	
Habana, Cuba	Dec. 23, 1898	Jan. 7, 1899	
Key West, Fla		Jan. 21, 1899	
Santiago de Cuba	Jan. 25, 1899	Jan. 27, 1899	
Key West, Fla		Feb. 6, 1899	
Habana, Cuba	Feb. 7, 1899	Mar. 1, 1899	
Lamberts Point, Va		Mar. 12, 1899	
Guantanamo Bay, Cuba	Mar. 19, 1899	Mar. 25, 1899	
Lamberts Point, Va		Nov. 23, 1901	
San Juan, P. R	June 15, 1902	June 20, 1902	

Name of vessels and stations	Date of arrival	Date of departure	Remarks
Leonidas:			
Guantanamo, Cuba	Oct. 18, 1898	Oct. 29, 1898	
Lamberts Point, Va		Sept. 14, 1901	
San Juan and other points in Puerto Rico	Sept. 20, 1901	June 26, 1902	
Machias:			
Tompkinsville, N. Y		Jan. 19, 1899	
Habana and other points in Cuba	Jan. 26, 1899	Mar. 28, 1899	
Key West, Fla		Apr. 19, 1899	
San Juan and other points in Puerto Rico	Apr. 24, 1899	May 8, 1899	
Nuevitas, Cuba	May 12, 1899	May 22, 1899	
Key West, Fla		July 16, 1899	
San Juan, P. R	July 21, 1899	July 30, 1899	
Gibara and other points in Cuba	Aug. 26, 1899	Sept. 14, 1899	Patrolling for filibusters.
Pensacola, Fla		Feb. 17, 1902	
San Juan and other points in Puerto Rico	Mar. 8, 1902	Apr. 4, 1902	General; Potomac Fleet.
Marblehead:			
New York, N. Y		Mar. 2, 1899	
Habana and other points in Cuba	Mar. 9, 1899	Mar. 25, 1899	
Marcellus:			
Boston, Mass		Oct. 27, 1898	
Habana, Cuba	Jan. 11, 1899	Feb. 5, 1899	
Marietta:			
Boston, Mass		Oct. 10, 1898	
Gibara and other points in Cuba	Oct. 17, 1898	Nov. 14, 1898	
Key West, Fla		Nov. 18, 1901	
San Juan and other points in Puerto Rico	Jan. 2, 1902	Jan. 23, 1902	Ship employed carrying mail and stores from San Juan. P. R. to Culebra. V. I., for vessels of the North Atlantic Squadron.
Massachusetts:			
New York, N. Y		Apr. 7, 1899	
San Juan, P. R	Apr. 25, 1899	Apr. 26, 1899	
Mayflower:			
Tompkinsville, N. Y		Dec. 6, 1898	
Caimanera and other points in Cuba	Dec. 11, 1898	Jan. 9, 1899	
New York, N. Y		June 23, 1900	Special service.
San Juan, P. R	June 30, 1900		
Boston, Mass		Aug. 14, 1900	
San Juan and other points in Puerto Rico	Aug. 20, 1900	Mar. 31, 1901	Surveying special service.
Nashville:			
Gibara, Cuba		Oct. 18, 1898	
Off San Key, Fla		Feb. 9, 1899	
Habana, Cuba	Feb. 9, 1899	....do	
Mobile, Ala		Feb. 18, 1899	
Cienfuegos and other points in Cuba; also in Puerto Rico.	Feb. 22, 1899	Apr. 11, 1899	
Newark:			
Guantanamo Bay, Cuba		Oct. 4, 1898	
Do	Oct. 12, 1898	Oct. 17, 1898	
San Juan, P. R	Oct. 21, 1898	Nov. 6, 1898	
Tompkinsville, N. Y		Nov. 26, 1898	
Guantanamo Bay, Cuba	Mar. 29, 1899	Mar. 29, 1899	
New York:			
Hampton Roads, Va		Dec. 3, 1898	
Habana, Cuba	Dec. 7, 1898	Dec. 19, 1898	
Tompkinsville, N. Y		Feb. 16, 1899	
Habana and other points in Cuba; also in Puerto Rico.	Mar. 1, 1899	Apr. 26, 1899	
Panther:			
Philadelphia, Pa		Nov. 26, 1898	
San Juan, P. R	Dec. 2, 1898	June 25, 1899	
Peoria:			
New York, N. Y		Nov. 3, 1898	
San Juan and other points in Puerto Rico	Nov. 9, 1898	Mar. 5, 1899	
Potomac: Guantanamo and other points in Cuba	Sept. 23, 1898	Nov. 8, 1898	
Resolute:			
Key West, Fla		Oct. 10, 1898	
Habana and other points in Cuba	Oct. 11, 1898	Apr. 29, 1899	
Sandoval: Gibara, Cuba	Nov. 5, 1898	Nov. 6, 1898	
Scorpion:			
Key West, Fla		Nov. 19, 1898	
Habana, Cuba	Nov. 20, 1898	Nov. 27, 1898	
Key West, Fla		Nov. 9, 1900	
San Juan, P. R	Dec. 23, 1900	Jan. 1, 1901	Special service for Navy Department.
San Juan and other points in Puerto Rico	Apr. 10, 1901	Apr. 15, 1901	Special service.

Name of vessels and stations	Date of arrival	Date of departure	Remarks
Solace:			
Ponce and other points in Puerto Rico	Oct. 1, 1898	Oct. 3, 1898	
Norfolk, Va		Nov. 1, 1898	
San Juan and other points in Puerto Rico	Nov. 5, 1898	Nov. 10, 1898	
Guantanamo Bay, Cuba	Nov. 12, 1898	Nov. 14, 1898	
Southery:			
Key West, Fla		Oct. 2, 1898	
Guantanamo and other points in Cuba	Oct. 6, 1898	Jan. 16, 1899	
Sterling:			
New York, N. Y		Oct. 11, 1898	
San Juan, P. R	Jan. 19, 1899	Jan. 28, 1899	
Supply:			
Key West, Fla		Aug. 16, 1898	
Gibara, Cuba	Aug. 18, 1898	Aug. 19, 1898	
Tompkinsville, N. Y		Sept. 12, 1898	
San Juan, P. R	Sept. 20, 1898	Sept. 25, 1898	
Guantanamo and other points in Cuba	Sept. 28, 1898	Oct. 3, 1898	
Texas:			
Hampton Roads, Va		Dec. 14, 1898	
Habana, Cuba	Dec. 17, 1898	Feb. 9, 1899	
Galveston, Tex		Feb. 17, 1899	
Habana and other points in Cuba	Feb. 20, 1899	Mar. 25, 1899	
San Juan, P. R	Apr. 25, 1899	Apr. 26, 1899	
Hampton Roads, Va		Dec. 13, 1899	
Habana, Cuba	Dec. 17, 1899	Dec. 21, 1899	Took on board remains of *Maine* dead.
Topeka:			
Key West, Fla		Nov. 27, 1898	
Habana, Cuba	Nov. 27, 1898	Jan. 1, 1899	
San Juan, P. R	Jan. 19, 1899	Jan. 28, 1899	
Uncas:			
Port Royal, S. C		Oct. 8, 1899	
San Juan and other points in Puerto Rico	Oct. 17, 1899	Aug. 25, 1901	Inspection of lighthouses. Taking passengers for U. S. Army.
San Juan, P. R	Feb. 2, 1902	Apr. 28, 1902	With mail and provisions to special detachment of marines.
Vicksburg:			
Hampton Roads, Va		Nov. 2, 1898	
Polominas Island and other points in Puerto Rico	Feb. 3, 1899	Feb. 18, 1899	
Guantanamo and other points in Cuba	Mar. 24, 1899	Apr. 3, 1899	
Wren:			
Key West, Fla		Feb. 4, 1900	
San Juan and other points in Puerto Rico	Feb. 8, 1900	Apr. 17, 1900	
Port Padre and other points in Cuba	Apr. 21, 1900	May 25, 1900	
Key West, Fla		Nov. 18, 1900	
Nuevitas and other points in Cuba	Nov. 20, 1900	June 25, 1901	Making passage and surveying.
Key West, Fla		Nov. 21, 1901	
Bahia Honda and other points in Cuba	Nov. 22, 1901	June 24, 1902	Do.
Wilmington:			
Norfolk, Va		Dec. 24, 1898	
San Juan, P. R	Dec. 30, 1898	Jan. 2, 1899	
Yankton:			
Palm Beach, Fla		Jan. 20, 1899	
Guantanamo Bay and other points in Cuba	Jan. 24, 1899	June 26, 1899	
Port Royal, S. C		Nov. 12, 1899	
Nipe and other points in Cuba	Nov. 19, 1899	June 29, 1900	Surveying duty.
Port Royal, S. C		Nov. 18, 1900	
Nipe Bay and other points in Cuba	Nov. 24, 1900	June 25, 1901	Surveying of Nipe Bay, Cuba.
Key West, Fla		Dec. 14, 1901	
Cape Corrientes and other points in Cuba	Dec. 16, 1901	June 9, 1902	Surveying work.

51. List of United States Army organizations which left the United States for service in Cuba or Puerto Rico between August 12, 1898, and July 4, 1902, as shown in report, Adjutant General, War Department July 1, 1909.

	Period	
	Years	Months
ENGINEER TROOPS		
COMPANY C (FORMERLY COMPANY E)		
Cuba: June 14 to Aug. 28, 1898	0	2
COMPANY E (FORMERLY COMPANY C)		
Cuba: June 14 to Aug. 28, 1898	0	1
CAVALRY		
FIRST U. S. CAVALRY		
Cuba: Headquarters and A, B, C, D, E, G, I, and K, June 14 to Aug. 15, 1898 (4 troops remained in Florida to August 1898)		2
SECOND U. S. CAVALRY		
Cuba:		
A, C, D, and F, June 14 to Aug. 28, 1898	0	2
Headquarters and B, Feb. 16, 1899, to Apr. 28, 1902	3	2
A, C, and D, Feb. 3, 1899, to Apr. 28, 1902	3	3
E and H, Feb. 16, 1899, to Jan. 22, 1902	2	11
F and G, Feb. 3, 1899, to Jan. 22, 1902	3	
I, K, and L, Feb. 16, 1899, to May 9, 1902	3	3
M, Feb. 3, 1899, to May 9, 1902	3	3
Puerto Rico: B, July 23 to Dec. 1, 1898 (7 troops remained in Florida to August 1898)		4
FIFTH U. S. CAVALRY		
Puerto Rico:		
Headquarters and K and L, Nov. 9, 1898, to Aug. 11, 1900	1	9
A, July 25, 1898, to Mar. 29, 1900	1	8
B and D, Nov. 9, 1898, to Mar. 29, 1900	1	5
C, Feb. 1, 1899, to Mar. 29, 1900	1	2
E and G, Nov. 9, 1898, to Dec. 4, 1900	2	1
F and H, Feb. 1, 1899, to Dec. 21, 1900	1	11
I and M, Feb. 1, 1899, to Aug. 11, 1900	1	6
SIXTH U. S. CAVALRY		
Puerto Rico: H, July 28 to Dec. 1, 1898 (3 troops remained in Florida to Aug. 1, 1898)	0	4
SEVENTH U. S. CAVALRY		
Cuba:		
Headquarters and E, G, I, and L, Jan. 13, 1899, to May 22, 1902	3	4
A, Jan. 13, 1899, to Apr. 22, 1902	3	3
B, Jan. 22, 1899, to Apr. 22, 1902	3	3
C, Jan. 13, 1899, to Apr. 17, 1902	3	3
D, Jan. 22, 1899, to Apr. 21, 1902	3	3
F, H, K, and M, Jan. 22, 1899, to May 22, 1902	3	4
EIGHTH U. S. CAVALRY		
Cuba:		
Headquarters and I and M, Nov. 13, 1898, to Mar. 2, 1902	3	4
A, B, and C, Nov. 13, 1898, to Jan. 23, 1900	1	2
D, Jan. 31, 1899, to Jan. 23, 1900	1	
E and H, Jan. 31, 1899, to May 26, 1902	3	4
F, Jan. 31, 1899, to Apr. 30, 1902	3	3
G, Nov. 13, 1898, to Apr. 30, 1902	3	6
K and L, Jan. 31, 1899, to Mar. 2, 1902	3	1
NINTH U. S. CAVALRY		
Cuba: Headquarters and A, B, C, D, E, G, H, and K, June 14 to Aug. 20, 1898 (4 troops remained in Florida to August 1898)		2
TENTH U. S. CAVALRY		
Cuba:		
Headquarters and A, B, C, D, E, F, G, and I, June 14 to Aug. 20, 1898 (4 troops remained in Florida to August 1898)		2
Headquarters and A, C, L, and M, May 1, 1899, to Apr. 30, 1902	3	
B, D, I, and K, May 17, 1899, to May 12, 1902	3	
E and F, May 17, 1899, to Jan. 10, 1900		8
G and H, May 1, 1899, to Jan. 10, 1900 (4 troops remained in Texas, January 1900 to April 1901)		8

	Period	
	Years	Months

FIELD ARTILLERY

FIRST FIELD ARTILLERY

Battery D (formerly Battery E, First Artillery, and First Battery Field Artillery)

Cuba: June 14 to Aug. 25, 1898 ---------- | | 2

Battery E (formerly Battery C, Third Artillery, and Fifth Battery Field Artillery)

Cuba and Puerto Rico: July 3 to Dec. 1, 1898 (sailed for Cuba July 3, and left there for Puerto Rico July 20, 1898) ---------- | | 5

Battery F (formerly Battery D, Fifth Artillery, and Ninth Battery Field Artillery)

Cuba and Puerto Rico: July 3 to Dec. 1, 1898 (sailed for Cuba July 3, and left there for Puerto Rico July 20, 1898) ---------- | | 5

THIRD FIELD ARTILLERY

Battery A (formerly Battery F, Third Artillery, and Sixth Battery Field Artillery)

Cuba and Puerto Rico: July 3 to Dec. 1, 1898 (sailed for Cuba July 3, and left there for Puerto Rico July 20, 1898) ---------- | | 5

Battery B (formerly Battery M, Seventh Artillery, and Fifteenth Battery Field Artillery)

Puerto Rico: July 23, 1898, to June 27, 1899 ---------- | | 11

Battery C (formerly Battery F, Fifth Artillery, and Tenth Battery Field Artillery)

Cuba: July 3 to Aug. 30, 1898 ---------- | | 2

Battery D (formerly Battery A, Second Artillery, and Third Battery Field Artillery)

Cuba, June 14 to Aug. 30, 1898 ---------- | | 3
Jan. 21, 1899, to Apr. 22, 1902 ---------- | 3 | 3

Battery E (formerly Battery F, Second Artillery, and Fourth Battery Field Artillery)

Cuba, June 14 to Aug. 23, 1898 ---------- | | 2
Jan. 21, 1899, to Aug. 12, 1900 ---------- | 1 | 7

Battery F (formerly Battery C, Seventh Artillery, and Fourteenth Battery Field Artillery)

Puerto Rico: July 23, 1898, to June 27, 1899 ---------- | | 11

FIFTH FIELD ARTILLERY

Battery C (formerly Twenty-ninth Battery Field Artillery)

Cuba: Sept. 22, 1901, to Jan. 7, 1902 ---------- | | 4

Battery D (formerly Battery F, Fourth Artillery, and Eighth Battery Field Artillery)

Cuba: July 3 to Aug. 30, 1898 ---------- | | 2

SIXTH FIELD ARTILLERY

Battery A (formerly Battery K, First Artillery, and Second Battery Field Artillery)

Cuba: June 14 to Aug. 30, 1898 ---------- | | 3

Battery D (formerly Battery B, Fourth Artillery, and Seventh Battery Field Artillery)

Cuba and Puerto Rico: July 3 to Dec. 1, 1898 (sailed for Cuba July 3 and left there for Puerto Rico July 20, 1898) ---------- | | 5

COAST ARTILLERY CORPS

THIRTEENTH COMPANY

Cuba: Dec. 29, 1898, to Oct. 18, 1899 ---------- | | 10

FOURTEENTH COMPANY

Cuba: Dec. 29, 1898, to Oct. 18, 1899 ---------- | | 10

FIFTEENTH COMPANY

Cuba: Jan. 21 to Oct. 18, 1899 ---------- | | 9

	Period	
	Years	Months
COAST ARTILLERY CORPS—Continued		
SIXTEENTH COMPANY		
Cuba: Dec. 29, 1898, to Oct. 18, 1899 _____	_____	10
SEVENTEENTH COMPANY		
Cuba: Jan. 21, 1899, to Feb. 8, 1904 _____	5	1
EIGHTEENTH COMPANY		
Cuba: Jan. 11, 1899, to Oct. 27, 1903 _____	4	10
NINETEENTH COMPANY		
Cuba: Jan. 11, 1899, to Feb. 8, 1904 _____	5	1
TWENTIETH COMPANY		
Cuba: Dec. 29, 1898, to Feb. 8, 1904 _____	5	1
TWENTY-FIRST COMPANY		
Cuba: Dec. 29, 1898, to Oct. 27, 1903 _____	4	10
TWENTY-SECOND COMPANY		
Cuba: Dec. 29, 1898, to Feb. 8, 1904 _____	5	1
TWENTY-THIRD COMPANY		
Cuba: Oct. 22, 1899, to Oct. 24, 1903 _____	4	_____
TWENTY-FOURTH COMPANY		
Cuba: Oct. 22, 1899, to Oct. 24, 1903 _____	4	_____
FORTY-FIRST COMPANY		
Cuba: June 14 to Aug. 22, 1898 _____	_____	2
FORTY-SECOND COMPANY		
Cuba: June 14 to Aug. 15, 1898 _____	_____	2
FIFTY-SECOND COMPANY		
Puerto Rico: Mar. 1, 1899, to Dec. 3, 1900 _____	1	9
FIFTY-THIRD COMPANY		
Puerto Rico: Aug. 3, 1898, to Dec. 3, 1900 _____	2	4
FIFTY-SIXTH COMPANY		
Puerto Rico: Nov. 14, 1900, to May 17, 1904 _____	3	6
FIFTY-NINTH COMPANY		
Puerto Rico: Nov. 14, 1900, to May 15, 1904 _____	3	6
INFANTRY		
FIRST U. S. INFANTRY		
Cuba:		
E and G, May 10 to 17, 1898 _____	_____	_____
Headquarters and A, B, C, D, E, F, G, and H, June 14 to Aug. 28, 1898 _____	_____	2
Headquarters and F, Dec. 30, 1898, to Aug. 12, 1900 _____	1	7
A and D, Dec. 30, 1898, to Sept. 19, 1899 _____	_____	9
B, Dec. 29, 1898, to Sept. 19, 1899 _____	_____	9
C, Jan. 8 to Sept. 19, 1899 _____	_____	8
E and G, Jan. 8, 1899, to Aug. 12, 1900 _____	1	7
H, Dec. 29, 1898, to Aug. 12, 1900 _____	1	7
I, Dec. 29, 1898, to Sept. 6, 1900 _____	1	8
K, Jan. 8, 1899, to Aug. 7, 1900 _____	1	7
L, Dec. 30, 1898, to Aug. 7, 1900 _____	1	7
M, Dec. 29, 1898, to Aug. 7, 1900 (4 companies in Kansas and Arkansas, September 1899 to April 1901) _____	1	7

	Period	
	Years	Months

INFANTRY—Continued

SECOND U. S. INFANTRY

Cuba:		
Headquarters and A, B, C, D, E, F, G, and H, June 14 to Aug 15, 1898		2
I, June 29 to Aug. 15, 1898		2
Headquarters and A, B, C, and D, Apr. 13, 1899, to July 24, 1900	1	3
E, F, G, and H, Apr. 13 to Sept. 25, 1899		5
I, K, L, and M, May 25, 1899, to July 24, 1900 (4 companies in Ohio and Kentucky, September 1899 to April 1902)	1	2

THIRD U. S. INFANTRY

Cuba: Headquarters and A, B, C, D, E, F, G, and H, June 14 to Aug. 25, 1898		2

FOURTH U. S. INFANTRY

Cuba: Headquarters and A, B, C, D, E, F, G, and H, June 14 to Aug. 19, 1898		2

FIFTH U. S. INFANTRY

Cuba:		
Headquarters and A, C, F, and G, Aug. 21, 1898, to July 25, 1900	1	11
B, D, E, and H, Aug. 21, 1898, to Aug. 9, 1900	2	
I, K, L, and M, Aug. 21, 1898, to Sept. 27, 1899	1	1

SEVENTH U. S. INFANTRY

Cuba: Headquarters and A, B, C, D, E, F, G, H, and I, June 14 to Aug. 27, 1898		2

EIGHTH U. S. INFANTRY

Cuba: Headquarters and A, B, C, D, E, G, and H, June 14 to Aug 20, 1898		2
Puerto Rico: F, July 28, 1898, to Dec. 1, 1898		4
Cuba:		
Headquarters and A, B, C, D, G, and H, Dec. 13, 1898, to July 24, 1900	1	7
E and F, Dec. 13, 1898, to July 21, 1900	1	7
I, K, L, and M, Dec. 13, 1898, to Sept. 19, 1899		9

TENTH U. S. INFANTRY

Cuba: Headquarters and A, B, C, D, E, F, G, and H, June 14 to Aug. 16, 1898		2
Cuba:		
Headquarters and E, F, and G, Dec. 11, 1898, to Feb. 28, 1901	2	3
A, Dec. 23, 1898, to Feb. 17, 1901	2	2
B, Dec. 11, 1898, to Feb 17, 1901	2	2
C and D, Dec. 17, 1898, to Feb. 17, 1901	2	2
H, Dec. 23, 1898, to Feb. 28, 1901	2	2
I and M, Dec. 23, 1898, to Sept. 25, 1899		9
K and L, Dec. 17, 1898, to Sept. 25, 1899 (4 companies in Nebraska and Wyoming, October 1899 to March 1902)		9

ELEVENTH U. S. INFANTRY

Puerto Rico:		
Headquarters and K, July 23, 1898, to Dec. 5, 1900	2	4
A, C, and D, July 22, 1898, to Aug. 12, 1900	2	1
B, July 23, 1898, to Aug. 12, 1900	2	1
E, F, G, and H, July 23, 1898, to Apr. 8, 1902	3	9
I, July 23, 1898, to Dec. 3, 1900	2	4
L and M, July 22, 1898, to Dec. 5, 1900	2	4

TWELFTH U. S. INFANTRY

Cuba: Headquarters and A, B, C, D, E, F, G, and H, June 14 to Aug. 23, 1898		2

FIFTEENTH U. S. INFANTRY

Cuba:		
Headquarters and A, B, C, D, I, K, L, and M, Nov. 28, 1898, to Jan. 9, 1900	1	1
E, F, G, and K, Nov. 28, 1898, to Oct. 20, 1899 (4 companies in New York from October 1899)		11

SIXTEENTH U. S. INFANTRY

Cuba:		
Headquarters and A, B, C, D, E, F, G, and H, June 14 to Aug. 18, 1898		2
I, July 14 to Aug. 18, 1898 (organized in Cuba)		1
K, July 13 to Aug. 18, 1898 (organized in Cuba)		1

SEVENTEENTH U. S. INFANTRY

Cuba: Headquarters and A, B, C, D, E, F, G, and H, June 14 to Aug. 21, 1898		2

NINETEENTH U. S. INFANTRY

Puerto Rico: Regiment, July 23, 1898, to June 5, 1899		10

	Period	
	Years	Months
INFANTRY—Continued		
TWENTIETH U. S. INFANTRY		
Cuba:		
Headquarters and A, B, C, D, E, F, G, and H, June 14 to Aug. 23, 1898		2
I, July 13 to Aug. 23, 1898		1
TWENTY-FIRST U. S. INFANTRY		
Cuba: Headquarters and A, B, C, D, E, F, G, and H, June 14 to Aug. 23, 1898		2
TWENTY-SECOND U. S. INFANTRY		
Cuba: Headquarters and A, B, C, D, E, F, G, and H, June 14 to Aug. 20, 1898		2
TWENTY-FOURTH U. S. INFANTRY		
Cuba: Headquarters and A, B, C, D, E, F, G, and H, June 14 to Sept. 3, 1898		3
TWENTY-FIFTH U. S. INFANTRY		
Cuba: Headquarters and A, B, C, D, E, F, G, and H, June 14 to Aug. 22, 1898		2

52. List of volunteer organizations which left the United States for service in Cuba or Puerto Rico between August 12, 1898, and July 4, 1902, as found in statistical exhibit of strength of volunteer forces called into service during the War with Spain issued by The Adjutant General's office in 1899.

TROOPS THAT WENT TO CUBA

Organization	Mustered in—	Mustered out—	Left the United States	Returned to the United States
Third Georgia Infantry	Aug. 24, 1898	Apr. 22, 1899	Jan. 14, 1899	Mar. 29, 1899
Second Illinois Infantry	May 16, 1898	Apr. 26, 1899	Dec. 9, 1898	Apr. 3, 1899
Fourth Illinois Infantry	May 19–20, 1898	May 2, 1899	Jan. 3, 1899	Apr. 5, 1899
Ninth Illinois Infantry	July 4–11, 1898	May 20, 1899	....do........	Apr. 21, 1899
One Hundred and Sixtieth Indiana Infantry.	May 12, 1898	Apr. 25, 1899	Jan. 8, 1899	Mar. 29, 1899
One Hundred and Sixty-first Indiana Infantry.	July 11–13, 1898	Apr. 30, 1899	Dec. 13, 1898	Mar. 31, 1899
Forty-ninth Iowa Infantry	June 2, 1898	May 13, 1899	Dec. 19, 1898	Apr. 11, 1899
Twenty-third Kansas Infantry (Colored).	July 2–19, 1898	Apr. 10, 1899	Aug. 25, 1898	Mar. 5, 1899
Third Kentucky Infantry	May 21–31, 1898	May 16, 1899	Jan. 18, 1899	Apr. 10, 1899
Second Louisiana Infantry	May 11–26, 1898	Apr. 18, 1899	Dec. 24, 1898	Mar. 22, 1899
Maine Volunteer Artillery, Batteries A, B, C, D.	May 17–July 20, 1898	Mar. 31, 1899	Jan. 17, 1899	Mar. 11, 1899
Eighth Massachusetts Infantry	May 11–14, 1898	Apr. 28, 1899	Jan. 7, 1899	Apr. 9, 1899
Thirty-first Michigan Infantry	May 8–11, 1898	May 17, 1899	Jan. 27, 1899	Apr. 16, 1899
Sixth Missouri Infantry	July 20–Aug. 6, 1898	May 10, 1899	Dec. 21, 1898	Apr. 11, 1899
Third Nebraska Infantry	July 1–17, 1898	May 11, 1899	Dec. 30, 1898	Apr. 12, 1899
Twelfth New York Infantry	May 13, 1898	Apr. 20, 1899	....do........	Mar. 26, 1899
Two Hundred and Second New York Infantry.	July 19–Aug. 8, 1898	Apr. 15, 1899	Dec. 5, 1898	Mar. 20, 1899
First North Carolina Infantry	May 3–11, 1898	Apr. 22, 1899	Dec. 8, 1898	Mar. 28, 1899
Sixth Ohio Infantry	May 12–July 2, 1898	May 24, 1899	Dec. 30, 1898	Apr. 26, 1899
Second South Carolina Infantry	May 14–Aug. 23, 1898	Apr. 19, 1899	Jan. 3, 1899	Mar. 28, 1899
Fourth Tennessee Infantry	July 1–13, 1898	May 6, 1899	Dec. 1, 1898	Apr. 1, 1899
First Texas Infantry	May 10–12, 1898	Apr. 18, 1899	Dec. 23, 1898	Apr. 2, 1899
Fourth Virginia Infantry	May 9–25, 1898	Apr. 27, 1899	Dec. 19, 1898 [1]	Mar. 29, 1899
Second U. S. Volunteer Engineers	June 28–July 12, 1898	May 16, 1899	Nov. 23, 1898	Apr. 17, 1899
Third U. S. Volunteer Engineers, Headquarters E, F, G, H.			Feb. 4, 1899	Do.
Companies A, B, C, and K	July 25–Aug. 20, 1898	May 17, 1899	Feb. 17, 1899	Do.
Companies D, I, L, and M			Dec. 20, 1898	Do.
Third U. S. Volunteer Infantry	June 11–July 9, 1898	May 12, 1899	Aug. 13, 1898	Apr. 2, 1899
Fourth U. S. Volunteer Infantry	June 2–15, 1898	June 8, 1899	Oct. 12, 1898	May 16, 1899
Ninth U. S. Volunteer Infantry (colored).	June 18–July 16, 1898	May 25, 1899	Aug. 17, 1898	Apr. 30, 1899

[1] Company F sailed on Dec. 13, 1898.

TROOPS THAT WENT TO PUERTO RICO

Organization	Mustered in—	Mustered out—	Left the United States	Returned to the United States
Forty-seventh New York Infantry.	May 24, 1898	Mar. 31, 1899	Oct. 10, 1898	Mar. 10, 1899
Sixth U. S. Volunteer Infantry	June 24–July 15, 1898	Mar. 15, 1899	do	Feb. 18, 1899

VESSELS WHICH PARTICIPATED IN THE OPERATIONS OF THE SECOND NICARAGUAN CAMPAIGN BETWEEN AUG. 27, 1926, AND JAN. 2, 1933: AND THE DATES BETWEEN WHICH THESE RESPECTIVE VESSELS WERE ENGAGED

53. List of vessels:

Name of vessel	Period of service, both dates inclusive		Name of vessel	Period of service, both dates inclusive	
	From—	To—		From—	To—
Asheville	Aug. 5, 1929	Aug. 12, 1929	Denver	Nov. 27, 1929	Nov. 28, 1929
Do	Dec. 26, 1929		Do	Mar. 29, 1930	Mar. 31, 1930
Do	Feb. 7, 1930	Feb. 9, 1930	Do	Apr. 22, 1930	May 7, 1930
Do	Jan. 31, 1931	Mar. 3, 1931	Do	Sept. 5, 1930	Oct. 10, 1930
Do	Apr. 14, 1931	Apr. 30, 1931	Detroit	Mar. 23, 1927	Apr. 17, 1927
Do	May 13, 1931	June 17, 1931	Edwards, J. D	Jan. 9, 1927	Jan. 9, 1927
Bainbridge	Apr. 26, 1927	June 4, 1927	Do	Jan. 17, 1927	Jan. 27, 1927
Barker	Jan. 10, 1927		Do	Jan. 31, 1927	Feb. 3, 1927
Do	Jan. 13, 1927	Jan. 31, 1927	Do	Feb. 7, 1927	Feb. 13, 1927
Barry	Dec. 19, 1926	Dec. 30, 1926	Flusser	Apr. 24, 1927	May 19, 1927
Do	Jan. 2, 1927	Jan. 9, 1927	Do	May 23, 1927	June 12, 1927
Borie	Jan. 9, 1927	Jan. 18, 1927	Galveston	Aug. 27, 1926	Nov. 1, 1926
Do	Jan. 24, 1927	Mar. 15, 1927	Do	Nov. 13, 1926	Dec. 7, 1926
Brooks	Dec. 18, 1926	Dec. 21, 1926	Do	Dec. 10, 1926	Dec. 20, 1926
Cincinnati	Jan. 11, 1927		Do	Jan. 5, 1927	Feb. 27, 1927
Do	Jan. 14, 1927	Jan. 27, 1927	Do	Mar. 4, 1927	Apr. 22, 1927
Cleveland	Dec. 12, 1926	Jan. 17, 1927	Do	Apr. 30, 1927	June 18, 1927
Do	Jan. 21, 1927	Mar. 22, 1927	Do	Sept. 26, 1927	Oct. 13, 1927
Do	Mar. 28, 1927	May 24, 1927	Do	Nov. 6, 1927	Nov. 20, 1927
Do	May 30, 1927	June 7, 1927	Do	Dec. 2, 1927	Dec. 20, 1927
Do	June 18, 1927	July 21, 1927	Do	Jan. 8, 1928	Jan. 23, 1928
Do	Aug. 4, 1927	Aug. 24, 1927	Do	Feb. 26, 1928	Mar. 31, 1928
Do	Sept. 16, 1927	Sept. 19, 1927	Do	Apr. 4, 1928	Apr. 11, 1928
Do	Sept. 23, 1927	Oct. 1, 1927	Do	Apr. 30, 1928	Apr. 30, 1928
Do	Oct. 11, 1927	Oct. 14, 1927	Do	May 15, 1928	June 18, 1928
Do	Oct. 28, 1927	Nov. 20, 1927	Do	Sept. 26, 1928	Oct. 19, 1928
Do	Mar. 24, 1928	Apr. 24, 1928	Do	Nov. 2, 1928	Nov. 15, 1928
Do	Apr. 29, 1928		Do	Feb. 18, 1929	Feb. 19, 1929
Do	May 15, 1928	June 14, 1928	Do	Apr. 18, 1929	Apr. 19, 1929
Do	July 11, 1928		Do	June 2, 1929	June 27, 1929
Do	July 23, 1928	July 26, 1928	Do	Aug. 2, 1929	Aug. 4, 1929
Do	July 31, 1928	Aug. 8, 1928	Do	Apr. 5, 1930	Apr. 22, 1930
Do	Aug. 25, 1928	Sept. 22, 1928	Gilmor	Sept. 25, 1926	Oct. 7, 1926
Do	Oct. 4, 1928	Oct. 15, 1928	Do	Oct. 11, 1926	Oct. 30, 1926
Do	Oct. 20, 1928		Goff	Jan. 15, 1927	Feb. 11, 1927
Do	Nov. 3, 1928	Nov. 8, 1928	Hatfield	Feb. 13, 1927	Feb. 27, 1927
Do	May 19, 1929	May 21, 1929	Do	Mar. 3, 1927	Mar. 21, 1927
Do	June 27, 1929	Aug. 2, 1929	Henderson	Mar. 7, 1927	Mar. 26, 1927
Coughlan	Feb. 18, 1927	Mar. 21, 1927	Humphreys	Nov. 21, 1926	Nov. 22, 1926
Denver	Sept. 18, 1926		James, Reuben	Jan. 31, 1927	Mar. 15, 1927
Do	Sept. 25, 1926	Nov. 16, 1926	Kane	Mar. 19, 1927	Apr. 4, 1927
Do	Nov. 27, 1926	Jan. 13, 1927	Do	Apr. 24, 1927	Apr. 24, 1927
Do	Jan. 17, 1927	Mar. 20, 1927	Kidder	June 13, 1927	June 27, 1927
Do	Mar. 26, 1927	May 30, 1927	King	Apr. 26, 1927	May 3, 1927
Do	June 2, 1927	June 29, 1927	Do	May 7, 1927	June 9, 1927
Do	July 15, 1927	Aug. 13, 1927	La Vallette	June 13, 1927	June 23, 1927
Do	Aug. 24, 1927	Sept. 6, 1927	Lawrence	Feb. 13, 1927	Mar. 11, 1927
Do	Dec. 29, 1927	Jan. 12, 1928	Do	Mar. 14, 1927	Mar. 21, 1927
Do	Jan. 21, 1928	Jan. 22, 1928	Litchfield	June 23, 1927	July 10, 1927
Do	Jan. 29, 1928	Feb. 19, 1928	Do	July 31, 1927	July 31, 1927
Do	Mar. 5, 1928	Mar. 28, 1928	Marblehead	Jan. 11, 1927	Jan. 29, 1927
Do	Apr. 9, 1928	May 15, 1928	Marcus	Aug. 11, 1917	Aug. 13, 1927
Do	June 17, 1928	July 22, 1928	McFarland	Mar. 19, 1927	Apr. 8, 1927
Do	Aug. 8, 1928	Aug. 12, 1928	Do	Apr. 12, 1927	Apr. 24, 1927
Do	Aug. 25, 1928	Aug. 27, 1928	Melvin	June 25, 1927	July 18, 1927
Do	Dec. 6, 1928	Dec. 14, 1928	Memphis	Oct. 26, 1932	Nov. 8, 1932
Do	Jan. 1, 1929	Jan. 4, 1929	Mervine	June 26, 1927	June 26, 1927
Do	Jan. 16, 1929	Jan. 21, 1929	Do	July 9, 1927	July 20, 1927
Do	Apr. 11, 1929	Apr. 14, 1929	Milwaukee	Jan. 29, 1927	Feb. 8, 1927
Do	Aug. 9, 1929	Aug. 9, 1929	Do	Feb. 11, 1927	Feb. 15, 1927
Do	Aug. 16, 1929	Sept. 30, 1929	Do	Feb. 19, 1927	May 2, 1927

Name of vessel	Period of service, both dates inclusive		Name of vessel	Period of service, both dates inclusive	
	From—	To—		From—	To—
Milwaukee	June 2, 1927	June 4, 1927	Sacramento	Mar. 14, 1930	Mar. 24, 1930
Do	June 9, 1927	June 13, 1927	Do	Jan. 3, 1931	Jan. 31, 1931
Mullany	July 30, 1927	Aug. 13, 1927	Do	Apr. 17, 1931	May 13, 1931
Osborne	Jan. 11, 1927	Jan. 16, 1927	Do	Aug. 14, 1931	Sept. 11, 1931
Overton	Aug. 30, 1932	Sept. 13, 1932	Selfridge	June 18, 1927	July 17, 1927
Paulding, J. K.	Nov. 1, 1926	Nov. 13, 1926	Do	July 23, 1927	July 26, 1927
Do	Nov. 16, 1926	Nov. 19, 1926	Shirk	July 2, 1927	July 23, 1927
Do	Mar. 19, 1927	Mar. 29, 1927	Sloat	June 25, 1927	July 9, 1927
Do	Apr. 3, 1927	Apr. 24, 1927	Do	July 22, 1927	Aug. 8, 1927
Philip	Jan. 31, 1932	Feb. 9, 1932	Smith, Robert	June 12, 1927	June 25, 1927
Do	Apr. 8, 1932	Apr. 11, 1932	Do	July 16, 1927	Aug. 9, 1927
Do	Apr. 30, 1932	Apr. 30, 1932	Sturtevant	Sept. 19, 1932	Oct. 4, 1932
Preston	Apr. 29, 1927	May 10, 1927	Thompson, Smith	Sept. 25, 1926	Sept. 30, 1926
Do	May 15, 1927	June 3, 1927	Do	Oct. 3, 1926	Nov. 1, 1926
Do	June 7, 1927	June 13, 1927	Do	Jan. 11, 1927	Jan. 16, 1927
Quail	Dec. 27, 1926	Jan. 31, 1927	Tracy	Nov. 22, 1926	Dec. 18, 1926
Do	Feb. 9, 1927	Feb. 12, 1927	Do	Mar. 15, 1927	Apr. 26, 1927
Raleigh	Feb. 5, 1927	Mar. 23, 1927	Trenton	Apr. 17, 1927	May 16, 1927
Reid	Apr. 24, 1927	May 22, 1927	Tulsa	Aug. 29, 1926	Sept. 28, 1926
Do	May 26, 1927	June 12, 1927	Do	Oct. 7, 1926	Oct. 8, 1926
Rochester	Aug. 31, 1926	Oct. 6, 1926	Do	Oct. 12, 1926	Oct. 16, 1926
Do	Oct. 15, 1926	Dec. 9, 1926	Do	Nov. 1, 1926	Dec. 14, 1926
Do	Dec. 22, 1926	Jan. 20, 1927	Do	Mar. 3, 1927	Apr. 30, 1927
Do	Jan. 27, 1927	Feb. 1, 1927	Do	May 7, 1927	July 19, 1927
Do	July 21, 1927	July 24, 1927	Do	Aug. 13, 1927	Sept. 24, 1927
Do	Aug. 2, 1927	Aug. 5, 1927	Do	Oct. 14, 1927	Nov. 7, 1927
Do	Oct. 10, 1927	Oct. 11, 1927	Do	Nov. 30, 1927	Dec. 20, 1927
Do	Nov. 6, 1927	Nov. 7, 1927	Do	Jan. 6, 1928	Feb. 16, 1928
Do	Jan. 7, 1928	Feb. 1, 1928	Do	Mar. 10, 1928	----------
Do	Feb. 16, 1928	Mar. 15, 1928	Do	June 14, 1928	July 2, 1928
Do	Mar. 24, 1928	Apr. 7, 1928	Do	July 7, 1928	July 11, 1928
Do	May 28, 1928	May 31, 1928	Do	July 21, 1928	July 25, 1928
Do	June 27, 1928	June 30, 1928	Do	Aug. 7, 1928	Aug. 21, 1928
Do	July 8, 1928	July 18, 1928	Do	Aug. 31, 1928	Sept. 16, 1928
Do	Aug. 21, 1928	Aug. 25, 1928	Do	Sept. 28, 1928	Oct. 4, 1928
Do	Sept. 22, 1928	Sept. 27, 1928	Do	Nov. 18, 1928	Dec. 9, 1928
Do	Oct. 19, 1928	Nov. 27, 1928	Whipple	Nov. 22, 1926	----------
Do	Dec. 31, 1928	Jan. 7, 1929	Do	Dec. 5, 1926	Dec. 5, 1926
Do	Feb. 4, 1929	Feb. 11, 1929	Do	Dec. 9, 1926	Dec. 19, 1926
Do	July 13, 1929	July 18, 1929	Do	Mar. 15, 1927	Apr. 27, 1927
Do	Nov. 25, 1929	Dec. 19, 1929	Wickes	Jan. 30, 1932	Feb. 9, 1932
Do	Oct. 9, 1930	Nov. 16, 1930	Williamson	Jan. 15, 1927	Jan. 29, 1927
Do	Apr. 3, 1931	Apr. 14, 1931	Do	Feb. 2, 1927	Feb. 18, 1927
Sacramento	Mar. 16, 1929	Mar. 27, 1929	Wood	June 27, 1927	July 16, 1927
Do	June 2, 1929	June 4, 1929	Yarborough	June 12, 1927	June 18, 1927
Do	Sept. 22, 1929	Sept. 24, 1929	Do	July 8, 1927	Aug. 5, 1927

VESSELS WHICH PARTICIPATED IN THE OPERATIONS IN THE VALLEY OF THE YANGTZE RIVER, CHINA, FROM SEPT. 3, 1926, TO OCT. 21, 1927, AND FROM MAR. 1, 1930, TO DEC. 31, 1932; AND THE DATES BETWEEN WHICH THESE RESPECTIVE VESSELS WERE ENGAGED

54. List of vessels:

Name of vessel	Period of service, both dates inclusive		Name of vessel	Period of service, both dates inclusive	
	From—	To—		From—	To—
Alava, General	Sept. 20, 1926	Nov. 6, 1926	Beaver	May 25, 1931	June 2, 1931
Do	Apr. 14, 1927	May 14, 1927	Do	Oct. 9, 1931	Oct. 10, 1931
Do	June 7, 1927	June 30, 1927	Bittern	Feb. 7, 1932	Mar. 9, 1932
Do	Aug. 24, 1927	Oct. 21, 1927	Do	May 27, 1932	June 3, 1932
Asheville	Nov. 3, 1926	Apr. 2, 1927	Do	Oct. 6, 1932	Oct. 9, 1932
Do	May 13, 1927	May 18, 1927	Black Hawk	Oct. 21, 1926	Oct. 28, 1926
Do	Aug. 2, 1927	Aug. 23, 1927	Do	Apr. 21, 1927	June 6, 1927
Do	Mar. 18, 1932	Mar. 23, 1932	Do	Apr. 21, 1931	May 3, 1931
Do	June 27, 1932	Oct. 9, 1932	Do	Sept. 15, 1931	Sept. 17, 1931
Avocet	Apr. 23, 1931	May 7, 1931	Do	Sept. 23, 1931	Sept. 24, 1931
Do	Oct. 9, 1931	Oct. 22, 1931	Do	Oct. 20, 1931	Nov. 2, 1931
Barker	Nov. 28, 1930	Jan. 12, 1931	Do	Feb. 9, 1932	May 23, 1932
Do	July 8, 1931	Aug. 21, 1931	Do	Oct. 5, 1932	Oct. 25, 1932
Do	Oct. 18, 1931	Nov. 2, 1931	Botie	May 19, 1930	July 16, 1930
Do	Feb. 5, 1932	Mar. 27, 1932	Do	Jan. 29, 1932	Mar. 10, 1932
Do	Oct. 4, 1932	Oct. 25, 1932	Bulmer	Jan. 7, 1927	Mar. 3, 1927

Name of vessel	Period of service, both dates inclusive		Name of vessel	Period of service, both dates inclusive	
	From—	To—		From—	To—
Bulmer	May 23, 1927	June 28, 1927	Isabel	Feb. 6, 1932	Feb. 25, 1932
Do	Aug. 21, 1927	Oct. 21, 1927	Do	May 3, 1932	June 7, 1932
Do	Feb. 1, 1930	Feb. 28, 1930	Do	Sept. 20, 1932	Sept. 24, 1932
Do	Aug. 4, 1930	Oct. 1, 1930	Do	Sept. 27, 1932	Oct. 1, 1932
Do	May 2, 1931	May 11, 1931	Do	Oct. 3, 1932	Oct. 8, 1932
Do	Aug. 27, 1931	Aug. 29, 1931	Do	Oct. 10, 1932	Nov. 10, 1932
Do	Oct. 24, 1931	Nov. 2, 1931	Jason	Apr. 23, 1931	May 7, 1931
Do	Feb. 2, 1932	Feb. 6, 1932	Do	Sept. 16, 1931	Sept. 28, 1931
Do	Feb. 8, 1932	Feb. 19, 1932	Jones, Paul	Oct. 20, 1926	Oct. 28, 1926
Do	Feb. 21, 1932	Feb. 21, 1932	Do	Mar. 11, 1927	June 1, 1927
Do	Apr. 15, 1932	May 2, 1932	Do	Sept. 7, 1927	Sept. 15, 1927
Do	May 6, 1932	May 9, 1932	Do	Apr. 14, 1930	June 30, 1930
Do	May 13, 1932	May 16, 1932	Do	Apr. 22, 1931	May 3, 1931
Do	May 19, 1932	May 23, 1932	Do	July 19, 1931	July 23, 1931
Do	Aug. 5, 1932	Aug. 7, 1932	Do	Oct. 19, 1931	Nov. 2, 1931
Canopus	May 16, 1931	June 30, 1931	Do	Feb. 2, 1932	Mar. 22, 1932
Do	May 8, 1932	May 16, 1932	Do	Mar. 24, 1932	May 23, 1932
Cincinnati	Apr. 4, 1927	Sept. 19, 1927	Do	Aug. 13, 1932	Aug. 14, 1932
Do	Sept. 27, 1927	Oct. 15, 1927	Do	Oct. 13, 1932	Oct. 27, 1932
Edsall	Jan. 10, 1927	Mar. 2, 1927	Luzon	Mar. 1, 1930	Dec. 31, 1932
Do	Apr. 18, 1927	July 2, 1927	MacLeish	Jan. 7, 1927	Mar. 10, 1927
Do	Aug. 21, 1927	Aug. 22, 1927	Do	Apr. 20, 1927	June 19, 1927
Do	Oct. 1, 1927	Oct. 21, 1927	Do	Aug. 21, 1927	Aug. 22, 1927
Do	Feb. 1, 1930	Feb. 28, 1930	Do	Jan. 29, 1931	Apr. 22, 1931
Do	July 16, 1930	Sept. 26, 1930	Do	Aug. 28, 1931	Nov. 2, 1931
Do	Apr. 15, 1931	Apr. 22, 1931	Marblehead	Apr. 3, 1927	June 10, 1927
Do	Aug. 27, 1931	Sept. 1, 1931	Do	Aug. 9, 1927	Aug. 27, 1927
Do	Feb. 2, 1932	Feb. 2, 1932	Do	Sept. 6, 1927	Oct. 18, 1927
Do	Feb. 4, 1932	Mar. 25, 1932	McCormick	Jan. 7, 1927	Mar. 2, 1927
Do	Mar. 27, 1932	May 2, 1932	Do	Apr. 18, 1927	June 19, 1927
Do	May 6, 1932	May 9, 1932	Do	Aug. 21, 1927	Oct. 21, 1927
Do	May 13, 1932	May 16, 1932	Do	Feb. 1, 1930	Feb. 28, 1930
Do	May 19, 1932	May 23, 1932	Do	Apr. 13, 1931	Apr. 20, 1931
Do	Oct. 4, 1932	Oct. 25, 1932	Monocacy	Sept. 3, 1926	Oct. 21, 1927
Edwards, John D	May 22, 1930	July 16, 1930	Do	July 1, 1930	Feb. 13, 1931
Do	July 7, 1931	July 8, 1931	Do	Apr. 23, 1931	Dec. 31, 1932
Do	Aug. 21, 1931	Sept. 2, 1931	Noa	Jan. 31, 1927	Feb. 2, 1927
Do	Oct. 19, 1931	Nov. 2, 1931	Do	Feb. 24, 1927	June 1, 1927
Do	Feb. 5, 1932	Mar. 13, 1932	Do	July 4, 1927	Aug. 27, 1927
Do	Mar. 15, 1932	Mar. 16, 1932	Oahu	May 1, 1930	Dec. 31, 1932
Do	May 10, 1932	May 23, 1932	Palos	Sept. 3, 1926	Oct. 21, 1927
Do	Oct. 4, 1932	Oct. 25, 1932	Do	July 1, 1930	Feb. 13, 1931
Elcano	Sept. 3, 1926	Oct. 21, 1927	Do	Apr. 23, 1931	Dec. 31, 1932
Finch	Feb. 7, 1932	Apr. 5, 1932	Panay	Mar. 1, 1930	Do.
Do	Apr. 8, 1932	Apr. 11, 1932	Parrott	Jan. 7, 1927	Jan. 20, 1927
Do	Apr. 15, 1932	May 24, 1932	Do	Feb. 22, 1927	Mar. 2, 1927
Ford, John D	Sept. 11, 1926	Jan. 18, 1927	Do	Apr. 18, 1927	June 9, 1927
Do	Mar. 28, 1927	July 7, 1927	Do	June 13, 1927	June 28, 1927
Do	May 2, 1931	June 17, 1931	Do	Aug. 21, 1927	Oct. 21, 1927
Do	July 6, 1931	July 13, 1931	Do	July 16, 1930	Aug. 22, 1930
Do	Oct. 5, 1931	Oct. 5, 1931	Do	Feb. 1, 1931	May 11, 1931
Do	Feb. 4, 1932	Mar. 10, 1932	Do	Aug. 25, 1931	Sept. 2, 1931
Do	Apr. 25, 1932	May 23, 1932	Do	Feb. 2, 1932	Feb. 6, 1932
Do	Oct. 4, 1932	Oct. 11, 1932	Do	Feb. 8, 1932	May 2, 1932
Guam	Mar. 1, 1930	Dec. 31, 1932	Do	May 6, 1932	May 9, 1932
Hart	Oct. 12, 1926	Dec. 1, 1926	Do	May 13, 1932	May 16, 1932
Do	Dec. 19, 1926	Jan. 9, 1927	Do	May 19, 1932	May 23, 1932
Do	May 25, 1927	Aug. 4, 1927	Do	Aug. 5, 1932	Aug. 6, 1932
Do	Oct. 11, 1927	Oct. 17, 1927	Do	Oct. 5, 1932	Oct. 25, 1932
Henderson	May 2, 1927	June 2, 1927	Peary	Sept. 15, 1926	Jan. 18, 1927
Do	June 23, 1927	June 29, 1927	Do	Mar. 28, 1927	July 2, 1927
Heron	Apr. 23, 1931	May 7, 1931	Do	July 13, 1927	July 22, 1927
Do	Oct. 18, 1931	Oct. 22, 1931	Do	Oct. 15, 1927	Oct. 21, 1927
Do	Sept. 23, 1932	Oct. 6, 1932	Do	Sept. 20, 1930	Nov. 28, 1930
Houston	Apr. 15, 1931	June 8, 1931	Do	June 4, 1931	July 15, 1931
Do	Aug. 22, 1931	Sept. 5, 1931	Do	Oct. 19, 1931	Dec. 11, 1931
Do	Sept. 24, 1931	Nov. 16, 1931	Do	Feb. 4, 1932	Mar. 10, 1932
Do	Feb. 3, 1932	May 5, 1932	Do	Oct. 4, 1932	Oct. 25, 1932
Do	May 31, 1932	June 7, 1932	Pecos	July 16, 1931	July 24, 1931
Do	Sept. 24, 1932	Sept. 24, 1932	Do	Aug. 29, 1931	Aug. 30, 1931
Do	Sept. 27, 1932	Oct. 12, 1932	Penguin	Sept. 3, 1926	Oct. 21, 1927
Do	Oct. 14, 1932	Nov. 10, 1932	Pigeon	...do...	Do.
Hulbert	Oct. 20, 1926	Oct. 28, 1926	Do	May 16, 1931	May 28, 1931
Do	Feb. 24, 1927	May 11, 1927	Do	June 22, 1931	June 23, 1931
Do	June 27, 1927	Aug. 23, 1927	Do	June 6, 1932	June 13, 1932
Huron	Sept. 20, 1926	Nov. 6, 1926	Pillsbury	Sept. 11, 1926	Jan. 16, 1927
Isabel	Sept. 3, 1926	Oct. 21, 1927	Do	Mar. 28, 1927	Apr. 1, 1927
Do	Apr. 5, 1931	June 5, 1931	Do	May 6, 1927	July 19, 1927
Do	Aug. 21, 1931	Sept. 20, 1931	Do	Oct. 15, 1927	Oct. 21, 1927
Do	Sept. 23, 1931	Sept. 25, 1931	Do	Mar. 1, 1930	Apr. 14, 1930
Do	Sept. 27, 1931	Nov. 16, 1931	Do	June 2, 1931	June 3, 1931

Name of vessel	Period of service, both dates inclusive		Name of vessel	Period of service, both dates inclusive	
	From—	To—		From—	To—
Pillsbury	Oct. 19, 1931	Oct. 21, 1931	S-41	May 15, 1931	May 28, 1931
Do	May 16, 1932	May 23, 1932	Do	May 8, 1932	May 16, 1932
Do	Oct. 5, 1932	Oct. 25, 1932	Sacramento	Nov. 1, 1926	Apr. 20, 1927
Pittsburgh	Jan. 13, 1927	June 30, 1927	Do	Aug. 28, 1927	Sept. 26, 1927
Do	Aug. 24, 1927	Oct. 21, 1927	Do	Apr. 13, 1932	May 2, 1932
Pope	Sept. 3, 1926	Sept. 20, 1926	Do	May 5, 1932	June 11, 1932
Do	Oct. 3, 1926	Mar. 17, 1927	Do	Sept. 2, 1932	Sept. 19, 1932
Do	May 3, 1927	July 16, 1927	Sicard	Oct. 20, 1926	Oct. 26, 1926
Do	Oct. 15, 1927	Oct. 21, 1927	Do	Mar. 2, 1927	May 2, 1927
Do	Mar. 1, 1930	Apr. 14, 1930	Do	June 8, 1927	June 10, 1927
Do	May 1, 1931	May 8, 1931	Do	July 4, 1927	Aug. 22, 1927
Do	May 17, 1931	May 25, 1931	Simpson	Jan. 7, 1927	Mar. 3, 1927
Do	July 14, 1931	July 15, 1931	Do	Apr. 18, 1927	June 20, 1927
Do	Oct. 19, 1931	Dec. 17, 1931	Do	Aug. 21, 1927	Sept. 21, 1927
Do	Feb. 5, 1932	Mar. 9, 1932	Do	July 16, 1930	Oct. 1, 1930
Do	May 6, 1932	May 23, 1932	Do	Dec. 11, 1931	Feb. 18, 1932
Do	Oct. 4, 1932	Oct. 8, 1932	Stewart	Sept. 3, 1926	Sept. 18, 1926
Preble	Oct. 20, 1926	Oct. 28, 1926	Do	Jan. 31, 1927	Feb. 2, 1927
Do	Feb. 24, 1927	May 30, 1927	Do	Mar. 11, 1927	July 13, 1927
Do	June 26, 1927	Aug. 4, 1927	Do	Sept. 17, 1930	Nov. 28, 1930
Preston, William B.	Oct. 20, 1926	Oct. 28, 1926	Do	May 2, 1931	July 15, 1931
Do	Mar. 2, 1927	Mar. 29, 1927	Do	Oct. 15, 1931	Oct. 15, 1931
Do	May 29, 1927	June 1, 1927	Do	Feb. 26, 1932	May 2, 1932
Do	June 26, 1927	Aug. 27, 1927	Do	May 6, 1932	May 9, 1932
Pruitt	Oct. 20, 1926	Oct. 28, 1926	Do	May 13, 1932	May 16, 1932
Do	Mar. 2, 1927	June 2, 1927	Do	May 19, 1932	May 23, 1932
Do	June 27, 1927	June 28, 1927	Do	Oct. 11, 1932	Oct. 25, 1932
Do	Aug. 12, 1927	Aug. 15, 1927	Thompson, Smith	July 1, 1930	July 16, 1930
Richmond	Apr. 3, 1927	June 2, 1927	Do	Nov. 20, 1930	Feb. 4, 1931
Do	June 22, 1927	July 29, 1927	Do	July 12, 1931	July 13, 1931
Do	Aug. 3, 1927	Sept. 19, 1927	Do	July 15, 1931	July 31, 1931
Rizal	Oct. 26, 1926	Jan. 9, 1927	Do	Aug. 29, 1931	Sept. 1, 1931
Do	June 5, 1927	Aug. 19, 1927	Do	Oct. 19, 1931	Nov. 2, 1931
Do	Oct. 11, 1927	Oct. 17, 1927	Do	Feb. 5, 1932	Mar. 29, 1932
Do	Sept. 18, 1930	Oct. 20, 1930	Do	Oct. 4, 1932	Oct. 25, 1932
Rochester	Apr. 29, 1932	Dec. 31, 1932	Tracy	Apr. 14, 1930	May 24, 1930
S-30	May 25, 1931	June 2, 1931	Truxtun	Sept. 15, 1926	Mar. 17, 1927
S-31	do	Do.	Do	May 16, 1927	July 22, 1927
Do	June 22, 1931	June 30, 1931	Do	Oct. 15, 1927	Oct. 21, 1927
Do	Aug. 12, 1931	Aug. 27, 1931	Do	Mar. 1, 1930	Apr. 14, 1930
S-34	May 25, 1931	June 2, 1931	Do	Jan. 21, 1932	Apr. 1, 1932
S-35	May 25, 1931	June 2, 1931	Tulsa	do	Apr. 14, 1932
S-36	May 15, 1931	May 28, 1931	Do	Oct. 15, 1932	Nov. 7, 1932
Do	May 8, 1932	May 16, 1932	Do	Nov. 10, 1932	Dec. 31, 1932
S-37	May 15, 1931	May 28, 1931	Tutuila	Mar. 1, 1930	Do.
Do	May 8, 1932	May 16, 1932	Villalobos	Sept. 3, 1926	Oct. 21, 1927
S-38	May 15, 1931	May 28, 1931	Whipple	Apr. 14, 1930	May 19, 1930
Do	Oct. 10, 1931	Oct. 16, 1931	Do	Nov. 28, 1930	Feb. 4, 1931
Do	May 28, 1932	June 2, 1932	Do	July 19, 1931	July 23, 1931
S-39	May 15, 1931	May 28, 1931	Do	Oct. 19, 1931	Nov. 2, 1931
Do	May 8, 1932	May 16, 1932	Do	Feb. 5, 1932	Feb. 26, 1932
Do	Sept. 23, 1932	Oct. 3, 1932	Do	Feb. 27, 1932	Apr. 23, 1932
S-40	May 15, 1931	May 28, 1931	Do	Oct. 4, 1932	Oct. 25, 1932
Do	June 6, 1932	June 13, 1932			

LANDING PARTIES

Name of vessel	From	To	Name of vessel	From	To
Chaumont	Dec. 23, 1926	Jan. 1, 1927	Pecos	Feb. 9, 1927	Apr. 23, 1927
Do	Feb. 24, 1927	May 5, 1927	Do	June 18, 1927	June 21, 1927
Do	May 20, 1927	May 30, 1927	Do	July 16, 1927	July 18, 1927
Do	June 13, 1927	June 25, 1927	Do	July 26, 1927	Aug. 13, 1927
Do	July 2, 1927	July 6, 1927	Do	Sept. 4, 1927	Sept. 6, 1927
Do	Oct. 16, 1927	Oct. 20, 1927	Do	Oct. 20, 1927	Oct. 21, 1927

Sixth Regiment of United States Marines on board the U. S. S. *Henderson* from May 2, 1927, to June 2, 1927.

Expeditionary detachment, Aircraft Squadron, Third Brigade United States Marines, who were on board the U. S. S. *Henderson*, at Shanghai, China, from June 23, 1927, to June 27, 1927.

Appendix C

Table of Distances
Related to Naval Operations in 1898

TABLE OF DISTANCES

ATLANTIC	NAUTICAL MILES	STATUTE MILES
Key West to Havana	·90	104
Key West to Cienfuegos	520	598
Key West to Tampa	220	253
Key West to Santiago de Cuba *via* Cape Maysi . .	610	702
via Cape Antonio . .	790	910
Key West to San Juan, P. R.	972	1,119
Cape Verde Islands to Martinique	2,070	2,385
Cape Verde Islands to San Juan, P. R.	2,350	2,707
Martinique to San Juan	380	438
Martinique to Curaçao	500	576
Curaçao to Santiago de Cuba	625	720
Curaçao to Cienfuegos	900	1,036
Cienfuegos to Santiago de Cuba	315	364
Santiago de Cuba to Guantánamo	40	46
Santiago to Mole S. Nicolas, Haiti	122	140
Santiago to Gonaives; Haiti	185	213
Santiago to San Juan, P. R.	580	668
Windward Passage to San Juan	450	519
New York to Cape Verde Islands	2,919	3,361
New York to Havana	1,215	1,398
New York to San Juan, P. R.	1,411	1,626
Sandy Hook to Capes of Virginia	240	276
Capes of Virginia to Havana	938	1,078
Santiago to El Caney	. . . .	4
Siboney to Las Guasimas	. . . .	2¾
Siboney to El Pozo	. . . .	7
Siboney to San Juan Hill	. . . .	8½
Siboney to Santiago	. . . .	9¾
Guantánamo to Santiago by land (about)	. . . .	75

PACIFIC	NAUTICAL MILES	STATUTE MILES
Hong-Kong to Manila	628	723
Subig Bay to Manila	55	63
Manila to Sangley Point	6½	7½
San Francisco to Honolulu	2,110	2,325
Honolulu to Guam	3,337	3,842
Guam to Manila	1,742	2,006
San Francisco to Manila *via* Honolulu and Guam . .	7,189	8,275
Suez to Manila *via* Singapore	6,358	7,321

Table of Distances Related to Naval Operations in 1898.
Source: French Ensor Chadwick, *The Relations of the United States and Spain: The Spanish-American War* (New York: Charles Scribner's Sons, 1911), I, facing p. 1.

Appendix D

List of Spanish Ships
Running the U.S. Blockade of Cuba, 1898

Harbor.	Name of ship.	Date.	Cargo.
Cienfuegos	Steamer Montserrat	Apr. 26	War material.
Do.............	Steamer Adula	June 17	50 barrels flour, 50 barrels corn, 50 sacks rice, 10 tubs butter, 15 barrels pork, 15 barrels beef, 10 barrels hard tack, 6 sacks beans, 5 sacks pease.
Do............	Steamer Reina Maria Cristina.	June 22	1,000 boxes bacon, 50 barrels bacon sides, 600 barrels codfish, 200 sacks beans.
Santiago de Cuba a.	Steamer Polaria	May 7	300 sacks barley, 14,000 sacks rice.
Caibarien a	Steamer Alava...............	July 4	2,500 sacks flour, 6 barrels codfish.
Do............	Steamer Franklin...............do ...		2,495 sacks flour, 3,056 sacks corn, 200 sacks spices, 333 sacks potatoes.
Manzanillo	Steamer Anita...............	b June 18	Small quantities flour, rice, and meat.
Sagua la Grande a..	Steamer Fritjof Nansen	July 3	Small quantities potatoes, onions, meat, and rice.
Matanzas..........	Steamer Montserrat	July 29	8,000 sacks rice, 805 sacks beans, 600 sacks pease, 500 sacks flour, 1,399 boxes bacon, 213 boxes codfish, a large quantity of smoked meat, 15 barrels drugs.
Cayo Frances a	Steamer Franklin	July 31	3,495 sacks flour, 1,350 sacks corn, 500 sacks rice, 165 sacks beans.
Batabano	Coast steamer Arturo.......	b June 13	800 sacks corn, 150 sacks flour, 20 sacks pease, 100 sacks beans, 80 cans lard.
Do.............	Coast steamer Sara.........	b June 24	35 boxes flour, 20 half boxes and 2,490 sacks corn.
Do.............	Bark Tres Hermanos........	b June 20	Beans, flour, and corn.
Do.............	......do	July 14	156 tubs bacon, 200 sacks rice, 160 sacks corn, 129 barrels flour, 60 boxes meat, 65 boxes condensed milk.
Do.............	Coast steamer Victoria	July 13	237 sacks corn, 20 sacks pease, 100 sacks flour, 200 sacks beans, 5 sacks lentils, 12 boxes salt meat, 120 cans, 2 barrels, and 4 tubs lard.
Do.............	Steamer Villaverde	b June 23	4,785 sacks flour, pease, coffee, beans, corn, and rice.
Do.............	Brig Bujia....................	July 26	6 barrels lard, 438 sacks rice, 22 sacks beans, 200 sacks flour.
Nuevitas a.........	Steamer Saffi	May 20	125 sacks pease, 95 sacks rice, 185 barrels wine, 650 sacks salt, 50 boxes oil, 5 boxes cheese, garlic, hard-tack, and pepper.
Do.............	Steamer Franklin............	June 11	2,266 boxes flour, 284 sacks rice, 2,593 sacks beans, 96 sacks spices, 50 sacks pease, 697 sacks corn, 72 sacks coffee.
Do.............	Steamer Chateau Lafitte....	June 17	50 barrels codfish, 6 barrels soup, 3,885 barrels flour, 9,295 sacks flour, 5,000 sacks rice.
La Isabella (seaport of Sagua la Grande). a	Steamer Regulus	July 19	6,573 barrels flour, 1,000 sacks wheat, 4,000 sacks corn, 450 boxes canned meat, 1,000 barrels pork, 500 barrels hard-tack, 30 boxes groceries, 1 box quinine.
San Cayetano.......	Steamer Pralrono...........	b Aug. 8	400 sacks flour, 100 sacks rice, 100 sacks beans, 200 sacks corn, 272 tubs lard, 20 baskets garlic, 10 baskets onions.

a These ports were never declared to be blockaded.
b These ports were not declared to have been blockaded until after these dates.

Only four of the above-mentioned ports were included in the President's proclamation declaring certain ports to be blockaded, viz, Cienfuegos and Matanzas on and after April 22, 1898, and Manzanillo and Batabano on and after June 27, 1898.

Out of the 22 instances given in the table of vessels entering Cuban ports during the war, there were but 9 of these which ran the blockade.

O. N. I.

List of Spanish Ships Running the U.S. Blockade of Cuba, 1898.

Source: *Sketches from the Spanish-American War By Commander J......* in U.S. Navy, Office of Naval Intelligence, *Notes on the Spanish-American War* (Washington, D.C.: Government Printing Office, 1900): 37.

INDEX

(Bold numbers indicate main entries.)

Morong Peninsula, Philippines 430

Moros (Philippine Muslims) 342, 422, 424, 427. *See also list of entries at front of book under* Moro Campaigns

Morro Castle, Havana, Cuba 63, 318, 440

Morrow, Charles Haskell 18, 19

Morúa law 134

Moscow, Russia 237, 570

Mosel Valley, Germany 598

Moses, Bernard 531

"Mosquito Squadron." *See* **Auxiliary Naval Forces in the Spanish-Cuban/American War**

Motion Pictures in the Spanish-Cuban/ American War 350–351

Moton, Robert Russa 351

Moton Commission, Haiti (1930) 223, **351–352,** 436

Motorized Supply for the Punitive Expedition 352–353

Mott, John R. 22

Móxica, Ambrosio 264, 569

Muda, Datu Raja 42

Mudge, J.E. 310

Mulinuu Peninsula, Samoa 310

Munro, Dana Gardner 212

Mura, Habib 42

Murfreesboro, Tennessee, Battle 274, 278, 595

Murmansk, Russia 314, 353, 354, 367, 368, 380, 382, 389, 434, 450, 571

Murmansk Railroad Front, North Russia (1919) 17, 314, **353–354,** 368, 382

Musahuas, Nicaragua 114

Mussolini, Benito 81

Muth, Lawrence 84

Myrick, Herbert 25

N

NAACP. *See* National Association for the Advancement of Colored People (NAACP)

NRA. *See* National Revolutionary Army (NRA) in China

Naco, Arizona 355, 503

Naco, Mexico 323, 355; **Battle (1914–1915) 355–356**

Nafarrete, Emiliano P. 431

Naic, Philippines 197

Nanjing (Nanking), China 183, 356, 357, 399, 605

Nanjing (Nanking) Incident, China (1927) 5, 183, **356–357,** 591

Nanshan (U.S. warship) 30, 102, 103, 306

Naón, Romulo S. 372

Napoleon III 340–341

Nashville (U.S. warship) 62, 104, 309, 367, 369, 370, 396, 397, 398

Nashville campaign, Civil War 123, 507

Natera, Ramón 23

Nation, The 441, 442, 444, 504, 552

National Association for the Advancement of Colored People (NAACP) 436, 441, 552

National Board of Sanitation, Cuba 292

National Citizens' Committee on Relations with Latin America 444

National City Bank of New York 65, 158

National Defense Act (1916) 129, 358

National Defense Act (1920) 130

National Grange 25

National Guard 103, 125, 287, 320, 328, 503, 553–555, 579; Nicaraguan. *See* **Guardia Nacional de Nicaragua;** Texas contingent 105

National Guard Association 554

National Guard Mobilization (1916–1917) 357–361

National Liberation Front of Vietnam 87, 543

National Revolutionary Army (NRA) in China 590, 591

Native Americans. *See names of tribes and names of chiefs*

Navajo Indians 502

Naval General Board. *See* United States Navy, General Board of the Navy

Naval Observatory, Washington, D.C. 482

Naval Operations at Samoa (1899) 361

Naval Operations in the Philippine Islands (1898–1903) 361–364

Naval Operations in the Puerto Rico Campaign (1898) 364–365

Naval Operations in the Spanish-Cuban/ American War 365–366

Naval Operations off Cuba (1912) 366–367

Naval Operations off North Russia (1918–1919) 367–368

Naval Operations off Siberia (1918–1922) 368–369

Naval Operations Relating to Panama (1903) 369–371

Naval War Board (1898) 173, 235, 295, **371–372**

Naval War College, Newport, Rhode Island. *See* United States Naval War College, Newport, Rhode Island

Navarre region, Spain 592

Navarro, Júan J. 565

Navy Yard, Mare Island, California 500, 588; New York 588; Philadelphia 367, 564

Neate, John 464

Nebraska 320

Nebraska (U.S. warship) 134

Neely, Charles F. 139

Negros Island, Philippines 334, 335, 414, 421, 422, 478, 569, 576

Neptune Mine, Nicaragua 114

Netherlands 342